At last — a revolutic
state-of-the-art antiqu
that puts scores of antiq
locations at your fing

The Antique Atlas™

You'll go farther, dig deeper, and discover more antique treasures with The Antique Atlas. It's your most comprehensive guide to antiquing in America, not only covering the shops themselves but the scenic, historic areas in which they are located.

YOU'LL FIND:

- Names, addresses and phone numbers for over 15,000 shops and malls in 48 states, many providing detailed information on days and hours of operation, special services, specific merchandise offered and "How To Get There" directions
- Includes reviews and locations of the most loved bed & breakfast, country inns and restaurants throughout America
- Easy-to-read travel maps for each state

PLUS SPECIAL FEATURES SUCH AS:

- Editorials on Historic Antiquing Towns — Including interviews with local shop owners
- Stories and locations for some very "surprising" side trips

AND THAT'S NOT ALL

- Antique shop/mall reviews
- Show and auction reviews
- NEW Specialty listings outlining shops/malls throughout the U.S. who specialize in specific antiques and collectibles

What they're saying about
The Antique Atlas

"Antique lovers should check out **The Antique Atlas,** *a listing of more than 15,000 shops in 48 states. The book includes reviews & travel maps."*
- - Jerry Shriver, *USA Today*

"The bible of unusual and rare articles."
- - Fred Petrucelli, *Log Cabin Democrat*

"It's a shopper's dream guide."
- - Ken Moore, *Naples Daily News*

"This book certainly fills a void in the antique business."
- - Terry Kovel, *Kovels on Antiques & Collectibles*

"Antique Atlas: A treasure map, the most complete listing anywhere at this moment."
- - Barbara Hertenstein, *St. Louis Post-Dispatch*

"The Atlas" makes life easy for antique hunters. You'll wonder how you ever did without it."
- - Ed Conrad, *Standard Speaker, PA*

"The most comprehensive guide to antiquing in America."
- - Bob Milne, *Travelwriter Marketletter*

"Finally, here is the long-awaited resource that antiquers and travelers everywhere will always want to keep by their sides. **The Antique Atlas** *has it all - an exhaustive state-by-state guide to shops, lodging, and even entertainment along with excellent regional maps. How did we ever live without it?"*
- - *New England Antiques Journal*

"A clever way to put information together."
- - Peggy Mooney, *The Emporia Gazette*

*"***The Antique Atlas** *is a book that will probably be treasured by tourist who are also collectors."*
- - Frank Miele, *Flathead Business Journal*

"Even if you are not into antiques big time, this guide is still most interesting just to have around and look through."
- - Edith Smith, *The Valdosta Daily Times*

"Up to now, we've had to depend on signs, area brochures and, if we're lucky, state and regional guides to point us toward antiques in unexplored territory. Now some enterprising dealers have come up with a book no collector should leave home without - **The Antique Atlas***."*
- - Peggy Welch Mershon, *About Antiques, Mansfield News Journal*

*"This isn't one (***The Antique Atlas***) just to browse through at the bookstore, it's one to carry around everywhere you go."*
- - Shanna Wiggens, *Argus Observer*

The **Antique Atlas** *has been featured in these fine publications:*

Antique Trader's Collector Magazine & Price Guide
The Antique Shopper
The Collector's Marketplace
Maine Antique Digest
Victoria
The (Memphis) Commercial Appeal
Women's News of the Mid-South
Springfield News-Leader
Victorian Homes
Colorado Homes & Lifestyles
Chicago Tribune
Los Angeles Times
New Yorker
American Airlines Inflight Magazine

The Antique Atlas™

The Guide to Antiquing in America

Written, Edited and Compiled by
Kim & David Leggett

Rainy Day Publishing

Rainy Day Publishing, Inc.
Cordova, TN

Rainy Day Publishing, Inc.
1740 N. Germantown Pkwy., Suite 18
Cordova, TN 38018
1-800-456-9326

Printed in the United States of America.

ISBN 0-9656920-2-7

Library of Congress Catalog Card Number 97-092488

Foreword

Of course, we are always looking for that out-of-the-way shop filled with unrecognized treasures, that $1,000 vase priced $75. But when does it pay to leave the turnpike and go off into a small town to visit the shops? Local dealers often have brochures listing nearby antiques stores, the farm papers sometimes include a section on shopping for antiques, and the dealers are usually happy to lead us to the next area with stores. But we need more.

The Antique Atlas is the first large national guide book that recognizes the problems of the out-of-state shopper searching for antiques. It has maps, places to stay, and a town-by-town guide to the shops and malls. We like to photocopy the pages about the states we plan to be in. That way we have some of the town history, detailed directions, and maps. There are antique show schedules so we can try to arrive in a town when the big show is on.

Thank you, Kim and David, for writing this book that helped us out of a very scary night. We were driving in a rural area, no houses in sight, when the fog made it almost impossible to see. Once in a while a street sign was visible. The book listed a phone number for a nearby shop. We hoped the owner lived there and was awake as we called from the car phone to explain our problem. Antiques people are the best! The shop owner talked us along the road and through the fog telling us where to turn...Thirty minutes later we were at a motel.

We know it is impossible to ever do a complete listing of antiques shops. They open and close daily. The Antique Atlas is as complete as any we have used, and the format makes it fun and interesting.

Ralph and Terry Kovel

Kovels' Antiques & Collectibles Price List

This book is dedicated to my mother, Linda Miller, who spent countless hours typesetting, correcting and doing "a lot of everything else" that was needed. Thanks for all your time and devotion.

And, to David and Jo Brandon, our friends, family and supporters. Thank you so much for believing in The Antique Atlas and for believing in us and our dreams.

With deepest love and appreciation
Kim & David

Introduction

Even as a child I loved to go "antiquing." Every Friday night my aunt and grandmother would take me along to a little country auction at "Peppermint Pond," where they often purchased incredible antiques at next to nothing prices. To this day my aunt still sleeps in a gorgeous six-foot-tall oak bed which she purchased for $20. Not one to be left out of a bargain-hunting, shopping excursion, I too purchased a fair amount of jumble and junk along with some "good stuff" (or so I thought). My room became the envy of cousins and friends who came to admire the long, sparkling strands of hippie beads, peace signs, strange-looking incense burners and other '60s memorabilia. Today, 30 years later, I prefer early American painted pieces over the "Partridge Family Does Dixie" look, but one thing has never changed - the intense desire to search and find "pieces of the past."

I was convinced that there were plenty of antique establishments all across America worth seeking out, but there was simply no handy way to find them. Because I couldn't find a book which provided such a listing, I resolved to research and write one myself. I am happy to say that most businesses were thrilled to be included in this book. Their personal stories are a testimony to their love and devotion to their business. Within these pages you will find a great mix of "antiquing" possibilities from the offerings of exclusive antique markets and group shops to the diverse selections of traditional antique and collectible shops and malls. All the antique shows listed in this book represent only the finest in antique furnishings and very early collectibles. Many of the bed and breakfasts, country inns, and hotels are listed on the National Register of Historic Places and offer exceptional overnight accommodations. You'll also find information on historical towns and suggestions for some very interesting "in-town" side trips to add to your "antiquing" adventures. Should all this shopping make you hungry, I've thrown in a few select dining establishments as well.

If in your travels you happen upon a shop/mall/market/show/auction/etc., which is not included please call us at Rainy Day Publishing - we would love to include them in our 1999 edition. Additionally, our bimonthly newsletter will keep everyone up-to-date on recent openings and closings, so your participation in keeping us informed will be greatly appreciated. And most importantly, when visiting any of these businesses please let them know you read about them in **The Antique Atlas**.

Happy hunting!
Call us any time - We would love to hear from you!
1-800-456-9326

Kim & David Leggett

Tips To Remember When Using This Book

1. The listings following the maps are in alphabetical order. Consequently, the numbers appearing on the maps will not be in numerical order.
2. The purpose of the maps is to direct you to a general location using major highways or interstates as references. Secondary highways and streets are intentionally omitted.
3. A listing is provided to those stores which specialize in specific antiques and collectibles.
4. The directions in this book were submitted to Rainy Day Publishing by the listed business. Rainy Day Publishing does not accept responsibility for incorrect directions.
5. At the time of publishing, the information in this book was verified to be correct. However, the publisher cannot be responsible for any inconvenience due to outdated or incorrect information.

NOTE: At the time of printing, we were experiencing a large volume of area code changes. If you should reach a number which appears to be disconnected, call the operator to verify if there has been an area code change.

R • I • V • E • R • C • H • A • S • E
ANTIQUE GALLERY

36,000 SQ. FT.
146 Dealers
110 Parking Spaces

$5 Million Inventory
Dealers Welcome
Visa-MC-Amex-Disc-Checks

3454 LORNA RD. BIRMINGHAM, AL 35216

A Division of Nix, Inc.

OPEN 7 DAYS

205-823-6433

6

Scott's

Antiques, Gifts & Accessories

(205) 931-2006
58 Main Street

Arab

2

Antique Warehouse

Retail

Located between Ashville and Pell City with easy access to I-20 and I-59.

1-800-951-5777

32765 U.S. Highway 231

Ashville

3

Alabama

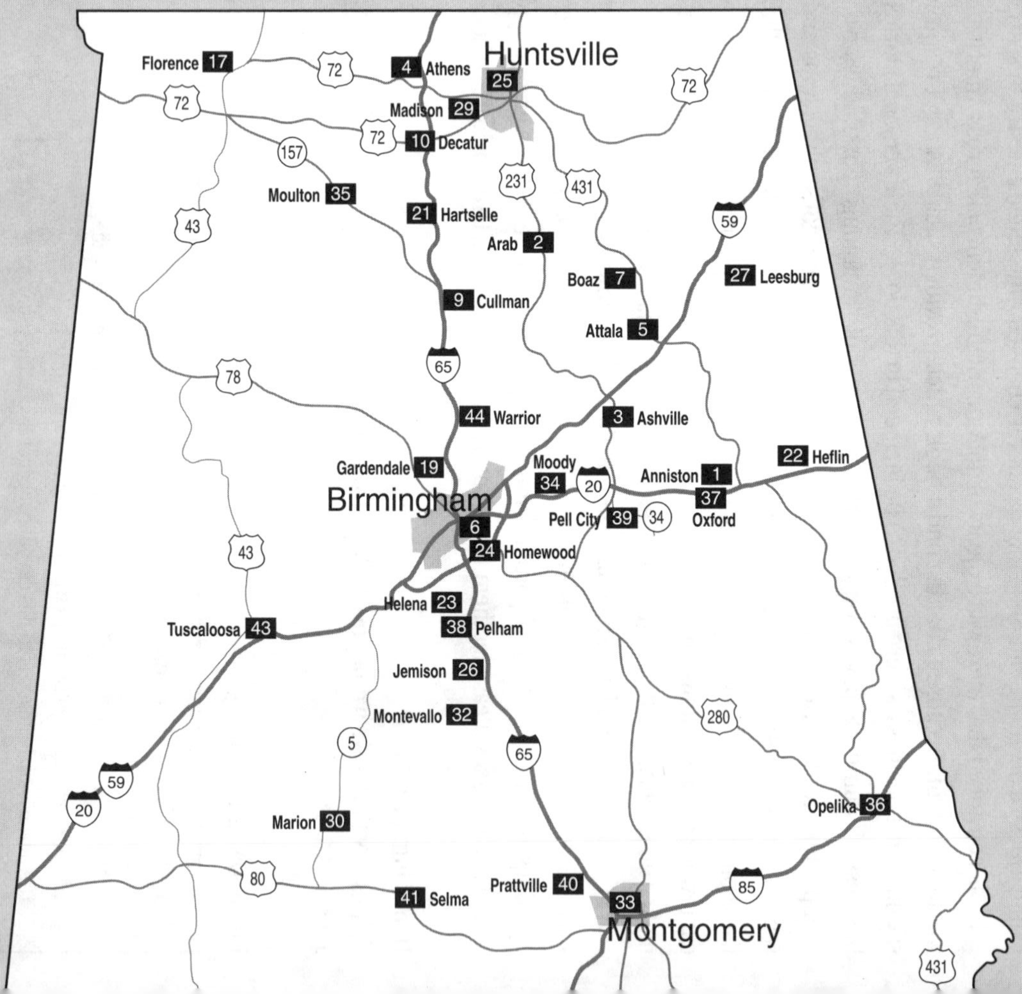

David Tims Wholesale Antiques

Highway 34, Pell City

Direct Importer from:
England • France • Belgium
Denmark • Indonesia
Philippines

39

Where Memories Linger

119 Main Street
Arab

2

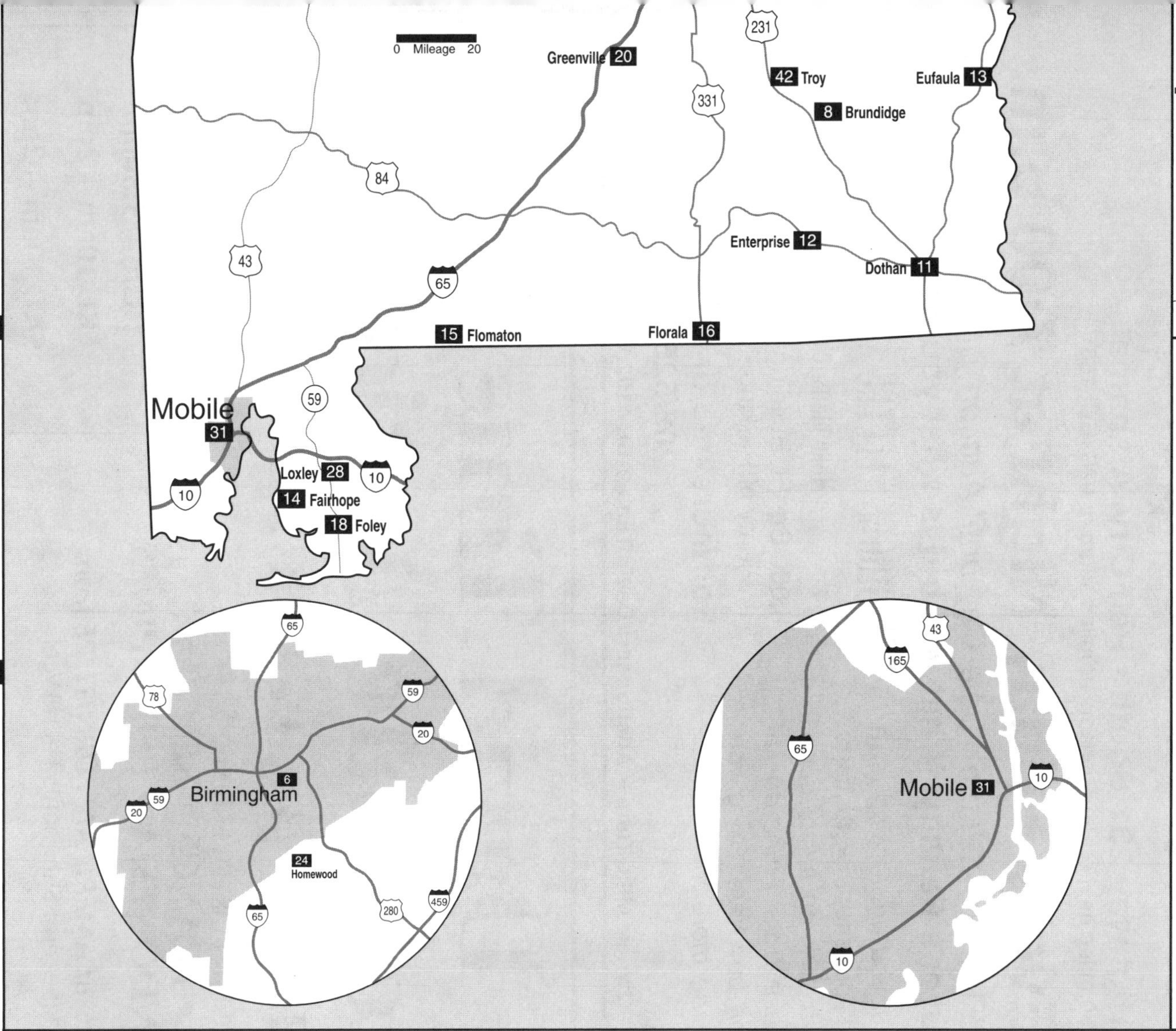
0 Mileage 20
Greenville 20
231
42 Troy
Eufaula 13
331
8 Brundidge
84
Enterprise 12
43
65
Dothan 11
15 Flomaton
Florala 16
59
Mobile
31
10
Loxley 28
10
14 Fairhope
18 Foley
65
78
59
20
6
Birmingham
59
20
24
Homewood
65
280
459
43
165
65
Mobile 31
10
10

Alabama

1 ANNISTON

Jamie's Antique Village
1429 Snow St.
205/831-2830

The Town Shop
908 Noble Street
205/237-7356

Treasures & Keepsakes
1900 Wilmer Ave.
205/235-2251

Apple Barrel Antique Mall
3320 Henry Road
205/237-0091

Anniston Galleries
906 Noble Street
205/236-3741

2 ARAB

Scott's Antiques, Gifts & Accessories

117 N. Main
205/931-2006
Open Tue., Wed., Fri., Sat., or by appointment

Directions: Hwy. 231, 30 miles south of Huntsville.

Scott's is the perfect place to shop for antique furnishings and decoratives to accessorize your home. From formal to simply "stylish," whatever your taste, Scott's extensive selection of antiques and accessories is sure to earn the appreciation of the discrimitive shopper. In addition you will find a sizable collection of depression era glassware, porcelain and china figurines.

Where Memories Linger

119 Main Street
205/931-2065
Open Mon.-Sat. 11-2

Directions: Located on Highway 231, 30 miles south of Huntsville

A "must stop" for anyone who loves the aroma of freshly roasted coffee and the smell of warm, just baked cookies. This Victorian-influenced tearoom offers a generous sampling of homemade tea cakes, fruit cake and gourmet coffees.

On the lunch menu you will find the house specialty, chicken salad, or choose from a number of other gourmet selections.

For a memorable experience to share with friends, take home a gift basket filled with samples of gourmet coffees and other treats.

Olde World Antique Gallery
2330 N. Brindlee Mt. Pkwy.
205/586-2185

Fine Things Antiques
303 Cullman Rd.
205/586-5685

Kelleys Supply
220 Ruth Rd.
205/586-4169

Jean's Antiques
2893 Highway 231
205/586-5007

Special Touchs
Highway 231 N
205/498-5504

3 ASHVILLE

Antique Warehouse

3276 U.S. Highway 231
205/594-5777 or 800/951-5777
Mon.-Fri. 9-5, Sat. 8-12

Directions: From I-59, exit east onto Highway 231. Located 5 miles beyond Ashville.

Antique Warehouse, as the name implies, is a huge warehouse full of everything and anything in the way of antiques and reproductions. Here you will find American, English, French, and Belgium oak, walnut, mahogany and maple. To complete your furnishings, Antique Warehouse also has an eclectic offering of bronzes, paintings, lamps, chocolate sets, tea sets and more.

4 ATHENS

Have time to stop and explore a few days in Alabama? Grab your shovels and head for the hills. Rumor has it that an undetermined amount of gold and silver coins are buried in the quaint little Southern town of Athens, Alabama. Located in the rolling foothills of the Appalachian Mountains in northern Alabama, Athens is blessed with an abundance of historic homes and sites, many dating back to the mid-1800s. It is here, in this charming historic town, that the story of buried treasures unfolds.

As the Civil War was ending, soldiers loyal to the South collected a large amount of gold and silver coins. The plan was to take the treasure to Montgomery, but Union forces interfered. Near Athens, the wagon carrying the treasure sank in the murky Alabama clay, becoming immobile. While working to free it, the Confederate band was surprised by a small Union patrol. Believing the wagon contained weapons and ammunition, the Union sergeant ordered the wagon unloaded. A skirmish erupted between the two groups. Three of the Yankee soldiers were killed, along with two of the three Confederates. A wounded Union soldier escaped, leaving the Confederate leader - known only as Hansen - behind to defend the treasure. Dumping the treasure in the adjacent bog to conceal it from the Union armies, Hansen made his way to the home of a friend, where he reported his misfortune, along with the general location of the treasure. Hansen was killed shortly afterward by a Union soldier. His friend never recovered the coins.

Sutton's Antiques
1010 N. Jefferson St.
205/233-0235

Athens Antique Mall
309 S. Marion St.
205/230-0036

Hickory House
23101 U.S. Highway 72
205/232-9860

Favorite Places To Eat

Cracker Barrel Old Country Store
I-65 & U.S. Hwy. 72, Exit 351
205/232-4141

5 ATTALLA

Howard House Antiques
420 5th Ave. NW
205/538-0461

Col. John's Auction
413 4th St. NW
205/538-7884

Memory Lane Antiques
420 4th St. NW
205/538-8594

Pembroke Antiques
307 5th Ave.
205/570-0041

Yesterday's Treasures Antiques
426 4th St. NW
205/538-3111

Courtyard Antiques
318 5th Ave. NW
205/538-3455

Days Gone By
424 4th St. NW
205/538-1920

Gramling Antiques
419 4th St. NW
205/538-2464

6 BIRMINGHAM

Riverchase Antique Gallery

3454 Lorna Road
205/823-6433
Mon.-Sat.: 10-6; Sun.: 1-6 (Closed Thanksgiving Day and Christmas Day)

Directions: Located at I-459 and Lorna Road, across from the Galleria, only 10 minutes south of Birmingham

The seasoned veteran, as well as the rookie, loves the thrill of the hunt. To an avid antiquer, the quest for that certain item, be it a Shaker cabinet or a Tiffany lamp, is often as exciting (and treasure-filled) as the find itself.

A fine spot to begin the hunt when traveling near Birmingham, Alabama, is Riverchase Antique Gallery. The 146 dealer gallery spans 36,000 square feet for your meandering pleasure.

An abundance of furniture in styles such as French, English, Mission, Primitive and Shaker is displayed throughout the gallery. Riverchase Antique Gallery hosts an impressive inventory of bedroom and dining room suites, armoires and sideboards, in addition to many other pieces of fine furniture.

At Riverchase Antique Gallery, the unusual is the norm. Dealers display juke boxes, refurbished telephones, lamps, glassware, china, paintings, pottery, toys and collectibles. Is it any wonder Riverchase Antique Gallery was voted "Best of Birmingham," ten years running?

Redmont Market Antiques
2330 7th Ave. S
205/320-0440

Peck & Hill Antique Furniture
2400 7th Ave. S
205/252-3179

Lakeview Antiques
2427 7th Ave. S
205/323-0888

Hanna Antiques Mall
2424 7th Ave. S
205/323-6036

Avon Antique Shop
2801 7th Ave. S
205/324-8353

5th Avenue Antiques
2410 5th Ave. S
205/320-0500

First Avenue Antiques
7315 1st Ave. N
205/833-6083

Christopher House Antiques
2921 18th St. S
205/870-7106

Interiors Market
2817 2nd Ave. S
205/323-2817

Shades Crest Antique Gallery
774 Shades Mountain Plaza
205/823-1166

On-A-Shoestring
601 Shades Crest Rd.
205/822-8741

Attic Antiques
5620 Cahaba Valley Rd.
205/991-6887

Elegant Earth
1907 Cahaba Rd.
205/870-3264

Urban Farmer
2809 18th St. S
205/870-7118

Estate Antiques
3253 Lorna Rd.
205/823-7303

Cather & Brown Books
3904 Clairmont Ave. S
205/591-7284

Oak Grove Antiques
609 Oak Grove Rd.
205/945-7183

Antiques & Dreams
9184 Parkway East
205/836-2411

Antique Mall East
217 Oporto Madrid Blvd. N
205/836-1097

Maryon Allen Co.
3215 Cliff Rd.
205/324-0479

Birmingham Antique Mall
2211 Magnolia Ave. S
205/328-7761

Chinaberry
1 Hoyt Lane
205/879-5338

Lamb's Ears Ltd.
3138 Cahaba Heights Road
205/969-3138

Favorite Places To Eat

Ollie's Barbeque
515 University Blvd.
205/324-9485

Memphis, Tenn., has long been recognized as the home of the bar-b-qued pig, but Ollie's Barbeque in Birmingham, Alabama, is sitting right on the doorstep.

Since 1926, the McClung family has been serving smoked meat not only to the hometown crowd, but to folks from as far away as Sacramento, California. Their original establishment on Birmingham's south side is gone, but their new pork place on University Boulevard displays a swanky pit built in the middle so customers can see just what it takes to make meat taste this good.

Sliced pork with crunchy edges is the most popular choice. On a plate or piled high in a sandwich, these tender wedges are topped with the McClung family recipe, a vinegar-tomato sauce. A choice of tossed salad, beans, french fries, or coleslaw comes with the meal. If you've saved room for dessert, you're in for a treat of homemade pies (chocolate, coconut, lemon and apple), a yummy end to a great meal!

Interesting Side Trips

Arlington
331 Cotton Avenue SW
205/780-5656
Tue.-Sat. 10-4; Sun. 1-4 (Closed Mondays and city holidays)

Directions: Located 1 1/2 miles west of downtown Birmingham on 1st Avenue North which becomes Cotton Avenue. From I-65 South, take the 6th Avenue North exit; from I-65 North, take the 3rd Avenue North exit. Then follow the signs.

In 1953, this many-times-renovated family home became the property of the City of Birmingham. Arlington is located in Elyton, one of the oldest sections of the city. Incorporated in 1821, Elyton was the first permanent county seat of Jefferson County.

Neither the exact date of Arlington's construction nor the builder's name are known, but construction of the present structure occurred sometime after purchase in 1842 by Judge William S. Mudd. The style of architecture is Greek Revival, easily identified by the central hallways upstairs and down, as well as the symmetry of rooms on either side of the hallways.

Today, the property has been restored to a grandeur reminiscent of its finest era. Arlington possesses an excellent collection of decorative arts, mostly 19th century American. Additional collections throughout the home have been made available through the generosity of local donors.

7 BOAZ

Sana's Antiques on Main
111 S. Main St.
205/593-8009

Gazebo Antique Gallery
106 Thomas Ave.
205/840-9444

Downtown Antique Gallery
102 S. Main St.
205/593-0023

Boaz Antique Mall
102 Thomas Ave.
205/593-1410

Almost Antiques
104 Thomas Ave.
205/593-1412

Adams Antique Mall
225 E. Mill Ave.
205/593-0406

Southern Heritage
285-C U.S. Hwy 4315
205/593-1132

8 BRUNDIDGE

City Antiques
108 E. Troy St.
334/735-5164

Green's Antiques
794 S. Main St.
334/735-2247

Rue's Antique Mall & Deli
123 S. Main
334/735-3125

9 CULLMAN

Cullman Antique Alley
500 County Rd. 1170
205/739-1900

Magnolias & Lace
1716 2nd Ave. NW
205/734-9639

Yesterday's Antiques & Gifts
105 2nd Ave. SW
205/739-3972

Southern Accents Arch Antqs.
308 2nd Ave. SE
205/737-0554

South Wind Antiques
301 3rd Ave. SE
205/737-9800

Plantation Designs
202 1st Ave. SE
205/734-0654

Craig's Antiques & Gifts
220 1st Ave. SE
205/734-2252

Antiquities
308 3rd St. SE
205/734-9953

Judy's Antiques
407 Cleveland Ave. SW
205/734-8300

Golden Pond
2045 County Rd. 222
205/739-0850

Fireside Antiques
1133 County Rd. 222
205/737-5135

Favorite Places To Eat

Cracker Barrel Old Country Store
I-65 & Hwy. 157, Exit 310
205/739-6950

10 DECATUR

London's
114 Moulton St.
205/340-0900

Sykes Antiques
726 NE Bank St.
205/355-2656

Sarah's Gifts & Antiques
302 2nd Ave. SE
205/351-1451

Nebrig-Howell House Antiques
722 Bank St. NE
205/351-1655

Hummingbird Antiques
721 Bank St. NE
205/351-1451

Riverwalk Antique Mall
818 Bank St. NE
205/340-0075

Antique Jungle
219 E. 2nd Ave.
205/351-6278

Southland Collectibles, Ltd.
3311 Old Moulton Road
205/350-7272

Rhodes Ferry
502 Bank Street NE
205/308-0550

11 DOTHAN

Miz Minnie's Antiques
450 S. Oates St.
334/794-2061

King's Clocks & Antiques
1015 Headland Ave.
334/792-3964

Wildot Inc.
409 S. Oates St.
334/794-8372

Alabama Antq. Mall/Auc. Ctr.
14341 S. U.S. 231 Suite 2
334/702-0720

Antique Attic
5037 Fortner St.
334/792-5040

12 ENTERPRISE

Country Matters & Antiques
905 E. Park Ave.
334/347-4649

Ronald Evans Antiques
204 N. Main St.
334/347-4944

Special Accents
102 N. Main St.
334/347-0887

Gaston's Antiques
528 Glover Ave.
334/347-0285

Country Matters & Antiques II
1241 Shellfield Rd.
334/347-4649

13 EUFAULA

Directions: From Montgomery, U.S. 82 southeast through Union Springs to Eufaula

Eufaula, Alabama, is home to a little more than 13,000 citizens; however, this modest-sized city brags of being constructed of over 700 historic buildings. Situated along the banks of the Chattahoochee River, Eufaula was at one time a prosperous riverport town for planters throughout the states of Alabama, Georgia, and Florida. This town, blossoming in spring with dogwood and azaleas, is blessed with an abundance of antebellum homes characteristic of the deep South. The wealthy families of the 1840's and 1850s put their show of money into the exquisite and lavishly-presented homes, churches, and other buildings.

Unlike many of its sister cities whose beauty and grace

were interrupted during the Civil War, Eufaula was fortunate that the Confederacy conceded before Union forces could occupy or destroy it. This resulted in the preservation of many hundreds of historic structures. In addition, during the post-war era, many other attractive homes and buildings rose in Eufaula. The tradition of admiration of fine craftsmanship and architecture set the stage for the preservation of these magnificent structures as well. Alabama is host to the finest 19th century small-town commercial district. Moreover, guests of the town discover the state's most luxurious and plentiful collection of domestic Italianate architecture. Seth Lore-Irwinton Historic District boasts many of the town's historic homes. Shorter Mansion (1884), Fendall Hall (1860), Holleman-Foy Home (1907), Hart-Milton House (1843) and Kendall Manor offer some of the best examples of Neoclassical and Italianate mansions. Waterford chandeliers, hand-stenciled walls and murals breathe the grace and style of times past within the walls of these homes. Broad Street possesses many of the historic commercial buildings. The Tavern, an inn in the 1830's, later a Confederate hospital, is presently a studio and private home listed on the National Register of Historic Places.

The Eufaula tourism council supplies brochures for walking and driving tours of the homes within the historic district. Although most homes are private, during Eufaula's Pilgrimage in April, many homeowners open their doors inviting visitors to enjoy the rooms and family heirlooms inside. The pilgrimage, furthermore, greets guests with open-air art exhibits, tea gardens and concerts. If not enough, one of the major antique shows in the state opens during the pilgrimage, occurring each year during the second weekend of April.

Memory Lane
106 S. Eufaula Ave.
334/616-0995

Walker's Antiques
149 S. Eufaula Ave.
334/687-5362

Fagins Thieves Market
317 S. Eufaula Ave.
334-687-4100

Attic Treasures
2908 S. Eufaula Ave.
334/687-3438

14 FAIRHOPE

Bay Antiques & Collectibles
328 De La Mare Street
334-928-2800
Mon.-Sat. 10-5

Directions: 20 miles east of Mobile; 50 miles west of Pensacola; off I-10. Located on Mobile Bay; 30 miles west of Gulf Shores, Ala. De La Mare is 1 block south of Fairhope Avenue.

Tucked away in the intimate and romantic downtown village of Fairhope, Alabama, Bay Antiques & Collectibles is surrounded by a lovely garden of blooming seasonal flowers. The store's name as well as its aura are derived from its nearness to Mobile Bay.

Antique linen and lace along with jewelry made from old buttons are the speciality of this quaint little shop. Silver pieces, antique books and some select furniture are also presented.

Lunch is served in the nearby courtyard overlooking the gardens.

15 FLOMATON

Flomaton Antique Auction
277 Old Highway 31
334/296-3059

16 FLORALA

Stateline Mini Mall
1517 W. Fifth Ave.
334/858-2741

Florala Flea Mkt. & Antq. Mall
1511 W. Fifth Ave. (Hwy. 331)
334/858-7000

17 FLORENCE

Antiques on Court
442 N. Court St.
205/766-4429

Bellemeade Antique Mall
Highway 72 E.
205/757-1050

Estate Antique Mall
3803 Florence Blvd.-Hwy. 72
205/757-9941

Taylor's Treasures
5136 Hwy. 17
205/764-7172

Southern Antique Mall
3801 Florence Blvd.
205/757-8288

Gifford's Antiques & Gifts
1202 N. Wood Ave.
205/766-7340

18 FOLEY

Old Armory Mall
812 N. McKenzie St
334/943-7300

Gas Works Antique Mall Inc
818 N. McKenzie St.
334/943-5555

Southern Belle Antique Mall
1000 S. McKenzie St.
334/943-8128

Perdido Antiques Inc.
323 S. Alston St.
334/943-5665

Gift Horse Antique Stalls
201 W. Laurel Ave.
334/943-7278

Brown Mule Antique Mall
8340 Highway 59 S.
334/943-4112

Hollis "Ole Crush" Antique Mall
200 S. McKenzie (Hwy. 59)
334/943-8154

19 GARDENDALE

Favorite Places To Eat

Cracker Barrel Old Country Store
I-65 & Fieldstown Rd., Exit 271
205/631-8011

20 GREENVILLE

Favorite Places To Eat

Cracker Barrel Old Country Store
I-65 & AL. 185, Exit 130
334/382-2691

21 HARTSELLE

Southern Antiques
103 Railroad St. SW
205/773-3923

Jeanette's Jazzy Jk & Antiques
115 Railroad St. SW
205/773-2299

Jeff Sandlin's Antiques
219 Main St. W
205/773-4774

Holladay Hill Antiques
1807 Highway 32 NW
205/773-0116

Hartselle Antique Mall
209 Main St. W
205/773-0081

Heavenly Treasures & Gifts
221 Main St. W
205/773-4004

Country Classic Antiques
303 Main St. W
205/773-9559

Golden Oldies Antiques
109 Main St. W
205/773-1508

Railroad Street Antique Mall
113 Railroad Street SE
205/773-2299

22 HEFLIN

The Willoughby Street Mall
91-A Willoughby Street
205/463-5409
Mon.-Sat. 10-5; Sun. 1-5 (Closed New Year's Day, Easter, Mother's Day, Thanksgiving and Christmas Day)

Directions: Traveling I-20, 70 miles from Atlanta, Ga., or Birmingham. Ala., exit 199. Turn north on Highway 9. Go 1 1/2 miles to Highway 78. Turn right on 78. Go approximately 3 blocks. Turn right on Coleman Street. Go 1 block. Turn left on Willoughby Street. Go 1/2 block. Old red brick high school building on right.

Back in 1936, The Willoughby Street Mall was the Cleburne County High School of Heflin, Alabama. The red paint outside is original and the owners are restoring the building's interior to better represent its school days.

Today, this 35,000-square-foot mall is filled with a collage of antiques and collectibles that includes pottery (Hull, Roseville, Shawnee), depression glass in a variety of patterns and colors, furnishings from Victorian to primitive and a list that goes on and on.

If you're in the market for Alabama art, be sure to visit the art gallery where local artist market their works.

23 HELENA

Antique Monger
5274 Helena Rd.
205/663-4977

Our Place Antiques & Things
Hwy 261 Main St.
205/620-9361

The Basket Cottage
5281 Helena Rd.
205/664-4033

24 HOMEWOOD

Edgewood Antiques
731 Rear Broadway St.
205/870-3343

Little House Art Center
2915 Linden Ave.
205/879-4186

Michael's Antiques
1831 29th Ave. S
205/871-2716

Europa Antiques Inc.
1820 29th Ave.
205/879-6222

Frankie Engel Antiques
2949 18th St. S
205/879-8331

Carriage Antique Village
88 Green Springs Hwy.
205/942-8131

25 HUNTSVILLE

Cotton Pickin Antiques
8402 Whitesburg Dr. S
205/883-1010

Madison Square Antiques
1017 Old Monrovia Rd.
205/430-0909

Hart Lex Antique Mall
1030 Old Monrovia Rd.
205/830-4278

Packards Antiques
11261 Memorial Pkwy. SW
205/881-1678

Wilma's Antiques
515 Pratt Ave.
205/536-7250

Railroad Station Antique Mall
Natl. Historic Lombardo Bldg.
315 N. Jefferson St.
205/533-6550

Old Town Antique Mall
820 Wellman Ave. NE
205/533-7002

Golden Griffin
104 Longwood Dr. SE
205/535-0882

Darwin Antiques
320 Church St. NW
205/539-9803

Ashton Place
410 Governors Dr. SW
205/539-5464

Red Rooster Antique Mall
12519 Memorial Pkwy. SW
205/881-6530

Haysland Antique Mall
11595 Memorial Pkwy
205/883-0181

Valerie Fursdon Inc.
2212 Whitesburg Dr.
205/533-6768

Pratt Avenue Antique Mall
708 N.E. Pratt Ave.
205/536-3117

Kay's Kupboard
515 Fountain Row
205/536-1415

Gallery Antiques
209 Russell St. NE
205/539-9118

Bulldog Antique Mall
2338 Whitesburg Dr. S
205/534-9893

Antiques Etc.
2801 Memorial Pkwy.
205/533-0330

26 JEMISON

The Jemison Inn
212 Highway 191
205/688-2055
Open year round

Old-time style in a small town setting describes The Jemison Inn of Jemison, Alabama. The intimate inn provides three guest rooms, so reservations are a must to assure you a place to stay. The former family home, built in the 1930's, has been refurbished and now boasts many heirloom antique furnishings. Southern charm and hospitality abound in this delightful inn. Fresh flowers grace each room. The full breakfast provided to lodgers is accompanied by fresh fruits in season. On fine spring and fall evenings, you can sit on the wrap-around porch enjoying an afternoon refreshment, compliments of the inn. A further touch of Southern style is punctuated by turned-down beds and mints on the pillows. The intimate, hospitable charm of The Jemison Inn makes it a great wind-down stop.

Touch of the Past
120 Old Main
205/688-4938

27 LEESBURG

the secret-Bed & Breakfast Lodge
2356 Highway 68 West
205/523-3825
Open year round
Reservations requested

Directions: From I-59 take the Collinsville exit (exit 205). Follow Highway 68 east for 9.2 miles. Located on the left side of the street.

"the secret" sits cozily among twelve acres of garden and wilderness atop Lookout Mountain. On a clear day you can see seven cities, including the skyline of Gadsden, the lights of Anniston and the industrial smokestacks of Rome, Georgia. It is perfectly situated on the edge of a mountain top so the sunrises and sunsets are spectacular.

Carl and Dianne Cruickshank, the owners and innkeepers, found "the secret" almost by accident. "We were looking at possible locations for a bed and breakfast," Diane said. "We had gone all through Etowah and Dekalb counties one Sunday, and we decided to take a look at this. It was love at first sight."

You might say Carl and Dianne rescued the house from despair. Originally built by People's Telephone Company owner Millard Weaver as a family home, the place had changed owners several times in the years following Weaver's death. It was then empty for a long time. The Cruickshanks came along at the right time while restoration was still possible. Carl performed most of the reconstruction himself.

Today, "the secret" provides a romantic atmosphere throughout the home with such amenities as an enormous central stone fireplace, a 22-foot vaulted living room/dining room ceiling and four spacious guest rooms. The home is furnished throughout with antiques, art, copper, brass, tile and rare woods. The 10-foot Lazy Susan table from which breakfast is served, has become quite a conversation piece among guests.

In addition to providing breath-taking scenery, the gardens and grounds are also home to two treasured peacocks.

28 LOXLEY

Plunderosa Antiques
Highway 59
334/964-5474

Woodland's Antique Mall
Highway 59
334/964-4301

29 MADISON

Cracker Barrel Old Country Store
I-565 & Wall-Triana, Exit 7
205/461-7670

30 MARION

Browsabout Antqs. & Things
105 E. Jefferson St.
334/683-9856

Twink's Antiques & Gifts
212 Washington St.
334/683-4770

Pappy's Porch
106 E. Green St.
334/683-9541

La Mason
215 Washington Street
334/683-9131

31 MOBILE

Mobile Antique Gallery
1616 South Beltline Highway
334/666-6677
Mon.-Sat. 10-6; Sun., 1-6

Directions: Located on the west side service road of I-65 at exit 1B. One mile north of I-10

Voted "Best of Mobile" for three consecutive years, Mobile Antique Gallery presents an outstanding market of antiques and collectibles in a 21,000 square feet gallery. This bustling showplace houses the wares of well over 100 quality antique dealers offering exquisite furnishings, linens, silver, china, porcelains, depression era glassware, antique toys and much, much more. A snack bar is located in the gallery.

1848 Antiques
356 Dauphin St.
334/432-1848

Bentley's
22S Florida St.
334/479-4015

Cotton City Antique Mall
2012 Airport Blvd.
334/479-9747

Red Barn Antique Mall
418 Dauphin Island Pkwy.
334/473-9227

Gallery Old Shell
1803 Old Shell Rd.
334/478-1822

Antoinette's Antiques
4401 Old Shell Rd.
334/344-7636

Plantation Antique Galleries
3750 Government Blvd.
334/666-7185

Yellow House Antiques
1902 Government St.
334/476-7382

Kearney Antiques
1004 Government St.
334/438-9984

Cobweb
422 Dauphin Island Pkwy.
334/478-6202

Dogwood Antiques
2010 Airport Blvd.
334/479-9960

E & J Galleries
1421 Forest Hill
334/380-2072

Mary's Corner
2602 Old Shell Rd.
334/471-6060

Antique Shop Inc.
3510 Cottage Hill Rd.
334/661-1355

Mobile Antique Gallery
1616 S Beltline Hwy.
334/666-6677

Criswell's Antiques
4103 Moffat Rd.
334/344-4917

Favorite Places To Eat

Cracker Barrel Old Country Store
I-65 & Dauphin St., Exit 4
334/473-6761

Interesting Side Trips

Oakleigh House Museum
350 Oakleigh Place
334/432-1281
Mon.-Sat. 10-4, (Closed legal holidays and Christmas week)

Directions: 2 1/2 blocks South of Government Street between Roper Street and George Street.

Oakleigh Period House Museum and Historic Complex is operated by the Historic Mobile Preservation Society. The 3 1/2 landscaped acres consist of Oakleigh, the city's official ante-bellum period house museum, the Cox-Deasy House, and the Archives Building, which also houses the administrative offices of the Society.

Oakleigh, which was begun in 1833 by Mobile merchant James W. Roper, is included in the American Buildings Survey and the National Register of Historic Places. Mr. Roper was his own architect and incorporated unique and practical features into the design of his home. It is beautifully furnished with fine period collections of furniture, portraits, silver, china, jewelry, interesting kitchen implements and toys. The museum gift shop is on the ground floor of Oakleigh.

The Cox-Deasy House, circa 1850, is a contrast to Oakleigh. It is a raised Creole Cottage, typical of the modest middle-class city dwellers along the Gulf Coast. It is furnished in simple 19th-century antiques.

Guided tours of Oakleigh and the Cox-Deasy House are conducted by members of the Society.

32 MONTEVALLO

Cedar Creek Antiques
2979 Hwy 119 S
205/665-2446

Montevallo Antiques
615 Main St.
205/665-4142

33 MONTGOMERY

Nicole Maleine Antiques
121 N. Goldwiate St.
334/834-8530

Unique Treasures
1712 Upper Wetumpka Rd.
334/834-0437

Herron House Antiques
422 Herron St.
334/265-2063

Bodiford's Antique Mall
919 Hampton St.
334/265-4220

Emily Dearman Antiques
514 Cloverdale Rd.
334/269-5282

Frances Edward's Antiques
1010 E Fairview Ave.
334/269-5100

Louise Brooks Antiques
1034 E. Fairview Ave.
334/265-8900

Mulberry House Antiques
2001 Mulberry St.
334/263-5131

Old Cloverdale Antiques
514 Cloverdale Rd.
334/262-6234

May-Bell's Corner Antiques
1429 Bell St.
334/265-3298

Montgomery Antique Galleries
1955 Eastern Blvd.
334/277-2490

Favorite Places To Eat

Cracker Barrel Old Country Store
I-85 & Eastern Blvd., Exit 6
334/271-4308

34 MOODY

Favorite Places To Eat

Cracker Barrel Old Country Store
I-20 & S.S. 411, Exit 144
205/640-2478

35 MOULTON

Heirloom Antiques
Court St.
205/905-0602

Hilda's Attic
538 Lawrence St.
205/974-0470

The Shelton House Antiques
2020 Morgan St.
205-974-1444

Memories Antiques & Ideas
716 Main St.
205/974-4301

Blue Willow Antiques & Gifts
607 County Rd. 217
205/974-3888

Town Square Antique Mall
Main St.
205/974-2345

36 OPELIKA

Highway 280 Antique Mall
4730 Alabama Hwy. 147 N
334/821-8540

Olde Towne Antiques
805 Geneva St.
334/745-0580

Magnolia House
807 Geneva St.
334/749-9648

Blue Iris Antiques
400 2nd Ave.
334/745-6756

Favorite Places To Eat

Cracker Barrel Old Country Store
I-85 & U.S. 280/431, Exit 62
334/749-2363

37 OXFORD

Favorite Places To Eat

Cracker Barrel Old Country Store
I-20 & Morgan Road, Exit 188
205/835-6700

38 PELHAM

Favorite Places To Eat

Cracker Barrel Old Country Store
I-65 & Cahaba Valley Rd., Exit 246
205/987-1555

39 PELL CITY

David Tims Wholesale Antiques
Highway 34
205/338-7929
Mon.-Thurs. 10-5:30; Fri.-Sat. 10-2

Directions: Located south of Pell City on Hwy. 34.

It's quite a surprise to find a super-sized jumbo antique market located in the midst of a little country town. With a huge showroom and several more warehouses filled to the rafters, David Tims Wholesale Antiques has everything, literally, in the way of antiques and fine reproductions.

Imports from 11 different countries (England, France, Belgium, Holland, etc.) arrive weekly to this antique metropolis. In addition, David receives several antique shipments each week from the New York area. It would not be out of the ordinary to find outstanding American heirlooms offered for sale from some of the New York area's finest estates. I'm not offering a listing or even a partial list on this one. As a matter of fact, any endeavor on my part to attempt such a listing would, without a doubt, fall short of its intended goal. Therefore, plan a day - two are suggested - to explore the showroom and warehouses of David Tims Wholesale Antiques. If you can't find what you're looking for here, it has probably never been made.

Pell City Auction Company
Highway 231 South
205/525-4100
Auction: Fridays, 7 p.m./Preview: Fridays -7 p.m.

Directions: Located 30 miles east of Birmingham, 10 miles south of I-20 (Exit 158).

Dubbed by its owner Mike Tims as "The biggest little auction in Alabama," Pell City Auction Company presents its wares in a spacious 8,000 square foot building. This gracious Southern business boasts to housing "hundreds of items every sale." Many of the "good, desirable pieces" arrive as estate merchandise selectively collected from all across the United States.

Shoppers are encouraged to bring their trucks to this auction house overflowing with chairs, wardrobes, wall clocks, hangings, bedroom suites, dining tables and chairs plus many unusual items.

40 PRATTVILLE

Favorite Places To Eat

Cracker Barrel Old Country Store
I-65 & State Hwy. 14, Exit 181
334/365-9600

41 SELMA

Selma Antique & Art Mall
1410 Water Avenue
334/872-1663

Gordon Antiques
705 Dallas Avenue
334/875-2400

42 TROY

Hillside Antiques
4839 Highway 231 N
334/735-5567

43 TUSCALOOSA

Favorite Places To Eat

Cracker Barrel Old Country Store
I-59 & Skyland Blvd., Exit 76
205/562-8282

44 WARRIOR

B. Cooper's Antqs. & Cllbls.
133 Louisa Street
205/647-2272

Currier Antiques
110 E. 5th Street
205/647-8048

Victorian Rose
125 Louisa Street
205/647-1600

Garden Gate Antiques
110 E. 5th Street
205/647-8048

Notes

Arizona

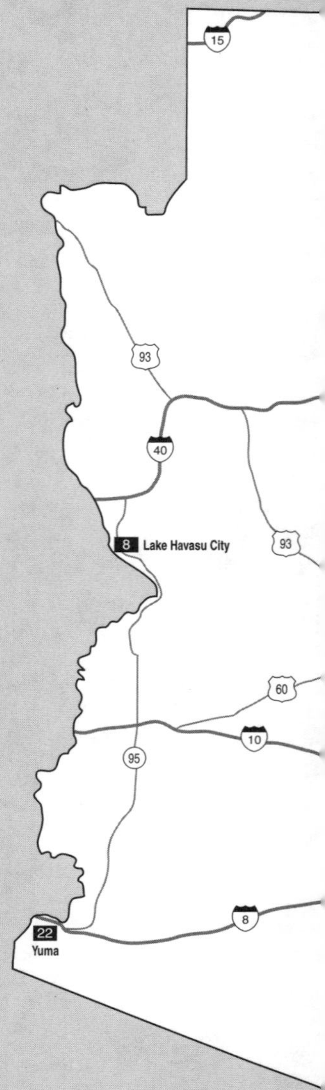

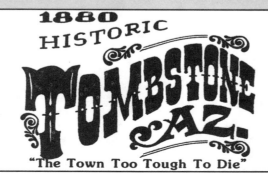

ANTIQUE PLAZA

114 West Main Street
(602) 833-4844

20,000 Square Feet
with Over 100 Dealers

Mesa

Antique Plaza

10

EIGHT BALL ANTIQUES

And Other Stuff

Specializing in Antique Telephones

1050 S. Page Springs Rd. • P.O. Box 884 • Cornville, AZ 86325
Jim Niccum, Owner

2

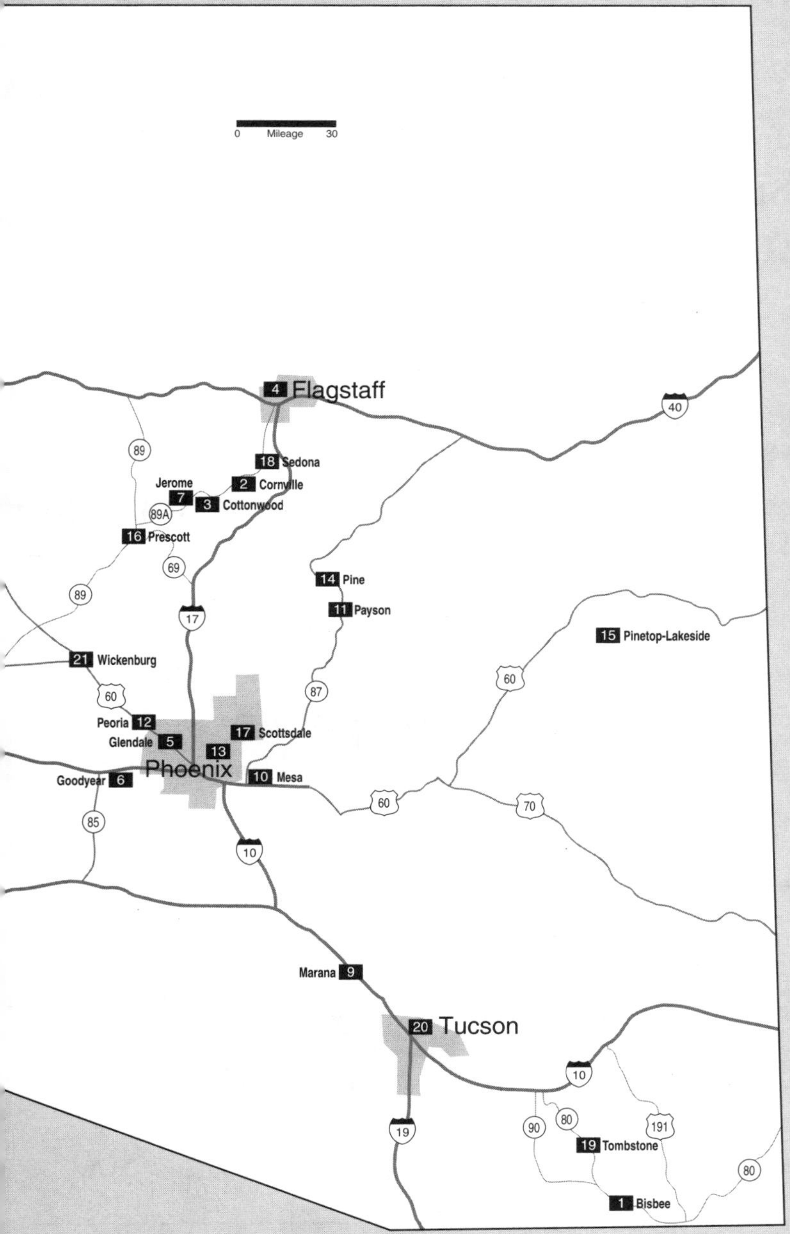

Apple Tree

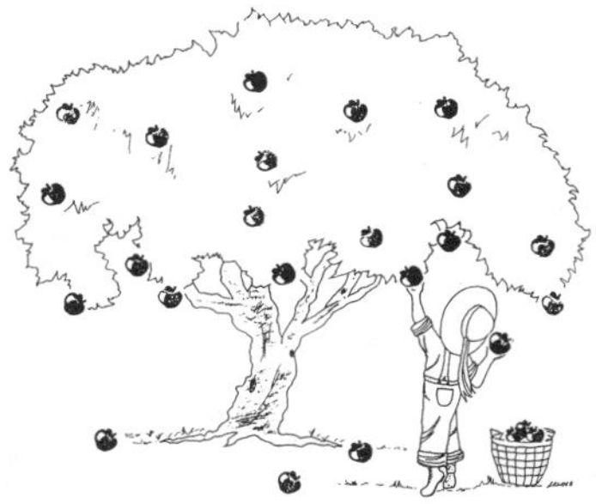

5811 West Glendale Ave.
(602) 435-8486

Glendale

5

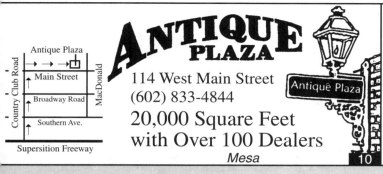

Arizona's Antique Capital

HISTORIC DOWNTOWN GLENDALE

Historic Catlin Court Shops

More than 80

Antiques

& Specialty Shops plus

unique eateries

5

Circa 1898

GHOST CITY INN

BED & BREAKFAST

AN OVERNIGHT TRADITION

Jerome

7

Pinecrest Lane Antiques

&

Billings Country Pine Antiques

Invites you to shop in Beautiful Pinetop

15

Glendale - Arizona's Antique Capital

- Just west of Phoenix in the Valley of the Sun -

Visit a turn-of-the-century town center.

Discover the history, character and charm of Old Towne & Historic Catlin Court Shopping Districts. More than 80 antique stores, specialty shops and unique eateries, all nestled together within a four-block radius. Parking is free and walking is easy and convenient.

Sample some of Glendale's spectacular events.

Glendale Glitters Holiday Light Display
Glendale Chocolate Affaire
Glendale Jazz Festival
Glendale's Celebration of
Art & Antiques

Venture to other Glendale attractions.

Tour Historic Sahuaro Ranch and Glendale Xeriscape Garden. Or hop on the free town trolley to Cerreta Candy Factory.

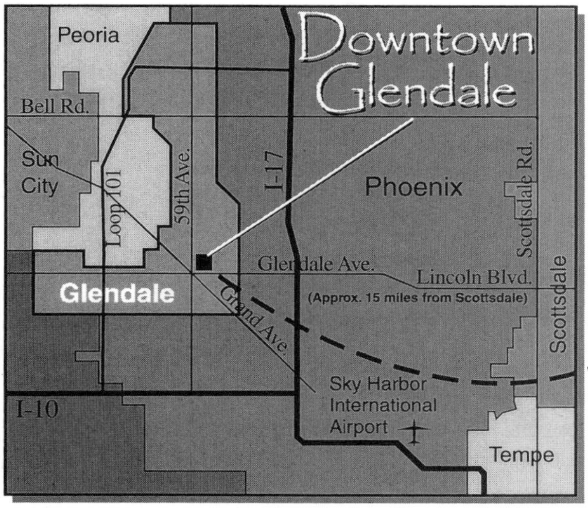

Call today to receive a FREE brochure and calendar of events, 602-930-2957.

www.arizonaguide.com/glendale

City of Glendale Tourism Division, 5850 W. Glendale Ave., Glendale, AZ 85301. FAX: 602-915-2696.

Arizona

1 BISBEE

Coming into mile-high Bisbee takes you back to the turn of the century. Situated in southeastern Arizona near the Mexican border, Bisbee gained prominence as a mining center in the late 19th century. Today Bisbee preserves this atmosphere by offering a variety of lifestyles set in a matrix of the West's once extensive copper kingdom.

As you walk amidst the solid, stately brick buildings downtown, you can feel the wealth generated by the city's copper mines that were founded to answer the call of the Age of Electricity. As you drive the narrow, twisting streets, or walk endless flights of stairs, you will marvel at the early residents' ingenuity in adapting their lives to the steeply sloping canyons.

Don't leave town without a visit to the Bisbee Mining and Historical Museum, where you will see firsthand why Bisbee, once "Queen of the Copper Camps," is now a thriving community that draws tourists from around the world to experience turn-of-the-century life in an urban center on the frontier. Then go underground on the guided Queen Mine Tour, through what was once a working copper mine, and talk to former miners as they explain life in the dark underground shafts.

The Bisbee Inn
45 OK Street
888/432-5131 or 520/432-5131
Alfred & Elissa Strati, Proprietors

Directions: For specific directions to The Bisbee Inn from your location, please call the Innkeepers.

Originally built in 1917 as a miner's hotel, today the Inn is a certified historic restoration containing 20 guest rooms, most with private baths, original oak and period furnishings, and a charming dining room serving complimentary country breakfasts. It is located in the downtown historic district in close proximity to Brewery Gulch and other Bisbee points of interest.

On Consignment In Bisbee
100 Lowell Traffic Cr.
520/432-4002
Open Tue.-Sat. 10:30-5:30 and 1st Sun. each month 12-5

Directions: Located 1/4 mile south of the Lavender Pit Mine on the Traffic Circle (the only building right on the circle).

Antiques and glass, tools, brass, vintage kitchenware, jewelry and lots of ??? On Consignment boasts of having something for every taste and budget. Once described as "The Attic of Cochise County", this 12,000 sq. ft. store is jam-packed with an amazing mix of old, new and the unusual. Strange things happen at On Consignment in Bisbee. A woman customer came in and recognized, high on the wall, a seascape painted by her husband's long-deceased great-aunt, who never left San Francisco. Like most of the great-aunt's paintings, it had been sold at a gallery. The family had only a few of her works and the woman was thrilled to find one for $25.

Bisbee Antiques & Collectibles
3 Main St.
520/432-4320

Pentimento
24 Main St.
520/432-2752

Johnson's Antiques & Books
45 Main St.
520/432-2736

Flying Saucers Antqs. & Cllbls.
26A Brewery Ave.
520/432-4858

Main Street Antiques
67 Main St.
520/432-4104

Second Love Antiques
21 Subway St.
520/432-5597

Good Goods
54 Brewery Gulch
520/432-2788

Acorn Gift Shoppe & Antiques
Hwy. 80, 1 Mile E. Of Tunnel
520/432-7314

Attractions

Bisbee Mining and Historical Museum
Located in downtown Historic Bisbee
Open 10-4, seven days, fee charged, senior discount
520/432-7071

Queen Mine Tours
Hwy. 80 interchange entering Old Bisbee
520/432-2071

Restaurants

Cafe Roka - contemporary Italian
(listed in "One Hundred Best Restaurants in Arizona")
35 Main Street
520/432-5153

2 CORNVILLE

Eight Ball Antiques
1050 S. Page Springs Rd.
520/634-1479
Open Wed.-Sun. 10-5, Mon. & Tue. by chance

Directions: Located 80 miles north of Phoenix or 45 miles south of Flagstaff. Take I-17 to McGuireville Exit #293. Travel west 9 miles on Cornville Road to Page Springs Road. Turn right on Page Springs Road. Go 1/4 mile, building is on left.

"If you build it, they will come" - a commonly heard phrase originally coined by several "claim to fame" baseball teams. I borrowed it because it is so appropriate for Eight Ball Antiques. Nestled away in the sleepy little community of Cornville, Jim and his wife, Kristin, have successfully attracted collectors of the unusual from all over the U.S. You will understand this curious following the minute you enter the 4,500 square-foot building filled to the rafters with oddities such as service station memorabilia, wagon wheels, large games, peddle toys, Lincoln Log building sets, old tools, primitives and lots more. If one of the antique cars offered for sale won't fit into your trunk, you can opt for a scaled-down version. Jim has quite an assortment of collectible cars from which to choose.

Not your traditional antique "stop," I figured Jim must have some "highly guarded" sources for acquiring such offerings.

He clarified my misconception by explaining that his forte for gathering this hodge-podge of gizmos and gadgets was a result of his 30 years of collecting. Looks like Jim and Kristin had one heck of a spring cleaning when they decided to open up shop!

3 COTTONWOOD

Colleen's Antiques Mall
720 N. Balboa St.
520/639-2032

Home Sweet Home
303 S. Main St.
520/634-3304

Old Town Antiques
712 N Main St.
520/634-5461

4 FLAGSTAFF

The Inn at 410 Bed & Breakfast
410 North Leroux Street
520/774-0088
Rates $110-155

Built at the turn of the century, this Craftsman house was the home of a wealthy banker, businessman and cattle rancher. Now it offers eight guest rooms with private baths filled with a blend of antiques and contemporary furnishings in a variety of styles, like the Southwest Room (Santa Fe decor), the Sunflower Fields Room (vibrant country motif), and the Dakota Room (rustic twig furniture and cowboy decor). Three rooms have fireplaces and two have whirlpool tubs. The rest of the inn is filled with stained glass and local antiques, and fresh home-baked cookies appear each afternoon!

Carriage House Antq. Mall
413 N. San Francisco St.
520/774-1337

Golden Memories
101 S. Milton Rd.
520/774-5915

Collection Connection
901 N. Beaver
520/779-2943

Incahoots
9 E. Aspen Ave.
520/773-9447

Mountain Christmas
14 N. San Francisco St.
520/774-4054

Old Highway Trading Post
698 E. Route 66
520/774-0035

Favorite Places To Eat

Cracker Barrel Old Country Store
I-40 & Lucky Ln., Exit 198
520/773-1524

5 GLENDALE

Directions: Downtown Glendale is located at 59th and Glendale Avenues, just 4 miles west of I-17. Take the Glendale Avenue exit and drive approximately 20 minutes from downtown Phoenix, 40 minutes from Scottsdale Road and Lincoln Drive, and 30 minutes from downtown Tempe.

Known as Arizona's "Antique Capital," historic Glendale offers more than 80 antique and specialty shops, plus unique eateries and tea rooms in the Historic

Downtown area.

See review this section for specific information.

The Apple Tree
5811 W. Glendale Avenue
602/435-8486
Mon.-Sat. 10-5, Sun. 11-4

Directions: (Phoenix Metro Area) From I-17, exit #205, Glendale Ave., go West 4 miles. From I-10, Exit #138. 59th Avenue, go North 5 miles to Glendale Avenue, turn right (East) on Glendale Ave. Shop is on South Side of Glendale Ave. Between 59th and 58th Avenues.

This 6,000-square-foot multi-dealer mall has just entered its 7th year showcasing quality antiques and collectibles from smalls to large furniture. There is truly something for everyone here - pottery, depression and fine glass, old toys, quilts, kitchenware, crockery, redware, vintage jewelry and much more. A large portion of the shop is devoted to some of the best early country pieces and primitives in the area. A must on all antiquing trips, The Apple Tree was voted "Favorite Antique Shop" in the NW Valley by readers of the *Arizona Republic* newspaper.

Shaboom's
5533 W. Glendale Ave.
602/842-8687

Adventures Thru Looking Glass
5609 W. Glendale Ave.
602/930-7884

Purple Elephant
5734 W. Glendale Ave.
602/931-1991

Nifties Antiques
5745 W. Glendale Ave.
602/930-8407

Ramblin Roads
5747 W. Glendale Ave.
602/931-5084

Lois Lovables Antiques
5748 W. Glendale Ave.
602/934-8846

Antique Arena
5825 W. Glendale Ave.
602/930-7121

Larry's Antiques
7120 N. 55th Dr.
602/435-1133

Strunk's Hollow
6960 N. 57th Dr.
602/842-2842

Old Mill Stream Antiques
7021 N. 57th Dr.
602/939-2545

Now Then & Always Inc.
7021 N. 57th Dr.
602/931-1116

Gatehouse Antiques
7023 N. 57th Dr.
602/435-1919

Antique Treasurers
7025 N. 57th Dr.
602/931-8049

Back to the Classic Antiques
7031 N. 57th Dr.
602/939-5537

Memories Past Antiques
7138 N. 57th Dr.
602/435-9592

Antique Emporium
6835 N. 58th Dr.
602/842-3557

Century House Antiques
6835 N. 58th Ave.
602/939-1883

Mr. Peabody's Antiques
6835 N. 58th Ave.
602/842-0003

Lamps by Shirley
6835 N. 58th Ave.
602/842-3306

Glendale Square Antiques
7009 N. 58th Ave.
602/435-9952

Grandma's House Antiques
7142 N. 58th Ave.
602/939-8874

Sandy's Dream Dolls
7154 N. 58th Ave.
602/931-1579

Hometown Antiques
5745 W. Palmaire Ave.
602/931-8790

Second Debut
5851 W. Palmaire Ave.
602/939-3922

ABD/Murphy Park Place
5809 W. Glendale Ave.
602/931-0235

Casa De Lao
5803 W. Glendale Ave.
602/937-9783

Cooper Street Antiques
5757 W. Glendale Ave.
602/939-7731

Shady Nook Books & Antiques
5751 W. Glendale Ave.
602/939-1462

House Of Gera
7025 N. 58th Ave.
602/842-4631

Arsenic & Old Lace
7157 N. 59th Ave.
602/842-9611

Remember That? Antiques
5807 W. Myrtle Avenue
602/435-1179

Antique Apparatus Exchange
5802 W. Palmaire Avenue
602/435-1522

Antique Etc.
5753 W. Glendale Ave.
602/939-2732

6 GOODYEAR

Favorite Places To Eat

Cracker Barrel Old Country Store
I-10 & Litchfield, Exit 128
602/856-5161

7 JEROME

Almost a mile high in the center of Arizona, the town of Jerome is a historic National Landmark. Once a roaring copper mining camp and a boom town of 15,000 people, Jerome was built on Cleopatra Hill above a vast deposit of copper. The mines, the workers and those who sought its wealth - miners and smelter workers, freighters and gamblers, bootleggers and saloon keepers, storekeepers and assorted Europeans, Latins and Asians, prostitutes and preachers, wives and children - all made Jerome, Arizona, what it was.

Prehistoric Native Americans were the first miners. The Spanish followed, seeking gold but finding copper. Anglos staked the first claims in the area in 1876, and United Verde Mining Operations began in 1883, followed by the Little Daisy chain. Americans, Mexicans, Croatians, Irish, Spaniards, Italians and Chinese added to the increasingly cosmopolitan mix that caused Jerome to grow rapidly from tent city to prosperous company town.

Billions of dollars of copper were extracted from the earth under Jerome. Changing times in the Arizona Territory saw pack burros, mule-drawn freight wagons and horses replaced by steam engines, autos and trucks. Fires ravaged the clapboard town again and again, but Jerome was always rebuilt.

In 1918, underground mining was phased out after uncontrollable fires erupted in the 88 miles of tunnels under the town. Open pit mining brought dynamiting. The hills rattled and buildings cracked. The earth's surface began to shift and sections of the business district slid downward. Jerome's notorious "sliding jail" moved 225 feet and now rests across the road from its original site.

Dependent on the ups and downs of copper prices, labor unrest, depressions and wars, Jerome's mines finally closed in 1953. After the mines closed and "King Copper" left town, the population went from a peak of 15,000 in the 1920s to some 50 hardy souls in the late 1950s. The 1960s and '70s were the time of the counter culture, and Jerome offered a haven for artists, who renovated homes and opened abandoned shops to sell their wares. Soon newcomers and a few remaining Jerome old-timers were working together to bring Jerome back to life.

Today, Jerome is very much alive with writers, artists, artisans, musicians, historians, and families. The town is chock-full of shops and galleries, and about 95% of all the town's remaining buildings date from 1895 to the 1920s.

Ghost City Inn Bed and Breakfast
541 North Main Street
520/63GHOST (520/634-4678)
Open all year, rates $75-95, full breakfast included

Built in 1898, the historically registered Ghost City Inn Bed & Breakfast offers a veranda view from each guest room that scans the Verde Valley and the terraced red rocks of Sedona - a view that some say challenges the views of the Grand Canyon in magnificence. All five guest rooms contain an artful blend of Victorian and early American. A full-service breakfast and afternoon tea are provided, as well as a turn-down service with chocolates, and assistance with recreational plans.

8 LAKE HAVASU CITY

Boulevard Mall
2137 McCulloch Blvd. N
520/855-7277

Country Memories
1850 McCulloch Blvd. N. -B3
520/680-0655

Pieces of Olde Antq. Shoppe
2018 McCulloch Blvd.
520/453-6533

9 MARANA

Favorite Places To Eat

Cracker Barrel Old Country Store
I-10 & Cortaro, Exit 246
520/579-1845

10 MESA

Carole & Maxine's Antiques
2353 E. Brown Road
602/964-6006
E-mail CAAUGUSTIN@aol.com
url address: http://www.quikpage.com/C/carole
Open Tue.-Sat. 11-5

Directions: Traveling Highway 60 east of Phoenix, take Gilbert Rd. exit north to Brown Rd. Turn east 1/2 mile on south side. Mesa is approximately 18 miles east of Phoenix. The shop is on E. Brown Road in Mesa.

Ms. Augustin has been importing 18th and 19th century pine furniture and accessories from the U.K. for 35 years. The shop and the Augustin home is located on historical property. The farmhouse dates back to 1918 and the antique shop is situated in the two-story barn in back. Ms. Augustin was originally in business with her mother, but today she runs this elegant, "with the feel of country," upscale shop herself. Her knowledge of fine quality antiques is evident in the selections she has displayed throughout the shop. Along with the pine furnishings you'll find a delightful array of flow blue, as well as other fine blue and white pieces, Victorian glass, a sampling of decorative accessories, and "hard to find" exceptional copper and brass items.

Antique Plaza
114 W. Main Street
602/833-4844
Open daily 10-5:30

Directions: From Superstition Freeway, take Country Club Rd.. north to Main Street. Turn right on Main Street. Antique Plaza is located on the left.

Offering an enormous variety of antiques and collectibles since 1988, Antique Plaza is housed in a fifty year old building in downtown Mesa. With 20,000 square feet and over 100 dealers, this mall is sure to provide plenty of bounty for antique treasure hunters.

Stewart's Military Antiques
108 W. Main St.
602/834-4004

Mini Antique Mall
46 W. Main Street
602/833-5355

Downtown Antiques
202 W. Main St.
602/833-4838

New Again Antiques
212 W. Main St.
602/834-6189

Glass Urn
456 W. Main St. #G
602/833-2702

Almost Anything
3015 E. Main St. #101
602/924-6260

Treasures From Past Antqs.
106 E. McKellips Rd.
602/655-0090

Beyond Expressions Antiques
3817 E. McKellips Rd.
602/854-7755

Mesa Antique Mart
1455 S. Stapley
602/813-1909

Pam's Place
1121 S. Country Club Dr.
602/827-9637

Ron & Soph Antiques
1060 W. Broadway
602/964-7437

Collectors Corner Antiques
919 E. Broadway Rear
602/969-0081

Interesting Side Trip

The Lost Dutchman

Located in the Superstition Mountains just outside of Mesa

There have been hundreds of reported claims to the Lost Dutchman treasure dating back as far as the 1870s. Perhaps the first recorded claim was made by The Dutchman, a man named Jacob Waltz who was actually of German descent. The gold is believed to be stashed away in the Superstition Mountains somewhere near the landmark known as Weaver's Needle. Additional clues published in the *Phoenix Gazette* during the late 1800s indicates that a lost cabin plays a significant part in the claim's location.

The question of whether this gold is, in fact, from a mine or the remains of some earlier expedition, is as much a mystery as the treasure itself. One of the many legends surrounding the Lost Dutchman indicates that in the 1840s a Mexican cartel unearthed the treasure from the mine. However, the miners were attacked by Apaches and never got out with the gold. Unaware of the importance of the yellow metal, the Indians ripped apart the sacks containing the gold, spreading it across the area.

If this story is true, then the Lost Dutchman isn't a mine at all. This would also mean Jacob Waltz wasn't digging; he was gathering the gold scattered by the Apaches. His claim was merely a cover for protection against other prospectors seeking the lavish bounty. According to Waltz, the same map used by the Mexican expedition led him and another German, Jacob Weiser, to discover the mine. Once again, their extraction of the gold was cut short by an Apache ambush similar to the one staged against the Mexicans in 1840. It is unclear whether Jacob Weiser survived, but Waltz made it out alive.

There is no indication that Waltz returned to collect his fortune prior to the earthquake on May 3, 1887. The gold, whether still in the mine or scattered on the ground, would have disappeared in the shifting of rock and earth. If, in fact, Waltz had located the Lost Dutchman, the identifiable landmarks which served as clues would have been dramatically altered by the quake.

Nevertheless, Jacob Waltz definitely knew something about this mysterious lost treasure - too much of his life was consumed by its existence. On his deathbed on October 25, 1891, Waltz spoke one last time about the infamous Lost Dutchman. He told his caretaker, Mrs. Julia Thomas, the story of the fabulous mine he had discovered in the Superstition Mountains.

Given all the information reported by Jacob Waltz and countless others who have followed in his footsteps, it seems somewhat reasonable to believe the Lost Dutchman, in whatever form, exists.

11 PAYSON

Glass Slipper Antiques
603 S. Beeline Hwy.
520/474-6672

Granny's Attic
800 E. State Hwy. 260
520/474-3962

Hopi House
102 S. Beeline Hwy.
520/474-4000

Payson Antique Mall
1001 S. Beeline Hwy.
520/474-8988

12 PEORIA

Favorite Places To Eat

Cracker Barrel Old Country Store
Loop 101 & Bell Road

13 PHOENIX

Antique Gems
2305 N. 7th Ave.
602/252-6288

Spine
1323 E. McDowell Rd.
602/252-4858

Vintage Classics
2301 N. 7th St.
602/252-7271

Consignment Gallery
330 E. Camelback Rd.
602/631-9630

Mussallem Fine Arts Inc.
5120 N. Central Ave.
602/277-5928

Xavier Square Antiques
4700 N. Central Ave.
602/248-8208

Alcuin Books
115 W. Camelback Rd.
602/279-3031

Antique Gallery
5037 N. Central Ave.
602/241-1174

Central Antique Gallery
36 E. Camelback Rd.
602/241-1636

Pink Flamingo Antiques
2241 N. 7th St.
602/261-7730

Arizona Hist. Cache Antqs.
5807 N. 7th St.
602/264-0629

Bobbi's Antiques
3838 N. 7th St.
602/264-1787

Empire Antiques
5003 N. 7th St.
602/240-2320

Second Hand Rose
1350 E. Indian School Rd.
602/266-5956

Central Outpost
9405 N. Central Ave.
602/997-2253

Antique Gatherings
3601 E. Indian School Rd.
602/956-8203

Sweet Annie Doodle's
5025 N. 7th St.
602/230-1058

Travel Thru Time
5115 N. 7th St.
602/274-0666

Nook & Kranny
4302 N. 7th Ave.
602/241-0228

Valley Toys & Collectibles
11725 N. 19th Ave.
602/678-5130

Antiquary
3044 N. 24th St.
602/955-8881

Do Wah Diddy
3642 E. Thomas Rd.
602/957-3874

Antique Outpost
10012 N. Cave Creek Rd.
602/943-9594

Ark Room Inc.
539 E. Glendale Ave.
602/266-7368

Nickelodeon
110 W. Seldon Ln.
602/943-3512

Scott D Gram Arts & Antiques
1837 W. Thunderbird Rd.
602/548-3498

Pzaz
2528 E. Camelback Rd.
602/956-4402

Antique Accents
2515 E. Bell Rd.
601/493-1956

Brass Armadillo
12419 N. 28th Drive
888/942-0030

Interesting Side Trips

The Heard Museum
22 East Monte Visa Road
One block east of Central Ave., and three blocks north of McDowell Rd.
602/252-8840 or 602/252-8848 (message)
Open (9:30-5 Mon.-Sat.) (9:30-8 Wed.) (noon-5 Sun.)
closed on major holidays
Admission charges

Since first opening its doors in 1929, the Heard Museum has earned an international reputation for its outstanding representation of the culture and heritage of Native Americans in the Southwest, plus its unique exhibits and innovative programming. It is internationally recognized for its collections of artifacts and art documenting the history of native cultures, especially Southwestern Native Americans. The Heard Museum was founded in 1929 by Dwight B. and Maie

Bartlett Heard, a prominent Phoenix couple who had moved to the Valley of the Sun in the mid-1880's from Chicago. The Heards were avid collectors of Native artifacts and art, especially those of Southwestern Native American cultures. The couple built the Heard Museum in order to share their collection. More than 250,000 people visit the Heard Museum each year - more than any other museum in Arizona. About 25,000 visitors are school children.

Located in central Phoenix, the Heard Museum is home to more than 35,000 objects, as well as an extensive 24,000-volume reference library. The variety of exhibits contain objects that run the gamut from 800 A.D. to pieces made in the 1990's. The Spanish Colonial Revival building was especially designed on Heard property to house their renowned family collection. Today, visitors can enjoy the Heard's seven exhibit galleries and grounds. Frequently, Native American artists demonstrate beadworking, weaving or carving. Visitors have an opportunity to talk with the artists as they work.

The Hall of Flame
6101 East Van Buren Street
Located near the Phoenix Zoo, east of Phoenix
602/275-3473
Open Mon-Sat, 9-5
Admission is charged

What's loud and red and ever so appropriately located in Phoenix, Arizona? It has helmets, uniforms, ladders, vehicles, and alarms and is the brainchild of the late Chicago industrialist George Getz, Jr. If you haven't Getzed already, Phoenix is the perfect spot for the Hall of Flame, the world's largest fire-fighting museum.

With over 130 restored vehicles dating from 1725 through 1961, the galleries cover almost an acre and have nearly everything relating to fire fighting. Memorabilia ranges from 19th-century parade carriages that look great on the Fourth of July, but are useless in fighting fires, to about 450 rare insurance company marks, a "hot" collectible; from lithographs, photographs, paintings, and drawings to leather hats and buckets from colonial times; and from "hands on" exhibits of a 1916 American La France engine and special safety displays devised for children, to a 1725 Newsham pumper, the first and oldest fire rig in the United States.

Designed to ignite understanding of America's most dangerous occupation, the museum re-creates the history of man's eternal war against conflagration. "In England, fire-fighting brigades were privately run by insurance companies," points out Dr.. Peter Molloy, the Hall of Flame's executive director and resident historian. "By the late 17th century, the companies began to post fire marks on homes."

In the colonies, volunteers often fought blazes by throwing water on buildings surrounding the one that had caught fire (it was usually already lost by the time the brigade arrived). One rather unimpressive-looking long pole utilized an attached hook to peel first the roof and then the walls from burning structures. "Back then, houses were made of wood and packed closely together, with shingled roofs and wooden or plaster chimneys." Teams of men patrolled the city at night, sounding a rotating wooden rattle similar to a New Year's noisemaker to alert the populace of a pending inferno. These are on display along with klaxons, Model T horns and other alarms, making this one museum where visitors don't have to worry about keeping quiet.

According to Molloy, fire-fighting men (and later women) are a pretty inflammatory bunch: "They're tough, aggressive and see their company as the best in the area. Before the onset of centralized battalions, ethnic-based gangs would often conduct turf wars over who should fight the fire." In order to collect insurance money, a brigade would send bullies to lay claim to the fireplug, giving rise to the expression "plug ugly."

Hence, each brigade tried to outdo the other in purchasing and flaunting glamorous but impractical equipment like the Hall of Flame's delicate, elaborate 1870 Hotchkiss parade vehicle, which is currently valued at about $100,000. "One of my favorite displays is a fancy 1909 gasoline-powered buggy used by a fire chief in Indiana," relates Molloy. "One day a youngster on a bicycle passed him on the way to a blaze." Shortly afterwards the chief purchased a Model T Ford.

Still, most of the items on display have seen honorable service and have been painstakingly refurbished. "We've tried to restore them to their original condition, sometimes even researching newspaper archives or contacting descendants of the original designer in our search for accuracy," comments Molloy. The hand pumps are particularly swell: in addition to the Newsham model, which required six firemen to operate the handles, and 1844 pumper used in Philadelphia necessitated a force of *50* to get enough pressure into an air chamber to shoot a stream of water 200 feet. "It was so arduous that teams had to rotate every few minutes."

Until his early 80's, when declining health forced him to quit, George Getz drove a 1930 Ahrens Fox in Phoenix's annual Fiesta Bowl Parade. With 8.5 tons of hose, pump, water tank, and ladders, the vehicle lacked power steering and reminded an often-forgetful populace of those who take the heat. The Hall of Flame continues to carry their torch.

Favorite Places To Eat

Cracker Barrel Old Country Store
I-17 & Deer Valley, Exit 215

14 PINE

Gingerbread House
Hwy. 87 & Randell Dr.
520/476-3504

Apple Annie's
Hardscrabble Rd.
520/476-4569

Old Settler's Trading Post
Hwy. 87
520/476-3500

Pineberry Antiques & Cllbls.
86 Hwy. 87
520/476-2219

15 PINETOP/LAKESIDE

Billings Country Pine Antiques
103 W. Yaeger Ln.
520/367-1709

White Mountain Antiques
1691 W. White Mt. Blvd.
520/368-6266

Pinecrest Lane Antiques
50 E. Pinecrest Ln.
520/367-0943

16 PRESCOTT

Historic Prescott, established in 1864, is one of the oldest communities in Arizona. Located nearly a mile high on a pine-covered basin at the base of the Bradshaw Mountains, Prescott was the only United States territorial capital founded in a wilderness. It was spawned from gold fever after mountain man Joseph Reddeford Walker led the first prospectors to the site in 1863. What began as a ramshackle mining camp grew into the central Arizona territory's hub for trading and freighting. Miners, ranchers and cowboys found solace in the gambling halls and saloons that soon peppered the city's streets.

Prescott's first courthouse was built in 1867; its first hanging occurred in 1875 (the doomed man's innocence was proven 60 years later). Twice named territorial capital, it lost the honor first to Tucson in 1867, and finally to Phoenix in 1889. A devastating fire in 1900 all but leveled downtown, razing homes, hotels and businesses along the streets of Gurley, Montezuma and North Cortez. Undaunted, the citizens of Prescott rebuilt their lost structures in much finer fashion than those that had stood before.

Traces of Prescott's earlier days abound throughout the downtown area, from saloons boasting hand-carved mahogany bars to historic hotels, from the Hassayampa Inn to Sharlot Hall Museum. Take a turn up North Cortez, where an entire row of antique emporiums offer collections ranging from the distinctive to the whimsical. Step off the beaten path and you may discover that singular treasure of your dreams tucked inside one of the Alley shops.

The depths of downtown Prescott's commitment to the cultural arts was firmly established with the laying of the cornerstone of the Elks Opera House April 4, 1904. This Grand Lady of Gurley Street has graciously hosted live performances for more than 90 years, echoing with the footfalls of famous vaudeville troupes, distinguished actors from the Royal Shakespeare Company, and Broadway stars. On Gurley Street, the Sharlot Hall Museum opens the door on the color and excitement of the Arizona Territory. The museum bears the name of the first woman to hold public office in Arizona (1909), a local poet and historian whose life was an adventure in itself. Resting gracefully on three acres, Sharlot Hall Museum's historic buildings house a fascinating collection of artifacts which help bridge the span of time between Prescott's modern life and that of the past.

Mount Vernon Inn
204 North Mount Vernon Avenue
520-778-0886
Rates $90-120

Built in 1900, the Mount Vernon Inn is nestled among shade trees in the center of the Mount Vernon Historical District, Arizona's largest Victorian neighborhood. The grand house, with its candle snuffer turret, gables, pediments and Greek Revival porch, proudly recalls a time when imagination and frontier self-confidence expressed itself in an architecture best described as whimsical.

Each main house guest room has a private, bath and all are tastefully decorated and furnished with period furniture. The guest cottages (originally the carriage and tack houses) and the studio house are separate from the main house. Completely private, cottage guests can prepare breakfast in the convenient kitchen or stroll to any of the wonderful restaurants within easy walking distance. All guests are invited to use the main house parlor and sitting room.

Book Nook
324 W. Gurley St.
520/778-2130

Collector's Mart
133 N. Cortez
520/776-7969

Lil Bit O'Everything
103 N. Cortez
520/445-6237

Emporium on Cortez
107 N. Cortez
520/778-3091

Prescott Antiques & Crafts
115 N. Cortez St.
520/445-7156

Pennington's Antiques
117 N. Cortez St.
520/445-3748

131 North Cortez Antiques
131 N. Cortez St.
520/445-6992

Deja Vu
134 N. Cortez St.
520/445-6732

Merchandise Mart
205 N. Cortez
520/776-1728

Arizona Territory Antiques
211 W. Aubrey St.
520/445-4656

Young's Antiques & Collectibles
115 W. Willis St.
520/717-1526

17 SCOTTSDALE

The Song of the Balladeer

Back in the 1880s Chaplain Winfield Scott heard the siren song of the unexplored. The irresistible melody, which had already lured thousands to the California gold mines, called him to travel. Gazing at a vast stretch of undeveloped country, Scott proclaimed it "unequaled in greater fertility or richer promise." What would soon become an agricultural community, christened Scottsdale, recorded its first official historic moment.

That strong tie to a frontier past still exerts itself, with great charm and persistence, in modern Scottsdale. Cowboys, horses, a reverence for the land, and a respect for Western tradition are very much a part of the contemporary scene. Visitors come here today, as they did years ago, to explore the possibilities.

So what's the most direct way to experience the Old West? A guided horseback ride or jeep tour over desert trails, the snug fit of your cowboy hat's brim, the drowsy warmth of the sun, or the brilliant streaks of vermilion reddening the Western horizon, evoke a deeply nostalgic response. A mesquite campfire carrying the aroma of sizzling steaks, and the lonesome melodies of a cowboy balladeer will beckon you back in time and in spirit.

The ultimate immersion in life on the trail, however, is the dude ranch. Straying from authenticity just enough to keep guests happy, the ranch experience embraces the rowdy fun of haywagon rides, songfests, cookouts, trap and skeet shooting and of course, daily horseback excursions.

Most unusual, though, may be an overnight pack trip in the nearby Superstition Mountains. Here you can pan for gold and search like thousands of wild-eyed prospectors before you, for the legendary Lost Dutchman's Mine. (See #2 Mesa for more information on the Lost Dutchman's Mine.)

Scottsdale's truest, proudest passion, however, is reserved for the arts. This glorious environment inspired master architects Frank Lloyd Wright, Paolo Soleri and Bennie Gonzales, whose studios and works have helped to create the aesthetic appeal of the city.

With more than 120 galleries, studios and museums, Scottsdale shines as an internationally known art center. You'll want to plan an evening around the Scottsdale Art Walk held in downtown Scottsdale every Thursday night, year-round. The galleries stay open late, serve refreshments, and encourage you to meet their guests - artists, art critics, writers, musicians, dancers, and performers of all types.

Antiques Super-Mall
(formerly Arizona Antique Gallery)
1900 N. Scottsdale Road
602/874-2900
Open Mon.-Sun. 10-6, Thurs. 10-8

Antique Centre
2012 N. Scottsdale Rd.
602/675-9500

Antique Trove
2020 N. Scottsdale Rd.
602/947-6074

For more specific information, see full page this section.

The Phoenician Resort
6000 East Camelback Road
602/941-8200
800-888-8234 (U.S. and Canada)
(a property of the ITT Sheraton Luxury Collection)

An all-encompassing, international luxury resort harmoniously covering 250 acres at the base of Camelback Mountain. The Phoenician has only been in operation eight years, yet has garnered every possible award in all categories offered by national and international ratings surveys. An elegant vacation retreat, it offers an unparalleled combination of luxury accommodations, appointments, amenities and service.

Brown House Antiques
7001 E. Main St. #4
602/423-0293

Carriage Trade Antiques Inc.
7077 E. Main St.
602/970-6700

J. H. Armer Co
6926 E. Main St.
602/947-2407

J. Scott Antiques
7001 E. Main St.
602/941-9260

Gray Goose Antiques
7001 E. Main St.
602/423-5735

Richard II Antiques
7004 Main St.
602/990-2320

Rose Tree Antiques
7013 E. Main St.
602/949-1031

Irontiques
7077 E. Main St. #4
602/947-9679

Crystal Crown Antiques
7077 E. Main St.
602/994-5034

Collectors' Finds Antiques Inc.
7077 E. Main St.
602/946-9262

Christopher's Galleries
7056 E. Main St.
602/941-5501

Circa Galleries
7056 E. Main St.
602/990-1121

Music Box Shop Inc.
7236 E. 1st Ave.
602/945-0428

Mollard's
7127 E. 6th Ave.
602/947-2203

Bradbury's Antique Bazaar
6166 B Scottsdale Rd. #603
602/998-1885

Gallery 10 Inc.
34505 N. Scottsdale Rd.
602/945-3385

Pewter & Wood Antiques
10636 N. 71st Way
602/948-2060

Rustique Collections
23417 N. Pima Rd. Ste. 165
602/473-7000

Impeccable Pig
7042 E. Indian School Rd.
602/941-1141

John C. Hill Antique Indian Art
6962 E. 1st Avenue
602/946-2910

Ye Olde English Antiques Co.
6522 E. Mescal Street
No Phone # Available

18 SEDONA

Greentree Stocks
2756 W. Hwy. 89A
520/282-6547

Claire's Sweet Antiques
Basha's Center
520/204-1340

Compass Rose Gallery
671 State Route 179
520/282-7904

Hollywood Collectibles
30 Adante Dr.
520/204-1965

Claire's Sweet Antiques
251 Highway 179
520/204-1340

19 TOMBSTONE

How Tombstone Came To Be

Tombstone, Arizona, is one of the most recognizable names in American history. About 70 miles southeast of Tucson and 30 miles from the Mexican border in southeastern Arizona, Tombstone is one of the most famous of the silver boomtowns of the Old West. But it was actually named in ironic humor of a man's impending death!

With a prospector's outfit and $30, Edward Schieffelin headed for Apache country, east of Fort Huachuca, Arizona, to look for silver. When soldiers at the fort heard of his folly, they laughed and told him all he would find in those hills would be his tombstone...meaning that the Indians would surely get him. In late August, 1877, Schieffelin made his first of many silver strikes and named his rich vein "The Tombstone." He realized around $1 million from his claims in the early 1880s, and soon the town of Tombstone arose, the mightiest city between El Paso and San Francisco. Some reports go as far as to state that the population in the 1880's reached nearly 15,000 - larger than Los Angeles or San Francisco at the time! But the silver mines closed in 1889 and the population disappeared. Today about 1,600 people live in Tombstone, but hundreds of thousands of tourists visit each year.

On May 14, 1896, Schieffelin died in Oregon. In accordance with his wishes, he was buried in Tombstone, covered by a monument three miles west of town. On this monument is a marker inscribed, "This is my Tombstone."

Interesting Side Trips

The Bird Cage Theatre

Downtown Tombstone, Arizona
Admission charged

The last of a bygone era of western history, the Bird Cage was the most famous honky-tonk in America between 1881 and 1889. The *New York Times* referred to it in 1882 as the wildest, wickedest night spot between Basin Street and the Barbary Coast! Tombstone was in its prime mining boom during the 1880s. At the same time, the Bird Cage was making a reputation for the town that would never be forgotten. In nine years this lusty den of iniquity never closed its doors 24 hours a day. Before its operation would end in 1898, it would be the sight of 16 gunfights. The 140 bullet holes that riddle the walls and the ceilings are mute evidence of these happenings.

The Bird Cage was named for the 14 bird cage crib compartments that are self-suspended from the ceiling overhanging the gambling casino and dance hall. It was in these compartments that the prostitutes (or ladies of the night, as they were called) plied their trade. The refrain from the song, *"She's Only A Bird In A Gilded Cage"* became one of the nation's most popular songs. These bird cages remain today with their original red velvet drapes and trimmings.

The entertainment on stage at the Bird Cage ranged from its nightly French circuit cancan dancers to risque performances for the male gender, to national headliners such as Eddie Foy, Lotta Crabtree and a host of others. The ladies of the town, and there were some, never entered the Bird Cage - or, for that matter, even walked on the same side of the street. The hand painted stage with its original curtain, retains its faded luster today, as in 1881.

Directly below the stage are the wine cellar, the dressing rooms and the poker room. Here the longest poker game in western history occurred. It was a house game and players had to buy a $1,000 minimum in chips for a seat in the game.The game ran continually for eight years, five months and three days! Today that poker table still stands as it was left, with its chairs on the dirt floor. Some of the most famous characters of western history came to the Bird Cage to gamble, drink and be entertained by its lovely ladies.

Wyatt Earp met his third wife, Sadie Marcus, at the Bird Cage. Red-coated bartenders poured nothing but Tombstone's best at a custom-made cherrywood bar and back bar. The bar is flanked by a dumb-waiter that sent drinks upstairs to the ladies of the night and their men friends. Today it exists as Tombstone's only remaining bar of the 1880s in its original building.

When you look into the original French mirror of the back bar, you see the famous bar painting of Fatima, who has been hanging in the same location since 1882. She carries the scars of six bullet holes and stands nine feet high. When disaster struck Tombstone by the folding of the mines, the Bird Cage was sealed and boarded up with all its fixtures and furnishings intact. For almost 50 years it stood closed, its contents touched only by the passing of time. In 1934 the Bird Cage Theatre became a historic landmark of the American West, when it was opened for the public to visit. The Bird Cage stands today as an adolescent old maid in her infancy for all to see and to feel the nostalgia of the past. It is Tombstone's only historic landmark in its original state, preserved from its beginning in 1881, maintaining its lighting fixtures, chandeliers, drapes and gambling tables on the casino floor. Its massive grand piano is still in the orchestra pit. The coin operated juke box still plays today as in 1881. You also see Tombstone's most valuable individual antique - The Black Moriah. This original Boothill hearse is trimmed in 24K gold and sterling silver.

A big draw today for the Bird Cage is its ghosts - dozens, maybe even hundreds of them-that manifest themselves on a daily basis to just about everyone who comes to town. It seems that the paranormal is the "normal" order of modern Tombstone, complete with sights, sounds, smells, ghostly appearances, and objects that mysteriously and inexplicably appear and disappear. Bill Hunley (whose family built, owned and operated the Bird Cage), his family and friends, plus hundreds of tourists, have all documented these strange but (to Tombstone residents) normal occurrences. So have numerous parapsychologists, psychics and professional photographers. Some years ago, Duke University even sent a team of parapsychologists to conduct research at the Bird Cage where they counted 27 spirits and even took their photographs! So when people say that the past comes back to haunt us, they mean it literally in Tombstone!

20 TUCSON

American West Primitive Art
363 S. Meyer Ave.
520/623-4091

Antiques & Indian Art
27 S. 5th Ave.
520/791-9091

Fronas
312 E. Congress
520/798-1624

Saguard Moon Antiques Co-op
45 S. 6th Ave.
520/623-5393

Booked Up
2828 N. Stone Ave.
520/622-8238

Hammerblow Mining Museum
1340 W. Glenn St.
520/882-7073

Treasure Shop
24 E. 15th St.
520/622-5070

Firehouse Antiques Center
6522 E. 22nd St.
520/571-1775

A Treasure Chest
4041 E. Grant
520/327-9001

Christine's Curiosity Shop
4940 E. Speedway Blvd
520/323-0018

Eisenhut Antiques
2229 N. Country Club Road
520/327-9382

Antique Center of Tucson
5000 E. Speedway Blvd.
520/323-0319

Medicine Man Gallery
7000 E. Tanque Verde Rd.
520/722-7798

Antique Mall
3130 E. Grant Rd.
520/326-3070

Antique Mini-Mall
3408 E. Grant Rd.
520/326-6502

Arizona Mall
3728 E. Grant Rd.
520/770-9840

Cat House Collectibles
2924 E. Broadway Blvd.
520/795-2181

Country Trading Post
2811 N. Country Club Rd.
520/325-7326

Primitive Arts Gallery
3026 E. Broadway Blvd
520/326-4852

Sunland Antiques Inc.
2208 N. Country Club Rd.
520/323-1134

Phyliss' Antiques
1918 E. Prince Rd.
520/326-5712

Antique Presidio
3024 E. Grant
520/323-1844

21 WICKENBURG

Head-West Barber Shop and Antique Shop

605 W. Wickenburg Way (Highway 60)
520/684-3439
Open 9-5 daily, closed Wed.

Directions: Travel west 3/4 of a mile from downtown Wickenburg's one and only traffic light, on the left side of 60 West (which is also West Wickenburg Way), next to The Sizzling Wok.

When have you had the opportunity to shop for antiques and get an old-fashioned barber shop hair cut all in one stop? This unusual concept is the brainchild of the Burketts, who own and operate Head-West. Now, I haven't actually seen the place, but George, the owner, tells me the shop is complete with an old-fashioned barber pole. The Burketts opened the barber shop 12 years ago and added antiques in 1993. They carry great western pieces like an old cowboy bathtub, spurs, etc., plus a selection of Hummels, Royal Doulton, quality glassware, antique dolls and butter churns, antique furniture and much, much more.

Arizona

An Antique Store
272 E. Wickenburg Way
520/684-3357

Antique Village
280 E. Wickenburg Way
520/684-5497

22 YUMA

Packrat's Den
1360 S.. 3rd. Ave.
520/783-4071

Ron & Dean's Emporium
261 S. Main St.
520/782-1933

Bargain Spot
385 S. Main St.
520/783-5889

Britain's Antiques
4330 W. Riverside Dr.
520/783-4212

Favorite Places To Eat

Cracker Barrel Old Country Store
I-8 & Highway 95, Exit 297
520/343-1988

Notes

Arkansas

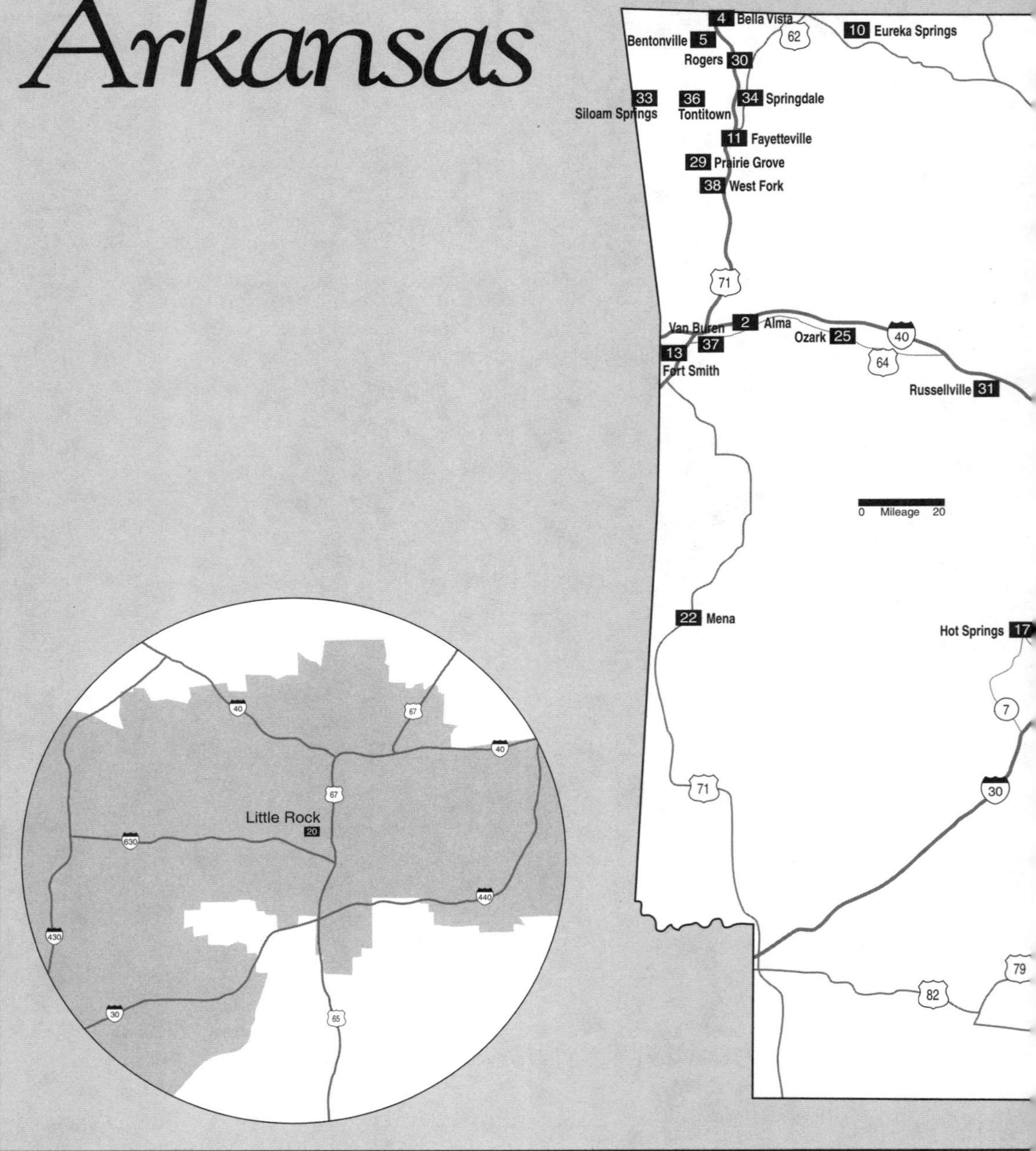

4 Bella Vista
62
10 Eureka Springs
Bentonville 5
Rogers 30
33 Siloam Springs
36 Tontitown
34 Springdale
11 Fayetteville
29 Prairie Grove
38 West Fork
71
Van Buren 37
2 Alma
Ozark 25
40
64
13 Fort Smith
Russellville 31
0 Mileage 20
22 Mena
Hot Springs 17
7
71
30
79
82
40
67
40
67
Little Rock 20
630
440
430
30
65

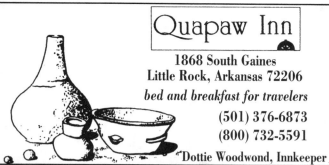

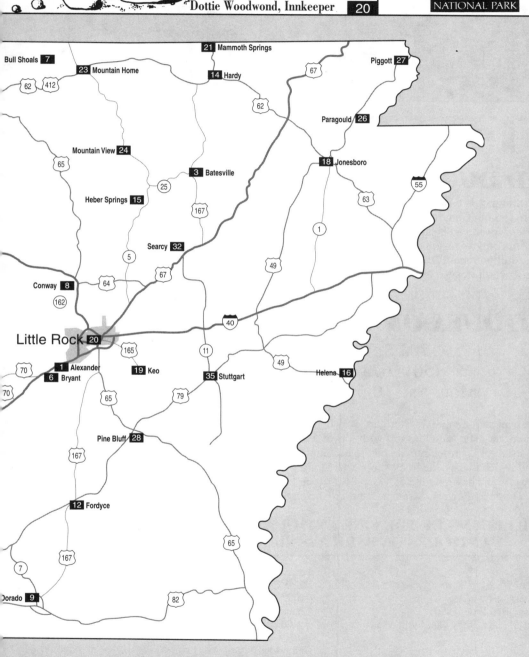

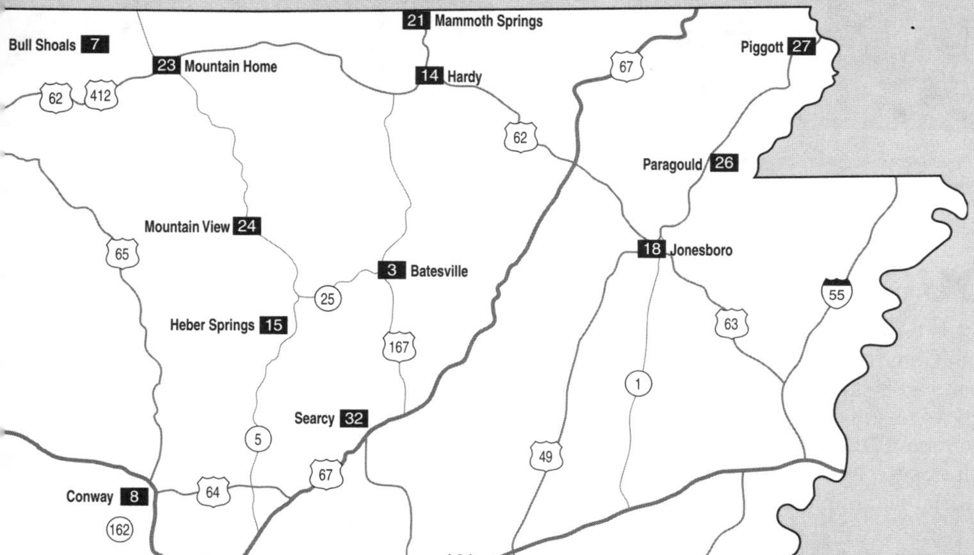

Bull Shoals 7
23 Mountain Home
21 Mammoth Springs
14 Hardy
Piggott 27
Paragould 26
Mountain View 24
3 Batesville
18 Jonesboro
Heber Springs 15
Searcy 32
Conway 8
Little Rock 20
1 Alexander
6 Bryant
19 Keo
35 Stuttgart
Helena 16
Pine Bluff 28
12 Fordyce
Dorado 9
62
412
67
62
65
25
167
55
63
1
5
49
67
64
162
40
165
11
49
70
70
65
79
167
65
167
7
82

STUTTGART

RICE AND DUCK CAPITAL OF THE WORLD

Although not a large city, the town of Stuttgart is bustling with activity. Probably best noted, by those living outside of town, as the home of the World's Championship Duck Calling Contest, Stuttgart has other attractions as well. The Agricultural Museum provides its visitors with an understanding of the history of the tools and methods of farming, as well as a glimpse of the life style of days gone by, after all Stuttgart is the Rice Capital. A recent expansion documents the agricultural and transportation equipment that was used by local farmers in the past, and another addition records the history of duck hunting in the area. Stuttgart boasts an Art Center which provides year-round exhibits and related activities such as classes. The duck calling contests draw visitors to the area several times a year, but Stuttgart also has a nationally-acclaimed miniature art show with representatives from more than a dozen states.

ANTIQUES ON PARK AVENUE

1703 S. Timber
(501) 673-1179
Mon.-Sat. 10-5; Sun. 1-5

Earleen and Dwight were the first to open an antique mall in Stuttgart, which grew out of Earleen's love for collecting old things. After she had furnished two old homes with antiques, she found herself with lots of wonderful things, but nowhere to put them. That's when she convinced Dwight to renovate a portion of his truck repair shop to accommodate an antique mall. The entrance to the two-story shop is around and behind the building which houses the truck shop. She, along with several other dealers, carries a general line of antiques, but includes the unusual as well. The day I visited the shop I was delighted to find a stunning Victorian Renaissance baby cradle and a very different, hand-crocheted bedspread.

A PARTIAL LISTING OF THE FINE ANTIQUES OFFERED AT ANTIQUES ON PARK AVENUE

Price Guides
Furniture (Including Barley Twist Chair W/Needlepoint Upholstery
King Size Hand Carved Mahogany Bed From 1890s
Lamps (Including Cordey, Horn, Aladdin, Ruby Cut, Etc.)
Carnival Glass
Depression Glass
Milk Glass
Blue Chrysanthemum Sprig Custard
Hand Painted China
Old Blown Christmas Ornaments
Green Stoneware Corn Pitcher
Neck Tie Boxes and Hankie Boxes
Books
Costume Jewelry
Primitives
Postcards
Large Oak Art Nouveau Mantle Of Stickley Style
Chairs
Art Glass
Pattern Glass
Cambridge
Bisque
Green Blown Champagnes W/Enamel
Staffordshire Lady Flower Vase
43 Pc. Villeroy & Boch "Holly" China
Flemish Art & Burnt Wood Boxes
Charming Old Framed Prints
Rugs
Pottery
Old Lg. Handmade Copper Hanging Pot

Special invitation to dealers. To assist with your travels, we offer after hours showing: Call the mall at (870) 673-1159 during open hours, or call Dan at (870) 673-1364 or Hotsey at (870) 673-6640 after 5 P.M.

Arkansas

1 ALEXANDER

Blackwell Antiques
23650 I-30
501/847-2191

Partain's Antique Mall
25014 I-30
501/847-4978

Wornock's Antiques
12590 I-30
501/847-8222

2 ALMA

"The" Flea Market
1727 Highway 71 N
501/632-2551

Sisters 2 Too Antique Mall
702 Highway 71 N
501/632-2292

Neva's Collectibles
Highway 71 North
501/632-5450

Favorite Places To Eat

Cracker Barrel Old Country Store
I-40 & State Rd. 71, Exit 13
501/632-0767

3 BATESVILLE

AARON's Antiques
1382 Bates St.
870/793-7233

Back In Time Antiques
217 E. Main St.
870/793-6445

Diamann's Antiques
4401 Heber Springs Rd.
870/251-9151

Ramsey Mt. Treasures
553 Batesville Blvd.
870/793-5714

Patterson Antique Shop
535 White Dr.
870/793-1139

Carousel Antiques
2080 Harrison Street
870/612-5555

4 BELLA VISTA

The Bella Vista Flea Market
130 The Plaza - Hwy. 71
501/855-6999

Treasures at Wishing Springs
Wishing Springs Road
501/271-1991

Steven Whysel, L.L.C.
3403 Bella Vista Highway (Hwy. 71)
501/855-9600

5 BENTONVILLE

Sunshine Glassworks & Antqs.
206 Hwy. 72 East
501/273-9218

Then & Now Home Furnishings
610 SW "A"
501/273-7551

6 BRYANT

Saugey's Antiques
@ Galarena Antique Mall
22430 I-30-Exit 123
501/847-6173

The Black Horse
@Collectors Market
501/847-6899

Ann Greer Collectibles
@ Finders Keepers Antique Mkt.
23650 I-30
501/847-4647

Days Gone By
23650 I-30
501/847-4647

Favorite Places To Eat

Cracker Barrel Old Country Store
I-30 & State Route 183, Exit 123
501/847-7878

7 BULL SHOALS

Interesting Side Trip

Bull Shoals Caverns and Mountain Village 1890
Located just off Highway 178 in Bull Shoals
501/445-7177 or 1-800-445-7177

In north central Arkansas you can see what life was like for turn-of-the-century settlers back to prehistoric man. Mountain Village 1890 is an authentically restored Ozark town that was retrieved from neglect and decay and completely resurrected as a living tribute to a hardy, resourceful and gentle people – the Ozark mountain folk. See life as it was over 100 years ago, then move to Bull Shoals Caverns, and visualize how prehistoric man, then indigenous Native Americans, and finally Ozark mountaineers lived in some of the world's oldest caverns. You'll see natural formations, an underground stream, underground rivers, a miniature lake and an underground waterfall, while learning how the caverns were formed.

8 CONWAY

Antiques In The Red Barn
IH-40 at Hwy. 64
501/329-9608

Antiques-Antiques of Conway
713 Oak St.
501/327-2185

Carmen's Antiques
1017 Van Ronkle St.
501/327-6978

Bobbie's Antiques
1015 Oak St.
501/327-7125

Honey Hole Antiques
382 Hwy. 65 N
501/336-4046

Quattlebaum Antiques
1010 Van Ronkle St.
501/329-8671

Sybella's
286 Hwy. 65 N
501/329-8847

Treasure Hunt
5 D Gapview Road
501/329-6007

Conway Antique Mall
925 Oak Street
501/450-3909

Favorite Places To Eat

Cracker Barrel Old Country Store
I-40 & U.S. 65, Exit 125
501/327-6107

9 EL DORADO

Peggy's Hobby House
2908 Oak Ln.
501/863-9553

Gene's Junktiques
825 W. Elm St.
501/862-7068

Marian's Downstairs Attic
301 S. Madison Ave.
501/862-9580

Main St. Antique Mall
209 E. Main St.
501/862-0028

Blewster's
1603 W. Hillsboro St.
16 Eureka Springs

Friendship District
800 E. Spring St.
501/863-3913

Blann's
320 W. Main
501/863-9302

Attic Treasures
520 N. Jackson
501/862-6331

10 EUREKA SPRINGS

The Victorian era of the late 1800s and the Ozark Mountains in northern Arkansas have combined to create a beautifully unique town that has the distinction of having its entire downtown shopping district and residential area listed on the National Register of Historic Places. In Eureka Springs not only will you find hundreds of Victorian buildings, but there are narrow, winding mountain streets and lovely limestone walls built from Arkansas stone. Streets are sometimes hundreds of feet higher or lower than adjacent streets, and no streets cross at right angles. The town grew from belief in the legendary healing powers of its spring waters, as thousands of people traveled to the springs for their health. Today Eureka Springs is a world-famous Victorian resort town of native limestone buildings, gingerbread houses, shaded trails, springs and gazebos. The best way to explore this fascinating town is by trolley and on foot. Six trolley routes service most of the town's lodgings, each designated by a color displayed on a sign in the front window. Just west of town on U.S. 62 W. are two particularly fascinating attractions: the exquisitely beautiful Thorncrown Chapel, an architectural masterpiece, and the 33-acre Eureka Springs Botanical Gardens. Eureka Springs is also home to the nationally famous Passion Play, a spectacular outdoor drama depicting the life, death and resurrection of Christ. And from its roots as an artists' colony in the 1930s and 40s, the town is now one of the most respected fine arts centers for the Mid-South. The Eureka Springs and North Arkansas Railway offers a four-mile excursion (departing hourly) through the Ozarks. A more leisurely tour of the mountains is available by cruise boat on the scenic Beaver Lake.

Crescent Cottage Inn
211 Spring Street
501/253-6022
www.eureka-usa.com/crescott
$93-130, includes breakfast

Directions: For specific directions to Crescent Cottage Inn, please call the Innkeeper.

Built in 1881 for Powell Clayton, the first governor of Arkansas after the civil war, Crescent Cottage Inn is a famous historic landmark. This "Painted Lady" with three stories, turned posts, spindelwork on front and back porches, a tower capped by a pointed hipped roof, curved topped tall windows, cut-out gable decorations and sunbursts is located at the residential beginning of the historic loop known in Governor Claytons day as the "Silk Stocking District." It is the most historic and photographed house in town and appears in the famous book American Painted Ladies. Its photograph also graces the pages of Victorian Express.

The house and guest rooms are filled with European antiques dating from 1770 to 1925. The living and dining rooms are separated by a great arch (the only one remaining by the English architect Bouell) and offers high coffered ceilings. A hand-pressed flower chandelier from 1882 hangs in the living room. There are four guest rooms, all with private baths, Jacuzzis, queen size beds, TV, VCR and telephones.

Two of the guest rooms, Miss Adaline's Room and Charlotte's Room have double Jacuzzi spas, refrigerators and beautiful fireplaces along with unique hand-painted ceilings. The doors of the rooms open onto a porch with swings for enjoying the panoramic view while providing access to the lovely English gardens complete with a waterfall. The Sun Room, named from its origin as a sun porch, includes a Jacuzzi as well as for the Cranberry Suite with a sitting room and hand-painted ceilings. All guest rooms along with the two back verandas overlook a rare, largely unobstructed view of a valley and totally forested mountain range. Complimentary soft drinks are available for all guests.

A great full breakfast is served on the upper porch when possible (usually April through October), or in the dining room. Fresh local fruits, berries and melons, baked bananas, Belgian waffles, salsa souffle, oven baked puff pancakes, smoke ham, bacon, sausages, juices, rich coffees, teas and hot chocolates are a part of the menu offered at the inn.

Crescent Cottage Inn is a short walk to historic downtown attractions. A trolley stop is located across the street from the inn for those of you who prefer to tour the city by trolley. The area is known for two large lakes offering great swimming, boating and fishing, hiking trails, summer opera, art galleries, shops, restaurants, folk art and craft fairs and is home to The Great Passion Play. The town swells with tourist in the fall, mainly October, for a glimpse of the beautifully colored leaves and again in spring for the wild flowering dogwood and redbud trees.

The inn, featured in such publications as *Country Living, Southern Living, Country Inns* and numerous newspapers throughout the U.S., has a three-diamond AAA rating, is Mobile quality rated and is also a member of and inspected by The Association of B&Bs of Arkansas. For more information on Crescent Cottage Inn, visit their website at the above address and/or call for a color brochure.

Old Sale Barn Antiques
Hwy. 23 S. & 62 E
501/253-5388

Eureka Emporium
Hwy. 187
501/253-9346

Garrett's Antique Print
125 Spring St.
501/253-9481

Main St. Traders Gallery
35 N. Main St.
501/253-6159

Melinda's Memories
49 Kingshighway
501/253-7023

Memories Past Antiques
Highway 62 E.
501/253-5747

Victorian Sampler
33 Prospect
501/253-8374

Pump & Circumstance
77 Mountain St.
501/253-6644

Forgotten Treasures Antique
53 B Spring St.
501/253-9989

Crystal Gardens Antiques
190 Spring St.
501/253-9586

Country Antiques
Stadium Rd.
501/253-8731

Uncle Shelby's Gntlmen's Antqs.
127 1/2 Spring St.
501/253-9883

Springs Antiques
6 S. Main St.
501/253-6025

Jack's Antiques
R 1 Box 66 Hwy. 235
501/423-3725

Bustopher Jones Antiques
#5 Van Buren Hwy 62 E
501/253-6946

Yesteryears Antique Mall
Highway 62 East
501/253-5100

11 FAYETTEVILLE

Calico Counter
601 W. 6th St.
501/443-0155

Dickson Street Bookshop
325 W. Dickson St.
501/442-8182

Gift House
525 Mission Blvd.
501/521-4334

Long Ago Antiques
1934 Huntsville Rd.
501/443-3435

Long Ago Antiques
102 N. School Ave.
501/521-3459

Heritage House Antiques
351 N. Highland Ave.
501/582-5653

Sara Kathryn's
600 Mission Blvd.
501/444-9991

All My Treasures Flea Market
2932 E. Huntsville Rd. (Hwy. 16 E)
501/575-0250

Meadow Street Marketplace
22 East Meadow Street
501/521-3181

Feather Your Nest
17 N. Block
501/443-3355

Home Place
701 North Street
501/443-4444

Miss Phydella's Art & Antique
434 N. College
501/587-1207

Footprints
4294 W. 6th
501/267-3951

12 FORDYCE

From a Civil War battleground and cemetery and vintage trains to antiques, Paul "Bear" Bryant, and a bakeshop/deli of national renown, Fordyce, Ark., is an intriguing little town in southern Arkansas. Although its present claim to fame is a vast pine forest, resources for Georgia-Pacific Industries, Fordyce has preserved a good portion of its colorful past.The town was named after Civil War Colonel Samuel Fordyce, who later built the Fordyce Bath House in Hot Springs. Even the first direct-dial long distance telephone call in the U.S. was made from Allied Telephone Company in Fordyce in 1960! There's a large historic district and a great many antique shops. The Dallas County Museum features the county's history and includes displays and memorabilia of one of its famous sons: the late, legendary Paul "Bear" Bryant, football coach for decades at the University of Alabama. The Wynne Phillips House Bed & Breakfast, a National Historic Register listing, is still owned and operated by one of the children whose parents bought the house in 1914. Hampton Springs Cemetery, near Carthage, is the only segregated burial site in the state, with graves dating back to 1916 and bearing primitive markings and accents of African heritage. And, of course, there's Klappenbach Bakery, offering a full menu of baked goods and a terrific sandwich shop next door. Then there's the annual Fordyce on the Cotton Belt Festival, a full week of fun in April with a parade, arts and crafts, food, antique cars and vintage trains on display.

Wynne Phillips House Bed & Breakfast
412 West Fourth Street
501/352-7202
Rates: $55-60, including full breakfast

This rambling, pale apricot-colored clapboard home set in isolated splendor in the middle of an immaculately manicured lawn, is one of the most impressive bed & breakfasts you will encounter. It is surrounded by a complete walkaround-porch—a veranda of incredible size and style. The second story is completely ringed with a balcony that follows the perimeter of the veranda, making the entire second story as accessible for strolling and sitting as the ground floor!

Built around 1904, this Colonial Revival style home was purchased in 1914 by Colonel Thomas Duncan Wynne, an attorney and three-time mayor, for his wife and the seven children who would be born there. The youngest of those seven children—Agnes Wynne Phillips—owns the house today with her husband, Colonel James H. Phillips, and operates it as a B & B. Agnes inherited the house in 1985 and turned it into a B & B because it was so large. It took her and Jim three years to restore the huge property. Drawing on the original house plans from archives in the Old State House in Little Rock, old photographs, newspaper clippings, and the memories of family and friends, Agnes and Jim have recreated the ambience of the home's earlier years.

There are five guest rooms with private baths, a glass-enclosed game room at the back of the house, and a 60-foot lap pool. The house is furnished from all different eras and styles, and includes antiques and family heirlooms. The downstairs boasts Chippendale chairs with needlepoint seats in the dining room, gas fireplaces in the parlor and a Mission-furnished library, with a scattering of Asian rugs and interesting pieces from the Phillips' travels (during Jim's army career they were posted in Pakistan and Germany, and moved 30 times). Upstairs each guest room is named after one of Agnes' siblings, and each is decorated with treasures from their childhood. Breakfast is prepared for guests by Walter, the house butler, who formerly was an army cook. Two types of grapes found only in the South are grown in the inn's arbor, and are offered in the inn's breakfast jelly.

13 FORT SMITH

Coming Home
809 S. Greenwood Ave.
501/782-4438

Phoenix Village Antique Mall
4600 Towson Ave.
501/648-9008

Packrat's Antiques
319 Rogers Ave.
501/783-3330

14 HARDY

Old Hardy Town Mall
Main St.
501/856-3575

Oldies N Goodies Shoppe
Johnston & 1st St.
501/856-2994

Simply Collectibles
709 Main St.
501-856-3545

Steele's Antiques
Main St.
501/856-3247

Donnie's Antiques
Hwy. 62 & 63 E
501/966-7401

Victorian Lace
703 Main Street
501/856-2902

15 HEBER SPRINGS

If you like beautiful lakes and rivers, scenic mountains, all kinds of water sports and outdoor activities, antiques, and general exploring, then Heber Springs, Ark., is tailor-made for you. The town hugs the eastern end of shimmering Greers Ferry Lake, a 40,000-acre U.S. Corps of Engineers facility. Just below the dam at Heber Springs is the Little Red River, one of America's best trout fishing streams. All around the lake and river are parks, resorts, accommodations and full-service marinas for all sorts of water-related activities.

The Heber Springs area is noted for its numerous antique, gift and collectibles shops, ranging from Depression glassware to 19th century European furniture. In addition to the antiques, there are Ozark crafts that represent an era when the Arkansas hill people had to produce the things necessary for survival in this isolated and primitive frontier. In October each year, Heber Springs hosts craftsmen from a wide geographical area for a three-day show and sale. Art is also an important aspect of the offering to tourists coming to this mountain community.

Heber Springs is also home to two nationally known producers of potpourri and fragrances, as well as another famous firm that sells framed prints of original paintings and decorative accessories. These companies supply gift shops all over the country and, to some extent, internationally. And there are festivals every year, from April through December. Nearby attractions to Heber Springs include the Ozark Folk Center in Mountain View, Blanchard Springs Caverns (just up the road from the Ozark Folk Center), Batesville (the state's oldest surviving town), and Little Rock.

Annabelle Antiques
202 W. Front St.
501/362-9948

Antique Market Place Mall
306 W. Main St.
501/362-2111

Somewhere In Time
304 W. Main St.
501/362-9429

Finishing Touch Intrs. & Antqs.
312 W. Main
501/362-7207

Browsing Post
Hwy 25 S
501/362-5560

16 HELENA

Antique Mall of Helena
428 Cherry St.
501/338-8612

Sue Matthews Gifts & Antiques
430 Cherry St.
501/338-6071

Between Friends
517 Cherry St.
501/338-3150

On The Levee Antiques & Gifts
107 Perry St.
501/338-8500

17 HOT SPRINGS

Buckstaff Bathhouse
Bathhouse Row
501/623-2308

Only in Hot Springs can you take a whirlpool bath and get a massage courtesy of the U.S. National Park Service! Buckstaff Bathhouse, a tradition on world-famous Bathhouse Row in Hot Springs, is operated under the regulation of the U.S. Dept. of the Interior, National Park Service. So relax and enjoy the ultimate bathing experience. Buckstaff has served bathers since 1912. A top-flight staff offers outstanding service, top facilities and famous Hot Springs thermal mineral water baths - an unbeatable combination for therapeutic bathing or just plain relaxing. Placed on the National Register of Historic Places in 1974, and declared a National Historic Landmark in 1987, Buckstaff offers massages, bathing packages, bathing supplies, separate men's and women's departments, and men's and women's sun decks.

Seller's Showcase Antique Mall
2138 E. Higdon Ferry Rd.
501/525-2098

Antq. & Collector's Showroom
1100 Malvern Ave.
501/623-6278

Three Sisters Antiques
821 Hobson Avenue
501/623-1909

Kathern's Antiques
2230 Malvern Ave. Ste. E
501/624-4781

Fabulous Finds, Inc.
2025 Central Ave.
501/623-9003

Adele's Antiques & Yesteryear
1704 Albert Pike
501/623-3573

Shepard's Old Time Shop
1 Carmona Ctr.
501/922-3215

Cosmo's Classy Collectibles
114 Central Ave.
501/623-2404

Tillman's Antiques
118 Central Ave.
501/624-4083

Historic District Antiques
514 Central Ave.
501/624-3370

Yum-Yum Antiques
1313 Central Ave.
501/624-7046

Shaw's Antiques
1526 Central Ave.
501/624-0163

Morris Antique Mall
1700 Central Ave.
501/623-4249
Morris Antique Mall is also located in Keo and Little Rock

Watson Antiques
1819 Central Ave.
501/623-6061

Central Ave. Antiques
2025 Central Ave.
501/623-9003

Anderson Antiques
3400 Central Ave.
501/321-1252

Peculiar Treasures
2025 Central Ave.
501/623-9003

Quilt House Antiques
5841 Central Ave.
501/525-1567

Papa's Antiques
308 Whittington Ave.
501/624-4211

Jay's Uniques
309 Whittington Ave.
501/623-5911

Bath House Row Antiques
202 Spring St.
501/623-6888

Interesting Side Trips

The Witness: A Dramatic Musical Passion Play
501/623-9781

The Witness is the story of the birth, life, death and resurrection of Jesus Christ, as told and sung by the Apostle Peter. Everyone can see a little of themselves in this common fisherman, whose life was changed by the miraculous events he witnesses. You, too, will find yourself caught up in the struggles, human doubts and eventual great faith of the disciples, as each panoramic scene unfolds.

The Witness is performed outdoors in the Mid-America Amphitheatre, nestled in a beautiful wooded area of the Ouachita Mountains. Call for dates and times.

Bathhouse Row
(Located in the Heart of Hot Springs)

Visit the Fordyce Bathhouse Museum to experience the grandeur of the golden age of spas. Enjoy a luxurious bath for yourself in one of several bathhouses located on Bathhouse Row. You'll be relaxed and ready to "antique" in the many shops located adjacent to the bathhouses.

18 JONESBORO

Bridge St. Antqs. & Cllbls.
600 Kate
501/932-5007

Edwina's Antiques
324 S. Main
501/935-1358

Nettleton Antiques
4920 E. Nettleton Ave.
501/932-8580

Tymes Past Antiques
305 S. Main St.
501/972-9444

Forty Niner Antiques
3105 Southwest Dr.
501/972-8536

19 KEO

Morris Antiques
306 Highway 232 W
501/842-3531 Fax: 501/842-2858
Open Mon.-Sat. 9- 5, Sun. 12-5

Directions: Take I-440 to Exit 7. Follow Highway 165 South towards England. Go 13 miles to Keo. Turn right on Highway 232 at the flashing caution light. Go 3 blocks and turn right behind the Methodist Church.

With 50,000 square feet and 8 buildings full of an extensive inventory of American, English, French and Italian, Morris Antiques in the tiny town of Keo has something for everyone.

If you're looking for "big stuff" this is the place-beautiful canopy beds, Teesters, large ornate dining room suites, armoires, complete bedroom sets and more. They also offer a nice selection of accessories that includes silver, porcelain, cut glass, lamps, chandeliers and some works of art.

20 LITTLE ROCK, NORTH LITTLE ROCK

Dr. Witt's Quapaw Inn

1868 Gaines
501/376-6873 or 1-800-732-5591
Check-in between 5-10, exceptions by prior arrangement
Reservations requested but not always necessary

Directions: From I-30 take I-630 to the Broadway-Central Exit (IB). Follow the access road to Broadway. Turn left onto Broadway, go 8 blocks to 18th St., go 2 blocks to Gaines, turn left onto Gaines. The inn is 1-1/2 blocks from where you turned onto Gaines - the big pink house on the right.

Guests at Dr. Witt's Quapaw Inn not only get a good night's rest, but can also get the "inside scoop" on America's first family! Innkeeper Dottie Woodwind says that since Bill, Hillary and Chelsea were their neighbors during President Clinton's tenure as governor of Arkansas, the Woodwinds have dozens of Clinton family stories to tell, even some about Socks, the First Cat! Guests at Little Rock's original bed and breakfast can also get information on boarding the family horse, making theater and dinner reservations, and getting directions to the best places to visit. Breakfast at the inn is served to guests only.

Pasha Bass Antiques
5811B Kavanaugh Blvd.
501/660-4245

Dauphine
5819 Kavanaugh Blvd.
501/664-6007

Abingworth
5823 Kavanaugh Blvd.
501/663-5554

Cottage Collection
701 N. Ash St. (@Kavanaugh)
501/664-0883

Crystal Hill Antique Mall
5813 Crystal Hill Rd.
501/753-3777

New Town Antique Shoppes
5913 Crystal Hill Rd.
501/753-3460

Marshall Clements Corp.
1509 Rebsamen Park Rd.
501/663-1828

Grand Finale
1601 Rebsamen Park Rd.
501/661-9242

Pflugrad Antiques
5624 R St.
501/661-0188

My Husband's Treasures
4401 Camp Robinson Rd.
501/791-3628

Train Station Antiques
In Historic Union Station
1400 W. Markham
501/376-2010

Fabulous Finds Antique Mall
1521 Merrill Dr. Ste. D175
501/224-6622

Lorenzen & Co. Booksellers
7509 Cantrell Rd.
501/663-8811

Hogan's Antique Furniture
14600 Cantrell Rd.
501-868-9224

Old Stuff Store
4811 Jones Loop Rd.
501/821-3178

Bowman Curve Antiques
11600 Mara Lynn Rd.
501-228-4898

Jordan's Antiques
4705 Frazier Pike, College Station
501/490-1391

General Store Antiques
12227 Macarthur Dr.
501/851-6202

Collector's Haven Antiques
12819 Macarthur Dr.
501/851-2885

Homestead Antiques
4823 Rixie Rd. #B
501/833-8676

English Antiques Gallery
5500 Landers Rd.
501/945-6004

I-40 Antique Mall
Exit 142-13021 Long Fisher Rd.
End-East Bound Service Rd.
501/851-0039

Garden of Eden Simply Silks
Pleasant Valley Plaza
501/225-5171

Antiques on the Wharf
2310 Cantrell Rd
501/376-6161

Kavanaugh Antiques
2622 Kavanaugh
501/661-0958

LaVien Rose
5800 R St. Ste. 101
501/661-1620

Classic Collections
301 N. Shackleford E-1
501/219-2527

Twin City Antique Mall
5812 Crystall Hill Road
501/812-0400

Height of Fashion
3625 Kavanaugh
501/664-0301

Argenta Antique Mall
201 E. Broadway
501/372-7750

Steen Walnut Company
116 East "E" Street
Off 3500 JFK Road
501/753-4344

Private Treasures by Etta
701 Parkdale Street
501/945-5314

Brown's Clock Shop
3500 Parker Street (Levy)
501/753-0859

21 MAMMOTH SPRING

Country Store Antiques
314 Main St.
501/625-3844

Michael's Variety
304 Main
501/625-3254

Ozark Heritage
301 Main St.
501/625-7303

Cedar Jctn. Craft & Flea Mkt.
Hwy. 63
501/625-3017

22 MENA

Depot Antiques Mall
519 Sherwood
501/394-1149

Doc's Emporium
905 Mena St.
501/394-5742

Mena Street Antique Mall
822 Mena Street
501/394-3231

Misty Mountain Antiques
592 Highway 375 E
501/394-3082

23 MOUNTAIN HOME

Located in north central Ark., Mountain Home is cradled in the gentle slopes of the Ozark Mountains.

With each moderate but distinct season, the Ozarks unfold to present a new panorama of color and beauty. Winter's light blanket of snow covers the forest floor during its brief hibernation. Although much of the plant life will temporarily succumb to winter's presence, the pines and cedars remain evergreen throughout the year. After a two to three month winter reprieve, the hills spring to life with pinks and whites of blossoming redbuds and dogwood trees and colorful wildflowers. Set against a new pale green cover, spring's blooms remind us of a water color palette of subtle, pastel colors.

Under a sky of intense blue, summer brings its own plethora of color to the forest - deep greens of the cedar glades compliment the various greens of the hardwoods. The cool temperatures of autumn drastically change the color scheme of the mountains, and the forest bursts into the fire-like colors of red, orange and gold.

The Ozarks offer miles of natural beauty any time of the year. You can wander the past while contemplating the present and dreaming of the future. It all combines to give you a wonderful time and place for "antiquing" in the picturesque setting of Mountain Home.

The Farm House Antique & Craft Mall

824 Club Blvd.
870/425-7211
Open 9-5:30. Mon.-Sat., April 1 to Nov. 1; 9-5 Nov. 1-April 1; 1-5 Sundays.

Directions: Located one block off of Highway 62 NE.and Highway 412. In town (Mountain Home) turn at the red light off Highway 62 NE. onto Highway 178. The Farm House is one block down on the right behind Pizza Inn and the Twin Lakes Twin Cinema, and across the highway from the golf course.

The name of this business fits it well. Although The Farm House Antique and Craft Mall isn't actually a farm house, it has the look and feel of one. The front porch provides a perfect "rest stop" while inside 8,000 square feet of antiques & collectibles awaits the antique enthusiast. The shop offers a large selection of Franciscan pottery, Glossine, depression glass and many unusual pieces. Quality furnishings from primitive to Victorian are also presented.

Earl's Antiques

3348 Hwy. 62 W.
870/425-8578
Open 10-5, Mon.-Sat. and by chance or appointment on Sun.

Directions: Earl's Antiques is located on Hwy. 62 W., 2 miles west of the city limits on the left-hand side, across from White River Pottery.

If you are looking for something a little bit out of the ordinary in antiques, try Earl's Antiques in Mountain Home. Robert and Carol Earl specialize in unique restored back bars, country store fixtures, Victorian walnut and oak furniture, barber shop and post office memorabilia.

Dolls of Yesteryear
6601 Highway 62 E
870/492-4010

Antique Mall of Mt. Home
686 Hwy. 62 E
870/424-2442

Magnolia House Antiques
6417 Hwy. 62 E
870/492-6730

Once Upon A Time Antiques
625 Hwy. 62 E
870/425-1722

Ox Yoke Antiques
4689 Hwy. 62 & 412 E
870/492-5125

Char's Place
4588 Hwy. 62 E
870/492-6644

Ozark Mountain Mall
1330 Hwy. 62 E
870/425-5618

24 MOUNTAIN VIEW

Interesting Side Trips

The Ozark Folk Center
Spur 382 off AR Hwy. 5
501/269-3851 (information)
1-800-264-FOLK or 501/269-3871 (lodging and conference facilities)

Instead of buying antiques, here's the chance of a lifetime to see just how those antiques you love were crafted and to make some heirlooms yourself! A one-of-a-kind place, the Ozark Folk Center is America's only facility that works at preserving the heritage and way of life of the Ozark mountain people. There is such an incredible array of things to do, see, hear, and experience that visitors really should plan to spend at least a few days at the Center. Not only are there dozens of things going on at the Center from early mornings to very late at night, but you can also see the awesome Blanchard Springs Caverns just a few miles away, or go trout fishing in some of the best waters in the country, picnic and hike in the Ozarks, and then rest a day or two at Greers Ferry Lake before returning home.

The Center offers a full season of events, and hands-on activities, and Dry Creek Lodge offers comfortable rooms right at the facility. You can also design your own custom crafts workshops and enroll for private or group lessons in such old-time arts as: broom making, corn shuckery, natural dyes, spinning, weaving, herb gardening, blacksmithing, needlework, quilting, photography, pottery, hominy making, lye soap making, sorghum making, woodstove cookery, basket making, bowl carving, coopering, chair making, chair seat weaving, hickory bark peeling, shingle making, spoon carving, and woodcarving.

25 OZARK

Located in the picturesque mountain area known as the Ozarks and surrounded by beautiful lakes and countryside, the little town of Ozark was established in 1835. It got its name from French explorers who called this area "aux arc," meaning "big bend," a likely reference to the 19-mile bend in the Arkansas River on which this town is bordered.

A quaint little town, Ozark's history is rich with Civil War happenings. Originally built in the 1800s, the beautiful Franklin County Courthouse played host during the Civil War to Union troops who captured the courthouse, built gun ports in its walls and used it for supply storage. A Confederate raid destroyed its beauty and, in fact, when the last smoke cleared, all the houses in Ozark were burned except three. The structure was rebuilt in 1945 and is now listed on the Register of Historic Places.

There are several excursion possibilities in Ozark, a town which is a veritable "old attic" of discoveries for the collectibles and antiques enthusiast. Its charming square has shops to be explored and interesting spots to get a bite to eat. A "must see" is the old jail, built in 1914 out of locally quarried stone cut in random size blocks. Five public hangings, viewed by thousands, took place near this building - all hanged for murder.

Stu's Web Antiques & Ozark-Abillia
300 Commercial
501/667-4542
Open 10-5 Wed.-Sat. ("We may be here any day at anytime—just call!")

Directions: From I-40 take exit 37 (Highway 29). Go 2 miles south to the stop light (at the intersection of Highways 219 and 64). Stu's Web is the two-story brick building on the right.

Specializing in folk art and the hard-to-find collectibles, Stu's Web & Ozark-Abilia carries hand-carved canes, old photographs, movie memorabilia and nautical antiques in an old building that used to be a hardware store. One of his most recent unusual finds is a pair of chairs supposedly from Marilyn Monroe's estate. The chairs purchased from a Hollywood decorator are Beregres in style. The two very ornate armchairs are upholstered in fabric suited to Marilyn's personality.

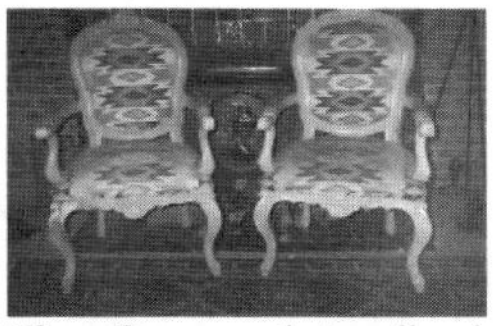
These Beregres chairs offered by Stu's Web once belonged to the late Marilyn Monroe.

26 PARAGOULD

Faulkner County Place
6205 W. Kingshighway
501/239-3301

Paragould Antique Mall
6312 W. Kingshighway
501/239-4485

Williams Glass Barn
330 Greene Rd. 796
501/236-3610

Victorian Lace
120 N. Second St
501/236-7673

27 PIGGOTT

Sugar Creek Antiques
126 S. 2nd Street
501/598-3923

Victorian Roses & Lace
221 W. Main St.
501/598-1219

Enchanted Forrest
193 West Main St.
501/598-3663

28 PINE BLUFF

White House Antiques
4005 Camden Rd.
501/879-1336

Memories and More
2603 S. Cherry St.
501/536-3116

Jo-Be's Antiques
402 Portea Cr.
501/534-1362

Amo's Antiques & Things
1323 S. State St.
501/535-7500

Caroline's Victorian Country
9404 Hwy. 270
501/247-4258

Chapel Plaza Antique Mall
1 Chapel Plaza Hwy. 79 S
501/879-4402

Sissy's Log Cabin Inc.
2319 Camden Road
501/879-3040

29 PRAIRIE GROVE

Country Charm Antiques
16781 W. Hwy. 62
501/846-2689

Long Ago Antiques
206 N. Pittman St.
501/267-3083

Ozark Mercantile
116 N. Mock St.
501/846-4456

Antique Emporium
107 E. Buchanan
501/846-4770

30 ROGERS

The Rose Antique Mall
2875 W. Walnut St.
501/631-8940

Vintage Antique Mall
108 W. Walnut St.
501/631-3930

Shelby Lane Mall
719 W. Walnut
501/621-0111

Miss Judi's Passion
103 W. Walnut
501/636-7758

Back Street Antiques & Such
722 W. Maple
501/621-9979

Clark's Depression Glass
1003 North 8th
501/636-4327

Country House
1007 N. 2nd St.
501/631-9200

Mrs. L. G. Matthew, Sr.
707 E. Hilltop
501/636-2917

Bear Creek Antiques
15790 E. Highway 12
501/925-2327 (Bear)

McGregor's Antiques
2143 W. Olive St.
501/636-6829

Robert's Flea Market and Antique Mall
3704 W. Walnut
501/636-9273

31 RUSSELLVILLE

Antique Mall
1712 N. Arkansas Ave.
501/968-3449

Emporium
214 W. Main St.
501/968-1110

P J's Corner
903 W. Main St.
501/968-1812

This N That & Something Else
519 S Arkansas Ave.
501/968-5356

What-A-Deal
1410 E. Main St.
501/890-5069

Treasure House Antiques
Highway 7
501/968-3652

Sweet Memories Antique Mall
212 W. Main Street
501/967-5354

Glen Powell's Red Barn
42 Jacob Lane
501/968-2971

Dubois Antiques
2614 W. Second Lane
501/968-8370

Buford Smith's Finer Things
418 E. 5th St.
501/968-3820

Favorite Places To Eat

Cracker Barrel Old Country Store
I-40 & St. Hwy. 7, Exit 81

32 SEARCY

Memory Lane Antiques
1006 S. Main St.
501/268-2439

Bob's Antqs. & Classic Car Parts
3317 Hwy. 36 W.
501/268-3198

Jessica Ray Antiques
410 N. Oak St.
501/279-0611

Frances Antiques
701 W. Race St.
501/268-2154

Arkansas

Searcy Emporium
3015 E. Race Avenue
501/279-7025

Room Service Antique Mall
2904 East Race Avenue
501/279-0933

33 SILOAM SPRINGS

Washington Street Antiques
1001 S. Washington St.
501/524-9722

The French Hen
120 South Broadway
501/524-3788

Fantasy Land Flea Market
1490 Highway 412 W.
501/524-6681

34 SPRINGDALE

Famous Hardware Antq. Mall
113 W. Emma Ave.
501/756-6650

Gallery Antiques
3905 S. Thompson St.
501/751-7773

Pat's Antiques
2500 Melody Ln.
501/751-6703

Best Yet Flea Market
633 Sanders
501/751-4642

Barker's Antiques
Elm Springs & Oak Grove Rds.
501/750-2305

Jennifer's Antique Mall
No address listed
501/750-4646

Magnolia House Flea Mkt. Inc.
312 S. Thompson
501/751-1787

Discount Corner Flea Market
418 E. Emma
501/756-0764

35 STUTTGART

Antiques On Park Avenue
1703 S. Timber
501/673-1179
Mon.-Sat. 10-5; Sun. 1-5

Directions: From I-40 take the Hazen exit (#193). Travel South 2 to 3 miles on Highway 11 until the highway T's into Highway 70. Take a left at the T, travel 2 miles to Highway 11 S., continue South on Highway 11 into Stuttgart. To get to Antiques On Park Avenue., turn left at the red light when you come into Stuttgart which is Highway 79. Go through the next light to the 2nd light which is 165 and Park. Take a right, travel approximately 3 miles, Antiques On Park Avenue is located on the right across from the car wash on the left.

For additional information see review in this section.

Walt Krisell
512 E. Second St.
501/673-3558

Carol's Country Collectibles
316 South Main
501/673-6593

Ponders Auction
1504 South Leslie
501/673-6551

36 TONITOWN

Tonitown Flea Market
Highway 412 W.
501/361-9902

Yesteryears Antique Mall
Highway 412 W.
501/361-5747

Historic Mercantile Flea Market
136 Henri De Tonti Blvd.
501/361-2003

37 VAN BUREN

Just across the river from Ft. Smith, Ark., and right at the Oklahoma state line, Van Buren is an antique lover's dream. Its restored Victorian Main Street is a smorgasbord of tiny shops and warehouses filled with furniture, including the largest importer of European antique furniture in the Southwestern U.S. The shops are also filled with rare glass treasures, vintage hats and clothing, Coca-Cola and other trademark collectibles, antique toys, porcelain and china dolls, Victorian prints, and old tins and canisters. And since it's one of the original entryways to the Southwest, you can also shop for anything "southwestern," including turquoise and sterling silver jewelry, Navaho rugs and blankets, hand-thrown pottery, and western art of all kinds.

If you tire of shopping, you can take the "scenic route" and enjoy Ozark beauty from the Ozark Scenic Railway vintage train, or the Frontier Bell excursion river boat that travels along the Arkansas River. Top it all off with a couple of nights at the Old Van Buren Inn on Main Street, and you've got a great little vacation!

Old Van Buren Inn
633 Main Street, corner of 7th and Main
501/474-4202
Rates: $65-110

Formerly the Crawford County Bank building, the Old Van Buren Inn was purchased in 1988 by Jackie Henningsen, who while on vacation from California, saw the building and fell in love with it. She and her family and friends spent hours renovating the building and turning the ground floor into an excellent California-style restaurant.

The second floor was then transformed into a bed-and-breakfast. There are just three bedrooms; each is filled with hand-picked Victorian antique furniture. The beds are soft and comfortable. Rocking chairs and a selection of books in each room complete the relaxing atmosphere. The sunny bathroom, which has a double tub, is shared by the three rooms.

Henningsen lives on the property, which was described as "the ultimate building" when it was erected in 1889. A new high-pressure brick was used in its construction, and the fixtures and fittings included Tennessee Valley marble, hardwoods from around the world, and ornate tin work.

The restaurant is Henningsen's pride and joy. Open and sunny, it serves food as Californian as the South can get. Meals are light and flavorful: crisp light salads, bean sprouts and avocados, quiche, seafood sandwiches, and hot Texas Chili. Desserts are homemade. Don't miss the apple dumpling. The restaurant is open all week, from 9:00 a.m. to 5:00 p.m.weekdays and from noon to 4:00 p.m. on Sundays.

The ghost of the Old Van Buren Inn is an unidentified but roaming spirit that inhabits the second story of the former bank building. Henningsen describes the spirit as an "unseen presence." But, she says, "He's friendly," and suggests that her guests should introduce themselves to him.

It would be surprising if such a building did not have a ghost. The former bank survived several attempted hold-ups and other robberies and was closed down in the Great Depression. It ended up as the local gas company's offices. During Prohibition it had another role. The third floor was a speakeasy. At least that's how the local stories go. Why else would there still be a peephole cut in the door?

The old building went on to become a dance hall and then a club before Henningsen began her loving restoration. Now, it is somewhere you can "bank" on for having a nice visit.

From *Haunted Hotels* Copyright 1995 by Robin Mead
Published by Rutledge Hill Press, Nashville, Tennessee

Antique Mall of Van Buren
415 Main St.
501/474-7896

Antique Warehouse & Mall
402 Main St.
501/474-4808

Bridgewater's Antiques
614 Main St.
501/474-8616

Country Cellar
606 Main St.
501/474-1700

Grapevine Shoppe, Inc.
615 Main St. #A
501/474-5800

Somewhere In Time
1307 N. Hills Blvd.
501/474-4600

T J's Treasures & Bevie's
715 Main St.
501/474-7678

Victoria's Antiques
13 S. 5th St.
501/474-5299

Whiteaker Ark. Oil Stone
708 Main St.
501/474-6416

Country Corner Antiques
815 B Main St.
501/783-8216

Victorias Antiques
514 Main St.
501/474-6299

38 WEST FORK

West Fork Antiques
34 McGee Road
501/839-8202

Notes

Established 1978
ANTIQUES
and Goodies

1128 Third Street
Eureka

(707) 442-0445

44

Old Owl Inn
Cottages
A Bed & Breakfast
and
Cottontail
Antiques
& Gifts

701 Hwy. 395
Red Mountain

137

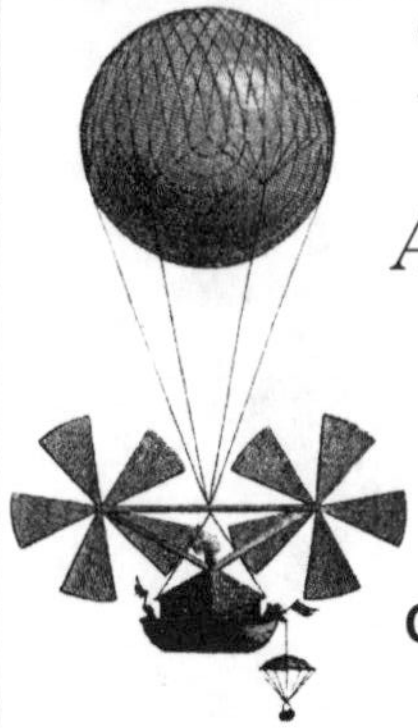

The ***Hangar***

Antiques & Collectibles

Central Coast Outdoor
Antique & Collectible Market

(805) 481-9095
Oceano Airport 561 Air Park Drive
Oceano

117

BATHROOM
Machineries

Antique Plumbing Fixtures.
Original lighting, hardware and old keys
495 Main Street • (209) 728-2031
Murphys

108

Enjoy
Antiquing
In the Spirit of
the old West

Main Street
Chowchilla

offers seven fine
antique shops all
within a four
block area

29

California

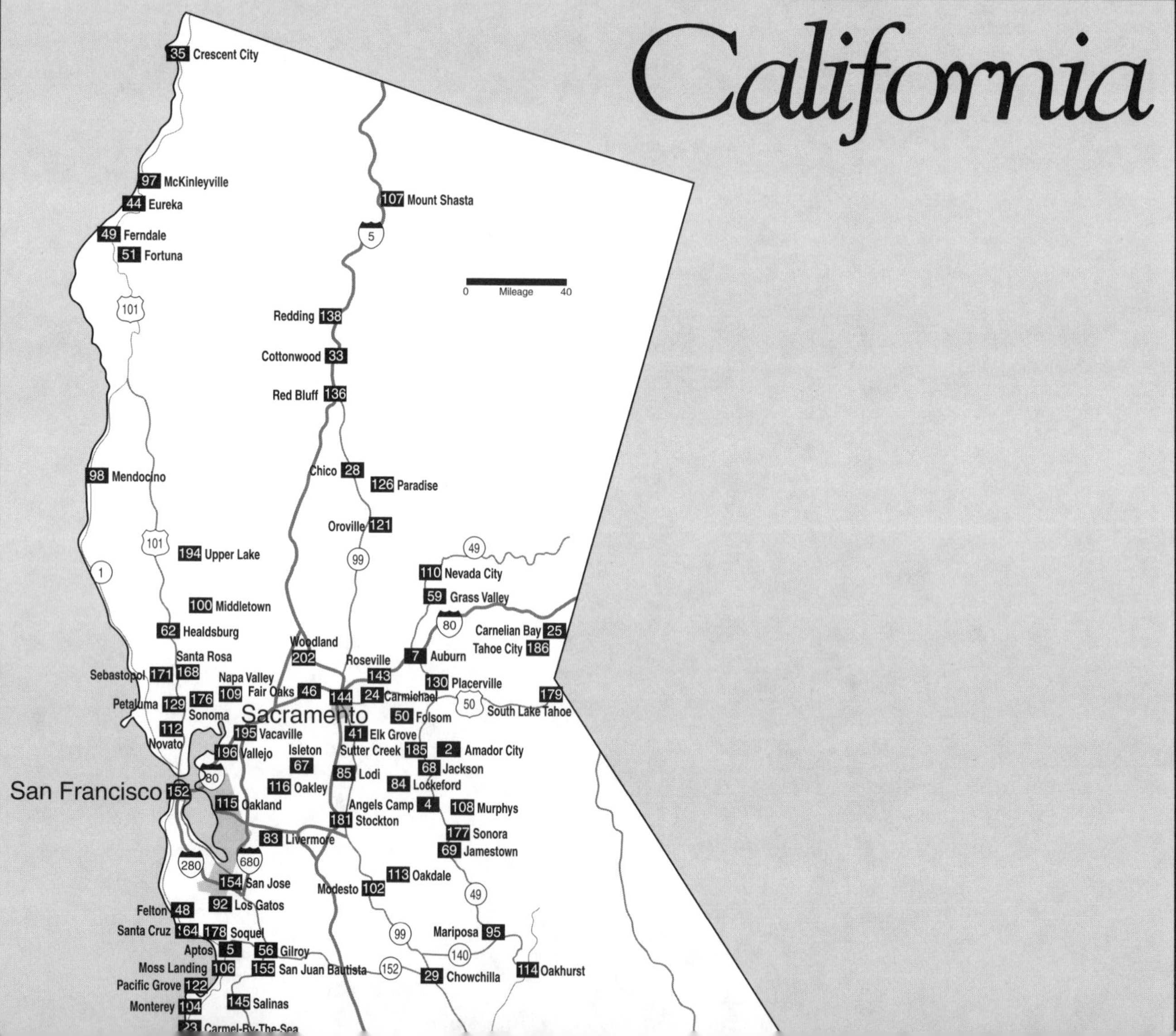

YESTERDAY'S
PAPER®

PAPER
ANTIQUES

SPECIALIZING IN PAPER
AMERICANA, OLD
STOCKS & BONDS, &
ANTIQUARIAN BOOKS

31815 CAMINO CAPISTRANO
STE. C11
(714) 248-0945 SHOP
(714) 583-1899 FAX
OPEN DAILY 11-5

SAN JUAN CAPISTRANO

156

Haulbaurs
Timeless
Treasures

Antiques &
Clock Repair
3207 Marysville Blvd.
(916) 924-1371
Sacramento

144

Yesteryear's
Marketplace

9,500 sq. ft.
of Antiques

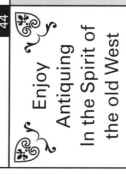

433 Georgia Street
(707) 557-4671
Vallejo

A Pier at the Past
ANTIQUES

With a Look at the Present... —And a Glance at the Future

368 Pier Avenue
(805) 473-1521
Oceano

117

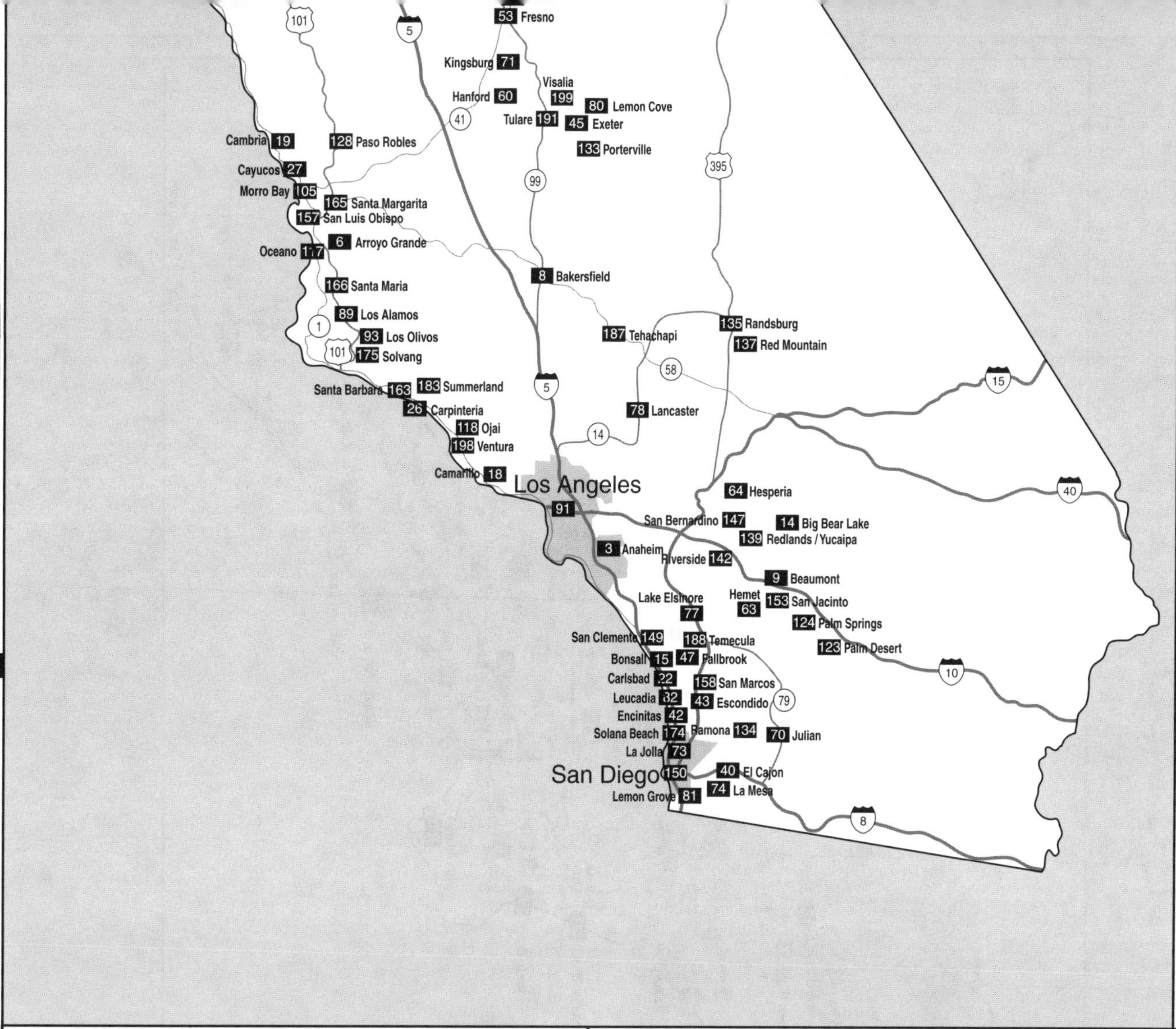

The Cranberry House
ANTIQUE CENTER
Established 1992

15,000 Square Feet of
SHOPPING HEAVEN

ANTIQUES & COLLECTIBLES
WE PURCHASE FROM 1 ITEM TO ESTATES

12318 Ventura Boulevard
Studio City, CA 91604
818-506-8945

182

AANTEEK AAVENUE MALL

3 mi. W. of I-5
2832 State St.
Open 11-5
Carlsbad

22

Swan Song

197 E. Second St.
(on antique row)
(909) 620-5767
4 floors of Victorian, country primitive, traditional, quilts, porcelain, paintings

"an upscale antique market"

Pomono

132

Mom & Apple Pie
A · N · T · I · Q · U · E · S

789 Tucker Road, #2 (Corner of Tucker Rd. & Hwy. 202)
(805) 822-8765
Tehachapi

187

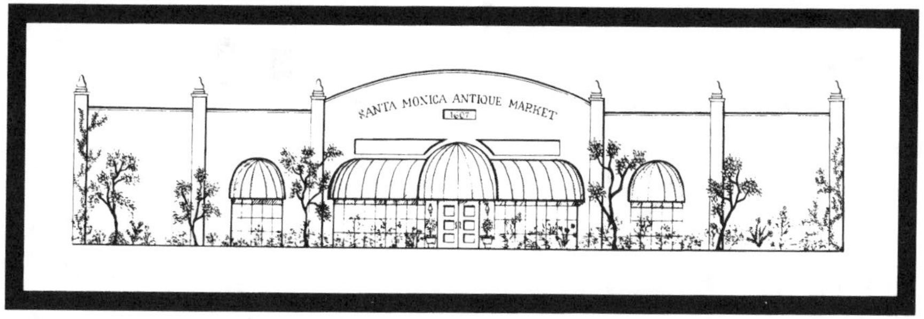

Santa Monica Antique Market

167

California
Los Angeles Area

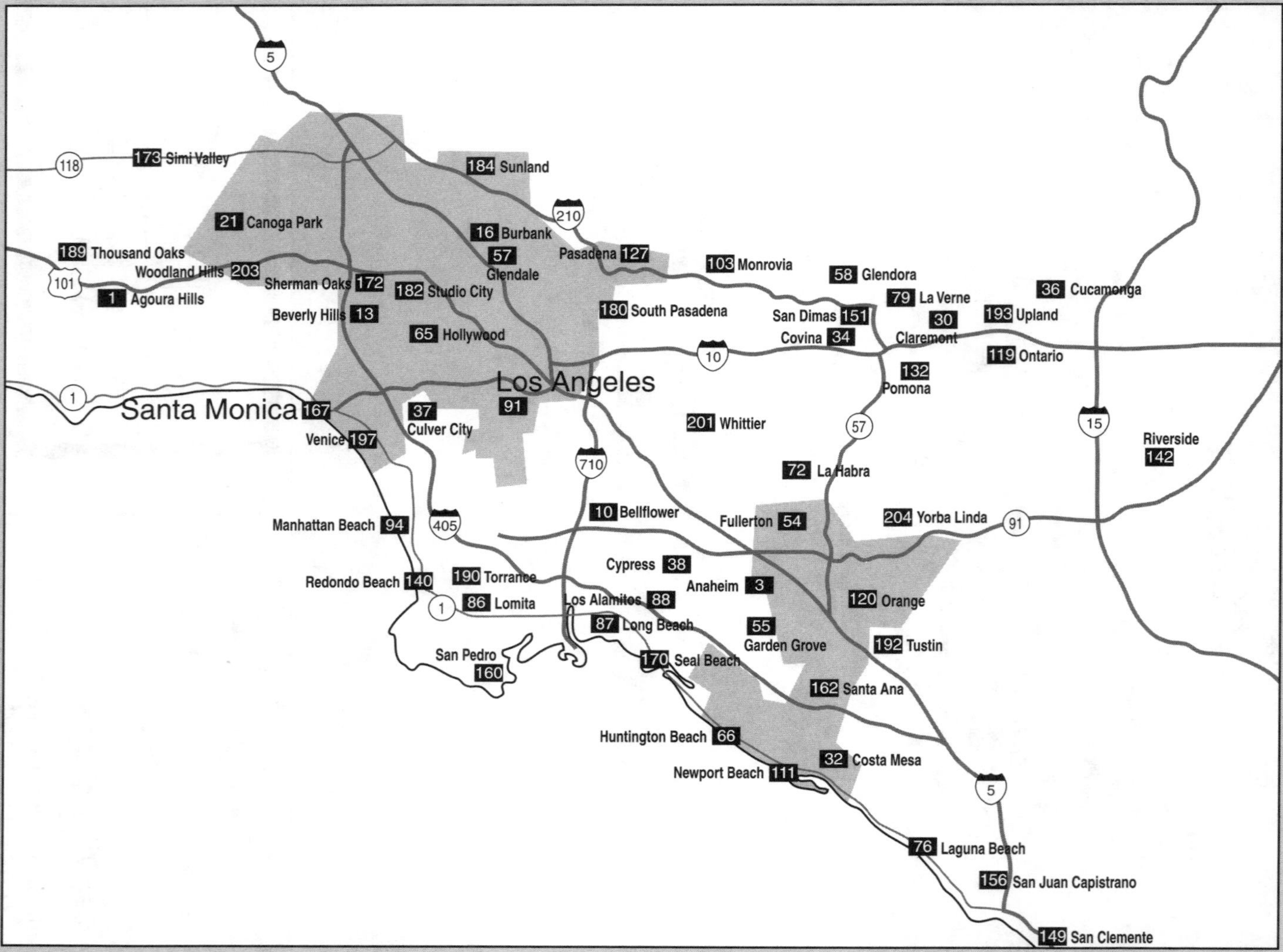

California San Francisco Area

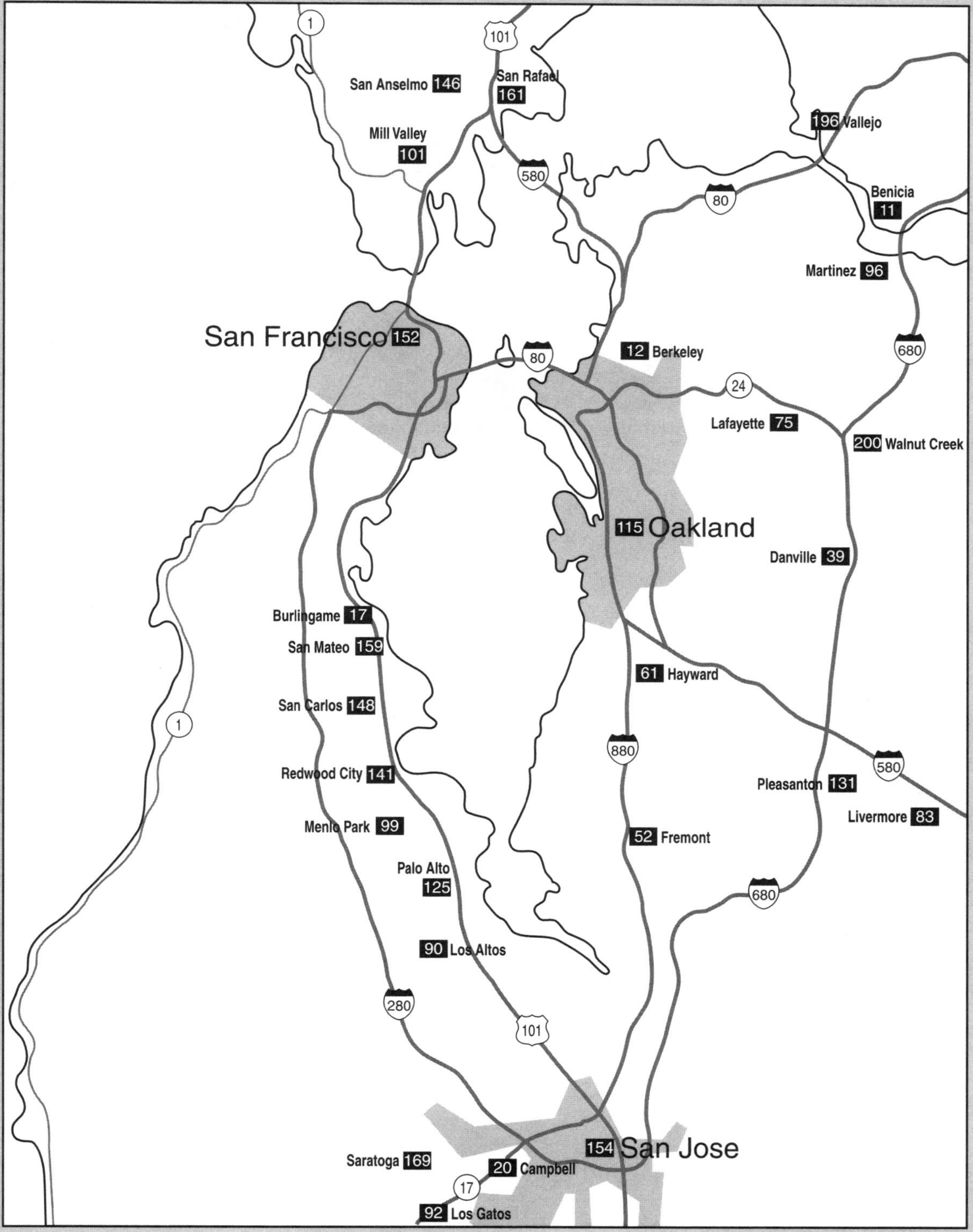

California

Cottontail Antiques, Old Owl B & B

The Old Owl Inn, originally owned by Slim Riffle, was at one time a library in the town of Atolia. Slim moved it to Red Mountain in 1918. He then added on to the building and turned it into a bar, brothel and gambling saloon.

The Owl witnessed many shoot-outs, bar-room brawls and two fisted poker games. Legend has it that the ladies of the evening along with illegal booze was hidden in tunnels below out of sight of the watchful eye of the local Sheriff.

Cottontail Antiques is located at the Old Owl Inn.

Today, The Owl Cottages is a bed and breakfast decorated with antiques throughout. Guests can stay in Slim's Cottage, a spacious two-bedroom with kitchen, living room and old-fashioned bath, which was the private home of Slim Riffle. Bessie's Honeymoon Cottage is also available for that special romantic night or weekend – with kitchenette and private bath.

The newly expanded Cottontail Antiques is located on the property providing antiquers with treasures to take home as a momento of their stay at the Old Owl Inn, including Fenton, angels and needlework items.

Bessie's Honeymoon Cottage.

Antique Shopping in California's European Village

Travels through California wouldn't be complete without a stop in the charming European village of Solvang.

Located in California's beautiful, unspoiled Central Coast region just 30 minutes north of Santa Barbara, Solvang was founded by Danish immigrants just after the turn of the century. Today this small, old world community is one of California's most popular tourist attractions, attracting 3,000,000 visitors annually from around the world with its unique, friendly atmosphere.

While the scent of Danish pastries wafting from any one of Solvang's 18 bakeries may attract the visitor the first time — the area's natural beauty, live theater, wonderful new restaurants, horse ranches and wineries, factory outlet shopping, along with the town's 350 unique retail shops and great antique stores — keep the visitor, as well as locals, coming back time and time again.

The area's largest and most prestigious antique shop is the **Solvang Antique Center**, now in its 16th year of operation. Located right in the heart of the shopping village, the Solvang Antique Center features 65 carefully-selected, quality antique dealers in the historic Old Mill Shops building. The award-winning building provides a unique shopping environment, with natural lighting from arch-top windows and skylights and museum-style display cases, with thousands of decorative and specialty items mixed throughout the furniture galleries.

The Solvang Antique Center has rapidly gained the reputation among collectors and antique dealers as one of the finest multiple-dealer galleries in California, praised by many as one of the best in the country. As a result of their quality merchandising techniques, service-oriented staff, state-of-the-art computerized inventory control system, locator services and worldwide delivery, the Solvang Antique Center now displays the merchandise of participating dealers from as far away as England, France, China and Russia.

There's something at the Solvang Antique Center for everyone from the casual browser to the serious collector – from silver, porcelain, cut glass, estate jewelry, print, paintings and collector items to fine furniture, antiquities, automatic pianos, and museum-quality investment items.

Featured within the Solvang Antique Center is Hrs. Antique Clocks, offering one of the largest selections of restored clocks and music boxes in the country. **Hrs. Antique Clocks** features more than 300 quality restored antique clocks of all types, fine pocket watches and vintage wristwatches, cylinder and disc music boxes, musical clocks and automata, nickelodeons and automatic grand pianos.

Special items recently on display include an animated Dutch Musical Tall Case, c. 1830 from the Henry Ford Museum, playing 18 tunes on 18 bells; and a beautifully enameled pocket watch in its original carrying case, believed to have been owned originally by Benjamin Franklin.

The Solvang Antique Center also provides full restoration services of quality clocks, watches, music boxes, scales, and furniture for dealers and private collectors.

Renaissance Design Center, open by appointment in the same building, offers reproductions of 18th and 19th century furniture, clocks, lighting and accessories at designer-wholesale prices, as well as a full range of quality architectural and building products.

The Solvang Antique Center is located at 486 First Street in Solvang, Calif., opposite Solvang Park, and is open seven days a week from 10 a.m. until 6 p.m.

California

1 AGOURA HILLS

Agoura Antique Mart
28863 Agoura Rd.
818/706-8366

Showcase Antiques
5021 Kanan Rd.
818/865-8268

Sandy Lane Antique Mall
28878 Roadside Dr.
818/991-0229

Antique Mall
28826 Roadside Drive
818/991-8541

2 AMADOR CITY

Sherrill's Country Store
14175 State Hwy. 49
209/267-5578

Mac Clan Antiques
14215 State Hwy. 49
209/267-1032

Jensen's Antique Dolls Bears
14227 State Hwy. 49
209/267-5639

Roth Van Anda Antiques
14461 W. School
209/267-5411

Victorian Closet
14170 State Hwy. 49
209/267-5250

3 ANAHEIM

Len & Kathy's Collectible Toys
1215 S. Beach Blvd. Ste. E & F
714/995-4151

Treasure Cliff
1783 W. Lincoln Ave.
714/491-2830

Lincoln Antique Mall
1811 W. Lincoln Ave.
714/778-2522

Antique Alley
10351 Magnolia St.
714/821-1576

4 ANGELS CAMP

Calaveras Coin & Collectibles
1255 S. Main St.
209/736-2646

Angels Camp Mercantile
1267 S. Main St.
209/736-4100

Grandmothers Antiques
1273 S. Main St.
209/736-0863

5 APTOS

A Backward Glance
417 Trout Gulch Rd.
408/462-9559

Arabesque Antiques
417 Trout Gulch Rd.
408/688-9883

Ardyce's
417 Trout Gulch Rd.
408/476-5296

Village Fair Antiques
417 Trout Gulch Rd.
408/688-9883

Wilwood Antiques
417 Trout Gulch Rd.
408/684-9407

6 ARROYO GRANDE

Rich Man-Poor Man Antq.
106 W. Branch St.
805/489-8511

Branch St. Antique Mall
126 E. Branch St.
805/473-3276

Village Antique Mart
126 E. Branch St. #A
805/489-6528

Glance at the Past
410 E. Branch
805/489-5666

Village Antique House
146 Traffin Way
805/474-1660

7 AUBURN

Fine's Antique Mall & Gallery
337 Commercial St.
916/888-7607

Old West Trail Antiques
343 Commercial St.
916/823-2784

Sweet Sue Old & New
345 Commercial St.
916/885-5537

Antiques International
4035 Grass Valley Hwy.
916/888-0324

Betty Nelson Antiques
1586 Lincoln Way
916/823-2519

Mercantile Antiques
875 Nevada St.
916/888-8740

Serendipity
135 Sacramento St.
916/885-1252

Treasure's
218 Washington St.
916/888-6229

8 BAKERSFIELD

Forever Yours
2594 Brundage Ln.
805/322-9646

Cleo's Attic Antiques
1888 S. Chester Ave.
805/832-8202

Edison Antiques
2227 Edison Hwy.
805/322-6174

Collectorium
2414 Edison Hwy.
805/322-4712

Antique Loft
6 H St.
805/325-2402

Fond Memories
151 H St.
805/322-9326

Season's
166 H St.
805/323-7673

Pidgeon Hill
167 H St.
805/323-1226

Renaissance
168 H St.
805/327-2902

Art & Antiques
231 H St.
805/633-1008

Childhood Memories Antiques
1106 H St.
805/326-0346

Grandma's Trunk
1115 H St.
805/323-2730

Betty's Barn of Antiques
4811 Morro Dr.
805/366-5620

Great American Antiques
625 19th St.
805/322-1776

Central Park Antique Mall
701 19th St.
805/633-1143

Nothin' New
1310 19th St.
805/327-9664

Somewhere In Time
1312 19th St.
805/326-8562

Timeless Treasures
1320 19th St.
805/327-5052

Five & Dime Antiques
1400 19th St.
805/323-8048

Golden Carousel
1407 19th St.
805/326-8252

Curiosity Shop Antiques
1607 19th St..
805/324-7112

As Time Goes By/Costume Shop
1631 19th St.
805/325-5222

Woody's Antiques
1656 19th St.
805/324-1994

Old World Emporium
731 16th St.
805/861-0940

Johnny Crow's Garden
5635 Taft Hwy.
805/836-9828

9 BEAUMONT

Larry Nelson's Antiques
136 E. 6th St.
909/769-1171

Chatterbox
350 E. 6th St.
909/769-1071

Beaumont Antique Mall
450 E. 6th St.
909/845-1397

Decorating Addict Antiques
480 E. 6th St.
909/845-5856

Browning's
504 W. 6th St.
909/845-8608

L & M Coins & Collectibles
725 A Beaumont Ave.nue
909/769-2800

Legacy Antiques
442 E. Sixth Street
909/845-5600

10 BELLFLOWER

Fischer Antiques
17041 Lakewood Blvd.
310/633-6718

J & B Antiques & Decor
17418 Clark Ave.
310/804-1174

11 BENICIA

This That N Whatever
129 1st St.
707/745-8706

Benicia Antique Shop
305 1st St.
707/745-0978

Kindred Spirits
632 1st St.
707/745-6533

Dials Antiques
190 W. J St.
707/745-2552

12 BERKELEY

Lorne Gay Antiques
2990 Adeline St.
510/649-8550

Jack's Antiques
3021 Adeline St.
510/845-6221

Betty Jane's Collectibles
3192 Adeline St.
510/652-4586

Kalway Antiques
305 The Uplands
510/848-5177

Military Artifacts & Collectibles
1601 Ashby Ave.
510/841-2244

Louis A Capellino Antiques
1987 Ashby Ave.
510/845-5590

Hudson Antiques
1999 Ashby Ave.
510/848-4916

Trout Farm Antiques
2179 Bancroft Way
510/843-3565

Berkeley Collectibles Shop
2280 Fulton
510/848-3199

Grove Antiques (Sat. only)
1417 MLK Jr. Way #A
510/525-9120

It's About Time Antiques
1621 San Pablo Ave.
510/526-0626

Brent's Unique Shop
1824 San Pablo Ave.
510/841-9051

It's Her Business Junque Funk
2508 San Pablo Ave.
510/845-1663

Rosebud Gallery
1857 Solano Ave.
510/525-6454

Laurent Bermudez Prim Arts
1859 Solano Ave. #B
510/527-1042

June Kadish Antiques
1878 Solano Ave.
510/528-2785

13 BEVERLY HILLS

Sherwoods Spirit of America
325 N. Beverly Dr.
310/274-6700

Auntie Barbara's Antiques
238 S. Beverly Dr.
310/285-0873

Roth & Co.
9511 Brighton Way
310/271-5485

Amphora Arts & Antiques
212 N. Canon Dr.
310/273-1433

Royal-Athena Galleries
9478 W. Olympic Ste. #304
310/277-0133

Amphora Arts & Antiques
308 N. Rodeo Dr.
310/273-4222

Krono's
421 N. Rodeo Dr.
310/205-0766

Jake's Place
309 N. Robertson Blvd.
310/288-0287

Barakat Antiques Gallery
9876 Wilshire Blvd.
310/859-0676

14 14 BIG BEAR LAKE

Mud Hen Antiques
40143 Big Bear Blvd.
909/866-8313

M & B Antiques
40700 Village Dr.
909/866-4200

15 15 BONSALL

This Old House
30158 Mission Road
760/631-2888

16 16 BURBANK

Tower Trading Co.
1314 W. Magnolia Blvd.
818/848-3950

Mary La Shaum's Antique Shop
2110 W. Magnolia Blvd.
818/842-0210

Flashback Antique Mart
2624 W. Magnolia Blvd.
818/563-2121

Best of Times
2918 1/2 W. Magnolia Blvd.
818-848-5851

Renaissance Antiques
3317 W. Magnolia Blvd.
818/567-0935

Madrid Antiques
3416 W. Magnolia Blvd.
818/845-9028

Victorian Rose Antiques
3421 W. Magnolia Blvd.
818/842-3201

White Elephant
3422 W. Magnolia Blvd.
818/842-0721

Antique Attic
4005 W. Riverside Dr.
818/566-7155

Magnolia House Antiques
3910 W. Magnolia Blvd.
818/843-8750

17 BURLINGAME

Carol Ann Antiques
1215 Burlingame Ave.
415/344-7003

Fat Cat Antiques
247 California Dr.
415/348-1119

Red House Antiques
1101 Douglas Ave.
415/344-4658

Burlingame Antiques
915 Howard Ave.
415/344-4050

Whistling Sevan Antiques
359 Primrose Rd.
415/343-1419

Wood Duck Antiques
363 Primrose Rd.
415/348-0542

Heirloom's Antique Mall
783 California Drive
415/344-8800

18 CAMARILLO

Unique Antiques
65 Palm Drive
805/484-4100

The Antique Mall of Camarillo
58 Palm Drive
805/484-7710

Ingersoll's Antiques
62 Palm Drive
805/482-9936

Augusta's Showroom
2280 Ventura Blvd.
805/987-9883

Abagail's Attic Antiques
2633 Ventura Blvd.
805/388-0334

Savannah West
2235 Ventura Blvd.
805/383-6836

The Yellow House Antiques
2369 Ventura Blvd.
805/482-0330

One More Time Antique Mall
2433 Ventura Blvd.
805/388-0229

19 19 CAMBRIA

Morning Song
4210 Branch St.
805/927-7101

Once Upon A Time
555 Main St.
805/927-5554

Granny Had One Antiques
712 Main St.
805/927-7047

Fairey's Antiques
715 Main St.
805/927-3665

Urban Roots
768 Main St.
805/927-7234

Cambria Antique Center Mall
2110 Main St.
805/927-2353

Antiques on Main
2338 Main St.
805/927-4292

Country Collectibles
2380 Main St. #A
805/927-0245

Moonstone Antique Emporium
5620 Moonstone Beach Dr.
805/927-5624

20 20 CAMPBELL

Donna's Antiques
301 E. Campbell Ave.
408/866-1252

Second Time Around
327 E. Campbell Ave.
408/379-7240

Yesteryears Antiques & Cllbls.
379 E. Campbell Ave.
408/379-1864

Woodworks Antiques
841 Union Ave.
408/377-9778

21 CANOGA PARK

Collector's Eye
21435 Sherman Way
818/347-9343

Now & Then
21501 Sherman Way
818/340-4007

Antique Co.
21507 Sherman Way
818/347-8778

Claudia's Collectibles
21511 Sherman Way
818/702-6261

Sadie's Corner Antiques
21515 Sherman Way
818/704-7600

Jeanne's Antiques & Cllbls.
21523 Sherman Way
818/702-9266

Old Country Road
21529 Sherman Way
818/340-3760

Affordable Antiques
21612 Sherman Way
818/348-2909

22 CARLSBAD

AANTEEK AAVENUE MALL
2832 State Street
760/434-8742
Open 11-5 daily, closed major holidays only.

Directions: Take I-5 to Carlsbad Village Drive, then turn west and go 5 blocks to State Street. Turn north (right) and go 1 full block, cross over Grand Ave.nue, and count 6 stores on the right (east) side of State Street.

AANTEEK AAVENUE MALL is 5000 square feet of extra clean, well lighted, well stocked antiques and collectibles. Dresden, Flow Blue, Roseville, Bauer, cut glass, sterling, art, mirrors, steins, furniture, paper, books, Royal Doulton, Hummels, extensive selection of display aids and reference books, reproduction silk and stained glass lamp shades, lamps, windows, jewelry, California Pottery, flatware, china sets, rare Franciscan, cigarette lighters, lanterns, patches, pens, hood ornaments, toys, inkwells, book ends, perfumes, purses, paperweights, photos, figurines, collector plates, and much more. Very eclectic, you won't be sorry! — Friendly and helpful staff who feel it is their pleasure to open cases for their customer.

From Clara's Attic
561 Carlsbad Village Dr.
760/720-9384

Black Whale Lghting & Antqs.
562 Carlsbad Village Dr.
760/434-3113

Carlsbad House of Antiques
2752 State St.
760/720-1061

Olde Ivy Antiques
2928 State St.
760/729-8607

De Witts Antiques
2946 State St.
760/720-1175

Roseboro House
2971 State St.
760/729-3667

Mulloy's Estate Jewelry
2978 State St.
760/729-5774

Backroads Antiques
2988 State St.
760/729-3032

Antiques Junction
3021 State St.
760/434-2332

Almost State Street Antiques
3087 State St.
760/434-7502

Byrnes Antqs. Restoration Co.
2698 State St.
760/434-7800

Postal's Antiques
2825 State St.
760/729-7816

Tom Vigne Antiques
505 Oak Avenue
760/729-7081

Treasures of Carlsbad
2921 Roosevelt St.
760/729-6010

Great Places To Eat

Neimans
2978 Carlsbad Boulevard
760/729-4131

Dine luxuriously in the elegant home of German immigrant Gerhard Schutte, one of the driving forces behind the development of Carlsbad. From 5 p.m. every evening enjoy the pasta, salad, soup and shrimp buffet, or prime rib, steaks and fresh fish. A cafe menu is served daily from 11:30 a.m. to 11 p.m., and Sunday champagne brunch from 8:30 a.m. to 2 p.m.

23 CARMEL

Nestled in a pine forest above a spectacular white sand beach, the one-square-mile village of Carmel is reminiscent of European charm. There is no mail delivery: homes are known only by name and have no addresses. Winding streets, secluded alleyways, courtyards and arcades are highlighted by 70 art studios and galleries, numerous antique shops, specialty boutiques and small cafes.

Carmel is also the home of Mission Ranch Restaurant, owned by actor and two-term Carmel mayor, Clint Eastwood. Clint bought the historic Mission Ranch property in 1986. The ranch, built in the mid-1880s, was a dairy farm until the '20s. What is now the restaurant was once the dairy's creamery.

The dining room has a cozy ranch decor, complete with checkered tablecloths and a large stone fireplace. For views of the scenic pastoral grounds, one can eat outside on a wide deck with umbrella tables.

The basic menu is ranch-style: prime rib, steaks and BBQ ribs. If this doesn't arouse your tastebuds, Chef Craig Ling offers other house specialities from which to choose: loin of lamb, salmon, fresh seafood, roasted chicken, beef brochette and meatless lasagna for vegetarians. Dinners include soup or salad, twice-baked potatoes and fresh vegetables. The restaurant offers an appetizer, a la carte and a homemade dessert menu as well.

Mission Ranch Restaurant

26270 Dolores
408/625-9040
Hours:
Dinner, 4:30-10:00 - 7 days
Lunch, 11:30-3, Sat. only
Brunch, 9:30-2:30 - Sunday

The Stonehouse Inn

8th below Monte Verde
408/624-4569, 800/748-6618
Open Daily 10-9
Rates $99-199

Directions: Traveling Hwy. 1 south or north, take Ocean Ave.nue exit. Travel Ocean Avenue to Junipero, turn left, proceed to 8th, turn right, travel five blocks to Monte Verde. Located on the left side (south side) of block between Monte Verde and Casanova.

This charming inn has a complete stone exterior, hand-shaped by local Indians when it was built in 1906. Through the years, Mrs. "Nana" Foster, the original owner, often invited notable artists and writers from the San Francisco Bay area to stay in her Carmel home. Sinclair Lewis, Jack London and Lotta Crabtree were among these guests. Rooms are named in their honor.

A glass enclosed front porch provides the entrance and sets the mood for the warmth and ambiance you are soon to experience.

Guests often gather in the living room in front of the large stone fireplace to enjoy not only the warmth of the fire, but the pleasure of meeting new friends from around the world.

The restful bedrooms are light and airy, some having a view of the ocean through the trees. Each room is decorated in soft colors and features antiques, cozy quilts, fresh flowers, fruit and special touches.

A generous breakfast is served each morning in the sunny dining room, the peaceful garden or before the fire.

Anna Beck Antiques
26358 Carmel Rancho Lane
408/624-3112

Villa Antiga
Delores
408/626-6207

Langer's Antiques
Delores (Between Ocean & 7th)
408/624-2102

Robertson's Antiques
Delores & 7th
408/624-7517

Trappings
W. Juniper & N/W 6th
408/626-4500

Anderle Gallery
Lincoln, Ocean & 7th
408/624-4199

Robt Cordy Antiques
Lincoln & 6th
408/625-5839

Magpie Antiques
Ocean Ave. & Lincoln
408/622-9341

Great Things Antiques
Ocean Ave.
408/624-7178

Retrospect
San Carlos
408/624-8245

Antiques Francais
3742 The Barnyard
408/624-7444

24 CARMICHAEL

Queen Anne Cottage
2633 El Camino Ave.
916/481-4944

For Olde Type Sake
6030 Fair Oak Blvd.
916/978-9818

Antiques Unlimited
6328 Fair Oaks Blvd.
916/482-6533

Hovis Antiques
7800 Fair Oaks Blvd.
916/944-4736

25 CARNELIAN BAY

The Meadows Collection
By Appointment Only
530/546-5516

26 CARPINTERIA

Angels
4846 Carpinteria Ave.
805/684-8148

Seaside Gallery & Cafe
4945 Carpinteria
805/684-8582

Antique Delights
771 Linden Ave.
805/684-2717

Art In 'Teriors An' Tiques
865 Linden Ave.
805/684-6034

Magpie Collections
961 Linden Ave.
805/684-6034

27 CAYUCOS

Cayucos Antiques
151 Cayucos Dr.
805/995-2206

Cayucos Trading Post
98 N. Ocean Ave.
805/995-3453

Rich Man - Poor Man Antique
146 N. Ocean Ave.
805/995-3631

Remember When
152 N. Ocean Ave.
805/995-1232

American Pie
890 S. Ocean Ave.
805/995-0832

28 CHICO

Country Squyres' Antiques
164 E. 3rd Street
916/342-6764

Trends & Traditions
126 W. 3rd
916/891-5622

American Antiques
1355 Guill St.
916/345-0379

Sixpence
225 Main St.
916/891-6706

8th & Main Antiques Center
745 Main St.
916/893-5534

Antique Annex
1421 Carnaby Street
916/893-8823

Hidden Treasure Antiques
2234 Park Ave.
916/893-5773

29 CHOWCHILLA

While driving through Central California, look for the quaint agricultural town of Chowchilla, an easy and convenient exit off of State Freeway 99 and State Highway 152, where you and your family can park your R.V. and rest and relax in a palm shaded park. Adjacent is a cluster of seven antique shops within a four block area located on the main street through town. Enjoy this low key pioneering atmosphere where you can take your time to shop and browse among friendly small town people. There are also numerous restaurants and sandwich shops with a variety of cuisines available.

Chowchilla has an unusual history in its development. This small city named after an Indian tribe, did not explode in population as did most early California settlements. However, it sits in the geographical center of the state and requires only a short drive west to the ocean front attractions and a short drive east to the high Sierra Nevada Mountains and to the entrance of the beautiful Yosemite Valley. (The Sierras offer many scenic routes that include Redwood forests, mountain lakes, streams and camping.) It is located in the most productive agriculture area in the world. The Central Valley boasts the production of 250 agricultural commodities.

The Parrott Shop

535 Robertson Blvd.
209/665-4311
Open 10:30-5:00, 7 days a week

Harvey & Geri Parrott, owners of The Parrott Shop, have been antique collectors for 25 years. Their shop on Robertson St. is filled with over 10,000 items within its 4,000 square feet. A large selection of prints, glassware (including carnival and depression), crystal, china, pottery such as Roseville, Weller, Hull, Bauer, Fiesta and McCoy can be found among this eclectic offering of antiques. Military items, costume jewelry, tools, kitchenware, fishing items, books, cookie jars, decanters, bird cages, musical instruments, lighting, furnishings of several periods and styles are also available. They even have a section devoted to oriental pieces along with a special area for quilters.

Frontier Towne

521 Robertson Blvd.
209/665-3900
Open: 10:30-5:00 daily, closed Thursday
Owner: Sandy Batey

Frontier Towne opened its doors in 1985 as one of the first collectives in the San Joaquin Valley. The interior resembles the main street of an old western town, complete with settings of an old general store, bank, saloon, boarding house and blacksmith shop. This 5,000 sq. ft.

shop offers a huge variety of antiques and collectibles. Western collectibles are a speciality of the owner as she is a ranch raised cowgirl and still rides and competes in rodeos (in her spare time!). A very interesting stop on your antique trail.

The 2nd Frontier
529 Robertson Blvd.
209/665-3900
Open: 10:30-5:00 daily, closed Thursday

The 2nd Frontier which opened in 1997 is the sister shop to Frontier Towne. Specializing in retro furniture and large items, the shop has a quickly changing inventory - mostly due to its exceptionally low prices.

His & Hers Antiques
527 Robertson Blvd.
209/665-1911
Open: 11-5, 7 days a week

Noted as one of the fun places to shop in Chowchilla, His & Hers Antiques offers something for everyone from primitive to formal. Twelve dealers from Fresno to San Francisco supply the wares which make up this eclectic inventory.

Village Antiques
510 Robertson Blvd.
209/665-1487
Open: Thurs.-Mon., 9-5, Tue. 9-2

For the past ten years, Brigette Brooks has offered her customers a unique blend of antiques and collectibles. In addition to the usual and the unusual, she also carries old paper items.

The Glasstique Shoppe
331 Robertson Blvd.
209/665-5676
Open: Daily, 10-5, closed Wed.

This shoppe, which is 1700 square feet in size, specializes in flow blue porcelain, beautiful furniture, and a general line of antiques and collectibles.

The owners have been collecting antiques for thirty-five years and have operated The Glasstique Shoppe for ten years at this location.

Gray Duck Antique Mall
216 Robertson Blvd.
209/665-3305
grammy@madnet.net
Open: Daily 10-5, closed Wed.

Gray Duck Antique Mall has established itself over the past fifteen years as a special place to shop. This 3,000-square-foot showcase mall specializes in advertising, war memorabilia, toys and western tack along with a general line of antiques and collectibles.

30 CLAREMONT

Cat In The Window
206 W. Bonita Ave.
909/399-0297

Cambridge Row Antiques
206 W. Bonita Ave.
909/625-1931

Back Bay Antiques
206 W. Bonita Ave.
909/621-9917

31 CLOVIS

Osterberg's Mercantile
460 Clovis Ave.
209/298-4291

Clovis Antique Mall 1&2
530 & 532 Fifth St.
209/298-1090

Antiques N'More
536 Fifth St.
209/322-1781

Peacock Alley Antiques
614 Fifth St.
209/299-1186

Days of Yore Antiques & Cllbls.
618 Fourth St.
209/322-6265

Donnie Lu's Gifts & Treasures
320 Pollasky
209/299-5538

Olde Time Antique Mall
328 Pollasky
209/299-2575

Melton's Carousel World
425 Pollasky
209/298-8930

Treasured Memories
457 Pollasky Ave.
209/299-4266

4th Street Antique Mall
461 Pollasky Ave.
209/323-1636

32 COSTA MESA

Panier De Fleurs
2915 S. Bristol
714/979-1819

Castle Antiques
112 E. 18th St.
714/722-6779

Jack & Gloria's Antiques
1304 Logan Ave. #E,F,G
714/546-5450

Fanfare Tiffany Lamps
1765 Newport Blvd.
714/642-6692

Newport Antique Center
2384 Newport Blvd.
714/631-2411

Zazy Goona Antique Mall
1770 Orange Ave.
714/646-4561

Heirloom Galleries
369 E. 17th St.
714/631-4633

Crofton Antiques
670 W. 17th St.
714/642-4585

Cottage Company
1686 Tustin Ave.
714/722-0777

Treasures on Consignment
2220 Fairview Rd.
714/645-5477

Art & Antique Row
130 E. 17th St.
714/722-1177

Consignment Gallery
270 E. 17th St.
714/631-2622

Instant Replay
369 E. 17th Ste. 6
714/642-8898

Stix & Stones
333 E. 17th Unit b-12
714/646-7233

Old Stones
711 W. 17th St. Unit a-5
714/574-8033

Normandy Metal
1603 Superior Ave.
714/631-5555

Decor delux
444 W. 19th S
714/722-6074

Jack & Gloria's II
2981 Fairview Road
714/751-3809

33 COTTONWOOD

The Pidgeon Hole
20832 Front St.
916/347-9605

Cottonwood Antiques
3306 Main Street
916/347-0692

Country Lane Antiques
20839 Front St.
916/347-5598

Abbey Gayle's Fine Things
20840 Front St.
916/347-9669

34 COVINA

Signs Of The Times Antiques
110 N. Citrus Ave.
818/966-7101

Nostalgia Nook Antiques
112 N. Citrus Ave.
818/339-8699

Collector's Alley
225 N. Citrus Ave.
818/858-9964

Vestige Antiques
312 N. Citrus Ave.
818/967-8970

Looking Back
316 N. Citrus Ave.
818/966-8842

Ivy & The Rose
113 W. College St.
818/967-1171

Old Covina Antique Emporium
514 N. Citrus
818/859-9972

G & L Collectibles
332 N. Citrus
818/966-6829

35 CRESCENT CITY

Antiques Etc.
280 U.S. Highway 101 S
707/464-9012

Sunset House Antiques
1060 Sunset Circle
707/464-6631

Eclectic
305 U.S. Highway 101S
707/464-7907

36 CUCAMONGA

A's Antiques
8078 Archibald
909/989-8017

37 CULVER CITY

Beaded Bird
3811 Bagley Ave.
310/204-3594

Aunt Iris's Antiques
10762 Washington Blvd.
310/838-5349

38 CYPRESS

Cora & Mac's Glass Antiques
5012 Ball Road
714/229-8325

Anne Michael's
5917 Cerritos Avenue
714/821-7990

39 DANVILLE

Antiques Du Coeur
391 Hartz Ave.
510/837-5049

Rue 137
398 Hartz Ave.
510/837-1148

Danville Antiques
111 Town & Country Rd.
510/837-4784

40 EL CAJON

El Cajon Antiques
161 E. Main St.
619/441-8804

Main Street Antique Mall
237 E. Main St.
619/447-0800

Flinn Springs Country Store
14860 Olde Hwy. 80
619/443-1842

Magnolia Antique Mall
456 N. Magnolia Ave.
619/444-0628

41 ELK GROVE

Dalin Jewelers
8765 Elk Grove Blvd.
916/685-6530

Country Blend
9084 Elk Grove Blvd.
916-686-8223

Bells Cookie Jar
9086 Elk Grove Blvd.
916/685-7810

Country Grove Antiques
9098 Elk Grove Blvd.
916/685-2082

42 ENCINITAS

Acanthus Fine Antiques
1010 1st St.
619/633-1515

Rose Petal Cottage
536 N. Hwy. 101
619/632-0032

Caldwell's Antiques
1234 N. Hwy. 101
619/753-2369

ABC Trading Co.
1240 N. Hwy. 101
619/753-5160

Simply Nostalgia
162 S. Rancho Sante Fe Rd.
619/943-1328

43 ESCONDIDO

Victorian Garden Antiques
115 W. Grand Ave.
619/737-9669

121 Grand Antiques
121 W. Grand Ave.
619/489-0338

Escondido Antique Mall
135 W. Grand Ave.
619/743-3210

Memory Lane Antiques
158 E. Grand Ave.
619/480-1215

In The Cave
227 E. Grand Ave.
619/739-9117

Art's Antiques & Collectibles
252 E. Grand Ave.
619/746-7104

Cornucopia Antiques
317 E. Grant Ave.
619/745-9792

Hidden Valley Antique Empor.
333 E. Grant Ave.
619/737-0333

44 EUREKA

Antiques and Goodies
1128 3rd St.
707/442-0445
Mon.-Sat.10-5, Sundays during the summer.

Directions: Traveling south on U.S. 101 turn right on M Street, left on 3rd; shop is on the left/ traveling north on U.S. 101 turn left on L Street, right on 3rd; shop is on the right.

Antiques and Goodies offers seven rooms of imported furnishings and smalls. The shop specializes in English, French and Japanese furniture, Victorian housewares, tools and clocks. You will also find a large selection of Quimper, Mottoware, Majolica, and British commemoratives.

Antique Annex
208 F St.
707/443-9113

Old Town Antiques
318 F St.
707/442-3235

Eureka Antique Mall
533 F St.
707/445-8835

Hexagram Antiques
426 3rd St.
707/443-4334

The Hose Company
1401 3rd St.
707/445-4673

45 EXETER

Exeter Antiques
216 East Pine
209/594-4221
Open 10-6 every day except Tuesdays
(after hours phone number for out-of-town dealers: 209/747-3558)

Directions: From Highway 99 travel east on Highway 198 for 15 miles to Highway 65 (Exeter Porterville turnoff). Go south 2 miles to Pine Street (at the water tower), turn right. Go 4 blocks and Exeter Antiques is located on the left next to a small park and giant orange grove mural. There are eight antique shops within walking distance.

Brian Barton has been around the antique business almost all his life. His grandparents were collectors, his mother an interior designer, and his dad an architect. So it was nothing out of the ordinary when Brian decided to turn the old dry goods store into an antique shop. And, being the son of an architect, it was only natural that he wanted to restore it to its original design. The building was actually constructed around 1909, but the earliest photo Brian could find was taken in 1911.

And so it stands, just as gracefully as it stood in 1911. a charmingly restored building full of genuine early American antiques. Brian and his wife, Susan, have filled this two-story dream shop with some of the finest antiques in the country. They respectfully offer authentic painted pieces, American pottery, a large dairy advertising section, old lighting, folk art and loads of furniture. The Bartons have stressed that you will find only the "real McCoy" here - absolutely no reproductions.

46 FAIR OAKS

House Of Uniquities
10147 Fair Oaks Blvd.
916/863-0111

Blue Eagle Antiques
10201 Fair Oaks Blvd.
916/966-4947

Mary Scott Antiques
10211 Fair Oaks Blvd.
916/967-2493

47 FALLBROOK

Ruthy's
205 N. Main St.
619/723-8043

Millies Antique N Old Lace
3137 S. Mission Rd. #A
619/723-9206

Country Elegance
3137 S. Mission Rd. #B
619/723-3417

Ivy House Antiques
3137 S. Mission Rd. #B
619/728-7038

Tin Barn Antiques
3137 S. Mission Rd. #D
619/723-1609

Kirk's Antiques
321 N. Orange Ave.
619/728-6333

48 FELTON

Carousel Gallery Antiques Dolls
6931 Highway 9
408/335-3076

Huckleberry House
Antiques By Appointment
408/335-1395

49 FERNDALE

Gingerbread Mansion Inn
400 Berding Street
707/786-4000
Rates $100-205
Four-Diamond Rated

Located in a well preserved Victorian Village, The Gingerbread Mansion Inn is one of northern California's most photographed homes. The Inn is a striking display of superior Victorian architecture surrounded by immaculately groomed English gardens.

Originally built in 1899 for a local doctor, the mansion had doubled in size by the 1920s.

Throughout the years, it has been a haven for the sick and wounded, a resting quarters for the elderly, a meeting place for war veterans, and the place several families called home.

Today, this completely restored estate pampers guests with such amenities as bubble baths in the his-and-her claw foot tubs, bathrobes and bedside chocolates.

Exploring and experiencing the sights and sounds of the village is the principal pastime of the guests. A delightful little surprise offered by the innkeeper is the use of one of the bicycles painted in colors to match the inn. Umbrellas are offered if it rains.

Oh, and there's one more little intriguing detail that I haven't told you about - the surprise visitors at Gingerbread Mansion Inn. Robin Mead, a London resident and writer explored the mansion and wrote of these "unannounced visitors" in a book entitled *Haunted Hotels.* Here is Robin's story:

THE GHOSTS at the Gingerbread Mansion Inn are presumed to be a couple of mischievous Victorian children, although nobody is quite sure who exactly they were, when they lived there, or what they are doing. Suffice it to say they have picked wonderful surroundings, for the Gingerbread Mansion is one of the best-preserved and most beautifully kept Victorian houses in the United States.

"When I bought the house, it had been empty for years," innkeeper Ken Torbert says. A former corporate planning analyst, he used to visit inns on his own holidays, and when he was driving past the Gingerbread Mansion and saw a For Sale sign up outside, he simply fell in love with it. "When I first walked into the place, even though I am a Victorian buff, it had a sense of space and balance-and I knew I wanted to live here. I love it," Torbert says.

There was a problem, however. Local people, especially youngsters, avoided the derelict old house, a former nursing home, because they believed it was haunted.

"Every town has a haunted house, and in Ferndale it was this one." says Larry Martin, who grew up in the town and now works as the inn's chef.

Undaunted, Torbert started a painstaking and extremely thorough restoration—and the house is now immaculate. The ghostly youngsters, if they are still around, should be pleased with their home-but odd things happen. a picture which Torbert hung in the front parlor mysteriously moved itself into the lounge.

Guests walking up the main staircase have slipped on the slightly short thirteenth stair and claimed they were pushed. And one guest, Christopher Earls, spending the night of his twentieth birthday in a suite, awoke "too frightened to turn over" because he "thought there was something there."

Torbert's wife, Sandie, tells of two women guests who arrived from San Francisco saying they had come to the Gingerbread Mansion because their friends had "talked about the children."

Children? Sandie has just one daughter. But Torbert can add to the story: "We had some touched-up photos of Victorian children with somber faces," he recalls. "Sometimes, guests would stay up late and write long entries in the guest books which we have in each room. They wrote about the children, who came alive at night."

It is hard to imagine a more peaceful and comfortable inn. Relax, and the mind plays tricks. And there can be few more relaxing places than the Gingerbread Mansion Inn.

From *Haunted Hotels* Copyright 1995 by Robin Mead
Published by Rutledge Hill Press, Nashville, Tennessee

Foggy Bottoms
563 Main St.
707/786-9188
Mon.-Sat. 12-5, Sun. 12-4

Directions: Take the Ferndale exit from Highway 101. Cross over Fernbridge Drive into Ferndale. Foggy Bottoms is in the first block of the business district on Main St.. near Shaw Ave.

Foggy Bottoms Antiques, named for the foggy veil which often descends upon this quaint valley town, is located in a State Historic Landmark town, on a National Historic Landmark street.

The shop, housed in a 1,000-square-foot turn-of-the-century building, may be small but is richly blessed with notable charm. "It's all I can handle," says Jacque Ramirez, who is both shopkeeper and owner of Foggy Bottoms. She is also co-owner (with her husband, Richard) of Grandmother's House Bed and Breakfast located just seconds away from the shop at 861 Howard St.

Foggy Bottom's "claim to fame" is its offering of many old radio program cassettes. The shop stocks a hodge-podge of unusual smalls; china, porcelains, a nice selection of salt and pepper shakers, early rolling pins, pottery and just about anything old that Jacque finds interesting.

For some unknown reason, Ferndale happens to be the home to many avid sweater knitters, and for that reason Foggy Bottoms offers an ample selection of yarns, patterns and accessories for the genteel looper.

After a long day of antiquing and sight-seeing in this "picture postcard" valley, you're always welcome to stay at Grandmother's House. Built in 1901, this bed and breakfast offers gracious accommodations with all the romance and charm of the turn of the century. The three guest rooms are decorated with antique furnishings, as is the rest of the house. The dining room provides a parlor with wood-burning fireplace.

Enjoy the peaceful back porch while watching Buffalo graze in a nearby pasture. Located in a quiet residential neighborhood.

Golden Gait Mercantile
421 Main St.
707/786-4891

Cream City Mall
1400 Main St.
707/786-4997

50 FOLSOM

As Time Goes By Antiques
306 Rile St.
916/985-6206

Sheepish Grin Antique Market
625 Sutter St.
916/885-0257

Thistle & Rose Scottish Antqs.
722 Sutter St.
916/353-1936

Dal Bello Antiques Collective
727 Sutter St.
916/985-3772

Williams Carriage Hse. Antqs.
728 Sutter St.
916/985-7416

Emily's Antique Corner
732 Sutter St.
916/985-6222

Curiosity Shoppe
801 Ω Sutter St.
916/985-0534

Olde Towne Antiques
809 Sutter St.
916/985-2853

Colonies
813 Sutter St.
916/985-3442

Cottage In The Mall
813 Sutter St.
916/985-0496

Setnik's In Time Again
815 Sutter St.
916/985-2390

51 FORTUNA

Fernbridge Antique Mall
597 Fernbridge Dr.
707/725-8820

Rundells Antiques & Cllbls.
569 Main St.
707/725-9175

Fortuna Florist
1006 Main St.
707/725-1133

Fortuna Art & Old Things
1026 Main St.
707/725-3003

Linda's Antiques
1116 Main St.
707/725-5664

52 FREMONT

Cherished Memories
121 I St.
510/792-3634

Our Corner
151 I St.
510/791-9077

The Clock Man
120 J St.
510/794-5928

Antiques Junction
37312 Niles Blvd.
510/793-3481

With a Little Help My Friends
37313 Niles Blvd.
510/797-2088

Shelby's
37357 Niles Blvd.
510/790-0544

Morning Glory Antiques
37372 Niles Blvd.
510/790-3374

Woodhaven
37396 Niles Blvd.
510/745-7666

The Store
37415 Niles Blvd.
510/797-8471

Shades Of The Past
37495 Niles Blvd.
510/791-2415

Ma Mere Intl.
37501 Niles Blvd.
510/793-8043

Les Belles Antiques
37549 Niles Blvd.
510/794-4773

Bite & Browse
37565 Niles Blvd.
510/796-4537

Lost In The Attic
37663 Niles Blvd.
510/791-2420

Old And New
37675 Niles Blvd.
510/792-4757

East Bay Dolls & Bears
37721 Niles Blvd.
510/792-2559

Carlson's
37761 Niles Blvd.
510/794-3560

Jean & Bea's Toys U-NU
37769 Niles Blvd.
510/793-2848

Timeless Treasures
37769 Niles Blvd.
510/795-7755

53 FRESNO

Treasure of Sierra Madre
463 E. Belmont Ave.
209/264-9343

Dug 'O' Vic's European Antqs.
1310 N. Blackstone Ave.
209/442-8494

Chesterfield Antiques
5092 N. Blackstone Ave.
209/225-4736

Stacy's Antiques
2686 N. Clovis Ave.
209/292-8403

Lina's Antiques
1918 N. Echo Ave.
209/497-9767

Alice's Palace
22 E. Olive Ave.
209/485-4408

Fulton's Folly Antique Mall
920 E. Olive Ave.
209/268-3856

54 FULLERTON

Greer's Antique Mall
118 E. Commonwealth Ave.
714/879-3999

Antique Mine
124 E. Commonwealth Ave.
714/526-2200

George's Antiques
201 W. Commonwealth Ave.
714/871-4347

Back Home Antiques
509 W. Commonwealth Ave.
714/526-3553

Doll Trunk
531 W. Commonwealth Ave.
714/526-1467

Jones Mercantile
531 W. Commonwealth Ave.
714/879-3501

Farm Bell Antiques
912 E. Commonwealth Ave.
714/526-4080

Antique Gallery
110 N. Harbor Blvd.
714/871-3850

Amerage Avenue Antiques
122 N. Harbor Blvd. Ste. 110
714/525-6383

Kindred Co
202 N. Harbor Blvd.
714/879-2324

Antique Companion
204 N. Harbor
714/525-2756

Old Towne Fullerton Antiques
206 N. Harbor
714/447-9046

Harbor Antique Mall
207 N. Harbor Blvd.
714/680-0532

Park Place Antiques & Cllbls.
209 N. Harbor Blvd.
714/447-1050

55 GARDEN GROVE

Private Collections
12931 Main St.
714/539-4419

Garden Grove Merc.
12941 Main St.
714/534-1857

L C & Sally's Antiques
12951 Main St.
714/530-3035

Sleepy Hollow Antique Mall
12965 Main St.
714/539-9187

56 GILROY

Final Frontier
7411 Monterey St.
408/847-1050

Gilroy Antiques
7445 Monterey St.
408/842-1776

Monterey St. Antiques
7511 Monterey St.
408/848-3788

Classic Cottage Antiques
7515 Monterey St.
408/842-0399

Garbos Antiques & Collectibles
7517 Monterey St.
408/848-6722

Hampton Court Antiques
7542 Monterey St.
408/847-2455

Antique Avenue
7562 Monterey St.
408/842-0673

Lindsey & Friends Antique Mall
7888 Monterey St.
408/842-5586

Littlejohns Fine Jewelry
8220 Monterey St.
408/842-1001

57 GLENDALE

Weed's Antqs. & Clock Repair
3427 Ocean View Blvd.
818/249-1508

About Antiques
3533 Ocean View Blvd.
818/249-8587

Fiona's
3463 N. Verdugo Rd.
818/249-6776

58 GLENDORA

Millie's Dolls
140 N. Glendora Ave.
818/963-8311

Owl Antiques & Collectibles
160 N. Glendora Ave. #1
818/963-5616

Country Village Antiques
163 N. Glendora Ave.
818/914-6860

Orange Tree
216 N. Glendora Ave.
818/335-3376

Anything Goes Emporium
218 N. Glendora Ave.
818/963-3939

Old Packing House
243 S. Vermont Ave.
818/963-8171

59 GRASS VALLEY

Grass Valley Antique Empor.
150 Mill St.
916/272-7302

Duck Soup
160 Mill St.
916/477-7891

Al's Attic Antiques
11671 Maltman Dr.
916/272-1777

Auntie's Attic
504 Whiting St.
916/273-1095

60 HANFORD

Country Bazaar
7090 N. Douty St.
209/584-8798

Livery Stable Shops
113 S. Douty St.
209/582-0356

Anna's Antiques
119 S. Douty St.
209/582-6897

Hanford Antique Emporium
108 E. 8th St.
209/583-8202

Corner
102 E. 6th St.
209/584-7097

61 HAYWARD

Hayward Faire Antiques
926 B St.
510/537-7823

Incurable Collector
944 B St.
510/733-5122

Jeannie's Antiques
1013 B St.
510/582-1773

Ryan's Country Farm Antiques
1019 B St.
510/881-7755

Antique Connection
1033 B St.
510/889-8608

B Street Antiques
1037 B St.
510/889-8549

62 HEALDSBURG

Antique Harvest
225 Healdsburg Ave.
707/433-0223

Healdsburg Classic Antiques
226 Healdsburg Ave.
707/433-4315

Vintage Antiques Etc.
328 Healdsburg Ave.
707/433-7461

Irish Cottage Antiques
112 Matheson St.
707/433-4850

Going Vintage Antqs. & Cllbls.
44 Mill St.
707/433-4501

Vintage Plaza Antiques
44 Mill St.
707/433-8409

63 HEMET

Hermitage Antiques
910 E. Florida Ave. #B2
909/925-1968

Fond Memories
123 N. Havard St.
909/652-2511

Second Time Around
699 N. San Jacinto St.
909/652-6798

64 HESPERIA

Carousel Faire
15800 Main St.
619/244-2336

Antiques By Janie
15885 Main St. #220
619/244-9797

Apple Pie Antiques
15885 Main St.
619/947-4474

Miss Jenny's
15885 Main St. #170
619/947-4020

Sonja's Treasures
15885 Main St.
619/947-6642

Eufemia's Antiquery
11605 Mariposa Rd.
619/244-4828

Silvia's Boutique
15885 Main St.
619/244-0796

Making Memories
15885 Main St. #160
619/947-6259

Cobblestone Square Antiques
15885 Main St.
619/244-5301

Miss Jenny's II
15885 Main St. #260
619/947-2229

65 HOLLYWOOD/WEST HOLLYWOOD

Radisson Hollywood Roosevelt Hotel
7000 Hollywood Boulevard
213/466-7000 or for reservations 1-800-833-3333

Situated right in the heart of Hollywood, The Radisson Hollywood Roosevelt Hotel is a stylish property built in 1927 as the centerpiece of the film world - a role it still fulfills. Always the place to see and be seen, it staged the first-ever Academy Awards ceremony in its Blossom Ballroom in 1929, and it has hosted a variety of major movie premieres and opening night galas during the following four decades.

Then in 1983, the hotel - named after President Theodore Roosevelt - began a two-year, $40 million restoration. Original features such as the classic Spanish revival style exterior and the famous Blossom Room remained as they had always been. Hand-painted ceilings were restored; Spanish wrought-iron grilles were renovated. Finally, in March 1986, her dignity regained, the hotel was declared open again at a gala ceremony attended by fifteen hundred of Hollywood's rich and famous.

Today the hotel features 335 beautifully appointed rooms, including twenty luxury suites. Among the suites are a Grand Suite, the Celebrity Suite, ten movie-themed suites, and nine three-room Hollywood suites. There are also 65 cabana rooms in a tropical garden setting bordering an Olympic-sized heated swimming pool, Jacuzzi, and the Tropicana Bar.

The hotel restaurant, Theodore's, offers fine dining in the California/continental style. It's open for breakfast, lunch, and dinner seven days a week and serves an elaborate champagne brunch on Sundays. The cabaret nightclub, Cinegrill, hosts top-name entertainers. Cover charges and show times vary.

Hollywood's "Walk of Fame," where the past and the present have their names engraved in stars on the sidewalk, is right outside the hotel on Hollywood Boulevard. The renowned Mann's Chinese Theater is also at the doorstep, and attractions such as Universal Studios, Disneyland, Beverly Hills, and the Hollywood Bowl are all within easy reach.

The ghost at the Radisson Hollywood Roosevelt Hotel is Marilyn Monroe. She's joined there by Montgomery Clift and a number of other stars.

The renovation of the property seemed to disturb all sorts of spirits. Even the hotel's publicity material admits, "Yes, this property is haunted. There are many ghosts and spirits we know about, and probably a lot more that we don't know."

The easiest to check out is in the Blossom Ballroom. In mid-December 1985, just two weeks before the hotel's unofficial reopening, actor Alan Russell, working as personal assistant to the general manager, discovered a cool spot in the ballroom. Lots of staff and guests have experienced it, and it has even been investigated scientifically. It's a circle, about thirty inches in diameter. The temperature in the circle is about ten degrees cooler than the rest of the room. There is no obvious explanation for this, and although the cool spot dissipates when the room is crowded, it soon returns when the room is empty. Psychics say there is a man in black there, showing a lot of anxiety.

Cleaner Suzanne Leonard had plenty of cause for anxiety herself on the same day Alan Russell discovered the cool spot. She was dusting the tall, dark-framed mirror in the general manager's office when she saw the reflection of a blond girl in the glass. She turned around to speak to her but there was no one there. Puzzled, Leonard reported the incident to her boss, who revealed that the mirror had once belonged to Marilyn Monroe and had been removed from the pool side suite Marilyn occupied at the hotel when the film star died. The mirror has now been moved to the lower level elevator landing, so curious guests can keep their own lookout for Marilyn's ghost.

Stay at the hotel long enough and you could even cast your own film. Montgomery Clift, who spent three months in Room 928 while filming *From Here to Eternity*, has been felt brushing past people in the corridor outside the room where he once paced for hours, learning his lines. There's a "ghost writer" in the personnel office, who taps away at the electric typewriter after the empty office is locked up for the night; a lighting man who turns the lights on and off in Star Suite 1101/1102, and a sound man who makes telephone calls to the switchboard from empty rooms. There are even cast parties. Guests quite often call to complain about noisy neighbors in the room next door to theirs, only to be told the room is empty.

It would all make a thrilling film. But Montgomery Clift does not seem to welcome modern film makers to Room 928 and has caused all kinds of problems. Marilyn's mirror doesn't want to be filmed, and the cool spot in the ballroom is cold enough to affect audio equipment.

Research psychic, Peter James, spent some time investigating the hotel's phenomena in the spring of 1992. He felt the presence of numerous film stars: Carmen Miranda in a hallway on the third floor; Humphrey Bogart near the elevator; Errol Flynn, Edward Arnold, and Betty Grable in the Blossom Room, and Montgomery Clift up in Room 928. As he walked into the Tropicana Bar, James exclaimed, "Marilyn Monroe is here, right here, and her presence is very strong."

So who needs to go to the movies? It's all there in the Hollywood Roosevelt Hotel, the stuff of which a publicity man's dreams are made. And, quite coincidentally, the hotel has felt moved to put out an eight-page press release detailing its phantom film stars and their latest personal appearances.

From *Haunted Hotels*, copyright 1995 by Robin Mead,
Published by Rutledge Hill Press, Nashville, Tennessee

Rye Byers Antiques
8424 Melrose Ave.
West Hollywood
213/655-2095

City Antiques
8444 Melrose Ave.
West Hollywood
213/658-6354

Villa Medici
8687 Melrose Ave.
West Hollywood
310/659-9984

Papillion Gallery
8818 Melrose Ave.
West Hollywood
310/659-9984

W. Antiques
8925 Melrose Ave.
West Hollywood
310/275-5099

Antiques & Design
610 N. Robertson Blvd.
West Hollywood
310/659-0946

Ashby's Antiques
638 N. Robertson Blvd.
West Hollywood
310/854-1006

John Alan Antiques
644 N. Robertson Blvd.
West Hollywood
310/854-5438

Gregory's Country Home
8747 Sunset Blvd.
West Hollywood
310/652-7288

Last Moving Picture Co.
6307 Hollywood Blvd.
213/467-0838

66 HUNTINGTON BEACH

Way Back When
8901 Atlanta Ave.
714/960-5335

Country Cottage
18211 Enterprise Ln. #B
714/842-5959

Back In Tyme Antiques
517 Walnut Ave.
714/536-2194

67 ISLETON

Country Cupboard
15 Main
916/777-6737

Junk & Treasures
112 2nd
916/777-4828

Windmill Antiques Etc.
15041 State Highway 160
916/777-6112

68 JACKSON

Amador Antique Emporium
12311 Martell Rd.
209/223-2030

Water Street Antiques
11101 State Highway 88
209/223-4189

National Hotel Antiques
2 Water St.
209/223-3447

Specialty Shop
5 Main St.
209/223-3036

69 JAMESTOWN

Main St. Mercantile
18138 Main St.
209/984-6551

Bear Essentials Antiques
18145 Main St.
209/984-5315

Butterfield House Century Gifts
18158 Main St.
209/984-3068

Over The Hill Antiques
18205 Main St.
209/984-3237

Crackel & Co.
18210 Main St.
209/984-4080

Pine Tree Peddlers
18211 Main St.
209/984-3647

Jamestown Mercantile Antqs.
18255 Main St.
209/984-5148

Mostly Pennsylvania
18278 Main St.
209/984-0533

Daisy Tree II
18280 Main St.
209/984-0661

Now & Then Antiques
17775 State Hwy. 108
209/984-4224

70 JULIAN

Eden Creek Orchard Bed & Breakfast

1052 Julian Orchards Drive
619/765-2102 or 619/753-4603
Fax: 619/943-7959
Open all hours, all days
Rates from $90

Directions: Highways 78 and 79 both go through downtown Julian. Turn north at the four-way stop on Main Street, the only four-way stop in town. Go 2 miles (Main Street turns into Farmer Road) and cross Wynola Road, where Farmer Road turns into Julian Orchards Drive. Pass the Menghini Winery on the left and 500 feet farther down on the left is Eden Creek Orchard Bed & Breakfast.

A little bit different, in an interesting romantic setting, is the Eden Creek Bed & Breakfast. It's set in a 10-acre apple orchard, just 500 feet from a winery and 2 miles from the historic gold mining town of Julian. Eden Creek offers two suites. The smaller one is upstairs in the "barn" and caters to one couple in complete privacy. This suite's focal point is the custom queen canopy bed; the bath holds an antique clawfoot tub with shower, and a sink made from an antique sewing machine. The larger Eden Creek suite is a two-bedroom, one-bath accommodation on the ground floor of the house next to the barn. With a queen canopy bed in one room and a double in the second bedroom, this suite can accommodate two couples or a family. Both suites have wood-burning stoves, antique furnishings, down pillows and comforters, and share access to the semi-private Jacuzzi on the back deck of the barn.

Guests are offered bottled water, a split of Menghini wine, snacks, and meal tickets redeemable for breakfast or lunch at Mama's Cafe in Julian. There is a nearby dinner theater and numerous restaurants in the Julian area. Eden Creek Orchard is a short distance from the Volcan Preserve Trail, where strollers can see dozens of species of birds, wild turkey, deer and coyote, and even Bighorn sheep have been closely observed in the nearby Anza Borrego Desert State Park.

Wynola Timeless Treasures
4355 Hwy. 78 #C
619/765-3113

Antique Boutique
2626 Main St.
619/765-0541

Applewood & Co.
2804 Washington
619/765-1185

71 KINGSBURG

Swedish Village Antiques
1135 Draper St.
209/897-4419

Apple Duplin Antiques
1440 Draper St.
209/897-5936

Granny's Attic
1513 Draper St.
209-897-4203

72 LA HABRA

Su Casa Antiques
310 E. Whittier Blvd.
310/694-3108

Ragtime Antiques
901 W. Whittier Blvd.
310/694-5414

Clockworks
2204 W. Whittier Blvd.
310/694-5608

73 LA JOLLA

McGee's Antiques Of La Jolla
7467 Cuvier St.
619/459-1256

Renaissance Art & Antiques
7715 Fay Ave.
619/454-3887

Antiques Of Europe
7437 Girard Ave.
619/459-5886

Glorius Antiques
7645 Girard Ave.
619/459-2222

Silver Store
7909 Girard Ave.
619/459-3241

Circa
7861 Herschel Ave.
619/454-7962

Bird Rock Antiques
5623 La Jolla Blvd.
619/459-4091

Angelique's
1237 Prospect St. Ste. U
619/459-5769

Alcala Gallery
950 Silverado St.
619/454-6610

Taylor Antique Gallery
1000 Torrey Pines Rd.
619/456-1041

La Jolla Consignment & Mall
7509 Girard
619/456-0936

Early American Numismatics
P.O. Box 2442
619/459-4159

74 LA MESA

Antique Elegance
8363 Center Dr. #5B
619/697-8766

Grossmont Antique Mart
8379 Center Dr.
619/466-2040

Country Loft
8166 La Mesa Blvd.
619/466-5411

Rocking Horse Antique Mall
8223 La Mesa Blvd.
619/469-6191

Time & Treasures
8290 La Mesa Blvd.
619/460-8004

Granny's Antiques
8360 La Mesa Blvd.
619/465-9641

La Mesa Village Antiques
8371 La Mesa Blvd.
619/461-7940

Image Maker
8219 La Mesa Blvd.
619/461-9490

75 LAFAYETTE

Antiquary
1020 Brown Ave.
510/284-5611

Brown Ave. Collective
1030 Brown Ave.
510/284-7069

Clocks Etc.
3401 Mount Diablo Blvd.
510/284-4720

76 LAGUNA BEACH

Wild Goose Chase-Sweet William
1936 South Coast Highway
714/376-9388
Open Mon.-Sat. 10:30-5, Sun. 12-5

Directions: Take the 405 freeway from Los Angeles to Laguna Canyon Road, which is Highway 133. Take Highway 133 to the Pacific Coast Highway, turn left, and continue past Center Street. Sweet William is between Center Street and Diamond Avenue.

Situated in an old 1929 cottage on the beach, Wild Goose Chase-Sweet William offers the antique shopper authentic Americana. They specialize in old quilts, folk art pieces, bird houses and original painted period furniture. They also have original oil paintings (florals and landscapes) by artist Andrea Dern, wife of actor Bruce Dern. But the eyecatching display at Sweet William's is the gigantic model of a barn from Monticello, Iowa, that was used as an instructional tool to teach farmers how to build barns back in the 1930s. It is still covered in its original grey paint and comes complete with horses in their stalls. They also have two rare movie props: three-foot exact replicas of the New York Central and the Pacific Fruit Express trains, that were used in the old silent movies. If you're into the unusual, you're sure to find it here.

Laguna Antiques & Consign.
330 N. Coast Hwy.
714/497-9744

Gallery One of Laguna
1220 N. Coast Hwy.
714/494-4444

Ruins Antiques
1231-33 N. Coast Hwy.
714/376-0025

Melange
1235 N. Coast Hwy.
714/497-4915

Antiqua
1290 N. Coast Hwy.
714/494-5860

Antiques & Interiors
448 S. Coast Hwy.
714/376-2005

Family Jewels
490 S. Coast Hwy.
714/494-2436

Richard Yeakel Antiques
1099 S. Coast Hwy.
714/494-5526

Antique Boutique
1432 S. Coast Hwy.
714/494-1571

Iron Maiden
1524 S. Coast Hwy.
714/497-0414

Redfern Gallery
1540 S. Coast Hwy.
714/497-3356

Kaehler's Fine Arts
332 Forest Ave.
714/494-3864

Consignment Corner
888 Glenneyre St.
714/497-1010

Roberta Gauthey Antiques
1166 Glenneyre St.
714/494-9925

Jerry's Antiquities N Things
1295 Glenneyre St.
714/494-0019

77 LAKE ELSINORE

Enchanted Treasures
169 N. Main Street
909/674-8336
Open 10-5 daily, including holidays

Directions: Traveling I-15, exit Main Street, between Franklin and Peck.

Cindy's shop, Enchanted Treasures, is in an early 1900s building that began life as a bus depot, then later became the local hardware store. Today this 8,000-sq.-ft. shop offers a nice selection of porcelain dolls, Fenton, unique jewelry, quality furnishings, and a large selection of decorative accessories.

Antique Corner
106 W. Graham Ave.
909/674-7989

Chimes
201 W. Graham Ave.
909/674-3456

Grand Antique Mall
18273 Grand Ave.
909/678-5095

Antique Emporium
101 S. Main St.
909/245-3977

78 LANCASTER

Antiques & Things
44625 Sierra Hwy.
805/945-0504

Buffy's Antiques & Collectibles
3606 E. Avenue I
805/946-0335

79 LAVERNE

Generations
2343 D Street
909/593-4936

Yesterday's Antiques
2320 D Street
909/593-4456

Sweet Memories
2336 D Street
909/596-2944

Ken's Olden Oddities
1910 White Avenue
909/593-1846

80 LEMON COVE

Mesa Verde Plantation Bed & Breakfast
33038 Sierra Highway 198
209/597-2555 or 1-800-240-1466
Web Site:http://www.psnw.com/~mvpbb
E.-mail: mvpbb@psnw.com
Rates $70-125

Directions: Take Highway 99 to the town of Visalia. Go 23.5 miles east on Highway 198.

Scott and Marie Munger operate their bed & breakfast at an old citrus plantation in the foothills of the Sierra Nevada Mountains. To carry out the plantation theme, Scott and Marie have named and decorated all eight guest rooms after characters from *Gone With The Wind*. There's the Melanie, the Scarlett O'Hara, the Belle Watling, the Rhett Butler, the Ashley Wilkes, Mammy's Room, Prissy's Room, and the Aunt Pitty Pat. From the descriptions of the rooms they sent us, they are right on the mark for matching decor to personalities!

The Mesa Verde also offers guests orange groves for meandering, a spa, heated pool, gazebo, hammocks under the trees, verandas and fireplaces. Guests can also enjoy a gourmet breakfast in the elegant dining room or outside in the courtyard garden, where you can dine with the hummingbirds.

Walker House Antiques
33513 Sierra Dr. Hwy. 198
209/597-2361

81 LEMON GROVE

Years of Yesterday Antiques
7895 Broadway
619/464-3892

Lemon Grove Antique Mall
7919 Broadway
619/461-1361

Broadway Antique Mall
7945 Broadway
619/461-1399

Vivian's
7968-7970 Broadway
619/461-2728

82 LEUCADIA

Leucadia Inn-By-The-Sea
960 North Highway 101
619/942-1668
Open seven days

Directions: From Highway 5 (south to San Diego or north to Los Angeles), go west on Leucadia Blvd., then right on N. Highway 101. Take the first left on Jasper, and the inn is on the corner of Jasper and N. Highway 101.

Here's a bed and breakfast with a twist: Leucadia Inn bills itself as "a theme room bed and breakfast," with uniquely decorated rooms featuring an African safari, New Orleans, Hollywood nostalgia, a bit o'country, tropical, and Nantucket. Just one block from the beach, the inn also offers guests sunset baskets, breakfast in room or tickets to the patio restaurant just 100 feet from the inn.

83 LIVERMORE

Livermore Trading Post
250 Church St.
510/443-2822

Cleo's Memory Lane Antiques
2041 1st St.
510/443-2536

Adams Family Antiques
2047 1st St.
510/443-9408

Yesterday's
2053 1st St.
510/373-1817

Anne Marie's Antqs. & Things
2074 1st St.
510/454-9870

Forget Me Not
2187 1st St.
510/606-6330

Bill's Antiques & Collectibles
2339 1st St.
510/449-9002

Blue Door Antiques
321 N. L St.
510/449-2111

84 LOCKEFORD

Foxglove Antiques
13333 Highway 88
209/727-3008
Mon.-Sun. 10-5, Closed Tuesday

Directions: Traveling south from Sacramento on Hwy. 99 to Lodi (or traveling north from Stockton on Hwy. 99), take Hwy. 12 east, travel approximately 6 miles to Hwy. 88, follow Hwy. 88 northeast to Lockeford. Located next to Post Office.

It will come as no surprise that Foxglove Antiques offers a nice selection of Roseville pottery. The owner, Gloria Mollring, is the author of *Roseville Pottery Collector's Price Guide.* If pottery is not your fancy, Gloria and her husband, Jim, provide an eclectic selection for any curious shopper. Exceptional period pieces, jewelry, books, dolls, and paper collectibles are just a few of the many antiques available at this shop.

85 LODI

Old Friends Antiques
225 N. California St.
209/367-0607

Grave's Country Antiques
15 N. Cherokee Ln.
209/368-5740

Grand J D Antiques
440 E. Kettleman Ln.
209/334-1140

Moehring's Antiques
440 E. Kettleman Ln.
209/369-1818

Victoria
1894 Victorian House
861 E. Pine St.
209/333-1762

Mickey's Antqs. & Cllbls. Mall
14 N. School St.
209/369-9112

86 LOMITA

A & D Antiques
2055 1/2 Pacific Coast Hwy.
310/326-2434

Anna Vocka's Antiques
1856 Pacific Coast Hwy.
310/325-2574

Gloria's Antiques
2032 Pacific Coast Hwy.
310/530-5060

87 LONG BEACH

Quick's Antiques
2545 E. Broadway
562/433-8038

William J Hossack Antiques
2720 E. Broadway
562/439-4195

Outre' Antiques
2747 E. Broadway
562/439-0339

Kelly's Place
412 Cherry Ave.
562/438-2537

Antique Clock Gallery
2122 E. 4th St.
562/438-5486

Millie's Place
144 Linden Ave.
562/435-8566

Kathy's Antiques
1340 E. Market St.
562/422-6987

Long Beach Antique Mall
3100 E. Pacific Coast Hwy.
562/494-2526

Sleepy Hollow Antique Mall
5689 Paramount Blvd.
562/634-8370

Antiques & More
327 Pine Ave.
562/432-1173

Redondo House
274 Redondo Ave.
562/434-5239

Antique Adoption
4160 N. Viking Way
562/420-1919

Village Vault Antiques
5423 E. Village Rd.
562/425-7455

Julie's Antique Mall
1133 East Wardlow Road
562/989-7799

88 LOS ALAMITOS

Whiskers & Co Antiques
10670 Los Alamitos Blvd.
310/493-4700

Los Alamitos Antique Shop
10702 Los Alamitos Blvd.
310/493-5911

Estate Store
10899 Los Alamitos Blvd.
310/430-8819

Coliseum Antiques
10909 Los Alamitos Blvd.
310/598-0811

89 LOS ALAMOS

Gussied Up
349 Bell St.
805/344-2504

General Store Antiques
458 Bell St.
805/344-2123

Krall Antiques
515 Bell St.
805/344-6311

The Prop Shop
Bell St.
805/344-3121

Los Alamos Depot Mall
515 Leslae
805/344-3315

90 LOS ALTOS

Patrician Antiques
197 1st St.
415/948-5218

Oriental Corner
280 Main St.
415/941-3207

Maria's Antiques Of Los Altos
288 1st St.
415/948-1965

Geranium House Antiques
371 1st St.
415/941-2620

Maria's Antiques Of Los Altos
393 Main St.
415/941-9682

91 LOS ANGELES

Art Spectrum
2151 Avenue of the Stars
310/788-0720

Bus Stop
5273 1/2 E. Beverly Blvd.
213/728-6720

Fainting Couch
7260 Beverly Blvd.
213/930-0106

Houle Rare Bks. & Autographs
7405 Beverly Blvd.
213/937-5858

Futurama
7956 Beverly Blvd.
213/651-5767

Beverly Hills Antiquarian
8840 Beverly Blvd. #32
310/278-0120

Marc Navarro Antiques
8840 Beverly Blvd.
310/285-9650

918 Antique Gallery
8840 Beverly Blvd.
310/271-0404

Antiquarius Center
8840 Beverly Blvd.
310/274-2363

Angele Hobin
8840 Beverly Blvd.
310/276-4449

European Antiques
8840 Beverly Blvd.
310/274-3089

Excalibur Antique Jewelry
8840 Beverly Blvd.
310/859-2320

London Imports
8840 Beverly Blvd.
310/858-7416

Lief
8922 Beverly Blvd.
310/550-8118

Catchell Five
1740 Colorado Ave.
213/256-0114

Circa Antiques
3608 Edenhurst Ave.
213/662-6600

Farmer's Market Arts & Antqs.
140 S. Fairfax Ave. #N
213/931-4804

Showcase Gallery
140 S. Fairfax Ave.
213/939-7403

Menyea's Decor
3113 W. Florence Ave.
213/752-9326

Penny Lane
2820 Gilroy St.
213/667-1838

Caravan Book Store
550 S. Grand Ave.
213/626-9944

La Maison Du Bal
705 N. Harper Ave.
213/655-8215

Antique Guild
Helms Bakery Bldg.
310/838-3131

Antique Guild
Helms Bakery Bldg.
310/838-3131

Rosetta Gallery
1958 Hillhurst Ave.
213/913-0827

Simply Unique Collbls
1903 Hyperion Ave.
213/661-5454

Fat Chance
162 N. La Brea Ave.
213/930-1960

Repeat Performance
318 N. La Brea Ave.
213/938-0609

Iron N' Antique Accents
342 N. La Brea Ave.
213/934-3953

Retro Gallery
524 1/2 N. La Brea Ave.
213/936-5261

Virtue
149 S. La Brea Ave.
213/932-1789

Francesca Dona
665 S. La Brea Ave.
213/933-0433

Consignment Collections
355 N. La Cienega Blvd.
310/657-2590

Dagmar
514 N. La Cienega Blvd.
310/652-1167

Gregorius-Pineo
653 N. La Cienega Blvd.
310/659-0588

Blake's Antiques
665 N. La Cienega Blvd.
310/289-0970

Quatrian
700 N. La Cienega Blvd.
310/652-0243

Therien & Co.
716 N. La Cienega Blvd.
310/657-4615

Remains To Be Seen Antiques
735 N. La Cienega Blvd.
310/659-3358

Pat McGann Antiques
748 N. La Cienega Blvd.
310/358-0977

Blackman Cruz
800 N. La Cienega Blvd.
310/657-9228

Nina Schwimmer Antiques
804 N. La Cienega Blvd.
310/657-4060

Ralf's Antiques
807 N. La Cienega Blvd.
310/659-1966

Richard Gould Antiques
808 N. La Cienega Blvd.
310/657-9416

Abraham Larry Antiques
810 N. La Cienega Blvd.
310/651-4834

Christianne Carty Antiques
814 N. La Cienega Blvd.
310/657-2630

Chateau Allegre
815 N. La Cienega Blvd.
310/657-7259

Evans & Gerst Antiques
910 N. La Cienega Blvd.
310/657-0112

Baldacchino Antiques
919 N. La Cienega Blvd.
310/657-6810

Smith & Houchins
921 N. La Cienega Blvd.
310/652-0308

Antique Rug Co.
928 N. La Cienega Blvd.
310/659-3847

Niakin Gallery
935 N. La Cienega Blvd.
310/652-6586

Lifetime Arts & Crafts Gallery
7111 Melrose Ave.
213/939-7441

Circa 1910 Antiques
7206 Melrose Ave.
213/965-1910

Denny Burt Modern Antiques
7208 Melrose Ave.
213/936-5269

Off The Wall Antiques
7325 Melrose Ave.
213/930-1185

Pictorial Antiques
7965 Melrose Ave.
213/951-1060

Grumps Antiques & Cllbls.
7965 Ω Melrose Ave.
213/655-3564

Pine Mine
7974 Melrose Ave.
213/852-1939

Napolean Antiques
8050 Melrose Ave.
213/658-7853

Burke's Country Pine Inc.
8080 Melrose Ave.
213/655-1114

Hays House of Wicker
8253 Melrose Ave.
213/653-2999

Thanks For The Memories
8319 Melrose Ave.
213/852-9407

Archipelago
8323 Melrose Ave.
213/653-7133

Recollections II
8377 W. Melrose Ave.
213/655-6221

Marshall Galleries
8401 Melrose Ave.
213/852-6630

French Antiques
8404 Melrose Ave.
213/653-5222

J F Chen Antiques
8414 Melrose Ave.
213/655-6310

Marshall Galleries
8420 Melrose Ave.
213/852-1964

Blue House
8440 Melrose Ave.
213/852-0747

Empire Gallery
8442 Melrose Ave.
213/655-9404

CBH Antiques
8452 Melrose Ave.
213/653-3939

French Antique Clock
8465 Melrose Ave.
213/651-3034

J P Hemmings Antiques USA
8471 Melrose Ave.
213/655-7823

Charles Gill, Inc.
8475 Melrose Ave.
213/653-3434

Cota's Antiques
8573 Melrose Ave.
310/659-1822

Dassin Gallery
8687 Melrose Ave. #B131
310/652-0203

Deanna Yohanna Antiques
8908 Melrose Ave.
310/550-0052

Rosh Antique Galleries
8400 Melrose Pl.
213/655-6969

Mehran Antiques
840 Melrose Pl.
213/658-8444

B Nagel Antiques
8410 Melrose Pl.
213/655-0115

Museum Antiques
8417 Melrose Pl.
310/652-3023

La Maison Francaise Antiques
8420 Melrose Pl.
213/653-6534

Karl The XII Swedish Antiques
8428 Melrose Pl.
213/852-0303

Licorne Antiques
8432 Melrose Pl.
213/852-4765

Sabet Antiques
8451 Melrose Pl.
213/651-5222

R. Tarlow Antiques
8454 Melrose Pl.
213/653-2122

Villa Medici
8460 Melrose Pl.
213/951-9172

Connoisseur Antiques
8468 Melrose Pl.
213/658-8432

Trent Antiques
8469 Melrose Pl.
213/651-1234

Charles Pollock Antiques
8478 Melrose Pl.
213/651-5852

R M Barokh Antiques
8481 Melrose Pl.
213/655-2771

Recollections I
140 S. Orlando Ave.
213/852-7123

Other Times Books
10617 W. Pico Blvd.
310/475-2547

Blagg's
2901 Rowena Ave.
213/661-9011

Hideaway House Antiques
143 N. Robertson Blvd.
310/276-4319

Camille Chez Antiques
513 N. Robertson Blvd.
310/276-2729

Chelsea Antiques
117 S. Robertson Blvd.
310/859-3895

Gazebo Antiques
120 S. Robertson Blvd.
310/275-5650

Collection
315 S. Robertson Blvd.
310/205-3840

Acquisitions
1020 S. Robertson Blvd.
310/289-0196

An Antique Affaire
2600 S. Robertson Blvd.
310/838-2051

Paladin Antiques
7356 Santa Monica Blvd.
213/851-8222

Big White Elephant
7974 Santa Monica Blvd.
213/654-1928

Ramon's Antique Store
8250 Santa Monica Blvd.
213/848-2986

Antique Way
11729 Santa Monica Blvd.
310/477-3972

Antiques Plus
11914 1/2 Santa Monica Blvd.
310/826-1170

Portabella
11715 San Vincente Blvd.
310/820-3599

Ragtime
11715 San Vincente Blvd.
310/820-3599

Family Tree
8655 S. Sepulveda Blvd.
310/641-2122

Westchester Faire
8655 S. Sepulveda Blvd.
310/670-4000

London Bridge Antiques
8655 S. Sepulveda Blvd.
310/216-7677

Stephen Hilliger Antiques
8655 S. Sepulveda Blvd.
310/670-9306

Rose Antiques
8655 Sepulveda Blvd.
310/641-6967

Rubbish
1627 Silver Lake Blvd.
213/661-5575

Arthur Green
2201 W. Sunset Blvd.
213/413-3427

Minnette's Antiques Etcetera
2209 W. Sunset Blvd.
213/413-5595

Wells
2209 Sunset Blvd.
213/413-0558

Arts & Antiques
2211 W. Sunset Blvd.
213/413-5964

Peron Antiques & Collectibles
2213 W. Sunset Blvd.
213/413-7051

China House Funky Junk
5652 W. 3rd St.
213/935-9555

Giermo Antique Lighting
8405 W. 3rd St.
213/653-3450

Electica
8745 W. 3rd St.
310/275-1004

Harry Studio Antqs. Warehouse
8639 Venice Blvd.
310/559-7863

High Noon
9929 Venice Blvd.
310/202-9010

Joe's Antiques
3520 1/2 Washington Blvd.
213/737-4267

92 LOS GATOS

Main Street Antiques
150 West Main Street
408/-395-3035
Mon.- Sat., 10-5, Sun. 12-5

Directions: Traveling Hwy. 17 from San Jose to Santa Cruz, turn right on Los Gatos/Saratoga Rd., left at the first red light (University Avenue), right on Main St., four doors down on the right.

Main Street Antiques has been offering exceptional wares to antiquers for the past 20 years. The shop offers an eclectic line of fine antiques such as estate jewelry, flow blue, Roseville, Rookwood, Nippon, Limoges, majolica, formal and early furnishings and bronze statuary. Whether a serious shopper or an occasional browser, you won't be disappointed with what you find here.

Curious Book Shoppe
23 E. Main St.
408/354-5560

Patterson's Antiques
88 W. Main St.
408/354-1718

Antiquarium
98 W. Main
408/354-7878

Jean Newhart Antiques
110 W. Main
408/354-1646

Main St. Antiques
150 W. Main St.
408/395-3035

Les Poisson Antiques
25 N. Santa Cruz Ave.
408/354-7937

Maria's Antiques of Los Gatos
112 N. Santa Cruz Ave.
408/395-5933

93 LOS OLIVOS

Linrich Antiques & Collectibles
2879 Grand Ave.
805/686-0802

Haywire
2900 Grand Ave.
805/688-9911

Maria Tatiana Gallery
2920 Grand Ave.
805/688-9622

94 MANHATTAN BEACH

Once Upon a Quilt
312 Manhattan Beach Blvd.
310/379-1264

95 MARIPOSA

Downtown Mariposa offers a historic glimpse of the gold rush days. Many buildings evident of the era now house antiques, art galleries and fine dining establishments. Mariposa is the home of the oldest continuously operating courthouse west of the Rocky Mountains.

Restful Nest Bed & Breakfast Resort
4274 Buckeye Creek Rd.
209/742-7127
http://www.yosemite.net/mariposa/mhotels/restful/
Rates $85-95

Directions: From Merced (37 miles); from Highway 99 take I-40 East. Make a right on Yaqui Gulch Road. Go about 3 1/2 miles,Yaqui Gulch turns into Buckeye Road. Follow Buckeye Road for approximately 1 mile. Make a left on Buckeye Creek Road. The Restful Nest is 3/10 mile on the right.
From Fresno & Oakhurst: From Fresno, take 41 North to Oakhurst. From Oakhurst, take 49 North. Go 30 miles to Ben Hur. Make a left on Ben Hur. Follow Ben Hur to Buckeye Road.
Make a right to Buckeye Creek Road. The Restful Nest is 3/10 mile on the right.

Nestled in the beautiful foothills of the Sierra Nevada mountains in the heart of California Gold Country, the Restful Nest offers an experience of olden California hospitality with the flavor of Provence.

Three tastefully appointed guest rooms promise pleasant relaxation and refreshment. Each room has a private entrance, a private bath and fresh air windows, overlooking majestic oaks and rolling hills.

The aroma of freshly baked brioche and other breads (rated tops by visitors from France and Belgium) will lure you to the country dining room where, along with these delicious breads, you will enjoy homemade sausages, luscious California fruits, country jams, preserves, juice, freshly brewed coffee and a variety of teas.

Jailhouse Square Gifts/Antqs.
5018 Bullion St.
209/966-3998

Chocolate Soup/Jailhouse Too
Corner 6th & Bullion
209/966-5683

Correia's Antiques
5031 B Hwy. 140
209/966-5448

Campbell's Antiques
Corner 4th & Hwy. 140
209/966-4660

Anita's Antiques
Corner Hwy. 140 & 4th
209/966-2433

Princeton Empor Antiques
4976 Mt Bullion Cutoff
209/966-2372

Fabled Kottage
5029 State Hwy. #C
209/742-7075

96 MARTINEZ

Antique Connection
817 Arnold Dr.
510/372-8229

Another Time
911 Alhambra Ave.
510/229-5025

Nature's Way Doll Center
917 Alhambra Ste. A
510/228-5263

Cobweb Antiques
735 Escobar St.
510-229-9038

Ferry Street Antiques
413 Ferry St.
510/370-9091

Antique Corner
500 Ferry St.
510/372-9330

Olde Towne Antiques
516 Ferry St.
510/370-8345

Our Shoppe
606 Ferry St.
510/228-9919

Asilee's Victorian Antiques
608 Ferry St.
510/229-0653

Sheila a Grilli Bookseller
610 Ferry St.
510/228-6422

Crance's Antiques
605 Main St.
510/229-2775

Bill & Mike's Antiques
609 Main St.
510/229-3664

First Street Antiques
613 Main St.
510/228-7560

Lipary Sports Collectibles
617 Main St.
510/370-6032

Shannon's Olde & Goodies
623 Main St.
510/372-6045

The Military Store
625 Main St.
510/372-5897

B J's Antiques & Collectibles
627 Main St.
510/228-1202

Attic Child Antiques
653 Main St.
510/228-3072

Molly's Collectibles
718 Main St.
510/370-7466

Martinez Antiques & Cllbls.
724 Main St.
510/335-0939

Bayol's Antiques & Collectibles
728 Main St.
510/372-3398

Plain & Fancy Antiques
802 Main St.
510/229-4288

Family Traditions
810 Main St.
510/229-4331

Annie's Unique Antiques
814 Main S.
510/228-0394

97 MCKINLEYVILLE

Almost All Antiques
2764 Central Ave.
707/839-0456

98 MENDOCINO

Golden Goose
45094 Main Street
707/937-4655

Primrose Lane
44770 Larkin Road
707/937-2107

99 MENLO PARK

Millstreet Antiques
1131 Chestnut St.
415/323-9010

Mary J Rafferty Antiques
1158 Chestnut St.
415/321-6878

Conversation Piece
889 Santa Cruz Ave.
415/327-9101

100 MIDDLETOWN

Middletown Antqs. Collective
21207 Calistoga
707/987-2633

Cobb Mountain Antiques
17140 Highway 175
707/928-5972

Dorothy's Antiques
21304 Hwy. 175
707/987-0325

101 MILL VALLEY

Luck Would Have It
14 Locust Ave.
415/380-8625

Nellus Antiques
357 Miller Ave.
415/388-2277

Via Diva Antiques
27 Throckmorton Ave.
415/389-0911

Capricorn Antiques
100 Throckmorton Ave.
415/388-1720

Dowds Barn
157 Throckmorton Ave.
415/388-8110

102 MODESTO

Chelsea Square Antiques
305 Downey Ave.
209/578-5504

Hatch Road Antique Mall
2909 E. Hatch Rd.
209/538-0663

Marie Antoinette's Antiques
500 Scenic Dr.
209/524-9446

The March Hare
321 Downey Ave.
209/524-8336

Retro Antiques
502 Scenic Dr.
209/522-2959

Looking Back Antiques
1136 Tully Rd.
209/523-1443

103 MONROVIA

Patty's Antiques
109 W. Foothill Blvd.
818/358-0344

Monrovia West Antique Mall
925 W. Foothill Blvd.
818/357-5235

Kaleidoscope Antiques
306 S. Myrtle Ave.
818/303-4042

Through The Years
401 1/2 S. Myrtle Ave.
818/305-5259

Frills
504 S. Myrtle Ave.
818/303-3201

104 MONTEREY

Alicia's Antiques
835 Cannery Row
408/372-1423

Treasure Bay
801 Lighthouse Ave.
408/656-9303

Pieces of Olde
868 Lighthouse
408/372-1521

Cannery Row Antique Mall
471 Wave St.
408/655-0264

105 MORRO BAY

Antiques Et Cetera
1141 Main St.
805/772-2279

Glass Basket
245 Morro Bay Blvd.
805/772-4569

Wits End
257 Morro Bay Blvd.
805/772-8669

O Susanna
325 Morro Bay Blvd.
805/772-4001

Madam & The Cowboy
333 Morro Bay Blvd.
805/772-2048

Scruples Antiques
450 Morro Bay Blvd.
805/772-9207

Woody's Antiques
870 Morro Bay Blvd.
805/772-8669

Cindi's Antiques
820 Morro Bay Blvd.
805/772-5948

106 MOSS LANDING

Then & Now
Moss Landing Rd.
408/633-4373

Potter Palmer Antiques
Moss Landing Rd.
408/633-5415

Moss Landing Antique Co.
Moss Landing Rd.
408/633-3988

Life In The Past Lane
Moss Landing Rd.
408/633-6100

Harbor House Antiques
7092 Moss Landing Rd.
408/633-8555

Zyanya Collectibles
7981 Moss Land Rd. #a
408/633-4266

Moss Landing Merc Antiques
7981 Moss Landing Rd.
408/633-8520

Up Your Alley
8011 Moss Landing Rd.
408/633-5188

Little Red Barn Antiques
8045 Moss Landing Rd.
408/633-5583

Paul Messer Antiques
8461 Moss Landing Rd.
408/633-4361

Waterfront Antiques
7902F Sandholdt Rd.
408/633-1112

107 MOUNT SHASTA

Mount Shasta Black Bear Gllry.
201 N. Mount Shasta Blvd.
916/926-2334

Halfords Antiques
407 N. Mount Shasta Blvd.
916/926-3901

Antiques Etc.
612 S. Mount Shasta Blvd.
916/926-2231

108 MURPHYS

D.E.A. Bathroom Machineries
495 Main St.
209/728-2031
1-800-255-4426

Porcelain glistens from five showrooms in the former Odd Fellows Hall. You will find antique bathroom fixtures from soap dishes to sitz baths, bathroom scales to bathroom sinks, lighting fixtures, wash basins, clawfoot tubs, drinking fountains, brass hooks to brothel tokens. Showrooms are filled with spittoons, wooden toilet tanks, steam radiators, antique mail boxes, medicine cabinets, rib-cage showers (bigger than some bathrooms), and toilets. Toilets made back when toilet making was an art. Gorgeous toilets with sculptured tanks and bowls, gracefully and flowing bulbous, some hand-painted, some with raised ornamentation.

The most decorative bowl, called "The Deluge" is the rarest of the collection. Sorry, it's not for sale. It's an original, manufactured by Thomas Twyford, who worked in Victorian England for the most renowned toilet maker of them all, Thomas Crapper.

If you can't make it to the showroom, D.E.A. offers two mail order catalogues featuring their supply of the above plus much, much more in antique and reproduction fixtures and accessories. Video catalogues are also available to provide clients a better idea of their hundreds of antique products.

The company boasts a rather impressive client list: Ted Turner, Mark Harmon, Sally Jesse Raphael, Lloyd Bridges and Ralph Lauren have all purchased fixtures from D.E.A. Museums, bed and breakfasts, public and private restoration projects from all over the country have also looked to D.E.A. for their architectural needs.

The store has become quite a tourist attraction over the past 20 years. Sightseers have been known to wander into the store just for a peek at the unusual "stuff" offered there. And more unusual "stuff" is always on the way. The owner, Tom Schellar, travels across the United States looking for deals on all kinds of antiques. Anything interesting, he buys it, only 1 — and in his delightful store, he'll probably sell it.

All That Glitters
434 Main St.
209/728-2700

Sue's Antiques
466 Main St.
209/728-9148

109 NAPA VALLEY

There are approximately 184 wineries dotting the picturesque countryside known as the Napa Valley. Many were established well over 100 years ago and are still operating today. Most offer samplings in the tasting rooms located in the elegant mansions once owned by the founding winemakers.

One such estate is the Beringer Vineyards. Established in 1876 by Jacob and Frederick Beringer, it is the oldest continuously operated winery in the Napa Valley. The tasting room is located in Frederick's mansion (The Rhine House) and is elegantly decorated with stained glass, carved oak wainscoating, slate roof and wood floors. The excellent guided tour of the St.. Helena Winery leads you through the wine caves tunneled deep into the hillside where Beringer vintages age in oak cooperage.

California's first three-story stone gravity-flow winery, Far Niente, was completed in 1885 and the words "Far Niente" were carved into its stone face. A loose translation from the Italian phrase "In Dolce Far Niente" suggests "life without a care." The winery's operation ceased with prohibition and Far Niente lay sleeping for 60-odd years until it was purchased and renovated by the present owners.

Winemaking at Freemont Abby in St.. Helena dates from the fall of 1886 when Josephine Tychson, the first woman to build a winery in California, began operating on the site. The present owners began their enterprise in 1967. The wines, Chardonny, Merlot, Cabernet Sauvignon, Cabernet Bosche and Johanniskerg Riesling, have won international acclaim. The tasting room is furnished with antiques and Oriental rugs.

It was in the stone cellar of St.. Clement Vineyards' historic Rosenbaum House that the eighth Napa Valley winery was established before the turn of the century. It is in that same hundred-year-old cellar that St.. Clement wines are aged today.

The Rosenbaum House, a landmark Victorian, has been meticulously restored and is now open to visitors for the first time since 1878. The parlor now serves as an intimate tasting room. The porch swing on the veranda, picnic tables on the shaded patio and the expansive gardens offer a nostalgic vantage from which to view the valley.

Established in 1890, Sutter Home has been owned since 1947 by the Trinchero family. It is renowned for its rich, robust Amador County Zinfandel and its pale pink White Zinfandel, the best-selling premium wine in America. Sutter Home also produces a full line of high-quality varietal wines sold under the Sutter Home Fre brand name.

The Sutter Home Victorian house and gardens are landmarks in Napa Valley-featuring over 800 varieties of plant life, including 100 varieties of roses, 50 different daylilies, a dazzling array of camellias, lupines, columbines, begonias, century-old palm and orange trees and an extensive herb garden. Sutter Home's Visitor's Center, housed in the original winery building, features special exhibits evoking 19th century Napa Valley, as well as complimentary tastings.

For a complete listing of Napa Valley wineries and tour information, contact The Napa Valley Visitors Bureau or call 1-800-651-8953.

ANTIQUING IN THE NAPA VALLEY

CALISTOGA

The Tin Barn Collective
At the Gliderport
1510 Lincoln Ave.
707/942-0618
Open daily, 10-5

Offers a distinctive array of antiques and collectibles including china and crystal, vintage lighting, art pottery, prints and paintings, silver and linens, wicker and wrought iron, jewelry, arts and crafts, country primitives, French antiques, Orientalia, art deco and a new garden center.

NAPA

Antiques Etc.
3043 California Blvd. off Trancas
707/255-4545
"The Estate Shop" Open Tue..-Sat. 11-5 or by appointment

Thousands of collectibles, memorabilia, paintings, textiles, musical instruments, Indian baskets, rugs, art glass, cut glass, dolls, furniture, lamps, clocks, jewelry, pottery and more in a warehouse setting. Appraisal service.

Gullwigg & Thacker Antiques
1988A Wise Dr.
707/252-7038
Open daily 10-5

Not a "My grandmother had one of those" shop (unless, of course, she was 200 years old). Decidedly different. Varied in content. Compassionately priced, 17th, 18th, 19th, 20th century antiques.

The Irish Pedlar
1988A Wise Dr.
707/253-9091
Open daily 10-5

Offers an extensive selection of one-of-a-kind, old country pine and a large variety of accessories to accent the pine—linens, quimper, French wine related items, decoys.

Napa Coin Gallery
3053 Jefferson (Sam's Plaza)
707/255-7225
Hours Tue.-Fri., 11-5, Sat. 11-4, closed Sunday and Monday

"The One Stop Shop" for gold and silver coins and all supplies. Estate jewelry as well as coin jewelry items. Small antiques. Old postcards and other interesting historical items.

Red Hen Antiques
5091 St. Helena Hwy.
707/257-0822
Open every day 10-5

Situated in the vineyards on Highway 20 between Napa and Yountville, Red Hen Antiques houses more than 65 quality antique dealers. It features an extensive array of well-displayed collectibles, antiques and gifts. A landmark antique showplace.

Riverfront Antique Center
805 Soscol Ave. below 3rd St.
707/253-1966
Open daily 10-5:30

75+ dealers, 24,000 square feet. Napa's newest multi-dealer antiques mall offers a large selection of unique and affordable antiques and collectibles.

ST. HELENA

Elrod's Antiques
3000 St. Helena Hwy.
707/963-1901
Open Daily 11-5

European Country Antiques
1148 Main St.
707/963-4666
Open Mon.-Sat. 10-5, Sunday 12-4

Specializes in German pine wood antiques.

St. Helena, St. Helena Antiques
1231 Main St.
707/963-5878
Daily 11-5 and by appointment

Rare and unusual antiques, antiquities and collectibles. Tools, rugs, corkscrews, quilts, primitives, garden appointments, ethnic objects, masks, furniture, clocks, china, decanters, guns, paintings. Buy and sell.

YOUNTVILLE

Antique Fair
6412 Washington St.
707/944-8440
Open 10-5 daily
http://www.antiquefair.com

An impressive selection of French furniture and accessories.

BED AND BREAKFASTS IN THE NAPA VALLEY

ANGWIN

Forest Manor
415 Cold Springs Rd.
707/965-3538, 800/ 788-0364

Secluded 20-acre English Tudor estate tucked among forest and vineyards above St. Helena. Described as "one of the most romantic country inns . . .a small exclusive resort," the three-story Manor features high vaulted ceilings, massive hand-carved beams, fireplaces, verandas. The romantic honeymoon suite has a fireplace and a private jacuzzi for two.

CALISTOGA

Brannan Cottage Inn
109 Wapoo Ave.
707/942-4200

Delightful gardens surround this quiet 6-room gingerbread Victorian, winner of the 1985 Napa Landmarks Award for historic preservation in Napa County. Known for its original wild flower stencils, the Inn offers a sunny courtyard & parlor with fireplace. Listed on the National Register of Historic Places, this is the only guest house left on its original site built for the "Calistoga Hot Springs Resort" in 1860.

Calistoga Country Lodge
2883 Foothill Blvd.
707/942-5555

Secluded lodge in the western foothills of Calistoga. Beautifully decorated with American antiques, bleached pine, lodgepole furniture and Indian artifacts.

Calistoga Inn/Napa Valley Brewing Co.
1250 Lincoln Ave.
707/942-4101

A landmark building built at the turn of the century, the Calistoga Inn is located on the main street of town. The Inn features a fine restaurant, an outdoor patio-grill and beer wine garden, and an in-house pub brewery where Calistoga Lager is brewed and served fresh.

Calistoga Wayside Inn
1523 Foothill Blvd.
707/942-0645

A 1920s Spanish style home situated in a secluded park-like setting on half acre with decorative gardens. Relax in the hammock.

Calistoga Wishing Well Inn
2653 Foothill Boulevard (Hwy. 128)
707/942-5534

A three-story farmhouse, situated among vineyards on four acres with a breathtaking mountain view.

Christopher's Inn
1010 Foothill Blvd.
707/942-5755

Original 1930'scottages have been transformed into intimate rooms, interiors by Laura Ashley and antique furnishings, many with fireplaces. Some rooms have patio gardens.

Culver's, a Country Inn
1805 Foothill Blvd.
707/942-4535

This completely restored country Victorian home, circa 1875, is a registered historical landmark. Each of the bedrooms has period furniture, including a uniquely designed quilt. Living room with fireplace, porch with view of Mount St. Helena.

The Elms
1300 Cedar St.
707/942-9476, 800/235-4316

A three-story French Victorian built in 1871 and on the National Register of Historic Places, The Elms offers charm and elegance within walking distance of Calistoga. Located on a quiet street next to a park, it has antique filled rooms with fireplaces, feather beds, down comforters, and bathrobes. Complimentary wine and cheese and a large gourmet breakfast are served in the dining room.

Falcons Nest
471 Kortum Canyon Road
707/942-0758

A secluded hilltop estate nestled on 7 acres. Panoramic views overlooking the Napa Valley. Just minutes to the wineries and spas. All rooms have Country French decor with queen beds, and you can enjoy the spa under the stars. Breakfast is served on the balcony.

Fanny's
1206 Spring St.
888-942-9491

Built in 1915 as a comfortable family home, Fanny's has now been renovated and named for Robert Louis Stevenson's bride. The exterior of the house has a full length porch ready with rocking chairs and a swing. Inside, bedrooms feature plank floors, feather comforters and window seats that will take you back to grandma's attic. The living room and dining room are rich with charm. An old fireplace, numerous soft quilts, sofas and an array of nooks and crannies are perfect for hiding away or meeting new people.

Foothill House
3037 Foothill Blvd.
707/942-6933, 800/942-6933

Nestled among the western foothills just north of Calistoga, the Foothill House began as a simple farmhouse at the turn of the century. The cozy yet spacious rooms are individually decorated with country antiques, and a queen or king four poster bed. Gourmet breakfast, complimentary wine; hors d'oeuvres served in the evening.

Hill Crest B&B
3225 Lake County Hwy.
707/942-6334

Located near the base of Mt. St. Helena, this rambling country home is filled with cherished family heirlooms. Antique silver, china, oriental rugs, books and other furnishings are the legacy of the Tubbs and Reid families. There's a small lake for fishing, and you may hike on 36 hilly acres, take a dip in the pool or relax in the sun and take in the breathtaking view.

Meadowlark Country House
601 Petrified Forest Rd.
707/942-5651

Built in 1886 and situated on 20 forested acres, this two-story country home has been remodeled for modern comfort and retains its relaxed country atmosphere. Each room has queen bed and view of forest, gardens or meadows. California breakfast included.

Mount View Hotel
1457 Lincoln
707/942-6877 Fax 707/942-6904
800/861-6877

A National Historical Landmark, this romantic hotel has been Calistoga's celebrated hotel for over seventy years. A private courtyard with outdoor pool and jacuzzi invite you to ease back, or dive in. The complete European-style spa, located in the hotel, offers a full range of services including mud wraps, massages, herbal baths and facials. The Mount View is also home to Jan Birnbaum's Catahoula restaurant and saloon, serving Jan's famous Southern-inspired American cuisine for lunch and dinner. The cottages each have a private patio, hot tub, and wet bar.

The Pink Mansion
1415 Foothill Blvd.
707/942-0558

Painted pink in the 1930's by Aunt Alma, this 120-year-old Calistoga landmark offers a combination of Victorian elegance and modern luxury. The formal living room with fireplace, as well as the dining room and game room, are for guests' use. Each room has a postcard view of the hills and local landmarks, and downtown Calistoga is within walking distance. Full gourmet breakfast. Three acres of landscaped gardens and wooded escapes. For those who enjoy a late night swim, the indoor heated pool and jacuzzi are a must.

Quail Mountain Bed & Breakfast
4455 North St., Helena Hwy.
707/942-0316

A secluded, luxury romantic estate located on 26 acres, 300 ft. above Napa Valley on a heavily forested mountain range with a vineyard and orchard on the property. Full breakfast is served in the sunny solarium common room or formal dining room in winter months.

Scarlett's Country Inn
3918 Silverado Trail
707/942-6669

Three exquisitely appointed suites set in the quiet mood of green lawns and tall pines overlooking the vineyards. Breakfast under the apple trees or in your own sitting room. Close to wineries and spas.

Scott Courtyard
1443 2nd St.
707/942-0948

Just two blocks from downtown Calistoga, Scott Courtyard resembles a Mediterranean villa with latticed courtyard and private gardens. The large social room has been described as "tropical Art Deco" with a bistro kitchen where a full breakfast is served pool side.

Silver Rose Inn
351 Rosedale Rd.
707/942-9581

Located near the end of picturesque Silverado Trail at Rosedale Road, high on a rocky outcropping and surrounded by centuries-old live oak trees, this lovely retreat has a panoramic view of the upper Napa Valley with its spreading vineyards and the towering Palisade mountains. All nine tastefully decorated guest rooms have private baths and some have balconies, fireplaces and whirlpool tubs. The Silver Rose has recently added a new hot springs spa. For the exclusive use of guests staying at the inn, the new spa includes mud, seaweed, herbal baths, hydro massage, facials and massage services.

Stephen's Wine Way Inn
1019 Foothill Blvd.
707/942-0680 800/572-0679

A restored 1915 home where the atmosphere is casual and the innkeepers are like old friends. You can enjoy a glass of wine on the spectacular multi-level deck or by the fire in the parlor. Enjoy a full gourmet breakfast from an ever-growing collection of recipes. Each room is individually decorated in antiques and quilts. a cottage offers privacy for those who prefer it.

Trailside Inn
4201 Silverado Trail
707/942-4106

This charming 1930 farmhouse in the country has three suites, each with private entrance, porch-deck, bedroom, kitchen, bath and living room with fireplace.

Complimentary wine, mineral water, fresh baked bread and breakfast fixings provided.

Triple S. Ranch
4600 Mt. Home Ranch Rd.
707/942-6730

Rustic cabins and a homey atmosphere make this mountain hideaway a pleasant place to relax and unwind. There's a swimming pool, restaurant and cocktail lounge and many scenic mountain trails to hike. Nearby are the Old Faithful Geyser of California and the Petrified Forest.

Zinfandel House
1253 Summit Dr.
707/942-0733

A private home located in a wooded setting above the valley floor between St. Helena and Calistoga. The 1,000-square-foot deck offers a spectacular view of the valley. Two tastefully decorated rooms. Wine is offered and a lovely breakfast is served in the morning.

NAPA

Arbor Guest House
1436 G Street
707/252-8144

This 1906 Colonial transition home and carriage house have been completely restored for the comfort of guests. Rooms are beautifully appointed with antiques. Two rooms have spa tubs. For guests seeking privacy and seclusion, the carriage house bed/sitting rooms, both with fireplaces, are most fitting. A charming garden motif is featured throughout the inn, with the wallpaper, window coverings and the medley of period furniture in brass, iron, oak, mahogany, wicker and carved and beveled glass.

Beazley House
1910 First Street
800/559-1649

Napa's first bed and breakfast is located in central Napa in a fine old neighborhood. The shingle style/colonial revival mansion of over 4,400 square feet was built in 1902. It has six guest rooms, all with private baths. Behind the mansion the carriage house has been reproduced and has five rooms, all with private baths, fireplaces and private, two-person spas. a full breakfast of home-baked muffins, fresh fruit and crustless cheese quiche is served in the mansion's formal dining room. In the spacious living room, complimentary tea is available to guests each afternoon.

The Blue Violet Mansion
443 Brown St.
707/253-BLUE

A large, elegant 1886 Queen Anne Victorian, the mansion was built for Emanuel Manasse, an executive at the Sawyer Tannery. Lovingly restored, and winner of the 1993 Landmarks Award of Merit for historical restoration. Located in the historic district of Old Town Napa, it is within walking distance of downtown shops and restaurants. The home now offers large, cheerful rooms with queen or king beds, fireplaces, balconies, spas and private baths. Outside is a garden gazebo with a swing, a shaded deck and rose garden. Full country breakfast and afternoon and evening refreshments are included.

Brookside Vineyard
3194 Redwood Rd.
707/944-1661

This gracious country bed and breakfast is also a picturesque working vineyard. a tree shaded lane leads you to the serene creek setting of this comfortable California mission-style inn. The three spacious guest rooms each have adjoining baths, and are tastefully furnished with antiques and collectibles. One room has a private patio, fireplace and sauna. Guests enjoy complimentary afternoon wine on the deck with a glorious view, or in the living room next to the fireplace. After dinner cordials are available in the cozy library. a full breakfast is served in the gazebo overlooking a stand of Douglas fir and the natural beauty of a creek lined with oak and bay trees.

The Candlelight Inn
1045 Easum Dr.
707/257-3717

This English Tudor, built in 1929 on one park-like acre in the city of Napa, has nine romantic rooms, one with its own sauna. The elegant living room features high contoured ceilings and a fireplace, and the innkeepers serve an exquisite breakfast and provide an afternoon social hour in the dining room, where the view through the French doors into the garden will delight you.

Cedar Gables Inn
486 Coombs St.
707/224-7969

Built in 1892, Cedar Gables is styled after 16th Century English Country homes. Six beautifully appointed guest rooms are furnished with antiques - some have whirlpool tubs and fireplaces. All have private baths. Each evening, innkeepers Margaret and Craig Snasdell welcome you with a spread of fruit, cheeses and wine. a bountiful breakfast is served in the cheerful sunroom.

Churchill Manor
485 Brown Street
707/253-7733

An 1889 National Landmark, Churchill Manor is the largest home of its time in the Napa Valley. The mansion rests amid lush grounds and is surrounded by an expansive veranda with twenty-two gleaming white columns. Entering through leaded-glass doors, guests are surrounded by magnificent woodwork, fixtures, and antique furnishings. While lavish in appointments, Churchill Manor is also warm and inviting. Guests enjoy afternoon fresh-baked cookies and refreshments, and a two-hour wine and cheese reception in the evening, and gourmet breakfast in the marble-tiled solarium.

Country Garden Inn
1815 Silverado Trail
707/255-1197

Situated on one and a half acres of mature woodland riverside property, the inn was built in the 1850s as a coach house on the Silverado Trail. The building is surrounded by trees and flowers, brick and stone pathways, a garden terrace, and there's a circular rose garden with a lily pond, fountain and large aviary. Each spacious room is furnished with antiques. Several have private jacuzzis and fireplaces. Full breakfast, afternoon tea and evening hors d'oeuvres are included.

Cross Roads Inn
6380 Silverado Tr.
707/944-0646

Offering unparalleled views and complete privacy from its 20-acre vantage point high in the eastern hills of the Napa Valley, Crossroads Inn has spacious, individually decorated suites with wine bars and jacuzzi spas. Breakfast can be served in your suite or on your private deck. Afternoon tea, wine and cocktails are served around the native stone fireplace, and brandies are offered before retiring.

The Hennessey House
1727 Main St.
707/226-3774

This Eastlake-style Queen Anne Victorian was once the residence and office of Dr. Edward Zack Hennessey, an early, prominent Napa County physician. The house is now listed on the Register of Historic Places. Rooms have private baths, and some have canopy or feather beds, fireplaces and whirlpool tubs. The house is furnished with English or Belgian antiques, and the dining room features a hand painted, stamped ceiling.

Hillview Country Inn
1205 Hillview Lane
707/224-5004

Enjoy the country life at Hillview Country Inn, a spectacular 100-year-old estate where you can stroll the beautifully manicured grounds amid fruit trees, herb garden, lavish lawns and the Old English Rose Garden.

In the inn's gracious parlor, you can start your morning with a sumptuous country breakfast. Each guest suite is distinctly decorated, and includes a fruit and wine basket upon arrival and a sweeping view of the Napa Valley.

Inn on Randolph
411 Randolph St.
707/257-2886

A showcase for area artists, every room in this restored 1860 Gothic Revival has been embellished with original designs - from handpainted murals and faux finishes to a distinctive willow canopy bed. Each generously proportioned guest room offers a sitting area, private bath and robes. Some feature a double or deep soaking whirlpool tub, gas fireplace or private deck. Comfortable sitting areas have marble fireplaces. The one-half acre of landscaped grounds provides a sundeck, gazebo and hammock.

La Belle Epoque
1386 Calistoga Ave.
707/257-2161

A Queen Anne Majesty built in 1893, with its multi-gabled dormers and high-hipped roof, La Belle Epoque is one of the finest examples of Victorian architecture in the wine country. Decorative flat and molded carvings can be seen in the gables and bays, and the original stained glass windows remain in the transoms and semi-circular windows. Guest rooms are decorated with fine period furniture, and several have fireplaces. Generous gourmet breakfast. Complimentary wine and hors d'oeuvres served in wine tasting room.

La Residence
4066 St. Helena Hwy.
707/253-0337

A French barn and 1870 mansion in its own 2 acre park-like setting, beautifully restored and furnished. The spacious rooms and suites have private baths, fireplaces, French doors, verandas or patios, and are luxuriously appointed. a spa and heated pool are framed by heritage oaks and towering pines. Full breakfast in sun-filled dining room with classical piano and fireplace included, as are sunset wine and hors d'oeuvres.

The Napa Inn
1137 Warren
707/257-1444, 800/435-1144

A three-story Queen Anne Victorian located on a quiet tree-lined street in a historic section of the town of Napa, the inn is furnished with turn-of-the-century antiques in each of the six guest rooms, parlor and formal dining room.

Oak Knoll Inn
2200 E. Oak Knoll Ave.
707/255-2200

A romantic, elegant, all-stone French country inn secluded within an expansive vineyard preserve. Features pool and hot tub and rooms with Italian marble fireplaces, private baths, vaulted ceilings, king-size brass beds and separate French door entrances, providing views of Stag's Leap Palisades and the surrounding oak-studded hillsides. A full breakfast in the morning, and wine and hors d'oeuvres in the evening are served on the deck overlooking the vineyards, or in front of the fireplace in the dining room.

The Old World Inn
1301 Jefferson
707/257-0112

A unique and memorable Victorian, decorated in the bright Scandinavian colors of artist Carl Larsson. Afternoon tea and cookies, nightly hors d'oeuvres, and an evening gourmet dessert buffet are offered.

Stahlecker House Bed & Breakfast Country Inn And Gardens
1042 Easum Dr.
707/257-1588

A secluded, quiet country inn, Stahlecker House is located just minutes from the wineries. Canopy beds, antique furnishings and a comfortable gathering room with fireplace, contribute to a relaxed, homey atmosphere. a quiet, restful deck overlooks lawns, gardens and shade trees. Complimentary lemonade, coffee, tea and cookies.

Trubody Ranch
5444 St. Helena Hwy.
707/255-5907

Built in 1872, Trubody Ranch is a Gothic Revival Victorian home with water tower. Surrounded by 120 acres of family-owned vineyard land, the ranch is located in the center of Napa Valley. Rooms are furnished in family antiques of the period. Guests enjoy garden and vineyard strolls. There are views from both rooms. Breakfast is freshly baked breads, home-grown fruit in season, fruit juice, tea and coffee.

ST. HELENA

The Ambrose Bierce House
1515 Main St.
707/963-3003

Ambrose Bierce, famous witty author of *The Devil's Dictionary* and many short stories, lived in this house on the main street of St.. Helena until 1913, when he mysteriously vanished into Mexico. His former residence, now a luxurious bed and breakfast inn, was built in 1872. Like Bierce himself, the inn is an intriguing blend of ingredients—luxury, history and hospitality. Bedroom suites are furnished with antiques, including comfortable queen-sized brass beds and armoires. Bathrooms have brass fittings, clawfoot tubs and showers. Suites are named for the historical figures whose presence touched Bierce and the Napa Valley in the late 1800s: Ambrose Bierce himself; Lillie Lantry, the era's most scandalous woman; Edward Muybridge, acclaimed "father of the motion picture", and Lillie Hitchcock Coit, the legendary "Belle of San Francisco." Complimentary gourmet breakfast of coffee, juice, fruits and pastries.

Asplund Conn Valley Inn
726 Rossi Rd.
707/963-4614

Nestled in lush garden surroundings with views of the vineyards and rolling hills, the inn is truly in the country, yet just five minutes away from Main Street, St.. Helena. Antique furnishings, garden views, library and fireplace. Complimentary fruit, cheese and wine and a full breakfast. Country roads for strolling. Fishing nearby.

Bartels Ranch and Country Inn
1200 Conn Valley Rd.
707/963-4001

Peaceful, romantic, 60-acre country estate with 10,000 acre views-amidst vineyards! Award-winning "3 star" accommodations feature 3 guest rooms and one champagne suite with spa, sauna, and fireplace. Private baths include robes. Full breakfast served til noon in choice view settings. Unique entertainment room offers fireside billiards, chess, piano and library. Evening social hour, dessert, tea, coffee & cookies served 24 hrs.

Bylund House Bed & Breakfast Inn
2000 Howell Mtn. Rd.
707/963-9073

Secluded country estate in the tradition of the Northern Italian Villa just minutes from downtown St. Helena. Two very private rooms with private baths, balconies and custom appointments. Complimentary wine, hors d'oeuvres and lavish continental breakfast.

Chestelson House
1417 Kearney St.
707/963-2238

Victorian home in a quiet residential neighborhood away from the busy highways. Gracious hospitality, delicious full breakfast and afternoon social hour. View of the mountains from the wide veranda.

The Cinnamon Bear
1407 Kearney
707/963-4653

This charming bed & breakfast home is just a 2-block walk to St. Helena's Main St. shops and restaurants. Antiques, quilts and teddy bears fill the rooms. Afternoon refreshments and dessert in the evening are followed by a full gourmet breakfast. Read by the fireplace or relax on the spacious porch of this quaint place to stay.

Creekside Inn
945 Main St.
707/963-7244

Located in the heart of St. Helena, yet sheltered from the hustle and bustle of town by ancient oaks and by the murmurs of White Sulphur Creek rippling past its secluded rear garden patio, Creekside offers three guest rooms furnished in a Country French theme. There's a fireplace in the common room, and a full breakfast is served in the sunroom or on the creekside patio.

Deer Run
3995 Spring Mtn. Rd.
707/963-3794

A truly secluded, peaceful mountain, four-acre retreat, Deer Run is nestled in the forest on Spring Mountain above the valley vineyards, affording the quiet serenity of a private hideaway. All units have fireplaces and antique furnishings. And there's a heated swimming pool. A full breakfast is served in the dining area.

Erika's Hillside
285 Fawn Park
707/963-2887

This hillside chalet, just two miles from St. Helena, has a peaceful, wooded country setting and a view of vineyards and wineries. The grounds are nicely landscaped. The rooms are spacious, bright and airy with private entrances and bath, fireplace and hot tub. Continental breakfast is served in the solarium. The structure - more than 100 years old - has been remodeled and personally decorated by German-born innkeeper, Erika Cunningham.

Glass Mountain Inn
3100 Silverado Trail
707/963-3512

In the midst of the Napa Valley's vineyards, yet snuggled among century-old redwoods, pines and oaks, proudly stands the majestic Victorian Glass Mountain Inn. Towers, turrets and stained glass enhance the inn, where amenities include hand carved oak fireplaces, whirlpool and Roman soaking tubs. A full breakfast is served in a stone dining room viewing a candlelit wine cave built in the 1800s.

Harvest Inn
1 Main St.
707/963-9463

This elegant AAA Four Diamond English Tudor-style inn has spacious and secure cottages furnished with original antiques. Many cottages also include elaborate brick fireplaces, wet bars and vineyard views. Deluxe spa suites are available. 24-hour pool and Jacuzzi, wine bar and conference rooms with cobblestone fireplaces and stained glass windows are available.

Hilltop House
9550 St. Helena Road
707/963-8743

Just minutes from St. Helena, Hilltop House is a peaceful mountain hideaway on 135 acres of unspoiled wilderness on the Napa County line, which offers a hang glider's view of the historic Mayacama Mountains.

Hotel St. Helena
1309 Main St.
707/963-4388

Victorian hotel located on St. Helena's Main Street. Offers richly furnished antique filled-rooms with private or shared baths. The Hotel is within walking distance of St. Helena's many fine restaurants and wineries.

Ink House
1575 St. Helena Hwy.
707/963-3890

A traditional Italianate Victorian built by Theron H. Ink in 1884. This historic valley home offers four charming guest bedrooms complete with era furnishings with private baths. In the parlor, guests are invited to read or play the antique pump organ. a glass-walled observatory features a 360-degree view of the vineyards.

Judy's Ranch House
701 Rossi Rd.
707/963-3081

At Judy's country-style bed and breakfast, surrounded by a 3-acre Merlot vineyard, you can enjoy the oak trees and seasonal creek that run through the seven acres, or take a walk down a peaceful country road.

La Fleur B&B
1475 Inglewood Ave.
707/963-0233

This Victorian, nestled among the vineyards, features three beautifully appointed rooms, all with fireplaces and private baths. a deluxe full breakfast is served in the solarium overlooking the surrounding vineyards. a private tour of Villa Helena Winery comes with your stay.

Oliver House Bed & Breakfast
2970 Silverado Trail
707/963-4089

A Swiss chalet nestled in the hills with a panoramic view of the Napa Valley. There are four bedrooms with antiques; one has a 115-year-old brass bed. Another bedroom has its own private fireplace.The focal point of the cozy living room parlor is a large stone fireplace. Breakfast of muffins, fruit and pastries is served. Visitors are welcome to stroll around the lovely grounds of the four-acre estate.

Rustridge Ranch
2910 Lower Chiles Valley Rd.
707/965-9353

A family-owned and operated estate where grapes and horses grow together, Rustridge Ranch and Winery is seven miles east of the Silverado Trail in the picturesque rolling hills of the Chiles Valley. Thoroughbred racehorses graze among the oak trees and along the hillsides, while vineyards envelop the valley. The rambling Southwestern ranch-style house has been remodeled and converted into a gracious, contemporary Bed and Breakfast Inn.

Shady Oaks Country Inn
399 Zinfandel Lane
707/963-1190

Old-fashioned elegance and warm hospitality welcome you to this country inn. Secluded and romantic on 2 acres and nestled in the vineyards among some of the finest wineries and restaurants in the Napa Valley. The guest rooms and their country comforts are housed in a 1920s home and a winery built in the 1800s. The rooms are furnished with antiques, fine linens and private baths. a full champagne gourmet breakfast is served fireside, in bed or on the garden veranda. Wine and cheese are served each evening.

Spanish Villa Inn
474 Glass Mountain Rd.
707/963-7483

Nestled in a wooded valley on Glass Mountain Road, the villa is a short scenic drive from St. Helena and Calistoga. Each room includes a king-size bed, private bath and Tiffany lamps. Breakfast is served in the galleria. Neatly manicured grounds with ancient oak trees, palms and flower gardens surround the villa.

Sutter Home Winery B&B
277 S. St. Helena Hwy.
707/963-3104

Situated on the beautifully landscaped grounds of this historic old winery, Sutter Home's guest rooms offer Victorian elegance and a central location convenient for fine dining, shopping and relaxed wine country touring. Accommodations include antique furnishings, fireplaces, as well as, an expanded continental breakfast featuring freshly baked goods, fruit juices, cereals and coffee.

Vigne Del Uomo Felice
1871 Cabernet Lane
707/963-2376 .

Situated on the west side of Napa Valley surrounded by the peace and quiet of the vineyards, Vigne del Uomo Felice is, appropriately translated, Ranch of the Happy Man. The completely furnished stone cottage with bedroom, bath and studio offers guests the opportunity to shed their cares.

Villa St. Helena
2727 Sulphur Springs Ave.
707/963-2514

A grand Mediterranean-style villa located in the hills above St. Helena. This secluded 20-acre wooded estate combines quiet country elegance with panoramic views of beautiful Napa Valley. Built in 1941 to accommodate elaborate entertaining with its spacious courtyard and view-filled walking trails, the Villa has a comfortable interior featuring period-style furniture.

White Sulphur Springs Resort
3100 White Sulphur Springs Rd.
707/963-8588

California's first resort, established 1852, White Sulphur Springs has two small inns and nine cottages, outdoor sulphur soaking pool, massage, mud wraps and jacuzzi, and hiking trails. It is a rustic old-world retreat with 330 acres of redwood, fir and madrone forests—secluded, yet only 3 miles from St. Helena.

Wine Country Inn
1152 Lodi Lane
707/963-7077

Perched on a knoll overlooking manicured vineyards and nearby hills, this country inn offers 24 individually decorated guest rooms. The Smiths used local antiques and family-made quilts to create an atmosphere of warmth and comfort. Fireplaces and balconies add charm.

Wine Country Victorian and Cottages
707/963-0852

This classic Victorian beauty is situated amid majestic oaks, elms and pines. In the adjoining gardens the estate also offers WINE COUNTRY COTTAGE, originally guest quarters for the main residence, now a cozy self-contained unit. You'll find "country quiet" here, as well as many delightful surprises in Napa Valley's oldest Bed & Breakfast.

Zinfandel Inn
800 Zinfandel Lane
707/963-3512

Burgundy House
6711 Washington
707/944-0889

A stone two-story brandy distillery built in 1891 of local fieldstone and river rock now houses the country inn. Five comfortable and cozy rooms, each with private bath, welcome you, as does a decanter of local wine. Antique country furniture and period furnishings complement the rugged masonry. a full breakfast is served in the "distillery" or in the beautiful garden outside.

Maison Fleurie
6529 Yount St.
707/944-2056, 1-800-788-0369

The Maison Fleurie, Four Sisters Inns newest inn, is a luxurious haven of French country romance. Two-foot-thick brick walls, terra cotta tile and paned windows are reminiscent of a farmhouse in Provence. The inn has 13 beautifully decorated guest rooms, a swimming pool and outdoor spa, spacious landscaped grounds and a cozy dining room serving a gourmet breakfast to each guest. Wine tastings, dinner reservations, balloon rides, spa services and sightseeing itineraries are carefully planned by the inn's attentive staff. In the afternoon, wine and hor d'oeuvres are served, as well as cookies, fruit and beverages throughout the day.

Napa Valley Railway Inn
6503 Washington St.
707/944-2000

Rekindling the nostalgia evoked by names like Burlington Route, Great Northern RR and Southern Pacific, the inn consists of nine turn-of-the-century railroad cars — three cozy cabooses and six spacious railcars restored to their original glory. Interiors are furnished to suggest the opulence of the era, with the added comfort of contemporary amenities. Each suite has a brass bed, sitting room with a loveseat for relaxing, and a full bath. Adjacent to Vintage 1870, Yountville, with its restaurants, shops and galleries.

Oleander House
7433 St. Helena Hwy.
707/944-8315

Comfortable, elegant, sun-drenched and carefree, this Country French two-story B & B combines old-world design with modern amenities. Guests enjoy spacious rooms with queen-size beds, high ceilings, private bath, balcony, fireplace, antiques and Laura Ashley decor. Landscaped patio garden. A full gourmet breakfast is served. Knowledgeable innkeepers assist with advice on the valley's best attractions. Within walking distance of Mustards Restaurant.

Vintage Inn, Napa Valley
6541 Washington St.
707/944-1112

Created by California artist Kip Stewart, the inn features spacious, exquisitely appointed guest rooms, each with wood-burning fireplace, refrigerator, whirlpool bath spa, in-room brewed coffee and terry robes. An elaborate California Champagne breakfast is included, along with afternoon tea and nightly turn-down service. Recipient of AAA's prestigious Four Diamond Award. Walk to Vintage 1870 and many fine restaurants.

The Webber Place
6610 Webber St.
707/944-8384

Surrounded by a white picket fence, The Webber Place is a red farmhouse built in 1850. It is now a homey and affordable bed and breakfast inn decorated in Americana Folk Art style. Artist Diane Bartholomew bought the place seven years ago, and she has her studio next door. On sunny afternoons she serves sun tea and cookies on the front porch, and in the morning the farmhouse kitchen smells of coffee, biscuits and bacon as she sets to work making a real country breakfast. Guest rooms have ornate iron and brass beds covered with antique quilts. Two rooms share a deep old-fashioned tub with brass fixtures, and the other two rooms have tub alcoves right in the room. The Veranda suite is much larger, with a hammock on its own sheltered veranda and entrance.

Favorite Places to Eat

Spring Street
1245 Spring St.
St. Helena
707/963-5578

This bungalow-turned-restaurant on Spring Street, St. Helena, was the home for nearly 50 years of opera singer Walter Martina and his wife, Dionisia, who moved to St.. Helena in 1915 to manage the popular William Tell Hotel. The Martina's loved to entertain. Their guests gather for gourmet cooking, fine wine and music in the lush adjoining garden with its vine-covered trellis beside the oval fountain. Spring Street Restaurant carries on the tradition of good food and wines, serving Saturday and Sunday brunch that features fresh baked biscuits, sweet rolls, muffins, special omelettes and homemade preserves; weekday lunches featuring special sandwiches, salads and homemade desserts, and delicious, American fare dinners daily. Everything is available for takeout and may be ordered ahead by calling the restaurant.

Trilogy
1234 Main St.
707/963-5507

You enter this small, intimate restaurant through an iron gate and a courtyard off St. Helena's Hunt Street and find yourself in a quiet dining room with gracious furniture, elegant chandeliers, flowers on cloth-covered tables and classical stereo music. The California French cuisine of chef Diane Pariseau is delicious to the palate and delightful to the eye. Trilogy's wine list is exciting and cosmopolitan and goes far beyond the choices you find in many larger wine country restaurants. Local produce and fresh fish and poultry, never frozen, are featured and the sauces — French — are prepared in the restaurant's own kitchen. People watchers will enjoy watching the passing parade on St.. Helena's quaint Main Street from the dining room, and those who enjoy outdoor dining will find the courtyard a pleasant place in fair weather.

Triple S Ranch
4600 Mt. Home Ranch Rd.
North of Calistoga
707/942-6730

A ranch and restaurant operated by the Schellenger family for more than 30 years. Triple S Ranch serves up nostalgia along with mouth-watering meals. Perched high in the Sonoma Mountains near Petrified Forest, The Triple S Restaurant was converted from the ranch's original redwood barn built more than a century ago. Thick homemade soup or large salads with plenty of French bread accompany each dinner, and there's a choice of delicious country specialties. The portions are generous. Onion rings at Triple S are legendary, and the ranch has become famous for them. They also have french fried frog legs! After dinner, you might enjoy a game of bocci ball or horseshoes.

110 NEVADA CITY

Nevada City Warehouse
75 Bost Ave.
916/265-6000

La Cache
218 Broad St.
916/265-8104

Assay Office Antiques
130 Main St.
916/265-8126

Shaw's Antiques
210 Main St.
916/265-2668

Main Street Antique Shop
214 Ω Main St.
916/265-3108

2nd Time Around
548 Searls Ave.
916/265-8844

Tinnery
205 York St.
916/265-0599

111 NEWPORT BEACH

Vallejo Gallery
1610 W. Coast Hwy.
714/642-7945

Jane's Antiques
2811 Lafayette Rd.
714/673-5688

Antiques 4 U
312 N. Newport Blvd.
714/548-4123

Old Newport Antiques
477 N. Newport Blvd.
714/548-8713

A Secret Affair
3441 Via Lido Ste. a & B
714/673-3717

Grandma's Cottage
400 Westminster Ave.
714/645-9258

Jeffries Ltd.
852 Production Place
714/642-4154

112 NOVATO

Consignment Shop
818 Grant Ave.
415/892-3496

Now & Then
902 Grant Ave.
415/892-0640

Black Pt. Antiques Collectibles & Gifts
35 Harbor Dr.
415/892-5100

113 OAKDALE

Past & Present Antiques
219 E. F St.
209/847-1228

Twice Treasured
231 E. F St.
209/848-2750

Two Gals Trading Post
1725 E. F St.
209/847-3350

Peddler's Attic
223 S. Sierra Ave.
209/847-4710

114 OAKHURST

Good Oldaze
Hwy. 41 & 426
209/683-6161

Oakhurst Frameworks
49027 Road 426
209/683-7845

Collectors Mall
40982 N. State Highway 41
209/683-5006

115 OAKLAND

Tim's Antiques & Collectibles
5371 Bancroft Ave.
510/533-7493

Williamsburg Antiques
5375 Bancroft Ave.
510/532-1870

Deerfield's Collectibles
5383 Bancroft Ave.
510/534-6411

Good The Bad & The Ugly
5322 & 26 College Ave.
510/420-1740

Rockridge Antiques
5601 College Ave.
510/652-7115

Avenue Antiques
6007 College Ave.
510/652-7620

Garcia's Antiques
2278 E. 14th St.
510/535-1339

Richard a Pecchi Antiques
30 Jack London Sq. #110
510/465-9006

Lost and Found Antiques
4220 Piedmond Ave.
510/654-2007

116 OAKLEY

Lena's Antiques
3510 Main St.
510/625-4878

Norcross Timeless Treasures
3639 Main St.
510/625-0193

Country Courthouse
3663 Main
510/625-1099

117 OCEANO

A Pier At The Past
368 Pier Ave.nue
805/473-1521
(Open during summer 10-6 Wed.-Sun.) (during winter 11-5 Wed.-Sun.)-Mon. & Tue. by chance.

Directions: From Highway 101 North: Take Los Barros Rd. exit to Oceano. From Highway 101 South: Take 4th Street exit to Grand, right to Highway 1, left to Pier Ave.nue, right to the shop and the beach. a Pier At The Past is on State Highway #1, 3 miles south of Pismo Beach and 2 miles north of Nipomo.

I don't know which you'll love the most - the antique shop or George Kiner himself. He is the epitome of the "laid back" California lifestyle. George set up shop on the beach at Oceano in 1994, but he has been in business in California for 35 years. Starting out in the 1960s, before the major rekindling of interest in antiques took hold, George was one of the early Union Street dealers. He owned several shops in various San Francisco locations - one of which was the ever-popular Varietorium. It was dubbed "the" place to shop for antiques, and George, with his myna bird Susie, became quite well known.

George opened two more shops in California, one in the San Fernando Valley and one in Studio City. Both were destroyed by earthquakes. These events prompted his move to Oceano, where he opened a fun little shop call a Pier At The Past.

It is, according to George, right at the entranceway for the tricycles and A.T.V.s heading for the Oceano Dunes, "the only place on the West Coast where you can drive down and find 1,000 campsites." There used to be a pier at the beach years ago, but it was lost in a storm. The gutted building that houses a Pier At The Past had been a building block restaurant. George rented it, put up temporary walls for his paintings, hung some lighting and was in business. He knows how temporary things can be, having weathered the earthquakes and lost stores over the years. George also lives in the shop, which visitors often don't realize as they browse. He keeps everything open. "You can walk through into the living room and on into the bedroom," says George. "If someone wants to buy my bed, I'll sell it and sleep on a futon until I find something I like."

Besides his bed, George carries lots of cups and saucers, paintings from all periods, costume jewelry and accessories, beaded purses, compacts and barber bottles, Indian pottery, unusual furniture pieces, lots of little tables, Oriental decorative items, English Bristol china, German Royal Bonn porcelain and kitchen items to the 1930s.

If you know you're going to stop by, you might want to call first - George is often out on the beach taking a walk.

Central Coast Outdoor Antique & Collectible Market
Oceano Airport
561 Air Park Drive
805/481-9095 (Dealer Information)
2nd Saturday of each month 7-2

Directions: Off Highway 1, South of Pismo Beach.

On the second Saturday of every month, the Oceano Airport parking lot is transformed into an antique mecca. This open air market is only one and a half blocks from Pismo Beach and is part of the beautiful tourist area of San Luis Obispo County. The Market features free admission and parking.

The Hangar Antiques & Collectibles
Oceano Airport
561 Air Park Drive
805/481-9095
Open Fri., Sat., & Sun. Or By Appointment

This unusual setting for antiques was once an old airplane hangar. Today, it is packed with quality antiques and collectibles ranging from gas and oil memorabilia, airplane related items, many big boy toys, as well as wonderful items for the ladies. Constantly changing inventory.

118 OJAI

Gracies Antique Mall
238 E. Ojai Ave.
805/646-8879

Antique Collection
236 W. Ojai Ave.
805/646-6688

Treasures of Ojai
110 N. Signal St.
805/646-2852

119 ONTARIO

Ontario Antiques Annex
127 W. B St.
909/391-8628

Ontario Antiques
203 W. B St.
909/391-1200

Inland Empire Antiques
216 W. B St.
909/986-9779

Martha's Antique Mall
326 N. Euclid Ave.
909/984-5220

Golden Web
235 N. Euclid
909/986-6398

Treasures 'N' Junk
215 South San Antio
909/983-3300

120 ORANGE

S & E Gallery
227A E. Chapman Ave.
714/532-6787

American Roots
105 W. Chapman Ave.
714/639-3424

Daisy's Antiques
131 W. Chapman Ave.
714/633-6475

Country Roads Antiques
204 W. Chapman Ave.
714/532-3041

Tony's Architectural & Garden
123 N. Olive
714/538-1900

Treasures From The Past
611 W. Chapman Ave.
714/997-9702

Mulherin & O Dell's Antiques
106 N. Glassell St.
714/771-3390

Anthony's Fine Antiques
114 N. Glassell St.
714/538-1900

George The Second
117 N. Glassell St.
714/744-1870

Rocking Chair Emporium
123 N. Glassell St.
714/633-5206

Happiness By The Bushel
128 N. Glassell St.
714/538-3324

It's About Time
131 N. Glassell St.
714/538-7645

Grand Avenue Antiques
140 N. Glassell
714/538-3540

Antique Place
142 N. Glassell St.
714/538-4455

Encore Presentations
144 N. Glassell St.
714/744-4845

Jim & Shirley's Antiques
146 N. Glassell St.
714/639-9662

Mr C's Rare Records
148 N. Glassell
714/532-3835

Antiques & Me
149 N. Glassell St.
714/639-4084

A & P Collectables
151 N. Glassell
714/997-1370

Attic Delights
155 N. Glassell
714/639-8351

Lucky Find Antiques
160 N. Glassell St.
714/771-6364

Antiques Antiques
165 N. Glassell St.
714/639-4084

Woody's Early Misc.
169 & 173 N. Glassell St.
714/744-8199

Le Chalet Antiques & Doll Shop
277 N. Glassell St.
714/633-2650

Rick Sloane Antiques
2055 N. Glassell St.
714/637-1257

Watch And Wares
108 S. Glassell St.
714/633-2030

Antique Annex
109 S. Glassell
714/997-4320

Partners Eclectic Antiques
110 S. Glassell St.
714/744-4340

Jewelry & Gift Mart
110 1/2 S. Glassell
714/633-2325

Dorothy & Friends Antiques
114 1/2 Glassell St.
714/771-5087

Orange Circle Antique Mall
118 S. Glassell St.
714/538-8160

Uncle Tom's Antiques
119 S. Glassell St.
714/538-3826

Someplace In Time
132 S. Glassell St.
714/538-9411

Muff's Antiques
135 S. Glassell St.
714/997-0243

Nick Schaner Antiques
136 S. Glassell St.
714/744-0204

Just For Fun
140 S. Glassell
714/633-7405

Plaza 42 Antiques
141 S. Glassell St.
714/633-9090

Summerhill Limited
142 S. Glassell St.
714/771-7782

Victoria Co.
146 S. Glassell St.
714/538-7927

Antique Station
178 S. Glassell
714/633-3934

Ruby's Antique Jewelry
111 N. Olive
714/538-1762

Old Towne Orange Antq. Mall
119 N. Olive
714/532-6255

Willard Antiques
143 S. Olive St.
714/771-7138

Rothdale's Fine Antiques
40 Plaza Square
714/289-6900

J & J Antiques
55 Plaza Square
714/288-9057

Tea Leaf Cottage
60 Plaza Square
714/771-7752

China Terrace Antiques
1192 N. Tustin Ave.
714/771-4555

121 OROVILLE

Day Dreams
1462 Myers St.
916/534-8624

Old Town Emporium
2034 Montgomery St.
916/533-7787

Lock Stock & Barrell
2061 Montgomery
916/534-7515

Carousel Antiques
2421 Montgomery
916/534-8433

Miners Alley Collective
1354 Myers St.
916/534-7871

122 PACIFIC GROVE

Patricks
105 Central
408/372-3995

Woodenickle
529 Central
408/646-8050

Antique Warehouse
2707 David Ave.
408/375-1456

Camden & Castleberry Antqs.
2711 David Ave.
408/375-0701

Trotter's Antiques
301-303 Forest Ave.
408/373-3505

Antique Clock Shop
489 Lighthouse Ave.
408/372-6435

Front Row Center
633 C Lighthouse Ave.
408/375-5625

Interesting Side Trip

Point Pinos Lighthouse
Asilomar Ave. off Ocean View Blvd.
408/648-3116

Built in 1856, oldest continuously operating lighthouse on the West Coast.

123 PALM DESERT

Treasure House
73199 El Paseo Ste C & D
619/568-1461

124 PALM SPRINGS

Casa Cody Bed & Breakfast Country Inn
175 South Cahuilla Road
619/320-9346
Fax: 619/325-8610
Rates vary by season

A romantic, historic hideaway nestled against the spectacular San Jacinto Mountains in the heart of Palm Springs Village, Casa Cody is the oldest operating hotel in Palm Springs. It was founded in the 1920s by the beautiful Hollywood pioneer, Harriet Cody, cousin to the legendary Buffalo Bill. The inn has 23 single-story accommodations in five early California hacienda-style buildings, all decorated in Sante Fe decor, and all surrounded by bougainvillaea and citrus-filled courtyards. Guests have a choice of single or double rooms, studios, and one or two bedroom suites, all with private baths and entrances. There's a one-bedroom cottage and a historic two-bedroom adobe for those who desire seclusion. The inn also offers two pools and a tree-shaded whirlpool spa.

Palm Springs Art Gallery
170 E. Arenas Rd.
619/778-6969

Pars Gallery
353 S. Palm Canyon #A
619/322-7179

Irene's Antiques
457 N. Palm Canyon Dr.
619/320-6654

Robert Kaplan Antiques
469 N. Palm Canyon Dr.
619/323-7144

Campbell's Estate Gallery
886 N. Palm Canyon Dr.
619/323-6044

Carlan Collection
1556 N. Palm Canyon Dr.
619/322-8002

125 PALO ALTO

Antique Emporium
4219 El Camino Real
415/494-2868

Adele's Antiques
231 Hamilton Ave.
415/322-7184

Kimura Gallery
482 Hamilton Ave.
415/322-3984

Antiques Unlimited
542 High St.
415/328-3748

Hilary Thatz Inc.
38 Stanford Shopping Center
415/323-4200

Di Capi Ltd.
10 Town & Country Village
415/327-1541

Alan Jay Co.
14 Town & Country Village
415/462-9900

Cotton Works
500 University Ave.
415/327-1800

126 PARADISE

19th Century Antique Shop
5447 Skyway
916/872-8723

Time Was
5610 Skyway
916/877-7844

Penny Ante Antiques
5701 Skyway
916/877-0047

Patti's Snoop Shoppe
7357 Skyway
916/872-4008

Attic Treasures
7409 Skyway
916/876-1541

Deloris' Antiques - Collectibles
7639 Skyway
916/872-2828

127 PASADENA

Carol's Antiques
1866 N. Allen
818/798-1072

Chuck's Antiques
23 N. Altadena
818/564-9582

Jay's Antiques
95B N. Arroyo Pkwy.
818/792-0485

Jane Warren Antiques
832 E. California Blvd.
818/584-9431

Carlson-Powers Antiques
1 W. California Blvd. Ste. 411
818/577-9589

Dovetail Antiques
1 W. California Blvd. Ste. 412
818/792-9410

On The Twentieth Century
910 E. Colorado Blvd.
818/795-0667

Time Recyclers
2552 E. Colorado Blvd.
818/440-1880

Tiffany Tree
498 Del Rosa Dr.
818/796-4406

Antiques & Objects
446 S. Fair Oaks Ave.
818/796-8224

Georgene's Antiques
448 S. Fair Oaks Ave.
818/440-9926

Marc's Antiques
460 S. Fair Oaks Ave.
818/795-3770

Pasadena Antique Center
480 S. Fair Oaks Ave.
818/449-7706

Blackwelders Antqs. & Fine Art
696 E. Colorado Blvd.
818/584-0723

Oliver's Antiques Fine Arts
597 E. Green St.
818/449-3463

Kelley Gallery
770 E. Green St. #102
818/577-5657

Green Dolphin St. Antiques
985 E. Green St.
818/577-7087

J & N. Antiques
989 E. Green St.
818/792-7366

Pasadena Antique Mall
44 E. Holly St.
818/304-9886

Showcase Antiques
60 N. Lake Ave.
818/577-9660

Marco Polo Antique Shop
62 N. Raymond Ave.
818/356-0835

Design Center Antiques
70 N. Raymond Ave.
213/681-6230

A Matter of Taste
328 S. Rosemead Blvd.
818/792-2735

128 PASO ROBLES

Antique Emporium
1307 Park St.
805/238-1078

Great American Antiques
1305 Spring St.
805/239-1203

Homestead Antiques & Cllbls.
1320 Pine St.
805/238-9183

Sentimental Journey
1344 Pine St.
805/239-1001

129 PETALUMA

R & L Antiques
3690 Bodega Ave.
707/762-2494

Kentucky Street Antiques
127 Kentucky St.
707/765-1698

Waddles-N-Hops
145 Kentucky St.
707/778-3438

Dolores Hitchinson Antiques
146 Kentucky St.
707/763-8905

Doris's Antiques
152 Kentucky St.
707/765-0627

Fraley's Antiques
110 Petaluma Blvd. N #A
707/763-4087

Chanticleer Antiques
145 Petaluma Blvd. N
707/763-9177

Chelsea Antiques
148 Petaluma Blvd. N
707/763-7686

Antique Market Place
304 Petaluma Blvd. N
707/765-1155

Antique Collector
523 Petaluma Blvd. S
707/763-7371

130 PLACERVILLE

Jennings Way Antiques
3182 Center St.
916/642-0446

Treasure Tent Antiques
376 Main St.
916/626-9364

Empire Antiques
420 Main St.
916/626-8931

The Loft
420 Main St.
916/626-8931

Olde Dorado Antique Empor.
435 Main St.
916/622-4792

Placerville Antiques & Cllbls.
440 Main St.
916/626-3425

Beever's Antiques & Books
462-464 Main Street
916/626-3314

Memory Lane Antiques
460 Main St.
916/626-9207

131 PLEASANTON

Olde Towne Antiques
465 Main St.
510/484-2446

B J Gardner Fine Period Furn.
531 Main St.
510/484-5456

Main St. Antiques & Cllbls.
641 Main St.
510/426-0279

Cattelan's Antique Furn.
719 Main St.
510/485-1705

Clutter Box
99 W. Neal St.
510/462-8640

132 POMONA

Swan Song
197 E. Second Street (Antique Row)
909/620-5767
562/433-1033 (Appt.)
Open: By Appointment

Swan Song is an exceptional, upscale antique shop with a unique setting. Primitives and country furnishings fill the basement of what once was the old department store. The main floor is reserved for oil paintings, art glass, silver, oriental, and fine china. The second story is filled (over 100 pieces) with Victorian furniture, vintage clothing, along with American and Indian pottery. The third and final floor of this shop features quilts, traditional antique furnishings along with designer pieces. If you're not in the market to purchase these exquisite items, you can rent them. Everything in the store is available for rental. Sounds like a great place to plan a wedding or party.

Pfeiffer's Collectibles
147 E. 2nd St.
909/629-8860

Girl's Antiques
151 E. 2nd St.
909/622-5773

Jack's Antiques
161 E. 2nd St.
909/633-5589

Pomona Antique Center
162 E. 2nd St.
909/620/7406

My Way Antiques
175 E. 2nd St.
909/620-6696

Persnickity Antiquity
180 E. 2nd St.
909/620-8996

Ralph's Inland Empire Antqs.
185 E. 2nd St.
909/622-0451

Robbins Antique Mall
200 E. 2nd St.
909/623-9835

Grandpa's Antiques
205 E. 2nd
909/629-5854

Grandma's Goodies
211 E. 2nd
909/629-3906

Collector's Choice
104 S. Locust
909/865-7110

Dragon Antiques
216 E. 2nd St.
909/620-6660

Kaiser Bill's Military Shop
224 E. 2nd St.
909/622-5046

Lila's Place
233 E. 2nd St.
909/620-7270

Empire House Antiques
237 E. 2nd St.
909/622-9291

Olde Towne Pomona Mall
260 E. 2nd St.
909/622-1011

McBeth's Antiques
263 E. 2nd St.
909/622-0615

Nothing Common Antiques
265 E. 2nd St.
909/620-1229

Harrie's General Store
269 E. 2nd
909/629-1446

Hobbs & Fried Merc.
275 E. 2nd
909/629-1112

Sanders Antiques
279 E. 2nd St.
909/620-8295

China Closet
290 E. 2nd St.
909/622-2922

Southwest Antiques
198 E. 2nd St.
909/620-8334

133 PORTERVILLE

Now & Then Country Mall
19230 Avenue 152
209/783-9313

Jerico Antique Emporium
134 N. Main St.
209/784-2211

Sandie's
32 W. Mill Ave.
209/781-6740

Junk N Tique
36 W. Mill Ave.
209/783-2448

J. Fox Antiques
40 W. Mill Ave.
209/784-1737

Irene's Antiques
33 W. Putnam Ave.
209/782-8245

Downing Antiques
1522 West Putnam Ave.
209/784-1465

134 RAMONA

Ye Olde Curio Shoppe
738 Main St.
619/789-6365

Old Town Antiques
760 Main St.
619/788-2670

Ramona Antiques & Cllbls.
872 Main St.
619/789-7816

Peterson's Antiques & Cllbls.
2405 Main St.
619/789-2027

135 RANDSBURG

Cottage Hotel Bed & Breakfast & Antiques
130 Butte Avenue
760/374-2285
Open 11-5, Thurs.-Mon., closed Tue.-Wed. (sometimes) and during Christmas/New Year.

This is the place to go to be pampered - a quiet getaway with an enclosed Jacuzzi for all-season use. Hidden away in the California High Desert in the historical gold mining town of Randsburg, the Cottage Hotel Bed & Breakfast began at the turn of the century with the gold boom in Randsburg. Today all the rooms have been restored to reflect that era, with period furnishings being the key. There are common areas for relaxing and viewing the desert, and even accommodations in the Housekeeping Cottage next door for families with small children. Located conveniently between Highways 14 and 395, the Cottage Hotel Bed & Breakfast is also listed in the Auto Club (AAA) tour book for California and Nevada, and the Bed & Breakfast Guide *Gateway To Death Valley*. According to innkeeper Brenda Ingram, Randsburg is called "The Living Ghost Town," but she assures us that all the ghosts are very friendly!

136 RED BLUFF

Antiques N Things
339 Ash St.
916/527-7098

Great American Antiques
613 Main St.
916/529-4340

Stelle's Main St. Antiques
623 Main St.
916/529-2238

Kramer's Antiques
644 Main St.
916/527-1701

Hunt House Antiques
718 Main St.
916/527-6104

Kelco Antiques & Collectibles
1445 Vista Way
916/529-3245

Washington St. Antiques
610 Washington St.
916/528-1701

137 RED MOUNTAIN

Old Owl Inn Cottages a Bed & Breakfast
Cottontail Antiques, Collectibles & Gifts
701 Highway 395
760/374-2235 or 1-888-653-6954 (toll free)
Antique shop open daily except Wed. from 10-5
Bed and Breakfast open daily

Directions: 25 miles north of intersections Highway 395 and 58. Twenty miles south of Ridgecrest.

The Old Owl Inn is located in the historic Rand Gold Mining District of the California High Desert and 1/2 mile from the Death Valley turnoff. The Owl, founded in 1918, was originally a gambling hall, saloon and brothel with many original furnishings.

The Owl witnessed many shoot-outs, bar-room brawls and two fisted poker games. Legend has it that the ladies of the evening, along with illegal booze, was hidden in tunnels below, out of sight of the watchful eye of the local sheriff.

Today, the Owl Cottages is a bed and breakfast and decorated with antiques throughout. Guests can stay in Slims Cottage, which is a spacious two bedroom with full kitchen, living room and old fashioned bath, perfect for families with children. Or in Bessie's Honeymoon Cottage for that special romantic night or weekend with a kitchenette and private bath. The Owl is also listed in the auto club (AAA) Southern California Bed & Breakfast Guide.

The newly expanded Cottontail Antiques is located on the property providing antiquers with treasures to take home as a momenta of their stay at the Owl Cottages.

138 REDDING/SHASTA LAKE CITY

Absolutely Wonderful Antiques
2948 Cascade Blvd.
916/275-4046

Barabara's Antiques
3266 Cascade Blvd.
916/275-6879

Antiques & Accents
3266 Cascade Blvd. #12
916/275-2619

Hollibaugh Antiques
3266 Cascade Blvd.
916/275-2990

I-5 Antique Mall
3270A Cascade Blvd.
916/275-6990

139 REDLANDS\YUCAIPA

Ila's Antiques and Collectibles
215 East Redlands Blvd.
(located in the Packing House Mall, in "The Cellar")
909/793-8898
Open Mon.-Sun., 11-5:30

Directions: Traveling I-10, exit at Orange Street and go south 3 blocks, turn left to 7th and Redlands Blvd.

Ila's Antiques is located in "The Cellar" of the old Banner Packing House. In the early days of the 1900s, this historic building housed a citrus packing company which shipped sweet California oranges to markets all across the U.S.

To get to Ila's, you must first pass through the Packing House Mall (a separate business) which houses 80 dealers offering a wide variety of antiques and collectibles. Once inside, take the stairs to "the cellar," where you'll discover 3,000 square feet of the finest antiques in the area. This shop undoubtedly has one of the largest costume jewelry collections in the U.S. - over 5,000 pieces! In addition, you'll find silver, crystal, Czechoslovakian glass, china, antique dolls and some select furniture pieces.

Laurel Jones China
409 N. Orange
909/793-8611

Emma's Trunk
1701 Orange Tree Lane
909/798-7865

Carriage Barn Antiques
31181 Outer Hwy. 10 S.
909/794-3919

Antique Exchange Mall
31251 Outer Hwy. 10
909/794-9190

Sandlin's Antiques
31491 Outer Hwy. 10
909/794-4311

Marion Side Door Antiques
31567 Outer Hwy. 10
909/794-1320

Fiddler's Cove
31567 Outer Hwy. 10 #1
909/794-6102

Cripe's Antiques
31583 Outer Hwy. 10 S.
909/794-5355

Raney's Freeway Antiques
31597 Outer Hwy. 10
909/794-4851

Out Back Antiques
31599 Outer Hwy. 10
909/794-0530

Antique Gallery
31629 Outer Hwy. 10 Unit E
909/794-0244

Ellen's Antiques
31629 Outer Hwy. 10 Unit F
909/794-9340

Cathy's Cottage Antiques
31843 Outer Hwy. 10
909/389-9436

Keepsake Antique Mall
31933 Outer Hwy. 10
909/794-1076

Last Stop Antique Shop
32019 Outer Hwy. 10 S
909/795-5612

The Packing House
215 E. Redlands Blvd.
909/792-9021

Precious Times Antiques
1740 W. Redlands Blvd.
909/792-7768

Eclectic Art Gallery
516 Texas St.
909/793-7016

Paul Melzer Rare Books
12 E. Vine St.
909/792-7299

Gatherings
330-A N. Third St.
909/792-1216

The Blues
114 E. State Street
909/798-8055

C. B. Antiques
316 E. Citrus Avenue
909/792-0017

Antique Arcade
31159 Outer Hwy. 10 S
909/794-5919

Vintage Clothing & Books
31629 Outer Hwy. 10*B
909/794-1785

Chandlers Cove
1512 Barton Road
909/307-0622

Olde Hollow Treet
38480 Oak Glen Rd.
909/797-5032

Memory Lane Antiques
31773 Outer Highway 10 S
909/794-3514

Antiques Unlimited
31567 Outer Hwy. 10 S
909/794-4066

Anne's Yesteryear's
31663 Outer Hwy. 10 S
909/795-5446

140 REDONDO BEACH

Patina
1815 1/2 S. Catalina Ave.
310/373-5587

Antique Corral
145 S. Pacific Coast Hwy.
310/374-0007

Le Grange Country Furn
719 S. Pacific Coast Hwy.
310/540-7535

Vicki's Antiques & Collectibles
1221 S. Pacific Coast Hwy.
310/540-6363

Antique Doll Closet
1303 S. Pacific Coast Hwy.
310/540-8212

141 REDWOOD CITY

Athena Antiques Inc.
926 Broadway St.
415/363-0282

Palace Market Antiques
825 Main St.
415/364-4645

Finders Keepers Antiques
837 Main St.
415/365-1750

Redwood Cafe & Spice Co.
1020 Main St.
415/364-1288

Eclectric Antiques
1101 Main St.
415/364-1549

142 RIVERSIDE

Abbey's Antiques
3671 Main St.
909/788-9725
Open Mon.-Sat.10:00-5:30, Sun. by chance.

Offering 2,000 sq ft of fine antiques, vintage clothing, linens, jewelry, silver and more.

Mission Antiques
4308 Lime St.
909/684-5639

Cinnamon Lane Antique Mall
6056 Magnolia Ave.
909/781-6625

Katy's Collectibles
6062 Magnolia Ave.
909/369-9030

Karen's Antiques
9631 Magnolia Ave.
909/358-0304

Amazing Grace Antiques
3541 Main St.
909/788-9729

R R Antiques
3583 Market St.
909/781-6350

Darlene Nemer
3596 Main St.
909/684-9010

Mrs. Darling
4267 Main St.
909/682-0425

Seventh Heaven Antiques
3605 Market St.
909/784-6528

Petey's Place
4212 Market St.
909/686-4520

Beasley's Antiques
3757 Mission Inn Ave.
909/682-8127

Crystal's Antique Mall
4205 Main St..
909/781-9922

The Gas Pump
9637 Magnolia
909/689-7113

Victorian Rose Antique Mall
3784 Elizabeth St.
909/788-5510

Mr Beasley's Auction
3878 6th Street
909/682-4279

143 ROSEVILLE

Roseville Antique Mall
106 Judah St.
916/773-4003

Around Again Antiques
342 Lincoln St.
916/783-8542

Terri Andrus' Treasures
1304 Buttercup Ct., Section D #5
916/782-6158

Tin Soldiers
222 Vernon St.
916/786-6604

Pepper Tree
223 Vernon St.
916/783-1979

Antique Store
226 Vernon St.
916/774-0660

Home Passage Antiques
229 Vernon St.
916/782-5111

Velvet Purse Antiques
230 Vernon St.
916/784-3432

Antique Trove
238 Vernon St.
916/786-2777

This N That
243 Vernon St.
916/786-7784

Julie's Antique Mall
625 Vernon St.
916/783-3006

Memories Past Antiques
801 Vernon St.
916/786-2606

144 SACRAMENTO

Historic Old Sacramento

The Old Sacramento historic area, a registered national landmark and state historic park, is a 28-acre site on the banks of the Sacramento River. It is a vital historic, business, residential, shopping, and dining district with a fascinating past and the greatest concentration of historic buildings in California.

John Sutter arrived in 1839 and founded the first permanent settlement in the area. After the gold discovery in 1848, businesses sprang up along the riverfront in what is now Old Sacramento. There were hotels, saloons, bathhouses, the first theatre in California, and a variety of shops where would-be miners could outfit themselves for the gold fields.

Transportation has always figured prominently in Sacramento's history. The city was the western terminus of the short-lived Pony Express and the transcontinental railroad. Today, Old Sacramento is home to the largest interpretive railroad museum in North America-the California State Railroad Museum. The 100,000-square-foot museum displays 21 meticulously restored locomotives and cars, and over 40 one-of-a-kind exhibits tell the fascinating story of railroad history from 1850 to the present.

Historic equipment and exhibits on the transcontinental railroad and 19th century rail travel are housed in the reconstructed 1876 Central Pacific Railroad Passenger Station.

About one mile from the California State Railroad Museum, just on the edge of Old Sacramento, is another spectacular facility dedicated to transportation-the Towe Ford Museum. The world's most complete antique Ford automobile collection includes every year and model produced by Ford between 1903 and 1953. There are more than 150 cars and trucks, with many in excellent original condition and others that have been beautifully and authentically restored. The collection also includes an array of original and restored cars from the late '50s, '60s, and '70s.

Other museums include the California Military Museum, the Discovery Museum and the Crocker Art Museum. Explore historic Old Sacramento with a self-guided "Walking Tour," which is available from the Visitor Information Center at 2nd and K streets. One hundred unique shops and 20 eclectic restaurants will satisfy even the most discerning visitor. Numerous special events take place here year-round including the Sacramento Jazz Jubilee, Festival de la Familia, Pacific Rim Festival and a couple of collectors' fairs.

Riverboat Delta King Hotel
1000 Front St. (on the Sacramento River)
Old Sacramento
916/444-5464

This magnificently restored dockside paddlewheeler has been entertaining guests since 1927. Spend the night in one of 44 elegant staterooms on the shores of the Sacramento River.

If murder and suspense intrigue you, you will enjoy the Suspects Murder Mystery Dinner Theatre on the Delta King Friday and Saturday evenings. Match wits with a master detective searching for clues and interrogating guests. Look out, you may be a suspect yourself!

Haulbaurs Timeless Treasures
3207 Marysville Blvd.
916/924-1371
Mon.-Sat. 10-5:30

Directions: Traveling business 80 from San Francisco to Sacramento, take the Marconi exit, head West.

Marconi becomes Arcade, Arcade takes you to Marysville Blvd. Located near the corner of Arcade and Marysville Blvd.

Haulbaurs Timeless Treasures has been in operation for four years. It is amazing how that many treasures can be up for grabs in 1,700 square feet of space. The shop is literally filled to the brim with some of the most unusual collectibles west of the Mississippi.

Do you collect antique fishing gear? They have it—lots of it! What about old telephones? Yes, they have those, too. Cookie jars, bird cages, books, musical instruments, tools? - yes, all there. European army collectibles, European beer steins - (you won't be bored). Oh, and did I mention German pencil sharpeners and German toys? - Got Em! It's one of those, "It's no telling what you'll find in here" kind of shops.

Anna's Collectibles
1905 Capitol Ave.
916/441-1310

Old World Antiques
6313 Elvas Ave.
916/456-9131

Antique's Etc.
4749 Folsom Blvd.
916/739-1483

Memory Lane
1025 Front St.
916/488-0981

Closet
1107 Front St.
916/442-3446

River City Antique Mall
10117 Mills Rd.
916/362-7778

Lovell's Antique Mall
2114 P St.
916/442-4640

Bookmine
1015 2nd St.
916/441-4609

Slater Antiques & Collectibles
609 N. 10th St.
916/442-6183

Antique Tresors Legacy
1512 16th St.
916/446-6960

Wee Jumble Shop
1221 19th St.
916/447-5643

Swanberg's Antqs. & Cllbls.
2673 21st St.
916/456-5300

Grandpa's Antiques
1423 28th St.
916/456-4594

Chez Antique
855 57th St.
916/455-7504

Discovery Antiques
855 57th St.
916/739-1757

Windmill Antiques
855 57th St.
916/454-1487

Gravy Boat Antiques
855 57th St.
916/457-1205

Every Era Antiques
855 57th St.
916/456-1767

Elaine's Jewel Box
866 57th St.
916/451-6059

Bagwell's Antiques
866 57th St.
916/455-3409

Sullivan's Antiques
866 57th St.
916/457-9183

Fifty-Seventh St. Antiques
875 57th St.
916/451-3110

Interesting Side Trips

Exploring Gold Country

Sacramento was the original jumping off point for the goldminers, and today it's the perfect base for exploring the Gold Country, an area so rich in lore that you may easily find yourself transported back to that era. Remnants of this exciting time in California history are still visible all around. To reach the northern mines, take Interstate 80 east from Sacramento toward the town of Auburn, a quaint gem with great antique stores and a variety of restaurants. From here head north on Highway 49 to the Empire State Mine in Grass Valley.

From Auburn you may also head south on Highway 49 to Coloma, the original gold discovery site in 1848. Continue south on 49 through Placerville and stop at one of the many El Dorado or Amador County wineries for a taste. On to Calaveras County and Angels Camp, home to the Jumping Frog Jubilee during the third week in May. Other well-preserved Gold Rush era towns include Murphys, San Andreas, Mokelumne Hills and Copperopolis. Don't miss Calaveras Big Trees State Park with its giant sequoias. Have you every tried spelunking? Moaning, California and Mercer Caverns are just the places for it. There're dozens of eclectic art galleries, quaint antique shops and excellent eateries all around the area. Take an hour to ride the train in the breathtaking foothills scenery at Railtown State Park near Jamestown, or pan for gold in a clear mountain stream. Sonora, Columbia State Park and Groveland are other draws for Gold Country visitors.

Heading south on Highway 49 stop in Coulterville, one of the best-preserved Gold Rush towns in the Sierra foothills. Enjoy boating and fishing at Lakes McClure and McSwain, and visit the oldest continuously operating courthouse west of the Rocky Mountains in the quaint town of Mariposa. At the end of a long day relax in the pine-covered community of Fish Camp located at the southern entrance to Yosemite National Park.

145 SALINAS

Echo Valley Antiques
849 Echo Valley Rd.
408/663-4305

Bonanza Antiques
467 El Camino Real
408/422-7621

Lily's Odds & Ends
10 W. Gakilan St.
408/757-4562

Hall Tree Antique Mall
202 Main St.
408/757-6918

Generation Gap
338 Monterey St.
408/751-6148

Country Peddler Antiques
347 Monterey St.
408/424-2292

146 SAN ANSELMO

Greenfield Antiques
8 Bank St.
415/454-4614

C Fetherston Antiques
10 Bank St.
415/453-6607

Center Market
Center Blvd. & Saunders
415/454-3127

Antique Habit
10 Greenfield Ave.
415/457-1241

Oveda Maurer Antiques
34 Greenfield Ave.
415/454-6439

Antique World
216 Greenfield Ave.
415/454-2203

Roger Barber Asian Antiques
114 Pine St.
415/457-6844

Modern I Gallery
500 Red Hill Ave.
415/456-3960

Michael Good Fine & Rare Bks.
35 San Anselmo Ave.
415/452-6092

Shadows
429 San Anselmo Ave.
415/459-0574

Vintage Flamingo
528 San Anselmo Ave.
415/721-7275

Yanni's Antiques
538 San Anselmo Ave.
415/459-2996

Second Hand Land
703 San Anselmo Ave.
415/454-5057

Dove Place Antiques
160 Sir Francis Drake Blvd.
415/453-1490

Legacy Antiques
204 Sir Francis Drake Blvd.
415/457-7166

Sanford's Antiques
2 Tunstead Ave..
415/454-4731

Aurora Gallery
306 Sir Francis Drake Blvd.
415/459-6822

Kisetsu & The French Garden
310 Sir Francis Drake Blvd.
415/456-9070

San Anselmo Country Store
312 Sir Francis Drake Blvd.
415/258-0922

Collective Antiques
316 Sir Francis Drake Blvd.
415/453-6373

Pavillion Antiques
610 Sir Francis Drake Blvd.
415/459-2002

147 SAN BERNARDINO

Mueller's Vintage Collectibles
363 S. Arrowhead Ave.
909/384-8110

Treasure Mart Antiques.
293 E. Redlands Blvd.
909/825-7264

Old Fashion Shop West
1927 N. E St.
909/882-5819

Heritage
1520 S. E St.
909/888-3377

A Touch of Class
214 W. Highland Ave.
909/883-1495

AEL Antique Mall
24735 Redlands Blvd.
909/796-0380

148 SAN CARLOS

Antiques Trove
1119 Industrial Rd.
415/593-1300

Felicity's Collectibles
600 Laurel St.
415/593-9559

Antique Collage Collective
654 Laurel St.
415/595-1776

Laurel Antiques
671 Laurel St.
415/593-1152

149 SAN CLEMENTE

Plum Precious Antiques
101 Avenida Miramar
714/361-0162

Stanford Court Antiques
106 Avenida Del Mar
714/366-6290

San Clemente Antiques
214 Avenida Del Mar
714/498-2992

Zachery's Crossing
307 N. El Camino Real
714/498-1148

Three Centuries Antq. Gallery
408 N. El Camino Real
714/492-6609

Pacific Trader
1407 N. El Camino Real
714/366-3049

Patrice Antiques
1602 N. El Camino Real
714/498-3230

Victoria's Antiques
101 N. El Camino Real
714/366-6232

Garden Antiques
109 S. El Camino Real
714/492-8344

Penny N Sue's
218 Ave. Del Mar
714/492-6027

Antiques & Collectibles
159 Ave. Del Mar
714/369-7321

Blue Moon Antiques
111 W. Avenida Palizada #10A
714/498-4907

Forgotten Dreams
1062 Call Del Cerro Bldg. #1226
714/361-0054

150 SAN DIEGO

Adams Ave. Consignment
2873 Adams Ave.
619/281-9663

Country Cousins
2889 Adams Ave.
619/284-3039

Alouette Antiques
2936 Adams Ave.
619/284-9408

Antique Seller
2938 Adams Ave.
619/283-8467

Sign of The Whales Antiques
4121 Ashton St.
619/275-6122

Pacific Beach Antiques
4675 Cass St.
619/483-4001

St. Vincent De Paul Ctr. Shoppe
3137 El Cajon Blvd.
619/624-9701

Palace Antiques
363 5th Ave. #104
619/234-4004

Paper Antiquities
1552 5th Ave.
619/239-0656

Fifth Ave. Antiques
2452 5th Ave.
619/544-9040

Circa a. d.
3867 4th Ave.
619/293-3328

Beverlee's Antiques
1062 Garnet Ave.
619/274-1933

Vest Pocket
4015 Harney
619/291-9199

Country Craftsman
2465 Heritage Park Row
619/294-4600

5th & J Antique Mall
502 J St.
619/338-9559

Antique Mall
704 J St.
619/239-6255

Elon
704 J St.
619/235-9191

Unicorn Antiques
704 J St.
619/232-1696

Empire Enterprises
704 J St.
619/239-9216

Antique Castings
8333 LaMesa Ste B
619/466-8665

Whooping Crane Antiques
1617 W. Lewis St.
619/291-9232

Lincoln Roberts Gallery
411 Market St.
619/702-5884

Gaslamp Books,Prints & Antqs.
413 Market St.
619/237-1492

Second Floor Antique Mall
448 W. Market
619/236-9484

Memories Antiques
448 W. Market St.
619/231-9133

Legacy's Antiques
448 W. Market St.
619/232-7236

Bobbie's Paper Dolls
448 W. Market St.
619/233-0055

Burton's Antiques
448 W. Market St.
619/236-9484

Third Floor Antiques
448 W. Market
619/238-7339

Bert's Antiques
448 W. Market St.
619/239-5531

Elite Antiques
448 W. Market
619/238-1038

Oriental Treasure Box
448 W. Market
619/233-3821

English Garden
4140 Morena Blvd. #B
619/456-1793

House of Antiques
4901 Morena Blvd.
619/273-8054

Vignettes-Antiques
4828 Newport Ave.
619/222-9244

Newport Ave. Antique Center
4864 Newport Ave.
619/222-8686

Decades Antique Mall
4873 Newport Ave.
619/226-6711

Ocean Beach Antique Mall
4878 Newport Ave.
619/222-1967

What Mama Had
4215 Park Blvd.
619/296-7277

Rocky's Antqs., Books, Cllbls.
4608 Park Blvd.
619/297-1639

Miscellanea
4610 Park Blvd.
619/295-6488

Now & Then
4655 Park Blvd.
619/298-1022

Antique Alley Mall
1911 San Diego Ave.
619/688-1911

T & R Antiques Warehouse
4630 Santa Fe St.
619/272-2500

Lost Your Marbles Too
3933 30th St.
619/291-3061

House of Heirlooms
801 University Ave.
619/298-0502

Papyrus Antqs. & Unusual
116 W. Washington St.
619/298-9291

Olde Cracker Factory
448 W. Market St.
619/233-1669

Mission Gallery
320 W. Washington St.
619/692-3566

151 SAN DIMAS

Just Us Antiques
120 W. Bonita Ave.
909/599-0568

Old Towne Antique Mall
125 W. Bonita Ave.
909/394-1836

Jabberwocky Antiques
138 W. Bonita Ave. #101A
909/394-0084

Heart Of The Village Antique
155 W. Bonita Ave.
909/394-0628

Annie's Antiques & Cllbls.
161 W. Bonita Ave.
909/592-2616

Two Eager Beavers Antiques
165 W. Bonita Ave.
909/592-3087

Frontier Village Antiques
115 N. Monte Vista Ave.
909/394-0628

152 SAN FRANCISCO

Clyde & Eva's Antique Shop
3942 Balboa St.
415/387-3902

Antique Traders
4300 California St.
415/668-4444

Browsers Nook
530 Castro St.
415/861-2216

Brand X Antiques
570 Castro St.
415/626-8908

Lovejoy's Antqs. & Tea Room
1195 Church St.
415/648-5895

Schlep Sisters
4327 18th St.
415/626-0581

Grand Central Station Antqs.
595 Castro St.
415/863-3604

Homes of Charm
1544 Church St.
415/647-4586

Alley Cat Jewels
1547 Church St.
415/285-3668

Old Stuff
2325 Clement St.
415/668-2220

Garden Spot
3029 Clement St.
415/751-8190

Mureta's Antiques
2418 Fillmore St.
415/922-5652

Other Shop
112 Gough St.
415/621-1590

Deco to 50's
149 Gough St.
415/553-4500

Decodence
149 Gough St.
415/553-4500

Modern Era Decor
149 Gough St.
415/431-8599

Vintage Modern
182 Gough St.
415/861-8162

Henry's Antiques & Art Gallery
319 Grant Ave.
415/291-0319

J C's Collectables
564 Hayes St.
415/558-6904

Foster-Gwin Antiques
38 Hotaling Place
415/397-4986

Jekyll's On Hyde
1044 Hyde St.
415/775-3502

Hyde & Seek Antiques
1913 Hyde St.
415/776-8865

Thomas Livingston Antiques
414 Jackson St.
415/296-8150

Louis D Fenton Antiques
432 Jackson St.
415/398-3046

Lotus Collection
434 Jackson
415/398-8115

Edward Marshall Antiques
441 Jackson St.
415/399-0980

Dora Mauri Antichita
455 Jackson St.
415/296-8500

Daniel Stein Antiques
458 Jackson St.
415/956-5620

Challiss House
463 Jackson St.
415/397-6999

Hunt Antiques
478 Jackson St.
415/989-9531

Sen's Antiques Inc.
200 Kansas
415/487-3888

Antiques Antiques
245 Kansas St.
415/252-7600

D Carnegie Antiques
601 Kansas St.
415/641-4704

Willmann Country Pine
650 King St.
415/626-6547

North Beach Antqs. & Cllbls.
734 Lombard St.
415/346-2448

Golden Gate Antiques
1564 Market St.
415/626-3377

Browsers Nook
1592 Market St.
415/861-3801

Grand Central Station Antiques
1632 Market St. #A
415/252-8155

Isak Kindenauer Antiques
4143 19th St.
415/552-6436

In My Dreams
1300 Pacific Ave.
415/885-6696

Four Corners Antiques
90 Parnassus Ave.
415/753-6111

La Belle Antiques
2035 Polk St.
415/673-1181

Russian Hill Antiques
2200 Polk St.
415/441-5561

Alexander Collections
309 W. Portal Ave.
415/661-5454

Lupardo
3232 Sacremento St.
415/928-8662

Woodchuck Antiques
3597 Sacramento St.
415/922-6416

Every Era Antiques
3599 Sacramento St.
415/346-0313

Harvey Antiques
700 7th St. 2nd Floor
415/431-8888

Sixth Ave. Antiques
189 6th Ave.
415/386-2500

Quality First
608 Taraval St.
415/665-6442

Biscuit Jar Antiques
2134 Taraval St.
415/665-4520

Telegraph Hill Antiques
580 Union St.
415/982-7055

Tampico
2147 Union St.
415/563-3785

Collective Antiques
212 Utah St.
415/621-3800

Upstairs/Downstairs
890 Valencia St.
415/647-4211

Decorum
1400 Vallejo St.
415/474-6886

153 SAN JACINTO

Country Heritage Antiques
2385 S. San Jacinto Ave.
909/658-8468

Corner Antiques
2525 S. San Jacinto Ave.
909/925-1799

Anns Attic
2547 S. San Jacinto Ave.
909/925-0272

154 SAN JOSE

Time Tunnel Vintage Toys
532 S. Bascom Ave.
408/298-1709

William B. Huff Antiques
999 Lincoln Ave.
408/287-8820

Past & Presents
1324 Lincoln Ave.
408/297-1822

Willow Glen Collective
1349 Lincoln Ave.
408/947-7222

Gold Street Antiques
2092 Lincoln Ave.
408/266-9999

Ancora Ancora
751 W. San Carlos St.
408/977-1429

Antique Village
1225 W. San Carlos st
408/292-2667

San Carlos St. Antiques
1401 W. San Carlos St.
408/293-8105

Laurelwood Antiques & Cllbls.
1824 W. San Carlos
408/287-1863

Briarwood Antiques & Cllbls.
1885 W. San Carlos
408/292-1720

Annette's Antiques
1887 W. San Carlos St.
408/289-1929

Antique Colony
1915 W. San Carlos St.
408/293-9844

Antique Dreams
1916 W. San Carlos St.
408/998-2339

Antique Decor/Treasure of Joy
1957 W. San Carlos St.
408/298-5814

Antique Memories & Cllbls.
2314 Steven Creek Blvd.
408/977-1758

Rosewood Antiques
1897 W. San Carlos St.
408/292-1296

Interesting Side Trips

The Winchester Mystery House

525 S. Winchester Boulevard
408/247-2000

Was widowed heiress, Sarah Winchester, a few bricks shy of a full load, believing she'd ward off the spirits of hostile Indians and others by the continuous thirty-eight-year construction of what eventually became her 160-room, $5.5 million mansion? Or was she merely a frustrated architectural genius, the first to discern the value of many late nineteenth-century innovations, who, rather than using a blueprint, sketched as the "spirits" moved her? Her home was among the first in the country to have elevators, wool insulation, gas lights and stove, an "annunciator" intercom with which she could page her many servants from anywhere in the house, and built-in scrub boards and soap holders, which she patented.

This is the puzzle posed to visitors of the Winchester Mystery House in San Jose, California, which was built and rebuilt from 1884 until practically the moment after Sarah Winchester's death in 1922. At 24,000 square feet, it has 10,000 windows, 2,000 doors, 52 skylights, 47 fireplaces (one of which is hand carved), 40 staircases and bedrooms, 13 bathrooms, six kitchens, three elevators, two basements, and one shower.

Only the best was used, and this Victorian home boasts parquet floors with multifaceted inlaid patterns of precious hardwoods; gold and silver chandeliers; exquisite art glass windows, and doors with hinges and designs of silver, bronze, and gold. Storerooms still contain tens of thousands of dollars worth of Tiffany doors and windows, as well as precious silks, satins, linens, and other fabrics. a glass-lined conservatory not only guaranteed sunlight but also had a metal sub-flooring that could be drained to the garden below whenever the servants watered the plants. An accoustically balanced ballroom that cost the then-outrageous sum of $9000 was put together using carpenter's glue and wooden pegs, with tiny nails used only in moldings and floorings.

But the mansion, which rambles over nearly six acres and is four stories (down from seven before the San Francisco earthquake), brims with oddities. Stairways lead to ceilings, and doors open into walls. Pillars on fireplaces are installed upside down, ostensibly to confuse evil spirits. One $1500 Tiffany window will never see the light of day because it's blocked off by a wall. Skylights shoot up from the floor, and a five-foot door, just right for the diminutive (four feet, ten inches, one hundred pounds) Sarah, stands next to a normal-sized one that leads nowhere. One cabinet opens up to one-half inch of storage space, while the closet across from it reveals the back thirty rooms of the home.

The number thirteen abounds. Several rooms have thirteen panels with the same number of windows, which, in turn, have "guess how many" panes. a baker's dozen can be found in the lights in the chandeliers, in the cupolas in the greenhouse, and in the palms that line the front driveway.

Sarah's last will and testament consisted of thirteen parts and was signed thirteen times, and legend has it that when she dined, it was on a gold service set for herself and twelve invisible guests. To further encourage ghost busting, the house had only two mirrors.

In order to better understand the house, one needs to delve into the enigma that was Sarah Pardee Winchester. Born in 1839, in New Haven, Connecticut, she married William Winchester in 1862. He was the son of Oliver Winchester, inventor and manufacturer of the repeating rifle that allegedly won the West. According to several accounts, Sarah was an attractive, cultured musician who spoke four languages.

But her life was far from normal. Her only daughter, Anna, died in infancy, and a few years later in 1881 her husband succumbed to pulmonary tuberculosis. "Sarah had never fully recovered from the first loss, so this further intensified her anguish," states Shozo Kagoshima, director of marketing for the museum. Sarah was now incredibly wealthy, thanks to the invention that had the dubious honor of having killed more game, Indians, and U.S. soldiers than any other weapon in American history. She inherited $20 million and nearly 50 percent of the stock in the Winchester company, the latter of which gave her a tax-free (until 1913) stipend of about $1000 *a day*. So money was no object.

To ease her grief, Sarah went to a "seer" in Boston, who told her that "the spirits of all those the Winchester rifles had killed sought their revenge by taking the lives of her loved ones," relates Kagoshima. "Furthermore, they'd placed a curse on her and would haunt her forever." But Sarah could construct her own escape hatch, the medium said, by "moving West, buying a house, and continually building on it as the spirits directed." That way, she could escape the hostile ones (particularly Indians), while providing a comfortable respite for friendly ghosts (including perhaps Casper), and possibly guaranteeing eternal life.

So Sarah traveled to San Jose and plunked down nearly $13,000 in gold coins to buy an eight-room farmhouse from a Dr. Caldwell. Thus an exquisite behemoth was born.

Renovated in 1973, the rambling structure has 110 rooms open to the public, about 20 more than were in use when Sarah was alive. "The rest were damaged by the 1906 earthquake or are offices," explains Kagoshima. Other than normal restoration to maintain the status quo "the house is to remain the same as when she died."

"Sarah was an eccentric, although she had many good ideas about building and modern conveniences," sums up Kagoshima. The Winchester Mystery House may never be solved, but it—and everyone connected with it—has had a long, strange trip.

From *America's Strangest Museums*

Published by arrangement with Carol Publishing Group. A Citadel Press Book

155 SAN JUAN BAUTISTA

Lillian Johnson Antiques
405 3rd St.
408/623-4381

Gerrie's Collectibles Etc.
406 3rd St.
408/623-1017

Golden Wheel Antiques
407 3rd St.
408/623-4767

156 SAN JUAN CAPISTRANO

Old Mission San Juan Capistrano

There is one historic place in Southern California where visitors gather, only to return again and again. It is the famous old Spanish Mission at San Juan Capistrano, the quaint little town located above the shores of the Pacific, halfway between San Diego and Los Angeles along the old Camino Real.

Mission San Juan Capistrano is beautiful, old and romantic. You can hear the tolling of its centuries old bells and walk down its time worn paths. Its serenity and peace amid lush gardens and cool fountains, cloistered by old adobe walls, offers visitors seclusion from the sounds and sights of a busy world.

Founded over two centuries ago, the Mission is a monument to California's multi-cultural history, embracing its Spanish, Mexican, Native American and

European heritage. Originally built as a self-sufficient community by Spanish padres and Indian laborers, the Mission was a center for agriculture, industry and education. The spiritual and cultural heritage of the Mission is owed to the legendary Fr. Junipero Serra, who founded over eight missions in California and earned heroic stature as the "Father of California", becoming its first citizen in July of 1769.

Today, you'll discover many areas of interest within the Mission walls, including the museum, founding documents, early soldiers barracks, friars quarters, an olive millstone, cemetery, and an aqueduct system. Then, continue with a walk through the renowned gardens to the majestic ruins of the great Stone Church, and along the path to beautiful little Serra Chapel, oldest building in California.

You can see the little adobe church, "Father Serra's Chapel", the oldest building still in use in California. Constructed in 1777, it houses a magnificent Baroque altar which is over 350 years old. The famous "Golden Altar" was shipped from Spain to California in 10 large crates containing 396 pieces. Originally intended for use in the Los Angeles Cathedral, the altar piece was given to the Mission in 1922. Crafted of Spanish cherry wood covered with gold leaf, the 22 feet high and 18 feet wide golden altar features 52 carved angels who watch over visitors today.

The setting is very spiritual. Light falls on it from a long narrow window above. Viewed through the hundred foot nave which is usually in semi-darkness, the shimming golden sight is one not easily forgotten.

There are many romantic legends about the Mission. The most popular are about the swallows of Capistrano. Swallow's Day is celebrated annually on March 19. Visitors from all over the world come to witness the return of the swallows to Capistrano. Legend says the swallows, seeking sanctuary from an innkeeper who destroyed their nests, took up residence at the old Mission. They return to the site each year to nest, knowing their young can be safe within the Mission walls.

You'll also learn about the legend of Magdalena, whose penance was to walk up and down the church aisle with a lighted candle to atone for disobeying her father, who had forbidden her from courting a man beneath her station in life. On her first day of penance, December 8, 1812, an earthquake destroyed the great Stone Church and buried her in the ruins. It is said that on certain nights in December her candlelight can still be seen shining out of the church ruins.

General Information: The Mission is open from 8:30 AM to 5:00 PM daily except on Thanksgiving, Christmas and Good Friday afternoon. Admission is $5 for adults and $4 for seniors and children. Members free. There is usually no extra charge for exhibitions or special events.

Location: The Mission is conveniently located one block from the Ortega exit off the 5 freeway, at the corner of Camino Capistrano and Ortega Hwy.

Visitors Center: To book a guided tour or arrange a special event, call 714/248-2049. To write for information, please send inquiry to P.O. Box 697, San Juan Capistrano, CA 92693.

Yesterday's Paper
31815 Camino Capistrano Ste. C11
714/248-0945
Open: Daily 11-5, (7 days a week)

Directions: From I-5 take Hwy. W. exit 2 blocks to Camino Capistrano, turn left, shop is on the right. Located in the Historic District.

For ten years this shop has specialized in everything old made of paper. Antiquarian books, documents, magazines, newspapers, prints, illustrations, posters, pinups and more.

Sentimental Journey West
31843 Camino Capistrano
714/661-4560
Open 11-5 every day except Wednesdays. Call first if traveling.

A really different "antiquing adventure" awaits the visitor to Sentimental Journey West. It's the place where the "Wild West" comes alive in touchable, buyable, take-home living color! Owners Ron and Eila Turner offer any and everything that is genuine Old West from the 1800s. Their 6,000 items include - but certainly aren't limited to - Cowboy and Indian lodge furniture and decor; gold mining equipment; Wells Fargo memorabilia; vintage clothing, including an 1880s bear coat; Indian jewelry; signed gambling items from the 1800s; covered wagons; benches; guns and rifles; Roy Rogers and Hopalong Cassiday collectibles; badges, holsters and spurs; a signed printing press; movie memorabilia and props from the Old West movies; kettles and barrels; Montery furniture and western oils. They even have three mint condition Dead Wood Dick 1899 comics!

The shop is located in the oldest two-story adobe building in town, with the original three-foot thick walls and wooden plank floors. It was originally a French hotel in the 1840s and later a 20,000 head cattle ranch. Don't miss this rare look into part of our country's most colorful history!

Majorca of San Juan
31815 Camino Capistrano
714/496-7465

Durenberger & Friends
31531 Camino Capistrano
714/240-5181

Old Barn Mall
31792 Camino Capistrano
714/493-9144

Encore Antiques
31815 Camino Capistrano
714/661-3483

Just Perfect Antiques
31815 Camino Capistrano
714/240-8821

Curiosity Antiques
31107 Rancho Viejo Rd. #B2
714/240-1553

Decorative Arts Villa
31431 Camino Capistrano
714/488-9600

Studio Five Design
31511 Camino Capistrano
714/240-1474

Gifts For The Home Int'l
31681 Camino Capistrano
714/443-3913

Ye Old Collector Shop
31815 Camino Capistrano
714/496-6724

Grand Avenue Antiques
33208 B Paseo Cerveza
714/661-1053

Favorite Places To Eat

Capistrano Depot
26701 Verdugo Street-Amtrak Station
714/488-7600

L'Hirondelle French Cuisine
31661 Camino Capistrano-Mission Hacienda
714/661-0425

Ramos House Cafe
31752 Los Rios Street-Historic District
714/443-1342

Sidewalk Cafe
31882 Del Obispo-Plaza Del Obispo
714/443-0423

157 SAN LUIS OBISPO

Treasure Island Antiques
645 Higuera St.
805/543-0532

Showroom
1531 Monterey St.
805/546-8266

158 SAN MARCOS

Antique Village
983 Grand Ave.
760/744-8718

Vicki Harman, Antiques-Estates
1440 Grand Ave.
760/591-4746

Burdock Victorian Lamp Co.
757 N. Twin Oaks Valley Rd. #5
760/591-3911

159 SAN MATEO

Hoosier-Town Antiques
726 S. Amphlett Blvd.
650/343-3673

B Street Collective
710 S. B St.
650/342-0993

Camelot Antiques & Art
714 S. B St.
650/343-7663

Come C Interiors
807 S. B St.
650/344-5899

Ellsworth Place Antiques
115 S. Ellsworth Ave.
650/347-5906

Canterbury Antiques
1705 Gum St.
650/570-7010

Shawn's
2218 Palm Ave.
650/574-2097

Alberts Antiques
310 S. San Mateo Ave.
650/348-2369

Come C Antiques
159 South Blvd.
650/344-5899

Look What I Found
168 South Blvd.
650/573-7113

Memory House Antiques
74 E. 3rd Ave.
650/344-5600

160 SAN PEDRO

South Bay Antiques
100 W. 1st St.
310/833-2578

161 SAN RAFAEL

English Country Pine & Design
2066 4th St.
415/485-3800

Bargain Box Sunny Hills
508 Irwin St.
415/459-2396

Collier Lighting
3100 Kerner Blvd.
415/454-6672

Twenty Ross Common
20 Ross St.
415/925-1482

162 SANTA ANA

Steven-Thomas Antiques
800 E. Dyer Rd.
714/957-6017

Lyman Drake Antiques
2901 S. Harbor Blvd.
714/979-2811

Charles Wallace Antiques Inc.
2929 S. Harbor Blvd.
714/556-9901

Second Season
2380 N. Tustin
714/835-0180

163 SANTA BARBARA

Collector's Corner
701 Anacapa St.
805/965-8915

Adobe Antiques
707 Anacapa St.
805/966-2556

Awalk in the Woods
15 E. Anapamu
805/966-1331

Peregrine Galleries
508 Brinkerhoff Ave.
805/963-3134

Elders
512 Brinkerhoff Ave.
805/962-0933

Hightower & Russell
528 Brinkerhoff Ave.
805/965-5687

Mary's on the Avenue
529 Brinkerhoff Ave.
805/962-8047

Robert Livernois Art
533 Brinkerhoff Ave.
805/962-4247

Corner Cottage
536 Brinkerhoff Ave.
805/962-7010

Peregrin
1133 Coast Village Rd.
805/969-9671

Main Antiques
39 E. DeLa Guerra St.
805/962-7710

Moriarty's Lamps
305 E. Haley St.
805/966-1124

Mackey Anqs./Pine Trader
410 E. Haley St.
805/962-0250

State St. Antique Mall
710 State St.
805/965-2575

Mingei
736 State St.
805/963-3257

Indigo
1323 State St.
805/962-6909

164 SANTA CRUZ

Chateau Victorian
118 First St.
408/458-9458
Open Daily
Rates $110-140

Directions: Hwy. 17 drops onto Ocean St./Beaches. Go to the end of Ocean St.. which forms a "T" at the light. Right on San Lorenzo to next light; left on Riverside, go over bridge through the light to the next stop sign; right on 2nd St., next stop sign left on Cliff St.; go one block; right on 1st St.; just past the first building on the left is parking. House is on the right.
From Hwy. 1, coming from the north. Coming in on Mission St., go to 4th stop light; right on Bay St. to the end, forming a "T"; left on West Cliff Dr., which drops onto Beach St.; bottom of small hill is a stop sign; continue straight to next stop sign; left on Cliff St.; go one short block; left on First St.
From Hwy. 1, coming from the south; ends in a fish hook and drops onto Ocean St./Beaches, and as above.

Replete with decorative cornices, bay windows and gingerbread trim, Chateau Victorian, a national historic landmark, was built around 1885. It was turned into an elegant bed & breakfast in 1983. The inn was originally a single-family residence for a family that obviously enjoyed the beach and the ocean. Within a block of Chateau Victorian is a beautiful beach, stretching for nearly a mile from the San Lorenzo River to beyond the wharf.

Wood-burning fireplaces adorn all seven rooms and each room offers its own special touch of Victorian-styled themes. The Garden View Room contains an original Victorian bay window and a four-poster canopy bed. The Ocean View Room, appropriately named for its overlook of Monterey Bay, has a marble fireplace and a clawfoot tub. The Pleasure Point Room has a bay window seat overlooking a garden of flowers. Old-fashioned armoires, and private entrances to The Patio Room and Sunrise Room, provide an intimate "home away from home" atmosphere. There is a Lighthouse Room and a Natural Bridges Room with high ceilings and redwood crossbeams. From this room guests will also enjoy a small view of Loma Prieta Mountain.

A breakfast of fresh fruits, croissants, muffins, preserves, juices, coffee and teas are available from 9:00 to 10:30 a.m. in the lounge, on the secluded deck or on the terrace.

Modern Life
925 41st Ave.
408/475-1410

Mr. Goodie's
1541 Pacific Ave.
408/427-9997

Lovejoys
2600 Soquel Ave.
408/479-4480

Hall's Surrey House Antiques
708 Water St.
408/423-2475

Possibilities Unlimited
1043 Water Street
408/427-1131

165 SANTA MARGARITA

Gasoline Alley Antiques
2200 El Camino Real
805/438-5322

Kathy's Antiques
2324 El Camino Real
805/438-3542

Faded Glory Antiques
2719 El Camino Real
805/438-3770

Carriage House Antiques
22302 El Camino Real
805/438-5062

Little Store Antiques
22705 El Camino Real
805/438-5347

166 SANTA MARIA

Little Store Antiques
22705 El Camino Real
805/438-5347

Golden Retriever Antiques
111 W. Main St.
805/349-1038

Antique Mall
1573 Stowell Center Plaza
805/922-6464

167 SANTA MONICA

Santa Monica Antique Market
1607 Lincoln Boulevard
310/314-4899
Open daily Mon.-Sat., 10-6, Sun., 12-5
free valet parking

Santa Monica Antique Market is located on Los Angeles's fashionable West Side and houses over 150 dealers and 20,000 square feet of merchandise. The inventory comes from all over the world and includes all types of furnishings and collectibles. Rediscover the Age of Romance with distinctive antique and custom-made decorative accessories from the Victorian through the Art Deco periods. You'll find exquisite lamps and chandeliers, signature jewelry, figurines, cherubs, pottery and assorted items of uncommon beauty reminiscent of Victorian times.

Create the pleasure of outdoor living in your garden room or terrace with gilded wooden columns, statues, fountains, handsomely crafted wrought iron pieces and neo-classical accents.

If you enjoy and cherish America's textile arts, accessories and furnishings, then you're in for a treat. The Market offers lovely antique quilts dating from 1870-1940, stunning iron and brass beds, a 1910 white wicker high chair, bird houses from 1920-1940, and many fine and unusual folk art pieces. You'll also find a superb representation of country primitives such as Shaker and Mennonite shutters, mantels, pie safes, windows, and old watering cans.

The Market displays some wonderful American arts and crafts movement pieces. Furniture bearing the distinguished names of Stickley, Limberts, Lifetime, and Harden can be found along with hand-hammered copper lighting and metalwork by Roycroft and Dirk Van Erp.

Travel through American Modernism to Italian Baroque with architectural fragments: pediments, finials and columns, Paladian mirrors, tin work, mercury glass, paints, iron work and Latin American furniture.

One of the Market's greatest successes has been an ability to tailor services to the different needs of its diverse customer base. Santa Monica Antique Market offers a layaway plan, 48-hour at-home trial period, delivery, international shipping, item searches, restoration and appraisal referrals, bridal registry, gift certificates, free gift wrapping, and off-hours shopping - popular among celebrity clientele. Other bonuses include a book section, an espresso bar, and free valet parking.

House of Yorke
549 11th St.
310/395-2744

Clifford Antiques
1655 Lincoln Blvd.
310/452-7668

Main Street Antiques
2665 Main St.
310/392-4519

Raintree Antiques
2711 Main St.
310/392-7731

British Collectibles Ltd.
1727 Wilshire Blvd.
310/453-3322

Quilt Gallery
1025 Montana Ave.
310/393-1148

Rosemarie McCaffrey
1203 Montana Ave.
310/395-7711

Brenda Cain Store
1211 Montana Ave.
310/395-1559

Montana Country
1311 Montana Ave.
310/393-3324

Prince of Wales
1316 Montana Ave.
310/458-1566

Country Pine & Design
1318 Montana Ave.
310/451-0317

Twigs
1401 Montana Ave.
310/451-9934

Blue House
1402 Montana Ave.
310/451-2243

Federico's
1522 Montana Ave.
310/458-4134

Caswell Antiques
1322 2nd St.
310/394-3384

168 SANTA ROSA

Pygmalion House
331 Orange Street
707/526-3407
Open Year Around

Directions: For specific directions from your location, please call the innkeepers.

If you're looking for the perfect romantic getaway that won't cost you a fortune, you need look no further than Pygmalion House in Santa Rosa, California. Pygmalion House is nestled in a quiet neighborhood just a couple of blocks from Santa Rosa's Old Town. It is within walking distance to the various antique shops as well as some wonderful restaurants and coffee houses.

Pygmalion House, one of Santa Rosa's historical landmarks, is a fine example of Victorian Queen Anne architecture. This charming home was built in the 1800s on land owned by one of the city's leading developers, Mr. Thomas Ludwig. This house withstood the great earthquake and fire of 1906 which devastated much of Santa Rosa's heritage.

Pygmalion House derives its name from an ancient Greek myth, which was the basis for George Bernard Shaw's play 'Pygmalion' and the musical 'My Fair Lady'. The name reflects the transformation, brought about by painstaking renovation, from an old dilapidated house to the grand lady it is today.

You'll find this gracious Bed and Breakfast full of antiques from the collection of the famous stripper, Gypsy Rose Lee and the famous madam and past Sausalito mayor, Sally Stanford. Each of the guest rooms are quiet and nicely decorated, including private bath, and a queen or king-size bed. The main room, or "double parlor" includes a beautiful fireplace as well as an offset sitting area that looks out from octagon-shaped windows.

Each morning you'll feast on the full breakfast that is served from 8:00 a.m. to 9:30 a.m. Breakfast includes fresh fruit or melon, fresh baked muffins and croissants, and eggs with either ham, bacon, or sausage. Fresh squeezed orange juice is also served as well as Pygmalion House's fresh ground blend of five different kinds of coffee, including Kona coffee from Hawaii.

With all of these special touches that Pygmalion House offers you would think that a nights stay would be expensive. Well the best thing about this B&B is their prices. You can get a room with a queen-sized bed for only $75.00 per night and a king-sized bed for $85.00. Considering that B&B's can run a much as $100-$200 a night, Pygmalion House offers it's guests true value for their money as well as a wonderful experience that is sure to bring you back time and time again.

Antiques Apples & Art
105 3rd St.
707/578-1414

Marianne Antiques
111 3rd St.
707/579-5749

Whistle Stop Antiques
130 4th St.
707/542-9474

Blue Goose Antiques
60 W. 6th St.
707/527-8859

C & H Antiques
204 Wilson St.
707/527-7421

Treasure House
700 Wilson St.
707/523-1188

169 SARATOGA

Carol's Antique Gallery
14455 Big Basin Way
408/867-7055

M E. Benson's Antiques
14521 Big Basin Way
408/741-0314

Bit O Country
14527 Big Basin Way
408/867-9199

McKenzie House Antiques
14554 Big Basin Way
408/867-1341

Front Window
12378 Saratoga Sunnyvale Rd.
408/253-2980

Blue Candlestick
14320 Saratoga Sunnyvale Rd.
408/867-3658

170 SEAL BEACH

Audrey's Antiques
132 Main St.
310/430-7213

Antique Gallery
217 Main St.
310/594-4985

Finders Keepers Unlimited
406 Marina Dr.
310/493-4952

171 SEBASTOPOL

Carol's Curios
961 Gravenstein Hwy.
707/823-8334

Country Cottage Antiques
1235 Gravenstein Hwy.
707/823-4733

Antique Society
2661 Gravenstein Hwy.
707/829-1733

Ed's Antiques
2661 Gravenstein Hwy.
707/829-5363

Willow Tree Antiques
2701 Gravenstein Hwy.
707/823-3101

Lone Pine Antiques
3598 Gravenstein Hwy.
707/823-6768

Llano House Antiques
4353 Gravenstein Hwy.
707/829-9322

Sebastopol Antique Mall
755 Petaluma Ave.
707/823-1936

172 SHERMAN OAKS

Outer Limits
13542 Ventura Blvd.
818/906-8133

Marilyn Hirsty Antiques
13627 Ventura Blvd.
818/995-4128

Piccolo Pete's
13814 Ventura Blvd.
818/990-5421

Sherman Oaks Antique Mall
14034 Ventura Blvd.
818/906-0338

Aunt Teeks
4337 Woodman Ave.
818/784-3341

173 SIMI VALLEY

A Collectors Paradise - Penny Pinchers
4265 Valley Fair Street
805/527-0056
Open Mon.-Sat. 10-5 and Sun. 11-5

Directions: From the 405 Freeway: Take Highway 118 West to the Tapo Cyn. exit, make a left to Cochran, make another left and go three blocks to Winifred, make a right and go about 10 blocks to Valley Fair. OR from Highway 101, take 23 North, which changes into the 118 East. Go to Tapo Cyn. exit, make a right, go to Cochran, make a left, go three blocks to Winifred, make a right and go about 10 blocks to Valley Fair.

In business for 30 years, Penny Pinchers offers Empire furniture and Depression glass, plus all types of nostalgic antiques and collectibles. They also offer the very hard, but not frequently found, services of furniture repair, jewelry repair and custom work, and appraisals. Also a full antique and collectible book library is available for the customers' use.

Memories Antiques
4325 Valley Fair St.
805/526-6308

Pine Haven Antiques
4371 Valley Fair St.
805/520-3801

Antiques At Willie's
4345 Valley Fair St.
805/584-2580

174 SOLANA BEACH

Antique Warehouse
212 S. Cedros Ave.nue
619/755-5156

Appleby Intl. Art
143 S. Cedros Ave.
619/259-0404

Geissmann Rudolf Oriental Carpet
143 S. Cedros Ave.
619/481-3489

175 SOLVANG

California is noted for having a little bit of everything in the state, but what about the title of "Danish Capital of America"? In the gently rolling Santa Ynez Valley, Solvang (which means *sunny field* in Danish) was founded in 1911 by Danes from the Midwest seeking to establish a West Coast Danish colony and folk school. Over the years the town began to look more and more Danish as the townspeople, perhaps encouraged by visits from Danish royalty, turned increasingly to Danish-style architecture. Today, visiting Danes say the town looks more like Denmark than the original country, with buildings of timber-framed white stucco, sloping green copper or wood shingle roofs, gables, dormer and towers, cobblestone sidewalks, outdoor cafes, and shops with leaded-glass windows. There are even four windmills - one still turns.

Specific Danish sites in Solvang include a half-scale replica of the Little Mermaid (the original sits in the Copenhagen harbor), and the Bethania Lutheran Church, a typical rural Danish church with hand-carved pulpits and a scale model of a Danish sailing ship hanging from the ceiling. The Elverhoy Museum preserves the history of Solvang with old photographs, crafts, period rooms, and other exhibits, and the Hans Christian Anderson Museum honors the life and work of the father and master of the modern fairy tale.

But Solvang's most historic site is, ironically, not Danish. It is the beautifully restored adobe Mission Santa Ines, established in 1804 as the 19th of the 21 missions built in California by Spanish Franciscan priests. The chapel, in continuous use since 1817, is decorated with murals by Indian artists and masterpieces of Moorish art and architecture.

But for the shopper, Solvang is Valhalla! There are 350 shops, noted for their antiques, paintings and Danish goods (pastries, music boxes, porcelain figurines, knotted sweaters, folk art, handmade lace, and Danish costumes.) After shopping, visitors can tour the town by carriage or on the Honen, a replica of a turn-of-the-century Copenhagen streetcar pulled by a pair of Belgian draft horses. And to tour the picturesque valley, hang gliders and bicycles are the only way to go!

Solvang Antique Center
486 First Street
805/686-2322
Open 7 days a week 10-6
Cafe/Bistro in same building, open daily 11-9

Directions: From the south (Los Angeles, Santa Barbara): Highway 101 North to Buellton. Take Solvang Exit (Highway 246) east into Solvang (3 miles). Just past Solvang Park in the center of the village turn right onto First Street. The Solvang Antique Center is on the left in the middle of the block.
Highway 101 North to Santa Barbara. Take Highway 154 Exit (San Marcos Pass) past Lake Cachuma. Take Solvang Exit (Highway 246) west into Solvang. Once in the Solvang village, go one block past the stop light at Alisal Road. The Solvang Antique Center is on the left in the middle of the block.
(Both of the above routes are scenic. The first route is a divided highway. The second route is about 15 minutes shorter, but the road is a winding mountain road through the Los Padres National Forest.
From the north (San Francisco, Hearst Castle): Highway 101 South to Buellton. Take Solvang Exit (Highway 246) east into Solvang (3 miles). Just past Solvang Park in the center of the village turn right onto First Street. The Solvang Antique Center is on the left in the middle of the block.

For specific information see review in the color section.

Home Ranch
444 Atterdag Rd.
805/686-0069

Frogmore House Antiques
1676 Oak St.
805/688-8985

176 SONOMA

Buffy Antique
414 1st St.
707/996-5626

Antique Center of Sonoma
120 W. Napa St.
707/996-9947

D Tenenbaum Antiques
128 W. Napa St.
707/935-7146

Cat & The Fiddle
153 W. Napa St.
707/996-5651

Curry & I Antiques
17000 Sonoma Hwy.
707/996-8226

177 SONORA

Antique Passions
8 S. Washington St.
209/532-8874

Antiques Etcetera
18 S. Washington St.
209/532-9544

Carriage Trade Antiques
36 S. Washington St.
209/532-0282

Castagnola's Empor. Antiques
93 S. Washington St.
209/533-8443

Baer's 1851 Antiques
105 S. Washington St.
209/533-2460

Pine Tree Peddlers
107 S. Washington St.
209/533-2356

178 SOQUEL

Wayne's Antiques
2940 S. Main St.
408/462-0616

Crawford Antiques
4401 Soquel Dr.
408/462-1528

Frank's Antiques
4900 Soquel Dr.
408/462-3953

Country Garden Antiques
4904 Soquel Dr.
408/462-5188

After Effects
4920 Soquel Dr.
408/475-5991

Edward & Sons Antiques
5025 Soquel Dr.
408/479-7122

179 SOUTH LAKE TAHOE

Auntie Q's 2nd Hand Treasures
800 Emerald Bay Rd.
916/542-2169

Hanifins Art & Antiques
855 Emerald Bay Rd.
916/542-4663

Hannifins Antiques
868 Emerald Bay Rd.
916/544-6769

Sierra Bookshop
3445 Lake Tahoe Blvd.
916/541-4222

180 SOUTH PASADENA

Isn't It Romantic
950 Mission St.
818/441-4824

Yoko
1011 Mission St.
818/441-4758

Mission Antiques
1018 Mission St. #3
818/799-1327

And Etc.
1110 Mission St.
818/799-6581

181 STOCKTON

Ivy
209 Dorris Place
209/466-6652

A & B Antiques
216 W. Harding Way
209/946-4337

Peckler's Antiques
220 W. Harding Way
209/462-7992

Lions Den Antiques
230 W. Harding Way
209/547-0433

House of Clocks
311 Lincoln Center
209/951-1363

Memory's Antiques & Cllbls.
2220 Pacific Ave.
209/462-5258

Trotting Horse Antiques
9177 Thornton Rd.
209/477-0549

Mardel's Antique Annex
917 N. Yosemite St.
209/546-0926

Mardel's Antiques
926 N. Yosemite St.
209/948-8948

182 STUDIO CITY

The Cranberry House
12318 Ventura Blvd.
818/506-8945
Open 11-6 daily

Directions: Take Highway 405 North to Highway 101 East (to Los Angeles). Exit at Coldwater Canyon, turn right to Ventura Blvd., then turn left. Cranberry House is on the right about 2 miles. OR take Highway 5 North to Highway 134 West, take Highway 134 West to Highway 101 West, take Highway 101 West to Laurel Canyon, turn left onto Ventura Blvd., then right and go about 3 blocks. Cranberry House will be on the left. Look for the 100-foot cranberry awning on the front!

Designers, prop masters, serious collectors, flea market fanatics and avid antique perfectionists all declare The Cranberry House as their source for the best in treasure hunting. One hundred forty dealers in 15,000 square feet offering Americana, fine and costume jewelry, linens and quilts, smoking collectibles, vintage accessories and silver, toys, and the best in furniture of domestic and European heritage from Rococo to Moderne. Still can't find it? Register for the Wish List and their friendly, knowledgeable staff will assist with a no obligation search and notify you when your "wish" arrives. Worldwide shipping, layaway, bridal registry, custom gift wrap, 24 hour approval program, and gift certificates are all part of the excellent customer service.

Be sure to attend the annual Birthday Sale the third weekend in May with discounts up to 50%. Also not to be missed is the Holiday Open House the second weekend in December. The breathless holiday decor, free gourmet eats and 10% off everything sale create an unforgettable shopping experience. Get your personal invitation to both events by adding your name to the guest registry.

Ivy Cottage
12206 Ventura Blvd.
818/762-9844

Fables Antiques
12300 Ventura Blvd.
818/506-2904

Mother of Pearl & Sons
12328 Ventura Blvd.
818/505-8057

Ferret
12334 Ventura Blvd.
818/769-2427

Pearl River
13031 Ventura Blvd.
818/986-5666

King's Cross
13059 Ventura Blvd.
818/905-3382

183 SUMMERLAND

Mary Suding Fine Antiques
2173 Ortega Hill Rd. 2nd Floor
805/969-4324

Christian-Tevis Antiques
2173 Ortega Hill Rd.
805/969-0966

Summerland Antq. Collective
2194 Ortega Hill Rd.
805/565-3189

Summerland Antique Annex
2240 Lillie Ave.
805/565-5226

Urban Hunter
2272 Lillie Ave.
805/969-7987

Antico II
2280 Lillie Ave.
805/565-4899

Summerhill Antiques
2280 Lillie Ave.
805/969-3366

Lillie Antiques & Accessories
2560 Lillie Avenue
805/565-1271

Heather House Antiques
2448 Lillie Ave.
805/565-1561

Gentlemen Antiquarians
2560 Lillie Ave.
805/565-1271

184 SUNLAND

Cathy's Cottage
8417 Foothill Boulevard
818/353-7807
Open 11-5, Tue.-Sat.

Directions: Off the 210 Freeway at Sunland Blvd. (Right next to Jack-N-Box).

Boy, if this building could talk, what stories it could tell! It was a beauty shop for 50 years - can you imagine the decades of gossip that soaked into those walls? Today it still offers much to talk about. Cathy, the shopkeeper and owner, keeps the place comfortably packed with all kinds of great "old stuff." She has Hummels, Sebastians, porcelains, dolls, kitchenware, some western and railroad memorabilia, plus much more.

Interesting Story

Adventure In Postcards
8423 Foothill Boulevard
818/352-5663
Open 10-5, Wed.-Sat., unless out of town buying or selling.

Directions: Located just 1/2 mile east of the #210 Freeway at the Sunland Blvd. offramp (Sunland becomes Foothill one block east of the freeway).

If you are looking for a very small, portable, inexpensive piece of Americana, Lee Brown's emporium in Sunland may have just what you need. The shop is truly an adventure in postcards.

With something like a quarter of a million postcards in stock, covering everything imaginable, most of Lee's cards are in the $1-$5 range and are dated pre-World War I. Although some signed cards can pull $100 or so, and a few rare ones can fetch $1,000 at an art auction, thousands of the little pictures sell for just 20 cents, making postcards one of the most affordable and interesting collectibles available.

The Sunland shop stocks everything from depictions of natural disasters, like the 1906 San Francisco earthquake, to one-eyed cows and nudes reading books. Other paper ephemera and some miscellaneous smalls are also offered.

It was three years ago that Brown discovered a very special holiday card that stood out among the thousands she was sorting. "I seldom read the backs of postcards, there's just not time; but I noticed some handwriting that I recognized," Brown said. "Then I spotted my grandmother's name, Mabel Holdefer, on a card dated 1908. She had sent it to a relative." Her grandmother raised her, so finding the card was a real treasure. I'm sure that's one postcard that will never be sold.

Antiques Etc.
7906 Foothill Blvd.
818/352-3197

185 SUTTER CREEK

Klima's Antiques
94 Boston Alley
209/267-5318

Creekside Shops
22 Main St.
209/267-5520

Alicia's
26 Main St.
209/267-0719

Somewhere In Time
34 Main St.
209/267-5789

Columbian Lady
61 Main St.
209/267-0059

Old Hotel Antiques
68 Main St.
209/267-5901

Water Street Antiques
78 Main St.
209/267-0585

Arnolds Antiques
80 Main St.
209/267-0603

Cobweb Collection Antiques
83 Main St.
209/267-0690

O'Neill's Antiques
84 Main St.
209/267-0450

Jackson Antiques
28 Main Street
209/223-0188

186 TAHOE CITY

Girasole
319 W. Lake Blvd.
916/581-4255

187 TEHACHAPI

Mom & Apple Pie Antiques
798 Tucker Road #2
805/822-8765
Open Tue.-Fri. 10-5, Sat. 10-5:30, Sun. 12-5, closed Mon. Open late or open early if needed for you out-of-towners!

Mom & Apple Pie Antiques began business September 1, 1996. Courtney Kearnes, owner, decided to open up shop after the antique store she managed closed in July of 1996. With the help of husband Brent, son Jarred (3) and daughter Taylor (1), Mom got the store up and running in a month. The business is now a REAL family affair, as her moms and dads (2 of each) are involved in the business with her!

The 2000 square foot shop is home to 12 dealers from all around the area. Most of the dealers have 20+ years of experience in the business and deal in QUALITY, QUALITY, QUALITY merchandise. The shop specializes in vintage jewelry (Victorian through 60s), timepieces, vintage linens & lace, quilts, sewing implements, Victorian smalls of all kinds, country primitives including furniture, and so much more! They dabble in just about everything and will do mail order business on most items. Visit their website for a firsthand look.

The atmosphere is inviting, with fresh hot coffee or apple cider in the cool months, and refreshing iced tea in the summer. They offer special presentations for local clubs or groups on request. Come see it to believe it - Mom would love to show you some down home hospitality!

Kathy's Mini Mall
104 W. Tehachapi Blvd.
805/822-6691

Apple Country Antiques
114 W. Tehachapi Blvd.
805/822-7777

Grace's Antiques
20300 Valley Blvd. #E.
805/822-5989

188 TEMECULA

Across the River Antiques
28418 Felix Valdez Ave.
909/699-9525

Granny's Attic
28450 Felix Valdez Ave. #C
909/699-9449

Always Wanted Antiques
28545 Felix Valdez Ave.
909/695-1136

Chaparral Antique Mall
28465 Front St.
909/676-0070

A To Z Antiques
28480 Front St.
909/699-3294

Loft
28480 Front St.
909/676-5179

Old Town Antique Faire
28601 Front St.
909/694-8786

Mr. R's Antiques
28635 Front St.
909/676-2002

Gramma Audrey's Antqs. Too
28636 Front St.
909/699-9338

Shire Limited
28656 Front St.
909/676-9233

Nana's Too
28677 Front St. #C
909/699-5292

Country Seller & Friends Antqs.
42050 Main Street
909/676-2322

Treasures You'll Cherish
42012 Main St.
909/694-6990

Timeless Treasures
28475 Front Street Ste. A
909/695-2926

Nancy's Antique Mall
42030 Main St. #BF
909/699-3889

Packard's Antiques
42031 Main St. #C
909/693-9442

Gramma Audrey's Antiques
42031 Main St.
909/699-9139

Morgan's Antiques
42049 Main St.
909/676-2722

Temecula Trading Post
42081 Main St.
909/767-5759

Juliet's Collectibles
44060 Margarita Rd.
909/693-1410

189 THOUSAND OAKS

2nd Edition
368 E. Thousand Oaks Blvd.
805/497-9727

Antique Suites Mall
783 E. Thousand Oaks Blvd.
805/373-0366

Maggie & Me Antiques
783 E. Thousand Oaks Blvd.
805/496-1603

Antiques of Tomorrow
3075 E. Thousand Oaks Blvd.
805/494-4095

190 TORRANCE

Kasden's Antiques
24548 Hawthorne Blvd.
310/378-8132

Dunk Antiques
4164 Pacific Coast Hwy.
310/375-6175

Janson & Son Antiques
1325 Sartori Ave.
310/787-1670

Collector's Gallery
833 Torrance Blvd.
310/532-2166

Pieces of the Past Antique Mall
19032 S. Vermont Ave.
310/324-6767

191 TULARE

Old Town Emporium
207 S. K St.
209/688-8483

192 TUSTIN

Tustin Consignments
474 El Camino Real
714/730-5037

Angels Garden
486 El Camino Real
714/669-1337

Bruce Cole Noland Antiques
500 El Camino Real
714/730-5502

Step Back In Time
528 El Camino Real
714/734-9093

Not Just Antiques
546 El Camino Real
714/731-8813

Gerdas Antiques
550 El Camino Real
714/832-4932

Olde Town Tustin Antique Mall
650 El Camino Real
714/838-1144

Van Dorens Consignments
17321 17th St.
714/505-3141

Schafer's Antiques
171 N. Tustin Ave.
714/541-5555

193 UPLAND

Calico Reflections
130 E. 9th St.
909/981-2135

Collectors Cottage
243 E. 9th St.
909/920-1136

Antique Alley
257 E. 9th St.
909/985-5563

Myra's Antiques
139 N. 2nd
909/981-7002

Carriage House Antiques
152 N. 2nd Ave.
909/982-2543

Kiosk Corner
188 N. 2nd Ave.
909/981-2876

Alphenaar's Antiques
251 N. 2nd Ave.
909/949-7978

Sideboard
170 N. 2nd Ave.
909/981-7652

Classic Collectibles
136 E. 9th St.
909/985-9543

The Art Room Antiques
291 N. 2nd Avenue
909/946-8160

Upland Ole ' Town
270 N. 2nd Ave.
909/981-2408

194 UPPER LAKE

Vintage Store
375 N. Highway 2
707/275-0303

First & Main
9495 Main St.
707/275-3124

195 VACAVILLE

Bygone Shoppe Antiques
143 McClellan St.
707/449-3575

Past & Presents
333 Merchant St.
707/449-0384

Vasquez Antiques & Collectibles
357 Merchant St.
707/447-9434

196 VALLEJO

Yesteryear's Marketplace
433 Georgia St.
707/557-4671
Mon.-Sat., 10-5
Sunday afternoon by chance - Knock if light is on.

Directions: From I-80 take Georgia St.. exit, go west; 30 yards past Sonoma Blvd.

This 9,500 square foot antique marketplace is located in Redman's Hall. In the 1930's it housed the National Dollar Store. For the past seven years it has been the home of a wonderful shop filled to the brim with fine antiques. You'll be delighted to find crystal, china, Roseville, Weller and other potteries, as well as furnishings from early American to elegant formal. Lamps, prints, porcelains and other accessories are also offered for the discriminating shopper.

Interesting Side Trips

St. Peter's Chapel at Mare Island
328 Seawind Dr.
707-557-1538

Famous for its 29 stained glass windows, most designed by the Tiffany Studios of New York.

197 VENICE

Revival
1356 Abbot Kinney Blvd.
310/396-1360

Neptina
1329 1/2 Abbot Kinney
310/396-1630

Bountiful
1335 Abbot Kinney Blvd.
310/450-3620

198 VENTURA

Antique Alley
263 S. Laurel St.
805/643-0708

Antique Accents
315 E. Main St.
805/643-4511

Heirlooms Antique Mall
327 E. Main St.
805/648-4833

Attic Treasures
337 E. Main St.
805/641-1039

Antiques Etc. Mall
369 E. Main St.
805/643-6983

Main Street Antique Mall
384 E. Main St.
805/648-3268

Nicholby Antique Mall
404 E. Main St.
805/653-1195

My Last Hurrah/Attic Trunk
451 E. Main St. #9
805/643-6510

Times Remembered
467 E. Main St.
805/643-3137

Sevoy Antiques
494 E. Main St.
805/641-1890

Red House Antiques
1234 E. Main St.
805/643-6787

Sherlock's Antique Lighting
8672 N. Ventura Avenue
805/649-4683

Garden Angel Collective
1414 E. Main
805/643-1980

Park Place Collectibles
1416 E. Main
805/652-1761

Bid Time Return
1920 E. Main St.
805/641-2003

Oak Street Antiques
27 South Oak St.
805/652-0053

Curio Cottage
64 S. Oak St.
805/648-5508

Sevoy Antiques
1501 Palma Dr.
805/642-8031

America Antiques
2459 Palma Dr.
805/650-6265

199 VISALIA

Spit 'n' Polish Antiques
15361 Ave.nue 280
209/247-3558
Open by appointment only ("That just means phone first, we're open when we're home!")

Directions: From Highway 99, go east on Ave.nue 280 (Exeter Farmersville turn off) exactly 9 miles (watch your odometer!). On the south side of the road is a big yellow sign that says "Spit 'n' Polish" Antiques. Phone to catch us at home.

At Spit 'n' Polish, Brian and Susan specialize in antique bathroom fixtures, including a big selection of toilets, sinks, tubs, accessories, towel bars, medicine cabinets and lighting fixtures. They also tell a funny story involving some of their inventory:

"At a crowded antique show in Fresno, California, an adorable little girl in a pink dress must not have wanted to bother her folks who were looking at some furniture across the aisle. Before we knew it, she had her panties around her ankles and was using our circa 1900 pull chain toilet that was on display. Totally unabashed (we, of course, let her finish), she probably wondered at the absence of toilet paper. When she was finished, off she went - her parents had mysteriously disappeared - and an amused customer marched right up and plunked down the purchase price - as long as we agreed to wash out the toilet bowl before loading it in her car!"

Planning Mill Mall
515 E. Center Ave.
209/625-8887

Stuff N Such
1214 E. Houston
209/734-4114

Cottage
15472 E. Mineral King
209/734-8996

Carriage House Antiques
15484 E. Mineral King
209/635-8818

White's House Antiques
4628 W. Mineral King
209/734-2128

Showcase Mall
26644 S. Mooney Blvd.
209/685-1125

200 WALNUT CREEK

Sundance Antiques
2323 Boulevard Circle
510/930-6200

Our Showroom Antiques
2363 Boulevard Circle
510/947-6844

Quail Country Antiques
1581 Boulevard Way
510/944-0930

Walnut Creek Antiques
2050 N. Broadway
510/947-4900

201 WHITTIER

Virginia's Antiques
6536 Greenleaf Ave.
310/696-2810

Treasure Chest Antiques
6718 Greenleaf Ave.
310/696-6608

Uptown Antiques
6725 Greenleaf Ave.
310/698-1316

Yesterdays Memories
12310 Penn St.
310/696-6124

Yellow Pipe Antiques
13309 Philadelphia
310/945-2362

Pepe's Antiques
13310 Philadelphia St.
310/945-1676

Elegant Elephant
6751 Washington Ave.
310/698-7037

King Richard's Antique Mall
12301 Whittier Blvd.
310/698-5974

All The Kings Toys
12323 Whittier Blvd.
310/696-3166

202 WOODLAND

Bee's Antiques & Collectibles
1021 Lincoln Ave.
916/662-3246

Old Depot Antiques
1021 Lincoln Ave.
916/662-1215

Tinkers Antiques & Cllbls.
338 Main St.
916/662-3204

House Dresser
518 Main St.
916/661-9596

Antiques on Main
528 Main St.
916/668-1815

203 WOODLAND HILLS

Affordable Antiques
4870 Topanga Canyon Blvd.
818/888-2568

Joseph Wahl Arts
5305 Topanga Canyon
818/340-9245

Antique Frames & Furniture
22845 Ventura Blvd.
818/224-4845

204 YORBA LINDA

C. P. McGinnis & Co.
4887 Main St.
714/777-8990

Susan Tanner Antiques
4884 Main St.
714/693-1913

Dixie Lee's Antiques
4900 Main St.
714/779-3905

Gifts N Treasures
4897 Main St.
714/777-8371

Notes

·C·O·L·O·R·A·D·O·
ANTIQUE GALLERY
5501 S. Broadway • Littleton
23

Off Her Rocker
Antiques

In the Heart
of the Rockies
Nederland
29

Eagle's Nest
Bed & Breakfast
206 N. Colorado
(970)641-4457
Gunnison
2

Return to Yesteryear
in
COLORADO SPRINGS
20 Shops to Explore
9

ANIMAS
MUSEUM
Visit Durango's
History Museum

31st St. & West 2nd Ave.
Durango
12

Ride the Original
Narrow Gauge
SILVERTON TRAIN
Durango
12

STRATER HOTEL
SINCE 1887
DURANGO, COLORADO
12

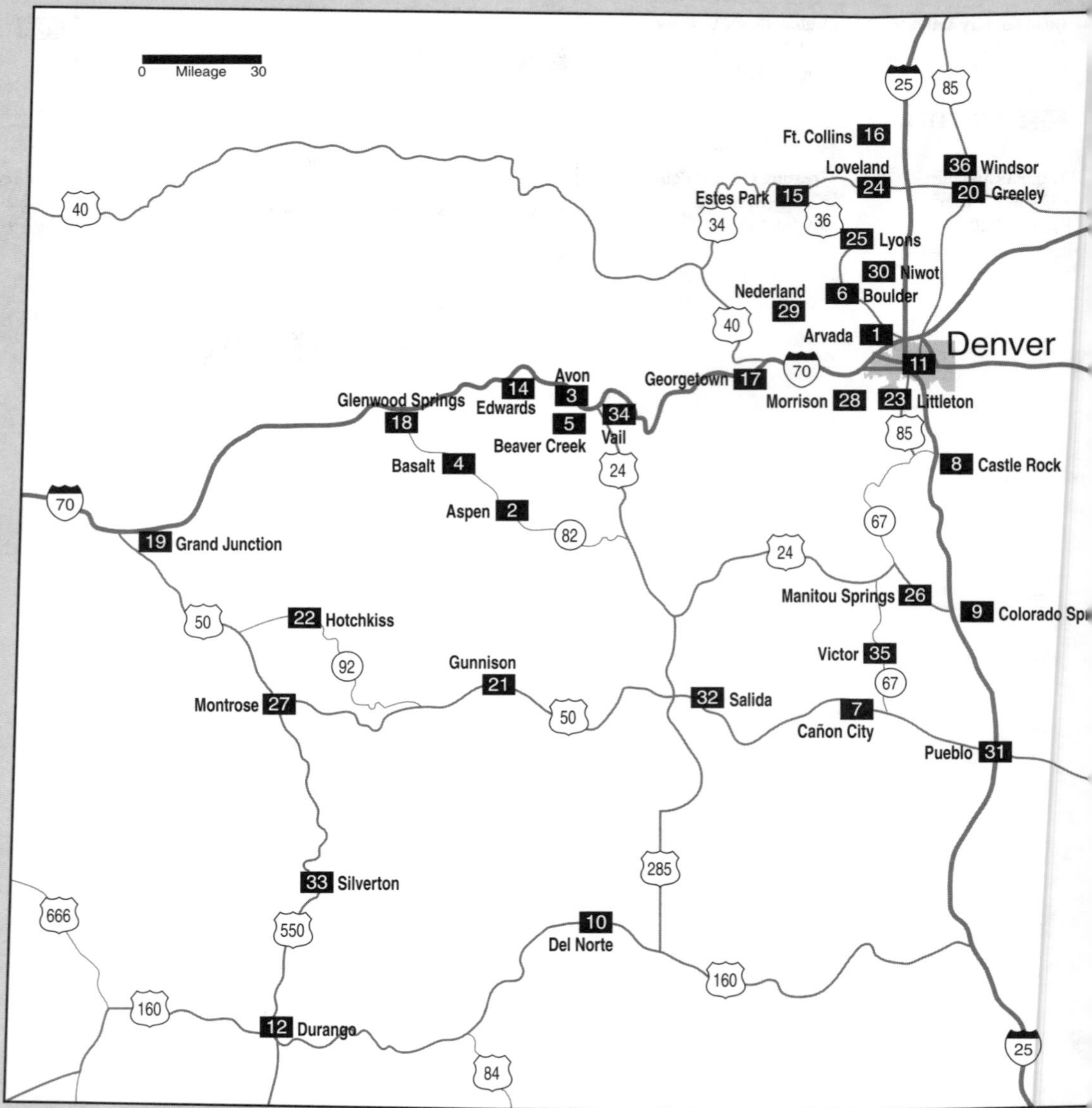

LA GARITA CREEK RANCH
Del Norte
10

WELCOME TO THE
NORTHPOLE
SANTA'S WORKSHIP
AT THE FOOT OF PIKE'S PEAK
9

Blue Lake Ranch
A Country Inn

Also featuring Cabins, Cottages & Suites
Durango
1

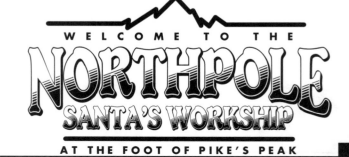

Assay Antiques

Victor 35

Van Dyke's Antiques

Largest selection of Flow Blue west of the Mississippi

Englewood 13

Architectural Salvage

1215 Deleware St.
Antiques Only
No Reproductions
(303) 615-5432

Denver 11

HOTCHKISS ANTIQUE DEALERS

Invite you to spend the day antiquing

Welcome

22

Colorado

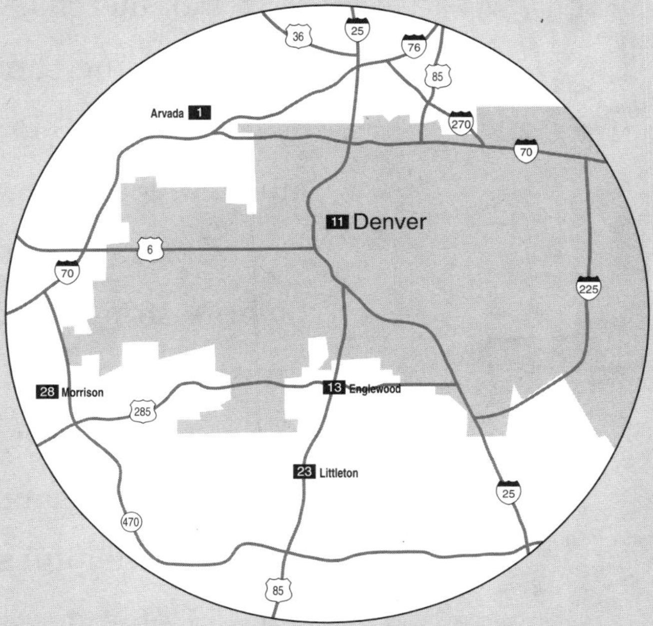

Experience the peace & quiet of a different time.

1868 Homestead
1890s Working Farm

Listed on National Register of Historic Places

Colorado Springs 9

VAN BRIGGLE ART POTTERY

During your visit to the Pikes Peak Region, we hope you'll include a free tour of our studios in your travel plans.

600 South 21st Street
Colorado Springs

9

8th & Pearl Antiques

Boulder 6

Do-it-ur-self

ANTIQUE PLUMBING SUPPLY

3100 Brighton Boulevard Denver

1-800-286-0455

11

GIUSEPPE'S®

OLD DEPOT RESTAURANT

Enjoy it all in the 107-year-old historically restored former Denver and Rio Grande Railroad Station.

Colorado Springs 9

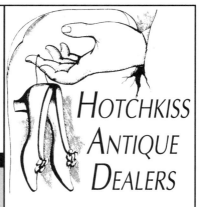

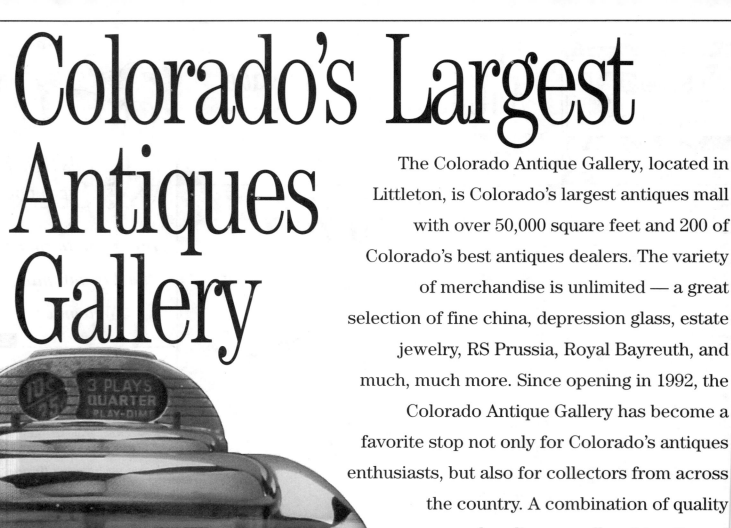

Colorado

1 ARVADA

D & J Antiques
5678 Olde Wadsworth Blvd.
303/422-4650

Arvada Antique Emporium
7519 Grandview Ave.
303/422-6433

Cabin Antiques
7505 Grandview Ave.
303/467-7807

Elegant Glass Antiques
7501 Grandview Ave.
303/424-9330

Foxhaven Farms Antiques
7513 Grandview Ave.
303/420-2747

House of Rees
7509 Grandview Ave.
303/424-0663

Olde Wadsworth Antiques
7511 Grandview Ave.
303/424-8686

2 ASPEN

Alderfer's Antiques of Aspen
309 E. Main St.
970/925-5051

Country Flowers
433 E. Cooper St.
970/925-6522

MC Hugh Antiques
431 E. Hyman Ave.
970/925-5751

Katie Ingham Antique Quilts
257 Glen Eagles Dr.
970/925-2595

Fetzer's
308 S. Hunter
970/925-5447

3 AVON

Shaggy Ram
1160 W. Beaver Creek Blvd.
970/949-4377

4 BASALT

Churchill's Limited
148 E. Homestead St.
970/927-3485

Double D Lazy T Trading Co.
22826 Hwy. 82
970/927-9679

Old Paint & Memories
50 Sunset Dr.
970/927-8096

5 BEAVER CREEK

Note: Below is a wonderful story submitted by the Vail Valley Tourism & Convention Bureau.

A bear in Beaver Creek was yearning for a spa vacation. Earlier, he'd secretly watched vacationers soaking, enjoying wine and sharing stories of mountain hikes and river rafting adventures, Swedish massages and mud treatments. Long after they departed, he climbed atop the floating cover of a bubbling hot tub and swatted at the delicious-looking hummingbird feeders above.

Locals in the valley like to enjoy the good life, too, you know.

Grammy's Attic
41131 U.S. Hwy. 6 & 24
970/949-6099

Sagebrush Antiques
210 Offerson
970/949-0519

Sagebrush Antiques
34925 Hwy. 6 Unit C3
970/949-0519

Shaggy Ram
1060 W. Beaver Creek Blvd
970/926-4663

6 BOULDER

8th & Pearl Antiques
740 Pearl
303/444-0699
Tue.-Sat. 11-5:30, Sun. 12-5

Directions: From Denver take I-25 North to the Boulder exit—U.S. 36. Continue to Boulder and stay on 36 to Canyon Blvd., across from the shopping center turn left to 9th St., then right to Pearl; go 2 blocks left to 8th & Pearl.

8th and Pearl Antiques is a seven dealer co-op. It's a general line shop, but each dealer has something special to offer the discriminating shopper. Consequently, they feature a broad spectrum of furniture from the late 18th century through the 1950s. You'll find accessories to compliment any decor, such as fine china, glassware, pottery, textiles, lighting, folk art, prints, and oils. They offer a nice selection of sterling silver and feature estate and Indian jewelry. In addition, you'll find holiday collectibles, ephemera, antique toys and primitives.

Note: Great lunching spots and coffee cafes are within a two-block walk from the shop, as well as the famous Boulder Downtown Mall.

8th & Pearl Antiques
740 Pearl St.
303/444-0699

Classic Facets
2010 10th St.
303/938-8851

Indochine
2525 Arapahoe Ave. E31
303/444-7734

Sage Gallery Antiques
5360 Arapahoe Ave.
303/449-6799

7 CAÑON CITY

Carriage House Antiques
840 S. 1st St.
719/269-9428

Greenhorn Enterprises
1434 Pine St.
719/275-1444

Lone Tree Antiques
429 S. 9th St.
719/275-0712

Sherrilyn Antiques
202 Main St.
719/275-5849

8 CASTLE ROCK

Auntie Lisa's Antiques
1647 Park St.
303/688-7552

Claudia's Cupboard
522 Wilcox St.
303/688-9725

Country Palace Antiques
400 3rd St.
303/688-6775

9 COLORADO SPRINGS

It was in 1870 that Civil War hero and retired army general, William Jackson Palmer, caught his first glimpse of what is now Colorado Springs. After the war, the rapidly growing railroad industry had captured his interest, and he had come to the Pikes Peak region to investigate the possibilities of expansion.

In 1871, enchanted by the beauty of the region, Palmer began laying out the city of his dreams. He fancied to build a tourist resort on the region's reputation as a healthful climate. He dubbed the town Colorado Springs, although the closest mineral springs were six miles away in Manitou Springs, several hours by buggy.

In the 1800s only the very wealthy could afford to tour, so Palmer saw to it that the finest hotels and private mansions were built. Attracting Europeans in droves, Colorado Springs earned the nickname "Little London."

In 1893, an eastern school teacher making her first visit to the young city was captivated, as General Palmer had been, by the area's grandeur. After a trip to the top of Pikes Peak, teacher and poet, Katharine Lee Bates, wrote what would become her most famous work. Later set to music, "America the Beautiful" has become perhaps the nation's most beloved patriotic anthem.

In the years that followed the founding of Colorado Springs, thousands of others have been inspired by the beauty of the region. From that inspiration the citizens of the Pikes Peak region have grown to appreciate their rich cultural heritage. Today the city boasts many fine historical homes, museums, a living history farm and some of the most spectacular views in the world.

Antique Gallery
21 N. Nevada Ave.
719/633-6070

Antique Merchants
14 S. Tejon St.
719/442-6928

McIntosh Weller Antiques
1013 S. Tejon St.
719/520-5316

Kaya Gaya
1015 S. Tejon St.
719/578-5858

Jug & Basin Antiques
1420 W. Colorado Ave.
719/633-9346

Chuck's Furniture
1502 W. Colorado Ave.
719/634-5631

Villagers Antiques & Cllbls.
2426 W. Colorado Ave.
719/632-1400

Avenue Antiques & Collectibles
2502 W. Colorado Ave.
719/520-9894

Martin's Gallery of the West
2513 W. Colorado Ave.
719/633-4884

Dean & Co. Antiques
2607 W. Colorado Ave.
719/635-3122

Antique Legacy
2624 W. Colorado Ave.
719/578-0637

Adobe Walls
2808 W. Colorado Ave.
719/635-3394

My Mothers Attic Antiques
207 W Rockrimmon Blvd. #F
719/528-2594

Country Pines Antiques
6005 Templeton Gap Rd.
719/596-4004

NuNN Art & Antiques
717 N. Union Blvd.
719/473-4746

Nevada Avenue Antiques
405 S. Nevada Ave.
719/473-3351

Antiques Unique on 8th Street
1515 S. 8th St.
719/475-8633

Legend Antiques
2165 Broadway St.
719/448-9414

Iron Pump Antiques
1024 S Royer St.
719/636-3940

Colorado Country Antique Mall
2109 Broadway St.
719/520-5680

Interesting Side Trips

Van Briggle Art Pottery
600 South 21st St.
719/633-7729
Tours: Mon.-Sat. Call for times

Directions: Five minutes west of downtown Colorado Springs at 21st Street and Highway 24.

Van Briggle Art Pottery has been mixing clay, water and fire with the potter's magic since 1899. It is one of the oldest active art potteries remaining in the United States. The company was founded by acclaimed potter and sculptor Artus Van Briggle, together with his wife, Anne, who was also an accomplished artist. The Van Briggles designed their creations by incorporating flowing floral motifs, carefully patterned to enhance the graceful shapes of the pottery, and then finishing the pieces with the soft "matte" glazes which have come to represent the Van Briggle style. These beautiful glazes grace a variety of designs, from Art Nouveau to current Southwestern styles. You will also find figurines, distinctive lamp shades, bowls, vases and lamps made at the studio.

Rock Ledge Ranch
1805 30th St.
719/578-6777
Call for hours June-August

Located near the Gateway Rocks to the Gardens of the Gods, the Rock Ledge Ranch, formerly the White House Ranch, provides a living history of an early Colorado Springs ranch, with exhibits and demonstrations of old-time ranching.

Ghost Town Museum
Hwy. 24
719/634-0696
Open year round

Ghost Town Museum is an authentically reconstructed Old West town built from the very buildings abandoned after the Pikes Peak Region's gold mining era. Explore the boardwalk that connects the saloon, jail, blacksmith and merchants of "Main Street" to the livery (which houses stagecoaches, buggies, carriages of the day, and turn-of-the-century automobiles) and the Victorian Home. Each exhibit displays a fascinating array of valuable collectibles such as those actually used by our ancestors—your great-grandparents!

North Pole
Santa's Workshop
North Pole, CO.
719/684-9432
Open mid-May through December

Directions: Drive 10 miles west of Colorado Springs on Highway 24 to Cascade (Exit 141 from I-25) and follow the signs.

Imagine a place where every day is Christmas. Where your children can meet and talk to Santa Claus himself. Where your family can ride a mountaintop ferris wheel, a swinging space shuttle, an antique carousel, an aerial tram through the treetops, a miniature train and more. Where you can enjoy tasty foods and snacks, and picnic in an evergreen forest. Where your kids can feed live deer, create their own colorful candle, watch a magician perform and play in a game-packed arcade. Where you can mail cards postmarked "The North Pole".

You don't have to imagine such a place because it really exists...at the North Pole, home of Santa's Workshop...at the foot of Pikes Peak. Call for exact days and times.

Favorite Places To Eat

Cracker Barrel Old Country Store
I-25 & Hwy. 83 at Academy Blvd., Exit 150A
719/260-7721

Giuseppe's Old Depot Restaurant
10 South Sierra Madre
719/635-3111

Directions: Downtown, 1 block west of Antlers/ Doubletree.

On October 26, 1871, the first passenger train from Denver stopped at the site of the soon-to-be Denver & Rio Grande Western Railroad Station in the infant city of Colorado Springs. The history of Colorado can hardly be considered without the history of the railroad. Rich in timber and minerals, the new territory attracted adventurous souls filled with optimism as well as foresight.

Perhaps nothing reflects the courage and glamour of those times more than this Denver Rio Grande Western Railroad Station. Constructed of "glass stone" found near Castle Rock, Colorado, the Depot still shakes to the freight and coal trains of today. The last passenger train pulled out of the Depot in 1966, but the memories have been preserved in the many photographs and memorabilia gracing the walls of the station. The original oak doors still open wide to welcome today's guests. The floor of the main Dining Room still bears the original tiles that have been polished smooth by millions of feet since 1887. Colorado Spruce was used for the twenty- foot ceiling in the former passenger waiting room. The cherubim overlooking the north and south ends of this room have been preserved from a less fortunate structure, The Burns Theater.

The Depot has provided a whistle stop for former presidents, Theodore and Franklin Roosevelt, as well as Harry Truman during campaigns for the presidency.

Today the customers inside this 107-year-old historically restored station aren't passengers. They are diners feasting upon such specialties as stonebaked pizza and lasagna, savory ribs and steak, prime rib, spaghetti, or one of the many other scrumptious choices offered by Giuseppe's Old Depot Restaurant.

10 DEL NORTE

La Garita Creek Ranch
38145 Cty. Rd. 39-E
719/754-2533

Directions: 17 miles south of Sayuache or 18 miles north of Monte Vista on Hwy. 285—turn west at La Garita sign (Road G). Continue approximately 6 miles past La Garita Store to fork in road. Take left fork. Continue approximately 4 miles to the next fork. You will see La Garita Creek Ranch sign. Take right fork for 1 mile. Turn right at sign onto the property.

If you're feeling energetic after all that antique shopping, you've come to the right place. La Garita Creek Ranch offers plenty of activities for further explorations. You might try horseback riding along the scenic trails or fishing in a nearby creek. The true adventurists can test their skills in Penitente Canyon, the world renowned rock climbing area. Then end your perfect day in a quiet mountain cabin, complete with fireplace and hot tub. The ranch offers a full bar and restaurant.

11 DENVER

Architectural Salvage, Inc.
1215 Delaware St.
303/615-5432
Open Mon.-Sat. 10-5, Sun. 12-5

Directions: Traveling I-25, take exit 210 A (Colfax exit), east 1 mile, south on Delaware 2-1/2 blocks. (Delaware runs south only from Colfax between Rocky Mountain News Building and The Denver Mint.)

No reproductions here. For 10 years, Architectural Salvage has provided customers with outstanding antique doors, lighting, windows, leaded glass, clawfoot tubs, shutters, gates, columns and more. Everything is neatly arranged indoors for your convenience.

Do-It-Ur-Self Antique Plumbing & Heating Supply
3120 Brighton Blvd.
303/297-0455
Open Mon.-Fri. 8-5:30, Sat. 8-5, closed Sun.

Directions: Located 1.5 miles south of I-70 on Brighton Blvd. Brighton Blvd. Is exit 275B (exit for Stock Shows Complex and Denver Coliseum). The business is in lower downtown Denver.

Outfitting a new bathroom in grand old style? Restoring a once proud but now dated bathroom? The eye-catching charm of this company's stock exists within the Antique Plumbing Showroom where you'll find restored vintage clawfoot tubs, 4 foot servants' tubs, dainty slipper tubs for ladies' and ample 6 foot tubs, all displayed for purchasing. Some tubs originally appeared with paint detailing or wood accents which have survived on most pieces. Ornate pedestal and fluted sinks, original toilets, some two-piece models with oak tanks and porcelain pull chains stand in the showroom. These Victorian period fixtures date back to the early 1900s. Also in stock are many varieties of Victorian bathroom accessories, or Victorian fixture and faucet reproductions. As an added bonus, the repair/parts department can help with the "impossible to find" parts.

The Gallagher Collection
1298 South Broadway
303/756-5821
Mon.-Sat. 10-5:30, Sun. 12-5

Directions: Take I-25, exit 207, 4 blocks south to the corner of Louisiana and South Broadway.

Located in the old potato chip factory amidst Denver's Antique Row, The Gallagher Collection offers an outstanding array of unusual books in all fields. You'll find significant selections in Western, Americana, Children's, Illustrated, Decorative Binding, History, Biography, Natural History, Hunting and Fishing, and Cookbooks, plus additional fine books in other fields. They even offer antiques for the library. Many other curiosities can be found there as well.

Maggie May's Sandbox
212 S. Broadway
303/744-8656

Gateway Antiques & Art
357 Broadway
303/744-8479

Amsterdam Antiques
1428 S. Broadway
303/722-9715

Antique Market
1212 S. Broadway
303/744-0281

Antique Mercantile
1229 S. Broadway
303/777-8842

Antique Center on Broadway
1235 S. Broadway
303/744-1857

Antique Alcove
1236 S. Broadway
303/722-4649

Talisman Antiques
1248 S. Broadway
303/777-8959

Denver Antique Guild
1298 S. Broadway
303/722-3359

Lee's Antique Emporium
1321 S. Broadway
303/722-1741

Rosalie McDowell Antiques
1400 S. Broadway
303/777-0601

Warner's Antiques
1401 S. Broadway
303/722-9173

Hooked on Glass
1407 S. Broadway
303/778-7845

Uniquittes
1415 S. Broadway
303/777-6318

Al's Collectables & Antiques
1438 S. Broadway
303/733-6502

Calamity Jane Antiques
1445 S. Broadway
303/778-7104

A International Antiques
1448 S. Broadway
303-722-0671

Antiques by Corky
1449 S. Broadway
303/777-8908

Somewhere In Time
1417 S. Broadway
303/777-3659

Vintage Classics/Upland Intrs.
1460 S. Broadway
303/777-1728

Aspen Antiques
1464 S. Broadway
303/733-6463

Antique Exchange Co-op
1500 S. Broadway
303/777-7871

Glass Roots Antiques
27 E. Dakota
303/778-8693

Antiques of Denver
1534 S. Broadway
303/733-9008

Wazee Deco
1730 Wazee St.
303/293-2144

Sleepers Antiques
1564 S. Broadway
303/733-8017

Foxy's Antiques
1592 S. Broadway
303/777-7761

Packrat Antiques
1594 S. Broadway
303/778-1211

Times Shared
1160 E. Colfax Ave.
303/863-0569

Reckollections Indoor
5736 E. Colfax Ave.
303/329-8848

Decorables & Antiques Best
5940 E. Colfax Ave.
303/399-8643

Treasured Scarab
25 E. Dakota Ave.
303/777-6884

Country Club Antiques
408 Downing St.
303/733-1915

East West Designs
600 Ogden St.
303/861-4741

Artifact Room
2318 S. Colorado
303/757-2797

Antique Zoo
1395 S. Acoma St.
303/778-9191

Buckboard
3265 S. Wadsworth Blvd.
303/986-0221

Hampden Street Antiques
8964 E. Hampden Ave.
303/721-7992

Wayside Antiques
3795 S. Knox Ct.
303/781-1422

Collectible Chair Co.
2817 E. 3rd Ave.
303/320-6585

Borgman's Antiques & Things
1700 E. 6th Ave.
303/399-4588

Starr Antiques
2940 E. 6th Ave.
303/399-4537

Stuart-Buchanan Antiques
1530 15th St.
303/825-1222

Grandpa's Depot & Caboose
1616 17th St. #267
303/892-1177

Hill Antiques
3631 W. 32nd Ave.
303/477-9042

Precious Memories
4020 Tennyson St.
303/455-3383

Mountain Man Antiques
3977 Tennyson St.
303/458-8447

Feathered Nest
935 E. Cedar Ave.
303/744-6881

Country Line Antiques
1067 S. Gaylord St.
303/733-1143

Way We Were Antiques
1211 E. Alameda Ave.
303/777-1776

Victoriana Antique Jewelry
1512 Larimer St. #39R
303/573-5049

APIRY
585 Milwaukee St.
303/399-6017

Red's Antique Galleries
5797 E. Evans Ave.
303/753-9187

Denver Doll Emporium
1570 S. Pearl St.
303/733-6339

Interesting Side Trips

Byers-Evans House
Corner of 13th Ave. & Bannock St.
303/620-4933

The Byers-Evans House was built in 1883 by Rocky Mountain News publisher, William Byers. It was sold in 1889 to the family of William Gray Evans, an officer of the Denver Tramway Company. Guided tours take visitors through this elegant residence, richly filled with original family furnishings.

12 DURANGO

Blue Lake Ranch
16000 Highway 140
(Hesperus)
970/385-4537
E Mail Address: bluelake @frontier.net
Web Site: http://www.frontier/nbluelake
Rates: $65-245
Reservations taken Mon.-Sun. 8 a.m.-8 p.m.

Directions: Blue Lake Ranch is 15 minutes west of Durango. To protect the guests' privacy, there is no highway signage for Blue Lake Ranch. Use your odometer to find the gravel driveway. From the north, east or west: Take Highway 140 south at Hesperus. Go 6.5 miles to find the driveway to the right. From the south: Take Highway 170 in New Mexico north, which turns into Colorado Highway 140 at the state line. Continue north and note the junction of Highway 141 and Highway 140. Blue Lake Ranch is 1.3 miles north of this junction on the left.

Blue Lake Ranch has evolved from a simple 1910 homestead into a luxurious European-style Country Estate. From the elegantly appointed Main Inn to the secluded garden cottages, there are unsurpassed views of Blue Lake, and the gardens of the 13,000-foot La Plata Mountains. A year-round destination acclaimed for its spring and summer gardens, the ranch offers spectacular fall color and becomes a winter wonderland with the first snowfall. There is absolute privacy and quiet without another house in sight. Guests enjoy fishing for trophy trout in the lake, strolling in the gardens, where over 10,000 iris bloom annually, and exploring the ranch's private wildlife preserve.

The Main Inn is the original restored homestead house and serves as Ranch headquarters. In the summer a European-style breakfast buffet is served in the dining room and on the garden patios. The buffet offers a delicious selection of cheeses, meats, cereals, fruits, seasonal berries, pastries, juices, Southwestern dishes and fresh roasted coffee or tea. Afternoon tea is served at 5 p.m. on the garden patios.

The four guest rooms in the Inn are all comfortably separated from one another. The Garden Room entered through the library hall has a window seat, fireplace and private deck in a garden overlooking the lake. The Oriental-style bath has a shower room with a deep-soaking tub. Situated at the top of a circular staircase, The Rose Room provides 360-degree views of the lake, gardens and mountains through dormer windows, has a queen bed and sitting area. The Victorian Room is furnished with an 1850s handcarved four poster canopied double bed and has a Dutch door to the garden. The private unattached bath has a six-foot-long claw footed tub.

In addition to the four rooms in the Inn, Blue Lake Ranch has a 3 bedroom, 3 bath log cabin on the lake, a cottage in the woods, two suites in a renovated barn and a turn of the century homestead house on the banks of the La Plata River.

Note: Dr. Shirley Isgar, Innkeeper at Blue Lake Ranch, delights in recounting this amusing tale. At the Country Inn, an illusive trout lured a first-time fisherman physician in waders a bit too far out into the lake. While concentrating on landing an incredible rainbow trout, he didn't realize he had sunken into the soft mud up to his thighs. Meanwhile, a guest (a malpractice lawyer) was watching from the cabin directly on the lake. Finally the physician, not being able to move, cried for help and the lawyer pulled him into shore...minus his boots. Who gets the bill?

Strater Hotel
699 Main Avenue
1-800-247-4431 or 970/247-4431
Open year round

Built in 1887 and furnished throughout with authentic Victorian antiques, the Strater Hotel has been catering to travelers for 108 years. Selected by *Diversion Magazine* as "Colorado's finest Victorian Hotel," the Strater offers 93 beautiful guest rooms, a restaurant, and a saloon all set in the melodramatic aura of the 1800s gold rush days.

Southwest Book Trader
175 E. 5th St.
970/247-8479

Time Traveler
131 E. 8th St.
970/259-3130

Wildflowers Antiques
742 Main Ave.
970/247-4249

Interesting Side Trips

Durango & Silverton Narrow Gauge Railroad
479 Main Ave./Durango & Silverton Train Depot
970/247-2733
Call for schedule & tickets

When you ride the DURANGO & SILVERTON NARROW GAUGE RAILROAD, you'll experience a legacy of mountain railroading history that has remained virtually unchanged for over a century.

This historic steam-powered train once carried food, provisions and silver. Today the Silverton takes visitors on a spectacular scenic trip through the San Juan Mountains. Witness relics of the 1800s that line the railroad's tracks, or even catch a glimpse of bears, elk, bald eagles, and many other species of Rocky Mountain wildlife. It's one train ride you won't soon forget.

Animas Museum
31st St & West 2nd Ave.
970/259-2402
Mon.-Sat. 10-6 May through Oct.

Located in the residential neighborhood in the old Animas City section of town, Durango's only history museum is somewhat out of the public eye. But what surprises are in store for those who venture off the beaten path of north Main to visit the museum! Cloistered within the sandstone walls of the 90-year-old museum building are untold treasures of the San Juan Basin's rich and colorful heritage. Does an 1880s hand-crafted saddle made in Animas City intrigue you? Perhaps a porcelain Victorian doll, a D&RG railroad lantern, a pair of Buckskin Charlie's beaded moccasins or a Zuni polychrome olla is more to your liking. These objects and many more can be seen in the museum's exhibits.

13 ENGLEWOOD

Van Dyke's Antiques
3663 S. Broadway
303/789-3743
Mon.-Sat. 10-5, Sun. 1-4
303/973-0110 for after hour appointments

Directions: Denver Metro Area—Take I-25 to Hwy. 85 (Hampdon Ave) west to Broadway, exit south on Broadway, 1/2 block on west side of street.

If you are a flow blue collector, Van Dyke's is a "must shop." Here you will find the largest selection of flow blue west of the Mississippi. In addition, this shop is filled with quality antiques: Victorian glass, American and European furniture, silver, depression glass, dolls, paintings, prints, period pieces, lighting and more.

14 EDWARDS

Sagebrush Antiques
34925 Hwy. 6 Unit C3
970/949-0519

15 ESTES PARK

Bountiful
125 Moraine Ave. #B
970/586-9332

Cottage & Gardens
7461 County Rd. 43
970/586-0580

Little Victorian Attic
157 W. Elkhorn Ave.
970/586-8964

16 FORT COLLINS

Nostalgia Antiques
2216 Northridge Ct.
970/221-5139

Bell Tower Antiques
2520 N. Shields St.
970/482-2510

Happenstance
136 W. Mountain Ave.
970/493-1668

Collins Antique Mart
6124 S. College Ave.
970/226-3305

Front Range Antique Mall
6108 S. College Ave.
970/282-1808

17 GEORGETOWN

Antique Emporium
501 Rose St.
303/569-2727

Cobweb Shoppe of Georgetown
512 6th St.
303/569-3112

Nora Blooms' Antiques
614 6th St. #B
303/569-0210

Powder Cache Antiques
612 6th St.
303/569-2848

Stuff & Such
601 14th St.
303/569-2507

18 GLENWOOD SPRINGS

Anita's Antiques & Elegant
1030 Grand Ave.
970/928-9622

Forever Elegant
815 Grand Ave.
970-928-0510

Glenwood Books & Collectibles
720 Grand Ave.
970-928-8825

19 GRAND JUNCTION

Guy Kelly Washburn Antiques
600 White Ave.
970/241-6880

Antiques of the Old West
140 W. Main St.
970/242-1563

American Heritage Antiques
117 N. 6th St.
970/245-8046

Great American Antiques Store
439 Main St.
970/242-2443

Finders Trove
558 Main St.
970/245-0109

20 GREELEY

Antiques At Lincoln Park
822 8th St.
970/351-6222

Blossom Tyme Gifts & Antiques
1201 11th Ave.
970/352-4379

Create Antiques
2200 Reservoir Rd.
970/353-1712

Foster's Antiques & Clock Shop
1329 9th Ave.
970/352-9204

Gingerbread Antiques
725 10th Ave.
970/356-0818

Grandma's Attic
1113 8th Ave.
970/350-0932

21 GUNNISON

Eagle's Nest Bed and Breakfast
206 N. Colorado
970/641-4457
Open every day

Directions: Take Hwy. 50 to the Holiday Inn in Gunnison. Located directly behind the Holiday Inn on the corner of Colorado and Virginia.

Hugh and Jane McGee are retired school teachers from a northern Chicago suburb. They now enjoy their new vocation as proprietors of the Eagles Nest B&B in Gunnison.

The upstairs of the McGee home has a large suite, private bath and breakfast nook or reading room for relaxing. The front porch beautifully displays Hugh's own works of art—stained glass. Hugh's superb culinary masterpieces - Western Eggs Benidict, Vegetable Omelets and French Toast "keeps folks raving!" Jane also finds time to be a Mary Kay cosmetics consultant. It is advisable to call well ahead for reservations.

Colorado

22 HOTCHKISS

Beulah B's
1091 A Hwy. #133
970/872-3051

Cowboy Collectibles
448 Bridge St.
970/872-3025

The Ark II
101 W. Bridge St.
970/872-2226

Country Home Store
264 W. Bridge St.
970/872-4647

Cowboy Collectibles
448 Ridge St.
970/872-3025

23 LITTLETON

Colorado Antique Gallery
5501 S. Broadway
303/794-8100
Open Mon.-Sat. 10-6, Thurs. 10-8, Sun. 12-6

For more specific information see full page this section.

Creamery
2675 W. Alamo Ave.
303/730-2747

Olde Littleton Antique Co-op
2681 W. Alamo Ave.
303/795-9965

Olde Towne Antqs. & Vintage
2500 W. Main St.
303/347-9258

Remember When Antiques
2569 W. Main St.
303/798-2989

Colorado Antique Gallery
5501 S. Broadway
303/794-8100

24 LOVELAND

Lynn Allee Down Antiques
1220 Langston Ln.
970/667-9889

Bonser Antique Mall
315 E. 4th St.
970/669-8005

Canyon Collectibles
5641 W. U.S. Hwy. 34
970/593-9227

Country Shed Antiques
136 E. 4th St.
970/667-9448

Country Wishes & Wants
120 E. 4th St.
970/635-9132

Diamonds & Toads
137 E. 4th St.
970/667-9414

Grandma's Attic
214 E. 4th St.
970/667-1807

Kottage
333 Cleveland Ave.
970/667-1110

Nostalgia Corner
140 E. 4th St.
970/663-5591

Rocky Mtn. Antiques Inc.
3816 W. Eisenhower Blvd.
970/663-7551

Favorite Places To Eat

Cracker Barrel Old Country Store
I-25 & U.S. Hwy. 34, Exit 257
970/593-9947

25 25 LYONS

Kollars Copper Kettle Antqs.
422 Main
303/823-5495

Left-Hand Trading Co.
405 & 228 Main
303/823-6311

Left-Hand's Antq. & Western
228 E. Main
303/823-5738

Ralston Brothers Antiques
426 High St.
303/823-6982

26 MANITOU SPRINGS

Nothing New
116 Canon Ave.
719/685-9353

Interesting Side Trips

Miramont Castle
Capitol Hill Ave. off Ruxton Ave.
719/685-1011

Are you fascinated by old buildings? Do you love history? Are you interested in the unusual? If so, tour Miramont Castle! The world-famous "castle" was constructed in 1895, and currently hosts more than 42,000 visitors annually. The four-story structure has 46 rooms (28 of them open to the public), two-foot-thick stone walls, and incorporates nine distinctly different styles of architecture over 14,000 square feet of floor space!

Miramont Castle has played an important role in the history of Manitou Springs. Originally built by a wealthy French priest, over the years the castle has been both a sanitarium and an apartment house.

Today you can tour the historic Miramont Castle and marvel at the Drawing Room with its gold ceiling and 200-ton Peachblow sandstone fireplace. You can enjoy a quiet moment in the eight-sided Montcalm Chapel, visit the new miniature museum, or take in the grandeur of the 400-square-foot Marie Francolon bedroom. Relax in the Queen's Parlor enclosed tearoom, which offers tasty menu items and striking views of the surrounding mountains.

27 MONTROSE

Black Bear Antiques
62281 Hwy. 90
970/249-5738

C & D Antiques
1360 Townsend Ave.
970/249-6155

Cat's Meow
843 E. Main St.
970/249-4243

Pattie's Antiques
17086 S. Hwy. 550
970/240-9642

Traders Way Antiques
17656 Hwy. 550
970/249-3745

28 MORRISON

El Mercado
120 Bear Creek Ave.
303/697-8361

Little Bits of Yesterday
309 Bear Creek Ave.
303/697-8661

Morrison Antiques
307 Bear Creek Ave.
303/697-9545

Western Trail Antiques & Gifts
205 Bear Creek Ave.
303/697-9238

29 29 NEDERLAND

Off Her Rocker Antiques
4 East First St.
303/258-7976
Hours: 10-6 daily (Summer), 10-5 daily (Winter), closed New Year's Day, Thanksgiving Day, Christmas Day

Directions: Located on a National Designated Scenic Byway at the intersection of Hwy. 119 and Hwy. 72 between Black Haiok/Central City and Estes Park. The shop is located on the southeast corner of the intersection of Hwy. 119 and First St., which is the main street in Nederland.

Customers frequently ask Mrs. Warren how she came up with the unusual name "Off Her Rocker" for her business. With a smile, she tells them of the day (eight years ago) when she informed Mr. Warren of her plans to open an antique shop in Nederland. He promptly turned to her and said, "Are you off your rocker?" In honor of his obvious enthusiasm for her new venture she proudly replied, "Thank you—we're ready to do business."

You'll find this shop as delightful as the shopkeeper. Mrs. Warren offers a unique collection of everything under the sun in a charming, historical building located in the heart of the Rocky Mountains.

30 NIWOT

Lockwood House Antiques
198 2nd Ave.
303/652-2963

Niwot Antique Emporium
136 2nd Ave.
303/652-2587

Wise Buys Antiques
190 2nd Ave.
303/652-2888

Niwot Trading Post
149 2nd Ave.
303/443-0184

31 PUEBLO

Silver Lining Antiques
27050 U.S. Highway 50 E
719/545-3575

Blazing Saddle Antiques
118 S. Union Ave.
719/544-5520

Mid 30's Glass Shop
225 S. Union Ave.
719/544-1031

Cardinelli's Antiques
525 N. Santa Fe Ave.
719/544-9016

Oldies But Goodies Antq. Shop
113 W. 4th St.
719/545-4661

Victorianna's
213 S. Union Ave.
719/583-8009

A Touch of the Past
3369 S. Interstate 25
719/564-1840

Lane's House of Glass Inc.
111 Colorado Ave.
719/542-2210

Quilt Shop Antiques
111 E. Abriendo Ave.
719/544-4906

Trail Antiques
28018 E. U.S. Hwy. 50
719/948-2001

Silver Lining Antiques
27050 US Hwy. 50 E
719/545-3575

Favorite Places To Eat

Cracker Barrel Old Country Store
I-25 & Eagleridge, Exit 102
719/595-0711

32 32 SALIDA

Carriage House Antiques
148 N. F St.
719/539-4001

Jacobson's Antiques
7535 W. U.S. Hwy. 50
719/539-2093

Old Log Cabin Antiques
225 E. Rainbow Blvd.
719/539-2803

Colorado

33 SILVERTON

Silverton, Colorado, and its surrounding countryside are a playground where the scenery uplifts the spirit and sends energy levels climbing. The town is a National Historic Landmark, representing the Victorian era.

Having never suffered the catastrophic fires that most old mining towns have endured, Silverton is one of the best preserved, with most of its original homes and businesses still standing. Among the original buildings to explore is the San Juan County Historical Society Museum, a 1902 structure that once housed the county jail. The museum provides an excellent introduction to the town and its history.

On the "wilder" side of town is Blair Street, infamous for once offering Silverton and its visitors 40 saloons and brothels. These businesses appeared in abundance in mining and railroad towns at the turn of the century. Now serving as a location for many western movie shots, the street has earned an additional reputation since the heyday of its original activities.

Tantalized by the history and the longing for gold that the town and its premises encourage, you should be well prepped for the Old Hundred Gold Mine Tour. Local miners have established this one-hour train ride tour into an authentic gold mine deep within a mountain. Experienced miners guide the tours.

For the adventurous, a trip can be planned aboard a coal-fired, steam-operated train of the Durango & Silverton Narrow Gauge Railroad, which has served Silverton since 1882. Part of the year a railroad-operated bus shuttles passengers from Silverton to Durango for return the same day by rail, allowing a new perspective of the fabulous views offered by the surrounding landscape. Another option is to make the complete Durango-Silverton-Durango loop, stopping over for one or more nights in Silverton.

The French Bakery
1250 Greene Street
970/387-5423

Directions: From Denver, take I-70 West to exit 37 (before Grand Junction), CO 141 South to U.S. 50 South to U.S. 550 (at Montrose), U.S. 550 South to Silverton. Located on the first floor of Teller House Hotel.

The French Bakery is located on Greene Street, which just happens to be the main fairway through the tiny town of Silverton. Along this street, attractive Victorian period buildings and homes patiently pass the years.

The building housing the bakery is also home to the Teller House Hotel, which is on the second floor of the two-story brick building. Built by Silverton Brewery owner, Charles Fischer, the upstairs has been a hotel since its construction in 1896. It is listed as a National Historic Landmark and retains its original woodwork, high ceilings and many of its original Victorian furnishings.

The French Bakery, on the first floor below, serves a hearty southwestern breakfast, soup, deli sandwich or gourmet pizza for lunch. The bakery has long been hailed as a favorite dining spot by hotel guests and drop-ins.

Alma House
220 East 10th Street
970/387-5336
Open year round.

Directions: From Denver, take I-70 West to exit 37, then CO 141 South to U.S. 50 south to U.S. 550 at Montrose. Continue along U.S. 550 South into Silverton.

European in style, this hotel presents Victorian charm in its authentic decor. Restoration efforts have created a step back in time with furnishings and fixtures, style and atmosphere, without sacrificing modern convenience. Superb European and Southwestern cuisine is served at Christine's, located on the Alma House property.

34 VAIL

Englishman Fine Art & Antqs.
143 E. Meadow Dr. #205
970/476-3570

Finishing Touch of Vail Inc.
122 E. Meadow Dr.
970/476-1656

Lodge & Cabin Dry Goods Co.
100 E. Meadow Dr.
970/476-1475

Olla Podrida Gallery
100 E. Meadow Dr.
970/476-6919

35 VICTOR

Assay Office Antiques
113 South Third
719/689-2712
Open 7 days a week end of May to September 15, 11-5; open by appointment in the winter

Directions: Take Highway 67 to Victor. At the corner of Victor Avenue and 3rd Street, turn right. The shop is situated in the middle of the block on the west side.

Assay Office Antiques gets its name from the building's younger days as an assayer's office. For those of you who haven't a clue what an assayer is, here's an explanation. Back in the gold rush days, Victor was the largest gold mining district in the United States. The miners, speculators, the hopeful and the lucky, would bring their samples to the local assayer's office where it was tested for its true gold content.

Today within the walls of this turn-of-the-century building, trades of the past can still be found (and offered for sale). The shop carries a nice selection of gold mining gear, such as picks, pans, weights and measuring devices. Apart from the relics related to the history of the town, you can turn up old railroad items, some nice primitives, old toys, glassware and other interesting collectibles.

36 WINDSOR

Memory Lane Antiques
426 Main St.
970/686-7088

Windsor House of Antiques
414 Main St. #B
970/686-7913

37 YUMA

The Farmstead
46999 County Rd. E
970/848-2643

Albany Street Antique & Gift
203 S Albany St.
970/848-5214

Kaliko Kreations
419 S. Houston
970/848-0807

Peach Tree General Store
220 W. 8th Ave.
970/848-5216

Notes

Wayne Pratt, Inc.

American Antiques

346 Main Street South
Woodbury, CT 06798
(203) 263-5676
Fax (203) 266-4766

78

Derby Antique Center Inc.

Quality antiques bought and consigned

181 Main Street • Derby

15

Antique & Artisian Center

69 Jefferson St.
(203)327-6022
Stamford

66

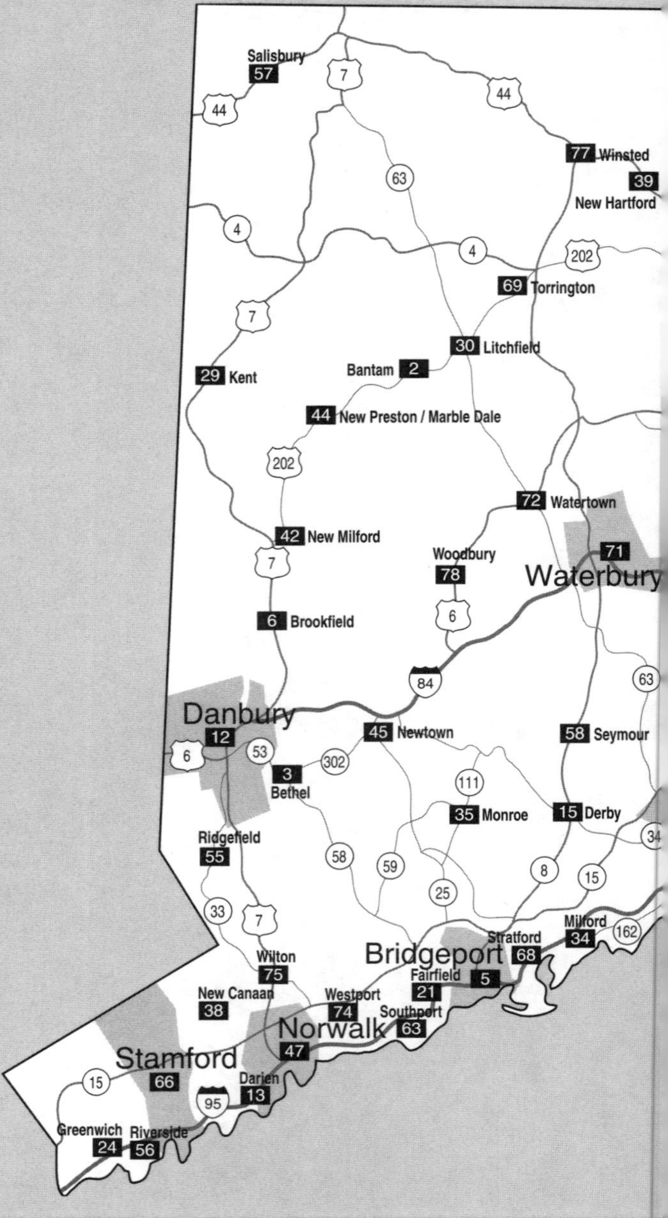

MYSTIC SEAPORT
THE MUSEUM OF AMERICA AND THE SEA™

Mystic

36

OLD LYME INN

Old Lyme

48

100 Lyme Street
Old Lyme

48

Riverside Antiques

- ANTIQUES -
- COLLECTABLES -
- BOUGHT & SOLD -
- CLOCK REPAIR -
Wed-Sun 10 - 5

Suite 101, Bldg. 2A
58 Pomfret Street
Putnam

George & Cathy
(860) 928-6020

54

THE INN AT NATIONAL HALL

A New World Manor House with an Old World Grace

Two Post Road West
Westport
1-800-Nat-Hall

74

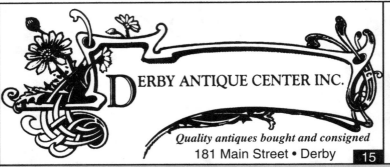

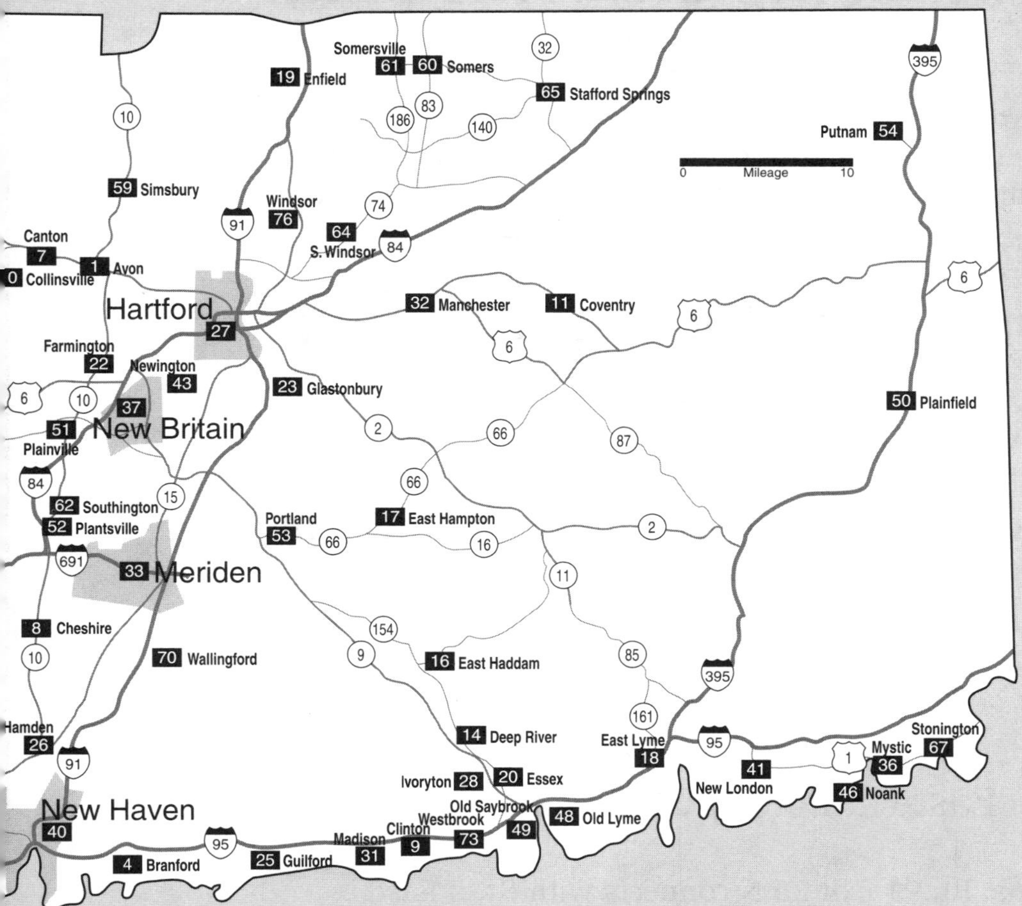

Connecticut

Connecticut

NOTE: Telephone area codes are changing. Fairfield & New Haven Counties will remain area code 203. All other cities and towns will change to 860.

1 AVON

D & W Collectibles
13 E. Main St.
860/676-2180

Moosavi Persian Rugs
45 E. Main St.
860/676-0082

2 BANTAM

Bradford House Antiques
895 Bantam Rd.
860/567-0951

Gooseboro Brook Antiques
38 Old Turnpike Rd.
860/567-5245

Old Carriage Shop Antq. Ctr.
920 Bantam Rd.
860/567-3234

Weston Thorn
940 Bantam Rd.
860/567-4661

3 BETHEL

Saltbox Antiques
123 Greenwood Ave.
203/744-6097

4 BRANFORD

Yesterday's Threads Vintage
206 Meadow St.
203/481-6452

Oldies But Goodies
781 E. Main St.
203/488-7230

Taken For Granite Antiques
409 Leetes Island Rd.
203/488-0557

C & R Antiques
62 Knollwood Dr.
203/488-9860

Clock Tower Antiques
824 E. Main St.
203/488-1919

5 BRIDGEPORT

Sweet Memories
2714 Fairfield Ave.
203/330-0558

Tinker's Treasures
2980 Fairfield Ave.
203/579-4243

Olivia's Attic
3004 Fairfield Ave.
203/332-0253

All That Glitters
3000 Fairfield Ave.
203/333-5836

6 BROOKFIELD

Sugar Hollow Antiques
797 Federal Rd.
203/775-5111

Antiques International
934 Federal Rd.
203/740-2336

Old Favorites Antiques
9 Arrowhead Rd.
203/775-3744

7 CANTON

Canton Barn Antiques-Auctions
75 Old Canton Road (located off Route 44)
860/693-0601

If you like the excitement and drama of antique auctions, then be sure to visit the weekly Saturday night auctions at Canton Barn. They hold a preview at 5 p.m. on the day of the sale, and the auction begins at 7:30 p.m. Bring your money, but don't bring the kids, because like many establishments, they don't accept children during the auction!

Balcony Antiques
81 Albany Turnpike
860/693-6440

On The Road Bookshop
163 Albany Turnpike
860/693-6029

Canton Green Antique Store
181 Albany Turnpike
860/693-0008

Antiques at Canton Village
Canton Village Rte. 44
860/693-2715

Lila Sklar Antiques
Canton Village-Rte. 44
860/651-9111

Griffin Brothers & Co.
10 Front
860/693-9007

Cob-Web Shop
20 Dyer Cemetery Rd.
860/693-2658

8 CHESHIRE

Cartophilians
430 Highland Ave.
203/272-1143

Chez Angele
115 Knobhill Road
203/271-9883

Granny's Attic
192 S. Main St.
203/272-8262

Magnolia Shoppe
908 S. Meriden Rd.
203/272-3303

9 CLINTON

Clinton Antique Center
78 E. Main St.
860/669-3839

Antiques on Main St.
104 E. Main St.
860/664-9163

Waterside Antiques & Gifts
109 E. Main St.
860/669-0809

Square-Riggers Antique Center
350 E. Main St.
860/664-9001

John Street Antiques
23 W. Main St. #A
860/669-2439

Loft
59 W. Main St.
860/669-4583

Hey-Day Antiques
9 Rocky Ledge Dr.
860/669-8800

Van Carter Hale Fine Art
36 W. Main St.
860/669-4313

10 COLLINSVILLE

The Collinsville Antiques Co.
Historical Collins Axe Factory
P. O. Box 473
860/693-1011

11 COVENTRY

CCS Antiques & Gifts
2799 Boston Turnpike
860/742-6099

Memory Lanes Country Side
2224 Route 44 #A
860/742-0346

12 DANBURY

Red White & Blue White Gllry.
49 South Street
203/778-5085

Antiques & Collectibles
49 South Street
203/791-1275

13 DARIEN

Knock On Wood
355 Post Rd.
203/655-9031

Antiques of Darien
1101 Boston Post Rd.
203/655-5133

Emy Jane Jones Antiques
770 Post Rd.
203/655-7576

Sebastian Gallery
833 Post Rd.
203/656-3093

Windsor Antiques Ltd.
1064 Post Rd.
203/655-2330

14 DEEP RIVER

Detour
Old Piano Factory
860/526-9797

Irish Country Pine
246 S. Main
860/526-9757

James E. Elliott Antique
453 Winthrop Rd.
860/526-9455

Riverwind Antique Shop
68 Main St.
860/526-3047

Way We Wore
116 Main St.
860/526-2944

15 DERBY

The Derby Antique Center, Inc.
181 Main Street
203/734-7614
Open Tue.-Thurs. 10-2, Fri.-Sat. 10-5, closed Sun.-Mon.

Directions: The Derby Antique Center is located on Connecticut Route 34N., 500 feet from Exit #15 North or Route 8 South. Route 8 runs north and south through Connecticut. The shop is on the right side traveling north on Main Street in Derby, which is also Connecticut Route 34 North and South.

There's lots of expertise in antiques here at The Derby for shoppers to draw on as they browse through this large store. Although owner Peter Petrino has had the store only four years himself, he grew up working with the past owner and learned the business inside-out before taking the reins. The former owner also comes back from Florida in the summers to work in the store and greet old, familiar faces. The Derby handles "everything," as Peter says, but seems to get in a lot of musical instruments, besides the furniture, china, collectibles, jewelry, etc.

**Note: An amusing story as told by The Derby Antique Center.*

"One day we received a call from a woman who was interested in selling an item to us. Rather than waste everyone's time, we always ask pertinent questions, one specific as to the age of items, as we only buy antiques. Her reply to my question of 'Is it old?' was simply yes. In trying for more information I asked "'How old?' 'I don't know' was the reply. I then asked how she knew it was old, and she said, 'I know it's old because I bought it from some old guy, and it smells old.' This is now our benchmark to determine age of items, and we have this quotation posted in our shop."

Favorite Places To Eat

Vonete's Palace of Sweets
262 Main Street
203/734-2061

"The store that time forgot" is generally how folks describe the small, timeworn storefront of Vonete's (pronounced "von-ET-ees") in downtown Derby. It's been serving truly old-fashioned ice cream and candy treats since 1905 - how many calories have been served in 92 years? Real egg creams, orange flips, banana royales, tutti-fruitti sundaes, aristocratic chocolate sauce, hot fudge topping...all this and more is served within the tin ceiling, walls painted in Easter-egg pastels, teeny-tiny tiles on the floor, a counter and a few tables in the back. Candy is still weighed in an antique scale that is the real McCoy. In addition to candy, ice cream, and an awesome repertoire of soda fountain specialties, you can also get skinny hamburgers cooked on a tiny, old-fashioned grill.

But the house specialty, according to many long-standing customers, are the sundaes, particularly ones that are topped with chocolate sauce or hot fudge. Be sure to order a glass of seltzer to wash down that hot fudge, because it's so intensely fudgy that it will cause a powerful thirst. Chocoholics, beware!

16 EAST HADDAM

Howard & Dickinson Antiques
48 Main St.
860/873-9990

Jim Miller Antiques
Town
860/873-8286

17 EAST HAMPTON

Nestled in the south central hills of Connecticut lies the quaint, historic town of East Hampton. Formerly known as Chatham, the area was originally famous for its ship-making and bell industries. Today, the old town center has developed into a cluster of antique shops and eateries making for a pleasant afternoon of antique shopping.

Old Bank Antiques
66 Main Street
860/295-9416
Open Wed.-Sun. 10-5, Fridays until 8 p.m., or by appointment

Directions: Route 91 exit 25 N.; connects with Route 2 East, exit 13, right onto Route 66, left at 3rd light.

Old Bank Antiques is just as its name implies, an old bank. I have always been fascinated with buildings such as these, mostly because they hold something I would like to have - *A Lot Of Money*.

Years ago if you had walked into this "Old Bank," the vaults would have been shut and tightly locked, protecting the loot from bank-robbing bandits who often rode into town unexpectedly. Today, the doors are opened wide, welcoming all to view a different kind of bounty. Displayed within are small antique pieces such as flow blue, limoges, lamps, sterling, china, music boxes, toys, firearms and art.

Throughout this three-story building, thirty antique dealers offer a distinguished collection of 18th-20th century furnishings and smalls, with over 300 pieces of furniture ready to go in oak, mahogany, pine and wicker. The shop is also one of the few places that always has big tables and *sets* of chairs.

Antiques at Seventy Main St.
70 Main St.
860/267-9501

Past & Present Antiques
81 Main St.
860/267-0495

18 EAST LYME

Judy's Unfound Treasures
180 Boston Post Rd. #A
860/739-7440

Country Life Antiques
55 W. Main
860/739-8969

Book Barn
41 W. Main
860/739-5715

19 ENFIELD

Hazard Antique Center
287 Hazard Ave.
860/763-0811

Growth Co.
167 Hazard Ave.
860/749-9237

20 ESSEX

Arne E. Ahlberg Antiques
145 Westbrook Rd.
860/767-2799

American Heritage Antiques
251 Westbrook Rd.
860/767-8162

Francis Bealey American Arts
3 S. Main St.
860/767-0220

Hastings House
4 N. Main St.
860/767-8217

Phoenix Antiques
10 Main St.
860/767-5082

Valley Farm Antiques
134 Saybrook Rd.
860/767-8555

21 FAIRFIELD

Reminisce with Kathy
238 Post Rd.
203/254-0300

James Bok Antiques
1954 Post Rd.
203/255-6500

Winsor Antiques
43 Ruance St.
203/255-0056

22 FARMINGTON

Farmington Lodge Antiques
185 Main St.
860/674-1035

Samovar Antiques
780 Farmington Ave. #F
860/677-8772

23 GLASTONBURY

Always Buying Antiques
By Appointment Only
860/646-6808

Tobacco Shed Antiques
119 Griswold St.
860/657-2885

Black Pearl Antiques
2217 Main St.
860/659-3601

Perfect Finish
27 Commerce St. #C
860/657-2295

24 GREENWICH

Elaine Dillof Antiques
71 Church St.
203/629-2294

Church Street Antiques
77 Church St.
203/661-6309

Greenwich Ave. Antiques
369 Greenwich Ave.
203/622-8361

Henri-Burton French Antiques
382 Greenwich Ave.
203/661-8529

Guild Antiques
384 Greenwich Ave.
203/869-0828

Michael Kessler Antiques
40 E. Putnam Ave.
203/629-1555

Manderley Antiques
134 E. Putnam Ave.
203/861-1900

Provinces De France
22 W. Putnam Ave.
203/629-9798

Rue Fauborg
44 W. Putnam Ave.
203/869-7139

Hallowell & Co.
340 W. Putnam Ave.
203/869-2190

Eggplant & Johnson Inc.
58 William St. #A
203/532-0409

Consign It Inc.
115 Mason St.
203/869-9836

Maison La Belle
15 E. Elm St.
203/622-0301

Classic Antique Consignment
173 Hamilton Ave.
203/869-0916

Antan Antiques
E. Putnam Ave.
203/698-3219

Surrey Collectibles
563 Steamboat Rd.
203/869-4193

Fieldstone Antiques
260 Mill St.
203/531-0011

25 GUILFORD

Arne E. Ahlberg Antiques
1090 Boston Post Rd.
203/453-9022

Guilford Antique Center
1120 Boston Post Rd.
203/458-7077

Gustave D. Balacos
2614 Boston Post Rd.
203/488-0762

26 HAMDEN

Donald Barese Fine Art
47 Wakefield St.
203/281-7438

T Melillo Antiques
2373 Whitney Ave.
203/281-3787

27 HARTFORD

The Unique Antique
Hartford Civic Center
860/522-9094
Open 10-7:30 Mon.-Sat., Sundays by chance

Directions: Located right in the center of Hartford, the Hartford Civic Center adjoins the Sheraton Hotel. Exit I-91 at the downtown exit. The high-rise Sheraton is visible from either I-84 or I-91.

This is the place to stop if you are in the market for very high-end antique and estate jewelry. The Unique Antique is an antique shop in a mall and carries one of the largest selections of antique/estate jewelry in the East. Owner Joanne Douglas brings a lifetime of experience in this field to her shop and customers. She has been in the business for 20 years, but her grandmother was an antique jewelry dealer, and Joanne grew up with an antique store in the house. She gets her stock from sources in New England, mainly through dealers and individuals who bring pieces in to her. If you want anything from "diamonds down to costume," The Unique Antique is a "must."

Carol's Antiques & Collectibles
453 Washington St.
860/524-9113

Bacon Antiques
95 Maple Ave.
860/524-0040

Unique Antiques
1 Civic Center Plaza #1
860/522-9094

Interesting Side Trips

The Mark Twain House
351 Farmington Avenue
860/493-6411
Open year round with peak season and off-season hours.

From sun-dappled days of playing on the Mississippi River at Hannibal, Missouri, to the winter wonderland of Hartford, Connecticut, is a long way, but American author and humorist Mark Twain (Samuel Langhorne Clemens), built a Victorian mansion in Hartford for his family, where they all lived from 1874 to 1891. Now a National Register Historic Landmark (since 1963), the Mark Twain House is a showplace, a museum, a piece of American history and a very rare piece of American decorative art.

Twain wrote seven major works (including *Tom Sawyer, Adventures of Huckleberry Finn, The Prince and the Pauper, Life on the Mississippi*, and *A Connecticut Yankee in King Arthur's Court*) while living in this remarkable High Victorian building. Designed by Edward Tuckerman Potter, the 19-room mansion features an important collection of fine and decorative arts, and the only remaining domestic interiors by Louis Comfort Tiffany and his design firm, Associated Artists. Now restored to its 19th century glory, the house is a museum and research center with a collection of some 10,000 objects, and offers a full program of literary, musical, family oriented, scholarly, and educational programs.

Mark Twain's Carriage House, also designed by Potter, was home to the Clemenses' coachman and his family, along with horses, carriages and a sleigh. For a time, Twain did his writing in a makeshift study in the Carriage House. The buildings share a lawn with the home of 19th century author Harriet Beecher Stowe, who was Clemens' neighbor.

28 IVORYTON

Copper Beech Inn
46 Main Street
860/767-0330
Open year round, except first week of January
Rates $105-165

The Copper Beech Inn takes its name from the magnificent copper beech tree that fronts the property, one of the oldest and largest of its kind in Connecticut. The 1880s home was built as an elegant Victorian country cottage, complete with carriage barn, root cellar, and terraced landscaping. Surrounded by turn-of-the-century gardens and native woodlands, the house was rescued from disrepair and vacancy in the 1970s, and restored and opened as the Copper Beech Inn. The guest rooms in the main house are decorated with country and antique furnishings; the old-fashioned baths have been left intact. Guest rooms in the renovated carriage house have four-poster beds, whirlpool baths, and French doors leading to decks. French country style dining is available in the restaurant on the premises.

29 KENT

Company Store Antiques
30 Kent Cornwall Rd.
860/927-3430

R.T.Facts Garden & Architrl.
22 S. Main St.
860/927-5315

Foreign Cargo & Amer. Antqs.
Main St.
860/927-3900

Golden Thistle
Main St.
860/927-3790

Harry Homes Antique
3 Carter Rd.
860/927-3420

Kent Antiques Center
Kent Station Square
860/927-3313

30 LITCHFIELD

Linsley Antiques
499 Bantam Rd.
860/567-4245

Barry Strom Antiques
595 Bantam Rd.
860/567-9767

Thomas M. McBride Antiques
62 West St.
860/567-5476

Jeffrey Tillou Antiques
33 West Street
860/567-9693

31 MADISON

Crescent Antiques
60 Boston Post Rd.
203/245-9145

Mildred Ross
294 Boston Post Rd.
203/245-7122

K. H. Crump Clockmaker
387 Boston Post Rd.
203/245-7573

Madison Trust Antique
891 Boston Post Rd.
203/245-3976

Fence Creek Antiques
916 Boston Post Rd.
203/245-0151

Nosey Goose
33 Wall St.
203/245-3132

32 MANCHESTER

Yesterday's Treasures
845 Main St.
860/646-8855

Lest We Forget Antiques
503 E. Middle Turnpike
860/649-8187

33 MERIDEN

Dee's Antiques
600 W. Main St.
203/235-8431

Fair Weather Antiques
763 Hanover Rd.
203/237-4636

Hanover Antiques
819 Hanover Rd.
203/639-1002

34 MILFORD

The Stock Transfer
554 Boston Post Road
203/874-1333
Open Tue.-Sat. 10-4

Directions: From I-95 North: Take Exit 37 (High Street) and turn right to Route 1. Turn left and go Ω block. The shop is on the right. From I-95 South: Take Exit #36 (Plains Road) to Route 1. Turn left and go Ω mile. The shop is on the right. From Merritt Parkway: Take Exit 54 to the first Milford Exit and go to Route 1. Turn right and go 1/2 block. The shop is on the right in "The Courtyard."

Nanci has been in business for 15 years at The Stock Transfer. With 2400 square feet of space, it is the largest shop of its kind in the area, and, says Nanci, they carry "everything." Shoppers can find furniture, crystal, china, jewelry, oriental rugs, paintings and lots more.

Ray's Antiques
16 Daniel St.
203/876-7720

New Beginnings
107 River St.
203/876-8332

Antiques of Tomorrow
93 Gulf St.
203/878-4561

Something of Bev's
400 Bost Post Rd.-Colony Center
203/874-4686

Favorite Places to Eat

Cracker Barrel Old Country Store
I-95 & Woodmont Rd., Exit 40
203/877-7595

35 MONROE

Addie's Cottage
144 Main St.
203/261-2689

Barbara's Barn
418 Main St.
203/268-9805

Strawberry Patch Antiques
418 Main St.
203/268-1227

36 MYSTIC

Pequot Hotel Bed & Breakfast
Burnett's Corner
711 Cow Hill Road
860/572-0390
Open year round
Rates $95-130

It just doesn't seem like stagecoaches ever ran anywhere but the old West-certainly not through New England-but the Pequot Hotel Bed & Breakfast is an authentically restored 1840 stagecoach stop. This stately Greek Revival landmark, located in the center of the Burnett's Corners historic district, still has its original hardware, moldings and fireplaces. Two of the three guest rooms, all with private baths, have 12-foot-high coved ceilings and Rumford fireplaces. There is a rare book collection in the library, wicker furniture on the screened porch, and two parlors for guests' use. More than 20 acres of trails and woods, open fields, ponds, spacious lawns, and gardens surround the hotel.

Briar Rose Antiques
27 Broadway Ave.
860/536-4135

Tradewinds Gallery
20 W. Main St.
860/536-0119

Interesting Side Trips

Mystic Seaport
75 Greenmanville Avenue
860/572-5331
WebSite: www.mystic.org
Open daily year round except Christmas Day

Directions: Mystic Seaport is located midway between New York and Boston in Mystic, Connecticut. Take I-95 to Exit 90. Proceed one mile south on Route 27.

This place is absolutely fascinating! You don't even have to like sailing to be amazed by all the glimpses into our country's history that are preserved here at this private museum. In 1929 three residents of Mystic - Dr. Charles K. Stillman, Edward E. Bradley and Carl D. Cutler - formed the Marine Historical Association, Inc., in order to establish a museum and preserve the rapidly disappearing remnants of America's maritime past. The museum's name was changed in 1978 to Mystic Seaport. So, Mystic Seaport is an indoor/outdoor museum which includes historic ships, boats, buildings and exhibit galleries relating to American maritime history. The exhibit area is located on 17 acres along the Mystic River. Primary emphasis is on the maritime commerce of the Atlantic coast during the 19th century. The village area architecture, gardens, and demonstrations depict life in a maritime community from 1850 to 1921. Located on an estuary three miles from the open sea, the Museum is divided into three main areas: Preservation Shipyard, where museum staff maintain the Museum's unique historic ships and small boats, while preserving the traditional skills of wooden shipbuilding; the outdoor Village Exhibits, representing elements of life and work in 19th century New England seaport communities, and aboard the ships that sailed from them; and the Gallery exhibits, presenting fabulous collections of maritime art and artifacts, and special changing exhibitions on important aspects of America's relationship with the sea.

37 NEW BRITAIN

Vintage Shop
61 Arch St.
860/224-8567

Universal Stamp & Coin
304 Broad St.
860/827-9439

38 NEW CANAAN

Evans-Leonard Antiques
114 Main St.
203/966-5657

Silk Purse
118 Main St.
203/972-0898

Main St. Cellar Antiques
120 Main St.
203/966-8348

New Canaan Antiques
120 Main St.
203/972-1938

Sallea Antiques
66 Elm St.
203/972-1050

Courtyard Antiques
150 Elm St.
203/966-2949

English Heritage Antiques Inc.
13 South Ave.
203/966-2979

Elisabeth De Bussy Inc.
By Appointment Only
203/966-5947

39 NEW HARTFORD

Rose Marie
202 Main St.
860/693-3979

New Hartford Junction
510 Main St.
860/738-0689

40 NEW HAVEN

Edwin C. Ahlbery Antiques
441 Middletown Ave.
203/624-9076

W. Chorney Antiques
827 Whalley Ave.
203/387-9707

Antiques Market
881 Whalley Ave.
203/389-5440

Antique Corner
859 Whalley Ave.
203/387-7200

Second Time Around
970 State St.
203/624-6343

Patti's Antiques
920 State St.
203/865-8496

Village Francais
555 Long Wharf Dr.
203/562-4883

41 NEW LONDON

Captain's Treasures
253 Captains Walk
860/442-2944

42 NEW MILFORD

Chamberlain's Antiques
469 Danbury Rd.
860/355-3488

Retro
267 Kent Rd.
860/355-1975

Accent Antiques
Church St.
860/355-7707

This N That Shop
27 Old State Rd.
860/350-4001

Ida's Antiques
329 Danbury Rd.
860/354-4388

43 NEWINGTON

Connecticut Antique Wicker
1052 Main Rear
860/666-3729

Doll Factory Vintage Clothing
2551 Berlin Turnpike
860/666-6162

Trellis Antiques & Gifts
39 Market Square
860/665-9100

44 NEW PRESTON/MARBLE DALE

Earl Slack Antiques
Wheaton Rd. (Marble Dale)
860/868-7092

Grampa Snazzy's Log Cabin
270 Litchfield Tpk. (New Preston)
860/868-7153

Martell & Suffin Antiques
1 Main St. #A (New Preston)
860/868-1339

Reece Antiques
15 E. Shore Rd. (New Preston)
860/868-9966

Room With A View
13 E. Shore Rd. (New Preston)
860/868-1717

Recherche Studio
166 New Milford Tpk. (New Pres.)
860/868-0281

45 NEWTOWN

McGeorgi's Antiques
129 S. Main
203/270-9101

Poverty Hollow Antiques
78 Poverty Hollow Rd.
203/426-2388

Van Tassell Tole House
Route 34
203/426-4889

Jack & Gloria Bethune Antqs.
P.O. Box 602
203/426-5211

46 NOANK

Palmer Inn
25 Church Street
860/572-9000
Open year round
Rates $125-185

On a prime piece of real estate just off Long Island Sound is a soaring, magnificent home that reveals the extravagance and superb craftsmanship of turn-of-the-century architecture. Two miles from Mystic Seaport, shipyard craftsmen built a grand seaside mansion for shipbuilder Robert Palmer in 1906. The house, described by the architects as a "Classic Colonial Suburban Villa," features a hip roof with dormers, a balustrade, dentil cornices, pilasters, Palladian windows, and a huge portico with two-story Ionic columns. These architectural details remain intact on the outside, while inside guests enjoy and marvel at 13-foot ceilings, a mahogany staircase and beams, brass fixtures, intricate woodwork, stained-glass windows, and original wall coverings, all of which have been restored. The six guest rooms with private baths are filled with family heirlooms and antiques, as well as modern luxuries. Balconies offer views of Long Island Sound, while fireplaces warm the chilly Connecticut winter evenings.

The Antiquary
215 Park
860/928-4873

Favorite Places To Eat

Abbott's Lobster in the Rough
117 Pearl Street
860/536-7719

A no-frills, outdoor, summertime tradition and icon, Abbott's is *the* place to eat lobsters, clams, and its legendary clam chowder. Villagers from Noank, summer residents and even tourists flock to Abbott's for the unimprovable pleasure of a shore dinner in the rough, served on plastic trays, eaten on picnic tables, al fresco seating, with salt air, sea breezes and seagulls for decor.

But the main focus is lobsters - any size, steamed while you wait; clam chowder - in true southern New England style, and Abbott's lobster rolls, one of the few regional specialties unique to Connecticut. Sheer summer luxury!

47 NORWALK

Pak Trade
14 Wall St.
203/857-4165

Eagles Lair Antiques
565 Westport Ave.
203/846-1159

Old Well Antiques
135 Washington St.
203/838-1842

Koppels Antique Warehouse
24 1st St.
203/866-3473

48 OLD LYME

Old Lyme Inn

85 Lyme Street
800/434-5352
Open year round except for first two weeks of January
Rates $86-158

Directions: Going south on I-95, take Exit 70 and turn right off of the ramp. Going north on I-95, turn left off of the ramp, right at the second light. Follow this road (Rte. 1) to the second light and the inn is on the left.

Situated on the main street in Old Lyme's historic district, Old Lyme Inn represents the classic traditions of excellence in dining and lodging that is the very heart of a small Connecticut town. The original building, constructed around 1850 by the Champlain family, was a 300-acre working farm until the Connecticut Turnpike cut through Old Lyme in the early 1950s. Some guests still remember when the place housed a riding academy in the 1920s, where it is reputed that Jacqueline Bouvier Kennedy Onassis took lessons. Prior to that, around the turn of the century, many of Old Lyme's famous impressionist artists hauled their painting wagons into the beautiful fields and Connecticut woodlands behind the inn. Townspeople also remember lively square dancing in the old barn that burned (only the foundation remains) about 300 yards behind the still remaining 1850s yellow barn.

When the turnpike arrived, the Champlain family home was sold and became the Barbizon Oaks, named after the Barbizon School for painters that Old Lyme emulated, and the 300-year-old oak tree that still stands on a hill behind the inn. It became a boarding establishment, and survived a major fire that was the beginning of a spiral into disrepair. Its staircase and interior walls disappeared, and it became an Italian restaurant of questionable reputation. When Diana Field Atwood bought it in 1976, the second floor was still charred and the building was ready for demolition. The kitchen, then in the basement, was a hazard to its occupants - including the dead rat found in one of the ovens. The only access to the second floor was up a rickety fire escape supported by a metal milk crate and pulled down with one hand!

But when Diana bought it, she restored the inn to its current beauty. Walls and staircases were rebuilt, marble fireplaces were found and everything was redone from the basement to the attic. Now it offers not only fine dining, but 13 guest rooms with private baths and Empire and Victorian antiques. The inn's facilities include four separate dining rooms and a cocktail lounge, with seating from 2 to 70. In combination with the guest rooms, the inn handles conferences, wedding parties, rehearsal dinners and other special events.

Guests can spend time in the Victorian Bar that came out of one of Pittsburgh's oldest taverns. It has never been refinished, retaining its original beveled glass mirrors and scores of dart holes from many games in the past. The mirror over the bar's fireplace was purchased at an auction for $5 - no one else wanted it! The marble mantles in the bar and parlor came from a lady in Wetherfield who had saved them when her family's home was being razed.

Many of the paintings in the inn represent the Old Lyme School of artists who resided up the street at Florence Griswold's home (now the Lyme Historical Society) at the turn of the century. There are also paintings purchased from current artists at Lyme Art Association shows, and some lovely watercolors in the Champlain rooms, from unknown artists of Old Lyme, found at tag sales.

The Empire Room (the main dining room) was an addition to the original building, added around the time of the Barbizon Oak period. The large pier mirror was found in an old Norwich mansion undergoing the wrecker's ball. Curly maple balustrades from an old Pennsylvania home march up the front staircase. Nineteenth century chestnut paneling covers the walls in the private dining room. In the front hall, the original paintings and stenciling were done by Gigi Horr-Liverant. This type of wall painting was done quite often during the mid-1800s by itinerant artists; they usually painted local scenes, so the inn's wall murals represent several of the old buildings on Lyme Street, and going up the stairs - Hamburg Cove in Lyme and Tiffany's Farm, the only working dairy farm owned by one of Connecticut's former legislators.

Over the years the inn has been awarded multiple prestigious awards and tributes: three star reviews by the *New York Times* on three separate visits; three stars from *Connecticut Magazine;* five stars from the *Norwich Bulletin;* wonderful stories in *Signature, Travel & Leisure, Redbook, Town & Country,* and many more; feature billing in *Bon Appetite* and on a separate cover of the same magazine; feature stories in *Connoisseur, Food & Wine,* and *NewYork Magazine.* And for three years in a row, the inn's pastry chef won the "Ultimate Chocolate Dessert" contest in Hartford.

Bee and Thistle Inn

100 Lyme Street
860/434-1667 or 1-800-622-4946
Rates $75-210

Directions: By Amtrak from Boston or New York: Train stops at Old Saybrook Station. By car from Boston or Providence: Take I-95 South to Exit 70, turn right off the ramp. The inn is the third house on the left. From New York City: Take the New England Thruway (I-95 North) to Exit 70. At the bottom of the ramp turn left. Take the first right onto Halls Road (Route 1 North). to the "T" in the road and turn left. The inn is the third house on the left. From Hartford: Take I-91 South to Route 9 South to I-95 North. Take Exit 70 and turn left off of the ramp. Take the first right onto Halls Road (Route 1 North). Go to the "T" in the road and turn left. The inn is the third house on the left.

The Bee and Thistle is somewhat more formal than many bed and breakfasts, but the effort is worth it. With landscaped and natural areas along the Lieutenant River in the historic district of Old Lyme, the inn states that it is "a return to early American gracious living." The house was built in 1756 for Judge Noyes, very close to the Post Road. Around the turn of the century the Hodgson family moved it back from the road to its present location. They added the lovely sunken garden, the porches and the kitchen area. It remained a private home until the late 1930s, when Henrietta Greenleaf Lindsay found herself a widow with a large house to support. Her friend, Elsie Ferguson, an actress at the Goodspeed Opera House, suggested Henrietta take in boarders. Because it was Elsie's idea, Henrietta named her boarding house the Bee and Thistle after the Ferguson clan emblem in Scotland. The logo is still used today.

Dining is a highlight and specialty of the house, with appropriate evening dinner attire required and jackets required on Saturdays. But for that little extra effort, guests will enjoy four star creative American cuisine that has been voted the "Best Restaurant" and "Most Romantic Place" to dine in Connecticut by *Connecticut Magazine* Readers' Choice Poll. Candlelit dining areas showcase the food; wine comes from a large selection; desserts are award-winning; it is an experience many visitors enjoy simply as an evening out. Breakfast is served either on the porches or in the privacy of individual rooms. Luncheon is the chance for the chefs to use their imaginations.

To work off the excesses of the dining room, a walk down Lyme Street leads to historic homes, museums, galleries, fine antique shops, and beautiful private homes. A short drive away are numerous attractions and sites.

Antique Associates-Old Lyme
11 Halls Rd.
860/434-5828

Elephant Trunk
11 Halls Rd.
860/434-9630

Treasures
95 Halls Rd.
860/434-9338

49 OLD SAYBROOK

Antiques at Madison
869 Middlesex Turnpike
860/388-3626

Antiques Depot
455 Boston Post Rd.
860/395-0595

Corner Cupboard Antiques
853 Middlesex Turnpike
860/388-0796

Essex-Saybrook Antqs. Village
345 Middlesex Turnpike
860/388-0689

Joseph Goclowski Antiques
223 Hidden Cove Rd.
860/399-5070

Old Saybrook Antiques Center
756 Middlesex Turnpike
860/388-1600

Connecticut

Presence of the Past
488 Main St.
860/388-9021

Sweet Pea Estate Jewelry
851 Middlesex Turnpike
860/388-0289

Van's Elegant Antiques
998 Middlesex Turnpike
860/388-1934

Essex Town Line Antqs. Village
985 Middlesex Turnpike
860/388-5000

50 PLAINFIELD

Plainfield Trading Post
260 Norwich Rd.
860/564-4115

51 PLAINVILLE

Winter Associates
21 Cooke St.
860/793-0288

March Hare Antiques
188 W. Main St.
860/747-2526

52 PLANTSVILLE

Village Antique Shop
61 Main Street
860/628-2498

West Main Antiques
9 W. Main St.
860/620-1124

Nothing New
69 W. Main St.
860/276-0143

Plantsville General Store
780 S. Main St.
860/621-5225

Al Judd & Associates
40 W. Main St.
860/628-5828

G. W. G. Antiques
758 Main Street
860/620-0244

Ginny's Country Cupboard
Main Street
No Phone

53 PORTLAND

Robert T. Baranowsky Antiques
66 Marlborough
860/342-2425

54 PUTNAM

Riverside Antiques
Bldg. 2A Suite 101
58 Pomfret St.
860/928-6020
Open: Wed.-Sun. 10-5:00

Directions: From Interstate 395 take exit 95. Go right onto Kennedy Drive. At the first traffic light, left onto Pomfret St., 200 yards on the left directly across from WINY Radio Studio.

Located on the western edge of the extensive Putnam Antiques District, Riverside Antiques is housed in the Wilkinson Mill (Hale Mfg. Co.) ca. 1830, a stone and brick structure formerly used for the manufacture of woolen goods. Riverside Antiques is a co-op featuring 20+ dealers selling a full range of quality antiques and collectibles, complimented by an on-site Clock Repair Shop.

Grams & Pennyweights
626 School St. Rt 44
860/928-6624

Grandpa's Attic
10 Pomfret St.
860/928-5970

Antiques Marketplace
109 Main St.
860/928-0442

Brighton Antiques
91 Main St.
860/928-1419

J B Antiques
37 Front St.
860/928-1906

Antique Corner
112 Main St.
860/963-2445

Toys In The Attic
4 Pomfret St.
860/928-2525

Art & Antiques
88 Main St.
860/963-0105

55 RIDGEFIELD

The Red Petticoat Antiques
113 West Lane, Route 35
203/431-9451
Open Tue.-Sat. 10-5:30, Sun. 12-5:30, closed Mondays

In April, 1777, a young girl saved her home (which is now The Red Petticoat Antiques) on West Lane, Ridgefield from being burned and plundered, and protected a wounded Patriot from being captured by British soldiers, by waving her red petticoat from the window in pretended sympathy with the Tories. The wounded Patriot had an important message to deliver to General George Washington, but was too weak to travel, so the girl sewed the message into the red petticoat and delivered it to Dobb's Ferry. Soon after, Washington expressed his gratitude by sending her some lovely red silk for a new petticoat, hoping it would replace the one she had sacrificed so bravely for her country...or so the story is told.

Continuity and tradition are important parts of the fabric of the Northeast, and The Red Petticoat antique store is built on American history and its own tradition, making it a perfect setting in which to sell historical objects. To begin with, the building itself is a home that was built in 1740, in one of the most beautiful settings in New England. For another, antiques have been sold at the sign of The Red Petticoat for as long as most people can remember. One of the oldest owners and sellers was Florene Maine, who knew and taught people about some of the finest English furniture ever made. After her death, the house remained an antique shop and the present owners, Ralph and Gloria Pershino, bought it. Now the antique selection is much more eclectic, with seven rooms of 18th and 19th century antique furnishings, folk art, iron and wicker, ephemera, oriental rugs, lamps, and fine furniture reproductions by Douglas Dimes.

A specialty of the house is advertising ephemera, which draws a great number of the shop's customers. Many people come to The Red Petticoat just for this. They have customers who are either employed by companies or whose families have started major companies, and the Perschinos call them when particular advertisements come in, usually items from the late 1800s to the early 1900s. A major part of the Perschinos' business is repeat customers, who particularly like to shop at the store for accessories and gifts. They cater to a varied clientele, who either shop by phone, or who come into the store and browse through the room settings. There is a beautiful sunroom filled with antique wicker, a huge fireplace where the old kitchen once was, decked out with tools and iron from the past. There is a staircase leading to a cozy room upstairs, with the entire stairway furnished with Wallace Nutting vintage pictures - seven rooms of 18th and 19th century antique furnishings and much more, all in a beautiful country setting in this historical antique house.

Hunter's Consignments
426 Main St.
203/438-9065

Horologists of London Clocks
450 Main St.
203/438-4332

Consignments by Vivian
458 Main St.
203/438-5567

Silk Purse
470 Main St.
203/431-0132

Attic Treasures Ltd.
58 Ethan Allen Hwy
203/544-8159

Country Gallery Antiques
346 Ethan Allen Hwy
203/438-2535

Route 7 Antiques
659 Danbury Rd.
203/438-6671

Ridgefield Antiques Center
109 Danbury Rd.
203/438-2777

56 RIVERSIDE

Classiques Antqs. & Consign.
1147 E. Putnam
203/637-8227

Estate Treasures of Greenwich
1162 E. Putnam
203/637-4200

Maury Rose Antiques
1147 E. Putnam Ave.
203/698-2898

57 SALISBURY

Buckley & Buckley
84 Main St.
860/435-9919

Salisbury Antiques Center
46 Library St.
860/435-0424

58 SEYMOUR

Seymour Antique Co.
26 Bank St.
203/881-2526

Chrisandra's
249 West St.
203/888-7223

59 SIMSBURY

Simsbury Antiques
744 Hopmeadow St.
860/651-4474

Back Fence Collector
1614 Hopmeadow St.
860/651-4846

William III Antiques
21 Wolcott Rd.
860/658-1121

60 SOMERS

Antiques & Folk Art Shoppe
62 South Rd. - Rt 83
860/749-6197

Somer House Designs & Antqs.
62 South Rd. - Rt 83
860/763-4458

Genora's Furn. & Antiques
40 Maple St.
860/749-3650

Olde Tavern Antiques
491 Main St.
860/763-3688

61 SOMERSVILLE

The Old Mill Inn Bed & Breakfast
63 Maple Street
860/763-1473
Open daily
Rates $85-95

Directions: From the north or south: Take I-91 to Exit 47E, then proceed east on Route 190 five miles to the Somersville traffic signal. Turn right on Maple street, past the old mill (red brick buildings with a waterfall on the left), to the second house on the left, #63 Maple Street. From the west: Take Route 190 east under I-91, then follow the above directions. From the east: Take Route 190 west through Somers, then go 2 miles to the traffic signal at Somersville, then south to #63 Maple Street.

This warm and inviting private home was originally built in the mid-1800s. It was enlarged and renovated 100 years later by an owner of the Mill, who raised a family of seven in its gracious rooms. The second floor guest wing has five bedrooms complete with down comforters, full-size robes and bath sheets, fresh fruit and purified drinking water. There is a quiet, comfortable reading room, a large sun deck which is perfect for soaking up rays or star gazing by telescope at night. Downstairs is another guest room, a parlor with fireplace, and a dining room with hand-painted walls of flowering shrubs and trees, which merge with a similar vista through the window wall that overlooks a deep expanse of lawn bordered by flowering shrubs and trees. The entire property is surrounded by giant maple trees that open onto the green, and guests can wander down the path through the woods to the private beach on the Scantic River. There they'll find hammocks, swings, canoes, picnic tables, fishing and bicycles, and a spa for evening soaking of any sore muscles from the day's activities.

Nearby attractions are only minutes away and include antique shops, restaurants, numerous museums and historic homes. In the immediate area are two golf courses, an equestrian center and a motor speedway.

*Note: David and I stayed with Stephanie and Jim during our antiquing tour to Brimfield, Massachusetts. These guys are so much fun and made our stay something special to remember. We definitely recommend The Old Mill Inn.

62 SOUTHINGTON

Now & Then
1173 Queen St.
860/793-8451

63 SOUTHPORT

Chelsea Antiques
293 Pequot Ave.
203/255-8935

Ten Eyck-Emerich
342 Pequot Ave.
203/259-2559

Pat Guthman Antiques
340 Pequot Ave.
203/259-5743

64 SOUTH WINDSOR

Treasure Trunk Antiques
1212 Sullivan Ave.
860/644-1074

Country Barn Collectibles
1135 Sullivan Ave.
860/644-2826

65 STAFFORD SPRINGS

Mallard's Nest
17 Crystal Lake Rd.
860/684-3837

Smith's Collectibles
107 W. Stafford Rd.
860/684-5844

66 STAMFORD

Antique & Artisan Center
69 Jefferson Street
203/327-6022
Open Mon.-Sat., 10:30-5:30; Sunday 12-5

Directions: Traveling North on I-95 take Exit 8, turn right at second light on Canal Street. Take first left onto Jefferson Street. Antique & Artisan Center is located in second building on the right.

Antique & Artisan Center is housed in a converted historic ice house. Catering to the discriminating shopper, the market is considered to be one of New England's finest. Within 22,000 square feet, over 100 dealers display their wares in spacious room settings. Period and decorative furnishings, exquisite porcelains, glass, silver, art and bronzes are just a sampling of the fine quality pieces you will find here.

Finders Keepers
22 Belltown Rd.
203/357-1180

United House Wrecking
535 Hope St.
203/348-5371

67 STONINGTON

Water Street Antiques
114 Water St.
860/535-1124

Collections
119 Water St.
860/535-9063

Grand & Water Antiques
135 Water St.
860/535-2624

Mary Mahler Antiques
144 Water St.
860/535-2741

Peaceable Kingdom Antiques
145 Water St.
860/535-3434

Orkney & Yost Antiques
148 Water St.
860/535-4402

Neil Bruce Eustace
156 Water St.
860/535-2249

Pendergast N Jones
158 Water St.
860/535-1995

Quester Maritime Gallery
77 Main St.
860/535-3860

Marguerite Riordan
8 Pearl St.
860/535-2511

Findings-A Collection by Patrick Gallagher
68 Water St.
860/535-1330

68 STRATFORD

4 Seasons Antiques
427 Honeyspot Rd.
203/377-5086

Main Street Antiques
2399 Main St.
203/380-2450

Natalie's Antiques & Cllbls.
2403 Main St.
203/377-1483

Stratford Antique Center
400 Honeyspot Rd.
203/378-7754

69 TORRINGTON

Remember When
66 Main St.
860/489-1566

Americana Mart
692 S. Main St.
860/489-5368

Northwood Antiques
47 Main St.
860/489-4544

Wheatfield Antiques
83 Main St.
860/482-3383

70 WALLINGFORD

Wallingford General Antiques
202 Center St.
203/265-5567

Curiosity Shop
216 Center St.
203/294-1975

Wallingford Center St. Antqs.
171 Center St.
203/265-4201

Connecticut Coin Gallery
428 N. Colony St.
203/269-9888

Images-Heirloom Linen
32 N. Colony St.
203/265-7065

Hunt's Courtyart Antiques
38 N. Main St.
203/294-1733

Antique Center of Wallingford
28 S. Orchard St.
203/269-7130

71 WATERBURY

Brass City Antiques
2152 E. Main St.
203/753-1975

Mattatuck's Antiques
156-158 Meriden Rd.
203/754-2707

Century Antiques
1015 W. Main St.
203/573-8092

72 WATERTOWN

Treasures & Trash
755 Thomaston Rd.
860/274-2945

Corner Curio
413 Main St.
860/945-9611

Fannie Rose Vintage Clothing
737 Main St.
860/274-0317

73 WESTBROOK

Westbrook Antiques
1119 Boston Post Rd.
860/399-9892

Shops at Tidewater Creek
433 Boston Post Rd.
860/399-8399

Trolley Square Antiques
1921 Boston Post Rd.
860/399-9249

74 WESTPORT

The Inn at National Hall

Two Post Road West
203/221-1351 or 1-800-NAT-HALL
WebSite:http://www.integra.fr/relaischateaux/nationalhall
Rates $195-475, including breakfast

Neither its sensible name nor its formidable red-brick exterior prepares guests for the delightful mix of whimsy, privacy, history, elegance and luxury that is found in this magnificent 15-bedroom Bed & Breakfast, first-class restaurant, boardroom/conference room and residents' drawing room. The Italianate structure was built in 1873 by Horace Staples, chairman of the First National Bank of Westport, founder of Staples High School and owner/operator of a lumber and hardware business with offices at National Hall, and a fleet of commercial sailing vessels. The Saugatuck River was an active waterway in those days and this sailing fleet was berthed alongside National Hall. The building originally housed the First National Bank on the first floor, the local newspaper on the second floor, and the town's meeting hall on the third floor - hence its unofficial name, National Hall.

In 1884 the third floor public space was converted into classrooms for a short while until Staples High School was completed. The third floor, with its panoramic views of the Saugatuck River, served as the town's location for graduations, dances, theatrical productions, as well as public meetings. At the turn of the century, the space was even large enough for basketball games and other athletic events. National Hall remained the focal point of Westport's business district and social scene until the 1920s. In 1926 the hall was sold for $25,000 (the National Bank had moved by then) and by 1929 the Connecticut State Police maintained offices in the building, sharing it with many of the first tenants. In 1946 the building was renovated and reopened as the Fairfield Furniture Store on all three floors. This business remained for 34 years, closing its doors in 1980.

In 1987 Arthur Tauck, president of Westport-based Tauck Tours, purchased the 120-year-old structure and began its meticulous, five-year, $15 million renovation. Local artists were recruited to do the elaborate stenciling and hand-painted decor throughout the structure. After taking a masterclass from the renown English artist Lyn Le Grice, the local artists were assigned individual rooms and areas to work on. San Francisco-based artists John Wullbrandt and Jeff Patch, with Joszi Meskan Associates, supervised the local artists and are personally responsible for the hand-painted decor in several of the rooms, as well as the mural and interior artwork in the restaurant. One of the most notable features - and everybody's favorite - is the tiny elevator decorated with a *trompe l'oeil* library!

George Subkoff

260 Post Road East
203/227-3515

Ultra-quality upscale is about the only way to describe one of the most famous dealers in Manhattan and in Connecticut collecting circles. George Subkoff's tony showroom is on Post Road in Westport, just past Main Street and the central downtown area, across from a picture postcard New England church. His antiques are not for the faint of heart nor light of wallet. Most are of Continental provenance, with a few early American pieces.

George has been in the business for 35 years, a third-generation antique dealer. He specializes in, as he puts it, "quality, quality, quality" - mostly furniture of the 17th through the mid-19th centuries. A world renown dealer who sells to very well known decorators, George is an avid collector of trompe l'oeil. He often buys privately at auctions and has multiple sources who offer him the select pieces they receive. You never know what you're going to find in his showroom as you browse through the two floors of paintings, lighting fixtures, etc. As George is fond of saying, "Every day is an adventure," whether buying, selling, or hunting.

Jordan Delhaise Gallery
238 Post Rd. E
203/454-1830

Todburn
243 Post Rd. W
203/226-3859

Family Album
283 Post Rd. E
203/227-4888

Glen Leroux Collections
68 Church Ln
203/227-8030

Riverside Antiques Center
265 Riverside Ave.
203/454-3532

Bungalow
4 Sconset Square
203/227-4406

Leslie Allen A Home
3 Kings Hwy N
203/454-4155

Favorite Places To Eat

Coffee An'

343 North Main Street
203/227-3808

This is the end of the line for donut nuts! Go between 7 and 9 a.m., mingle with the crowds, and watch the regulars at the twin counters on either side of the store and at the seats along the front window. They've got their dunking-sipping-reading-the-paper-routine down to a science - you'd never guess there were so many ways to dunk and eat donuts! And take your appetite - there's no way you can eat just one!

The genius responsible for this morning ritual is Derek Coutouras, who starts cooking in the back room every morning at 4 a.m., working at the fry kettles, hanging freshly cooked donuts on dowels to cool, drizzling on the glaze and sprinkling sugar. Up front, Mrs. Coutouras and a team of speed-demon waitresses man the counters and cash register. They can barely keep up with the demand for chocolate, glazed, plain, jelly-filled and powdered sugar donuts, but the real *piece de resistance* is the cinnamon buns - about six inches wide and three inches high, veined with lodes of dark, sweetened cinnamon, with a faintly brittle glaze of sugar - billowing, yeasty spiral too big for dunking or even picking up whole. It takes half an hour just to work your way through it, washed down with three or four cups of good coffee. To die for!

75 WILTON

Wilton Antiques Shows

Managed by Marilyn Gould
MCG Antiques Promotions, Inc.
10 Chicken Street
203/762-3525

The most exciting antiques venue in the east...where more fine dealers show more notable antiques covering a broader spectrum of the market and at a range of prices than can be found anywhere. These outstanding shows offer the opportunity for significant buying; making a trip to Wilton always worthwhile. For a complete listing of show dates and locations call for brochure.

Connecticut Trading Co.
72 Old Ridgefield Rd.
203/834-5008

Old & New Collectibles
146 Danbury Rd.
302/762-8359

Wayside Exchange Antiques
300 Danbury Rd.
203/762-3183

Simply Country
392 Danbury Rd.
203/762-5275

Vallin Galleries
516 Danbury Rd.
203/762-7441

Frances Hills Antiques
1083 Ridgefield Rd.
203/762-3081

Greenwillow Antiques
26 Cannon Rd.
203/762-0244

Emerald Forrest
951 Danbury Rd.
203/544-9441

76 WINDSOR

Charles R. Hart House

1046 Windsor Avenue
860/688-5555
Rates $65 and up
WebSite: http://www.ntplx.net/~harthous

Directions: Take I-91 north or south to Exit 36. Proceed east on Route 178 to Route 159 (.7 mile). Turn right on Route 159 south, proceed .2 mile to Country Lane on the left, enter the first driveway on the left.

Tucked away in Connecticut's oldest town, the Charles R. Hart House was first constructed as a simple farmhouse. It was later added to and embellished with Queen Anne fixtures and appointments. In 1896 Charles R. Hart, a well-known Hartford merchant, carefully restored the house in the colonial revival style by adding luxurious Lincrustra wall coverings, ceramic tiled fireplaces and an elegant Palladian window. The Hart family maintained ownership until the 1940s, when it became the homestead for a pheasant farm! Today it has been fully restored and furnished with period antiques, including an extensive collection of clocks.

Nadeau's Auction Gallery
184 Windsor Ave.
860/246-2444

Olde Windsor Antique Gallery
184 Windsor Ave.
860/249-4300

Patti's Treasures & Antiques
73 Poquonock
860/687-1682

77 WINSTED

Laurel City Coins & Antiques
462 Main St.
860/379-0325

Verde Antiques & Books
64 Main St.
860/379-3135

78 WOODBURY

Wayne Pratt, Inc.
346 Main Street S
203/263-5676
Open daily 10-5, Sun. 12-5

Wayne Pratt, owner of Wayne Pratt Antiques, has long been recognized as one of the most prestigious antique dealers in America and abroad. On occasion, you may find Wayne exhibiting his wonderful "finds" at upscale antique shows across the country. On any other day, you can visit his showroom where you are assured of finding authentic and distinctive pieces of furniture, silver, rugs, art, porcelains, decorative lamps and other antique accessories.

Art & Peggy Pappas Antiques
113 Main St. S
203/266-0374

Gothic Victorian Antiques
137 Main St. S
203/263-0398

Tucker Frey Antiques
451 Main St. S
203/263-5404

Frank Jensen Antiques
142 Middle Road Turnpike
203/263-0908

Country Bazaar
451 Main St. S
203/263-2228

Country Loft
557 Main St. S
203/266-4500

Jean Reeve Antiques
813 Main St. S
203/263-5028

Grass Roots Antiques
12 Main St. N
203/263-3983

British Country Antiques
50 Main St. N
203/263-5100

Woodbury Antiques
745 Main St. N
203/263-5611

Mill House Antiques
1068 Main St. N
203/263-3446

Monique Shay Antiques
920 Main St. S
203/263-3186

Antiques on the Green
6 Green Circle
203/263-3045

Joel Einhorn
819 Main St. N
203/266-9090

Eagle Antiques
615 Main St. N
203/266-4162

Madeline West Antiques
373 Main St. S
203/263-4604

Carriage House
403 Main St. S
203/266-4021

Le Manoir Ctry. French Antqs.
428 Main St. S
203/263-2709

Daria of Woodbury
82 Main St. N
203/263-2431

Taylor Manning Antiques
107 Main St. N
203/263-3330

West Country Antique
334 Washington Rd.
203/263-5741

Rosebush Farm Antiques
267 Good Hill Rd.
203/266-9114

Visiting Historic Lighthouses of Connecticut

Living in a lighthouse ranks right up there with running away to join the circus. Although automation has replaced the jobs of lighthouse keepers, many lighthouses of all shapes and sizes can still be found in Connecticut.

Old Lighthouse Museum, Stonington. A photographic journey to other lighthouses is among the exhibits in the Stonington light station on the east side of the harbor. The stone tower and the keeper's house attached to it were built in 1840.

Sheffield Island Lighthouse, South Norwalk. The slate-roofed granite lighthouse, on a 53-acre island bird sanctuary, has ten rooms on four levels that you can explore. A picnic area outside and regular ferry service to the island make the adventure even more fun.

Several boat operators, such as Captain John's of Waterford/Old Saybrook, provide harbor tours and visits to lighthouses.

The New London Ledge Light, a mile offshore at the entrance to New London's harbor, is among other lighthouses that can be reached by boat. Its beacon and eerie foghorns are automated now, but local legend says that the ghost of an old lighthouse keeper still keeps watch there.

The New London Light, at the entrance to the harbor, is the fifth-oldest in the country, dating from 1760. The original building was replaced by the present structure, an 80-foot octagonal tower, in 1801. Its Fresnel lens, now automated, has flashed its warning signals since before the Civil War.

Other lighthouses a short boat ride away from New London are at Great Captain Island, off Greenwich; Penfield Reef, off Fairfield; Stratford Shoal, off Stratford; Southwest Ledge, off New Haven, and Morgan Point, off Noank.

Avery Point Light, on the Groton campus of the University of Connecticut, was built in 1941 and was never lit. It services the Coast Guard today as a research and development center, finding ways to make every lighthouse do its job better.

For additional information
Call: 1-800-CT-BOUND, 1-800-282-6863

Notes

Delaware

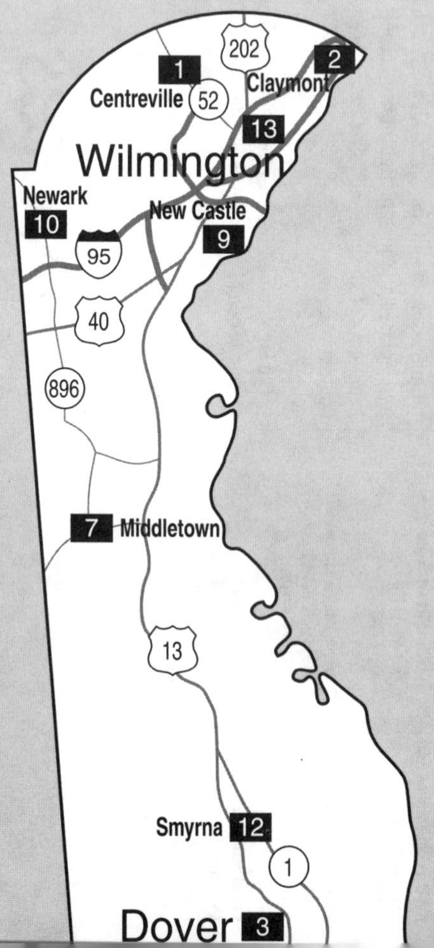
1
Centreville
52
202
2
Claymont
13
Wilmington
Newark
10
New Castle
9
95
40
896
7
Middletown
13
Smyrna
12
1
Dover
3

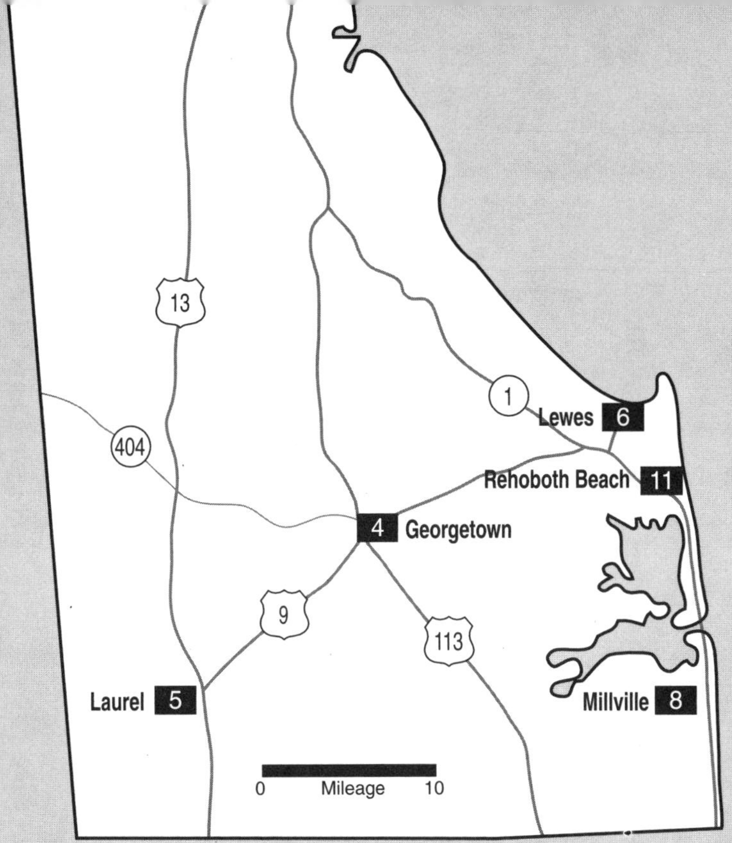

13
404
1
Lewes 6
Rehoboth Beach 11
4 Georgetown
9
113
Laurel 5
Millville 8
0 Mileage 10

Delaware

1 CENTREVILLE

Twice Nice Antiques
5714 Kennett Pike Ste. 22
302/656-8881

Kenneth Lindsey Antiques
5811 Kennett Pike
302/654-3054

Barbara's Antiques & Books
5900 Kennett Pike Ste. 52
302/655-3055

2 CLAYMONT

AAA Claymont Antiques
2811 Philadelphia Pike
302/798-1771

Lamb's Loft
16 Commonwealth Ave.
302/792-9620

3 DOVER

Ancestors Inc.
1025 S. Dupont Hwy.
302/736-3000

Delaware Made
214 S. State St.
302/736-1419

Dover Antique Mart
4621 N. Dupont Hwy.
302/734-7844

Then Again
28 W. Loockerman St.
302/734-1844

Paul's Antique Furniture
4304 N. Dupont Hwy.
302/734-2280

Antiques Art & Collectibles
329 W. Loockerman St.
302/736-0739

Heart Strings
136 W. Loockerman St.
302/674-9016

Kilvington Antiques
103 S. Bradford St.
302/734-9124

4 GEORGETOWN

Bailey's Bargains
Route 113
302/856-2345

Brick Barn Antiques
Route 9
302/684-4442

Candlelight Antiques
406 N. Dupont Hwy.
302/856-7880

Collector's Corner
101 E. Market St.
302/856-7006

Gas Station
546 N. Dupont Hwy.
302/855-1127

Georgetown Antiques Market
105 E. Market St.
302/856-7118

Passwaters Antiques
6 Primrose Lane
302/856-6667

Generations Antiques
Route 9
302/856-6750

5 LAUREL

Front Street is Laurel's oldest street, following an old Indian trail along Broad Creek. The town was plotted in 1802 after the sale of the Indian reservation that had occupied much of the land. The town was named for the abundance of laurel growing in nearby woods. Today it is the site of a rapidly expanding flea market—the largest in Delaware—that complements the traditional farmers' markets and auctions of the region. Laurel is the site of an annual Watermelon Festival.

O'Neal's Antiques
Route 13 & 466
302/875-3391

Delmar Antiques
Route 13
302/875-2200

Golden Door
214 E. Market St.
302/875-5084

6 LEWES

Settled by the Dutch in 1631, Lewes (pronounced "Lewis") is Delaware's oldest settlement and is located on the Delaware Bay rather than on the Atlantic Ocean. Known for its fishing marinas, Lewes is also the southern terminal of the Cape May-Lewes Ferry that crosses the mouth of the Bay between Delaware and New Jersey. Lewes is the site of an enclave of historic buildings and homes, many carefully restored. (see Lewes Historical Complex below)

Lewes Historical District

Burton-Ingram House
Oldest section built ca. 1789. Furnished with Chippendale and Empire antiques.

Blacksmith Shop
An old frame building, now an extension to the gift shop.

Doctor's Office
Greek Revival structure showing a turn-of-the-century doctor's office.

Early Plank House
Early Swedish-style construction, furnished as a settler's cabin. May be the oldest surviving building in the area.

Ellegood House
Serves as a gift shop.

Hiram Burton House
Ca. 1780 and furnished with items from the collection of John Farrace.

Rabbit's Ferry House
An early 18th-century Sussex County farmhouse.

Thompson Country Store
Built around 1800 in Thompsonville, DE. Operated continuously by the Thompson family from 1888 to 1962. Moved to Lewes, repaired and reopened in 1963.

The entrance fee for the Lewes Historical Complex also includes the Lightship Overfalls Museum. A sea-going lightship, like the one that was anchored on the Overfalls Shoal, this lightship used to be the Boston Light. It was given to Lewes in the 1960s. Located on the canal in Lewes by the U.S. Lifesaving Station.

Walking tours of the historic area begin at the Thompson Store, Shipcarpenter St. and W. Third St. Reservations required for groups. Open mid-June until Labor Day, Tuesday-Saturday. For information call the Lewes Historical Society, 302/645-7670.

Chatelaine's Antique Jewelry
108 2nd St.
302/645-1511

Classic Country Antiques
Route 9
302/684-3285

Antique Corner Downtown
142 3rd St.
302/645-7233

Auntie M's Emporium
116 W. 3rd St.
302/644-1804

Auntie M's Emporium
203 B Second Street
302/644-2242

Art & Antiques
130 Highway One Booth #8
302/645-2309

7 MIDDLETOWN

Butler & Cook Antiques
13 E. Main St.
302/378-7022

G. W. Thomas Antiques
2496 N. Dupont Pkwy.
302/378-2414

Daniel Bennett Shutt Inc.
123 W. Main St.
302/378-0890

8 MILLVILLE

Hudson's General Store
Rt. 26 & Road 348
302/539-8709

9 NEW CASTLE

New Castle, on the Delaware River just south of Wilmington, is an undiscovered jewel of the Eastern Seaboard. Cobblestone streets date from the Colonial era, as do the proud homes that line them. "A Day in Old New Castle" is held annually in May, and there are also Christmas time candlelight tours.

New Castle was founded by the Dutch on their way up the Delaware River. It was later conquered by the Swedes and then by the British. In 1682, it was the first landing site in North America of William Penn.

William Penn Guest House
206 Delaware Street
302/328-7736

Named in honor of Pennsylvania's Quaker founder, William Penn, this guest house was built in the same year of Penn's arrival to New Castle in 1682. In fact, Penn himself once stayed at the home as an overnight guest. Constructed of brick, this three-story building has been restored to its original architectural features, including wide-planked floors. Three guest rooms are available overlooking the green in the center of town. Revolutionary War sites, walking tours, shopping and dining are within walking distance.

Armitage Inn
2 The Strand
302/328-6618

The Armitage Inn sets on the bank of the Delaware River only a few feet from the spot where William Penn first stepped into the new world. Built in 1732, the inn includes the main house, a wing, and a garden cottage. It is believed that the inn began life as a one-room dwelling built during the 1600s. The room was incorporated into its expansion in 1732. Within this room is an original brick walk-in cooking fireplace. Guest rooms are historically decorated and furnished with period antiques. Guests are welcome to enjoy the common areas including the parlor, library, screened porch and garden.

Bittersweet
419 Delaware St.
302/324-1808

Yesterday's Rose
204 Delaware St.
302/322-3001

Lynch Antiques
1 2nd St.
302/328-5576

Cobblestones
406 Delaware St.
302/322-5088

Raven's Nest
204 Delaware St.
302/325-2510

10 NEWARK

Chapel Street Antiques
195 S. Chapel St.
302/366-0700

Classic Crafter
5 Polly Drummond Shopping Ctr.
302/369-1160

Yesterdays Treasures
2860 Ogletown Rd.
302/292-8362

11 REHOBOTH BEACH

Affordable Antiques
4300 Highway One
302/227-5803

Antiques Village Mall
221 Highway One
302/644-0842

Treasure House
3406 Highway One
302/227-2401

12 SMYRNA

Smyrna began about 1700 as an English Quaker settlement called Duck Creek Village, one mile north of the current town. The Smyrna Landing wharfs were centers of commerce in the 1800s. Many examples of Federal and Victorian architecture can be found in the town. Smyrna is eight miles west of the Delaware Bay and Bombay Hook Wildlife Refuge.

A Bit of the Past
3511 S. Dupont Blvd.
302/653-9963

Attic Treasures
2119 S. Dupont Blvd.
302/653-6566

Eileen Gant Antiques
5527 Dupont Pkwy.
302/653-8996

Smyrna Antiques Mart
3114 S. Dupont Blvd.
302/659-0373

Tin Sedan
12 N. Main St.
302/653-3535

C & J Antiques
Route 13
302/653-4903

What Nott Shop
5786 Dupont Hwy.
302/653-3855

13 WILMINGTON

Sheepish Grin, Inc.
Nancy and Bill Settel
Open by appointment
302/995-2614
Fax: 302/995-2899

I first met Bill and Nancy at the Heart of Country Show in Nashville, Tennessee. For those of you who read about Sheepish Grin in last years edition, I had mistakenly called Nancy's husband by the wrong name-"George"-instead of Bill. I wanted to set the record straight before the rumors started flying-Nancy was at that time and still is married to Bill. There has been no divorce and re-marriage in the family, although Nancy jokingly says that George could be the name of her husband in her next life and that I'm just ahead of my time. None-the-less, for now it's BILL. And BILL and NANCY are a great team.

They specialize in early painted country furniture and accessories such as old tins, iron, pantry boxes, rag dolls and primitive angels. They also are the manufacturers of the original Colonial Grunge Nubbie Candles (18th-century-looking candles). These candles are fabulous decorator items, and the Settels sell them wholesale to shops all over the world and to folks like me - I have 3 of each scent. (I still think Bill looks like "a George").

"sweet potato cabin" antiques and mighty fine folk art
Shop: 302/995-2614
Home: 302/995-1808
Open By Appointment

Directions: One block off I-95.

Nancy and Bill Settel, owners of the Sheepish Grin, have just opened one of the best shops, or should I say "warehouses," for early country furnishings in the U.S. and quiet possibly the world! Okay, so I'm getting a little carried away with that one, but their "stuff" is so wonderful! Sugar buckets, blanket chests, baskets, cupboards, cabinets and much, much more - most in original paint. An absolute must stop-but don't forget to call first.

Golden Eagle
1905 N. Market St.
302/651-3480

Brandywine Treasure Shop
1913 N. Market St.
302/656-4464

Next To New Shop
2009 Market St.
302/658-0020

Holly Oak Corner Store
1600 Philadelphia Pike
302/798-0255

Brandywine Antiques
2601 Pin Oak Dr.
302/475-8398

Country Corner
641 W. Newport Pike
302/998-2304

Wright's Antiques
802 W. Newport Pike
302/994-3002

Doyle Antiques
601 S. Maryland Ave.
302/994-1424

Merrill's Antiques
100 Northern Ave.
302/994-1765

Vintage Records
604 N. Market Street Mall
302/656-2444

Interesting Side Trips

Winterthur
Museum Garden Library
1-800-448-3883

Henry Francis du Pont's world-renowned collection of decorative arts made or used in America from 1640-1860, are showcased in two buildings on the property. The Galleries at Winterthur offer an introductory exhibition, Perspectives on the Decorative Arts in Early America. The Period Rooms offer visitors guided tours of rooms decorated as they might have been in days gone by. Spread over almost 1,000 acres, the Garden features native and exotic plants, ponds, woods and meadowland. Year-round programming includes the annual Point-to-Point races in May and the Yuletide tour. Reservations required for some tours. Located on DE 52, six miles northwest of Wilmington.

Hagley Museum
302/658-2400

Features the original du Pont mills, estate and gardens on 230 acres along the Brandywine River. Daily demonstrations and exhibits depict American life at home and at work in the 19th century. First du Pont family home, French garden, antique automobiles, first Dupont Company office and working machine shop highlight the visit. Three miles northwest of Wilmington via DE Routes 52 and 141.

Florida

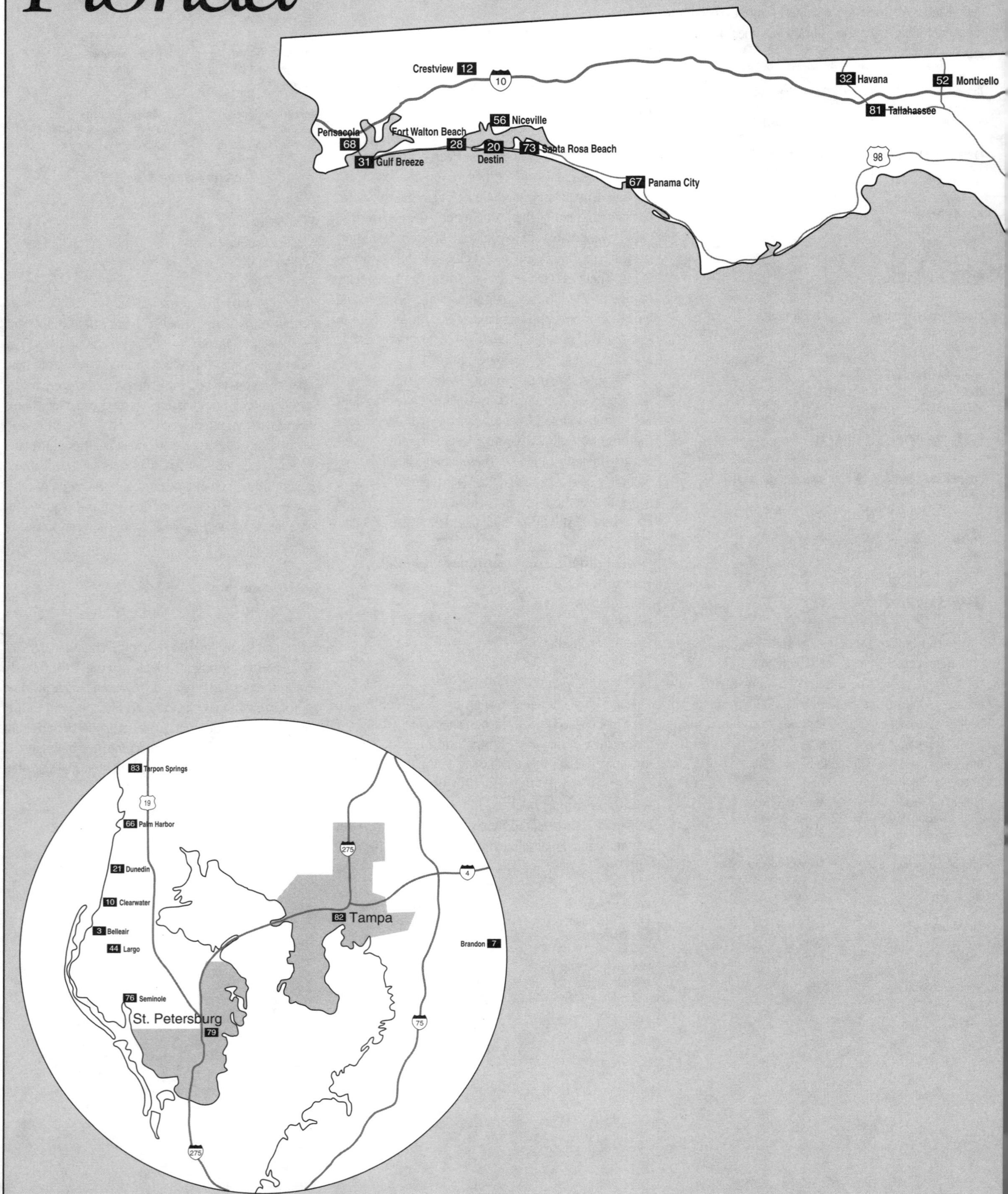
Crestview 12
10
32 Havana
52 Monticello
81 Tallahassee
56 Niceville
Pensacola
68
Fort Walton Beach
28
20
73 Santa Rosa Beach
31 Gulf Breeze
Destin
98
67 Panama City
83 Tarpon Springs
19
66 Palm Harbor
275
21 Dunedin
4
10 Clearwater
82 Tampa
3 Belleair
44 Largo
Brandon 7
76 Seminole
St. Petersburg
79
75
275

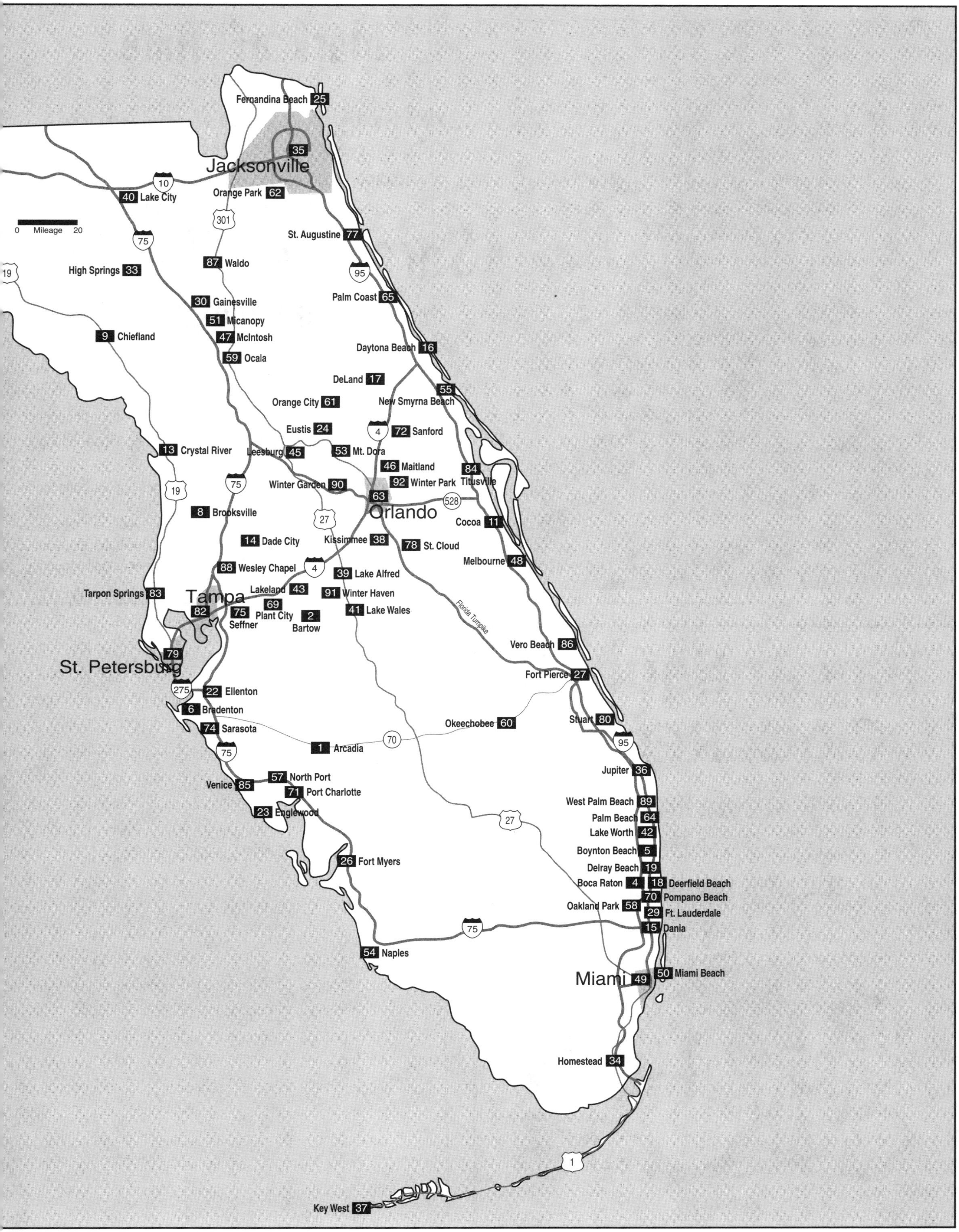

Fernandina Beach 25
35
Jacksonville
10
40 Lake City
Orange Park 62
301
0 Mileage 20
75
St. Augustine 77
87 Waldo
19
High Springs 33
95
30 Gainesville
Palm Coast 65
51 Micanopy
47 McIntosh
9 Chiefland
59 Ocala
Daytona Beach 16
DeLand 17
55
Orange City 61
New Smyrna Beach
Eustis 24
4
72 Sanford
13 Crystal River
Leesburg 45
53 Mt. Dora
46 Maitland
84
Winter Garden 90
92 Winter Park
Titusville
19
75
63
528
8 Brooksville
Orlando
27
Cocoa 11
14 Dade City
Kissimmee 38
78 St. Cloud
Melbourne 48
88 Wesley Chapel
4
39 Lake Alfred
Tarpon Springs 83
Tampa
Lakeland 43
91 Winter Haven
82
69
75 Plant City
2
41 Lake Wales
Seffner
Bartow
Florida Turnpike
Vero Beach 86
79
St. Petersburg
Fort Pierce 27
275
22 Ellenton
6 Bradenton
Okeechobee 60
Stuart 80
74 Sarasota
1 Arcadia
70
95
75
Jupiter 36
57 North Port
Venice 85
71 Port Charlotte
West Palm Beach 89
23 Englewood
Palm Beach 64
27
Lake Worth 42
Boynton Beach 5
26 Fort Myers
Delray Beach 19
Boca Raton 4
18 Deerfield Beach
70 Pompano Beach
Oakland Park 58
29 Ft. Lauderdale
75
15 Dania
54 Naples
50 Miami Beach
Miami
49
Homestead 34
1
Key West 37

1 ARCADIA

Townsend Antiques
5 E. Oak St.
941/494-2137

Hitching Post Antiques
24 W. Oak St.
941/993-9963

Maddy's Antiques
101 W. Oak St.
941/494-2500

Orange Blssm. & Picket Fence
15 S. Polk Ave.
941/491-0008

Glacier Melt Antqs. & Unusuals
114 West Oak St.
941/993-4489

Old Opera House Museum
106 West Oak St.
941/494-7010

Hidden Treasures
33 W. Magnolia Hwy. 70
941/491-0060

Forgotten Things
132 West Oak St.
941/491-0053

The Crested Duck
121 W. Oak St.
941/491-8600

Mary's Attic
12 W. Oak St.
941/993-2533

The Collectors Addict
109 West Oak St.
941/993-2228

My Friend & Me
305 W. Oak St.
941/993-4438

Arcadia Tea Room
117 W. Oak St.
941/494-2424

Three Amish Shoppe & More
12 N. Desoto Ave.
941/993-4151

2 BARTOW

Dolene's Downtown
290 E. Main St.
941/534-3311

Apple Blossom
318 E. Main St.
941/534-1717

Philip's Antiques
330 E. Main St.
941/533-2365

Yates Antiques
875 E. Main St.
941/533-7635

Bartow Antiques
280 S. Wilson Ave.
941/534-1094

3 BELLEAIR

Belleair Bluffs Antiques
428 Indian Rocks Rd. N
813/586-1488

Treasures & Dolls
518 Indian Rocks Rd. N
813/584-7277

Collum Antiques
580 Indian Rocks Rd. N
813/581-6585

Posh Pineapple Antiques
560 Indian Rocks Rd. N
813/586-3006

Royal Crown Antiques Etc.
562 Indian Rocks Rd. N
813/584-6525

Merndale Antiques
562D Indian Rocks Rd. N
813/581-1100

Encore Events
562 E. Indian Rocks Rd. N
813/585-7242

Lejan's Antiques
570 Indian Rocks Rd. N
813/586-7515

Neil's Furniture/Antique Shop
568 Indian Rocks Rd. N
813/586-3232

Antiques & Specialities
566 Indian Rocks Rd. N
813/584-4370

Jean's Locker Collectibles
596 Indian Rocks Rd. N #17A
813/585-8460

Elaine's Antiques
596 Indian Rocks Rd. N
813/584-6143

Back Door Antiques
596 Indian Rocks Rd. N
813/581-2780

Antiques & Design
560 Indian Rocks Rd. N
813/584-8843

Victoria's Parlour
596 Indian Rocks Rd. N
813/581-0519

Belleair Coins
730 Indian Rocks Rd. N
813/581-6827

Music Box
784 Indian Rocks Rd. N
813/581-1359

Jewel Antiques Mall
2601 Jewel Rd.
813/585-5568

Provence Art & Antiques
2620 Jewell Rd.
813/581-5754

4 BOCA RATON

Village Rose
7044 Beracasa Way
561/750-7070

Country Tyme Antiques
672 Glades Rd.
561/391-7749

Art Nouveau Antiques
6000 A Glades Rd. #168
561/347-2885

Find A Deal Antiques Gallery
2621 N. Federal Hwy.
561/362-9022

C-Trois & Co.
2831 N. Federal Hwy.
561/347-1169

Unusual Usuals
2831 N. Federal Hwy.
561/367-6083

Maybe Shop Antiques
221 E. Palmetto Park Rd.
561/392-5680

Luigi's Objects D'Art Gallery
6018 SW 18th Street, Ste. C9
561/394-4968

Country Pine
161 N.W. 11th St.
561/368-8470

5 BOYNTON BEACH

Favorite Places To Eat

Cracker Barrel Old Country Store
I-95 & Woolbright Road, Exit 43
561/736-6001

6 BRADENTON

Leach-Wells Galleries Antqs.
316 12th St. W
941/747-5453

Dotty's Depot
1421 12th Ave. W
941/749-1421

Antiques on the Avenue
2931 Manatee Ave. W
941/749-1360

George M. Hicks Antiques
5206 Manatee Ave. W
941/749-1866

Favorite Places To Eat

Cracker Barrel Old Country Store
I-75 & State Rd. 64, Exit 42
941/746-7886

7 BRANDON

Nostalgia Station Antiques
514 Limona Rd.
813/681-5473

Victoria's Attic Antiques
714 W. Lumsden Rd.
813/685-6782

Somewhere In Time
720 W. Lumsden Rd.
813/684-0588

Remember When Antiques
408 N. Parsons Ave.
813/654-8323

About Antiques
728 W. Lumsden Rd.
813/684-2665

Sweet Memories Antiques
608 N. Parsons Ave.
813/685-3728

Cottage Corner Antiques
616 N. Parsons Ave.
813/654-2193

American Country Antiques
745 Sandy Creek Dr.
813/681-9592

8 BROOKSVILLE

Barnette's Antique Mall
2 N. Broad St.
352/544-0910

Antiques at the Corner
10431 Broad St.
352/796-7518

Hillhouse Antiques
406 E. Liberty St.
352/796-8489

Cabin Creek Antiques
770 E. Jefferson St.
352/799-8770

Red Rooster Antiques & Cllbls.
838 E. Jefferson St.
352/799-4636

Old World Antiques
31 S. Main St.
352/796-2729

Favorite Places To Eat

Cracker Barrel Old Country Store
I-75 & S.R. 50, Exit 61
352/799-3101

9 CHIEFLAND

Kip's Trading Post
914 North Young Blvd. (U.S. 19)
352/493-1083
Mon.-Sat. 9:30-5, Sat. 9:30-2

Directions: Located on U.S. 19/98, at the intersection of 129, 27, 19/98. The middle of Chiefland between White Ford and the high school.

Kip's Trading Post is one of those hunt and dig kind of stores. It's especially suited for dealers who often find the prize amidst all the other items available. The store is noted for turning up some pretty neat "stuff" since a lot of their merchandise comes from local folks (you never know what granny had stuffed in her attic.). And, if you buy too much, you can even rent a U-Haul from Todd to get it all back home.

10 CLEARWATER

Able Antiques
1686 Clearwater Largo Rd.
813/581-5583

Banyan Tree's Trunk
1775 Clearwater Largo Rd.
813/587-0799

Pack Rat Corner
617 Cleveland
813/443-2721

Singletree Antiques
1411 Cleveland
813/447-1445

Iron Gate Antiques
703 Court St.
813/443-4730

Savoy Antiques
924 N. McMullen Booth Rd.
813/726-1111

Antique Pine Imports
13585 49th St. N
813/572-0956

11 COCOA

Country Life
313 Brevard Ave.
407/639-3794

Forget-Me-Not
404 Brevard Ave. #A
407/632-4700

Antiques & Old Lace Mall
1803 N. Cocoa Blvd.
407/631-5787

Gould's Old Time Gen. Store
307 Delannoy Ave.
407/632-2481

Past Gas Co.
308 Willard St.
407/636-0449

12 CRESTVIEW

Favorite Places To Eat

Cracker Barrel Old Country Store
I-10 & State Rd. 85, Exit 12
904/682-8804

13 CRYSTAL RIVER

Heritage Antiques Mall
103 N.W. U.S. Highway 19
352/563-5597

Trader Jack's Antiques
706 S.E. U.S. Highway 19
352/795-5225

Crystal River Antiques
756 N.E. U.S. Highway 19
352/563-1121

Cobblestone Alley Antiques
657 Citrus Ave.
352/795-0060

14 DADE CITY

Ivy Cottage
14110 7th St.
352/523-0019

Remember When Antq. Mall
14129 7th St.
352/521-6211

Church Street Antiques
14117 8th St.
352/523-2422

Corner Emporium
14136 8th St.
352/567-1990

Sugarcreek Antiques
37846 Meridian Ave.
352/567-7712

15 DANIA

Mark First Antique Guns
1 N. Federal Hwy.
954/925-0856

Antique Center of Dania Inc.
3 N. Federal Hwy.
954/922-5467

Antique Jewels by Paula
3 N. Federal Hwy.
954/926-1060

E & F Antiques & Collectibles
3 N. Federal Hwy.
954/929-3119

Gallery Picture Frames, Inc.
3 N. Federal Hwy.
954/920-2086

Goldie Kossow Antiques, Inc.
3 N. Federal Hwy.
954/921-5569

Linda's Antique Collectibles
3 N. Federal Hwy.
954/920-2030

M. France's Past Pleasures
3 N. Federal Hwy.
954/921-0022

Michael T. Pye
3 N. Federal Hwy.
954/922-5467

Murray's Antiques
3 N. Federal Hwy.
954/921-0470

Crown Antiques
10 N. Federal Hwy. #A
954/923-4764

Lorraine's Collectibles
13 N. Federal Hwy.
954/920-2484

Memorable Moments Antiques
15 N. Federal Hwy.
954/929-7922

Rose Antiques
17 N. Federal Hwy.
954/921-0474

Cameo Antiques
18 N. Federal Hwy.
954/929-0101

Athena Gallery
19 S. Federal Hwy.
954/921-7697

Collectomania
19 N. Federal Hwy.
954/926-7999

Daddy's Antiques & Cllbls.
19 N. Federal Hwy.
954/920-4001

Dania Antq. & Jewelry Arcade
19 N. Federal Hwy.
954/925-9400

Doe's Treasures
19 N. Federal Hwy.
954/923-3081

Glass Antique Or Not
19 N. Federal Hwy.
954/925-7667

Jackie's Fine Things
19 N. Federal Hwy.
954/456-5655

Antique Tony's & Furniture
24 N. Federal Hwy.
954/920-4095

Dania Antique Emporium
25 N. Federal Hwy.
954/927-1040

Tamara's Treasures
25 N. Federal Hwy.
954/927-1040

Pyewackett's Antiques
26 N. Federal Hwy.
954/926-7975

The Garden Path
27A N. Federal Hwy.
954/929-7766

Attic Treasures
32 N. Federal Hwy.
954/920-0280

Aries Antiques
47 N. Federal Hwy.
954/923-2239

Audrey Arovas Antiques
47 N. Federal Hwy.
954/920-0706

Grand Central Station
47 N. Federal Hwy.
954/925-8181

Memory Lane
52 N. Federal Hwy.
954/922-0616

Davidson Antiques
53 N. Federal Hwy.
954/923-8383

Beaudet Antiques
56 N. Federal Hwy.
954/922-5040

Royal Red Antiques
56 N. Federal Hwy.
954/925-6111

English Accent Antiques
57 N. Federal Hwy.
954/923-8383

Allison Jaffee Antiques
60 N. Federal Hwy.
954/923-3939

Antique Fancies
60 N. Federal Hwy.
954/929-4473

Antique Galleries Mall
60 N. Federal Hwy.
954/920-2801

Celia & Louis Kleinman Antqs.
60 N. Federal Hwy.
954/920-2801

Iris Fields of Dania
60 N. Federal Hwy.
954/926-5658

F & N Antiques
63 N. Federal Hwy.
954/923-3910

Scintillations Antiques Ltd.
67 N. Federal Hwy.
954/921-8325

Wilburn's Inc.
68 N. Federal Hwy.
954/922-3188

Gordon's of London
71 N. Federal Hwy.
954/927-0210

Hattie's Antiques & Collectibles
3 N. Federal Hwy.
954/929-4290

Ambiance Antiques & Design
19 N. Federal Hwy. Booth #7
954/925-9400

Antiquety Farms Antiques
6 N.W. 1st Avenue
954/925-0402

A to Z Antiques
11 N. Federal Hwy.
954/927-2707

Aunty Q's, Inc.
27 N. Federal Hwy.
954/925-3446

Barbra's Place, Inc.
249 S. Federal Hwy.
954/927-8083

Connie's Place
3 N. Federal Hwy.
954/922-5467

Dick's Toys & Collectibles
3 N. Federal Hwy.
954/922-5467

Friendly Shoppers
3 N. Federal Hwy.
954/922-5467

Gary Slade
47 N. Federal Hwy.
954/925-8181

House of Hirsch Antiques
75 N. Federal Hwy.
954/925-0818

J. J. Haag, Ltd.
3 N. Federal Hwy.
954/922-5467

Maurizio's Antiques
8 N. Federal Hwy.
954/929-9954

Murray's Antiques
3 N. Federal Hwy.
954/921-0470

Talya's Antiques
3 N. Federal Hwy.
954/923-6512

Anzardo's Fine Arts & Antiques
14 N.W. 1st Avenue
954/922-6140

16 DAYTONA BEACH

Favorite Places To Eat

Cracker Barrel Old Country Store
I-95 & U.S. 92, Exit 87
904/248-0034

17 DE LAND

Cratina's Frameshop & Antqs.
108 S. Woodland Blvd.
904/736-8392

Muse Book Shop
112 S. Woodland Blvd.
904/734-0278

Rivertown Antique Mall
114 S. Woodland Blvd.
904/738-5111

De Land Antique Mall
142 S. Woodland Blvd.
904/740-1188

Sylva's Antiques
428 S. Woodland Blvd.
904/734-4821

Angevine & Son
2999 S. Woodland Blvd.
904/734-6347

Estate Furniture
114 N. Woodland Blvd.
904/740-1104

Our Hearts In The Country
136 N. Woodland Blvd.
904/736-4528

Outhouse Antiques
1765 N. Woodland Blvd.
904/736-1575

Florida Victorian Archtl
112 W. Georgia Ave.
904/734-9300

18 DEERFIELD BEACH

A Moment In Time Antiques & Collectibles
3575 West Hillsboro Blvd.
954/427-7223
Tue.-Sat. 10:30-5:30

Directions: From I-95 go to Hillsboro Blvd., then head west to Powerline Road in the Shoppes of Deer Creek.

Shellee grew up in the art business. Her dad was a 3rd generation art dealer, so it was only natural that she follow in his footsteps. In her shop, the art is carefully blended with a selection of other wonderful things. Her exquisite taste and flair for decorating are evident throughout this beautifully arranged store. In settings reminiscent of *Country Living* magazine, you'll find country, early American and painted furniture accented with pottery, copper pots, old tools, washboards and other old iron and rustic pieces. If you're not into country, there are plenty more offerings of limoges, Royal Dalton, vintage jewelry and such.

Absolutely Fabulous
337 S.E. 15th Terrace
954/725-0620

Antiques Unusual
100 S. Federal Hwy.
954/421-8920

Cove Cottage Antiques Inc
1645 S.E. 3rd St.
954/429-0408

Joyce M Dudley Antiques
839 S.E. 9th St.
954/428-8500

19 DELRAY BEACH

Martha T Bartoo
430 E. Atlantic Ave.
561/279-0399

Estate Galleries
1201 N. Federal Hwy.
561/276-0029

Antique Buying Center
1201 N. Federal Hwy.
561/379-7360

Second Chance Emporium
2101 N. Federal Hwy.
561/276-6380

Finders Keepers Antiques
88 S.E. 4th Ave.
561/272-7160

Antiques Plus
130 N. Federal Highway
No Phone Listed

20 DESTIN

Smith's Antique Mall
12500 Emerald Coast Pwy.
904/654-1484

Clements Antiques of Fla.
9501 U.S. Hwy. 98 W.
904/837-1473

Antiques on the Harbor
202 Hwy. 98 E. (Near the Harborwalk)
904/837-6463

21 DUNEDIN

P Kay's Downtown
359 Scotland St.
813/734-1731

The Highlands
362 Scotland St.
813/547-1637

Cindy Lou's
330 Main St.
813/736-3393

Vyctoria's
365 Main St.
813/736-0778

22 ELLENTON

Old Feed Store Antique Mall
4407 Highway 301
941/729-1379
Mon.-Sat. 10-5 (closed Sun.)

Directions: Traveling I-75, take exit 43. Go west 9/10 mile on Highway 310. Turn left on 45th Avenue.

You'll never guess where this shop got its name. Okay, so I gave you a hint. Somewhere in the early to mid 1920s, the Old Feed Store Antique Mall was just as its name implies, the old feed store in Ellenton. Today, you'll find no evidence of grains, seeds or beans. What you will find are 65 dealers displaying a wide selection of oak, mahogany and walnut furnishings, exquisite glass and crystal items, jewelry, mirrors, china and much more.

(The Gamble Plantation, a historic mansion and grounds is located approximately 200 yards from the mall.)

23 ENGLEWOOD

Rujean's Cllbls. Past & Present
Corner Rt. 41 & Biscane Dr.
941/426-5418

Linda's Charming Choices
145 W. Dearborn St.
941/474-1230

The Paisley Pelican Artisan
447-449 W. Dearborn St.
941/473-2055

Coins, Jewelry & Antiques
140 N. Indiana Ave. (S.R. 776)
941/475-4740

"A Bull in a China Shop"
395 W. Dearborn St.
941/474-5004

24 EUSTIS

Cowboys
120 N. Bay St.
352/589-1449

Merry's Silver Vault
32 S. Eustis St.
352/589-4321

Old South Antique Mall
320 S. Grove St.
352/357-5200

Palm Village Shoppes
100 E. Magnolia Ave.
352/589-7256

Ye Olde Kracker House
517 E. Orange Ave.
352/357-3291

25 FERNANDINA BEACH

Yesterday's Child
14 N. 4th St.
904/277-0061

Fleur De Lis
14 S. 2nd St.
904/261-1150

Eight Flags Antq. Warehouse
21 N. 2nd St.
904/277-7006

Country Store Antiques
219 S. 8th St.
904/261-2633

Plantation Shop
4828 First Coast Hwy.
904/261-2030

Amelia Island Antique Mart
1105 S. 8th St.
904/277-3815

26 FORT MYERS

Old Times Antiques
1815 Fowler St.
941/334-7200

Yesterday & Today
1609 Hendry St.
941/334-6572

Flowers To Fifties
2229 Main St.
941/334-2443

Margie's Antique Market Place
2216 Martin Luther King Blvd.
941/332-3321

Heartland Antiques
12680 McGregor Blvd.
941/482-3979

Valerie Sanders Antiques
12680 McGregor Blvd.
941/433-3229

Blough's Antiques
12680 McGregor Blvd. #3
941/482-6300

Era Antiques
12691 McGregor Blvd.
941/481-8154

Bayview Collectibles & Antique
12695 McGregor Blvd.
941/432-0988

Absolutely The Best Antq. Emp.
12695 McGregor Blvd. #1
941/489-2040

Judy's Antiques
12710 McGregor Blvd.
941/481-9600

George Brown Antiques
12710 McGregor Blvd.
941/482-5101

Tit For Tat This & That
12717-2 McGregor Blvd.
941/489-3255

Laura's Aura
2218 1st Street
941/334-6633

Pappy Antique N' Good Junque
1079 N. Tamiami Trl
941/995-0004

Bea's Antique Shop
1535 N. Tamiami Trail
941/995-0130

Favorite Places To Eat

Cracker Barrel Old Country Store
I-75 & State Road 80, Exit 25
941/693-2244

27 FORT PIERCE

Fredericks Antiques
2872 N. U.S. Highway 1
561/464-0048

Red Rooster Attic
3128 N. U.S. Highway 1
561/466-8344

Treasure Coast Antique Mall
4343 N. U.S. Highway 1
561/468-2006

Red Barn Antiques Mall
4809 N. U.S. Highway 1
561/468-1901

Antiques Etcetera
211 Orange Ave.
561/464-7300

Olde Town Antique Mall
116 N. 2nd St.
561/468-9700

Favorite Places To Eat

Cracker Barrel Old Country Store
I-95 & State Road 70, Exit 65
407/595-9393

28 FORT WALTON BEACH

King Arthur Classic's
30 Eglin Pkwy. SE
904/243-9197

Rose Harbor Interiors
85A Eglin Pkwy. NE
904/664-0345

Garden Gate Antique Mall
85B Eglin Pkwy. NE
904/664-0164

Fran's Treasure Trove
167 A&B Eglin Pky. NE
904/243-2227

Willow Tree
169B Elgin Pkwy. NE
904/243-4991

Abrams Antiques
86 N. Eglin Pkwy.
904/664-0770

Bailey's Antiques
136 Miracle Strip Pkwy.
904/244-2424

Darby Mitchell Antiques
158 Miracle Strip Pkwy.
904/244-4069

White Sands Antiques
161 Miracle Strip Pkwy.
904/243-6398

Country Junkshun
1303 Beverly St.
904/864-4735

Abrams Antique Cottage
147 Hollywood Blvd. NE
904/664-0011

Rose Garden Antiques
151 A Elgin Parkway
904/243-2268

Fort Walton Beach Antq. Mall
167 Miracle Strip Parkway SE
904/243-6255

Magnolia Tree
151 Eglin Parkway SE
904/244-2727

Village Emporium
149 Hollywood Blvd. NE
904/302-0111

Abrams Antiques
86 N. Eglin Parkway
904/664-0770

Li'l Darlings by JW
100 Beal Parkway SW
904/244-2551

29 FT. LAUDERDALE

Carl Stoffers Antiques
3699 N. Dixie Hwy.
954/564-9077

Gemini Antiques
4117 N. Dixie Hwy.
954/563-9767

Jims Antiques Ltd
1201 N. Federal Hwy.
954/565-6556

June Sharp Antiques
3000 N. Federal Hwy.
954/565-8165

Lilywhites Antiques & Interior
3020 N. Federal Hwy.
954/537-9295

Down East Antiques
3020 N. Federal Hwy.
954/566-5023

Malouf Tower Antiques
2114 S. Federal Hwy.
954/523-5511

Teddy Bear Antiques
4136 SW 64th Ave.
954/583-7577

Antiques Limited
2125 S. Federal Hwy.
954/525-3729

Glausiers Antiques
2130 S. Federal Hwy.
954/524-3524

Las Olas Arts & Antiques
611 E. Las Olas Blvd.
954/527-2742

Coo-Coo's Nest
1511 E. Las Olas Blvd.
954/524-2009

Lomar Collectibles
3291 W. Sunrise Blvd.
954/581-1004

Victorian Reflections Inc.
1348 Weston Rd.
954/389-4498

Perry & Perry
3313 N.E. 33rd St.
954/561-7707

30 GAINESVILLE

Browse Shop
433 S. Main St.
352/378-5121

Reruns
807 W. University Ave.
352/336-0063

My Mother's Place
Thornebrook Vlg.
2441 N. W. 43rd St. #24A
352/376-4580

Favorite Places To Eat

Cracker Barrel Old Country Store
I-75 & Archer Rd., Exit 75
352/375-2424

31 GULF BREEZE

Annais Antique Mall
4531 Gulf Breeze Parkway
904/916-1122

32 HAVANA

Antique Center
104 N. Main St.
904/539-0529

Berry Patch
117 6th Ave.
904/539-6988

H & H Antiques
302 N. Main St.
904/539-6886

Antiques & Accents
213 N.W. 1st St.
904/539-0073

My Secret Garden
127 E. 7th Ave.
904-539-8729

McLauchlin House
201 W. 7th Ave.
904/539-0901

Hallway Annex
110 E. 7th Ave.
904/539-8822

Sticks 'N Stitches
108 E. 7th Ave.
904/539-8070

Kudzu Plantation
102 E. 7th Ave.
904/539-0877

Cannery
115 E. 8th Ave.
904/539-3800

Antique Center
104 N. Main Street
904/539-0529

33 HIGH SPRINGS

Bus Stop Antiques
205 N.W. Santa Fe Blvd.
904/454-2478

Burch Antiques Too
60 N. Main St.
904/454-1500

High Springs Antiques Center
145 N. Main St.
904/454-4770

Sophie's Antiques & Gifts
215 N. Main St.
904/454-2022

Wisteria Corner Antq. Mall
225 N. Main St.
904/454-3555

Main St. Antique Mall
10 S. Main St.
904/454-2700

Palm Springs Antiques
220 S Main St.
904/454-5389

Platz Antiques & Collectibles
625 S. Main St.
904/454-4193

Victorian Village
1700 U.S. 441 S
904/454-1835

34 HOMESTEAD

Bayleaf Peddler
813 N. Homestead Blvd.
305/247-9200

Renaissance Interiors
69 N.W. 4th St.
305/247-5283

Albury Rd. Antiques
115 N. Krome Ave.
305/242-1366

Book Nest
115 N. Krome Ave.
305/242-1366

Forever Antiques
115 N. Krome Ave.
305/248-0588

Sian San Antiques & Cllbls.
115 N. Krome Ave.
305/246-8010

Yesterday's Memories
115 N. Krome Ave.
305/247-0191

Time Line Vintage Clothing
115 N. Krome Ave.
305/248-6511

Jo Crafton Antiques
123 N. Krome Ave.
305/245-1700

Crouse's Homestead Antiques
137 N. Krome Ave.
305/247-5555

Cam's Antiques
140 N. Krome Ave.
305/245-3320

Jacobsen's Antiques & Cllbls.
144 N. Krome Ave.
305/247-4745

Autumn Leaf Cottage
229 N. Krome Ave.
305/246-3513

Roby's Antiques & Collectibles
229 N. Krome Ave.
305/246-3513

Cobblestone Antiques
501 N. Krome Ave.
305/245-8831

Antique Clocks & Gifts
1316 N. Krome Ave.
305/247-9555

Ages Ago
102 S. Krome Ave.
305/245-7655

35 JACKSONVILLE

Carriage House Antique Mall
8955 Beach Blvd.
904/641-5500
Mon.-Sat. 10-6, Sun. 12-6

Directions: Located on Beach Blvd. at Southside Blvd.

Carriage House Antique Mall offers visitors that "Jack-of-all-trades" atmosphere with its spectrum of items and services. Once inside the mall, you can roam through aisles of glassware including decanters, goblets, china, crystal, and depression pieces. A wide selection of collectibles and gifts are also housed within the mall.

Tappin Book Mine
705 Atlantic Blvd.
904/246-1388

Gallery of Antiques
7952 Normandy Blvd. #1
904/783-6787

Antique House
1841 Dean Rd.
904/721-0886

Audrey's Attic at Five Points
1036 Park St.
904/355-8642

Somewhere In Time Antiques
1341 University Blvd. N.
904/743-7022

Olde Gallery
3921 Hendricks Ave.
904/396-2581

Springfield Antiques
1755 N. Pearl St.
904/355-2897

Canterbury House Antiques
1776 Canterbury St.
904/387-1776

Little Shop of Antiques
2010 Forbes St.
904/389-9900

Antiques Are Forever
2 Independent Dr.
904/358-8800

Ina's Antiques
3572 Saint Johns Ave.
904/387-1379

Judy Judy Judy
1633 San Marco Blvd.
904/396-1537

Frontier
5161 Beach Blvd.
904/398-6055

Grandma's Things
5814 St. Augustine Rd.
904/739-2075

Uncle Davey's Americana
6140 St. Augustine Rd.
904/730-8932

Olde Albert's
5818 St. Augustine Rd.
904/731-3947

White House Antiques
214 4th Ave. S
904/247-3388

Shop of M. Miller
1036 Park St.
904/384-3724

China Cat Antiques
226 4th Ave. S
904/241-0344

Bayard Country Store
12525 Phillips Hwy.
904/262-2548

Orange Tree Antiques
4209 St. John Ave.
904/387-4822

Antique Wooden Horse
6323 Phillips Hwy.
904/739-1008

Interiors Market
5133 San Jose Blvd.
904/733-2223

Annie's Antiques
9822 Beach Blvd.
904/641-3446

Avonlea Antiques
11000 Beach Blvd.
904/645-0806

Lovejoy's Antique Mall
5107 San Jose Blvd.
904/730-8083

Don's Antiques
5121 San Jose Blvd.
904/739-9829

Favorite Places To Eat

Cracker Barrel Old Country Store
I-95 & J. Turner Butler Blvd.

36 JUPITER

Axe Antiques
275 AH A 1A (SR811)
561/743-7888

Patricia Ann Reed Fine Antqs.
126 Center Street Ste. B-7
561/744-0373

37 KEY WEST

Wanted Store
1219 Duval St.
305/293-9810

Sam's Treasure Chest
518 Fleming St.
305/296-5907

Joseph's Antiques
616 Greene St.
305/294-9916

China Clipper
333 Simonton St.
305/294-2136

Commodore Antiques
500 Simonton St.
305/296-3973

Just Good Stuff
1100 White St.
305/293-8599

38 KISSIMMEE

Favorite Places To Eat

Cracker Barrel Old Country Store
I-4 & S.S. Hwy. 192, Exit 25A
407/396-6521

39 LAKE ALFRED

Biggar Antiques
140 W. Haines Blvd.
941/956-4853

Potpourri Antiques
144 W. Haines Blvd.
941/956-5535

Picket Fence
135 E. Pierce St.
941/956-3471

Barn Antiques
State Rd. 557
941/956-1362

40 LAKE CITY

Favorite Places To Eat

Cracker Barrel Old Country Store
I-75 & Hwy. 90, Exit 82
904/755-5638

41 LAKE WALES

Inglenook Antiques & Cllbls.
3607 Alt. 27 N
941/678-1641

Bittersweet Memories
113 E. Park Ave.
941/676-4778

Liberty Antiques
130 E. Park Ave.
941/678-0730

Once Upon A Tyme Antiques
201 N. Scenic Hwy.
941/676-0910

Bruce's Antiques
201 N. Scenic Hwy.
941/676-4845

Wisteria Cottage
229 E. Stuart Ste. 11
941/676-6730

42 LAKE WORTH

Mickey's Antiques
12 S. J St.
561/582-7667

Ada's Olde Towne Antique Mall
25 S. J St.
561/547-1700

P & G Antiques
702 Lake Ave.
561/547-6326

Lake Avenue Antiques
704 Lake Ave.
561/586-1131

Tuesday Gallery
705 Lake Ave.
561/586-1180

Hawkins Antiques & Art
712 Lake Ave.
561/582-4215

Yesterday's Antique Mall
716 Lake Ave.
561/547-3816

Roussos & Sons Antiques
801 Lake Ave.
561/585-2100

Antique Palace
808 Lake Ave.
561/582-8803

Carousel Antiques Center
813 Lake Ave.
561/533-0678

Heritage Antiques
621 Lake Ave.
561/588-4755

43 LAKELAND

Agape Antique Center
243 N. Florida Ave.
941/686-6882

Silver Cloud Shop
701 N. Florida Ave.
941/687-4696

Celebration Gallery
1037 S. Florida #106
941-686-9999

Somewhere In Time-Nonstalgia
1715 S. Florida Ave.
941/688-9472

Peacock Antiques
234 N. Kentucky Ave.
941/686-7947

A Keslinger Antiques Complex
244 N. Kentucky Ave.
941/683-4444

Sissy's Gallery
314 N. Kentucky Ave.
941/687-6045

My Cottage Garden
327 N. Kentucky Ave.
941/688-9686

Bubba's Country Store
3720 County Line Rd.
941/647-5461

Frog Pond
3403 Providence Rd.
941/858-1979

Roger A Cheek Gallery
218 E. Pine St.
941/686-5495

Casey Lynn Antiques
214 Traders Alley
941/682-2857

Reflections Of The Past
215 Traders Alley
941/682-0349

Favorite Places To Eat

Cracker Barrel Old Country Store
I-4 & Socrum Loop Rd., Exit 19
941/853-5405

44 LARGO

Nearly New Shop
623 W. Bay Dr.
813/586-2196

Time & Again
814 W. Bay Dr.
813/586-3665

Details
1260 W. Bay Dr.
813/585-6960

Brenda's Styling
39 Clearwater Largo Rd.
813/582-9839

Country Village
11896 Walsingham Rd.
813/397-2942

T & T Antiques
12790 66th St. N
813/531-8072

45 LEESBURG

Leesburg Antique Mall
403 W. Main St.
352/323-3396

Victorian Rose
415 W. Main St.
352/728-8388

Smith's Antiques & Collectable
717 W. Main St.
352/787-1102

Ruth's Antiques
1223 W. Main St.
352/787-7064

Mary's Treasure Chest
2300 W. Main St.
352/326-3181

Curiosity Shop
1310 N. Shore Dr.
352/787-6870

Morning Glori Antique Mall
1111 S. 14th St. (Hwy. 27)
352/365-9977

46 MAITLAND

Cranberry Corners
203 E. Horatio Ave.
407/644-0363

Pence & Pound House
630 S. Maitland Ave.
407/628-4911

Bestenwurst Antiques
145 S. Orlando Ave.
407/647-0533

Halley's Antiques Mall
473 S. Orlando Ave.
407/539-1066

47 MCINTOSH

Creekside Antiques/Collectible
Highway 441 & Ave. E
352/591-4444

Book Barn/O. Brisky's
Highway 441 & Ave. F
352/591-2177

Fort McIntosh Armory
Highway 441 & Ave. G
352/591-2378

Harvest Village
22050 N. U.S. Highway 441
352/591-1053

48 MELBOURNE

Hometown Expressions
712 E. New Haven Ave.
407/676-0692

Born Again
724 E. New Haven Ave.
407/768-8442

Melbourne Antique Mall
806 E. New Haven Ave.
407/951-0151

Finders Keepers
809 E. New Haven Ave.
407/676-5697

Antiques Anonymous
811 E. New Haven Ave.
407/724-5666

Effie's Antiques & Collectibles
819 E. New Haven Ave.
407/728-7345

Red Lion Antiques
821 E. New Haven Ave.
407/726-8777

Eclectibles Unlimited
825 E. New Haven Ave.
407/768-9795

Just For You
829 E. New Haven Ave.
407/768-2636

Helen's Antique & Modern
847 E. New Haven Ave.
407/723-8830

Age of Elegance
932 E. New Haven Ave.
407/728-8870

Antique Mall & Collectibles
3830 W. New Haven Ave.
407/727-1761

Antique Connection
568 W. Eau Gallie Blvd.
407/255-1333

Betty's Antiques
2001 Melbourne Ct.
407/951-2258

Favorite Places To Eat

Cracker Barrel Old Country Store
I-95 & Wickham Rd., Exit 73
407/242-0350

49 MIAMI/NORTH MIAMI

Aunt Hattie's Attic
10828 N.E. 6th Ave.
305/751-3738

Echoes of the Past Antiques
12325 N.E. 6th Ave.
305/895-8462

Len's 7th Ave. Antiques
4950 N.W. 7th Ave.
305/754-5601

Manetta's Antiques
5531 S.W. 8th St.
305/261-8603

J R Antiques
5987 S.W. 8th St.
305/264-6614

Harris Antique Shop
8747 N.W. 22nd Ave.
305/693-0110

Gloria's Place
2231 S.W. 22nd St.
305/285-2411

Antiques Paradise
2371 S.W. 22nd St.
305/285-7885

Escala Antiques & Gifts
2385 S.W. 22nd St.
305/857-9955

Ralph's Antiques
3660 S.W. 22nd St.
305/441-1193

Hidden Place
1092 S.W. 27th Ave.
305/644-0469

Arenas Antiques
1131 S.W. 27th Ave.
305/541-0900

Antique Center
2644 S.W. 28th Ln.
305/858-6166

Charlotte's International
2650 S.W. 28th Ln.
305/858-9326

ITO
2685 S.W. 28th Ln.
305/856-1361

Twery's Inc.
160 N.E. 40th St.
305/576-0564

Antiques & Gifts by Roses
6350 S.W. 40th St.
305/667-8703

Nostalgiaville
6374 S.W. 40th St.
305/669-1608

Well Design
6550 S.W. 40th St.
305/661-1386

Beall's Antiques & Collectibles
6554 S.W. 40th St.
305/663-2103

Robin's Nest Antiques
6703 S.W. 40th St.
305/666-7668

Old Paris
7125 S.W. 47th St.
305/666-7008

Antiques & Tribal
7165 S.W. 47th St. #B319
305/661-1094

Gloria Allison Antiques
7207 S.W. 48th St.
305/666-3900

Suarez Graciela
7209-7217 S.W. 48th St.
305/667-3431

Antiquario Fine Furniture
7219 S.W. 48th St.
305/663-8151

Pine Mine
7262 S.W. 48th St.
305/663-4432

Gilbert's Antiques Inc.
7265 S.W. 48th St.
305/665-2006

Dietel's Antiques
2124 S.W. 67th Ave.
305/266-8981

Ceramic By Design
4664 S.W. 72nd Ave.
305/663-5558

1800's Antiques & Accessories
4666 S.W. 72nd Ave.
305/668-9777

British Connection Antiques
4669 S.W. 72nd Ave.
305/662-9212

Drummond of Perth Antiques
4691 S.W. 72nd Ave.
305/665-3345

Bonnin Ashley Antiques, Inc.
4707 S.W. 72nd Ave.
305/667-0969

Antiques & Country Pine
4711 S.W. 72nd Ave.
305/665-7463

General Consignment
4762 S.W. 72nd Ave.
305/669-0800

Malina's Victorian Country
4836 S.W. 72nd Ave.
305/663-0929

General Consignment
4215 S.W. 75th Ave.
305/261-3200

Ideas & More Inc.
4467 S.W. 75th Ave.
305/265-8538

Eclectique
6344 Bird Road
305/666-7073

Joylot Antiques
921 N.E. 79th St.
305/754-9136

F. & D. Lopez-Del Rincon Art
803 82nd St.
305/861-5997

Golden Era Antiques
1640 N.E. 123rd St.
305/891-1006

Tania Sante's Classic
6556 Bird Rd.
305/662-4975

Dietel's Antiques
6572 Bird Rd.
305/666-0724

A & J Unique Antiques
2000 Biscayne Blvd.
305/576-5170

Spencer Art Gallerie
4441 Collins Ave.
305/532-7577

Midori Gallery Antique
3170 Commodore Plz.
305/443-3399

Alhambra Antiques Center
3640 Coral Way
305/446-1688

Alba Antiques
3656 Coral Way
305/443-5288

Oldies But Goodies
17842 S. Dixie Hwy.
305/232-5441

Ye Olde Cupboard
17844 S. Dixie Hwy.
305/251-7028

B & H Antiques
12777 W. Dixie Hwy.
305/899-0921

Washington Square Antiques
19090 W. Dixie Hwy.
305/937-0409

Victoria's Armoire Country
4077 Ponce De Leon Blvd.
305/445-3848

Stone Age Antiques
3236 N.W. South River Dr.
305/633-5114

Olde Tyme Shoppe
1549 1/2 Sunset Dr.
305/662-1842

Antiques & Art
10143 SW 79th Ct.
305/663-3224

Valerio Antiques
2901 Florida/Coconut Grove
305/448-6779

50 MIAMI BEACH

Collectors Art Gallery
730 Lincoln Rd.
305/531-4900

Circle Art & Antiques
1014 Lincoln Rd.
305/531-1859

Bolero
1688 Meridian Ave.
305/534-3759

Senzatempo
815 Washington Ave.
305/534-8882

51 MICANOPY

The Shop
Cholokka Blvd.
352-466-4031

Chateau Des Antiques
Cholokka Blvd.
352/466-4505

Among The Ivy
Cholokka Blvd.
352/466-8000

Delectable Collectibles
Cholokka Blvd.
352/466-3327

Smiley's Antique Mall
17020 County Road 234
352/466-0707

Baytree Antiques Inc.
Cholokka Blvd.
352/466-3946

Sun Glo Farm Antiques
16319 S.E. County Rd. 234
352/466-3037

Micanopy Country Store
108 Cholokka Blvd.
352/466-0510

Antique Alley
110 Cholokka Blvd.
352/466-0300

Savino's Antiques
203 Cholokka Blvd.
352/466-3663

Elena's Antiques
206 E Cholokka Blvd.
252/466-4260

Roberts Antiques
208 Cholokka Blvd.
352/466-3605

House of Hirsch Too Antiques
209 E. Cholokka Blvd.
352/466-3774

52 MONTICELLO

Southern Friends Antique Mall
I-10, exit 33 (U.S. Highway 19)
904/997-2559
Mon.-Sat. 10-6, Sun. 1-6

Directions: From I-10, take exit 33 (U.S. Highway 19). The store has no street number.

The name suggests true Southern hospitality. Southern Friends Antique Mall opened its doors in March of 1997 and has done a wonderful job of filling this 7,500-square-foot store with quality antiques. No reproductions or crafts are accepted by the 50 dealers who work to create an authentic representation of glassware, pottery, porcelain, quilts, linens, books, clocks and more. For you Civil War buffs, Southern Friends has a nice offering of Civil War memorabilia as well.

Bush Baby
280n N. Cherry St.
904/997-6108

Rosewood Flowers & Antiques
Highway 19
904/997-6779

Mister Ed's
Highway 27
904/997-5880

Court House Antiques
205 E. Washington St.
904/997-8008

53 MT. DORA

Mt. Dora Antique Mall
315 N. Donnelly St.
352/383-0018

Iris' Attic Antiques
317 N. Donnelly St.
352/735-2189

Caroline's Antiques
331 N. Donnelly St.
352/735-4003

Oliver Twist Antique Furniture
404 N. Donnelly St.
352/735-3337

Corner Nook Antiques
426 N. Donnelly
352/383-9555

Verandah Antique Galleries
427 N. Donnelly
352/735-0330

Old Village Antiques
439B N. Donnelly
352/383-1820

Olde Bostonian Antiques & Gift
442 N. Donnelly
352/383-3434

Frog's of Donnelly
100 W. 3rd Ave.
352/383-3553

Wild Rose Antique Mini Mall
140 E. 4th Ave.
352/383-6664

Southern Exotic Antiques
116 W. 5th Ave.
352/735-2500

Renninger's Antique Center
20651 U.S. Highway 441
352/383-8393

Cottage Artwork & Antiques
605 N. Donnelly Ave.
352/735-2700

Courtyard Antiques
142 E. 4th Ave.
352/735-1915

Rosecreek Antiques & Gifts
418 N. Donnelly St.
352/735-0086

Di Antiques
122 E. 4th St.
352/735-1333

Stairway to the Stars
411-203 Donnelly
352/383-9770

54 NAPLES

Lovejoy Antiques
960 2nd Ave. N
941/649-7447

Rocking Horse Antiques
950 3rd Ave. N
941/263-6997

Antiques-Glenna Moore
465 5th Ave. S
941/263-4121

Gabriel's South
555 5th Ave. S
941/643-0433

Baldwin's at Fifth
604 5th Ave. S
941/263-2234

Thompson-Strong Antiques
605 5th Ave. S
941/434-6434

Naples Trading Co.
810 6th Ave. S
941/262-0376

Yahl Street Antique Mall
5430 Yahl Street
941/591-8182

Ivy House Antiques
639 8th St. S
941/434-9555

Bailey's Antiques & Country
606 9th St. N
941/643-1953

Margie's Antiques
153 10th St. S
941/262-3151

Antique Guild
183 10th St. S
941/649-0323

Catherine's Collectibles Inc.
255 13th Ave. S
941/262-4800

Recollections New & Old
639 8th Street S
941/649-1954

Barney's Island Antiques
348 Capri Blvd.
941/394-2848

Lovejoy Antiques
950 Central Ave.
941/649-7447

Granny's Attic
1971 County Road 951
941/353-0800

Wizard of Odds II
4584 Mercantile Ave.
941/261-4459

Debbie's Monkey Business
2033 Pine Ridge Rd. #3
941/594-8686

Black Bear Cove Inc.
1661 Trade Center Way
941/598-1933

Favorite Places To Eat

Cracker Barrel Old Country Store
I-75 & County Rd. 951, Exit 15
941/455-6588

55 NEW SMYRNA

Victoria Station
402 Canal St.
904/426-8881

New Smyrna Antiques
419 Canal St.
904/426-7828

Coronado Antiques
512 Canal St.
904/428-3331

Kelly's Country Store
569 Canal St.
904/428-2291

Jeff's Antiques
507 S. Dixie Fwy.
904/423-2554

Lion D'or Antiques
511 N. Orange St.
904/428-1752

56 NICEVILLE

Steven's Yesterday's Furn.
98 Nathey @ Hwy. 85 N
904/678-6775

Little Ole Lady Trading Post
314 Bayshore Drive
904/678-7424

Gee Gee's Antiques
1209 N. Partin Highway 285
904/678-2689

The Early Attic
119 Jones Avenue
904/678-9089

57 NORTH PORT

Rujan's Antiques & Collectibles
13640 Tamiami Trail
941/426-5418

58 OAKLAND PARK

C Strange Antiques
3277 N. Dixie Hwy.
954/565-6964

Antique Exchange
3493 N. Dixie Hwy.
954/564-3504

Yesteryears Today
3689 N. Dixie Hwy.
954/568-0362

Vintage Fabrics & Etc.
3500 C N.E. 11th Ave.
954/564-4392

Affordable Treasures
1051 N.E. 45th St.
954/938-4567

59 OCALA

Frazer Coal Co. Antiques
6200 South Pine Avenue
352/368-7678
Tue.-Sat. 10:30-5, Sun.-Mon. Noon-5

"Unusual Accessories For the Country Lifestyle" is the offering at Frazer Coal Co. Within the shop you'll always find a nice selection of primitives, pie safes, wooden chests, trunks, stoneware, graniteware, quilts, jars, painted cupboards and quality oak pieces. Everything you need for a beautifully decorated country home.

Stuf N Such
1310 Highway 484
352/245-7744

ABS Antiques Co.
4185 W. Highway 40
352/351-1009

Ocala Antique Mall
3700 S. Pine Ave.
352/622-4468

Camellia House Antiques
1317 S.E. Fort King Street
352/629-8085

Antique Attic
507 S.E. Fort King St.
352/732-8880

Antique Emporium Inc.
6500 S. Pine Ave.
352/351-1003

A Corner of Yesterday
521 S.E. Fort King St.
352/622-1927

Favorite Places To Eat

Cracker Barrel Old Country Store
I-75 & State Rd. 200, Exit 68
352/854-7870

60 OKEECHOBEE

Peddlers Cove
216 S.W. 4th St.
941/467-1939

My Other House
10017 N. Hwy. 441
941/357-3447

Fort Drum Antique Mall
30950 Highway 441 N
941/763-6289

Curiosity Shop
118 S.E. Park St.
941/467-6411

Silver Spoon
401 S.W. Park St.
941/763-0609

61 ORANGE CITY

Curiosity Corner Furniture
746 N. Volusia Ave.
904/775-3122

Orange City Mighty Mall
747 N. Volusia Ave.
904/775-1666

Antiques & Things
1427 S. Volsia Ave.
904/775-4900

62 ORANGE PARK

Favorite Places To Eat

Cracker Barrel Old Country Store
I-295 & U.S. 17, Exit 3
904/264-2292

63 ORLANDO

Butterpat's
2439 Edgewater Dr.
407/423-7971

Myrtee B's Antiques
321 Ivanhoe Blvd. N.
407/895-0717

Swanson's Antiques
1217 N. Orange Ave.
407/898-6050

Penny Edwards Antiques
1616A N. Orange Ave.
407/896-2499

William Moseley Gallery
1221 N. Orange Ave.
407/228-6648

Troy's Treasures
1612A N. Orange Ave.
407/228-6648

Designer House, Inc.
1249 N. Orange Ave.
407/895-9060

Fee Fi Fauk
1425 N. Orange Ave.
407/895-9060

Antique Exchange
1616 N. Orange Ave.
407/896-3793

Marge Leeper Collection
1618 N. Orange Ave.
407/894-2165

A & T Antiques
1620 N. Orange Ave.
407/896-9831

Flo's Attic
1800 N. Orange Ave.
407/895-1800

Allison's Antiques
1804 N. Orange Ave.
407/897-6672

Antiques Arcade
1806 N. Orange Ave.
407/898-2994

Jack Lampman Antiques
1810 N. Orange Ave.
407/897-1144

Two Timer
1815 N. Orange Ave.
407/894-4342

Rock & Roll Heaven
1814 N. Orange Ave.
407/896-1952

Floraland
1808 N. Orange Ave.
407/898-2301

1817 Antiques
1817 N. Orange Ave.
407/894-6519

D L Times Two Antiques
1827 N. Orange Ave.
407/894-6519

DeJavu Vintage Clothing
1825 N. Orange Ave.
407/898-3609

Backstreet Bodega
1909 N. Orange Ave.
407/895-9444

Golden Phoenix
1826 N. Orange Ave.
407/895-6006

Oriental Unlimited & Antiques
2020 N. Orange Ave.
407/894-2067

A. J. Lillun Antiques
1913 N. Orange Ave.
407/895-6111

Back Street
2310 N. Orange Ave.
407/895-1993

Red's Antiques & Collectibles
1827 N. Orange Ave.
407/894-6519

White Wolfe Cafe & Antiques
1829 N. Orange Ave.
407/895-9911

Victorian Gallery
1907 N. Orange Ave.
407/896-9346

Annie's Antique Alley
2010 N. Orange Ave.
407/896-0433

Pieces of Eight Antq. Empor.
2021 N. Orange Ave.
407/896-8700

Bangarang
2309 N. Orange Ave.
407/898-2300

Corner Cupboard
4797 S. Orange Ave.
407/857-1322

And So On
1807 N. Orange Ave.
407/898-3485

B's Antiques
1214 N. Mills Ave.
407/894-6264

College Park Antique Mall
1317 Edgewater Dr.
407/839-1869

Millie's Glass & China Shop
5512 Edgewater Dr.
407/298-3355

Virginia Rose
542 Virginia Dr.
407/898-0552

Backstreet Bodega
817 Virginia Dr.
407/895-9444

Laughing Gargoyle Antiques
322 W. Colonial Dr.
407/843-8070

Apple Core Antiques & Gifts
3327 Curry Ford Rd.
407/894-2774

Antique Mall
361 E. Michigan St.
407/849-9719

A Antq. Shop By Flo's Attic
310 E. New Hampshire St.
407/894-0607

Em's Attic
1530 S. Primrose Dr.
407/896-0097

Orlando Antique Exchange
420 W. 27th St.
407/839-0991

Favorite Places To Eat

Cracker Barrel Old Country Store
I-4 & Kirkman Rd., Exit 30B
407/248-6260

Florida

64 PALM BEACH

Deco Folies
210 Brazilian Ave.
561/822-8960

Island Trading Co.
105 N. County Rd.
561/833-0555

Art & Antiques
117 N. County Rd.
561/833-1654

Rose Pennm, Inc.
301 S. County Rd.
561/835-9702

Kofski Antiques
315 S. County Rd.
561/655-6557

F. S. Henemader Antiques
316 S. County Rd.
561/835-9237

R.J. King & Co.
6 Via Parigi
561/659-9029

Lars Bolander Ltd.
375 S. County Rd.
561/832-2121

Bellon Antiques
309 Peruvian Ave.
561/659-1844

Fleur-De-Lis Antiques
326 Peruvian Ave.
561/655-2295

Christian Du Pont Antqs. Inc.
353 Peruvian Ave.
561/655-7794

Vilda B. De Porro
211 Worth Ave.
561/655-3147

Spencer Gallerie
240 Worth Ave.
561/833-9893

Meissen Shop
329 Worth Ave.
561/832-2504

L'Antiquaire
329 Worth Ave.
561/655-5774

Yetta Olkes Antiques
332 S County Rd.
561/655-2800

Brighton Pavillon
340 Worth Ave.
561/835-4777

Devonshire
340 Worth Ave.
561/833-0796

Barzina
66 Via Mizner
561/833-5834

Galerie Haga Antiques
2 Via Parigi
561/833-2051

Letitia Lundeen Antiques
5 Via Parigi
561/833-1087

65 PALM COAST

Favorite Places To Eat

Cracker Barrel Old Country Store
I-95 & Palm Coast Pkwy., Exit 91C
904/445-2127

66 PALM HARBOR

Generations Antiques
1682 Alt. 19 N
813/787-0067

Miss B's Antiques & Cllbls.
1710 Alt. 19 N
813/787-0388

Cierra-Jordan Antique & Gift
1026 Florida Ave. Ste. C
813/781-0305

The Gift Connection
1001 Omaha Cir.
813/781-0103

67 PANAMA CITY

Antique Cottage
903 Harrison Ave.
904/769-9503

Shady Oaks Antiques
3706 W. Hwy. 98
904/785-3308

68 PENSACOLA

American Antique Mall
2019 N. T St.
904/432-7659

Turn of the Century Antiques
2401 N. T St.
904/434-1820

Heirlooms
2706 N. T St.
904/438-2279

Burch Antiques
3160 N. T St.
904/433-5153

Hamilton House Antiques
4117 Barrancas Ave.
904/456-2762

Warehouse Antiques
60 S. Alcaniz St.
904/432-0318

Ragtime Antiques
3113 Mobile Blvd.
904/438-1232

Dusty Attic
1113 N. 9th Ave.
904/434-5568

Baily Attic
9204 N. Davis Hwy.
904/478-3144

9th Ave. Antiques Mall
380 N. 9th Ave.
904/438-3961

East Hill Antique Village
805 E. Gadsden St.
904/435-7325

Cleland Antiques-Seville Sq.
412 E. Zarragossa St.
904/432-9933

L L Sloan Antiques
115 S. Florida Blanca St.
904/434-5050

Status Symbol
698 Hindberg Ste. 106
904/432-6614

Lind House Estate Jewelers
217 S. Alcaniz St.
904/435-3213

This Ole House
712 S. Palafax St.
904/432-2577

Favorite Places To Eat

Cracker Barrel Old Country Store
I-10 & Pine Forest Rd., Exit 2
904/944-2090

69 PLANT CITY

Bay Antiques & Clock Repair
109 East Reynolds Street
813/759-6638
Hours: Tue.-Sat. 10-5

Directions: Traveling I-4 between Tampa and Lakeland, exit at # 13. Go south on Highway 39. Turn left on Reynolds Street (U.S. 92 East). Pass through 2 traffic lights. The shop is the second on the right.

If old clocks are your forte then stop for a visit at Bay Antiques & Clock Repair. Tom Smiley, known as the resident clock "Doc", can answer all your questions (or at least try to) and even repair your old clock if needed. If you're in the market to purchase an old timepiece the shop has a nice selection to choose from.

Glyn (Tom's better half) is the antique addict. She brings to the shop not only some very nice antique pieces from which to choose, but a wealth of knowledge. She can answer most any question you may have about your selection of glassware, jewelry, furniture or linens. With a large library of reference books as her guide, Glyn will share plenty of information with you.

If you're an animal lover, be sure to say hello to "Sweet," the dedicated and lovable dachshund who greets customers at the door (unless he happens to be taking a nap).

The Olde Village Shoppes Mini Mall and Le Bistro Cafe
108 S. Collins Street
813/752-3222
Open: Tue.-Sat. 10-5:30, Closed Sun. & Mon.

It takes a person of great vision to take an old, dilapidated building and turn it into a thing of beauty. That is just what Victoria Hawthorne has accomplished. She saw beyond the crumbling bricks, broken windows and littered interior. Hawthorne envisioned an enclosed European Style Shopping Village. She and her husband purchased the historic building in 1996 and began the work to fulfill her dream. The results are spectacular.

The quaint shops are connected by a red brick walkway with overhead ceilings of sky blue and big puffy clouds. All the shops have European facades or are a part of a beautiful English garden with a bubbling fountain. The 56 shops are filled with such eclectic treasures as stained glass pieces, antique Victorian lamps, *Gone With The Wind* memorabilia, paintings, fine antique furnishings, glassware, vintage jewelry, imported tiles from around the world and porcelain dolls, just to name a few.

Le Bistro Cafe gives shoppers a respite from the day's hectic pace. Chef Christopher, trained at the American Culinary Art Institute, prepares fresh soups, sandwiches, salads and seafood. Catering is available as well as High Tea, by reservation.

Vickie Hawthorne's dream to promote the revival of downtown Plant City is off to a remarkable start. Take some time to discover for yourself The Olde Village Shoppes and enjoy the beautiful surroundings of historic Plant City.

Dale Gardner contributed to this story.

70 POMPANO BEACH

Heritage Clock Shop
713 E. Atlantic Blvd.
954/946-4871

Antique Market Place
721 E. Atlantic Blvd.
954/943-6221

Emporium Antiques
1642 E. Atlantic Blvd.
954/946-0120

Memories
2692 E. Atlantic Blvd.
954/785-1776

Purnie's Antiques
25 N. Ocean Blvd.
954/941-6154

71 PORT CHARLOTTE

Favorite Places To Eat

Cracker Barrel Old Country Store
I-75 & Kings Hwy., Exit 31
941/624-4994

72 SANFORD

Arts & Ends
116 E. 1st St.
407/330-4994

Granny Squares
118 E. 1st St.
407/323-3919

Granny's on Magnolia
201 E. 1st St.
407/322-7544

Junk Exchange
118 Palmetto Ave.
407/330-7748

Two Doves & A Hound Antqs.
205 E. 1st St.
407/321-3690

Antiques Etc.
205 E. 1st St. Ste. C
407/330-1641

Yester Years
205 E. 1st St. #A
407/323-3457

Bennington & Bradbury Antqs.
210 E. 1st St.
407/328-5057

Somewhere In Time
222 E. 1st St.
407/323-7311

Delilah's
301 E. 1st St.
407/330-2272

Sanford House Inc
616 W. 1st St.
407/330-0608

Sanford Antiques
700 W. 1st St.
407/321-2035

Helen's Den
205 N. Palmetto Ave.
407/324-3726

Park Avenue Antique Mall
1301 S. Park Ave.
407/321-4356

Favorite Places To Eat

Cracker Barrel Old Country Store
I-4 & State Rd. 46, Exit 51
407/324-1020

73 SANTA ROSA BEACH\GRAYTON BEACH\SEASIDE\SEAGROVE BEACH

Bayou Arts & Antiques
105 Hogtown Bayou Ln.
904/267-1404

Martha's Plantation Shop
1727 S. County Hwy. 393
904/267-2944

Gunby's
4415 Scenic Rt. 30-A E
904/231-5958

Grandma's Stuff
35 Musset Bayou Rd.
904/267-1999

Ole Outpost
687 S. Church Street
904/267-2551

Tidewater Antiques
Emerald Coast Plaze Ste. 33
904/267-9599

Hogtown Landing
Hwy. 393 N. & Cessna Park
904/267-1271

Tea Tyme Antiques
Hwy. C-30A & Tanglewood Dr.
904/267-3827

"S" House Antiques
3866 W. Hwy. C-30A & Satinwood
904/267-2231

Fernleigh, Ltd.
Hwy. C-30A (Seaside Town Center)
904/231-5536

74 SARASOTA

Mark of Time
24 South Lemon Avenue
800/277-5275
Mon.-Thurs. 10:30-5:30, Fri. 11-4, Sat. 10-2

Directions: Traveling on I-75, take exit 39 onto Fruitville Road (SR 780), going west for 5 miles into downtown. Turn left onto Lemon Avenue, and proceed through two STOP signs and a traffic light. The shop is on the right.

Located in the heart of Sarasota's antique district, Mark of Time specializes in rare antique clocks. The shop recently acquired a Ferdinand Lapp Centennial Clock, circa 1876. This one-of-a-kind clock and cabinet was created by Ferdinand Lapp especially for the Centennial International Exhibit in Philadelphia. Mark of Time also offers expert clock and watch repair. Antique furnishings and accessories are available along with the many fine selections of clocks.

Bargain Box Consign. Shoppe
4406 Bee Ridge Rd.
941/371-1976

Daddy Franks
907 Cattleman Rd.
941/378-1308

Miller's Antiques
970 Cattleman Rd.
941/377-2979

Talk of the Town
4123 Clark Rd.
941/925-3948

Alley Cat Antiques
1542 4th St.
941/366-6887

Treasures & More
1466 Fruitville Rd.
941/366-7704

Shadow Box
1520 Fruitville Rd.
941/957-3896

Li Lou
1522 Fruitville Rd.
941/362-0311

Sarasota Antqs. & Upholstery
1542 Fruitville Rd.
941/366-9484

Dotty's Accents & Antiques
1555 Fruitville Rd.
941/954-8057

Queen Anne's Lace Antiques
2246 Gulf Gate Dr.
941/927-0448

Sanders Antiques
22 N. Lemon Ave.
941/366-0400

Design Shop
34 S. Lemon Ave.
941/365-2434

A. Parker's Books
1488 Main St.
941/366-2898

A World Coin & Jewelry Exch.
1564 Main St.
941/365-5415

Rosie O'Grady's Antiques
32 S. Palm Ave.
800/793-4193

Hartman, William
48 S. Palm Ave.
941/955-4785

Apple & Carptr. Gllry. Fine Art
64 S. Palm Ave.
941/951-2314

Kevin L. Perry, Inc.
127 S. Pineapple Ave.
941/366-8483

New England Antiques
500 S. Pineapple Ave.
941/955-7577

Beverly's Antiques & Cllbls.
510 S. Pineapple Ave.
941/953-6887

Sarasota Trading Co.
522 S. Pineapple Ave.
941/953-7776

Creative Collections
527 S. Pineapple Ave.
941/951-0477

Orange Pineapple
533 S. Pineapple Ave.
941/954-0533

Jack Vinale's Antiques
539 S. Pineapple Ave.
941/957-0002

Avenue Antiques
606 S. Pineapple Ave.
941/362-8866

Yesterday's Browse Box
2864 Ringling Blvd.
941/957-1422

Antiques & Collectibles Vault
1501 2nd St.
941/954-4233

Bacon & Wing
1433 State St.
941/371-2687

Raymond's 2nd Hand World
5624 Swift Rd.
941/925-7253

Remember Gallery
1239 S. Tamiami Trl.
941/955-2625

Caroline's Used Furn. & Antqs.
4511 S. Tamiami Trl.
941/924-7066

British Pine Emporium
4801 S. Tamiami Trl.
941/923-7347

Shah Abba's Fine Oriental Rugs
4801 S. Tamiami Trl.
941/366-6511

Antiques and Country Pine
5201 S. Tamiami Trl.
941/921-5616

Coral Cove Antique Gallery
7272 S. Tamiami Trl.
941/927-2205

Franklin Antiques & Cllbls.
3512 N. Lockwood Ridge Road
941/359-8842

Methuselah's Antiques
322 S. Washington Blvd.
941/366-2218

Crissy Galleries
640 S. Washington Blvd. Ste. 150
941/957-1110

Robert A. Blekicki Antiques
640 S. Washington Blvd.
941/365-4990

Yellow Bird of St. Armands
640 S. Washington Blvd. Ste. 230
941/388-1823

Century Antiques
3626 Webber St.
941/921-0056

Steven Postan's Antiques
2305 Whitfield Park Dr.
941/755-6063

Coco Palm Glty. Art & Antiques
1255 N. Palm Ave.
941/955-1122

Cherubs of Gold
2245 Ringling Blvd.
941/366-0596

Franklin Antiques & Cllbls.
3512 N. Lockwood Ridge Rd.
941/359-8842

75 SEFFNER

Favorite Places To Eat

Cracker Barrel Old Country Store
I-4 & State Rd. 579, Exit 8
813/621-7323

76 SEMINOLE

Cobweb Antiques
7976 Seminole Blvd.
813/399-2929
Mon.-Sat. 10-5, closed Mondays May through September

Directions: Traveling I-275, take exit 15; go west on Gandy Blvd. (Becomes Park Blvd.) to Seminole Blvd. (Alt. 19). Turn right onto Seminole Blvd. Drive two blocks north. Make a left into Temple Terrace. Located on the northwest corner of Seminole Blvd. and Temple Terrace.

Cobweb Antiques is one of those "have all," "do all," "be all" kind of shops. They carry antique furniture, pottery, jewelry, watches, clocks, china, silver, books, postcards, prints, paintings, mirrors, lamps, linens, vintage clothing, antique firearms and related items. And if that weren't enough, they do estate liquidations, appraise firearms, real estate and antique automobiles. I wonder if these guys ever take a vacation.

The Fox Den
6020 Seminole Blvd.
813/398-4605

Vintage Antiques
6920 Seminole Blvd.
813/399-9691

Cobwebs Antiques
7976 Seminole Blvd.
813/399-2929

Adams Emporium
8780 Seminole Blvd.
813/397-7938

Evon's Antiques
7480 90th St.
813/391-3586

The Hen Nest
5485 113th St. N
813/398-1470

77 ST. AUGUSTINE

The Cedar House Inn
79 Cedar Street
800/233-2746
Open year round. Reservations taken from 10-8:30 daily

Directions: Northern: From I-95 S, take SR 16 (exit 95) east to U.S. 1 (Ponce de Leon Blvd.). Turn right and go to the third traffic light. Turn left on King Street and go through two traffic lights. Turn right on next street (Granada Street) and go one block to Cedar Street. Turn right. The Inn is the second house on the left. Southern: From I-95 N, take SR 207 (exit 94) east to U.S. (Ponce de Leon Blvd.). Turn left and go to the second traffic light. Turn left on King Street and go through two traffic lights. Turn right on the next street (Granada Street) and go one block to Cedar Street. Turn right. The Inn is the second house on the left.

The Cedar House Inn is located in St. Augustine, the oldest town in the United States. Built in 1893, this Victorian inn has been characterized by family lore and love. As a remembrance to Russ and Nina Thomas' grandparents, each of the six guest rooms are named in their honor. Additionally, the rooms are decorated with family heirlooms and memorabilia from the particular grandparent's life. Tess' Room, often called the "angel room" by guests, was named for Russ' maternal grandmother. During the 1920s, she was an actress on early radio, the co-founder of the first Girl Scout troop in Paterson, N.J., and known to many as an "angel." "Tess's room reflects her life and love of people," explains Russ. It is often requested by new brides and grooms.

On one such occasion, a honeymoon couple booked the suite for a one night's stay between their wedding reception and their departure for the Bahamas the next day. They arrived late at night and departed early, apparently never needing to use the key nor ever having glanced at the key's name tag. Departing in a rush, they forgot to turn in the key. For the next week, Russ and Nina joked about how Tess' key was on a honeymoon.

Meanwhile, on the islands, the honeymooners were in quite a dismay. It seems upon checking into their hotel the groom had slipped the room key into his pocket. When they reached the room, try as he might, the key he took out of his pocket wouldn't open the door. He and his bride promptly marched down to the hotel lobby, confronted the desk clerk and displayed the offending key. One glance, and the clerk explained that this was not his hotel's key and asked who is "Tess" anyway. Which is exactly what the bride wanted to know "...and who is Tess??!!" Fortunately, after a few embarrassing moments, the groom fished into his other pocket, found the real hotel key, unraveled the mystery, and saved his new marriage.

Centuries Past
9C King St.
904/824-9588

Carriage House Antiques
5A Sanchez Ave.
904/829-8505

Bettye's Baubles & Books
60 Cuna St.
904/823-9363

Riverside Antiques
58 Charlotte St.
904/824-5424

Antique Warehouse
6370 U.S. Hwy. 1N.
904/826-1524

Barclay-Scott Antiques
4 Rohde Ave.
904/824-7044

Conch House Antiques
600 Anastasia Blvd.
904/825-1255

Anastasia Antique Center
201 Anastasia Blvd.
904/824-7126

Second Hand Rose
13 Anastasia Blvd.
904/824-7800

Lovejoy's Antique Mall
1302 N. Ponce De Leon Blvd.
904/826-0200

Joy's Antiques
72 San Marco Ave.
904/823-0706

Wolf's Head Books
48 San Marco Ave.
904/824-9357

Down Memory Lane
56 San Marco Ave.
904/823-1228

Grandma's Attic
60 San Marco Ave.
904/829-9871

San Marco Antique Mall
63 San Marco Ave.
904/824-9156

Country Store Antiques
67 San Marco Ave.
904/824-7978

Ravenswood Antiques
81 San Marco Ave.
904/824-1740

First Encounter Antiques
216 San Marco Ave.
904/823-8855

Debra Williams
Back of Lightner Museum
904/824-1552

Blue Max Antique Shop
Lightner Mall
904/826-0963

North Country Antiques
Lightner Antique Mall
904/829-2129

Second Time Around Antiques
Lightner Antique Mall
904/825-4982

All Precious & Pleasant Riches
203 S Ponce De Leon Blvd.
904/824-3156

Favorite Places To Eat

Cracker Barrel Old Country Store
I-95 & State Rd. 16, Exit 95
904/829-9222

78 ST. CLOUD

A & D Antiques & Collectibles
1032 New York Ave.
407/891-0331

Troy's Treasures
1037 New York Ave.
407/957-0588

Caesar's Treasure Chest
1116 New York Ave.
407/892-8330

Forget Me Not Antiques
1122 10th St.
407/892-7701

79 ST. PETERSBURG

Nana's Other Place
260 1st Ave. N
813/827-0813

Nana's Place
428 4th St. N
813/823-4015

Rosemary's Antiques
770 4th Ave. N
813/822-1221

B & G Antiques
1018 4th St. N
813/823-2452

4th Street Antique Arcade Inc.
1535 4th St. N
813/823-5700

Sunken Gardens Antq. Gallery
1825 4th St. N
813/822-5117

Dessa Antiques
2004 4th St. N
813/823-5006

More Friends Antiques
1219 9th St. N
813/896-5425

Patty & Friends Antiques
1225 9th St. N
813/821-2106

Person's Antiques Too
1250 9th St. N
813/895-1250

Memory Lane
2392 9th St. N
813/896-1913

Suzette's Antiques
3313 W. Maritana Dr.
813/360-2309

Main House Antique Center
4980 38th Ave. N.
813/522-2492

Carrousel Antiques
7033 46th Ave. N
813/544-5039

Bennie's Barn
3700 58th Ave. N
813/526-4992

Ma's Glass Barn
5822 60th Ave. N
813/546-2459

Tudor Antiques
601 Central Ave.
813/821-4438

Elephant Trunk
627 Central Ave.
813/823-2394

Stuart Galleries
647 Central Ave. #1
813/894-2933

David Ord Antiques & Fine Art
649 Central Ave.
813/823-8084

Jackie's Place
657 Central Ave.
813/544-1844

Urbana
665 Central Ave.
813/824-5669

Hauser Antiques
7204 Central Ave.
813/343-5511

Burr Antiques
7214 Central Ave.
813/345-5727

Blue Bear Antiques
7214 Central Ave.
813/345-8851

Cappy's Corner Antiques
7215 Central Ave.
813/345-4330

Antique Shoppe
7223 Central Ave.
813/341-1199

Harpies' Bazaar
7240 Central Ave.
813/343-0409

Antique Depot
2835 22nd Ave. N
813/327-0794

Park Street Antique Center
9401 Bay Pines Blvd.
813/392-2198

Beach Drive Antiques
134 Beach Dr. NE
813/822-3773

Abbey Road Antiques
1581 Canterbury Rd. N
813/345-6852

Karen's Place
9999 Gandy Blvd. N
813/576-0764

Pink House of Collectibles
1515 4th St. N
813/894-2746

Gas Plant Antique Arcade
1246 Central Avenue
813/895-0368

Echo Antiques
1209 Central Ave.
813/898-3246

80 STUART

Pastimes Furniture
2380 N.W. Bay Colony Dr.
561/335-0590

Custom Woods
650 N.W. Buck Henry Way
561/692-0702

A Certain Ambiance
522 Colorado Ave.
561/221-0388

Beckoning Antiques
614 Colorado Ave.
561/288-5044

Partners Antique Mall
6124 S.E. Federal Hwy.
561/286-6688

Time Will Tell
3 S.W. Flagler Ave.
561/283-6337

Collections
53 S.W. Flagler Ave.
561/288-6232

Bon Bon Antiques
2681 S.E. Ocean Blvd.
561/288-0866

Partners Mall
6124 S. East Federal Highway
561-286-6688

Favorite Places To Eat

Cracker Barrel Old Country Store
I-95 & State Rd. 76, Exit 61
407/781-0097

81 TALLAHASSEE

Grant's Collectibles
2887 W. Tharpe St #C
904/575-2212

Early American Antiques
2736 Pecan Rd.
904/385-2981

Killearn Antiques
1415 Timberland Rd.
904/893-0510

Old World Antiques
929 N. Monroe St.
904/681-6986

Country Collection
1500 Apalachee Pkwy.
904/877-0390

Favorite Places To Eat

Cracker Barrel Old Country Store
I-10 & North Monroe, Exit 29
904/385-9249

82 TAMPA

Paris Flea
3115 W. Bay to Bay Blvd.
813/837-6556

Hunter's Find Antiques
3224 W. Bay to Bay Blvd.
813/251-6444

L'Exquisite Antiques
3413 W. Bay to Bay Blvd.
813/837-8655

Your Treasures
3413 W. Bay to Bay Blvd.
813/837-8655

Cox/Feivelson
3413 W. Bay to Bay Blvd.
813/837-8655

Neta Winders
3901 W. Bay to Bay Blvd.
813/839-0151

A Silver Chest
203 S. Dale Mabry Blvd.
813/228-0038

Antique Mall of Palma Ceia
3300 S. Dale Mabry Blvd.
813/835-6255

Flo's Antiques
4301 W. El Prado Blvd.
813/837-5871

Larry R. Engle Antiques
4303 W. El Prado Blvd.
813/839-0611

Tureville Antiques
4303 W. El Prado Blvd. #A
813/831-0555

Grandma's Place
4305 W. El Prado Blvd.
813/839-7098

Antique & Art by Patty
4305 W. El Prado Blvd. #A
813/832-6129

Ceia Palma Porcelain & Art
1802 S. Macdill Ave.
813/254-7149

Frantiques
1109 1/2 W. Waters Ave.
813/935-3638

South Mac Dill Antique Mall
4004 S. Macdill Ave.
813/832-3766

The Antique Room
4119 S. Macdill Ave.
813/835-8613

Cracker House
4121 S. Macdill Ave.
813/837-2841

Decades Ago-go
1514 E. 7th Ave.
813/248-2849

Uptown Threads
1520 E. 8th Ave.
813/248-5470

Grandma's Attic
1901 N. 13th St.
813/247-6878

Lorene's Antiques & Cllbls.
9840 Angus Dr.
813/249-0901

Antique Mall of Tampa
1102 E. Busch Blvd.
813/933-5829

Red Rooster Antiques
6420 N. Central Ave.
813/238-2615

Floriland Antique Cntr.
9309 N. Florida Ave.
813/935-9257

Greg's Unique Antiques
708 E. Grove Ave.
813/977-1990

Smith's Trading Post
1781 W. Hillsborough Ave.
813/876-2292

Boyd Clocks
937 S. Howard Ave.
813/254-7862

Timeless Treasures
2305 W. Linebaugh Ave.
813/935-8860

Huckleberry's Cottage Antiques
3808 W. Neptune St.
813/258-0707

Brushwood
3006 W. Swann Ave.
813/873-8022

83 TARPON SPRINGS

Angelic Antiquities & Accents
104 E. Tarpon
813/942-8799

Beehive
104 E. Tarpon
813/942-8840

Carter's Antique Asylum
106 E. Tarpon
813/942-2799

Antiques on the Main Inc.
124 E. Tarpon Ave.
813/937-9497

Thru The Looking Glass Antqs.
132 E. Tarpon Ave.
813/942-2851

Menzer's Antiques
134 E. Tarpon Ave.
813/938-3156

Antiques Forever
143 E. Tarpon Ave.
813/938-0078

Victorian Ivy
151 E. Tarpon Ave.
813/942-6080

Court of Two Sisters
153 E. Tarpon Ave.
813/934-9255

Tarpon Avenue Antiques
161 E. Tarpon Ave.
813/938-0053

Vintage Department Store
167 E. Tarpon Ave.
813/942-4675

84 TITUSVILLE

Favorite Places To Eat

Cracker Barrel Old Country Store
I-95 & State Rd. 50, Exit 79

85 VENICE

Buttercup Cottage
227 Miami Ave. West
941/484-2222

Albee Antiques
602 E. Venice Ave.
941/485-0404

Treasures In Time
101 W. Venice Ave.
941/486-1700

Favorite Places To Eat

Cracker Barrel Old Country Store
I-75 & Jacaranda Blvd. Exit 35
941/480-9200

86 VERO BEACH

Red Barn Antiques
5135 N. U.S. Highway 1
561/778-9860

Gaslight Collectibles
6235 U.S. Highway 1
561/569-0033

Company Store & Antq. Mall
6605 N. U.S. Highway 1
561/569-9884

Antique Alley
1171 Commerce Ave.
561/569-5068

Olde Towne Antiques
1708 Old Dixie Hwy.
561/778-5120

Antique Time
3600 69th St.
561/567-0900

Favorite Places To Eat

Cracker Barrel Old Country Store
I-95 & State Rd. 60, Exit 68
407/563-0066

87 WALDO

Waldo Antique Village
17805 N.E. U.S. Hwy. 301
352/468-3111

Red Barn of Waldo
455 S.W. 3rd Way
352/468-2880

Casa Las Brujas Antiques
State Road 24
352/468-2709

Laura's Antiques & Collectibles
State Highway 24
352/468-2016

Past Reflections
250 N. Main St.
352/468-2528

88 WESLEY CHAPEL

Favorite Places To Eat

Cracker Barrel Old Country Store
I-75 & State Rd. 54, Exit 58
813/973-4884

89 WEST PALM BEACH

Boomerang Modern
3301 South Dixie Highway
561/835-1865
Tue.-Sat. 11-5 and by appointment

Directions; On I-95, take exit 50 (Southern Blvd.). Go east 1 mile to South Dixie Highway. Then go north 1/2 mile to Boomerang Modern located on the left.

Boomerang Modern offers mid-20th style and design within the largest collection of blonde, streamline Heywood Wakefield furniture in the Southeast. Early and rare pieces designed by Gilbert Rhode, Leo Jiranek and renowned streamline automotive designer, Count Alexis de Sakhnoffsky, are featured.

Also offered are decorative objects and accessories by leading artisans and designers of the mid-twentieth century, along with funky, 50s lamps, ceramics and glass.

Tinson Antique Galleries
718 S. Dixie Hwy.
561/833-0700

Argosy
1913 S. Dixie Hwy.
561/832-5753

Cassidy's Antiques
3621 S. Dixie Hwy.
561/655-2313832-8017

Antique Row's Little House
3627 S. Dixie Hwy.
561/833-1552

Bittersweet of Palm Beach
3630 S. Dixie Hwy.
561/655-2313

Land's End Antiques
3634 S. Dixie Hwy.
561/833-1751

James & Jeffrey Antiques
3703 A S. Dixie Hwy.
561/832-1760

Cashmere Buffalo
3709 S. Dixie Hwy.
561/659-5441

E. Nelson Antiques
3715 S. Dixie Hwy.
561/659-4726

Old-Timers Antique Mall
3717 B Dixie Hwy.
561/832-5141

Lu Lu's Stuff
3719 S. Dixie Hwy.
561/655-1529

Dennis Joel Fine Arts
3720 S. Dixie Hwy.
561/835-1991

Brass Scale
3721 S. Dixie Hwy.
561/832-8410

ART Lane's Time and Again
3725 S. Dixie Hwy.
561/655-5171

Time And Again
3725 S. Dixie Hwy.
561/655-5171

Elephant's Foot
3800 S. Dixie Hwy.
561/832-0170

Michael Maclean Antqs. & Est.
3803 S. Dixie Hwy.
561/659-0971

Greta S. Decorative Antiques
3803-1/2 S. Dixie Hwy.
561/655-1533

Floral Emporium
3900 S. Dixie Hwy.
561/659-9888

Time Worn Treasures
4211 S. Dixie Hwy.
561/582-8064

Real Life Antiques
5105 S. Dixie Hwy.
561/582-8064

Deco Don's
5107 S. Dixie Hwy.
561/588-2552

R. B. Antiques
5109 S. Dixie Hwy.
561/533-5555

John Cantrell & Margaret
7729 S. Dixie Hwy.
561/588-8001

Favorite Places To Eat

Cracker Barrel Old Country Store
I-95 & 45th St., Exit 54
407/686-0660

90 WINTER GARDEN

Shirley's Antiques
12900 W. Colonial Dr
407/656-6406

Winter Garden Country Store
403 S. Dillard St.
407/656-0023

Trailside Antiques
12 W. Plant St.
407/656-6508

Page's Pastiques Inc.
741 Tildenville School Rd.
407/877-3845

Antiques
1075 S. Vineland Ave.
407/656-5166

91 WINTER HAVEN

Classic Collectibles & Antqs.
279 W. Central Ave.
941/294-6866 or 1-800-287-6866

Robert Holley Antiques & Gifts
318 W. Central Ave.
941/299-3131

Antique Mall Village
3170 U.S. Highway 17 North
941/293-5618

Mimi's Bargain Corner
3240 Dundee Rd.
941/324-5275

Joan Alach Antiques
326 W. Central Ave.
941/293-8510

92 WINTER PARK

Per Se Antiques & Collectibles
116 E. Park Ave.
407/628-5231

American Antiques
1500 Formosa Ave.
407/647-2260

Antique Buff
334 Park Ave. N
407/628-2111

Chintz & Co.
515 Park Ave. N
407/740-7224

Mimi's Antiques
535 Park Ave. N
407/645-3499

Ferris-Reeves Galleries
140 E. Morse Blvd.
407/647-0273

Carols Antiques & Collectibles
171 E. Morse Blvd.
407/645-2345

Ginger's Antiques
2695 W. Fairbanks Ave.
407/740-8775

Our Antiques Market
5453 Lake Howell Rd.
407/657-2100

Winter Park Antique Mall
2335 Temple Trail
407/628-5384

Notes

Georgia

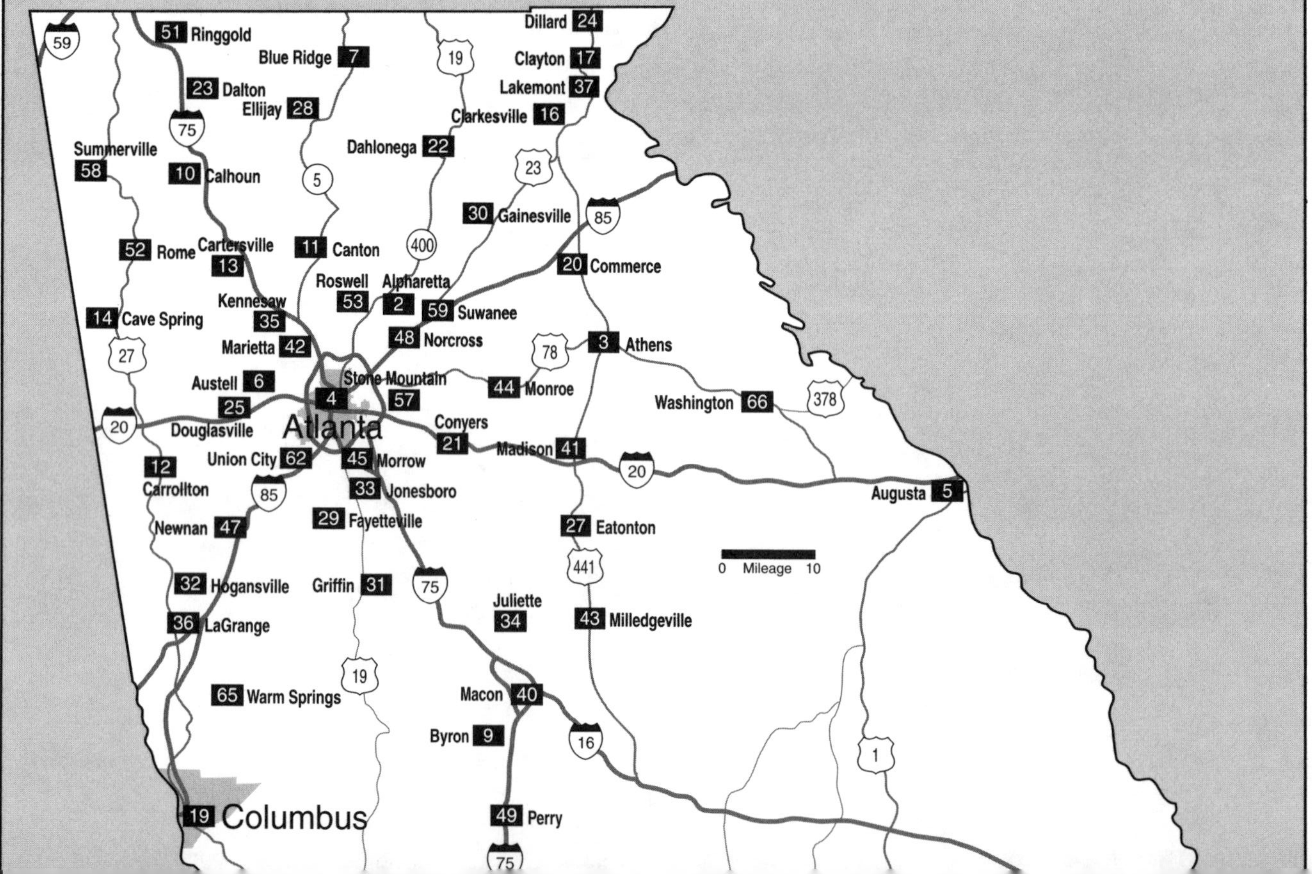
51 Ringgold
Blue Ridge 7
23 Dalton
Ellijay 28
Dillard 24
Clayton 17
Lakemont 37
Clarkesville 16
Summerville 58
10 Calhoun
Dahlonega 22
30 Gainesville
52 Rome
Cartersville 13
11 Canton
Roswell 53
Alpharetta 2
20 Commerce
14 Cave Spring
Kennesaw 35
59 Suwanee
48 Norcross
3 Athens
Marietta 42
Austell 6
25
Stone Mountain 57
4
44 Monroe
Washington 66
Douglasville
Atlanta
Conyers 21
Madison 41
Union City 62
45 Morrow
12 Carrollton
33 Jonesboro
Augusta 5
Newnan 47
29 Fayetteville
27 Eatonton
0 Mileage 10
32 Hogansville
Griffin 31
Juliette 34
43 Milledgeville
36 LaGrange
65 Warm Springs
Macon 40
Byron 9
19 Columbus
49 Perry
59
19
75
5
23
85
400
78
27
378
20
85
441
75
19
16
1

Plan to spend several hours if you want to see all of the

Big Shanty
ANTIQUE MALL

100 + dealers 50,000 sq ft

Open 7 days
M-S 10-6, Sun 12-6

Huge selection of antiques and collectibles

Quality consignments arriving daily

Auction gallery on premises

Visit Jackie's Cafe

1720 N Roberts Rd.
(15 mi NW of Atlanta)

I-75 exit 116, west on Barrett Pkwy to Hwy 41, turn right & go to 2nd light. We're on the right in Kennesaw Crossing Shopping Center next to "Cowboys".

(770) 795-1704

For those interested in U.S. history, we're 1/2 way between Kennesaw Mountain National Park and The Kennesaw Civil War Museum, home of "The General".

Kennesaw

35

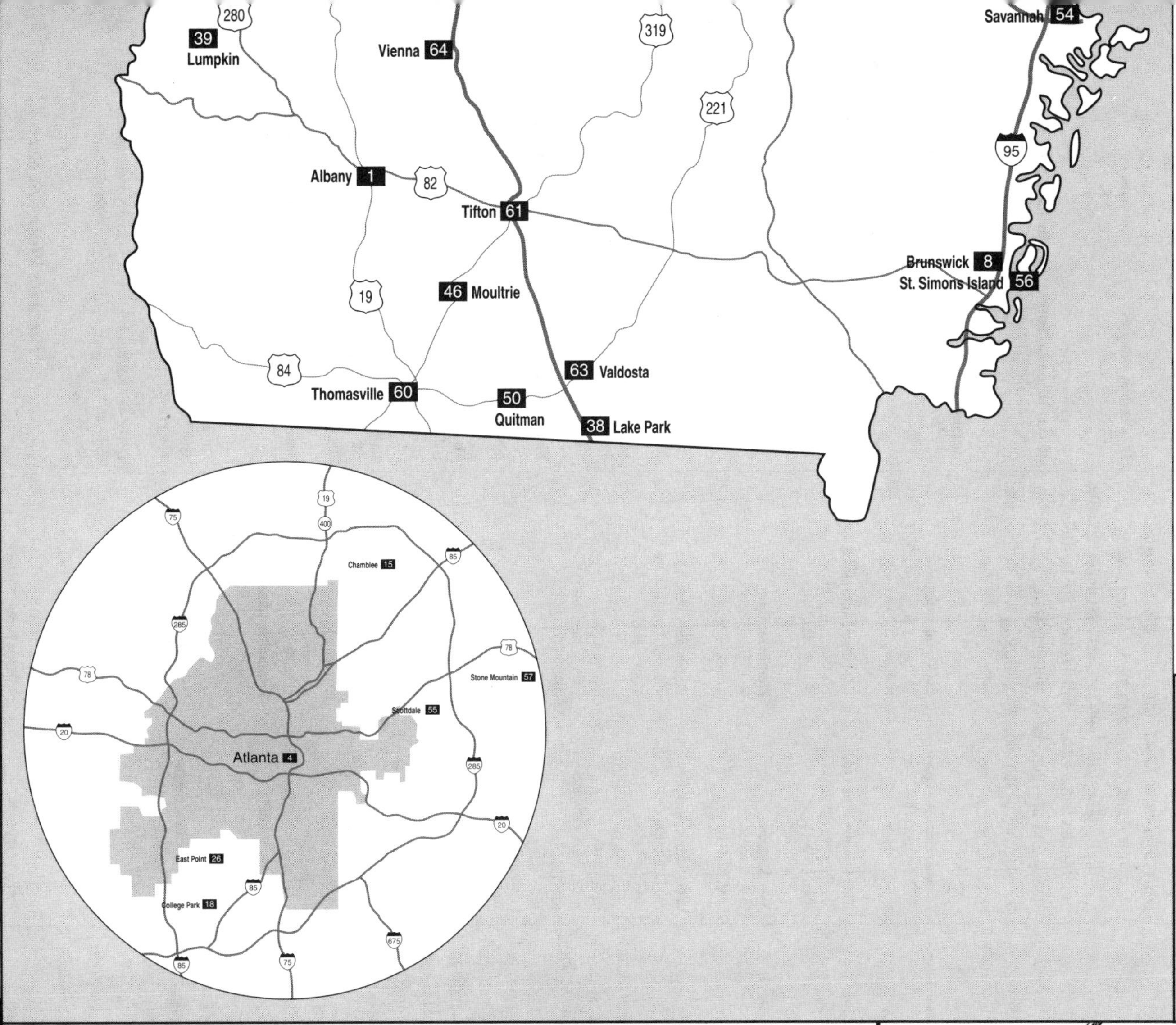

Nana's Nook

South Side of Courthouse Square

(912) 838-4131

Lumpkin

39

Cheshire Antiques

1859 Cheshire Bridge Rd.

(404) 733-5599

Atlanta

4

Roswell Antique Gallery

- *30,000 Sq. Ft.*
- *240 Dealer Spaces*
- *$6 Million Inventory*
- *Kids Korner*
- *Concession Area*
- *276 Parking Spaces*
- *Clean Rest Rooms*

Dealers Welcome
Discounts Available

10930 Crabapple Road
(Crabapple Square Shopping Center)
Roswell, Georgia 30075

770-594-8484

Toll Free 1-888-JACK NIX • FAX 770-594-1511

VISA-MC-AMEX
DISCOVER
CHECKS
LAY-AWAYS

OPEN 7 DAYS

Monday-Saturday
10A.M. - 6P.M.
Sunday
1P.M. - 6P.M.

53

THE LAKEHOUSE on Lake Rabun

Antiques & Mountain Furniture
Specializing in Adirondack Furnishings

(706) 782-1350

Lakemont

37

Georgia

1 ALBANY

Treasure House Antiques
800 N. Slappey Blvd.
912/436-9874

Bennett's Home Place
910 N. Slappey Blvd.
912/436-0040

Cottage Antiques
526 Pine Ave.
912/435-7333

2 ALPHARETTA

Old Milton Antique Mall
27 S. Main St.
770/752-0777

Main St. Antiques
53 S. Main St.
770/663-1355

A Flea Antique
222 S. Main St.
770/442-8991

Murf's Applecart Market
735 Mayfield Rd.
770/740-0308

Crabapple House Antiques
765 Mid Broadwell Rd.
770/343-9454

Crabapple Home Place Antqs.
12680 Crabapple Rd.
770/475-2799

Crabapple Corners
790 Mayfield Rd.
770/475-4545

Laura Ramsey Antiques
220 S. Main St.
770/475-2085

Sweetapple Antqs. Crabapple
780 Mayfield Rd.
770/663-6555

Shops of the Gin
780 Mayfield Rd.
770/475-3647

3 ATHENS

One of Athens' most cherished landmarks is a unique failure. The double-barreled cannon was cast at the Athens Foundry in 1862 to the specifications of John Gilleland, a local house-builder.

Each barrel was to be loaded with a cannonball connected to the other by an eight-foot chain. When fired, the balls were supposed to separate, pull the chain taut and sweep across the field, mowing down Yankees.

A contemporary reported that when test-fired, the projectile "had a kind of circular motion, plowed up an acre of ground, tore up a cornfield, mowed down saplings, then the chain broke sending the two balls in opposite directions. One of the balls killed a cow in a distant field, while the other knocked down a chimney on a log cabin." The observers "scattered as though the entire Yankee army had been turned loose in that vicinity," end of quote.

Athens displays its unusual weapon in a special park on the City Hall lawn, with the cannon pointing north, "just in case."

Another beloved landmark is a "Tree that Owns Itself," perched atop a hill approached by a cobblestone street.

Antiques Etc.
Perimeter Square
10 Huntington Rd. #3B
706/354-7863

Archipelago Antiques
1676 S. Lumpkin St.
706/354-4297

Hill Street Galleries
524 Hill St.
706/543-4172

Young's Antiques
1379 Prince Ave.
706/353-6997

4 ATLANTA

Cheshire Antiques

1859 Cheshire Bridge Road
404/733-5599
Open: Daily 11-7, closed Christmas & Thanksgiving

Directions: Located 1 mile from I-85. Take Monroe Drive or Lenox Road exit, go 2 blocks north from Pedmont Road. Located in the Shopping Center.

Within 7,000 sq. ft. of space, 35 dealers offer exceptional sought-after items such as Hull, Fostoria, Fiesta, Roseville, McCoy and fine porcelains and glassware. In addition, the shop has dealers who specialize in toys, sterling and exquisite glassware.

Turnage Place Antiques
3097 Piedmond Rd.
404/239-0378

Buckhead Antiques
3207 Early St.
404/814-1025

Irish Country Pine Ltd.
511 E Paces Ferry Rd.
404/261-7924

Jeff Littrell Antiques & Interior
178 Peachtree Hills Ave.
404/231-8662

Now & Again
56 E. Andrews Dr.
404/262-1468

Plantation Shop
96 E. Andrews Dr.
404/841-0065

Reed Savage Antiques
110 E. Andrews Dr.
404/262-3439

Regals Antiques
351 Peachtree Hills Ave.
404/237-4899

Toby House
517 E. Paces Ferry Rd.
404/233-2161

Antiques Etc.
1044 N. Highland Ave.
404/874-7042

Providence
1409 N. Highland Ave.
404/872-7551

Boomerang
1145 Euclid Ave.
404/577-8158

Allan Arthur Oriental Rugs
25 Bennett St.
404/350-9560

Beaman Antiques
25 Bennett St.
404/352-9388

Bittersweet Antiques
45 Bennet St.
404/351-6594

H Moog Antique Porcelains
2300 Peachtree Rd. Ste. B 105
404/351-2200

Interiors Market
55 Bennett St.
404/352-0055

Jacqueline Adams Antiques
2300 Peachtree Rd. Ste. B-110
404/355-8123

John Eric Riis Designs Ltd.
875 Piedmont Ave. NE
404/881-9847

Nottingham Antiques
45 Bennett St.
404/352-1890

Peurifoy Antiques
2300 Peachtree Rd. Ste. C103
404/355-3319

Robuck & Co. Antiques
65 Bennett St.
404/351-7173

Shelton Antiques
2267 Peachtree Rd. NE
404/351-5503

Stalls At Bennett Street
116 Bennett St.
404/352-4430

J Michael Stanley
2265 Peachtree Rd. NE
404/351-1863

Walker McIntyre Antiques
2300 Peachtree Rd. Ste. B101
404/352-3722

Woodward & Warwick
45 Bennett St.
404/355-6607

House of Treasures
1771 Centra Villa Dr. SW
404/752-7221

Anne Flaire Antiques
900 Huff Rd. NW
404/352-1960

Atlanta Antiques Exchange
1185 Howell Mill Rd. NW
404/351-0727

Bull & Bear Antiques
1189 Howell Mill Rd. NW
404/355-6697

Garwood House Ltd.
1510 Ellsworth Indus. Blvd. NW
404/892-7103

Howell Mill Antiques
1189 Howell Mill Rd. NW
404/351-0309

Pine Cottage
1189 Howell Mill Rd. NW
404/351-7463

O'Callaghan Antiques
1157 Foster St NW
404/352-2631

Provenance
1155 Foster St. NW
404/351-1217

Robert Mixon Antiques
1183 Howell Mill Rd. NW
404/352-2925

Another Time-Antiques
1382 Dresden Dr. NE
404/233-2500

Acquistions
631 Miami Cr. NE
404/261-2478

Antique Collections
1586 Piedmont Rd. NE
404/875-0075

Antique Paintings
631 Miami Cr. NE
404/264-0349

Morehouse & Graham Antqs.
631 Miami Cr. NE #15
404/237-0599

Bobby Dodd Antiques
695 Miami Cr. NE
404/231-0580

Canterbury Antiques Ltd.
660 Miami Cr. NE
404/231-4048

Granny Taught Us How
1921 Peachtree Rd.
404/351-2942

Dearing Antiques
709 Miami Cr. NE
404/233-6333

Milou's Market
1927 Cheshire Bridge Rd. NE
404/892-8296

Out of the Attic Antiques
1830 Cheshire Bridge Rd. N
404/876-0207

Pine & Design Imports
721 Miami Cr. NE
404/266-3741

Red Baron's Private Reserve
631 Miami Cr. NE
404/841-1011

Thames Valley Antiques
631 Miami Cr. NE
404/262-1541

Twickenham Gallery, Inc.
631 Miami Cr. Ste. 24 & 26
404/261-0951

Williams Antiques
699 Miami Cr. NE
404/231-9818

Antiquities Historical Gallery
3500 Peachtree Rd. NE
404/233-5019

Sandy Springs Galleries
233 Hilderbrand Dr. NE
404/252-3244

Antiques of Vinings
4200 Paces Ferry Rd. NW #230
770/434-1228

The Levison & Cullen Gallery
2300 Peachtree Rd. Ste. C101
404/351-3435

20th Century Antiques
1044 N Highland Ave.
404/892-2065

Designer Antiques Ltd.
25 Bennett St.
404/352-0254

Gallery Momoyama
2273 Peachtree Rd.
404/351-0583

Favorite Places To Eat

Mary Mac's Tea Room

224 Ponce de Leon Avenue NE
404/876-1800

There seems to be something inversely proportional in the more of a lack of sophistication and elegance, to the more enjoyable and tasty cooking of food. Such is the case at Mary Mac's in Atlanta. It's a lunchroom with no frills and low prices where you write your own order for the waitress to pick up. But it is one of the tops in regional cuisine in the South. They even have a dessert called Carter Custard, made with peanuts and named after a well-known Georgia resident!

Mary Mac's is most noted for its fast service, fried chicken, and vegetables. Once you are seated at one of the plain laminated tables, you check the day's menu (printed on pastel paper), then write your order on a tiny pad. The waitress flies by, grabs the order, and is instantly back with the food! Do order the fried chicken, and eat as many different vegetables as you can get down. It is a breathtaking, belt-tightening experience.

5 AUGUSTA

Antique World Mall Inc.
1124 Broad St.
706/722-4188

Marketplace Antiques
1208 Broad St.
706/724-6066

Broad Street Antique Mall
1224 Broad St.
706/722-4333

Downtown Antique Mall
1243 Broad St.
706/722-3571

Attic Antiques
2301 Peach Orchard Rd.
706/793-1839

Quaint Shop
1918 Central Ave.
706/738-7193

Antiques & Furnishings
1421 Monte Sano Ave.
706/738-4400

Aunt Sissy's Antiques
421 Crawford Avenue
706/736-0754

Riverwalk Antique Depot
505 Reynolds St.
706/724-5648

Ann Spivey Antiques
2611 Central Ave.
706/733-5889

E E Neely Antiques
2053 Walton Way #B
706/667-9714

Antique Gallery of Augusta
2055 Walton Way
706/667-8866

Favorite Places To Eat

Cracker Barrel Old Country Store
I-20 & Belair Rd., Exit 63
706/650-2414

6 AUSTELL

Grapevine
2787 Bankhead Hwy.
770/944-8058

Ramona's Antiques & Things
2805 Bankhead Hwy.
770/941-2993

Whistle Stop Antiques
2809 Bankhead Hwy.
770/739-8366

Wishful Thinking
5850 Bankhead Hwy.
770/745-1194

7 BLUE RIDGE

Sammy's Antiques
662 E. Main St.
706/632-3991

Blue Ridge Antique Mall
285 Depot St.
706/632-5549

Blue Ridge Antiques
631 E. Main St.
706/632-7871

Main Street Antiques
631 E. Main St.
706/632-7788

8 BRUNSWICK

Favorite Places To Eat

Cracker Barrel Old Country Store
I-95 & U.S. 341, Exit 7A
912/267-7905

9 BYRON

Lord Byron Antiques & Cllbls.
100 W. Heritage Blvd.
912/956-2789

Big Peach Antq. & Cllctbl. Mall
Highway 49
912/956-6256

Little Peach Antiques & Gifts
Highway 49
912/956-4222

10 CALHOUN

Calhoun Antique Mall
1503 Red Bud Rd. NE
706/625-2767

Showcase Antiques
1017 Hwy. 53 East SE
706/602-1233

Magnolia House
309 Belwood
706/625-2942

11 CANTON

Beaver's Antiques
370 E. Marietta St.
770/720-2927

Cherokee Antiques
210 Lakeside Dr.
770/345-2989

Chamberhouse
145 W. Main St.
770/479-2463

12 CARROLLTON

Antiques & Stuff
4552 Carrollton Villa Rica Hwy.
770/832-1855

Linda's Antiques
269 Cross Plains Hulett Rd.
770/836-8051

Antique Mall
106 Adamson Sq.
770/832-2992

Cotton Gin Antiques
4640 E. Hwy. 166
770/834-3196

Red Door Gallery
150 Bankhead Ave.
770/830-0025

Oak Mountain Mall
2093 S. Hwy. 16
770/838-0037

Ben's Antiques & Collectibles
4098 N. Hwy. 27
770/832-8050

13 CARTERSVILLE

Favorite Places To Eat

Cracker Barrel Old Country Store
I-75 & Hwy. 20, Exit 125
770/386-6973

14 CAVE SPRINGS

Asbury House
4 Rome Rd.
706/777-0330

Appletree Antiques
24 Broad St.
706/777-8060

County Roads Antique Mall
19 Rome Rd.
706/777-8397

Crowe's Nest
6 Broad St.
706/777-1439

411 Antiques & Uniques
22 Alabama St.
706/777-0411

15 CHAMBLEE

Eugenia's Authentic Antique Hardware
5370 Peachtree Road
770/458-1677 or 1-800-337-1677
Fax: 770/458-5966
Open Mon.-Sat. 10-6 (EST)

This is a store that should be invaluable to anyone who buys antiques. Eugenia's specializes in one-of-a-kind, hard-to-find hardware items. But what sets them apart is that all their hardware is authentic—no new pieces or reproductions. Owners Eugenia and Lance Dobson search out every piece, clean and polish everything they buy for the store. They carry an extensive line of authentic antique door hardware, both interior and exterior, dating back to the 19th century, primarily 1840-1960. Here is just a short list of some of the items Eugenia's carries.

* bath and powder room accessories: soap, cup and toothbrush holders, towel bars, faucets, cast iron claw feet, wire soap baskets, cabinet latches and hinges
* furniture hardware: handles, pulls and knobs in Hepplewhite, Queen Anne, arts and crafts, Art Deco, Victorian, colonial, Eastlake, Art Nouveau, Chippendale
* door hardware, both interior and exterior: thumb latch entry sets, glass rosette sets, Victorian cast iron dead bolts, mortise locks, rim locks, elbow locks, door plates
* other accessories: sconces, door knockers, mechanical door bells, curtain/drapery tie-backs, hooks, letter slots, finials, switch/receptacle plates, pocket door hardware, brass bed finial balls, trunk/chest hardware, casters, decorative wrought iron pieces, old keys, door stops
* fireside shop: andirons, firesets, fire fenders, firescreens, cast iron grates

A Little Bit Country Antiques
5496 Peachtree Rd.
770/452-1726

Happy Happy Shoppe
5498 Peachtree Rd.
770/458-8700

Pennsylvania John's
5459 B Peachtree Rd.
770/451-8774

Way We Were Antiques
5493 Peachtree Rd.
770/451-3372

24 Carat Antiques
5360 Peachtree Industrial Blvd.
770/451-2224

Antique City
5180 Peachtree Industrial Blvd.
770/458-7131

Blue Max Antiques
5180 Peachtree Industrial Blvd.
770/455-3553

Atlanta Antq. Ctr. & Flea Mkts.
5360 Peachtree Industrial Blvd.
770/458-0456

Cannon Mall Antiques
3509 Broad St.
770/458-1662

Antique Haus
3510 Broad St.
770/455-7570

Blanton House Antiques
5449 Peachtree Rd.
770/458-1453

Broad Street Antique Mall
3550 Broad St.
770/458-6316

Rust & Dust Co.
5486-92 Peachtree Rd.
770/458-1614

Helen's Antiques & Collectibles
5494 Peachtree Rd.
770/454-9397

Moose Breath Trading Co.
5461 Peachtree Rd.
770/458-7210

Biggar Antiques
5576 Peachtree Rd.
770/451-2541

End of the Row Antiques
5485 Peachtree Rd.
770/458-3162

Liza's Cafe
2201 American Industrial Blvd.
770/452-7001

The Cameo Estate Jewelry
3535 Broad St.
770/457-9925

Baby Jane's
5350 Peachtree Rd.
770/457-4999

Antique Asylum
5356 Peachtree Rd.
770/936-0510

16 CLARKESVILLE

Barbara's Antiques
Hwy. 197
706/947-1362

Dixie Galleries Antiques
1404 Washington Sq.
706/754-7044

Wonders' Antiques
On The Square-Washington St.
706/754-6883

Parker Place Antqs. & Gifts
On The Square-Washington St.
706/754-5057

Once Upon A Time Co.
1440 N. Washington
706/754-5789

Nostalgia Antiques & Cllbls.
1417 Washington St.
706/754-3469

Miss Mary's Antqs. on Square
135 Grant St.
706/754-1742

Habersham Antique Shop
135 Grant St.
706/754-5454

17 CLAYTON

Berry Patch Antiques
Hwy. 441 N
706/782-7216

Heritage Antiques
Hwy. 441 S
706/782-6548

Second Hand Rose Antiques
Charlie Mountain Rd.
706/782-1350

Favorite Places To Eat

Green Shutters Tea Room
Old Highway 441 south of Clayton
706/782-3342

If you've never experienced the utter delight and pure pleasure of eating great food in the absolute "quiet" of the real, undisturbed country, then take a break and eat at the Green Shutters Tea Room. Hidden in the mountains of north Georgia, this little jewel has been serving three meals a day for the past forty or so years. Get there early and enjoy breakfast on the back porch overlooking a meadow with a split-rail fence, and watch the sunrise slowly paint the dewy grass with tiny jewels of light while the rooster crows. Eat crisp-crust biscuits slathered in homemade jelly and honey fresh from the hive; crispy pan-fried country ham; grits swimming in butter, eggs any way you like and steaming hot coffee.

Stop for lunch or dinner in the indoor dining room, and sink into crunchy fried chicken, country ham, biscuits, and all the southern-style vegetables you can imagine. Everything is served country/family style, in bowls that are passed whenever needed. Green Shutters is open from the day school closes until the day school starts, or until it gets too cold, so call first to see if they're cooking.

18 COLLEGE PARK

Mu Mac Antiques
3383 Main St.
404/768-6121

Royal Touch Antiques
3395 Main St.
404/669-9525

Sarah's Antiques
2815 Roosevelt Hwy.
404/761-2881

Gallen's Antiques
1682 Virginia Ave.
404/761-5166

19 COLUMBUS

English Patina
1120 10th Ave.
706/576-4300

That Added Touch of Columbus
1103 13th St.
706/327-2330

The Tea Caddy
1231 Stark Ave.
706/327-3010

Glass Porch Antiques
3852 Gentian Blvd.
706/569-7777

Keeping Room
4518 Reese Rd.
706/563-2504

Charles & Di Antiques
7870 Veterans Parkway
706/324-3314

Peaches & Cream
1443 17th St.
706/327-7485

20 COMMERCE

Favorite Places To Eat

Cracker Barrel Old Country Store
I-85 & U.S. 441, Exit 53

21 CONYERS

Favorite Places To Eat

Cracker Barrel Old Country Store
I-20 & State Rd. 138, Exit 42
770/785-7600

22 DAHLONEGA

Do-Drop-In Antiques
87 N. Chestatee St.
706/867-6082

Golden Memories Antiques
8 Public Square
706/864-7222

Rockhouse Market Place
Highway 52 E. & Rockhouse Rd.
706/864-0305

Favorite Places To Eat

The Smith House
84 S. Chestatee
706/864-3566

The Smith House is a first-come, first-served, no holds barred kind of place; no reservations are accepted, and on weekends the place is packed. It's an elbow-to-elbow kind of atmosphere, with communal tables, shared by whomever is fortunate enough to get a seat! Pay one price and eat all you want. There is no menu, no choices. Everything that the kitchen has prepared that day is brought to the tables in large serving dishes, and it's a constant passing game. You can always count on fried chicken, bolstered either by Brunswick stew or catfish and hushpuppies, plenty of southern-style vegetables and warm breads.

The history of The Smith House began before the Civil War, during Georgia's gold rush—yes, I mean Georgia! This southern love affair with the golden stuff attracted prospectors from all over America, one of whom was wealthy Vermonter Captain Frank Hall. Hall staked a claim just east of Dahlonega's public square, and struck a fashionably rich lode. Dahlonega authorities, so the legend goes, would not allow their town's heart to be stripped open, so the stubborn Yankee decided if he couldn't have the wealth, nobody could. He promptly built an ostentatious mansion, complete with carriage house and servants' quarters, right on top of the vein! In 1922, long after Captain Hill's feud with Dahlonega had ended, Henry and Bessie Smith bought the house to operate it as an inn. For $1.50 travelers got a room and three meals! Mrs. Smith was a sensational cook, and praise for her culinary creations soon spread far and wide, especially about her fried chicken, country ham and fresh vegetables. When Fred and Thelma Welch took over ownership in 1946, The Smith House became known for its family-style offerings. Today, although the rooms have been spruced up a little, the food has not changed. It's still old-fashioned north Georgia cooking. As of yet, nobody has tried to dig up Captain Hall's gold.

23 DALTON

Favorite Places To Eat

Cracker Barrel Old Country Store
I-75 & Walnut Ave., Exit 136
706/226-5231

24 DILLARD

Black Rock Antiques
Hwy. 441
706/746-2470

Dillard Mini Mall
Hwy. 441
706/746-5194

Pine Cone Antiques of Dillard
Hwy. 441
706/746-2450

Stikeleather's
Hwy. 441
706/746-6525

Treasures Old & New Antiques
Hwy. 441
706/746-6566

Village Peddler
Hwy. 441
706/746-5156

Yesterday's Treasures
6 Depot St.
706/746-3363

25 DOUGLASVILLE

Antiques Plus
6554 Church St.
770/489-1669

Homespun & Sweet Antqs.
6118 Fairburn Rd.
770/949-1020

Your Cup of Tea
5848 Bankhead Hwy.
770/489-7908

Favorite Places To Eat

Cracker Barrel Old Country Store
I-20 & Hwy. 92, Exit 10
770/949-0999

26 EAST POINT

East Point Antiques
1595 White Way
404/767-2555

Sara Goen's Antiques
1603 White Way
404/762-1234

Dragon's Lair
1605 White Way
404/762-7020

Amazing Grace Elephant Co.
1613 White Way
404/767-2423

27 EATONTON

Welcome to Eatonton and Putnam County, home of Brer Rabbit and the Uncle Remus Tales. As you drive through the tree-lined streets, you will witness some of the most unique styles of Antebellum architecture in the South, or you might even catch a glimpse of Sylvia, the ghost that occupies Panola Hall, the former home of Dr. Benjamin Hunt. Eatonton is proud of the many people it has produced. Two of the most famous are Joel Chandler Harris, creator of the Uncle Remus Tales; and Alice Walker, author and Pulitzer Prize winner for her book, *The Color Purple.*

Fox Hunt Antiques
109 N. Jefferson Ave.
706/485-6402

Crystal Palace Flea Market
1242 Madison Rd.
706/485-9010

28 ELLIJAY

Betty's Primatiques
19 River St.
706/635-6262

Victorian Attic
40 N. Main St.
706/636-3700

Trading Post Inc.
54 N Main St.
706/276-1699

Old Hotel Antique Mall
11 North Ave.
706/276-2467

Antiques & More
6 River St.
706/635-7738

Ole Harper's Store
3 miles out 52 W
706/276-7234

Coosawattee Mini Mall
215 S. Main St.
706/636-4004

Cartecay Trading Post
Big Creek Rd.
706/635-7009

29 FAYETTEVILLE

Brannon Antiques
165 W. Lanier Ave.
770/461-9160

Attic Treasures Antiques
235 S. Glynn St.
770/460-8114

Fayette Collectibles
105 E. Stonewall Ave.
770/460-6979

Olde & Crafty Antiques & Gifts
125 Fisher Ave.
770/460-8101

30 GAINESVILLE

Antiquities In Time
330 Bradford St. N
770/534-3689

Select Accents
1037 Thompson Bridge Rd.
770/503-7032

Antiques & Uniques
2145 Cleveland Rd.
770/536-1651

Antique Nook
1740 Cleveland Rd.
770/536-0646

Brickstore Antiques
1744 Cleveland Rd.
770/532-8033

Curiosity Shop
2714 Old Cornelia Hwy.
770/536-7088

31 GRIFFIN

Dovedown Antique Mall
315 W. Solomon St.
770/412-6121

Complements
522 W. Solomon St.
770/229-2561

J Newton Bell Jr Antiques Inc.
417 S. 6th St.
770/227-2516

Solomon House Antiques
103 N. 13th St.
770/229-5390

Nearly New Store
1003 W. Taylor St.
770/229-8397

Country Cottage
1975 Atlanta Rd.
770/227-0476

Treasures Antiques & Furniture
233 N. Hill St.
770/228-0053

32 HOGANSVILLE

Cheatham's Antiques
302, 304 & 306 E. Main
706/637-4130

Ray Cheatham's Enterprises
308 E. Main
706/637-6227

Liberty Hill Antiques
301 S. Hwy. 29
706/637-5522

Potpourri Antiques
302 E. Main St.
706/637-5564

Treasure Chest
307 S. Hwy. 29
706/637-9999

33 JONESBORO

Marianne's Collectables
7488 Tara Blvd.
770/471-0571

Sweet Memories
181 N. Main St.
770/478-7100

Jonesboro Antique Shoppe
203 N. Main St.
770/478-4021

34 JULIETTE

In Juliette the primary color is green, as in *Fried Green Tomatoes*. They are now served hot at The Whistle Stop Cafe, the actual film location of the movie. Other notable stops in this area include the Piedmont Wildlife Refuge, Lake Juliette and the 1847 Jarrell Plantation Historic Site.

Garments Praise & Antiques
McCrackin Rd.
912/994-0011

35 KENNESAW

Big Shanty Antique Mall
1720 North Roberts Rd.
770/795-1704
Open Tue.-Sat. 10-6, Sun. 12-6, closed Mondays.

Directions: Take I-75 to exit 116. Go west to Highway 41, turn right and go to the second light. Turn right, and the mall is in Kennesaw Crossing Shopping Center, 15 miles northwest of Atlanta.

Big Shanty Antique Mall has something to please both genders. In their huge 50,000-square-foot space you'll find everything in the way of antiques and collectibles. They carry glassware, china, dolls, furniture, rugs, jewelry, art, prints and so on and so on. And for the men (no, I didn't forget you), Big Shanty holds monthly gun shows. In fact, last year they had eight gun shows, one every month from May through December! They also have monthly auctions, so call ahead for dates and times.

By-Gone Treasures
2839 S. Main St.
770/428-2262

Garner's Antiques
2950 Moon Station Rd.
770/428-6481

Kennesaw Mountain Military
1810 Old Highway 41
770/424-5225

Favorite Places To Eat

Cracker Barrel Old Country Store
I-75 & Chastain Rd., Exit 117
770/429-1524

36 LA GRANGE

B J's Quiet Country Barn
29 Old Hutchinson Mill Rd.
706/845-7838

Lemon Tree Shoppes
204 Morgan St.
706/882-5382

Water Wheel Antiques
1751 New Franklin Rd.
706/883-8242

Greenville Street Antiques
606 Greenville St.
706/883-8539

37 LAKEMONT

THE LAKEHOUSE on Lake Rabun
Lake Rabun Road
706/782-1350
404/351-5859
Open: Fri., Sat., and Sun. 11-6 May 1-Oct. 30. Closed Winter Months.

Directions: From Clayton, GA. go south on Hwy. 441 approximately 4 miles to Wiley Junction. Turn sharp right and go 50 yards to old Hwy. 441. Turn left and go approximately 1 mile to Alleys Store in Lakemont. Continue approximately 1/4 mile to a fork in the road. Take the right fork (Lake Rabun Road) and go approximately 2 miles to THE LAKEHOUSE antique shop. (On the left across from the historic Rabun Hotel.)

THE LAKEHOUSE antique shop on beautiful Lake Rabun in the northeast Georgia mountains is a multi-dealer shop with two floors of antiques and mountain (rustic) furniture. The shop specializes in Adirondack furnishings for the mountain cabin and lake home. They also carry a line of mountain twig furnishings by Buz Stone. Bamboo fly rods, outboard motors, old camp paddles, blankets, birchbark items along with local folk ark and paintings complete the inventory at this unique mountain shop.

38 LAKE PARK

Favorite Places To Eat

Cracker Barrel Old Country Store
I-75 & Lake Park, Exit 2
912/559-0864

39 LUMPKIN

Nana's Nook
South Side of Court House Square
912/838-4131
Open: Tue.-Sat. 11-5, Sunday by Chance and Closed Mondays

Directions: Nana's Nook is located on the South Side of the Court House Square, Lumpkin, Ga. Lumpkin is 35 miles south of Columbus, Ga on U.S. 27.

Nana's Nook, owned and operated by Dolores Harris and Gina Mathis, a mother and daughter team, has no consignors or dealers. It was a life-long dream of Dolores (Nana) to own an antique shop when she retired after having taught 30 years of elementary school music. Daughter Gina, talked here into opening the shop. Their goal is to have affordable antiques and collectibles for everyone taste and budget. The two have "decorated" the shop as we would our own homes and have been complimented numerous times by customers on its "at home" feel and "no dust" atmosphere. While visiting Lumpkin, be sure to enjoy the other shops and tourist sights such as Westville Historic Village and Providence Canyon State Park. The town of Lumpkin offers two great places to eat, Dr. Hatchett's Drugstore Museum and Michele's Country Cooking Buffet.

Interesting Side Trips

The Village of Westville
Intersection of U.S. 27 and GA. 27
912/838-6310
Open: Tue.-Sat. 10-5, Sunday 1-5

Westville is a functioning living history village of relocated, authentically restored, original buildings and landscape. The Village of Westville realistically depicts Georgia's pre-industrial life and culture of 1850 for your educational benefit.

Stroll down the streets and watch craftsmen at work producing items for their neighbors in the Village. Hear the "clang" of the blacksmith's hammer and anvil, and smell the gingerbread and biscuits cooking on the stove and fireplace. Try your hand at making seasonal crafts, such as candles, syrup, and soap. Here, you family will "glimpse the forgotten dreams" of 150 years past.

40 MACON

Welcome to America's Dreamtown, historic Macon, your southernmost stop on Georgia's Antebellum Trail. Founded in 1823 on the banks of the Ocmulgee River, Macon is a dreamtown for those looking for a wealth of antebellum treasures. Wide avenues, created by Macon's original town planners, lead you through what has been called "a city in a park." In fact, Macon was designed to resemble the ancient gardens of Babylon, providing for large parks and garden squares. Today, some 200,000 Yoshino cherry trees throughout the city make Macon the Cherry Blossom Capital of the World!

Village Antique Mall
2390 Ingleside Avenue
912/755-0075
E-mail: vam2@mindspring.com
Open: 7 days a week until 6. Extended hours at Christmas. Accepts all major credit cards.

Directions: Located only three minutes from I-75 in the heart of Georgia. Northbound, take exit 52, cross 41 South, turn left onto 41 North, turn right at the 5th traffic light (Rogers Avenue) come to the next traffic light and turn left onto Ingleside Avenue. You will find Village Antique Mall at the end of the block on the left. From exit 54 southbound, go to second traffic light and turn right onto Ingleside Avenue. They will be on the left after the first traffic light at the end of the block.

Specializing in pieces rarely found in the area, Village Antique Mall offers the discriminating shopper items from the arts and crafts era, such as Stickley, Limbert, Van Briggle and Niloak. Twenty-five expert antique dealers specialize in fine china, oil paintings, 30s & 40s Mahogany furnishings as well as period pieces offered by Sherwood Antiques. Considered by its customers to be one of the finest antique malls in the middle Georgia area, this shop prides itself as offering only the finest in true antiques and collectibles.

*Dealer of quality care products for your antiques: Howards Products, Kramers Antiques Improver, Bri-Wax and more.

Eclectic Era Antique Place
1345 Hardeman Ave.
912/746-1922

Piddlers Canopy Antiques
217 Emery Hwy.
912/743-0309

Catherine Callaway Antiques
3164 Vineville Ave.
912/755-9553

McLean Antiques
2291 Ingleside Ave.
912/745-2784

Exmoor Antiques
2370 Ingleside Ave.
912/746-7480

Vine Villa Antique Mall
119 Marshall Ave.
912/471-7804

Yellow House Antiques
2176 Ingleside Ave.
912/742-2777

Wildwood Cottage
2195 Ingleside Ave.
912/741-4005

Collectables Unlimited
6717 Hawkinsville Rd.
912/788-0005

Mallard Nest Antiques
5860 Bankston Lake Rd.
912/788-8606

A-OK Antiques Etc.
5296 Riverside Dr.
912/477-1422

Great Places To Eat

Cracker Barrel Old Country Store
I-475 & Hwy. 80, Exit 1
912/477-4848

Cracker Barrel Old Country Store
I-75 & Arkwright Riverside Dr., Exit 55A
912/474-7029

41 MADISON

Madison Antique Mall
1291 Eatonton Rd.
706/342-3753

Attic Treasures Antiques
121 S. Main St.
706/342-7197

Old Madison Antiques
184 S. Main St.
706/342-3839

Step Back In Time, Inc.
130 W. Washington St.
706/342-3311

42 MARIETTA

Railway Antqs. & Design Cntr.
472 N. Sessions St. NW
770/427-8505

Antique Accents
67 Church St.
770/426-7373

Keeping Room
77 Church St.
770/499-9577

Hill House Antiques
85 Church St.
770/425-6169

Southern Traditions Antiques
93 Church St.
770/428-6005

Heather's Neste
95 Church St.
770/919-8636

Willow Antiques
105 Church St.
770/426-7274

Mountain Mercantile
107 Church St.
770/429-1663

Mountain Mercantile
115 Church St.
770/429-1889

Antique Store of Marietta
113 Church St.
770/428-3376

Avery Gallery
390 Roswell Rd.
770/427-2459

Emporium at Marietta
547 Roswell Rd.
770/919-8087

Trading Memories
686 Roswell Rd.
770/421-9724

Back Home Antiques
1450 Roswell Rd.
770/971-5342

Red Geranium
1460 Roswell Rd.
770/578-4527

Marietta Antiques Exchange
1505 Roswell Rd.
770/565-7460

Abe's Antiques
1951 Canton Rd.
770/424-0587

Water Spaniel Collectibles
7 Whitlock Ave.
770/427-0277

Du Pre's Antique Market
17 Whitelock Ave. NW
770/428-2667

Lamps of Yesteryear, Inc.
5 Powder Springs St.
770/424-6015

Ari's I Antiques
19 Powder Springs St.
770/425-0811

Juniper Tree Cllbls. & Antiques
15 West Park Square
770/427-3148

Ari's II Antiques
18 Powder Springs St.
770/425-4153

Victoria's Garden
21 West Park Square
770/419-0984

Antique Corner
110 S Park Square
770/428-4294

Antiques on the Square
146 S. Park Square
770/429-0434

Antiquity Mall
815 Pine Manor
770/428-8238

Favorite Places To Eat

Cracker Barrel Old Country Store
I-75 & Delk Rd., Exit 111
770/951-2602

43 MILLEDGEVILLE

J & K Fleas Antiques
2937 N. Columbia St.
912/454-3006

Jeans Antique Shop
2205 Irwinton Rd.
912/452-1550

Sugartree
1045 N. Jefferson St. NE
912/452-7914

Browsing Barn
169 Sparta Hwy. NE
912/452-7740

Carolyn's Antiques
1415 Vinson Hwy. SE
912/453-9676

44 MONROE

Primitive Touch
136 N. Broad St.
770/267-9799

Road Side Bargain Shop
2183 Hwy. 78 NW
770/267-6227

Vinegar Hill Antique Mall
120 N Broad St.
770/267-3350

45 MORROW

Favorite Places To Eat

Cracker Barrel Old Country Store
I-75 & Jonesboro Rd., Exit 76
770/961-4533

46 MOULTRIE

Olde Harmony Antiques
15 2nd Ave. SE
912/985-5679

R & R Antiques
4246 Tallokas Rd.
912/985-3595

Southland Country Antiques
123 1st St. SE
912/985-7212

Southland Antiques & Gifts
120 1st St. SE
912/890-2092

Sid's
112-114 1st St. NE
912/985-8300

47 NEWNAN

Homespun Heart
50 Farmer St.
770/253-0480

R J's Antiques & Collectibles
17 Augusta Dr.
770/251-0999

Whistle Stop Antique Shop
1002 Hwy. 16 W
770/251-6759

Three Crowns Antiques Ltd.
733 Bullsboro Dr.
770/253-4815

Amelia's Collectables
182 Jefferson St.
770/251-6467

48 NORCROSS

Georgia Antique Ctr. & Mkt.
6624 Dawson Blvd.
770/446-9292

Pride of Dixie Antique Market
1700 Jeurgens Ct.
770/279-9853

Favorite Places To Eat

Cracker Barrel Old Country Store
I-85 & Jimmy Carter Blvd., Exit 37
770/446-1313

49 PERRY

Favorite Places To Eat

Cracker Barrel Old Country Store
I-75 & State Road 127, Exit 42
912/987-2242

50 QUITMAN

Malloy Manor Bed & Breakfast
401 West Screven Street
912/263-5704 or 1-800-239-5704
Rates: $55-85

Directions: Go west on U.S. Highway 84 off I-75 at the Quitman, Georgia Exit, about halfway between Atlanta and Orlando.

Malloy Manor is the place to go to experience a unique blend of Victorian elegance and Old South southern hospitality! At this three-story, 1905 Victorian home listed on the National Register of Historic Places, you can literally stop and smell the roses, or any other flowers for that matter, because this city is situated in the middle of a "fragrance zone." Quitman is Georgia's camilla city; Valdosta, Georgia's azalea city, and Thomasville, Georgia's rose city.

You can imagine yourself in pre-Civil War times enjoying the balmy days on the large wraparound porch outfitted with rockers and a swing, or gliding gracefully across the entrance that features leaded glass in sidelights and transom, with more leaded glass sidelights in the upper sitting room. All the staircases, wainscoting and moldings are original, and each room holds not only antiques and lace curtains, but a working fireplace! The parlor features a windup Victrola, and the music room houses an old upright piano. Three suites are available, each with sitting room and private bath. Also there is a pair of rooms that share a sitting room and bath. Gourmet lunches and dinners are served next door at The Booth House restaurant, in a restored Victorian home.

Antiquers can explore all of Quitman—the entire town is on the National Historic Register!—and there are multiple antique shops and fascinating old homes. The Brooks County Cultural Arts Museum, open every afternoon, features local artistry and Civil War and local artifacts.

51 RINGGOLD

Gateway Antiques Center
4103 Cloud Springs Road
706/858-9685
Open: 9 a.m.-8 p.m., 7 days a week

Directions: Last exit in Georgia or first exit south of Chattanooga, I-75 exit 142 - 200 yards on right.

Gateway Antiques Center, appropriately named for its location in Georgia, is a whopping 40,000 sq. ft. wonderland of antiques and collectibles. Considered by some to be the South's largest antique mall (I certainly won't argue that), the store has 300 dealers, 400 showcases and a true sampling of every antique imaginable. The mall specializes in offering a large variety of smalls for the traveler.

Autumn Oak Antique Mall
383 Bandy Ln.
706/965-7222

Barn Gallery Antiques
Alabama Rd.
706/935-9044

Joel's Antiques
4192 Bandy Rd.
706/965-2097

My Favorite Things
7839 Nashville St.
706/965-8050

Huskey's Antiques
3218 Boynton Dr.
706/937-4881

52 ROME

Apple Cart Antiques
1572 Burnett Ferry Rd.
706/235-7356

Antique Musique
2358 Old Kingston Hwy.
706/291-9230

Heritage Antique Mall
174 Chatillon Rd.
706/291-4589

Masters Antiques
241 Broad St.
706/232-8316

Northside Antiques
1203 Calhoun Ave.
706/232-6161

Smart Shop
1007 N. Broad St.
706/234-5667

Three Rivers Antique Shop
109 Broad St.
706/290-9361

Grandpa's Attic
516 Shorter Ave.
706/235-8328

Unique Ideas Antqs. & Cllbls.
405 Mount Alto Rd.
706/235-4787

West Rome Trading Post
1104 Shorter Ave.
706/232-3525

Skelton's Red Barn Antiques
10 Burton Rd.
706/295-2713

53 ROSWELL

Roswell Antique Gallery
10930 Crabapple Road (Crabapple Square Shopping Center)
770/594-8484 or 1-888-JACK NIX
Fax: 770/594-1511
Open daily, Mon.-Sat. 10-6, Sun. 1-6, closed Thanksgiving Day and Christmas Day

Directions: Located 2.8 miles west of Highway 400 at the intersection of Crabapple Road and Crossville Road (next to Van Gogh's Restaurant).

For specific information, see review this section.

Arts & Antiques
938 Canton St.
770/552-1899

Victorian Dreams
944 Canton St.
770/998-9041

Cotton Blossom Inc.
944 Canton St.
770/642-2055

Trade Winds
952 Canton St.
770/587-4993

Roswell Clock & Antique Co.
955 Canton St.
770/992-5232

Mulberry House Antiques
1028 Canton St.
770/998-6851

Moss Blacksmith Shop
1075 Canton St.
770/993-2398

Cottage
1132 Canton St.
770/641-9422

Elizabeth's House
1072 Alpharetta St.
770/993-7300

Historic Roswell Antique Mkt.
1207 Alpharetta St. #C
770/587-5259

Shops of Distinction
11235 Alpharetta Hwy.
770/475-3111

Brown & Co. Antiques & Gifts
650 Holcomb Bridge Rd.
770/993-3991

Nottingham Antiques
1085 Holcomb Bridge Rd.
770/518-4855

Maude's Antiques
957 Canton St.
770/594-1400

Smith's Antiques & Consignments
1154 Alpharetta St.
770/518-9689

54 SAVANNAH

Alex Raskin Antiques
441 Bull St.
912/232-8205

Alexandra's Antique Gallery
320 W Broughton St.
912/233-3999

An English Accent
509 Lincoln St.
912/233-9589

Antique Alley
121 E. Gwinnett St.
912/236-6281

Arthur Smith Antiques
1W. Jones St.
912/236-9701

Blatner's Antiques
347 Abercorn St.
912/234-1210

Bozena's European Antiques
230 W. St. Julien St. #A
912/234-0086

Carriage House Antiques
135 Bull St.
912/233-5405

Contents
205 W. River St.
912/234-7493

Japonica
13 W. Charlton St.
912/236-1613

Jere's Antiques
9 N. Jefferson St.
912/236-2815

Jimmie's Attic Antiques
14 C Bishop Ct.
912/236-9325

Kenneth Worthy Antiques Inc.
319 Abercorn St.
912/236-7963

Jacqueline Levine
By Appointment Only
912/233-8519

Historic Savannah Antq. & Mkt.
220 W. Bay St.
912/238-3366

Melonie's
202 E. Bay St.
912/231-1878

Memory Lane Antiques & Mall
230 W. Bay St.
912/232-0975

Mulberry Tree
17 W. Charlton St.
912/236-4656

Old Arch Antiques & Cllbls.
235 W. Boundary St.
912/232-2922

Once Possessed Antiques
130 E. Bay St.
912/232-5531

Pinch of the Past
109 W. Broughton St.
912/232-5563

Scrooge & Marley Antiques
137 Bull St.
912/236-9099

V & J Duncan Antique Maps
12 E. Taylor St.
912/232-0338

Willows
101 W. Broughton St.
912/233-0780

Schie's Olde Shoppe
2204 Skidaway Rd.
912/234-6662

Seventh Heaven Antique Mall
3104 Skidaway Rd.
912/355-0835

Treasure Trove
3301 Waters Ave.
912/353-9697

Waters Avenue Antique Mall
3405 Waters Ave.
912/351-9313

Misty's Antiques
5794 Ogeechee Rd.
912/921-1202

17 South Antiques
4401 Ogeechee Rd.
912/236-6333

Peddler Jim's Antiques
38 Montgomery St.
912/233-6642

Junk House Antiques
5950 Ogeechee Rd.
912/927-2354

Great Places To Eat

Cracker Barrel Old Country Store
I-95 & Hwy. 204, Exit 16
912/927-6559

55 SCOTTDALE

Old Mill Antiques
3240 E. Ponce De Leon Ave.
404/292-0223

Yesterday's Antiques
3252 E. Ponce De Leon Ave.
404/292-3555

Grandma's Treasures
3256 E. Ponce De Leon Ave.
404/292-6735

56 ST. SIMONS ISLAND

Low Country Walk
1627 Frederica Rd.
912/638-1216

Antiques & Interiors Inc.
1806 Frederica Rd.
912/638-9951

Shaland Hill Gallery
3600 Frederica Rd.
912/638-0370

Franklin's Antique Folly
3600 Frederica Rd.
912/634-0606

D'Amico's
208 Redfern Village
912/638-2785

Frederica Antiques
10 Sylvan Dr.
912/638-7284

Sainte Simone's
536 Ocean Blvd.
912/634-0550

Island Annex
545 Ocean Blvd.
912/638-4304

One of a Kind
320 Mallory St.
912/638-0348

Village Mews
504 Beachview Dr.
912/634-1235

Village Exchange
315 15th St.
912/638-6373

Tabby House
105 Retreat Ave.
912/638-2257

57 STONE MOUNTAIN

Country Manor Antiques
937 Main St.
770/498-0628

C M Becker Ltd. Antiques
1100 2nd St.
770/879-7978

Paul Baron's Antiques
931 Main St.
770/469-8476

Remember When Collectibles
6570 Memorial Dr.
770/879-7878

58 SUMMERVILLE

Soon after retiring as a Baptist preacher in 1965, the Reverend Howard Finster received instructions from the Lord to convert the swampland surrounding his lawnmower and bicycle repair shop in Summerville into "Paradise Garden." Working with cast-off materials, Finster created sculpture illustrating Scriptural messages, sidewalks embedded with glass and tools, edifices composed of bicycle parts and bottles, and a "Wedding Cake" chapel. He also began to paint in response to God's instructions. His distinctive sermon art combines visual imagery with texts from the Bible and other sources.

Now one of America's most popular self-taught artists, Finster's works came to the world's attention through exhibitions, as well as a 1980 *Life* magazine article that included his work.

The National Endowment for the Arts recognized Finster's work with a 1982 visual Artist Fellowship in Sculpture, which he used to enhance his "Paradise Garden." Since then, the Garden has become a popular site for art lovers, tourists and advocates of self-taught artists. In October 1994, Finster made several major pieces from the Garden available to the High Museum of Art in Atlanta to ensure their long-term preservation.

Cherokee Antique Market
132 South Commerce St.
706/857-6788
Open daily Mon.-Sat. 10-5, Sun. 1:30-5

Directions: From the north: 40 miles south Chattanooga, Tennessee on U.S. Highway 27. Exit I-75 at Ringgold (exit 140). Go south on Georgia 151 to U.S. 27. From the south: 25 miles north of Rome, Ga., on U.S. Highway 27. Exit I-75 at Adairsville (exit 128). Follow Georgia 140 west to U.S. 27, then north to Summerville. The store is located at the junction of U.S. Highway 27 and Georgia Highway 48 in Summerville.

In the heart of Confederate territory, Cherokee Antique Mall deals in rare Civil War documents and antiques, as well as fine furniture, porcelains, primitives, quilts, linens and collectibles.

Farm House Antiques
Hwy. 27 N
706/857-4822

TLC Antiques
5 N. Commerce St.
706/857-6723

59 SUWANEE

Favorite Places To Eat

Cracker Barrel Old Country Store
I-85 & Lawrenceville/Suwanee Rd., Exit 44
770/932-5692

Georgia

60 THOMASVILLE

Thomasville Antique Mall
132 S. Broad
912/225-9231

Firefly Antiques
125 S. Broad
912/226-6363

Cabin Fever Antiques
311 S. Broad St.
912/227-0024

Collector's Corner
326 S. Broad St.
912/228-9887

James S. Mason Antiques
309 W. Remington Ave.
912/226-4454

Town & Country Antiques
119 S. Madison St.
912/226-5863

Times Remembered
209 Remington Ave.
912/228-0760

Brass Ring
124 S. Stevens St.
912/226-0029

Ross' Woodshop
Hwy. 319 S.
912/226-8786

Southern Traditions
302 Gordon St.
912/227-0908

61 TIFTON

Favorite Places To Eat

Cracker Barrel Old Country Store
I-75 & U.S. 319, Exit 18
912/386-4412

62 UNION CITY

Favorite Places To Eat

Cracker Barrel Old Country Store
I-85 & Hwy. 138, Exit 13
770/964-9996

63 VALDOSTA

Vintage Shoppe
1905 Baytree Place
912/245-0201

Martha's Antiques
1915 Baytree Place
912/241-8627

Odds & Ends Antique
1919 Baytree Place
912/244-6042

Favorite Places To Eat

Cracker Barrel Old Country Store
I-75 & St. Augustine Rd., Exit 5
912/244-5258

64 VIENNA

Exit 36 Antique Mall
1410 E. Union St.
912/268-1442

Hidden Treasures
109 E. Union St.
912/268-1127

Antiques Etc.
109 E. Union St.
912/268-1127

Joel's Antiques & Collectibles
215 N. 6th St.
912/268-2919

Olde Shoppe Upstairs
108 A Union St.
912/268-9725

Vienna Antiques
101 N. 7th St.
912/268-2851

65 WARM SPRINGS

"It was the best holiday I ever had..."—Franklin D. Roosevelt, commenting upon returning from Warm Springs, Georgia in March 1937. President Franklin D. Roosevelt made Warm Springs world-famous when he became a regular visitor and built his only home, The Little White House, there. He was often seen riding around Meriwether County in his little blue roadster. Even before Roosevelt's day, visitors came seeking the warm mineral springs which were believed to have curative powers.

Antiques & Crafts Unlimited Mall
Santa Fe Art Gallery
Alternate 27
706/655-2468

Located two miles north of Warm Springs, Georgia on U.S. Highway 27 Alternate, Antiques & Crafts Unlimited Mall is open year long for your shopping pleasure. There are 114 shops, including the Santa Fe Art Gallery. Antiques & Crafts Unlimited Mall is open daily from 9:00 to 7:00 April through October and 9:00 to 6:00 November through March. Antiques & Crafts Unlimited Mall is closed on Christmas Day. You will find a wide variety of antiques & collectibles including quality furniture, depression glass, elegant glass, collectibles of all kinds, plus a few quality crafts.

The Sante Fe Art Gallery is located inside of Antiques & Crafts Unlimited Mall. You will be able to view and purchase art by regional artist Arthur Riggs. His work is very unique and much sought after. Don't miss this Art Gallery when you are in the area. Also you will find art by Roberta Geter in the Santa Fe Art Gallery. Roberta is a young budding artist, who is proving to be very talented.

You will also find art located elsewhere in the building by Roberta Jacks of Monroe, Louisiana. Roberta has a unique style of her own. You must see her art to really appreciate it.

Visit them on the World Wide Web at: http://www.users.dircon.co.uk/~andyc/ANTIQUES

Llewellyn's
5634 Spring Street
706/655-2022

Veranda
10 Broad St.
706/655-2646

66 WASHINGTON

Colonial Antiques
721 E. Robert Toombs Ave.
706/678-2635

Sunny Daze Antq. & Gift Shop
4151 Lexington Rd.
706/274-3286

Green Barn Antiques
105 Wills Memorial Dr.
706/678-7286

Heard House Gallery
32 E. Robert Toombs Ave.
706/678-3604

Carl's Antiques & Collectibles
722 E. Robert Toombs Ave.
706/678-2225

Ye Olde Lamplighter
222 E. Robert Toombs Ave.
706/678-2043

Roswell Antique Gallery

Are you looking for something a little different in the way of an antiquing experience? Roswell Antique Gallery will be worth your stop.

The gallery has 30,000 square feet, 240 quality dealer spaces, and plenty of room outside to accommodate even the lavish traveler's bus-sized recreational vehicle. What makes the Gallery unique is the focus on quality and the assurance that the merchandise is period antique; no reproductions are allowed. If questionable, a product's authenticity is judged by three impartial experts before being added to inventory, giving the customer a quality selection dating prior to the 1950s.

Boasting 'something for everyone' would be appropriate for Roswell Antique Gallery. They offer a concession area, a Kid's Korner with a television, and a 'husband recovery area' for wives who cannot bear to leave before visiting every square foot the gallery has to offer.

The Roswell Antique Gallery is located in the Crabapple Square Shopping Center, 10930 Crabapple Road in Roswell.

Jack Nix and his son Bill can boast about their shop's variety.

Idaho

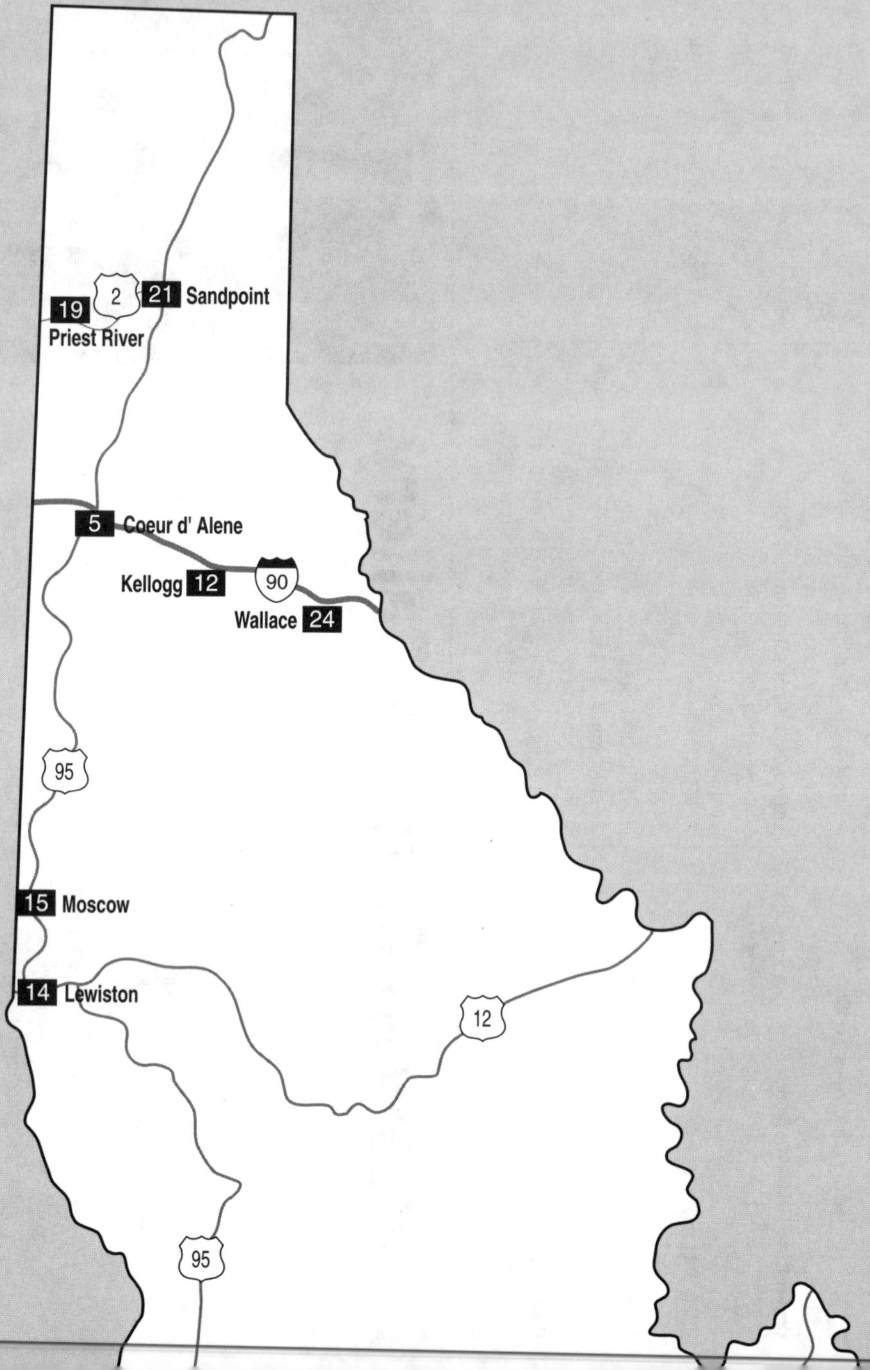

2
19
21
Sandpoint
Priest River
5
Coeur d' Alene
Kellogg
12
90
Wallace
24
95
15
Moscow
14
Lewiston
12
95

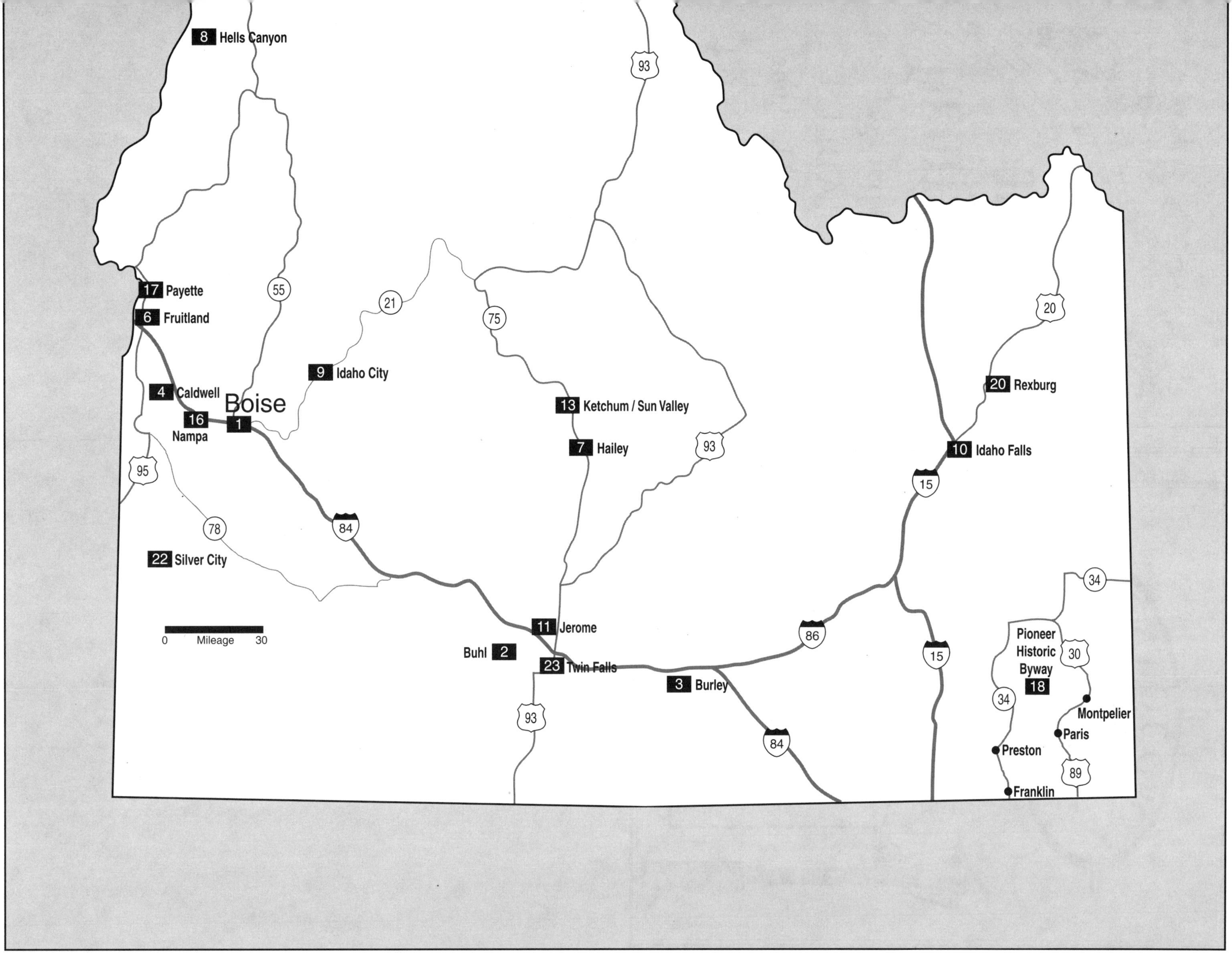
8 Hells Canyon
17 Payette
6 Fruitland
4 Caldwell
Boise
1
16
Nampa
9 Idaho City
22 Silver City
13 Ketchum / Sun Valley
7 Hailey
11 Jerome
Buhl 2
23 Twin Falls
3 Burley
20 Rexburg
10 Idaho Falls
Pioneer
Historic
Byway
18
Montpelier
Paris
Preston
Franklin
0 Mileage 30
93
55
21
75
95
84
78
93
86
15
20
34
30
89

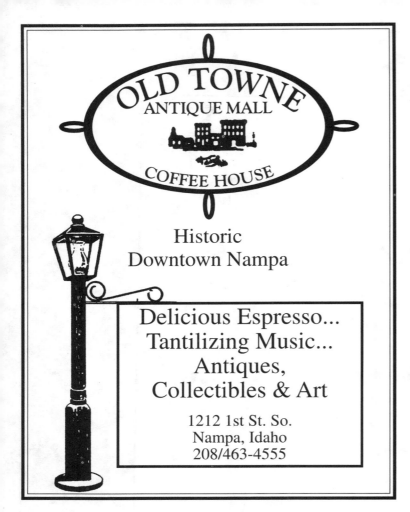

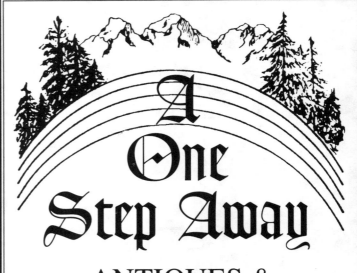

Idaho

1 BOISE

Idaho Heritage Inn
109 West Idaho
208/342-8066
Open year round. Reservations requested.

Directions: Exit I-84 at Broadway in Boise; then follow north to Idaho Street.

The Idaho Heritage Inn was built in 1904 for one of Boise's early merchants, Henry Falk. It remained in the Falk family until it was purchased in 1943 by then governor Chase A. Clark. Lovingly restored by its present owners, the Inn is now listed on the National Register of Historic Places.

All rooms at the Inn have been comfortably and charmingly provided with private baths, period furniture and crisp linens. The spacious main floor common rooms include a formal dining room, living room and sunroom, featuring diamond-paned French doors, oak flooring and Oriental carpets.

Guests of the Inn enjoy a complimentary breakfast of fresh-squeezed juice, choice of beverage, fresh fruit in season, and a delectable entree which may include baked German pancakes, apricot cream cheese stuffed French toast, or apple skillet cake.

Surrounded by other distinguished turn-of-the-century homes, the Inn is conveniently located within walking distance of downtown, 8th Street Marketplace and Old Boise (a historic shopping district).

Acquired Again
1306 Alturas St.
208/338-5929

Forget Me Not Antiques
1603 N. 13th St.
208/344-0678

Blue Moon Antiques
1611 N. 13th St.
208/3356-5954

Collection Connection
1612 N. 13th St.
208/343-6221

American Nostalgia Antiques
1517 N. 13th St.
208/345-8027

Antique Village
944 Vista Ave.
208/342-1910

Early Attic
2002 Vista Ave.
208/336-7451

Hobby Horse Antiques
231 Warm Springs Ave.
208/343-6005

Antiques Hub
2244 Warm Springs Ave.
208/336-4748

Carol's Antiques & Collectibles
10670 Overland Rd.
208/322-5059

Collector's Choice
5150 Franklin Rd.
208/336-2489

Collector's Choice Too
5284 Franklin Rd.
208/336-3170

Elliott's Great Stuff
1006 Main St.
208/344-9775

Nifty 90's Antique Shop
2422 Main St.
208/344-3931

Rigby's Antiques
106 N. 6th St.
208/386-9961

5th Street Antiques
225 N. 5th St.
208/344-7278

Victoria's Antiques
9230 Ustick Rd.
208/376-8016

Wild Hare Bookshop
3397 N. Cole Rd
208/377-5070

2 BUHL

Claudia's Country Cabin
3917 N. 1500 E
208/543-5315

Granny's Drawers
219 Broadway Ave. N
208/543-6736

3 BURLEY

South of Burley is an eerie and dreamlike landscape where people have been doing a double-take for centuries. It's called City of Rocks and it's now a national reserve.

There's little warning of what is to come as you drive the gravel road over rolling hills of desert sage. Suddenly, huge granite columns loom up 60 stories high!

The area has a poignant history that can still be glimpsed. Here is where would-be Californians parted from the Oregon Trail and headed southwest over desert plains and high mountain passes. The impressive spires became a memo board of hope, fear and determination; many of the inscriptions written in axle grease can still be read.

Rumor has it that there's gold among the mammoth rocks. On his deathbed, a stagecoach robber confessed to burying his treasure at the City of Rocks. It has never been found.

The City of Rocks is a bit out of the way, but well worth the effort. Oakley, a village en route, is listed on the National Register of Historic Places because of its many intricate stone and wood structures built before the turn of the century. No other town in Idaho has such a concentration of old buildings.

A good starting point is the Oakley Co-op Building on the corner of Main and Center Streets. Near the city park is a jail cell that once held the noted outlaw, "Diamondfield" Jack Davis.

Monica's Antique & Unique
1336 Overland Ave.
208/677-3929

Golden Goose
1221 Overland Ave.
208/678-9122

4 CALDWELL

Alan Vulk Auction Service
523 Main Street
208/454-2910

Caldwell Auction
4920 Cleveland Boulevard
208/454-1532

5 COEUR D'ALENE

Wolf Lodge Inn
Frontage Road
208/664-6665

Wolf Lodge Inn has been serving up the biggest steaks in the West for twenty years. The smallest is the "Lil Dude" (a one-pounder), but if you're really hungry, you can opt for the two-pound T-bone or the majestic two-and-a-half-pound porterhouse. Cooked over a hardwood fire in an impressive steak pit, the heavy-textured beef, aged eighteen days and never frozen, develops a sizzling blackened crust to contain its juices.

There are other wonderful delicacies on the menu as well. Lobster tails, shrimp, Rocky Mountain oysters (testicles of bulls in case you didn't know) all served up with incredible side dishes of Belgium bakers (the potato), beans, salads and a wonderful German bread call krekel.

The Roosevelt Inn
105 Wallace Avenue
208/765-5200
Open year round

Directions: Call ahead.

The Roosevelt Inn, named after the 26th president, Theodore Roosevelt, was built in 1906. Included in the National Register of Historic Places, this beautiful red brick building with its steeple shaded by maple trees, offers traditional elegance and Hungarian hospitality.

Two charmingly furnished parlors and dining area featuring lovely leaded glass windows and a hand-painted mural welcome you on the main floor. Each of the cozy guests rooms are decorated with antiques and provide views of the lake.

The Roosevelt Inn is located within a short walking distance to area restaurants, shops and boutiques. The nature trails of beautiful Tubbs Hill are also within easy access.

Coeur D'Alene Antique Mall
3650 N. Government Way
208/667-0246

Coeur D'Alene Antique Mall
408 W. Haycraft Ave. #11
208/664-0579

Good Things
204 N. 3rd St.
208/667-6958

Crow's Nest Antiques
416 E. Sherman Ave.
208/667-1679

Lake City Antique Mall
401 N. 2nd St.
208/664-6883

Sherman Antiques & Cllbls.
1116 E. Sherman Ave.
208/666-1809

Sherman Arms Antiques
412 E. Sherman Ave.
208/667-0527

Timeless Treasures Antiques
823 N. 4th St.
208/765-0699

Wiggett Antique Mall
119 N. 4th St.
208/664-1524

6 FRUITLAND

Elm Hollow Bed & Breakfast
4900 Highway 95
208/452-6491
Open year round

Directions: Traveling I-84, take Exit 3. Drive toward Parma. Elm Hollow is at the bottom of the dip between Glenway and Fairview. Make a left onto the driveway, just before milepost 58. Only two and one half miles south of I-84; makes for a convenient stop-over for travelers.

Nestled against a hillside overlooking fertile Idaho farms and orchards, Elm Hollow Bed & Breakfast gives the weary traveler a true taste of home. Guests to this country retreat experience the relaxing atmosphere of old-fashioned hospitality and good Dutch cooking.

The Guest Room offers spacious comfort with queen

size beds and loveseat, and a full bookcase provide the touches of home for a cozy evening.

For a romantic getaway, the Barn (a renovated section of the old dairy barn) offers privacy and a great view of the countryside.

Mornings at Elm Hollow start with a choice of Continental breakfast with home-baked breads and sweet rolls, or a full and hearty country meal, served family style in the dining room.

Now & Then
7190 Elmore Rd.
208/452-5500

Riverview Antiques & Cllbls.
1125 N.W. 16th St.
208/452-4365

Suzy's Nu-2-U
200 S.W. 3rd
208/452-5878

7 HAILEY

Hailey's Antique Market
P.O. Box 1955
208/788-9292
Locations: Inside—Hailey Armory/Outside—Roberta McKercher Park
Call For Dates

Lone Star Designs
109 S. Main St.
208/788-9158

8 HELLS CANYON

Seven Devils and A Hell of A Canyon
Over one mile deep, Hells Canyon is North Americas deepest river gorge, deeper even than the Grand Canyon. Walls of black, crumbling basalt thrust straight up, forcing boaters and fishermen on the Snake River to crane their necks for blue sky. Looking down upon the canyon are the mighty Seven Devils, an awe-inspiring mountain range that crests over 1 1/2 miles above the river.

9 IDAHO CITY

Idaho City was, at one time, the largest city in the Northwest-a rough and tumble, rip-roaring mining town that epitomized the "boom or bust" lifestyle of Gold Rushers. Gold often took precedence over human life. It's said that of the 200 men and women buried in picturesque Boot Hill, only 28 died of natural causes.

A One Step Away Bed and Breakfast and Antique Shop
112 Cottonwood Street
208/392-4938

Nestled on a quiet little street on the south side of town, "One Step Away" is a quaint bed and breakfast with an exquisite antique shop adjoining it. Rooms are tastefully furnished in 1800s elegance and named after early settlers of Idaho City. The Jenny Lynn Chamber is dedicated to the famous lady of the Nightingale Theater; the Miner's Room is named in honor of all the men who left their native homes in search of fortunes and were the first to settle in the area, and the Beth Parkinson Suite serves as a tribute to the previous owner of the house.

A gourmet breakfast is served on antique china and silver pieces of the era. The antique-filled dining room is available for meals, or room service is provided if you prefer.

Idaho City Hotel
Corner of Montgomery and Walulla
208/392-4290

In 1929, the Idaho City Hotel was a boarding house run by Mrs. Mary Smith. Since that time it has been completely renovated to retain its quaint charm and rustic flavor. Five guest rooms are available. The hotel has a wonderful wraparound porch and a tin roof.

10 IDAHO FALLS

A spectacular waterfall provides the scenic centerpiece for Idaho Falls, a growing city surrounded by gold and green croplands and rustic barns.

This community of 50,000 people is further blessed by 39 parks ranging from small corner parks, where business people stop to chat and eat lunch, to large parks such as Tautphaus Park which houses a nationally renowned zoo.

The Rotary International Peach Park located along the greenbelt features granite lanterns, gifts to the city from its sister city in Japan.

Cross Country Store
4035 Yellowstone Hwy.
208/529-0766

Antique Gallery
341 W. Broadway St.
208/523-3906

Scavenger Shop
202 1st St.
208/523-7862

A Street Village
548 Shoup Ave.
208/528-0300

11 JEROME

Frontier Antiques
149 W. Main
208/324-1127

Antiques & Things
137 E. Main St.
208/324-8549

Few Seconds More
1000 N. Lincoln Ave.
208/324-4869

Rose Antique Mall
130 E. Main St.
208/324-2918

12 KELLOGG

Driving east on I-90 from Coeur d'Alene, you'll find yourself in the Silver Valley, the largest silver producing area in the world and a bonanza for history buffs.

Silver Valley has been transformed not once but twice, first by the ambition and sacrifice of intrepid miners. Today, Kellogg offers different treasures—a Bavarian-theme village, murals, statues, a mining museum, and unique events.

Willows Antiques
119 McKinley Avenue
208/556-1022

13 KETCHUM-SUN VALLEY

Antique Peddlers' Fairs
Location: Warm Spring Resort
208/344-6133

Directions: At the base of Bald Mountain
Call for specific dates

Antiques Etc.
431 Walnut Ave. N
208/726-5332

Legacy Antiques & Imports
491 10th St.
208/726-1655

Polly Noe Antiques
471 Leadville Ave. N
208/726-3663

14 LEWISTON

Bargain Hunter Mall
1209 Main St.
208/746-6808

Somewhere in Time
628 Main St.
208/746-7160

15 MOSCOW

Second Hand/First Hand
107 S. Main
208/882-5642

16 NAMPA

Old Towne Antique Mall-Coffee House
1212 1st Street South
208/463-4555
Open Mon.-Sat., 10-6; Sun. 10-3 (seasonal)
Coffee House: Mon.-Fri. 8-6; Sat. 10-6; Sun. 10-3 (seasonal)

Directions: Traveling I-84 Exit 36. Travel South on Franklin Blvd. to stop sign. Turn right on 11th Avenue. Drive approximately 1 1/2 miles, then under railroad overpass. Immediately turn left on 1st Street south at light. Located 1 1/2 blocks on left (Historic Downtown). We are 25 miles east of Boise, Idaho.

Located in historic downtown Nampa, Old Towne Antique Mall is more than just an antique shop. It has a coffee shop inside serving delicious espresso. The dealers who display their wares are usually on hand to answer any questions you may have.

A wide variety of merchandise is available such as nostalgic paper goods, vintage clothing, china, pottery, along with a complete line of furnishings from early country to Victorian to depression.

Yesteryear Shoppe
1211 1st St. S.
208/467-3581

Hogey's Antique & Restoration
4203 Garrity Blvd.
208/466-9461

Village Square Antiques
1309 2nd St. S.
208/467-2842

17 PAYETTE

Lambsville Collectibles
101 S. 16th Street, Hwy. 95
208/642-1727

Yesterdays Cupboard
220 N. Main St.
208/642-3711

18 PIONEER HISTORIC BYWAY

Southeast Idaho's Pioneer Historic Byway gives motorists a nostalgic glimpse, through rustic ranches and roadside communities, of a West long past. The route begins in Franklin, Idaho's oldest white settlement, and retraces the steps of Idaho's earliest pioneers. Franklin's center is now designated by the state as a historic district, and two buildings are on the National Historic Register—the Franklin Co-op Building built in the 1860s, and the Hatch home, a classic of pioneer architecture.

Nearby are the remnants of Idaho's first flour mill and one of the oldest homes in the state, a two-story edifice built almost entirely of rock.

After passing through the rustic town of Preston, you'll come to the Bear River Massacre Site, now a national landmark. More Indians were killed here in one battle than in any other in the United States.

The byway continues on to Montpelier, home of the fascinating Rails and Trails Historical Museum. Just south of Montpelier is the small town of Paris. The Romanesque Mormon Tabernacle, complete with intricate wood ceilings and stone carvings, was built in 1889 of red sandstone snow-sledded to Paris from a quarry 18 miles away.

Between Montpelier and the Utah border, Butch Cassidy made a quick but impressive visit by robbing the local bank.

Another astounding drive is the Bear Lake-Caribou Scenic Byway running through Paris. It begins on Highway 89 at the Utah state border and passes mammoth Bear Lake.

The Scenic Byway continues at Montpelier on Highway 30 and at Soda Springs on Highway 34. The drive, in its entirety from the Utah border to the Wyoming border, is 111 miles or 2 1/2 hours. Along the way are numerous attractions—Bear Lake State Park, the Paris Museum, the Cache National Forest, the Caribou Forest, the carbonated waters and spouting geysers of Soda Springs and the Blackfoot Reservoir.

19 PRIEST RIVER

Nancy's Antiques & Cllbls.
204 Treat
208/448-2680

Joodle Bug's
120 Wisconsin
208/448-2442

Mercer's Memories
221 Main St.
208/448-1781

20 REXBURG

North of Idaho Falls on Highway 20 is the historic and charming town of Rexburg, home to several diverse and noteworthy attractions.

Just a block off Main Street you'll find a gray stone Tabernacle now listed on the National Register of Historic Places. At Porter Park is the only restored authentic wooden carousel in Idaho.

But Rexburg is probably best known for a nearby, unusual tourist site: a dam which collapsed in June 1976, dumping eight billion gallons of roaring flood water into the unsuspecting valley below. A visit to the dam site on the Teton River will give you an idea of the power that was unleashed. An understanding of the flood's effect on local people, and their ability to rebuild their fertile valley, can be gained at a unique museum outside Rexburg.

Rexburg is also home to the Idaho International Folk Dance Festival. The week-long event features dance groups from around the world. Dancers and musicians gather here from Europe, Asia, South America and the south Pacific to share the vibrant and expressive spirit of their homelands. Perhaps no other event in Idaho boasts such international flavor. The dancing begins July 26th and concludes August 3rd each year.

Country Keepsakes
12 E. Main St.
208/359-1234

Mainstreet Antiques Mall
52 E. Main St.
208/356-5002

21 SANDPOINT

Antique Arcade
119 N. 1st Ave.
208/265-5421

22 SILVER CITY

Silver City, high in the Owyhee Mountains, is an evocative ghost town chock-full of historic buildings and atmosphere. This "Queen of Idaho Ghost Towns" appears just as she was during her boom times with over 70 rustic buildings remaining intact.

23 TWIN FALLS

The Oregon Trail pioneers, who trudged through South Central Idaho on their way to Oregon, would be astounded at the sight of present day Twin Falls. Poised near the edge of spectacular Snake River Canyon, the city is the commercial center of scenic Magic Valley, one of America's most productive agricultural areas.

Driving down inside the canyon is an experience, a world apart from the terrain high above. The Perrine Bridge spanning the canyon is 1,500 feet long and 486 breathtaking feet above the river. This is the location of Evil Knievel's attempted jump across the canyon in a rocket cycle.

In town are two museums of note. The Herrett Museum on the College of Southern Idaho campus has in its collection over 3,000 North and Central Native American artifacts, ranging from 12,000-year-old relics to contemporary Hopi Kachina Dolls.

Anne Tiques Etc.
325 Main Ave. E.
208/736-0140

Second Time Around
689 Washington St. N
208/734-6008

Snow's Antqs. & Sleigh Works
136 Main Ave. N
208/736-7292

Treasures from the Past
227 Main Ave. E
208/733-2976

24 WALLACE

The Jameson
304 6th Street
208/556-1554

The historic Jameson Restaurant and Saloon opened its doors in 1900 as a small-town hotel and traditional saloon. It is now restored to its former elegance, offering guests the charm of the Victorian era. The bedrooms are on the third floor, and are very Victorian in appearance with heavy wooden furniture, chunky hand-carved wooden headboards and carpets in Victorian patterns. It is in Room Three that Maggie, who once stayed at the Hotel as a long-term guest in the early part of the century, often returns for a visit. The hotel staff knew very little about Maggie except that she often received letters from New York and London. The letters arrived frequently for years until one day early in the 1930s, Maggie checked out of the hotel headed for the East Coast. A few weeks later, word was received that she had either been murdered in a train robbery or died violently in an accident.

Several months later the staff noticed room fans and lights were turned off by an invisible hand. Hot showers turned cold and guests found themselves locked in their rooms with the key on the outside! Strangest of all, someone was using the sheets and towels in Room Three despite the fact it was locked and empty.

The puzzled owners decided to consult a psychic who agreed there was a spirit at the hotel: a woman who had died violently and who, because she had no home of her own, had "checked back in." To this day, Maggie makes her presence known. She still steals keys, turns off the water and joins guests for social gatherings. She is always friendly and welcomed by the current hotel owners and their guests.

The Wallace Corner
525 Cedar Street
208/753-6141

ROUTE 59 ANTIQUE MALL

3 S 450 Rt. 59
Warrenville
(1 mile N. of I-88)

Premier Mall in Area

• 60 Dealers •

• Excellent Variety •

• 1 mile N. of Cracker Barrel•

630-393-0100

117

COUNTRY FAIR MALL
ANTIQUES & COLLECTIBLES

2 Buildings of

Antiques

&

Collectibles

504 First Ave.

Coal Valley

309-799-3670

630-262-0959
307 W. State St. (Rt. 38) • Geneva, IL 60134

Findings of Geneva Antiques

vintage linens & laces, men's collectibles,
old books & other wonderful stuff!

regular hours:
Tues-Sat 10:30-6 Sun 12-5

40

Uniques Antiques, Ltd.

3,000 sq. ft. of Antiques and Collectibles

1006 W. Jefferson St. • 815-741-2466

Joilet

51

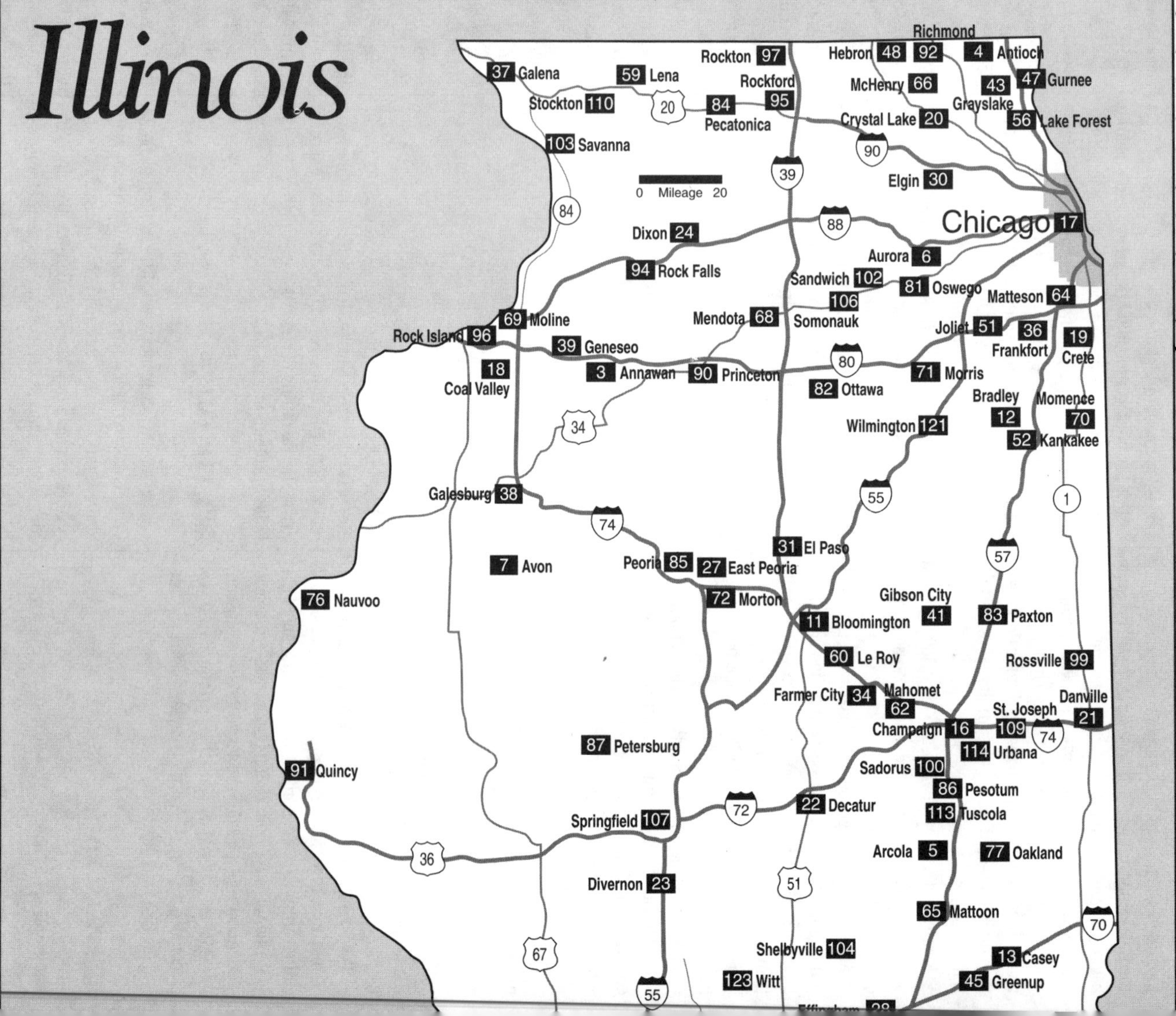

Wildflower Antique Mall

Our dealers have many years of experience purchasing quality antiques for you, our customers. Come in & discover the treasures they have found.

I-57 Exit 220 at Rt. 45

217-867-2704

Mon.-Sat. 9-6
(extended summer hours)
Sun. 10-5

PESOTUM

86

Antique Association of Lemont Invites you to Visit

Historic Downtown Lemont

8 Antique Shops
Unique Restaurants
Specialty Stores

Mueller's
Antiques & Collectibles

6 Farm Buildings
Full of Antiques

Shiloh

105

The Pulford Opera House Antique Mall

27,000 sq. ft. of
Antiques in a
turn-of-the-century
Opera House

Savanna

103

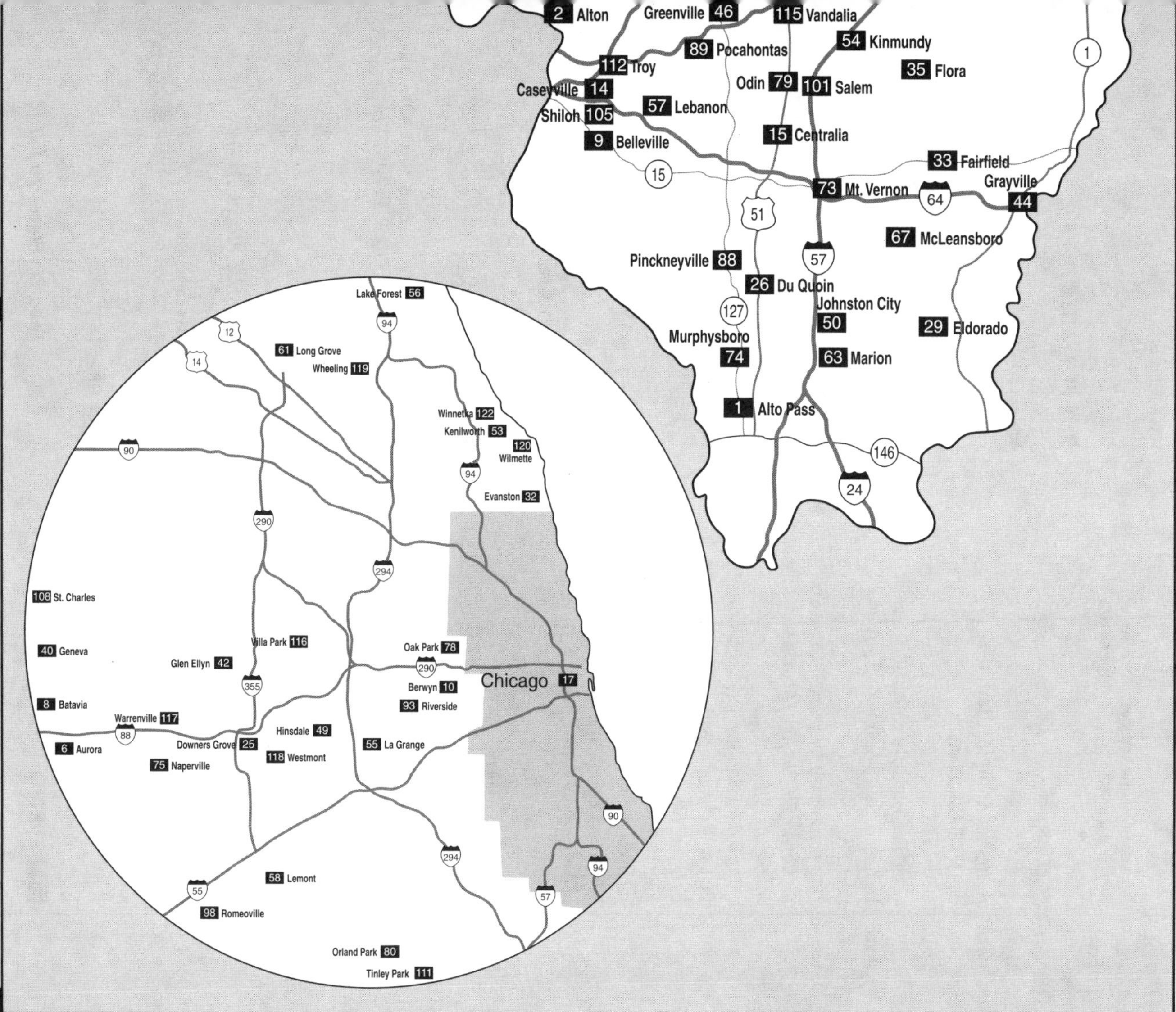

Wilmington

Antique Dealers Association

Six unique shops
on one street

Wilmington

121

ANNAWAN ANTIQUE ALLEY

Antiques,
Collectibles & More

309 North Canal St.
309-935-6220

Annawan

3

Lil' Red Schoolhouse Antiques

35463 Batavia Rd.

Warrenville

117

Lisa's I & II ANTIQUE MALLS

OVER 40,000 SQ. FT. • 200 PLUS DEALERS

Divernon

OPEN 7 DAYS
10 A.M. TO 6 P.M.
I-55 & RT. 104
(EXIT 82)
LISA'S I
(217) 628-1111
LISA'S II
(217) 628-3333

23

Gramma's Attic Antique Mall

4 floors in an old
150 yr. old Hotel

Ottawa

82

1 ALTO PASS

Austin's of Alto Pass
Route 127 and Alton Pass Road
618/893-2206
Open Sat., 10-5; Sun., 1-5; other times, call for appointment.

Directions: Alto Pass, Ill., is located on Illinois Highway 127. Travel 16 miles south from Murphysboro, Illinois, or 8 miles north from Jonesboro, Illinois, on Highway 127. To reach Alto Pass from Carbondale, Illinois, take Route 51 south to Makanda Road; turn right; then make a quick left onto Old Highway 51 South. Travel approximately 5 miles to Alto Pass Road and turn right to stop sign at Skyline Drive. Turn right onto Skyline and follow through town to old grade school building on the left.

This one-owner shop is located in a beautifully restored brick grade school built in 1927. A large selection of hand-picked, restored furniture and lots of unusual old wares are available to the discriminating shopper.

2 ALTON

Gabriel's Old Post Office Mall
300 Alby St.
618/462-8204

Dormann's Gifts & Interiors
330 Alby St.
618/462-2654

Alton Landing Framery
100 Alton St.
618/465-1996

Alton Landing Antiques
110 Alton St.
618/462-0443

1900's Antiques Co.
7 E. Broadway
618/465-2711

Prairie Peddler
200 State St.
618/465-6114

Carol's Corner/Frank's Steins
16 E. Broadway
618/465-2606

Cane Bottom My Just Desserts
31 E. Broadway
618/462-5881

Cracker Factory Mini Mall
203 E. Broadway (2nd Floor)
618/466-9008

Thames on Broadway
205 E. Broadway (Lower Floor)
618/462-1337

Country Meadows
207 E. Broadway
618/465-1965

Antiques & Collectibles
301 E. Broadway
618/462-3656

Simple Treasures
301 E. Broadway
618/462-3003

Jim's Attic
301 E. Broadway
618/463-7699

River Bend Replicas
301 E. Broadway
618/462-8206

The Second Reading
301 E. Broadway
618/462-2361

Unusual Place
301 E. Broadway Ave.
618/474-2128

Wildwood
301 E. Broadway
618/465-4012

Mississippi Mud Pottery
310 E. Broadway
618/462-7573

Granny's Time
319 Broadway
618/462-5440

Jack's Cllbls./Jeanne's Jewels
319 Broadway
618/463-0451

Heartland Antiques
321 E. Broadway
618/465-6363

Jan's Antiques
323 E. Broadway
618/465-2250

Steve's Antiques
323 E. Broadway
618/465-7407

Sloan's Antiques
401 E. Broadway
618/463-0808

Alton Antique Center
401 E. Broadway (Lower)
618/463-0888

Old Bridge Antique Mall
435 E. Broadway
618/463-9907

Rubenstein's Antiques
724-26 E. Broadway
618/465-1306

Debbie's Decorative Antiques
108 George & Broadway
618/465-6018

River Winds
117 Market St.
618/465-8981

3 ANNAWAN

Annawan Antique Alley
309 North Canal Street
309/935-6220
Open (Jan.-March; Mon.-Sat., 10-5; Sunday, 12-4) (April-Dec., Mon.-Sat., 9-5:30; Sun., 12-4)

Directions: From Interstate 80, take Exit 33. Go south on Illinois 78. The first left driveway (about 1 block from Exit 33).

Tucked away in the quiet, small town of Annawan, Illinois, the Annawan Antique Alley adopted its name from its former life as a bowling alley. Located just one block from I-80 the "alley" is a convenient "antique stop." This multi-dealer antique mall offers furnishings, quilts, Tiffany and Tiffany-style lamps, statuary, and a lot more of the items you would expect to find in a quality antique mall.

4 ANTIOCH

Green Bench Antiques
924 Main St.
847/838-2643

Collection Connection
400 Lake St.
847/395-8800

Antioch Antique Mall
42189 N. Lake Ave.
847/395-0000

Williams Brothers Emporium
910 Main St.
847/838-2767

Park Avenue Antique Mall
345 Park Ave.
847-838-1624

5 ARCOLA

Green Barn Antiques
111 N. Locust St.
217/268-4754

Emporium Antiques
201 E. Main St.
217/268-4523

6 AURORA

Treasures Old & New
355 East End Trail
630/896-0161

Peddler Showcase
566 Parker Ave.
630/851-4200

7 AVON

Avon Antique Mall
Main St. Rt. 41
309/465-7387

8 BATAVIA

Yesterdays
115 S Batavia Ave.
630/406-0524

Savery Antiques
14 N. Washington
630/879-6825

Just Good Olde Stuff Inc.
8 E. Wilson St.
630/879-2815

Kenyon & Co.
215 E. Wilson St.
630/406-0665

Village Antiques
416 E. Wilson St.
630/406-0905

9 BELLEVILLE

Antiques & Things
704 N. Douglas Ave.
618/236-1104

Traditional Manor
1101 N. Illinois St.
618/235-4683

Eagle Collectibles Inc.
22 E. Main St.
618/257-1283

Belleville Antique Mall
208 E. Main St.
618/234-6255

Ben's Antique Mall
225 E. Main St.
618/234-0904

10 BERWYN

BBMM Antiques
6710 Cermak Rd.
708/749-1465

Silver Swan Antiques
6738 16th St.
708/484-7177

Antique Treasure Chest
6746 16th St.
708/749-1910

Past Time Antiques
7100 16th St.
708/788-4804

Josie's Antiques & Collectibles
2135 Wisconsin Ave.
708/788-3820

11 BLOOMINGTON

Bloomington Antique Mall
102 N. Center St.
309/828-1211

Antique Mart/J. Williams Inc.
907 S Eldorado Rd.
309/662-4213

A Gridley Antiques
217 E. Front St.
309/829-9615

Favorite Places To Eat

Cracker Barrel Old Country Store
I 55/74 & Market Street, Exit 160A
309/829-3155

12 BRADLEY

Favorite Places To Eat

Cracker Barrel Old Country Store
I-57 & Hwy 50, Exit 315
815/936-6022

13 CASEY

Perisho's Antiques
104 E. Colorado Avenue
217/932-4493

14 CASEYVILLE

Favorite Places to Eat

Cracker Barrel Old Country Store
I-64 & State Rd. 157, Exit 9
618/397-1599

15 CENTRALIA

Kim Logan
1829 Gragg St.
618/532-8495

Lofty Affair
Walnut Hill Road
618/532-0186

Cedar House Antqs. & Cllbls.
I-57 & Hwy. 161 (Exit 109)
618-533-0399

J & M Resales
1180 Medlin Rd.
618/532-6031

16 CHAMPAIGN

First Street Antiques
206 S 1st St.
217/359-3079

Good Time Antiques
1519 N. Highland Ave.
217/359-6234

Carrie's
204 N. Neil St.
217/352-3231

Partners In Time Antiques
311 S Neil St.
217/352-2016

Capricorn Antiques
720 S. Neil St.
217/351-6914

Gray's Antiques & Collectibles
723 S. Neil St.
217/351-9079

Vintage Antiques
117 N. Walnut St.
217/359-8747

17 CHICAGO

Salvage One Architectural Artifacts
1524 South Sangamon Street
312/733-0098
Open Tue.-Sat., 10-5; Sun., 11-4

Directions: From O'Hare Airport, downtown Chicago, north and west Suburbs, take Dan Ryan Expressway, 90/94 east; exit 18th Street Exit and turn right (west); right (north) on Halsted; left (west) on 16th Street; go three blocks and right (north) on Sangamon Street. From Midway, Indiana, Michigan, and South Chicago, take Dan Ryan Expressway 90/94 West; exit Canalport/ Cermak Road Exit; proceed north on access road (Ruble Street); left (west) on 16th Street, go five blocks and right (north) on Sangamon Street.

Salvage One was founded in 1980 and purchased in 1986 by Leslie Hindman Auctioneers, the Midwest's leading auction house. It has since grown to be the largest architectural salvage company in the country. "Today the popularity of using salvaged architectural materials is not limited to people restoring vintage homes or even choosing to construct a historically accurate design. The vast majority of people buying architectural elements are adding them to enhance their homes or surroundings," says Anne McGahan, of Salvage One.

The staff at Salvage One travels the continent in search of the finest architectural treasures available. At the time of this printing the group had purchased a stunning collection of 13,

14th-century Italian pink marble columns and capitals, a late 17th-century Chinese pottery water carrier, an early French pine butcher's table, a pair of cast iron garden urns with elaborate rococo designs and a Chinese teakwood lantern with hand-painted glass panels.

Salvage One offers over 6,000 interior and exterior doors, an enormous selection of vintage hardware, stained, leaded and beveled glass windows and doors, garden ornaments, fabricated furniture, bathroom fixtures, lighting, and one of the nation's largest inventories of period American and Continental fireplace mantels and accessories, acquired from across the U.S.., England, and France.

Brochures, photographs, condition reports and worldwide shipping are available for Salvage One customers.

Turtle Creek Antiques
850 W. Armitage Ave.
773/327-2630

Armitage Antique Gallery
1529 W. Armitage Ave.
773/227-7727

Daniels Antiques
3711 N. Ashland Ave.
773/868-9355

Lincoln Antique Mall
3141 N. Lincoln Ave.
773/244-1440

Ray's Antiques
1821 W. Belmont Ave.
773/348-5150

Antique House
1832 W. Belmont Ave.
773-327-0707

S & F Johnson Antiques
1901 W. Belmont Ave.
773/477-9243

Nineteen Thirteen
1913 W. Belmont Ave.
773/404-9522

Kristina Maria Antiques
1919 W. Belmont Ave.
773/472-2445

Belmont Antique Mall
2039 W. Belmont Ave.
773/549-9270

Phil's Antique Mall
2040 W. Belmont Ave.
773/528-8549

House of Nostalgia
2047 W. Belmont Ave.
773/244-6460

Father Time Antiques
2108 W. Belmont Ave.
773/880-5599

Danger City
2129 W. Belmont
773/871-1420

Good Old Days
2138 W. Belmont Ave.
773/472-8837

Kaye's Antiques
2147 W. Belmont Ave.
773/929-8187

Belmont Antique Mall West
2229 W. Belmont Ave.
773/871-3915

Olde Chicago Antiques
2336 W. Belmont Ave.
773/935-1200

Quality Antiques & Gifts
6401 N. Caldwell Ave.
312/631-1134

Stanley Galleries Antiques
2118 N. Clark St.
773/281-1614

Wrigleyville Antique Mall
3336 N. Clark St.
773/868-0285

Acorn Antiques & Uniques Ltd.
5241 N. Clark St.
773/506-9100

Camden Passage Antiques Mkt.
5309 N. Clark St.
773/989-0111

Collectables on Clybourn
2503 N. Clybourn
773/871-1154

Michael Fleming Antiques
5221 N. Damen Ave.
773/561-8696

Shop Front Antiques
5223 N. Damen Ave.
773/271-5130

Wallner's Antiques
1229 W. Diversey Pkwy.
773/248-6061

International Antiques
2300 W. Diversey Ave.
773/227-2400

Stanley Antiques
3489 N. Elston Ave.
773/588-4269

Pilsen Gallery Arch
540 W. 18th St.
312/829-2827

Aged Experience Antiques
2034 N. Halsted St.
773/975-9790

Silver Moon
3337 N. Halsted St.
773/883-0222

Hyde-N-Seek Antiques
5211 S. Harper Ave. #D
773/684-8380

Sandwich Antiques Market
1510 N. Hoyne Ave.
773/227-4464

Portals Limited
230 W. Huron St.
312/642-1066

Antiques Centre at Kinzie Sq.
220 W. Kinzie St.
312/464-1946

Tompkins & Robandt
220 W. Kinzie St. 4th Floor
312/645-9995

Griffins & Gargoyles Ltd.
2140 W. Lawrence Ave.
773/769-1255

Haily's Antiques & Collectibles
5508 W. Lawrence Ave.
773/202-0555

Gibell's & Bits
5512 W. Lawrence Ave.
773/283-4065

Steve Starr Studios
2779 N. Lincoln Ave.
773/525-6530

Time Well
2780 N. Lincoln Ave.
773/549-2113

Urban Artifacts
2928 N. Lincoln Ave.
773/404-1008

Chicago Antique Center
3045 N. Lincoln Ave.
773/929-0200

Red Eye
3050 N. Lincoln Ave.
773/975-2020

Harlon's Antiques
3058 N. Lincoln Ave.
773/327-3407

Gene Douglas Antiques
3419 N. Lincoln Ave.
773/561-4414

Zigzag
3419 N. Lincoln Ave.
773/525-1060

Lake View Antiques
3422 N. Lincoln Ave.
773/935-6443

Lincoln Ave. Antique Co-op
3851 N. Lincoln Ave.
773/935-6600

Benkendorf Antique Clocks
900 N. Michigan Ave.
312/951-1903

Antiques on the Avenue
104 S. Michigan Ave. 2nd Floor
312/357-2800

U.S. #1 Antique
1509 N. Milwaukee Ave.
773/489-9428

Modern Times
1538 N. Milwaukee Ave.
773/772-8871

Crossings Antiques Mall
1805 W. 95th St.
773/881-3140

Little Ladies
6217 N. Northwest Hwy.
773/631-3602

Malcolm Franklin Inc.
34 E. Oak St.
312/337-0202

Russell's Antiques
2404 W. 111 St.
773/233-3205

David McClain Antiques
2716 W. 111th St.
773/239-4683

Therese Chez Antiques
3120 W. 111th St.
773/881-0824

Decoro
224 E. Ontario St.
312/943-4847

Time Square Ltd.
6352 S. Pulaski Rd.
773/581-8216

Architectural Artifacts Inc.
4325 N. Ravenswood Ave.
773/348-0622

Gallery 1945
300 N. State
312/573-1945

Garrett Galleries
1155 N. State St.
312/944-6325

First Arts & Antiques
7220 W. Touhy Ave.
312/774-5080

Sara Breiel Designs
449 N. Wells St.
312/923-9223

Rita-Bucheit Ltd.
449 N. Wells St.
312/527-4080

Pimlico Antiques Ltd.
500 N. Wells St.
312/245-9199

O'Hara's Gallery
707 N. Wells St.
312/751-1286

Chicago Riverfront Antq. Mkt.
2929 N. Western Ave.
773/252-2500

Rich Oldies & Goodies
4642 N. Western Ave.
773/334-7033

Penn Dutchman Antiques
4912 N. Western Ave.
773/271-2208

A & R
8024 S. Western Ave.
773/434-9157

Memories & More
10143 S. Western Ave.
773/238-5645

Cluttered Cupboard
10332 S. Western Ave.
773/881-8803

Grich Antiques
10857 S. Western Ave.
773/233-8734

R J Collectibles
11400 S. Western Ave.
773/779-8828

An Antique Store
1450 W. Webster Ave.
773/935-6060

Jazz'e Junque
3831 N. Lincoln Ave.
773/472-1500

18 COAL VALLEY

Country Fair Mall
504 West 1st Avenue (Hwy. 6)
309/799-3670
Open Mon. & Thurs., 10-6; Tue., Fri., & Sat., 10-5; Sun., 12-5 (Closed Wednesdays)

Directions: Traveling I-280 west to Exit 5B (Moline Airport) to Highway 6 east. Mall is 1 and 3/4 mile on the north side of the highway.

No one goes away emptied handed at Country Fair Mall. Kent Farley, the owner, has created a two-star attraction for antiquers. For the discriminating shopper, one location provides upscale antiques; no reproductions, no sifting through the ordinary. The second location houses 150 to 170 booths of a "Shopper's Haven." Treasure hunters should be prepared to dig!

19 CRETE

Third Generation Antiques
831 W. Exchange
708/672-3369

Farmer's Daughter
1262 Lincoln St.
708/672-4588

Season's
1362 Main St.
708/672-0170

Indian Wheel Co.
1366 Main St.
708/672-9612

Gatherings
1375 Main St.
708/672-9880

The Marketplace
550 Exchange
708/672-5556

Village Antiques & Lamp Shop
595 Exchange
708/672-8980

The Finishing Touch
563 Exchange
708/672-9520

Woodstill's Antiques
610 Gould St. (Beecher)
708/946-3161

20 CRYSTAL LAKE

Way Back When Antiques
4112 Country Club Rd.
815/459-1360

Penny Lane Antiques
6114 Lou St.
815/459-8828

Railroad Street Market
8316 Railroad St.
815/459-4220

Aurora's Antiques
8404 Railroad St.
815/455-0710

Carriage Antiques & Cllbls.
8412 Railroad St.
815/455-0710

Country Church Antiques
8509 Ridgefield Rd.
815/477-4601

Carriage's Antiques
5111 E. Terra Cotta Ave.
815/356-9808

21 DANVILLE

Queen Ann's Cottage
407 Ann St.
217/443-5958

Treasures Unique
1327 Main St.
217/443-4280

Bob's Antiques
53 N. Vermilion St.
217/431-3704

Two's Company
109 N. Vermilion St.
217/446-7553

22 DECATUR

China House Antiques
801 W. Eldorado St.
217/428-7212

Collector's Shop
2345 S. Mount Zion Rd.
217/864-3000

Nellie's Attic Antique Mall
3030 S. Mount Zion Rd.
217/864-3363

Calliope House
560 W. North St.
217/425-1944

Favorite Places To Eat

Cracker Barrel Old Country Store
I-72 & U.S. 51, Exit 38
217/876-8036

23 DIVERNON

Lisa's I & II Antique Malls
I-55 and Route 104
217/628-1111; 217/628-3333
Open 7 days a week from 10a.m.-6p.m.; closed Thanksgiving and Christmas.

Directions: Both Lisa's I & II Antique Malls are located on Interstate 55 at Route 104 (Exit 82), 10 miles south of Springfield, Illinois.

Promising 40,000 square feet of rambling room, these two malls exhibit a full array of antiques and collectibles. No crafts are to be found among the quality selection of antiques which includes: furniture (oak, cherry, walnut, pine, mahogany), early American, glassware, old toys, jewelry and much, much more.

If you are looking for something "large" to take home, the old Stagecoach is for you. It's quite a showpiece and it's FOR SALE! Delivery is available at Lisa's I & II (I wonder if that means the Stagecoach, too?).

Country Place Antiques
RR1 Frontage Rd.
217/628-3699

24 DIXON

Brinton Ave. Antique Mall
725 N. Brinton Ave.
815/284-4643

Dixon Antique Station
1220 S. Galena Ave.
815/284-8890

E & M Antique Mall
1602 S. Galena Ave.
815/288-1900

25 DOWNERS GROVE

Mr. Chips Crystal Repair
743 Ogden Ave.
630/964-4070

Asbury's
1626 Ogden Ave.
630/769-9191

Country Cellar
2101 Ogden Ave.
630/968-0413

26 DUQUOIN

Main Street Antiques Mall
211 E. Main
618/542-5043

The Mulberry Tree Antiques,
24 S. Mulberry St.
618/542-6621

27 EAST PEORIA

Charley's
1815 Meadows Ave.
309/694-7698

Pleasant Hill Antique Mall
315 S. Pleasant Hill Rd.
309/694-4040

Southern Knights
125 E. Washington St.
309/694-4581

Cowboy Antiques
1107 E. Washington St.
309/699-3929

Antiques Inclusive
2469 E. Washington St.
309/699-0624

28 EFFINGHAM

Favorite Places To Eat

Cracker Barrel Old Country Store
I-70/57 & Ave. of Mid-America, Exit 160
217/347-7130

29 ELDORADO

Eldorado Antique Mall
935 4th Street
618/273-5586

Little Egypt Antiques
1212 State St.
618/273-9084

30 ELGIN

Favorite Places To Eat

Cracker Barrel Old Country Store
I-90 & Hwy. 31, Exit 25
847/742-2500

31 EL PASO

Century House Antiques
11 & 2nd St./ I-39 Exit 14
309/527-3705

El Paso Antique Mall
I-39 & Rt. 24
309/527-3705

32 EVANSTON

Eureka!
705 West Washington
847/869-9090
Open Tue.-Sat., 11-5

Directions: From Chicago, take any main artery north

to Evanston. Evanston is the first suburb north of Chicago along the lake. When going north or south along the Tri-State (Route 294) or on the Edens Expressway (Route 94), exit at Dempster (east). Go east 15-20 minutes to Ridge Avenue in Evanston (stoplight). Turn right (south); go 1 street past Main Street. Turn left onto Washington, and go 3 blocks to 705. Located 1 block south of Main, 1 block west of Chicago Avenue, 3 blocks east of Ridge.

Now, this shop could quite possibly be a first - "No Repro's" in the way of collectibles. The owner claims "this is the best nostalgia shop in Chicagoland! Early advertising, paper ephemera, world's fair collectibles, black memorabilia, and odd ball items can all be found throughout this fun shop. Men will love it!

Harvey Antiques
1231 Chicago Ave.
847/866-6766

Another Time Another Place
1243 Chicago Ave.
847/866-7170

Pursuit of Happiness
1524 Chicago Ave.
847/869-2040

Sarah Bustle Antiques
821 Dempster St.
847/869-7290

Village Bazaar
503 Main St.
847/866-9444

Edward Joseph Antiques
520 Main St.
847/332-1855

Rusty Nail
912 1/2 Sherman Ave.
847/491-0360

33 FAIRFIELD

Riverside Antiques
Highway 15 E
618/842-3570

Robinson's Antiques
Route 15
618/842-3626

Dickey's Antiques
Highway 15 E Rt. 5
618/842-2820

La Jean's Country Antiques
U.S. 45 South
618/847-4525

34 FARMER CITY

Main Street Antiques
115 S. Main St.
309/928-9208

Margaret's Attic To Basement
117 S. Main St.
309/928-3023

Salt Creek Emporium
120 Main St.
309/928-2844

Farmer City Antiques Center
201 S. Main St.
309/928-9210

Renaissance Art Studio
211 S. Main St.
309/928-2213

The Junction
E. Rt 150 & 54
309/928-3116

35 FLORA

Eileen's Antiques
526 E. Fourth St.
618/662-6171

Wallace Antiques
504 E. North Ave.
618/662-8252

36 FRANKFORT

Antiques Unique
100 Kansas St.
815/469-2741

The Trolley Barn
11 S. White Street
815/464-1120

37 GALENA

Directions: From Chicago, travel I-90 (Northwest Tollway) to U.S. 20 at Rockford. Follow U.S. 20 west to Galens: also from Chicago, take I-88 to I-39. Travel I-39 north to U.S. 20 at Rockford. Go U.S. 20 west to Galena.

Once mired in decay and forgotten river routes, Galena, Illinois, has been revived. Some of America's most enticing countryside surrounds this small town of historic manor houses, handsome brick mercantile and business buildings, and churches accented with the craft and love shown in hand-carved altars and pulpits. The enchanting qualities of Galena are echoed in the fact that many leading Chicago CEOs have chosen to retire to this spot.

Galena and Jo Daviess County swell with more than 50 antique shops (making this the main Midwestern antiquing center), 50 bed and breakfasts, 12 galleries, 25 private studios, along with 150 specialty shops. Billed and living up to fame, Galena is one of the most popular destinations in the Midwest. Weekends find bed and breakfasts booked, so travelers should make reservations early. November and March are the only reliably slow months during the year.

Glick Antiques
112 N. Main St.
815/777-0781

Reds Antiques & Collectibles
11658 W. Red Gates Road
815/777-9675

Hawk Hollow
103 S. Main St.
815/777-3616

Galena Shoppe
109 Main St.
815/777-3611

My Favorite Things
116 S. Main St.
815/777-3340

Touch-Banowetz Antiques
117 S. Main St.
815/777-3370

Karen's
209 S. Main St.
815/777-0911

Cedar Chest
213 S. Main St.
815/777-9235

Sparrow
220 S. Main St.
815/777-3060

J G Accent Unlimited
221 S. Main St.
815/777-9550

Village Merchantile
225 S. Main St.
815/777-0065

Beneath the Dust
302 S. Main St.
815/777-3202

Tin-Pan Alley
302 S. Main St.
815/777-2020

EGK Collectibles
305 S. Main St.
815/777-0180

Belle Epoque
306 S. Main St.
815/777-2367

Crickets
404 S. Main St.
815/777-6176

A Peace of the Past
408 S. Main St.
815/777-2737

Galena Antique Mall
8201 State Route 20 W.
815/777-3440

38 GALESBURG

East Main Antiques
125 E. Main St.
309/342-4424

Rug Beater Antiques
137 E. Main St.
309/343-2001

Highway Antique Shop
224 E. Main St.
309/343-1931

Rail City Antiques
665 E. Main St.
309/343-2614

Antique Corporation
674 E. Main St.
309/342-9448

General Store Antiques
940 E. North St.
309/342-2926

Attic Antique Shop
169 E. Water St.
309/342-7956

Ziggy's Antiques
674 E. Main St.
309/342-9448

Galesburg Antique Mall
349 E. Main St.
309/343-9800

39 GENESEO

Geneseo Antique Mall
117 E. Exchange
309/944-3777

Heartland Antique Mall
4169 S. Oakwood Avenue
309/944-3373

40 GENEVA

Findings of Geneva Antiques

307 W. State Street (Rt. 38)
630/262-0959
E-mail: findings g@aol.com

"Findings" has been opened approximately two years at the busy intersection of Route 38 (State Street) and Third Street, in Geneva's beautiful Downtown shopping district. It is owned by Marv and Jan Barishman, who operate it on a daily basis; from 10:30 to 6:00 pm Tuesday through Saturday, 12:00 to 5:00 Sunday, and closed on Mondays.

The shop has become well known for its finer and unusual older books, covering a wide range of collectable topics. Sharing the spotlight are collectable glass, pottery, sterling and finer linens. It is not unusual to find prints hanging on the walls, done by collected artists; as well as a wide selection of older postcards, world's fair items, paper collectibles, magazines, pocket knives, and toys.

The customer is always dealing with the owners in this shop, and has an opportunity to source information, as well as friendly discussion surrounding the items displayed here. Buying and selling items is a daily occurrence in this old-fashioned environment, and one can hear a pleasant interchange of price negotiating during many of the purchase and sales transactions.

The Store is actively buying many items regularly. The most sought after items are pre 1900 leather bound and "marbleized" books, fancy cut-work tablecloths, whitework bed linens, table scarves and Damask napkins. Active buying is always taking place in Franciscan Pottery's "Dessert Rose", "Ivy" and "Apple" dinnerware; Hall china's "Crocus" pattern, and McCoy Pottery; Fostoria, Heisey, and Cambridge glass; and illustrated children's books like "Little Black Sambo" and those illustrated by N. C. Wyeth or Jessie Wilcox Smith.

A Step in the Past
122 Hamilton St.
630/232-1611

Geneva Antiques Ltd.
220 S. 3rd St.
630/208-7952

Geneva Antique Market
227 S. 3rd St.
630/208-1150

Fourth Street Galleries
327 Franklin
630/208-4610

41 GIBSON CITY

Wil E. Makit Antiques
305 E. 1st
217/784-4598

Red Barn Antiques
620 E. 11th St. (Rt. 54 & 11th)
217/784-8752

The Silver Lion
107 N. Sangamon
217/784-8220

42 GLEN ELLYN

Patricia Lacock Antiques
526 Crescent Blvd.
630/858-2323

Stagecoach Antiques
526 Crescent Blvd.
630/469-0490

Finders Keepers
558 Crescent Blvd.
630/469-5320

Marcia Crosby Antiques
477 Forest Ave.
630/858-5665

Royal Vale View Antiques
388 Pennsylvania Ave.
630/790-3135

Pennsylvania Place
535 Pennsylvania Ave.
630/858-1515

43 GRAYSLAKE

Grayslake Trading Post
116 Barron Blvd.
847/223-2166

Yesterday Once More
299 W. Belvidere Rd.
847/223-4944

Duffy's Attic
22 Center St.
847/223-7454

Antique Warehouse
2 S. Lake St.
847/223-9554

44 GRAYVILLE

Antiques & More
1 Mile N. of I-64
618/375-4331

Prairie Town Antiques
101 N. Main
618/375-7306

45 GREENUP

Cumberland Road Collectibles
100 W. Cumberland
217/923-5260

Western Style Town Antq. Mall
113 E. Kentucky St.
217/923-3514

46 GREENVILLE

County Seat Mall Inc.
105 N. Third Street
618/664-8955

47 GURNEE

Favorite Places To Eat

Cracker Barrel Old Country Store
I-94 and Grand Ave., Exit 70
847/244-1512

48 HEBRON

Prairie Avenue Antiques
9936 Main St.
815/648-4507

Hebron Antique Gallery
10002 Main St.
815/648-4080

Grampy's Antique Store
10003 Main St.
815/648-2244

Lloyd's Antiques & Restoration
10103 Main St.
815/648-2202

Nancy Powers Antiques
12017 Maple Ave. (Rt. 173)
815/648-4804

Scarlet House
9911 Main St.
815/648-4112

Back In Time Antiques
10004 Main Street
815/648-2132

Watertower Antiques
9937 Main Street
815/648-2287

49 HINSDALE

Yankee Peddler
6 E. Hinsdale Ave.
630/325-0085

Aloha's Antique Jewelry
6 W. Hinsdale Ave.
630/325-3733

Griffin's In The Village
16 E. lst St.
630/323-4545

Fleming & Simpson Antqs. Ltd.
53 S. Washington St.
630/654-1890

50 JOHNSON CITY

"Little Shop in the Woods"
Corinth Road
618/982-2805

Seagle's Creative Collectibles
Liberty School Road
618/983-8130

Shamrock Antiques
306 W. Broadway
618/983-6661

Some Things Special Antiques
1805 Benton Avenue
618/983-8166

51 JOLIET

Uniques Antiques, Ltd.
1006 West Jefferson Street
815/741-2466

Uniques Antiques, Ltd. at 1006 W. Jefferson Street in Joliet, Illinois is conveniently located near two interstates. You can reach it from I-55 at the Rt. 52 east exit 253 and go straight east for 4.8 miles; Rt. 52 is W. Jefferson St. as it goes through Joliet. You can also reach it from I-80 at the Larking Ave. North exit 130B. Take Larkin Ave. North, turn right (east) at the 3rd stoplight and go 1.5 miles to Uniques.

Uniques Antiques, Ltd. is a single-owner shop that has 3,000 sq. ft. of a wide variety of clean, quality, and well-displayed antiques and collectibles. Everything is guaranteed to be what it is represented as; 99% of the merchandise is 30 years old or older. The owner, Ron Steinquist, stands behind the authenticity of his merchandise. You will find everything from smalls to furniture: advertising items and signs, china, clocks, cameras, crocks, dolls, glassware, jugs, lamps, mirrors, military items, milk bottles, phonographs, pocket watches, pottery, prints, political pins, radios, sheet music, toys, telephones, vases, wristwatches from the 40s, World's Fair items, and much more. In addition there is one room of "Boys Toys" that specializes in auto-related items, hunting, fishing, etc. You can almost smell the testosterone in this room!

Special services that are available at Uniques Antiques, Ltd. are: clock and watch repair, chair caning, radio repair, and stain removal from porcelain and pottery. China repair will be available in the near future.

Joliet is home to four Riverboat Casinos, the historic Rialto Theatre and is situated on the Heritage Corridor of the I&M Canal that runs from Chicago to La Salle-Peru, Illinois. There are numerous restaurants in the area that run the gamut from fast food to fine dining. There are a large number of motels at the Houbolt Road and Larkin Ave. exits off of I-80 and at the Rt. 30 exit off of I-55.

The largest and best antique show in the Midwest is the Sandwich Antiques Market, about 30 miles from Joliet. There is one show a month from May to October; you can call the Chicago office for the 1998 show dates (773/227-4464) or contact them on the internet at this address: http://www.antiquemarkets.com

Favorite Places To Eat

Cracker Barrel Old Country Store
I-80 & Houbolt Rd.., Exit 127
815/744-0985

52 KANKAKEE

Kankakee Antique Mall
145 S. Schuyler Ave.
815/937-4957

Bellflower Antique Shop
397 S. Wall St.
815/935-8242

Blue Dog Antique
440 N. 5th Ave.
815/936-1701

53 KENILWORTH

Smith & Ciffon
626 Green Bay Rd.
847/853-0234

Kenilworth Antique Center
640 Green Bay Rd.
847/251-8003

Federalist Antiques
515 Park Dr.
847/256-1791

54 KINMUNDY

Buckboard Antiques
253 S. Madison
618/547-3731

Lil's Antiques
301 E. Third Street
618/547-3604

55 LA GRANGE

Corner Shop
27 Calendar Ct
708/579-2425

Patterns of the Past
15 W. Harris Ave.
708/579-5299

Victorian Vanities
19 W. Harris Ave.
708/354-1865

Rosebud Antiques
729 W. Hillgrove Ave.
708/352-7673

Antiques & More
2 S. Stone Ave.
708/352-2214

Another Time Around
10 S. Stone Ave.
708/352-0400

56 LAKE FOREST

Country House
179 E. Deerpath Rd.
847/234-0244

Lake Forest Antiquarians
747 E. Deerpath Rd.
847/234-1990

Samlesburg Hall Ltd. Antiques
730 Forest Ave.
847/295-6070

Spruce Antiques
740 N. Western Ave.
847/234-1244

Lake Forest Antique Inc.
950 N. Western Ave.
847/234-0442

Anna's Mostly Mahogany
950 N. Western Ave.
847/295-9151

On Consignment Ltd. Antiques
207 E. Westminster Rd.
847/295-6070

Snow-Gate Antiques Inc.
234 E. Wisconsin Ave.
847/234-3450

57 LEBANON

General Store Antique Mall
112 E. St. Louis St.
618/537-8494

The Shops at 111
111 W. St. Louis St.
618/537-4162

Grandma's Attic
119 W. St. Louis St.
618/537-6730

Mom & Me
200 W. St. Louis St.
618/537-8343

The Cross Eyed Elephant
201 W. St. Louis St.
618/537-4491

Town & Country
205 W. St. Louis St.
618/537-6726

Peddler Books
209 W. St. Louis St.
618/537-4026

And Thistle Dew
210 W. St. Louis St.
618/537-4443

Heritage Antiques
218 W. St. Louis St.
618/537-2667

Owings Antiques
326 W. St. Louis St.
618/537-6672

58 LEMONT

Thirty minute southwest of Chicago, Lemont has over 40 dealers in 8 antique stops. Specialty stores display the works of local craftsmen and artisans. A cookie jar museum and historical museum are located nearby.

ANTIQUES ON STEPHEN STREET

Carroll & Heffron Antiques & Collectibles
206 Stephen Street
630/257-0510
Open Mon.-Sat., Sun. 12-4

Proud to be a part of the little international village of Lemont, the store has an always-changing inventory of almost everything: furniture, toys, glassware, books, artwork, and more.

Myles Antiques
119 Stephen Street
630/243-1415
Open 10-4, 7 days a week

Affordable elegance with a fine selection of European and American furniture, quality home decorating accessories, and Fenton art glass. Discover treasures from the past or that special something for that special someone.

Bittersweet Antiques & Country Accents
111 Stephen Street
603/243-1633
Open 7 days, 10-4

Located in an 1885 Limestone building filled with country primitives, painted furniture, decoys, fishing lures and woodenware. In addition they offer antique country decorator items, candles, lamps, wreaths, silks, etc. Sourcing available to find your special "wants."

Pacific Tall Ships
106 Stephen Street
1-800-690-6601

Unique maritime gallery specializing in handcrafted museum quality sailing ships of the world. Included with the ships are your choice of several different custom-built cases to enhance the decor of your home or office.

ANTIQUES ON MAIN STREET

Greta's Garrett
408 Main
603/257-0021
Hours: Tue.-Sat. 11-4

Antiques, collectibles, art pottery, fine glass, jewelry, Lenox china, linens, jewelry, old books, etc. Specializing in appraisal service and estate sales. We buy. Free Estimates.

Lemont Antiques
228 Main Street
630/257-1318
Open 7 days weekly, usually 10-5 or by appointment

Set in the restored 1862 Gerharz Funeral Store. Restoration and referral service, clock repair, antiques & collectibles, furniture, china, glass, clocks, dolls, jewelry, salt and pepper shakers, linens, lamps, cookie jars, collector plates, Russian curios and primitives.

Main Street Antique Emporium
220 Main Street
630/257-3456
Open Mon.-Fri., 11-8; Sat. 10-5; Sun. 11-5

Two stores in one, filled with antiques, collectibles, stamps, postcards, lamps, toy trains, and unique things. We also refurbish lamps. Multi-dealer shop.

ANTIQUES ON CANAL STREET

Antique Parlour
316-318 Canal Street
630/257-0033
Open Tue.-Sun. 11-5

Set in the 2400-square-foot 1928 Dodge Car Showroom. Engraved with the "Bicentennial Mural" wall. Victorian & Country fine furniture and homethings, 1840s to 1940s, antique guide books, plate holders, Victorian paper goods, silk lampshades.

Karen Adams
310 Canal Street
815/485-9660

Unique dealer specializing in complete & partial estates, architectural salvage removal and demolition, acquisition of advertising and photographic collection and unusual art.

Great Places to Eat

Lemont's Famous Christmas Inn
107 Stephen
630/257-2548
Hours: Tue.-Sat. starting at 11 a.m., Sun 9 a.m.-2 p.m.

Lunch and dinner in a Christmas atmosphere. Featured in "Best Decorations in Chicagoland." Sunday's breakfast buffet is a great way to start your antiquing day in Lemont.

Old Town Restaurant
113 Stephen Street
630/257-7570
Hours: Tue.-Sun, 11-8, Closed Monday

Lunch, dinner, family-style European cuisine, including Polish, Lithuanian, Hungarian, German. Carry-outs. Homemade bakery the specialty. Sunday brunch.

The Strand Cafe & Ice Cream Parlor
103 Stephen Street
630/257-2112
Hours: Weekdays 11a.m.-10p.m. Weekends 8a.m.-10p.m.

Fantastic food, breakfast, lunch or dinner! Serving the best Cajun food outside New Orleans. Best ice cream parlor in the U.S.A. and the best chocolate soda in the world. Bob Gerges plays the concert piano, honky tonk piano and accordion Fri.-Sun., 6 p.m. to closing. Tony Price plays the concert piano and sings every day for lunch.

Nick's Tavern
221 Main Street
630/257-6564
Open Mon.-Sat., 11a.m.-10:30p.m.

An antique in its own right, Nick's Tavern has been serving Lemont for more than 50 years. Home of "The Best Biggest Cheeseburger" in the state.

Interesting Side Trip

The Cookie Jar Museum
111 Stephen Street
708/257-2101

In 1975, Lucille Bromberek successfully completed a treatment program for alcoholism. Although she had no idea what to do with her life now that she'd recovered, she bolted up in bed one night "because a little voice inside my head told me to start collecting cookie jars." Four years later, she opened the only known cookie jar museum in the civilized world.

"I traveled throughout the country and found them at garage sales, antique shows, and flea markets," she remembers. As her reputation grew, people began sending her C-jars, as she fondly calls them, from all over the United States and abroad. Soon her home was overflowing, not unlike one of her overfilled collectibles.

Today the museum is in an office building and boasts a Wedgewood jar that's over a century old; rare Belleek china shamrock-and-pineapple containers from Ireland; a Crown Milano jar worth $3000 and petite, hand decorated biscuit jars, some of which have gold filigree, and others of which are made of exquisite cranberry glass.

"Most C-jars cost from $1 to $2,000, although prices have risen dramatically since I started. Jars I paid $5 for are now worth at least $125." For instance, those made from Depression glass, which was cheap in the thirties, can now fetch up to $8,000. "a few go for as high as $23,000, such as the McCoy 'Aunt Jemima' that belonged to Andy Warhol." That's a lot of dough for something that holds empty calories. Most in the two-thousand-plus collection are from twenty to fifty years old.

But the real fun of the museum is the perusal of Bromberek's piquant groupings. In the Pig Sty, Miss Piggy shares shelf space with peers dressed in black tie, chef's togs, and a nurse's uniform. There's even a jar depicting a farmer giving slop to the porkers.

Other cookie jar menagerie members include dogs, owls, turkeys, bears, camels, cows, fish, and a whale. "The lambs and the lions and the cats and mice are shelved together and get along beautifully." One of Bromberek's favorites is the "Peek-a-Boo" jar, a ceramic rabbit in pajamas. "They made only a thousand."

The museum has cookie jar trolleys, ships, trains, cars, airplanes, and even a gypsy wagon and a spaceship to help visitors along on their journeys. And, of course, there are the usual seasonal themes: a jack-o'-lantern, a Santa Claus, and a jar commemorating the annual downfall of many a dedicated dieter, Girl Scout cookies.

Nursery rhyme characters range from the old woman who lived in the shoe to the cow who jumped over the moon, and visitors will find Dennis the Menace, Howdy Doody, and WC. Fields as well. Bromberek has devoted three shelves to a Dutch colony and its population. Some of her arrangements tell a story, such as the one in which Cinderella is followed by a castle and then a pumpkin coach. "Turnabouts," with different faces on each side, include Mickey/Minnie Mouse, Papa/Mama Bear, and Pluto/Dumbo.

No cookie jar museum would be complete without homage paid to the treats they hold. a giant Oreo and a Tollhouse cookie, bags depicting Pepperidge Farm and Famous Amos munchies, and the Keebler elf are all represented here. Other enterprising containers include the Quaker Oats box, a Marshall Field's Frango Mint bag, the real-estate logo for Century 21, and an Avon lady calling on a Victorian-style house. For the health conscious, there are strawberry and green-pepper-shaped jars (at least the *container's* nonfattening). And you can really get caught with your hand in cookie jars that play music when opened.

Although Bromberek collects cookie cutters, cookie cook books, cookie plates, and measuring spoons that work for other comestibles besides cookies, the jars remain her true passion. "If they could talk, the stories they'd tell!" she half-jokes. "They come alive when I'm not there. The chefs and grannies stir up their favorite recipes for a grand gala affair. They come out of their little house C-jars, go to the barn, turn on the radio C-jar and dance up a storm." She claims she sometimes finds them in different spots in the morning. Well, okay.

Leave the appetite at home, however. "There's not a cookie on the premises."

From *America's Strangest Museums*

Published by arrangement with Carol Publishing Group, a Citadel Press Book

59 LENA

St. Andrew's Antiques
12075 W. Oak St.
815/369-5207

Rebecca's Parlor Antiques
208 S. Schuyler St.
815/369-4196

Cubbie's Bull Pen
211 N. Schuyler St.
815/369-2161

Raccoon Hollow Antiques
7114 US Route 20 W.
815/233-5110

60 LE ROY

On The Park Antiques Mall
104 E. Center St.
309/962-2618

Party Line Antiques
301 W. Oak
309/962-8269

61 LONG GROVE

Mrs. B & Me
132 N. Old McHenry Rd.
847/634-7352

Curiosity Shop
350 N. Old McHenry Rd.
847-821-9918

Emporium of Long Grove
227 Robt Parker Coffin
847/634-0188

Especially Maine Antiques
231 Robt Parker Coffin
847/634/3512

Carriage Trade
427 Robt Parker Coffin
847/634-3160

62 MAHOMET

Country Crossroads
103 S. Lincoln St.
217/586-5363

Olde Town Gallery
401 E. Main
217/586-3211

Victorian House
408 E. Main St.
217/586-4834

Tin Rabbit
415 E. Main St.
217/586-4178

Willow Tree Antiques
421 E. Main St.
217/586-3333

63 MARION

Collector's Choice
500 S. Court St.
618/997-4883

Old Homeplace
112 E. Deyoung St.
618/997-2454

Treasure Trove
1616 Emory Lane
618/993-2213

Kerr's Antiques
213 N. Hamlet St.
618/993-6389

Spotlight Antiques
1301 Interprise Way
618/993-0830

Oldies But Goodies
503 N. Madison St.
618/993-0020

Guesswhat & Co.
103 N. Market St.
618/997-4832

Jenny Lee Antiques
314 Red Row
618/993-5054

B & a Collections & Antique Clock Repair
1420 Julianne Dr.
618/997-2047

Favorite Places To Eat

Cracker Barrel Old Country Store
I-57 & Main St., Exit 53
618/993-6306

64 MATTESON

Favorite Places To Eat

Cracker Barrel Old Country Store
I-57 & Rt. 30, Exit 340
708/503-4000

65 MATTOON

Country Charm Antiques
816 Charleston Ave.
217/235-0777

Mattoon Antique Mart
908 Charleston Ave.
217/234-9707

Patti Re's Artistic Creations
Rt. 4 Box 11A
217/235-4857

Maple Tree Corner Antiques
1316 Lafayette Ave.
217/235-4245

66 MCHENRY

The Crossroad Merchant
1328 N. Riverside Drive
815/344-2610

67 MCLEANSBORO

Melba's Antiques
601 S. Washington St.
618/643-3355

Southfork Antique Mall
105 E. Broadway
618/643-4458

68 MENDOTA

Prairie Trails Antique Mall
704 Illinois Avenue
815/539-5547

Apple Tree Junction
701 Illinois Avenue
815/539-5116

Heartland Treasures
714 Illinois Avenue
815/538-4402

Little Shop On the Prairie
702 Illinois Avenue
815/538-4408

69 MOLINE

Mostly Old Stuff
1509 15th St.
309/797-3580

Victorian House Antiques
1925 6th Ave.
309/797-9755

Mississippi Manor Antique Mall
2406 6th Ave.
309/764-0033

70 MOMENCE

Cal-Jean Shop
127 E. Washington
815/472-2667

Days of Yesteryear
Hwy I-17
815/472-4725

71 MORRIS

Judith Ann's
117 W. Jackson St.
815/941-2717

Morris Antique Emporium
112 W. Washington St.
815/941-0200

72 MORTON

Favorite Places To Eat

Cracker Barrel Old Country Store
I-74 & Morton Ave., Exit 102
309/263-2103

73 MT. VERNON

Darnell's Antiques
Route 148
618/242-6504

Flota's Antiques
901 S. 10th Street
618/244-4877

Olde World Antiques
2515 Broadway
618/242-7799

Variety House Antiques
410-412 S. 18th St.
618/242-4344

Favorite Places To Eat

Cracker Barrel Old Country Store
I-57/I-64 & State Hwy. 15, Exit 95
618/242-9110

74 MURPHYSBORO

Virginia's Antiques
1204 Chestnut St.
618/687-1212

Old & In The Way
1318 Walnut St.
618/634-3686

Phoebe Jane's Antiques
1330 Walnut St.
618/684-5546

75 NAPERVILLE

Nana's Cottage
122 S. Webster
800/690-2770

Favorite Places To Eat

Cracker Barrel Old Country Store
I-88 & Rt. 29, Exit 59
630/778-6699

76 NAUVOO

Country Cottage Antiques
1695 Knight St.
217/453-6478

Old Nauvoo Antique Mall
1265 Mulholland St.
217/453-6769

Rita's Romantiques
2592 N. Sycamore Haven Dr
217/453-6480

77 OAKLAND

Outback Antique Store
2 E. Main
217/3462584

78 OAK PARK

Treasures N Trinkets
600 Harrison St.
708/848-9142

Antiques Etc. Mall
125 N. Marion
708/386-9194

79 ODIN

Lincoln Trail Antiques
U.S. Highway 50
618/775-8255

Vernon's Antiques
Box 57, Rt. 50
618/775-8360

80 ORLAND PARK

Beacon Hill Antique Shop
14314 Beacon Ave.
708/460-8433

Old Bank Antique Shop
14316 Beacon Ave.
708/460-7979

Emporium Antique Shop
14320 Beacon Ave.
708/460-5814

Favorite Things
14329 Beacon Ave.
708/403-1908

Olde Homestead Ltd.
14330 Beacon Ave.
708/460-9096

Cracker Barrell Antiques
9925 W. 143rd Pl
708/403-2221

General Store
14314 S. Union Ave.
708/349-9802

Station House Antique Mall
12305 W. 159th St. (Lockport)
708/301-9400

81 OSWEGO

Bob's Antique Toys
23 W. Jefferson St.
630/554-3234

Oswego Antiques Market
72 S. Main St.
630/554-9779

Oswego Antiques Market II
78 S. Main
630/554-9779

Old Oak Creek Shoppes
4025 US Highway 34 #B
630/554-3218

82 OTTAWA

Gramma's Attic Antique Mall
219 West Main Street
815/434-7332
Open Mon.-Sat., 9:30-5

Directions: From Interstate 80, take the Ottawa Exit south on Highway 23 to Main Street. Located south of Downtown courthouse, go right (west) 1/2 block, south side of the street.

From the name given to this establishment, one might come to the conclusion that it is a cozy little place filled with great "old things." But you can't judge a book by its title! This building swells to four floors and is a restored 150-year-old former hotel. That would date its existence back to 1847, when Illinois was the Pioneer West in still young America. It was a time when gunbelts were slung over bedposts, "ladies of the night" were escorted upstairs, whiskey flowed and bar-room brawls extended out into the streets. Today, thanks to the restoration efforts of Woody Jewett, Gramma's Attic, one of Ottawa's newest antique malls is a "gem" of a place to shop. Thirty-four dealers present a large selection of antique glassware, furniture, quilts, dolls, jewelry, collectibles, books and more.

83 PAXTON

Cheesecloth & Buttermilk
124 S. Market St.
217/379-3675

Antique Mall & Tea Room
931 S. Railroad Avenue
217/379-4748

84 PECATONICA

Antiques at Hillwood Farms
498 N. Sarwell Bridge Road
815/239-2421

85 PEORIA

Mia's Antiques & Uniques
1507 E. Gardner Lane (Heights)
309/685-1912

U Name It
3205 W. Harmon Hwy.
309/677-6710

Whaley's Clock Shop
218 W. McClure Ave.
309/682-8429

Abe's Antiques
2001 N. Wisconsin Ave.
309/682-8181

Backdoor Antiques & Cllbls.
725 SW Washington
309/637-3446

The Illinois Antique Center
308 SW. Commercial St.
309/673-3354

86 PESOTUM

Wildflower Antique Mall
511 S. Chestnut
217/867-2704
Open: Mon.-Sat. 9-6, Sun. 10-5

Directions: Exit 220 - I-57 & Rt. 45

Wildflower Antique Mall is your "last chance for antiques" - that is if you're traveling near Pesotum, Illinois. It is the only antique shop within a 300 mile radius. Presently the shop includes 43 experienced and dedicated dealers filling 5500 sq. ft. of space. But, since Wildflowers has become such a popular stop for traveling antiquers, the mall is expanding. Within you'll find a nice, neatly arranged selection of antiques and collectibles to add to your collection or for your home decorating needs.

87 PETERSBURG

Salem Country Store
Route 97 S.
217/632-3060

Petersburg Peddlers
113 S. 7th St.
217/632-2628

Fezziwig's
110 E. Sheridan St.
217/632-3369

Estep & Associates
320 N. 6th St.
217/632-4154

Stanis Sayre Antique Store
511 S. 6th St.
217/632-7016

88 PINCKNEYVILLE

Oxbow Bed & Breakfast
Route 1, Box 47
618/357-9839

Open year round from 7 a.m. to 11 p.m.

Directions: Oxbow is located on Highways 13/127, 1 and 3/4 miles south of Perry County Courthouse. If traveling I-64, take Exit 50 (Highway 127), and drive approximately 23 miles south. If driving I-57, take Exit 77 (Highway 154), then go 28 miles east.

A true vision of craftsmanship, Oxbow Bed & Breakfast was created by taking old barns and silos and turning them into perfect retreats for anyone in search of the more relaxed life. The barns were moved from various sites throughout the area to the present property, then painstakingly reconstructed and restored.

An older barn (settled behind the main house) is a retreat for honeymooners or others wanting to escape the crowds. During the summer months, take a dip in the swimming pool creatively constructed from old silo staves.

89 POCAHONTAS

Annabelle's Antiques Academy
Academy & National
618/669-2088

T G Antiques Mall
IH 70 & Hwy 40
618/669-2969

Wagon Wheel Antiques
202 National St.
618/669-2918

Village Square Antiques
202 State St.
618/669-2825

90 PRINCETON

Midtown Antique Mall
I-80 exit 56
815/872-3435

Sherwood Antique Mall
1661 N. Main St.
815/872-2580

91 QUINCY

Broadway Antique Mall
1857 Broadway
217/222-8617

Pawnee
501 Hampshire St.
217/222-8090

R & W Antiques
117 N. 4th St.
217/222-6143

June's Antiques
121 N. 4th St.
217/223-9265

Old Town Antiques
2000 Jersey St.
217/223-2963

Brocks Antiques
516 Main St.
217/224-7414

Yester Year Antique Mall
615 Maine St.
217/224-1871

Carriage House Antiques
805 Spring St.
217/228-2303

Vintage Home Furniture
208 S. 10th
217/224-5166

92 RICHMOND

A Little Bit Antiques
5603 Broadway
815/678-4218

Happy House Antiques
5604 Broadway
815/678-4076

Once Upon a Time
5608 W. Broadway
815/678-6533

Old Bank Antiques
5611 Broadway
815/678-4839

Hiram's Uptown Antiques
5613 Broadway
815/678-4166

A Step Above
5626 Broadway
815/678-6906

Cat's Stuff
5627 Broadway
815/678-7807

Serendipity Shop
9818 Main St.
815/678-4141

Antiques On Broadway
10309 N. Main St.
815/678-7951

Emporium-1905
10310 N. Main St.
815/678-4414

Marilyn's Touch
10315 N. Main St.
815/678-7031

Ed's Antiques
10321 N. Main St.
815/678-2911

93 RIVERSIDE

Riverside Antique Market
30 East Ave.
708/447-4425

J P Antiques
36 East Ave.
708/442-6363

Arcade Antiques & Jewelers
25 Forest Ave.
708/442-8110

Arcade Antiques & Furniture
7 Longcommon Rd.
708/442-8999

94 ROCK FALLS

Rock River Antique Center
2105 East Rt. 30
815/625-2556

95 ROCKFORD

Homestead Antiques
3712 N. Central Ave.
815/962-7498

Peddler's Attic
2609 Charles St.
815/962-8842

Houtkamp Art Glass Studio
120 N. Main St.
815/964-3785

Krenek's Clock Haven
2314 N. Main St.
815/965-4661

Eagle's Nest Antiques
7080 Old River Rd.
815/633-8410

Forgotten Treasures
4610 E. State St.
815/229-0005

East State St. Antique Mall #2
5301 E. State St.
815/226-1566

East State St. Antique Mall
5411 E. State St.
815/229-4004

Favorite Places To Eat

Cracker Barrel Old Country Store
I-90 & State Street, Exit 63
815/226-1944

96 ROCK ISLAND

Rock Island Antique Mart
1608 2nd Ave.
309/793-6278

Old Hat Antiques
1706 3rd Ave.
309/794-9089

Iron Horse Antiques & Gifts
533 30th St.
309/793-4500

Jackson's Antiques
1310 30th St.
309/793-1413

97 ROCKTON

Big D's Antiques
110 N. Blackhawk Rd.
815/624-6300

Nichols Antiques
212 W. Main St.
815/624-4137

98 ROMEOVILLE

Favorite Places To Eat

Cracker Barrel Old Country Store
I-55 & Weber Road, Exit 263
630/759-6171

99 ROSSVILLE

Fife & Drum
15 E. Attica St.
217/748-4119

Scarce Glass
101 S. Chicago St.
217/748-6352

Hall Closet
103 S. Chicago St.
217/748-6766

Heritage House
104 S. Chicago St.
217/748-6681

Market Place
106 S. Chicago St.
217/748-6066

Smith's Antiques & Collectibles
107 S. Chicago St.
217/748-6728

Freeman's Folly
110 S. Chicago St.
217/748-6720

100 SADORUS

Antique & Curiosity Shop
101 S. Vine Street
217/598-2200

This 'N That Shop
119 E. Market Street
217/598-2462

101 SALEM

Freeman Creek Antiques
3242 Hotze Road
618/548-6677

Little Lulu's
216 E. Main Street
618/548-0219

102 SANDWICH

Sandwich Antique Market
2300 E. Rt. 34
Village East Plaza
815/786-6122

Quackers Country Accents
127 S. Main
815/786-6429

Sandwich Antiques Mall
108 N. Main St.
815/786-7000

103 SAVANNA

Pulford Opera House Antiques Mall/J.T. Bradley's
324 Main Street
815/273-2661
Open Mon.-Thurs., 10:30-5:30; Fri.-Sat., 10:30-8: Sun., 11-6
Memorial Day through Labor Day: Mon.-Sat., 9:30-8; Sun., 11-6

Directions: Highway 84, "Great River Road," is a major highway running north/south along the Mississippi River. (Savanna is mid-distance between the Quad cities and Dubuque, Iowa.) Route 84 is called Main Street in downtown Savanna. The mall is located on Main Street.

The Pulford Opera House Antique Mall was built at the turn of the century and is the largest antique mall in northwestern Illinois. In 1905, the Opera House was the site of the murder of a local attorney, followed by the suicide of the Opera House owner, Botworth Pulford, a week later. Some folks attribute the occasional strange noises and occurrences throughout the house to their "ghosts." Apart from the spiritual visitors that frequent the Pulford Opera House are thousands of antique enthusiasts who flock to this 27,000-square-foot establishment, noted for its quality antiques. Located four doors south is J. T. Bradley's, the mall's companion store. This restored 1880s eatery offers soups, sandwiches, a salad bar, pastries and many entrees along with 30 more booths of antiques. a total of 120 dealers from Illinois, Iowa and Wisconsin provide the fine antiques displayed for purchase throughout both locations.

104 SHELBYVILLE

Hidden Antiques at the Hub
111 E. Main St.
217/774-2900

Pat's Antiques
133 E. Main St.
217/774-4485

Wooden Nickel Antiques
140 E. Main St.
217/774-3735

Auntie Darling's Daydreams
225 N. Morgan St.
217/774-5510

Jake's Antiques
W. Route 16
217/774-4223

Kinfolk
RR 1
217/774-2557

Jakes Warehouse
1501 W. South 8th St.
217/774-4201

105 SHILOH

Mueller's Antiques & Collectibles

522 North Main Street
618/632-4166
Open Thurs.-Sun., 1-5

Directions: Traveling Interstate 64, exit at #19 B (SR. 158). Go north to traffic lights (Old SR. 50). Turn left, and go approximately 1/4 mile to Shiloh Road (Main Street). Turn left going 1/4 mile to shop on the left.

Some of us collect antique glassware, linens, primitives, etc. but the owners at Mueller's Antiques collects buildings. Not necessarily buildings of a historic nature, but buildings full of history. On the main street of town in Shiloh, Ill., you'll find six farm buildings filled to the rafters with antiques. Everything imaginable can be found in here, so bring a big truck and a hefty wallet - you won't go away empty handed.

106 SOMONAUK

House of 7 Fables

300 East Dale Street
815/498-2289
Open 10-5 daily, but call ahead to avoid disappointment.

Directions: Somonauk is on U.S. Route 34 (Ogden Avenue) which runs parallel to and between Interstates 80 and 88, approximately 22 miles east of Interstate 39. The shop is at the corner of North Sagamore and Dale Streets, 1/2 block north of Route 34. The shop is a red house with white trim, white letters "ANTIQUES."

House of Seven Fables is, itself one of those treasures that collectors love to find. The half dozen or more buildings that make up the shop are all painted brick red with white trim and are rescued antiques themselves.

Owner Merwin Shaw got hooked on antiques back in the 1930s, when he "dusted, polished and steel-wooled antiques for a lady here in Somonauk." as he tells it.

Not only is the store, with all its items for sale, crammed to the rafters with finds in just about every category, but the repair areas - yes, repair areas - are just as interesting, because much of the repair work done here is a lost or dying art. There are hobby horse and toy restoration workshops, a wicker repair workshop, and an antique picture framing area. The shop handles vintage lighting, but they also do restoration and wiring of old pieces.

Inside one of the buildings, stuffed among the Windsors and firkins stacked in front of a window area, are several moonshine jugs, and green glass sits on the window ledge. Another window holds pink and red glass, with rockers, tables and baskets in front.

Antique chandeliers and bird cages hang from the ceiling in another corner over a hodgepodge of furniture covered with paintings and potted plants. Another corner, with shelves and cabinets running floor to ceiling, holds hundreds of vintage tins: coffee, tea, milk, liquor, all shapes, sizes, colors, configurations. Another wall is more elegant in tone, with framed pictures of all kinds hung in an orderly arrangement over a few choice pieces of furniture. Then there are the showcases - antiques themselves - filled with colored pressed glass cruets, rose bowls, toothpick holders, butter molds, complete sets of dishes, and perfume bottles, all arranged by color. It's a visual feast!

Bigger pieces of early American furniture that shoppers will find include Colonial pine cupboards, Shaker rockers, and hutch-top dry sinks decorated with accessories like salt glaze pottery, apothecary items and Norwegian tins.

There's usually something for everyone, and more importantly, there is a place to bring your treasures when they need tender loving care.

107 SPRINGFIELD

Old Georgian Antique Mall
830 S. Grand Ave. E
217/753-8110

Antiques Antiques
2851 Green Valley Rd.
217/546-1052

AAron's Attic Antiques
1525 W. Jefferson St.
217/546-6300

Renaissance Shop
2402 W. Jefferson St.
217/787-8125

Silent Woman Antique Shop
2765 W. Jefferson St.
217/787-3253

Eastnor Gallery of Antiques
700 E. Miller St.
217/523-0998

House Of Antiques
412 E. Monroe St.
217/544-9677

Antiques Unique
617 E. Monroe St.
217/522-0772

Springfield Antique Mall
3031 Reilly Dr
217/522-3031

Barrel Antique Mall
5850 S. 6th St.
217/585-1438

Ruby Sled-Antiques & Art
1142 S. Spring St.
217/523-3391

Pastime Antiques
6279 N. Walnut St.
217/487-7200

Murray's Oxbow Antiques
2509 S. Whittier Ave.
217/528-8220

Favorite Places To Eat

Cracker Barrel Old Country Store
I-55 & Toronto Rd., Exit 90
217/529-2290

108 ST. CHARLES

Riverside Antiques
410 S. 1st St.
630/377-7730

Consign-Tiques
214 W. Main St.
630/584-7535

Brown Beaver Antiques
219 W. Main St.
630/443-9430

Antique Market III
413 W. Main St.
630/377-5599

Studio Posh
17 N. 2nd Ave.
630/443-0227

Market
12 N. 3rd St.
630/584-3899

Memory Merchant Antiques
15 S. 3rd St.
630/513-0340

Antique Market I
11 N. Third St.
630/377-1868

Antique Market II
303 W. Main (Rt. 64)
630/377-5798

109 ST. JOSEPH

Peach's Antiques
228 E. Lincoln
217/469-8836

Pine Acres Trees & Herbs
E. of Sidney on 2300 E.
217/688-2207

The Village Shoppe
228 E. Lincoln
217/469-8836

110 STOCKTON

Grandpa & Grandma Antiques
118 W. Front Ave.
815/947-2411

Cornerstone Creations
101 N. Main St.
815/947-2358

Tredegar Antique Market
208 E. North Ave.
815/947-2360

Glick's Antiques
3602 E. Woodbine St.
815/858-2305

111 TINLEY PARK

Favorite Places To Eat

Cracker Barrel Old Country Store
I-80 & Hwy. 43, Exit 148
708/614-8066

112 TROY

Favorite Places To Eat

Cracker Barrel Old Country Store
I-70/55 & Rt. 162, Exit 18
618/667-2021

113 TUSCOLA

Wood Tin & Lace
604 S. Main St.
217/253-3666

Prairie Sisters Antique Mall
102 W. Sale St.
217/253-5211

Prairie Church Antique Mall
568 36th E.
217/253-3960

114 URBANA

Favorite Places To Eat

Cracker Barrel Old Country Store
I-74 & Hwy. 45, Exit 184
217/344-9087

115 VANDALIA

Back When Antiques
118 N. Elm
No Number Listed

Cuppy's Antique Mall
& Old Fashioned Soda Fountain
618/283-0080

Treasure Cove Antique Mall
302 W. Gallatin
618/283-8704

Wehrle's Antiques
Rt. 51
618/283-4147

116 VILLA PARK

Astorville Antiques
51 S. Villa Ave.
630/279-5311

Memories from the Attic
119 S. Villa Ave.
630/941-1517

117 WARRENVILLE

Lil' Red Schoolhouse Antiques and Cllbls.
3 South 463 Batavia Road
630/393-1040
Open Mon.-Sat., 10-5; Sun., 11-5

Directions: From Chicago, take 290 (Eisenhower Expressway) west to I-88. Continue on I-88; exit at Winfield Road. Travel north to second stoplight (Amoco and Mobile stations); turn left, go 2 blocks to STOP sign. Turn right, 4th building on the right (opposite the fire station). Coming on Route 59, turn east on Butterfield Road, to Batavia Road. Turn right (south) to shop on left hand side.

Settled among a grove of wonderful trees which give way to a lawn tumbling down to the Du Page River, sets the Lil' Red Schoolhouse. It was built in 1836 when teachers were required to be single ladies. There are ten rooms and two porches which make up the schoolhouse's construction. The desk, the chalkboard, the pencils and the rulers have all been replaced with quality antiques. You'll find tables, chairs (many dating to the early 1900s and beyond), lamps, glassware, early tools and a hodgepodge of other wonderful things.

The Lil' Red Schoolhouse schedules it outdoor sales for the second Sunday of each month (dealers take note).

Rt. 59 Antique Mall
3 S. 450 Rt. 59
630/393-0100
Open: Mon.-Sat. 10-6, Sun. 11-4:30

Directions: 1 mile north of I-88, 1 mile from Cracker Barrel

Rt. 59 Antique Mall features 60 dealers offering a nice selection of pottery, exquisite glassware, primitives, architectural pieces, '50s items, art deco, distinctive furnishings, lamps and Star Wars collectibles. The shop provides a "kids place" with books, toys and games - perfect for Moms who love to shop. Stop and see why Rt. 59 Antiques Mall is a favorite spot for local antiquers.

118 WESTMONT

Tony's Collectibles
141 S. Cass Ave.
630/515-8510

Elite Repeat
123 E. Ogden Ave.
630/960-0540

Old Plank Rd. Antiques
233 W. Ogden Ave.
630/971-0500

Zeke's Antiques & Leo's Lamps
135 W. Quincy St.
630/969-3852

119 WHEELING

Kerry's Clock Shop
971 N. Milwaukee Ave.
847/520-0335

Lundgren's
971 N. Milwaukee Ave.
847/541-2299

The Crystal Magnolia
971 N. Milwaukee Ave.
847/537-4750

Shirley's Dollhouse
971 N. Milwaukee Ave.
847/537-1632

My Favorite Place
971 N. Milwaukee Ave.
847/808-1324

O'Kelly's Antiques
971 N. Milwaukee Ave.
847/537-1656

County Faire Antiques
971 N. Milwaukee Ave.
847/537-9987

Antiques of Northbrook
971 N. Milwaukee Ave.
847/215-4994

Coach House Antiques
971 N. Milwaukee Ave.
847/808-1324

Antiques Center of Ill.
1920 S. Wolf Rd.
847/215-9418

120 WILMETTE

Shorebirds
415 1/2 4th St.
847/853-1460

Buggy Wheel
1143 Greenleaf Ave.
847/251-2100

Collected Works
1405 Lake Ave.
847/251-6897

Raven & Dove Antique Gallery
1409 Lake Ave.
847/251-9550

Heritage Trail Mall
410 Ridge Rd.
847/256-6208

Josie's
545 Ridge Rd.
847/256-7646

121 WILMINGTON

Wilmington Antique Dealers Association

Wilmington offers days of treasure hunting in the century old buildings of N. Water Street. There are 3 multi-level antique malls and 9 additional antique shops featuring over 100 dealers with a wide variety of antiques and collectibles. These shops along with a diner and "The best burgers in Will County" at RTM's, specialty shops with bakery, coffee, teas and ice cream make N. Water Street an enjoyable and rewarding adventure.

Snuggled within 20 minutes of three major interstate routes on the Kankakee River, Wilmington is easily accessible. From I-80 take the I-55 exit south to sixth 238, then left on Strip Mine Rd. to Rte. 53, left again to second light then left on Water St. From I-57 take the Peotone/Wilmington exit 327 to Rte. 53 then left to second light, and left on Water St.

Mill Race Emporium
110 N. Water Street
Multi-level, multi-dealer – Antiques and collectibles
815/476-7660

Water Street Mall
119-121 N. Water St.
Multi-level, multi-dealer
Full line-Fenton-Heisey-carnival-pottery-toys
Discover-Visa-Mastercard
815/476-5900

Abacus Antiques
113-115 N. Water St.
Art Deco-50s items-furniture-more
815/476-5727

The Opera House Antiques
203 N. Water St.
Antiques-Collectibles-Primitives
Discover-Visa-Mastercard
815/476-0872

R. J.'s Relics
116-118-120 N. Water St.
Multi-level, multi-dealer
Space and showcase rental
Knives-Military-Books-Sports cards-Jewelry-Vintage clothing-Furniture and much more
Discover-Visa-Mastercard
815/476-6273

Paraphernalia Antiques
112-114-124 N. Water St.
Jewelry-Irish Pine-European Imports
815/476-9841

Stuff-N-Such
Antiques-collectibles-crafts
815/476-0411

O'Koniewski's Treasures
General Line-anything unusual and interesting
815/476-1039

122 WINNETKA

Jack Monckton Gallery
1050 Gage St.
847-446-1106

West End Antiques
619 Green Bay Rd.
847-256-2291

Arts 220
895 1/2 Green Bay Rd.
847/501-3084

Antique Heaven
982 Green Bay Rd.
847/446-0343

Pied a Terre
554 Lincoln Ave.
847/441-5161

Robertson-Jones Antiques
569 Lincoln Ave.
847/446-0603

Knightsbridge Antiques
909 Green Bay Rd.
847/441-5105

M Stefanich Antiques Ltd.
549 Lincoln Ave.
847/446-4955

Heather Higgins Antiques
567 Lincoln Ave. #A
847/446-3455

Stuart Antiques
571 Lincoln Ave.
847/501-4454

Country Shop
710 Oak St.
847/441-8690

123 WITT

Hole in the Wall
3 E. Broadway
217/594-7132

Mystique Antiques
510 N. Main St.
217/594-2802

Country Store Antiques
411 E. Ford St.
217/594-7275

Notes

THE
B·O·O·K I·N·N

Bed & Breakfast

Quality Used Bookstore (Bought & Sold)

508 West Washington
(219) 288-1990
Fax (219) 234-2338
Internet Address:
http://members.aol.com/bookinn/

South Bend 70

Bill's Clockworks

Antique Clocks • Cuckoo Clocks
Clock Repair & Restoration

8 West Columbia St. (Hwy. 18) • Flora, IN
Phone (219) 967-4709 • Toll Free 1-888-742-5625
http://www.qklink.com/clockworks
Monday - Friday 9-6 • Saturday 9-5
MAJOR CREDIT CARDS ACCEPTED • FREE LAYAWAY 22

WELCOME
TO NAPPANEE, INDIANA

Come Visit Borkholder
Mall and Marketplace
Antiques, Craft Mall & Dutch Kitchen
Over 500 Vendors
Open All Year Mon. thru Sat.••Summer 9-5; Winter 10-5
Antique & Miscellaneous Auction
Every Tuesday at 8 a.m.
Flea Market Monday thru Saturday
CR 101, North of U.S. 6, 1-1/2 mile West of S.R. 19

BORKHOLDER
DUTCH VILLAGE
MALL & MARKETPLACE
NAPPANEE, INDIANA
(219) 773-2828 49

Indiana

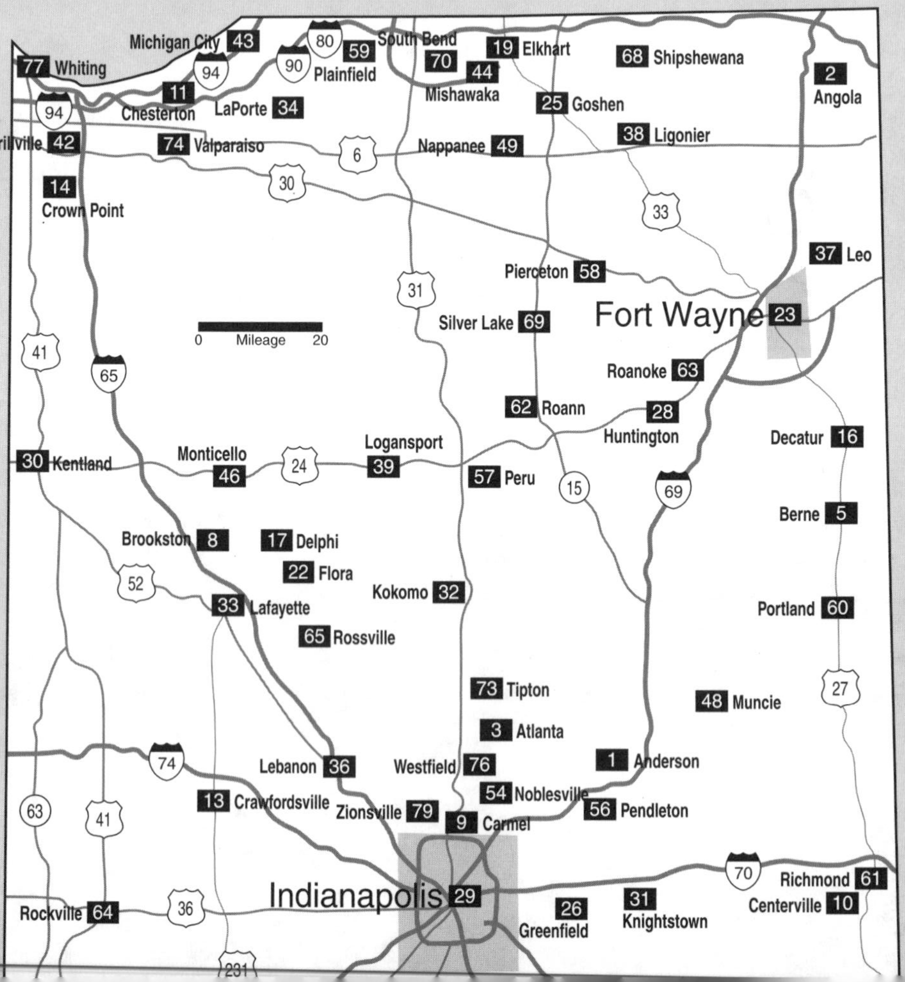

Visit
Nashville
in Brown County

The Perfect
Antiquing
Get-A-Way

50

HOOSIER ANTIQUES & CLOCKS

1630 S. 3rd St.
812-238-0562

Terre Haute

BROWN HEN ANTIQUE & CRAFT MALL

Rt. 11, Junct. 50 & 37
(812) 279-9172

Bedford

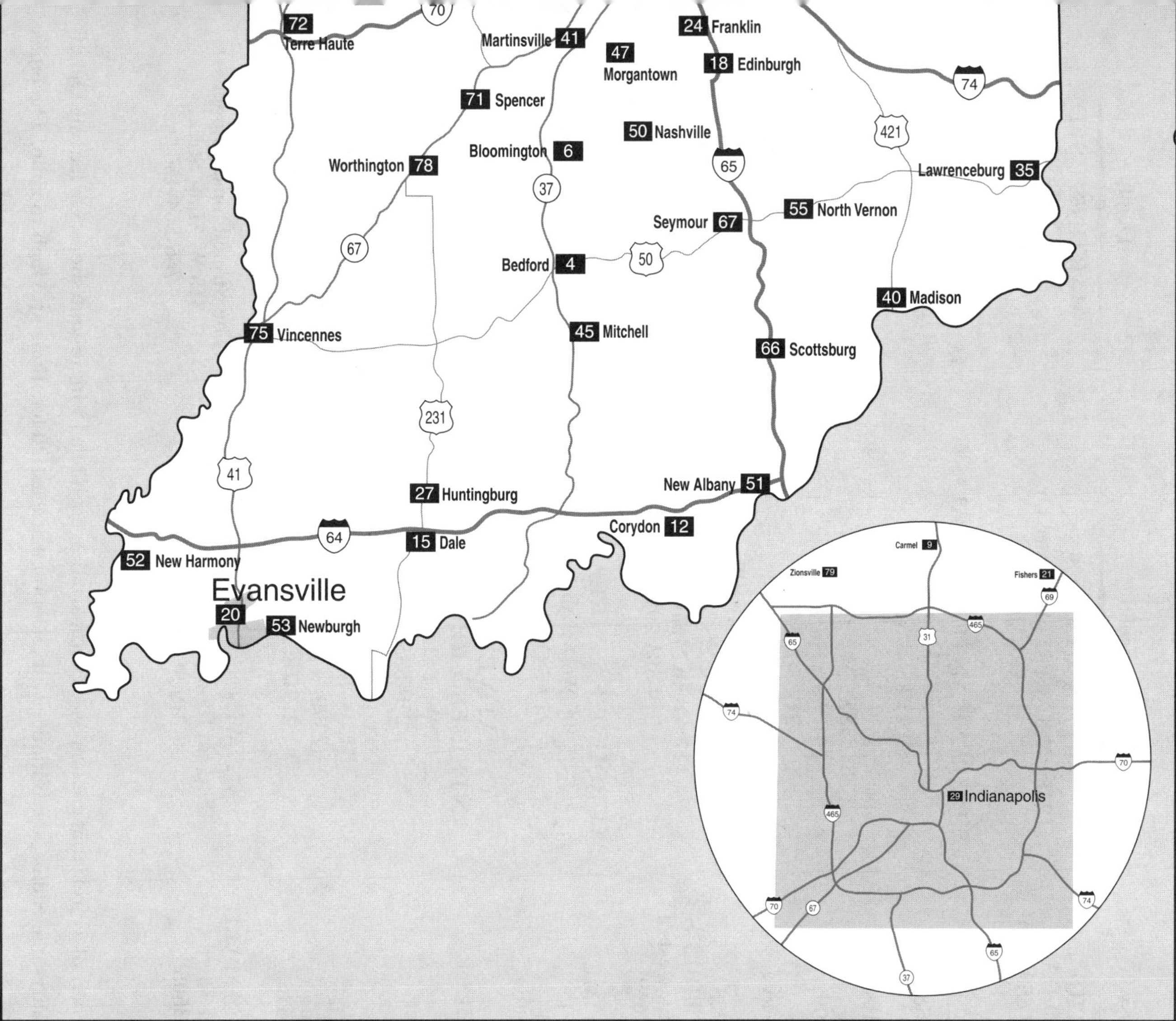

72 Terre Haute
70
Martinsville 41
47 Morgantown
24 Franklin
18 Edinburgh
74
71 Spencer
50 Nashville
421
Worthington 78
Bloomington 6
65
Lawrenceburg 35
37
Seymour 67
55 North Vernon
67
Bedford 4
50
40 Madison
75 Vincennes
45 Mitchell
66 Scottsburg
231
41
27 Huntingburg
New Albany 51
64
15 Dale
Corydon 12
52 New Harmony
Evansville
20
53 Newburgh
Carmel 9
Zionsville 79
Fishers 21
69
65
31
465
74
70
29 Indianapolis
465
70
67
74
65
37

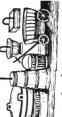

Indiana Directory of Antique & Unique Shops

Flora, Brookston, Rossville

JOHN'S TOYS & ANTIQUE
4160 N. County Road O.E.V.
Frankfort • 765-659-9017 / 659-3519

WERTZ ANTIQUES
IN 18 W of IN 75
Flora • 219-967-3056

BILL'S CLOCKWORKS
8 West Columbia
Flora • 219-967-4709
888-742-5625
http://www.qlink.com/clockworks

ROLLING WHEELS
ANTIQUES & COLLECTIBLES
8136 West St. Rd. 26 or 4 mi. west of
Rossville • 765-379-2649

BACK THROUGH TIME
ANTIQUES MALL
9 West Main (at Flasher)
Rossville • 765-379-3299

STEWART'S ROSSVILLE
ANTIQUE MALL
54 East Main Street
Rossville • 765-379-9000

BURGET'S LOFT
Rt. 1 Box 293 A
Brookston • 765-563-6866

BROOKSTON ANTIQUES MALL
St. Rd. 43 North Edge of Town
Brookston • 765-563-3505

Monticello

BETH'S ANTIQUES
12355 N. Upper Lake Shore Dr.
219-583-3002

UPTOWNE ANTIQUES MALL
134 South Main Street
219-583-3202

BLOSSOM STATION
101 West Broadway
219-583-5359

MAIN STREET
ANTIQUES MALL
127 North Main Street
219-583-2998

TURQUOISE 'N' TREASURES
400 West Fisher
219-583-8143

CREATIVE CLUTTER
ANTIQUES & REFINISHING
2702 West Shafer Drive
219-583-3336

BLACK DOG INN
2390 N. Untaluti
219-583-8297

INNTWINNED INN TIME
Second Floor Sportsman Inn
219-583-5133

Delphi

MARTIN'S USED
FURNITURE
North Market Street
765-564-3813

J&B FURNITURE STORE
113 S. Washington Street
765-564-9204

DELPHI ANTIQUES MALL
117 S. Washington Street
765-564-3990

LIL' BIT OF COUNTRY
125 S. Washington St.
765-564-6231

TEDDY'S EMPORIUM
115 East Main Street
765-564-3742

TOWN SQUARE MALL
110 West Main Street
765-564-6937

TIMES PAST ANTIQUES
& ART ACCENTS STUDIO
124 East Main Street
765-564-6317 OR 564-3424

CROUCH'S
VICTORIAN ANTIQUES
404 East Main Street
765-564-4195

The Stone House Shoppes
315 W. Main Street
765-564-4663

Delphi, Indiana, is the center of a circle that encompasses several cities, each filled with unique shops. On leaving Delphi in any direction within a twenty-mile radius, the antiquer will encounter at least 20 locations at which to shop. The cities within the circle have organized a co-op to promote themselves, a membership list that is ever-growing, but includes shops within or between the cities of Flora, Brookston, Rossville, Monticello and Delphi.

Each city wihin the co-op recognizes the others' ability to draw a crowd. Monticello is home of the famous Indiana Beach; Brookston has an annual popcorn and apple festival; Rossville has a summer's end festival with roads closed and street vendors in operation; and Flora has an annual pork producer cook-off, with an old car "cruise in," oldies music, and a lot of activity. The area also has the Walbash and Erie Canal digs every summer. Visit the area, you'll be a satisfied antiquer!

T•H•E B•O•O•K I•N•N

Built by Martha and Albert Cushing in 1872, this home was one of the earliest residences in the historic district of South Bend. Cushing was a local businessman with interests in several enterpises, including a drug and bookstore at 101 North Michigan Street. The house is listed as an outstanding example of Second Empire architecture by the Indiana Historic Site Preservation Committee. Sometimes called French Victorian, the mansard roof with ornamental arched dormer windows creates an impression of massive elegance. The entry doors with double leaf wood and applied decoration reportedly won first place for design at the 1893 Columbian Exposition in Chicago.

Inside you will find twelve foot ceilings and handhewn, irreplaceable butternut woodwork that welcome you into this elegant mansion. THE BOOK INN has been a designer showcase and every room offers comfortable bed and breakfast accommodations. The five sleeping rooms all have private bathrooms.

THE BOOK INN is located in the historic West Washington District of downtown South Bend, Indiana. The original owners, the Cushings, must have watched in wonder when Clement Studebaker built his home, *Tippecanoe Place*, "right next door" in 1888. Studebaker's forty-room 'feudal castle' is now an elegant restaurant where you can explore the mansion and enjoy a wonderful meal.

"High ceilings, large comfortable beds with beautiful linens, lovely antique furnishings, picture books, novels, cozy reading chairs, fresh flowers, lush terry robes, private bath - everything I could possible want. The entire house, from the well-stocked library and kitchen to the dining room table set with crystal, linen, great coffee, and tasty breakfast fare, is a weary traveler's dream. Peggy and John made me feel welcome, relaxed and pampered."

(Guest) Suzanne Peck
America's Favorite Inns, B&Bs & Small Hotels

Also recommended in:
Best Places to Stay
AAA Three Diamond Inn

The Book Inn
508 West Washington
South Bend, Indiana
(219) 288-1990
Fax. (219) 234-2338
Internet Address: http://members.aol.com/bookinn/

Indiana

1 ANDERSON

Jerry's Junkatique
509 E. 8th St.
317/649-4321

Harold's Hideaway
2023 Lindberg Rd.
317/642-7880

Anderson Antique Mall
1407 Main St.
317/622-9517

Abby's
1231 Meridian St.
317/642-8016

Antiques by Helen Marie
909 Raible Ave.
317/642-0889

Favorite Places To Eat

Cracker Barrel Old Country Store
I-69 & Scatterfield Rd., Exit 26
765/642-6424

2 ANGOLA

Angola Mini Mall
109 W. Gale St.
219/665-7394

Olde Towne Mall
101 W. Maumee St.
219/665-9920

Then & Now Mini Mall
200 W. Maumee St.
219/665-6650

Angola Antique Depot
208 W. Maumee St.
219/665-2026

Angola Antique Depot
611 W. Maumee
219/665-2026

3 ATLANTA

The Wooden Indian Antiques
115 W. Main Street
765/292-2722
Open: Summer (April-December. Sat.-Wed. 11-5), Winter (January-March, Fri.-Sun. 12-5), other times by chance or appointment

Directions: Located in downtown Atlanta next to the railroad tracks. Atlanta is 5 miles south of Tipton on State Route 19 and 12 miles north of Noblesville on State Route 19. U.S. 31 is 5 miles west of Atlanta. The road to Atlanta from U.S. 31 (approximately 296th Street) is 20 miles north of I-465 (on north edge of Indianapolis) and 20 miles south of Kokomo.

As you might have surmised, The Wooden Indian Antiques shop specializes in wood. They stock from 800 to 1,000 pressed back chairs and although they are not always in pristine condition, choices are limitless. There is something for everyone; including the do-it-yourselfer. They also do chair caning, a diminishing art.

The next time someone asks, "It that chair taken," you can tell them, "yes but there are many, many more where that one came from at The Wooden Indian Antiques."

4 BEDFORD

Brown Hen Antique & Craft Mall
Route 11, Box 646
812/279-9172
Open Mon.-Sat. 10-5, Sun. 12-5.

Directions: Located three miles south of 16th Street in Bedford on Highway 37/50 just south of Hickory Hill Restaurant & Dalton's RVs.

Brown Hen Antiques & Craft Mall definitely has something to cackle about. The "old" Brown Hen Mall was leveled by a tornado in 1991; however, hanging over the check-out counter was a large painting of a brown hen. An inspection of damage found the shop completely gone, but the brown hen survived with only minor damage. Hopefully, this "brown hen" has a place of honor in the new Brown Hen shop, which offers an eclectic array of antiques and collectibles.

Zollman's Finery
917 15th St.
812/275-2216

5 BERNE

Berne Antique Mall
105 W. Water St.
219/589-8050

Karen's Treasures
444 E. Main St.
219/589-2002

6 BLOOMINGTON

The Garret
403 W. Kirkwood
812/339-4175
Hours: Mon.-Wed., Fri. & Sat. 9-6, Thurs., Sun. By appointment or chance

Directions: Highways 37, 45, 48 and 446 all go into Bloomington. Go to the Court House Square in downtown. One street south is Kirkwood (also called 5th Street). The Garret is 2 blocks west on the corner of Kirkwood and Madison.

The Garretts have been in the antiquing business nearly forty years and, according to them, their shop is "simply the largest, oldest, and most diversified shop in the area." The three floors of this unique shop, house not only a world of wonderful antiques, but a rock and mineral shop as well. The specialties of The Garret are lighting and furniture.

Cowboys & Indians
110 E. Kirkwood Ave.
812/323-1013

Grant St.
213 S. Rogers St.
812/333-6076

Odds & Olds
2524 S. Rogers St.
812/333-3022

Bloomington Antique Mall
311 W. 7th St.
812/332-2290

Elegant Options Antique Gallery
403 N. Walnut St.
812/332-5662

7 BRAZIL

Brazil Antique Mall
105 E. National Ave.
812/448-3275

Crestline Antiques
531 E. National Ave.
812/448-8061

Stuff N Things Antiques
U.S. Hwy. 40 E.
812/448-3861

His & Hers
RR 12
812/448-3153

8 BROOKSTON

There are two antique shops located in Brookston as well as others in the immediate area. See review at the end of this section for a complete listing.

9 CARMEL

Matty's Antiques
210 W. Main St.
317/575-6327

Heritage of Carmel
250 W. Main St.
317/844-0579

Acorn Farm Country Store
15466 Oak Rd.
317/846-6257

Antique Emporium
1055 S. Range Line Rd.
317/844-8351

10 CENTERVILLE

Tom's Antique Center
117 E. Main St.
765/855-3296

Now & Then Antiques
139 E. Main St.
765/855-2806

Wheeler's Antiques
107 W. Main St.
765/855-3400

Webb's Antique Mall
200 Union St.
765/855-2489

11 CHESTERTON

Antiques 101
101 Broadway
219/929-1434

Kathy's Antique Shop
530 Indian Boundary Rd.
219/926-1400

Yesterday's Treasures Antiques
700 Broadway
219/926-2268

Russ & Barb's Antiques
222 W. Lincoln Ave.
219/926-4937

Emma's Antiques & Gifts
428 S. Calumet Rd.
219/929-4427

12 CORYDON

Kinter House Inn
101 South Capitol Avenue
812/738-2020
Fax: 812/738-7430
Open year round

All the elements which made Kinter House Inn the finest hotel in Corydon are still preserved today. The current owners have restored this three-story brick Italianate to its 1873 grandeur.

Griffin Bldg. Antique Mall
113 E. Beaver St.
812/738-3302

John's Try'Al
110 N. Elm St.
812/738-1924

Red Barn Antique Mall
215 Highway 62 W
812/738-2276

13 CRAWFORDSVILLE

Cat's Meow
4030 State Road 32 E
317/362-0053

Fireside Antique Mall
4035 State Road 32 E
317/362-8711

Cabbages & Kings
124 S. Washington St.
317/362-2577

14 CROWN POINT

Gard Gallery Antiques
700 N. Sherman St.
219/663-0547

Dan's Antiques
8703 E. 109th Ave.
219/663-4571

Antique Shoppe
Old Courthouse Shops
219/663-1031

Antique Mall of Crown Point
103 W. Joliet St.
219/662-1219

15 DALE

Lincoln Heritage Antiques
Highway 231
812/357-1993

16 DECATUR

Family Tree Antiques
618 Adams St.
219/728-2880

Memories Past Antique Mall
111 E. Jefferson St.
219/728-2643

Red Duck Antiques
132 N. 2nd St.
219/728-2224

Town House Antiques
222 N. 2nd St.
219/724-2920

Yvonne Marie's Antique Mall
152 S. 2nd St.
219/724-2001

17 DELPHI

There are nine antique shops located in Delphi as well as others in the immediate area. See review at the end of this section for complete listing.

18 EDINBURGH

Favorite Places To Eat

Cracker Barrel Old Country Store
I-65 & U.S. 32, Exit 76
812/526-7968

19 ELKHART

Caverns of Elkhart
111 Prairie Ct.
219/293-1484

Elkhart Antique Mall
51772 State Road 19
219/262-8763

Favorite Places To Eat

Cracker Barrel Old Country Store
I-80 & Cassopolis St., Exit 92
219/264-6963

20 EVANSVILLE

River's Inn Bed and Breakfast
414 S.E. Riverside Drive
812/428-7777 or 1-800-797-7990
Fax: 812/421-2902
Open year round

Built in 1866 and furnished throughout with fine antiques and collectibles this three-story Italianate home overlooks the Ohio River. Third floor rooms have balconies from which you can view the river or the beautiful gardens below. Johnny Walker potato pie is often served at breakfast.

Different Things
2107 W. Franklin St.
812/423-3890

A King's Antique Shoppe
504 N. Garvin St.
812/422-5865

Em Siler Antiques
513 N. Green River Rd.
812/476-2656

Daylight Country Store
12600 N. Green River Rd.
812/867-6932

Lori's Antiques
12747 N. Green River Rd.
812/867-7414

Pack Rat
305 N. Main St.
812/423-7526

American & European Antqs.
402 N. Main St.
812/421-1720

Walkway Mall
518 Main St.
812/421-9727

1001 Antiques
711 N. Main St.
812/422-0291

Rick Tremont Antiques
608 S.E. 2nd St.
812/426-9099

Bill's Antiques
601 E. Virginia St.
812/422-0810

Paxson's Antiques
1355 Washington Ave.
812/476-6790

Franklin Street Antique Mall
2123 W. Franklin St.
812/428-0988

Inside Out
12747 N. Green River Rd.
812/867-7414

Puckett's Treasures & Cllbls.
Washington Square Mall
812/473-2988

The Tuesday Shop
7521 Old State Road
812/867-6332

Whispering Hills Antiques
10600 Highway 65
812/963-6236

Favorite Places To Eat

Cracker Barrel Old Country Store
I-164 & Lloyd Expressway, Exit 7
812/479-8788

21 FISHERS

Favorite Places To Eat

Cracker Barrel Old Country Store
I-69 & 96th St., Exit 3
317/842-2766

22 FLORA

There are four antique shops located in Flora as well as others in the immediate area. See review at the end of this section for a complete listing.

Bill's Clockworks
8 W. Columbia Street (Hwy. 18)
219/967-4709
1-888-742-5625
http://www.qklink.com/clockworks
Open: Mon. - Fri. 9-6, Sat. 9-5

Owner Bill Stoddard has had a lifelong interest in clocks. When he was a small boy, his grandfather, who had a small clock collection, showed Bill how to wind and regulate clocks. At the age of eight he acquired his first time-piece and so began his love for collecting. Bill and his mother, while cleaning out an attic, discovered a broken Waterbury octagon lever wall clock, ca. 1880. Several years later, he saved up money mowing lawns and had the clock repaired.

Throughout his teen years, Bill's love for collecting clocks grew. In April, 1991 Bill opened his own clock shop in his home in Indianapolis. By 1995 Bill had moved to Flora where he opened shop in the former Rainbow Cafe. He enjoys repairing many different types of clocks, particularly early American weight driven clocks. Bill says he enjoys his work because he gets to repair each clock, treating it as if it were his own, enjoying it while it's in the shop, then seeing the smile on the customers face when their time-piece is clean, shiny and repaired. And the best part - he gets paid for doing something he truly loves.

23 FORT WAYNE

Betty's Antiques
1421 Broadway
219/424-0504

Candlelight Antiques
3205 Broadway
219/456-3150

Old Clock Shop & Antiques
3331 Butler Ct.
219/483-2061

Wagenhaus Furniture Gallery
3920 N. Clinton St.
219/484-9420

Karen's Antique Mall
1510 Fairfield Ave.
219/422-4030

Favorite Places To Eat

Cracker Barrel Old Country Store
I-69 & Rt. 3, Exit 111B
219/489-1855

24 FRANKLIN

Jeri's Antiques
56 E. Jefferson St. #C
317/738-3848

Lighthouse Antique Mall
62 W. Jefferson St.
317/738-3344

Peddler's II
90 W. Jefferson St.
317/736-6299

Town Square Antiques
104 W. Jefferson St.
317/736-9633

25 GOSHEN

Carriage Barn Antiques
1100 Chicago Avenue
219/533-6353
Open Mon.-Fri. 9:30-5, Sat. 9:30-4

Directions: From 80/90 Indiana Toll Road, Exit 101 at Bristol. Turn south on State Road 15 to Goshen. Go right (west) on U.S. 33 to K.F.C. (Indiana Avenue). Turn right and continue for 2 Ω blocks to the old Bag Factory. Park behind the log house. Look for arched entry into brick building.

Looking for a piece of furniture like "Grandma" used to own? Unless Grandma is 125-225 years old, you're not likely to find it here in the Carriage Barn. Their circa 1780-1890 furniture is displayed in room settings with appropriate accessories and quilts.

Fine replica tin, copper, and brass lighting accentuate these fine old furnishings. If you are a true antique enthusiast, you can't help but feel a pang for the past as you browse through this truly unique antique haven.

Goshen Antique Mall
107 S. Main St.
219/534-6141

26 GREENFIELD

Carriage House Antiques
210 Center St.
317/462-3253

Reflections of Time
14 W. Main St.
317/462-3878

Red Ribbon Antiques
101 W. Main St.
317/462-5211

J W. Riley's Emporium
107 W. Main St.
317/462-5268

Bob's Antiques
113 W. Main St.
317/462-8749

The Red Rooster
1001 W. Main St.
317/462-0655

Sugar Creek Antique Mall
2244 W. U.S. Highway 40
317/467-4938

27 HUNTINGBURG

Mulberry Tree Antiques and Collectibles

4625 S. State Route 162
812/482-1822
Hours: Wed.-Sun. 10-5, Mon.-Tue. by appointment

Directions: Traveling I-64, take Exit 63 north approximately 7 miles. The Mulberry Tree is centrally located in the county, 1/2 mile north of State Highways 162 and 64, 5 miles north of Ferdinand, 5 miles south of Jasper, or 5 miles east of Huntingburg.

This shop's "claim to fame" is their quality antiques and excellent dealers. Mulberry Tree is owner-operated and friendly, providing two good reasons to stop in for a visit!

Parker House Antiques
307 E. 4th St.
812/683-5352

B-K Antiques
507 E. 4th St.
812/683-2534

Goodthings
517 E. 4th St.
812/683-4815

Antique Boutique
3582 S. 75 W.
812/683-2850

Country Corner
3rd & Geiger St.
812/683-4849

Green Tree Antiques
312 E. 4th St.
812/683-4448

Locker Antiques
314 E. 4th St.
812/683-4149

Yesterdays Antiques & Cllbls.
320 E. 4th St.
812/683-4422

Enchantingly Yours
330 E. 4th St.
812/683-5437

Gene's Antiques
330 4th St.
812/683-4199

Judy Ann's Antiques
SE Corner 4th & Main
812/683-4993

Lamb's 'n Ivy
421 E. 4th St.
812/683-5533

28 HUNTINGTON

S & B Antiques & Collectibles
434 N. Jefferson St.
219/356-1302

29 INDIANAPOLIS

Colonial Antiques

5000 West 96th Street
317/873-2727
Hours: Fri.-Sat. 10-5; other days by appointment

Directions: Take I-465 north to Michigan Road (Exit 421). Exit north and go 1 block to 96th Street. Colonial Antiques is 1 miles west on the right.

Once, not long ago, architectural treasures were destroyed, fallen prey to the wrecking ball in order to build society's latest needs—a new high rise, a service station, a grocery store, or even a cement parking lot. Today these treasures have been sought after and salvaged by decorators, builders and collectors. Colonial Antiques specializes in these unique, mostly one-of-a-kind finds including lighting, mantels, hardware and more.

Bluemingdeals Antiques
4601 N. College Ave.
317/924-4765

Margie's Menagerie
4905 N. College Ave.
317/931-1400

Neat Antiques & More
4907 N. College ave
317/921-1916

Recollections Antiques
5202 N. College Ave.
317/283-3800

Barn Village Antiques
5209 N. College Ave.
317/283-5011

A Rare Find Gallery
4040 E. 82nd St. #10C
317/842-5828

D T Hollings Antiques Inc.
1760 E. 86th St.
317/574-1777

Finds Antiques
1764 E. 86th St.
317/571-1950

North Indy Antique Mall
7226 E. 87th St. #E.
317/578-2671

Sayger Antiques
711 E. 54th St.
317/251-1936

Hope's Shop
116 E. 49th St.
317/283-3004

Trash to Treasures
5505 N. Keystone Ave.
317/253-2235

Abe's Attic Treasures
1431 S. Meridian St.
317/636-4105

Midland Arts & Antiques
907 E. Michigan St.
317/267-9005

Red Barn Galleries
325 E. 106th St.
317/846-8928

Blue Sun Gallery
922 E. Westfield Blvd.
317/255-8441

Antique Centre
3422 N. Shadeland Ave.
317/545-3879

Antiques N More
3440 N. Shadeland Ave.
317/542-8526

Antique Mall
3444 N. Shadeland Ave.
317/542-7283

Quality Antiques
1105 Shelby St.
317/686-6018

Nostalgia
7501 Somerset Bay #B
317/926-0097

Southport Antique Mall Inc.
2028 E. Southport Rd.
317/786-8246

Indianapolis D/Town Antique
1044 Virginia Ave.
317/635-5336

Mobile Merchant
1052 Virginia ave
317/264-9968

Fountain Square Antique Mall
1056 Virginia Ave.
317/636-1056

D & D Antique Mall
6971 W. Washington St.
317/486-9760

Favorite Places To Eat

Cracker Barrel Old Country Store
I-65 & Southport Rd., Exit 103
317/784-7691

Cracker Barrel Old Country Store
I-465 & 38th St., Exit 17
317/298-8908

Cracker Barrel Old Country Store
I-70 & Post Road, Exit 91
317/897-1042

30 KENTLAND

Pastyme Peddlers
210 & 213 N. 3rd St.
219/474-9306

Dad's Trash & Treasures
506 E. Seymour St.
219/474-3231

31 KNIGHTSTOWN

Knightstown Antique Mall
136 W. Caret St.
317/345-5665

Olde Town Hall Antiques
19 N. Franklin St.
317/345-5381

Lindon's Antique Mall
32 E. Main St.
317/345-2545

Heartland Antique Mall
121 E. Main St.
317/345-5555

Abigail's Antique Mall
416 E. Morgan Street
317/345-5950

32 KOKOMO

Cathey's Corner
5966 N. Country Rd. 00 EW
317/868-7346

Roninger's Then & Now Store
4410 S. 00 EW
317/453-0521

C & L Antiques
841 S. Main St.
317/452-2290

Cricket Box
907 S. Main St.
317/459-8790

Ol' Hickory & Lace Antiques
913 S. Main St.
317/452-6026

Down Memory Lane
1704 E. Alton Road
317/452-4140

33 LAFAYETTE

Buck's Collectibles & Antiques

310 South 16th Street
317/742-2192
Hours: Mon.-Sat. 10-5

Directions: Enter Layfayette on I-65. Travel west on South Street to 16th Street at 5 points intersection. Turn left on 16th Street. Bucks is on the corner of 16th and Center Streets.

Filled to the brim with antiques and collectibles supplied by a mix of 45 dealers, this mall is definitely a must stop if you are interested in browsing or purchasing the unique and the unusual.

Leonard's Antiques & Books
1324 N. 14th St.
317/742-8668

Pack Rat Antiques
424 Main St.
317/742-7490

Alley Gifts & Collectibles
638 Main St.
317/429-5758

Antique Mall of Lafayette
800 Main St.
317/742-2469

Lee-Weises Antiques
1724 N. 9th Street
317/423-2754

Chesterfield Antiques & Cllbls.
210 N. 6th St.
317/742-2956

Koehler Bros. General Store
3431 Stae Road 26 E.
317/447-2155

Lamb & Heart Americana
3433 State Road 26 E.
317/447-1863

Favorite Places To Eat

Cracker Barrel Old Country Store
I-65 & State Rd. 26, Exit 172
765/447-9544

34 LA PORTE

Corner Cupboard
108 Lincolnway
219/326-9882

Coachman Antique Mall
500 Lincolnway
219/326-5933

It's A Wonderful Life
708 Lincolnway
219/326-7432

Antique Junction Mall
711 Lincolnway
219/324-0363

Walnut Hill Antiques
613 Michigan Ave.
219/326-1099

35 LAWRENCEBURG

Shumways Olde Mill Antique
232 W. High St.
812/537-1709

Livery Stable Antique Mall
318 Walnut St.
812/537-4364

36 LEBANON

Cedars of Lebanon Antiques
126 W. Washington St.
317/482-7809

37 LEO

Leo Antique Exchange
11119 Grabill Rd.
219/627-2242

Cellar Antique Mall
15004 A State Rd. 1
219/627-6565

Shades of Country
51004 State Rd. 1
219/627-2189

38 LIGONIER

Creative Visions
115 S. Cavin St.
219/894-3449

Mad Hatter Antiques
254 W. US Highway 6
219/894-4995

39 LOGANSPORT

A-1 Preowned Items
112 Burlington Ave.
219/739-2121

Market Street Antiques
222 E. Market St.
219/735-0131

Yesteryear Antiques & Cllbls.
525 E. Market St.
219/753-7371

Homewood Antiques
1075 N. State Road 25
219/722-2398

40 MADISON

Schussler House Bed and Breakfast
514 Jefferson Street
812/273-2068 or 1-800-392-1931
Open year round
Rates $75-120

The Schussler House was built in 1849 for Charles Schussler a local physician who used the residence for his office and home.

Today, this Federal and Greek Revival home is an elegant bed and breakfast featuring antique and reproduction furniture throughout the three guest rooms and common areas. A gourmet breakfast is served in the dining room.

Broadway Antique Mall
701 Broadway St.
812/265-6606

Lumber Mill Antique Mall
721 W. 1st St.
812/273-3040

Wallace's Antiques
125 E. Main St.
812/265-2473

Antiques On Main
129 E. Main St.
812/265-2240

Best Friends
133 E. Main St.
812/265-5548

Main St. Antique Mall
210 E. Main St.
812/273-5286

Antiques Etc.
224 E. Main St.
812/273-6768

Old Town Emporium
113 E. 2nd St.
812/273-4394

Madison Antique Mall
401 E. 2nd St.
812/265-6399

41 MARTINSVILLE

Emporium
110 N. Main St.
317/349-9060

Morgan Co. Auc. & Flea Market
128 N. Main St.
317/342-8098

Gateway Collectibles
96 E. Morgan St.
317/342-8983

Creative Accents, Inc.
166 E. Morgan St.
317/342-0213

42 MERRILLVILLE

Favorite Place To Eat

Cracker Barrel Old Country Store
I-65 & 61st St., Exit 255
219/947-2617

43 MICHIGAN CITY

The Antique Market
3707 North Frontage Road
219/879-4084
Hours: Mon.-Sat. 10-5, Sun. 12-5, closed major holidays

Directions: Take I-94 to Exit 34B and U.S. Highway 421 north. Go 1 block to stoplight and turn right, then take another quick right onto Frontage Road (access road toThe Antique Market).

Easily accessible from I-94 and Highway 142, The Antique Market with its more than 85 dealers is one of the few remaining markets or malls that has not conformed by adding crafts and reproductions to its line of antiques and collectibles. If you are a true antique enthusiast, you will enjoy shopping among the fine old treasures.

Road House Antiques
3900 W. Dunes Hwy.
219/878-1866

Mona's Treasure Chest
4496 Wozniak Road
219/874-6475

E. T World Antiques
7326 Johnson Rd.
219/872-9002

Days Gone By Antiques
10673 W. 300 N
219/879-7496

Stocking Bale Antiques Mall
227 W. 7th St.
219/873-9270

44 MISHAWAKA

Antiques Etc.
110 Lincoln Way E
219/258-5722

Interiors Etc.
301 Lincolnway E
219/259-7717

Pack Rat Pats
3005 Lincoln Way E
219/259-5609

Ed's Collectables
126 N. Main St.
219/255-5041

45 MITCHELL

Ma Nancy's Antiques
609 W. Main St.
812/849-2203

Checkerberry
615 W. Main St.
812/849-3784

Persimmon Tree Antiques
619 W. Main St.
812/849-5300

Mitchell Antique Mall
706 W. Main St.
812/849-4497

46 MONTICELLO

There are eight antique shops located in Monticello as well as others in the immediate area. See review at the end of this section for a complete listing.

47 MORGANTOWN

Morgantown Antiques
49 E. Washington St.
812/597-0412

Miller's Antiques
Route 1 Box 5A
812/597-6024

Yesterday's Antique & Auction Service
149 W. Washington St.
812/597-5525

48 MUNCIE

Off-Broadway Antique Mall
2404 N. Broadway Ave.
317/747-5000

Walker Antiques
4801 E. Memorial Dr.
317/282-0399

49 NAPPANEE

Borkholder Dutch Village
71945 C. R. 101
219/773-2828, fax 219/773-4828
Hours: Mon.-Sat. 10-5 winter, 9-5 summer

Directions: Located 1/4 mile north of U.S. 6, 1 1/2 miles west of State Rd. 19; or 13 miles east of U.S. 31, then 1/4 mile north off U.S. 6.

Indiana

In 1987, Freeman Borkholder, owner of Borkholder American Vintage Furniture, decided to purchase a facility to showcase the local crafts and antiques for which Nappanee is well known. He bought, believe it or not, high rise chicken houses, completely renovated them, and created Borkholder Dutch Village. It is an authentic country-style marketplace, complete with a flea market, an arts and crafts mall, a restaurant, antique mall, events center and village shops.

The Dutch Village is open six days a week (see hours above) and a huge antique auction is held every Tuesday at 8 a.m. At the auction and throughout the antique mall, you can find quality furniture, including bedroom and dining room suites, dry sinks, roll-top desks, iceboxes, hall trees, and buffets. And you can add a taste of the past to your life with antique dinnerware, jewelry, dolls, vintage clothes—and more!

Stroll through the arts and crafts mall, where you'll find quilts, wood carvings, shelving, dolls, framed artwork, knitted and crocheted items, new and used household goods, floral arrangements and many other hand-crafted items.

For lunch, visit the Dutch Kitchen, where you can indulge in a soda fountain treat, like a Green River or a Phosphate, enjoy a homemade lunch and top it off with Amish Apple Dumplings or another scrumptious dessert.

AAA Antique Shop
Hwy 6 W
219/773-4912

Main Street Antiques Mall
160 N. Main St.
219/773-5158

Antiques on the Square
106 S. Main St.
219/773-5770

Nappanee Antique Mall
156 S. Main St.
219/773-3278

Amishland Antique Mall
106 W. Market St.
219/773-4795

50 NASHVILLE

Lee's Antiques
S. Jefferson #45 A
812/988-1448

Brown County Antique Mall II
3288 E. State Rd. 46
812/988-1025

Grandma Had One Antique Center
216 S. Van Buren St.
812/988-1039

51 NEW ALBANY

Old New Albany Antique Mall
225 State St.
812/948-1890

52 NEW HARMONY

New Harmony Antique Mall
500 Church
812/682-3948

Donna Smith's Heirlooms Etc.
527 Church
812/682-5027

Antique Showroom in Mews
531 Church St.
812/682-3490

Treasure Trove
514 S. Main St.
812/682-4112

53 NEWBURGH

Rivertown Antiques
1 W. Jennings St.
812/853-2562

Generations
218 W. Jennings St.
812/853-7270

Little Red Barn Antiques
10044 W. State Route 662
812/853-8096

Country Gentleman Antiques
103 State St.
812/858-9544

54 NOBLESVILLE

Durwyn Smedley Antiques
853 Conner St.
317/776-0161

Olde House Antiques
293 S. 8th St.
317/773-6951

Lazy Acres Antiques
77 Metsker Lane
317/773-7387

Noblesville Antique Mall
20 N. 9th St.
317/773-5095

Bound To Be Found Antiques
74 N. 9th St.
317/776-1993

55 NORTH VERNON

Country Corner Market
4250 N. State Hwy 7
812/346-1095

Olde Store Antiques
162 E. Walnut St.
812/346-1925

Cornett's
246 E. Walnut St.
812/346-8995

North Vernon Antique Mall
247 E. Walnut St.
812/346-8604

56 PENDLETON

Bob Post Antiques
104 W. State St.
317/778-7778

Pendleton Antique Mall
123 W. State St.
317/778-2303

Grandma's Treasures
128 W. State St.
317/778-8211

57 PERU

Annie's Attic
57 N. Broadway
317/473-4400

Peru Antique Mall
21 E. Main St.
317/473-8179

58 PIERCETON

Beebe's Antique Shop
Downtown Pierceton
219/594-2244

Old Theater Antique Mall
103 N. 1st St.
219/594-2533

Antiques at Sign of Gas Light
130 N. 1st St.
219/594-2457

Curiosity Shop
112 S. 1st St.
219/594-2785

Gregory's Antiques
State Road 13
219/594-5718

59 PLAINFIELD

Gilley's Antique Mall
5789 E. U.S. Hwy. 40
217/839-8779

Avon Antiques
7673 E. U.S. Hwy. 36
317/272-4842

Little Dave's Everything Store
10107 W. Washington
317/839-6040

Favorite Places To Eat

Cracker Barrel Old Country Store
I-70 & Hwy. 267, Exit 66
317/838-9198

60 PORTLAND

Farmstead Antiques
Hwy. 275
219/726-4930

Carlson's Antiques
212 N. Meridian St.
219/726-7919

61 RICHMOND

Scott Lure Co. & Trading Post
1449 E. Chester Rd.
317/935-5091

Fosters E Street Gallery
825 N. E St.
317/935-9055

Ft. Wayne Furniture Store
193 Fort Wayne Ave.
317/966-9372

The Silhouette Shop
126 S. 4th St.
317/935-7887

Top Drawer Antique Mall
801 Promenade
317/939-0349

John's
823-825 Promenade
317/962-0214

Kate's Furniture
131 Richmond Ave.
317/966-5246

At The Garden Gate
111 S. 3rd
317/939-0777

Favorite Places To Eat

Cracker Barrel Old Country Store
I-70 & U.S. 40, Exit 156A
765/935-0881

62 ROANN

Covered Bridge Merc. Co.
165 N. Chippewa Rd.
765-833-7473

Mom & Pop's Jazzy Junk
175 N. Chippewa Rd.
765/833-2233

Royal Attic Design
180 N. Chippewa St.
765/833-5333

Roann Antique Mall
200 N. Chippewa St.
765/833-6242

63 ROANOKE

Antiques from BC At Lonsdale
10979 North Roanake Road
219/672-9744
Open daily 10-5, by chance and any time by appointment

Directions: Just 7 miles south of I-69, take Exit 102 to Highway 24 South until you reach 1100 North, then turn right and go to the next corner. The shop is located in the front of the school building on the southeast corner.

Located in a 1915 school building, this shop specializes in quality country and formal furniture dating from the 18th-20th century. Additionally, they offer decorative paintings and accessories to enhance your home.

64 ROCKVILLE

Covered Bridge Mall
115 S. Jefferson St.
317/569-3145

Rockville Antique Mall
411 E. Ohio St.
317/569-6873

Aunt Patty's Antiques
U.S. Route 36
317/569-2605

Bart's Corner
Walker Ramp Rd.
317/344-6112

65 ROSSVILLE

There are three antique shops located in Rossville as well as others in the immediate area. See review at the end of this section for a complete listing.

66 SCOTTSBURG

Country Cousins Antiques
Hwy 31 S.
812/752-6353

Scottsburg Antique Mall
4 N. Main St.
812/752-4645

67 SEYMOUR

Broadway Antiques
219 N. Broadway St.
812/522-9538

Remember When Antiques
317 N. Broadway St.
812/522-5099

Lucille's House of Antiques
603 S. Chestnut St.
812/522-5541

Crossroads Antique Mall
311 Holiday Sq
812/522-5675

Favorite Places To Eat

Cracker Barrel Old Country Store
I-65 & Hwy. 50, Exit 50B
812/522-3122

68 SHIPSHEWANA

Log House Country Store
255 Depot
219/768-4652

Berry's Hitching Post
250 E. Middlebury
219/768-7862

Fisher's Antiques
155 Morton
219/768-4213

Haarer's Antiques
165 Morton
219/768-4787

69 SILVER LAKE

Attic Antiques
107 N. Jefferson
219/352-2744

D & J Antiques
102 S. Jefferson
219/352-2400

Twin Lakes Antiques
7208 W. State Road 114
219/982-2939

70 SOUTH BEND

The Book Inn
508 West Washington
219/288-1990
http://members.aol.com/bookinn/

Directions: Exit #77 off the I-80/90 Toll Road.

For specific information on The Book Inn see review this section.

Thieves Market Mall
Crossroad Shopping Center
219/273-1352

Anthony's Country Villa
1606 W. Ewing Ave.
219/287-8180

A-Antiques Ltd.
1009 N. Frances St.
219/232-1134

Antiques & Things
2210 Huron St.
219/282-2550

Light Owl Antiques
529 Lincoln Way W.
219/287-1184

Victorian Galleries
2011 Miami St.
219/233-3633

AAA Quality Antiques
1763 Prairie Ave.
219/232-1099

Unique Antique Mall
50981 US Highway 33
219/271-1799

71 SPENCER

River Valley Sales
27 E. Franklin St.
812/829-4948

Hillside Cottage and Antiques
870 W. Hillside Ave.
812/829-4488

Maxine's
56 E. Jefferson
812/829-6369

Spencer Antique Mall, Inc.
165 S. Main St.
812/829-0785

Robinson House Galleries
3 N. Montgomery St.
812/829-9558

72 TERRE HAUTE

Hoosier Antiques & Clocks
1630 S. 3rd Street
812/238-0562
Open Mon.-Sat. 10-5, Sunday by chance or appointment

Directions: Traveling I-70 exit at U.S. 41 (Exit 7) and proceed 1.2 miles North on 3rd Street. Turn right at either Hulman Street or Osborne Street. Parking is at the rear off the alley. Traveling U.S. 40 drive 1.2 miles south of the Court house at Wabash Avenue and 3rd Street. In Terre Haute, 3rd Street is U.S. 41 and Wabash is U.S. 40.

Hoosier Antiques & Clocks is located in a charming, shingled cottage built in the early 1900s. The shop carries a general line of antiques and collectibles and specializes in antique clocks. All clocks are in running condition.

Swank Antiques
1126 N. 8th St.
812/235-7734

Antiques Crafts & Things
137 W. Honey Creek Pkwy.
812/232-8959

E. Bleemel Flour & Feed
904 Poplar St.
812/232-2466

Lowry's Antiques
1132 Poplar St.
812/234-1717

Ancient Tymes Antiques Mall
1600 S. 3rd St.
812/238-2178

Antiques Inc.
2000 S. 3rd St.
812/235-4829

Gatherings
1429 S. 25th St.
812/234-8322

Shady Lane Antique Mall
9247 S. U.S. Hwy. 41
812/299-1625

Granny's Daughter
11746 S. U.S. Hwy. 41
812/299-8277

Nancy's Downtown Mall
600 Wabash Ave.
812/238-1129

North Side Collectables
2323 Lafayette Ave.
812/466-9091

Colonial Antiques
Farmersburg, S. on U.S. 41
812/696-2600

Anderson Antiques
1612 S. 3rd St. (U.S. 41)
812/232-2991

Antiques, Tim Weir
1641 S. 25th St.
812/234-6515

Kasameyer Antiques & Collectibles
5149 S. U.S. 41 (7th & 41)
812/299-1672

Favorite Places To Eat

Cracker Barrel Old Country Store
I-70 & U.S. 41, Exit 7
812/235-6593

73 TIPTON

Dezerland
114-116 S. Main
317/675-8999

Foster's Last Stand
122 N. Main St.
317/675-3391

74 VALPARAISO

Sydow Antiques
153 W. Lincolnway
219/465-1777

Accents Etc.
202 E. Lincolnway
219/464-3739

Valparaiso Antique Mall Inc.
212 E. Lincolnway
219/465-1869

75 VINCENNES

Yesteryear
305 Main St.
812/882-2459

Hitching Post
1717 Washington Ave.
812/882-9372

Old Town Attic Antiques
1804 Washington Ave.
812/882-0903

76 WESTFIELD

Antiques Galore & More
110 E. Main St.
317/867-1228

Welcome House Antiques Etc.
202 E. Main St.
317/867-0077

Jonathan Westfield Co.
120 N. Union St.
317/896-3566

R Beauchamp Antiques
16405 Westfield Blvd.
317/897-3717

77 WHITING

Granny's General Store
1309 Community Ct.
219/659-7538

Blue Ribbon Antiques
1858 Indianapolis Blvd.
219/659-4502

Just Little Things
1600 119th St.
219/659-3438

78 WORTHINGTON

Carriage House Antiques
318 S. Jefferson St.
812/875-3219

79 ZIONSVILLE

Brown's Antique Shop
315 N. 5th St.
317/873-2284

Zionsville Antiques
75 N. Main St.
317/873-1761

Sow's Ear
76 S. Main St.
317/873-2785

Indiana Folkart & Antiques
120 S. Main St.
317/873-4424

Captain Logan
150 S. Main St.
317/873-9999

Helen Kogan Antqs. & Lighting
195 S. Main St.
317/873-4208

Iowa

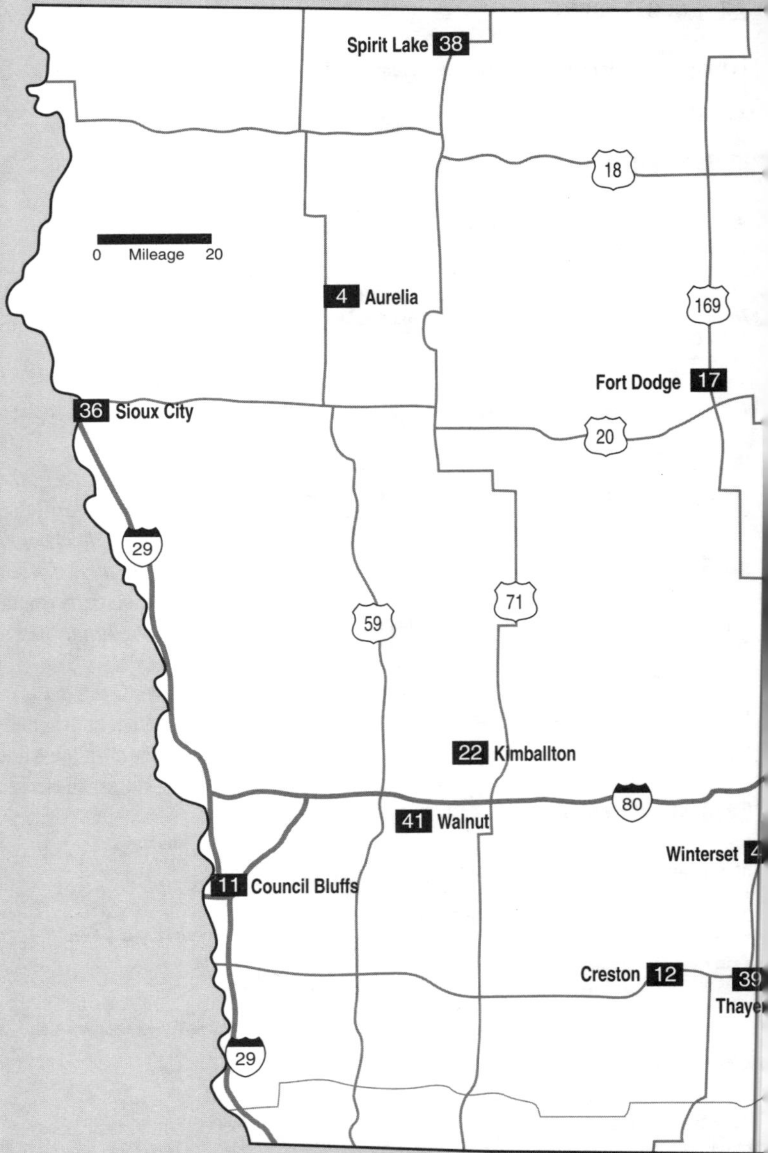
Spirit Lake 38
18
0 Mileage 20
4 Aurelia
169
Fort Dodge 17
36 Sioux City
20
29
71
59
22 Kimballton
80
41 Walnut
Winterset
11 Council Bluffs
Creston 12
39
29

Kalona Antique Co. at 4th & C

ANTIQUES - QUILTS - COLLECTIBLES

Furniture Warehouse
1 Block South

19 Dealers Covering
2 Floors

Specializing in Oak,
Pine, and Walnut

Housed in an 1890's
Baptist Church

Wholesale to dealers

(319) 656-4489 / Days
(319) 656-5157 / Evenings

20

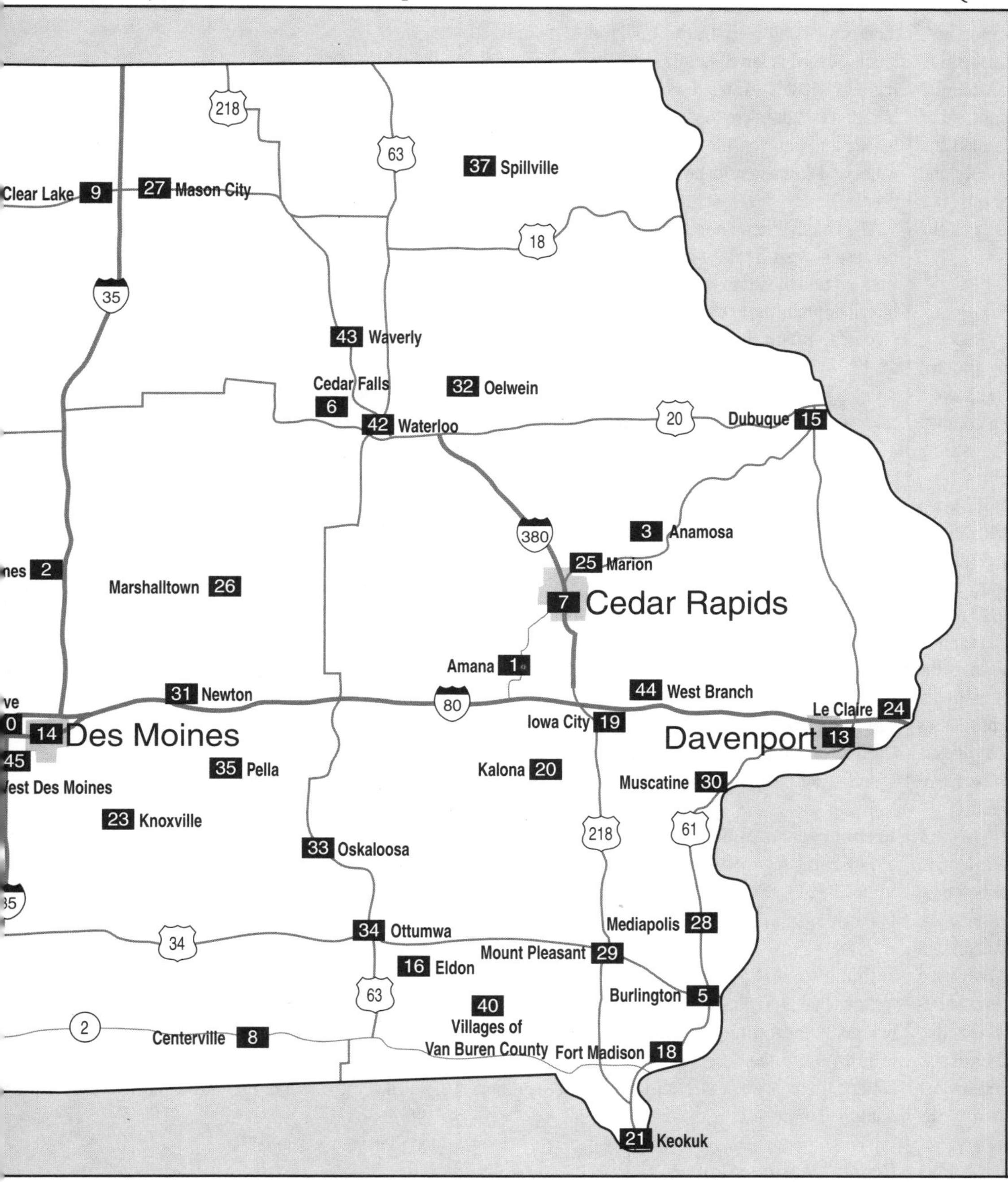

L & H Antique Mall

4300 Sq. ft.
of Antiques
and Collectibles

28 Dealers with a
wide array of items

Thayer

39

MAIN STREET
IOWA

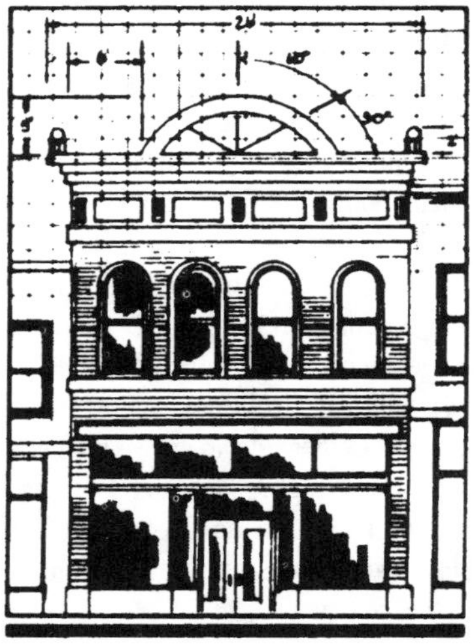

MEMORIES ON MAIN

Antique Mall & Old-Time Ice Cream Parlor

80 Dealers - 11,000 sq. ft. • OPEN 7 DAYS

203 Main Street • 515-233-2519 • Downtown Ames

2

Let's take a trip through history and celebrate the 10th anniversary of "Main Street" Iowa. Over the past decade, the preservation-based downtown revitalization program of the National Trust for Historic Preservation has helped Iowa not only to preserve, but celebrate and share its heritage and culture through the "Main Street" program. All across the state each year, "Main Street" towns keep their pasts alive. Annual heritage festivals help Iowans and visitors appreciate the lifestyles of our ancestors with food, costumes, events and music of times past. Visiting these "Main Street" communities is like an annual vacation in a time machine! You'll see unique shops intermingled with historic buildings...festivals, food and fun from America's Heartland...pride, personality and friendliness of hearty, happy people. Consider this your special invitation to stop by, stay a while and catch the spirit on "main streets" all across Iowa.

1 AMANA

Iowa's Amana Colonies are seven closely situated villages that comprise a unique settlement running along the Iowa River valley, through lush farming country. Amana's early settlers left Germany in 1842 seeking religious freedom. They settled near Buffalo, New York, but in 1855 they moved to Iowa and established seven villages known as the Amana Colonies on 26,000 acres of wooded hills. There they lived under a religious communal system, sharing work, meals, worldly goods and religious services. In 1932 the villagers voted to end the communal way, and they created the Amana Church Society to direct their faith, which is now known as the Community of True Inspiration. They created the Amana Society to operate the 26,000 acres of land and businesses that were formerly held by the commune. All the villagers became stockholders in the Society, bought their own homes, and some founded their own businesses.

The first village to be settled was named "Amana," from the Song of Solomon (4:8), which means "to remain true." There were seven villages in the original Colonies; today there are a total of nine. Visitors may recognize the name Amana from an appliance they may own. Amana Refrigeration was founded by Amana people and is located in the village of Middle Amana! Just 93 miles east of Des Moines, the other villages are West Amana, East Amana, South Amana, High Amana, and Homestead. There is also a section of South Amana called Upper South, and another village called Little Amana, that were not part of the original colony.

Colony villagers have all remained true to a simpler way of life that still revolves around old-world craftsmanship and handcrafted furniture, clock-making, black smithing, world-famous cooking, and locally manufactured goods. These items are sold in numerous stores and shops, including the many quality antique shops that are an added attraction of the Colonies. For the past 150 years, Amana residents have quarried their own sandstone, made their own bricks, and cut their own timber for more than 400 buildings that cover the villages. They farmed, built woolen and calico mills for clothing and fabric, established cabinet shops to build furniture, and craft shops to supply daily necessities. Today they still produce products at the furniture factories, the woolen mill, and in most of the craft shops, where artisans make baskets, brooms, candles, ironwork, pottery and more.

Community life called for community kitchens, and the Amana Colonies have become well-known for superb food, wines and beer. In the tradition of communal kitchens, food is served family style. German specialties include Wienerschnitzel and Sauerbraten, as well as traditional Midwestern food. The bakeries are known for breads and pastries, the many wineries for their fruit wines, and the brewery for award-winning "German style" beer.

The Colonies remain Iowa's leading visitor attraction because of their heritage and hospitality. People come from around the world to see the historic villages and to buy their products, to tour the museums and to enjoy a piece of Germany in the American colonies.

Great Places To Shop (Antiques in the Amana Colonies)

Main Amana

Antiques and Things
F Street (next to Colony Cone)
319/622-6461
Open daily 9-5
Antiques, collectibles, doll house and crafts

Carole's
4521 220th Trail (Main Street)
319/622-3570
Open daily Summer 9-6/Winter 10-5
Upstairs: old-new-used-abused

Erenberger Antiques
4514 F Street
319/622-3230
Open Mon.-Sat. 11-5, Sun. 12-5

Primitives and pine furniture are the main items featured in this original Amana home built in 1856. Early pine and painted furniture are displayed, along with small primitive antique accessories including greenware, pottery, tin, copper, pewter, stickware, baskets, decoys, quilts and more.

Renate's Antique Gallery
4516 F Street
319/622-3859
Open Mon.-Sat. 10-5, Sun. 12-5

Eight rooms of exploring fun are in this original, two-story Amana home built in 1870. Each room displays something different. In the entry room Renate has her loom where she makes rag rugs (some days visitors can watch). There's china and glass in the dining room, bowls in the kitchen, furniture in the bedroom and primitives in the family room. Renate's specializes in pottery and antiques from the Amana Colonies.

Smokehouse Square Antiques
4503 F Street
319/622-3539
Open Mon.-Sat. 10-5, Sun. 11-5, Summer 9:30-5:30, Sun. 11-5

Smokehouse Square Antiques has added a new dimension to antiquing in the Colonies. The mall is home to more than 29 of eastern Iowa's finest antique dealers. The inventory is constantly changing, but you will always find furniture, glassware, china, pottery, stoneware, graniteware, silver, jewelry, quilts and linens, books and paper, pictures and mirrors, and many advertising items, plus toys and children's collectibles, primitives, folk art, tools, decoys, fishing collectibles, 1950s memorabilia and railroad items.

Tick Tock Antiques
220th Trail (across from Amana General Store)
319/622-3730

Collectibles, glassware, primitives

West Amana

Cricket on the Hearth Antiques
404 6th Avenue West
319/622-3088
Wed.-Sun. 10-5 May-Oct.

Unique country gifts, collectibles and antiques

West Amana General Store
511 F St.
Located on top of the hill
319/622-3945
Open daily 10-5, Summer 9-5

Antiques, furniture and a nice line of gifts

South Amana

Fern Hill Gifts and Quilts
103 220th Trail
Located at the corner of Highway 6 and 220
319/622-3627
Mon.-Sat. 9:30-5, Sun. 12-4

Antiques, quilts, supplies, dolls, bears and everlastings

Granary Emporium
1063 4th Avenue
319/622-3195
Open daily 10-5

Antiques, glassware, furniture, primitives

High Amana

High Amana Store
1308 G Street
Located on Highway 220 (Amana Colonies Trail, 4 miles west of Main Amana)
319/622-3797
Open daily

Built in 1857 of sandstone quarried at the edge of high Amana, the high Amana Store was the original "one stop" shopping center of its time for local residents and area farmers. Over the years it has sold everything from fabric and notions to bicycles and appliances to kerosene, and even served as the local post office. In a setting of original pressed tin ceilings, glass display showcases and comb-painted drawer fronts, the store today offers traditional Amana Colonies arts and crafts, quilts, products of Iowa, glassware, unique toys and books, cards, gourmet food products, herbs, spices and more.

Great Places To Stay In The Amana Area

Babi's B & B
2788 Highway
South Amana
319/662-4381

Baeckerei B & B
6 Trail, Box 127
South Amana
319/622-3597 or 1-800-391-8650

Corner House B & B
404 F St.
West Amana
319/622-6390 or 1-800-996-6964

Die Heimat Country Inn
Box 160, 4430 V St.
Homestead
319/622-3937

Dusk To Dawn B & B
2616 K St. Box 124
Middle Amana
319/622-3029

Rawson's B & B
Box 118
Homestead
319/622-6035 or 1-800-637-6035

Interesting Side Trips

Herbert Hoover Presidential Library and Birthplace
Located in West Branch just 30 miles east of Amana Colonies just off of I-80
Open daily
319/643-5301

Kalona: Amish and Mennonite community that offers an opportunity to see the differences between the Amanas (not Amish) and Kalona, which is "Amish-land."

Located about 30 miles south and east of the Amana Colonies 319/656-2519

2 AMES

Memories On Main Antique Mall & Old-Fashioned Ice Cream Parlor
203 Main Street
515/233-2519
Open daily Memorial Day-Labor Day 10-8; Labor Day-Memorial Day 10-6, Mondays until 8, special Christmas hours

Directions: Located 3 miles from I-35. From exit 111 B: Take Highway 30 west, Duff Avenue north, then left on Main Street. From exit 113: Take 13th Street west, Duff Avenue south, right on Main Street.

Great ice cream, great antiques and collectibles, an unbeatable combination! You get both at M.O.M.'s, as it's known in Ames. The 1940s soda fountain serves great ice cream treats made the old-fashioned way, while *Fancy That Lamp Shop* features fine fabric and glass shades suitable for antique and vintage lamps. The mall itself offers a constantly changing array of items, from fine furniture to fun collectibles like lamps, glass, china, dinnerware, linens, pottery, figurines, decorative accessories, kitchen collectibles, primitives, crocks, cast iron, dolls, children's items, vintage clothing, records, books, sheet music and more!

Pak-Rat
110 S. Hyland Ave.
515/296-0230

Coin Castle II, Inc.
236 Main St.
515/232-7527

3 ANAMOSA

This Old Farm Antiques
110 S. Elm St.
319/462-2856

Country Creek Cove
110 E. Main St.
319/462-3788

Antiques of Anamosa
122 E. Main St.
319/462-4195

4 AURELIA

C & M Antiques
Highway 7 W.
712/434-2217

Brown's Antiques
116 Main St.
712/434-2337

Forgotten Favorites
128 Main St.
712/434-2069

Vogt's Antiques & Toys
141 Main St.
712/434-5380

Cedars Antiques
2235 W. 9th St.
712/434-2244

5 BURLINGTON

A-1 Antiques & Uniques
1234 Agency St.
319/752-5901

Privy Antiques
2500 Division St.
319/752-8320

Call & Haul Antiques
401 N. Front St.
319/754-6389

Antique Mall
800 Jefferson St.
319/753-6955

Antiques & Things
806 Jefferson St.
319/753-5096

Old Shoppe
601 S. Main St.
319/753-0166

Casey's World Antiques
6212 Summer St.
319/752-3265

6 CEDAR FALLS

Jackson's
2229 Lincoln St.
319/277-2256

Gilgens Consignment Furniture
115 W. 16th St.
319/266-5152

Cellar Antiques
4912 University Ave.
319/266-5091

7 CEDAR RAPIDS

Parlor City Antiques & Cllbls.
301 F Ave. NW
319/366-7500

Wellington Square Antq. Mall
1200 2nd Ave. SE
319/368-6640

Gingerbread
92 16th Ave. SW
319/366-8841

Prospector Antique Mall
5907 16th Ave. SW
319/396-5573

Yester Years
308 3rd Ave. SE
319/362-1777

Antique Wicker & Collectibles
1038 3rd Ave. SE
319/362-4868

8 CENTERVILLE

Summer Antiques
1099 N. 18th St.
515/856-2680

Taste of Country
300 W. State St.
515/856-5705

9 CLEAR LAKE

Yesteryear House of Antiques
112 N. 8th St.
515/357-4352

Whispering Oaks Antiques
2510 S. 8th St.
515/357-5094

Good Olde Days
809 5th Pl. N.
515/357-6575

Keepsake Antiques
308 Main Ave.
515/357-7553

Antiques on Main
309 Main Ave.
515/357-3077

Jada Consignment Shop
309 Main Ave. #B
515/357-2555

Jo's Antiques
311 Main Ave
515/357-8120

Legacy Antiques
315 Main Ave.
515/357-4000

Antique Alley
19 S. 3rd Street
515/357-7733

Kraemer's Antiques
412 Main Ave.
515/357-3786

Cornerstone Antiques
22 S. 3rd St.
515/357-3899

10 CLIVE

Favorite Places To Eat

Cracker Barrel Old Country Store
I-35/80 & University Avenue
515/226-9603

11 COUNCIL BLUFFS

Collins Antiques
607 S. Main St.
712/328-2598

Jantiques
729 S. Main St.
712/323-6624

Favorite Places To Eat

Cracker Barrel Old Country Store
I-29/80 & S. Expressway, Exit 3
712/366-6076

Iowa

12 CRESTON

Jessie's Antique Gems
R.R. 1
515/782-5366

Creston Power Plant Antiques
902 N. Sumner
515/782-7035

Two Bricks Shy Antiques
804 E. Tylor
515/782-2725

13 DAVENPORT

Trash Can Annie Antiques
421 Brady St.
319/322-5893

Riverbend Antiques
425 Brady St.
319/323-8622

Lampsmith Antique
5102 W. Locust St.
319/391-8552

Bird In Hand
1121 Mound St.
319/322-1082

Antiques By Judy
401 E. 2nd St.
319/323-5437

Antique America
702 W. 76th St.
319/386-3430

Favorite Places To Eat

Cracker Barrel Old Country Store
I-80 & Hwy. 61/Brady St., Exit 295A
319/386-4847

14 DES MOINES

Brass Armadillo Inc.
701 N. E. 50th Ave.
515/282-0082

R & S Enterprises
1601 E. Grand Ave.
515/262-9384

Soda City Collectables
1244 2nd Ave.
515/282-0345

15 DUBUQUE

Bob's Antiques
3271 Central Ave.
319/583-6061

Collector's Corner
340 W. 5th St.
319/588-0886

Harbor Place Antiques
98 E. 4th St.
319/582-6224

Antiques at the Schoen's
144 Locust St.
319/556-7547

Antiques on White
902 White St.
319/557-2141

16 ELDON

American Gothic Antiques & Tearoom
408 Elm Street
515/652-3338

For a nostalgic antiquing experience American Gothic Antiques & Tearoom offers antiques in the front 1500 square feet of the store, and a restaurant and ice cream shop in the back. Homemade pies are the house specialty. Everything is housed in an historic old hardware store that is over 100 years old - a true antique itself!

17 FORT DODGE

Antique Emporium
Crossroads Mall
515/955-4151

Old Harvester Gifts & Antiques
1915 1st Ave. N
515/955-6260

Downtown Antiques Mall
102 S. 14th St.
515/573-3401

Michehl's Memory Furniture
RR 5
515/576-0148

Pine Cupboard
25 S. 12th St.
515/576-7463

18 FORT MADISON

For an old army post, Fort Madison is a swinging, adventurous place even today! It was the site of the first outpost west of the Mississippi River, when flintlock rifles and cannons were the main armaments. Today visitors can take the narrated Olde Towne Express and buy antiques galore in the Downtown Riverfront district. You can watch—and maybe walk—the world's longest double-deck swingspan bridge in action, or take your chances on firmer ground at the Catfish Bend Casino.

Mississippi Rose & Thistle Inn
532 Avenue F
319/372-7044
Open daily 8:00 a.m.-10:00 p.m.
Rates: $70-90

Directions: Fort Madison is easily reached by U.S. 61, a major connection to I-80 and I-70. The Inn is located between Burlington, Iowa (18 miles north) and Keokuk, Iowa (20 miles south). Both are reached by U.S. 61, and the Inn is located 2 blocks north of the highway. Turn on 5th St., go 2 blocks, turn left on Avenue F (a one-way street). Go 1 block and the Inn is on the left side at the corner of Avenue F and 6th St.

This lovely, historic brick Italianate mansion was built in 1881 by Dennis A. Morrison, a partner in Morrison Plow Works. The Morrison family owned the first automobile in Fort Madison, a 1902 Stanley Steamer. Today, the Inn has been carefully restored to its past splendor, extravagance and elegance. Guests can gaze upon ornate woodwork and marble fireplaces, walk on Oriental carpets, and enjoy period antiques. After a day exploring, riverboat gambling, antiquing, golfing, and picnicking, guests can return to the Inn for afternoon wine and hors d'oeuvres in the parlor or on the wraparound porch, then choose a book from the library and retire with a glass of sherry from your own private stock! Candlelight dinners and gourmet picnic baskets are available with advance notice.

Each bedroom has its own distinctive charm and decor. The Lillian Austin room is furnished with an old-fashioned brass bed, antique oak dresser and clawfoot tub. The Celsiana Room holds an old-fashioned white and brass bed, antique walnut dresser and clawfoot tub. The Mary Rose Room offers a clawfoot tub, white and brass bed and antique Eastlake dresser. And the Tara Allison Room charms guests with a white and brass bed, sitting alcove, balcony and whirlpool.

Sixth & G Antique Mall
602 Avenue G
319/372-6218

Memory Lane Antique Mall
820 Avenue G
319/372-4485

Wishing Well Antiques
3510 Avenue L
319/372-5237

19 IOWA CITY

Granny's Antique Mall
315 E. 1st St.
319/351-6328

Antique Mall of Iowa City
507 S. Gilbert St.
319/354-1822

Watt's Antiques & Collectibles
1603 Muscatine
319/337-4357

20 KALONA

Kalona Antique Co. Plus
Antique Furniture Warehouse
Corner of 4th & C.
211 4th St.
319/656-4489 Days
319/656-5157 Evenings
Open Mon.-Sat. 9am-5pm
Closed Sundays & Major Holidays

Directions: Located just 18 miles south of Iowa City, IA. on Highway 1, or 9 miles west of Highway 218 (The Avenue of the Saints) on Highway 22.

The Kalona Antique Company is housed in an old 1890s Baptist Church in downtown Kalona, Iowa, the home of the largest Amish settlement west of the Mississippi River. The Kalona Antique Co. showcases the wares of 19 dealers on 2 floors offering a quality selection of antiques, quilts and collectibles. Ken and Brenda Herington own and operate the Kalona Antique Co. and Furniture Warehouse. They specialize in oak, pine and walnut furniture. The Furniture Warehouse, just one block south of the Kalona Antique Co. features original finish furniture. The shop offers wholesale prices to dealers and will open after hours for dealers traveling through the area.

Main Street Antiques
413 B Ave.
319/656-4550

Courtyard Square
417 B Ave.
319/656-2488

Woodin Wheel Antqs. & Gifts
515 B Ave.
319/656-2240

Fifth Street Antiques
303 5th St.
319/656-2080

Heart of the Country Antqs.
203 5th St.
319/656-3591

Weathervane
411 5th St.
319/656-3958

Yoder's Antiques
435 B Ave.
319/656-3880

21 KEOKUK

Showcase Antique Mall
800 Main St.
319/524-1696

Treasures & Trash
1803 S. 7th St.
319/524-1112

22 KIMBALLTON

Attic Antiques
114 N. Main
712/773-3255

Mama Bear
117 N. Main
712/773-2430

Mercantile
122 N. Main St.
712/773-3777

Country Corner
200 N. Main St.
712/773-2300

D Johnson Antiques
209 N. Main
712/773-3939

23 KNOXVILLE

Antiques Or Others
1253 Highway 14
515/842-4644

24 LE CLAIRE

Riverview Antiques
510 Cody Rd.
319/289-4265

Rare Find Antiques
114 N. Cody Rd.
319/289-5207

Memory Lane
110 S. Cody Rd.
319/289-3366

25 MARION

Country Corner Antiques
786 8th Ave.
319/377-1437

Remember When Antiques
847 8th Ave.
319/373-3039

Antiques of Marion
1325 8th Ave.
319/377-7997

Scott's Antiques Furniture
1060 7th Ave.
319/377-6411

Park Place Hotel Antiques
1104 7th Ave.
319/377-2724

Marion Center Antique Mall
1150 7th Ave.
319/377-9345

Eckhart's Antique Furniture
560 10th St.
319/377-1202

Sanctuary Antique Center
801 10th St.
319/377-7753

Harmening Haus
915 10th St.
800/644-3874

Cooper's Antiques
997 10th St.
319/377-3995

26 MARSHALLTOWN

Charley's Antiques
3002 S. Center St.
515/753-3916

Marshall Relics
14 E. Main St.
516/752-7060

Main Street Antique Mall
105 W. Main St.
515/752-3077

Granny's Country Mall
3201 Village Cir.
515/752-6966

27 MASON CITY

Olde Central Antique Mall
317 S. Delaware Ave.
515/423-7315

Wilson Antiques
317 S. Delaware Ave.
515/423-5811

Cobweb Corners Antiques
715 N. Federal Ave.
515/423-2160

North Federal Antique
1104 N. Federal Ave.
513/423-0841

28 MEDIAPOLIS

Patriot Antiques
Hwy. 61
319/394-9137

Heirloom Antiques
Hwy. 61 S
319/394-3444

Lamp Post Antiques
318 Wapello St. N.
319/394-3961

29 MOUNT PLEASANT

Iris City Antique Mall
Highway 34 West
319/385-7515

Old & New Things
110 S. Main Street
319/385-8937

Broadway Auction
N. Broadway
No Phone Listed

30 MUSCATINE

River Bend Cove
418 Grandview Ave.
319/263-9929

Market Place
1919 Grandview Ave.
319/263-8355

Annsarts & Antiques
208 Iowa Ave.
319/263-6411

Old Blue Bldg. Antiques
821 Park Ave.
319/263-5430

Melon City Antique Mart
200 E. 2nd St.
319/264-3470

River's Edge Antiques
331 E. 2nd St.
319/264-2351

Manley's Antiques
417 E. 2nd St.
319/264-1475

Lost Treasures
419 E. 2nd St.
319/262-8658

31 NEWTON

Pappy's Antique Mall
103 1st Ave. W
515/792-7774

Tripp Thru The Past
3928 N. 4th Ave. E
515/792-5514

Skunk Valley Antique Mall
7717 Hwy. F 48 W
515/792-2361

32 OELWEIN

Amish Settlement

Rural Buchanan County
319/283-1105
Open 8-5 Mon.-Sat. Year round, closed New Year's, Epiphany, Good Friday, Ascension Day, Thanksgiving Day and Christmas Day

Visitors to the Amish Settlement are given a glimpse of the life that fascinates most Americans. The Amish teach separation from the world, which includes living without modern conveniences, something most Americans find unbelievable. The Amish till the soil with horse-drawn equipment, and their doctrine forbids the use of electricity and telephones. They make most everything they need on a daily basis, and they sell baked goods, quilts, and handmade furniture at their farm homes in the Settlement.

Century House Antiques
720 S. Frederick Ave.
319/283-3591

West Charles Antiques
17 W. Charles St.
319/283-3591

33 OSKALOOSA

Rock & Shell Shop
117 A Ave. W
515/673-3816

Tyme & Again
113 High Ave. E
515/673-5857

Antique Shop
117 High Ave. E
515/673-0895

Old Friends Antiques
123 N. Market
515/673-0428

34 OTTUMWA

Phil Taylor Antiques
224 Fox Sauk Rd.
515/682-7492

35 PELLA

When you drive into Pella, Iowa, you'll probably double check the map, because you'll feel like a giant wind has blown you across the ocean to Holland! It looks and sounds like Holland, with windmills and wooden shoes, Dutch pastries and Klokkenspel, courtyards and sunken gardens, and acres and acres of tulips! In Pella the Old and New worlds combine completely every May and December at the Tulip Time Festival and Sinterklass (Santa Claus) Day. And the recently renovated and reopened Pella Opera House, built in 1900, provides year-round musical and theatrical performances by nationally known performers.

Beekhuizen Antiques
913 W. 8th St.
515/628-4712

Country Lane Antqs. & Cllbls.
752 190th Ave.
515/628-2912

Red Ribbon Antique Mall
812 Washington St.
515/628-2181

36 SIOUX CITY

Red Wheel Furn. & Antiques
By Appointment Only
712/276-3645

Old Town Antiques & Cllbls.
1024 4th Hwy. 712/258-3119
712/258-3119

Heritage House Antiques
3900 4th Ave.
712/276-3366

Gas Light Antiques
1310 Jennings Hwy.
712/252-2166

Collectors Cupboard
500 S. Lewis Blvd.
712/258-0087

Shirley's Stuff & Antiques
1420 Villa Ave.
712/252-1565

37 SPILLVILLE

The Bily Clocks

Joseph and Frank Bily truly mastered time, carving intricate wooden clocks with moveable figures and music. Their father, John, thought they were slightly cuckoo and felt they should devote themselves entirely to their "real" jobs of farming and carpentry. But the brothers persisted in their carving during the long, idle Iowa winter afternoons and evenings. Although they passed away in the mid-1960s, their artistry remains on permanent display in a Victorian-era home once occupied by Czech composer, Antonin Dvorak, when he stayed in Spillville, Iowa.

With its well-kept streets, manicured parks, tidy public square, and bandstand that's hosted innumerable tributes to returning war heroes, this picturesque village is a hotbed of Americana. Founded in 1854 by Joseph Spielman, and settled mostly by fellow Czechs, the town's name was later Americanized from Spielville to Spillville. It was here that Antonin Dvorak, "tired from a year's work as director of the New York Conservatory of Music and homesick for the companionship of his countrymen," (according to a descriptive brochure), came in the summer of 1893 with his family. Along with adding the finishing touches to his *New World Symphony*, he is said to have found inspiration for his *Humoresque* pianofortes, and to have composed the lesser-known *American Quartette* while in Spillville, too. He liked it so much, he returned the following summer for a two-week vacation.

Visitors might not be enthusiastic about Spillville - how many hours can one spend staring at a rock with *Humoresque* engraved on its side at the Dvorak Memorial in Riverside Park, or meandering around the gothically imposing St. Wenceslas Church, with its 1876 pipe organ that was played by Dr. Dvorak himself. But the 40 clocks and two model churches in the Bily exhibit are sure to be fascinating.

The Bily brothers' tools were nearly all homemade, while almost all of their clockworks and chimes came from a factory. Although they primarily used native walnut, butternut, maple and oak, some of their earliest attempts are made of imported cherry, mahogany, boxwood and white holly. Many of the clocks are several feet tall, weighing hundreds of pounds. They built the first one around 1913, so some musical discs are nearly one hundred years old.

"You truly can't appreciate the clocks until you see them in action," states exhibit manager, Joyce, Fuchs. The Bily's initial tickers, such as the *Grand Tower Clock* and the *Creation Clock*, were quite ornate, patterned after the European Gothic cathedral style. Later endeavors represented specific persons, places or events. In the *Apostle Clock*, the twelve apostles parade every hour within a large church like structure. The *American Pioneer History Clock* has fifty-seven panels showing symbols of United States history: the Liberty Bell, the Mayflower, cowboys on the range, and many others. While playing "America," the moving part depicts the four ages of humans, from childhood to geezerdom.

An airplane-shaped *Lindbergh Clock*, with a carving of the aviator's head inside it, commemorates his historic flight. The *Parade of Nations Clock* features a moving globe with people holding hands; the *Statuary Clock* offers busts of Thomas Edison, Michelangelo, and local notables. Obviously the brothers admired these folks: a small orchestra inside the clock performs "Praise to the Lord."

Among the cream of the clocks is the *Village Blacksmith*, their last major project, which was done between 1942 and 1943. Based on the poem of the same name by Henry Wadsworth Longfellow, it has a realistic-looking bellows, forge, and anvil, a collection of tools that were carved before being placed individually on the back wall, and a hat that can be removed from the farmer's head and put on the blacksmith's. "You can even see the stitches in the patch on the farmer's pants," points out Fuchs. "My Old Kentucky Home" is rendered while the blacksmith hammers on the plowshares.

The Bily brothers did not want to sell or break up their collection. Upon their deaths they had arranged to donate it to the town of Spillville, where it remained in the Dvorak building. As if to cement the deal, they carved a violin-shaped clock featuring Dvorak's head. What a harmonious bunch.

38 SPIRIT LAKE

Spirit Lake Antique Mall
2015 18th St.
712/336-2029

Heritage Square Antiques
1703 Hill Ave.
712/336-3455

Rubarb Antiques
2009 Hill Ave.
712/336-2154

39 THAYER

L & H Antique Mall
301 South 3rd Avenue (mailing address)
Highway 34 (shop location)
515/338-2223
Open Tue.-Sat. 10-5, Sun, 12-5, closed Mondays, holidays and the week between Christmas and New Year's.

Directions: Located on Highway 34, 14 miles west of Osceola and 17 miles east of Creston.

Lee and Helen Spurgeon, the owners of L & H Antique Mall, celebrate their sixth anniversary in their shop this year. They started out with 3200 square feet and 20 dealers. Last year they added 1100 square feet and eight more dealers. Who knows how high they'll go? And if you look closely in the shop, among the depression glass, Hull pottery, furniture, tools, black memorabilia, Fox and Parrish prints and country crafts, you'll see an engraved walnut plaque congratulating Helen on her selection to the National Directory of Who's Who in Executive and Professionals. Congratulations to the Spurgeons!

40 VAN BUREN COUNTY

The Villages of Van Buren County
1-800-868-7822
E-mail: Villages@netins.net
WebSite: http://www.netins.net/showcase/villages

These former riverboat ports, located along the Des Moines River in the southeast corner of Iowa just north of the Missouri border, are quaint, quiet villages that still maintain the atmosphere and relaxed lifestyle of the past century. Populated today with resident artists and craftspeople, antiques sellers and history buffs, these villages offer visitors relaxation and renewal in a setting that preserves and illuminates our history.

The villages in Van Buren Country include Selma, Birmingham, Stockport, Douds, Leando, Kilbourn, Lebanon, Pittsburg, Milton, Cantril, Keosauqua, Bentonport, Vernon, Mount Sterling, Bonaparte and Farmington, plus several lakes and state parks.

Bentonport National Historic District
Scenic Byway J-40 in Van Buren County
319/592-3579
Open Tue.-Sun. 10-5, April-October. Some businesses open daily or for longer season.

This 1840s river town, with its 100-year-old bridge and walkway, was already thriving when Iowa became a state. Mormon craftsmen, on their western trek to Utah, helped construct some of its buildings; the ruins of old mills along the Des Moines River are evident even today. Visitors can stroll through shops in historic buildings that feature antiques, locally made handcrafted items from working artisans, and American Indian artifacts. Then they can camp at riverside parks and campgrounds or stay at the historic bed and breakfast, eat at the cafe, view the rose garden, or launch into the river at the boat ramp and dock that are available.

Great Places to Shop, Eat and Stay in Bentonport

Greef General Store
Downtown Bentonport
319/592-3579

Antique mall features quality furniture, primitives, etc., plus art and a collection of Indian artifacts.

Country Peddlers
Downtown Bentonport
319/592-3564

Specializes in originally designed folk art.

The Hot Pot Cafe
Downtown Bentonport
319/592-3579

Sandwich shop serves soup and sandwiches, drinks, homemade goodies, ice cream and Dutch treats.

Mason House Inn and Antique Shop of Bentonsport
Route 2, Box 237
1-800-592-3133
Rates: $54-74

The Mason House Inn was built by Mormon craftsmen on their way to Utah in 1846, the year Iowa became a state. It remains the oldest steamboat river inn in the Midwest still serving overnight guests, quite a record when you consider that it has been in continual service to travelers for 150 years! With the state's only fold-down copper bathtub (that really raises questions, doesn't it!), it has, according to local legend, hosted such notables as John C. Fremont, Abraham Lincoln and Mark Twain. The Inn offers nine guest room, five with private bath.

Outback Antiques is also located on the premises.

Bonaparte National Historic Riverfront District

The history of Iowa's riverboat era is predominant in Bonaparte. The historic buildings in its downtown district have been carefully preserved and restored in a renaissance of cultural revival. Two of the 1800s mills are still in existence. The old flour and grist mill of 1878 is now the location of one of southeast Iowa's finest restaurants, The Bonaparte Retreat. Bonaparte Mill Antiques is next door in the former Meek's Woolen Mill, and other historic buildings in the district house a variety of businesses. The Aunty Green Museum is just down the street, where visitors can see a collection of historic memorabilia.

Great Places to Shop and Eat in Bonaparte

Bonaparte Mill Antiques
319/592-3274
Open 11-7 Tue.-Sun.

Antiques and collectibles

Bonaparte Retreat Restaurant
319/592-3339
Lunch served 11-1 every day except holidays; dinner served at 5 every day except holidays and Sundays.

Located in a restored grist mill.

Milton, Cantril, Lebanon Triangle
Van Buren County

Another opportunity for people to see firsthand the simple but beautifully crafted life of the Amish and Mennonites is available in the villages of Milton, Cantril and Lebanon, a triangular area in the western end of Van Buren County. Mennonites have settled in the Cantril community, offering several businesses that are open to visitors, including a general store that features bulk groceries and yard goods. In the Milton and Lebanon areas, visitors can watch the Amish practice the trades of horseshoeing, blacksmithing, buggy and harness making, furniture making, sawmill work, and other old world crafts that are a daily part of the Amish lifestyle. Candy and dry goods stores are open to visitors in the Milton area.

Daughtery's Coffee Shop
Cantril
319/397-2100
Open 7-5 Mon.-Fri.

Antiques, lunch, coffee and donuts

Great Places to Shop and Eat in Farmington

Borderline Antiques
103 Elm
319/878-3714
Open Thurs.-Sat. 10-4:30

Bridge Cafe and Supper Club
319/878-3315
6-4 Mon. & Tue. 6-9 Wed.-Sat., 7-2 Sun.

"Traditional Iowa fare since 1932"

Great Places to Shop, Eat and Stay in Keosauqua

Hotel Manning
100 Van Buren Street
319/293-3232 or 1-800-728-2718
Open year round
Rates $35-65

Hotel Manning, named for a founder of Keosauqua, was built in 1839 to house a bank and general store. The second and third stories were added in the 1890s and the entire edifice took on a style known as "steamboat gothic," with verandas spanning the width of the first two floors. The grand hotel opened on April 27, 1899 and has been in continuous use as a hotel since then! Guests and visitors can marvel at the lobby's ceilings, original pine woodwork and antique fixtures. The lobby also holds a rare Vose rosewood grand piano, a specially commissioned grandfather clock, and outstanding examples of early pine and oak furniture. The 18 guest rooms, 10 with private bath, are filled with handsome antiques.

Top of the Hill Antiques
319/293-3022

Their antiques can also be found at the Greef Store in Bentonsport.

The Village Creamery
319/293-3815
Summer: 11-10 daily/Winter 11-5 daily

Soft ice cream products, sandwiches, etc.

41 WALNUT

Farm Fresh Antiques
200 Antique City Dr.
712/784-2275

Country Treasure's Mall
202 Antique City Dr.
712/784-3090

Heart of Country
207 Antique City Dr.
712/784-3825

Everybody's Attic Antiques
210 Antique City Dr.
712/784-3030

Corn Country Antiques
212 Antique City Dr.
712/784-3992

Victorian Rose Antiques
216 Antique City Dr.
712/784-3900

Antique Furniture Emporium
226 Antique City Dr.
712/784-3839

Walnut Mercantile Co.
230 Antique City Dr.
712/784-2225

Simple Pleasures-Antiques
309 Antique City Dr.
712/784-3999

Don's Antiques
310 Antique City Dr.
712/784-2277

Bear Trap Antiques
608 Highland St.
712/784-3779

Barn Mall
615 Highland St.
712/784-3814

Walnut Antique Mall
514 Pearl St.
712/784-3322

Granary Mall
603 Pearl St.
712/784-3331

Village Blacksmith
610 Pearl St.
712/784-3332

42 WATERLOO

Calico Hen's House
1022 Alabar Ave.
319/234-1266

Tovar's Hidden Treasures
1642 Burton Ave.
319/232-0769

Grandpa Harry's
620 Commercial St.
319/232-5900

Hobby Horse Antiques
622 Commercial St.
319/233-6506

Pilot House Antiques
1621 Falls Ave.
319/232-5414

Pink Pig (Washburn)
7114 Laporte Rd.
319/296-3000

Black's Antiques
501 Sycamore St.
319/235-1241

Antique Galleries
618 Sycamore St.
319/235-9945

Buehner's Antiques
627 Sycamore St.
319/232-5710

43 WAVERLY

Apple Cottage Gifts & Antiques
103 Bremer Ave.
319/352-0153

Round Barn Antiques
R.R. 2
319/352-3694

44 WEST BRANCH

Memories Restored
111 E. Main
319/643-7330

Main Street Antiques & Art
110 W. Main
319/643-2065

45 WEST DES MOINES

Antique Jamboree

Valley Junction
5th Street area
Call for dates.

For more than 18 years, important antique dealers from across the Midwest have presented their wares at the West Des Moines Antique Jamboree. The show promoters insist upon exceptional antiques; no reproductions or crafts. Therefore, the discriminating shopper will be delighted to find nice porcelains, art glass, period to formal furnishings and more.

Valley Junction

Directions: Take I-235 to the 63rd Street exit. Go south and follow the Valley Junction signs.

In 1893 Valley Junction bustled with horse-drawn traffic, a trolley line, eight-foot wooden sidewalks, and dirt streets lined with three banks, three drug stores and several "boarding houses" of questionable character! By 1900 the Chicago, Rock Island and Pacific Railroad made Valley Junction a popular stop, with 26 passenger trains arriving and departing daily. Today visitors can enjoy more than 120 specialty stores, art galleries, antique shops and restaurants, each with a unique historic character.

One of the places in Valley Junction that is an absolute "must see" for anybody, any age, is the Valley Junction Train Station and Toy Train Museum. Centerpiece of the museum is the colossal 1,000 square foot toy train layout, designed by renowned Broadway set designer Clarke Dunham, and built in New York by Dunham Studios. Eleven Lionel trains, powered by state-of-the-art electronics, run on four different elevations where viewers of all sizes can watch and discover minute details at every eye level. There's the candy factory with its arteries of pipes, valves, tanks and Life Saver watertower. There are animated figures working and playing in a four-season wonderland, concrete arch viaducts, tunnels through spectacular mountains, towns and villages where tiny figures recreate daily life and fun all across America. Over 2,000 feet of track, connected by bridges and viaducts, loop through a scale-model of America's rural and urban landscapes. You'll see freight trains hauling grain and delivering goods to industrial areas; passenger trains carrying workers and tourists to the layout's metropolitan cities. Surrounding the central layout are dozens of custom-built oak and glass showcases where museum owner Doug DuBay displays his personal, extensive collection of antique trains, tiny houses and railroad memorabilia.

From there visit the Valley Junction Toy Train Station—a collector and hobbyist shopping paradise! Shelf after shelf of Lionel equipment and layout accessories are there for viewing, dreaming and buying. After seeing the museum and its fantastic possibilities, it's no wonder that most visitors don't leave the Toy Train Station empty-handed! The museum and Toy Train Station are open Mon.-Sat. 10-5 and Sun. 12-5. The address is 401 Railroad Place, 515/274-4424.

Fifth Street Mall

115 5th St.
515/279-3716

Fifth Street Mall presents quality antiques and collectibles with showcases full of great merchandise. They also have a 1940s original soda fountain.

Bill & Sharon's Antiques
510 Elm St.
515/279-7719

"Prezzies"
513 Elm St.
515/255-1915

Addie's Antiques
100 5th St.
515/274-8866

Elinor's Wood 'N Wares
102 5th St.
515/274-1234

Station
104 5th St.
515/255-6331

Joy's Treasures
108 5th St.
515/279-5975

Antique Mall
110 5th St.
515/255-3185

Diane's Antiques
110 5th St.
515/255-3185

Cherry Stone
111 5th St.
515/255-6414

Country Caboose Antiques
113 5th St.
515/277-1555

David Meshek Antq. Lighting
115 5th St.
515/277-9009

Time Passages Ltd.
980 73rd St.
515/223-5104

A Okay Antiques
124 5th St.
515/255-2525

Collectables, Etc.
125 5th St.
515/274-1401

Especially Lace
202 5th St.
515/277-8778

Alverdas Antiques
211 5th St.
515/255-0931

Pegasus Gallery
218 5th St.
515/277-3245

Valley Junction Mall
333 5th St.
515/274-1419

Lanny's
404 5th St.
515/255-0700

Willoughby Station
415 Railroad Place
515/255-6331

Antique Collectors Mall
1980 Grand Ave.
515/224-6494

46 WINTERSET

Madison County Mercantile
58 W. Court Ave.
515/462-4535

East Coast Connection
116 S. 1st Ave.
515/462-1346

Notes

Kansas

36
70
83
283
50
9 Dodge City
54
23 Liberal

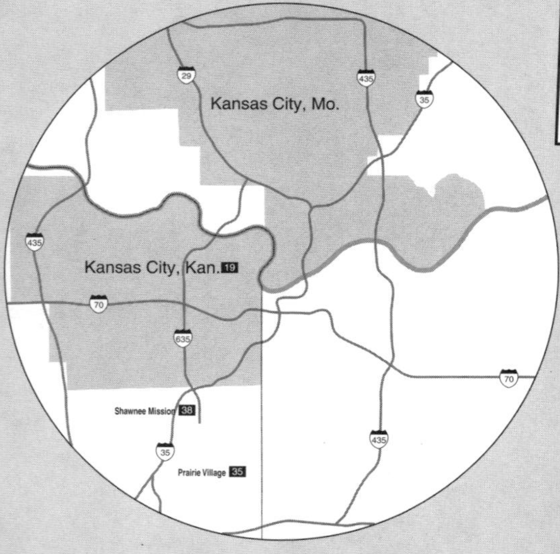

29
435
35
Kansas City, Mo.
435
Kansas City, Kan. 19
70
635
70
Shawnee Mission 38
435
35
Prairie Village 35

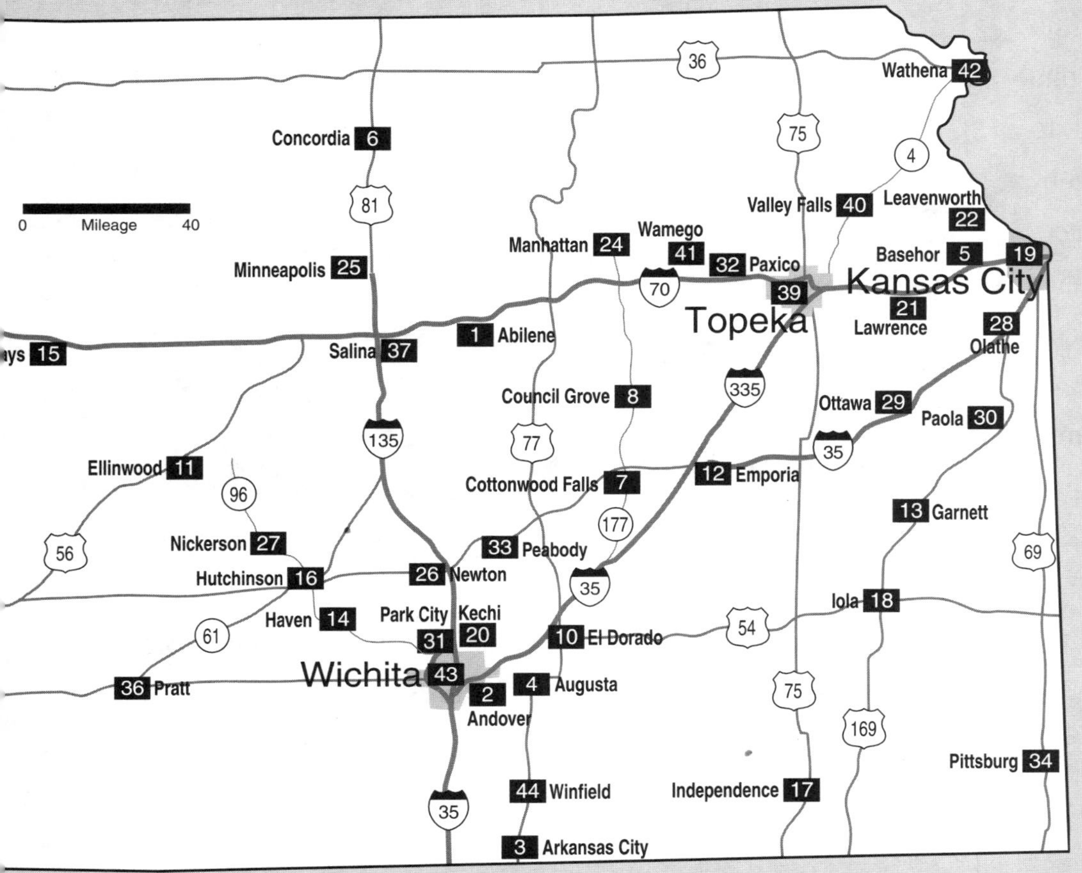

Wathena 42
Concordia 6
Valley Falls 40
Leavenworth 22
0 Mileage 40
Manhattan 24
Wamego 41
32 Paxico
Basehor 5
19
Minneapolis 25
39
Kansas City
Topeka
21 Lawrence
28 Olathe
1 Abilene
ys 15
Salina 37
Council Grove 8
Ottawa 29
Paola 30
Ellinwood 11
Cottonwood Falls 7
12 Emporia
13 Garnett
Nickerson 27
33 Peabody
Hutchinson 16
26 Newton
Iola 18
Haven 14
Park City
Kechi
31
20
10 El Dorado
36 Pratt
Wichita 43
2 Andover
4 Augusta
Pittsburg 34
44 Winfield
Independence 17
3 Arkansas City
36
75
4
81
70
335
135
77
35
96
177
56
69
61
54
169

Kansas

Wichita castle has European touch

Salve...

This Latin message greets all the guests to the Castle Inn Riverside. Carved in stone over the drive, it is one of the many details that will speak to you during your stay. Built in 1888 by Burton Harvey Campbell, this architectural masterpiece was fashioned after a castle located in the foothills of Scotland. It is more than mortar and limestone, it is the result of one man's dream and several architects' expertise.

The 28-room castle was built from 1886-88 for a cost of $90,000 by Colonel Burton Harvey Campbell. At the time, Campbell was one of Wichita's wealthiest residents, and he spared no expense in building the castle.

The stonework is known as "rough rock face," a style that presents the roughest natural surface of the gray limestone, which came from the Butler Country quarry. Materials also came from farther away. The original floors were created in Chicago by Behl and Company; the hardware was ordered directly from the factory in New York, and the stairwell, fireplaces, lamps and fixtures were imported from Europe.

For 20 years, the mansion remained the property of Campbell. In 1910 Walter Morris purchased the estate for less than a third of what it cost to build.

Fifty years later it became the property of Maye Crumm, who began calling it Crumm Castle. For a time it housed the Belle Carter High School, an institution begun and operated by Crumm.

In April 1973, the castle was entered on the National Register of Historic Places as "a building of architectural significance."

The high ceilings, the spaciousness of the grand foyer, and the 250-year-old staircase (imported from London) all combine with the 650-year-old Grecian fireplace to add history and hospitality.

In the '70s, the upkeep of the castle became a constant struggle. To raise funds for its survival, the 19-room mansion was opened to the public for tours of all but the rooms occupied by the Crumm family.

In 1994, the castle, a historic and beloved member of the Wichita community, was existing on borrowed time. It was then that Terry and Paula Lowry purchased the property. Out of respect for Campbell and his vision, they returned his name to the castle.

This room derives its name from the legendary "fiery" Queen of Scotland, whose image appears in the middle of the Scottish fireplace.

They invested all their time, energy and resources into restoring this majestic structure to its original beauty.

Damaged stones were painstakingly taken apart and replaced with pieces created by expert masons. The woodwork and floors have been brought back to their original luster. The roof has been reslated with tiles from Vermont. The plumbing was replaced with safer materials and the upstairs ballroom has been converted into five luxurious suites.

Like many before them, the Lowrys had a dream of making the castle their home, but their dream is much larger. They want to share its beauty with the rest of the world.

The parlor is decorated in salmon-colored walls, a hand-carved and mirrored fireplace, a grand piano, and rich tapestry designs highlight the furnishings.

This luxury inn features 14 uniquely appointed guest rooms, each a distinctive theme based on the heritage of the castle.

Amenities include jacuzzi tubs for two (six rooms), fireplaces (12 rooms), complimentary wine and hors d'oeuvres, and an assortment of homemade desserts and gourmet coffees served each evening.

The Castle Inn Riverside is located less than five minutes from downtown Wichita and approximately 15 minutes from Mid-Continent Airport. For your meeting needs, the castle offers a carefully designed conference area in the original castle cellar.

Please call (316) 263-9300 for reservations. In the meantime, Salve ... the castle bids you welcome!

1 ABILENE

If you "like Ike," you're in the right place. After he returned from World War II, General Dwight D. Eisenhower told a hometown crowd "the proudest thing I can claim is that I am from Abilene." At the Eisenhower Center in Abilene, visit the home, library and final resting place of the former president and five-star general.

And don't miss Kirby House, a fully restored 1855 gingerbread mansion that is now a wonderful family restaurant, and the Seelye Mansion, a twenty-five room Georgian mansion built in 1905.

Downtown Antique Mall
313 N. Buckeye Ave.
913/263-2782

Chisholm Trail Antiques
1020 S. Buckeye Ave.
913/263-2061

Liddle Shoppe
306 N. Cedar St.
913/263-0077

Abilene Antique Plaza
418 N.W. 2nd St.
913/263-4200

Family Antiques
1449 2700th Ave.
913/598-2356

2 ANDOVER

Andover Antique Mall
656 N. Andover Rd.
316/733-8999

3 ARKANSAS CITY

Antiques Plus Mall
120 N. Summit St.
316/442-5777

Summit Antique Mall
208 S. Summit St.
316/442-1115

Mylissa's Garden Antiques
309 S. Summit St.
316/442-6433

4 AUGUSTA

White Eagle Antique Mall
10187 SW U.S. Highway 54
316/775-2812
Open Mon.-Sat., 10-9; Sun. 12-7
7 days a week

Directions: Located 2.5 miles west of Augusta on the south side of U.S. Hwy. 54. Travelers on U.S. Hwy. 77 take U.S. Hwy. 54 west at Walnut Street stoplight in Augusta.

White Eagle Antique Mall, billed as "A Collector's Dream Come True," is no disappointment. The mall features that hard-to-find, early petroleum and gas station memorabilia. With over 100 dealers, this place is attractively filled to the brim with high quality glassware, primitives, vintage clothing, old books, jewelry, lamps, old toys, pottery, tools, large and small furniture and other exceptional antiques.

Like A Rose
343 Main St.
316/775-5860

Circa 1890
10257 SW River Valley Rd.
316/775-3272

Two Fools Antiques
429 State St.
316/775-2588

Pigeon's Roost Mall
601 State St.
316/775-2279

5 BASEHOR

Bedknobs & Biscuits
15202 Parallel
913/724-1540
Rates: $50-70

A little bit of country close to Bonner Springs and Kansas City. A warm, inviting beamed gathering room; walls covered in hand-painted vines. Stenciling throughout the house, lovely quilts, lace curtains and colorful stained glass to enjoy. Complimentary cookies in the evening and a huge country breakfast in the morning.

6 CONCORDIA

General Store Antiques
317 W. 5th St.
913/243-7280

Dan's Antiques
101 E. 6th St.
913/243-3820

Chapter I Books
120 E. 6th St.
913/243-1423

Antique Mall
128 E. 6th St.
913/243-2313

7 COTTONWOOD FALLS

Grand Central Hotel
215 Broadway
316/273-6763 or 1-800-951-6763

Most of us rarely think of hills in connection with Kansas, but hidden among the state's Flint Hills is an elegant hotel that is a luxurious surprise when you stumble across it. The Grand Central Hotel bills itself as "very exclusive, very distinctive, very, very special." Located one block west of National Scenic Byway 177 in historic Cottonwood Falls, the hotel was built in 1884 and has been fully restored to its original grandeur. It offers ten suites, each beautifully appointed and oversized, and decorated with a western flair. In fact, each suite is "branded" with historic brands of the area's local ranchers! It offers full dining and complete catering services, and is often the suite of choice for weddings, receptions, small board and business conferences, corporate outings, and, of course, private accommodations. It caters to the business trade with concierge and room service, plus V.I.P. robes and a business center; but the hotel also offers hunting trips, bicycle tours, horseback riding, and tours of the surrounding Flint Hills.

1874 Stonehouse Bed & Breakfast on Mulberry Hill
Rural Route 1, Box 67A
316/273-8481
Rates $75

If you've ever wondered about the landscape that nurtured Dorothy and Toto, here's your chance to spend some time at one, possibly. The 1874 Stonehouse on Mulberry Hill offers three lovely rooms with private baths on the second floor, with two common rooms and a stone fireplace. But that's not nearly all. On its 120 acres guests can spend all day, or several days, exploring old stone fences, a river valley that crosses the property, acres of woods (more than 10 acres), a pond, the ruins of an old stone barn and corral, an abandoned railway right-of-way, and a decrepit "hired hands place." The inn and its grounds are a magnet for fishermen and hunters, equestrians and naturalists, antiquers and photographers, cyclists and hikers, bird watchers and historians, and maybe even a little girl in pigtails and her funny little dog.

8 COUNCIL GROVE

Council Grove was the last outfitting post between the Missouri River and Santa Fe on the Santa Fe Trail. In 1825, the U.S. government negotiated with the Osage Indians for a passage across their lands. The stump of Council Oak still stands where the treaty was signed. At the Last Chance Store, you can still visit the last supply stop on the Santa Fe Trail. And if you're hungry, try some tasty family recipes at the Hays House Restaurant, the oldest continuously operated restaurant west of the Mississippi.

Prairie Pieces
217 W. Main St.
316/767-6628

Faded Roses
307 E. Main
316/767-5217

Union Street Antiques
103 N. Union St.
316/767-6015

Hays House 1857 Restaurant
112 West Main Street
316/767-5911
Summer: 7 a.m.-9 p.m.
Winter: 7 a.m.-8 p.m.

Oldest restaurant west of the Mississippi; National Register Historic Landmark; nationally acclaimed restaurant featured in many magazines and newspapers; outstanding steaks, breads and dessert made from scratch daily.

9 DODGE CITY

Ole Jem's
212 S. 2nd Ave.
316/227-6162

Collector's Cottage
106 E. Wyatt Earp Blvd.
316/225-7448

Curiosity Shoppe
1102 W. Wyatt Earp Blvd.
316/227-3340

Interesting Side Trips

Relive the 1870s heyday of the rip-snortin', gun-slingin' Wild West at Dodge City's Boot Hill Museum and Front Street complex. More than five million Texas longhorn cattle were driven to the "Cowboy Capital." Miss Kitty still runs the Longbranch Saloon, gunslingers have "high noon" shootouts and an authentic stagecoach still boards passengers for a ride along Front Street.

10 EL DORADO

North Ward Junction Antiques

518 North Star
316/321-0145
1-800-286-0146
Open seven days a week; Mon.-Sat., 10-5:30; Sun. 1-4
Accepts all major credit cards - offers dealer discounts.

Directions: From I-35 exit 71 (East); turn left on Central, go 2.5 miles into El Dorado. Turn left at the courthouse onto Star. Go five blocks north. From Highway 54 east of El Dorado, come into town on Central heading west, turn right at the courthouse; go five blocks north.

This shop began life in 1884 as the North Ward School. No longer catering to the educational concerns of fidgety boys and girls, this 4,000-square-foot shop provides fifteen quality antique dealers the opportunity to display their wares in decorated room-like settings. A large selection of furniture is available along with accent pieces of porcelain, china, glassware, elegant table settings, linens, prints and much, much more.

Cinnamon Tree
1417 W. Central Ave.
316/321-0930

Leather Works
1630 W. Central Ave.
316/321-7644

Blast from the Past
527 N. Washington St.
316/321-3434

11 ELLINWOOD

James J. Elliott Antiques
1 N. Main
316/564-2400

Our Mother's Treasures
14 N. Main
316/564-2218

Starr Antiques
104 E. Santa Fe
316/564-2400

12 EMPORIA

Emporia is a city with over 130 years of history as an agricultural and railroad community. It still maintains its small town Middle American charm, exemplified by brick streets, tree-lined avenues and many beautiful old Victorian homes.

Emporia was also the home of two-time Pulitzer Prize winner, William Allen White, owner of The Emporia Gazette. White became famous overnight for his opposing editorial reviews against the Populist Party.

Plumb House Bed and Breakfast

628 Exchange Street
316/342-6881
Rates $35-75
Directions: Call from your location.

Built in 1910 and once the home of George and Ellen Plumb, this bed and breakfast offers classic Victorian charm. Its original beveled glass windows and pocket doors are still intact, and the home is furnished throughout with Victorian era antiques.

Guests may choose from the Horseless Carriage with large windows overlooking a garden; the Garden Suite offering views from a balcony; the Rosalie Room, the Loft, or Grannie's Attic filled with over 250 dresses, hats, gloves, shoes, and jewelry. Everything you need for dress-up tea parties.

Wild Rose Antique Mall

1505 East Road 175
316/343-8862
Open Tue.-Sat., 11-5; Sun. 1-5; closed Monday

Directions: 3 miles East of Emporia on I-35 at exit #135 (Thorndale exit)

Terry McCracken, owner and shopkeeper at the Wild Rose Antique Mall, has collected antiques since her childhood. Up until seven years ago, she had never sold a one of them. When she decided to retire as a real estate broker (she added that she's not that old); she opened a booth at a mall in Topeka. Her success prompted her to open her own shop in Emporia where she presented high-end antique glassware, quilts, jewelry, china, pottery, linens, primitives and furnishings. Today, thanks to all the folks who enjoyed shopping at Wild Rose, Terry has expanded. Her new shop allows space for more dealers with a broader selection of antiques. Three dealers specialize in items from the Victorian era. Congratulations, Terry!

13 GARNETT

Country Peddler
146 E. 5th Ave.
913/448-3018

Corner Stone Antiques
146 E. 5th Ave.
913/448-3737

Goodies Antiques
121 E. 4th Ave.
913/448-6712

Emporium on The Square
415 S. Oak St.
913/448-6459

14 HAVEN

The Home Place Antiques

7619 South Yoder Road
316/662-1579
Open Tue.-Sat.; 10-5

Directions: 4 1/2 miles south of Highway 50; 1 1/2 miles north of Highway 96.

The Home Place Antiques is located in a barn built in 1909 and sets on a fourth-generation farm, thus creating the perfect atmosphere for selling antiques. The "old barn" is full of antiques, from furniture (lots of it) to dishes, to pottery, to a little of everything.

15 HAYS

Antique Mall
201 W. 41st St.
913/625-6055

Little's Antiques
717 Vine St.
913/628-3393

Interesting Side Trips

Old Fort Hays was built to protect military roads, guard the mails and defend construction gangs on the Union Pacific Railroad. See the original blockhouse, guardhouse and officers' quarters. "Buffalo Bill" Cody supplied the fort with buffalo meat, and General Custer's ill-fated 7th cavalry was stationed here.

16 HUTCHINSON

Antique Memories
25 E. 1st St.
316/665-0610

Unique Antiques
1831 E. 4th Ave.
316/669-8678

Yesterday's Treasures
436 Hendricks St.
316/662-0895

Cow Creek Antiques
127 S. Main
316/663-1976

Nu-Tu U
201 S. Main St.
316/662-4357

Book Collector
404 N. Main St.
316-665-5057

Finders Keepers II
412 N. Main St.
316/663-5457

Broker's Antiques
820 S. Main St.
316/665-7040

GAI Marche Ltd.
2528 N. Main St.
316/662-6323

17 INDEPENDENCE

If you're a fan of "Little House on the Prairie," visit a replica of the house where Laura Ingalls Wilder lived and found inspiration for her books. The cabin was rebuilt where it originally stood near Independence.

The Rosewood Bed and Breakfast

417 W. Myrtle
316/331-2221
Rates: $50-60

Directions: Located 1 block north of Hwy. 75/169 at 11th Street and Myrtle.

This stately home was built in 1915 for William Gates, general manager of Prairie Oil and Gas. Leaded glass windows and wrap-around porches still embrace the home. Decorated throughout in period antiques, the Victorian Rose room creates a picture of a romantic time gone by. A white iron bed piled high with pure white and soft pink dressings is the focus of the room, with a large bay window providing the morning sun. The Royal Orchid, preferred by honeymooners, has a black canopy bed. The Desert Blossom is the whimsical room, decorated in a Southwestern flair.

Breakfast is served in the dining room near the bay windows and fireplace.

Attic Treasures
211 E. Main St.
316/331-6401

Southwest Wood Shop
1813 W. Main St.
316/331-1400

18 IOLA

Northrup House Bed & Breakfast
318 East Street
316/365-8025
Rates: $60-70

The Northrup House, a Queen Anne Victorian, was built in 1895 by Lewis Northrup, a prominent Iola businessman and community leader. The interior features stained glass windows, beautiful oak woodwork, crystal chandeliers and pocket doors. The house is furnished with elegant antiques. The guests are welcome to use the parlors, dining room and porches.

19 KANSAS CITY

Palmer's Antiques
761 Central Ave.
913/342-8299

Glenn Books
1710 Central Ave.
913/321-3040

Happy House Antiques
1712 Central Ave.
913/321-8909

Treasures from Granny's Attic
6000 Leavenworth Rd.
913/334-0824

Antique & Craft City Mall
1270 Merriam Lane
913/677-0752

Adventure Antiques
1306 Merriam Lane
913/831-6005

Anderson's General Store
1713 Minnesota Ave.
913/321-3165

Old World Antiques
4436 State Line Rd.
913/677-4744

Show Me Antiques
4500 State Line Rd.
913/236-8444

State Line Antique Mall
4510 State Line Rd.
913/362-2002

Collector's Emporium
3412 Strong Ave.
913/384-1875

Past Renewed
4356 Victory Dr.
913/287-2817

Favorite Places To Eat

Cracker Barrel Old Country Store
I-70 & 78th St., Exit 414
913/788-2412

20 KECHI

Country Antiques Kechi
201 E. Kechi Rd.
316/744-0932

Anderson Antiques
309 E. Kechi Rd.
316/744-8482

Cherishables
311 E. Kechi Rd.
316/744-9952

Primitives Plus
127 Foreman
316/744-1836

21 LAWRENCE

Quantrill's Antique Mall & Flea Market
811 New Hampshire Street
913/842-6616
Open every day 10 to 5:30

Directions: Located 3 miles south of the I-70 East Kansas Turnpike Exit. One block east of Massachusetts Street. Two blocks from Riverfront Outlet Mall.

Quantrill's is the oldest antique mall in the state of Kansas. This massive 3-story natural limestone structure dates back to 1863. With 150 dealers covering 20,000 square feet, their inventory list is just as impressive. You'll find furniture, toys, jewelry, glassware, pottery, books, lunch boxes, dolls, advertising memorabilia, buttons, crocks and Fiesta. From their list of the unusual, they offer retro '60s and '70s items, tobacco, military and '50s dinettes and other nostalgic items.

Topiary Tree Inc.
15 E. 8th St.
913/842-1181

Antique Mall
830 Massachusetts St.
913/842-1328

B & S Antiques
1017 Massachusetts St.
913/843-9491

Strong's Antiques
1025 Massachusetts St.
913/843-5173

22 LEAVENWORTH

Caffee's Leavenworth Antique Mall
505 Delaware
913/758-0193
Open: Mon.-Wed., 10-6, Thurs.-Sat. 10-9

Directions: Located in Historic Downtown Leavenworth.

Caffee's Antique Mall is housed in the old J.C. Penny department store. This historic building provides three floors offering a wide variety of antiques from Primitive to Victorian to Deco. The shop specializes in a large selection of furniture with one dealer specializing in old and rare coins.

Caffee's has a tea room within the mall, a welcome spot for serious antiquers. The Tea Room is open Mon.-Sat. 10:30 a.m.-4 p.m. and Thurs.-Sat. 6 p.m.-9 p.m.

Bob's Antiques
511 Delaware St.
913/680-0101

Ginny's Antiques
206 S. 5th St.
913/651-8426

Carol's Cupboard
207 S 5th St.
913/651-0400

Weakley's Antq. Furniture
1433 Kingman St.
913/682-5816

River Front Antique Shop
401 S. 2nd St.
913/682-3201

Trumpet Vine
1700 2nd Ave.
913/651-8230

June's Antiques
612 Cherokee
913/651-5270

23 LIBERAL

Randy's Antiques
1 S. Kansas Ave.
316/624-0641

Yesterday's Treasure
406 E. Pancake Blvd.
316/624-1683

Interesting Side Trips

Take a stroll along Dorothy's Yellow Brick Road in Liberal. See the original miniature farmhouse used in the 1939 classic film "The Wizard of Oz," or go through a full-sized replica of Dorothy's house. Liberal also is the home of Kansas' largest aviation museum, the Mid-America Air Museum. There are more than 80 vintage aircraft on display. And the world-famous International Pancake Race is held in Liberal each Shrove Tuesday.

24 MANHATTAN

Pop's Collectables
315 S. 4th St.
785/776-1433

Gumbo Hill Antique Shop
6590 Gumbo Hill Rd.
785/539-5778

On The Avenue
405 Poyntz Ave.
785/539-9116

Antq. Emporium of Manhattan
411 Poyntz Ave.
785/537-1921

Under the Avenue Antq. Mall
413 Poyntz Ave.
785/537-1921

Zeandale Store
RR 3
785/537-3631

Tuttle's Antique Market
2010 Tuttle Creek Blvd.
785/537-4884

Time Machine Antique Mall
4910 Skyway Drive
785/539-4684

25 MINNEAPOLIS

Griffin's Antqs. & Cllbls.
703 E. 10th
913/392-2821

Blue Store Emporium
307 W. Second St.
913/392-3491

26 NEWTON

Wharf Road
413 N. Main St.
316-283-3579

Stuart's Antique Gallery
709 N. Main St.
316/284-0824

27 NICKERSON

Hedrick Exotic Animal Farm/Bed and Breakfast
7910 N. Roy L. Smith Rd.
316/422-3245
1-800-618-9577
Open 8-10; seven days a week.

Directions: 50 miles NW of Wichita on Highway 96; 8 miles west of Hutchinson on Highway 96. From I-70, go south on 135 at Salina to McPherson. Take Highway 61 to Hutchinson, Take Highway 96 west 8 miles. Located on the north side of Highway 96.

Looking for a little bit out of the ordinary place to stay? Then book your reservations here. Hedrick's Bed and Breakfast offers a relaxing, country atmosphere in a picturesque Old West town front nestled in the midst of a farm. But cows and horses aren't the only animals you'll find here. It wouldn't be out of the ordinary to find camels, zebras, llamas, kangaroos, and ostriches. And Jeffrey, the tallest animal found on the farm, will practically kiss you for an apple slice. In case you haven't guessed, Jeffrey's a giraffe.

You can arrange for the staff to take you on a guided tour where you can actually touch and feed the animals. Camel rides, pony rides, hayrack rides and campfire weiner roasts can also be arranged.

The decor of each guest room depicts an animal on the farm, with personal touches such as zebra sheets, rugs from Peru and much more. True to the western heritage of Kansas, the Inn reflects the image of Main Street in the Old West, complete with swinging "bar" doors. An outside balcony which completely surrounds the Inn is accessible from each room. A great place to bring the kids.

28 OLATHE

Rosebriar Limited
11695 S. Black Bob Rd.
913/829-3636

Heirloom Antiques
2135 N.E. 151 St.
913/780-3478

Aggie's Attic Antiques
301 1/2 W. Park St.
913/768-0058

Flutterby
1313 E. Santa Fe St.
913/780-1644

Favorite Places To Eat

Cracker Barrel Old Country Store
I-35 & 119th St., Exit 220
913/780-9108

29 OTTAWA

Over The Hill Collectibles
120 S. Main St.
785/242-8016

Down Home Antiques
202 S. Main St.
785/242-0774

Gable's Antiques
503 N. Main St.
785/242-7144

Outback Antiques
534 N. Main St.
785/242-1178

Silver Arrow Trading Post
1630 S. Main St.
785/242-0019

Ottawa Antique Mall & Rest.
202 S. Walnut St.
785/242-1078

30 PAOLA

Park Square Emporium
18 S. Silver St.
913/294-9004

Magdelena's Antqs. & Cllbls.
8 S. Silver St.
913/294-5048

Special Occasions
23 W. Wea St.
913/294-8595

31 PARK CITY

Recollections
1530 S. 61st St.
316/744-8333

Poor House Antiques
1542 N. 61st St.
316/744-9935

Teddy's Antiques & Cllbls.
1550 E. 61st St.
316/685-0435

Annie Antiques & Collectibles
1600 S. 61st St.
316/744-1999

32 PAXICO

Paxico Variety Shop
203 Main St.
913/636-5292

Main Street Antiques
204 Main St.
913/636-5200

Time Warp Antiques
207 Main St.
913/636-5553

Mill Creek Antiques
109 Newbury
913/636-5520

Paxico Antiques
111 Newbury Ave.
913/636-5426

33 PEABODY

This little town of 1,400 probably has preserved its architectural heritage better than any other community in the state. Gutted by two fires in its first 14 years of existence, Peabody was rebuilt in 1885 with limestone fire walls between the buildings.

"That's what saved our town," said the town historian, Koni Jones. "You can see that the buildings are still the way they were in the 1880s. One of our slogans is 'It really is a step back in time.'"

The town was named for a railroad executive who donated a library to the fledgling community in 1874. It was the first free library in Kansas, and today the original building is the Peabody Historical Museum.

Visitors downtown can also browse an antique store, try a phosphate at a 1920s soda fountain, enjoy flavored coffees and teas at the Jackrabbit Hollow Bookstore, or dine in restaurants that once were a bank in 1887 and a chicken hatchery in 1885.

Tumbleweed Antiques
101 N. Walnut Street
316/983-2200

Sharon's Korner Kitchen
128 N. Walnut
316/983-2307

Turkey Red Restaurant
101 S. Walnut
316/983-2883

Jack Rabbit Hollow Books
113 N. Walnut
316/983-2600

34 PITTSBURG

Marilyn's Ceramics Crafts
710 W. Atkinson Rd.
316/231-4131

George's Antiques
210 S. Broadway St.
316/232-6340

Treasure Village Antiques
212 S. Broadway St.
316/231-4888

Browsery-Collector Antiques
216 S. Broadway St.
316/232-1250

Friday's Child
615 N. Broadway St.
316/235-0403

Antique Shop
2305 N. Broadway St.
316/231-4090

35 PRAIRIE VILLAGE

Mission Road Antique Mall
4101 W. 83rd Street
913/341-7577

36 PRATT

Peggy's Antiques
208 S. Main St.
316/672-5648

Brick Street Antique Mall
212 S. Main St.
316/672-6770

Mom's Attic
607 S. Main St.
316/672-7656

37 SALINA

Auld Lang Syne & Auld Lang Syne, Too

101 N. Santa Fe too-110 N. Santa Fe
913/825-0020 913/827-4222
Open: Mon.-Sat. 10-5, Sun. 1-5

Directions: Corner of Santa Fe and Iron

Two shops to double your antiquing pleasure. Auld Lang Syne is located in the former First National Bank Building complete with a center courtyard for relaxing. Auld Lang Syne, too is across the street. Both shops display the wares of ninety dealers offering a selection of antiques and collectibles of various styles and periods

Treasure Chest of Salina
N. Broadway
913/827-9371

Furniture Clinic
405 S. Clark St.
913/827-5115

Stan & June's Heirlooms
201A S. 5th St.
913/823-6627

Fourth Street Mini Mall
127 S. 4th St.
913/825-4948

Forever & Ever Antiques & Collectibles
108 N. Santa Fe Ave.
913/827-4222

38 SHAWNEE

Old Shawnee Town

As visitors pass through the gates into Old Shawnee Town, they are enveloped by the 1880s atmosphere of the town. From the blacksmith's shop to the sod house, the setting makes visitors become a part of life on the Kansas frontier.

Furniture, tools and household items are just a few of the goods to see on the walk through town. The original Shawnee jail - the first in Johnson County - stands in Old Shawnee Town for people of all ages to explore.

For those who decide to make it a day at the site, the central grassy area serves as an ideal spot for picnics and group gatherings.

Johnson County Historical Museum

From pioneer trail utensils to the coming of the television, the Johnson County Historical Museum brings the area's history to life.

The experiences of prairie pioneers come alive at the Hands-on History display in the museum. After donning the traditional attire of calico dresses or overalls, kids can try their hand at mixing pretend biscuits or discovering how to harness an oxen team.

O'Neill's Classics - Antiques & Uniques

11200 Johnson Drive
913/268-9008
Open: Tue.-Fri. 10-5:30, Sat. 10-4:30, Closed Sun. & Mon.

Directions: One mile from I-35, on the north side of Johnson Drive, just a block west of its intersection with Nieman Road.

Located in the historic town of Shawnee, O'Neill's carries a general line of antiques and collectibles. Antique chairs, tables, dressers, pictures, elegant glassware and the such are just a few of the items one may find in this quaint 1400 sq. ft. store. The oldest piece in the store dates to around 1830 with collectibles up through 1960s.

Local residents frequent the store often, but the owners, Mike & Cyndee Bohaty, love meeting new antique friends who stop in while traveling. Cyndee grew up around antiques and was once a member of Questers, a national association of people interested in antiquing. When

Cyndee and Mike were married they loved going to auctions - Cyndee jokingly laughs that they couldn't afford anything else. Today, they still love auctions as evidenced by the wonderful pieces available in their store.

Gene Switzer Antiques
6711 Antioch Rd.
913/432-3982

Consignment Shop
4740 Rainbow Shop
913/384-2424

Armoires & More
12922 W. 87th Street
913/438-3868

Mission Road Antique Mall
4101 W 83rd St.
913/341-7577

Memory Lane Antiques
5401 Johnson Dr
913/677-4300

Lincoln Antiques
5636 Johnson Dr.
913/384-6811

Past & Present Antiques
5727 Johnson Dr.
913/362-6995

Drake's Military Antiques
8929 Johnson Dr.
913/722-1943

Peterson's Antiques
7829 Marty St.
913/341-5065

Antiques & Oak
10464 Metcalf Ave.
913/381-8280

J & M Collectables
7819 W. 151st St.
913/897-0584

Zohner's Antiques
10200 Pflumm Rd.
913/894-5036

June's Antiques
612 Cherokee
913/651-5270

39 TOPEKA

Shade Tree Antiques
1300 S.W. Boswell Ave.
913/232-5645

B & J Antique Mall
1949 S.W. Gage Blvd
913/273-3409

Cobweb
2508 S.W. 15th St.
913/357-7498

Antique Elegance
2900 S.W. Oakley Ave.
913/273-0909

Antiques Unique
1222 S.W. 6th Ave.
913/232-1007

Pastense
3307 S.W. 6th Ave.
913/233-7107

Packrat Antiques
3310 S.W. 6th Ave.
913/232-6560

Kansan Relics & Old Books
3308 S.W. 6th Ave.
913/233-8232

Reflections Antiques
2213 S.W. 10th Ave.
913/232-4619

History House
215 S.W. Topeka Blvd
913/235-1885

Antique Plaza of Topeka
2935 S.W. Topeka Blvd
913/267-7411

Rose Buffalo Antiques & Cllbls.
3600 S.W. Topeka Blvd
913/267-7478

Darlas World Antqs. & Cllbls.
3688 S.W. Topeka Blvd
913/266-4242

Wheatland Antique Mall
2121 S.W. 37th St.
913/266-3266

Topeka Antique Mall
5247 S.W. 28th Ct.
913/273-2969

Washburn View Antique Mall
1507 S.W. 21st Street
913/234-0949

Dickerson Antiques
5331 S.W. 22nd Pl.
913/273-1845

Saltbox
507 S.W. Washburn Ave.
913/233-6264

Favorite Places To Eat

Cracker Barrel Old Country Store
I-470 & Wanamaker/Huntoon St., Exit 1B
913/273-3393

40 VALLEY FALLS

Valley Falls Antiques
423 Broadway
913/945-3666
Open Tue.-Sat., 10-5; Sun. 12-5; closed Monday

Directions: Located halfway between Topeka and Atchison, Kansas, 30 miles either direction, via Highway 4. In Valley Falls, go downtown. The store is easily found at the corner of Walnut and Broadway.

Halfway between Topeka and Atchison, Kansas, sits Valley Falls, "Antique Capital of Jefferson County." Among the three established shops and the one opening this year, Valley Falls Antiques presents its shoppers the expected assortment of goods, in addition to some not-so-usual items.

The shop is housed in a historic bank building built in 1872, and within its walls you can shop for antique furniture, primitives, glassware and collectibles. Delores Werder, owner and shopkeeper, admits that original artwork is a passion for her. She prefers to purchase pieces with some unusual quality. Among her display of art, you will find prints, paintings and block prints.

41 WAMEGO

Carriage House Antqs.
210 Lincoln St.
913/456-7021

Wagon Wheel Antiques
409 Lincoln St.
913/456-8480

Antq. Emporium of Wamego
511 Lincoln St.
913/456-7111

Fulkerson's Antiques
206 Maple St.
913/456-917

42 WATHENA

Carousel Bed & Breakfast
Route 1
913/989-3537
Open year round; 7-10 p.m.

Directions: Approximately 15 miles west of I-29 and Highway 36 interchange. The B&B driveway comes off of Highway 36 three miles west of Wathena and 4 miles east of Troy, Kansas. (60 miles north of Kansas City and 9 miles west of St. Joseph, Missouri.)

Located on a country hillside with a gorgeous panoramic view of the glacial hills, the Carousel Bed and Breakfast has been beautifully restored to its 1917 splendor by innkeeper Betty Price, her husband, and her sister, Ginnie. The trio was the restoration crew responsible for the Victorian elegance evident throughout the home. Ginnie was the painter, Betty hung all the wallpaper while Mr. Price ran all the errands. If you look closely at the stairway spindles, you might observe a rather heavy coating of paint on them. It seems that Ginnie, in her efforts to perform the perfect task, got carried away and painted them five times! That night she dreamed that the stairway reached all the way to heaven and that she was painting every one of them.

This labor of love is especially evident in the Victorian parlor where personal touches have created a soothing environment for guests to relax. Victorian furnishings are placed throughout the home, further enhancing its aura.

Breakfast is served beginning at 7 a.m. for early birds who are eager to venture out into the beautiful surroundings that embrace The Carousel.

43 WICHITA

In 1865, Jesse Chisholm and James Mead established Wichita near a village of grass lodges built by the Wichita Indians. The settlement around their trading post soon attracted passing drovers along the Chisholm Trail, and Wichita boomed into a wide-open cowtown. Today you'll find remnants of Western history almost everywhere you look. Step back to the early years of the booming cattle town at Old Cowtown Museum. The 44 restored buildings and authentic characters will give you a true sense of Wichita in the 1870s. Visitors can see Wichita's first jail, a fully stocked general store, a one-room school, a saloon, a railroad depot, and also watch a blacksmith demonstrate his craft.

Across town is the historic Old Town District. It's one part of town you won't want to miss. This newly renovated warehouse district is packed full of antique shops, a variety of delightful restaurants, galleries and great night spots. And from May through October enjoy the Wichita Farm and Art Market, an open-air market of fresh produce, arts, and crafts.

Wooden Heart Antiques
141 S. Rock Island St.
316/267-1475
Open: Daily, evenings by appointment

Directions: 7 blocks off I-135 in the old town business district.

Wooden Heart Antiques is comprised of a large building filled to the rafters with oak, walnut, and mahogany furniture along with antique accessories and collectibles. The shop caters to the wholesale and retail customer.

White Eagle Antique Mall
10187 SW U.S. Highway 54
316/775-2812
Open Mon.-Sat., 10-9; Sun. 12-7
7 days a week

Directions: Travelers through Wichita on I-135 should take the East 54 (Kellogg) exit. Go east on U.S. Highway 54 (Kellogg) 16 miles. The mall is located on the south side of U.S. Highway 54. Travelers on I-35 (Kansas Turnpike) use exit 50 and go east on U.S. Highway 54 (Kellogg) 11 miles. The mall is located on the south side of U.S. Highway 54.

White Eagle Antique Mall billed as "A Collector's Dream Come True," is no disappointment. The mall features that hard-to-find, early petroleum and gas station memorabilia. With over 100 dealers, this place is attractively filled to the brim with high quality glassware, primitives, vintage clothing, old books, jewelry, lamps, old toys, pottery, tools, large and small furniture and other exceptional antiques.

The Castle Inn Riverside
1155 North River Boulevard
316/263-9300
1-800-580-1131

For specific information on The Castle Inn Riverside, see review this section.

Green Dragon's Books
2730 Boulevard Plaza
316/681-0746

Gay '90s Antique Shop
1303 N. Broadway St.
316/263-7421

Park City Antique Mall
6227 N. Broadway St.
316/744-2025

M. Ballard & Co.
920 Buffum St.
316/267-7831

River City Basket Co.
509 E. Douglas Ave.
316/265-1068

Douglas Avenue Antiques
517 E. Douglas Ave.
316/263-6454

Santa Fe Hse. /Old Town Glly.
630 E. Douglas Ave.
316/265-4736

S A Phillip Company
1109 E. Douglas Ave.
316/267-5730

Legacy Antiques
105 S. Emporia St.
316-267-2730

Variety Plus & Mills Stream
110 W. Harry St.
316-262-4299

Paradise Antique Mall
430 E. Harry St.
316/269-4441

KIS Antiques
724 N. Main St.
316/267-1357

A & A Antique Mall
2419 Maple St.
316/945-4250

Hewitt's Antiques
228 N. Market St.
316/264-2450

A Little Everything Antiques
2301 S. Meridian Ave.
316/945-3150

Reflections
550 North Rock Road
316/267-7477

Ice House Antiques
136 S. Oliver Rd. (Kechi)
316/744-2331

Somewhere In Time
30 N.W. Pkwy.
316/681-1007

Dorothy's Antqs. & Cllbls.
1515 E. Pawnee St.
316/265-6035

Yesterdays
535 N. Woodlawn St.
316/684-1900

Vanderkellen Galleries
701 E. 2nd St. N
316/264-0338

Country Sentiments
200 S. 61st St.
316/744-9403

Hephner Antiques
737 S. Washington St. #3
316/264-3284

Granny's Shanty
405 N. West St.
316/942-6222

44 WINFIELD

B & B Antiques
1102 E. 5th
316/221-0457

Virginia Jarvis Antiques
701 Main St.
316/221-1732

Antique Mall of Winfield
1400 Main St.
316/221-1065

Antiques Plus Mall
1820 Main St.
316/221-6699

Jenny's Treasures
919 Manning St.
316/221-9199

Notes

Kentucky

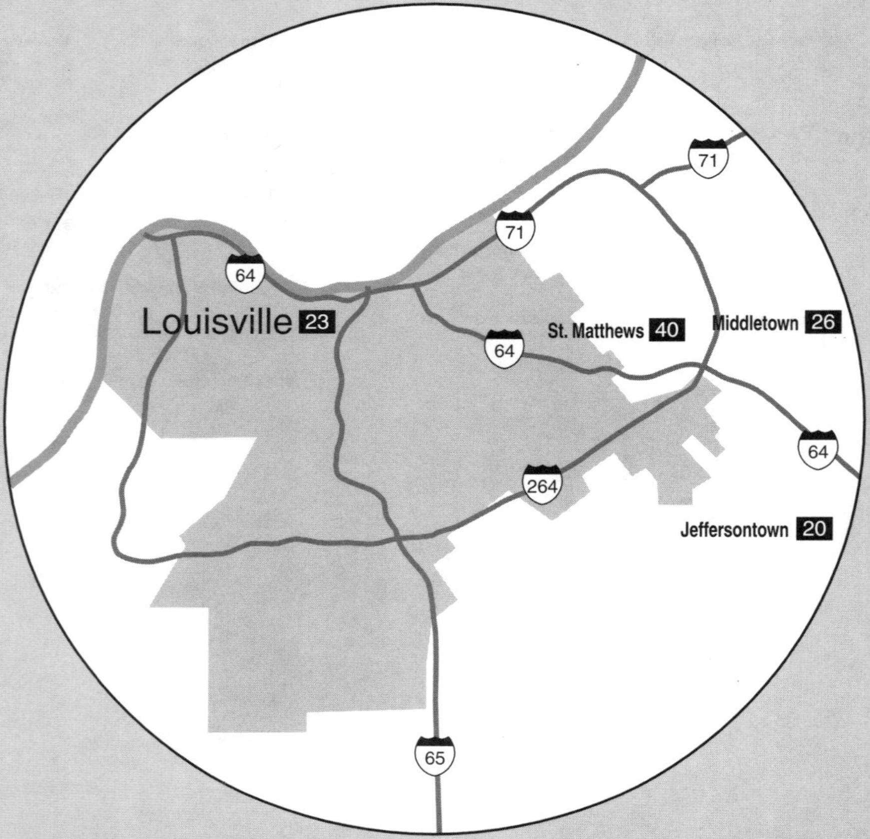

71
71
64
Louisville 23
St. Matthews 40
Middletown 26
64
64
264
Jeffersontown 20
65

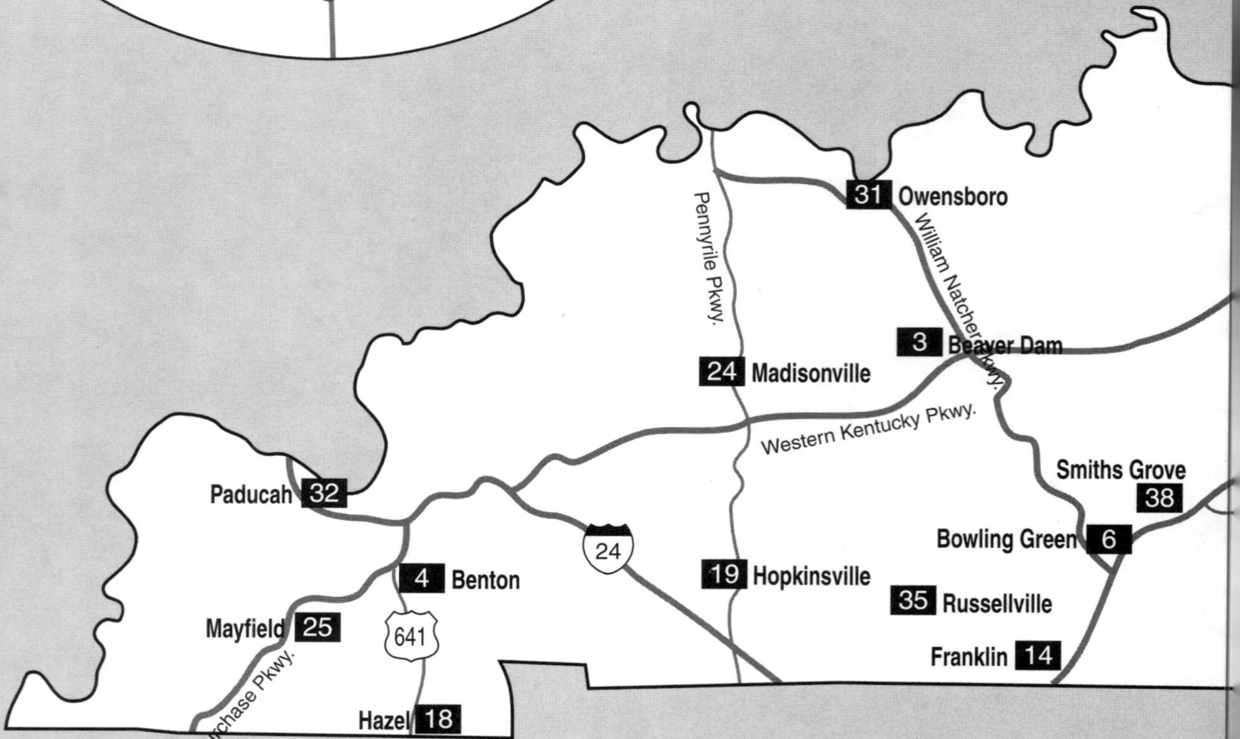

31 Owensboro
Pennyrile Pkwy.
William Natcher Pkwy.
3 Beaver Dam
24 Madisonville
Western Kentucky Pkwy.
Smiths Grove 38
Paducah 32
Bowling Green 6
24
19 Hopkinsville
4 Benton
35 Russellville
Mayfield 25
641
Franklin 14
Purchase Pkwy.
Hazel 18

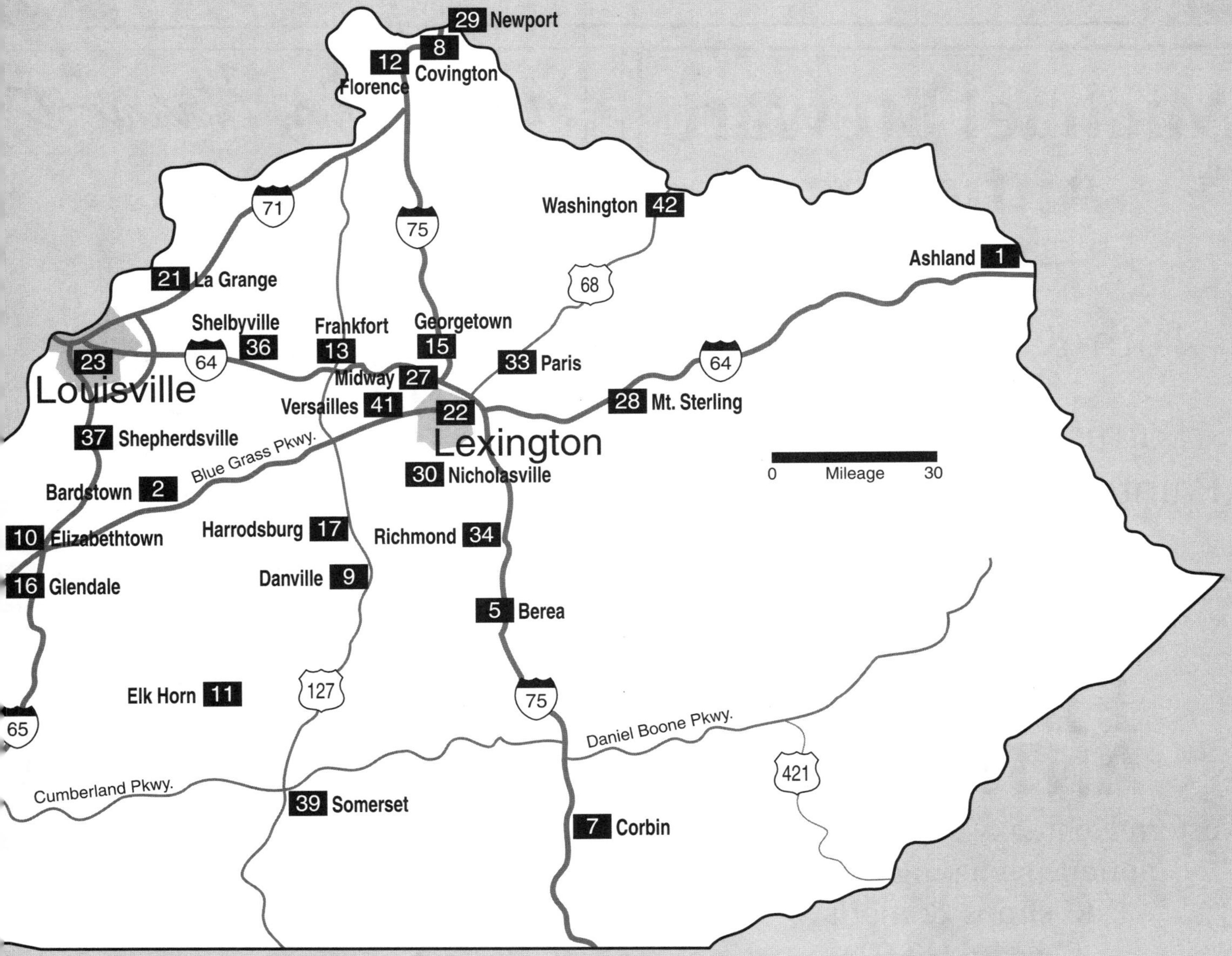

29 Newport
8
12
Covington
Florence
71
75
Washington 42
Ashland 1
68
21 La Grange
Shelbyville
Frankfort
Georgetown
36
13
15
23
64
33 Paris
Midway 27
64
Louisville
Versailles 41
22
28 Mt. Sterling
37 Shepherdsville
Lexington
Blue Grass Pkwy.
0 Mileage 30
30 Nicholasville
Bardstown 2
Harrodsburg 17
Richmond 34
10 Elizabethtown
16 Glendale
Danville 9
5 Berea
Elk Horn 11
127
75
65
Daniel Boone Pkwy.
421
Cumberland Pkwy.
39 Somerset
7 Corbin

Past Times

ANTIQUE MALL

14,000 sq. ft. of antiques & collectibles
135 W. Cumberland Gap Pkwy.
(606) 528-8818

Corbin

7

Michael Stewart Antiques

Featuring
18th & 19th Century

Furnishings • Books
Paintings • Accessories

Paducah

32

American Harvest Antiques

632 N. 6th & Park
Located in Historic
Downtown Paducah

502-442-4852

Specializing in Early Country
Furniture & accessories with
original paint or finish

Paducah

3

HAZEL ANTIQUES

Western Kentucky's oldest and largest
antique shopping district.
13 shops & malls

Find us on US Hwy 641 between
Murray, KY and Paris, TN
Open 7 days a week

Hazel

18

Farmer's Daughter Antiques

502-444-7619
Exit 3 Off I-24 —
Hwy 305 South —
6330 Cairo Road

Paducah

32

CENTRAL LOUISVILLE'S BEST ANTIQUE SHOPS AND MALLS

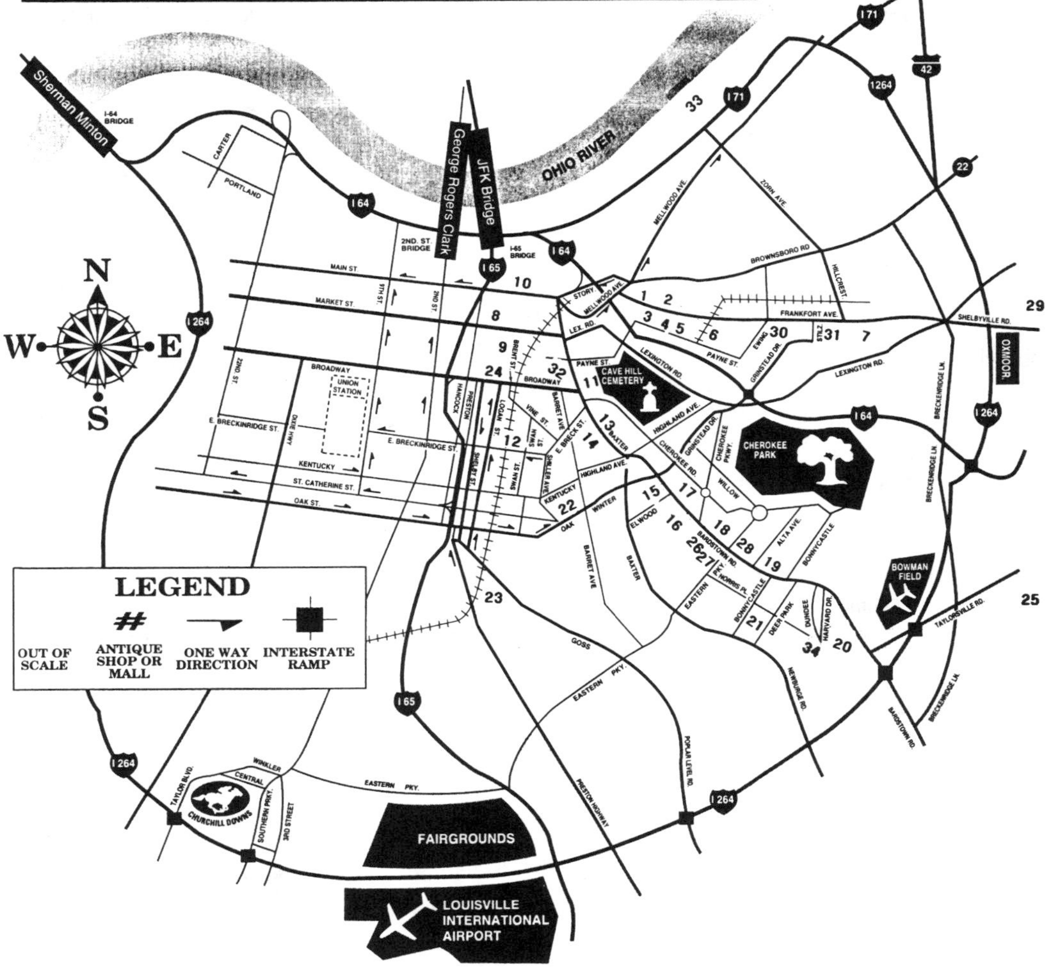

1. **Charmar Galleries**
   2005 Frankfort Avenue
   502/897-5565
2. **2023 Antiques**
   2023 Frankfort Avenue
   502/899-9872
3. **Scott F. Nussbaum Antiques**
   2036 Frankfort Avenue
   502/894-9292
4. **Henderson Antiques**
   2044 Frankfort Avenue
   502/895-6605
5. **Elizabeth's Timeless Attire**
   2050 Frankfort Avenue
   502/895-5911
6. **John Henry Sterry Antiques**
   2144 Frankfort Avenue
   502/897-1928
7. **Annie's Attic**
   3812 Frankfort Avenue
   502/897-1999
8. **Joe Ley Antiques**
   615 E. Market St.
   502/583-4014
9. **Nanny Goat Strut Antiques & Collectibles**
   638 E. Market St.
   502/584-4417 x104
10. **Bittners**
    731 E. Main Street
    502/584-6349
11. **Baxter AvenueAntique Mall**
    623-625 Baxter Ave.
    502/568-1582
12. **Swan Street Antique Mall**
    947 E. Breckinridge St.
    502/584-6255
13. **Steve White Gallery**
    945 Baxter Avenue
    502/458-9581
14. **Highland Antiques**
    940 Baxter Avenue
    502/583-0938
15. **Hanna's Place Antiques**
    1126 Bardstown Rd.
    502/589-3750
16. **Steve Tipton Antiques**
    1327 Bardstown Road
    502/451-0115
17. **Zigafoos...Antiques & Beyond**
    1287 Bardstown Road
    502/458-2340
18. **David Friedlander Antiques**
    1341 Bardstown Road
    502/458-7586
19. **Another Antique Shop**
    1565 Bardstown Road
    502/451-5876
20. **Antiques at the Loop**
    1940 Harvard Drive
    502/584-4248
21. **Forevermore**
    1734 Bonnycastle Avenue
    502/473-0021
22. **J. C. & Co. Dreamlight**
    1004 Barret Avenue
    502/456-4106
23. **Louisville Antique Mall**
    900 Goss Avenue
    502/635-2852
24. **Antiques on Broadway**
    821 E. Broadway
    502/584-4248
25. **Schumann Antiques**
    4545 Taylorsville Road
    502/491-0134
26. **Frances Lee Jasper Rugs**
    1330 Bardstown Road
    502/459-1044
27. **The Eclectic Jones**
    1570 Bardstown Road
    502/473-0396
28. **Children's Planet**
    1349 Bardstown Road
    502/458-7018
29. **Annie's Attic**
    12410 Shelbyville Road
    502/244-0303
30. **The Weekend Antiques**
    2910 Frankfort Avenue
    502/897-1212
31. **Mary Lou Duke**
    2916 Frankfort Avenue
    502/893-6577
32. **Attic Treasures**
    600 Baxter Avenue
    502/587-9543
33. **Louisville Visual Art Assoc.**
    3005 River Road
    502/896-2146
34. **Red Geranium Shop**
    1938 Harvard Drive
    502/454-5777

Kentucky

1 ASHLAND

Tunnel Hill Antique Shoppe
1827 6th St.
606/324-6880

Miners Coins & Antiques
830 29th St.
606/325-9425

Vintage Hall
By Appointment Only
606/329-1173

2 BARDSTOWN

Jailer's Inn
111 West Stephen Foster Avenue
502/348-5551 or 800/948-5551
Open February through December, closed January

Ever wondered what it would be like to spend a night or two in jail? Well you can—sort of—if you stay at the Jailer's Inn in Bardstown! This 1819 building (listed on the National Register) was originally built as a jail, with prisoners housed and the jailer living below. In 1874 prisoners were moved to a new jail built right behind this old one, and the old building became the jailer's official permanent residence. Believe it or not, both buildings were used for the original purposes until 1987! The complex was then declared the oldest operating jail in the state of Kentucky! Now the 1819 building has been completely renovated into six individually decorated guest rooms filled with antiques, original rugs and heirlooms. Guest quarters range from the Victorian Room and the Garden Room to the former women's cell, which is decorated in prison black and white and features two of the original bunk beds plus a more modern waterbed. One room even has a jacuzzi. Guests are treated to a filling continental-plus breakfast and refreshments.

Town and Country Antiques
118 N. 3rd St.
502/348-3967

3 BEAVER DAM

Ohio County is older than the Commonwealth of Kentucky and was named for the Ohio River, which was originally its northern boundary. It is the fifth-largest county in Kentucky—located 23 miles south of Owensboro, 40 miles north of Bowling Green, 100 miles southwest of Louisville, and 90 miles north of Nashville, Tenn.

Downtown Antique Mall
103 N. Main
502/274-4774

Casey's Antiques & Collectibles
116 N. Main
No phone listed

Past & Presents Antiques
930 N. Main
502/274-3360 or 502/274-7124

Tomorrow's Trsr. Doll Shop
108 N. Main
502/274-7946

Knob Hill Antiques
282 Knob Hill Road
502/274-3065

Pat's Antiques & Collectibles
Highway 269 off of Highway 231
502/274-3076

Flower Land Antiques
1202 N. Main
502/274-4488

Hotel Tillford
101 N. Main
502/274-4701

Reflections of the Old & New
340 S. Main
502/274-7980

Beaver Dam Auction
200 E. 3rd
502/274-3349

Papa's Playhouse
724 Buttermilk Lane
502/274-7558

Lee's
116 Main
502/274-3108

Capp's Mini Mall
110 W. 3rd
502/274-7367

4 BENTON

Answer
321 Main
502/527-1078

The Antique Mall
600 Main
502/527-2085

Antiques Et Cetera
1026 Main St.
502/527-7922

Treasured Memories
1207 Main St.
502/527-0039

Benton Antiques & Collectibles
103 W. 13th St.
502/527-5424

5 BEREA

Berea Antique Gallery
408 Chestnut St.
606/986-7722

Chestnut St. Antique Mall Inc.
420 Chestnut St.
606/986-2883

Bay Window Antiques
436 Chestnut St.
606/986-2345

Something Olde
437 Chestnut St.
606/986-6057

Bratcher's Antiques
438 Chestnut
606/986-7325

Place In Time
440 Chestnut St.
606/986-7301

Todd's Antique Mall
7435 Highway 21 E
606/986-9087

Impressions of Berea
116 McKinney Dr.
606/986-8177

Howard's Antique Mall
573 Mount Vernon Rd.
606/986-9551

Appletree Antiques & Cllbls.
621 Mount Vernon Rd.
606/986-6121

Teresa's Antiques & Art Gallery
702 Prospect St.
606/986-9147

6 BOWLING GREEN

River Bend Antique Mall
315 Beech Bend Rd.
502/781-5773

Ax Handle Antiques
2441 Stonebridge Lane
502/782-1541

Daniel's Wicker
2125 Bill Dedmon Rd.
502/842-6926

Precious Memories
1224 Indianola St.
502/842-3201

Loulees Memory Lane
2926 Louisville Rd.
502/781-0653

Nedas Antiques & Collectibles
5397 Louisville Rd.
502/843-9656

Kreisler Antiques & Gifts
422 E. Main St.
502/843-1400

Greenwood Mall
Scottsville Rd.
502/781-9655

Werner-Lowe Ltd.
1232 U.S. 31 W. Bypass
502/796-2683

Timeless Treasures
1058 U.S. 31 W. Bypass
502/781-3698

Favorite Places To Eat

Cracker Barrel Old Country Store
I-65 & Hwy. 231, Exit 22
502/843-8087

7 CORBIN

Past Times Antique Mall, Inc.
135 W. Cumberland Gap Parkway
606/528-8818
Open daily 9-6 Mon.-Sat., 11-6 Sun.

Directions: From I-75: take Exit 29 east. At the first traffic light make a right turn. Past Times is located behind Burger King and Super 8 Motel.

Past Times houses some interesting things in its 14,000 square feet of space. Its 95 booths hold the general consignment of furniture, primitives, collectibles, etc., with a great deal of glassware, plus railroad and mining memorabilia, plus a very active trade in antique knives, period safety razors, etc.

Meadow Land Antiques & Collectibles
3475 Cumberland Falls Hwy.
606/523-2803

Favorite Places To Eat

Cracker Barrel Old Country Store
I-75 & Hwy. 25 East, Exit 29
606/523-0522

8 COVINGTON

The World's Largest Outdoor Sale
August 14-17

Covington is the northern starting point...and the roadside bargains extend south to Alabama! Pack a lunch and hop in the car for this 450-mile shopping adventure. 513/357-MAIN.

Sentimento Antique & Cllbls.
525 Main St.
606/291-9705

Philadelphia Street Antiques
526 Philadelphia St.
606/431-6866

Mertacks Ltd.
440 Scott St.
606/431-3311

9 DANVILLE

History abounds in the picturesque community of Danville, 35 miles southwest of Lexington. The Rhodes House (305 North Third, where *Raintree County* was filmed in 1956) is just one of the 50 sites on the city's walking tour. The visitor center is in the beautiful Greek Revival McClure-Barbee House (304 South Fourth, Monday through Friday, 9 a.m. to 4 p.m., 800/755-0076). Danville's internationally recognized Great American Brass Band Festival is in mid-June.

Ten constitutional conventions took place at Constitution Square State Historic Site (134 South

Second) between 1784 and 1792. The park includes the original pre-1792 post office (the first west of the Alleghenies!), Governor's Circle, and replica meetinghouse, courthouse and jail. You'll also see the 1817 Fisher's Row houses, now an art gallery; the historical society museum in the Watts-Bell House featuring a great collection of vintage clothing.

A Leigh & Company
128 S 4th St.
606/236-2137

Antique Mall of Hist. Danville
158 N. 3rd St.
606/236-3026

Annies Loft
By Appointment Only
606/236-6735

10 ELIZABETHTOWN

Elizabethtown, 35 miles south of Louisville, has a wealth of American history including ties to Abraham Lincoln's family. The walking tour on Thursdays (free, June through September, 7:00 p.m.) has costumed characters from the town's past such as Carrie Nation, General George Custer and Sarah Bush Lincoln.

Around the corner is the 1825 Brown-Pusey House, the town's first haven for travelers. This stately Georgian colonial building housed General Custer and his wife in the 1870s.

Back Home
251 W. Dixie Ave
502/769-2800

Irene's Antiques
407 E. Dixie Ave
502/737-2552

Antiques & Things
618 E. Dixie Ave
502/769-9691

Buckboard Antiques
125 Hillsdale Drive
502/737-0589

Heartland Antique Mall
707 E. Dixie Ave
502/737-8566

Touch of the Past Antiques
9 Houchens Plaza
502/765-2579

Goldnamers
210 N. Main St.
502/766-1994

Elizabethtown Antique Mall
516 N. Main St.
502/769-3959

Addington Antiques
711 W. Park Rd.
502/765-6456

Favorite Places To Eat

Cracker Barrel Old Country Store
I-65 & Hwy. 62, Exit 94
502/765-5525

11 ELKHORN

Piece of the Past
466 Elkhorn
502/465-3171

12 FLORENCE

Favorite Places To Eat

Cracker Barrel Old Country Store
I-75 & Turfway Rd., Exit 182
606/283-0101

13 FRANKFORT

Frankfort, chosen the state capital in 1792, is nestled among the rolling hills of the Bluegrass in a beautiful Kentucky River valley. Much of Kentucky's history has been written here—old frontiersman Simon Kenton pleaded relief from taxes, Henry Clay practiced his oratory, former Vice President Aaron Burr was charged with treason—the stories go on and on.

Button Box
123 Brighton Park Blvd.
502/695-7108

Ron-Jo's Antiques & Cllbls.
227 Broadway St.
502/223-5466

Poor Richard's Books
233 W. Broadway St.
502/223-8018

Old Capitol Antiques
239 W Broadway
502/223-3879

Treadle Works
333 W Broadway St.
502/223-2571

Rail Fence Antiques
415 W Broadway St.
502/875-5040

Kelliance Antiques
950 Louisville Rd.
502/223-4770

Gift Box
1500 Louisville Rd.
502/223-2784

14 FRANKLIN

A surveyor's mistake created the Kentucky-Tennessee "Triangular Jag," a small piece of land that forms Simpson County's southern border. The muddy waters of legal ownership made the area a safe place for duelists to avoid the law. The Sanford Duncan Inn, six miles south of Franklin, was a popular overnight stop for guests such as General Sam Houston, before meeting at nearby Linkumpinch to settle their "gentlemanly disputes."

Franklin's downtown historic district includes the Simpson County Archives & Museum in the old jailer's residence, with wall drawings left by Civil War soldiers held prisoner here (free, Monday-Friday, 206 North College, 502/586-4228).

Strickly Country Antique Mall
5945 Bowling Green Rd.
502/586-3978

Main St. Antiques & Cllbls.
207 N. Main St.
502/586-6104

Miss Penny's Antique Mall
272 Trotters Lane
502/586-9951

Heritage Antique Mall
111 W. Washington St.
502/586-3880

Favorite Places To Eat

Cracker Barrel Old Country Store
I-65 & 31 West, Exit 2
502/586-4675

15 GEORGETOWN

Georgetown was founded in 1790 by the Baptist minister Elijah Craig. He is best known for his world famous invention, "bourbon" whiskey. You'll see where he drew water when you visit Royal Spring Park (Water and West Main). Also see the mini-local history museum in an authentic 1874 log cabin built by former slave Milton Leach. Don't miss great antique shopping downtown in one of the most picturesque Victorian areas in the state.

Blackridge Hall
4055 Paris Pike
502/863-2069 or 1-800-768-9308
Rates: $89-159

Staying at Blackridge Hall gives guests a taste of the elegance of Southern lifestyle in Kentucky's fabled Bluegrass region. This is a luxurious Southern Georgia-style mansion on five acres in Bluegrass horse country. There are five guest rooms, all with private baths, and all filled with antiques and reproductions. Two of the master suites have jacuzzis. Every morning a full gourmet breakfast is served in either the dining room or on the veranda. And it's all located just minutes to Lexington, Keeneland and Red Mile Racetracks, University of Kentucky, Toyota Motor Corporations Tours, and all those historic Georgetown antique shops.

Den of Antiquity
100 W. Main St.
502/863-7536

Central Kentucky Antique Mall
114 E. Main St.
502/863-4018

Pooh's Place
122 E. Main St.
502/867-3930

Georgetown Antique Mall
124 W. Main St.
502/863-9033

Trojan Antiques Gallery
130 N. Broadway St.
502/867-1823

Wyatts Antique Center
149 E. Main St.
502/863-0331

Favorite Places To Eat

Cracker Barrel Old Country Store
I-75 & Hwy. 62, Exit 126
502/863-5670

16 GLENDALE

Don't miss the charming Historic Register community of Glendale, 7 miles south of Elizabethtown off I-65, Exit 86. Antique malls, shops and a country store line the street bisected by the L & N railroad crossing. Enjoy great food at The Whistle Stop, 502/369-8586, or The Depot, 502/369-6000. Most shops are open Tuesday through Saturday 11 a.m.-6 p.m. The annual Glendale Crossing Festival is in October.

Log Cabin Antique Shop
101 Jaggers Rd.
502/369-6001

Ivy Gate
120 E. Main St.
502/369-6343

Crow's Nest
138 Main St.
502/369-6060

Side Track Shops
212 E. Main St.
502/369-8766

Sisters
1 Block off Main
502/369-8604

A Step Back Antiques
College Street
502/369-6122

Through the Grapevine
1 Block off Main
502/369-7925

Bennies Barn
434 E. Main St.
502/369-9677

Glendale Antique Mall
103 W. Railroad Ave
502/369-7279

Ramona's Antiques
122 E. Railroad
502/369-9652

17 HARRODSBURG

Once a frontier territory, Harrodsville was founded in 1774 as the first permanent English settlement west of the Allegheny Mountains. On the walking and driving tours, spanning more than 200 years of history, you'll pass by stately pre-Civil War homes, churches and businesses representing various architectural styles. Morgan Row, 220-232 S. Chiles, is the oldest rowhouse standing in Kentucky. While on Main, don't miss a stroll through Olde Towne Park featuring a cascading fountain.

A highlight of the historic community is Beaumont Inn, built on the site of the Greenville Springs Spa. It was constructed in 1845 as one of the South's most prestigious girls schools. Since 1919, it has operated as a country inn under four generations of the same family (638 Beaumont Inn Drive, 606/734-3381).

North Main Center Antique Mall
520 North Main Street
606/734-2200
Open Mon.-Sat. 10-5, Sun. 1-5, closed Wednesdays

Owner Nena Inden has loved antiques since she was a teenager, so what better business to get into than owning an antique store? She has over 22,000 square feet filled with Victorian pieces, primitives, china, glassware, '50s collectibles, jewelry, silver, old prints, frames, and children's toys.

But the real treat would be to see Nena and husband Christian's home, fabulous Ashfeld Manor. This 1891 stone mansion, complete with a four-story tower, is about 8,000 square feet of breathtaking old-world craftsmanship and opulence. Every room is made of a different wood, with hand-carved fireplaces, French chandeliers, and original wainscotting.

Old Kentucky Restorations
122 W. Lexington St.
606/734-6237

Granny's Antique Mall
1286 Louisville Rd.
606/734-2327

J Sampson Antiques & Books
107 S. Main St.
606/734-7829

Harrodsburg Antique Mall
123 S. Main St.
606/733-9555

Main Street Antiques
221 S. Main St.
606/734-2023

Tomorrows Another Day
117 Poplar St.
606/734-9197

18 HAZEL

Easily reached by antique hounds in four states (Tennessee, Kentucky, Arkansas and the Missouri Bootheel), Hazel is western Kentucky's oldest and largest antique shopping district. Located on U.S. Highway 641 at the Kentucky/Tennessee state line just east of the fabulous Land Between The Lakes, this tiny turn-of-the-century community has been transformed into an antique shopper's heaven. Almost all the storefronts are now antique shops or malls, offering a smorgasbord of antiques and collectibles.

There are several annual festivals and open houses in Hazel targeted for antique lovers.

* Freedom Fest-July 4, 1997, with decorations, fireworks, and special deals on antiques throughout town.

* Hazel's Celebration-Oct. 4, an old-time country street festival. Hazel's population is 500; this festival draws 8,000! There's food, entertainment, art, cloggers, even the winning lottery ticket is drawn here!

* Christmas Open house (sponsored by the Antique Dealers Association)-Saturday after Thanksgiving, all the shops in town have refreshments, decorations and carolers.

Miss Bradie's Antiques and Christmas
304 Dees Street (Dees and Main)
502/492-8796
Open daily except Thanksgiving Day and Christmas Day, Mon.-Sat. 10-5, Sun. 12:30-5

Here's a good stop for early Christmas shoppers. Miss Bradie's specializes in antiques and decorative accessories and also features a year-round Christmas room. Owner Jo McKinley is an authorized dealer for Christopher Radko glass ornaments, Old World Christmas, Annalee Dolls and Boyds Bears. Indulge your shopping habit and get those pesky Christmas shopping chores out of the way at the same, enjoyable time!

Ginger's Antiques and Refinishing
310 Main Street, P.O. Box 37
502/492-8138
Open daily Mon.-Sat. 10-4:30, Sun. 1-4:30

Among the many antique shops in Hazel is Ginger's. They offer not only the wares of 12 dealers, but folks can visit Ginger's 3rd Floor Candy Store. The candy store is like an old-fashioned general store, with big glass jars full of Mrs. Burton's Gourmet candy, lots of jams and jellies, different kinds of honey, and all the luscious things that used to fascinate kids in an old-fashioned candy store! They also have a soda fountain in the candy store, so shoppers can quench their thirst after all that buying!

Miss Martha's Antiques
302 Main Street
502/492-8145
Open daily 10-4:30

Bill Price has been offering a general variety of antiques, including primitives, kitchen collectibles and furniture, to the public for 14 years. During these years, he has had the opportunity to see and hear lots of funny stories from his customers and shoppers. Here's one of the stories he has to tell:

Two ladies came into my shop several years ago late on a Saturday afternoon. They had spent the day at the Heart of Country Show in Nashville and had decided to come to Hazel on their way home. They had obviously had a good time and had probably stopped somewhere for a lunch that had included a couple of Bloody Marys. One of the ladies immediately began picking up items and talking about how much cheaper things were here than at the show (naturally!). She began making a pile of things on my check-out counter. She would put something on the counter then go back for more. Each time she put something in her pile, her friend would say, "Oh, Roger's gonna kill you!" The first lady would find something else she wanted and her friend would say, "Oh, Roger's gonna kill you!" This went on for a while, and after about three or four of these comments, the happy shopper stopped and looked at her friend. "Listen," she said, "When I first started going out on these shopping trips, Roger used to worry about how much money I had with me or whether or not I had the checkbook with me. Later, he'd be nervous if I went out and took the credit card with me. Now when I get home, the only thing Roger asks is, "Is anybody shipping anything?"

Country Collectibles
Main Street, P.O. Box 258
502/492-8121
Open Tue.-Sat. 10-4:30, Sun. 1-4:30, closed Mondays

This collection cache offers the shopping public Victorian furnishings, primitives and glassware.

Hazel Antique Mall & Flea Market
Route 2, Box 169AAA
502/492-6168
Open Mon.-Sat. 8-5

An all-purpose, well-rounded antique shop and flea market, the mall is located approximately 2 miles north of Hazel's antique district on U.S. Highway 641.

Horse's Mouth Antiques
308 Main Street, Box 207
502/492-8128
Open daily 10-4:30

The name of the shop makes you grin, but if you're into crystal, silver, china, old kerosene lamps and Aladdin lamps, you won't want to miss this stop!

Decades Ago Antique Mall
317 Main Street
502/492-8140
Open year round 10-4:30 Mon.-Sat., 1-4:30 Sun.

Decades Ago—it sounds like the beginning of a bedtime story, doesn't it? It is a multi-dealer mall with more than 90 exhibitors plus showcases filled with wonderful antiques and collectibles.

Memory Lane Antiques
P.O. Box 155
502/492-8646
Open daily 10-4:30 Mon.-Sat., 1-4:30 Sun.

For the past two years Larry Elkins' mall has offered 25 booths that carry a variety of furniture, glass, collectibles, primitives and other items, catering to both the individual shoppers and to dealers.

Tooters Antique Mall
209 3rd Street
502/492-6111
Open daily Mon.-Sat. 10-4:30, Sun 1-4:30 (winter) and Mon.-Sat. 10-5:30, Sun. 1-4:30 (summer)

Snacks and drinks are available when you take a break from strolling through this 8,000 square foot, multi-dealer mall with showcases and more than 40 booths.

Retro-Wares
306 Main Street, P.O. Box 251
502/492-8164
Open daily, Mon.-Sat. 10:30-4:30, Sun. 1-4:30

Situated in the heart of Hazel's antique district, this is the place to find those neat chrome and vinyl retro things. The shop specializes in mid-century furnishings and art deco, with a large collection of costume jewelry, limited edition Barbies, and fashion flashbacks.

Vintage Selections
312 Center Street
Open Wed.-Sun. 11-5

If you still like to "play" dress up, or if you like to do more than imagine yourself in the clothes of days gone by, Vintage Selections has a wide variety of vintage clothing, ranging from the very old through the hippy days of the 1970s.

Idle Hour Antiques
Main Street, P.O. Box 42
502/492-8180
Open by appointment or by chance

Idle Hour Antiques is another Hazel Shop that specializes in Victorian furnishings and collectibles.

Charlie's Antique Mall & Soda Fountain
303 Main Street
502/492-8175
Open daily 10-4:30 Mon.-Fri., 10:30-5 Sat., 1-4:30 Sun.

This 60-dealer mall offers not only an appealing variety of antiques, but an assortment of fountain treats as an added dividend. They serve ice cream, sodas, shakes, and malts at the old-fashioned soda fountain, so you can rest and revive between browsing and buying!

19 HOPKINSVILLE

The Antique Mall
Main St.
502/887-9363

The Snoop Shop
Main St.
502/889-0360

Country Boy Stores
Newstead Rd.
502/885-5914

Quidas Antiques
1301 E 9th St.
502/886-6141

Rubadues Variety Store
8410 Princeton Rd.
502/886-3974

Forget-Me-Nots Antiques
110 E. 6th St.
502/885-5556

20 JEFFERSONTOWN

Favorite Places To Eat

Cracker Barrel Old Country Store
I-64 & Blankenbaker Rd., Exit 17
502/266-8895

21 LA GRANGE

Heirlooms
110 E. Main St.
502/222-4149

Iron Horse Antiques
119 E. Main St.
502/222-0382

Primrose Antiques
123 E. Main St.
502/222-8918

Three Peas In Pod
125 E. Main St.
502/222-2139

Favorite Places To Eat

Cracker Barrel Old Country Store
I-71 & State Route 53, Exit 22
502/222-1156

22 LEXINGTON

Boone's Antiques of Kentucky, Inc.
4996 Old Versailles Road
606/254-5335
Open Mon.-Sat. 8:30-5:30

Directions: From Highway 75: Follow all the signs to the airport, then pass the entrance on Man-of-War. Stay on Highway 60 west. Boone's is located on Highway 60 west, 1 1/2 miles from the airport, 3/4 miles from Keeland Race Track. From Highway 64: Take Highway 60 east when approaching Castle. Go to the top of the hill to the caution light, then right on Old Versailles Road.

Boone's offers 27,000 square feet of English, French and American Antiques. They carry everything from furniture and rugs to porcelains and unusual accent pieces.

Pless Antiques
247 N. Broadway St.
606/252-4842

Lutes Antiques
807 E. Euclid Ave.
606/266-1109

Country Antique Mall
1455 Leestown Rd.
606/233-0075

Gift Box
171 N. Lowry Lane
606/278-2399

Heritage Antiques
380 E. Main St.
606/253-1035

Gallery One
401 W. Main St.
606/225-1247

Zee Faulkner Antiques
509 E. Main St.
606/252-1309

Antiquities
636 W. Main St.
606/255-5912

Lexington Antique Gallery
637 E. Main St.
606/231-8197

Eclections
320 W. 2nd St.
606/225-5177

Clock Shop
154 W. Short St.
606/255-6936

Antique Mall at Todds Square
535 W. Short St.
606/252-0296

Mike Maloney Antiques
303 Southland Dr.
606-275-1934

O'Loves Cllbl Antiques
410 W. Vine St. #149
606/253-0611

Cowgirl Attic
220 Walton Ave.
606/225-3876

Blue Grass Bazaar
246 Walton Ave.
606/259-0303

Favorite Places To Eat

Cracker Barrel Old Country Store
I-75 & Newtown Pike, Exit 115
606/233-7684

Cracker Barrel Old Country Store
I-75 & Winchester Rd., Exit 110
606/293-2555

23 LOUISVILLE

Some people call is "Louaval," others say "Louieville," but regardless of how you pronounce it, you'll find plenty of things to see and do in Kentucky's largest city. Louisville is a blend of restored historic sites and sparkling new structures, fine arts and architecture, horses and sports, and more park acreage than any other city in the country.

The excitement in Louisville comes to a fevered pitch each year during the Kentucky Derby Festival, one of the country's largest civic celebrations, beginning with the "Thunder Over Louisville" fireworks extravaganza and ending with the "Run for the Roses," the one and only Kentucky Derby (April 19 through May 5, 502/584-6383).

Louisville is a treat for antique shopping. The largest malls are Den of Steven, Joe Ley Antiques, and Louisville Antique Mall.

St. James Court Art Show
October 3-5
For more information call: 502/635-1842

Historic Old Louisville marks the spot for this treasure hunting adventure also known as one of the largest outdoor art shows in the nation! Explore tree-lined streets of this grand 'ole Victorian neighborhood to unearth a king's ransom of trinkets and treasures. This one is more than a must-see, it's a must-BE!

Tin Horse Antiques
1040 Bardstown Rd.
502/584-1925

Archibald Geneva Galleries
1044 Bardstown Rd.
502/587-1728

Alines Antiques
1130 Bardstown Rd.
502/473-0525

As Time Goes By
1310 Bardstown Rd.
502/458-5774

Kentucky

Steve Tipton Ltd
1327 Bardstown Rd.
502/451-0115

Discoveries
1315 Bardstown Rd.
502/451-5034

David R Friedlander Antiques
1341 Bardstown Rd.
502/458-7586

Blanches Antiques
1416 Bardstown Rd.
502/452-2209

All Booked Up
1555 Bardstown Rd.
502/459-6348

Another Antique Shop
1565 Bardstown Rd.
502/451-5876

Century Shop
1703 Bardstown Rd.
502/451-7692

Den of Steven Antiques Gallery
945 Baxter
502/458-9581

Swan Street Antique Mall
947 E. Breckinridge St.
502/584-6255

Architectural Salvage
618 E. Broadway
502/589-0670

Antiques on Broadway
821 Broadway
502/584-4248

Isaacs & Isaacs
3937 Chenoweth Square
502/894-8333

Louisville Antique Mall
900 Goss Ave.
502/635-2852

Kathryn's
1008 Goss Ave.
502/637-7479

Red Geranium Shop
1938 Harvard Dr.
502/454-5777

Candyjacks Antique Store
703 Lyndon Lane
502/429-6420

Jan's Antique Shop
704 Lyndon Lane
502/426-0828

Madalyn's Antiques
712 Lyndon Lane
502/425-9700

Antique Galleries
8601 W Manslick Rd.
502/363-3326

Towne House Antiques
612 E Market St.
502/585-4456

Joe Ley Antiques Inc.
615 E Market St.
502/583-4014

Middletown Antiques
11509 Old Shelbyville Rd.
502/244-1780

Annie's & Mine
12123 Old Shelbyville Rd.
502/254-9366

Pieces of Olde Antiques
11405 Old Shelbyville Rd.
502/244-3522

Red Barn Mall
12125 Old Shelbyville Rd.
502/245-8330

Schumann Antiques
4545 Taylorsville Rd.
502/491-0134

Holland House
129 D Saint Matthews Ave.
502/895-2707

Annie's Attic
104 Cannons Lane
502/894-0606

24 MADISONVILLE

Ole House Antique Mall
343 E Center St.
502/821-4020

Kesterson's Antiques
502 Hall St.
502/821-7311

Country Store Antiques & Crafts
455 S Madison Ave.
502/825-1556

25 MAYFIELD

Mayberry Antique Mall
114 W. Broadway St.
502/247-1979

Country Corner
Hwy. 97/Sedalia Rd.
502/247-9361

Remember When Antiques
Paris Rd.
502/247-7228

Collector's Shop
104 W. South St.
502/247-1706

26 MIDDLETOWN

Annie's Attic
12410 Shelbyville Road
502/244-0303

27 MIDWAY

Gordon H. Greek Antiques
204 N. Gratz St.
606/846-4336

Midway Antiques Gallery
138 E. Main St.
606/846-5669

Eagles Nest Antiques
126 Railroad St.
606/846-4652

D Lehman & Sons
100 Winter St. N
606/846-4513

28 MT. STERLING

Favorite Places To Eat

Cracker Barrel Old Country Store
I-64 & W.S. 460, Exit 110

29 NEWPORT

R & L Collectibles & Etc.
602 Monmouth St.
606/431-2230

471 Antique Mall
901 E. 6th St.
606/431-4753

Peluso Antique Shop
649 York St.
606/291-2870

30 NICHOLASVILLE

Rockinghorse Antique Mall
120 N. Main St.
606/885-7893

Coach Light Antique Mall
213 N. Main St.
606/887-4223

Antiques on Main
221 N. Main St.
606/887-2767

31 OWENSBORO

Spend A Buck Galleries
210 Allen St.
502/685-5025

Three Generations Antiques
223 Saint Ann St.
502/688-5991

Peachtree Galleries Antiques
104 W. 2nd St.
502/683-6937

Peachtree Galleries
105 W. 2nd St.
502/926-1081

Plantation Antiques
113 E. 2nd St.
502/683-3314

Owensboro Antique Mall
500 W. 3rd St.
502/684-3003

Downstairs Attic Country Store
2753 Veach Rd.
502/684-1819

Antiques & Collectibles
724 W. 2nd St.
No Phone

Antiques & Reproductions
818 E. Fourth St.
502/685-1554

Second Avenue Antiques
109 E. 2nd St.
502/683-0308

32 PADUCAH

Michael Stewart Antiques
136 Lone Oak Road
502/441-7222
Open by chance or appointment

Directions: From I-24 take Exit 7. Travel east on Lone Oak Road 1 1/2 miles. The shop is located on the right side of the street, a 1/2 block before Broadway.

Michael Stewart specializes in 18th and 19th century furniture, paintings, books, maps and accessories. The shop handles primarily English and American furniture, and occasionally French. Civil War and 19th century maps, 19th century American and European paintings, and leather-bound 19th century books, either in complete sets or single volumes, are found here.

The 1857s Bed and Breakfast
127 Market House Square
502/444-3960 or 1-800-264-5607
Rates: $65-85

This three-story, friendly-featured brick Victorian home offers everything needed for a complete and secluded weekend getaway. Listed on the National Register of Historic Places, the first floor holds Cynthia's Ristorante. Two guest rooms and a bath are on the second floor, and the third floor holds a family room and game room with hot tub and billiards table. All this is located in the downtown historic district, with antique stores, carriage rides, a quilt museum, lots of restaurants, and the Market House Cultural Center within walking distance. Guests may choose to book the entire second floor with private bath, if they want true privacy.

American Harvest Antiques
632 N. 6th Street
502/442-4852
Wed. 10-5 and Sat. 10-4 or anytime by appointment

Directions: Traveling I-24: Take Exit 4. Travel east approximately 5 miles toward historic downtown Paducah. Turn left on North 6th Street. American Harvest is located at the end of the block on the corner of North 6th and Park Avenue.

This interesting arrangement was originally a four-dealer group that has now, unfortunately, had to become three because of one member's health. The four women who started the shop have all been dealers and friends for many years, traveling and buying together all over the region. They decided to open the shop together because their tastes and ideas are similar and because, as one said, "We just love it!"

Lisha Holt, Sharon Clymer and Brenda Jones, along with retired member/dealer Wilma Becker, opened American Harvest antiques in historic downtown Paducah in an old grocery building. They also have the historic shotgun house next door filled with antiques. These ladies specialize in early American country furniture and accessories-from large pieces on down-with original paint or surface.

Farmer's Daughter Antiques
6330 Cairo Road
502/444-7619 or 502/443-5450
Open Wed.-Sat. 10-5, Sun. 1-5, closed Mon.-Tue.

Directions: From I-24 take Exit 3 onto Highway 305 South. The shop is just 1 1/2 miles from I-24 on Cairo Road.

This cutely-named shop holds 2,400 square feet of browsing pleasure for all who stop to look around. Noted for its wide variety of quality antiques such as oak and country furniture, kitchen wares, tools, old toys, fishing collectibles, decoys, quilts, linens, advertising memorabilia and more. Jane's love for "old things" is evident in her creative design of display throughout the store. This is a "must stop" for the decorator who loves country furnishings and accessories at a reasonable price.

American Quilter's Society National Show and Contest
Held in April each year.
For more information call: 502/898-7903

More than $80,000 in prizes draws the best quilters and their heirlooms to this national competition. Exhibits and workshops complete this quilt-crazy festival in Paducah, home of the museum of American Quilter's Society.

Antiques Cards & Cllbls., Inc.
203 Broadway St.
502/443-9797

Romantique
209 Broadway St.
502/575-0271

Broadway House Antiques
229 Broadway St.
502/575-9025

Rayburn-Smith, Inc.
2205 Broadway St.
502/444-0668

Market Antqs. & Cllbls. Shop
401 Jefferson St.
502/443-6480

Grandma & G'pa's Treasures
200 Kentucky Ave.
502/443-6505

Sherry & Friends Antique Mall
208 Kentucky Ave.
502/442-4103

Once Upon A Time Antiques
212 Kentucky Ave.
502/443-1062

Anthony Barnes Antiques
111 Market House Sq.
502/442-1891

Market Square Antiques
113 Market House Sq.
502/444-9253

Wood Whittlers
201 Ohio
502/443-7408

Affordable Antiques, Inc. II
933 S. 3rd St.
502/442-1225

Things Unique & Antique
133 S. 3rd St.
502/575-4905

Chief Paduke Antiques Mall
300 S. 3rd St.
502/442-6799

Favorite Places To Eat

Cracker Barrel Old Country Store
I-24 & Hwy. 60, Exit 4
502/443-9331

33 PARIS

Lea Loch Antiques
410 Main St.
606/987-7070

Green Apple Gift Shop
600 Main St.
606/987-7512

Antiques Arts & Collectibles
627 Main St.
606/987-0877

34 RICHMOND

Historic Richmond, off I-75 south of Lexington, has a variety of attractions to enjoy. This was Daniel Boone's site for his wilderness outpost, the birthplace of Kit Carson, and home of the fiery abolitionist Cassius Marcellus Clay. Civil War buffs will want to take the Battle of Richmond driving tour (800/866-3705). And, along the way, stop at the 1780 Valley View Ferry on Kentucky 169.

Lena's Antiques
2047 Berea Rd.-U.S. Hwy 25
606/623-4325

Waterstreet Mall
129 S. 1st St.
606/625-1524

Gift Box
139 N. Keeneland Dr.
606/624-0025

Olde Tyme Toys
209 W. Main St.
606/623-8832

Memories Antiques
401 North St.
606/625-0909

Favorite Places To Eat

Cracker Barrel Old Country Store
I-75 & Hwy. 25, Exit 90
606/623-0037

35 RUSSELLVILLE

For a community of its size, Russellville boasts the largest historic district in Kentucky. The Southern Bank of Kentucky at Sixth and Main was the site of the first documented bank robbery by Jesse James, with a re-enactment each October during the Logan County Tobacco Festival.

The Bibb House Museum, a circa 1822 Georgian mansion, was built by Major Richard Bibb, an early abolitionist and Revolutionary War officer. The collection of antebellum antiques includes Belter and Duncan Phyfe originals (183 West 8th, 502/726-2508).

Check out Libby's Family Entertainment, eight miles west on U.S. 68. Friday night is the Country Jamboree, while Saturday nights' "Live at Libby's" show is syndicated to more than 65 radio stations in the United States and Canada.

Diamond D Auction
208 North Bethel Street
502/726-7892
Call for auction dates

David and I first heard about the Diamond D Auction from Leon Tyewater (a great auctioneer with a wife who can really cook). We were stuck in Nashville, Tennessee, for a few days so we decided to check out this little country auction which was only an hour's drive away. It's one of those "sleeper" auctions. You know the kind—when you walk in and at the first glance you see nothing—then about 30 minutes into the sale something pops up that you can't live without! I'm sitting there minding my own business when out of the blue the most wonderful cupboard crosses the auction block. An authentic Tennessee piece from Piney Flats with its original dark oak finish, yellow paint inside, complete with perfect rat holes, and old glass doors— a true "virgin." Of course I bought it! For $550 wouldn't you?

Russellville Antique Mall
141 E. 5th St.
502/726-6900

Russellville Flower Shop
104 S. Franklin St.
502/726-7608

Interesting Side Trip

Shaker Museum
South Union (U.S. 68)
502/453-4167
Open March-December 15: Mon.-Sat. 9-5, Sun. 1-5

Shaker Museum at South Union, 15 miles east of Russellville on U.S. 68, is the site of the last Western Shaker community (1807-1922). The 1824 Centre House showcases the fine craftsmanship of this inventive communal group with hundreds of original artifacts. Have lunch at Shaker Tavern, 502/542-6801, Tuesday through Saturday from 11:30 a.m. to 2:00 p.m.; Sunday and dinner by reservation; also a bed and breakfast. Events include the Shaker Festival in late June.

36 SHELBYVILLE

You'll find a charming area of antique and specialty shops amid the late-Victorian, National Register downtown district at I-64, Exit 35 between Louisville and Frankfort. Shelbyville is home to world-renowned Wakefield-Scearce Galleries, located within the historic Science Hill buildings, with an outstanding inventory of English and European antiques (Washington Street, 502/633-4382).

The area is also known for wonderful regional restaurants. There's Science Hill Inn, 502/633-2825; the Claudia Sanders Dinner House, originally operated by the Colonel, at 3202 Shelbyville Road/U.S. 60 West, 502/633-5600; and the Old Stone Inn in Simpsonville, once a stagecoach inn, on U.S. 60 East, 502/722-8882.

Country Cottage Collectibles
137 Frankfort Rd.
502/633-5341

Main St. Antique Mall
514 Main St.
502/633-0721

Shelbyville Antique Mall
524 Main St.
502/633-0720

Things Worth Keeping
526 Main St.
502/633-0025

Antiques For You Mall
528 Main St.
502/633-7506

Tam Antiques
610 Main St.
502/633-3106

Old Mill Shop Antiques
117 7th St.
502/633-2733

Wakefield Scearce Antqs. Gllry.
525 Washington St.
502/633-4382

Corner Collectibles & Antqs.
629 Washington St.
502/633-4838

Something Unique
By Appointment Only
502/633-3621

37 SHEPHERDSVILLE

Favorite Places To Eat

Cracker Barrel Old Country Store
I-65 & Brooks Rd. Exit 121
502/955-4008

38 SMITHS GROVE

Smiths Grove Antique Mall
604 S. Main
502/563-4921

The Corner Cupboard
133 S. Main
502/563-6221

Pony Express
105 S. Main
502/563-5130

Ye Olde Bank Antiques
108 E. First Street
502/563-9313

Wright House Antiques Etc.
124 First Street
502/563-9430

Wanda's Antiques & Cllbls.
131 N. Main
502/563-6444

Anytime Antiques
133 N. Main
502/563-9111

Village Grove Antiques
135 N. Main
502/563-9100

Martin's Antiques
Hwy. 68-80
502/563-2575

Cotton Corner
Main Street
No Phone #, New Shop

39 SOMERSET

North 27 Antique Mall
3000 N. Hwy. 27
606-679-1923

Remas Antiques
450 S. Hwy. 27
606/679-7698

Southern Furniture & Antqs.
4810 S. Hwy. 27
606/678-0230

Cumberland Antique Mall
6494 S. Hwy. 27
606/561-8622

Pitman Creek Antique Mall
6940 S. Highway 27
606/561-5178

Gift Box Uniques Inc.
207 E. Market St.
606/679-8041

Somerset Antique Mall
209 E. Market St.
606/679-4307

Annies Antiques & Crafts
209 Oak Hill Rd.
606/678-6544

40 ST. MATTHEWS

Elaine Claire
211 Clover Lane
502/895-0843

Charmar Galleries Ltd.
2005 Frankfort Ave.
502/897-5565

Scott F Nussbaum Antiques
2036 Frankfort Ave.
502/894-9292

Henderson Antiques
2044 Frankfort Ave.
502/895-6605

Elizabeths Timeless Attire
2050 Frankfort Ave.
502/895-5911

Sarah Few McNeal Co.
2866 Frankfort Ave.
502/895-2752

41 VERSAILLES

Irish Acres
4205 Fords Mill Rd.
606/873-6956

Mason Antiques
408 Lexington Rd.
606/873-4792

Olde Towne Antique Mall
161 N. Main St.
606/873-6326

Farm House Antiques & Gifts
175 N. Main St.
606/873-0800

Farm House Antiques
825 Scotts Ferry Rd.
606/873-5100

42 WASHINGTON

House of Three Gables
2027 Old Main St.
No Phone #

Alice's Antiques & Jewels
2028 Old Main St.
606/564-4877

Peiis
2029 Old Main St.
606/759-5533

Iron Gate
2103 Old Main St.
606/759-7074

Strawberry Patch Antqs. & Gifts
2109 Old Main St.
606/759-7001

Washington Hall Antiquities
2111 Old Main St.
606-759-7409

Phyllis Antq. Lamp/Dollhouse
2112 Old Main St.
606/759-7423

1790 Row House Mall
2117 Old Main St.
606-759-7025

Notes

Louisiana

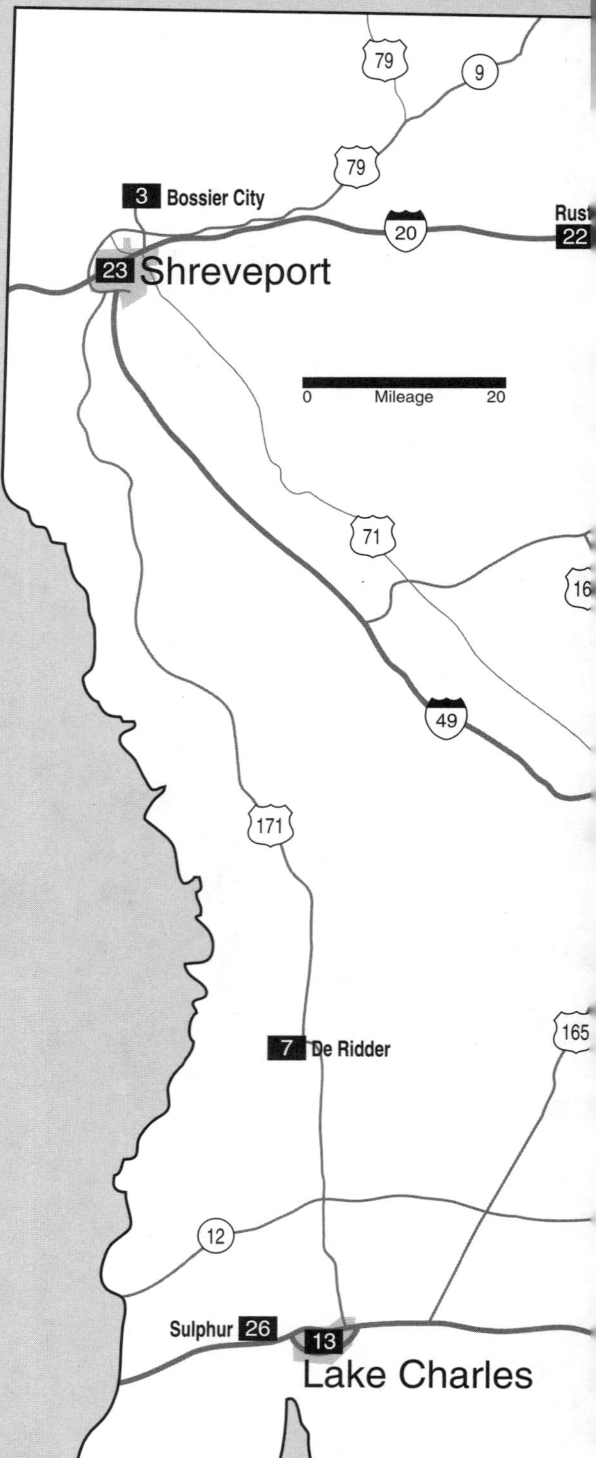

79
9
79
3 Bossier City
20
Rus
22
23 Shreveport
0 Mileage 20
71
16
49
171
165
7 De Ridder
12
Sulphur 26
13
Lake Charles

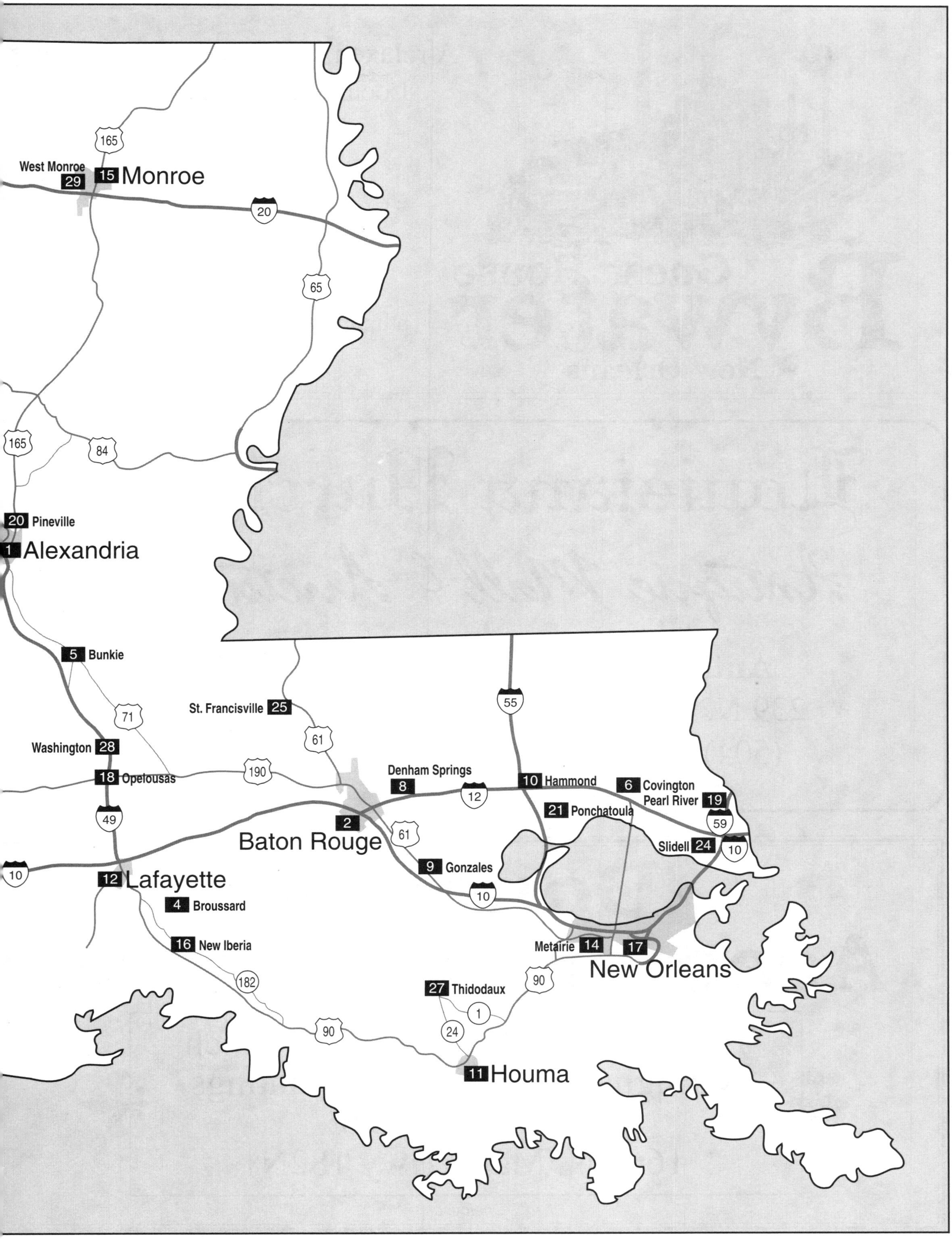
165
West Monroe
29
15 Monroe
20
65
165
84
20 Pineville
1 Alexandria
5 Bunkie
71
St. Francisville 25
55
61
Washington 28
18 Opelousas
190
Denham Springs
8
10 Hammond
6 Covington
Pearl River 19
12
21 Ponchatoula
59
49
2
61
Baton Rouge
Slidell 24
10
9 Gonzales
10
12 Lafayette
10
4 Broussard
16 New Iberia
Metairie 14
17
New Orleans
182
90
27 Thidodaux
1
24
90
11 Houma

Louisiana

1 ALEXANDRIA

Ancient Slots
3609 N. Bolton Ave.
318/473-2184

Hirsch House Antiques
1216 Jackson St.
318/442-7764

Eclectic
5528 Jackson St. Ext.
318/487-1728

Dantzlers Flea Market
5416 Masonic Dr.
318/443-1589

Eclectic II
5416 Masonic Dr.
318/487-1728

Miss Lily's
1900 Rapides Ave.
318/448-0186

B & N. Collectibles Antiques
2000 Rapides Ave.
318/487-8910

Sally Foster Designs
1307 Windsor Pl.
318/445-5480

2 BATON ROUGE

Louisiana Purchases Auction Company
637 St. Ferdinand Street
504/346-1803

The company specializes in on-site estate auctions and tag sales. Clients should call for the next auction date because, as owner Wayne Welch says, "We never know when it will be!" He never knows what customers will do, either, as this story he tells proves:

"I once had a lady wanting to buy a piece of stained glass. At the time I had over 180 pieces. She arrived around 10 a.m. and by 2 p.m. she finally decided on one. She really wanted this piece, knowing full well it would not fit. But she bought it anyway. About 20 minutes later she came back, crying like a baby. 'It just won't fit,' she sobbed. As everyone knows, all sales are final, but this lady had already bought more glass from me than she had windows, so I asked her if she had brought the piece back. She said "no" because of our policy. I then asked if she would be home after I closed the shop that day. After work I went over to her house and looked at the space she wanted to use the newly purchased piece of glass in. I told her to come by the store the next afternoon and I took the piece back and cut it down to fit. She came that afternoon, got it, took it home, and it fit perfectly. She is now my greatest advertisement!"

Cavalier House
8655 Bluebonnet Blvd.
504/767-9007

Lagniappe Antiques
2175 Dallas Dr.
504/927-0531

Jean Petit Antiques
3280 Drusilla Lane
504/924-3801

Great Heritage Antiques
5905 Florida Blvd.
504/923-1861

Kornmeyer Furniture Co. Inc.
7643 Florida Blvd.
504/926-0137

AAA Antiques
9800 Florida Blvd.
504/925-1664

Merchant's Landing
9800 Florida Blvd.
504/925-1664

Country Time Clocks & Gifts
11242 Florida Blvd.
504/272-4663

Guillot's Furn. Repair Co.
1906 N. Foster Dr.
504/357-6033

I M Causey and Co. Inc.
501 Government St.
504/343-3421

Aladdin's Lamp Resale Shop
2714 Government St.
504/338-1933

Confederate States Mlty. Antqs.
2905 Government St.
504/387-5044

The Antique Group
2963 Government
504/387-5543

Audubon Station & Co.
3153 Government
504/383-3599

Estate Auction Gallery
3374 Government
504/383-7706

River City Books
3374 Government
504/383-1003

Shades of the Past Antiques
3374 Government
504/383-6911

Westmoreland Antique Gallery
3374 Government
504/383-7777

The Decorator's Gallery
3378 Government
504/383-7708

Lynn's Antiques & Cllbls. Inc.
3582 Government
504/334-9048

Blue Pearl Antiques
3875 Government
504/346-8508

Designers Custom Lamps
4375 Government
504/344-4674

Atkinson Antiques
8868 Greenwell Springs Rd.
504/924-1941

Hearth & Home Antiques
10136 Greenwell Springs Rd.
504/272-7544

Potluck Antiques
10044 Hooper Rd.
504/262-8311

Collectors Choice
13612 Hooper Rd.
504/261-1835

Best Kept Secrets
5425 Highland Rd.
504/763-9066

Highland Road Antiques
16257 Highland Rd.
504/752-8446

Farm and Village
6636 Florida Blvd. Ste. 10
504/924-7555

Fetzer's Intrs. & Fine Antiques
711 Jefferson Hwy.
504/927-7420

Absolutely Genius
7317 Jefferson Hwy.
504/929-9862

Barker's Antique Jewelry
7565 Jefferson Hwy.
504/927-4406

Keepsake Antiques & Cllbls.
10912 Joor Rd.
504/261-3540

Dixon Smith Interiors
1655 Lobdell Ave.
504/927-4261

Wayside House Antiques Inc.
1706 May St.
504/344-2633

Classic Jewelers Inc.
7610 Old Hammond Hwy.
504/927-6299

Goudeau Antiques
1284 Perkins Rd.
504/383-7307

Antique Emporium
4347 Perkins Rd.
504/344-5856

Stewarts Inessa Antiques
8630 Perkins Rd.
504/769-9363

Sylvia's
12648 Perkins Rd.
504/769-7143

Country Bumpkin Antiques
13166 Perkins Rd.
504/769-5138

Fireside Antiques
14007 Perkins Rd.
504/752-9565

Eagles Nest Antiques
15127 Perkins Rd.
504/753-4748

Plank Road Antiques
11728 Plank Rd.
504/778-0280

Grandpa's Cellar
832 St. Phillip St.
504/344-7030

Landmark Antique Plaza Inc.
832 St. Phillip St.
504/383-4867

Country Emporium
10349 Sullivan Rd.
504/261-6959

Lum's Place
7607 Tom Dr.
504/923-0745

Favorite Places To Eat

Cracker Barrel Old Country Store
I-12 & Airline Hwy. Exit 2
504/926-1328

3 BOSSIER CITY

Cajun Crafters Junction
1882 Airline Dr.
318/747-6555

4 BROUSSARD

La Grande Maison
302 E. Main Street
318/837-4428
Open year round

Directions: 10 miles south of I-10 or 5 miles south of the airport, exit at Broussard, turn left at light. It is the large Victorian building on the right.

Built in 1911, the La Grande Maison was once the residence of the Paul and Lawrence Billeaud family. This Victorian style home features several lovely porches and is situated on a beautifully landscaped lot with large oak trees.

The home was purchased in 1994 by Norman and Brenda Fakier. It has been completely restored to its current grand style and is listed on the National Historic Register.

The bed and breakfast offers several lovely rooms, all with private bath. A full breakfast is included.

5 BUNKIE

By-Gone Days Antiques
105 W. Magnolia St.
318/346-4940

Griffins Antiques
228 S.W. Main St.
318/346-2806

6 COVINGTON

French House Antiques
735 E. Boston at Lee Lane
504/893-4566

Antiques On Consignment
315 N. Columbia St.
504/898-0955

Antique Obsession
421 N. Columbia St.
504/898-3667

Merlyn Fine Antiques
609 E. Gibson
504/892-6099

Country Corner Shop
205 Lee Lane
504/892-7995

Walker House Ltd.
221 Lee Lane
504/893-4235

A Few of My Favorite Things
316 Lee Lane
504/867-9363

Lee Lane Antique Mall
326 Lee Lane
504/893-4453

Claiborne Hill Antiques
72022 Live Oak St.
504/892-5657

Chocolate Tulips
714 E. Rutland St.
504/893-5506

Countryside
828 E. Rutland
504/893-7622

Chimes Antiques
125 N. Theard St.
504/8892-8836

Homespun Antiques
204 W. 21st Ave.
504/892-3828

Past Restored
2380 W. 21st Ave.
504/892-7475

Louisiana

7 DERIDDER

Secret Attic
109 S. Washington St.
318/463-4649

Uptown Deridder
113 N. Washington St.
318/463-7200

8 DENHAM SPRINGS

Louisiana Purchases Antique Mall
239 N. Range Avenue
504/665-2803
Open daily, Mon.-Sat. 10-5, Sun. 12-5
(after hours appointments available by calling 504/346-1803)

Directions: Located off of I-12 in Denham Springs. Take I-12 to Exit #10 and go north about 2 miles. When you cross a railroad track, you will be in "Antique Village." The mall is the last shop on the left at the traffic light.

Louisiana Purchases is one of two malls and a restaurant located under one roof, and shoppers can walk through each shop to get to the other one. In all there are 27 dealers, with several specializing in different items such as antique copper, primitives and antique stained glass. The other mall is La Maison Antique Mall, and the Brass Lantern Restaurant serves the biggest burger in town.

Romantique
104 N. Range Ave.
504/667-2283

Live Oak Antiques
111 N. Range Ave.
504/665-0488

Benton Brothers Antique Mall
115 N. Range Ave.
504/665-5146

Enchanted Attic
123 N. Range
504/664-3655

Diamond Mine
201 N. Range Ave.
504/664-6463

Way Back When Antiques
208 N. Range Ave.
504/667-4169

Painted Lady Antiques
215 N. Range Ave.
504/667-1710

Hart To Heart Antiques
219 N. Range Ave.
504/667-4018

La Maison Antiques
235 N. Range Ave.
504/664-4001

Backward's Glance
222 N. Range Ave.
504/667-9779

Antiques Plus
226 N. Range Ave.
504/664-3643

Theater Antiques
228 N. Range Ave.
504/665-4666

9 GONZALES

Favorite Places To Eat

Cracker Barrel Old Country Store
I-10 & Hwy. 30, Exit 177
504/647-5277

10 HAMMOND

Favorite Places To Eat

Cracker Barrel Old Country Store
I-55 & Hwy. 190, Exit 173
504/542-1828

11 HOUMA

Heritage House
1714 Barrow St.
504/872-3017

Bayou Antiques
2011 Bayou Blue Rd.
504/873-7500

Country Antiques
2036 Coteau Rd.
504/868-4646

Antique Gallery of Houma Inc.
3382 Little Bayou Black
504/857-8237

12 LAFAYETTE

Gateway Antiques, Inc.
200 Northgate Drive
318/235-4989
Open Mon.-Sat. 10-5, closed Sundays

Directions: Traveling I-10: Take Exit #103A to the first traffic light (East Willow). Take a left at the East Willow light and make another left behind Montgomery Ward in the Northgate Mall. This is Northgate Drive and the shop is in back of the Montgomery Ward parking lot. It can be seen at the East Willow light if you look to your left.

Gateway Antiques concentrates mostly on smalls and glassware, pottery, toys, perfume bottles, jewelry, jars and boxes, pieces of Roseville, Hull and Fiestaware, with some tools added for good measure.

Accent Studios Inc.
805 W. University Ave.
318/233-0186

Coin & Treasure Co.
2474 W. Congress St.
318/237-2646

Stewart's
1000 Coolidge Blvd.
318/232-2957

Bouligny Interiors Inc.
331 Doucet Rd.
318/984-2030

Clock House
326 Duhon Rd.
318/984-1779

Fazy's
1416 Eraste Landry Rd.
318/269-5800

Ole Fashion Things
402 S.W. Evangeline Thruway
318/234-4800

Ruins and Relics
900 Evangeline Dr.
318/233-9163

Antiques & Interiors Inc.
616 General Mouton Ave.
318/234-4776

Kings Rowe Antiques
326 Heymann Blvd.
318/261-5934

Auntie Em's
410 Jefferson St.
318/233-9362

Gert's Antiques Etc.
1306 Jefferson St.
318/261-2311

Lafayette Antique Market
2015 Johnston St.
318/269-9430

Antiques Et Cie
3601 Johnston St.
318/981-9847

Julia Martha Antiques Et Cie
3601 Johnston St.
318/981-9847

Artisans of Louisiana
3603 Johnston St.
318/988-4280

Gala's Unique Antiques & Gifts
922 Kaliste Saloom Rd.
318/235-7816

Treasures
924 Kaliste Saloom Rd.
318/234-9978

Granny's Attic
410 Mudd Ave.
318/237-6418

Gateway Antiques Inc.
200 Northgate Dr.
318/235-4989

Renaissance Market
321 Oil Center Dr.
318/234-1116

La Jolie
1326 W. Pinhook Rd.
318/233-5319

Graham's Antiques & Accents
1891 W. Pinhook Rd.
318/234-5045

Crowded Attic
512 N. University
318/237-5559

Hallmark Interiors & Antiques
412 Travis St.
318/234-5997

Crowded Attic
512 N. University Ave.
318/233-0012

Accent Studios Inc.
805 W. University Ave.
318/233-0186

Favorite Places To Eat

Cracker Barrel Old Country Store
I-10 & University, Exit 101
318/233-4220

13 LAKE CHARLES

Harry's Hodge Podge
701 14th St.
318/436-6219

Bayou Furniture Inc.
1104 Alamo St.
318/477-6456

Chapman Antiques & Cllbls.
748 Bank St.
318/436-2726

Somewhere In Time
2802 Hodges St.
318-494-0176

Curiosity Antique Mall
831 Kirkman St.
318/491-1170

Antics & Attics
1908 Kirkman St.
318/436-5265

Lacey Jade & Co.
3612 Kirkman St.
318/478-4304

My Sister's Closet
3735 Kirkman St.
318/474-4733

Kelly's Flea Market
332 N. Martin Luther King Hwy.
318/439-0382

Yesterday Today & Tomorrow
138 W. Prien Lake Rd.
318/478-1010

Reflections
608 A E. Prien Lake Rd.
318/479-1974

My Favorite Things
216 S. Ryan St.
318/439-1900

Nantiques
2508 Ryan St.
318/439-0366

14 METAIRIE

Sisters Antiques
114 Codifer Blvd.
504/828-6701

Rare Bits
800 Metairie Rd.
504/837-6771

Olde Metairie Antique Mall
1537 Metairie Rd.
504/831-4514

Steve M Burgamy
2011 Metairie Rd.
504/831-9265

Unique Galleries & Auction
4040 Veterans Memorial Blvd.
504/885-9000

15 MONROE

B & W Antiques
407 Desiard St.
318/387-9025

Clarence's Old Stuff
424 Desiard St.
318/323-1306

Collectiques
815 Desiard St.
318/387-5974

Cottonland Crafters Mall
1119 Forsythe Ave.
318/323-2325

R J Wills Antique Shop
1907 S. Grand St.
318/323-6150

Camille Wood Antiques
217 Hudson Lane
318-323-8979

16 NEW IBERIA

Jaja's Just Things
609 Charles St.
318/367-2141

Rose Antique Ville
2007 Freyou Rd.
318/367-3000

Magnolia Antiques
203 E. Main St.
318/365-5285

Bo's Attic Antiques
231 Pollard Ave.
318/364-1093

Janie's Vintage Jewelry
105 E. Saint Peter St.
318/365-8323

Kimberly Interiors Inc.
105 E. Saint Peter St.
318/365-8323

Lantiques
311 W. Saint Peter St.
318/364-8517

17 NEW ORLEANS

Bywater Guest House

908 Poland Avenue
504/949-6381
1-888-615-7498
E-mail: bywatergh@aol.com
URL: http://members.aol.com/bywatergh

Directions: A relaxed, comfortable atmosphere in an 1872 Eastlake Victorian home located in the Bywater National Historic District, 1 mile from the French Quarter.

Located on the site of the Audey Plantation, later known as the Faubourg Washington, Bywater Guest House is located one and one-half miles down river from the French Quarter. The house was built in 1872, in the Victorian style by Michael Darby, an American engineer. The main building construction shows styles influenced by Charles Eastlake. The site also holds the original kitchen, or cookhouse, which by law had to be a separate structure, and one of the first three car garages in the City of New Orleans. The house is furnished in antique and reproduction appointments and original artwork.

The Innkeepers at Bywater Guest House take pride in providing a relaxed, comfortable environment for their guests. Amenities for the three guest rooms include; comfortable queen size beds with feather mattresses and down duvets, writing tables and Queen Anne style chairs. The full breakfast includes a hot entree, fresh fruit and juice, coffee, tea and breads.

Dusty Mansion

2231 General Pershing Street
504/895-4576
Open year round
Rates $50-75

Just six blocks from the St. Charles Avenue streetcar, Dusty Mansion is ideally located for weekend exploration and enjoyment of New Orleans. This is a homey, casual inn on a quiet residential street just on the edge of the Garden District in the historic Bouligny Plantation District. It's a turn-of-the-century, two-story frame house with wide front porch and porch swing, original hardwood floors and cypress woodwork and doors. The four guest rooms (two with private bath) have romantic ceiling fans and are filled with antiques and reproduction pieces. The four beds are queen-sized and are either brass, canopied, sleigh or white enameled iron. A continental-plus breakfast is served in the dining room, and afterwards you can explore, relax and catch some rays on the sundeck, read or nap on the shaded patio, play pool or table tennis, and later, ease into the hot tub secluded in the gazebo.

Didier, Inc.

3439 Magazine Street
504/899-7749

This exclusive shop on Magazine Street specializes in period American furniture (1800-1840) and the accompanying decorative arts. Primarily the furniture is from Boston, Philadelphia, New York City and Baltimore. Everything is housed in an 1850s period home, completely restored to that era. The shop has clients who have been with them since 1970. Their decorative arts consist of period prints, paintings, glass and porcelain - absolutely no reproductions.

Bienville Antique Shoppe
4600 Bienville St.
504/488-2428

Whisnant Galleries
222 Chartres St.
504/524-9766

Cass-Garr Company
237 Chartres St.
504/522-8298

Blackamoor Antiques Inc.
324 Chartres St.
504/523-7786

Button Shoppe
328 Chartres St.
504/523-6557

Ray J Piehet Gallery-Antiques
608 Chartres St.
504/525-2806

Lucullus
610 Chartres St.
504/528-9620

Molieres Antique Shop
612 Chartres St.
504/525-9479

Animal Art Antiques
617 Chartres St.
504/529-4407

Adrian's Antiques
618 Conti St.
504/525-4615

OSuzanna's
1231 Decatur St.
504/581-5006

Collectible Antiques
1232 Decatur St.
504-566-0399

Legarage Antiques & Clothing
1234 Decatur St.
504/522-6639

Tomato Warehouse
1237 Decatur St.
504/524-2529

Framboyan
624 Dumaine St.
504/558-9241

Ruebarb Gallery
1101 First at Magazine
504/523-4301

Antiques by Ruppert
1018 Harmony St.
504/895-6394

Kohlmaier & Kohlmaier
1018 Harmony St.
504/895-6394

Ole Hickory Antq. Clock Rpr.
216 Hickory Ave.
504/737-2937

Antiques Etc.
8400 Jefferson Hwy.
504/737-3503

Stan Levy Imports Inc.
1028 Louisiana Ave.
504/899-6384

Charbonnet & Charb. Antqs.
2929 Magazine St.
504/891-9948

Java Nola
1313 Magazine St.
504/558-0369

Lee Ali Inter. Unlimited
1800 Magazine St.
504/586-8325

Shop of Two Sisters
1800 Magazine St.
504/586-8325

Antebellum Antiques
2011 Magazine St.
504/558-0208

Aarons Antique Mall
2014 Magazine St.
504/523-0630

Hands
2023 Magazine St.
504/522-2590

Audubon Antiques
2025 Magazine St.
504/581-5704

Antiques Magazine
2028 Magazine St.
504/522-2043

Dodge-Fjeld Antiques
2033 Magazine St.
504/581-6930

Miss Edna's Antiques
2035 Magazine St.
504/524-1897

Jim Smiley Vintage Clothing
2001 Magazine St.
504/528-9449

Attic Treasures
2039 Magazine St.
504/588-1717

Anthony's Town & Co. Antqs.
2049 Magazine St.
504/451-7314

Bep's Antiques
2051 Magazine St.
504/525-7726

Renaissance Shop
2104 Magazine St.
504/525-8568

Mona Mias
2105 Magazine St.
504/525-8686

Shades of Light
2108 Magazine St.
504/524-6500

Bush Antiques
2109 Magazine St.
504/581-3518

Eclectique Antiques
2112 Magazine St.
504/525-4668

Antique Vault
2123 Magazine St.
504/523-8888

Belle Mina Antique
2127 Magazine St.
504/523-3222

Magazine Antique Mall
2205 Magazine St.
504/524-0100

Bernard Regenbogen Furn.
2208 Magazine St.
504/522-6351

Dombourian Orntl. Rugs Inc.
2841 Magazine St.
504/891-6601

Christopher's Discoveries
2842 Magazine St.
504/899-6226

Antiques & Things
2855 Magazine St.
504/897-9466

Susan Taylor Interiors
3005 Magazine St.
504/891-0123

Magazine Arcade Antiques
3017 Magazine St.
504/895-5451

As You Like It Silver Shop
3029 Magazine St.
504/897-6915

Shaker Shop
3029 Magazine St.
504/895-8646

The Private Connection
3927 Magazine St.
504/593-9526

Finders Keepers
3118 Magazine St.
504/895-2702

Grand Antiques
3125 Magazine St.
504/897-3179

Esfahani Oriental Rugs
3218 Magazine St.
504/895-5550

Empire Antiques
3420 Magazine St.
504/897-0252

French Collectibles
3424 Magazine St.
504/897-9020

Blackamoor Antiques Inc.
3433 Magazine St.
504/897-2711

Didier Inc.
3439 Magazine St.
504/899-7749

Custom Linens
3638 Magazine St.
504/899-0604

K & K Design Studios
3646 Magazine St.
504/897-2290

Brass Image
3801 Magazine St.
504/897-1861

Uptowner Antiques
3828 Magazine St.
504/891-7700

Louisiana

Wirthmore Antiques
3900 Magazine St.
504/899-3811

Collector Antiques
3901 Magazine St.
504/895-7375

Jean Bragg Antiques
3901 Magazine St.
504/895-7375

Orient Expressed Imports Inc.
3905 Magazine St.
504/899-3060

Aux Belles Choses
3912 Magazine St.
504/891-1009

Mimano
3917 Magazine St.
504/895-9436

C Susman-Estate Jewelry
3933 Magazine St.
504/897-9144

Anne Pratt
3937 Magazine St.
504/891-6532

Judy, A Gallery
3941 Magazine St.
504/891-7018

Jacqueline Vance
3944 Magazine St.
504/891-3304

Country at Heart
3952 Magazine St.
504/891-5412

The Sitting Duck Gallery
3953 Magazine St.
504/899-2007

Dellwen Antiques
3954-56 Magazine St.
504/897-3617

Mac Maison Ltd.
3963 Magazine St.
504/891-2863

Davis Gallery
3964 Magazine St.
504/897-0780

Neal Auction Co.
4038 Magazine St.
504/899-5329

Gizmos
4118-4122 Magazine St.
504/897-6868

Emil Moore & Co. LLC
4119 Magazine St.
504/891-1198

Talebloo Oriental Rugs
4130 Magazine St.
504/899-8114

Berta's and Mina's Antiquities
4138 Magazine St.
504/895-6201

Sigi Russell Antiques
4304 Magazine St.
504/891-5390

Top Drawer Auction & Apprsl.
4310 Magazine St.
504/832-9080

Custom Woodwork & Antiques
4507 Magazine St.
504/891-1664

Fraza Framing & Art Gallery
4532 Magazine St.
504/899-7002

Carol Robinson Gallery
4537 Magazine St.
504/899-6130

Modell's Rostor & Polsg Inc.
4600 Magazine St.
504/895-5267

Jon Antiques
4605 Magazine St.
504/899-4482

Melange Sterling
5421 Magazine St.
504/899-4796

19th Century Antiques
4838 Magazine St.
504/891-4845

Pettie Pence Antique
4904 Magazine St.
504/891-3353

Wirthmore Antiques
5723 Magazine St.
504/897-9727

The Tulip Tree
5831 Magazine St.
504/895-3748

Enoch's Framing & Gallery
6063 Magazine St.
504/899-6686

Le Wicker Gazebo
3715 Magazine St.
504/899-1355

Apropos
3806 Magazine St.
504/899-3500

Driscoll Antqs. & Restoration
8118 Oak St.
504/866-7795

Au Vieux Paris Antiques
7219 Perrier St.
504/866-6677

French Antique Shop Inc.
225 Royal St.
504/524-9861

Diane Genre Orntl. Art /Antqs.
233 Royal st
504/525-7270

Brass Monkey
235 Royal St.
504/561-0688

Dixon & Dixon
237 Royal St.
504/524-0282

Rothschild's
241 Royal St.
504/523-5816

Royal Antiques Ltd.
309 Royal St.
504/524-7033

Robinson's Antiques
313 Royal St.
504/523-6683

Jack Sutton Antiques
315 Royal St.
504/522-0555

Rothschild's
321 Royal St.
504/523-2281

Keil's Antiques
325 Royal St.
504/522-4552

Royal Co.
325 Royal St.
504/522-4552

J Herman Son Galleries
333 Royal St.
504/525-6326

Waldhorn - Adler
343 Royal St.
504/581-6379

Manheim Galleries
409 Royal St.
504/568-1901

Moss Antiques
411 Royal St.
504/522-3981

Cynthia Sutton
429 Royal St.
504/523-3377

Jack Sutton Co. Inc.
501 Royal St.
504/581-3666

Gerald D Katz Antiques
505 Royal St.
504/524-5050

Le Petit Soldier Shop
528 Royal St.
504/523-7741

Royal Art Gallery Ltd.
537 Royal St.
504/524-6070

Harris Antiques Ltd.
623 Royal St.
504/523-1605

M S Rau Inc.
630 Royal St.
504/523-5660

L M S Fine Arts & Antiques
729 Royal st
504/529-3774

Regency House Antiques
841 Royal St.
504/524-7507

Patout Antiques
922 Royal St.
504/522-0582

Barakat
934 Royal St.
504/593-9944

Sigles Antiques & Metalcrafts
935 Royal St.
504/522-7647

W M Antiques
1029 Royal St.
504/524-1253

Centuries Old Maps & Prints
517 Saint Louis St.
504/568-9491

Riccas Architectural Sales
511 N. Solomon St.
504/488-5524

Nina Sloss Antiques & Interiors
1001 State St.
504/895-8088

Harper's Antiques
610 Toulouse St.
504/592-1996

The Westgate
5219 Magazine St.
504/899-3077

18 OPELOUSAS

Doucet's Acadiana Antiques
1665 N. Main
318/942-3425
Open 9:30-5 Mon.-Fri., 9-3:30 Sat., closed Sun.-Mon.

Directions: From I-49 take the Opelousas exit and follow the signs to Hwy.. 182 North (Main is also known as Hwy..182 N). The shop is located across from Soileau's Dinner Club.

Doucet's is a well-heeled shop that has been providing superior pieces since 1928. They handle only fine 18th and 19th century antiques, paintings and collectibles from France and England. This is truly a shop to visit if you are looking for high end French or English period pieces.

19 PEARL RIVER

Ann's Place Antiques
39613 Pecan Drive
504/641-2754

20 PINEVILLE

Peck's Antiques
706 Pearce Road
318/640-0006

Jessie's Antique Barn
5632 Hwy. 28 E
318/473-8347

Beaten Path Antiques
6892 Hwy. 28 E
318/445-9425

Handmaiden & Friends
318 Maryhill Rd.
318-640-3727

Peck's Antiques
706 Pearce Rd.
318/640-0006

21 PONCHATOULA

Remember When Antiques
223 West Pine Street
504/386-6159
Open Wed.-Sun. 10-5

This large and spacious mall carries everything from Victorian to primitives, but concentrates primarily on furnishings and glassware accessories.

Ponchatoula Antiques
400 West Pine Street
504/386-7809
Open Wed.-Sun. 10-5

This mall carries antiques, but their main focus is on fountains and statuary! They handle new fountains (not antique ones) and statuary in a variety of themes, and have at least 200 fountains on display at all times. The statuary is the free-standing yard and garden variety. If you're looking to add a touch of the exotic or a touch of luxury to your yard and garden, look here first.

Alford's General Store
114 E. Pine St.
504/386-0111

Layrisson Walker Ltd.
123 E. Pine St.
504/386-8759

Yesteryear Antiques
165 E. Pine St.
504/386-2741

Ellen's Antiques & Collectibles
179 E. Pine St.
504/386-3564

Country Market
10 W. Pine St.
504/386-9580

Needful Things
101 W. Pine St.
504/386-2918

Memory Lane
105 W. Pine St.
504/386-2812

Country Carosel Antiques
120 W. Pine St.
504/386-2271

Oldies and Goodies
138 W. Pine St.
504/386-0150

Red Baron Antiques Inc.
139 W. Pine St.
504/386-8792

Louisiana

Wholesale Antiques
152 W. Pine St.
504/386-8086

Courtyard Antiques
155 W. Pine St.
504\386-9569

Ma Meres
165 W. Pine St.
504/386-0940

Roussels Specialty Shop
177 W. Pine St.
504/386-9097

Remember When
223 W. Pine St.
504/386-6159

Ponchatoula Antiques Inc.
400 W. Pine St.
504/386-7809

C J's Antiques & Collectibles
160 SE Railroad Ave.
504/386-0026

Roussel's Annex
138 N. 6th St.
504/386-9096

22 RUSTON

Deep South Antiques
Hwy. 167 N
318/255-5278

Michael's Furniture Mart
305 W. Mississippi Ave.
318/251-9409

Railroad Depot
101 E. Railroad Ave.
318/255-3103

Acorn Creek Antiques
1323 S. Service Rd. W
318/255-1831

Times Past Antiques
103 N. Trenton St.
318/254-8279

Park Ave. Antique Mall
108 N. Vienna St.
318/255-4866

Pot Luck
202 N. Vienna St.
318/254-1331

23 SHREVEPORT

Hudson House Antiques
3118 Gilbert
318/865-2151

Bullock's
1723 Highland
318/226-9168

Nigel's Heirloom Antq. Gallery
3004 Highland Ave.
318/226-0146

Caloways Antiques & Bygones
811 Jefferson Pl.
318/221-5493

Hudson House Antiques
109 Kings Hwy.
318/868-9579

D&B Russell-Books
129 Kings Hwy.
318/865-5198

Kings Ransom
133 Kings Hwy.
318/865-4811

Enchanted Gardens
2429 Line Ave.
318/227-1213

Katie-Beths Antiques
3316 Line Ave.
318/868-5246

Arrangement
3322 Line Ave.
318/868-6812

Hinton Gallery
3324 Line Ave.
318/868-0018

Jack Farmer Antiques
6018 Line Ave.
318/869-3297

Then & Now
6030 Line Ave.
318/865-6340

Corrente Oriental Antqs. & Acc.
6401 Line Ave.
318/868-3833

Golden Pineapple
6104 Line Ave. #5
318/868-3691

London Gallery-Antiques
6401 Line Ave.
318/868-3691

Pilgrim's Progress
6535 Line Ave.
318-868-3383

Red Caboose Antiques
855 Pierremont Rd.
318/865-5376

Estate Sale Consignment
2847 Summer Grove
318/687-7525

Lost & Found Antiques
2847 Summer Grove
318/687-1896

Gozas Gallery Inc.
5741 Youree Dr.
318/868-3429

Antique Mall
546 Olive St.
318/425-8786

Favorite Places To Eat

Cracker Barrel Old Country Store
I-20 & Pines Blvd., Exit 10
318/688-6080

24 SLIDELL

Recollections
2265 Carey St.
504/641-9410

Barbara's Victorian Closet
124 Erlanger St.
504/641-6316

Magnolia House Antiques
228 Erlanger St.
504/641-3776

Bon MeNage Gallery
1922 1st St.
504/646-0488

La Jolie Maison
1944 1st St.
504/649-7055

Wishing Well
1952 1st St.
504/646-0801

Vintage Antiques & Cllbls.
1958 1st St.
504/649-5968

First Street Antiques
1960 1st St.
504/643-6727

Little Green House Antiques
1732 Front St.
504/643-5176

Slidell Trading Post
40137 Hwy. 190 E
504/643-1606

Slidell Antique Market
806 Cousin St.
504/649-0579

Victorian Tea Room
228 Carey St.
504/643-7881

Something Old/Something New
1929 2nd St.
504/649-8088

Parc Antique Mall
2019 2nd St.
504/649-0410

The Antique Store
1944 1st St.
504/649-7055

Horaist "A Design Experience"
1654 Front St.
504/643-3030

Favorite Places To Eat

Cracker Barrel Old Country Store
I-10 & Gause Blvd., Exit 266
504/645-9631

25 ST. FRANCISVILLE

Barrow House
524 Royal Street
504/635-4791

This beautiful, picturesque building is sitting right in the middle of the historic district of St. Francisville, a wonderful location for exploration. The two-story section was built in 1809 in the salt-box style, while the one-story wing and Greek Revival facade were added in 1855. The inn offers guests one suite and four double rooms, three of them with private baths. Antiques from the 1860s fill every nook and cranny of the historic building and guests are served wonderful dinners in the formal dining room.

C & D Collectible Now & Then
217 Ferdinand St.
504/635-3606

Honeysuckles
11739 Ferdinand St.
504/635-3367

Something Special
11911 Ferdinand St.
504/635-9804

Pretty Things Antiques
11917 Ferdinand St.
504/635-0308

26 SULPHUR

Miss Peggy's Antqs. & Cllbls.
208 S. Huntington St.
318/527-5027

Costwold
2223 Maplewood Dr.
381/625-3367

Sherry's Antique & Gift Shop
210 W. Napoleon St.
318/528-3346

Finders Keepers
414 E. Napoleon St.
318/527-7070

Favorite Places To Eat

Cracker Barrel Old Country Store
I-10 & Hwy. 108, Exit 23
318/626-9500

27 THIBODAUX

Dodge City Mall
1213 Canal Blvd.
504/447-4411

Erwin's Antique Bank
413 W. 4th St.
504/446-5827

Sweet Memories
602 Green St.
504/446-1140

Andree's Antiques
416 Jackson St.
504/447-5889

Angela's Antiques
517 Jackson St.
504/446-3641

Terry's Antiques
5504 W. Main St.
504/449-1600

Lafourche Antiques and Co.
424 Saint Mary St.
504/449-1635

Bryson's Angels
511 St. Phillip
504/447-1800

Mainstreet
606 W. 3rd St.
504/449-1001

Debbie's Antiques
705 W. Third
504/633-5680

28 WASHINGTON

O'Connors Antqs. School Mall
210 S. Church St.
318/826-3580

Cajun Antiques
400 S. Main St.
318/826-3710

29 WEST MONROE

Anderson Collection
204 Trenton St.
318/388-0366

Cotton's Collectables
255 Trenton St.
318/322-6479

River Run Antiques
303 Trenton St.
318/324-0517

Sanderson's Antiques
310 Trenton St.
318/325-0089

Martha's Unfinished Furniture
311 Trenton St.
318/323-1454

Trenton Street Images
312 Trenton St.
318/322-2691

O'Kelley's Antiques
313 Trenton St.
318/329-9409

Potpourri de Marie Tante
314 Trenton St.
318/325-0103

Imperial Galleries
317 Trenton St.
318/361-9458

Chandler's Antiques
318 Trenton St.
318/322-3925

Virginia's Antiques
320 Trenton St.
318/324-9885

Old Trenton Country Store
323 Trenton St.
318/323-7152

Louisiana

Sawyer's Antiques
4352 Whites Ferry Rd.
318/397-1292

Trenton Street Antique Mall
215 Trenton Street
318/325-9294

The Side Track
101 Trenton St.
318/323-9501

Marie's Antiques & Glass
224 Trenton Street
318/388-0908

Memory Lane Antiques
301 Trenton St.
381/323-3188

Trenton Street Gallery
319 Trenton St.
318/329-9200

Sanderson's Antique Mall
308 & 310 Trenton St.
318/325-0089

Favorite Places To Eat

Cracker Barrel Old Country Store
I-20 & Thomas Road, Exit 114
318/315-5505

Notes

HOUSTON-BROOKS AUCTION

"Quality Antique Auctions Since 1976"

Auction Every Sunday

Horseback Rd.

800-254-2214

Burnham

10

A MUST STOP SHOP • 103 QUALITY DEALERS PRESENT

FINE FURNITURE, PRIMITIVES, CHINA, POTTERY, PORCELAIN, TOYS, LINENS, JEWELRY, ART, BOOKS, COLLECTIBLES, DECORATOR ITEMS, CUT GLASS, PATTERN GLASS, DEPRESSION GLASS, ART GLASS, SILVER, COINS, EPHEMERA, DOLLS, AND MUCH MUCH MORE

REED'S

ANTIQUES & COLLECTIBLES

RTE. 1, **EXIT 2, ME TPKE**

OPEN YEAR ROUND, DAILY 10-5

ADDITIONAL QUALITY DEALERS ALWAYS WANTED

CALL 207-646-8010 OR 800-891-2017

Wells

33

THE GALEN C. MOSES HOUSE

A STYLISH VICTORIAN BED & BREAKFAST

Whatever the season... you will be pampered in this Victorian bed & breakfast staged in the past.

Reservations and information:
1009 Washington Street
(207) 442-8771
galenmoses@clinic.net.
http://www.bnbcity.com/inns/20028

Bath

5

Maine

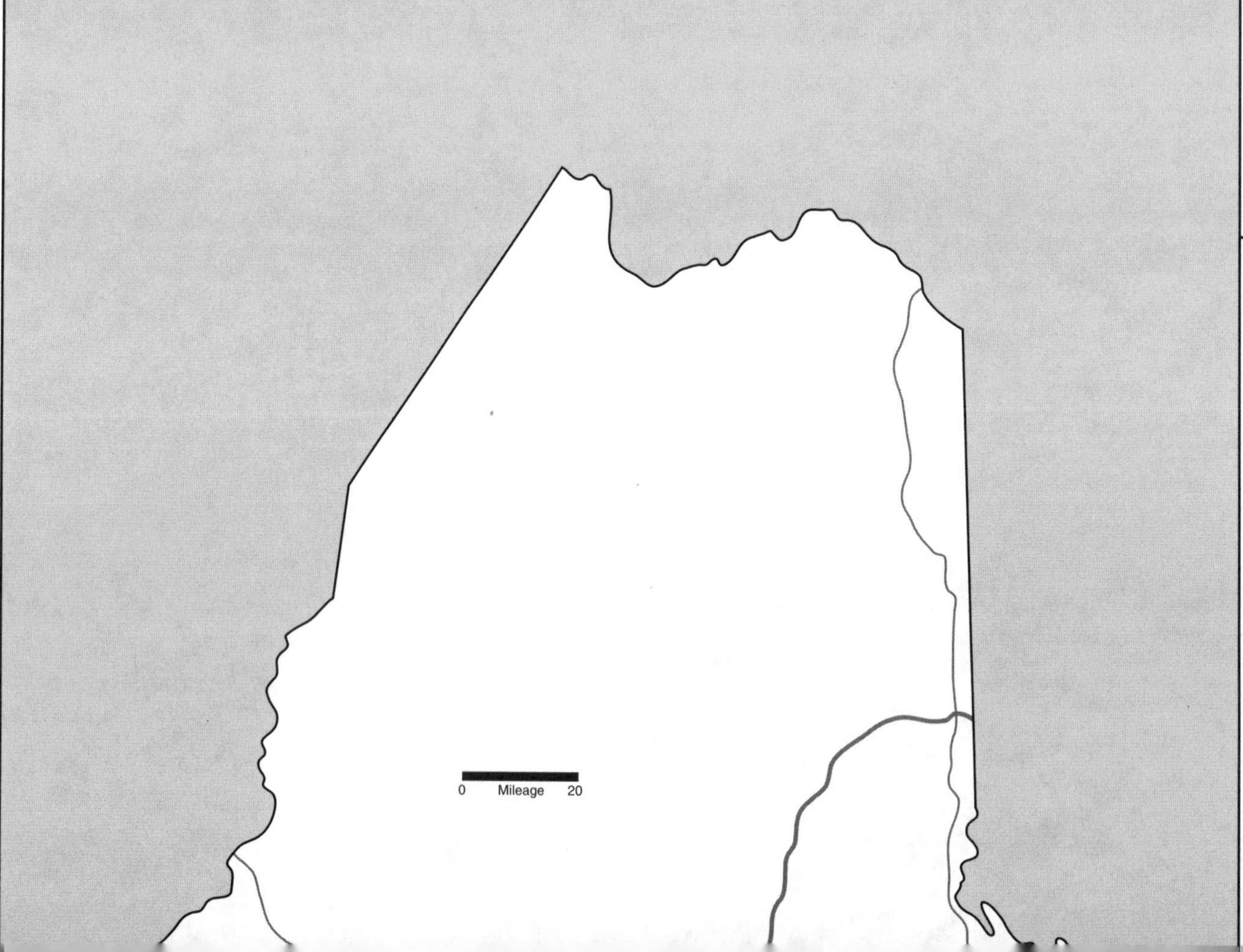

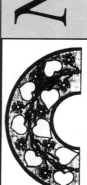

Brick House Antiques

Reverse Painted Lamps
Bohemian Glass
Art Nouveau
Fine Porcelain
Quality Furniture
Steins
Objects of Art

Corner Rt. 9 & Main St.

(207) 676-2885

No. Berwick

24

DAVID C. MOREY

AMERICAN ANTIQUES
103 MAIN STREET
(207) 354-6033

Thomaston

ORPHAN ANNIE'S

ART NOVEAU
ART DECO

Large quanity of art glass; French, American & Czeck, estate jewelry, vintage clothing, art pottery over 100 pieces of Roseville plus 2 story warehouse of furniture
96 Court St.
(207) 782-0638

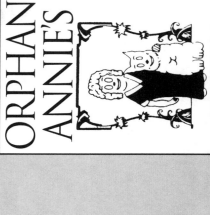

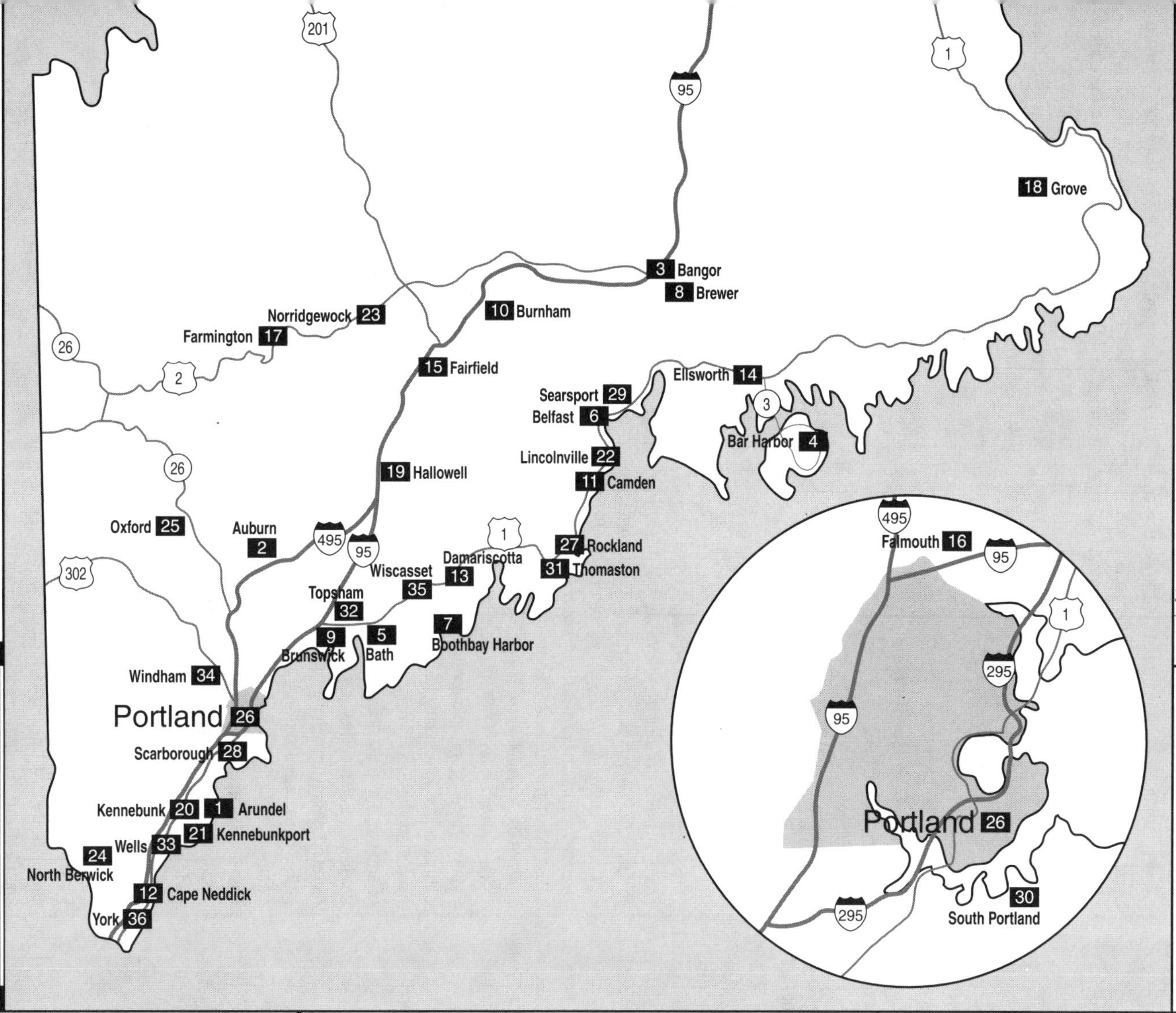

201
95
1
18 Grove
3 Bangor
8 Brewer
Norridgewock 23
10 Burnham
Farmington 17
26
15 Fairfield
2
Searsport 29
Belfast 6
Ellsworth 14
3
Bar Harbor 4
Lincolnville 22
11 Camden
19 Hallowell
26
Oxford 25
Auburn 2
495
95
1
27 Rockland
31 Thomaston
Damariscotta 13
Wiscasset 35
302
Topsham 32
9 Brunswick
5 Bath
7 Boothbay Harbor
Windham 34
Portland 26
Scarborough 28
Kennebunk 20
1 Arundel
21 Kennebunkport
Wells 33
24 North Berwick
12 Cape Neddick
York 36
495
Falmouth 16
95
1
295
95
Portland 26
295
30 South Portland

Maine

1 ARUNDEL

Arundel Antiques
1713 Portland Rd.
207/985-7965

Bacons
1740 Portland Rd.
207/985-1401

Nothing New Antiques
2796 Portland Rd. (Rt. 1)
207/286-1789

2 AUBURN

Orphan Annie's Antiques

96 Court Street
207/782-0638
Open daily Mon.-Sat. 10-5; Sun. 12-5

Directions: Take Exit 12 off the Maine Turnpike. Go left after the exit three miles into town. At the third stoplight, turn right onto Court Street. The shop is down 4 blocks on the right, across from the county courthouse.

For lovers of art glass, this is a shop you don't want to miss! Owner Dan Poulin has been in the antique business for 20 years, the last ten dealing primarily in art glass. This shop is full of such jewels as Tiffany, Stuben, Quezal, Imperial and numerous other styles in American glass; French glass pieces by Galle, Daum Nancy, D'Argental, Loetz and Czech glass. He specializes in art glass from the 1890s to the 1930s, getting most of the glass from private sources and some at auction.

The shop also offers over 100 pieces of Roseville, vintage clothing, along with a two-story warehouse filled to the brim with antique furnishings.

3 BANGOR

Alcott Antiques
30 Central St.
207/942-7706

Maritime International
547 Hammond St.
207/941-8372

4 BAR HARBOR

Bar Harbor Antiques
128 Cottage St.
207/288-3120

Olde Stuffe & Things
7 Everard Ct.
207/288-2203

Shaw Antiques
3 Cromwell Harbor Rd.
207/288-0114

Shaw Antiques & Fine Art
204 Main St.
207/288-9355

Supers Junkin Co.
Town Hill Route 102
207/288-5740

5 BATH

East of Brunswick along Coastal Route One is the shipbuilding city of Bath. Here is the site of Bath Iron Works, which produces many vessels for the United States Navy and the Merchant Marine. It is an impressive sight to see such massive ships under construction. Spectators can get a bird's eye view from the Route One Carlton Bridge, which spans the mighty Kennebec River. Bath is the business hub for many nearby resort areas along the Kennebec. Its downtown business district features wonderful brick sidewalks and street lamps reminiscent of the nineteenth century, while old sea captains' and shipbuilders' homes line the avenues. Visitors will also find a waterfront public park and several specialty and antique shops.

Between 1862 and 1902, Bath was the nation's fifth largest seaport, and nearly half of the United States' wooden sailing vessels were built here. During that era, more than 200 private shipbuilding firms flourished along a four-mile stretch of waterfront, producing large numbers of vessels. Exhibits describing the Maine shipbuilding traditions are displayed at the Maine Maritime Museum on the banks of the Kennebec in Bath. The Museum is a must for travelers interested in our nautical heritage.

The Galen C. Moses House

1009 Washington Street
207/442-8771
WebSite: http://www.bnbcity.com/inns/20028
E-mail: galenmoses@clinic.net.
Open year round
Rates $65-95

Directions: Take the Maine Turnpike (I-95) to Exit 6A (I-295). After Portland, I-295 rejoins I-95. Continue to Exit 22 (Route 1, Brunswick and Bath). Entering Bath, stay right for the last exit before the Bridge (marked "Historic Bath") and proceed to Washington Street. Turn left and drive 6 blocks to 1009 Washington, which is on the right.

The historic town of Bath offers both remarkable antique shopping and an incredible B&B. In 1994 former antique dealers James Haught and Larry Kieft moved from the antique business (except who ever really gets "out" of antiques!) into the bed and breakfast field - and they did it with a bang! They purchased the 1874 Galen C. Moses house and immediately made it the talk of the town.

The house was designed by Francis Fassett for Galen C. Moses (1835-1915) and redesigned in 1901 by John Calvin Stevens, one of Fassett's apprentices. The vernacular Italianate has an interior that is both Victorian and Colonial Revival. There are so many original, unique touches and finishes that I can't begin to list them all, but I will give you just a taste of what's in store when you visit: stained glass windows, elaborately carved mantels, window seats, arched windows, claw-foot tubs, and on the third floor, a full movie theater (vintage 1930s) complete with a projection booth and sixteen tiered seats facing a makeshift stage. During World War II, officers from the Brunswich Naval Air Station were invited to view movies (some of them supposedly "blue") as part of the local effort to build morale.

The three guest rooms, all with private baths, are upstairs (second floor) and continue the uniqueness of the house. The Victorian Room has bay windows and a white marble fireplace. The Moses Room holds an antique wash stand and the original plaster frieze on all four walls. The Vintage Room has been furnished with Oak and Walnut pieces of the period which compliment the 1874 built-in wash stand. And if all this doesn't overdose you on antiques, there are eight antique shops within blocks of the house, plus six antique shows per year in Bath.

Wait, there's more! Besides the rooms filled with antiques and the elegant gardens, the house contains a number of spirits, other than the sherry served at 5 p.m.! The ghosts are friendly and seem to make their presence felt on a regular basis. A full breakfast is served each morning, and the fare depends entirely on the cook's mood. Juice, coffee and muffins are always available for early risers or late sleepers, but the full meal can range from fresh fruit and blueberry pancakes to mushroom quiche or sour cream and chive omelets. It's an adventure all the way at the Moses House in Bath!

Brick Store Antiques
143 Front St.
207/443-2790

Countryside Antiques & Books
170 Front St.
207/442-0772

Cobblestone & Co.
176 Front St.
207/443-4064

Pollyanna's Antiques
182 Front St.
207/443-4909

Front Street Antiques
190 Front St.
207/443-8098

Atlantic Coast Antiques
Sanford Rd.
207/443-9185

6 BELFAST

Once a prosperous shipbuilding center, Belfast exhibits more than its share of exquisite Federal and early Victorian sea-merchants' mansions, many of them now operated as gracious inns and bed and breakfasts. White clapboard, aged brick, gingerbread trim, large lawns and enormous overarching oaks, elms and maples give the town a stately air. The charm is complimented by the "all-of-a-piece" flow of late 19th century brick shop fronts down Main Street to the bay and the attractive and neatly maintained Waterfront Heritage Park.

Anna's Antiques
Rt. 1
207/338-2219

Landmark Architectural Antqs.
4 Main St.
207/338-9901

Hall Hardware Co.
Searsport Ave., RR 1 Box 5138
207/338-1170

Avis Howell's Antiques
57 Pearl Street
207/338-3302

7 BOOTHBAY HARBOR

Bay Street Studio East Side
2 Bay St.
207/633-3186

Palabra Shops
85 Commercial St.
207/633-4225

Marine Antiques
43 Townsend Ave.
207/633-0862

Opera House Village Antiques
Townsend Ave.
207/633-6855

8 BREWER

Center Mall
39 Center St.
207/989-9842

Paul Noddin Antiques
171 Wilson St.
207/989-6449

9 BRUNSWICK

Robbins Antique & Art Gallery
343 Bath Rd.
207/729-3473

Dionne's Antique Shop
92 Merrymeeting Rd.
207/725-4263

Days Antiques
153 Park Row
207/725-6959

Antiques at 184 Pleasant
184 Pleasant St.
207/729-8343

10 BURNHAM

Houston-Brooks Auctioneers
Horseback Road
207/948-2214 or 1-800-254-2214
Fax: 207/948-5925

Directions: Off of I-95, take Exit #37 and take a right off the ramp. Follow the road 1 1/2 miles to Clinton Village. Take a right on Route 100 and follow for 7 miles to Burnham. Take a right at the store (signs are posted) and go 3.2 miles to the four corners. Take a right (signs are posted here, too) and the auction hall is the next place on the left.

Among the best-known auction houses in New England, Houston-Brooks is a family business that has been auctioning antiques for 27 years. Auctioneer and co-owner Pamela Brooks is one of the few practicing women auctioneers in the state. She's been at it 20 years herself; learning the art from working with her dad, who started the company. The auctions pull lots of customers from all over the region, especially from New England, upstate New York and Canada. Auctions are held every Sunday, and they offer a wide range of antique furniture, glass, collectibles, art and other items. According to Pam, they always have odd pieces come through. She says that the worst part of holding a weekly auction is that it's like running a never-ending race; you sell everything on Sunday and then wonder if you're going to have anything come in for the next week!

11 CAMDEN

Slightly larger than Kennebunkport - Camden's population is right at 4,000 - Camden is one of those rare places that is so stereotypical picturesque that it really looks "postcard perfect." Harbors, sailboats, softly mellowed houses, tree-lined streets and roads with dappled sunlight, breathtaking views around each bend in the road - this is Camden.

This is also sailboat country, and to really get a feel for the area, every visitor must spend a least a couple of hours out on Penobscot Bay. There are a variety of cruise options on both schooners and motor vessels, with trips running from just an hour to all day. If you are staying more than a little while, overnight, three-day and six-day cruises of the Maine coast are available on classic windjammers. You can also take weekend and week-long courses in sailing and earn a certificate that says "Learned to Sail in Maine."

When you shop, you'll find many more hand-loomed sweaters and handcrafted jewelry than you will tee shirts. And the food is not to be missed - all of the famous Maine fare, from lobsters, scallops and mussels to clams, haddock, salmon and swordfish. Here's a most interesting and refreshing end note: Camden has no fast-food franchises! So it really is "postcard perfect!"

Downshire House Clocks
49 Bayview St.
207/236-9016

Hard Alee
51 Bayview St.
207/236-3373

Star Bird
17 Main St.
207/236-8292

The Historic Inns of High Street

Edgecombe-Coles House
1-800-528-2336
Fax: 207/236-6227

A Little Dream
207/236-8742

Norumbega
207/236-4646
Fax: 207/236-0824
Internet: norumbeg@adadia.net

Whitehall Inn
207/236-3391 or 1-800-789-6565

Abigail's
1-800-292-2501
Fax: 207/230-0657

Hawthorne Inn
207/236-6181

12 CAPE NEDDICK

Columbary Antiques
RR 1
207/363-5496

Cranberry Hill Antiques
RR 1
207/363-5178

13 DAMARISCOTTA

Damariscotta is a classic Maine coastal village nestled along the eastern side of the Damariscotta River.

Oyster shell heaps, some reaching 30 feet in height, attest to this area being a centuries-old sanctuary for native American people. During the mid-1800s, Damariscotta was home to Metcalf and Norris, pioneer clipper ship builders. From their yards came the *Flying Scud*, famous for her 76-day passage to Melbourne.

1839 House
370 Bristol Rd.
207/563-2375

Patricia Anne Reed Fine Antqs.
148 Bristol Rd.
207/563-5633

Loons Landing Antiques
Courtyard Shops
207/563-8931

14 ELLSWORTH

Mill Mall Treasures
Bangor Rd., Route 1A
207/667-8055

His & Hers Antiques
Bucksport Rd.
207/667-2115

Eastern Antiques
52 Dean St.
207/667-4033

Sandy's Antiques
111 Oak St.
207/667-5078

Big Chicken Barn Books & Antiques
RR 3
207/667-7308

15 FAIRFIELD

Trading Post
194 Main St.
207/453-2526

Julia-Poulin Antiques
199 Route 201
207/453-2114

16 FALMOUTH

Scottish Terrier Antiques
89 Hillside Ave.
207/797-4223

Port 'N Starboard Gallery
53 Falmouth Rd.
207/781-4214

17 FARMINGTON

The Old Barn Annex Antiques
30 Middle Street #3
207/778-6908

Always presenting outstanding quality and exceptional antiques. If you can't visit them in Maine, be sure to watch for The Old Barn Annex Antiques on exhibit at finer antique shows.

18 GROVE

The Paul S. Noddin Antiques
171 Wilson St.
207/989-6449

19 HALLOWELL

Dealer's Choice Antique Mall
108 Water St.
207/622-5527

Berdam & Newsom Antiques
151 Water St.
207/622-0151

Brass & Friends Antiques
154 Water St.
207/626-3287

Acme Antiques
165 Water St.
207/622-2322

James Lefurgy Antqs. & Books
168 Water St.
207/623-1771

Johnson-Marsano Antiques
172 Water St.
207/623-6263

Josiah Smith Antiques
181 Water St.
207/622-4188

20 KENNEBUNK

Heritage House Antiques
10 Christensen Lane
207/967-5952

Rivergate Antique Mall
RR 1
207/985-6280

Antiques on Nine
75 Western Ave. (Rt. 9)
207/967-0626

Victorian Lighting
29 York St.
207/985-6868

21 KENNEBUNKPORT

Kennebunkport, with its little population of just 1,100, offers something for just about everyone, but especially for those who love the sea and a little seclusion. Scattered among its beaches, harbors, boat yards, rocky coasts, manicured streets, quaint shops and historic churches are the magnificent homes of 18th and 19th century sea captains, shipbuilders and wealthy summer residents. Many of these homes are now bed and breakfasts; indeed, few towns can match Kennebunkport for number, variety, and quality of its inns and the experience of the town's innkeepers. There are also several restored seaside hotels from another era that dot the scenic landscape of the town.

If you want a good introduction to the history of the Kennebunks(the name of the townsfolk), visit the Brick Store Museum. The museum shop features quality reproductions and books on local history and crafts. Another way to visit the area's past is to tour White Columns, a gracious Greek Revival mansion (1851-1853) with original furnishings that is maintained by the Kennebunkport Historical Society.

There's all sorts of things to do and see around Kennebunkport. Many of the historic buildings on Dock Square and elsewhere now house galleries and artists' studios, as well as many interesting little shops. The Seashore Trolley Museum has a collection of over 225 trolleys from around the world, and offers a three-mile ride on an antique electric trolley. And all visitors should take at least one off-shore excursion and indulge in whale-watching, sightseeing and cruising. There's also canoeing, golfing, cross-country skiing, hiking or biking.

Old Fort Inn
8 Old Fort Ave.
207/967-5353

Antiques USA
RR1
207/985-7766

22 LINCOLNVILLE

Blue Dolphin Antiques
164 Atlantic Hwy
207/338-3860

Deer Meadows
RR 1
207/236-8020

Painted Lady
RR 1
207/789-5201

23 NORRIDGEWOCK

Black Hill Antiques & Cllbls.
Main
207/634-5151

Victoria Shoppe Antique Mall
Main
207/634-3130

24 NORTH BERWICK

Brick House Antiques

Corner Rt. 9 & Main Street
207/676-2885
Open every day

Located seven miles from Wells and Ogunquit, Brick House Antiques is literally a treasure trove of hand picked antiques. Reverse painted lamps, Bohemian glass, Art Nouveau, fine porcelain, quality furniture, steins and objects of art are some of the examples that may be found in one of Maine's finest antique shops.

25 OXFORD

The Inn at Little Creek

Route 121
207/539-4046
Open year round
Rates $35-75

Directions: Take the Maine Turnpike to Exit 11 (Gray) to Route 26 North. Travel Route 26 North approximately 30 minutes to Oxford. Take Route 121 South. The inn is located on Route 121 South, 1 1/4 miles off of Route 26 in the village of Oxford.

This bed & breakfast truly stands out from all the others. It was started only two years ago by Ken Ward and Diane Lecuyer, and already has return guests from around the world. What sets it apart is that it is furnished in a Native American/Southwestern flavor, complete to the serving of buffalo meat and Native American teas for breakfast. And all this is tucked away in the southwestern end of Maine!

Running a B&B has been a dream of Ken's since he was 18 years old. When he and Diane decided to open the inn, they spent a year traveling around the country, visiting B&Bs, to see just what was available. They knew they wanted something totally different so, since Diane is part Native American, they decided to include her heritage as the main focus of their B&B. Although Diane is associated with the Iroquois Nation of the Northeast, they used the Southwestern feel because most non-Native Americans only know that side of the culture. The inn is furnished in the soft, muted pastel palette of the Southwest that is familiar to most people (as opposed to the harsher, more vivid palette that is also part of the Southwestern culture). But they have not focused on any specific tribes, using instead artifacts and accessories from all over North America. In this way, they use their B&B to help educate people about Native Americans in general. They are not yet selling Native American artifacts and antiques, but may in the future.

As to where one obtains buffalo meat in Maine? Well, surprise, there are two buffalo ranches in the state, one of which is conveniently near the inn and operated by a friend of Ken and Diane's. Diane is the cook and prepares all the buffalo meat dishes. The Native American teas are brought in from the Dakotas and served to the inn's guests for breakfast.

Although The Inn at Little Creek is new on the B&B scene, it has already established a following and is certainly a welcome addition and change of pace. So visit Ken and Diane and soak up a little culture and history while you relax in the "wilds" of Maine.

Kall Us Antiques
Rt. 26
207/743-9788

Meetinghouse Antiques
Rt. 26
207/539-8480

Undercover Antique Mall
Rt. 26
207/539-4149

26 PORTLAND

Shipwreck & Cargo Co.
207 Commercial
207/775-3057

Seavey's
249 Congress
207/773-1908

Annas Used Furn. & Cllbls.
612 Congress St.
207/775-7223

Antiques at Zinnias
662 Congress St.
207/780-6622

Venture Antiques
101 Exchange St.
207/773-6064

F. O. Bailey Co. Inc.
141 Middle St.
207/774-1479

Salty Professor Antique
4 1/2 Milk St.
207/772-4640

West Port Antiques
8 Milk St.
207/774-6747

27 ROCKLAND

Katrin Phocas Ltd. Antiques
19 Main
207/236-8654

Hall Antiques
432 Main
207/594-5031

Shore Village Antiques
474 Main St.
207/596-0077

Early Times Antique Center
Rt (90) in Rockport
207/236-3001

28 SCARBOROUGH

Centervale Farm Antiques

200 U.S. Route One at Oak Hill
207/883-3443 or 800/896-3443
Open year round, 10-5 (Nov.-June closed Mondays)

Directions: Maine Turnpike, Exit 6, then take Route 1 north 6 miles south of Portland via 295.

Delight in this New England barn filled with country antiques, furniture, paintings, rugs, lamps plus all sorts of accessories. An ell connected to the barn extends the wonderful selection to include porcelain, glassware, silver, toys up to and beyond "you-name-it."

Cliff's Antique Market
RR 1
207/883-5671

Centervale Farm Antiques
200 U.S. Route 1
207/883-3443

A Scarborough Fair Antiques
264 U.S. Route 1
207/883-5999

Top Knotch
14 Willowdale Rd.
207/883-5303

29 SEARSPORT

Pumpkin Patch Antiques
15 W Main St./Route 1
207/548-6047

Red Kettle Antiques
RR 1
207/548-2978

Searsport Antique Mall
RR 1
207/548-2640

30 SOUTH PORTLAND

Cherished Possessions
185 Cottage Rd.
207/799-3990

G L Smith Antiques Art Cllbls.
378 Cottage Rd.
207/799-5253

Mulberry Cottage
45 Western Ave.
207/775-5011

31 THOMASTON

Located on the St. George River is Thomaston, once an important port and home to many prominent sea captains. Beautiful homes still exist to mark the rich heritage of the town. General Henry Knox, chief-of-staff and Secretary of War for President George Washington, once resided in Thomaston. Today a replica of his mansion, Montpelier, offers visitors a chance to see the home as it was in the days when it housed the General's family.

David C. Morey American Antiques
103 Main Street
207/354-6033 or 207/372-6660
Open Wed., Fri. & Sat., 10-5 or by appointment anytime

Honoring the American craftsmen, David C. Morey Antiques presents 18th century American country furnishings and accessories in this 2,000 square foot shop.

Wee Barn Antiques
4 1/2 Georges St.
207/354-6163

Ross Levett Antiques
111 Main St.
207/354-6227

Anchor Farm Antiques
184 Main St.
207/354-8859

The Rose Cottage
187 Main St.
207/354-6250

32 TOPSHAM

Lisbon Road Antiques
1089 Lewiston Rd.
207/353-4094

Waterfall Corner Antiques
10 Main St.
207/725-0058

Red Schoolhouse Antiques
8 Middlesex Rd.
207/729-4541

Affordable Antiques
49 Topsham Fair Mall, #21
207/729-7913

33 WELLS

Reed's Antiques & Collectibles
U.S. Route 1
207/646-8010 or 1-800-891-2017
Open: Daily 10-5

Directions: Exit 2, ME Turnpike, Left on Route 1

In two short years Reed's has become known as the Number One multi-dealer shop in Maine for quality antiques and collectibles. Open year round, seven days a week, this customer-friendly store has merchandise ranging from Meissen to Mickey Mouse, Sevres to Star Wars, Neo-lithic artifacts to Nouveau art. Whether you are shopping for a personal treasure, a choice resale item or a special gift, you're sure to find it at Reed's. Come join the thousands of other satisfied customers from all over the world who have made Reed's their MUST STOP SHOP. When a Maine native says "This is the best shop in New England" they must be doing it right!

MacDougall-Gionet Antiques & Associates
U.S. Route 1; 2104 Post Road
207/646-3531
Open 9-5 daily, closed Mondays

Known as New England's most exciting period antiques center, MacDougall-Gionet's sixty quality dealers pack the barn full of names such as Hepplewhite, Chippendale and Sheraton. Here you will find items such as camphorwood chests, tavern tables, Pennsylvania dower chest in original salmon and smoked paint, an original mustard and stenciled dressing table, turquoise inlaid secretary desk and the list goes on. Stop in and see for yourself the marvelous inventory of fine antiques.

Farm
294 Mildram Rd.
207/985-2656

R Jorgensen Antiques
502 Post Rd., Rt #1
207/646-9444

Bomar Hall Antiques & Cllbls.
1622 Post Rd.
207/646-4116

Art Smith Antiques
1755 Post Rd.
207/646-6996

Peggy Carboni Antiques
1755 Post Rd.
207/646-4551

Smith-Zukas
1755 Post Rd.
207/646-6996

Wells Antique Mart
RR 1
207/646-8153

Country Mouse D & A
2077 Sanford Rd.
207/646-7334

Wells Union Antique Center
1755 Post Rd.
207/646-6996

34 WINDHAM

Barn
71 Route 115
207/892-9776

Smokey's Den Antiques
133 Roosevelt Trail
207/892-6775

35 WISCASSET

Wiscasset is an inspiring community for artists and writers, as well as shoppers and sightseers. Located on the west bank of the Sheepscot River at the western edge of Lincoln County, the town's attractions include two decaying four-masted schooners which were beached along the banks of the Sheepscot in 1932. *Luther Little* and *Hester*, as they are called, were built during World War I and saw active service during the 1920s as cargo vessels.

Other points of interest in this charming town are the distinguished and stately mansions which used to belong to sea captains and shipping merchants. Several of these are open to the public during the summer months. Scenic boat rides and train trips leave from the waterfront area to provide unique views of coastal wildlife and marvelous views.

Parkers of Wiscasset Antiques
Coastal Route One
207/882-5520
North and South Buildings open April-December
Seven days a week 9-5; after Columbus day, 10-4

A dream come true; two buildings filled to overflowing with anything you might desire in the antique line. At Parkers of Wiscasset Antiques, you will find folk art, toys, early pottery, quimper, country and primitives, furniture, quilts and rugs, paintings, Indian jewelry as well as the unusual; Irish lace baby bonnet, 18th century iron toaster, early brass trivet and human hair art in a frame are just a few of the recent offerings. If you're looking for the ordinary as well as the unique, we recommend you visit Parkers of Wiscasset Antiques.

Marston House Amer Antiques
Main
207/882-6010

Patricia Stauble
Main
207/882-6341

Two at Wiscasset
Main
207/882-5286

Nonesuch House Antiques
1 Middle St.
207/882-6768

Maine Antiques
RR 1
207/882-7347

Maine Trading Post
RR1
207/882-7400

36 YORK

York Antiques Gallery
Route 1
207/363-5002
Open daily 10-5 year round

Directions: Easy access from I-95, just 9/10 of a mile north from the Yorks, Ogunquit Exit (last exit before toll).

Intrigue and artistry are the hallmarks of the collection found at York Antique Gallery. Showcased in this multiple dealer shop are 18th and 19th century country and formal furniture in addition to accessories. Shoppers will also discover a surprising assortment of other goods including textiles, paintings/prints, nautical items, decoys/hunting, advertising, folk art, Indian, military/fire, as well as out of print reference books.

Marie Plummer & John Philbrick
44 Chases Pond Road
207/363-2515

Offerings of exceptional quality and a unique display of early antiques, makes this shop grandly unique. Just a sampling of the superior items available are: c. 1780 New England pine pipe box, an 18th century Westwald jug, and an 18th century New England maple rope bed.

Barn at Cape Neddick Antqs.
RR 1
207/363-7315

Bell Farm Antiques
RR 1
207/363-8181

Maritime Antiques
935 U.S. Route 1
207/363-4247

Olde Stuff Shop
RR 1
207/363-4517

York Village Crafts Antiques & Gifts
211 York St.
207/363-4830

1940s to 1990s Style:

JUKEBOXES • CLASSIC DINER FURNITURE
FAMILY GAME ROOM ITEMS

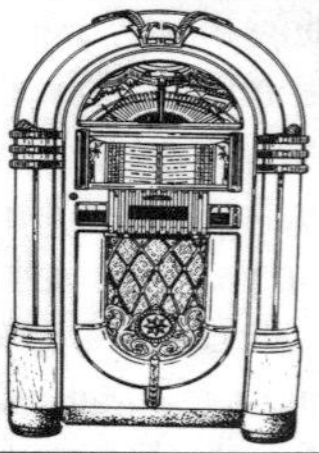

A-1 Jukebox & Nostalgia Company
208 South Pulaski Street • 4th Floor
Baltimore, MD • 1-888-694-9464
Web Site: jukebox50s@aol.com

2

Welcome to the
Antique Capital
of Maryland
New Market

38

Maryland's Largest
Antique Mall

AAA ANTIQUES MALL, INC.
2659 Annapolis Rd.
(Rts. 295 & 175)
410-551-4101
Over 58,000 Sq. Ft of Quality Antiques & Collectibles
Hanover

28

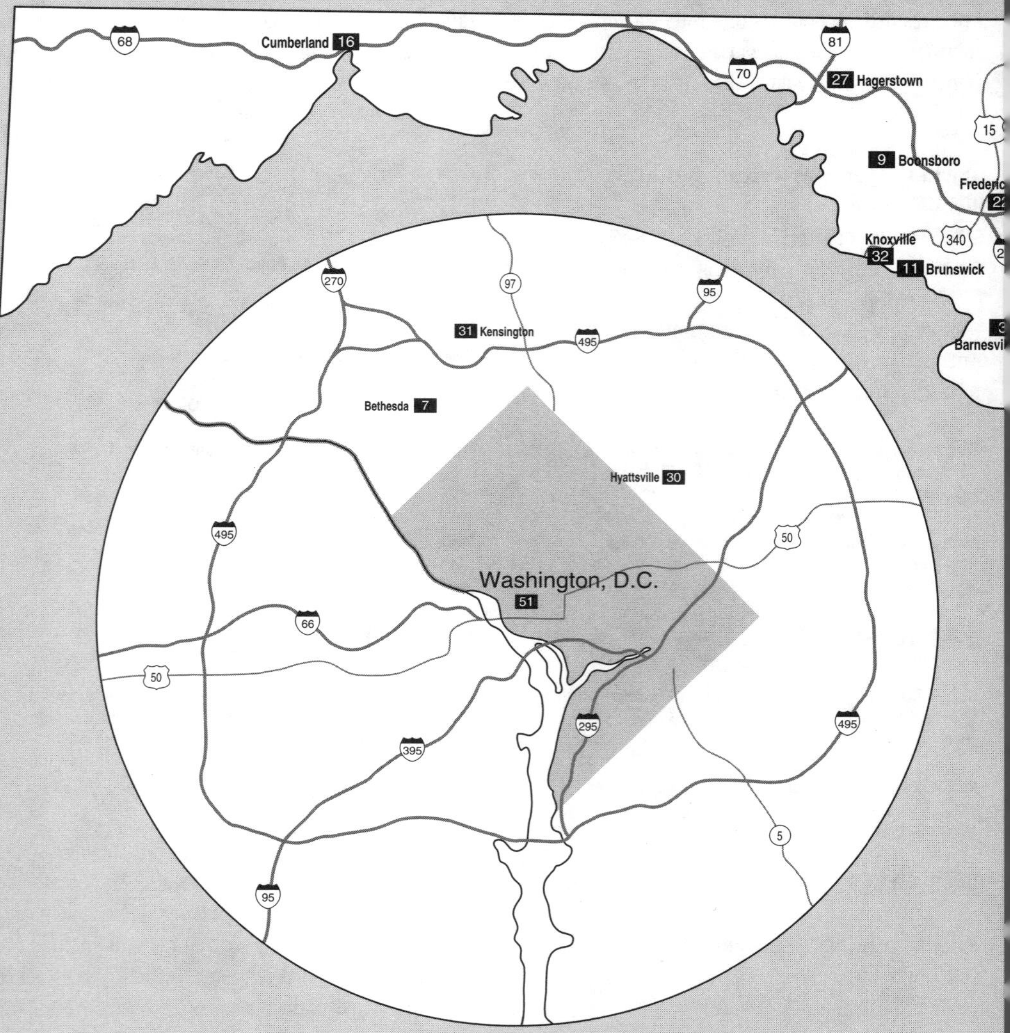

Maryland / D.C.

Off the Deep End
3,000 sq. ft. Show Room
Over 14,000 Books
Frederick, MD

22

MR. MOLE
BED & BREAKFAST
Near Antique Row
1601 Bolton Street • (410) 728-1179
Baltimore, MD

2

Shady Oaks of Serenity
Charles County's First Bed & Breakfast

(301)932-8864
800-597-0924
Bryantown, MD

12

Amaryllis
VINTAGE CO., INC.
Home Furnishings, Rugs, Decorative Arts
circa 1840-1940
4922 Wisconsin Ave. • (202) 244-2211
Washington, DC

51

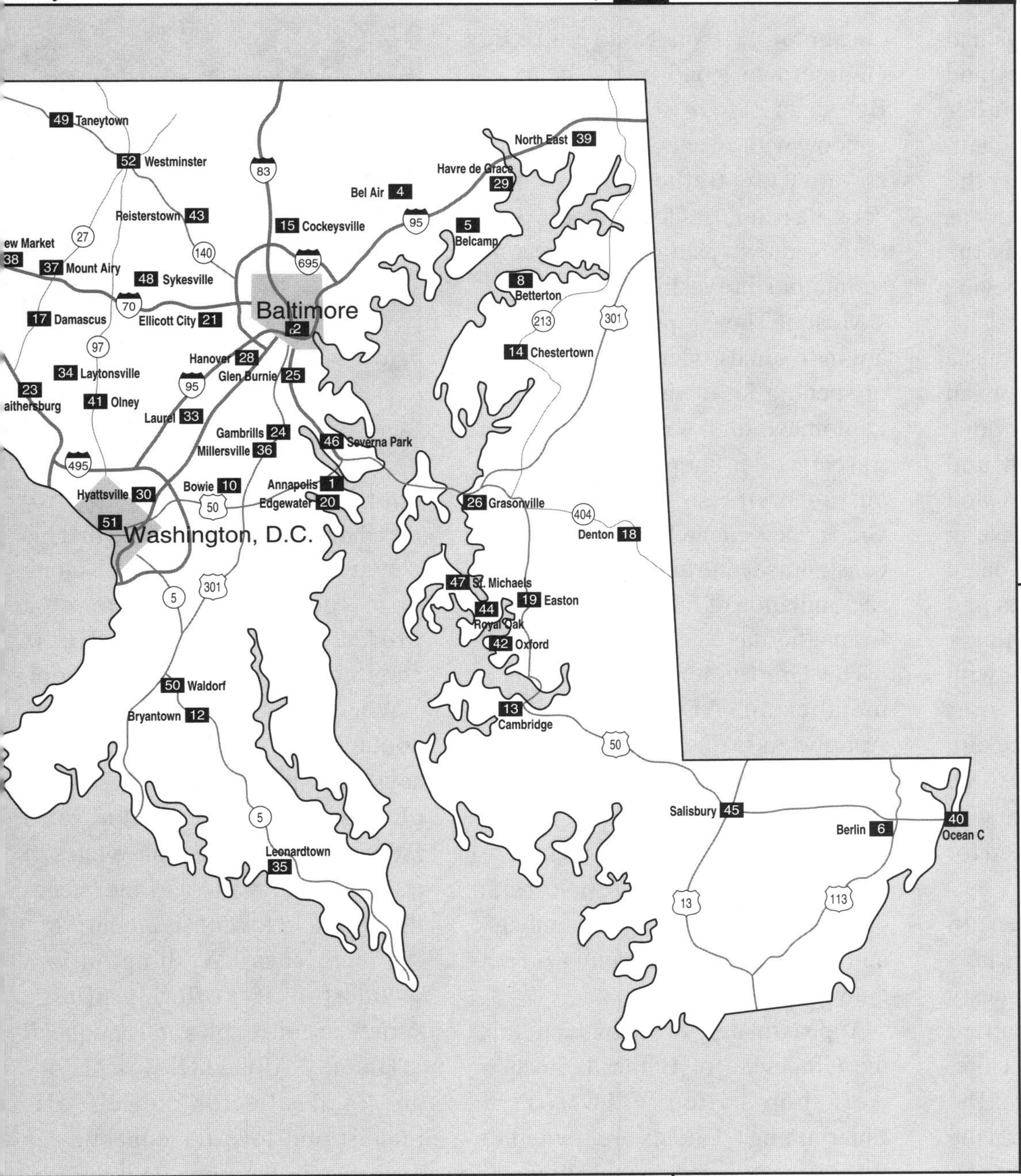

49 Taneytown
52 Westminster
83
North East 39
Havre de Grace 29
Bel Air 4
Reisterstown 43
15 Cockeysville
95
5 Belcamp
27
New Market 38
37 Mount Airy
140
695
48 Sykesville
8 Betterton
70
17 Damascus
Ellicott City 21
Baltimore
2
213
301
97
Hanover 28
14 Chestertown
34 Laytonsville
Glen Burnie 25
95
23
Gaithersburg
41 Olney
Laurel 33
Gambrills 24
Millersville 36
46 Severna Park
495
Hyattsville 30
Bowie 10
Annapolis 1
Edgewater 20
50
26 Grasonville
404
51
Washington, D.C.
Denton 18
47 St. Michaels
19 Easton
5
301
44
Royal Oak
42 Oxford
50 Waldorf
13
Cambridge
Bryantown 12
50
Salisbury 45
Berlin 6
40
Ocean City
5
Leonardtown
35
13
113

Making a Difference

Timothy Albrecht
Grapevine of Bethesda

Timothy Albrecht has always had a personal interest in antiques and tableware. He can remember collecting at the age of 10. Tim applied for a position at the Grapevine at the age of 16 and was turned down. Today, he owns the store now known as the Grapevine of Bethesda.

The Grapevine of Bethesda consigns and sells antiques, Persian rugs, and oil paintings. This antique store specializes in French and Continental furniture pieces as well as tableware. Most merchandise at the Grapevine of Bethesda is dated between 1850 and 1920. You can find anything from place plates to finger bowls at the Grapevine. Along with place settings of 12, the shop carries English and Continental porcelain. Beautiful oil paintings can also be bought or consigned here. Many of these paintings can be researched for history or has an auction trail.

The Grapevine has been in existence for fifty years. Past owners had impeccable qualities of honesty and fairness which traits are carried on today. First owned by Linda Gore, a very distant relative of Al Gore, The Grapevine was located on Brookville Road and then moved to Bethesda. Ms. Gore owned the business for 23 years before selling to the second owner, Mrs. Grant. Timothy Albrecht is the third owner and has operated this highly reputable business for three years.

This unique shop is located on the corner of Wilson Road and Old Georgetown Road in the heart of Bethesda. There is a store front window with an entrance at each side street. Cafe Bethesda, a French cooking school, is located next door (and is known as one of the best 50 restaurants in Washington, D.C.)

Most of The Grapevine's clientele are individuals interested in fine art or spend a lot of time entertaining. Diplomats, high society, and world travelers often shop at this reputable antique store. Many of The Grapevine's clientele bring pieces for consignment due to liquidation or the accumulation of fine pieces acquired from a heritage.

The Grapevine of Bethesda is a member of ADAM, Maryland Antique Association, an affiliate of Maryland Retail Association. Benefits of membership with the association, says Mr. Albrecht, are the "opportunities to share notes with other antique dealers and members, and the advantage of buying pieces among themselves."

Approximately every two months, the Grapevine of Bethesda hosts a workshop called "The Art of Entertaining." Clients are invited to listen to knowledgeable speakers talk on subjects such as Russian porcelain, English porcelain or style and tableware.

Mr. Albrecht's future goal for his antique business is to fine tune his collection and services; learn more about his fine collectibles; and to continue to look for quality merchandise and fine pieces that his clientele are searching for. His long term goal is to become a professional appraiser. He is currently attending appraisal school.

When asked what he enjoys most about his business, Mr. Albrecht says "the interesting people . . most of whom are mature, well traveled individuals who often have tales to tell of their travels and the pieces they bring in for consignment." Mr. Albrecht says "Washington is a wonderful city, offering a large variety of collectibles and antiques."

Timothy Albrecht loves history and is a collector himself. His interest and love for collecting is reflective in the fine quality pieces his store offers. The Grapevine of Bethesda's hours of operation are Tuesday through Saturday, 10 a.m.-5 p.m.; their address is 7806 Old Georgetown Road, Bethesda, MD 20814; and phone number (301) 654-8690.

1 ANNAPOLIS

Founded in 1649, Annapolis is often referred to as a "museum without walls," for the number of historic homes and buildings that have been restored and are open to the public. The city has served as Maryland's State Capitol since 1694, and was the nation's capital from November 1783 to August 1784.

A Absolutely A Fabulous Antqs.
14 Annapolis St.
410/268-8762

Country Finds
103 Annapolis St.
410/267-9366

Clockmaker Shop
Generals Hwy.
410/266-0770

Baldwin & Claude Antiques
47 Maryland Ave.
410/268-1665

Sixth Street Studio
422 6th St.
410/267-8233

Third Millennium Designs
57 Maryland Ave.
410/267-6428

Walnut Leaf Antiques
62 Maryland Ave.
410/263-4885

Maryland Ave. Antiques
82 Maryland Ave.
410/268-5158

DHS Designs Inc.
86 Maryland Ave.
410/280-3466

Annapolis Antique Gallery
2009 West St.
410/266-0635

Ron Snyder Antiques
2011 West St.
410/266-5452

2 BALTIMORE

A 14-block area in Eastern Baltimore, fronting on the Patapsco River with the deepest harbor in the area, this active post is one of the original communities that joined "Baltimore Town" to become the city of Baltimore. The first settlers came in 1724, and the grid plan was laid out by Edward Fell in 1761. Many of the cobblestone streets retain their English-inspired names, including Thames And Shakespeare. Fells Point's famed shipyards produced the renowned Baltimore clippers used as privateers, along with frigates and sloops used by the Continental Navy. The Broadway Market, along with scores of charming antiques shops and restaurants, still welcomes visitors from foreign lands—as well as locals intent on shopping or dining.

Antique Amusements

A-1 Jukebox & Nostalgia Co.
208 South Pulaski Street
Phone & Fax 410/945-8900
Toll Free Order Line 1-888-694-9464
Hours: 10am-5pm Mon. - Fri. and some Saturdays. Closed on Sundays
From 5:30pm-8:30pm Monday through Friday, they offer customers in home service and installation for the items they sell.

Directions: Located one mile west of Oriole Park at Camden Yards in West Baltimore. From Oriole Park take Lombard St., (it's one way west), 1 mile to Pulaski Street and turn left 1 1/2 blocks, on the right side side. From Interstate 91 northbound or southbound take exit #50 North to Wilkens Ave. and turn right. At the 5th traffic light turn left onto South Pulaski Street. 2 blocks north on the left side.

Antique Amusements A-1 Jukebox & Nostalgia Company has been in business for seventeen years selling and servicing jukeboxes. If you have a jukebox to sell they also buy jukeboxes. They will even rent a jukebox to you for your next party or company event. Their jukebox inventory consists of New Compact Disc Wurlitzer jukeboxes and Original Seeburg jukeboxes from the 50s, 60s, and 70s. It's important to know that more 45 R.P.M. records, (the 7 inch singles with the big hole), are currently being made now than at any time in the past and that's because so many folks are purchasing new Wurlitzer and original jukeboxes for their homes and businesses. Their $4.95 "Singles" Record Catalog lists ten thousand 45 R.P.M. records, and on any given order they can supply at least an 80% fill. They carry many replacement parts for Wurlitzer and Seeburg jukeboxes and all of the repair and parts manuals including schematics for: Rock-Ola; Rowe/Ami; Seeburg; and Wurlitzer jukeboxes. They also carry a complete line of classic style diner booths, chairs, stools, and tables. Some of the most unique items include: Edison Cylinder Machines from the turn of the last century, (they actually reproduce sound by playing a wax cylinder); reproduction barber poles which light-up and have a rotating pole, (made of glass and metal just like the originals); reproduction metal signs, (very limited production), mostly soft drink signs, some with thermometers; and a line of stained glass hanging light fixtures, (top quality). Antiques Amusements A-1 Jukebox & Nostalgia Company currently occupies 5,000 sq. ft. of space in a five story brick building known as the Cambridge Building. They are planning to move the entire business operation to Howard County, Maryland during 1998.

If you would like to see color pictures of their unique and beautiful items, please visit their Web Site at: jukebox50s@aol.com. The Web Site has taken the place of the old catalog, which they no longer use. Domestic and World Wide Shipping is available. Visa, Mastercard, and Personal Checks in U.S. Dollars are accepted.

Twin Gates B & B Inn

308 Morris Avenue
410/252-3131
Open year round

Soft music, fresh flowers, beautifully decorated rooms and unforgettable breakfasts are highlights of this inn nestled in a serene Victorian village. Voted "Baltimore's Best" by readers of *Baltimore* magazine.

Mr. Mole Bed & Breakfast

1601 Bolton Street
410/728-1179
Open year round

Awarded four stars by the Mobil Travel Guide, Mr. Mole offers five suites, some with two bedrooms and sitting room. Conveniently located near the opera, the symphony and antique row.

Another Period in Time

1708-1710 Fleet Street
410/675-4776
Open Mon.-Thurs., 9-5; Fri., 9-6; Sat., 10-6, Sun., 12-5 (Closed Easter Sunday, Thanksgiving Day and Christmas Day)

Directions: A short distance from the Inner Harbor.

Situated in the former Henry Sander & Sons Funeral Home (c. 1850), this multi-dealer emporium is located in the Historic Fells Point district of Baltimore. Truly representative of "another period," offerings from c. 1790 to 1950 include antique furniture, depression glass, costume jewelry, china, dolls and art.

Barbara's Collectibles
1707 Aliceanna St.
410/276-9702

Constance
1709 Aliceanna St.
410/563-6031

Along The Way, Ltd.
1719 Aliceanna
410/276-4461

Auntie Q's
1721 Aliceanna St.
410/276-7660

Saratoga Trunk
1740 Aliceanna St.
410/327-6635

Velveteen Rabbit
20 Allegheny Ave.
410/583-1685

Portebello Square Inc.
28 Allegheny Ave.
410/821-1163

Collectors Item
4903 Belair Rd.
410/483-2020

The Karmic Connection
508 S. Broadway
410/558-0428

The Pink Shack
602 S. Broadway
410/732-2919

Memory Lane Antiques
607 S. Broadway
410/276-0865

Off Broadway Antiques
614 S. Broadway
410/732-6522

Oh! Susanna
620 S. Broadway
410/327-1408

Hattie's Antiques & Collectibles
726 S. Broadway
410/276-1316

Max's Trading Co.
733 S. Broadway
410/675-6297

Craig Flinner Gallery
505 N. Charles St.
410/727-1863

Modest Rupert's Attic
919 S. Charles St.
410/727-4505

Silver Mine
1023 N. Charles St.
410/752-4141

Olde Touch
2103 N. Charles St.
410/783-1493

Sabina & Daughter
1637 Eastern Avenue
410/276-6366

Arbutus Bargain Market
5305 East Dr.
410-242/4050

A Squirrel's Nest
313 Eastern Blvd
410/391-3664

Thompson's Antiques
430 Eastern Blvd(Essex)
410/686-3107

Ramm Antiques & Collectibles
811 Eastern Blvd
410/687-5284

Reginald Fitzgerald Antiques
1704 Eastern
410/534-2942

John's Art & Antiques
1733 Eastern
410/675-4339

John's Antiques Inc.
1733 Eastern Ave.
410/576-0646

Antique Toy & Train World
3626 Falls Road
410/889-0040

Maryland/D.C.

Sunporch Antiques
6072 Falls Rd.
410/377-2904

The Book Miser
906 Fell
410/234-0482

American Pie
1704 Fleet St.
410/276-0062

J & M Antiques
1706 Fleet St.
410/732-2919

Davids-Gans Co., Inc.
910 W. 36th St.
410/467-8159

The Bowery of Antiques
1709 Fleet St.
410/732-2778

R & H Antiques
1720 Fleet St.
410/522-1621

Mystery Loves Company
1730 Fleet St.
410/276-6708

Antique Man
1731 Fleet St.
410/732-0932

In The Groove Antiques
1734 Fleet St.
410/675-7174

Antique Row
1922 Fleet St.
410/675-5291

Old Treasure Chest
3409 Greenmount Ave.
410/889-0540

Rag Picker Collection
5722 Harford Rd.
410/254-0033

Valley Gun
7719 Harford Rd.
410/668-2171

DJ's Antiques & Collectibles
7914 Harford Rd.
410/665-4344

Dusty Attic
9411 Harford Rd.
410/668-2343

Hamilton House Antiques
865 N. Howard St.
410/462-5218

Paean's Oriental Rugs
713 Howard St.
410/669-6690

Crosskeys Antiques
801 N. Howard St.
410/728-0101

Antiques at 805
805 N. Howard St.
410/728-8419

Dubeys Art & Antiques
807 N. Howard St.
410/383-2881

Antique Treasury
809 N. Howard St.
410/728-6363

Fisher Interiors P G
817 N. Howard St.
410/669-9292

Thaynes Antiques
823 N. Howard St.
410/728-7109

Heritage Antiques
829 N. Howard St.
410/728-7033

Imperial Half Bushel
831 N. Howard St.
410/462-1192

Angela R Thrasher Antiques
833 N. Howard St.
410/523-0550

Fox & Fox Antiques
837 N. Howard St.
410/523-6302

E. A Mack Antiques Inc.
839 N. Howard St.
410/728-1333

Amos Judd & Son Inc.
841-843 N. Howard st
410/462-2000

Wintzer Galleries
853 N. Howard St.
410/462-3313

Drusilla's Books
859 Howard St.
410/225-0277

Sindler Fine Arts & Antiques
859 Howard St.
410/728-3377

Yakov's Antiques
861 N. Howard St.
410/728-4517

Connoisseurs Connection
869 N. Howard St.
410/383-2624

Harris Auction Galleries Inc.
875 N. Howard St.
410/728-7040

L A Herstein & Co.
877 N. Howard St.
410/728-3856

Regency Antiques
893 N. Howard St.
410/225-3455

Antique Warehouse at 1300
1300 Jackson St.
410/659-0662

Antique Furniture Co.
3524 Keswick Rd.
410/366-2421

Gaines McHale Antiques
836 Leadenhall St.
410/625-1900

Nearly New
520 S. Marlyn Ave.
410/780-7490

Collectiques
1806 Maryland ave
410/539-3474

Nostalgia Too
7302 N. Point Rd.
410/477-8440

French Accents
3600 Roland Ave.
410/467-8957

Turnover Shop Inc.
3855 Roland Ave.
410/235-9585

A & M Antique & Mod. Jwlry.
708 N. Rolling Rd.
410/788-7000

Gold Exchange
708 N. Rolling Rd.
410/788-7086

China Sea Marine
903 S. Ann St. Wharf
410/276-8220

Japonaji
906 S. Ann St. Wharf
888/527-6625

Grrreat Bears
1643 Thames
410/276-4429

General Store
1734 Thames
410/675-0450

Heirloom Jewels
#14 Village Square
410/323-0100

Mel's Antiques
712 S. Wolfe St.
410/675-7229

Antique Exchange Inc.
318 Wyndhurst Ave.
410/532-7000

Alex Cooper Oriental Rugs
908 York Rd.
410/828-4838

Consignment Galleries Inc.
6711 York Rd.
410/377-3067

Michael's Rug Gallery
415 E. 33rd St.
410/366-1515

Keepers Antiques
222 W. Read St.
410/783-0330

3 BARNESVILLE

American Sampler
By Appointment Only
301/972-6250

4 BEL AIR

Country Schoolhouse Antiques
1805 E. Churchville Rd.
410/836-9225

Back Door Antiques
106 N. Main St.
410/836-8608

Antiques Bazaar
117 N. Main St.
410/836-7872

Bel Air Antiques Etc.
122 N. Main St.
410/838-3515

Oak Spring Antiques
1321 Prospect Mill Rd.
410/879-0942

5 BELCAMP

Favorite Places To Eat

Cracker Barrel Old Country Store
I-95 & MD543, Exit 80

6 BERLIN

Something Different
2 S. Main St.
410/641-1152

Brass Box
27 N. Main St.
410/641-1858

Sassafrass Station
111 N. Main St.
410/641-0979

Stuart's Antiques
5 Pitts St.
410/641-0435

Findings
104 Pitts St.
410/641-2666

7 BETHESDA

Grapevine of Bethesda
7806 Old Georgetown Rd.
301/654-8690
Open: Tue.-Sat., 10-5

Directions: Located in downtown Bethesda at the intersection of Old Georgetown Rd./Wilson Lane, Arlington and St. Elmo. Store has Georgetown entrance and Wilson Lane parking.

For specific information on this exclusive, upscale shop see review this section.

8 BETTERTON

Lantern Inn
115 Ericsson Avenue
410/348-5809
Open year round

Directions: Off of Maryland 213 between Chestertown and Galena. Turn north on Still Pond Road (Maryland 292) to Betterton's Beach. Left 2 blocks to inn.

The Inn was constructed in 1904 and is located in a small Victorian resort town. Thirteen guest rooms reflect the heyday of Betterton when excursion boats brought vacationers from Baltimore and Philadelphia. A large front porch offers relaxation in the beautiful surroundings. The Inn is conveniently located near Dixon's Furniture Auction and many fine antique shops.

9 BOONSBORO

Fits Place
7 N. Main St.
301/432-2919

Antique Partners
23 S. Main St.
301/432-2518

Gale Antiques at Sharpsburg
109 W. Main St.
301/432-4065

Auction Square Antqs. & Cllbls.
7700 Old National Pike
301/416-2490

10 BOWIE

Bets Antiques & Uniques
8519 Chestnut Ave.
301/464-1122

Fabian House
8519 Chestnut Ave.
301/464-6777

House of Hegedus
8521 Chestnut Ave.
301/262-4131

Welcome House
8604 Chestnut
301/262-9844

Keller's Antiques
8606 Chestnut Ave.
301/805-9593

Olde Friends & Memories
13006 9th St.
301/464-2890

Treasure House Antiques
13010 9th St.
301/262-2878

11 BRUNSWICK

Antiques N Ole Stuff
2 E. Potomac
301/834-6795

12 BRYANTOWN

Shady Oaks of Serenity Bed and Breakfast
7490 Serenity Drive
1-800-597-0924, 301/932-8864
Open year round

Directions: For specific directions to Shady Oaks of Serenity, please call the Innkeeper who will provide specific directions from your location.

Shady Oaks of Serenity is a six year old Georgia Victorian situated on three acres and surrounded by trees. This secluded home is off the beaten path, yet within a 45 minute drive of the nation's capitol and Annapolis, MD, home of the U.S. Naval Academy. Just down the road is the Amish country with antiques and unique shops, several historic churches, the renowned Dr. Mudd Home and Gilbert Run Park, a favorite county stop. Also, this retreat may be of interest to those visiting patients at the Charlotte Hall Veterans Home, only minutes away.

Decorated with an Amish theme, the Loveville room has a private bath and a king size bed for a peaceful night's rest. Visitors are welcome to gather in the Sitting Room, the front porch or enjoy an evening on the deck. Kathy and Gene cordially invite you to be a guest in their home and visit their historic county. The morning brings fresh coffee, homemade muffins or breads and a variety of fresh fruits.

13 CAMBRIDGE

Established in 1684 as a port on the Choptank River, Cambridge has a rich history as a ship building center, mill town, Civil War "underground railroad" stop, and internationally known packing and canning center. The historic district reflects the commercial and economic history of the town, with fascinating 18th and 19th century Georgian and Federal buildings clustered in the 100 and 200 blocks of High Street. Large mansion houses are located on Mill, Oakley and Locust Streets (many in the Queen Anne and Colonial Revival styles), while rhythmic rows of modest gable-front homes dating from the turn of the century are found along Vue de L'eau, West End, Willis and Choptank Streets. Skipjacks and other sailing vessels are often seen on scenic Cambridge Creek.

Heirloom Antique Gallery
419 Academy St.
410/228-8445

Packing House Antique Mall
411 Dorchester Ave.
410/221-8544

Bay Country Antique Co-op
415 Dorchester Ave.
410/228-3112

Jones Antiques
518 High St.
410/228-1752

A J's Antiques Mall
2923 Ocean Gtwy.
410/221-1505

Artwells Mall
509 Race St.
410/228-0997

14 CHESTERTOWN

The county seat of Kent County was created in 1706 and designated as one of Maryland's official ports in 1707. This river town had grown elegant, prosperous and daring by the 1770s. Residents angry over the Boston Port Act staged their own tea party—in broad daylight—against the British brigantine *Geddes* in 1774. This daring event is re-enacted each June as the Chestertown Tea Party. Chestertown is a wonderful place to explore on foot, and visitors may stroll past Federal town houses, Georgian mansions, a stone house supposedly constructed from a ship's ballast and many fine antiques and specialty shops. Chestertown is also home to Washington College, which was chartered in 1782 and named after George Washington with his expressed consent.

Crosspatch
107 S. Cross St.
410/778-3253

Red Shutters
337 High St.
410/778-6434

Seed House Gallery
860 High St.
410/778-2080

Childrens Exchange
306 Park Row
410/778-1467

Chestertown Antique & Furn. Center
6612 Churchill Road (Rt. 213)
410/778-5777

15 COCKEYSVILLE

Cuomo's Interiors & Antiques
10759 York Rd.
410/628-0422

Abundant Treasures Gallery
10818 York Rd.
410/666-9797

Pack Rat
10834 York Rd.
410/683-4812

Hunt Valley Antiques
10844 York Rd.
410/628-6869

Bentley's Antiques Show Mart
10854 York Rd.
410/667-9184

Alley Shoppes
10856 York Rd.
410/683-0421

Decorative Touch
11008 York Rd.
410/527-1075

Corner Cottage Antiques
11010 York Rd.
410/527-9535

Kendall's Antique Shop
3417 Sweet Air Rd.
410/667-9235

16 CUMBERLAND

Historic Cumberland Antique
55 Baltimore St.
301/777-2979

Yesteryear
62 Baltimore St.
301/722-7531

Ye Olde Shoppe
315 Virginia Ave.
301/724-3537

Auntie's Antiques & Cllbls.
328 Virginia Ave.
301/724-3729

Goodwood Old & Antique Furniture
329 Virginia Ave.
301/777-0422

17 DAMASCUS

Judy's
9861 Main St.
301/253-1688

Bea's Antiques
24140 Ridge Rd.
301/253-6030

Appleby's Antiques
24219 Ridge Rd.
301/253-6980

Flo's Antiques
28314 Kemptown Rd.
301/253-3752

18 DENTON

Attic Antiques & Cllbls. Mall
24241 Shore Hwy.
410/479-1889

Denton Antique Mall
24690 Meeting House Rd.
410/479-2200

19 EASTON

The Bishop's House
214 Goldsborough St.
410/820-7290

Situated in a historic district great for bicycle tours, this circa 1880 in-town Victorian inn is romantically decorated in period style. Fireplaces and whirlpool tubs relax spirits and soothe tired muscles. Antiques shops are only three blocks away.

Windsor Gallery
21 Goldsborough St.
410/820-5246

Wye River Antiques
23 N. Harrison St.
410/822-3449

Camelot Antiques Ltd.
7871 Ocean Gateway
410/820-4396

Sullivan's Antique Warehouse
28272 Saint Michaels Rd.
410/822-4723

Delmarva Jewelers
Tred Avon Square
410/822-5398

Foxwell's Antiques & Cllbls.
Rt. 50
410/820-9705

Stock Exch. Antq. & Consign.
Rt. 50
410/820-0014

American Pennyroyal
5 North Harrison Street
410/822-5030

Chesapeake Antique Center
29 South Harrison Street
410/822-5000

Easton Maritime Antiques
27 South Harrison Street
410/763-8853

Picket Fence Antiques
218 North Washington Street
410/822-3010

Kathe & Company
20 South Harrison Street
410/820-9153

Lanham Merida Antqs. & Ints.
218 N. Washington Street
410/763-8500

North Bend Galleries
28220 St. Michaels Road
410/820-6085

Oxford Antiques & Art Gallery
21-A North Harrison Street
410/820-0587

Tabot Antiques
218 North Washington Street
410/476-5247

Tharpe House Antiques
28 South Washington Street
410/820-7525

The Flo-Mir
23 East Dover Street
410/822-2857

Wings Antiques
7 North Harrison Street
410/822-2334

20 EDGEWATER

Rafters Antique Mini-Mall
1185 Mayo Rd.
410/798-1204

Londontown Antiques
1205 Mayo Rd.
410/698-6192

21 ELLICOTT CITY

Unique and well-preserved, this 19th-century mill town on the Patapsco River has sloping streets and sturdy granite buildings reminiscent of English industrial towns. Ellicott City was a summer destination for Baltimore residents and notable visitors who came by train, including Robert E. Lee and H. L. Mencken. Antiques shops, specialty boutiques and restaurants are abundant in this small town.

American Military Antiques
8398 Court Ave.
410/465-6827

Antique Depot
3720 Maryland Ave.
410/750-2674

Hall's Antiques & Collectibles
8026 Main St.
410/418-9444

Maxines Antiques & Cllbls.
8116 Main St.
410/461-5910

A Caplans Antiques
8125 Main St.
410/750-7678

Ellicott's Country Store
8180 Main St.
410/465-4482

Cottage Antiques
8181 Main St.
410/465-1412

Historic Framing & Collectibles
8344 Main St.
410/465-0549

Antique Mall @ Ellicott Mills
8307 Main St.
410/461-8700

Shops at Ellicott Mills
8307 Main St.
410/461-8700

Catonsville Village Antiques
787 Oella Ave.
410/461-1535

Oella Flea Market
787 Oella Ave.
410/461-1535

Rebel Trading Post
3744 Old Columbia Pike
410/465-9595

Wagon Wheel Antique Shop
8061 Tiber Aly
410/465-7910

22 FREDERICK

Antiques hunters and history lovers will find much to enjoy in Frederick. The city had a role in the Revolutionary War, War of 1812 and Civil War. Much of the historic district includes business and residences in and around the original 1745 city grid, with Market Street the north-south axis and Patrick Street the east-west axis. A wealth of commercial, residential, public and religious structures in the architectural styles spanning two centuries contribute to this historic and culturally significant city.

Off The Deep End
712 East Street
301/698-9006
Open Mon.-Sat., 10-7; Sun., 10-6

*Directions: *From Washington, D.C.: From Interstate 270 to Maryland Route 15 N., take 7th St. (East) Exit. Proceed to "Stop" sign at East St. Take a left onto East St. for 1/2 block. The shop is located on the right. From Baltimore: Interstate 70 W. To Route 15 N. Then proceed as above. From Pennsylvania: Maryland Route 15 S. to 7th St. (East) Exit. Then proceed as above.*

With over 3,000 square feet of space, a wide array of antique furniture and accessories are on display. Antique toys, collectibles, vintage clothing, plus intriguing 50s memorabilia and "bizarre" items form a part of this massive collection. You will also want to browse through the over 14,000 old and used books in stock.

The Turning Point Inn
3406 Urbana Pike
301/874-2421 or 301/831-8232
Rates: $75 weekdays, $85 weekends
Open year round

Shaded by four acres of trees and gardens, this exquisite antique-filled bed and breakfast country inn offers a delightful spot for a getaway or special occasion. With five spacious bedrooms having private baths, guests find additional comfort in the large living and dining room. A basket of fruit greets each guest, as well as the full country breakfast. Tuesday-Friday, lunch and dinner is served.

Warehouse Antiques
47 E. All Saints St.
301/663-4778

Catoctin Inn & Antiques
3619 Buckeystown Pike
301/831-8102

Brass & Copper Shop
13 S. Carroll St.
301/663-4240

The Consignment Warehouse
35 S. Carroll
301/695-9674

Cannon Hill Place
111 S. Carroll St.
301/695-9304

Carroll St. Mercantile
124 Carroll St.
301/620/4323

Gaslight Antiques
118 E. Church St.
301/663-3717

Homeward Bound
313 E. Church St.
301/631-9094

Collage Antiques
7 N. Court St.
301/694-0513

Antique Imports
125 East St.
301/662-6200

Eastside Antiques
221 East St.
301/663-8995

The Gallery
15 E. Packard
301/695-7376

Antique Galleries
3 E. Patrick St.
301/631-0922

Carroll Creek Antiques Etc.
14 E. Patrick St.
301/663-8574

J & T Antiques
29 E. Patrick St.
301/698-1380

Craftworks Antiques
55 E. Patrick St.
301/662-3111

Emporium At Creekside Antqs.
112 E. Patrick St.
301/662-7099

A & J Antiques
313 E. Patrick St.
301/695-1281

Family S. Choice Side Antiques
Rt 15 & Biggs Ford Rd.
301/898-5547

Flea Factory
Rt 15 & Biggs Ford Rd.
301/898-5052

Memory Lane Antique Mall
Rt 15 & Biggs Ford Rd.
301/898-5547

Brainstorm Comics
177 Thomas Johnson Dr.
301/663-3039

Old Glory Antique Mkt. Place
5862 Urbana Pike
301/662-9173

Frederick's Best
307 E. 2nd St.
301/698-1791

Favorite Places To Eat

Cracker Barrel Old Country Store
I-270 & Route 85, Exit 31 B
301/682-4405

23 GAITHERSBURG

Emporium of Olde Towne
223 E. Diamond Ave.
301/926-9148

Old Town Antiques
223 E. Diamond Ave.
301/926-9490

Becraft Antiques
405 S. Frederick Ave.
301/926-3000

Yesteryear Antique Farms Inc.
7420 Hawkins Creamery Rd.
301/948-3979

Peking Arts Inc.
7410 Lindbergh Dr.
301/258-8117

Days of Olde Antiques
710 State Route 3 Northbound
410/987-0397

Julia's Room
9001 A Warfield Rd.
301/869-1410

Gate House Antiques
21125 Woodfield Rd.
301/869-4480

24 GAMBRILLS

Holly Hill Antiques
382 Gambrills Rd.
410/923-1207

25 GLEN BURNIE

Rosie's Past & Present
7440 Balt Annapolis Blvd.
410/760-5821

Curiosity Unlimited Inc.
7450 Balt Annapolis Blvd.
410/768-8697

Neatest Little Shop
7462 Balt Annapolis Blvd.
410/760-3610

Fourth Crane Antiques
310 Crain Hwy. S.
410/760-9803

26 GRASONVILLE

Going Home Unique Gift Antqs.
3017 Kent Narrow Way S.
410/827-8556

Dutch Barn Antiques
3712 Main St.
410/827-8656

Enchanted Lilly
4601 Main St.
410/827-5935

Eastern Bay Trading Co.
4917 Main St.
410/827-9286

27 HAGERSTOWN

Halfway Antiques & Cllbls.
11000 Bower Ave.
301/582-4971

Beaver Creek Antique Market
40 East Ave.
301/739-8075

Ravenswood Antique Center
216 W. Franklin St.
301/739-0145

Cntry. Village of Beaver Creek
20136 National Pike
301/790-0006

Antique Crossroads
20150 National Pike
301/739-0858

Country Lanes
326 Summit Ave.
301/790-1045

28 HANOVER

AAA Antiques Mall, Inc.
2659 Annapolis Road
Rts. 295 & 175
410/551-4101

Be prepared to spend the day at Maryland's largest antiques mall offering over 58,000 square feet of quality, affordable antiques and collectibles.

You will find plenty of fine furniture from all periods as well as glassware from the brilliant, depression and elegant periods. The Mall also offers a fine selection of art glass and pottery. If you are in the market for military, movie, black memorabilia or any number of yesterday's treasures, this is the place to be.

Located only minutes from Baltimore and Washington, AAA Antiques Mall, Inc. offers plenty of free parking and welcomes bus tours. Wheelchair accessible-wheelchair on premises. If you need more information or require overnight accomodations, please feel free to call the Mall at 410/551-4101.

29 HAVRE DE GRACE

Eclections
101 North Washington St.
410/939-4917

Franklin St. Antiques & Gifts
464 Franklin St.
410/939-4220

Investment Antiques & Cllbls.
123 Market St.
410/939-1312

Splendor In Brass
123 Market St.
410/939-1312

Streets Uniques
2132 Pulaski Hwy.
410/273-6778

Bank of Memories
319 Saint John St.
410/939-4343

Wonder Back Antiques
331 N. Union Ave.
410/939-6511

Golden Vein
408 N. Union Ave.
410/939-9595

Washington St. Books & Antiques
131 N. Washington St.
410/939-6215

30 HYATTSVILLE

Annas Antqs. & Bits & Pieces
5312 Baltimore Ave.
301/864-5953

Ellington's
1401 University Blvd E
301/445-1879

Maryland Precious Metals
By Appointment Only
301/779-3696

31 KENSINGTON

Barrington Antique
10419 Fawcett St.
301/949-1994

Phyllis Van Auken Antqs. Inc.
10425 Fawcett St.
301/933-3772

Jantiques
10429 Fawcett St.
301/942-0936

James of Kensington
3706 Howard Ave.
301/933-8843

Kensington Station Antiques
3730 Howard Ave.
301/946-0222

Nancy T
3730 Howard Ave.
301/942-8446

Pen Haven
3730 Howard Ave.
301/929-0955

Villa Accents
3730 Howard Ave.
301/942-7944

ABS Consignment & Cllbls.
3734 Howard Ave.
301/946-9646

Oriental Antqs. by Susan Akins
3740 Howard Ave.
301/946-4609

Sally Shaffer Interiors
3742 Howard Ave.
301/933-3740

Jill Americana & Co.
3744 Howard Ave.
301/946-7464

Pritchard's
3748 Howard Ave.
301/942-1661

Antique Market II
3750 Howard ave
301/933-4618

Diane's Antiques
3758 Howard Ave.
301/946-4242

Mariea's Place
3758 Howard Ave.
301/949-2378

Antique Scientific Instruments
3760 Howard Ave.
301/942-0636

Kensington Antq. Mkt. Center
3760 Howard Ave.
301/942-4440

Antiques and Uniques
3762 Howard Ave.
301/942-3324

Antique Market
3762 Howard Ave.
301/949-2318

Paul Feng Antiques
3786 Howard Ave.
301/942-0137

European Antiques
4080A Howard Ave.
301/530-4407

Ambiance Galleries Ltd.
4115 Howard Ave.
301/656-1512

Sparrows
4115 Howard Ave.
301/530-0175

Paris-Kensington
4119 Howard Ave.
301/897-4963

Onslow Square Antiques
4125-4131 Howard Ave.
301/530-9393

Gonzales Antiques
4130 Howard Ave.
301/564-5940

Great British Pine Mine
4144 Howard Ave.
301/493-2565

Lighting by Est Gllry Antiques
4217 Howard Ave.
301/493-4013

Chelsea & Co.
4218 Howard Ave.
301/897-8886

Furniture Mill Inc.
4233 Howard Ave.
301/530-1383

Victoria Antiques
4265 Howard Ave.
301/530-4460

Time Frames
10408 Montgomery
301/929-8419

For Cats Sake Inc.
10513 Metropolitan Ave.
301/933-5489

All Books Considered
10408 Montgomery
301/589-2575

International Parade
10414 Montgomery Ave.
301/933-1770

Lionel Buy and Sell Repair
3610 University Blvd. W.
301/949-5656

Potomac Trade Post
3610 University Blvd. W
301/949-5656

32 KNOXVILLE

Schoolhouse Antiques
847 Jefferson Pike
301/620-7470

Garrett's Mill Antiques
1331 Weverton Rd.
301/834-8581

33 LAUREL

Antique Center
8685 Cherry Lane
301/725-9174

Dark Horse Antiques Mall
8687 Cherry Lane
301/953-1815

Antique Alley
99 Main St.
301/490-6500

David's Antiques & Gifts
353 Main St.
301/776-5636

Main St. Corner Shoppe Inc.
401 Main St.
301/725-3099

Geary's Antiques
508 Main St.
301/725-7733

L & L Antiques & Gifts
512 Main St.
301/725-7539

Antique Market
9770 Washington Blvd N
301/953-2674

34 LAYTONSVILLE

Griffith House Antiques
21415 Laytonsville Rd.
301/926-4155

Ludingtons Antiques
21520 Laytonsville Rd.
301/330-4340

Red Barn Antique Shops
6860 Olney Laytonsville Rd.
301/926-3053

35 LEONARDTOWN

Maryland Antiques Center
593 Jefferson St.
301/475-1960

Antiques on the Square
337 N. Washington St.
301/475-5826

36 MILLERSVILLE

Arundel Way Antiques
1004 Cecil Ave.
410/923-2977

Red Barn Antiques
241 Najoles Rd.
410/987-2267

37 MOUNT AIRY

Trading Post Antiques
13318 Glissans Mill Rd.
301/829-0561

Country House
309 N. Main St.
301/829-2528

38 NEW MARKET

Located on the old National Pike, New Market's Main Street was an important stop for 19th-century travelers headed west and for cattle drivers going to the eastern markets. Though the town was laid out in 1788 and patrolled by Confederate forces during the Civil War, it has survived the years well enough to be a largely intact rural town with many early buildings restored for combined use as antiques shops and homes. Unique buildings include the Prosser House, Ramsburg House and Fehr-Schriss House.

National Pike Inn
9 West Main Street
301/865-5055
Open year round

Located on Main Street amidst antique shops, this 1796-1804 Federal style inn offers five guest rooms decorated with individual themes. The large Federal Sitting Room surrounds guests in comfort. For a private outdoor retreat, step into the enclosed courtyard. The Colonial dining room is the location for the hearty morning breakfast. Create a memory in New Market.

Comus Antiques
#1 N. Federal St.
301/831-6464

Before Our Time
1 W. Main
301/831-9203

Fleshman's Antiques
2 West Main St.
410/775-0153

John Due Antiques
13 W. Main St.
301/831-9412

Jo's Antiques
21 W. Main St.
301/831-3875

Shaws of New Market
22 W. Main
301/831-6010

Victorian Jewelry
33 Main St.
301/865-3083

Arlenes Antiques
41 W. Main St.
301/865-5554

C W. Wood Books
42 W. Main
301/865-5734

Glen Moore & Violet
45 W. Main
301/865-3710

Main St. Antiques
47 W. Main St.
301/865-3710

1812 House
48 W. Main St.
301/865-3040

Tomorrow's Antiques
50 W. Main St.
301/831-3590

Mr Bob's
52 W. Main St.
301/831-6712

Browsery Antiques
55 W. Main St.
301/831-9644

Iron Bell
59 W. Main St.
301/831-9589

Thomas Antiques
60 W. Main St.
301/831-6622

Village Tea Room & Antq. Shop
81 W. Main St.
301/865-3450

Antiques Folly
105 W. Main St.
301/607-6513

Finch's Antiques
122 W. Main St.
301/685-3926

R P Brady Antiques
3 E. Main St.
301/865-3666

Thirsty Knight Antiques
9 E. Main St.
301/831-9889

Smith's Tavern Antiques
Main & Fifth St.
301/865-3597

Rossig's Frame Shop
1 N. Strawberry Alley
301/865-3319

Mimi's Antiques
3 Strawberry Alley
301/865-1644

Grange Hall Antiques
1 8th Ally
301/865-5651

39 NORTH EAST

The Mill House
102 Mill Lane
410/287-3532
Open year round

A tidal creek authenticates the early 1700 Mill House, which is filled with antique furnishings. Guests can take strolls through the spacious lawn, or settle back before the crackling fire in the parlor. Also, antique shops and restaurants are within an easy walk.

JB's Collectibles
32 S. Main St.
410/287-0400

40 OCEAN CITY

Bookshelf Etc.
8006 Coastal Hwy.
410/524-2949

Edgemoor Antiques
10009 Silver Point Lane
410/213-2900

GG's Antiques
9 Somerset St.
410/289-2345

Brass Cannon
204 S. Saint Louis Ave.
410/289-3440

41 OLNEY

Briars Antiques
4121 Briars Rd.
301/774-3596

Olney Antique Village
16650 Georgia Ave.
301/570-9370

Hyatt House Antiques
16644 Georgia Ave.
301/774-1932

Jimmy's Village Barn
16650 Georgia Ave.
301/570-6489

Liz Vilas Antiques
16650 Georgia Ave.
301/924-0354

Nicco's Antiques
16650 Georgia Ave.
301/924-3745

Barry Rogers
16650 Georgia Ave.
301/570-0779

42 OXFORD

Americana Antiques
111 S. Morris St.
410/226-5677

Anchorage House Antiques
Oxford Road
410/822-8978

Donald D. Donahue Sr.
111 S. Morris St.
410/226-5779

Oxford Salvage Co.
301 Tilghman St.
410/226-5971

Vintage Shop
202 S. Morris St.
410/226-5712

43 REISTERSTOWN

Curiosity Shoppes
17 Hanover Rd.
410/833-3434

Now N Then
208 Main St.
410/833-3665

New England Carriage House
218 Main St.
410/833-4019

Derby Antiques
222 Main St.
410/526-6678

Relics of Olde
222 Main St.
410/833-3667

Things You Love Antiques
234 Main St.
410/833-5019

Margie's Antiques & Dolls
237 Main St.
410/526-5656

Tinas Antiques & Jewelry
237 Main St.
410/833-9337

44 ROYAL OAK

Bellevue Store
5592 Poplar Lane
410/745-5282

Oak Creek Sales
25939 Royal Oak
410/745-3193

45 SALISBURY

Henrietta's Attic
205 Maryland Ave.
410/546-3700

Springhill Antiques
2704 Merritt Mill Rd.
410/546-0675

Peddlers Three
Old Quantico Rd.
410/749-1141

Holly Ridge Antiques
1411 S. Salisbury Blvd
410/742-4392

46 SEVERNA PARK

Antiques in the Park
540 Balto Anap Blvd.
410/544-2762

Taylor Antiques
557 Balton Anap Blvd.
410/647-1701

Memory Post Antique Boutique
Riggs Avenue
410/315-9610

Anatiues Market Place
4 Riggs Avenue
410/544-9644

Adair & Halligan
5 Riggs Avenue
410/647-0103

47 ST. MICHAELS

St. Michaels began in 1778 as a planned development backed by a Liverpool merchant firm, and was small but firmly established by the end of the Revolutionary War. Surrounded by tributaries of the Chesapeake Bay, St. Michaels is a delightful waterfront town and easy to explore on foot. Historic buildings span a period of two centuries, with many Federal period houses built in the early 19th century, including the Cannonball House, the Old Inn and the Kemp House. Many restaurants, specialty shops, bed and breakfasts, and inns welcome visitors to the town. The harbor has been developed into a marina, but commercial watermen also use it, as they have for generations.

Freedom House Antique
121 A S. Fremont St.
410/745-6140

Hodgepodge
308 S. Talbot St.
410/745-3062

Nina Lanham Ayres Antiques
401 S. Talbot St.
410/745-5231

Sentimental Journey Antiques
402 Talbot St.
410/745-9556

Pennywhistle Antiques
408 S. Talbot St.
410/745-9771

Saltbox Antiques
310 S. Talbot St.
410/745-3569

48 SYKESVILLE

Alexandra's Attic
7542 Main St.
410/549-3095

All Through The House
7540 Main St.
410/795-6577

Village Antique Shoppe
7543 Main St.
410/795-0556

My Bear-IED Treasures
7543 Main St.
410/795-0556

TLC Creations
7615 Main St.
410/549-1425

Yesterday Once More
6251 Sykesville Rd.
410/549-0212

Clocks & Collectibles
7311 Springfield Ave.
410/549-1147

49 TANEYTOWN

Margaret J. Maas
202 E. Baltimore St.
410/756-2480

50 WALDORF

Country Connection
2784 Old Washington Rd.
301/843-1553

Heritage Designs
3131 Old Washington Rd.
301/932-7379

Madatics Attic
3141 Old Washington Rd.
301/645-6076

51 WASHINGTON D.C.

Amaryllis Vintage Company, Inc.
4922 Wisconsin Avenue
202/244-2211
Open 7 days a week from 11-7.

Directions: Traveling I-495 take Exit #33. Travel south on Connecticut Avenue to Fessenden St. (approximately 3 and 1/2 miles). Turn right on Fessenden. Go to Wisconsin Avenue; turn left on Wisconsin, the shop is 1/2 block on the right.

With pieces from the 1840s to 1940s, this shop carries furniture and accessories. The most popular furnishing styles include Empire, Mission and Art Deco. Mirrors, lamps, rugs, paintings and jewelry add to the selection. Bridal Registry, gift certificates, and local delivery are available. A 90-day-same-as-cash credit line can be established for qualified applicants.

Dunnan's, Inc.
3209 O Street, NW
202/965-1614
Open 7 days a week, 11 a.m.-4 p.m.

Directions: Located in Historic Georgetown off Wisconsin Avenue.

With hundreds of antique items and accessories, this Historic Georgetown shop offers a wide selection and variety. Furniture, lamps, memorabilia, advertising, in addition to jewelry, collectibles and art, make up the eclectic array of wares. Inventory varies as a result of frequent deliveries.

Morris-Clark Inn
1015 L Street, NW
202/898-1200
Rates $115-185
Year-round accommodations

Built in 1864 and the only area inn listed independently in the National Register of Historic Places, it originally stood as two detached Victorian mansions. One presents an ornate Chippendale porch topped by a mansard roof. 1980s restoration united the structures creating an elegant small hotel. Original interior includes 12-foot-high mahogany-framed mirrors and elaborately carved marble fireplaces. All rooms offer Victorian, neoclassical, or country decor. *Gourmet* has featured the inn's well-respected restaurant.

Adams Inn
1744 Lanier Place, NW
202/745-3600
Year-round accommodations

This three-story townhouse built in 1908 nestles among antique shops in the surrounding blocks. Guest rooms have individual and distinctive home-style furnishings and accessories. Public rooms include breakfast room, parlor, television lounge. A seat amid the flowers of the garden patio, or taking in the view from the front porch, enhance each stay. Refreshments are complimentary.

Antiques-On The Hill
701 N. Carolina Ave. SE
202/543-1819

Tiny Jewel Box
1147 Connecticut Ave. NW
202/393-2747

Antiques Anonymous
2627 Connecticut Ave. NW
202/332-5555

Mission Possible
5516 Connecticut Ave. NW
202/363-6897

Mom & Pop Antiques
3534 Georgia Ave. NW
202/722-0719

Dalton Brody Ltd.
3412 Idaho Ave. NW
202/244-7197

Logan's Antiques
3118 Mount Pleasant St. NW
202/483-2428

Two Lions Antiques
621 Pennsylvania Ave. SE
202/546-5466

Justine Mehlman Antiques
2824 Pennsylvania Ave. NW
202/337-0613

Rooms & Gardens
3677 Upton St. NW
202/362-3777

Proud American (Georgetown)
1529 Wisconsin Ave. NW
202/625-1776

Julie Walters Antiques
1657 Wisconsin Ave. NW
202/625-6727

Rooms with a View
1661 Wisconsin Ave. N
202/625-0610

Blair House Antiques
1663 Wisconsin Ave. NW
202/338-5349

VIP Antiques
1665 Wisconsin Ave. NW
202/965-0700

China Gallery & Gifts
2200 Wisconsin Ave. NW
202/342-1899

Consignment Galleries
3226 Wisconsin Ave. NW
202/364-8995

Amaryllis Vintage Co. Inc.
4922 Wisconsin Ave. NW
202/244-2211

Chevy Chase Antique Center
5215 Wisconsin Ave. NW
202/364-4600

Antiques & Gifts Boutique
5300 Wisconsin Ave. NW
202/237-2060

Ruff & Ready Furnishings
1908 14th St. NW
202/667-7833

Brass Knob
2311 18th St. NW
202/332-3370

Retrospective Inc.
2324 18th St. NW
202/483-8112

Uniform
2407 18th St. NW
202/483-4577

Cherishables
1608 20th St. NW
202/785-4087

Adams Davidson Galleries Inc.
By Appointment Only
202/965-3800

Old Print Gallery Inc.
1220 31st St. NW
202/965-1818

Washington Dolls House
5236 44th St. NW
202/363-6400

Adam A Weschler & Son
909 E. St. NW
202/628-1281

Antique Textile Resource
1730 K St. NW, Ste .317
202/293-1731

Janis Aldrige Inc.
2900 M St. NW
202/338-7710

Frank Milwee
2912 M St. NW
202/333-4811

Cherub Antiques Gallery
2918 M St. NW
202/337-2224

Michael Getts Antiques
2918 M St. NW(Georgetown)
202/338-3811

Susquehanna Antiques Co. Inc.
3216 O St. NW
202/333-1511

Second Store Books & Antiques
2000 P St. NW
202/659-8884

Kelsey's Kupboard
3003 P St. NW
202/298-8237

Affrica
2010 R St. NW
202/745-7272

Interesting Side Trips

Washington Dolls' House & Toy Museum
5236 44th Street NW.
202/244-0024
Open Tue.,-Sat., 10-5; Sun., 12-5

Directions: One block west of Wisconsin Avenue between Jenifer and Harrison Streets.

The Washington Dolls' House and Toy Museum began as a private collection belonging to doll house historian, Flora Gill Jacobs. Her extensive antique collection of doll houses, toys and games were researched and dated; all are representative of either the architecture, decorative arts, or social history of the time of their creation.

52 WESTMINSTER

Seven East Main St.
7 E. Main St.
410/840-9123

Locust Wines & Antiques
10 E. Main St.
410/876-8680

Whites Bicycles
10 W. Main St.
410/848-3440

Ain't That A Frame
31 W. Main St.
410/876-3096

Westminster Antique Mall
433 Hahn Rd.
410/857-4044

Massachusetts

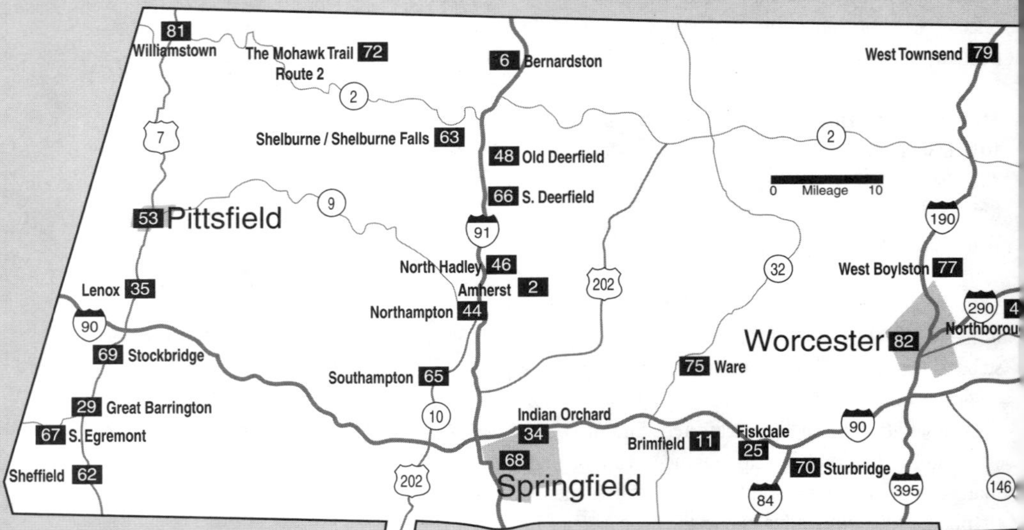

SEVEN HILLS COUNTRY INN

40 Plunkett St.
(800) 869-6518

Lenox

35

Diamond District

Breakfast Inn

A 3-diamond, 2-star. 3-crown historical bed & breakfast
(800) 666-3076

Lynn

38

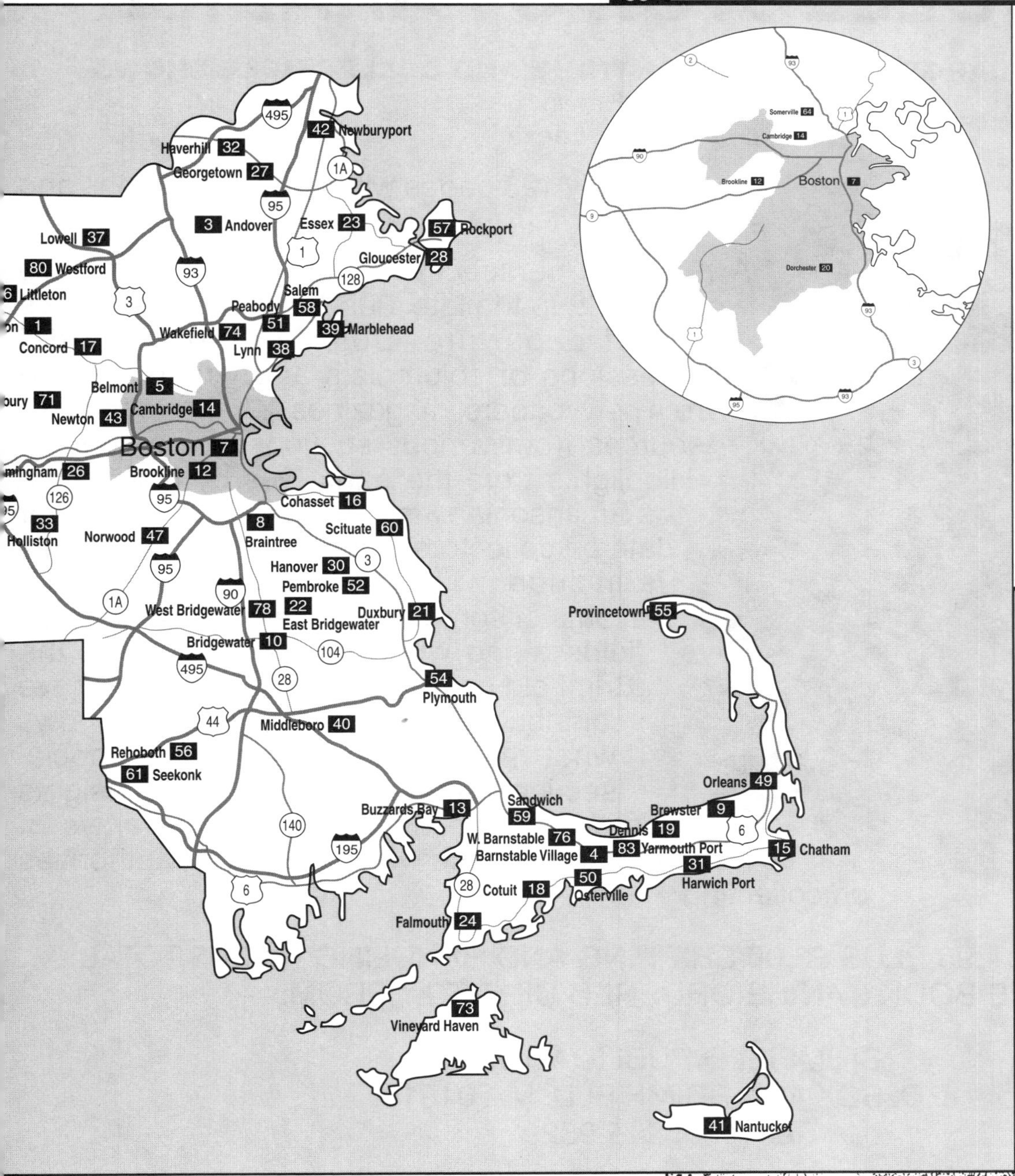

5&10 ANTIQUE GALLERY℠

70 Dealers
Open Daily 10-5

Rt. 5 & 10

413-773-3620

- *18th & 19th century furnishings*
- *Silver jewelry*
- *Dolls, toys*
- *Reference books*
- *Depression glass*
- *Primitives*

Old Deerfield

48

AN OLD-FASHIONED ANTIQUE SHOP WITH AFFORDABLE PRICES

ELMWOOD ANTIQUES

East Bridgewater

22

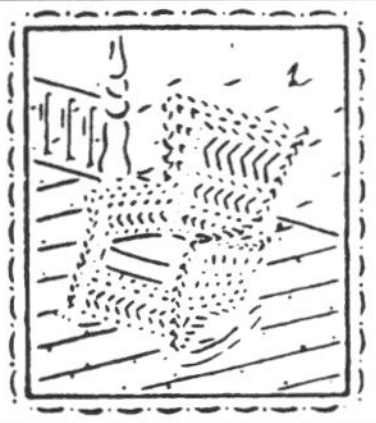

WICKER UNLIMITED

Specializing in antique wicker

Marblehead

39

A Romatic Victorian Inn in the heart of Cape Cod's Antique Row

Beautifully furnished with period antiques, fireplaces, private baths, water views.

BEECHWOOD

2839 Main Street (Route 6A)
(508) 362-6618
(800) 609-6618
www.virtualcapecod.com/market/beechwood

Barnstable

4

Hewins House

circa 1820

...a Bed & Breakfast on Falmouth's Village Green

Cape Cod

24

BEECHWOOD

Barnstable

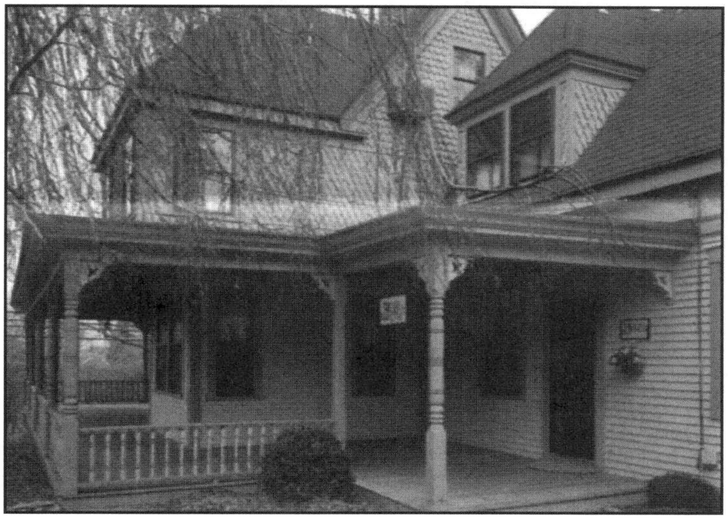

Innkeepers Debbie and Ken Traugot have made sure that the inn is as comfortable as it is pretty.

SOMETIMES YOU DREAM ABOUT GETTING away from it all—whiling away a summer afternoon with a glass of lemonade out on the porch, or relaxing in front of the fireplace with a mug of hot chocolate. Beechwood is the place where these fantasies become reality.

A tall hedge shields the gabled-roofed Victorian from Main Street, making it a peaceful respite. Two sprawling beech trees embrace the grounds, and a wide porch wraps around three sides of the house; a perfect spot for lounging, or even making friends with the resident golden retrievers, Hobbes and Star.

Innkeepers Debbie and Ken Traugot have made sure that the inn is as comfortable as it is pretty. The seven guest rooms are each strikingly different, from the elegant Rose Room with its canopy bed and fireplace, to the airy Lilac Room with its clawfoot bathtub, to the cozy third-floor Garret Room with its brass bed.

If you want to find out a bit more about the Cape Cod area on your visit, head down to the inn's parlor, where you will find an ample guide to local restaurants, information on sightseeing, and able advice from Debbie and Ken.

Location:
2839 Main St.
Barnstable Village, MA, 02630
Phone 508-362-6618

Rooms:
7 guest rooms, all with private baths, some have fireplaces. No telephones or televisions in rooms. No smoking

Rates:
In season $130-150

There's plenty to do in Barnstable, but the highlight is really antiquing. There are dozens of shops, craft stores, and the like, just a stone's throw away from Beechwood.

If you'd rather stay put, play croquet or badminton on Beechwood's broad lawn, or treat yourself to a few quiet moments on the porch swing. But before you decide, don't forget about breakfast.

Each morning, guests are served a bountiful breakfast in the dining room. Start with muffins or breads, followed by fresh fruit, and a hearty entree. It is here that guests gather for spirited conversation, to plan their days, or just slowly ease into the morning. And midday brings a respite of afternoon tea, with beverages and treats the civilized way.

Beechwood will feel like your home away from home.

Massachusetts

1 ACTON

Annals Antiques & Not
322 Central St.
508/263-8260

Encores Antiques
174 Great Rd.
508/263-1515

Seagull Antiques
481 Great Rd.
508/263-0338

2 AMHERST

Black Walnut Inn
1184 North Pleasant Street
413/549-5649
Fax: 413/549-5149
open 7-8, 365 days a year
Rates: $95-125

Directions: Traveling north on I-91: Take Exit 19 (marked Amherst) onto Route 9 East. Go 4.6 miles and turn left (Staples will be on your right) onto Route 116 North. Go 3 miles to the first traffic light and turn right onto Route 63 (Meadow Street). The next light is North Pleasant Street and Black Walnut Inn is the brick house on the right. Traveling South on I-91: Take exit 24, turn right onto Route 5; continue for 1 mile. Turn left on Route 116 South for 6 miles. Turn left at the first Amherst light onto Route 63 (Meadow Street). The next light is North Pleasant Street and Black Walnut Inn is on the right.

The Black Walnut Inn, a stately 1821 Federal style brick house shaded by tall black walnut trees, stands on the corner of North Pleasant and Meadow Streets in Amherst, just a few minutes from the campuses of Amherst College and the University of Massachusetts. Although the double doors, crowned with a large fan window, give the house an imposing facade, inside you'll find coziness and comfort. Each guest room is furnished with a mix of antiques and period-piece reproductions, all distinctive in size, furnishings, and history. Touches like the turn-of-the-century mulberry color chosen for the Mulberry Room, cherry Windsor-style and sleigh beds, antique dressing tables, a spinning wheel, a cast iron canopy bed, original wood wainscotting, exposed post and beam and fine wood floors all add rich, historical detail to an already historic house. A full breakfast, including homemade muffins and jams and fresh squeezed orange juice is genially served by hosts, Edd and Marie Twohig, who also offer guests tea, coffee and goodies from 2-8 p.m. on request. The barn that goes with the Black Walnut Inn is the last one in western Massachusetts of the scientific agricultural design.

Kay Baker's Antiques
233 N. Pleasant St.
413/549-4433

Main St. Antiques & Books
321 Main St.
413/256-0900

Grist Mill Antiques
Route 116 S
413/253-5926

3 ANDOVER

Andover Antiques Inc.
89 N. Main St.
508/475-4242

Alphabet Books & Antiques
68 Park St.
508/475-0269

Necessities
185 N. Main
508/475-7992

Bider's Antiques
6 Park St.
508/475-8336

4 BARNSTABLE VILLAGE

Beech Wood
A Romantic Victorian Inn
2839 Main Street, Rt. 6A
1-800-609-6618, 508/362-6618
E-mail: bwdinn@virtualcapecod.com
Website: www.virtualcapcod.com/market/beechwood/

Directions: For specific directions to Beech Wood please call the Innkeepers who will happy to provide specific directions from your location.

For specific information on Beech Wood Inn, see review this section.

5 BELMONT

Fancy That
4 Trapelo Rd.
617/489-3497

Cross & Griffin
468 Trapelo Rd.
617/484-2837

Antiques By Olde Mystic
367 Trapelo Rd.
617/489-4147

In Place
5 Bartlett Ave.
617/489-4161

Belmont Antique Exchange
243 Belmont St. #A
617/484-9839

6 BERNARDSTON

Carriage Barn Antiques
Route 5, 727 Brattleboro Road
413/648-9404

7 BOSTON

Devonia Antiques
43 Charles St.
671/523-8313

George Gravert Antiques
122 Charles St.
617/227-1593

Toad Hollow Antiques
121 Charles St.
617/742-9120

Commonwealth Antiques
121 Charles St.
617/720-1605

Bradstreet's Antiquarins
51 Charles St.
617/723-3660

Regeancy Antiques
70 Charles St.
617/742-3111

Eugene Galleries
76 Charles St.
617/227-3062

Antiques at 80 Charles
80 Charles St.
617/742-8006

Elegant Findings Antiques
87 Charles St.
617/973-4844

Upstairs Downstairs Antiques
93 Charles St.
617/367-1950

Towne & Country Home
99B Charles St.
617/742-9120

Antiques at 99 Charles
99A Charles St.
617/367-8088

Boston Antique Co-op 1
119 Charles St.
617/227-9810

Boston Antique Co-op II
119 Charles St.
617/227-9811

Marika's Antique Shop
130 Charles St.
617/523-4520

Danish Country
138 Charles St.
617/227-1804

Stephen Score
73 Chestnut St.
617/227-9192

Charles River St. Antiques
45 River St.
617/367-3244

Buddenbrooks Fine Books
31 Newbury St.
617/536-4433

Small Pleasures
142 Newbury St.
617/267-7371

Marcoz Antiques
177 Newbury St.
617/262-0780

Nostalgia Factory
336 Newbury St.
617/236-8754

Autrefois Antiques
125 Newbury St.
617/424-8823

Gallagher-Christopher Antqs.
84 Chestnut St.
617/523-1992

Newbury St. Jewelry & Antqs.
255 Newbury St.
617/236-0038

Brookline Village Antiques
1 Design Center Place, Ste. 325
617/734-6071

Akin Lighting Company
28 Charles St.
617/523-1331

Streamline Antiques
1162 Washington St.
617/298-3326

Great Places To Eat

Jasper's
240 Commercial Street
617/523-1126
Closed Sun. & Mon.

If you're not currently informed on the social status of American chefs, this tip's for you: don't miss eating at Jasper's, the restaurant of Jasper White, considered in many circles to be the single most famous chef in Boston and one of the most famous chefs in America. His namesake restaurant serves his distinctive new American cuisine, and reservations are a must.

No Name Restaurant
15-1/2 Fish Pier
617/338-7539

It's places like No Name Restaurant that you look for in every city you visit. Because you know that not only will you have a delightful dining experience, but the trip and the atmosphere alone will create memories that bear retelling over and over. No Name *is* the name. There is no sign outside; none is needed. It started years ago as a luncheonette with a counter and a few tables, strictly for wharf workers.

But word got around about its inexpensive, simple, fresh seafood, and No Name expanded. There is still a dingy luncheonette counter for single diners, but most tourists are seated in the new, paneled dining room with nautical decor and harbor view. Tables are crowded and communal. Customers yell out their orders, and waiters yell back and practically toss food from the kitchen. Start with the fish chowder—nothing but fish! Main course choices are scrod, sole, bluefish, scallops, clams or salmon. Side orders are homemade tartar sauce and fresh-cut slaw with a light, milky dressing. For dessert there's strawberry-rhubarb or blueberry pie, plain or a la mode. Very straightforward, very New England!

8 BRAINTREE

Second Thoughts Antiques
871 Washington St.
617/849-6750

Out of the Wood
230 Quincy Ave.
617/356-5030

Antiques & Things
826 Washington St.
617/843-4196

9 BREWSTER

Willaim Baxter Antiques
3439 Main St.
508/896-3998

Pflock's Antiques
598 Main St.
508/896-3457

Monomoy Antiques
3425 Rt. 6A
508/896-6570

William Brewster Antiques
2912 Main St.
508/896-4816

Mark Lawrence
1050 Main St.
508/896-8381

Kings Way Books & Antiques
774 Main (Rt. 6A)
508/896-3639

Homestead Antiques
2257 Main St.
508/896-2917

Heirloom Antiques
2660 Main St.
508/896-2080

Gaskill Antiques
134 Main St.
508/385-6663

Eve's Place
564 Main St.
508/896-4914

Breton House Antiques
1222 Stoney Brook Rd.
508/896-3974

Barbara Grant Antqs. & Books
1793 Main St.
508/896-7198

Donald B Howe's Antiques
1428 Main St.
508/896-3502

Black Brook Antiques
562 Stoney Brook Road
508/896-3387

10 BRIDGEWATER

Antiques Etc.
1278 Bedford St.
508/697-3005

Central Market
27 Central Square
508/697-2121

Fond Memories
34 Central Square
508/697-5622

11 BRIMFIELD

Brimfield Antiques & Collectibles Show

The Granddaddy of Them All!
May 12-17 - 1998
July 7-12 - 1998
Sept. 8-13 - 1998

The Brimfield "Strip" is a quarter of a mile long - and what a quarter of "land" it is! All adjacent to one another are 23 major fields offering both antique and collectible buyers the opportunity to select millions of items from any style and period. It's the one single place on earth where you can find both the familiar and unfamiliar in gizmos and gadgets, furniture, folk art, pottery, war memorabilia, garden decor, graniteware, books, toys, scores of glassware and other stuff! This monumental phenomenon started as a small show of about 60 to 75 dealers in 1959. Within a few short years it had grown to become the largest antique and collectible show in the world. And it certainly is not uncommon to find folks from around the world at Brimfield. Antiquers from countries such as Germany, England, Australia, and Canada (just to name a few) are seen throughout the week examining and purchasing the wonderful wares.

If you are a serious antiquer who loves the thrill of the hunt - you must make plans to attend the Brimfield Shows.

Submitted by Bob Brown, author of *Brimfield: The Collector's Paradise*

12 BROOKLINE

Turnip & Brig's
313 Washington St.
617/232-9693

Lost Engine Antiques
14 Harvard Ave.
617/254-4678

Erinn's Antiques
185 Corey Rd.
617/734-4522

Antiquers III
171 Harvard St. #A
617/738-5555

13 BUZZARDS BAY

Heirlooms Etc.
95A Main
508/759-1455

Almost Antiques
95B Main
508/759-2111

Grey Goose
95C Main
508/759-3055

Marketplace
61 Main St.
508/759-2114

Antediluvia Antiques
3241 Cranberry Hwy.
508/759-8775

14 CAMBRIDGE

European Country Antiques
146 Huron Ave.
617/876-7485

Easy Chairs
375 Huron Ave.
617/491-2131

James & Devon Booksellers
12 Arrow St.
617/868-0752

Penny Scale Antiques
1353 Cambridge St.
617/576-6558

Cambridge Antique Market
201 Monsignor O'Brien Hwy
617/868-9655

Sadye & Co.
182 Massachusetts Ave.
617/547-4424

Harvard Antiques
1654 Massachusetts Ave.
617/354-5544

Offshore Trading Co.
1695 Massachusetts Ave.
617/491-8439

City Lights Antique Lighting
2226 Massachusetts Ave.
617/547-1490

All & Everything
2269 Massachusetts Ave.
617/354-8641

Antiques on Cambridge Street
1076 Cambridge St.
617/234-0001

15 CHATHAM

Spyglass
618 Main St.
508/945-9686

Rose Cottage Antiques
1281 Main St.
508/945-3114

Agnes of Cape Cod
Balfour Lane 17C
508/945-4099

Carol's Antiques & Collectibles
1278 Main St.
508/945-1705

Aquitain Antiques
35 Cross St.
508/945-9746

16 COHASSET

3 A Antiques Center
130 Chief Justice Cushing Hwy.
617/383-9411

Victoria's by the Sea
87 Elm St.
617/383-2087

Reflections
808 Jerusaleum Rd.
617/383-6465

Lilac House Antiques
26 Elm
617/383-2598

Green Gage Plum
819 Chief Justice Cushing Hwy.
617/383-1778

Cohasset Antiques
Route 3A St.
617/383-6605

17 CONCORD

Upstairs Antiques
23 Walden St.
508/371-9095

Ford Crawford Antiques
1/2 Main
508/369-8870

North Bridge Antiques
45 Walden St.
508/371-1442

Concord Antiques
32 Main St. D/Stairs
508/369-8218

18 COTUIT

Acorn Acres Antiques
4339 Rt. 28
508/428-3787

Sow's Ear Antique Co.
4698 Rt. 28 & 130
508/428-4931

Remember When
4015 Rt. 28 Falmouth Rd.
508/428-5650

Cotuit Antiques
4404 Rt. 28 Falmouth Rd.
508/420-1234

Antiques of Tomorrow
45 Main St.
508/428-6262

1849 House
809 Main St.
508/428-2258

SMP Designs Beads
4766 Rt 28
508/420-0241

Paper Junction
215 Main St.
508/428-8061

Isaiah Thomas Books & Prints
4632 Rt 28
508/428-2752

19 DENNIS

Red Lion Antiques
601 Main St.
508/385-4783

Village Peddler Antiques
601 Main St.
508/385-7300

Antiques 608
608 Main St.
508/385-2755

Antiques Center of Cape Cod
243 Main St.
508/385-6400

Johanna
606 Main St.
508/385-7675

Old Town Antiques
593 Main St.
508/385-5202

Audrey's Antiques
766 Main (Rte 6A)
508/385-4996

Dovetail Antiques
543 Main (Rt. 6A)
508-385-2478

Gloria Swanson Antiques
632 B Main St.
508/385-4166

Antiques Center Warehouse
243 Main St. (Rt. 6A)
508/385-5133

20 DORCHESTER

Avenue Antiques
863 Dorchester
617/265-7100

Darkhorse Antiques
2297 Dorchester Ave.
617/298-1031

Lucy & Ethel's
1168 Washington St.
617/298-0501

21 DUXBURY

Gordon/Genev. Deming Antqs.
125 Wadsworth Road
617/934-5259

Wickham Books
285 Saint George St.
617/934-6955

Folk Art Antiques
447 Washington
617/934-7132

Simon Hill Antiques
453 Washington St.
617/934-2228

Duxbury Antiques
285 St. George St.
617/934-2127

22 EAST BRIDGEWATER

Elmwood Antiques & Country Store

734 Bedford Street
(Intersection of Routes 106 and 18)
508/378-2063
Open Tue.-Sat. 11-5, Sun. 12-5

Directions: Travel I-95 to Route 24 South. Take Exit 16, Route 106 East to Route 18. Elmwood Antiques is on the corner of Routes 106 and 18.

A 10-dealer group shop, Elmwood Antiques & Country Store offers mail order service from the U.S. to Europe. They carry a variety of items, including advertising, furniture, glass, china, Royal Doulton, Disney collectibles, toys, trains, dog collectibles, Coca-Cola memorabilia, military items and prints. While visiting, be sure to see their 132-year-old working post office.

23 ESSEX

Essex is a mecca for antiques hunters. But be warned: You'll find it impossible to resist the enticing aroma of fried clams that pervades the main street. Local restaurants pay homage to the tasty bivalve, which was first cooked here.

White Elephant's Shop
32 Main St.
508/768-6901

Chebacco Antiques
38 Main St.
508/768-7371

Main Street Antiques
44 Main St.
508/768-7039

Americana Antiques
48 Main St.
508/768-6006

As Time Goes By
63 Main St.
508/768-7479

Tradewinds Antiques
63 Main St.
508/768-3327

Ro-Dan Antiques
67 Main St.
508/768-3322

Annex Antiques
69 Main St.
508/768-7704

Emmons & Martin Antiques
163 Main St.
508/768-3292

Howard's Flying Dragon Antqs.
136 Main St.
508/768-7282

APH Waller & Sons
140 Main St.
508/768-6269

Golden Egg Antiques
140 Main St.
508/768-3922

Westerhoff Antiques
144 Main St.
508/768-3830

Neligan & Neligan
144 Main St.
508/768-3910

North Hills Antiques
155 Main St.
508/768-7365

Ellen Neily Antiques
157 Main St.
508/768-6436

L A Landry Antiques
164 Main St.
508/768-6233

Susan Stella Antiques
166 Main St.
508-768-6617

24 FALMOUTH

Hewins House Bed & Breakfast

20 Hewins Street, Village Green
508/457-4363 or 1-800-555-4366
Best time to call is 9-7 daily
Open year round

Directions: Take Route 28 south to Falmouth. Route 28 veers to the left at "Queens Byway" and becomes Main Street Falmouth. Make the left at "Queens Byway". (There is a pillar with a "Keep Right" sign in the middle of the road.) The next right is Hewins St., and Hewins House is right on the corner of Route 28 and Hewins.

Built around 1820 by John Jenkins, a wealthy merchant and sea captain, Hewins House today remains much as it was in the 19th century. The Federal era building, home of some of Falmouth's most prominent families, features wide pine floors, the original staircase, and a black and white floor cloth in the foyer that was made by current owner, Mrs. Albert Price, who also planned the formal gardens and restored a side porch to provide access to the garden area. Within easy walking distance are downtown shopping, restaurants, antique stores, tourist attractions, and a free shuttle that goes to the ferry docks that service Martha's Vineyard.

The Village Barn
606 Rt. 28A
508/540-3215

Enseki Antiques
73 Palmer Avenue
508/548-7744

Chrisales Country Home
550 W. Falmouth Hwy.
508/540-5884

Antiques in W. Falmouth
634 Rt. 28A
508/540-2540

Antiquarium
204 Palmer Ave.
508/548-1755

Beach Rose
35 N. Main St.
508/548-1012

25 FISKDALE

Commonwealth Cottage

See Sturbridge #70

26 FRAMINGHAM

Framingham Centre Antiques
931 Worcester Rd. (Rt. 9)
508/620-6252

Wex Rex Collectibles
Tropical Isle Plaza (Rt. 9 E)
508/620-6181

27 GEORGETOWN

A F Scala Antiques
28 W. Main St.
508/352-8614

Sedler's Antique Village
51 W. Main St.
508/352-8282

Elmwood Antiques
22 East St.
508/352-9782

28 GLOUCESTER

Tally's Trading Post
108 Eastern Ave.
508/283-8662

Beauport Antiques
43 Main St.
508/281-4460

Jer-Rho Antiques
352 Main Street
508/283-5066

Main St. Art & Antiques
124 Main St.
508/281-1531

29 GREAT BARRINGTON

The Coffman's Country Antiques Market

Jennifer House Commons
Stockbridge Road, Route 7
413/528-9282
Open 10-5 daily

Directions: Located in the southwestern "Berkshires," Coffman's is located on Route 7 between Great Barrington and Stockbridge.

A feast for serious, upscale antique lovers, Coffman's Country Antiques Market hosts over 100 quality antique dealers in room settings on three floors. Known for its distinctive, authentic American country antiques, Coffman's handles only merchandise produced before 1949 and only the upper end.

Elise Abrams Antiques
11 Stockbridge Rd.
413/528-3201

Olde-An Antiques Market
Rt. 7 Stockbridge Rd.
413/229-3131

Snyder's Store
945 Main St.
413/528-1441

Reuss Antiques Gallery
420 Stockbridge Rd. (Rt. 7)
413/528-8484

Bygone Days
969 Main St.
413/528-1870

Lion The Witch & The W/Robe
173 Main St.
413/528-6313

Memories
306 Main St.
413/528-6380

Antiques at the Red Horse
117 State Rd.
413/528-2637

Emporium Antique Center
319 Main St.
413/528-1660

Carriage House
389 Stockbridge Rd.
413/528-6045

Le Perigord
964 S. Main St. (Rt. 7)
413/528-6777

Paul & Susan Kleinwald Inc.
578 S. Main St. (Rt. 7)
413/528-4252

Donald McGrory Orntl. Rugs
12 Castle St.
413/528-9594

Mullin-Jones Antiquities
525 S. Main St. (Rt. 7)
413/528-4871

The Kahn's Antq. & Est. Jwlry.
38 Railroad St.
413/528-9550

Country Dining Room Antqs.
178 Main St. (Rte 7)
413/528-5050

Corashire Antiques
Rte 7 & 23 @ Belcher Sq.
413/528-0014

30 HANOVER

La Petite Curiosity Antiques
195 Washington Street
617/829-9599

31 HARWICH PORT

Seven South Antiques
7 South St.
508/432-4366

New To You Shop
543 Main St.
508/432-1158

Mews Antiques at Harwich Pt.
517 Main St.
508/432-6397

Maggie's Antiques Store
6 Cross St.
508/432-4299

32 HAVERHILL

Dovetail Antiques
133 River St.
508/374-4804

Paul Martin Antiques
266 River St.
508/521-0909

Graham & Sons Antiques
420 Water St.
508/374-8031

Antique World
108 Washington St.
508/372-3919

Tom's Place
4 Auburn St.
508/373-3820

Parker's Antiques
110 River St.
508/373-2332

33 HOLLISTON

Yankee Picker
86 Church Rear
508/429-9825

Wilder Shop
400 Washington St.
508/429-4836

Antiques Plus
798 Washington St.
508/429-9186

Holliston Antiques
798 Washington St.
508/429-0428

34 INDIAN ORCHARD

Cat's Paw Antiques
45 Parker Street
413/543-5254

35 LENOX

Seven Hills Country Inn
40 Plunkett Street
413/637-0060 or 1-800-869-6518
Open daily

Directions: Take Exit 2 off I-90 (Massachusetts Turnpike) and follow Route 20 West for approximately 3 miles. You will see a blue sign on the right that says "Seven Hills." That sign will be pointing to the left, which is Plunkett Street. Seven Hills Inn is 1 mile down Plunkett Street on the left.

Not just a fair-weather haven, Seven Hills Inn works year round to customize just about anything for vacations, banquets, weddings, business retreats and conferences. Furnished with care-worn antiques, and boasting hand-carved fireplaces, leaded glass windows and high ceilings, nothing has changed since the inn was originally built and known as Shipton Court, one of the original Berkshire cottages. The inn is comprised of 15 manor house and 37 terrace house guestrooms, including 3 handicapped accessible ones, on 27 acres in the heart of the Berkshires. There's also a 60-foot swimming pool and two hard-surface tennis courts. Ideally situated to take advantage of the Bershires' seasonal and cultural activities and scenery, Seven Hills Inn is surrounded with such offerings as fall foliage festivals, cider pressings, hayrides, downhill and cross-country skiing, historic homesites and museums. Tanglewood, Jacobs Pillow Dance Theatre, and, next door is the Edith Wharton estate, home of Shakespeare and Company.

Stone's Throw Antiques
51 Church St.
413/637-2733

Lavie En Rose
67 Church St.
413/229-3036

Charles L Flint Antiques
56 Housatonic St.
413/637-1634

36 LITTLETON

Van Wyck's Antiques
325 Great Rd.
508/952-2878

Upton House Antiques
275 King St.
508/486-3367

Sunflower Antiques
537 King St.
508/486-0606

Littleton Antiques
476 King St.
508/952-0001

Hamlet Antiques
161 Great Rd.
508/952-2445

Flowers & Spice & Everything
2 Mannion Pl
508/486-3687

Blue Cape Antiques
620 Great Rd.
508/486-4709

Frederic Gallery
510 King St.
508/486-9183

37 LOWELL

Whitney House Antiques
913 Pawtucket St.
508/458-0044

Hank Garrity Antiques
331 Broadway St.
508/453-6497

Vintage Co.
194 Middle St.
508/453-9096

James McKenna Antq. Clocks
1319 Middlesex St.
508/454-3521

38 LYNN

Diamond District Breakfast Inn
142 Ocean Street
617/599-4470 or 1-800-666-3076
Fax:617/599-2200

Directions: Located about 8 1/2 miles north of Boston and Logan International Airport, near the intersection of Routes 1A and 129.

Just 300 feet off of a 3.5 mile stretch of beach, the Diamond District Bed & Breakfast Inn offers guest rooms with private baths, ocean swimming, walking and biking paths, and business services. Recently listed on the National Register as a Historic District, the Inn is a 1911 Georgian style mansion with 17 rooms, sitting on one half acre in Boston's North Shore, also known as Lynn's "Diamond District." Once the private estate of P. J. Harney, a Lynn shoe manufacturer, the original house plans and specifications remain with the house, as do some original fixtures. Features include a three-story staircase, established gardens, hardwood floors, antiques and Oriental rugs, an 1895 rosewood Knabe concert grand piano, and a custom-made Chippendale dining room table and chairs.

Diamond District Antiques
9 Broad St.
617/586-8788

39 MARBLEHEAD

Wicker Unlimited
108 Washington St
617/631-9728
Open: Mon.-Sat. 10-5, Sun. Noon-6

Directions: Take Route 128 North from Massachusetts Turnpike (I-95) about 20 miles to Route 114 East (Exit 25 A Marblehead). Go east on 114 through Salem into Marblehead (Route 114 East becomes Pleasant Street). Follow Pleasant Street all the way to end "T" intersection. Turn left on Washington Street and look to your right. The store can be seen in old town. From 128 to Marblehead is 6 miles.

Marla Segal bought her first piece of wicker at the ripe old age of 15. The purchase of that single wicker rocker inspired her to the point of hopeless infatuation. After serving several years as an apprentice at a Boston firm, where she learned to repair wicker, Marla decided to open up her own shop. She quickly earned the reputation as an honest and knowledgeable dealer. Today, she supplies both veteran and new collectors with wicker she acquires from all parts of the country. "I try to match the lifestyle of the person to the right piece of wicker," she explains.

However, Marla's interests are unlimited, so a full array of American antiques and collectibles is also found in Wicker Unlimited. Quilts, Fiesta, Roseville, Limoges, linens, rugs, and even garden tools are just a small sampling of what might be available. Country pine, mahogany, oak or walnut—it's always a surprise to see what has been discovered in some of the great, old New England estates that surround the area.

Calico Country
92 Washington St.
617/631-3607

Old Town Antique Co-op
108 Washington St.
617/631-9728

Heeltapper Antiques
134 Washington St.
617/631-7722

Marblehead Antiques
118 Pleasant St.
617-859-8558

Honest Ladies-Good Buy
120 Pleasant St.
617-631-7555

Antiquewear-Buttons
82 Front St.
617/639-0070

40 MIDDLEBORO

51 Centre St. Antiques
51 Centre St.
508/947-9550

Middleboro Antiques Co.
11 N. Main St.
508/947-1844

Christina's Antiques
19 S. Main St.
508/947-5220

Milady's Mercantile
21 S. Main St.
508/946-2121

Barewood
282 W. Grove St.
508/947-4482

Acorn Hill Antique Shop
285 W. Grove St.
508/947-0982

41 NANTUCKET

Nantucket Island

Step off the ferry or the plane and you're in another world. Thirty miles off Cape Cod, this crescent-shaped island retains a quiet charm found in past days when whaling ships made the island haven their home. You'll find lots to explore on foot or on bicycle: unspoiled beaches and the solitary lighthouses, peaceful byways and lanes, historic mansions, and open-air farmers' stands.

Nantucket Town abounds with elegant restaurants and antiques, craft and specialty stores. Sea captains' houses line the cobblestone streets. The Whaling Museum, a former spermaceti factory, now overflows with artifacts and memorabilia from the island's once-thriving industry. Whale-watching trips, deep-sea fishing charters, and numerous excursion boats leave from Straight Wharf.

The island's magic continues year round. In late April, the Daffodil Festival features millions of yellow flowers planted by islanders as a celebration of spring.

Wayne Pratt, Inc.

28 Main Street
508/228-8788
(Seasonal)

Offering the discriminating shopper the opportunity to purchase antiques of exceptional quality and design. When traveling in Connecticut, be sure to visit their 3,000-square-foot showroom located in Woodbury.

Weeds
14 Centre St.
508/228-5200

Modern Arts
67 Old South Rd.
508/228-2358

Tonkin of Nantucket
33 Main Street
508/228-9697

Puss-N-Boots
18 Federal St.
508/228-5167

Nantucket House Antiques
1 S. Beach St.
508/228-4604

Jewelers Gallery of Nantucket
21 Center St.
508/228-0229

Frank Sylvia Jr. Antiques
0 Washington St.
508/228-2926

Frank Sylvia
6 Rays Ct.
508/228-0960

Antiques Depot
14 Easy St.
508/228-1287

Great Places To Eat

Atlantic Cafe

15 South Water Street
508/228-0570

Atlantic Cafe is one of those kinds of eating places where anybody can go at any time and feel comfortable, because it really doesn't matter how you look. They have a huge menu of all-American food, and eventually everyone you know will come in. You can bring the kids, the in-laws, the weekend guests, all in shorts, or grunge clothes, or whatever—it doesn't matter!

Jared Coffee House

29 Broad Street
508/228-2400

Jared Coffee House is a legend and a landmark in Nantucket—one of those "see and be seen" places. The formal dining room serves breakfast and dinner (steaks, fish, stuffed shrimp and desserts). An informal pub serves lunch and dinner (fish and chips, tuna, burgers, etc.). A must-do tourist destination.

42 NEWBURYPORT

Newburyport Estate Jewelers
7 State St.
508/462-6242

Olde Port Book Shop
18 State St.
508/462-0100

Flukes & Finds & Friends
37 State St.
508/463-6968

Lady Di's Antiques
21 Water St.
508/462-5858

Sam's Treasured Memories
39 Water St.
508/462-0024

Annex
49 Water St. #R
508/462-8212

Maiden Voyage Antiques
61 Water St.
508/465-9909

43 NEWTON

Marcia & Bea
1 Lincoln St.
617/332-2408

Sonia Paine Antiques Gallery
373 Boylston St.
617/566-9669

Give & Take Consignments
799 Washington St.
617/964-4454

Dining Room Showcase
833 Washington St.
617/527-8368

Treasure & Trivia
811 Washington St.
617/630-1780

44 NORTHAMPTON

Antiques Corner
5 Market St.
413/584-8939

Antq. Center of Northampton
9 1/2 Market St.
413/584-3600

American Decorative Arts
3 Oliver St.
413/584-6804

Up in the Attic
11 Market St.
413/587-3055

45 NORTHBOROUGH

Tins & Things
28 Main St.
508/393-4647

Elegant Junk
94 Main St.
508/393-8736

Elaine's Antiques
281 W. Main St.
508/393-0170

Bell Tower Antiques
56 W. Main St.
508/393-5477

Country Store
244 Main Street
508/393-4224

Cyrus Gale Antiques
20 Main Street
508/393-7300

Gramp's Attic
55 Hudson St.
508/393-1617

46 NORTH HADLEY

North Hadley Antiques
Route 47 - 399 River Drive
413/549-8776

47 NORWOOD

Norwood Antiques & Restor.
483 Washington St.
617/769-9198

Wise Owl
637 Washington St.
617/769-5255

Brenda's Antiques
644 Washington St.
617/762-3227

Applegate Antiques
721 Washington St.
617/769-8892

Norwood Trading Post
1182 Washington St.
617/762-2186

48 OLD DEERFIELD

In "Historic Deerfield, an Introduction," the author produces a setting of long ago:

"Deerfield is a beautiful ghost, haunted by the drama and violence of its early history as well as by more recent spirits who have witnessed the joys and sorrows of life in a small New England town over 300 years ago. Unlike other ghosts, Deerfield is no disembodied spirit eluding our sight and grasp. The town retains material evidence of Native American habitations from several millennia, the 17th century English town plan of compact village and broad meadows, 18th and 19th century houses filled with the relics of hearth and home that reveal to us so many intimate details of life in early New England. Twenty-four of the houses along The Street in Deerfield were here when revolution broke out against England in 1775. Another twenty-three buildings had been erected before 1850. Their contents date from the time of Deerfield's first English settlement in 1669 to the flourishing of the Arts and Crafts movement in the early 20th century."

In 1952 Mr. and Mrs. Henry N. Flynt, wanting to assure the future of the village of Deerfield, incorporated Historic Deerfield, Inc. (then known as the Heritage Foundation) to preserve Deerfield, open its old houses to visitors, and use the buildings and their collections to foster education in and understanding of the American past.

When the Flynts founded Historic Deerfield in 1952,

they had four houses open to the public in which they attempted to offer visitors a view of life in Deerfield in the colonial and early national periods. Although they had acquired a few choice antiques for display in these buildings, most of their furnishings were country pieces. In the 1950s their collection grew under the influence of antiques dealers, museum curators, and fellow collectors. They turned increasingly to high style furniture and began to form special collections of early American silver, English ceramics and Chinese export porcelain, and textiles, needlework, and costume. By the end of the decade the Flynts and Historic Deerfield had become widely recognized for the national importance of these collections. They are displayed in sympathetic settings in six historic buildings along The Street.

Today, Historic Deerfield offers workshops, lecture series, antiques forums, summer archaeological excavations and educational programs for students and visitors of all ages.

Daily guided museum tours and walking tours through the village highlight Deerfield and America's history for tourist and travelers from all over the world.

Among the accommodations for dining and lodging is the 1884 Deerfield Inn. The inn has 23 guest rooms, three dining rooms, a coffee shop and full-service bar. There are facilities on the premises for weddings, private parties and small business meetings. The inn is open throughout the year. (413) 774-5587.

All in all, there is plenty to see. Thirteen museum houses dating from circa 1720 to 1850 display more than 20,000 objects made or used in America from 1600 to 1900. Highlights of the collections include American furniture with special emphasis on the Connecticut River Valley; English and Chinese ceramics; American and English silver; and American and English textiles.

For further information, call (413) 774-5581

Contributed by *Southern Antiques Magazine*, May 1995

5 & 10 Antique Gallery
Rts. 5 & 10 (Old Deerfield)
413/773-3620
Website: http://antiques510.com
Open: Daily 10-5, Jan.-May, Closed Wed.

Directions: Exit 26 off I-91, 2A East, right at Dunkin' Donuts, right at first light, 1 1/4 mile on Rts. 5 & 10. Exit 24 off I-91, 7 miles North on Rts. 5 & 10, 1 mile North of Historic Deerfield, MA.

The 5 & 10 Antique Gallery is a bit of history within itself. The shop has provided quality antiques for the past 20 years. Featuring two levels of 18th, 19th and early 20th century furnishings, fine porcelain, china, glassware, silver, linens, primitives, toys, dolls, books, antique reference books, Sotherby catalogues, tools, kitchen ware, and showcases of smalls and collectibles all within the beautiful setting of Old Deerfield.

Lighthouse Antiques
Routes 5 & 10
No Phone Listed

49 ORLEANS/EAST ORLEANS

Lilli's Antique Emporium
225 Main St.
508/255-8300

Countryside Antiques
6 Lewis Rd.
508/240-0525

Continuum
7 Rt. 28
508/255-8513

East Orleans Antiques
204 Main St.
508/255-2592

50 OSTERVILLE

A Stanley Wheelock Antiques
870 Main St.
508/420-3170

Hollyhocks
891 Main St.
508/420-0484

Farmhouse
1340 Main St.
508/420-2400

51 PEABODY

Chuck Watts Antiques
18 Main St.
508/532-7400

Americana Antiques
22 Newbury St.
508/535-1042

A Lindsay Antiques
24 Winter St.
508/532-7544

52 PEMBROKE

Magic Garden Antiques
74 Congress
617/826-7930

Good Riddance Antiques
95 Church St.
617/826-8955

Antiques for Elyse
Rt. 27
617/293-3638

Endless Antiques
95 Church St.
617/826-7177

53 PITTSFIELD

Greystone Gardens
436 North St.
413/442-9291

Memory Lane Antiques
446 Tyler St.
413/499-2718

Potala
148 North St.
413/443-5568

Ralph & Heritage Fntain. Gllry.
348 Cloverdale St.
413/442-2537

Interesting Side Trips

Hancock Shaker Village
413/443-0188 or 1-800-817-1137

Hancock Shaker Village is located in western Massachusetts in the heart of the Berkshires. It is at the junction of Routes 20 and 41 west of Pittsfield. Convenient to the Massachusetts Turnpike, Taconic State Parkway and New York Thruway, it is a one-hour drive from Albany and a three-hour drive from New York or Boston. The Village is located near Tanglewood, the Norman Rockwell Museum, Clark Art Institute and many other major cultural attractions.

Shakers' "City of Peace," beckons you to discover the way of life of America's most successful communitarian society. Now a living history museum, the village was an active Shaker community from 1790 to 1960.

Members held all property in common and practiced celibacy, equality and separation of the sexes, and pacificism as they sought to create "heaven on earth". Putting their "hands to work and hearts to God", the Shakers created a society based in spirituality but rich in practicality and ingenuity. Discover their unique approach to life and the remarkable fruits of their labors at Hancock Shaker Village.

Explore the extraordinary 1826 Round Stone Barn, the remarkable 1830 communal Brick Dwelling, and eighteen other restored buildings which span three centuries. From the early water-powered laundry and machine shop to the heated 1916 automobile garage, you will marvel at Shaker design, workmanship, inventiveness and efficiency. Envision the Shakers worshiping in ecstatic dance and song in the sparse simplicity of the 1793 Meetinghouse. Learn about 20th-century Shaker life amidst the worldly decor and comforts of the Trustees' Office and Store.

Appreciate Shaker industriousness as you watch artisans and farmers at work. Chat with gardeners as they harvest herbs, vegetables, and seeds in the heirloom gardens.

Try a spinning wheel, loom, or quill pen in the Discovery Room. Enjoy a candlelight dinner in the quiet of the matches, sheep shearing and harvest activities. Explore Shaker archaeological sites. Savor the order and tranquility of the "City of Peace."

54 PLYMOUTH

Dillon & Co. English Country
12 North St.
508/747-2242

North Plymouth Antiques
398 Court St.
508/830-0127

Chiltonville Antiques
40 State Rd.
508/746-2164

Antiques at 108 Sandwich St.
108 Sandwich St.
508/747-3280

Plymouth Antiques Trading Co.
8 Court St.
508/746-3450

Antique Promendade
50 Court St.
508/830-0889

Antique House
184 Water St.
508/747-1207

Village Braider
48 Sandwich St.
508/746-9625

Interesting Side Trips

Plimoth Plantation
Plimoth Plantation Hwy.
Accessible via Route 3
508/746-1622

It's places like Plimoth Plantation and other living history museums that let us know just how remarkable our ancestors really were. Plimoth Plantation offers a chance to see Plymouth as it was when America's most famous immigrants, the Pilgrims, first colonized the New World. It also gives an in-depth look into the lives of the Wampanoag Indians, on whose land the Pilgrims settled. Key parts of the museum are the 1627 Pilgrim Village, where people represent actual Pilgrims in everyday life and settings, like house building, food preparation and gardening; the Carriage House Crafts Center, where you can watch period goods being reproduced using materials and tools like those of the 17th century; Hobbamock's Wampanoag Indian Homesite, where Native Americans describe the effects of the colonists' arrival on their own ancestors and how the events continue to affect their people today. Some of the staff are in native attire, and the area itself is a re-creation of one family's homesite. Don't forget to check out the *Mayflower II*, a reproduction of the ship that brought the Pilgrims to Plymouth, located on the waterfront adjacent to Plymouth Rock.

55 PROVINCETOWN

Provincetown Antique Market
131 Commercial St.
508/487-1115

West End Antiques
146 Commercial St.
508/487-6723

Scott Dinsmore Antiques
179 Commercial St.
508/487-2236

Clifford-William Antiques
225 Commercial St.
508/487-4174

Small Pleasures
359 Commercial St.
508/487-3712

Remembrances of Things Past
376 Commercial St.
508/487-9443

Alan's Attic
194 Commercial St.
508/487-4234

56 REHOBOTH

Madeline's Antiques
164 Winthrop St.
508/252-3965

Hornbine Antiques
183 Winthrop St.
508/252-3199

Sleepy Hollow Antiques
309 Winthrop St.
508/252-3483

Wooden Keyhole
582 Winthrop St.
508/336-7475

Mendes Antiques
Rt. 44 - 52 Blanding Road
508/336-7381

57 ROCKPORT

Hanna Wingate of Rockport
11 Main St.
508/546-1008

Woodbine Collection
35 Main St.
508/546-9324

Rockport Trading Co.
67 Broadway
508/546-8066

Rockport Quilt Shoppe
2 Ocean Ave.
508/546-1001

58 SALEM

Watts Antiques
32 West Ave.
508/744-0123

Museum Place
Museum Place Mall
508/745-4258

Salem Antiques
266 Canal St.
508/744-7229

Pickering Wharf Antiques
7 Pickering Way
508/741-3113

Filigree & Fancy Antiques
4 Wharf St.
508/745-9222

Burke Antiques
121 Essex St.
508/744-2242

Asia House
18 Washington Sq.
508/745-8257

AAA Olde Naumkeag Antiques
1 Hawthorne Blvd
508/745-9280

59 SANDWICH

Sandwich Antiques
131 Rt. 6A
508/833-8580

Paul Madden Antiques
16 Jarves St.
508/888-6434

Maypope Lane
161 Old Kings Hwy.
508/888-1230

H Richard Strand Antiques
2 Grove St./Town Hall Sq.
508/888-3230

Dillingham House
71 Main St.
508/833-0065

Alluring Antiques
121 Rt. 6A
508/888-7497

60 SCITUATE

Quarter Deck
206 Front St.
617/545-4303

Greenhouse Antiques
182 First Parish Rd.
617/545-1964

Echo Lake Antiques
366 Gannett Rd.
617/545-7100

Gatherings
131 Front St.
617/545-7664

61 SEEKONK

Antqs. at Hearthstone House
15 Fall River Ave.
508/336-6273

Vinny's Antiques Center
380 Fall River Ave.
508/336-0800

Consignment Barn
394 Fall River Ave.
508/336-3228

Ruth Falkinburg Doll Shop
208 Taunton Ave.
508/336-6929

Lost Treasures Antiques
1460 Fall River Ave.
508/336-9294

County Squire Antiques
1732 Fall River Ave.
508/336-8442

Grist Mill Country Store
879 Arcade Ave.
508/336-8232

62 SHEFFIELD

David M. Weiss
Main St. (Rte 7)
413/229-2716

Darr Antiques & Interiors
28 S. Main
413/229-7773

Corner House Antiques
Main St.
413/229-6627

1750 House Antiques
S. Main
413/229-6635

Frederick Hatfield Antiques
99 S. Main
413/229-7986

Anthony's Antiques
102 Main St. Rear
413/229-8208

Saturday Sweets
755 A N. Main (Rt. 7)
413/229-0026

Centuryhurst Berkshire Antqs.
Main St.
413/229-3277

May's Everything Shop
779 N. Main St.
413/229-2037

Avenue Antiques
1224 N. Main Ave.
413/229-2172

Cupboards & Roses
Rt. 7
413/229-3070

Ole T J's Antique Barn
Rt. 7
413/229-8382

Kuttner Antiques
Rt. 7
413/229-2955

Berkshire Gilders Antiques
15 Main St. (Rte 7)
413/229-0113

Jenny Hall Antiques
Rt. 7
413/229-0277

Dovetail Antiques
Rt. 7
413/229-2628

Classic Images Art & Antiques
527 Sheffield Plain
413/229-0033

Le Trianon
1854 N. Main (Rt. 7)
413/528-0775

Falcon Antiques
176 S. Undermountain Rd.
413/229-7745

63 SHELBURNE/SHELBURNE FALLS

Shea Antiques
69 Bridge St.
413/625-8353

Strawberry Field
1207 Mohawk Trail
413/625-2039

Rainville Trading Post
251 Main St.
413/625-6536

Orchard Hill Antiques
Colrain Rd.
413/625-2433

Yankee Pastime Antiques
Route 112 North Colrain
413/625-2730

64 SOMERVILLE

Londontowne Galleries
380 Somerville Ave.
617/625-2045

Karma Antiques
248 Beacon St.
617/864-5875

Warped
236 Elm St.
617/666-3129

65 SOUTHAMPTON

Southampton Antiques
172 College Hwy. (Rt. 10)
413/527-1022/Fax: 413/527-6056
Open Sat. 10-5. Appointments welcome, closed August

Meg and Bruce Cummings offer the largest selection of authentic antique American oak and Victorian furniture in New England — no reproductions, no imports and authenticity guaranteed. They have three large barns with five floors of merchandise for customers to browse through, sigh over, touch, examine and take home.

Instead of having a store catalog, they offer customers a custom-made video for $25, designed to meet particular specifications and needs. Each video is individually made and includes price quotes, style description, condition, approximate age and dimensions.

"We focus on high style American Victorian walnut, rosewood, mahogany, and turn-of-the-century oak," say the Cummings. "Furniture found in our barns is in three categories: 'as found' original varnish, superb original finish and refinished. We are very proud of our refinished product and feel that our refinishing process has reached a quality second to none."

Among the pieces regularly offered by the Cummings are curio cabinets, hall trees, desks, wicker, swivel chairs, bedroom suites, lockside chests, conference tables, clocks, bookcases, lamps, side-by-sides, library tables, beds, roll-top desks, Victorian sofas, marble-top furniture, sets of chairs, and square and round dining tables. Their specialties include Victorian Renaissance Revival, turn-of-the-century oak and Victorian Rococo.

66 SOUTH DEERFIELD

Yesterdays Antique Center
Routes 5 & 10
413/665-7226

Antiques at Deerfield
Routes 5 & 10
No Phone Listed

House of the Ferret
Routes 5 & 10
413/665-0038

Antiques by Sandra Pavoni
Routes 5 & 10
413/665-0511

67 SOUTH EGREMONT

Country Cat Antiques
Rte 23
413/528-4551

Howard's Antiques
Hillsdale Rd. (Rt. 23)
413/528-1232

Bruce & Sue Gventer: "Books"
1 Tyrrell Rd.
413/528-2327

Geffner/Schatzky Antiques
Rt. 23
413/528-0057

The Splendid Peasant Ltd.
Rte 23 at Sheffield Rd.
413/528-5755

Douglas Antiques
Douglas Levy, Rte 23
413/528-1810

68 SPRINGFIELD

Fancy That
699 Sumner Ave.
413/739-5118

Lady in Red Antiques
712 Sumner Ave.
413/734-6100

A-1 Antique Store
752 Summer Ave.
413/732-6855

Tri-Towne Collectibles
524 Main St.
413/543-5020

Patti's Antiques & Treasures
532 Main St.
413/543-8484

Market Place Antiques
2 Wilmont St.
413/732-0206

Prestige Antiques
435 White St.
413/739-2190

Cat's Paw Antiques
45 Parker St.
413/543-5254

69 STOCKBRIDGE

Inn at Stockbridge
P.O. Box 618, Rt. 7 N
413/298-3337
Open 8-9 daily
Rates:$75-225

Directions: On Route 7, 1 1/2 miles north of Stockbridge Center. Off the Massachusetts Turnpike, take Exit 2, Route 102 West to Route 7 North. Travel Route 7 North for 1 1/4 miles.

Graciously operated by Alice and Len Schiller, the Inn at Stockbridge offers eight guest rooms with private baths, including two suites. Settled on 12 secluded acres, the Colonial Revival style home, complete with Georgian detailing and classical columns, has remained structurally unchanged since its construction in 1906 as a vacation home for a Boston attorney. Each morning a full breakfast is served on a grand mahogany table set with china, silver, crystal, linen and lighted candles. Often after a refreshing dip in the pool, guests are treated to afternoon wine and cheese, and can spend a quiet evening browsing the inn's extensive library.

Interesting Side Trips

Charles H. Baldwin & Sons
1 Center Street
West Stockbridge
413/232-7785
Open 9-5 Tue.-Sat., occasionally open Sundays

As a counterpoint to overindulged chocoholics, West Stockbridge offers a vanilla lover's nirvana. In the tiny storefront of Charles H. Baldwin & Sons, vanilla connoisseurs can see vanilla being made according to the methods used by the Baldwin family since 1888. The shop itself dates back to the late 1700s; the oak barrels in which the extract is aged, over 100 years. The whole place smells like, well, vanilla. Shoppers can watch family members draw the spice from the casks into gallon jugs, then use the vintage, soldered-steel measuring cup with a spring-operated siphon to pour the fragrant brandy-colored liquid into tiny bottles, which are capped and labeled by hand. In the rear of the store is the "laboratory," where more family members blend almond, anise, peppermint and lemon extracts or their special vanilla sugar. Purchases are rung up on a 19th century cash register, and money is kept in a 100-year-old safe that opens with an antique brass key. A true piece of "living history."

70 STURBRIDGE

Showcase Antique Center, Inc.
At the entrance to Old Sturbridge Village
508/347-7190/Fax: 508/347-5420
Website: http://www.showcaseantiques.com
E-mail: showcase@hey.net
Open Mon., Wed.-Sat. 10-5, Sun. 12-5, closed Tue.

Directions: Located on Route 20 in Sturbridge, just one mile west from Exit 9 off I-90 (Massachusetts Turnpike) and from Exit 3B off I-84.

Linking history and the future through modern technology, Showcase Antique Center offers not only the physical, visual delight of strolling through selections of 160 showcase dealers, but modern conveniences of worldwide shipping, 24-hour fax, answering machine, E-mail, plus a website on the Internet.

Located at the entrance to Old Sturbridge Village, the selections feature art glass, china, pottery, silver, jewelry, paintings, Royal Bayreuth, primitives, Shaker and small furniture items. Some of the interesting items most recently found at the Showcase Antique Center are a Hull, Little Red Riding Hood cookie jar, oil on canvas painting of a child—American artist circa 1930, Civil War era tintype, pair of Rosenthal Rosari cobalt and gilt urns c. 1922, Tiffany Favoili compotes, blue splatter cup and saucer and a Kelva dresser box.

Commonwealth Cottage
11 Summit Avenue
508/347-7708
Open Mon.-Sun. All year
Rates: $85-145

Directions: From Massachusetts Turnpike (I-90): Take Exit 9 to Route 20 West towards Brimfield. After passing the intersection of Route 148 on the right, take the next left onto Commonwealth Avenue. At the "Heritage Green" sign, veer left and you'll see Commonwealth Cottage straight ahead. From I-84 East,: Take exit 3 B, (Route 20 W./Palmer). Follow Route 20 West and proceed as before. From Brimfield: Follow Route 20 East into Sturbridge. Make a right onto Commonwealth Avenue, then proceed as above. (Be careful—Commonwealth Avenue appears quickly. Just after the sign for 630 Main Street in front of the gray building of shops on the left, and a yellow clapboard house on the right.)

Sitting on a knoll surrounded by 200-year-old maple trees, almost in the heart of Sturbridge's attractions, is the charming Queen Anne Victorian home known as Commonwealth Cottage. Lovingly run by Wiebke and Bob Gilbert, the Commonwealh is comfortably furnished with period pieces and family hand-me-downs. A variety of guest rooms are available, most with queen-sized beds and private bath. Each room has its own personality, like the M&M Room, named after both Wiebke and Bob's grandmothers and furnished with many of their cherished belongings. Or Uncle Sam's baroque-themed room, and Mr. Bigelow's Room, named after Bob's dad and filled with lots of greens, wicker and an actual picket fence for the queen headboard. In addition to a sumptuous breakfast, complete with the house's own jams and jellies, guests are treated to afternoon tea.

Fairground Antique Center
362 Main St.
508/347-3926

Antique Center of Sturbridge
426 Main St.
508/347-5150

Sturbridge Antique Shops
200 Charlton Rd.
508/347-2744

This & That
446 Main St.
508/347-5183

Interesting Side Trips

Old Sturbridge Village
Route 20 West
508/347-3362
Website: http://www.osv.org

Directions: Route 20, Sturbridge, Massachusetts, Exit 2 off I-84. (After 7 p.m. use exit 3 B), exit 9 off the Massachusetts Pike.

Old Sturbridge Village is another amazing piece of living history. It is an extraordinary outdoor museum that brings to life a working community of the 1830s, down to the smallest details. The largest history museum in the northeast, Old Sturbridge is a re-created community on over 200 acres, with more than 40 restored structures, carefully relocated from as far away as Maine. The museum concept was conceived by a member of the Wells family in 1936 as the families of Albert B. And Joe Cheney Wells tried to decide what to do with both men's extensive collections of furniture, tools, utensils, paperweights, glassware, and 19th century clocks. After several major interruptions, including a hurricane and World War I, the museum opened to the public in 1946. In the ensuing 50 years the museum has grown and developed, been redefined and researched. Each exhibit and program is meticulously grounded in historical research, which provides a clearer understanding of the region's past.

By exploring the museum, visitors can experience daily life in an early 19th century country village in New England — from the rustic farmhouse kitchen to the elegant parlor in the finest house on the village common, from the blacksmith shop to a rural printing office and bookstore, examining along the way home furnishings and decorative arts, costume and dress, food and cooking utensils, and implements and devices of all sorts. By choosing to recreate the life and times of the 1830s, the museum founders have chosen a transitional era in New England when life was changing from an agrarian society to an industrial one, when water and steam power was replacing man and animal power, when exploration was increasing through better mass transportation, and the Northeast was moving into the industrial age. The exhibits show these changes in New England: farming with its seasonal tasks and customs; women's lives and their households; mill neighborhoods with their sawmills and gristmills; artisans and rural industry; the center village, more attuned to changes emanating from the cities; community events; and the story of Old Sturbridge Village itself, which celebrated its 50th anniversary in 1996 and is a major force in the field of historic preservation and restoration.

71 SUDBURY

Flashback Furnishings
88 Boston Post Rd.
508/443-7709

Pairs of Chairs, Etc.
345 Boston Post Rd.
508/443-3363

Sudbury Art & Antiques
730 Boston Post Rd.
508/443-0994

72 THE MOHAWK TRAIL

For an antidote to the hectic pace of modern life, travel the back roads of the northwest corner of Massachusetts, where you'll find charming villages, swimming holes, and covered bridges. The Mohawk Trail, now Route 2, began as a Native American trail, was widened by the early settlers, then was developed as America's first scenic automobile route. The trail is most spectacular in autumn, when the trees turn to brilliant crimsons, oranges and yellows.

A fragrant stop is Shelburne Falls, where the Bridge of Flowers, an old trolley bridge, is planted with masses of blossoms.

73 VINEYARD HAVEN

Once you've experienced the Vineyard's charm, you'll find it hard to leave. New England's largest island has soft sandy beaches, pine forests, rolling hills and moors, and a number of delightful towns.

Oak Bluffs is famous for its Methodist campground with brightly painted Victorian gingerbread cottages, built in the mid-1800s as a religious retreat. The town also features the Flying Horses, the oldest working carousel in America. Vineyard Haven is a picturesque turn-of-the-century community and a year-round ferry port. Edgartown, once a prosperous whaling port, is now a yachting center filled with stately mariners' homes. The town's Old Whaling Church is a performing arts center. All three towns have bistros, boutiques, and galleries.

Head "up island" and you'll discover the classic New England town of West Tisbury and the rolling hills of Chilmark. At the outermost point of the island are the dramatic color-streaked clay cliffs of Gay Head National Monument.

Backyard Store
Cromwell Lane
508/693-2320

Summer Old Summer New
76 Main St.
508/693-8333

Great Places To Eat

The Black Dog Tavern
Beach Street, Vineyard Haven Harbor
508/693-9223

The Black Dog Bakery
Water Street, Vineyard Haven Harbor
508/693-4786

Home of the Black Dog T-shirt, The Black Dog Bakery offers "only the best" breads, pies, cookies and more, while The Black Dog Tavern offers an eclectic menu of fresh seafood, pasta salads, and American ethnic thrown in.

74 WAKEFIELD

Iron Horse Antique Gallery
951 Main St.
617/224-1188

Back Track Antiques
239 North Ave.
617/246-4550

75 WARE

The Wildwood Inn Bed & Breakfast
121 Church Street
413/967-7798 or 1-800-860-8098
Open daily
Rates: $50-80

Directions: From Massachusetts Turnpike (I-90): Take Exit 8. Turn left off the exit ramp onto Route 32 North. Follow Route 32 North for 8 miles to Junction Route 32 North and Route 9 East. (A movie theater is in front of you.) Take a right onto Routes 32 North and 9 East. At the second light, take a left onto Church Street. (If you reach the fire station, you missed the left turn!) Wildwood Inn is on the right, 3/4 mile up Church Street, across from the Highland Street sign.

Midway between Boston and the Berkshires, near the southern gateway to New England, the town of Ware is located right on Highways 9 and 32, two of the beautiful foliage routes of New England, and just a short ride from exit 8 of the Massachusetts Turnpike.

Waiting to greet you in Ware is a homey, 1880 Victorian Inn furnished with American primitive antiques, handmade heirloom quilts, and early cradles. Located on a maple tree-canopied street lined with stately Victorian homes, Wildwood Inn offers a wrap-around porch for lazing away the afternoon, or two landscaped acres for strolling. You can even wander the adjacent 100-acre park, or canoe, bike or ski nearby. The Brimfield Antique Market is a 20-minute drive on "no traffic" back roads. It's also an easy drive to the Five College area, Old Sturbridge or Deerfield, Yankee Candle Complex, the Basketball Hall of Fame, or beautiful Quabbin wilderness. Seven of the nine guest rooms have private baths, and there is a two-bedroom suite with bath and parlor.

76 WEST BARNSTABLE

Bird Cage Inc.
1064 Main Street
508/362-5559

Maps of Antiquity
1022 Rt. 6A
508/362-7169

Salt & Chestnut
651 Rt. 6A
508/362-6085

77 WEST BOYLSTON

Robert & Co. Antiques
271 W. Boylston
508/835-6550

Yankee Heritage Antiques
44 Sterling St. (Jnct. 12 & 110)
508-835-2010

West Boylston Antiques
277 W. Boylston St.
508/835-8853

Obadiah Pine Antiques
160 W. Boylston St.
508/835-3806

Wexford House Gifts
9 Crescent St.
508/835-6677

78 WEST BRIDGEWATER

Upstairs Downstairs Antiques
118 S. Main St.
508/586-2880

West Bridgewater Antiques
220 S. Main St.
508/580-5533

One Horse Shay Antiques
194 S. Main St.
508/587-8185

Armen Amerigion Antiques
223 W. Center St.
508/580-1464

America's Attic
221 W. Center St.
508/584-5281

Carriage House Antiques
102 W. Center St.
508/584-3008

Massachusetts

79 WEST TOWNSEND

Delaney Clock Shop
443 Main St.
508/597-2231

Hobart Village Antique Mall
445 Main St.
508/597-0332

Delaney Bros. Antiques
519 Main St.
508/597-8340

Antq. Assoc. @ West Townsend
473 Main St.
508/597-8084

80 WESTFORD

Country Village Antiques
137 Littleton Rd.
508/392-0555

Antiques Orchard
83 Boston Rd.
508/692-7161

Antiques
301 Littleton Rd.
508/392-9944

Wolf's Den Antiques
139 Concord Rd. RM. 225
508/692-3911

81 WILLIAMSTOWN

Saddleback Antiques
Rt. 7 South
413/458-5852

Greenbrier
Rt. 7
413/458-2248

Village Flowers Country Store
Rt. 43, 112 Water Street
413/458-9696

The Amber Fox
622A Main Street (Rt. 2)
413/458-8519

The Library Antiques
70 Spring Street
413/458-3436

Collectors Warehouse
105 North Street
413/458-9686

82 WORCESTER

Pastiche
113 Highland St.
508/756-1229

Big Joes Antiques
6 Peabody St.
508/752-7961

Ragtime Ann-tiques
70 James St.
508/752-6638

83 YARMOUTH PORT

Design Works
159 Main St.
508/362-9698

Nickerson's Antiques
162 Main St.
508/362-6426

Ryan Cooper Maritime Antqs.
161 Main St.
508/362-0190

King's Row Antiques
175 Main St.
508/362-3573

Minden Lane Antiques
175 Main St.
508/362-0220

Lookout Farm Antiques
175 Main St.
508/362-0292

Notes

Michigan

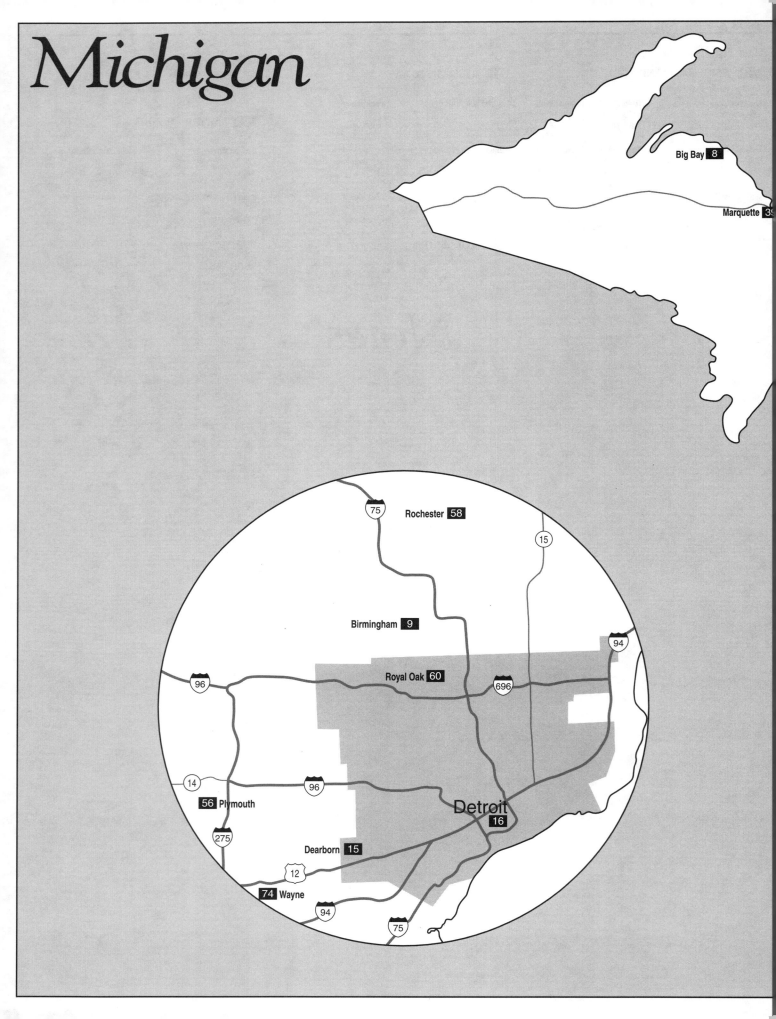

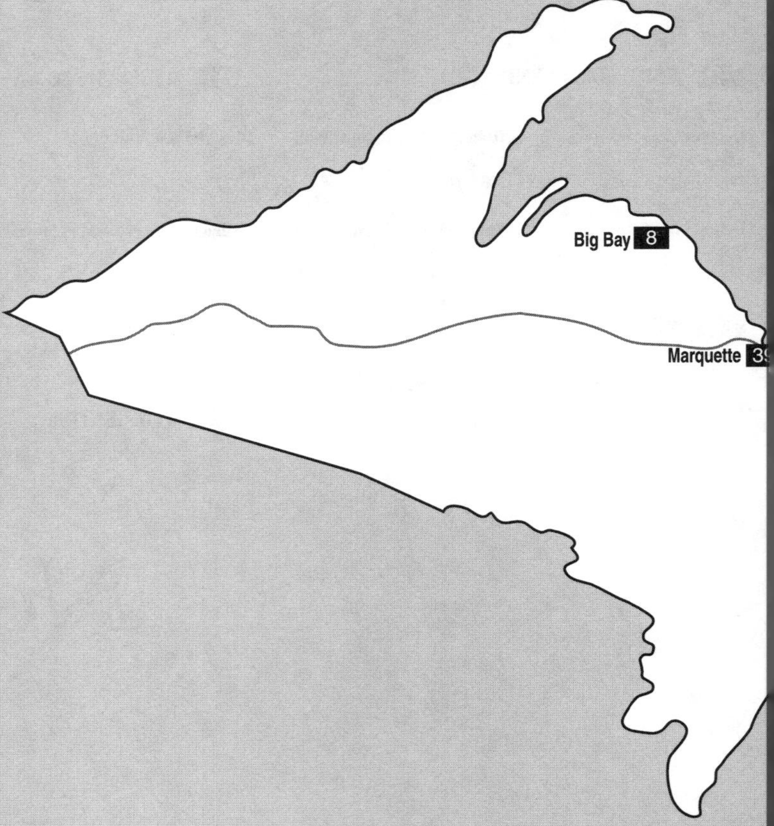
Big Bay 8
Marquette

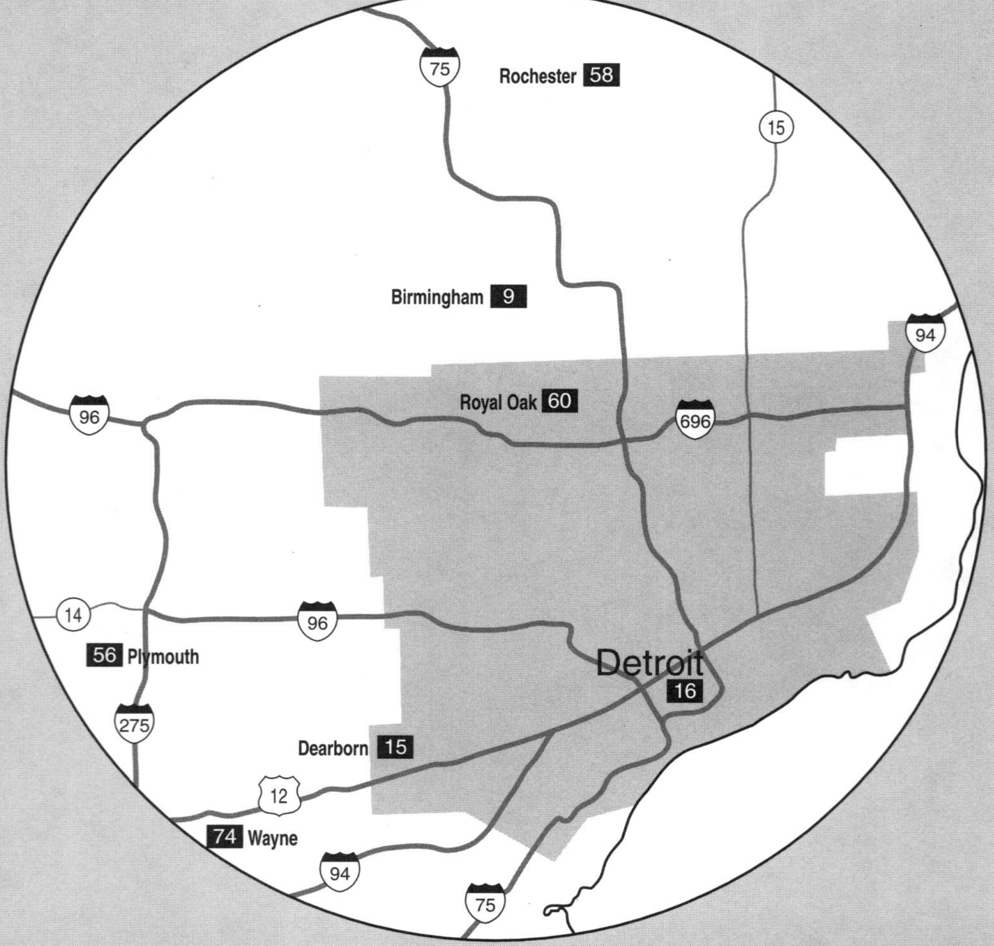
75
Rochester 58
15
Birmingham 9
94
96
Royal Oak 60
696
14
96
56 Plymouth
Detroit
16
275
Dearborn 15
12
74 Wayne
94
75

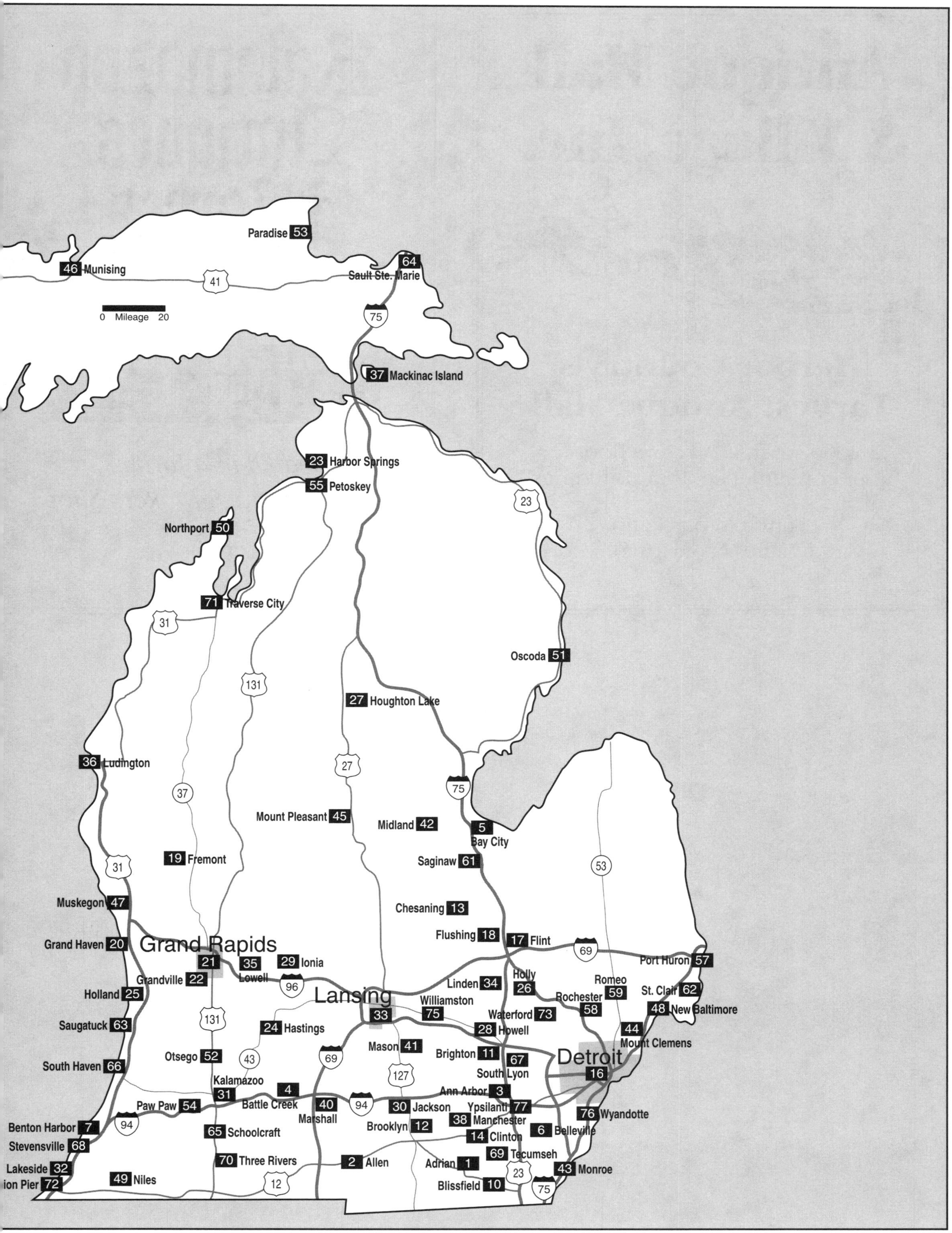

Paradise 53
46 Munising
41
64
Sault Ste. Marie
0 Mileage 20
75
37 Mackinac Island
23 Harbor Springs
55 Petoskey
23
Northport 50
71 Traverse City
31
Oscoda 51
131
27 Houghton Lake
36 Ludington
27
75
37
Mount Pleasant 45
Midland 42
5
Bay City
19 Fremont
31
Saginaw 61
53
Muskegon 47
Chesaning 13
Flushing 18
17 Flint
Grand Haven 20
Grand Rapids
69
21
35
29 Ionia
Port Huron 57
Lowell
Grandville 22
96
Linden 34
Holly
26
Romeo
59
Holland 25
Lansing
Williamston
75
Rochester
58
St. Clair 62
48 New Baltimore
131
33
Waterford 73
Saugatuck 63
24 Hastings
28 Howell
44
Mount Clemens
Mason 41
Brighton 11
67
South Lyon
Detroit
16
South Haven 66
Otsego 52
43
69
127
Kalamazoo
31
4
Ann Arbor 3
Paw Paw 54
Battle Creek
40
Marshall
94
30 Jackson
Ypsilanti 77
76 Wyandotte
38 Manchester
Benton Harbor 7
94
Brooklyn 12
6 Belleville
Stevensville 68
65 Schoolcraft
14 Clinton
69 Tecumseh
70 Three Rivers
2 Allen
Adrian 1
43 Monroe
Lakeside 32
23
49 Niles
12
Blissfield 10
75
ion Pier 72

1998 Michigan Antique Festivals

Midland Fairgrounds • US 10 at Eastman Ave.

Y'ALL COME!

May 30-31
July 25-26
Sept. 26-27

- **Special Interest Auto Show & Sales Lot**
- **Parts Swap Meet • Old Tractors & Engines**
- **Antique Show & Sale • Collectibles Market**
- **Memorabilia, Oddities & Folk Art**

Hundreds of cars & trucks on display & For Sale!
Join us for a FUN, Show & Shine Weekend with
Dash Plaques & Cash Prizes for the Show Cars!

1000 Outside & Inside Vendors! Held Rain or Shine	Gates Open 8 a.m. Admission $4.00 ea. Kids Under 11, FREE

NO PETS Allowed on Show Ground or in Buildings!

Info: 517-687-9001 (7 p.m. - 9 p.m., Mon. - Fri.)
MAF: 2156 Rudy Ct. Midland, MI 48642

1 ADRIAN

Birdsall Depot Antiques
4106 N. Adrian Hwy.
517/265-7107

Marsh's Antique Mall
136 S. Winter St.
517/263-8826

2 ALLEN

Michiana Antiques
100 W. Chicago Rd.
517/869-2132

Hand & Heart Antiques
109 W. Chicago Rd.
517/869-2553

Sandy's Simple Pleasures
109 W. Chicago Rd.
517/869-2875

Allen Old Township Hall Shops
114 W. Chicago Rd.
517/869-2575

Andy's Antiques
118 W. Chicago Rd.
517/869-2182

Peddlar's Alley
164 W. Chicago Rd.
517/869-2280

Olde Chicago Pike Antq. Mall
211 W. Chicago Rd.
517/869-2719

Antique East Side Mall
237 E. Chicago Rd.
517/869-2039

Greentop Country Antq. Mall
8651 W. Chicago Rd.
517/869-2100

Allen Antique Mall
9011 W. Chicago Rd.
517/869-2788

A Horse of Course
108 Prentiss
517/869-2527

3 ANN ARBOR

Ann Arbor Antiques Market
Margaret Brusher, Promoter
5055 Ann Arbor Saline Rd.
313/662-9453

Twenty-nine years ago, Margaret Brusher was a pioneer in the antique market, holding her first show at the local Ann Arbor Farmer's Market with 68 dealers participating. Nowadays, the monthly market draws over 350 dealers and a national (sometimes international) clientele.

So why has Ann Arbor stood the test of time? First is the Brusher's Market tough standards of authenticity, with every item guaranteed. Second, the market has shown a tendency to change as the antiques market in general changes. Where once, booth after booth was filled with country furniture and related accessories, desirous at the time, today's Ann Arbor represents variety and quality, irrespective of style or period to reflect the diversity of the customer. (For show dates, call the number listed above).

Rage of the Age
314 S. Ashley St.
313/662-0777

Treasure Mart
529 Detroit St.
313/662-1363

Past Presence Antiques
303 S. Division St.
313/663-2352

Antiques Market Place
210 S. 1st St.
313/913-8890

Antelope Antiques & Coins
206 S. 4th Ave.
313/663-2828

Graces Select Antiques
122 S. Main St.
313/668-0747

Arcadian Too Antqs. & Cllbls.
322 S. Main St.
313/994-8856

Maple Ridge Antiques
490 S. Maple Rd.
313/213-1577

Antique Mall of Ann Arbor
2739 Plymouth Rd.
313/663-8200

Kaleidoscope Books & Cllbls.
217 S. State St.
313/995-9887

Lotus Gallery
1570 Covington Dr.
313/665-6322

Dixboro General Store
5206 Plymoth Rd.
800/DIXBORO

Great Places To Stay

Woods Inn
2887 Newport Road
313/665-8394
Rates: $50-60

Here's a place to relax in the Michigan woods. The Woods Inn is an 1859, two-story wood and stone Early American home with four spacious guest rooms, plus an ample kitchen, dining room, parlor and large screened porch filled with wicker furniture. There are three acres of pine and hardwoods for guests' strolling pleasure, complete with sprawling gardens, a barn, and one of the few remaining smokehouses in Michigan. The inn is filled with Early American pieces and period collections of ironstone, colored art glass, and Staffordshire figurines.

4 BATTLE CREEK

Favorite Places To Eat

Cracker Barrel Old Country Store
I-94 & Beckley Rd., Exit 97
616/979-3900

5 BAY CITY

Mid Michigan Retail Sales
614 Garfield Ave.
517/893-6537

Everybody's Attic
606 E. Midland
517/893-9702

Owl Antiques
703 E. Midland St.
517/892-1105

Hen in the Holly
110 3rd St.
517/895-7215

Little House
924 N. Water St.
517/893-6771

Bay City Antiques Center
1010 N. Water St.
517-893-1116

Downtown Antiques Market
1020 N. Water St.
517/893-0251

6 BELLEVILLE

Favorite Places To Eat

Cracker Barrel Old Country Store
I-94 & Belleville Rd., Exit 190
313/697-5299

7 BENTON HARBOR

Good Old Times Antiques
3076 E. Napier Ave.
616/925-8422

Antique Exchange
4823 Territorial Rd.
616/944-1987

8 BIG BAY

Great Places To Stay

Big Bay Point Lighthouse Bed & Breakfast
3 Lighthouse Road
906/345-9957

Lighthouses have this mysterious pull and fascination for just about everybody, so imagine the thrill of staying in a lighthouse that's a B & B! In 1986, the two-story brick building and its adjoining 60-foot high square light tower at Big Bay Point were adapted to a bed and breakfast. It is now an 18-room inn with seven guest rooms (five with private bath) and a common living room with a fireplace, a dining room, a library, and a sauna in the tower. Not only do guests get great accommodations and a really nice place to poke around, but they can also go up in the tower and see the original 1500-pound Third Oder Fresnel Lens-the second largest ever used on the Great Lakes.

9 BIRMINGHAM

Hagopian World Of Rugs
850 S. Woodward
810/646-1850
Fax: 810/646-1850
Open: Mon. & Thurs. 10-9, Tue., Wed., Fri. & Sat. 10-6, Sun. 12-5

Directions: Hagopian's is located 4 miles north of I-75 on Woodward, between 14 Mile and 15 Mile Roads.

Hagopian's is the place to visit if you are interested in antique rugs. They handle only hand-knotted rugs - all shapes, sizes, colors, types - from India, Egypt, Turkey, Russia and about a dozen other countries. Their inventory runs in price from $100 to $100,000, and they offer complete rug cleaning and restoration services.

Watch Hill Antiques
330 E. Maple Rd.
810/644-7445

Cece's
335 E. Maple Rd.
810/647-1069

Lesprit
336 E. Maple Rd.
810/646-8822

Patrick Vargo Antiquarian
250 Martin St.
810/647-0135

Chase Antiques
251 E. Merrill St.
810/433-1810

Cowboy Trader
251 E. Merrill St.
810/647-8833

Leonard Berry Antiques
251 E. Merrill St.
810/646-1996

O'Susannah
570 N. Woodward Ave.
810/642-4250

Merwins Antiques Gallery
588 N. Woodward Ave.
810/258-3211

Chelsea Antiques Ltd.
700 N. Woodward Ave.
810/644-8090

Troy Corners Antiques
251 E. Merrill St.
248/594-8330

10 BLISSFIELD

Blissfield Antiques Mall
103 W. Adrian St.
517/486-2236

J & B Antiques Mall
109 W. Adrain St.
517/486-3544

Triple Bridge Antiques
321 W. Adrian St.
517/486-3777

Memories on Lane St.
104 S. Lane
517/486-2327

Greens Gallery of Antiques
115 S. Lane
517/486-3080

Estes Antiques Mall
116 S. Lane
517/486-4616

11 BRIGHTON

Nostalgia Days Gone By Antqs.
116 W. Main St.
810/229-4710

Mill Pond Antique Galleries
217 W. Main St.
810/229-8686

Entre Nous Antiques
323 W. Main St.
810/229-8720

Favorite Places To Eat

Cracker Barrel Old Country Store
I-96 & Grand River Rd., Exit 145
810/220-4977

12 BROOKLYN

Pine Tree Centre Antique Mall
129 N. Main St.
517/592-3808

Memory Lane Antique Shop
12939 South M-50
517/592-4218

Muggsie's Antiques
13982 U.S. Hwy. 12
517/592-2659

13 CHESANING

Fancy That Antiques & Uniques
324 W. Broad Street
517/845-7775 or 1-800-752-0532
Fax: 517/845-4190
Open April-December 10-6 Mon.-Sat., 12-5 Sun., January-March weekends 11-5 Sat., 12-5 Sun.; or by appointment

Directions: From I-75/U.S. 23, the shop is located north of Flint, Michigan. Use exit 131, which is M-57. Head west 18 miles on M-57. Located 2 miles east of M-52 on M-57, and 21 miles east of U.S. 27. 30 miles from Flint and Saginaw and 40 miles from Lansing.

Nothing but true antiques are allowed in the multi-level Fancy That Antiques & Uniques. No reproductions will be found among the crystal, china, silver, toys or two large cases of jewelry. You can also browse through art glass that includes Tiffany, French Cameo, Moser, Lotton and Loetz; cut glass and perfume bottles; American art pottery like Roseville and Rookwood; country primitives, quilts, linens, European porcelains and Nippon. An interesting and unique service that this shop offers is atomizer repairs-those squeezy bulbs on the ends of perfume bottles that squirt out the good-smelling stuff! The shop also offers estate sales and appraisal services.

14 CLINTON

First Class Antique Mall
112 E. Michigan Ave.
517/456-6410

Turn of the Century Light Co.
116 W. Michigan Ave.
517/456-6019

Wooden Box
141 W. Michigan Ave.
517/456-7556

15 DEARBORN

A & D Antqs. & Oriental Rugs
13333 Michigan Ave.
313/581-6183

Retro Image Co.
14246 Michigan Ave.
313/582-3074

Village Antiques
22091 Michigan Ave.
313/563-1230

Michelangelo Woodworking
1660 N. Telegraph Rd.
313/277-7500

16 DETROIT

Grand River Sales
4837 Grand River Ave.
313/361-3400

New World Antique Gallery
12101 Grand River Ave.
313/834-7008

Marketplace Gallery
2047 Gratiot Ave.
313/567-8250

Dumouchelle Art Galleries Co.
409 E. Jefferson Ave.
313/963-6255

Relics
10027 Joseph Campau St.
313/874-0500

Antique & Resale Shop
4811 Livernois Ave.
313/898-1830

Park Antiques
16235 Mack Ave.
313/884-7652

In-Between
16237 Mack Ave.
313/886-1741

Another Time Antiques
16239 Mack Ave.
313/886-0830

Xavier's
2546 Michigan Ave.
313/964-1222

Michigan Ave. Antiques
7105 Michigan Ave.
313/554-1012

Mikes Antiques
11109 Morang Dr.
313/881-9500

Mingles
17330 E. Warren Ave.
313/343-2828

17 FLINT

Favorite Places To Eat

Cracker Barrel Old Country Store
I-75 & Pierson Rd., Exit 122
810/230-0019

18 FLUSHING

Trudy's Antiques
113 N. McKinley Rd.
810/659-9801

Antq. Ctr. R & J Needful Things
G6398 W. Pierson Rd.
810/659-2663

19 FREMONT

Brass Bell Antique Mall
48 W. Main St.
616/924-1255

Rolling Ladder Antique Mall
10 W. Main St.
616/924-0420

20 GRAND HAVEN

Carriage House Antiques
122 Franklin Avenue
616/844-0580
Open: Tue.-Sat., 11-5; Sun. 1-5, Closed Monday, Closed January & February

Directions: From U.S. Hwy. 31 - travel west on Franklin in downtown Grand Haven. Parking and entrance in rear.

This quaint shop is located in a restored 1892 carriage house. The owners have been in the antiques business for 20 years so experience is a plus for shopping here. Specializing in true antiques from the 1830s to the 1930s, this two-story, 2,000 square feet shop offers quilts, linens, estate jewelry, glassware and a large selection of Victorian and country furnishings.

Whims and Wishes
216 Washington Ave.
616/842-9533

West Michigan Antique Mall
13279 168th Ave.
616/842-0370

21 GRAND RAPIDS

Antiques by the Bridge
445 Bridge St. NW
616/451-3430

Bygones
910 Cherry SE
616/336-8447

Heartwood
956 Cherry St. SE
616/454-1478

Classic Woods Refinishing
966 Cherry St. SE
616/458-3700

Turn of the Century Antiques
7337 S. Division Ave.
616/455-2060

Scavengers Hunt
210 E. Fulton St.
616/454-1033

Nobodys Sweetheart Vintage
953 E. Fulton St.
616/454-1673

Marlene's Antiques & Cllbls.
1054 W. Fulton St.
616/235-1336

Perception
7 Ionia Ave. SW
616/451-2393

Mary's Used Furnishings
732 Leonard St. NW
616/774-8792

Ms. Doll's Gifts & Collectibles
150 Madison Ave. SE
616/336-8677

Home Sweet Home
2712 Kraft SE
616/949-7788

Cherry Hill Antique Emporium
634 Wealthy St. SE
616/454-9521

Favorite Places To Eat

Cracker Barrel Old Country Store
I-96 & Alpine Ave. (Hwy. 37), Exit 30
616/785-0055

22 GRANDVILLE

Favorite Places To Eat

Cracker Barrel Old Country Store
I-196 & 44th St., Exit 67

Michigan

23 HARBOR SPRINGS

TLC Summer Place Antiques
811 S. Lake Shore Dr.
616/526-7191

Huzza
136 E. Main St.
616/526-2128

Joe De Vie
154 E. Main St.
616/526-7700

Lesprit
195 W. Main St.
616/526-9888

Pooter Olooms Antiques
339 State St.
616/526-6101

Elliott & Elliott
292 E. 3rd St.
616/526-2040

24 HASTINGS

Carlton Center Antique Market
2305 E. Carlton Center Rd.
616/948-9618

Daval's Used Furn. & Antiques
2020 Gun Lake Rd.
616/948-2463

Hastings Antique Mall
142 E. State St.
616/948-9644

25 HOLLAND

Dutch Colonial Inn
560 Central Ave.
616/396-3664

Antiques & Etc.
383 Central Ave.
616/396-4045

Nob-Hill Antique Mall
A1261 Graafschap Rd.
616/392-1424

Possessions Gifts & Antiques
287 Howard Ave.
616/395-8207

Twigs
184 S. River Ave.
616/392-2775

Stonegate Antiques & Gifts
1504 S. Shore Dr.
616/335-3646

Tulip City Antique Mall
3500 U.S. Hwy. 31
616/786-4424

Great Places To Stay

Dutch Colonial Inn Bed and Breakfast
560 Central Avenue
616/396-3664
Open year round

Directions:From Chicago: Take I-196 north to exit 44. Follow Business 196 to U.S. 31 (Muskegon). From U.S. 31, veer left on Central Avenue (1st stoplight). The Inn is 1 1/4 miles on the right. From Detroit: Take I-94 to U.S. 131 North, turn onto M 89 towards Allegan. Continue on M 89 to M 40. M 40 becomes State Street in Holland. Continue north on State Street until 23rd Street. Turn left from 23rd Street to Central Avenue. From Grand Rapids: Take I-196 to exit 52. Follow 16th Street west turning left onto Central Avenue.

What was once a wedding gift in 1928 is today a bed and breakfast inn offering Dutch hospitality. The decor is eclectic from Victorian Country to 1930s Chic. The Inn offers five guest suites (one a cozy hideaway), whirlpool tubs for two, a common area with fireplace and an open porch for relaxing.

26 HOLLY

Arcade Antiques
108 Battle Aly
810/634-8800

Balcony Row
216 S. Broad St.
810/634-1400

Holly Crossing Antiques
219 S. Broad St.
810/634-3333

Water Tower Antiques Mall
310 S. Broad St.
810/634-3500

Home Sweet Home
101 S. Saginaw St.
810/634-3925

Holly Antiques on Main
118 S. Saginaw St.
810/634-7696

27 HOUGHTON

Macvicar Antiques
9103 W. Houghton Lake Dr.
517/422-5466

Antique Mall
418 Shelden Ave.
906/487-9483

28 HOWELL

Adams Antique Mall
203 E. Grand River Ave.
517/546-5360

Egnash Antiques & Auctions
202 S. Michigan Ave.
517/546-2005

Lake Chemung Oldies
5255 W. Ri Circle
517/546-8875

Victorian Gardens
128 E. Sibley St.
517/546-6749

29 IONIA

Grand River Antiques
7050 S. State Road
616/527-8880
Open 10-5 daily

Directions: When traveling I-96, exit 3 67. Drive 1/4 mile north on M-66 to the light. Grand River Antiques is right there, across from The Corner Landing Restaurant.

Any day of the week antique hounds can visit the 20-plus dealers at Grand River Antiques. Housed in an old fresh fruit market, everything offered is authentic; no reproductions are allowed. There is a large collection of furniture, country primitives, vintage clothing, glassware and advertising collectibles. And Art Perkins, who owns Grand River antiques, along with wife Marcia, restores old trunks.

Ionia Antique Mall
415 W. Main St.
616/527-6720

Fire Barn Antiques
219 W. Washington St.
616/527-2240

30 JACKSON

Jackson Antique Mall
201 N. Jackson St.
517-784-3333

Gumper Antiques
3801 Stonewall Rd.
517-789-7982

Favorite Places To Eat

Cracker Barrel Old Country Store
I-94 & Airport Rd., Exit 137
517/783-5300

31 KALAMAZOO

Kalamazoo Antique Market
130 North Edwards
616/226-9788
Open Mon.-Sat. 11-6, Sun. 1-5

Directions: From U.S. 131, take exit 36 east to downtown. From I-94, take exit 78 north to downtown. Once in downtown, take Michigan Avenue to Edwards (behind Wendy's).

In the early 1890s the Kalamazoo Antique Mall was a carriage maker's shop. Today it holds the wares of 32 dealers who offer a broad selection of high quality antiques from Victorian to early country along with a great array of collectibles.

J P's Coins Cllbls. & Antiques
420 S. Burdick St.
616/383-2200

Alamo Depot Crafts
6187 W. D Ave.
616/373-3886

Emporium
313 E. Kalamazoo
616/381-0998

Souk Sampler
4614 W. Main St.
616/342-9124

Wild Goose Chase
4644 W. Main St.
616/343-5933

Crosstown Collectibles
7616 E. Michigan Ave.
616/385-1825

Red Wagon Antiques
5348 N. Riverview Dr.
616/382-5461

Warehouse Distributors
6471 Stadium Dr.
616/372-1175

Aldon Antiques
608 Summer St.
616/388-5375

Aaron & Associates
824 S. Westnedge Ave.
616/342-8834

Attic Trash & Treasures
1301 S. Westnedge Ave.
616/344-2189

Favorite Places To Eat

Cracker Barrel Old Country Store
I-94 & 9th Avenue, Exit 72
616/372-9698

32 LAKESIDE

Lakeside Antiques
14876 Red Arrow Hwy.
616/469-7717

Rabbit Run Antqs. & Interiors
15460 Red Arrow Hwy.
616/469-0468

33 LANSING

Antique Connection
5411 S. Cedar St.
517/882-8700

Tom's Furniture & Antiques
319 E. Grand River Ave.
517/485-8335

Classic Arms Company
1600 Lake Lansing Rd.
517/484-6112

Pennyless in Paradise
1918 E. Michigan Ave.
517/372-4526

Slightly Tarnished-Used Goods
2006 E. Michigan Ave.
517/485-3599

Triola's
1114 E. Mt. Hope Rd.
517/484-5414

Unique Furniture Store
1814 S. Washington Ave.
517/485-8404

Favorite Places To Eat

Cracker Barrel Old Country Store
I-96 & Rt. 43 (Saginaw St.), Exit 93
517/627-7755

34 LINDEN

Thimbleberry Antiques
100 W. Broad
810/735-7324

Linden Emporium
115 N.E. Bron Ave.
810/735-7987

Tangled Vine
131 N.E. Bron Ave.
810/735-4611

35 LOWELL

Cranberry Urn Antique Shop
208 E. Main St.
616/897-9890

Flat River Antique Mall
210 W. Main St.
616/897-4172

Main Street Antiques
221 W. Main St.
616/897-5521

Great Places To Stay

McGee Homestead Bed & Breakfast
2534 Alden Nash NE
616/897-8142
Open 24 hours daily Mar. 1-Dec. 31
Rates: $38-58

Directions: Take exit 52 off I-96 North. Go 7 miles through Lowell to Bailey Dr. Turn left at Alden Nash, then right for 2 miles to McGee Homestead.

Hosts Bill and Ardie Barger offer guests four spacious rooms individually decorated with antiques and all with private bath. The guest area of this 1880s brick farmhouse also has its own entrance, living room with fireplace, parlor and small kitchen. The five acres surrounding the house are filled with orchards, and there's even a barn full of petting animals. After the big country breakfast served each morning, guests can play golf at the course next door, go into Grand Rapids-only 20 minutes away, or visit Michigan's largest antique mall just five miles down the road!

36 LUDINGTON

Coles Antiques Villa
322 West Ludington Avenue
616/845-7414
(March-April & Nov.-Dec.) Fri.-Sat. 10-5, Sun. 1-5
(May-Aug.) Mon.-Sat. 10-6, Sun. 12-5

Directions: Going north on U.S. 31: From McKegon, exit for Old U.S. 31, turn left on Old U.S. 31 (Pere Marquette Road), follow to the intersection of U.S. 10. Turn left (west), head toward Lake Michigan. Go straight through downtown Ludington (3 stop lights 1 block apart). Cole's Antiques Villa is 2 blocks ahead on the right, just before House of Flavors Restaurant. Coming south on U.S. 31: from Traverse City, go west on U.S. 10 at Scottsville junction. Coming from the east: Take U.S. 10 straight west to downtown Ludington and follow the previous direction.

This group of dealers offers a great selection of furniture, glassware, china, pottery, quilts, linens, paper products, jewelry, fishing and military memorabilia, advertising collectibles, country decoratives, tools and kitchenware. They also hold two antiques shows and sales each year: one on the third weekend in October at the West Shore Community College, and another the first weekend in February at Lands Inn.

Antique Store
127 S. James St.
616/845-5888

Sunset Bay Antiques
404 S. James St.
616/843-1559

Country Charm Gifts & Antqs.
119 W. Ludington Ave.
616/843-4722

Sandpiper Emporium
809 W. Ludington Ave.
616/843-3008

Christa's Antiques & Cllbls.
1002 S. Madison St.
616/845-0075

Washington Antiques
102 2nd St.
616/843-8030

Great Places To Stay

The Inn at Ludington
701 East Ludington Avenue
616/845-7055
Rates: $65-85
Open year round

What is there about turrets and towers that fascinate us? The Inn at Ludington is an antique-laden Queen Anne, built in 1889, with a corner tower that is the focal point of the house. It still has its original leaded and stained glass windows, four working fireplaces and oak mantels, oak floors and a grand staircase. The six guest rooms with private baths have queen-sized poster or brass beds, handmade quilts and fresh flowers. Early risers will love it here because they get early morning coffee with homemade muffins, then get to eat a complete breakfast in the dining room with the late-rising sleepy heads! The inn also offers special occasion packages, picnic baskets and fall and winter weekend events.

37 MACKINAC ISLAND

Great Places To Stay

Haan's 1830 Inn
Huron Street
906/847-6244
Rates: $80-120
Open mid-May to mid-November
(Winter address: 3418 Oakwood Avenue)
708/526-2662

According to a survey conducted under the National Historic Preservation Act of 1966, Haan's 1830 Inn is the oldest example of Greek Revival architecture in the Northwest Territory. It is the oldest building used as an inn in the state of Michigan. Each of the seven guestrooms (five with private bath) is furnished with antiques from the mid-19th century and artifacts from the island's fur-trading period. The inn has been featured in numerous publications, including the *Chicago Tribune* and *Innsider*. It is located only a short distance from Mackinac Island's downtown area, old Fort Mackinac, and the ferry docks.

38 MANCHESTER

Manchester Antique Mall
116 W. Main Blvd.
313/428-9357

Eighteenth Century Shoppe
122 W. Main Blvd.
313/428-7759

Raisin Valley Antiques
201 E. Main St.
313/428-7766

39 MARQUETTE

Collector Lower Harbor Antqs.
214 S. Front St.
906/228-4134

Summer Cottage
810 N. 3rd St.
906/226-2795

Antique Village
2296 U.S. Hwy. 41 S
906/249-3040

Fagans
333 W. Washington St.
906/228-4311

40 MARSHALL

Marshall House Center
100 Exchange St.
616/781-7841

McKee Monument & Mercntl.
200 Exchange St.
616/781-8921

J H Cronin Antique Center
101 W. Michigan Ave.
616/789-0077

Hildor House Antiques
105 W. Michigan Ave.
616/789-0009

Keystone Antiques
110 E. Michigan Ave.
616/789-1355

Smithfield Banques
117 E. Michigan Ave.
616/781-6969

Little Toy Drum Antiques
135 W. Michigan Ave.
616/781-9644

J & J Antiques
206 W. Michigan Ave.
616/781-5581

Pineapple Lane Antiques
209 W. Michigan Ave.
616/789-1445

Heirlooms Unlimited
211 W. Michigan Ave.
616/781-1234

Finders Keepers Antiques
858 E. Michigan Ave.
616/789-1611

Cornwells Turkeyville USA
15 1/2 Mile Rd.
616/781-4293

Olde Homestead Antique Mall
15445 N Dr. N
616/781-8119

Great Places To Eat

Cornwell's Turkey House
18935 15 1/2 Mile Road
616/781-4293

Don't bother to stop at Cornwell's if you don't eat turkey, because that's all there is! At least to eat. It's a huge country-craftsy cafeteria-style eatery with an ice cream parlor, butcher shop, attached souvenir store, adjacent

Michigan

barn and outdoor dining. So you can eat turkey, shop, and get tomorrow's dinner all in one place! The Cornwell family raises its own turkeys, and you can get complete dinners with all the trimmings, turkey salads, turkey steaks, barbecued turkey, "sloppy Tom," turkey-Reubens, or the specialty: white meat turkey sandwich on a buttered bun. Oh, and hot caramel corn for dessert.

41 MASON

Art & Shirley's Antiques
1825 S. Aurelius Rd.
517/628-2065

Old Mill Antiques Mall
207 Mason
517/767-1270

Carriage Stop
208 Mason
517/676-1530

Front Porch
208 Mason
517/676-6388

Mason Antiques Market
208 Mason
517-676-9753

42 MIDLAND

Michigan Antique Festival
2156 Rudy Court
517/687-9001

For specific information on Michigan Antique Festivals, see full page this section.

Big Jim's Antiques
4816 Bay City Rd.
517/496-0734

Linda's Cobble Shop
2900 Isabella St.
517-832-9788

Dad's Antiques
3004 S. Poseyville Rd.
517/835-7483

Corner Cupboard
2108 E. Wheeler St.
517/835-6691

43 MONROE

Favorite Places To Eat

Cracker Barrel Old Country Store
I-75 & Dixie Hwy., Exit 15
313/243-0721

44 MOUNT CLEMENS

Estate Antiques
1142 Southbound Gratiot Ave.
810/468-9888

45 MOUNT PLEASANT

Riverside Antiques
993 S. Mission
517/773-3946

Mount Pleasant Antique Center
1718 S. Mission St.
517/772-2672

46 MUNISING

Bay House
111 Elm Ave.
906/387-4253

Old North Light Antiques
M 28 East
906/387-2109

47 MUSKEGON

Old Grange Mall
2783 E. Apple Ave.
616/773-5683

Country Peddler
2542 W. Bard Rd.
616/766-2147

D'town Muskegon Antq. Mall
30 W. Clay Ave.
616/728-0305

Airport Antique Mall
4206 Grand Haven Rd.
616/798-3318

Home Town Treasures
3117 Heights Ravenna Rd.
616/777-1805

Memory Lane Antique Mall
2073 Holton Rd.
616/744-8510

Kensington Antiques
2122 Lake Ave.
616/744-6682

Mandy's Antiques
1950 E. Laketon Ave.
616/777-1428

48 NEW BALTIMORE

Charlotte's Web Antiques
36760 Green St.
810/725-7752

Heritage Square Antique Mall
36821 Green St.
810/725-2453

Days Gone By
50979 Washington St.
810/725-0749

Washington Street Station
51059 Washington St.
810/716-8810

49 NILES

Michiana Antique Mall
2423 S. 11th St.
616/684-7001

Antiques and More
2429 S. 11th St.
616/683-4222

Bookouts Furniture
2439 S. 11th St.
616/683-2960

Niles Antique Mall
220 Front St.
616/683-6652

Yankee Heirlooms
211 N. 2nd St.
616/684-0462

Four Flags Antique & Craft Mall
218 N. 2nd St.
616/683-6681

River City Antique Mall
109 N. 3rd St.
616/684-0840

Old Time Outfitters, Ltd.
16 S. 12th St.
616/683-3569

50 NORTHPORT

Grandma's Trunk
102 N Mill St.
616/386-5351

Heathman Antiques & Finery
210 Mill St.
616/386-7006

5th St. Antiques
211 N. Mill St.
616/386-5421

Back Roads Antiques & Cllbls.
116 S. Nagonaba Ave.
616/386-7011

Bird N Hand
123 Nagonaba
616/386-7104

Cobweb Treasures Antiques
393 S. West
616/386-5532

51 OSCODA

McNamara Antique Mall
2083 N. U.S. Hwy. 23
517/739-5435

Ryland Company
2091 N. U.S. Hwy. 23
517/739-0810

Antique Mall
4239 N. U.S. Hwy. 23
517/739-4000

Wooden Nickel Antiques
110 E. Park Ave.
517/739-7490

52 OTSEGO

Otsego Antique Mall
114 W. Allegan St.
616/694-6440

Harry J's
123 W. Allegan St.
616/694-4318

Heritage Antique Mall
621 Lincoln Road
616/694-4226

Mercantile
504 Lincoln Rd.
616/692-3630

53 PARADISE

Great Places to Visit and Stay

Village of Sheldrake, near Paradise

Directions: Go west on Route 28 through Hiawatha National Forest, turn north on Route 123. Or take the scenic route along the shore of Lake Superior. From Paradise, Sheldrake can be reached by taking the Whitefish Point Road north.

Although Sheldrake is on the Michigan Historic Register, the village is no longer on the map. It's on Whitefish Bay, four miles north of Paradise, which is 60 miles north and west of Sault Sainte

Marie, the largest town on Michigan's Upper Peninsula. Sheldrake is an old logging village that once had about 1,500 people and about 150 buildings. Now only about a dozen buildings are still standing, and they are owned by Brent Biehl, an entrepreneur from Detroit who moved his family to Sheldrake in the 1960s and who has developed a small manufacturing plant for wood products that employs a dozen people. Biehl, his wife, and their six now-grown children have been, for the most part, the only year-round residents of the village, although they have renovated some of the wooden houses and do summer rentals.

Actually, that statement should be qualified: the Biehl family is the only *live*, year-round family in the village. Everybody else is a ghost! And there seem to be lots of them, mostly former residents. There's the old sea captain who stands on the dock, wearing a cap and cape smoking a pipe. There's the retired city engineer from Detroit who sits in a chair on the front porch of his old house and who turns on the lights in the house in the winter when nobody's home. There's the dark, bearded logger who used to walk through the older parts of one house and sit on the couch so people renting the house could see him. The ghost often opened and closed doors and walked around, but never did anything else.

The Biehls themselves have seen so many ghosts over the past 30 years that they have become rather blase about the whole situation. Figures appear and disappear regularly, voices are heard, pictures fall off walls, bathroom faucets turn on for no visible reason, smells of food cooking waft through the houses, "just the garden variety poltergeist things," says Biehl.

54 PAW PAW

Paw Paw Antique Gallery
404 E. Michigan Ave.
616/657-5378

55 PETOSKEY

Jedediah's Antiques & Cllbls.
422 E. Mitchell St.
616/347-1919

Joie De Vie
1901 M 119
616/347-1400

Joseph's World Art & Antiques
2680 U.S. 31 S
616/347-0121

Great Places To Stay

Stafford's Perry Hotel
Gaslight District, Bay at Lewis
616/347-4000 or 1-800-456-1917

Directions: From Detroit or the Upper Peninsula: Take I-75 to the Indian River exit, then take M 68 west to U.S. 31 and turn south. From Chicago: Follow I-94 to I-96 and then pick up U.S. 131 at Grand Rapids. U.S. 131 ends at Petoskey's northwest side.

The Perry Hotel opened in 1899 to the rave reviews of the thousands of summertime visitors who flocked to northern Michigan for its clean air, water and relaxing atmosphere. The Perry was built next to the downtown train depot, and many Perry guests spent the afternoons on the large front porch greeting friends and relatives as they arrived at the station. The hotel is now filled with antiques and reproductions that reflect the grandeur of the Edwardian era. Just out the back door is the Gaslight District, which has all manner of art studios, antique galleries and shops, or, for the more athletic, just 20 minutes away is world-class skiing, golf, boating, cross-country trails and beaches.

Stafford's Bay View Inn
2011 Woodland Avenue
616/347-2771 or 1-800-258-1886
Fax: 616/347-3413
Website: stafford @freeway.net or http://innbook.com/staffbay.html

Just a mile north of Petoskey, and owned and operated by the same Stafford family as the Perry Hotel in downtown Petoskey, is the Bay View Inn. Built in 1886, it is one of only three locations in the nation where guests can participate in a Chatauqua: a summertime educational program that includes lectures, concerts, plays, musicals, various spiritual speakers and Sunday church services. Encased in a sprawling, elegant, airy building, all 31 guest rooms have been decorated with Victorian antiques, wallpapers, quilts and modern amenities such as whirlpool tubs, fireplaces and private balconies overlooking the bayside gardens. The entire inn is filled with antiques, and with the staff dressed in period costumes, it's like walking back in time.

56 PLYMOUTH

Uptown Antiques
120 E. Liberty St.
313/459-0311

Upstairs Downstairs Antiques
149 W. Liberty St.
313/459-6450

In My Attic
157 W. Liberty St.
313/455-8970

Plymouth Antiques Mall
198 W. Liberty St.
313/455-5595

Memory Lane Antiques
336 S. Main St.
313/451-1873

Robin's Nest Antique Mall
640 Starkweather St.
313/459-7733

57 PORT HURON

Antique Collector's Corner
1603 Griswold St.
810/982-2780

Citadel Antique Gallery
609 Huron Ave.
810/987-7737

Yesterdays Treasures
4490 Lapeer Rd.
810/982-2100

Wooden Spool
2513 10th Ave.
810/982-3390

Favorite Places To Eat

Cracker Barrel Old Country Store
I-94 & Water St., Exit 274
810/982-1166

58 ROCHESTER

Antiques by Pamela
319 S. Main St.
810/652-0866

Watch Hill Antiques
329 S. Main St.
810/650-5463

Tally Ho!
404 S. Main St.
810/652-6860

Chapman House
311 Walnut Blvd.
810/651-2157

59 ROMEO

Village Barn
186 S. Main St.
810/752-5489

Town Hall Antiques
205 N. Main St.
810/752-5422

Romeo Antique Mall
218 N. Main St.
810/752-6440

60 ROYAL OAK

Royal Oak Auct. Hse. & Gllry.
600 E 11 Mile Rd.
810/398-0646

Antique Connection
710 E. 11 Mile Rd.
810/542-5042

Lovejoy's Antiques
720 E. 11 Mile Rd.
810/545-9060

White Elephant Antique Shop
724 W. 11 Mile Rd.
810/543-5140

Royal Antiques
1106 E. 11 Mile Rd.
810/548-5230

Decades
110 W. 4th St.
810/546-9289

Trumbulls Antique Emporium
112 E. 4th St.
810/584-0006

Dandelion Shop Antiques
114 W. 4th St.
810/547-6288

Red Ribbon Antiques
418 E. 4th St.
810/541-8117

Delgiudice Fine Arts & Antqs.
515 S. Lafayette Ave.
810/399-2608

Antqs. & Fine Jwlry. by Helen
107 S. Main St.
810/546-9467

Antiques on Main
115 S. Main St.
810/545-4663

Pinks-N-Lace
1000 N. Main St.
810/543-3598

Heritage Co. II Archl Artifacts
116 E. 7th St.
810/549-8342

Troy Street Antiques
309 S. Troy St.
810/543-0272

Yellow House Antiques
125 N. Washington Ave.
810/541-2866

North Washington Antiques
433 N. Washington Ave.
810/398-8006

Vertu
511 S. Washington Ave.
810/545-6050

Antiques & Rare Old Prints
516 S. Washington Ave.
810/548-5588

61 SAGINAW

Salt Marsh
220 N. Center Rd.
517/793-4861

Adomaitis Antiques
412 Court St.
517/790-7469

Antique Market Place
418 Court St.
517/799-4110

Dee Jay's Antiques
418 Court St.
517/799-4110

Little House
418 Court St.
517/792-9622

Ron's Antiques
12025 Gratiot Rd.
517/642-8479

Antique Warehouse, Inc.
1910 N. Michigan Ave.
517/755-4343

Favorite Places To Eat

Cracker Barrel Old Country Store
I-75 & Dixie Hwy., Exit 144
517/777-8443

62 SAINT CLAIR SHORES

Adams English Antiques
19717 9th Mile
810/777-1652

Jennifer's Trunk
201 N. Riverside Ave.
810/329-2032

Rivertown Antiques
201 N. Riverside Ave.
810/329-1020

John Moffett Antiques
1102 S. 7th St.
810/329-3300

Antique Inn
302 Thornapple St.
810/329-5833

63 SAUGATUCK

Country Store Antiques
120 Butler
616/857-8601

Taft Antiques
240 Butler
616/857-2808

Centennial Antiques
3427 Holland St.
616/857-2743

Handled With Care
403 Lake
616/857-4688

Fannies Antique Market
3604 64th St.
616/857-2698

Handled With Care-Everlasting
3483 Washington Rd.
616/857-3044

64 SAULT STE MARIE

Lagalerie Antiques
1420 Ashmun
906/635-1044

65 SCHOOLCRAFT

Fox Antiques Co.
113 N. Grand
616/679-4018

Ron's Grand St. Antqs. & More
205 N. Grand St.
616/679-4774

Schoolcraft Antique Mall
209 N. Grand St.
616/679-5282

Norma's Antiques & Cllbls.
231 S. Grand St.
616/679-4030

Prairie Home Antiques
413 N. Grand St.
616/679-2062

66 SOUTH HAVEN

Sunset Junque Antiques
856 Blue Star Memorial Hwy.
616/637-5777

Black River Antiques & Gifts
516 Phoenix St.
616/637-8042

Anchor Antiques Ltd.
517 Phoenix St.
616/637-1500

67 SOUTH LYON

South Lyon Corner Store
101 S. Lafayette St.
810/437-0205

Pegasus Antiques & Cllbls.
105 N. Lafayette St.
810/437-0320

Cabbage Rose
317 N. Lafayette St.
810/486-0930

68 STEVENSVILLE

Favorite Places To Eat

Cracker Barrel Old Country Store
I-94 & Lake Shore Dr., Exit 23
616/428-0550

69 TECUMSEH

Tecumseh Antique Mall
112 E. Chicago Blvd.
517/423-6441

Harold Robert Antiques
154 E. Chicago Blvd.
517/423-6094

Tecumseh Antique Mall II
1111 W. Chicago Blvd.
517/423-6082

Hitching Post Antiques Mall
1322 E. Monroe Rd.
517/423-8277

L & M Antique Mall
7811 E. Monroe Rd.
517/423-7346

70 THREE RIVERS

Antoinettes Gift Bkts. & Antqs.
51 N. Main St.
616/273-3333

Old Town Antique & Craft Hall
60 N. Main St.
616/273-2596

Links to the Past
52631 N. U.S. Hwy. 131
616/279-7310

71 TRAVERSE CITY

Devonshire Antiques
5085 Barney Rd.
616/947-1063

Antique Emporium
565 W. Blue Star Dr.
616/943-3658

Fascinations
140 E. Front St.
616/922-0051

Painted Door Gallery
154 E. Front St.
616/929-4988

Antique Company
4386 U.S. Hwy. 31 N
616/938-3000

Custer Antiques
826 W. Front St.
616/929-9201

Wilson's Antiques
123 S. Union St.
616/946-4177

Chums Corner Antique Mall
4200 U.S. Hwy. 31 S
616/943-4200

72 UNION PIER

Antique Mall & Village, Inc.
9300 Union Pier Road
616/469-2555
Open seven days a week 10-6

Directions: From Indiana and Illinois: Take I-94 to Union Pier Road, exit 6, then west (turn right) onto Union Pier Road. The Antique Mall & Village is 500 feet from exit 6 on the left, just past St .Julian Winery. From northern Michigan: Take I-94 to Union Pier exit 6, then turn left onto Union Pier Road. Antique Mall & Village is 100 feet from exit 6, immediately turn left.

At the Antique Mall & Village, dealers from four states bring together some of the finest Victorian, primitives and collectibles for your shopping pleasure. The Mall is the first installment of a complete Village close to Lake Michigan in the heart of Harbor County. It is the area's largest, offering 15,000 square feet of quality antiques. They have patio dining when you need to replenish your energy for more shopping, offering sandwiches and salads.

Plum Tree
16337 Red Arrow Hwy.
616/469-5980

Frog Forest Findings
16100 York Rd.
616/469-7050

73 WATERFORD

Great Midwestern Antique Emporium
5233 Dixie Hwy.
810/623-7460

74 WAYNE

Heritage Colonial
32224 Michigan Ave.
313/722-2332

J Wofford Co.
32536 Michigan Ave.
313/721-1939

Blue Willow Antiques
34840 Michigan Ave.
313/729-4910

Sanders Antiques
35118 Michigan Ave.
313/721-3029

75 WILLIAMSTON

Main Street Shoppe Antiques
108 W. Grand River Ave.
517/655-4005

Jolly Coachman
115 W. Grand River Ave.
517/655-6064

Old Plank Road Antiques
126 W. Grand River Ave.
517/655-4273

Corner Cottage Antiques
120 High St.
517/655-3257

Putnam Street Antiques
122 S. Putnam St.
517/655-4521

Canterbury Antiques
150 S Putnam St.
517/655-6518

Antiques Mkt. of Williamston
2991 Williamston Rd.
517/655-1350

Grand River Merchants
2991 N. Williamston Rd.
517/655-1350

76 WYANDOTTE

J & J Antiques
1836 Biddle St.
313/283-6019

Yesterdays Treasures
258 Elm St.
313/283-5232

Tony's Junk Shop
1325 Fort St.
313/283-2160

Thomas Antiques
93 Oak St.
313/283-1880

Lovejoy Antiques
95 Oak St.
313/282-3072

Etcetera Antiques
99 Oak St.
313/282-3072

Old Gray House Antiques
303 Oak St.
313/285-2555

77 YPSILANTI

R. Walker Design Associates
19 E. Cross St.
313/485-2164

Jim MacDonald Antiques
29 E. Cross St.
313/481-0555

Renewed Interest Antiques
33 E. Cross St.
313/482-4525

Thomas L Schmidt Antiques
7099 McKean Rd.
313/485-8606

Materials Unlimited
2 W. Michigan Ave.
313/483-6980

Schmidt's Antiques
5138 W. Michigan Ave.
313/434-2660

Griffin's Collectibles
629 Lynne Avenue
313/482-0507

Notes

Minnesota

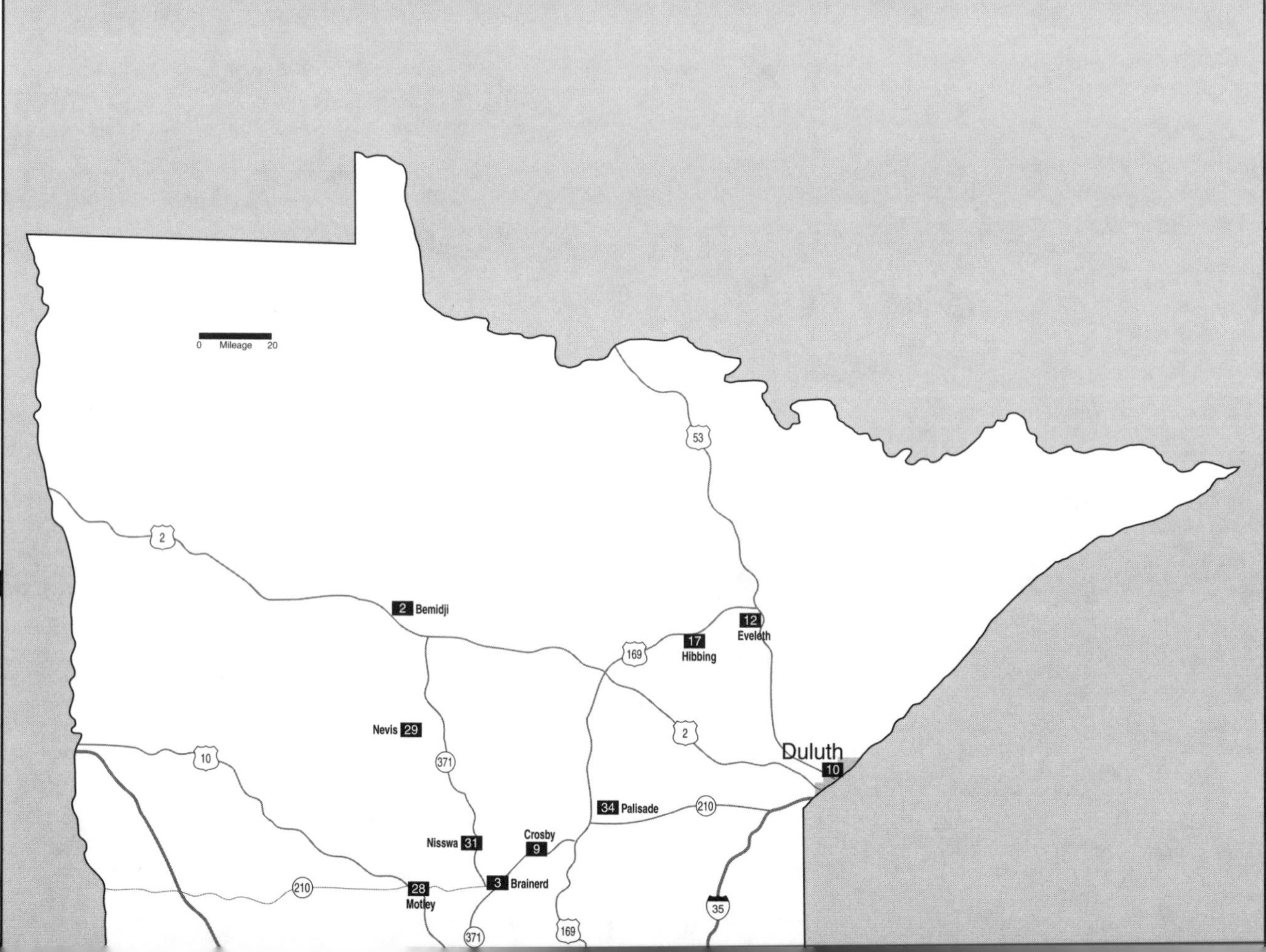

0 Mileage 20
53
2
2 Bemidji
12 Eveleth
17 Hibbing
169
Nevis 29
371
10
Duluth
10
34 Palisade
210
Nisswa 31
Crosby
9
3 Brainerd
28 Motley
35

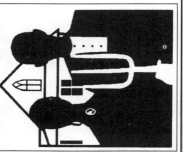

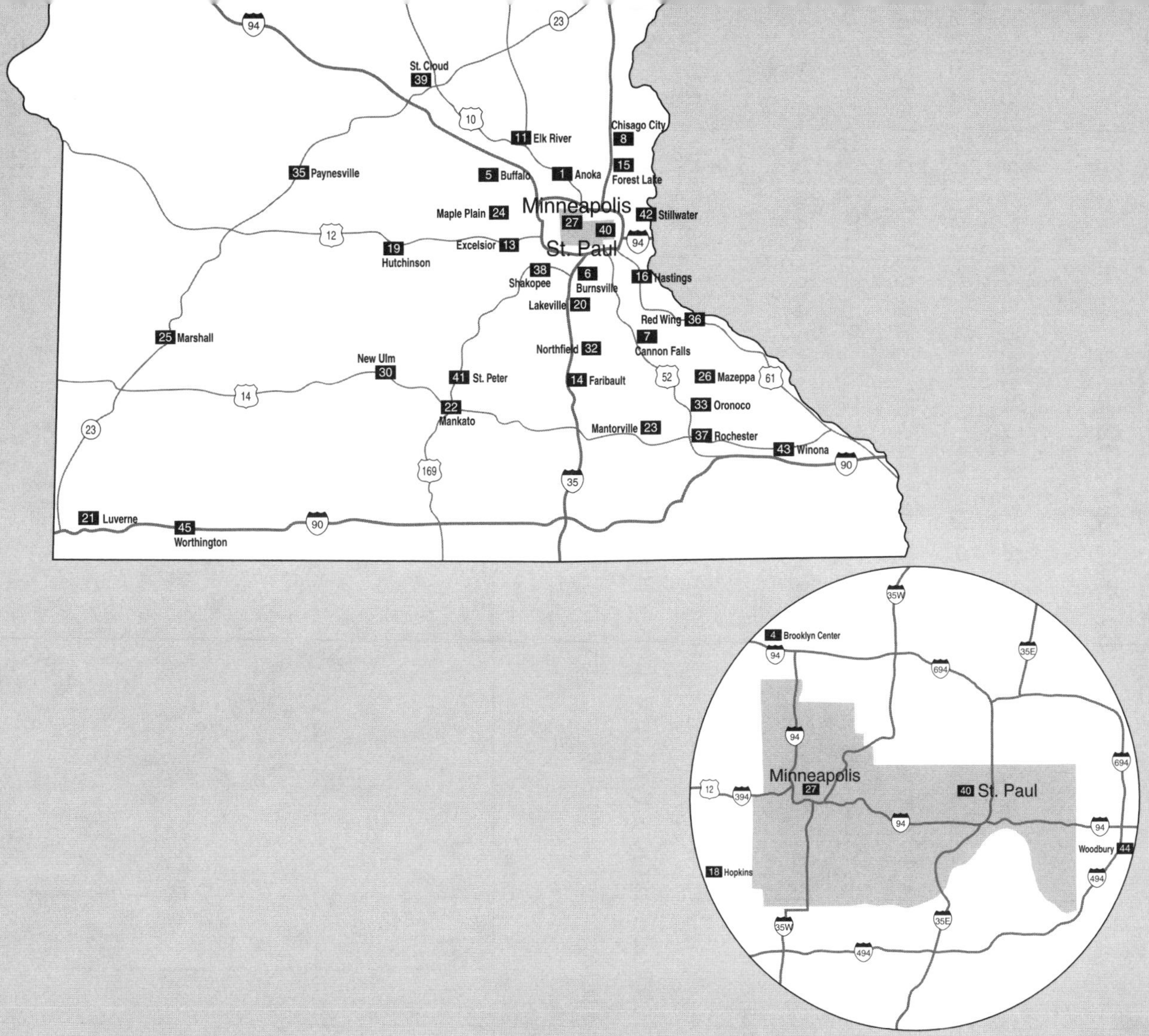

St. Cloud 39
Paynesville 35
Elk River 11
Chisago City 8
Buffalo 5
Anoka 1
Forest Lake 15
Maple Plain 24
Minneapolis 27
St. Paul 40
Stillwater 42
Excelsior 13
Hutchinson 19
Shakopee 38
Burnsville 6
Hastings 16
Lakeville 20
Red Wing 36
Marshall 25
Cannon Falls 7
New Ulm 30
Northfield 32
St. Peter 41
Faribault 14
Mazeppa 26
Oronoco 33
Mankato 22
Mantorville 23
Rochester 37
Winona 43
Luverne 21
Worthington 45
Brooklyn Center 4
Hopkins 18
Woodbury 44

AMERICAN GOTHIC ANTIQUES

236 S. Main St.
Stillwater, MN 55082
612-439-7709

This 45-plus dealer shop located in a lovely old building on Stillwater's main street was named from Grant Wood's famous 1930s painting entitled *American Gothic*. What's so unusual is the story behind the naming of this shop. The house in the painting's background belonged to Janie (Johnston) Eiklenborg's (the shop owner) great-grandmother. Janie says her "great granny" sat on the porch and actually watched as Mr. Woods doodled and sketched the details for this famous painting. The house, located in Eldon, Iowa, is still owned by the family, and Janie's sister Mari Beth lives there today. "It's been a fun story to share with customers," says Janie, "and we're so proud to have been a part of it."

Oh, my goodness, I got so carried away with this story that I almost forgot to tell you about the shop. Inside American Gothic Antiques, dealers display exquisite selections of Victorian and oak furnishings, country furniture and accessories, as well as a choice group of primitive items. On a smaller scale, there are generous offerings of vintage clothing and jewelry, glassware and other collectibles. "Thanks for sharing your story with us, Janie."

Recognize the house in this picture?
It is the house seen in Grant Wood's famous 1930s painting entitled "American Gothic".

Minnesota

1 ANOKA

Round Barn
3331 Bunker Lake Blvd. NW
612/427-5321

Antiques on Main
212 E. Main St.
612/323-3990

Amore Antiques
2008 2nd Ave.
612/576-1871

Yours Mine & Ours Antiques
2014 2nd Ave.
612/422-4959

2 BEMIDJI

Bargain Junction
3220 Adams NW/Hwy. 2 W.
218/751-5036

Back N Time Antiques
1105 15th St. NW
218/759-0206

Louise's Antiques
RR 8 #597
218/751-3577

Brier Patch Antiques
RR 3 #546
218/751-8832

Anntiques
301 3rd St. NW
218/751-2144

3 BRAINERD

Karen's Antiques & Things
Downtown
218/825-7355

Hyland Antiques
1466 Hwy. 371 N
218/828-8838

Antiques on Laurel
711 Laurel
218/828-1584

Bargains on 7th
211 S. 7th St.
218/829-8822

Antiques & Accents-Brainerd
214 S. 7th St.
218/828-0724

4 BROOKLYN CENTER

Favorite Places To Eat

Cracker Barrel Old Country Store
I-694 & Shingle Creek Pkwy., Exit 34
612/560-6808

5 BUFFALO

Behind The Picket Fence
30 Central Ave.
612/682-9490

Division Street Antiques
7 Division St.
612/682-6453

Vintage Mall
8 E. Division St.
612/682-0600

Buffalo Bay Antiques
11 E. Division St.
612/682-1825

Buffalo Nickel Antique Mall
Hwy. 55
612/682-4735

Waldon Woods Antiques
2612 State Hwy. 55 SE
612/682-5667

Annie's Attic
1205 State Hwy. 25 N
612/682-2818

6 BURNSVILLE

Robinson Cruise O Antiques
1509 West 152nd Street
612/435-7327
Available all hours and all days, call ahead

Directions: From Minneapolis, go south on Hwy. 35 West to Burnsville, to County Road 42 West. From County Road 42 West, go until exit onto County Road 5. Turn west on 152nd Street.

In Juanita Robinson's backyard in Burnsville, Minnesota, you will find a dry-docked 35-foot cruiser which has become Robinson Cruise O Antiques.

According to Mrs. Robinson, the boat was built in the late thirties by Mr. Olson, a steel worker by trade. It weighs between 12 and 18 tons and is all steel except the after cabin, which was a later addition. It was designed as a paddle wheeler, but with one critical problem: it would not back up! So the boat was hauled to the backyard until Mr. Olson's death.

In the '50s it was sold to Mr. Batcher who modified it, removed the paddle wheel, and built an after cabin. Proving to be too much to handle, the old boat was sold to the Robinson's who used it for weekend recreation.

After 15 years of use the *Robinson Cruise O* was dry-docked in the Robinson's 2-acre backyard. Time and disuse took their toll until Mrs. Robinson restored the old boat and converted it into an antique shop.

Primitives form a large part of her inventory, but she also displays dolls, hurricane lamps, dish and kitchen goods, as well as brass, stained glass and buttons. This old boat may not be seaworthy any more, but the old *Robinson Cruise O* is certainly worth seeing.

Hagens Furniture & Antiques
2041 W. Burnsville Pkwy.
612/894-5500

Touch of Countree
14150 Nicollet Ave.
612/435-3688

7 CANNON FALLS

Schaffer's Antiques Downtown
Downtown
507/263-5200

Fourth Street Antiques
106 4th St.
507/263-7249

Country Side Antique Mall
Old Hwy. #525
507/263-0352

8 CHISAGO CITY

Chisago Antique Co-op
10635 Railroad Ave.
612/257-8325

Kichi-Saga Antiques & Art
10645 Railroad Ave.
612/257-8273

Glyer Block Antiques
10675 Railroad Ave.
612/257-3043

9 CROSBY

Linda's Collectibles
10 W. Main St.
218/546-8233

Hallett Antique Emporium
28 W. Main St.
218/546-5444

Den of Antiquity
108 W. Main St.
218/546-5385

C & H Odds & Ends
425 Mesaba
218/546-5899

Alice's Antiques
22 First St. NW
218/546-6685

Iron Hills Antiques & Gun
128 W. Main St.
218/546-6783

Crosby Collectible Co-op
Main Street
218/546-5385

10 DULUTH

Brass Bed Antiques
329 Canal Park Dr.
218/722-1347

Antique Centre-Duluth
335 Canal Park Dr.
218/726-1994

Sunset Antiques
2705 E. 5th St.
218/724-8215

Greysolon Arms
1920 Greysolon Rd.
218/724-8387

Antiques on Superior St.
11 W. Superior St.
218/722-7962

Neil Shakespeare Antiques
38 E. Superior St.
218/723-8100

Antique Collectible Emporium
314 E. Superior St.
218/722-1275

Canal Park General Store
10 Sutphin St.
218/722-7223

11 ELK RIVER

Art Barn
20700 Hwy. 169
612/441-7959

Antiques Downtown
309 Jackson Ave.
612/441-1818

Antique Clock Doctor
7808 N.E. River Rd.
612/441-3456

Historical Fragments
7808 N.E. River Rd.
612/441-5889

12 EVELETH

Wildrose Antiques & Cllbls.
616 Grant Ave.
218/744-3053

Garden Cottage
7687 Wilson Rd.
218/744-4803

13 EXCELSIOR

Antiquity Rose & Dining Room
429 2nd St.
612/474-2661

John Ferm Coins
449 2nd St.
612/474-9223

Excelsior Coin & Collectibles
449 2nd St.
612/474-4789

Mary Oneal & Co.
221 Water St.
612/470-0205

Collectors Choice
227 Water St.
612/474-6117

Leipold's Gifts & Antiques
239 Water St.
612/474-5880

Country Look-In Antiques
240 Water St.
612/474-0050

14 FARIBAULT

Curiosity Shop Antiques
3052 Cedar Lake Blvd.
507/334-5959

Country Antiques
212 Central Ave. N
507/332-2331

Dimestore Antique Mall
310 Central Ave. N
507/332-8699

Keepers Antique Shop
403 Central Ave. N
507/334-7673

Collectors Antique Gallery
409 Central Ave. N
507/332-7967

Stoeckels Antq. Clocks & Dolls
615 3rd St. NW
507/334-7772

15 FOREST LAKE

Now Showing Antqs. & Cllbls.
119 Lake St. NE
612/464-2286

Muriel & Friends Antiques
1031 Lake St. SE
612/464-1954

Minnesota

16 HASTINGS

Carroll's Antiques
107 2nd St. E
612/437-1912

Cherished Treasures
116 2nd St. E
612/480-8881

Madeline's
205 2nd St. E
612/480-8129

Olde Main St. Antiques
216 2nd St. E
612/438-9265

Hastings Antique Market
375 33rd St. W
612/437-7412

Village General Antiques
14570 240th St. E
612/437-8150

17 HIBBING

Northland Antiques & Cllbls.
11192 Hwy. 37
218/263-4427

Ct Antiques
Hwy. 37
218/262-1891

Antique Treasure Trove
3798 S. Pintar Rd.
218/263-7246

Anties Attic Antiques
1621 13th Ave. E
218/262-3159

18 HOPKINS

K & C Trains
1409 Cambridge St.
612/935-5007

Blake Antiques
1115 Excelsior Ave. E
612/930-0477

Mary Francis
901 Main Street
612/930-3283

19 HUTCHINSON

Schaffer's Antiques
16457 Hwy. 7
320/587-4321

Main Street Antiques
122 Main St. N
320/587-6305

Barb's Country Collectibles & Antiques
12634 Ulm Ave.
320/587-9144

20 LAKEVILLE

Favorite Places To Eat

Cracker Barrel Old Country Store
I-35 & State Rd. 50, Exit 85
612/898-5151

21 LUVERNE

Duane's Glassware & Antiques
Brown Church/Estey and Main
507/283-2586

Hillside Antiques
County Rd. 4-RR 3, Box 22B
507/283-2985

Larry's Furniture Refinishing
RR 1 Box 84
507/283-2275

22 MANKATO

Arts & Antiques Emporium
1575 Mankato Place
507/387-6199

Northwind Antiques
110 E. Washington St.
507/388-9166

23 MANTORVILLE

This quaint little town in the picturesque valley of the middle fork of the Zumbro River, with its wealth of architectural heritage, Mantorville, Minn., was named to the National Register of Historic Places in 1975. A visit here opens the door to many historical pursuits.

This tiny town is probably most famous for one of its limestone buildings constructed in 1854, the Hubbell House Hotel. In its early days, the hotel was a 16x24-foot-long structure and was the only building in town having a double roof, thereby allowing room in the chamber for guests.

In 1856, the present three-story structure was built, and it immediately became an important stopping place along the trail from Mississippi to St. Peter. Senator Alexander Ramsey, General Ulysses S. Grant, Dwight D. Eisenhower, American journalist Horace Greeley, Roy Rogers and Mickey Mantle were but a few of the many guests who took relaxation in the pleasant facilities provided at the Hubbell House.

In 1946, Paul Pappas purchased the old hotel and opened its doors as a first-class restaurant. Although times have changed, early American hospitality is still available at the Hubbell House. Excellent food and outstanding service are still provided for the many visitors who happen upon this wonderful little town called Mantorville.

Grand Old Mansion B&B
507/635-3231
507/635-5690

Carl's Cut Crystal
5th Street

Pfeifer's Eden B&B
R.R. 1 (7 mi. from Mantorville)
507/527-2021

The Chocolate Shoppe
5th Street
507/635-5814

Memorabilia Antiques
5th Street
507/635-5419

24 MAPLE PLAIN

Country School House Shops
5300 U.S. Hwy. 12
612/479-6353
Open 7 days a week, 10-6

Directions: Located 25 miles west of Minneapolis. Go west from Minneapolis on Interstate 394 (U.S. Hwy. 12) to Maple Plain.

Plan to spend some time here because there is just so much to see. Set in an old 3-story schoolhouse are 100 dealers who have something for every shopper.

If collectibles and memorabilia are your forte, you'll find them here: toys, dolls, games, coins, glassware, china, books—you name it.

There are also antique household furnishings, rugs, clocks, and lamps, the latter of which can be repaired by their staff.

The Coffee Cabin Cafe located in the shop offers lunch, dessert, and gourmet coffee when you feel your energy flagging.

Gingerbread House of Antqs.
1542 Baker Park Rd.
612/479-1562

Steeple Antique Mall
5310 Main St.
612/479-4375

25 MARSHALL

Bev's Antiques
107 5th St.
507/537-1933

General Store
349 Main St. W
507/537-0408

Orphanage Antiques Strawberry
351 Main St. W
507/532-3998

26 MAZEPPA

Bed and Browse and Robby's Antiques
1st Street
507/843-4317
Open year round; call for reservation information.

Directions: From Minneapolis, head south on Minnesota Hwy. 52 until south of Zumbrota, Minnesota, then east on Country Road 60 to Mazeppa. Turn north on 1st Street to third block.

The Robinsons of Burnsville, Minnesota, lived a busy life as foster caregivers and were anxious to find a retreat from the visits of social workers, personal care attendants, and all of the comings and goings associated with such charitable works. They finally found asylum in an old building on a street corner in quaint Mazeppa, Minnesota.

Juanita Robinson recalls, "For 6 years of summer weekends, Luke, our adopted son, played while I hammered and sawed and painted...." It is a two-story building, the first floor of which is now *Robby's Antiques*. The second floor is now the "getaway."

The building, which is on the National Historic Register, has a brick front with stone walls on the interior, and has been an overnight haven for treasure hunters and weary travelers for the past three years. Guests bring their own food, or eat in nearby cafes.

There are some intriguing curiosities upstairs at the Bed and Browse, including a 100-year-old duck boat that has been converted to a display cabinet; an old English zinc bathtub that is now used for reading or napping, and the "in-house outhouse" door made of stained glass (backed by wood to insure privacy).

Downstairs at Robby's Antiques you'll find more treasures, such as stained glass, buttons and collectibles galore. Bed and Browse is also a convenient stopover for antiquing adventures in nearby Red Wing, Wabasha, Oronoco, Lake City and Rochester.

27 MINNEAPOLIS

Great Northern Antqs. & Vntg.
5159 Bloomington Ave. S
612/721-8731

J & H Used Furn. & Antiques
2421 W. Broadway Ave.
612/588-3049

Ross Frame Shop
4555 Bryant Ave. S
612/823-1421

Euro Pine Imports
4416 Excelsior Blvd.
612/929-2927

Hollywood North
4510 Excelsior Blvd.
612/925-8695

Park Avenue Antiques
3004 W. 50th St.
612/925-5850

Complements
3020 W. 50th St.
612/922-1702

Loft Antiques
3022 W. 5th
612/922-4200

Cupboard Collectables
3840 W. 50th
612/929-9244

Illyricun Antiques
430 1st Ave. N
612/338-3345

Tiques & Treasures Antiques
117 4th St. N
612/359-0915

Wooden Horse
3302 W. 44th St.
612/925-1148

Durr Ltd.
4386 France Ave. S
612/925-9146

A Anderson
3808 Grand Ave. S
612/824-1111

Plaza Antiques
1758 Hennepin Ave.
612/377-7331

Finishing Touches Antiques
2520 Hennepin Ave.
612/377-8033

H & B Gallery
2729 Hennepin Ave.
612/874-6436

J Oliver Antiques
2730 Hennepin Ave.
612/872-8952

Cobblestone Antiques Inc.
2801 Hennepin Ave.
612/823-7373

Battlefield Military Antiques
3915 Hwy. 7
612/920-3820

Shades on Lake
921 W. Lake St.
612/822-6427

Len's Antiques
1108 E. Lake St.
612/721-7211

Antiques Minnesota Inc.
1516 E. Lake St.
612/722-6000

Theatre Antiques
2934 Lyndale Ave. S
612/822-4884

Muzzleloaders Etcetra Inc.
9901 Lyndale Ave. S
612/884-1161

Sherrys Old Stuff Antiques
9139 Old Cedar Ave. S
612/854-5086

Spiderweb Antiques
6525 Penn Ave. S
612/798-1862

Antiques Riverwalk
210 3rd Ave. N
612/339-9352

Indigo
530 N. 3rd St.
612/333-2151

Architectural Antiques Inc.
801 Washington Ave. N
612/332-8344

American Classics Antiques
4944 Xerxes Ave. S
612/926-2509

Park Ave. Antiques
4944 Xerxes Ave. S
612/922-0887

Getchell's Antiques
5012 Xerxes Ave. S
612/922-6222

28 MOTLEY

Wilson House Antiques
Box 315
218/352-6629

Pat's Place
Box 173
218/352-6410

29 NEVIS

Danny's Arcade Ice Crm & Antiques
115 Main Street
218/652-3919

30 NEW ULM

New Ulm was established in 1848 by German settlers, and ties to the old country still run deep. Downtown shops sell delicious fudge and traditional German crafts. In the town square is a 45-foot *glockenspiel*, one of a few free-standing carillon clocks in the world. Outside of town is *Harkin Store*, an authentic restoration stocked with the goods, sights and smells of an 1870s general store.

Antiques Plus
117 N. Broadway St.
507/359-1090

Antique House
327 N. Broadway St.
507/354-2450

Cherry Lane Antiques
1440 Cherry St.
507/354-4870

Heritage Antiques
16 N. Minnesota St.
507/359-5150

Neidecker Antiques
1020 N. State St.
507/354-6459

31 NISSWA

International Country Antiques
Nisswa Square
218/963-0311

32 NORTHFIELD

Drive the *Outlaw Trail Tour* into Northfield, the escape route of notorious bank robbers Frank and Jesse James, who tried to rob Northfield bank but were foiled by alert townsfolk. The restored bank, one of many buildings in the historic downtown district, is now a museum.

Old Stuff Gallery
200 Division St.
507/645-7821

Terrell's Antiques
200 Division St.
507/645-5878

Three Acres Antiques
302 Division St.
507/645-4997

Cherubs Cove Inc.
307 Division St.
507/645-9680

Remember When Antiques
418 Division St.
507/645-6419

33 ORONOCO

Berg's Antique Store

50/420 Minnesota Avenue South
507/367-4413 or 507/367-4588
Open flexible days/hours. Call for appointment. (When possible, main buildings 9-5, Tue.-Sat.)

Directions: Traveling on State Hwy. 52 (6 miles North of Rochester). Exit onto Minnesota Avenue South (Main Street). Berg's is located next to the bridge in the largest (brick) building in town.

Berg's is an original in more ways than one. With the same owner and location since 1963, it specializes in original finishes and rough oak and pine pieces. "Nothing has been redone," boasts owner Mary Lou Berg.

These original finished pieces are exceptional, highly sought after, and hard to find—except here. You'll also find thousands of "smalls" to suit your fancy. What you *won't* find here are crafts, gifts, or reproductions.

Because the shop is so specialized, the hours vary, and Mary Lou recommends that you call ahead for an appointment. If you feel impulsive enough to just drop by, your best chances are between 9 and 5 Tuesday through Saturday.

Greta's Country Antiques
1005 1st St. SE
507/367-2315

Antiques Oronoco
Hwy. 52
507/367-2220

Cathi's Country Store & Antiques
230 S. Minnesota Ave.
507/367-4931

34 PALISADE

Old River Road Antiques

Route 2, Box 190
218/845-2770
Hours: By chance or appointment—open most days during the summer, and open most weekends during the spring and fall.

Directions: 4 miles north of the Hwy. 169 and Hwy. 210 junction toward Grand Rapids, Minnesota. 12 miles north of Aiken, Minnesota, on Hwy. 169.

Both this smaller version and the original barn built in 1913 are constructed of the salvaged wood from the old steamboat, Irene, which once traveled along the Mississippi River. It seems fitting that since its reconstruction in 1983, it has sat on the spot where the river road was once located.

The heritage of Old River Road Antiques provides an interesting introduction to the shop which carries many newly restored furnishings. Mr. Hlidek (the "h" is silent) restores the antique furniture, and the shop is a showcase for his work.

Other interesting items listed among what Ms. Hlidek terms her "fun junk" are Wade porcelain animals from England and her extensive button collection.

35 PAYNESVILLE

Koronis Antiques
26753 N. Hwy. 55
320/243-4268

Country Porch Antiques
399th Street-Hwy. 55
310/243-4027

Antique Cellar
104 Washburne Ave.
320/243-7605

Paynesville Antique Mall
104 Washburne Ave.
320/243-7000

Jeanne's Antiques & Collectibles
109 Washburne Ave.
320/243-7381

36 RED WING

In Red Wing shop for antiques, the latest fashions and more in the *Pottery District*, where *Red Wing Stoneware* was once made. On a self-guided walking tour, see the restored *T.B. Sheldon Auditorium Theatre*, a historic hotel and *Goodhue County Historical Museum*. More sights are visible from the river by excursion boat or from the *Red Wing Shoe Company Observation Deck*.

Pratt-Taber Inn

706 West Fourth Street
612/388-5945

As an elegant reminder of its heritage, the Pratt-Taber

Inn serves its guests a taste of Victorian style. Built in 1876, the interior is of fine woods like butternut and walnut. Particular attention was paid to rich details during construction, including the woodwork throughout and the trim on the wonderful porch, which is so representative of the style. Three fireplaces in the parlors are also expressive of such elegance. The richness continues in the inn's furnishings. The six bedrooms boast Renaissance Revival and Victorian style antiques.

Enjoy a gourmet breakfast before taking a walk to nearby downtown Red Wing, or to the banks of the Mississippi River. If you prefer, you can tour the area aboard an old San Francisco cable car that has been mounted to a truck chassis. If your timing is right, you can watch as eagles migrate through the area. An estimated 4,000 were sighted last year.

Mona Lisa Antiques & Gardens
1228 W. Main St.
612/388-4027

Memories
2000 W. Main St.
612/388-6446

Old Main Street Antiques
2000 W. Main St.
612/388-1371

Al's Antique Mall
1314 Old West Main St.
612/388-0572

Dorothy's Antiques
1604 Old West Main St.
612/388-7024

Tea House Antiques
927 W. 3rd St.
612/388-3669

Ice House Antiques
1811 Old West Main Street
612/388-8939

37 ROCHESTER

Old Stonehouse Antiques
1901 Bamber Valley Rd. SW
507/282-8497

Old Rooster Antique Mall
106 N. Broadway
507/287-6228

Sentimental Journeys Unlitd.
110 W. Center St.
507/281-6616

Peterson's Antqs. & Stripping
111 11th Ave. NE
507/282-9100

Timeless Treasures
7 1st Ave. SW
507/288-3398

Iridescent House
227 1st Ave. SW
507/288-0320

Mayowood Galleries
Kahler Hotel/ 2nd Ave. SW
507/288-2695

Mayowood Galleries
3705 Mayowood Rd. SW
507/288-6791

Collins Antq. Feed & Seed Ctr.
411 2nd Ave. NW
507/289-4844

Blondell Antiques
1408 1nd St. SW
507/282-1872

Just A Little Something
305 6th St. SW
507/288-7172

Antique Mall on Third
18 3rd St. SW
507/287-0684

John Kruesel's General Merchandise
22 3rd St. SW
507/289-8049

38 SHAKOPEE

Lady Di Antiques
126 South Holmes Street
612/445-1238
Open daily from 10-5

Downtown Shakopee, Minnesota, offers the discriminating shopper a superb selection at Lady Di Antiques. Owner Diane Sullivan, well known in Minnesota for her expertise in promoting high-end antique shows, has consolidated her sense of style and taste into this versatile shop.

Merchandise runs the gamut from vintage clothing to dolls and toys, to distinctive furnishings and decorative accessories.

Something Olde
120 Holmes St.
612/445-3791

Interesting Side Trips

Historic Murphy's Village
2187 East Hwy. 101
612/445-6900

Directions: On the banks of the Minnesota River, one mile east of Shakopee on Minnesota Hwy. 101—30 minutes from the Minneapolis/St. Paul International Airport and 23 minutes from the Mall of America.

In a quiet village nestled along the shores of the scenic Minnesota River, pioneers long ago learned to thrive in a sometimes hostile, sometimes hospitable new world. As they carved a life for themselves in the wilderness, the stories of their determination and dignity, and their spirit and ingenuity filled this new land.

Today, more than 100 years later, the spirit of that time lives on. Historic Murphy's Village is a unique living history museum that preserves and interprets 19th century life in the Minnesota River Valley. Dedicated to the lives of children and adults, both past and present, Historic Murphy's Village is not only a land that remembers time, but a land where history comes alive with each new day.

The idyllic wooded setting that stretches along one and a half miles of scenic river valley brings alive the charm and challenges of life in the 19th century. Families, history buffs and adventurers of all ages can step into this historic village, which features the rich diversity of early American life.

Each homestead, among the 40 different buildings at Murphy's, represents the coming together of the many groups that settled in the Minnesota River Valley between 1840 and 1890—Czech, Danish, English, French, German, Irish, Norwegian, Polish and Scandinavian. In addition, Murphy's Historic Village includes 16 Native American mounds that are estimated to be more than 2000 years old.

Visitors can stroll on their own or ride on horse-drawn trolleys. Their journey will cover the very early days of the fur trade era when people traveled by footpath and canoes, to the bustling village complete with its shops, homes, church, town hall and railroad depot. Throughout the village, costumed interpreters are prepared to spin a tale, demonstrate their craft and explain the daily life of the men, women and children who settled in the valley more than a century ago. Day-to-day activities such as cooking, weaving, spinning and woodworking take place in their homes and on their farmsteads. Visitors will hear how villagers lived and learned together during that rugged pioneer era.

Music and entertainment also often fill the daily Village routine. Musicians and crafts people are a common sight, while folks gather at the blacksmith shop or general store for a chat with tour guides and costumed interpreters.

39 SAINT CLOUD

Kay's Antiques
713 Germain
320/255-1220

Paper Collector Art Gallery
26 7th Ave. N.
320/251-2171

Depot Antique Mall
8318 State Hwy. 23
320/253-6573

40 SAINT PAUL

J & E Antiques
1000 Arcade St.
612/771-9654

Recollections
4754 Washington Square
612/426-8811

Victoria Grande Gardens
818 Grand Ave.
612/228-0228

Cottage Interiors
1129 Grand Ave.
612/224-2933

Anything & Everything Inc.
1208 Grand Ave.
612/222-7770

Oxford Antiques
58 Hamline Ave. S
612/699-1066

Antiques White Bear Inc.
4903 Long Ave.
612/426-3834

Wicker Shop
2190 Marshall Ave.
612/647-1598

Danny's Antiques
1076 Maryland Ave. E
612/776-6287

Granny Smith's Antqs. & Crafts
7600 147th St. W
612/891-1686

Antique Mart
941 Payne Ave.
612/771-0860

Antique Lane on Payne
946 Payne Ave.
612/771-6544

Golden Lion Antiques
983 Payne Ave.
612/778-1977

Emporium Antiques
1037 Payne Ave.
612/778-1919

Grand Old House
517 Selby Ave.
612/221-9191

Oldies But Goodies
1814 Selby Ave.
612/641-1728

Able Antiques
226 7th St. W
612/227-2469

Wescotts Station Antiques
226 7th St. W
612/227-2469

Alladdin's Antique Alley
239 7th St. W
612/290-2981

John's Antiques
261 7th St. W
612/222-6131

Ann & Larry's Antiques
2572 7th Ave. E
612/773-7994

Nakashian-Oneil Inc.
23 6th St. W
612/224-5465

Taylor & Rose
251 Snelling Ave. S
612/699-5724

French Antiques
174 W. 7th Street
612/293-0388

Antiques Minnesota Midway
1197 University Ave. W
612/646-0037

Robert J. Riesbery
343 Salem Church Rd.
612/457-1772

41 SAINT PETER

Collective Memories
216 S. Minnesota Ave.
507/931-6445

Tate Antiques
817 N. Minnesota Ave.
507/931-5678

42 STILLWATER

American Gothic Antiques
236 South Main Street
612/439-7709
Mon.-Thurs. 10-5, Fri. & Sat. 10-8, Sun. 11-5

Directions: On Interstate 94, 10 miles east of St. Paul, exit onto Hwy. 95 North at the Wisconsin border. Travel 8 miles north along the St. Croix River to Stillwater, Minn.

For specific information, see review this section.

DeAnna Zink's Antiques
9344 60th Street North
612/770-1987
Open Thurs.-Sat. 12-6, other days and hours by chance or appointment. Monday is "dealer day" from approximately 9-6 (discounts on everything).

Directions: Drive Interstate 694 to Hwy. 36 East. Take Hwy. 36 East 1 1/4 miles to Demontreville Trail. Get off to the left (north). Get on service road (60th Street), and continue east 1/2 mile to the big gray farmhouse on the hill. (From Stillwater: Take Hwy. 36 West to Keats; veer onto 60th Street; continue west for 1/2 mile.)

Once inside this 1870s farmhouse, you'll be delighted to find, not only what DeAnna refers to as a "general" line of antique furniture and accessories, but a choice selection of fine glassware, prints, and porcelains. Moreover, the display of Victorian and primitive pieces, which are DeAnna's specialty, are not to be missed.

Treat yourself to coffee and munchies while roaming the aisles of this charming shop.

One of a Kind
102 Main St. N
612/430-0009

Gabrielle
114 N. Main
612/439-5930

Main Street Antiques Stillwater
118 Main St. N
612/430-3110

Country Charm Antiques
124 Main St. S
612/439-8202

River City Antiques & Cllbls.
124 Main St. S
612/439-3889

Past And Present Antiques
208 Main St. S
612/439-6198

Stillwater Antiques
226 South Main
612/439-6281

St. Croix Antiquarian Books
232 South Main
612/430-0732

Mulberry Point Antiques
270 Main St. N
612/430-3630

Antique Radio Company
301 Main St. S
612/432-3919

Midtown Antique Mall
301 Main St. S
612/430-0808

More Antiques
312 Main St. N
612/439-1110

Architectural Antiques Inc.
316 Main St. N
612/439-2133

Mill Antiques
410 Main St. N
612/430-1816

Rivertown Antiques
501 Main St. N
612/439-8188

Battle Hollow Antiques
6148 Osgood Avenue
612/439-3414

43 WINONA

Markham's Antiques
1459 W. 5th St.
507/454-3190

A-Z Chair Caning
160 Main St.
507/454-0366

R D Cone Antiques Mall
66 E. 2nd St.
507/453-0445

Traveling Treasures
1161 Sugar Loaf Rd.
507/452-5440

Country Comfort Antiques
79 W. 3rd Street
507/452-7044

Haviland Matching Service
467 E. 5th Street
507/454-3283

44 WOODBURY

Favorite Places To Eat

Cracker Barrel Old Country Store
I-494 & Valley Creek Road, Exit 59
612/730-1233

45 WORTHINGTON

Hodgepodge Lodge
214 8th St.
507/376-4542

LBJ Antiques
760 W. Shore Dr.
507/376-5004

Margaret's Specialty Antiques
802 3rd Ave.
507/372-2239

Mississippi

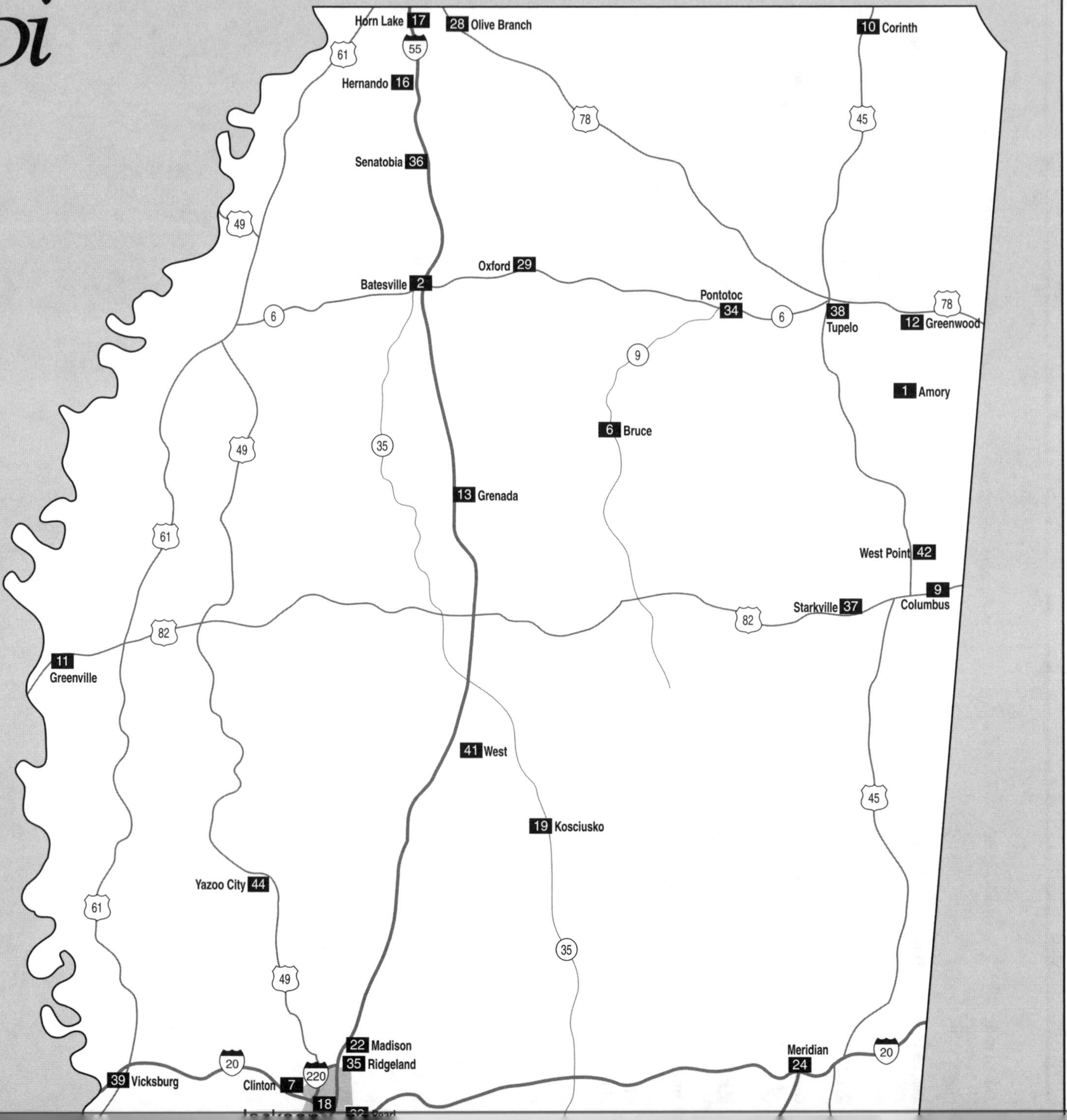

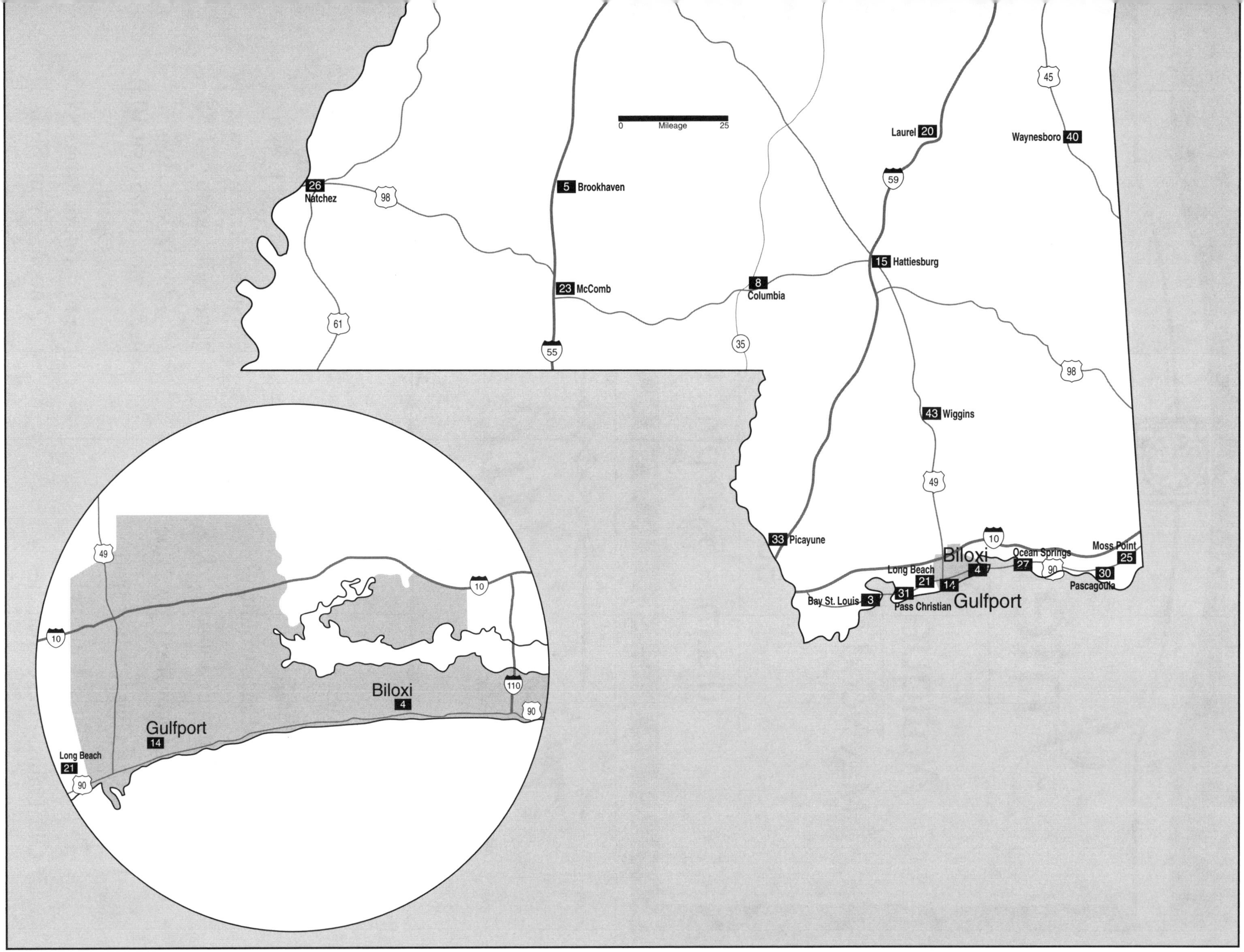

0 Mileage 25
26 Natchez
98
61
5 Brookhaven
23 McComb
55
8 Columbia
35
15 Hattiesburg
Laurel 20
59
Waynesboro 40
45
98
43 Wiggins
49
33 Picayune
Bay St. Louis 3
31 Pass Christian
Long Beach 21
14 Gulfport
Biloxi 4
10
Ocean Springs 27
90
Moss Point 25
30 Pascagoula
Gulfport 14
Biloxi 4
Long Beach 21
10
49
110
90

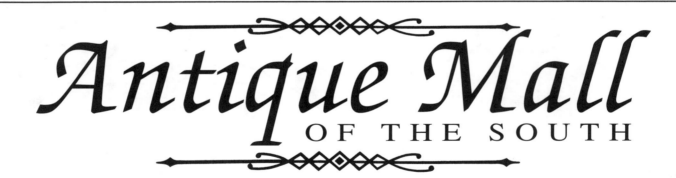

1 AMORY

Cotton Gin Antiques & Cllbls.
205 4th St. North
601/256-5905

Amory Mini-Mall
109 North Main St.
601/256-8003

The Park Antiques
109A South Main
601/257-2299

Jerry's Antiques & Collectibles
300 North Main
601/256-8790

2 BATESVILLE

Favorite Places To Eat

Cracker Barrel Old Country Store
I-55 & State Hwy. 6, Exit 243
601/563-6363

3 BAY SAINT LOUIS

Bay Town Inn
208 North Beach Boulevard
601/466-5870 or 1-800-467-8466

Circa 1900. National Register. Old historic turn-of-the-century home has waterfront view. Convenient to antique shops and restaurants. Seven guest rooms with private bath. Southern breakfast.

Palm House
217 Union Street
601/467-1665

Circa 1800s. National Register. West Indies-style planter's home surrounded by registered ancient live oaks and palms. Bikes, tennis, basketball, fishing trips. Beautiful veranda. Southern breakfast.

Beach Antique Mall
108 S. Beach Blvd.
601/467-7955

Rosebud Antiques & Cllbls.
506B S. Beach Blvd.
601/467-8351

The Magnolia Tree
1015 Hwy. 90
601/467-3410

Charters Antiques
125 Main St.
601/467-4665

Elena Cummings
131 Main St.
601/467-1648

Bay Shoppe Gallery, Inc.
136 Main St.
601/466-2651

Evergreen Antiques
201 Main St.
601/467-9924

M. Schon Antiques
110 S. 2nd St.
601/467-9890

Halcycon House
211 Main St.
601/466-0277

Lighthouse
212 Main St.
601/466-4344

Paper Moon
220 Main St.
601/467-8318

4 BILOXI

The Father Ryan House Bed and Breakfast
1196 Beach Boulevard
601/435-1189 or 1-800-295-1189

Circa 1841. National Register. One-time home and study of Father A. J. Ryan, poet laureate of the Confederacy. Private balconies overlooking white sand beaches and the Gulf. Nine rooms on 3 floors. Private bath. Period antiques. Pool and courtyard. Southern breakfast.

Memories Annex
546 Howard Ave.
601/374-6708

Hawksley's Fine Antiques
918 Howard Ave.
601/374-7058

Nixon Antique Gallery Ltd.
999 Howard Ave.
601/435-4336

Tu J's Treasures Ltd.
819 Jackson St.
601/435-5374

Russenes
128 Porter Ave.
601/432-0903

Spanish Trail Books
781 Vieux Marche Mall
601/435-1144

5 BROOKHAVEN

Brookwood Gifts & Antiques
706 Hwy. 51 N
601/833-3481

Brookhaven Flea Market
118 E. Monticello St.
601/835-1987

6 BRUCE

Collins Antiques
S. Tyson Rd.
601/983-7194

7 CLINTON

Collector's Cottage
307A Clinton Blvd.
601/925-0723

The Butter Churn
319 Clinton Blvd.
601/924-7971

Grannie's Attic
601 Hwy. 80 W
601/924-4352

Brick Street Antiques
312 N. Jefferson St.
601/924-5251

Pette's Place
300 Monroe
601/924-2147

Cindy's
406 Monroe
601/924-7078

Trash and Treasures
590 Springridge Rd.
601/924-3224

8 COLUMBIA

Neat Stuff
919 High School Ave.
601/736-5061

Main Street Frames & Antiques
706 Main St.
601/736-0820

The Tiger Lily
Main St.
601/731-2511

9 COLUMBUS

Amzi Love Bed and Breakfast Inn
305 Seventh Street South
601/328-5413

Circa 1848. National Register. Italian-style villa in Historic district. Romantic English garden. Five bedrooms with baths. Home is steeped in history and features original furnishings and old scrapbooks. Southern breakfast.

Liberty Hall
Armstrong Road
601/328-4110

Circa 1832. National Register. Nineteenth century portraits are displayed, along with such interesting documents as the old planter's diary that recounts the trials of running a 6,000-acre plantation. Picnic lunches, dinner with advance reservations, hiking and fishing.

White Arches
122 Seventh Avenue South
601/328-4568

Circa 1857. National Register. One of Columbus' most unique antebellum bed and breakfast inns. Historic District. Antiques, balcony, bath and comfortable seating areas. Relax on secluded verandas or with a book in the gentleman's library.

Phillips Antiques
1909 Hwy. 45 N
601/327-8955

Mad Horse Antiques
404 Main St.
601/327-0105

Vintage Vignettes & Framery
418 Main St.
601/327-5655

Riverhill Antiques
122 3rd St. S
601/329-2669

Stewarts Antiques Appraisals & Est.
925 3rd Ave. N
601/327-7110

10 CORINTH

The General's Quarters
924 Fillmore Street
601/286-3325

Circa 1872. Victorian home located in the Historic district of old Civil War town. Suite contains 140-year-old canopy bed. Lounge on second floor, veranda, parlor and beautiful garden. Furnished with period antiques. Evening snack. Southern breakfast.

Madison Inn
822 Main Street
601/287-7157

Turn-of-the-century house in downtown residential area. Four suites, with sitting room and private bath. Beautiful courtyard, aquarium, in-ground pool. Continental breakfast.

Robbins Nest Bed and Breakfast
1523 Shiloh Road
601/286-3109

Circa 1869. Southern Colonial-style home surrounded by oak, dogwood and azaleas. Situated on two acres. Three guest rooms with antiques and private baths. Generous breakfast served on the back porch where guests may relax in antique wicker furniture.

Junker's Parlor Antiques
2003 Hwy. 72 E.
601/287-5112

11 GREENVILLE

Dust & Rust
603 Hwy. 82 E
601/332-4708

Lina's Interiors
525 S. Main St.
601/332-7226

Wilson's Junk Tique & Woodwork
Hwy. 82 E.
601/335-7525

12 GREENWOOD

Russell's Antique Jewelry
229 Carollton Ave.
601/453-4017

Warehouse Antiques
229 Carrollton Ave.
601/453-0785

June's Junktiques
1718 Grenada Blvd.
601/455-2809

Patsy's Hodge Podge
511 Lamar St.
601/455-4927

Heritage House Antiques
311 E. Market St.
601/455-4800

Finchers, Inc.
512 W. Park Ave.
601/453-6246

Antique Wholesalers
527 W. Park Ave.
601/455-4401

Corner Collection
412 Walthall St.
601/453-8387

13 GRENADA

Maw & Paws Antiques
1079 Hebron Church Rd.
601/226-3672

Donna's Antiques & Gifts
N. Main St.
601/226-2595

14 GULFPORT

Old South Guest House
1911 Second Street
601/865-9325 or 800/633-6477

Circa 1926. Victorian four-plex guest house within walking distance of a casino and the beach. Sitting room, bath, bedroom, dining area and full kitchen.

Ronnie G's Antq. & Furn. Rest.
240 Courthouse Rd.
601/896-7391

Artiques
1130 Cowan Rd.
601/897-2273

Old Things
15415 Landon Rd.
601/832-6945

Dear Hearts
10425 Old Hwy. #49
601/832-6017

Back In Time Antique Mall
205 Pass Rd.
601/868-8246

Handsboro Trading Post
504 E. Pass Rd.
601/896-6787

Ward Antique Brass
711 E. Pass Rd.
601/896-5436

Right Stuff Antiques
1750 E. Pass Rd.
601/896-8127

Antique House
1864 E. Pass Rd.
601/896-3435

Capital Antiques Co.
2045 E. Pass Rd.
601/896-1741

Circa 1909 Antiques
2170 E. Pass Rd.
601/897-7744

Happy Everlasting
1221 31st Ave.
601/864-0609

Alston's Antiques & Gifts
2208 25th Ave.
601/868-3985

15 HATTIESBURG

Camellia Gardens
276 Monroe Road
601/544-7390

Circa 1917. Countryside estate offering two antique-filled bedrooms and a shared bath. Twenty-one acres of landscaping and various types of animals and birds to enjoy. Lunch and breakfast.

Tally House
402 Rebecca Avenue
601/582-3467

Circa 1907. National Register. Tally House has welcomed five Mississippi governors as overnight guests. The 13,000-square-foot home has an intriguing collection of antiques, cozy animals and birds to enjoy.

Tin Top Antiques
1005 Bouie St.
601/584-7018

Ruthie's Attic & Memory Lane
6196 Hwy. 49 N.
601/583-0429

Early Settler Antiques & Cllbls.
5330 Hwy. 42
601/582-8212

Old High School Antiques
846 N. Main
601/544-6644

Calico Mall
309 E. Pine St.
601/582-4351

The Antique Mall
2103 W. Pine St.
601/268-2511

Favorite Places To Eat

Cracker Barrel Old Country Store
I-59 & State Rd. 49, Exit 67A
601/296-7950

16 HERNANDO

Sassafras Inn Bed and Breakfast
785 Hwy. 51 South
601/429-5864 or 1-800-882-1897

Lovely English Tudor home with indoor pool, tropical gardens and waterfalls. Hot tub and recreation room. Large guest rooms and private baths. Perfect for honeymoons. Southern breakfast.

Shadow Hill
2310 Elm Street
601/449-0800

Originally opened as a tea room in 1923, this quiet country retreat is located on six acres and features large rooms, antiques, fireplaces and a wide front porch overlooking a deep, shaded lane.

Buddy's Antiques
151 Commerce
601/429-5338

Harper's Antiques
2610 Hwy. 51 S
601/429-9387

Treasures Old & New
2280 Hwy. 51 S
601/449-0560

Court Square Antiques
315 Losher
601/429-9300

17 HORN LAKE

Favorite Places To Eat

Cracker Barrel Old Country Store
I-55 & Goodman Rd., Exit 289
601/349-4203

18 JACKSON

Interior Spaces
Maywood Mart
1220 E. Northside Drive, Suite 120
601/981-9820
Mon.-Sat. 10-5:30

Directions: Traveling I-55, Exit 100. If traveling north on I-55: Take Exit 100. Go through the first stop light on Frontage Road. Located on the right in Maywood Shopping Center. If traveling south on I-55: Take Exit 100. Go to the first stop light. Turn left on Northside Drive. Then turn left on Frontage Road. Located on the right in Maywood Shopping Center.

This convenient Jackson shop hosts 35 dealers, who have their spaces filled with antiques, accessories, and art. Prices are affordable.

The staff also includes several interior decorators, ready to assist you at your request.

Interior Spaces also offers an "in home" decorating service, at a nominal cost, to help you complete your vision.

The Fairview Inn
734 Fairview Street
601/948-3429, 1-888-948-1908
Rates $100-150, $15 each additional person

Directions: I-55 exit #98A on Woodrow Wilson; left, first traffic light at North State; left, one block past second traffic light at Fairview Street. Inn is first property on left.

The Fairview Inn is a grand Colonial Revival home on the National Register of Historic Places and is located in the Belhaven Historic District neighborhood of Jackson, Mississippi. Whether you're hosting a gala or simply staging a luxurious getaway, The Fairview Inn's spacious facilities and Southern atmosphere are yours for the asking.

The Fairview Inn is a AAA Four Diamond Award winning bed and breakfast. For a closer look inside the Inn, visit them on the internet at: www.fairviewinn.com.

Oriental Shoppe
124 Highland Village
601/362-4646

Jo's Antiques
680 Commerce St.
601/352-3644

Primos Annelle & Associates
Highland Village
601/362-6154

Ax Antiques & Trading Post
3953 Hwy. 80 E (Pearl)
601/939-5887

Antique Mall of Richland
732 Hwy. 49 S
601/936-9007

Ye Olde Lamp Shoppe Ltd.
4505 I 55 N
601/362-9311

Reaves Oriental Rugs
420 Meadowbrook Rd.
601/362-7707

Caldwell Antiques
1048 Old Brandon Rd.
601/939-4781

Jim Westerfield Antiques
4429 Old Canton Rd.
601/362-7508

Grannie's Attic of Byram
6787 S. Siwell Rd.
601/371-6819

Stately Home Antiques
737 N. State St.
601/355-1158

C W. Fewel & Co.
840 N. State St.
601/355-5375

Elephant's Ear
3110 Old Canton Rd.
601/982-5140

High Street Collection
1217 Vine St.
601/354-5222

Interiors Market
Woodland Hills Shopping Center
601/981-6020

The Antique Market
3009 N. State Street
601/982-5456

Oliver Antiques
730 Lakeland Drive
601/981-2564

Barrington Antqs. & Access.
Woodland Hills Shopping Center
601/981-2035

Bobbie King Dressing Up
Woodland Hills Shopping Center
601/362-9803

Ann Hall Antiques Gallery
Woodland Hills II
601/981-0410

St. Martin's Gallery
2817 Old Canton Road
601/362-1977

Antique Market
3009 N. State St.
601/982-5456

Favorite Places To Eat

Cracker Barrel Old Country Store
I-55 & Beasley-Adkins Rd., Exit 102B
601/977-1055

19 KOSCIUSKO

Lucas Hill Bed and Breakfast
500 North Huntington Street
601/289-7860

Circa 1866. National Register. This Greek Revival planter's cottage is comfortable and elegant. Full of antiques and warm family history. Gift and antique shop. Short walk to Historic Court Square. Continental breakfast.

Redbud Inn
121 North Wells Street
601/289-5086 or 800/379-5086

Circa 1884. National Register. Queen Anne-style Victorian two-story, listed on Best Places to Stay in the South and top ten bed and breakfast inns in Mississippi. Furnished in period antiques. Antique shop. Tea Room. Near downtown Historic Square. Southern breakfast.

Antiques & Interiors Mall
301 W. Jefferson St.
601/289-3600

Peeler House Antiques
117 W. Jefferson St.
601/289-5165

20 LAUREL

The Mourning Dove Bed and Breakfast
556 North Sixth Avenue
601/425-2561 or 1-800-863-3683

Circa 1907. National Register. Classic four-square one block from the Lauren Rogers Museum of Art and located in the Historic District. Features two private cottages.

Southern Collections Mall
317 Central Ave.
601/426-2322

Miss Ann's House of Treasures
326 N. Magnolia St.
601/428-0607

Antiques Mart
427 Oak St.
601/425-0009

21 LONG BEACH

Red Creek Colonial Inn Bed and Breakfast
7416 Red Creek Road
601/452-3080 or 1-800-729-9670

Circa 1899. Situated on 11 acres of ancient live oaks and fragrant magnolias, this French cottage has seven bedrooms and five baths. A 64-foot front porch, usable antiques, old-fashioned wooden radios and porch swings.

Oak Leaf Shoppe
410 Jeff Davis Ave.
601/868-9433

22 MADISON

Anne-Tiques
118 Depot Dr.
601/853-4939

Alene's Antiques & Collectibles
180 Depot Dr.
601/853-1023

Talk of the Town
180 Depot Dr.
601/856-3087

Uptown Antiques Etc.
180 Depot Dr.
601/853-9153

Inside Story
2081 Main St.
601/856-3229

Madison Antiques Market
Main St.
601/856-8036

23 MCCOMB

Traditions-Art & Antiques
125 S. Broadway St.
601/249-3038

A J Sales
205 E. Georgia Ave.
601/684-8249

J & E. Antiques
127 S. Magnolia St.
601/249-3309

Whistle Stop Antiques
228 N. Railroad Blvd.
601/249-3990

Bell Remnants, Inc.
232 N. Railroad Blvd.
601/684-0529

24 MERIDIAN

Azalea Bed and Breakfast
601/482-5483 or 1-800-633-6477

Convenient to downtown Meridian. Home is filled with the host's collection of family heirlooms. Features a pre-Civil War mahogany-canopied bed, as well as a sun porch and patio.

Camellia Bed and Breakfast
601/482-5483

Charming guest suite with private entrance. Large bedroom with fireplace, private bath and living room. The suite has been decorated with antiques. Kitchen privileges.

A & I Place
2223 Front St.
601/483-9281

Old South Antique Mall
100 N. Frontage Rd.
601/483-1737

Booker's Antiques
Hwy. 19 S.
601/644-3272

Wayside Shop
5523 Poplar Springs Dr.
601/485-2205

Cabin Antiques
8343 Russell Topton Rd.
601/679-7922

House of Antiques & Cllbls.
1725 17th Ave.
601/485-5462

Z's Antiques
1607 24th Ave.
601/482-0676

Century House Antiques
2101 24th Ave.
601/482-5504

Flowers Unltd. Gifts & Access.
525 22nd Ave. S.
601/693-4865

McClain's Antiques
3834 York Rd.
601/679-5076

Favorite Places To Eat

Cracker Barrel Old Country Store
I-20 & U.S. 45, Exit 154
601/482-3003

25 MOSS POINT

Fisher's Antiques
5136 Elder St.
601/475-5731

Od's
7516 Hwy. 613
601/475-3612

Pass-Point Antiques
3806 Main St.
601/475-7863

Favorite Places To Eat

Cracker Barrel Old Country Store
I-10 & Hwy. 63, Exit 69
601/475-8856

26 NATCHEZ

Mark Twain Guest House
25 Silver Street
601/446-8023

Circa 1830. National Register. Three rooms, two rooms overlooking the Mississippi River and one with balcony and fireplace. Large shared bathroom. Entertainment downstairs in saloon on weekends. Near casino and restaurants.

Monmouth Plantation
36 Melrose Avenue
601/442-5852 or 1-800-828-4531

Circa 1818. National Register. Twenty-five rooms, including 13 suites. Sits on 26 acres with gardens, moss-draped oaks and small, clear pond. Voted most romantic place in the United States by *Glamour Magazine* and *USA Today*.

Lansdowne Plantation
1323 Martin Luther King Jr. Road
601/446-9401

Circa 1853. National Register. One large bedroom year-round, two during Natchez Pilgrimages. Furnished with antiques. House tour and complimentary wine. Quiet and secluded. Southern breakfast.

Linden Bed and Breakfast
1 Linden Place
601/445-5472 or 1-800-1-LINDEN

Circa 1880. National Register. Federal-style house has been in the Conner-Feltus family for six generations. Its front doorway was copied for Tara in *Gone With the Wind*. Seven bedrooms, heirlooms and canopied beds. Private bath. Southern breakfast.

Harper House
201 Arlington Avenue
601/445-5557 or 1-800-571-8848

Circa 1891. National Register. Victorian house, located in downtown Natchez within walking distance of many antebellum homes. Peach Suite—two bedrooms, sitting room and bath. Green Room—bay window, queen bed and bath. Southern breakfast.

High Point
215 Linton Avenue
601/442-6963 or 1-800-283-4099

Circa 1890. National Register. Victorian Queen Ann Country Manor home in a lovely Historic District. Three spacious rooms with private baths. Includes tour of home, afternoon social hour. Southern breakfast.

Clifton Heights Bed and Breakfast
212 Linton Avenue
601/446-8047

Turn-of-the-century Victorian. Natchez suite—one queen bed and two twin beds, full kitchen, private bath. Orleans suite—two bedrooms with double beds, shared bath. Swimming pool. Southern breakfast.

Dunleith
84 Homochitto
601/446-8500 or 1-800-446-2445

Circa 1856. National Register. The majestic mansion has been the backdrop for such films as *Huckleberry Finn* and *Showboat*. Eleven rooms. Wood-burning fireplaces. Southern breakfast.

Ravennaside
601 South Union Street
601/442-8015

Circa 1870. National Register. Ravennaside contains an extensive collection of Natchez Trace memorabilia. Private baths. Children welcome. Southern breakfast.

Shields Town House
701 North Union Street
601/442-7680 or 1-800-647-6742

Circa 1860. National Register. Exclusive suites in private setting with modern amenities, antique charm and landscaped courtyards. Garage parking adjacent to each suite. Main house courtyard features a large three-tier fountain and gardens.

T.A.S.S. House Bed and Breakfast
404 South Commerce Street
601/445-4663

Circa 1890. National Register. Two large luxurious suites located in a private home in the Historic Garden District. Walking distance to the Mississippi River and downtown. Authentic decor, antique furnishings, private bath. Southern breakfast.

Wensel House
206 Washington Street
601/445-8577

Circa 1888. National Register. Victorian, three bedrooms on second floor, each with private bath. Outstanding ornamental plaster ceilings and antique furnishings. Southern breakfast.

Weymouth Hall
One Cemetery Road
601/445-2304

Circa 1855. National Register. Greek Revival features a panoramic view of the Mississippi River. Remarkable architecture, fine millwork and brickwork. Completely furnished in period antiques. Private baths and entrances. Southern breakfast.

Audubon Gallery
103 S. Broadway St.
601/442-2329

Natchez Gun Shop
533 S. Canal St.
601/442-7627

As You Like It Silver Shop
410 N. Commerce St.
601/442-0933

Country Bumpkin
502 Franklin St.
601/442-5908

H Hal Garner Antiques
610 Franklin St.
601/445-8416

Antiquarian
624 Franklin St.
601/445-0388

Simonton Antiques
631 Franklin St.
601/442-5217

Mrs. Holder's Antiques
636 Franklin St.
601/442-0675

Antique Mall
700 Franklin St.
601/442-0130

Sharp Designs & Works of Art
703 Franklin St.
601/442-5224

Natchez Antiques & Cllbls.
705 Franklin St.
601/442-9555

Pippens Limited Antiques
708 Franklin St.
601/442-0962

Lower Lodge Antiques
712 Franklin St.
601/442-2617

Antiques-Washington Village
824 Hwy. 61 N
601/442-8021

B & B Flea Market
943 Hwy. 61 S
601/442-3505

Antique Lantern
145 Homochitto St.
601/445-0055

Rendezvous Antiques & Gifts
401 Main St.
601/442-9988

Tass House Antiques
111 N. Pearl St.
601/446-9917

27 OCEAN SPRINGS

Oak Shade Bed and Breakfast
1017 La Fontaine
601/875-1050

Spacious and completely private retreat situated amidst the quiet charm of old Ocean Springs. The room has a private entrance and a private bath. Library. Southern breakfast.

Who's Inn
623 Washington Avenue
601/875-3251

Gallery rooms are furnished with art and sculpture by Southern artists. Handicapped accessible. Located in the center of downtown Historic District. Stocked refrigerator in each room, private baths, three blocks from beach, bikes available. Continental breakfast.

The Wilson House Inn
6312 Allen Road
601/875-6933 or 1-800-872-6933

Circa 1923. Six guest rooms with private baths, white pine floors, fireplaces, 10-inch-wide wraparound porch, brick patio. One king bed, two queen beds, two full beds and one room with two twin beds. Southern breakfast.

Temptations
1508 Government St.
601/875-7896

Clocksmith
12401 Hanover Dr.
601/875-6613

28 OLIVE BRANCH

Frances Bargains
9059 Goodman Rd.
601/895-9272

Country Peddler Antique Mall
7711 Hwy. 178
601/895-0434

Old Towne Antiques & Gifts
9117 Pigeon Roost Rd.
601/893-2323

Olive Branch Bazaar
9119 Pigeon Roost Rd.
601/895-9496

Memes Attic
9121 Pigeon Roost Rd.
601/895-8616

29 OXFORD

Directions: From I-55 South toward Jackson, Mississippi, exit onto Hwy. 6 West. At South Lamar, you have reached downtown Oxford's antique district.

Bea's Antiques
1315 North Lamar
601/234-9405
Mon.-Sat. 9-5

Antiques, used furniture, quilts, glassware, mirrors, pictures, lamps and much more. Bea's buys estates.

The Bird In the Bush/The Oxford Collection
1415 University Avenue East
601/234-5784
Mon.-Sat. 9-5:30

A multi-dealer mall featuring affordable antiques and collectibles, nostalgic accessories, a variety of reproduction antiques, linens, quilts, and more.

Creme de la Creme
319 North Lamar
601/234-1463
Mon.-Sat. 10-5:30

A unique collection of shops featuring American, English, and French antiques and collectibles, distinguished home accessories, original art, children's furniture and gifts and a design and sew shop.

Inside Oxford
1220 Jefferson Avenue
601/234-1444
Mon.-Fri. 9-5:30, Sat. 10-5:30

French, English and American furniture both in the main showroom and in the warehouse. Oriental rugs, lamps, framed art, oil paintings and mirrors, chandeliers, accessories and gifts.

Material Culture, Inc.
405 South Lamar Boulevard
601/234-7055
Tue.-Sat. 10-5, Mondays by appointment

Featuring all things Southern, plus early to mid-nineteenth century American furniture and decorative arts, antique Persian carpets, folk art, fine crafts, vintage linens, handcrafted jewelry, antique architectural elements and materials, quilts and silver.

Barksdale-Isom House
1003 Jefferson Avenue
601/236-5600 or 1-800-236-5696

Circa 1838. National Register. Constructed entirely of native timber cut from the grounds and handworked by Indian and slave labor. Classic example of planter-style architecture.

Puddin Place
1008 University Avenue
601/234-1250

Circa 1892. Beautifully restored. Suite accommodations with private bath, fireplaces, antiques, collectibles and historic mementos. Short walk to historic town square, Ole Miss campus and Rowan Oak. Southern breakfast.

The Oliver-Britt House
512 Van Buren Avenue
601/234-8043

Circa 1905. Greek Revival. Five second-floor bedrooms, all with private baths and antiques. Breakfast at Smitty's, an Oxford tradition, on weekdays. Southern breakfast.

Tommy's Antiques & Imports
Hwy. 6 E
601/234-4669

Ruffled Feathers
Hwy. 6 W
601/236-1537

Old House Juntiques
Hwy. 30
601/236-7116

30 PASCAGOULA

Samuels Antiques
824 Denny Ave.
601/762-8593

Bernard Clark's W. Hse. Antqs.
2128 Ingalls Ave.
601/762-3511

Wixon & Co. Jewelers
1803 Jackson Ave.
601/762-7777

J & B Antiques
3803 Willow St.
601/769-0542

31 PASS CHRISTIAN

The Blue Rose Restaurant and Antiques
120 W. Scenic Drive
601/452-7004

The Blue Rose Restaurant and Antiques in Pass Christian sits majestically on Scenic Drive across from the Pass Christian Yacht Harbor.

The house, built in 1848, was originally a one-and-a-half story frame, five-bay coastal cottage with a gallery with square columns wrapped around three full sides of the house, and consoles carrying overhanging cornices over each bay. It has distinctive pilastered dormers and numerous rear ells attaching the former outbuildings and enclosing gallery.

Mr. Fitzpatrick, who built the home, was a merchant marine. He and his wife had four children, three girls and one boy. Their daughter, Nettie, was a nun and Kitty was the postmaster in the city of Pass Christian. Hugh was the supervisor for Beat 3 for many years and Lettie is believed to be a "ghost" at The Blue Rose. Lettie was mentally retarded and rarely allowed on the first floor of the house. It was rumored that at night, when everyone was asleep, Lettie would roam around the first floor with her terrier puppy. She died at the age of 11 or 12, of yellow fever. None of the other children had offspring and the house eventually went to a niece.

During World War II the house was converted into apartments and later sold to a man from Louisiana. The Blue Rose is now owned by Philip LaGrange, who is the fourth owner of the house in its history.

The house is listed on the National Register of Historic Places. The National Trust of Historic Preservation has described it as "the most significant antebellum home on the western portion of Pass Christian's beach front."

The broad front porch is now glassed in with breath taking views of the harbor and Gulf Coast waters. Interior areas are graced by stained glass, intricate woodwork, and high ceilings. The antique store, featuring fine antiques, estate silver and collectibles, is on the eastern portion of the house. The restaurant, featuring the finest cuisine on the Gulf Coast, is on the western portion of the house.

Inn At The Pass
125 East Scenic Drive
601/452-0333 or 1-800-217-2588

Circa 1879. National Register. On the beach of the Mississippi Gulf Coast. Victorian antiques, fireplaces, kitchenette, golf packages, restaurants and shops within walking distance. Original art in all rooms.

Wicker N Wood
254 E. Beach- Hwy. 90
601/452-4083

A-1 Trade World
8095 Menge Ave.
601/452-0590

Blue Rose Antiques
120 W. Scenic Dr.
601/452-7004

32 PEARL

Favorite Places To Eat

Cracker Barrel Old Country Store
I-20 & Pearson Rd., Exit 48
601/936-9990

33 PICAYUNE

Pirates Plunder
127 W. Canal St.
601/798-0885

Pineros Antiques
210 W. Canal St.
601/798-9615

Edwards Antiques & Gallery
335 W. Canal St.
601/798-3376

Abundant Treasures
111 N. Main St.
601/799-5871

34 PONTOTOC

Mason Jar Antique Mall
34 Liberty
601/489-7420

Court Square Antique Mall
42 Liberty
601/488-8844

35 RIDGELAND

Antique Mall of the South
367 Hwy. 51
601/853-4000
Mon.-Sat. 10-6, Sun. Noon-6

Directions: Located one mile north of I-55/County Road intersection (I-55 Exit 103). One mile north of Jackson, Mississippi.

This 14,000-square-foot antique mall is known to have the "finest quality antiques in the South." The inventory here will impress even the choosiest antique collector.

There is a distinct selection of furniture, including Early American, Country, Empire, Victorian, as well as "lots of oak." For collectors of fine glassware, they offer Fenton, flow blue, depression glass, and the finest cut glass pieces around. Hummel collectors will be delighted to find a selection of their favorite figurines available here. The locomotive hobbyist searching for that new locomotive to add to his collection just may find it here among the dandy selections of trains and accessories.

For an outstanding representation of quality antiques and collectibles, a "must stop" on your antiquing trail is the 50-dealer Antique Mall of the South.

Village Antiques
554 Hwy. 51, Ste. D
601/856-6021

Copper Kettle
637A Hwy. 51
601/856-7042

36 SENATOBIA

Spahn House
401 College Street
601/562-9853

Circa 1904. This gracious 15-room Southern mansion, situated on a picture-perfect shady street, is beautifully restored. Four guest rooms, jacuzzi baths, common areas. Honeymoon package. Lunch or dinner. Southern breakfast.

Dot Mitchell Antiques
123 Lively St.
601/562-4392

Sowell Antiques
104 E. Main St.
601/562-5785

Home Sweet Home
220 W. Main St.
601/562-0027

37 STARKVILLE

Carpenter Place
1280 Hwy. 25 South
601/323-4669

Circa 1835. National Register. Located on 120 acres which abound with wildlife, it is the oldest house in Oktibbeha County. Grounds have gardens for guests' enjoyment.

The Caragen House
1108 Hwy. 82 West
601/323-0340

Circa 1890. Steamboat Gothic design, the only one of its kind in Mississippi. Located inside the city limits on 22 acres. Five bedrooms with private baths, king beds, and refreshment center.

The Cedars Bed and Breakfast
2173 Oktoc Road
601/324-7569

Circa 1836. Antebellum plantation mansion surrounded by 183 acres of rolling pasturelands, woods and fishing ponds. Tour the historic house and grounds, or attend major sporting and cultural events at nearby Starkville.

Back Roads Antiques
Old Crawford Rd.
601/323-4763

Ginis Attic Antiques
1221 Old Hwy. 82 E
601/323-8790

Watson's Village Antiques
1237 Old High #82 E
601/323-5526

Tin Top Antiques
891 Old West Point Rd.
601/323-2032

38 TUPELO

The Mockingbird Inn
305 North Gloster
601/841-0286

Seven guest rooms represent the decor from different corners of the world. Private bath and queen-size beds. Common rooms. Evening soft drinks, coffee, tea, bottled water and juices are complimentary. Southern breakfast.

Red Door Antq. Mall & Cllbls.
1469 Coley Road
601/840-6777

Cottage Book Shop
214 N. Madison
601/844-1553

Main Attraction
214 W. Main St.
601/842-9617

Nostalgia Alley
214 W. Main St.
601/842-2757

Chesterfield's
624 W. Main St.
601/841-9171

George Watson Antiques
628 W. Main St.
601/841-9411

Murphey Antiques Ltd.
1120 W. Main St.
601/844-3245

My Granny's Attic
Appointment Only
601/844-4614

Pam Antiques & Lamp Shop
2229 W. Main St.
601/844-3050

Skyline Antiques
Old 78 E.
601/680-4559

Rain Station Antiques
202 S. Park St.
601/840-2030

Saltillo Antique Mall
832 Mobile St.
601/869-5292

The Treasure Chest
4097 W. Main
601/840-2015

Silver Web Antiques
810 Harrison #3
601/842-4022

Peppertown Antiques
Hwy. 78
601/862-9892

39 VICKSBURG

Balfour House
1002 Crawford Street
601/638-7113
Open year round

"Beneath the flickering glow of candlelight, elegant ladies and dashing Confederate officers danced one cold December evening in 1862, until a courier rushed in to announce that Union gunboats had been sighted on the Mississippi River. The officers bade their ladies a hasty good-bye and left to prepare for the defense of the city." (An eventful night at Balfour House)

Each December, Balfour House is host to a gala evening of music and festive re-enactment of the last grand ball before the siege of Vicksburg. Among Balfour House's other year-round accomplishments is its distinction as a National Register property and designated Mississippi landmark. Additionally, it is considered one of the finest Greek Revival structures in the state according to the Mississippi Department of Archives and History. This bed and breakfast establishment was certainly abuzz with activity during the siege of Vicksburg. In fact, and obviously so once you see, Balfour House became business headquarters for the Union Army after the fall of the city.

The 1982 restoration of the house complied obediently to the Secretary of the Interior's Standards for Rehabilitation, and in this obedience, the house's walls surrendered a cannonball and other Civil War artifacts. The three-story elliptical staircase and patterned hardwood floors were also restored in 1982. The work on these projects was honored with the 1984 Award of Merit from the state historical society.

With such a notable history, Balfour House would be a star stop for any Civil War, architectural or antique lover's tour of Vicksburg. Even so, the bed and breakfast offers delights matching the history of the home. The bedrooms are authentically decorated, and upon stepping out of your guest room each morning, you are invited to partake of a full Southern-style breakfast which is always generous and hearty. During the day, you might enjoy following the guided tour of the home, which will enlighten you on all of its history and beauty.

Yesterday's Treasures Antique Mall
1400 Washington Street
601/638-6213
Open Mon.-Sat. 10-5, closed Sun.

A multi-dealer mall in historic Downtown Vicksburg, offering furniture, glassware, Civil War relics, old books, pottery, quilts and linens, toys, collectibles, and much more!

Annabelle Bed and Breakfast
501 Speed Street
601/638-2000 or 1-800-791-2000

Circa 1868. Located in Vicksburg's Historic Garden District, this stately Victorian-Italianate residence is elegantly furnished with period antiques and rare family heirlooms. Private full baths. Southern breakfast.

The Corners
601 Klein Street
601/636-7421 or 1-800-444-7421

Circa 1872. National Register. Original parterre gardens, a 70-foot gallery across the front with a view of the Mississippi River, double parlor, formal dining room and library. Five rooms with fireplaces and eight rooms with whirlpool tubs, private bath. Southern breakfast.

Cedar Grove Mansion Inn
2200 Oak Street
601/636-1000 or 1-800-862-1300

Circa 1840. National Register. Greek Revival mansion overlooking the Mississippi River. Gardens, fountains and gazebos. Original antiques. Four-Diamond AAA Rating. Gourmet candlelight dining and piano bar.

Duff Green Mansion
1114 First East Street
601/636-6968 or 1-800-992-0037

Circa 1856. National Register. Used as a hospital for Confederate soldiers. Furnished with period antiques and reproductions. Honeymoon and anniversary package. Southern breakfast.

Floweree
2309 Pearl Street
601/638-2704

Circa 1870. National register. Fine example of Italianate architecture. Listed on Historic American Building Survey. Southern breakfast.

The Stained Glass Manor
2430 Drummond Street
601/638-8893 or 1-800-771-8893

Circa 1906. National Register. "The Stained Glass Manor" of Spanish design features 32 stained glass windows, fine oak paneling and spectacular staircase. The interior glows from the light through the delicate panes of rose, salmon, rust, gold, blue and green.

Old Feldhome Antiques
2108 Cherry St.
601/636-0773

River City Antiques
1609 Levee St.
601/638-4758

Washington St. Antique Mall
1305 Washington St.
601/636-3700

Yesterdays Treasures Antiques
1400 Washington St.
601/638-6213

Favorite Places To Eat

Cracker Barrel Old Country Store
I-20 & Clay St., Exit 5B
601/636-2115

40 WAYNESBORO

Four Generations
124 Mississippi Dr.
601/735-5721

Old French House
515 Mississippi Dr.
601/735-0353

41 WEST

The Alexander House
11 Green Street
800/350-8034
Open year round

Directions: From I-55, take Exit 164, between Jackson, Mississippi, and Memphis, Tennessee. Go 3 miles off the interstate. Located on the second paved road to the right after leaving the interstate exchange.

An incident from the rooms of The Alexander House as recounted by Ruth Ray and Woody Dinstel.

The Blinking Cat

Guests at The Alexander House often ask to photograph our rather elegant rooms and some of the more valuable or interesting antiques. We say, "Be our guests." One morning a guest was going through the rooms with a cam corder. She was in Miss Anne's room when she became excited and called everyone to her. She had a garbage can with an embossed cat as decoration in her viewfinder, and she cried out, "The cat blinked at me." We all gathered, but no one saw any blinking, no matter how hard we stared. A week or so later, this lady called from her home in Alabama to say when they showed the film on their television, the cat definitely blinked. Her husband even processed one frame that definitely showed the eyes closed! There is no streak of light across the frame. Needless to say, we have obtained a copy of the video, to show doubters the proof of the blinking cat.

Tucked lovingly into the heart of Mississippi is the town of West, which ironically is located east of Interstate 55. Among that town's historic buildings is The Alexander House. The unique events occurring in Miss Anne's room regarding "The Blinking Cat" are enough to entice the curious to spend a night or two peeping around corners to see embossed cats wink. Nevertheless, the opulent atmosphere and furnishings of this bed and breakfast allure anyone with a taste to be pampered and surrounded by the uncommon and exquisite. That pampered feeling certainly comes from being luxuriously housed within the historic district of West. The Alexander House was constructed as early as 1880. In 1994, the owners, Ruth Ray and Woody Dinstel, opened the restored home in its period grandeur. As a guest, you will be treated to a complimentary, Southern-style (hearty portions) breakfast in the authentically furnished, two-story home.

Gourmet lunches and dinners are available by reservation.

42 WEST POINT

Aunt Teeks
743 E. Brame Ave.
601/494-2980

Treasure Nook
111 Commerce St.
601/494-1103

Antique Mall
415 Hwy. 45 N
601/494-0098

Once Upon A Time Antiques
910 Hwy. 45 Alt St.
601/494-7811

Antiques on the Main
123 E. Main St.
601/494-2010

Tanglewood
125 E. Main St.
601/492-0074

Wisteria
411 E. Main St.
601/494-2010

43 WIGGINS

Serendipity Shop
203 E. Pine Ave.
601/928-5020

44 YAZOO CITY

Main Street Antiques
211 N. Main St.
601/746-9307

Chesire Cat
305 S. Main St.
601/746-8401

WHITE SQUIRREL HOLLOW
Bed and Breakfast Inn

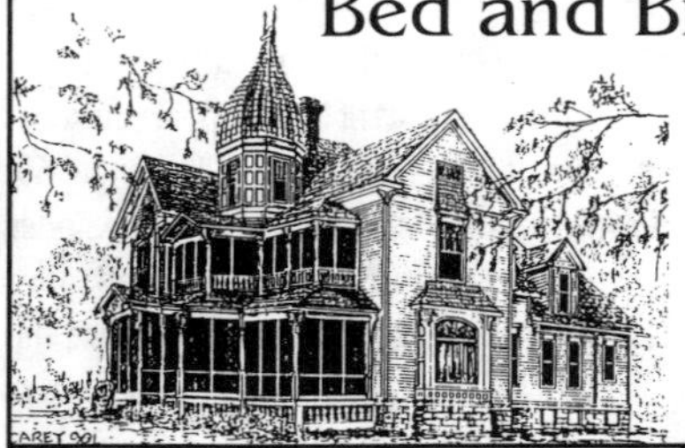

A historical, romantic, victorian 1896 home

Marionville

39

I-29 ANTIQUE MALL

Platte City, Missouri
located just 6 miles north of Kansas City International Airport on I-29 at exit #19
1-816-858-2921

- Open Daily 10:00 - 6:0
- Over 12,000 sq. feet
- 80+ quality dealers
- NO CRAFTS
- NO FLEA MARKET

4

Woodstock Inn

Bed & Breakfast

In the very heart of historic Independence

The Woodstock Inn Bed & Breakfast, a turn of the century Doll & Quilt Factory, invites you to enjoy gracious hospitality

(816) 833-2233

Independence

26

Missouri

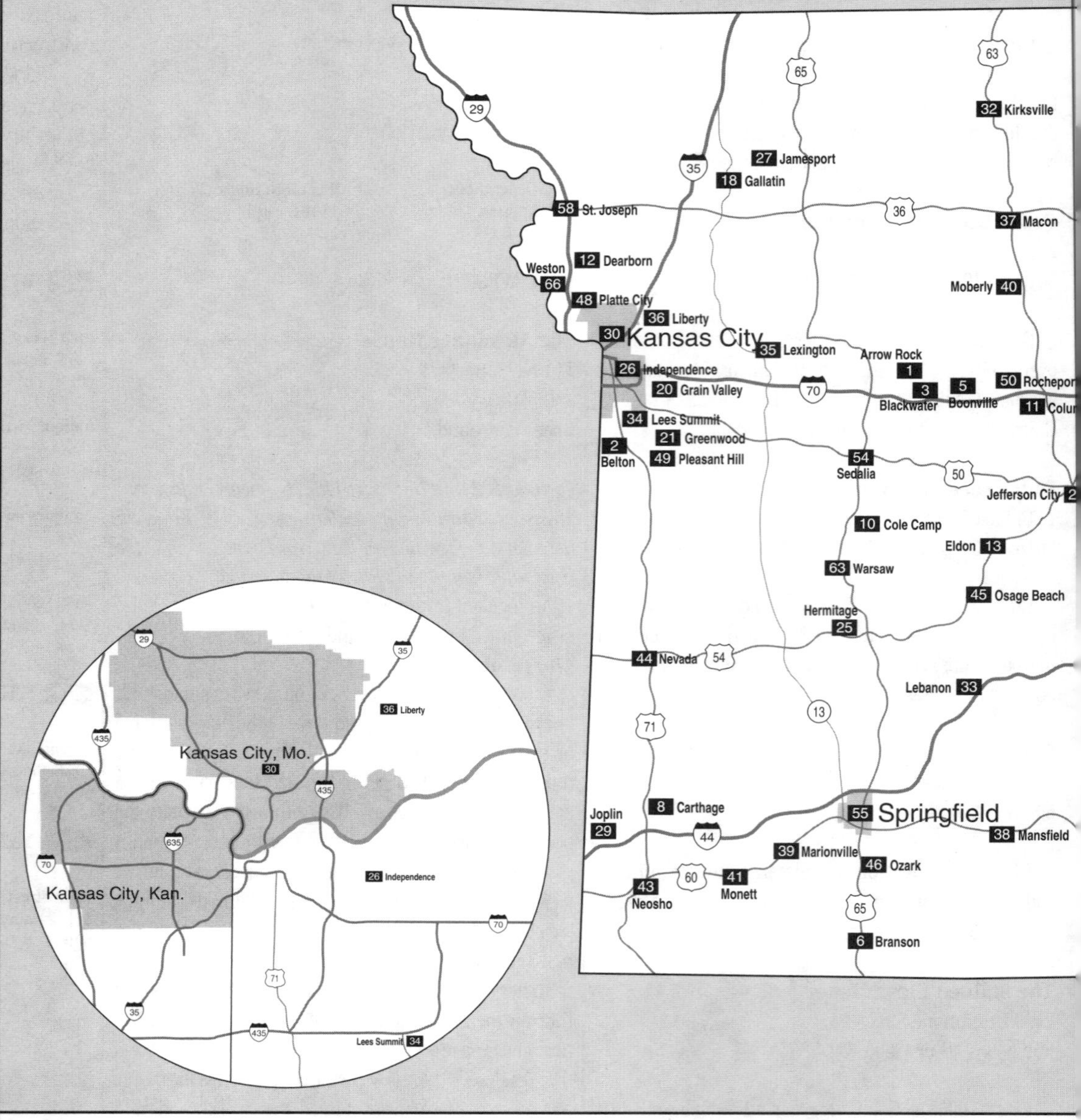

Country Meadows Antique Mall

Antiques Primitives & Collectibles

400 Dealers 40,000 sq ft.

4621 Shrank Drive
816/373-0410

Monday-Saturday: 9 - 9
Sunday: 9 - 6

Independence

26

Cherokee Antique Row

40 Unique Shops in a 4 Block Area

St. Louis

59

Ozark Antiques & Cllbls.

- 17,00 sq. ft.
- Over 100 dealers

S.W. corner of Highways 65 & 14

417-581-5233

see review this section

Ozark

46

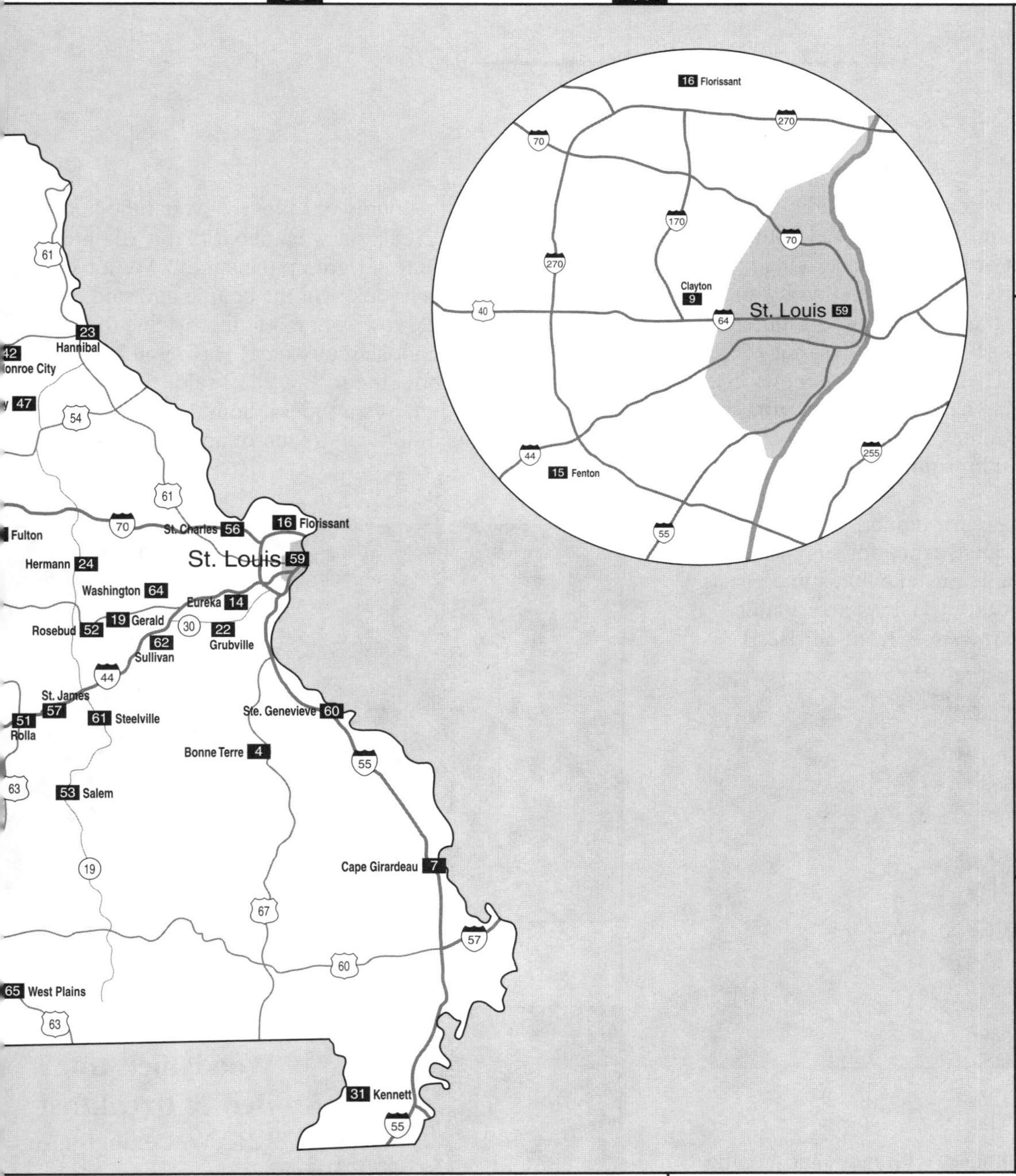
16 Florissant
270
70
170
70
270
Clayton
9
40
64
St. Louis 59
44
15 Fenton
255
55
61
23
Hannibal
42
Monroe City
47
54
61
Fulton
70
St. Charles 56
16 Florissant
St. Louis 59
Hermann 24
Washington 64
Eureka 14
19 Gerald
Rosebud 52
30
22
Grubville
62
Sullivan
44
St. James
57
51
Rolla
61 Steelville
Ste. Genevieve 60
Bonne Terre 4
55
63
53 Salem
19
Cape Girardeau 7
67
57
60
65 West Plains
63
31 Kennett
55

Woodstock Inn

Bed & Breakfast

Formerly a turn-of-the-century doll and quilt factory, the Woodstock Inn B&B is situated in the famous historical district of Independence. There are 11 guest rooms, each with a distinct personality and private bath. Guests start the morning off with the house specialty—gourmet Belgian waffles—or another special breakfast entree. Then it's off to visit the Truman Home, the Truman Library and Museum, the National Frontier Trails Center, the Old Stone Church, the RLDS Temple and Auditorium, Jackson Square, and all the rest.

But when you get ready for dinner, please ask innkeepers Todd and Patricia Justice for suggestions, or you might make the same mistake that some guests did in a story the Juctices tell: "There's a very nice-looking building right up the street from our B&B.

It looks like a very large house, with nice landscaping and green awnings over the windows. The sign by the door says 'Speaks.' Early one evening a pair of hungry and weary guests walked in our door wanting to check in. After the whole check-in process, the first words out of their mouths were, 'Where can we get something to eat? We are starving!' We suggested a few places just a couple of miles away, but the lady said right away, 'Oh, but what about that really nice restaurant on the left, right up the street?' We looked at each other, then looked at the couple and said, 'We really don't think you want to eat there!' She then asked, 'Why? It looks really nice! Have you heard anything bad about the food?' Todd said, 'It's a nice looking place but...it's a funeral home!' Needless to say our guests didn't eat dinner, or any other meal, there!"

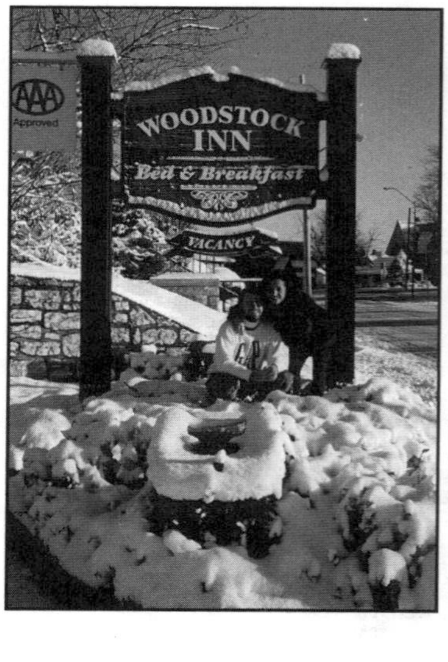

Woodstock Inn
Bed & Breakfast
1212 W. Lexington St.
Independence, MO
(816) 833-2233

Todd & Patricia welcome guests to the Woodstock Inn.

OZARK ANTIQUE MALL AND COLLECTIBLES

Wonderful advertising items can be found at Ozark Antiques.

Over 100 dealers have their wares displayed throughout the 17,000 square feet of Ozark Antiques. There is an endless variety of merchandise to choose from, with a very helpful staff happy to aid shoppers as they pour through large collections of primitives, pottery, furniture and thousands of pieces of depression glass. Other specialty lines include military items, fishing gear, gas pumps, Coca Cola memorabilia, toys, advertising, architectural salvage items, ball cards, Aladdin lamps, cookie jars, Ertl, radios, trains, tins, Fiestaware, marbles, knives and dolls.

Fine architectural pieces are available at Ozark Antiques.

Directions: At U.S. 65 and Highway 14 in Ozark, turn west and take first left, which is 20th Street. Look for Ozark Antique Mall on the right-hand side - it's the building with all the great old advertising signs and antiques out front in the southwest corner of Highways 65 and 14.

Ozark Antique Mall and Collectibles
200 S. 20th Street
Ozark, Mo.
417/581-5233
Open summer 9-6; winter 9-5, daily

1 ARROW ROCK

The year was 1804. Lewis and Clark were in the midst of their legendary explorations of the U.S. when they noted the bluff and the nearby salt licks in their journals and maps. Native Americans had for centuries gathered the flint from the bluff for arrowheads, hence the name Arrow Rock. After Lewis and Clark, westbound explorers and traders stopped at Arrow Rock Spring in 1829, some of them settled and founded the town. Today, Arrow Rock is basically untouched by time. The 70 people who currently live in the town are steeped in its history and in the recreation and preservation of its past.

Visitors to Arrow Rock can tour a restored 1834 tavern, a gunsmith's shop and home, the old print shop, frontier artist George Caleb Bingham's home, a museum dedicated to medical doctor John Sappington, who was a pioneer in the treatment of malaria, and more. Then you can experience live entertainment at Arrow Rock's award-winning Lyceum Theatre. Once a church, the theater is now a beautiful 420-seat complex where professional actors from around the country stage Broadway-caliber shows each summer. Also, visit shops filled with antiques, specialty gifts, and old-time crafts. Eat to your heart's content-everything from simple country fare to gourmet delights. Stay at a gracious bed and breakfast, or camp outdoors overlooking the Missouri River Valley.

Great Places To Shop

Arrow Rock Antiques
Located on Main Street
816/837-3333

18th and 19th century formal and high country furniture and accessories.

McAdams' Ltd.
816/837-3259
Open Apr.-Dec., Wed.-Sun., 10-5. or by appointment

Once the bank building in a bustling stop on the Sante Fe Trail, this historic building now holds a unique blend of European and American antiques with a distinctive line of new merchandise. Antique, estate and traditional new jewelry have been a McAdams' specialty for 20 years.

Pin Oak Antiques
301 Main Street, on the Boardwalk
816/837-3244
Open Wed.-Sun. Or by appointment

A full line of antique country furniture and accessories at reasonable prices. Two floors of antiques, including a basement "rough room."

The Village Peddler Antiques
One-half mile north of Arrow Rock on Highway 41
816/837-3392
Open Wed.-Sun. 10-5 or by appointment

A general line of furniture and smalls.

Great Places To Eat

Arrow Rock Emporium
Located on the Boardwalk
816/837-3364

A tea room atmosphere featuring home-cooked sandwich platters, flavored coffee, and delicious ice cream specialties.

Grandma D's Cafe
One block south of Main Street
816/837-3335

Enjoy dining surrounded by antiques and unique gifts. Sandwiches, salads, homemade soups, pies, and sweet breads.

The Old Arrow Rock Tavern
Located on Main Street one block from the Lyceum Theatre

Built in 1834, The Old Tavern continues to serve the public as it did in the glory days of the Sante Fe Trail. One of the oldest restaurants west of the Mississippi, the Old Tavern fare includes catfish, country ham, and fried chicken, with an ample selection in wine, beer and spirits. Reservations requested.

The Old Schoolhouse Cafe
Located in the Old Schoolhouse
816/837-3331

Enjoy homemade breakfast and lunch specialties located at the Westside basement entrance in The Old Schoolhouse.

The Evergreen Restaurant
Located one block north of Main Street on Highway 41
816/837-3251

Enjoy gracious dining with a European touch in a restored 1840s home.

2 BELTON

Dusty Attic Antiques & Cllbls.
319 Main St.
816/331-3505

1802
320 Main St.
816/322-7107

Jaudon Antique Mall
20406 S. State Rd. #D
816/322-4001

3 BLACKWATER

Rose Hill
21495 Hwy. 41
816/846-3031
Open Wed.-Sat., 10-5; Sun.-Tue., by chance or appointment

Directions: From I-70 west, exit #89. Travel 6 miles north through Blackwater on Route "K" to Hwy. 41, then go 1/2 mile north on Hwy. 41 to Rose Hill. From I-70 east, exit #98. Travel 7 miles north on Hwy. 41 toward Arrow Rock. Rose Hill is 1/2 mile on the right after you pass Route "K."

Visitors to Rose Hill get a special treat, so take your cameras. The shop of Rose Hill is located behind the Kusgen's home and is set up inside in fashion groupings, by rooms. They have bedrooms decorated with beds, wardrobes, chests and accessories; a living room with antique furniture and accessories; and a kitchen with a working model woodburning stove (not for sale). Kitchen items include old utensils, depression glass, and stoneware bowls.

The special treat is growing on the property at Rose Hill. It's Missouri's largest known sugar maple tree, recognized by the Missouri Dept. Of Conservation. The tree has a circumference of 13 feet 8 inches, soars 62 feet tall, and spreads out 88 feet. The Missouri Forestry Department estimates the tree to be 150 years old. A film about the tree has been televised in Missouri by PBS and a plaque was presented to the Kusgens by the Missouri Department of Conservation, attesting to the claim of the state's largest sugar maple tree.

4 BONNE TERRE

Victorian Veranda
207 E. School Street
573/358-1134 or 1-800-343-1134
Open daily 8-10:30 except Dec. 24-25
Rates $55-85

Directions: From St. Louis: Take I-55 South to U.S. 67. Turn south on U.S. 67 to Bonne Terre exit. Turn right on Hwy. 47, then left on Allen Street in Bonne Terre. Turn right on Main Street, then take an immediate left on East School Street to the inn. Only 45 miles from south St. Louis.

Just one of the unique and historic buildings and homes in Bonne Terre, Victorian Veranda is a large old home with a big wraparound porch and four guest rooms decorated in Victorian and country decor, all with private baths. Victoria's Room has six large windows and Victorian accessories, and a Jacuzzi for two. The Victorian Boot and Lace Room holds a wrought iron queen bed and is filled with Victorian high top boots and Battenburg lace. The Drake Room is furnished in the Mallard duck theme, all greens and burgundies, with a claw-foot tub for playing with your own rubber duckie; The Countryside

Room is bursting with Americana and country charm, complete with Charles Wysocki prints and country pine queen bed.

5 BOONVILLE

Itchy's Stop & Scratch Flea Mkt.
1406 W. Ashley Rd.
816/882-6822

Key to your Heart Antiques
1420 W. Ashley Rd.
816/882-8821

Hi-Way 5 Antique Mall
1428 W. Ashley Rd.
816/882-3341

Reichel and Co.
1436 W. Ashley Rd.
816/882-3533

Reichel Antique & Auct. Ctr.
1440 W. Ashley Rd.
816/882-5292

McMillan Ltd. Antiques
417 E. Spring St.
816/882-6337

6 BRANSON

Finders Keepers Flea Market
204 N. Commercial St.
417/334-3248

Apple Tree Mall
Hwy 76
417/335-2133

Somewhere In Time
Hwy 76
417/335-2212

Mothers & Mine Antiques
Mutton Hollow
417/334-2588

Apple Pie Ltd.
3612 Shepherd Hill Expressway
417/335-4236

Favorite Places To Eat

Cracker Barrel Old Country Store
Hwy. 76 & Little Pete Road
417/335-3003

7 CAPE GIRARDEAU

Campster School Antiques
3298 Bloomfield Rd.
573/339-1002

Another Time Another Place
715 Broadway St.
573/335-0046

Ohaira
1001 Independence St.
573/334-8020

Witness Designs
31 N. Main St.
573/334-0333

Antique Furniture & Crafts
18 N. Sprigg St.
573/339-0840

Peddlers Corner
111 N. Sprigg St.
573/334-1213

Heartland Antique Emporium
701 William St.
573/334-0102

Hansen's Collectibles
709 William St.
573/334-4410

A Antique Center Mall
2127 William St.
573/339-5788

Favorite Places To Eat

Cracker Barrel Old Country Store
I-55 & State Rt. K, Exit 96
573-651-4000

8 CARTHAGE

Goad Unique Antique Mall
111 E. 3rd St.
417/358-1201

Accent Angels & Antiques
342 Grant St.
417/359-5300

Jerdon Ltd.
311 S. Main St.
417/358-3343

Carthage Rt. 66 Antique Mall
1221 Oak St.
417/359-7240

9 CLAYTON

Listed as a part of St. Louis.

10 COLE CAMP

Stone Soup Antiques & Uniques
111 S. Maple Street
816/668-3624
Fax: 816/668-4458
Open Mon.-Sat., 10-5; Sun. 12-5

Directions: U.S. 65 20 miles south of Sedalia, east Hwy. 52, 1/2 block south of 4-way stop.

Here's a shop that takes its name - Stone Soup - from an old children's story. They offer an eclectic collection of antiques, collectibles, glassware (including depression glass, china and figurines), and country crafts in a "unique" 1906 lumber barn, complete with loft, that began its life as an old mercantile building. They also have a nice selection of furniture, including a bed that belonged to Walt Disney's parents!

11 COLUMBIA

Columbia Emporium
810 East Broadway
573/443-5288
Fax: 573/449-6782
Open Thurs.-Sat. and Mon. 11-5:30, Tue.-Wed. 11-4, closed Sun.

Directions: Travel west on I-70 (between St. Louis and Kansas City) to Columbia. Exit 126 south on Providence to Broadway. Turn left on Broadway. Columbia Emporium is located in downtown Columbia between 8th and 9th Streets. The shop is a lower level-one. Look for the black and gold sign.

This upscale emporium offers shoppers a large showroom of art, antiques and jewelry; specializing in large "ornate" 100-year-old furniture, and antique and estate jewelry.

Mary Watson Antqs. & Intrs.
923 E. Broadway Ave.
573/449-8676

Grandma's Treasures
2000 Business Loop
573/499-0883

Midway Antique Mall
I-70 & Hwy. 40 Exit 121
573/445-6717

Gates Antiques
11105 Mexico Gravel Rd.
573/474-4067

Museumscopes Antiques
2507 Old #63 S
573/449-8523

Ice Chalet Antique Mall
3411 Old #63 S
573/442-6893

McAdams Ltd.
32 S. Providence Rd.
573/442-3151

Itchy's Stop & Scratch
1907 N. Providence Rd.
573/443-8275

Favorite Places To Eat

Cracker Barrel Old Country Store
I-70 & Hwy. 63, Exit 128A
314/474-9977

12 DEARBORN

Lickskillet Antique Mall
214 Main
816/992-8776

Moore Antiques
108 W. 3rd
816/992-3788

Yesterday's Memories
110, 112, 114 W. 3rd
816/992-8941

Outpost Trading Co.
201 W. 3rd
816/992-3402

13 ELDON

Red's Antique Mall
Hwy. 52 & Bus 54 S
573/392-3866

Past & Present
106 S. Maple St.
573/392-2256

14 EUREKA

Remember When Antiques
126 S. Central Ave.
314/938-3724

Oldys & Goodys Antique Mall
127 S. Central Ave.
314/938-5717

Firehouse Gallery & Shops
131 S. Central Ave.
314/938-3303

Olde Thyme Shoppe
224 N. Central Ave.
314/938-3818

Ice House Antiques
19 Dreyer
314/938-6355

Eureka Antique Mall
107 E. 5th St.
314/938-5600

Great Midwest Antique Mall
100 Hilltop Village Center Dr.
314/938-6760

Accent on Antiques
120 S. Virginia Ave.
314/938-3200

Owl's Nest Antiques
128 S. Virginia Ave.
314/938-5030

Gingerbread House
138 S. Virginia Ave.
314/938-5414

Aunt Sadies Antique Mall
515 N. Virginia Ave.
314/938-9212

Wallach House Antiques
510 West Ave.
314/938-6633

15 FENTON

Favorite Places To Eat

Cracker Barrel Old Country Store
I-44 & Bowles Ave., Exit 274
314/349-3335

16 FLORISSANT

Gittemeier House Antiques
1067 Dunn Road
314/830-1133
Open daily Mon.-Sat. 10-4, Sun. 12-4

Directions: From Hwy. 270, take Exit 27 (New Florissant Road). Gittemeier House is located on the service road (1067 Dunn Road) behind the Shell Station.

It's always fun to visit an antique shop that is as old, or older, than the merchandise inside! Gittemeier House is a seven room, two-story 1860 Federal style house where the focus inside is on Victorian furniture - lots of impressive, towering wardrobes, marble topped pieces, glassware, all sorts of things from that elegant, extravagant age of Victoria!

17 FULTON

Cornerstone Antique Mall
537 Court St.
573/642-6700

Country Clipper Antiques
1225 S. Hwy. 54
573/642-0393

Kings Row Antiques
Jct Rt. F & Hwy. 54
573/642-5335

Willing House Antiques
211 Jefferson St.
573/642-7525

Lutz & Doters
505 Nichols St.
573/642-9350

18 GALLATIN

Towne Square Antiques
120 W. Grant St.
816/663-2555

Goat Mountain Antiques
Hwy. 6
816/663-2731

19 GERALD

The Bluebird Bed & Breakfast

For more specific information see listing under Rosebud #36

River House Bed & Breakfast

For more specific information see listing under Rosebud #36

20 GRAIN VALLEY

Sambo's Antiques
504 S. Main St.
816/224-4981

Primitives Plus
508A Main St.
816/224-3622

Main Street Mall Antiques
518 S. Main St.
816/224-6400

The Collector's Corner
513 Main St.
816/443-2228

21 GREENWOOD

Gate House Antqs. & Tea Room
302 Allendale Lake Rd.
816/537-7313

Country Heritage Antiques
16005 S. Allendale Lake Rd.
816/537-7822

Greenwood Antqs. & Tea Room
5th & Main on 150 Hwy.
816/537-7172

Traditions
5th & Main on 150 Hwy.
816/537-5011

Little Blue Antiques
409 W. Main St.
816/537-8688

Greenwillow Farm Antiques
15202 S. Smart Rd.
816/537-6527

22 GRUBVILLE

Grubville Guitars

314/274-4738
Fax: 314/285-9833
Open by appointment only

Directions: Located 35 minutes Southwest of St. Louis off Hwy. 30 on State Rd. Y between Highways 270 & 44.

A truly interesting shop on your antiquing trek, Grubville Guitars owned by Glenn Meyers, sells and restores used and vintage acoustic and electric guitars, basses, mandolins, banjos, violins and tube type amplifiers.

A musician for most of his life, Glenn thoroughly enjoys his work and has been interested in vintage instruments for 30 years. Most of his business is by word of mouth and his list of clients extends not only from the U.S. but from around the world.

Under Glenn's watchful eye the restoration and repair work is completed by two local guitar builders whose experience allows them to do any work necessary.

Being curious of this unusual fascination of Glenn's, I asked him what he considered to be a vintage instrument. He explains, "Vintage means certain instruments from the 1960s back to the 1700s. For instance, I recently worked on a style 1-42 Martin guitar that was made in 1898. A beautiful instrument with small body, ivory bridge, ivory tuners, Brazilian rosewood - back and sides - and abalone inlayed around the select spruce top. Martin began building guitars in the early 1800s and to this day builds some of the best instruments available." Glenn also noted that there is a difference in sound between the new and old instruments. "It has to do with the construction techniques used by the best makers, he says. Some of the woods available thirty years ago, are no longer available or are in short supply, such as Brazilian rosewood which is now banned as an import into the United States." Although Glenn prefers the sound of the old instruments, he says there are modern builders today who are reproducing the vintage sound and taking the art to a new level of excellence.

Sounds like Glenn really knows his business. Now we all know who to call the next time we pick up that old mandolin at an auction. You know the one you loved but passed up because it needed repairs.

23 HANNIBAL

Hannibal, Missouri, is synonymous with famous author and humorist Mark Twain. Twain's boyhood home, Hannibal, is the setting for the adventures of Tom Sawyer and Huck Finn. Near the riverfront is Twain's childhood home, restored to its exact mid-1800s appearance. The adjacent museum holds manuscripts and memorabilia, including one of his famous white suits. Nearby is the New Mark Twain Museum, featuring original Norman Rockwell paintings. Close by are Judge Clemens' law office, Becky Thatcher's House, and diorama and wax museums depicting Twain's famous characters.

Hannibal is full of interesting shops, and city tours take visitors into two impressive river mansions. The best way to see the sights is by river boat cruise or open-air tram, horse-drawn wagon or trolley. South of town, the Mark Twain Outdoor Theatre recreates some of his best-known works. Visitors can also explore the underground cave named for Twain, or visit the 18,600 acre Mark Twain Lake and the surrounding state park, where Twain's birthplace- - a two-room cabin- -is preserved.

Mrs. Clemens Antique Mall

305 N. Main Street
573/221-6427
Open daily Spring-Fall 9-5/Winter 9:30-4:30

Directions: Enter Hannibal on Route 79, 61, or 36. Mrs. Clemens Antique Mall is located 3 miles from I-72 in the Historic District, 1/2 block from the Mark Twain Home and Museum.

Mrs. Clemens Antique Mall has over 40 dealers displaying a large selection of dolls, advertising items, pottery, cut and pressed glass, period furniture and an electric train booth of 1950s and prior trains and accessories. Mrs. Clemens is also a franchised dealer of Anheuser-Busch collectibles and a member of the Anheuser Busch Collectors Club. When you need to take a break, you have at your fingertips an ice cream parlor and snack bar in the mall, with an old back board and marble top counters. Eight flavors of premium, hand-dipped ice cream, sodas and snacks are served at old ice cream tables with matching chairs.

Mark Twain Antiques
312 N. Main St.
573/221-2568

Smith's Treasure Chest LLC
315 S. 3rd St.
573/248-2955

24 HERMANN

Directions: Hermann is located between Hwy. 19 and Hwy. 100. If traveling I-70, Exit Hwy. 19, #175 and travel south for 14 miles to Hermann. If traveling west on I-44, Exit Hwy. 100, #251 (Washington exit) and travel west for 42 miles to Hermann. If traveling east on I-44, Exit Hwy. 19, #208 (Cuba exit) and travel north for 50 miles to Hermann. Hermann is 67 miles from St. Louis and 175 miles from Kansas City, and has daily Amtrak stops.

Hermann is a piece of the Old World in the middle of Missouri. The Germans who founded Hermann wanted a town that was "German in every particular." They carefully chose a site that reminded them of their beloved Rhine Valley and set about creating a city where German culture could flourish in the new world. Their vision was a grand one. Tucked away in the Ozark foothills, Hermann offers world-famous festivals, four thriving wineries, two historic districts, wonderful antique shops and delicious cuisine, served with a generous helping of Old World hospitality.

Great Places To Shop

Ace of Spades

112 E. First Street
573/486-3060

Garden art and handmade copper jewelry.

Antiques Unlimited
117 E. 2nd Street
573/486-2148

Large selection of refinished antique furniture, primitives and collectibles.

Burger Haus
Hwy. 19 and 13th Terrace
573/486-2828
Open daily

Furniture reproductions. Also handcrafted and painted items by local woodworker and artist, Os and Va.

Deutsche Schule Arts & Crafts
German School Building
573/486-3313
Open daily 10-5

Handmade crafts with 150 artisans from the area. Specializing in quilts. Many other items, including pottery.

Die Hermann Werks
214 E. 1st Street
573/486-2601
Open Mon.-Sat., 9-5, Sun. 11-4

Specializing in European giftware and Christmas ornaments.

J.H.P. Quilts and Antiques
101 Schiller Street
573/486-3069
Open Mon.-Sat. 10-4; Sun. 12-4

Specializing in country furniture, primitives, antique quilts, stoneware and accessories.

Jaeger Primitive Arms
415 E. 1st Street
573/486-2394
Open Mon.-Sat. 9:30-5:30; Sun. 11:30-5

Specializing in black powder guns.

Jewel Shop (Das Edelstein Geshaft)
230 E. 1st Street
573/486-2955
Open Tue.-Sat. 9-5

Fine jewelry.

Pottery Shop
108 Schiller Street
573/486-3552/3558

Handmade porcelain and stoneware by local potter. Special orders accepted for dinnerware, tiles, and mugs.

Rag Rug Factory
113 E. 5th Street
573/486-3735
Open daily or by chance/appointment

Rag rugs and other handwoven items.

Sweet Stuff & Shepardson's Antiques
210 Schiller Street
573/486-3903
Open Thurs.-Mon.

An eclectic blend of gourmet foods and coffees, antiques.

White House Hotel Museum & Antiques
232 Wharf Street
573/486-3200 or 573/486-3493
Open by chance or appointment

Antique collectibles, dolls.

Wilding's Antiques and Museums
523 W. 9th Street
573/486-5544

Country antiques. Museum houses permanent collection of Clem Wilding's wood carvings.

Wissmath Baskets
Rt. 1, Box 74
573/486-2090

Mail order or call for information. Specializing in handwoven baskets, deer antler baskets and 1-inch miniature baskets.

Wohlt House
415 E. First Street
573/486-2394
Open Mon.-Sat., 10-5

Antiques, locally handmade crafts, dried and fresh flower arrangements and wreaths.

Great Places To Stay

Drei Madel Haus
108 Shiller Street
573/486-3552 or 573/486-3558

1840s brick house in old town

Edelweiss B & B
800 18th Street
573/486-3184

Unique house with fabulous view.

Gatzmeyer Guest House
222 E. Second Street
573/486-2635 or 573/252-4380

Circa 1880s in Historic District

German Haus B & B
113 North Market
573/486-2222

Circa 1840s

Hermann Hill Vineyard & Inn
711 Wein Street
573/486-4455

Spectacular views and private balconies.

John Bohlken Inn
201 Schiller Street
573/486-3903

American country decor, homemade German pastries for breakfast.

Kolbe Guest House
214 Wharf Street
573/486-3453 or 573/486-2955

Circa 1850 with river view.

Market Street B & B
210 Market Street
573/486-5597

Turn of the century Victorian home.
Mary Elizabeth House
226 W. 6th Street
573/486-3281

1890s Victorian House

Meyer's Fourth Street B & B
128 E. Fourth Street
573/486-2917

Circa 1840s. Centrally located.

Mumbrauer Gasthaus
223 W. Second Street
573/486-5246

Circa 1885 in the heart of the Historic District.

Patty Kerr B & B
109 E. Third Street
573/486-2510

Circa 1840. Light breakfast. Outdoor tub.

Pelze Nichol Haus (Santa Haus)
Hwy. 100, 1.3 miles east of Missouri River bridge
573/486-3886

Primitive Christmas decor in 1851 Federalist brick home.

Reiff House B & B
306 Market Street
573/486-2994 or 1-800-482-2994

Circa 1871 in Historic District.

Schau-ins-Land
573/486-3425

Stone home that was once an 1889 winery.

White House Hotel B & B
232 Wharf Street
573/486-3200 or 573/486-3493

1868 historic hotel next to Missouri River with antique shop and ice cream parlor on premises.

Great Places To Eat

Buckler's Deli & Pizza
100 Schiller Street
573/486-1140 or 573/486-3514

See how the Bucklers turned an old bank into a unique deli.

Downtown Deli and Custard Shop
316 G; 1st Street
573/486-5002
Open daily until 10 p.m.

Featuring salads, sandwiches served on fresh baked breads and homemade pies. Hand-dipped and soft-serve ice cream.

Vintage 1847 Restaurant
Stone Hill Winery
573/486-3479
Open daily, lunch from 11 a.m.; dinner from 5 p.m.

Recommended by many food critics as one of America's finest restaurants. Casual dining in the original carriage house of the winery.

25 HERMITAGE

H. Bryan Western Collectables
Located at the corner of Spring Street and Hwy. 54
1-800-954-9911
Fax: 417/725-1572
Open daily 9-6

Directions: Hermitage is in southwest Missouri, and H. Bryan Western Collectables is on Hwy. 54 at the corner of Spring Street

"Real men shop at H. Bryan's Western Collectables," could be the motto at this Midwestern exchange. This home/shop combo was originally established during the 1940s as a watch repair/jewelry store. The present owners spent much of their formative years visiting the shop and learning the trade. It became a full-time profession when they purchased the business in 1995. Through the years, the shop has broadened its specialties to include the buying, selling and trading of vintage watches, collectible cigar lighters, Zippos, as well as antique and new knives for the collector or investor.

26 INDEPENDENCE

Woodstock Inn Bed & Breakfast
1212 West Lexington
816/833-2233
Open year round
Rates $54-99

Directions: From points north or the K.C. Airport: Take I-435 east (to St. Louis) to the 23rd Street Exit. Go left 2 1/2 miles to Crysler. Be in the left turn lane and go left 6 blocks. Crylser becomes Lexington and the Woodstock Inn is on the left at the end of the 6 blocks. From points west by way of I-70: Follow I-70 east through Kansas City to the I-435 North exit. Follow I-435 North to the first exit (23rd Street exit). Make a right turn and follow 23rd Street 2 miles to Crysler Street. After Crysler turns into Lexington, you will see a large auditorium on the right. The Inn is on the left. From Branson, Springfield and points southeast: Follow U.S. 30 North to I-70. Turn west on I-70 and follow it to Exit 12 or Noland Road. Turn right on Noland Road and follow it to 23rd Street (about 1.6 miles). Turn left on 23rd Street and go to Crysler Street (the first stop light). Turn right on Crysler. After about 7 blocks Crysler will turn into Lexington. After that, you will see a large auditorium on the right. The Inn is on the left.

For specific information, see review this section.

Country Meadows Antique Mall
4621 Shrank Drive
816/373-0410
Open: Mon.-Sat. 9-9, Sunday 9-6

Directions: From points North of K.C. Airport: South on I-435 to I-70 E. To Lee's Summit Rd. exit. South on Lee's Summit Rd. To 40 Hwy & East to Country Meadows Mall (3 blocks E. Of Lee's Summit Rd. on 40 Hwy). From points South of Grandview: Take 71 N. to I-470 (this becomes 291 N..). Exit at 40 Hwy. W. Country Meadows is approximately 1 mile W. of 291 on 40 Hwy. From points West, by way of I-70: Take Lee's Summit Rd. Exit S. to 40 Hwy E. Country Meadows is E. 3 blocks on 40 Hwy.

Country Meadows Antique Mall offers a stunning array of antiques and collectibles. This two-story mall is brimming with diverse treasures from the past and present. Antiques from over 400 dealers fill hundreds of booths and showcases at Country Meadows, where 40,000 square feet full of history will keep you shopping for hours. Stop in and enjoy lunch in the Tea Room, which is open daily. Convenient location, ample parking and friendly, knowledgeable staff will add to your shopping pleasure.

Sherman's Odds & Endtiques
109 W. Lexington Ave.
816/461-6336

Liberty House Antiques
111 N. Main St.
816/254-4494

Black Flag Antiques Inc.
118 S. Main St.
816/833-1134

Keeping Room
213 N. Main St.
816/833-1693

Classic Treasures
108 W. Maple Ave.
816/254-5050

Sermon-Aderson Inc.
210 W. Maple Ave.
816/252-9193

Sermon-Aderson Inc.
10815 E. Winner Rd.
816/252-9192

Adventure Antiques
11432 E. Truman Rd.
816/833-0303

Favorite Places To Eat

Cracker Barrel Old Country Store
I-70 & Lee's Summit Rd. Exit 14
816/373-3341

27 JAMESPORT

Founded in 1953 when the Amish first came to the area, Jamesport is the largest Amish community in Missouri. The town is home to numerous antique and crafts shops, including Amish stores that specialize in commodities particular to Amish needs. Other town attractions include the Harris Family Log Cabin, located in the city park. The cabin was built in 1836 by Jesse and Polly Harris, one of the first white couples to settle in the area. Great-grandsons Ray and Herb Harris, both in the their 70s now, reconstructed the cabin at its present site.

Great Places to Shop

Antiques Americana
One block north of 4-way stop next to library
816/684-5500 or 816/359-2408

Early American house contains antiques, collectibles, crafts, furniture, vintage clothing, primitives and gift items.

Balcony House Antiques
East of 4-way stop
816/684-6725
Open Mon.-Sat. year round, Sundays Apr. 1-Dec. 31.

Features a full line of quality antiques and collectibles: glassware, furniture, Indian artifacts, quilts, etc. In stock there are over 500 titles of reference books (with price guides) on antiques and collectibles.

The Barn Antiques & Crafts
826/684-6711

Large selection of antiques, collectibles, porcelain dolls, willow furniture, quilts, baskets, Christmas shop.

Broadway Pavilion Mall
South of 4-way stop
816/684-6655

Antiques, collectibles, furniture, glassware, pottery, jewelry, large selection of old books.

Carlyles & Pastime Antiques
East of 4-way stop
816/684-6222

Distinguished gifts, collectible items, antique furniture, home decorating ideas.

Colonial Rug and Broom Shoppe
2 1/2 blocks west of 4-way stop
1-800-647-5586
Open Sun. 8-6, summer and winter

See hand-woven rugs and brooms made daily. Purchase them already made or have them created to your own needs.

The Country Station
1 block east of 4-way stop
816/684-6454
Open Mon.-Sat. 10-4

Country furniture, needlework, dolls, doilies, antiques, collectibles and lots more.

Country Treasures
816/684-6338
Open Mon.-Wed. and Fri.-Sat., 10-4; closed Thurs. and Sun.

Baskets, old spools, Amish pictures, doilies, potpourris, candles, shelves, Amish made furniture, many items one of a kind.

Downtown Oak & Spice
816/684-6526
Open Mon.-Sat. 9-5

Woodcrafts, teas and spices, oak furniture, hand-dipped ice cream, baskets, Moser glass.

Ellis Antiques
Located at 4-way stop
816/684-6319
Open year round Mon.-Sat., 8-5: Sun. 1-4

Country furniture and accessories, glass, china, jewelry, etc.

Granny's Playhouse Antique Mall
East of 4-way stop
816/684-6599 or 816/359-3021

A unique selection of Jewel Tea, collectible jewelry, porcelain dolls, quilts, wall hangings, chimes, all in 33 booths.

Jamesport Antique Center
1 block east of 4-way stop
816/684-6171
Open all year

Furniture, glass, china, marbles, toys, advertising.

Iris Collectibles
Five blocks west of 4-way stop at corner of South and Elm
816/684-6626

Glassware, pottery, jewelry, and miscellaneous.

Leona's Amish Country Shop
816/684-6628
Open 7 days, 9-whenever

Dinner bells, Amish dolls and quilts, antiques and collectibles.

Marigolds
3 blocks west of downtown (The Orange House)
816/684-6122

Retail and wholesale. A house full of primitive country. Birdhouses, benches, mirrors, and lots of folk art.

Pastime Antiques I & II
816/684-6222

Antique furniture, finished and unfinished. Custom birdhouses, old fashion candies.

This-N-That
South Broadway
1 block north of 4-way stop
816/684-6594
Open Mon.-Sat. 9-5

Antique furniture, glassware, jewelry and collectibles.

Warren House Antiques
East of 4-way stop
816/684-6266
Open daily 10-5

Antique Mall, 27 booths, antiques and collectibles - dishes, furniture, tools, primitives and more.

Great Places To Stay

Country Colonial Bed & Breakfast
816/684-6711 or 1-800-579-9248

Originally built in the 1800s, this house has been restored to an era past with a veranda and three bedrooms, each with a private bath. Since the B&B is centrally located near the shops, you can spend your day shopping, and at night, relax by playing parlor games, reading one of the 500 antique books in the library, or playing the baby grand piano. In the morning awake to a full country breakfast.

Marigold's Inn
Located 3 blocks west of downtown next to Marigold's Shoppe
816/684-6122

Opening Spring of 1997. Twelve rooms, each individually decorated in folk art themes.

Oak Tree Inn Bed & Breakfast
4 miles on Hwy. "F" east of Jamesport
816/684-6250

Relax in an original 3-story Amish-built home set in a wondrous 20 acre grove of tall majestic oak trees.

Richardson House Bed & Breakfast
Northeast of 4-way stop
816/444-4355

At the end of a quiet lane, this turn of the century house on North Street will provide you with the perfect base for experiencing life in a simpler era. You will enjoy the complete privacy and exclusive use of this cozy, antique filled home which sleeps up to eight people. Hearty country breakfast is included.

Great Places To Eat

Anna's Bake Shop
Route 1, Box 34A, west end of town (Amish owned)
Open Mon.-Sat. 8-6, Closed Sun., closed from Christmas until Feb.

Fresh baked donuts, pies, breads, cinnamon and dinner rolls, cakes and much more.

Country Bakery
Located 1/2 mile south of Jamesport on Hwy. 190, Route 2, Box 177B
Closed Thursdays and Sundays (Amish owned)

Large selection of home-made baked goods.

Missouri

Gingerich Dutch Pantry and Bakery
Located at 4-way stop
Open Mon.-Sat. 6-9
816/684-6212

(Mennonites owned) Specializing in Amish style meals, homemade pies and baked goods, made fresh daily. Tasty sandwiches to home cooked dinner specials.

28 JEFFERSON CITY

Old Munichberg Antique Mall
710 Jefferson St.
573/659-8494

Twin Maples Collections
1125 Jefferson St.
573/636-2567

29 JOPLIN

Southside Antique Mall
2914 E. 32nd St.
417/623-1000

Uniform Shoppe
1052 S. Main St.
417/624-6650

Connie's Antiques & Cllbls.
3421 N. Range Line Rd.
417/781-2602

Country Heart Village
4901 S. Range Line Rd.
417/781-2468

Gingerbread House
RR 7
417/623-6690

Favorite Places To Eat

Cracker Barrel Old Country Store
I-44 & Hwy. 71, Exit 8A
417/782-9696

30 KANSAS CITY

Bellas Hess Antique Mall
715 Armour Rd.
816/474-4790

Belle Chelsea Antiques
4444 Bell St.
816/561-1056

Estate Pine Gallery
4448 Bell St.
816/931-6661

Olde Theatre Archl Salvage Co.
2045 Broadway St.
816/283-3740

Cummings Corner Antiques
1703 W. 45th Street
816/753-5353

River Market Antique Mall
115 W. 5th St.
816/221-0220

Molly & Otis O'Conner
1707 W. 45th St.
816/561-6838

Portobello Rd. & Camel Antqs.
1708 W. 45th St.
816/931-2280

Lloyd's Antiques
1711 W. 45th St.
816/931-7922

Elizabeth Gibbs
1714 W. 45th St.
816/561-7355

Joseph's Antiques
1714 W. 45th St.
816/756-5553

Parrin & Co.
1717 W. 45th St.
816/753-7959

Christopher Filley Antiques
1721 W. 45th St.
816/561-1124

Morning Glory Antiques
1807 W. 45th St.
816/756-0117

European Express
1812 W. 45th St.
816/753-0443

Anderson's Antiques
1813 W. 45th St.
816/531-1155

Brown's Emporium
1263 N. 47 St.
816/356-0040

Jewelry Box Antiques
2450 Grand Blvd
816/472-1760

Mom's Ole Stuff
10939 Hillcrest Rd.
816/765-6561

Asiatica Ltd.
4824 Rainbow Blvd
816/831-0831

J J McKee Antiquities
222 W. 7th St.
816/361-8719

Waldo Antiques & Imports
226 W. 75th St.
816/333-8233

Chabineaux's
334 W. 75th St.
816/361-1300

Waldo Galleria
334 W. 75th St.
816/361-2544

Waldo Galleria Antique Annex
336 W. 75th St.
816/361-2396

Remember When Antiques
349 NW 69 Hwy
816/455-1815

Old World Antiques Ltd.
1715 Summit St.
816/472-0815

Poor Richard's Antiques Object
401 E. 31st St.
816/531-4550

Boomerang
1415 W. 39th St.
816/531-6111

Darlene's Antiques & Cllbls.
5502 Troost Ave.
816/361-9901

Town Gallery
3522 N.E. Vivion Rd.
816/454-3570

Superlatives
320 Ward Pkwy.
816/561-7610

Twentieth Century Consortium
1004 Westport Rd.
816/931-0986

Smith & Burstert
1612 Westport Rd.
816/531-4772

Meirhoff's Antq. Stained Glass
210 Wyandotte St.
816/421-4912

River Market Antique Mall
115 W. 5th St.
816/221-0220

Sebree Galleries & Le Picnique
301 E. 55th St.
816/333-3387

31 KENNETT

Bank of Antiques & Special Finds
201 First Street
573/888-4663
Open: Mon.-Sat. 10-5, usually open til 8 on Thurs.

Directions: 17 miles from I-55 (Hayti exit) in downtown Kennett.

Bank of Antiques & Special Finds, gets its name from its former life as a bank in downtown Kennett, MO. Built in 1916, this historical establishment houses a fine selection of glassware, dolls, furniture, jewelry, some collectibles, and more. Within the bookstore located in the shop, you can browse for your favorite old title and enjoy a delicious box lunch and a cup of gourmet coffee.

The Treasure Chest
211 First Street
573/888-6772

32 KIRKSVILLE

Poor Richard's Gifts & Cllbls.
713 S. Baltimore St.
816/627-4438

Good Ole Days Antqs. & Cllbls.
1515 S. Baltimore St.
816/665-3540

Square Deal Antique Mall
Hwy. 63 Rt. 2
816/665-1686

Wood Rail Antique Mall
Hwy. 63 S
816/665-1555

Potpourri Antiques
106 W. Harrison St.
816/665-8397

33 LEBANON

Treasure Trove Antiques
1231 W. Elm St.
417/532-6945

Pleasant Memories Antq. Mall
25999 Hwy. 5
417/588-3411

Jefferson House Antiques
364 N. Jefferson Ave.
417/532-6933

Jennissa Antiques & Gifts
577 N. Jefferson Ave.
417/588-1029

Country Corner Antique Mall
585 N. Jefferson Ave.
417/588-1430

34 LEES SUMMIT

American Heritage Antq. Mall
220 S.E. Douglas St.
816/524-8427

Annie Sue's Antiques
302 S.W. Main St.
816/246-8082

Sandy's Mall
101 S.W. Market St.
816/525-9844

Exclusively M. Gifts & More
200 S.W. Market St.
816/525-5747

35 LEXINGTON

The Velvet Pumpkin
827 Main St.
816/259-4545

Victorian Peddler
900 Main St.
816/259-4533

Redgoose Antiques
914 Main St.
816/259-2421

36 LIBERTY

Liberty Square Antiques
2 E. Franklin St.
816/781-7191

Liberty Antique Mall
Town Square-1 E. Kansas
816/781-2796

Kansas Street Antiques
10 W. Kansas Ave.
816/781-1059

Liberty Antique Mall
1005 N. State Route 291
816/781-3190

Anna Marie's Antiques Gift
118 N. Water St.
816/792-8777

Sandy's Antiques Ltd.
131 S. Water St.
816/781-3100

Favorite Places To Eat

Cracker Barrel Old Country Store
I-35 & State Rt. 152, Exit 16
816/781-1444

37 MACON

The Weathervane
32429 Juniper Place
816/385-2941

Ednamay's Antiques
203 Jackson St.
816/385-3021

Ugly Duckling Antiques
1144 Jackson-Hwy. 63 N
816/385-6183

Colonel's Flea Market
312 S. Missouri Hwy. 63
816/385-2497

Carousel Antiques
127 Vine St.
816/385-4284

Antique Parlor & Coffee Bar
132 Vine St.
816/385-1168

38 MANSFIELD

Laura Ingalls Wilder, the greatly loved and internationally known authoress of the beloved "Little House" books, lived most of her life in Mansfield, Missouri. It is here at Rocky Ridge Farm that she wrote all nine of her famous books about her pioneer childhood and later life in Missouri. Her writing desk still stands in the home that Almanzo built for her. The home is on the National Register of Historic Places and is surrounded by apple, walnut and dogwood trees, many of which Laura planted.

Each year the residents of Mansfield relive the times of Laura Ingalls Wilder with their fall festival. There are costume and beard contests, a kiddie parade, a big parade, an arts and crafts fair, games for the children, surprises, entertainment from the bandstand, lots of good food, and gingerbread made from Laura's recipe. And of course, there are continuous tours all day through the Laura Ingalls Wilder Home and Museum. Call the Friendship House B&B for dates.

Friendship House Bed & Breakfast and Antique Boutique
210 West Commercial
417/924-8511
Open year around

Directions: For specific directions from your location, please call the Innkeepers.

Friendship House is the charming rock home where *Little House* author Laura Ingalls Wilder celebrated birthdays and other special occasions with her close friend, Neta Seals.

Built in 1939, by Mr. and Mrs. Seals, the 16-room home was planned as a rooming house advertising "Modern Rooms." Lovingly preserved by its present owners, the tree-shrouded brownstone wears the soft patina of age and bespeaks the tranquility of days past.

Friendship House is ideally located, one half block from the Mansfield Town Square, and is a five minute drive from the Laura Ingalls Wilder Home and Museum.

Yours hosts, Sharon and Charlie Davis, offer visitors old-fashioned hospitality and comfortable ambience. Guests may relax with a refreshing iced drink on the charming sun porch or head straight for the swimming pool. Tall fences, stately trees, and a landscaped patio envelop this lush backyard hideaway in peace and privacy.

The living room, with its lace-covered windows and rich blend of antiques and period reproductions, is an inviting place of repose. Breakfast is served in the adjoining formal dining room, where Laura and Neta gathered with their husbands and friends to share meals and celebrations.

Upstairs, visitors are transported in time to the boarding house days of the 1930s. Cozy sleeping rooms open onto the airy central hall. Its restful decor and gleaming woodwork are a welcome change from the sterility of modern day motels. Each room is individually decorated and has its original porcelain sink. A full bath and water closet are shared by the guests.

39 MARIONVILLE

Beautiful Victorian homes and a rare, urban white squirrel population are the hallmarks of Marionville, Missouri. According to town legend, around 1854 a circus came to town and brought rare white squirrels with them (were they part of an act?). When the circus left, their squirrels didn't! Now there are thousands of them. They don't cross the highway; they don't run off to the woods - they like living right in the middle of town!

White Squirrel Hollow Bed & Breakfast
203 Mill Street
417/463-7626
Open 24 hours a day, 7 days a week

Directions: White Squirrel Hollow B&B is located in Marionville at Mill Street and ZZ Hwy., west of U.S. Hwy. 60.

Step back in time when you visit the White Squirrel Hollow Bed and Breakfast. It's a historical, romantic Victorian home built in 1896 by one of the Ozarks first famous families, and it's filled with original antique photos, prints and furnishings. It's also a theme B & B, so its 5,000 square feet are filled with six different atmospheres decorated in antique, purist decor. Guests can choose from the Victorian Honeymoon suite with a full lace canopy bed and private screened balcony; the Gold Coast Room reminiscent of the 1849 California Gold Rush days; the Elizabethan Room, fit for royalty with it's flocked wall paper, satin canopy-covered bed, mink spread and English antiques; Turkish Corners, with a tented canopy bed, fabulous view and exotic touches; the Wild, Wild West Room, with an atmosphere from the days of western adventure; and a cottage that offers a night on African safari. The main house also boasts inlaid hardwood floors, beaded woodwork, a spiral staircase and doorway spandrels that are all original and lavish. The large music room was once a conservatoire, but now houses an antique baby grand and a 600-piece antique book collection. And of course there are the rare white squirrels rambling all across the property for your pleasure!

Ole Mill Around
Hwy. 60
417/463-7423

Kountry Korner Antqs. & Unqs.
Hwy. 60 & 265
417/463-2923

40 MOBERLY

Reed Street Antiques
303 W. Reed St.
816/263-7878

Jim's Country Barn Antiques
RR 4
816/263-6714

Moberly Plating & Antiques
512 W. Rollins St.
816/263-5371

Kierstle Haus Antiques
Route 1 Box 56
816/263-7828

41 MONETT

V. B. Hall Antiques
201 West Main Street
417/235-1110
Open daily Mon.-Sat. 9:30-5, Sunday 1-5

Directions: From intersection of Highways 60 and 37 in Monett, turn North on 37, 2 blocks turn right, one block - you're there!

The name V.B. Hall Antiques is very well known to the folks of Monett. Four generations of V. B.s have participated in the business community of this Missouri town, with V.B. Sr. even serving as town mayor for a term or two. The store, with 70 to 75 dealers in about 12,000 square feet of space, carries a large variety of items, from primitives to pottery, to glassware and a mixture of furnishings covering several periods and styles. The building itself is vintage 1947, beginning its life as a wholesale produce store.

Banks Antiques
103 N. Lincoln Ave.
417/235-6387

42 MONROE CITY

Downtown Antique Mall
208 S. Main St.
573/735-4522

Downtown Antique Mall
Business 36
573/735-3156

Country Mini Mall
Hwy. 24 & 36
573/735-4935

Over The Hill Antique Mall
101 S. Main St.
573/735-4966

43 NEOSHO

Neosho Gallery & Flea Market
900 N. College St.
417/451-4675

Four Seasons
322 S. Neosho Blvd
417/451-3839

44 NEVADA

Crossroads 71/54 Antq. Mall
1617 E. Ashland St.
417/667-7775

Louise Fanning Antiques
1231 E. Austin Blvd.
417/667-5903
Congratulations to Ms. Fanning on her 40th year in the antique business!

45 OSAGE BEACH

Osage Beach Flea Market
Hwy. 42 & 54
573/348-5454

Land of Yesteryear
Hwy. 54
573/348-3855

Osage River Co Store
Hwy. 54
573/348-0819

46 OZARK

Most of the thousands of antiquers who come to Ozark, Missouri every summer are, as one antique shop owner puts it, "just coming in to browse, but some people are on a mission." Another says that Ozark is known as *"the antique place to come,"* and that most of the visitors hit every store. There's plenty of stores to be found in Ozark, scattered throughout the city, but most are prominently collected at two sites: Missouri 14 and U.S. 65, and the Riverview Plaza locations on Missouri 14 northeast of the U.S. 65 intersections. Collectively all these stores contribute significantly to the city's tax revenues and tourism industry. Although the antique shops are not Ozark's only draw, they are important to the city's economy - so much so that the Ozark Chamber of Commerce promotes the shops on billboards and in tourist information mailings. Of course it doesn't hurt that Ozark is on the way to Branson, and picks up a great deal of traffic from that destination. From old dolls and battered school desks to yellowed newspaper front pages and expensive jewelry, any item you are looking for is likely to be somewhere among the booths of old stuff brought in from all over the country.

Antique Emporium
1702 West Boat Street
Located at 65 & CC (behind Lambert's Cafe)
417/581-5555
Open summer: Mon.-Sat. 9-9; winter; Mon.-Thurs. and Sat. 9-6, Fri. 9-9, Sun. 9-5

Directions: From I-44 exit 65 South. Antique Emporium is located approximately 9 miles south of I-44 on U.S. 65 on route to Branson, 9 miles south of Springfield.

All antiques and no crafts are what you'll find among the 100 dealers in the 12,000-square-foot mall of Antique Emporium. They don't carry a lot of bigger furniture, mostly small period pieces, but shoppers will find a great deal of glass, primitives and collectibles, including Roseville, Fiesta, Candlewick, Fenton, Heisey, china, and ladies artifacts. In addition you'll find clocks, quilts, gas pumps, railroad items, advertising, antique hunting and fishing items and western collectibles.

Ozark Antique Mall and Collectibles
200 S. 20th Street
417/581-5233
Fax: 417/581-5233 (Call first to have us plug in fax)
Open summer 9-6; winter 9-5, daily

Directions: At U.S. 65 and Hwy. 14 in Ozark, turn west and take the first left, which is 20th Street. Look for Ozark Antique Mall on the right-hand side - it's the building with all the great old advertising signs and antiques out front in the southwest corner of Highways 65 and 14.

The emporium is also home to an authentic Ozarks still. Sorry, the revenuers won't let them run it, but it is an interesting piece of American history you don't want to miss.

For specific information, see review this section.

Finley River Heirlooms, Inc.
105 North 20th Street
417/581-3253

Maine Streete Mall
1994 Evangel Street
417/581-2575

Pine Merchant Antiques
140 N. 20th Street
417/581-7333

Riverview Antique Center, Inc.
909 W. Jackson
417/581-4426

Scott's-Beckers' Hardware, Inc.
1411 S. 3rd Street
417/581-6525; 1-800-991-0151

47 PERRY

Huffman Trading Post
Hwy 19
573/565-3275

Price Emporium
113 W. Main St.
573/565-3159

Packrats Unlimited
124 E. Main St.
573/565-3594

Country Store Antiques
1007 E. Main St.
573/565-2822

Lick Creek Antiques
Main St.
573/565-3422

Miss Daisy's Antique Shop
Main St.
573/565-2737

Elam Antique Shoppe
110 S. Palmyra St.
573/565-2206

Arlington Antiques
Palmyra St.
573/565-2624

Perry Main Street Antiques
S. Palmyra
573/565-3246

48 PLATTE CITY

I-29 Antique Mall
Junction I-29 & H. H. Hwy.
816/858-2921
Open: Daily 10-6

I-29 Antique Mall is located in historic Platte City, Missouri just 30 minutes north of downtown Kansas City on Interstate 29. The Platte City area features some of the best antique shopping in the Midwest, with three large malls offering a wide range of quality furniture, glassware, advertising items and much more. A favorite stop for dealers and collectors from across the country, I-29 Antique Mall is just 6 miles north of K.C. International Airport, with abundant food and lodging close by. Visit the Platte City area and see some of the best antiquing Missouri has to offer!

W D Pickers Antique Mall
Exit 20 I-29
816/858-3100

Wellsbrooke Antiques
500 Main St.
816/858-5306

49 PLEASANT HILL

Cookie Jars & More
113 S. 1st St.
816/987-5244

First Street Antiques
121 S. 1st St.
816/987-5432

Sentimental Journey Antiques
100 Wyoming St.
816/987-3661

Downtown Antiques
115 Wyoming St.
816/987-5505

50 ROCHEPORT

Griffith's Antiques
405 Clark
573/698-3503

Richard Saunder's Antiques
Columbia & 2nd St.
573/698-3765

Missouri River Antqs. & Books
12851 W. High
573/698-2080

Whitehorse Antiques
12855 W. High
573/698-2088

Farm Road Antiques
370 N. Roby Farm Rd.
573/698-2206

River City Antique Mall
420 N. Roby Farm Rd.
573/698-2116

Henderson's Antiques
451 N. Roby Farm Rd.
573/698-4485

Widow Lister Antiques
405 2nd St.
573/698-2701

51 ROLLA

Antique Corner
606 Lanning Lane
573/368-5579

Mary's Antiques
13458 S. U.S. 63
573/364-5372

Totem Pole Trading Post
1413 Martin Spring Dr
573/364-3519

Hancock's Used Furniture
102 S. Rucker Ave.
573/364-2665

52 ROSEBUD

The Wild Rose Bed & Breakfast
Route 1, off Idel Road
573/764-2849
Rates $55-65

Directions: The Wild Rose is located off of Idel Road, the first mailbox on the left 1/4 mile east of Rosebud. Rosebud is just one hour west of St. Louis off I-44 on Hwy. 50.

The Wild Rose is a restored farmhouse filled with art and antiques, set on 25 beautifully landscaped acres just outside of Rosebud. The well-stocked lake is surrounded by pines and stately pin oaks, with trails winding through the woods and meadows. There are boats and fishing gear for the fishermen in the group (no license required), while anyone wanting to just unwind and commune with nature can sit by the peaceful Koi and goldfish pond near the house.

The library offers the beauty of stained glass windows, a fireplace and a collection of masks, with an additional fireplace in the cathedral-ceiling living room. Each bedroom has its own unique personality. The Victorian Rose is dominated by a high backed Victorian bed and rose-covered walls. The Rambling Rose combines wicker furniture and whimsical art work, dashed with tropical blues and pastels, plants and seashells. The English Rose has a wonderful 19th century English brass bed and antique camp table with two large wing chairs.

Apple Antiques
Hwy. 50
573/764-3148
Open Thurs.-Mon. 9:30-5, closed Tue.-Wed.

Directions: Apple Antiques is located 50 miles east of Jefferson City on Hwy. 50. From St. Louis, take I-44 west to the Union, Mo. exit, which is Hwy. 50.

Owner Edna Weatherford handles glassware, furniture and collectibles in her store, and tells a very interesting story about the shop's name, Apple Antiques. "The name of my antique shop is very unique, indeed. The customers usually tend to believe 'Apple' is my last name. Actually, it has nothing to do with my name. The last year I taught school, my students made a project of naming my shop. They came up with 'Apple Antiques' - an apple for the teacher, find the apple of your eye, etc. The parts of the apple are all divisions within the shop: the seed - beginning of goodness; the core - innermost and loved; the fruit - no serpents allowed; the peel - delicious value inside; the stem - attached and treasured; and last but not least; the apple orchard - ripe with age.

"There are apples everywhere you look, even on a shoplifting sign, the last line of which says, 'But Eve paid dearly when she stole an apple!' The name 'Apple Antiques,' has proven to be very...fruitful!"

Dinner Bell Antiques

Hwy. 50
573/764-3090
Open Mon.-Sat. 9:30-5, closed Sundays

Directions: Dinner Bell Antiques faces Hwy. 50 in Rosebud, halfway between St. Louis and Jefferson City.

Dinner Bell Antiques is nestled in a turn-of-the-century building full of antiques, collectibles, old tools, primitives, furniture, glassware and architectural antiques. According to owner Karen Jose, her store was the third building constructed in Rosebud when the railroad came through in 1900. In the past 96 years, the store has housed everything from shoe stores and farm implement stores to a drug store, a grocery, a barber shop, even the town post office.

Quilts By Shirley

249 Hwy. 50 (located at Shirley's House of Beauty)
573/764-2422

Shirley Rice, owner of Quilts By Shirley, is a true artisan, one of a dwindling group of women who still quilt by hand. She began quilting as a little girl, taught by her mother, and they quilted together for years. Shirley didn't really begin quilting part-time until about thirteen years ago, when she lost one of her little girls and went back to quilting as a means of therapy. She is a full-time hairdresser, so she quilts nights, weekends—anytime she has a few spare moments.

Shirley makes all of the tops for her quilts, table runners, baby quilts, Christmas tree skirts and wall hangings herself, and she has a couple of ladies who help her with the actual quilting. She can make most tops in a day's time, she says, but the quilting may take as long as two or three months. Her personal favorite pattern is the Wedding Ring, but she makes them all: Lover's Knot, Lone Star, Dresden Plate, Log Cabin. If customers who come to her shop don't see exactly what they want, Shirley will custom make anything to the exact size and color.

Her husband has gotten into the quilting business with her by making a special quilting frame that is much easier to handle, set up, use and store than the traditional giant frame. Mr. Rice's frame is made from square metal tubing and the frame is 10 feet long but only three feet wide; its special feature is a rolling florescent light that rolls along the edge of the frame, providing shadow-free lighting along the entire frame.

The Bluebird Bed & Breakfast

5734 Mill Rock Road
573/627-2515
Open all day, seven days a week

Directions: From State Hwy. 50 which runs through Gerald, go south on Route H, eight miles to the Bourbouse River. Go two miles across the river to Mill Rock Road. Turn left onto Mill Rock and the Bluebird is the first drive on the right; approximately 2/10 of a mile. Complete directions are provided with reservations.

The Bluebird Bed & Breakfast offers a peaceful English Country setting for city-dwellers in need of a little R & R.

Restful views, the chirping of birds, beautiful trees, flowering gardens and a well-stocked fishing pond provide the perfect escape.

There are four guest rooms, all comfortably appointed, each with its own unique theme. An old fashioned screened porch is ideal for bird watching, fish jumping, or simply cat-napping.

As is customary, continental and full breakfasts are served; gourmet dinners are available with 48 hours notice.

Only minutes from local flea markets, antique shops, caverns, and wine country, the Bluebird Bed & Breakfast can provide an effective reprise from an otherwise hectic world.

River House Bed & Breakfast

5339 Mill Rock Road
573/764-5262
Fax: 573/764-7262

Directions: From Hwy. 50 take Hwy. "H' from Gerald. Go 8 miles and cross the Bourbeuse River. Continue for 2 miles to Mill Rock Road, turn left, River House is 1.7 miles further down.

This bed and breakfast is appropriately named for the Bourbeuse River that flows through the property, with the bedroom window and side deck overlooking the river. The cottage includes a kitchen, full bath, living and dining areas, and bathroom, all completely furnished in antiques, Americana and accessories. The old Franklin wood stove can even be used. A very private, self-contained cozy getaway. Breakfast is served upon request.

53 SALEM

Bargain Barn
506 E. Center St.
573/729-7354

Antiques & Things
806 E. Center St.
573/729-4062

Gunny Sack
300 E. 4th St.
573/729-8797

Nina's Antique & Flea Market
Hwy 72 N
573/729-2958

Gateway Antiques
900B S. Main
573/729-7766

54 SEDALIA

Country Village Mall
4005 S. Limit Ave.
816/827-2877

Johns Used Furniture & Things
4011 S. Limit Ave.
816/826-7801

Millie's Pink Mall
Hwy. 65-5915 Limit
816/826-5894

Mapleleaf Antique Mall
106 W. Main St.
816/826-8383

Downtown Antiques
516 S. Ohio Ave.
816/826-2266

Sedalia Antique Shop
804 W. 16th St.
816/826-1472

55 SPRINGFIELD

Park Central Flea Market

429 Boonville
417/831-7516
Open daily Mon.-Sat. 10-5, Sun. 12-5

Directions: Traveling I-44 from the west, turn east on Chestnut Expressway, or traveling I-44 from the east, turn south on Glenstone and west on Chestnut Expressway, or exit Hwy. 65, and turn west on Chestnut Expressway. Take Chestnut Expressway to Boonville and turn south to 429 Boonville.

Having been in business for more than 20 years, Park Central Flea Market has lots of antiques and collectibles stashed in its two-story shop. They carry antique glassware, carnival glass, pottery, graniteware, pictures, primitives, toys and lamps.

Aesthetic Concerns Ltd.
326 N. Boonville Ave.
417/864-4177

Country Corner Flea Market
351 Boonville
417/862-1597

Treasure Chest
411 N. Boonville Ave.
417/863-1047

Centerfield Sportscards
427 Boonville
417/831-7675

Downtown Furn. Restoration
419 Boonville
417/865-3230

Fort No 5
425 N. Boonville Ave. #5
417/865-9966

By-Pass Antiques
535 B N West Bypass
417/865-4992

Bass Country Antique Mall
1832 S. Campbell Ave.
417/869-8255

Antique Warehouse & Mall
2139 S. Campbell Ave.
417/886-9776

Auction Barn
1435 W. College St.
417/831-2734

Another Man's Treasure
1700 W. College St.
417/864-2811

Nellie Dunn's Antiques
211 E. Commercial St.
417/864-6822

G & W Antiques & Collectibles
400 W. Commercial St.
417/869-0061

Great Discoveries
416 W. Commerical St.
417/869-9101

Century Galleries
1355 E. Commercial St.
417/869-4137

Mary II Antiques & Gifts
3747 S. Cox Rd.
417/888-3099

Antique Place
1720A S. Glenstone Ave.
417/887-3800

A Second Time Around Shoppe
1736 N. Glenstone Ave.
417/831-1666

Cottage & Provence
2744 S. Glenstone Ave.
417/887-1930

STD East Flea Market
651 S. Kansas
417/831-6331

Andrew's Collectibles
435 W. Kearney St.
417/831-3577

Coach House Antique Mall
2051 E. Kearney St.
417/869-8008

Touche Designs Inc.
2009 S. National Ave.
417/883-8633

Apple Barrel Antiques
2104 N. National Ave.
417/862-4635

Furniture Stripping Ozarks
1263 E. Republic Rd.
417/883-8313

Viles Swap Shop
3023 E. Republic St.
417/881-4042

Jerry's Antique Mall
309 South Ave.
417/862-4723

South Peer Antique Mall
317 South Ave.
417/831-6558

Knight's Stamps
323 South Ave.
417/862-3018

Springfield Antique Co.
406 South Ave.
417/866-6995

Sunshine Antiques
1342 W. Sunshine St.
417/864-0069

Anastasia & Co.
1700 E. Sunshine St.
417/890-1714

STD East Flea Market
1820 E. Trafficway
417/831-6367

History Antiques
1111 E. Walnut St.
417/864-8147

Collections
1112 E. Walnut
417/865-0552

Favorite Places To Eat

Cracker Barrel Old Country Store
I-44 & Glenstone Ave., Exit 80A
417/831-4600

56 ST. CHARLES

Saint Charles Antique Mall
1 Charlestowne Plaza
314/939-4178

Log House Antiques
2431 W. Clay St.
314/724-1889

Fifth Street Antique Mall
520 S. 5th St.
314/940-1862

Upstairs Market
837 1st Capitol
314/949-9271

Royal Antiques
101 N. Main St.
314/947-0537

Antiques & Oak
319 N. Main St.
314/946-1898

Aladdin's Lamp & Collectibles
321 S. Main St.
314/946-8865

Hobbitts Hole Antiques
323 N. Main St.
314/947-6227

Kuhlmann's Antique Empor.
324 N. Main St.
314/946-7333

Gina's at the Witt House
426 S. Main St.
314/946-6106

Mirabilia Gallery
524 S. Main St.
314/947-9077

Memories of Yesteryear
806 N. 2nd St.
314/724-2163

Mamie Maples Emporium
825 N. 2nd St.
314/947-0801

French Connection Antiques
826 N. 2nd St.
314/947-7044

Lauree's Vintage Jewelry
827 N. 2nd St.
314/940-1711

Bo's Primitive Peddler
901 N. 2nd St.
314/724-9366

Charlestowne Antiques
903 N. 2nd St.
314/946-7134

Little Hills Antiques
1125 N. 2nd St.
314/947-1770

Pioneer Antiques
1410 N. 2nd St.
314/724-1539

Wartimes Memorabilia
1501 N. 2nd St.
314/949-9929

Rachel's Antiques
1601 N. 2nd St.
314/925-1023

McKinley Antique Mall
1701 N. 2nd St.
314/946-8186

Favorite Places To Eat

Cracker Barrel Old Country Store
I-70 & Fifth St., Exit 229
314/947-6566

57 ST. JAMES

Kracker Barrell Antiques
108 N. Jefferson St.
573/265-3546

Forest City Popcorn Co.
124 N. Jefferson St.
573/265-3383

Old Mill Store
RR 2
573/699-4423

Heirlooms Past & Present
107 W. Springfield St.
573/265-7938

Treasure Nook
132 W. Washington St.
573/265-7416

58 ST. JOSEPH

No matter where you're bound, St. Joseph is the way to real adventure. Saddle up to glory at the Pony Express National Memorial, where "young, skinny, wiry fellows" like Buffalo Bill Cody and Johnny Fry started their 10-day relay dash to California with the mail. Follow the footsteps of 50,000 '49ers, who left here in the gold rush to "pick up a fortune." Walk in the front door of the house where Jesse James' infamous life came to an end and onto the recreated streets of ol' St. Jo at the Patee House Museum.

St. Jo isn't all rough and ready, though. Turn-of-the-century mansions are open for you to tour and even have high tea. Admire the works of the masters at the Albrecht-Kemper Museum of Art, and discover the secret gardens and stone bridges of the 26 miles of greenway linking the parks. Hunt through a nearly endless supply of beautiful antiques, and shop to your heart's content.

Located on the scenic river bluffs overlooking the Missouri River, born of the fur trade, nurtured by the "Westward Expansion," and brimming with a spirit of adventure, St. Joseph is a city you will never forget.

Somersby Antiques
501 N. Belt Hwy.
816/390-8864

Creverling's
1125 Charles St.
816/232-9298

Horns Antique Emporium
502 Felix St.
816/364-3717

Hatfield's Antique Mall
2028 Frederick Ave.
816/233-9106

Jerry's Antiques
2512 Frederick Ave.
816/232-9881

Coin-Jewelry-Antq. Exchange
3837 Frederick Ave.
816/232-8838

Dakon's Antiques
1801 Garfield Ave.
816/233-2971

Den of Antiquity
1919 Holman St.
816/279-0942

Penn Street Square
1122 Penn St.
816/232-4626

Corner Shoppe
1503 Penn St.
816/232-0045

Arnolds Antiques
644 S. 6th St.
816/233-4416

A & E Company
1213 S. 22nd St.
816/279-6206

Country House Antiques & Crafts
1801 N. Woodbine Rd.
816/232-4455

Favorite Places To Eat

Cracker Barrel Old Country Store
I-29 & Frederick Blvd., Exit 47
816/279-5191

59 ST. LOUIS

Cherokee Antique Row
2014 Cherokee Street
314/664-7916 or 314/773-8810
Open daily 11-4

Directions: Take I-55 to Arsenal Street (near the Anheuser-Busch Brewery), turn south on Lemp, go 4 blocks and turn west on Cherokee Street.

Here's your chance to shop from dawn till dusk in one spot! At Cherokee Antique Row you can visit 40 unique shops that sell many different varieties of items in a *four-block area.* Don't miss it!

Dapple-Gray Antiques
159 W. Argonne Dr.
314/965-0239

Stock Exchange Consign. Shop
2115 S. Big Bend Blvd.
314/645-3025

John's Furn & Antiques
7107 S. Broadway
314/351-6745

Phillips Antiques
8473 N. Broadway
314/867-0965

White Swan Antiques
7006 Bruno Ave.
314/781-7114

English Garden Antiques
1906 Cherokee St.
314/771-5121

Looking Glass
1915 Cherokee St.
314/773-1912

Panorama Antiques & Cllbls.
1925 Cherokee St.
314/772-8007

Neon Lady
1926 Cherokee St.
314/771-7506

Hammonds Books
1939 Cherokee St.
314/776-4737

Riverside Architectural Antqs.
1947 Cherokee St.
314/772-9177

Lealee Antiques
1950 Cherokee St.
314/772-9030

Remember When Antiques
1955 Cherokee St.
314/771-1711

My Friends Closet
2851 Cherokee St.
314/664-3993

Hartmann's Treasures
1960 Cherokee St.
314/773-5039

Purple Cow
2018 Cherokee St.
314/771-9400

Henderson Co.
2020 Cherokee St.
314/773-1021

Haffners Antiques
2100 Cherokee St.
314/772-6371

Odd Shop
2101 Cherokee St.
314/773-8566

TFA-Things From The Attic
2110 Cherokee St.
314/865-1552

Glass Turtle
2112 Cherokee St.
314/771-6779

Southside Antiques
2114 Cherokee St.
314/773-4242

Nostalgia Shop
2118 Cherokee St.
314/773-4907

Homemaker Antiques
2124 Cherokee St.
314/776-4267

Victorian Village Antiques
2125 Cherokee St.
314/773-8810

Frank & Julia's
2201 Cherokee
314/865-2995

Antiques by Art of the Ages
2205 Cherokee St.
314/776-0959

Debbie Fellenz Antiques
2224 Cherokee St.
314/776-8363

Penny's Collectibles
2307 Cherokee St.
314/771-2822

Haffner's Antiques
2847 Cherokee St.
314/771-3173

Claton Antiques
6403 Clayton Rd.
314/725-9878

Shaker Tree Antiques
7713 Clayton Rd.
314/726-3233

Legacy Antiques
7715 Clayton Rd. (Clayton)
314/725-2209

Regent Parade Consign. Shop
7721 Clayton Rd. (Clayton)
314/727-4959

Finches Consignment & Gifts
7729 Clayton Rd.
314/725-2622

Davis Place Antqs. & Consign.
7731 Clayton Rd.
314/727-9850

M J's Consignment Shop
7803 Clayton Rd. (Clayton)
314/863-8762

Mattis Antiques
7805 Clayton Rd. (Clayton)
314/721-5535

Small World Antiques
9752 Clayton Rd.
314/997-5854

Jules L Pass Antiques Ltd.
9916 Clayton Rd.
314/991-1522

Antique & Art Appraisers
9918 Clayton Rd.
314/993-4477

Kodner Gallery
9918 Clayton Rd.
314/993-4477

Braun Antiques
10315 Clayton Rd.
314/991-1798

Ziern Antiques
10333 Clayton Rd.
314/993-0809

The Original Cast Lighting Inc.
6120 Delmar Blvd
314/863-1895

Coyotes Paw Gallery
6388 Delmar Blvd.
314/721-7576

Rothschild's Antiques
398 N. Euclid Ave.
314/361-4870

Fellenz Antiques
439 N. Euclid Ave.
314/367-0214

Kodner Gallery
7501 Forsyth Blvd.
314/863-9366

Switching Post
7742 Forsyth Blvd.
314/725-7730

Books & Collectibles
3196 S. Grand Blvd
314/771-3196

J. Middleton Mid Century Mod.
3949 Gravois Ave.
314/773-8096

PSA Presentations
131 W. Jefferson Ave.
314/822-8345

Shackelford Antiques & More
4519 S. Kingshighway Blvd
314/832-6508

Alamo Military Collectables
716 Lemay Ferry Rd.
314/638-6505

A Country Place Antiques
2930 Lemay Ferry Rd.
314/892-6677

Ferrari's Consignment Shop
7314 Manchester Rd.-Maplewood
314/644-5755

European Country Antiques
9621 Manchester Rd.
314/968-2550

Post Card Shop
12024 Manchester Rd. (Des Peres)
314/822-7174

Four Seasons West Antiques
4657 Maryland Plaza
314/361-2929

Brilliant Antiques
8107 Maryland Ave. (Clayton)
314/725-2526

Tin Roof Antiques
2201 McCausland Ave.
314/647-1049

Clark Graves Antiques
132 N. Meramec Ave.
314/725-2695

This N That
3305 Meramec St.
314/353-2365

Tower Grove Antiques
3308 Meramec St.
314/352-9020

Alexander Furniture Co.
3309 Meramec St.
314/481-2111

Sambeaus Ltd.
4724 McPherson Ave.
314/361-4636

Golden Harvest
4732 McPherson
314/454-9330

West End Antiques Gallery
4732 McPherson Ave.
314/361-1059

Martin's Galleries
4736 McPherson Ave.
314/361-1202

West Monroe Antiques
132 W. Monroe Ave.
314/821-2931

Pierce House Antiques
139 W. Monroe (Kirkwood)
314/821-5140

Designs in Gold
11006 Olive Blvd.
314/567-3530

Vinegar Hill Antique
107 W. Pacific Ave.
314/962-0375

Now and Then Antiques
6344 S. Rosebury Ave.
314/721-3301

Remember Me Vintage Cloth.
1021 Russell Blvd
314/773-1930

Jack Parker Antiques
4652 Shaw Ave.
314/773-3320

Tommy T's
3010 Sutton Blvd.
314/645-7471

St. Louis Architectural Art
1600 S. 39th St.
314/773-2264

Harley's Harps
2271 Administration Dr.
314/567-1980 X206

Favorite Places To Eat

Cracker Barrel Old Country Store
I-55 & Meramec Bottom Rd., Exit 193
314/416-8880

60 STE. GENEVIEVE

Mill Antique Mart
301 N. Main St.
573/883-7333

Monias Unlimited
316 Market St.
573/883-7874

Sarah's Antiques
124 Merchant St.
573/883-5890

Mr. Frederic Ltd.
195 Merchant St.
573/883-2717

Kaegel's Country Collectibles
252 Merchant St.
573/883-7996

Zielinski's
288 Merchant St.
573/883-7004

Collagé
18 S. Third
573/883-9575

Odile's Linen & Lace Etc.
34 S. 3rd
573/883-2675

Joyce & Choyse's Antiques
58 S. 3rd St.
573/883-2358

The Summer Kitchen
146 S. 3rd St.
573/883-3498

Dalton's Treasure Chest
183 S. 3rd St.
573/883-9190

61 STEELVILLE

Nancy's Antique Dolls-N-Stuff
103 W. Main
573/775-3655

Willies Moles
105 E. Main
573/775-2722

Edies Backwoods Antiques
403 Main St.
573/775-2629

62 SULLIVAN

Country Collectibles
5054 Hwy. K
573/468-8170

White Lion Antiques
5 Maple St.
573/468-2437

Sullivan Showcase Antique Mall
201 N. Service Rd. W.
573/468-3943

63 WARSAW

This Old House Antqs. & Crafts
420 Commercial
816/438-3588

Swinging Bridge Antiques
Hwy. 7 & Main St.
816/438-7422

Mule Barn
Hwy 7. & Truman Dam
816/438-3186

Columns Antique Shop
1129 N. Lay Ave.
816/438-6032

Warsaw Antique Mall
245 W. Main
816/438-9759

Curiosity Shop
406 W. Main
816/438-5034

Molly's Antiques
616 W. Main
816/438-6911

Lou's Quilts & Buckley's Antqs.
702 W. Main
816/438-7853

64 WASHINGTON

Annie-Rose
1110 Clock Tower Plaza
314/239-1970

Waterworks Antiques
1 Elbert Dr.
314/390-2344

Feed Store Antique Mall
101 E. Main St.
314/390-0115

Tamm Haus Antiques
5 W. 2nd St.
314/239-9699

Attic Treasures
100 West Front St.
314/390-0200

65 WEST PLAINS

Elledge House Antiques
315 Broadway
417/256-2442

Aid Downtown Antique Mall
1 Court Square
417/256-6487

Jefferson St. Flea Market
310 Jefferson Ave.
417/256-4788

Looking Back
712 Porter Wagoner Blvd
417/256-8586

Antique Corner
313 Washington Ave.
417/256-2193

66 WESTON

J & L Antiques
Hwy 45 & P
816/386-2456

Tobacco Road
400 Main St.
816/386-2121

Missouri

J P's Antiques
509 Main St.
816/386-2199

Painted Lady Antiques
540 Main St.
816/386-5580

J P's Antiques
424 Main St.
816/386-2894

J P's Antiques
523 Main St.
816/386-2828

Tobacco Patch Country Store
18260 State Rt. 45 N
816/640-2627

Notes

Montana

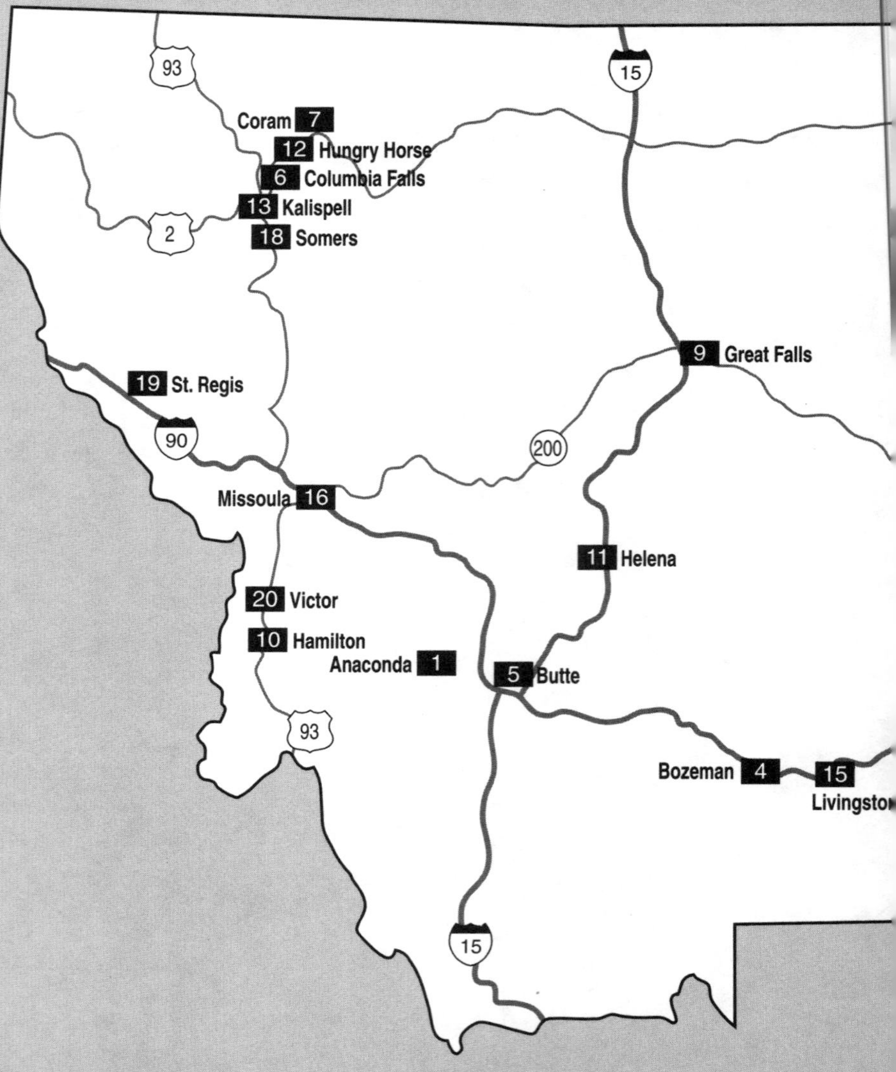
93
15
Coram 7
12 Hungry Horse
6 Columbia Falls
13 Kalispell
18 Somers
2
9 Great Falls
19 St. Regis
90
200
Missoula 16
11 Helena
20 Victor
10 Hamilton
Anaconda 1
5 Butte
93
Bozeman 4
15
Livingston
15

Fox Hollow
Bed & Breakfast
at Baxter Creek

The wonder of Montana's Big Sky awaits you...

545 Mary Rd.
For more information call: 800-431-5010

Bozeman 4

MT ANTIQUE

Located in the historic
Wassweiler Hotel & Bath House
4528 U.S. Hwy 12 West
406-449-3334

Helena 11

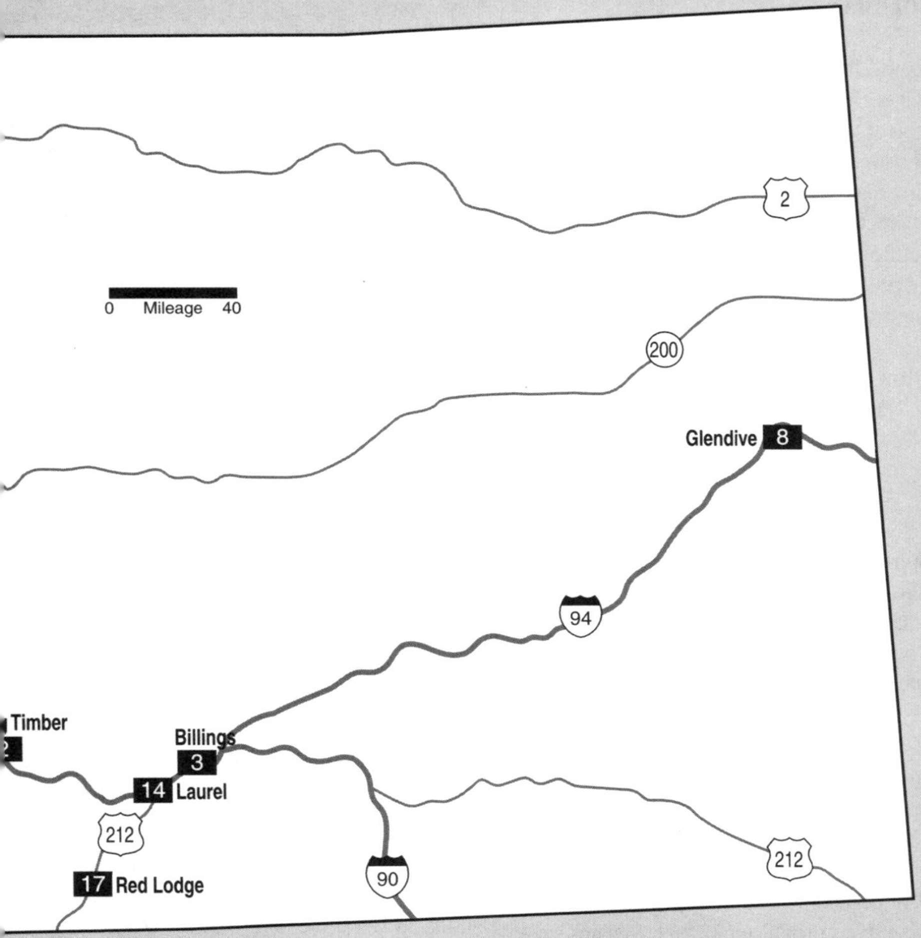

Experience Small Town Charm Antiquing in St. Regis

The Place of Antiques

Cold Creek Antiques

Someplace in Time

Downtown St. Regis 19

TORCH AND TOES

BED AND BREAKFAST
309 South Third Avenue
406/586-7285
800/446-2138
Bozeman

4

River Rock

elegant accommodations
179 Shrade Rd. • 800-477-0699
Kalispell

13

♡ Heartwood ♡

Home is where the heart is

A cheerful 1930's log cabin nestled among tall pines on 200 acres of secluded meadows & woodlands, surrounded by majestic mountains.

400 Seville Lane • (406) 387-5541

Coram 7

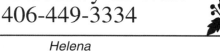

1 ANACONDA

Founded in 1883, this small town owes its existence to Marcus Daly and the Anaconda Copper Company. Smelting operations were suspended in 1980, but Anaconda has a firm grip on its role in Montana history. The town's landmark and a state park, "The Stack," stands 585 feet 1.5 inches tall. Visit the Copper Village Museum and Art Center for area history and a copper smelter display, and the Hearst Free Library, a classic 1889 period building donated to the city by George and Phoebe Hearst. Self-guided walking tour, brochure and bus tour of historic Anaconda begins at the Anaconda Visitor Center.

Brewery Antiques
125 W. Commercial St.
406/563-7926

Anaconda Antiques
208 Cottonwood St.
406/563-5770

Park St. Antique Mall in Anaconda
113 E. Park St.
406/563-3150

2 BIG TIMBER

Located at the foot of the Crazy Mountains, Big Timber offers a broad range of activities in a beautiful setting. Explore the Boulder Valley, fish blue-ribbon trout streams and stop by the Yellowstone River Trout Hatchery for an appreciation of cut-throat trout. Visit museums, galleries, antique shops and historic sites including Victorian Village, Montana Armory, Shiloh Rifle Manufacturing Co., Sweetgrass and Sage Gallery and the Crazy Mountain Museum.

Crazy Mountain Art & Antqs.
14 Anderson
406/932-4797

Village Antiques
Exit 367 Off I-90
406/932-4378

3 BILLINGS

Montana's largest city, Billings is a regional business hub, as well as a cultural, medical, educational and entertainment center. Museums, art galleries, theaters and shopping are all part of the appeal of this vibrant city. Discover the elegantly restored, turn-of-the-century Moss Mansion providing a glimpse into the life of Preston B. Moss, one of Billings' most prominent early residents. Bordered on the north by distinctive rock formations known as rimrocks, Billings is a gateway to Little Bighorn Battlefield National Monument, Bighorn National Recreation Area, Yellowstone Park, the Yellowstone River and the Abrasroka-Beartooth Wilderness.

Whispering Pines
12 S. Broadway
406/446-1470

Crackerjack's Antiques
Broadway & 1st Ave. N
406/259-5577

Heartland Marketplace
3405 Central Ave.
406/655-0747

Pickett Fence Antqs. & Cllbls.
645 Custer Ave.
406/254-1725

Waterwheel Antiques
2339 S. 56th Rd.
406/656-8350

Magic City Floral
1848 Grand Ave.
406/652-6960

Antique Peddler
1327 Main St.
406/256-7003

Oxford Hotel Antiques
2411 Montana Ave.
406/248-2094

Billings Nursery
2147 Poly Dr.
406/656-5501

A-l Attic Dreams Antiques
901 Terry Ave.
406/256-3051

Yesteryears
114-118 N. 29th St.
406/259-3314

Toni's Dool House
71 25th Street W
406/656-4864

Favorite Places To Eat

Cracker Barrel Old Country Store
I-90 & King Road, Exit 446

4 BOZEMAN

Visitors will find a small town atmosphere with big city amenities in Bozeman. This town, beautifully situated at the base of the Bridger Range, blends spectacular recreation with art galleries, museums, symphony, opera, history and many one-of-a-kind Western stores. Walk through the South Wilson Historic District, a residential area featuring houses that range from large mansions to small cottages. Visit the Gallatin Pioneer Museum for area history and artifacts.

Fox Hollow B & B
545 Mary Road
406/582-8440 or 1-800-431-5010
Open year round

At Fox Hollow B & B, the wonder of Montana's big sky awaits. Sunsets are spectacular from the wraparound porch of this country-style home. Settle into an oversized guest room, each with a private bath. Soak in the hot tub while gazing into the cool starlit Montana night. Wake to the aroma of coffee brewing and a delicious gourmet breakfast.

Torch and Toes Bed and Breakfast
309 South Third Avenue
406/586-7285 or 1-800-446-2138

This 1906 Colonial Revival home, found in the Bon Ton historic district, was built for Wilbur F. Williams, vice-president of the Bozeman Milling Company. Today, the Torch and Toes Bed and Breakfast retains its original high ceilings, oak wainscoting, and leaded-glass windows. Turn-of-the-century furnishings accentuate the house's original elements. Collections of gargoyles, mousetraps, and old postcards create a fanciful atmosphere. Each of four guest rooms (with private baths) presents an individual setting. During winter, a full breakfast is provided before the fireplace in the dining room. In summer, breakfast is served on the redwood deck.

Country Mall Antiques
8350 Huffine Ln.
406/587-7688

Davis Torres Furn. Collect
14 W. Main St.
406/587-1587

Cellar 105 Antiques & Gifts
105 W. Main St.
406/587-3013

Antq Mall-Downtown Bozeman
612 E. Main St.
406/587-5281

Country Charm
612 E. Main St.
406/587-5281

Antiques Etc.
25 N. Willson Ave
406/587-9306

The Attic
212 S. Wallace
406/587-2747

The Brass Monkey
370 Lodgepole Ln.
406/586-6855

Old World Antiques
1530 W. Main St.
406/582-1848

Pine Corner Antiques
144 W. Lamme
406/586-9230

Sack's of Bozeman
138 W. Mendenhall
406/587-7283

5 BUTTE

Once known as "the richest hill on earth," Butte is steeped in mining history. Copper, gold, silver were all found here, and Butte became a melting pot of ethnic diversity as immigrants flocked to the mines for employment. The Anselmo Mine Yard in uptown Butte is the best surviving example of surface support facilities that once served the mines. Butte is the home of Montana Tech of the University of Montana, which grew out of Butte's mining heritage. Its Mineral Museum displays 1,500 specimens, including a 27.5 ounce gold nugget. Walking tour brochures of this historic city are available at the Butte Chamber of Commerce. This is also the place to catch a tour of Butte on a replica of an early-day streetcar, "Old No. 1." Three-story, 34-room Copper King Mansion, home of former copper king/politician William A. Clark, has been preserved as it was in the 1880s.

The Scott Bed and Breakfast
15 West Copper
406/723-7030 or 1-800-844-2952

Built in 1897, this former boarding house for miners overlooking Butte's Historic Landmark District is today The Scott Bed and Breakfast. Extensively renovated, this historic setting offers the modern comforts of seven rooms, each with private baths. Explore nearby Copper King Mansion, as well as the World Museum of Mining.

Antiques on Broadway
45 W. Broadway
406/782-3207

Donut Seed Consignments
120 N. Main St.
406/782-7123

Rediscoveries Vintage Clothing
55 W. Park St.
406/723-2176

Rustic Montana Interiors
27 W. Park St.
406/723-1500

Debris Ltd.
123 N. Main St.
406/782-9090

6 COLUMBIA FALLS

A stop in this gateway city to Glacier National Park brings family fun and exploration. Enjoy championship golf in the summer; cross country skiing, ice skating and snowmobiling in the winter. The city also boasts a popular waterslide and whitewater rafting.

Bad Rock Country Bed & Breakfast
480 Bad Rock Drive
406/892-2829 or 1-800-422-3666

Badrock Country Bed & Breakfast is an elegant and charming home filled with Old West antiques, minutes from Glacier Park, on 30 acres in a gorgeous farming valley. Enjoy spectacular views of the 7200-foot-high Columbia Mountain, only 2 miles away. Experience the magic of quiet in the country and be pampered in the Bad Rock Bunny way. Soak in the secluded spa in a time reserved exclusively for you. Relax in one of the four new rooms made of hand-hewn square logs, with fireplaces and handmade lodgepole pine furniture, or settle into one of the four rooms in the home, all with private baths. Fantastic breakfasts are only one portion of the superb hospitality.

Charmaine's Antiques & Collectibles
35 5th St. W
406/892-3211

7 CORAM

Heartwood
400 Seville Lane
406/387-5541

The "Little Cabin" at Heartwood (a family homestead) is a cheerful, 1930s log cabin nestled among tall pines on 215 acres of secluded meadows and woodlands - completely surrounded by majestic mountains including views of the famous "Park Mountains" and located just seven miles from Glacier National Park. The "Little Cabin" is tastefully decorated with vintage furniture and accessories - yet remains very cozy and comfortable. The original (working) wood cookstove still occupies its place in the fully modern country kitchen. Accomodations include three bedrooms, living room, kitchen and large bathroom. Take advantage of nature trails, trout pond, nightly campfire, or just rest and relax.

8 GLENDIVE

"Helen's Stuff"
716 E. Bell St.
406/365-3405

Tin Shed
112 1/2 Country Club Road
406/365-4553

Alley Antiques
616 N. Kendrick
406/365-3330

Montana Antiques & Cllbls.
1111 West Bell
406/365-4691

Antiques & Such
614 North Meade
406/365-3018

9 GREAT FALLS

Great Falls is Montana's second-largest city, located on the Missouri River among the five falls that were both a magnificent spectacle and formidable barrier to early river travel. This area held significance for the Lewis and Clark Expedition. The explorers were forced to spend nearly a month portaging around the falls in June, 1805. Much of the Missouri River in this area remains as it was when Lewis and Clark first viewed it 190 years ago. The "Great Falls" of the Missouri is now the site of Ryan Dam, but may still be visited. Great Falls was also home of cowboy artist, Charlie Russell (1864-1926), whose original home and log studio are now part of the C. M. Russell Museum Complex. Soak up some local culture at the Montana Cowboys Bar and Museum or at Mehmke's Steam Engine Museum.

Browser's Corner
117 Central Ave.
406/727-5150

G P Trading Company
405 Central Ave.
406/727-0369

The Bet Art & Antiques
416 Central Ave.
406/453-1151

Accents & Antiques
1015 14th St. S
406/727-6049

Mary Beth Shop
500 4th Ave. N
406/452-4522

Bill's Time Center
827 9th St. S
406/761-1074

Bull Market Antq Mall
202 2nd Ave. S
406/771-1869

Lucky Lee's
8 1/2 7th St. S
406/452-0358

Now & Then Shop
718 13th St. N
406/452-0671

Far Out Antiques
301 24th St. NW
406/452-5211

Janet's General Store
115 Central Ave.
406/761-1655

10 HAMILTON

Located in the heart of the Bitterroot Valley, Hamilton is Montana's gateway to the Selway-Bitterroot Wilderness and a number of other recreational and historic attractions, including the Ravalli County Museum and Daly Mansion. Built in 1890 by Irish immigrant, Marcus Daly, one of Montana's colorful "copper kings," Daly Mansion with 42 rooms, 24 bedrooms, 15 baths and 5 Italian marble fireplaces, presides over 50 planted acres in Montana's scenic Bitterroot Valley.

Deer Crossing
396 Hayes Creek Road
406/363-2232 or 1-800-763-2232

Relax on the deck with a steaming cup of coffee and watch the sun rise over the Sapphire Mountains at Deer Crossing, a bed and breakfast with Old West charm. Enjoy a luxury suite with double jacuzzi tub, one of the three gracious guest rooms or the bunk house. The hearty ranch breakfast features garden fresh vegetables. Nearby adventures include fly fishing, rafting, hiking, horseback riding, skiing and snowmobile riding.

Clothes Tree
301 Main St.
406/363-7003

Hamtana
Pennsylvania
406/363-2482

Magpie Nest
247 State St.
406/363-3167

Howdy Antiques
383 Owings Lane SW
406/363-2186

11 HELENA

An 1864 gold strike touched off a boom era that transformed Helena into "Queen City of the Rockies" and Montana's capital city. Trace its history along Main Street, still known as Last Chance Gulch. View historic buildings and mansions dating back to the 1870s such as the Original Governor's Mansion built in 1888. This Victorian mansion was the official residence of nine governors between 1913 and 1959. Enjoy the Last Chance Tour Train, a one-hour narrated tour of historic downtown Helena.

MT Antique Mall
4528 U.S. Highway 12 West
406/449-3334
Open 7 days a week from 10 to 5:30

Directions: Located approximately 2 miles west of Helena on U.S. Highway 12 toward Missoula. From Interstate 15, go through Helena following the signs for Highway 12 West and Missoula.

Listed on the National Register of Historic Places, Wassweiler Hotel and Bath House, built in 1883, is home to MT Antique Mall. Over 30 dealers display a wide selection of antiques and collectibles offering a variety of quality furniture, accessories, glassware, pottery, plus much more inside this former stopover for the cattle drovers, gold dust rovers, and "strike-it-rich" elite of Helena's boom days.

Mo. River Chronicle Antiques
1125 Helena Ave.
406/442-7887

Days of Yore
25 S. Last Chance Gulch St.
406/443-7947

Chelsea's Place
38 N. Last Chance Gulch
406/442-0890

Quigleys Antiques
5944 U.S. Hwy. 12 W
406/449-8876

12 HUNGRY HORSE

Grandpa's Attic
8760 Highway 2 E
406/387-4166

13 KALISPELL

Founded in 1891, Kalispell is now a bustling small city and home to much history, culture, commercial activity and outdoor recreation. The city's natural beauty and pleasant lifestyle draw a wide variety of residents and tourists. Get acquainted with the city on a walking tour of historic buildings and enjoy regional culture at the Hockaday Center for the Arts.

Wander through Conrad Mansion's Victorian elegance, built in 1895 as the home of C. E. Conrad, Montana pioneer, Missouri River trader, freighter and founder of the city of Kalispell.

Creston Country Willows Bed & Breakfast
70 Creston Road
406/755-7517 or 1-800-257-7517

Near Glacier Park, wonder at the majestic mountain views and quiet charm of Creston Country Willows' rural setting. This bed & breakfast provides four guest rooms with private baths. In addition, head for area recreations, such as golfing, fishing or hiking, after the complimentary full country breakfast.

Stillwater Inn Bed & Breakfast
206 4th Avenue East
1-800-398-7024

Relax in the comfort of this lovely historic home built at the turn of the century. The Stillwater Inn offers four guest bedrooms, two with private bathrooms and two that share a bathroom. Start the day dining on the delicious gourmet breakfast. Within walking distance are antique shops, art galleries and the Charles Conrad Mansion.

End of the Trail Trading Post
1025 W. Center St.
406/756-3100

Idaho Street Antiques
110 E. Idaho
406/755-1324

Kalispell Antiques Market
48 Main St.
406/257-2800

Arts & Antiques Mall
40 2nd St. E
406/755-1801

Bazaar
154 2nd Ave.
406/257-1878

Antiques of Kalispell
175 6th Ave.
406/257-4415

Southside Consignments
2699 U.S. Hwy. 93 S
406/756-8526

Glacier Antique Mall
3195 U.S. Hwy. 93 N
406/756-1690

White Elephant
3258 U.S. Hwy. 93 S
406/756-7324

Demersville Mercantile
4010 U.S. Hwy. 93 S
406/755-0917

Stageline Antiques
2510 Whitefish Stage Rd.
406/755-1044

Moms Place
1023 W. S. Hwy. 2 W
406/257-4333

14 LAUREL

Located at the junction of great rivers and highways, Laurel is a convenient stop for travelers. The Chief Joseph Statue and Canyon Creek Battlefield Marker in downtown Fireman's Park commemorate the 1877 battle between the Nez Perce Indians, led by Chief Joseph, and the U.S. Cavalry under the command of Col. Samuel Sturgis.

Lind Antique Mall
101 W. 1st. St.
406/628-1337

Ye Olde Curiosity Shop
103 E. Main St.
406/628-7146

Blue Bell Antiques
210 E. Main St.
406/628-2002

15 LIVINGSTON

Downtown Livingston, a designated historic district on the National Register, encompasses 436 buildings, most within walking distance of one another. With the Yellowstone River flowing through town, Livingston is anglers' heaven, providing excellent floating and fishing access. Visit Park County Museum which is housed in a turn-of-the-century schoolhouse, featuring household displays, Indian artifacts, a stagecoach, sheep wagon and caboose. Located in a restored Northern Pacific Railroad station, Depot Center houses railroad and Western history exhibits and art shows.

Save The Pieces
119 W. Callender St.
406/222-8131

Island Antiques
1500 E. Park St.
406/222-8025

Livingston Merctl & Trade Co.
W. Park
406/222-3334

Doris Loomis Antiques
E. River Rd.
406/222-0427

Cowboy Connection
108 N. 2nd St.
406/222-0272

Authentic & Old Antique Mall
219 S. Main St.
406/222-9571

Grandma's Treasures
211 S. Main St.
406/222-2177

Jeannie's Alley Antiques
118 1/2 N. Yellowstone St.
406/222-1617

Need 'Ems-Uniquely Old & New
615 W. Park St.
406/222-0506

Vik's Antiques
Off Hwy. 89 S. at 05 Merrill
406/222-0128

16 MISSOULA

Montana's cultural superstar and third largest city, Missoula presides over the north end of the Bitterroot Valley. Best known as the home of the University of Montana, Missoula is an eclectic mix of students, independent business people, professors, foresters, artists and writers. At the head of five scenic valleys and the junction of three great rivers, Missoula has no shortage of recreational opportunities. Missoula is home to the Montana Repertory theatre, Missoula's Children's Theatre, String Orchestra of the Rockies and Garden City Ballet. Take a Trolley Tour through the historic downtown/university area or a carousel ride at A Carousel for Missoula in Caras Park beside the Clark Fork River. Soak up some western Montana history at the Historical Museum at Fort Missoula. Wonder with admiration at St. Francis Xavier Church, built in 1889, the year Montana became a state, outstanding for its graceful steeple, paintings and stained glass.

Ovilla
115 W. Front St.
406/728-3527

Jem Shoppe Jewelers
105 S. Higgins Ave.
406/728-4077

Birds Nest
219 N. Higgins Ave.
406/721-1125

Ma & Pa's Second Hand Store
531 N. Higgins Ave.
406/728-0899

Mr. Higgins Vintage Clothing
612 S. Higgins Ave.
406/721-6446

Herman's on Main Vint. Cllbls.
137 E. Main St.
406/728-4408

1776 Antiques
214 E. Main St.
406/549-5092

Montana Antique Mall
331 Railroad St. W
406/721-5366

Mountain Mama's Antiques
2002 S. Reserve St.
406/549-9281

Horse Trader Antiques
1920 S. Russell St.
406/549-6280

Opportunity Resources Inc.
2821 S. Russell St.
406/721-2930

Montana Craft Connection
1806 South Ave W
406/549-4486

Third Street Antiques
109 S. 3rd St. W
406/543-4428

Third Street Curiosity Shop
2601 S. 3rd St. W
406/542-0097

17 RED LODGE

This historic mining town has roots that reach back to the European homes of its diverse founders. Situated at the base of the Beartooth Mountains, Red Lodge is one of Montana's premier ski destinations in winter; in summer, it draws hikers, anglers, campers, sightseers and Yellowstone Park visitors via the nearby Beartooth Highway. Enjoy native North American animals and the children's petting zoo at the Beartooth Nature Center. Take in the area's history at the Carbon County Museum, housed in the homestead cabin of John Garrison, subject of the movie *Jeremiah Johnson*. Explore buildings and houses on and off Main Street that were built between 1883 and 1910 during the coal mining boom. Remnants of the ethnic groups that settled Red Lodge are preserved in "Hibug" Town, Finn Town and Little Italy, whose ethnic traditions are celebrated every August during the 9-day Festival of Nations.

Flower Shop
20 N. Broadway Ave.
406/446-2330

Mama Bear
217 S. Broadway Ave.
406/446-2207

Blue Door Antiques & Cllbls.
423 S. Broadway
406/446-2064

Montana Chinock
6 S. Broadway
406/446-1810

Whispering Pines
12 S. Broadway
406/446-1470

18 SOMERS

Laurie Levengood's Antiques
4834 Hwy. 93 S
406/857-3499

Somers Second Hand & Antqs.
210 Montana Hwy. #82
406/857-3234

19 ST. REGIS

Cold Creek Antiques
Cold Creek Road
406/649-2675

Discover a fine array of antique furniture, collectibles, glassware as well as a pleasing assortment of accessories and other items in Cold Creek Antiques, a cozy shop.

The Place of Antiques
Downtown St. Regis
406/649-2397
Open 7 days a week; 9-5

Directions: From I-90, take Exit #33 into St. Regis.

Featuring original finish and refinished antique oak furniture, The Place of Antiques prepares all of its refinished pieces. In addition to furniture, Red Wing items, depression glassware and advertising memorabilia enhance the shop's offerings brought together by over 70 dealers.

Someplace In Time
Hwy. 135
406/649-2637

For a nostalgic stroll, Someplace In Time offers antique dolls, furnishings, in addition to many other delightful and attractive items.

20 VICTOR

Named for a Flathead Indian chief and nestled in the Bitterroot Valley, Victor offers endless recreational opportunities. Explore the Victor Heritage Museum, housed in the railroad depot.

Antique Sellar
275 Dinger Lane
406/642-3386

Last Frontier Trading Post
2381 U.S. Hwy. 93 N
406/642-3940

Red Willow Dry Goods
111 Main St.
406/642-3130

Notes

A Store For All Seasons
SANTA MONICA ANTIQUE MARKET
1607 LINCOLN BLVD., SANTA MONICA, CA 90404
☎ (310) 314-4899 FAX (310) 314-4894

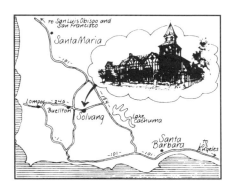

Houston's Largest...
Houston's Finest...
OVER 200 DEALERS • OPEN EVERY DAY
Just
2 Miles North
Of The Galleria
POST OAK RD.
THE ANTIQUE CENTER OF TEXAS
610 W. LOOP
OLD KATY RD.
EXIT POST OAK RD.
I-10
EXIT WASHINGTON
N
Open
Every Day
10AM - 6PM
Carolyn Thompson's
ANTIQUE
CENTER OF TEXAS
TEXAS' LARGEST
1001 WEST LOOP NORTH, HOUSTON
713/688-4211
Internet: www.txantiquemall.com

Jim Burk's Greater York Antique Shows

Jim Burk's Greater York Antiques Shows, held twice a year in the Memorial Building at the York, Pennsylvania fairgrounds, has been a favorite for serious "antiquers" for twenty-nine years. There are no previews, luncheons, lectures or hoopla planned before the show. All the frills are reserved for the "main event," which is the show itself. Much of the show's success can be attributed to the return year after year of some of the top antique dealers in America. Most of them come from Pennsylvania, Philadelphia, Connecticut, and Baltimore, although some have been spotted from Michigan, Virginia and New Jersey. But, no matter where they are from you can be assured that only the finest representations of antiques and collectibles will be displayed (or allowed, for that matter).

All of the dealers agree that Jim Burk is a pro when it comes to promoting antique shows. He knows what it takes to keep them happy: low booth rent, easy in and out access, and a no pressure setup. The combination of quality dealers and Jim's reputation for presenting a "class act" attracts buyers from all over the world. Long lines often form outside the building where anxious shoppers await the 8 a.m. opening. Then it's off to the races, as the isles begin to fill with collectors, decorators, dealers, housewives, and others, all who have come to see what is quite possibly the "Greatest Antique Show On Earth."

Presented by: Jim Burk Antique Shows
3012 Miller Road
Washington Boro, PA 17582
717/397-7209
Call for show dates

Featuring 150 dealers showing Americana at its best
The leader in quality antique shows for 30 years

BRANDYWINE

Bed and Breakfast and Antiques

Located in the center of Vermont's most ıarming village, Brandywine wraps you in the :ace of enjoying gorgeous surroundings in a ›untry-formal atmosphere.

It's a wonderful place to relax, or if you are oking for activity, you can enjoy many sports ıd hobbies right in town. The surrounding area fers many miles of fabulous hiking trails, bik- g, tennis, and beautiful streams for fishing. ıests can take a horse drawn carriage ride rough the charming village or enjoy a picnic lunch on one of the beautiful covered idges located on the property. For those who enjoy golf, there are several outstand- g courses in the immediate area.

Built in the 1830s, this spacious village inn is on the National Historic Register. It is beautifully furnished with period antiques, and it is as comfortable as it is elegant.

For those in love with the sport of antiquing, there is a 25 x 50 foot post and beam barn filled with a fabulous array of antiques for sale. The two floors of treasures are sure to please those who enjoy finding a bargain. From primitive through refined, you will discover one of Vermont's most interesting and eclectic antique shops.

Brandywine is always delighted to have families with ıildren and offers accommodations for your cat, dog r horse.

Brandywine Bed & Breakfast and Antiques
Main St. – Grafton, Vermont
(802) 843-2250
Open 7 days a week

Antique
Marketplace
of Collierville

Owner Barbara Ballard has created a showroom of elegant, yet versatile, antiques to grace your home or business. The Antique Marketplace of Collierville is a co-operative limited to quality dealers that offer no reproductions, only the authentic in furniture, light fixtures, silver, crystal, rugs, estate jewelry, and objects d'art. Their goal is to exceed your expectations in service and quality with presentations of American, European, or Country French. Additionally, special services are offered such as interior design, appraisals, and delivery. On-site refinishing and restoration are also available through The Retouchables shop, located within the Antique Marketplace.

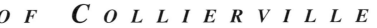

Antique Marketplace of Collierville offers to you, our discriminating clients, the opportunity to acquire antiques of exceptional quality and elegance in an atmosphere inspired by the Historic Square of Collierville, the history of our great nation, and the ancient past.

Antique Marketplace of Collierville
88 N. Main Street, Collierville, Tenn.
Phone: **901-854-8859**, Fax: 901-854-1814
Hours: Mon-Sat, 10-5, Sun., by appointment

Specializing In Upscale Country Furnishings and Accessories

Outstanding Architectural Doors

- Open by appointment anytime
- Offering unloading sales several times a year (call to be added to their mailing list)
- Watch for Kitty & Tony at finer antique shows nationwide

Kitty & Tony Ables
140 N. Main
Henning, TN
(901) 738-2381

1820s French Canadian Cupboard

Amish Clothing from Pennsylvania

Oak Country Cupboard c. 1800s

Early 1800s document box

Kitty (left) displays her wares at the Heart of Country Show twice a year

"The Mall With It All"

Franklin Antique Mall

In 1980, Joan and Archie Glenn opened the Franklin Antique Mall as their dream. Little did they know how successful the activity at the old "Icehouse" would become, as what started out as 35 booths, grew through three expansions to more than 100 dealers and 14,000 square feet. Located twenty miles south of Nashville, in a huge, handmade brick structure, the multi-level building, constructed in 1870, originally became a flour mill and was more widely known as Williamson County's Icehouse at the turn of the century. It has now become home to one of the area's most charming malls.

Inside amongst the wood and brick decor, collectors will find one of the South's biggest collections of furniture, from Early American to Victorian and turn of the century pieces in solid cherry, walnut, mahogany and oak. There is an ample supply of chests, tables, desks, beds, bookcases, sets of chairs and even a Jackson Press or two. There is a wide array of glassware from all periods, pottery, china, books, quilts, linens, clocks and pictures, and a booth of old lamps and replacement parts. Each booth is a treasure chest of nostalgia that collectively is an antique buff's bonanza.

The Franklin Antique Mall, multiple past winner of the Tennessean's Reader's Choice Award and former nominee of the Commercial Historical Preservation Award, just celebrated its 18th anniversary last year. The mall is now owned and operated by Amanda Glenn Pitts and Shawn Glenn with the death of their mother Joan last February. The success of the mall is due to the continued growth of traffic to more than 300,000 a year, the creativity and longevity of the dealers, and the chemistry of the sales staff, as a lot of the dealers and most of the sales staff have been at the business since its inception.

"The Mall With It All" dubbed by *Nashville Magazine* is located at the corner of Second Avenue South and South Margin Street in Franklin, Tennessee and is open 10:00 a.m. to 5:00 p.m., Monday through Saturday and 1 to 5:00 p.m. on Sunday. 615-790-8593.

Heart of Country®

Antiques Show
Nashville, Tennessee

Heart of Country Antiques Show: February 13, 14, 15, 1998
Opryland Hotel, Nashville, Tennessee

Show Hours:	Friday, February 13, 10 a.m. to 8 p.m.
	Saturday, February 14, 10 a.m. to 8 p.m.
	Sunday, February 15, 10 a.m. to 5 p.m.
Admission:	$8.00
Preview Party:	" A Valentine Preview Party," Feb. 12, 6:00 to 10:30 pm
	Admission, $60 includes a sumptious buffet, Nashville music, the first opportunity to buy antiques and FREE daily re-admission.

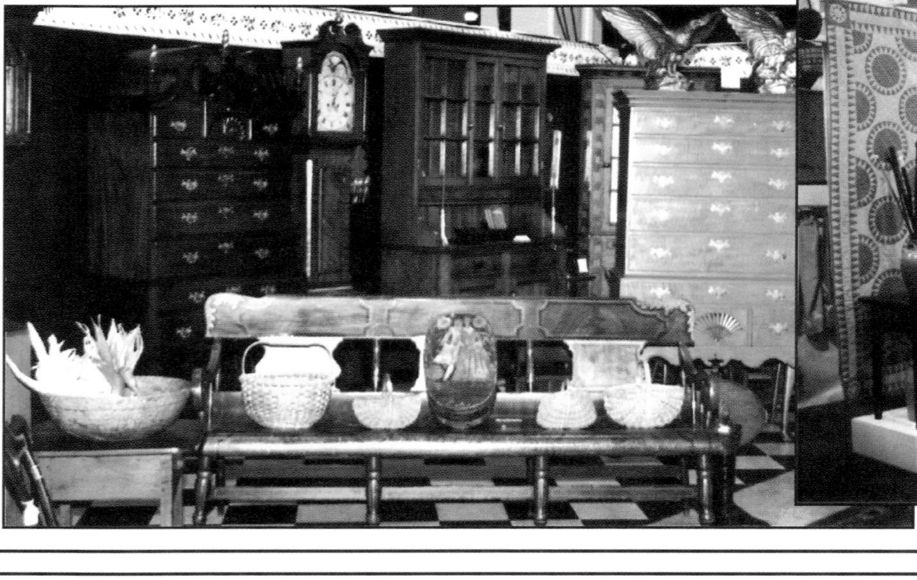

ANTIQUE MARKET
of Cordova
1740 N. Germantown Pkwy.
Cordova, Tenn.
(901) 759-0414
"A Quality Group Shop"

Nebraska

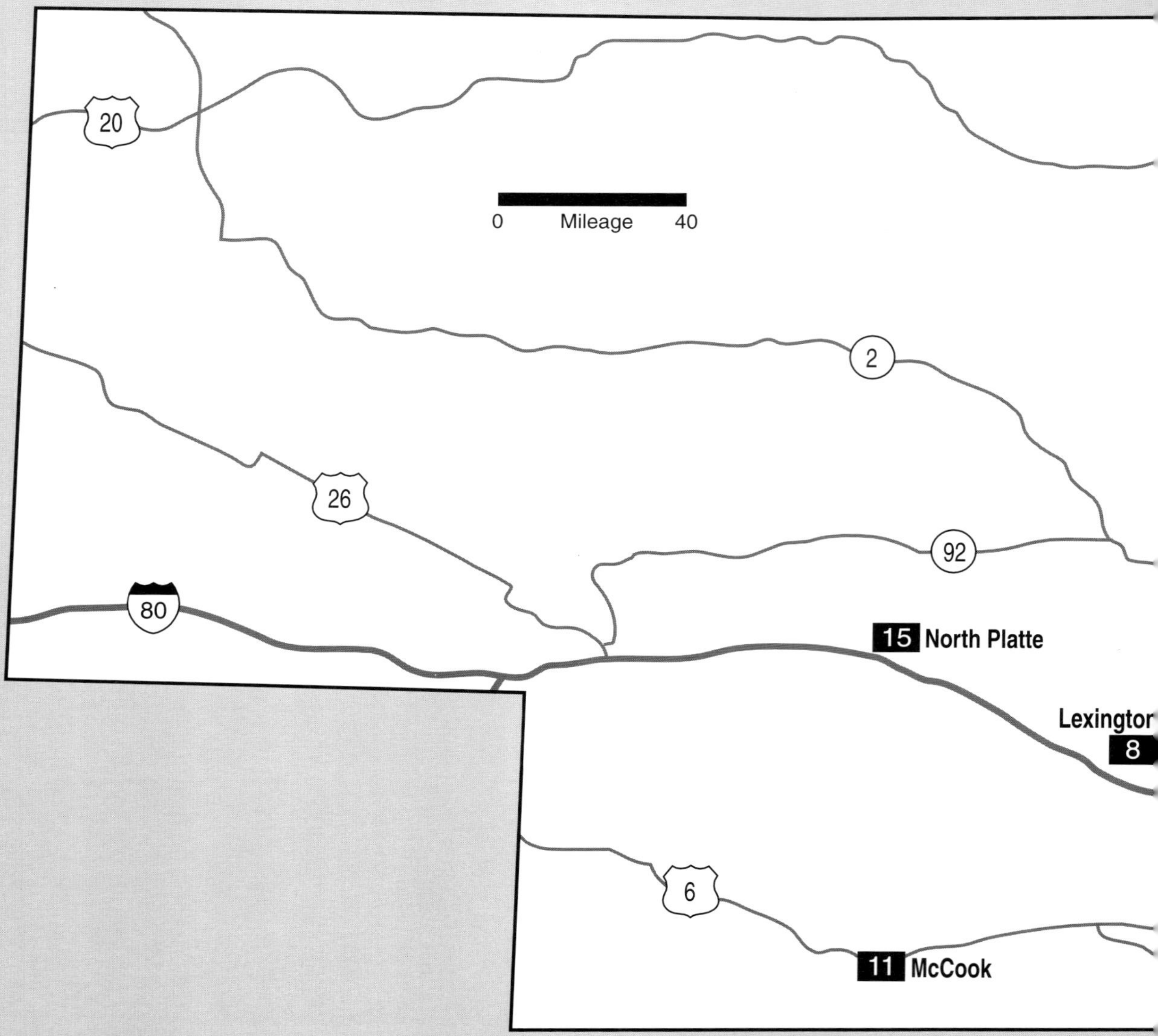

20
0
Mileage
40
2
26
92
80
15 North Platte
Lexingtor
8
6
11 McCook

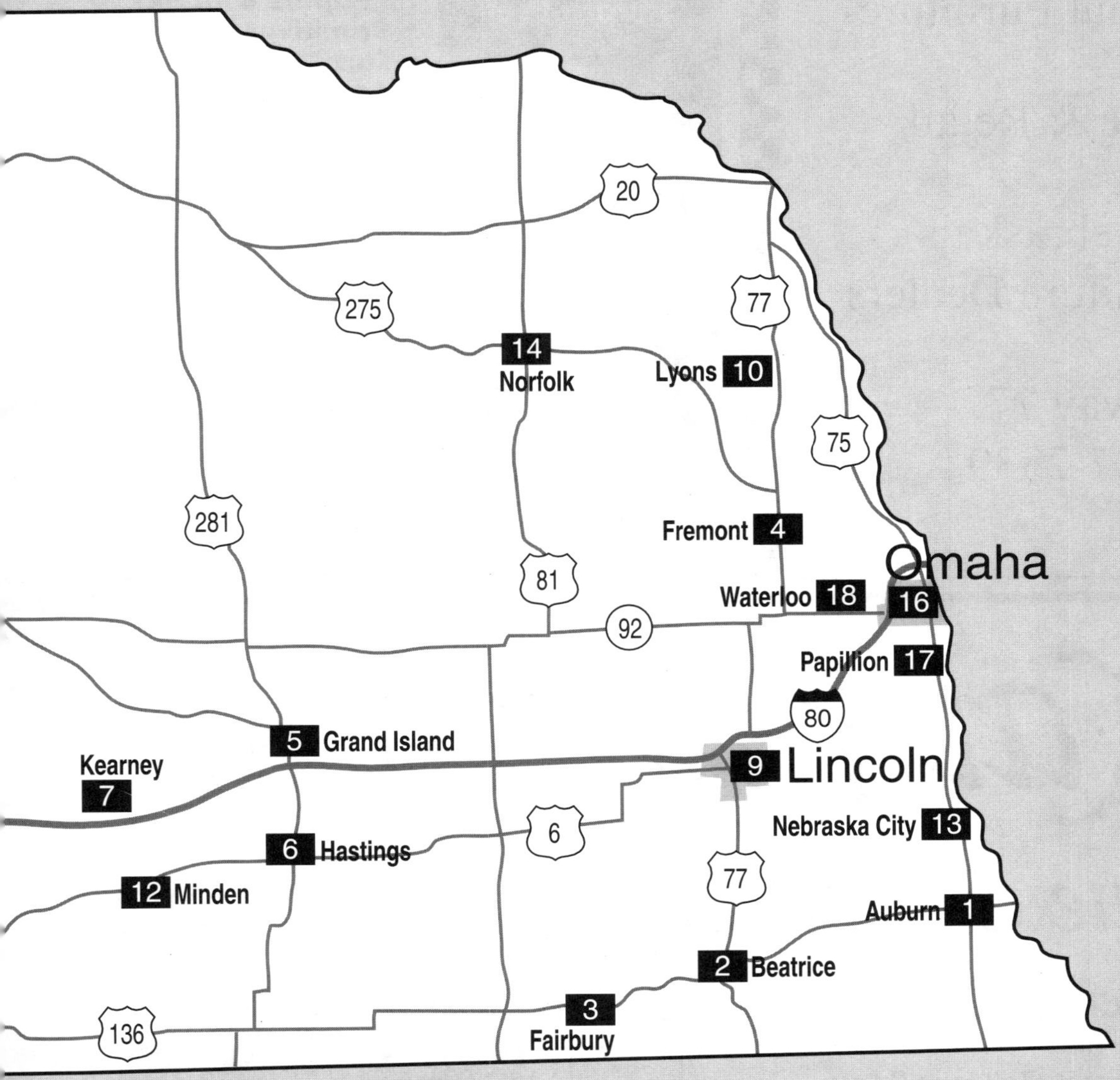

20
275
77
14
Norfolk
Lyons 10
75
281
Fremont 4
Omaha
81
Waterloo 18
16
92
Papillion 17
80
5 Grand Island
Kearney
7
9 Lincoln
6
Nebraska City 13
6 Hastings
77
12 Minden
Auburn 1
2 Beatrice
3
136
Fairbury

Kristi's Antiques, Inc.

Over 1,000 pieces
Oak & Walnut Furniture

Wholesale & Retail

One of Nebraska's
Largest Furniture Dealers

Highway 77
402-687-2339

Lyons

GREAT EXCHANGE
FLEA MARKET

Indoor • 12,000 Square Feet • 60 Dealers

Large Selection of Affordable
- **Antiques & Collectibles**
- **Furniture**
- **Advertising Items**
- **Vintage Magazines, Papers & Books**
- **Primitives**
- **Farm Toys**
- **And Much, Much More**

Hours:
10-5 Monday - Saturday
12-5 Sunday
(308) 381-4075

Ample Parkin

NE Corner South Locust & Hwy 34 Next to Desert Rose

Grand Island

Kaufmann's

Antique & Collectible Emporium

Lower Level Kaufmann Centre - Downtown

Kearney's Largest Antique Mall
Over 65 Dealers in over 8,000 sq. ft.
Old Variety Store from the 20's glassware, furniture, extremely nice old jewelry, dolls, early American. Plan to Spend 2 to 3 Hours

Open Monday - Saturday 10-5
Sunday 1-5
2200 Central Ave. • Kearney, NE 68847
(308) 237-4972

The Kirk Collection is fabric of Omaha

The next time you're watching a movie like *Forrest Gump* or the *Titanic*, pay special attention, you may be looking at fabric purchased from The Kirk Collection.

The Kirk Collection started dealing in antique quilts and only moved into antique fabrics when owner Bill Kirk brought two trunkloads of fabric home from an auction and the Kirks had to find a market for it.

After a textile show in L.A., Bill visited the set of Thirty-Something where the designer bought $500 in fabric in under a minute and the Kirks realized costume designers use a lot of fabric. That led to a four-year relationship with Quantam Leap, plus a lot of work with Homefront and Brooklyn Bridge on television. Nancy Kirk jokes "we don't lose customers, they get cancelled." Movie work followed with feature films including *Little Women, Wyatt Earp, Forrest Gump* and the new Tom Hanks film *That Thing You Do* and the *Titanic.*

"When setting the time period for a film or TV show, directors know that men recognize the cars on the street, and women recognize the fabric in the costumes," says Nancy.

It took the National Quilting Association show in Lincoln, Neb., to teach the Kirks that quilters also use a lot of fabric — but in little tiny pieces. They would come by the booth and ask for a quarter yard of fabric, and we would say "sorry, we don't cut fabric, because the costume designers wanted the longest lengths possible."

By the end of that three day show, we realized a quilter could spend $500 in nothing flat, but wanted it all in quarter yards. Needless to say, we cut fabric now. So much so, that the Kirks no longer do regular antique shows, but travel only for major quilt shows. They also send trunk shows of antique fabrics to quilt guilds and shops around the country. "That way the fabric can travel while we stay home," says Bill.

Now the majority of their business is done through their mail order catalog both nationally and internationally, and now on the World Wide Web at, http://www.auntie.com/kirk. But real live customers can shop in their real live shop in Omaha at 1513 Military Ave., Tue. through Sat. 10-5. For driving instructions, see their listing in The Antique Atlas.

19th century bear paw quilt.

1903s ocean waves variation

Bunting and street banners from a decorating company in Indiana form a patriotic display with a red-and-white quilt and a child's bunting dress.

Nebraska

1 AUBURN

Bobbi-Jon Antique Mall
923 Central Ave.
402/274-5548

Pioneer Antiques
1110 J St.
402/274-3681

2 BEATRICE

Bert's Bargains
515 Ella St.
402/228-2670

Riverside Antiques
321 N. 9th St.
402/228-2673

Third Street Antiques
123 N. 3rd St.
402/228-2200

3 FAIRBURY

Personett House Bed and Breakfast Inn
615 6th Street
402/729-2902
Rates from $35

This bed and breakfast takes its name from Susie Personett, who ran a boarding house in the home from 1916 to 1941. During World War II the Jefferson County Chapter of the Red Cross acquired the house and used it for various war-related purposes, such as assembling clothing and first aid articles to be sent to England.

Offering guests seven lovely rooms with shared baths, the Personett House is just one block from downtown Fairbury.

Stagecoach Mall
510 E Street
402/729-4034
Open Mon.-Sat. 9-6, Sun. 12-5

Directions: Stagecoach Mall is located 45 miles south of I-80 on Highway 15, at the intersection of Highway 136 and Highway 15.

Located in historic downtown Fairbury, award-winning Stagecoach Mall offers antiques, collectibles, crafts, gifts and goodies! They've been featured in *Midwest Living Magazine* and the book *Day Trips in the Heartland: A Get-Away Guide to Unique Places and Fun in the Heartland*. Don't miss them!

Linda's Attic
522 D St.
402/729-5180

Fairbury Antique Mall
222 W. 14th St.
402/729-5105

4 FREMONT

Visit historic downtown Fremont, eastern Nebraska's Antique Capital! There are seven antique shops within walking distance. Fremont is home of the May Museum that has a general store, a historic school room, an 1860 settler's log cabin, and a 25-room mansion filled with antiques. Fremont also is the home station of the Fremont and Elkhorn Railway's Fevr Dinner Train (402/727-0615).

John C. Antique Mall
544 N. Main
402/727-7092

A general line of antiques.

C & E Antiques
530 N. Main
402/721—2101

Twenty-five dealers who specialize in elegant glass.

Antique Alley
105 E. 6th Street
402/727-9542

Twenty dealers offering a general line of antiques.

Dime Store Days
109 E. 6th Street
402/727-0580

Forty dealers with something for everyone.

Park Avenue Antiques
515 Park Avenue
402/721-1157

Twenty-five dealers with a variety of items.

Memories Antiques
225 E. 6th Street
402/753-0578

Hen House Gallery
3305 N. Broad Street
402/721-5275

5 GRAND ISLAND

Great Exchange Flea Market
N.E. Corner of Hwy. 34 & S. Locust St.
308/381-4075
Open: Daily 10-5, Mon.-Sat.; Sun. 12-5

Directions: Eastbound on I-80, exit 312, go 4 1/2 miles north on Hwy. 281 to Hwy. 34, east 2 miles to S. Locust St. Westbound I-80, exit 318, go 4 miles north to Hwy. 34, west 6 miles to Locust St.

The Great Exchange Flea Market has over 12,000 sq. ft. of well lighted, clean floor area to browse. Certain areas are kept for specific themes, such as "The Paper Route" where you'll find new, used and collectible books, plus vintage magazines, newspapers, cookbooks, comics and tear sheets covering most of the paper collecting arena. A large area is set aside for furniture, mainly antique and collectible. A feature area of the market is Abby's Emporium which is the only craft area in the store.

In this shop is a trip down memory lane including the tin roofs and picket fences. You'll find everything here from cabinets to doilies. Shelves and benches are loaded with treasures to decorate your home or put a smile on a friend's face.

Billed as the finest flea market in Nebraska, the Great Exchange Flea Market has 60 dealers offering everything from Hummels to handcuffs, depression glassware, pottery, primitives, toys, collectibles and more.

Lana's Antique Mall
112 W. 2nd St.
308/384-9876
Open Mon.-Sat. 10-5, Sun. 12-5

Directions: From I-80, take Exit 281. Lana's is located 8 to 10 miles from I-80 on Highway 30 in Grand Island.

Nine dealers fill this two-story mall that specializes in country and primitive furnishings and accessories. It's easy to see how a piece will look in your home, since the individual rooms are set up as actual furnished areas with items from the mall.

Point of Interest: People from all over the country come to Grand Island from March through the first week of April to watch the sandhill cranes on their migratory route.

Country Trader
505 N. Pine
308/384-8277
Open Mon. and Wed. 12-5 or by appointment

Directions: Traveling I-80, take the exit to Highway 281. Travel north on 281 into Grand Island. Country Trader is located downtown.

Specializing in primitives, oak furniture and advertising items.

H & S Refinishing & Antiques
327 N. Cleburn St.
308/381-8737

General Store
420 W. 4th St.
308/389-4662

Second Time Around
Exit 318 I-80
308/886-2312

Time After Time
324 W. 3rd St.
308/384-7009

Keith's Red Lam Antiques
108 W. 3rd St.
308/384-6199

Heartland Antique Mall
216 W. 3rd St.
308/384-6018

Clutter Bug Antiques
219 W. 3rd St.
308/382-0369

Treasure Chest
216 S. Wheeler
308/382-8817

Second Time Around
Exit 318 I-80
402/886-2312

6 HASTINGS

VIP Antiques
1733 West 2nd Street
402/463-5055
Fax: 402/463-3038
Open Mon.-Fri. 8-5, Sat. 12-4

Directions: Traveling I-80, take Exit 312 to South Highway 281. Go 16.6 miles to 2nd and Burlington Streets and turn right (west) on 2nd Street. Go exactly 0.8 of a mile to the Total Convenience Store, which is on the left. Look up and you will see the VIP Antiques marquee. Turn left and go 1 short block and you are there.

Vicki and Paul Bergman love to cater to antique dealers and collectors, and their 5,000 square foot warehouse is filled with a full line of antiques and other treasures especially suited for both groups. The selection is varied, the quality is excellent and the price is right! Sounds like my kind of shop.

Grandma's Victorian Inn Bed & Breakfast
1826 West 3rd Street
402/462-2013
Rates from $60

An 1886 Victorian with a beautiful staircase and outstanding woodwork, Grandma's offers guests five rooms, each with private bath. The house is filled with antiques, with an accent on rocking chairs and queen-size beds in each guest room. Enjoy such simple, old-fashioned pleasures as sipping lemonade on the beautiful balcony, or relaxing on the front porch swings. Breakfast is served in the dining room, or, for an additional charge, can be served to you in bed!

Country Market Antiques
RR 1
402/462-6349

Old Bank Antiques
701 W. 2nd St.
402/463-8484

Antiques And
706 W. 2nd St.
402/463-8010

7 KEARNEY

Kaufmann's Antique & Collectible Emporium
2200 Central Avenue
308/237-4972
Hours: Mon.-Sat. 10-5, Sun. 1-5

Directions: Conveniently located off I-30. Go right 2 blocks from first stop light—over railroad overpass.

For specific information on Kearney's largest antique mall see 1/2 page this section.

Great Plains Art & Antique
131 S. Central Ave.
308/234-5250

Antique Co-op
229 Central Ave.
308/236-6990

Dady's Antiques & Collectibles
1622 Central Ave.
308/236-8319

8 LEXINGTON

Kugler Antiques
311 S. Washington Street
308/324-4267
Open daily 10-6

Directions: From I-80, take the Lexington exit, turn north and go 2 miles.

Located in a town that claims the title of "Antique Center of Nebraska," Kugler Antiques is unique in its inventory of antique furniture, primitives, glassware, pottery, crocks, silver, coins and old guns. The shop prides itself on providing shoppers with authentic antiques and is well known for its unusual collections. One of the most interesting is a collection of old mannequins that might remind you of the old department store days, when window dressing was an art in itself.

Bargain John's Antiques
700 S. Washington Street
308/324-4576
Open Mon.-Sat. 8-7, Sun. 12-6

Directions: Traveling I-80, take the Lexington exit to Highway 283. Follow Highway 283 into Lexington and turn left at the Pizza Hut off of Highway 283. The shop is located in the blue building.

Bargain John's has been Nebraska's largest supplier of quality antique furnishings since 1968. They specialize in Victorian furniture from the 1840s to 1910. They also carry a small quantity of Mission oak pieces and a grand selection of Victorian art glass and cameo glass.

Richardson Bargain Shed
951 W. Walnut
308/324-4786

Memories B&B & Antiques
900 Washington St.
308/324-3290

Tinder Box
909 N. Grant
308/324-3585

Memories Antique Shop
900 N. Washington
308/324-3290

Young's Furniture & Auction
1108 N. Adams St.
308/324-4594

Hofaker's Antiques
Hwy. 283
308/324-4719

Leif's Antique Mall
Van Buren
308/324-2242

Trinkets & Treasures
E. Hwy. 30 & Jefferson
308/324-5344

9 LINCOLN

Burlington Arcade
210 N. 7th Street
402/476-6067
Open Mon.-Wed. and Sat. 10-6, Thu.-Fri. 10-8, Sun. 1-5

Directions: From I-80, take the 9th Street exit to the historic Hay Market District, where Burlington Arcade is located.

Voted "Lincoln's Best Antique Mall" in 1996, Burlington Arcade Antique Mall is housed in the old Taxi Cab Building in Lincoln's historic Hay Market District. The 30-plus dealers fill the 7,000-square-foot building with a mix of fine furniture, glassware, linen and jewelry. Great restaurants in the immediate area, combined with Burlington's treasures, make a day's outing a must for avid antiquers and history buffs.

B B & R Antique Mall
1709 O Street
402/474-7505
Open Mon.-Fri. 10-6, Sat. 10-5, Sun. 12-5

Directions: From I-80, take the exit to 27th Street and travel south to O Street. Turn right and the shop is located approximately 10 blocks down, near the intersection of O Street and 17th Street. Parking is available behind the shop.

This 42-dealer mall is celebrating its second anniversary this year. They have a large variety of antiques ranging from jewelry to furniture to collectibles from the 1930s to the 1960s—just a big mix of everything.

Conner's Architectural Antiques
701 P Street
402/435-3338
Open Mon.-Sat. 9:30-6, Sun. 1-5

Directions: From I-80, take the 9th Street exit. Conner's is located in the historic Hay Market District of Lincoln, across the street from the old train depot.

Housed in the old Beatrice Creamery building, Conner's Architectural Antiques offers 20,000 square feet of any and everything you'll need to decorate your home. You'll find lighting, stained glass windows, doors, fireplace mantles, old hardware, garden accents, fencing, wrought iron tables and much, much more.

Additionally, the shop offers a matching service with over 20,000 pieces of china and crystal patterns.

Country Store
2156 S. 7th St.
402/476-2254

Indian Village Fl. Mkt. Empor.
3235 S. 13th St.
402/423-5380

Antique Corner Cooperative
1601 S. 17th St.
402/476-8050

Pack Rats A Cooperative
1617 S. 17th St.
402/474-4043

Coach House Antiques Inc.
135 N. 26th St.
402/475-0429

Continental Furniture Ltd.
400 N. 48th St.
402/464-0434

Applebee's Antiques
3911 S. 48th St.
402/489-6326

Scherer's Architectural Antqs.
6500 S. 56th St.
402/423-1582

Gatherings Antiques & Gifts
150 Armour Bldg.
402/476-1911

Cornhusker Mall Antiques
2120 Cornhusker Hwy.
402/438-5122

Raggedy Ann's Antique Shoppe
1527 N. Cotner Blvd.
402/464-0456

Bittersweet Antiques & Gifts
2215 N. Cotner Blvd.
402/466-4966

Capitol Beach Antique Mall
1000 W. O St.
402/474-1125

Second Wind
1640 O St.
402/435-6072

Johnson's Old Curiosity Shop
2420 Dudley St.
402/476-0393

Q Street Mall
1835 Q St.
402/435-3303

10 LYONS

Kristi's Antiques, Inc.

Hwy. 77
402/687-2339
Open Mon.-Sat. 10-5, by appointment for dealers

Dealers, take note! Kristi's caters to you, as well as to the general shopper. They specialize in wholesaling, with over 1,000 pieces of original finish oak and walnut furniture. They also handle quilts, graniteware, stoneware, country store items, and thousands of smalls.

11 MCCOOK

Kenny's Country Gifts & Antqs.
N. Hwy. 83
308/345-2817

Accents Etc.
307 Norris Ave.
308/345-7720

Huegels Hutch
401 Norris Ave.
308/345-7564

12 MINDEN

Minden could be the ideal picture of sweet, romantic middle America: all old town square charm with antique stores and little businesses surrounded by Victorian mansions on manicured lawns, surrounded yet again by rolling, lush farmland.

It really is a cozy little Nebraska prairie town with an old and imposing courthouse complete with a big white dome! There are lots of prosperous businesses in the downtown district, including four antique shops.

Minden also has the Harold Warp Pioneer Village, one of the top museums of its kind in the country. This is an award-winning museum with 26 buildings holding 50,000 items that trace the development of everything from lighting and bathtubs to motorcycles and musical instruments from 1830 onwards. Among the buildings are seven historic structures, including an original livery stable complete with harness shop, and an authentic replica of a sod house. The museum also presents daily weaving, broom-making and other craft demonstrations.

House of Antiques
320 E. 5th St.
308/832-2200

Treasure Chest Antiques
320 E. 5th St.
308/832-1770

Granny's Attic
353 E. 4th St.
308/832-2504

Vinegar Hill Antiques
1161 25 Rd.
308/743-2445

13 NEBRASKA CITY

Nebraska City Antique Mall

800 Central Avenue
402/873-9805
Open Mon.-Sat. 10-5 and Sun. 12-4

Directions: Nebraska City Antique Mall is located on Highway 75, approximately 2 miles from I-29 in Iowa.

At Nebraska City Antique Mall 12 dealers offer shoppers furniture, glassware, pottery and a "wide selection of everything!"

Peppercricket Farm Antiques

Hwys. 2 and 75
402/873-7797
Open daily 10-5

Directions: Peppercricket is located at the intersection of State Highways 2 and 75, just south of Nebraska City.

This shop, with the very unusual name, specializes in Victorian era furniture, flow blue china and New England smalls.

Carriage House
512 Central Ave.
402/873-7410

Grandma Lu's
705 Central Ave.
402/873-5799

Cindy's Dream Shop
705 Central Ave.
402/873-5799

The Antique Shop
820 Central Ave.
402/873-3937

14 NORFOLK

Norfolk Market Place

207 Norfolk Avenue
402/644-7824
Open Mon.-Sat. 10-5, closed Sundays

Directions: Norfolk Market Place is located directly on Business Highway 275. Actually, Norfolk Avenue is Business 275!

This is a year-round indoor flea market, so browsing doesn't have to wait for good weather! They specialize in antiques, collectibles, furniture, and (here's an unusual one!) old saddles, tack and buckles.

Nic-Nac Patty/Wac
800 Custer Ave.
402/379-4529

Antique Arcade
Hwy. 81
402/379-0533

Reals Clock Repair & Antqs.
127 Norfolk Ave.
402/371-4966

Main Street Antiques
715 Norfolk Ave.
402/371-6400

15 NORTH PLATTE

The Hayloft

2006 E. 4th Street
308/532-1300
Open Mon.-Fri. 10-5:30, Sat. 10-5, Sun. 1-5

Directions: Traveling I-80, take Exit 177 or 179 to East 4th Street.

The Hayloft (sounds like a wonderful Nebraska name) offers a nice selection of antiques, collectibles, handcrafts, art and gift items.

Antique Emporium
2019 E. 4th St.
308/532-9003

Dynamic Perfection
120 Rodeo Rd.
308/532-7420

16 OMAHA

Kirk Collection

1513 Military Avenue
1-800-398-2542 or 402/551-0386
Fax: 402/551-0971
Open Tue.-Sat. 10-5 and Monday by appointment

Directions: Take I-80 to I-480 North to 75 North to the Hamilton Street exit. Go left on Hamilton 15 blocks to Military Avenue. Take a right on Military Avenue, and the shop is the second building on the right.

For specific information see review this section.

McMillan's Old Market Antqs.
509 S. 11th St.
402/342-8418

Finders Keepers of Omaha
423 S. 13th St.
402/346-1707

A & A Antiques Co-Op Mall
1244 S. 13th St.
402/346-2929

Joe's 13th St. Co-op Antiques
1414 S. 13th St.
402/344-3080

Standing Bear Antiques
1904 S. 13th St.
402/341-4240

Lifes Luxeries
3127 N. 60th Street
402/554-0993

Cobweb Corners
1941 S. 13th St.
402/334-2091

Anchor Harbor Antqs. & Cllbls.
4815 S. 24th St.
402/731-0558

Oberman's Furniture
4832 S. 24th St.
402/731-8480

A Bit of the Past
6620 S. 36th St.
402/733-8832

Katelman Antiques
39th & Farnam
402/551-4388

Cherishables
1710 N. 120th St.
402/493-2948

Treasure Mart
8316 Blondo St.
402/399-8874

City Slicker Antiques & Such
4973 Dodge St.
402/556-8271

Omaha Auction Center
7531 Dodge St.
402/397-9575

Franx Antiques & Art Inc.
3141 Farnam St.
402/345-5266

Blue Ribbon Flea Market
6606 Grover St.
402/397-6811

Antiques & Fine Art
1215 Howard St.
402/341-9942

Honest John's Emporium
1216 Howard St.
402/345-5078

Cosgrove Auct. Furn. & Antqs.
3805 Leavenworth St.
402/342-5254

Ana's Attic
4833 Leavenworth St.
402/556-7366

Anderson O'Brien Gallery
8724 Pacific St.
402/390-0717

Meadowlark Antique Mall
10700 Sapp Brothers Dr.
402/896-0800

Antiques Plus
6570 Maple St.
402/556-9986

Brass Armadillo Antique Mall
1066 Sapp Brothers Dr.
800/896-9140

Vinton Street Antique Mall
1806 Vinton St.
402/345-4499

17 PAPILLION

Country at Heart
114 N. Washington St.
402/339-5988

18 WATERLOO

Venice Antiques
26250 W. Center Road
402/359-5782
Open Mon.-Sat. 10-5, Sun. 12-5

Located on Highway 92, just 8 miles from Omaha, Venice Antiques lives up to the image its name conjures up. This Venice has the best depression glass dealers in the area—six to eight of them—in 10,000 square feet of space that also carries a mix of other antiques.

Black Horse Antiques
301 3rd St.
402/779-2419

Notes

Nevada

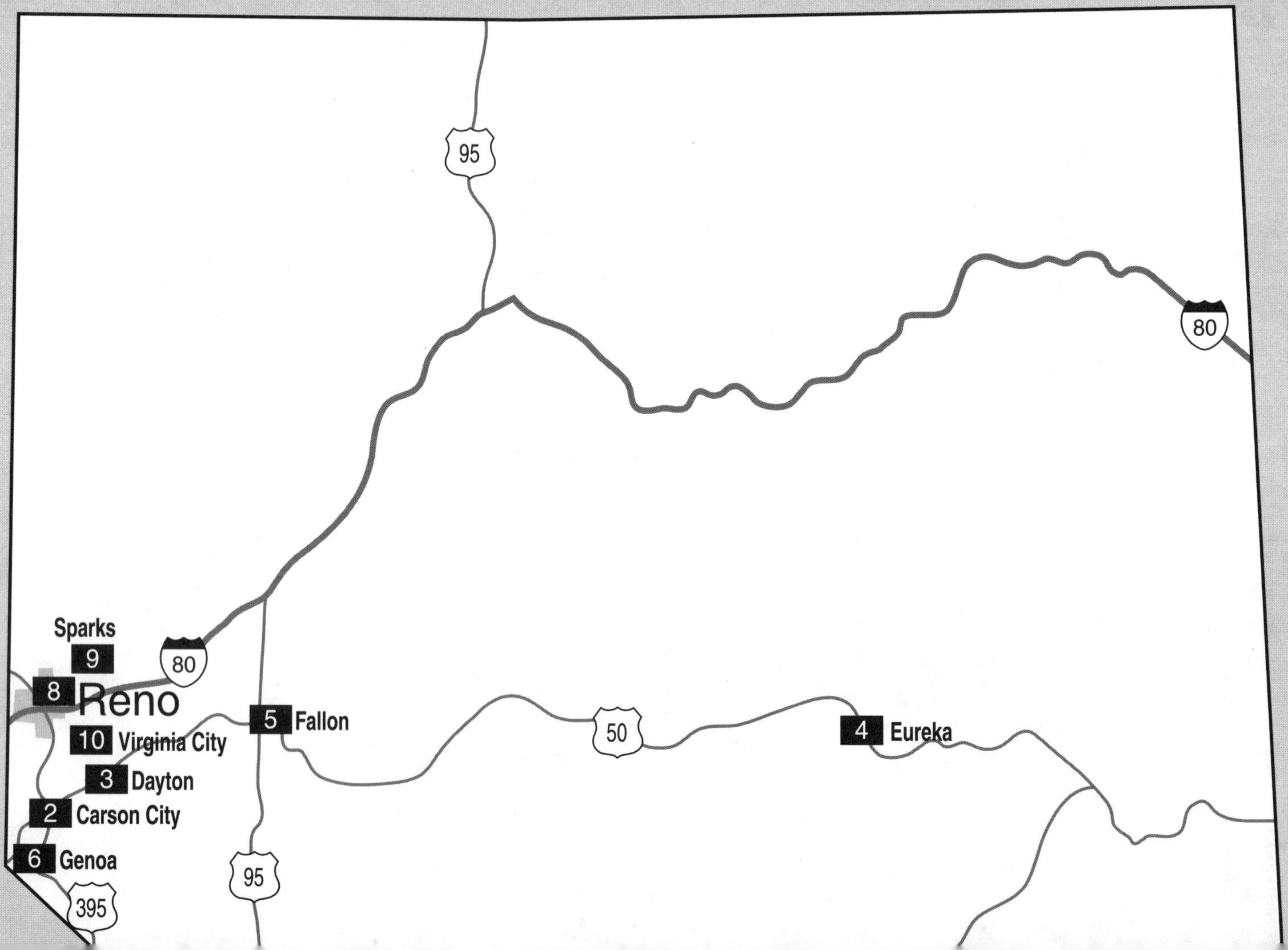
95
80
Sparks
9
80
8
Reno
5 Fallon
10 Virginia City
3 Dayton
2 Carson City
6 Genoa
95
395
50
4 Eureka

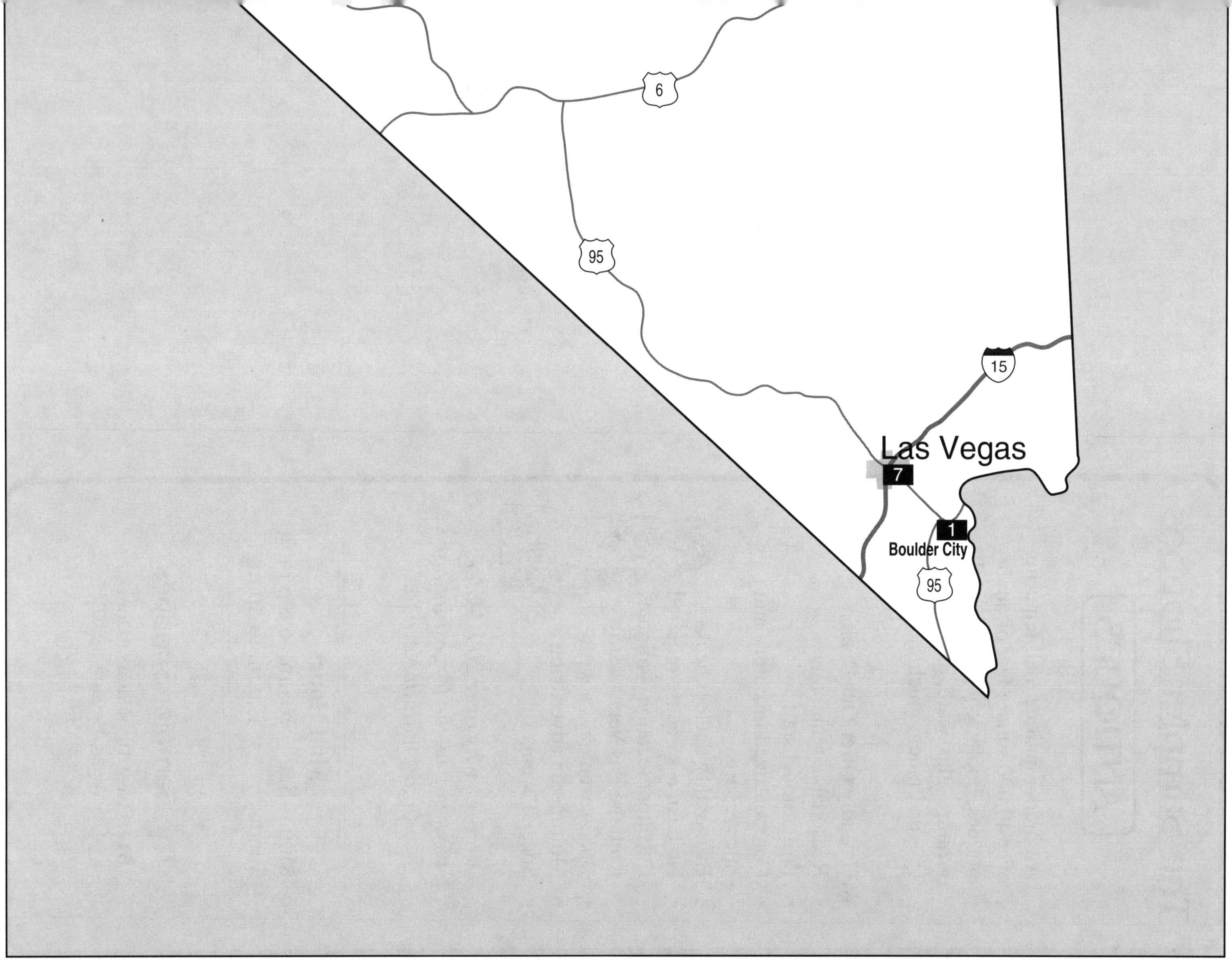

6
95
15
Las Vegas
7
1
Boulder City
95

1 BOULDER CITY

Ack's Attic
530 Nevada Hwy.
702/293-4035

Janean's Antiques
538 Nevada Hwy.
702/293-5747

Carole's Serendipity
544 Nevada Hwy.
702/293-7895

2 CARSON CITY

Deer Run Ranch Bed & Breakfast
5440 Eastlake Blvd.
Washoe Valley
702/882-3643
Rates: $80-95

"An Excerpt From the Archives of Deer Run Ranch"

The original ranch, called the Quarter Circle J P, was purchased in 1937 by Emily and Jim Greil (Muffy's parents) for back taxes of $2,400. It and the "Goat Ranch" at the foot of Jumbo Grade two miles north of here were the only residences on the one-lane dirt road around this side of Washoe Lake. All the children in the valley went to the one-room schoolhouse in Franktown, directly across the lake, grades 1-8, one teacher.

Legend has it that the ranch springs, including our spring and pond, watered small truck gardens, the produce being carried by wagon up "Deadman's" (our main driveway) and Jumbo Grades to Virginia City during the height of the mining boom on the Comstock in the late 1800s.

Sometime after the end of World War I, prohibition became the law of the land, and the "Moonshiners" gravitated to isolated lands with plenty of water to set up their stills. The spring tunnels here on the ranch were used for that purpose, and at some point before the repeal of prohibition in 1933, government agents blew up the stills, destroying the tunnel at our spring. Excavations for our house unearthed pipes and other distillery relics, as well as some of the old shoring from the original spring.

(Your hosts, David, an architect-builder, and Muffy Vhay, a professional artist-potter, are both longtime Nevada residents, and are knowledgeable about local lore and activities.)

"Deer Run Ranch As It Is Known Today"

Step out of the urban life, and into the peace and tranquility of one of the most idyllic spots in Nevada. Deer Run Ranch Bed and Breakfast is the perfect hideaway for a private, secluded getaway any time of the year. Alfalfa fields surround the complex, which has spectacular views of Washoe Lake and the Sierra Nevada mountains to the west. Tall cottonwoods shade the pond deck, a favorite spot for watching the abundant wildlife that call Deer Run home.

The private guest wing has two comfortable guest rooms with queen beds and private baths, and guest sitting room with private entry. In these tranquil guest rooms you can sit on the window seats and look out at the Sierras: or you might want to sit by the cozy fireplace in the sitting room, which is decorated with Navajo rugs and paintings, and enjoy the extensive library collection.

A full ranch breakfast, served at the handmade table in the sitting room, might include house specialties like omelets Florentine or Provencal. Enjoy fresh-brewed coffee and imported teas, home-baked specialty breads and muffins. Breakfast is served on pottery plates made on the ranch in the studio.

Country Castle
1210 N. Carson
702/887-7447

Bargain Barn
2106 N. Carson
702/883-3124

Great Basin Trading Co.
224 S. Carson St. Ste. 4
702/883-1183

Inglo Antiques & Collectibles
224 S. Carson St.
702/885-0657

Country House
4183 S. Carson St.
702/883-9796

Gasoline Alley
5853 S. Carson St.
702/884-4322

Chapel Antiques
112 N. Curry St.
702/885-8511

Callis Corner
202 N. Curry St.
702/885-9185

Harrington's Hall Closet
206 N. Curry St.
702/883-7707

Frontier Antique Mall
221 S. Curry St.
702/887-1466

Revelations
512 N. Curry St.
702/885-9645

Gold N Treasure
3110 Hwy. 50 E.
702/884-3777

Picard Et Cie
312 S. Carson St.
702/883-0323

Second Hand Rose
5891 U.S. Hwy. 50 E
702/883-6575

Art & Antiques
201 W. King St.
702/882-4447

Old West Antiques
111 Rice St.
702/882-4650

3 DAYTON

Butcher Block Antiques
45 Main
702/246-7056

Cottonwood Cottage
200 Main
702/246-5323

4 EUREKA

Situated on the "Loneliest Road in America," Eureka is the best preserved town on Hwy. 50 through Nevada. A stroll down Main Street in Eureka will take you back 100 years ago when Eureka was a thriving mining camp. Visit the historic courthouse, the Eureka Opera House, and the Eureka Sentinel Newspaper Building (now a fine museum). Explore the side streets and discover dozens of historic buildings, each with its own fascinating story.

Parsonage House Cottage
1023 Spring
702/237-5756
Year round accommodations.

Ease back into the past in this 1886 cottage where guests enjoy sole occupancy. Furnishings are antique and hand-crafted. Walnut and mahogany woods engulf guests in luxurious warmth and stately charm. A full kitchen and large six foot bathtub add further comforts.

5 FALLON

Beds & Spreads
203 S. Maine St.
702/423-2357

Just Country Friends
2180 Reno Hwy.
702/423-3315

Fallon Antique Mall
1951 W. Williams Ave.
702/423-6222

6 GENOA

Did you know Genoa is the home of the famous "Genoa Candy Dance?"

The "Candy Dance" originated in 1919 as an effort to raise money to purchase street lights for the community of Genoa. Lillian Virgin Finnegan, native born Genoan, and daughter of Judge D. W.. Virgin, suggested a dance with midnight supper at the Raycraft Hotel. As an added fundraiser, she encouraged the Genoa ladies to make a variety of candies to sell by the pound with samples passed around during the evening. The delicious candies proved to be the highlight of the evening and for the tiny town of Genoa, street lights became a reality.

The "Candy Dance" became an annual event, and each year the proceeds were used to keep Genoa's street lights burning. The dance and fair are held each year on the last full weekend in September.

Today, approximately 30,000 people attend this once-a- year, two day event when the Genoa candy makers and friends whip up approximately 3,000 lbs. of delicious candies such as nut fudge, plain fudge, turtles, almond roca, brittle, dipped chocolates, divinity and mints to name a few.

The "Genoa Candy Book," featuring prize winning candy recipes and a touch of Genoa's candy making history, is sold at the Candy Gazebo during the event.

Genoa House Inn
Jacks Valley Road
702/782-7075
Rates: $115-130

The Genoa House Inn is an authentic Victorian home on the National Register of Historic Places. Built in 1872 by A. C. Pratt, the town's first newspaper editor, the inn has a rich history of ownership.

The rooms here are distinct in their charm and individuality. One offers a private balcony, another a jacuzzi tub, yet another, a covered porch. All have private baths and are graced with period antiques and collectibles.

To add to the hospitality of the inn, innkeepers Linda and Bob Sanfilippo serve refreshments upon arrival. Early in the morning, coffee is delivered to your door, followed by a full breakfast served in the sunlit dining room; or if you prefer, in the privacy of your own room.

Genoa, the oldest settlement in Nevada, is nestled against the Sierra foothills with a panoramic view of

Carson Valley. Activities such as soaring, ballooning, or cycling are always available. For those who prefer to keep their feet on the ground, there are casual walks in the old town, tours of the various Victorian homes and buildings, or visits to Nevada's oldest saloon. There are also attractions in nearby Lake Tahoe and Virginia City.

Capture the charm of a simpler time in the place where Nevada began, at the Genoa House Inn.

Antiques Plus
2242 Main St.
702/782-4951

Westbrook Corner
2282 Main St.
702/782-3870

7 LAS VEGAS

The Sampler Shoppes Antiques
6115 West Tropicana
702/368-1170
Open Mon.-Sat., 10-6; Sunday 12-5

Directions: Taking Exit #37 from I-15 for Tropicana, go West on Tropicana 2 1/2 miles to Jones Boulevard. Located on the Southwest corner.

Just minutes from the Las Vegas "Strip" is the largest indoor antique mall in the state of Nevada. Occupying 40,000 square feet of floor space, this emporium displays a vast selection of quality furniture and antiques, books, toys, dolls, jewelry, and other collectibles.

With 200 dealers of distinction already represented, the mall is continuing to fill its available spaces, so there will be even more to delight the collector.

The "Pablo Picasso", located in the shoppes, serves coffee and light meals.

Yesteryear Mart
1626 E. Charleston Blvd.
702/384-6946

Josette's
1640 E. Charleston Blvd.
702/641-3892

Fields of Dreams
1647 E. Charleston Blvd.
702/385-2770

Silver Horse Antiques
1651 E. Charleston Blvd.
702/385-2700

Corner House Antiques
1655 E. Charleston Blvd.
702/387-0334

Fancy That
1909 E. Charleston Blvd.
702/382-5567

Antonio Nicholas Antiques
2016 E. Charleston Blvd.
702/385-7772

Yana's Junk
2018 E. Charleston Blvd.
702/388-0051

Antiques by Sugarplums Etc.
2022 E. Charleston Blvd.
702/385-6059

Nicholson & Oszadlo
2020 E. Charleston Blvd.
702/388-1202

A Estate Antiques
2026 E. Charleston Blvd. Ste A
702/388-4289

Granny's Nook & Cranny
2032 E. Charleston Blvd.
702/598-1983

Judy's Antiques
2040 E. Charleston Blvd.
702/386-9677

Antiques by Sara
3020 W. Charleston, Ste. 4
702/877-4330

Maudies Antique Cottage
3310 E. Charleston Blvd.
702/457-4379

Red Rooster Antique Mall
307 W. Charleston Blvd.
702/382-5253

Ratliffs Antiques
2532 E. Desert Inn Rd.
702/796-9686

Vintage Antique Mall
3379 Industrial Rd.
702/369-2323

House of Antique Slots
1236 Las Vegas Blvd. S
702/382-1520

Antiquities International
3500 Las Vegas Blvd. S
702/792-2274

Victorian Casino Antiques
1421 S. Main St.
702/382-2466

Anellos Collectibles All Kinds
1115 Western Ave.
702/366-1664

Maverick Antiques
3160 W. Sahara Ave.
702/253-7340

From China & Beyond
6336 W. Sahara Ave.
702/871-8801

Romantic Notions
6125 W. Tropicana Ave., Ste. F
702/248-1957

American Collectibles
6125 W. Tropicana Ave., Ste. F
702/248-1957

Valentino's Zootsuit Connection
906 S. Sixth St., Ste. B
702/383-9555

Great Places To Eat

Country Star American Music Grill
On the Strip at Harmon between Tropicana and Flamingo
702/740-8400

Food and drink lovers will find a delightful choice of exciting new menues at the Country Star. This restaurant, backed by Vince Gill, Reba McIntire, and Wynonna, offers high-quality American cuisine at moderate prices and features country music memorabilia, a huge video wall, and CD "listening post" where guests can check out the latest country hits.

8 RENO

Karen Hillary Antiques
418 California Ave.
702/322-1800

All R Yesterday Image of Past
125 Gentry Way
702/827-2355

Antique Collective
400 Mill St.
702/322-3989

Wells Avenue Antiques
719 E. 2nd St.
702/324-0100

Briar Patch Antiques
634 W. 2nd St.
702/786-4483

Antique Pleasure Palace
765 S. Virginia St.
702/324-7731

Antique Mall-Virginia St.
1215 S. Virginia St.
702/324-1003

Antique Marketplace
1301 S. Virginia St.
702/348-6444

Reno Antiques
677 S. Wells Ave.
702/322-5858

Times Past Antiques
855 S. Wells Ave.
702/329-0937

Grant's Tomb
721 Willow St.
702/322-6800

Past & Present Antiques
128 East Sixth St.
702/329-4370

9 SPARKS

Victorian Square Antique Mall
834 Victorian Ave.
702/331-2288

Heartfelt Handmade & Antqs.
1434 Victorian Ave.
702/356-8677

10 VIRGINIA CITY

Gold Hill Hotel
Hwy. 342
702/847-0111
Rates $35-135

Gracing the western countryside with quiet charm and elegance, Nevada's oldest hotel, Gold Hill Hotel, built in the late 1850s surrounds guests with period antiques. History and beauty combine in this setting where guests can relax in spacious rooms and soak in an antique claw foot tub. Some rooms have fireplaces—great for those chilly Nevada nights.

A wine list, with over 160 selections, compliments the wonderful meals served at the Gold Hill Hotel.

Comstock Antiques
408 N. A
702/847-0626

Notes

New Hampshire

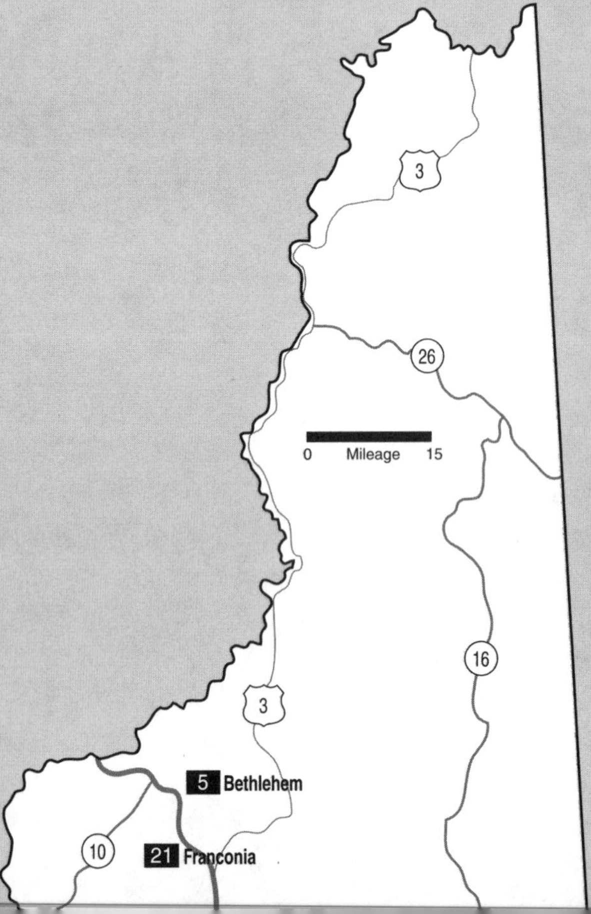

Wayside Inn

Riverside Lodging
in turn of century
New England
Country Inn

Bethlehem **5**

Blanche's

Bed & Breakfast
19th Century
Victorian Farmhouse
Artist's Studio
on premises

Franconia **21**

The Cliff Lodge

Romantic spot
overlooking
Newfound Lake.
Casual Dining

Newfound Lake **31**

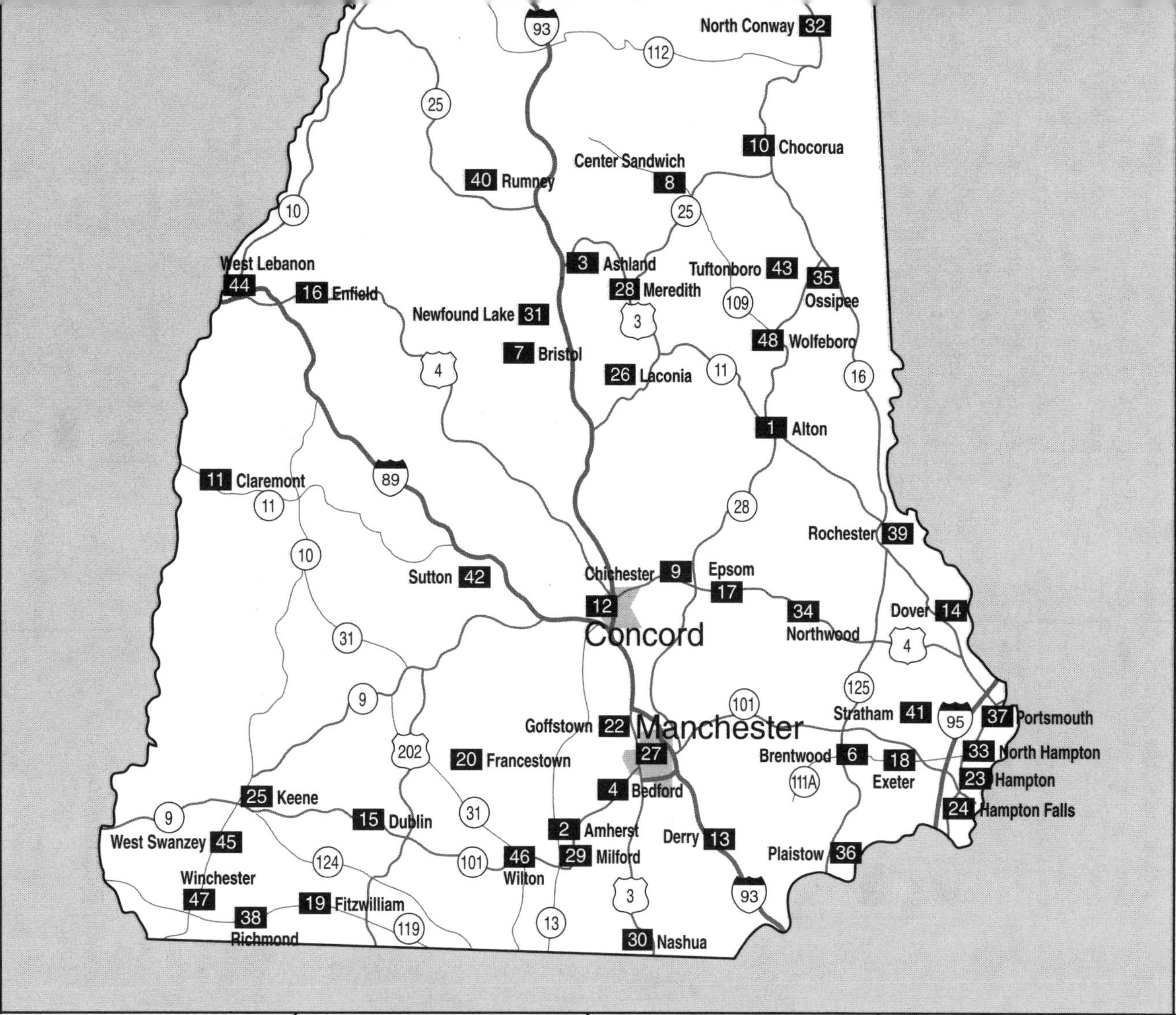

Wolfeboro Antiques Fair

45th Year

48

Start the Week Off Happy!

New England Antique & Collectibles Festival

Center Sandwich **8**

The Inn On Newfound Lake & Pasquaney Restaurant

Welcoming Travelers Since 1840
603-744-9111

Newfound Lake **31**

Checkered Past Antiques

Antique in an
Old 19th
Century Barn.

Bethleham **5**

Sutton Mills Antiques

Located in an
old 19th Century
General Store

Sutton **42**

Zahn's Alpine Guest House

HOSPITALITY IN THE STYLE OF ALPINE EUROPE

Extended European breakfast. Quiet, wooded location in the heart of Southern New Hampshire's Antique Trail. Moderately priced.
"Auf Wiedersehen Frau"

Milford **29**

1 ALTON

Cottontail Collectibles
Main - Rt. 11
603/875-5456

Homestead Place Antiques
Jct. Routes 11 & 23
603/875-2556

2 AMHERST

Tricorn Antiques
50 State Rt. 101A
603/672-2268

Consignment Gallery
74 State Rt. 101A
603/673-4114

Needful Things
112 State Rt. 101A
603/889-1232

101 A Antique Center
114 State Rt. 101A
603/880-8422

Antiques at Mayfair
119 State Rt. 101A
603/595-7531

Antiques at Mayfair
121 State Rt. 101A
603/598-9250

Iris Antiques
141 State Rt. 101A
603/882-2665

Mori Books
141 State Rt. 101A
602/882-2665

3 ASHLAND

Antique House
9 Highland
603/968-3357

Olde World Antiques
9 N. Main
603/968-9277

4 BEDFORD

Bell Hill Antiques
Rt. 101
603/472-5580

5 BETHLEHEM

Wayside Inn
Rt. 302, P.O. Box 480
603/869-3364 or 1-800-448-9557
Open daily 8-10; except Thanksgiving and Christmas

Directions: Take Exit #40 off I-93. Go east on Rt. 302 for 6.3 miles. The inn is on the right side.

Wayside Inn has a long and interesting history. It began in 1832, when the main building was built as a railroad boarding house for railroad workers (it sits across from the tracks). Around 1900 it became an inn for the general traveling public, and has remained open as such for nearly a century, making it the oldest continually operating inn in the area. The Victorian style building holds an extensive collection of antiques and quilts, and offers guests 28 rooms, all with private baths. There is an award-winning restaurant and lounge for guests' dining pleasure, and the restaurant gives diners a rare opportunity to enjoy Swiss specialties.

Checkered Past Antiques
154 Guider Lane
603/444-6628
Open year round, Mon.-Sat., 10-5; Sun., 12-4; closed Wednesdays Nov.-June.
E-mail: kscope@ConnRiver.net

Directions: Located at the junction of Rt. 302 and I-93 (Exit #40), Checkered Past is easily accessible. When exiting off I-93 or traveling Rt. 302 east, turn left at the Adair Country Inn sign and take Guilder Lane 4/10 of a mile to the end. When heading west on Rt. 302, immediately before the junction of I-93, turn right at the Adair Country Inn sign and follow Guilder Lane 4/10 of a mile to the end.

In addition to Checkered Past's (what a great name!) ever-changing array of antiques, their *heated* 19th century barn holds hand-crafted, custom-made reproduction furniture.

Curran's Antiques
Main St.
603/869-2089

Hundred Acre Wood
Main St.
603/869-6427

The Raven's Nest
Main St.
603/869-2678

3 of Cups
Main St.
603/869-2606

6 BRENTWOOD

Crawley Falls Antiques
159 Crawley Falls Road
603/642-3417

Directions: (From Massachusetts) Take I-495 North to Exit #51B (Rt. 125). Follow Rt. 125 for approximately 16 miles. Look for the blinking light at the intersection of Routes 125 and 111A. Turn right at light, then make immediate left and go about 300 yards to shop parking lot. Shop is on the hill behind Lindy's Country Store. (From Rt. 101): Take Rt. 125 exit. South approximately 5 miles to Rt. 111A, left at blinking light.

Visit this fabulous 18th Century homestead where the barn shop is filled with antique furniture and decorative accessories - primitive and vintage. The shop also features linens, china, artists' signed teddy bears (some made specially for the shop), ephemera and a wide selection of smalls. Displays not only show off the fine pieces in this shop, but are also artfully arranged to help you visualize ways to decorate your own home. Owner Donna Judah has created a warm and inviting atmosphere at Crawley Falls, complete with a children's area and sitting porch. No matter what your collecting interests, you surely will find something to take home with you at this wonderful shop.

7 BRISTOL

Tin Shoppe
13 Central Square
603/744-5723

New Hampton Antiques Center
Rt. 104
603/744-5652

Remember When
Rt. 104 - 52 Summer St.
603/744-2191

8 CENTER SANDWICH

New England Antiques & Collectibles Festival
"A Show, Sale & Celebration of Old Time Living"
Call number below for dates
Sandwich Fairgrounds, Junctions 113 & 109

New Hampshire's largest show, sale and celebration of old time living features over 200 exhibitors of antiques and collectibles. Emphasis is placed on family fun, live entertainment and nostalgia.

Great buys can be found on garden decorations, architectural details, fiesta ware, vintage toasters, radios, linens, tools, textiles, ephemera, robots, costume and bakelite jewelry, '50s kitsch, dolls, art pottery, series books and country furniture. Interactive demonstrations include hearthside cooking, bee keeping, blacksmithing, and soap making. Vintage car, truck and motorcycle show, sale and swap held simultaneously on 22-acre fairgrounds in a quaint New England village.

For more information call New England Antique Show Management, 603/539-1900.

9 CHICHESTER

Austin's Antiques
Rt. 4
603/798-3116

Teachers' Antiques at Thunder Bridge
11 Depot Road
603/798-4314

Two floors of painted country items, flow blue and Shaker smalls.

10 CHOCORUA

Michael Dam Bookseller
Rt. 16
603/323-8041

Lucky Acres
Rt. 16
603/323-8502

Chocorua View Farm Antiques
Rt. 16
603/323-8041

11 CLAREMONT

La Deaus Annex
38 Main St.
603/542-6352

Farmor's Group Shoppes
61 Main St.
603/542-2532

Scottish Bear's Antiques Inc.
54 Pleasant St.
603/543-1978

Antique Center
66 Pleasant St.
603/542-9331

12 CONCORD

House & House Collectibles
1 Eagle Square
603/225-0050

Ol' Speedway
374 Loudon Rd
603/226-0977

Interior Additions
38 N. Main St.
603/224-3414

B & M Trading Post
176 S. Main St.
603/753-6241

Whispering Birches Antiques
185 S. Main St.
603/753-8519

13 DERRY

Derry Exchange
132 W. Broadway
603/437-8771

GRS Trading Post
108 Chester Rd.
603/434-0220

Antique & Used Furniture
1 Pinkerton St.
603/437-4900

Log Cabin
182 Rockingham Rd.
603/434-7068

14 DOVER

Michael Bennet Antiques
917 Central Ave.
603/742-9955

Horse & Buggy Antiques
34 Freshet Rd.
603/742-2989

Flashbacks
10 Pierce St.
603/743-6542

Timeless Appeal
83 Washington St.
603/749-7044

15 DUBLIN

Hedge House
Main St. - Rt. 101
603/563-8833

Peter Pap Oriental Rugs
Rt. 101
603/563-8717

Seaver & McLellan Antiques
Rt. 101
603/563-7144

16 ENFIELD

Mary Keane House
Box 5, Lower Shaker Village
603/632-4241, 1-888-239-2153
http://mary.keene@valley.net
Open year round

Directions: From I-89, take Exit #17. Bear right on Rt. 4 (east) for 1 1/2 miles. Turn right at the blinker light on Rt. 4A and go 3 miles. The Mary Keane House is on the left in the heart of Lower Shaker Village.

Mary Keane House is a late Victorian style Bed & Breakfast located in the heart of historic Lower Shaker Village on the shore of Mascoma Lake. Expansive grounds, gardens, secluded beach and open and wooded hiking trails protected by 1200 acres of New Hampshire conservation district provide a peaceful and serene setting for a relaxing and stress-busting stay. Five spacious and light-filled one and two room suites (all with private baths) provide for your pleasure, antiques and comfort, elegance and whimsy. Watch the morning mist rise off the lake from your own balcony or enjoy the sunset from the glider swing on the west porch. The lakeside screened porch is the perfect spot to enjoy a summer afternoon conversation, book or nap while the living room with fireplace is the place to chase winter's chill. Full breakfast is served in the sunny dining room. They'll even pack you a picnic lunch for the antique trail or the hiking trail.

Interesting Side Trips

The Museum at Lower Shaker Village and Dana Robes' Workshop
Rt. 4A
For Museum information call 603/632-4346
For Dana Robes' Wood Craftsmen information call 603/632-5385

Here in 1793 the Shakers established their Chosen Vale, a village of quietly majestic buildings, gardens and fields. Today, the Shaker heritage is preserved at the Museum at Lower Shaker Village and the Dana Robes Wood Craftsmen. Walking tours, exhibits, craft demonstrations, workshops, special programs and events, and extensive gardens bring new life to Shaker culture at the Museum. Reproduction Shaker furniture, and furniture inspired by Shaker design, is made by hand at Dana Robes' workshop.

17 EPSOM

North Wind Antiques
56 Dover Rd.
603/736-9293

Chichester House of Antiques
146 Dover Rd.
603/798-4688

Epsom Trading Post
Rt. #28
603/736-8843

18 EXETER

Peter Sawyer Antiques
17 Court Street
603/772-5279
Open by appointment or by chance, but almost always open Mon.-Fri, 8-5

Offering appraisal and conservation services, Peter Sawyer Antiques specializes in important American clocks, particularly those of the New England area. They also offer a selection of fine 18th and 19th century New England furniture (emphasizing original state of preservation), American paintings, watercolors, drawing and folk art.

Decor Antiques
11 Jady Hill Circle
603/772-4538

Scotch Thistle
92 Portsmouth Ave.
603/778-2908

Dennis A. Waters
15 Oak St.
603/772-9065

19 FITZWILLIAM

Rainy Day Books
Rt. 119
603/585-3448
Fax: 603/585-9108
Open early April-mid November, 11-5 Thur.-Mon., and by appointment/chance, closed Tuesdays-Wednesdays.

Antiquarian books showcased in an antique setting in the center of New Hampshire - it's a true antique lover's paradise! Rainy Day Books is a used and antiquarian bookstore housed in a 19th century barn and adjacent house in Fitzwilliam, the antique center of the southern Monadnock region. There are five other antiquarian book shops within half an hour's drive of Fitzwilliam. Rainy Day has a general stock of over 30,000 books, and a good selection of old prints and maps. In addition to the general stock, they also have sizable collections in the following special areas: amateur radio, American History/Civil War, audio engineering, children's, computer technology, cookbooks, fiber arts, outdoors, polar/mountaineering, radar and antenna engineering, radio and wireless, radio broadcasting, royalty, steam engines, surveying, town histories, and transportation. (Oh, and by the way, they have a great name.)

Bloomin Antiques
Fitzwilliam
603/585-6688

Red Barn Antiques
Old Richmond Rd.
603/585-3134

Fitzwilliam Antiques
Rt. 12
603/585-9092

Clocks on the Common
Village Green
603/585-3321

20 FRANCESTOWN

Mill Village Antiques
195 New Boston Rd.
603/547-2050

Stonewall Antiques
532 New Boston Rd.
603/547-3485

21 FRANCONIA

Blanche's Bed & Breakfast
351 Easton Valley Road
603/823-7061
Open year round
Rates $40-85

Directions: From I-93: Take Exit 38 to Rt. 116 south for 5 miles. From I-91: Take Exit 17 to Rt. 302 east. Go 7 miles to Rt. 112 east, then go 9 miles to Rt. 116 north, then approximately 6 more miles to Blanche's.

Blanche's B&B gives guests a chance to relax in Victorian splendor while immersing themselves in an artistic atmosphere. Blanche's - named, by the way, for the family dog - is a restored 19th century Victorian farmhouse with views of the Kinsman Ridge. The artistic atmosphere is prevalent in the numerous decorative paintings scattered throughout the house, and an artist's working studio on the premises featuring hand painted canvas rugs. Steeped in the English B&B tradition,

Blanche's offers antiques throughout, to compliment the cotton linens, down comforters, comfortable beds and great breakfast for the five guest rooms, one with private bath.

22 GOFFSTOWN

Philip Davanza Clock Repair
Addison Rd.
603/668-2256

Griffin Watch & Antiques
5 S. Mast St.
603/497-2624

Country Princess Antiques
191 Mast
603/497-2909

23 HAMPTON

H G Webber
495 Lafayette Rd.
603/926-3349

24 HAMPTON FALLS

Antiques New Hampshire
Rt. 1 Lafayette Rd.
603/926-9603

Antiques One
Rt. 1 Lafayette Rd.
603/926-5332

Barn Antqs. at Hampton Falls
Rt. 1 Lafayette Rd.
603/926-9003

Antiques at Hampton Falls
Rt. 1 Lafayette Rd.
603/926-1971

25 KEENE

Classic Decorator
168 Emerald Street
603/355-4415

Good Fortune
114 Main St.
603/357-7500

Colony Mill Marketplace
222 West St.
603/357-1240

26 LACONIA

Agora Collectibles
373 Court St.
603/524-0129

Almost All Antiques
100 New Salem St.
603/527-0043

LKS Regn Flea Market & Antiques Exchange
38 Pearl St.
603/524-2441

27 MANCHESTER

End of Trail Antiques
420 Chestnut St.
603/669-1238

Postcards from the Past
571 Mast Rd.
603/668-5229

Thistle Stop Antiques
77 Pleasant St.
603/668-3678

N H Bargain Mart
334 Union St.
603/666-3644

28 MEREDITH

Etcetra Shoppe
Rt. 25
603/279-5062

Alexandria Lamp Shop
48 Main Street
603/279-4234

Burlwood Antique Center
Rt. 3
603/279-6387

Gordon's Antiques
Rt. 3
603/279-5458

Old Print Barn
Winona Road
603/279-6479

29 MILFORD

Zahn's Alpine Guest House

Rt. 13
603/673-2334
Fax: 603/673-8415
Located on Rt. 13 in Mont Vernon, New Hampshire on the Milford Town Line
Rates: Single $56, double $65 includes tax
WebSite: www.cinemagraphics.com/zahns

Directions: Zahn's Alpine Guest House is on a straight stretch of Rt. 13 with unimpeded visibility for almost a mile. On the left side (coming out of Milford, heading north) there is absolutely nothing at the roadside except the guest house's little cluster of signs (reflective at night), a lamp post (the only one), mail box, luminous green town line marker, and the mouth of the driveway. The building itself is obscured by trees, but there are five yard lanterns.

Here's a twist that's a really nice change from the usual bed and breakfast. Bud and Anne Zahn have spent a lot of time in Austria, Bavaria and the South Tirol (northern Italy) over the past 30 years while importing antiques and leading bike/ski groups to Alpine Europe. Over the years they stayed primarily in small, out-of-the-way lodging places where the style of hospitality was quite different from anything stateside. They enjoyed this European experience so much that they decided to recreate such a place in the states - and so Zahn's Alpine Guest House was born.

They chose pine post and beams for the outer structure, which not only gave the house the heavy, timbered look of the old Alpine farmhouses, but lent itself perfectly to the deeply overhung roof (you don't have to close the windows when it rains), and the perimeter balcony. They shipped in a sea container full of antique farm furnishings, Alpine-authentic carpets, lampshades, wrought-iron lanterns and accessories. One of the highpoints that all guests comment on are the specially made mattresses and appropriate bedding that are exact replicas of the Alpine style. There are eight double rooms with private baths. One room has a conventional double bed. The others have European twin beds (three inches wider and six inches longer than usual). The top cover is an untucked, European style comforter inside a sheeting cover. When these beds are pushed together, the effect is that of an oversized double bed, and the space between the mattresses is minimal.

The *Stube* (evening and breakfast room) is, as in Europe, at the disposal of all the guest. Worth a visit just to examine something every American homeowner should consider is the *Kachelofen* - the hand-made-on-site, hand-decorated, two-ton tile oven. Almost all dwellings in Alpine Europe utilize these marvelous heaters which exploit masonry characteristics of "quick absorption, slow release of heat." The Zahns were fortunate to find a Bavarian Master Builder fairly nearby who could create one for the guest house.

Antiquers' constitute a strong portion of the clientele at Zahn's due to the literally hundreds of antique shops located within 15-20 minutes of the house.

Elm Plaza Antique Center
222 Elm St. (Rt. 101A)
603/672-7846

Centurywood Antiques
571 Elm St. (Rt. 101A)
603/672-2264

New Hampshire Antique Co-op
Elm St. (Rt. 101A)
603/673-8499

Milford Antiques
40 Nashua St. (Rt. 101A)
603/672-2311

Golden Opportunities
326 Nashua St. (Rt. 101A)
603/672-1223

J C Devine Inc.
20 South St.
603/673-4967

30 NASHUA

House of Josephs Antiques & Collectibles

523 Broad Street
603/882-4118
Open Tue.-Sun., 10-5

Directions: From Rt. 3 North, take Exit #6 and bear left off the ramp onto Rt. 130 West. From Rt. 3 South, take Exit #6 and bear right off the ramp onto Rt. 130 West. Either way, go approximately 3 miles. The shop is a big red barn on the right.

Housed in an actual, traditional red barn on Broad Street, this multi-dealer shop offers the discriminating antiquer an assortment of fine furniture, china, glass and collectibles. The shop has been in business for over 25 years, and holds a large selection of furniture and, among its many dealers, several who specialize in either oriental items, beer memorabilia, and glass pieces.

Crown Hill Antiques
91 Allds St.
603/880-0966

A A Antiques & Memorabilia
214 Daniel Webster Hwy.
603/888-3222

L Morin Treasures
191 W. Hollis St.
603/883-2809

Past & Present
202 Main St.
603/880-7991

31 NEWFOUND LAKE

The Inn On Newfound Lake and Pasquany Restaurant

Rt. 3A
603/744-9111 or 1-800-745-7990 (reservations only)
Fax: 603/744-3894
Open daily 9-9
Rates $55-105

Directions: Take I-93 North (from Boston) to Exit 23. At the bottom of the ramp continue north on Rt. 104. At the small town of Bristol (approximately 6 miles) bear to the right (Rt. 3A). Continue on Rt. 3A approximately 6 miles, until you reach the inn, which is between the towns of Bristol and Plymouth.

The Inn on Newfound Lake has been welcoming

travelers since 1840. Formerly known as the Pasquaney Inn, it was the midway stop on the stage coach route from Boston to Montreal and now is the only remaining inn on the lake - at one time there were seven or eight. Located on seven and a half acres of lush New Hampshire countryside, the inn hugs the shore of Newfound Lake, the fourth largest lake in New Hampshire, and rated as one of the purest and cleanest bodies of fresh water in the world. As you can imagine, there is something to do outdoors in every season at the inn. Or if relaxation is what you're looking for, just kick back in one of the 31 extensively refurbished rooms. The main inn has 19 rooms, eleven with private baths and a common sitting room. Elmwood Cottage, which adjoins the main building by the veranda, contains 12 rooms, all with private baths and adjoining daybed rooms if needed. The cottage parlor has a full fireplace for added enjoyment. Besides the myriad outdoor activities and sports, indoor activities at the inn include shuffleboard, basketball, billiards, and table tennis, and a Jacuzzi and weight room.

When guests work up and appetite, they can go to the full-service Pasquaney Restaurant and tavern at the inn. The restaurant, complete with wood-burning stove, overlooks the lake for added atmosphere. Continental breakfast, lunch, dinner and Sunday brunch are available.

The Cliff Lodge
Rt. 3A
603/744-8660

Directions: Take I-93 north to Exit #23. At the bottom of the ramp take Rt. 104 North. When you reach the town of Bristol (approximately 6 miles), bear right on Rt. 3. Head north on Rt. 3 about 4 miles to the lodge.

Here is a restaurant and cabins offering wonderful, casual country dining in a lodge perched on the side of a hill overlooking Newfound Lake. What better view could you ask for! It's a very romantic spot, and cabin rentals are available in the summer. A perfect weekend getaway, where you can enjoy the lake and surrounding countryside, eat great meals at your leisure, and never have to fight traffic!

32 NORTH CONWAY

Sedler's Antiques
Kearsarge
603/356-6008

Antiques & Collectibles Barn
Rt. 16
603/356-7118

Aunt Aggie's Attic
Rt. 16
603/356-0060

Expressions By Robt. N. Waldo
Rt. 16
603/356-3611

Richard M Plusch
Rt. 16
603/356-3333

John F Whitesides Antiques
Rt. 16
603/356-3124

33 NORTH HAMPTON

North Hampton Antq. Center
1 Lafayette Rd.
603/964-6615

Silver & Sontz
30 Lafayette Rd.
603/964-6043

John Piperhouse
Sandy Point Rd.
603/778-1347

34 NORTHWOOD

Parker-French Antique Center
1st New Hampshire Turnpike
603/942-8852

R S. Butler's Trading Co.
1st New Hampshire Turnpike
603/942-8210

White House Antiques
1st New Hampshire Turnpike
603/942-8994

Willow Hollow Antiques
1st New Hampshire Turnpike
603/942-5739

Country Tavern Antiques
Rt. 4
603/942-7630

Coveway Corner Antiques
Rt. 4
603/942-7500

The Hay Loft Antique Center
Rt. 4
603/942-5153

Town Pump Antiques
Rt. 4
603/942-5515

35 OSSIPEE

Lakewood Station Antiques
Rt. 16
603/539-7414

Mark R Burns Antiques
Old Rt. 16
603/539-2489

Red Pine Antiques
Rt. 16
603/539-6834

Mountain Road Antiques
Norman Drew Hwy.
603/539-7136

Grant Hill Antiques
53 Main St. (Center Ossipee)
603/539-2431

Antler Antiques
Chickville Road
603/539-6822

The Stuff Shop
Rt. 171
603/539-7715

36 PLAISTOW

Granny's Attic
160 Plaistow
603/382-9195

Plaistow Commons Antiques
166 Plaistow
603/382-3621

37 PORTSMOUTH

Antiques Etc.
85 Albany St.
603/436-1286

Trunk Shop
23 Ceres St.
603/431-4399

Ed Weissman
110 Chapel St.
603/431-7575

Olde Port Traders
275 Islington
603/436-2431

Margaret Carter Scott Antiques
175 Market St.
603/436-1781

Victory Antiques
96 State St.
603/431-3046

Antiques & Art
116 State St.
603/431-3931

38 RICHMOND

The Yankee Smuggler Antiques
122 Fitzwilliam Road
603/239-4188
Fax: 603/239-4653
Open daily by chance or by appointment

Directions: Located 1/2 mile east of Rt. 32 (Richmond Four Corners). From I-91: Take Exit 28 (Northfield) to Rt. 10 to Winchester. Take a right on Rt. 119 and go 6 miles to Richmond Four Corners (blinking light). Yankee Smuggler is the sixth house on the left.

Ted and Carole Hayward are nearing their 40th year in the antique business and are still actively buying and selling quality country antiques, folk art and related accessories. Specializing in 18th and 19th century American country antiques with original painted surfaces, they carry large pieces of furniture like cupboards, tables, chest of drawers, desks, etc., as well as related accessories such as firkins, pantries, bowls, and picture frames, all in original paint - blue, red, green, mustard, and salmon, and grain, feather and sponge decorated. Visitors to The Yankee Smuggler can browse through two rooms in Ted and Carole's circa 1815 home, plus a large barn adjacent to the house. They are open year round by chance or appointment, but they suggest visitors call ahead first - that way they can start a fresh pot of coffee!

39 ROCHESTER

Elkins Trash & Treasures
26 & 28 N. Main St.
603/332-1848

Four Corners Antiques
204 Estes Rd.
603/332-1522

Signal St. Antiques
5 Signal St.
603/335-0810

40 RUMNEY

Courtyard Antiques
Rt. 25
603/786-2306

Willow Tree Antiques
Rt. 25
603/786-2787

41 STRATHAM

Compass Rose Antiques
17 Winnicut Road
603/778-0163

Directions: Compass Rose is located 10 miles west of Portsmouth, just off Rt. 33.

This charming shop carries a wide range of antiques with a focus on accessories. A few select furniture pieces are available, but what's lacking in furnishings is made up in the enormous offering of smalls. They carry exquisite lighting fixtures, glass, china, jewelry and much, much more. Antique weapons are also included among their inventory. Owners, Charles and Laurie Clark, have been in business for seventeen years, and the shop is actually located at their home. All of their items are "really" old (nothing modern) antiques from the 1800s.

Among the Clark's specialties are glass and china from the 1800s, "no depression or collectibles," says Laurie. Charles is the antique weapons expert and is a licensed gun dealer. Lighting fixtures, mainly whale oil lamps and lanterns, are also his forte.

The Wingate Collection
94 Portsmouth
603/778-4849

42 SUTTON

Sutton Mills Antiques
90 Main Street
603/927-4557
Open Tue.-Sat. 10-6; Sun., 12-5; closed Mondays

Directions: From I-89 North and South: Take Exit #10 and follow 114 south for 4 miles. Turn right on Main Street and the store is 1/2 mile on the right.

Sutton Mills is located in 1,900 square feet of an old, 19th century general store. This ten-dealer group features furniture, glass, old tools, estate and costume jewelry, coins and Americana.

43 TUFTONBORO

Dow Corner Shop
Rt. 171
603/539-4790

Golden Past Shop
Rt. 109A
603/569-4249

Treasure Hunt
Rt. 171
603/539-4863

Log Cabin Antiques
Rt. 109 A Ledge Hill Rd.
603/569-1909

The Ewings
65 Federal Corner
603/569-3861

44 WEST LEBANON

Terry's Antiques
Colonial Plaza-Airport Rd.
603/298-0556

Colonial Antique Markets
Rt. 12 A
603/298-7712

45 WEST SWANZEY

Knotty Pine Antiques Market
Rt. 10
603/352-5252

46 WILTON

New England Antiques
101 Intervale Rd.
603/654-5674

Here Today
71 Main
603/654-5295

Noah's Ark
Rt. 101
603/654-2595

47 WINCHESTER

Latchkey Antiques
4 Corners Plaza
603/239-6777

Hearthside
858 Keene Rd.
603/239-8697

48 WOLFEBORO

The 44th Annual Wolfeboro Antiques Fair
Call number below for dates
10 a.m.-4 p.m.
Brewster Academy, South Main Street

Held for 44 continuous years, this show highlights 75 dealers in room settings and outdoors in a courtyard. Exhibitors offer high quality antiques ranging from estate jewelry, Oriental rugs, quilts, books and prints, to rustic, primitive and formal furniture, glass, paintings and silver. Located in Wolfeboro at Brewster Academy overlooking Lake Winnipesaukee & The Belknap Mountain Range. This picturesque community of New England white houses and country churches is also known as the "Oldest Summer Resort in America." This traditional antique fair and sale caters to tourists and summer residents alike.

For more information, call New England Antique Show Management, 603/539-1900.

1810 House
Rt. 28
603/569-8093

Chicken Coop Antiques
Rt. 109
603/569-4320

Northline Antiques
Northline Road
603/569-2476

Moniques Antiques
5 Brummih Ct.
603/569-4642

The Swan's Bonnett
N. Main St.
603/569-3595

Barbara's Corner Shop
67 N. Main St.
603/569-3839

Hutchin's Antiques
Center St.
603/569-3203

Notes

Great Andover Antiques

124 Main St.
- *18th & 19th Century Furnishings*
- *Edison Players • Textiles*
- *Large Selection Stained Glass*

(973) 786-6384

Andover

2

The Henry Ludlam Inn

"this National Historic Inn claims 250 years of history!"

1336 Route 47

(609) 861-5847

Dennisville

22

Peddler's Shop

71 W. Blackwell St.
Dover
973-361-0545

Antiques And...

Watch Fobs   Dolls

23

John Wesley Inn

"Grand Old Victorian Lady"

30 Guerney St.
(609) 884-1012

Cape May

15

New Jersey

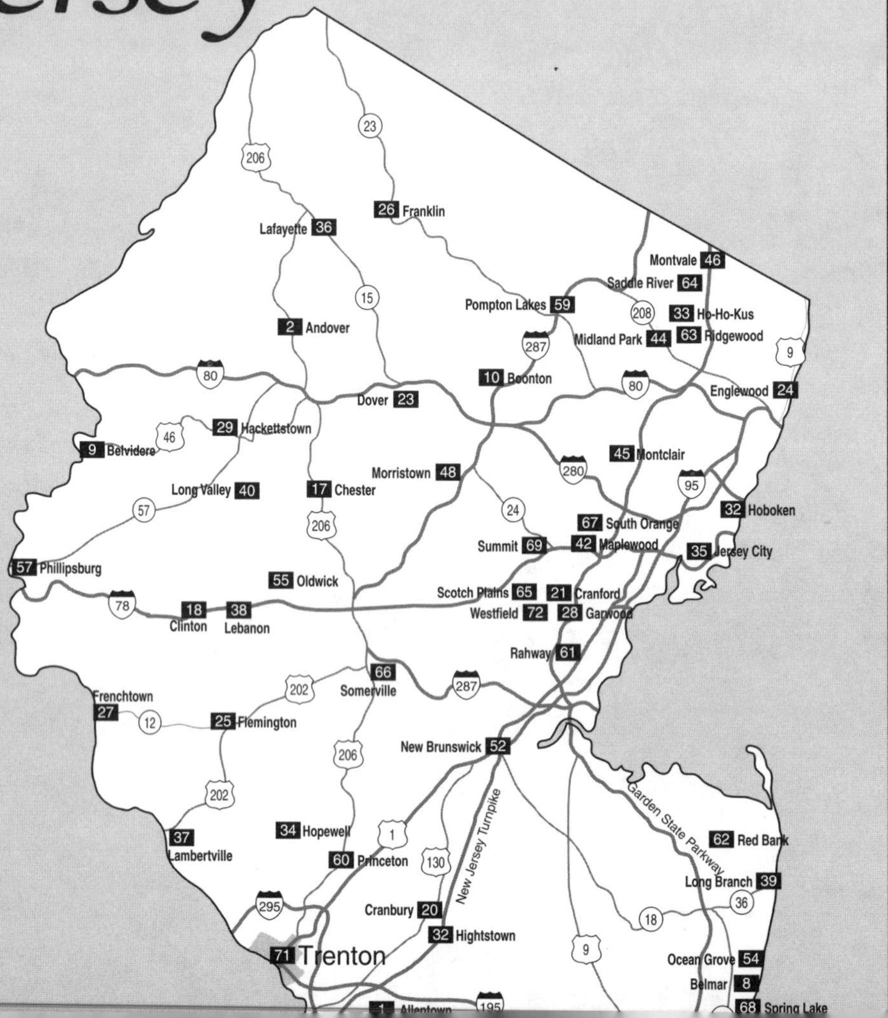

Stoneman of the Delaware

Located in the Lambertville Antique Market
Rt. 29
Civil War
Revolutionary
Colonial
Victorian
Historical
Frontier
Plus

Lambertville

37

Cordova Hotel

26 Webb Ave.
(908) 774-3084

Ocean Grove

Conti's

Antiques and Figurines

Trenton

DAVID RAGO
Auctions, Inc.
ART & ANTIQUE AUCTIONS

Buy • Sell • Consignment
Specializing in 20th Century Mission, Deco, and Postwar decorative arts and furnishings.
333 North Main Street
609.397.9374
Lambertville 37

Perrault-Rago Gallery

Fine Antiques Gallery
17 S. Main
609-397-1802
Lambertville 37

Lambertville
ANTIQUE AND AUCTION CENTER

Presenting Year-round High-end Arts & Crafts, Modern and General Line Antiques
Lambertville 37

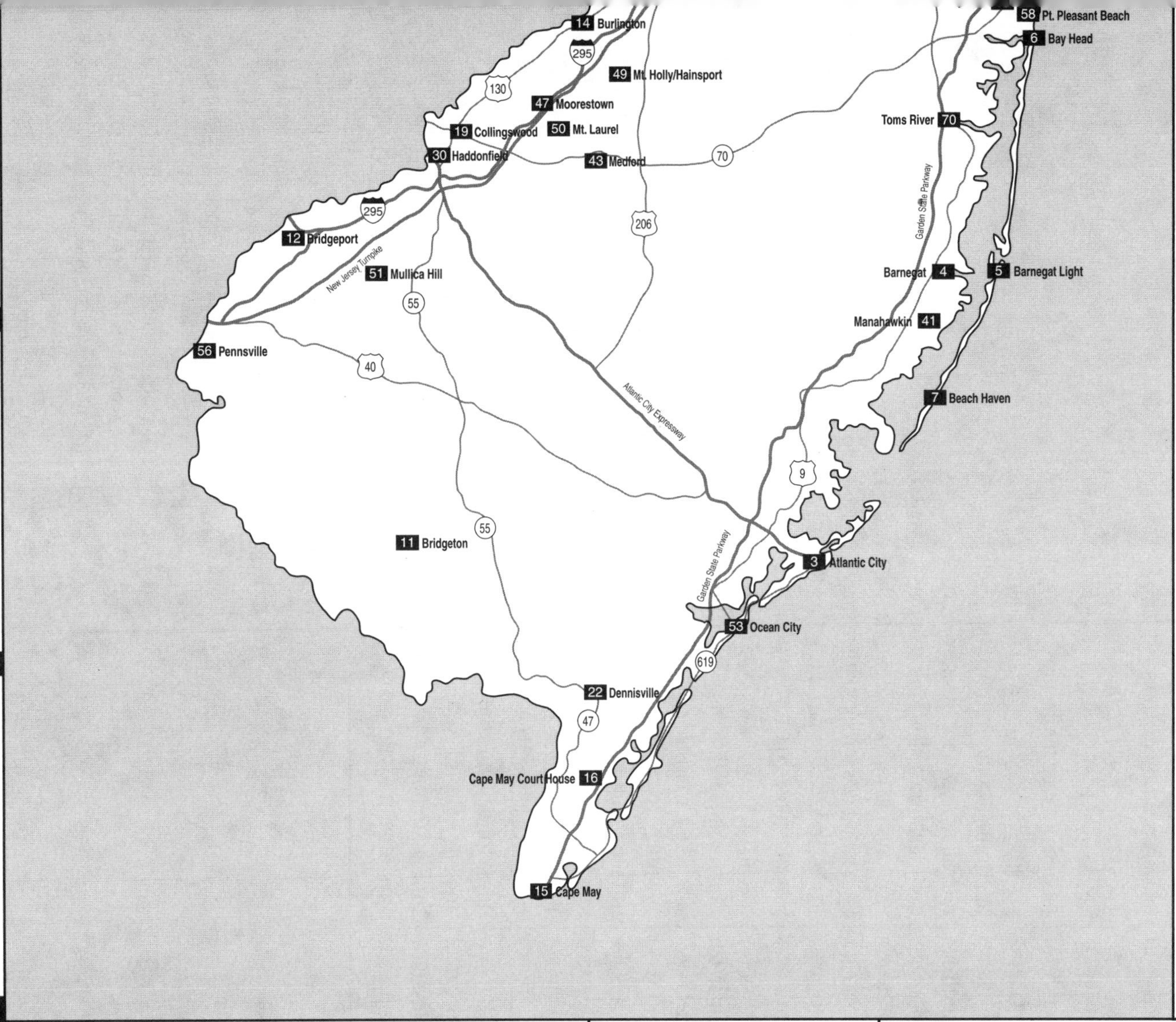

COUNTRY ANTIQUE CENTER
ANTIQUES • COLLECTIBLES

Over 90 Dealers Antiques & Collectibles Only

Featuring:
Primatives
Jewelry
Cut Glass
Depression Glass
Heisey Glass
Roseville Pottery
Clevenger Glass
Dolls
Furniture
Post Cards
Paper Products

Route 38
609-261-1924

Rt. 38 • Hainesport
Mt. Holly 49

York Street House
Exceptional In-Town Accommodations
Providing Bed & Breakfast
In An Historical Setting

No. 42 York Street
(609) 397-3007
Visit our Website at:
http://www.virtualcities.com
Lambertville

37

The Warehouse
• Antique Shop
• Art Gallery
• Candy Store
• Showcase Shop
• Cafe & Tea Room
Mullica Hill 51

RACCOON CREEK Antiques
5 Miles West of N.J.T.P. Exit 2
Just Off Rt 322,
1 Mile East of Commodore Barry Bridge
(609) 467-3197

Americana • Quilts • Folk Art
Bridgeport 11

David Rago Auctions

David Rago Auctions moved a year ago from its newly renovated facility in Lambertville, New Jersey, having previously spent 12 years holding arts and crafts and modern specialty auctions in the New York City area. The new 12,500-square-foot auction hall, once a hoisery mill, includes business offices, warehousing, and the offices of *Style: 1900*, the arts and crafts magazine published by the firm.

The Lambertville facility is at the north end of a town already famous for hundreds of antique shops and art galleries, as well as a large weekly antiques flea market. The city was a Revolutionary-era river crossing, joined by a bridge to New Hope, Pennsylvania, in Bucks County. As big industry vacated the city midway through the 20th century, the town gradually fell into disrepair. In the 1980s, it experienced a revival, fueled primarily by the influx of numerous arts and antiques dealers. It is the antiques-friendly atmosphere that encouraged Rago's decision to move his entire operation to New Jersey.

Rago's first auction, in June of 1984 in New Jersey's Meadowlands, was a modestly successful event with 400 lots grossing $88,000. At that time there were only two sales a year, but it grew steadily over the next decade and expanded to include 20th-century modern decorative arts and furniture and American impressionist paintings. The calendar year 1995 included nine auctions which grossed over $3 million, a record for the firm.

The tremendous cost of holding auctions in Manhattan was the overriding reason for the move of the well-established New York auctions. "Not only did we have to consider the high rental fees for appropriate space in New York," explained Rago, "but it was even more expensive to truck the material in and out of the city." He cited as an example the firm's June, 1995 sale, which consisted of 1,000 lots. The "pack-in" took a crew of 15 men two days to load 122 running feet of truck, an additional two days to set up the auction room in New York, and another two days after the sale to truck it back to New Jersey.

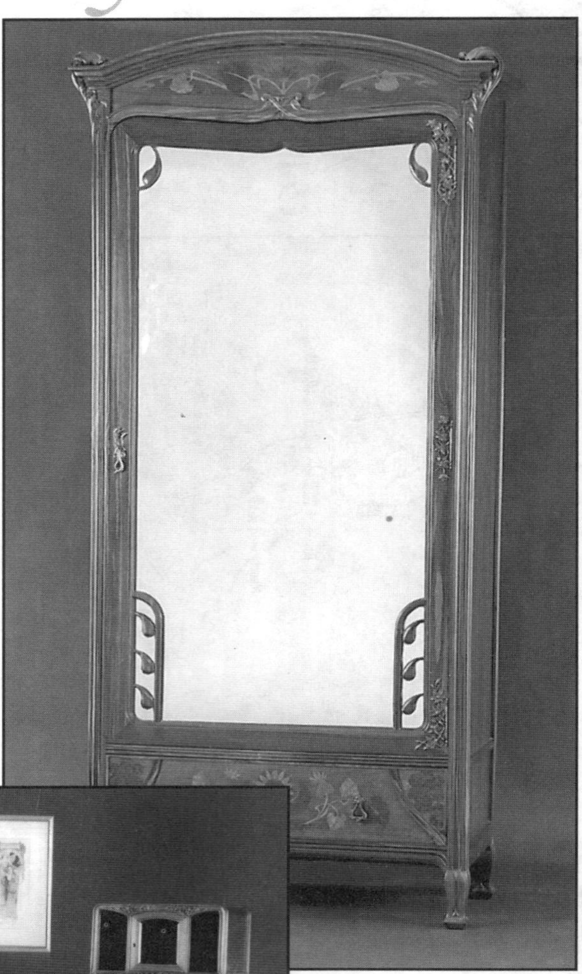

Above: Gallé and Majorelle marquetry furniture featured in auctions.

Above left: David Rago Auctions, Inc. _Above right:_ French Art Nouveau lithograph poster, Fine Majorelle marquetry table, Majorelle display cabinet, and a Loetz glass floor vase.

Additionally, almost half of what Rago sells at every auction is either by phone or absentee bid, and another 35% is sold to collectors and dealers who fly in from other parts of the country. While recognizing the importance of a savvy New York crowd, Rago knew that many from the city wanting to view and buy his merchandise didn't mind making the 80-minute trip, and even used such trips as occasions to spend a weekend antiquing in the country. "Lambertville is full of bed & breakfasts and fine restaurants. Our gallery has been in this town for years, and most people who visit for the first time are pleasantly surprised at how nice it is here," Rago said.

Another advantage in moving the entire

operation to Lambertville has been that, by having both the auctions and warehouses on site, sales previews can be extended by as much as a month before each event. In Manhattan, previews are restricted to two or three days prior to the sale, and there were even a few auctions where there was a preview only on the day of the auction. "Someone might not be able to attend the auction, but at least now, they can preview the sale weeks in advance if their schedule allows and then bid by phone or proxy," Rago stated.

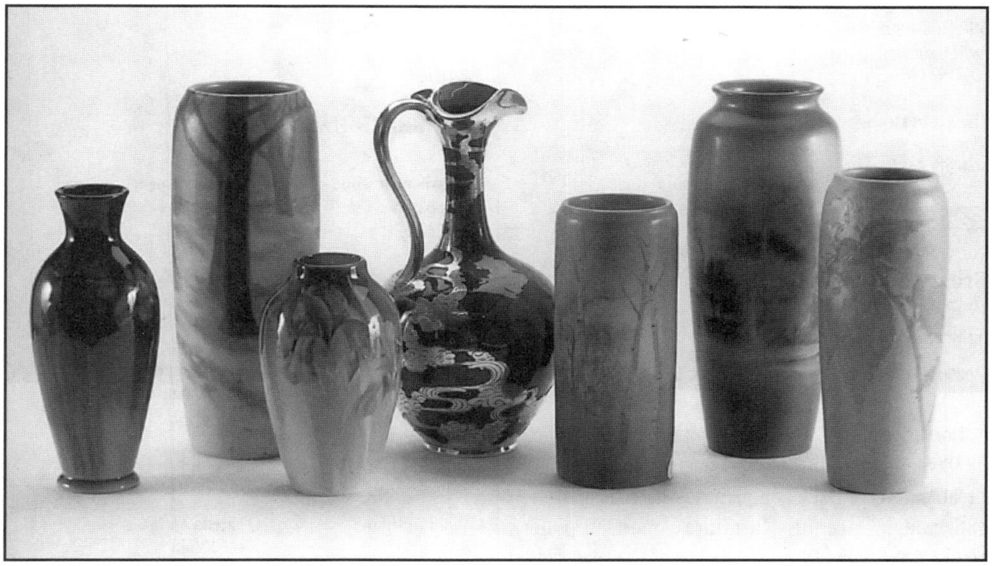

A fine selection of Rookwood Pottery.

A December 1996 auction held in the Lambertville facility gives a prime example of the types of goods that pass through Rago Auctions. A glance at the listing shows the complete research library of New York Modern Gallery 50/Fifty, a session of over 350 lots of Post War and Art Deco design, nearly 100 lots of European Art Nouveau, and an additional 400 lots of arts and crafts furnishings. Specific items within these lots included: 200-plus pieces of furniture by all of the major Post War designers, including Frank Lloyd Wright for Henredon, Bel Geddes, Eames, Saarinen, Nelson, Evans, Nakashima and others; Italian glass by Salviati, Barouvier, Venini, Cedenese, Seguso, and others; and modern ceramics by both American and European producers such as Natzler, Autio, Pillin, Wood, Poor, Scheier, Longwy and Boch Freres.

The Art Nouveau portion of the auction featured pieces of Galle and Majorelle marquetry inlaid furniture, glass by Mueller Freres, Rousseau, Daum, Lalique and Mount Joy, plus Loetz glass and Tiffany bronze. The American arts and crafts session featured nearly 125 pieces of furniture by all major period masters, including Greene & Greene, the Stickleys, Roycroft, and Limbert. The American art pottery selection was extremely memorable, with a Van Briggle Lorelai vase and 200 pieces of Grueby pottery, Rookwood, Newcomb, Fulper, Robineau, SEG, Marblehead, and others. To accommodate buyers from New York or Philadelphia who are without cars, Rago auctions provides a free shuttle service to and from the Trenton train station, which is approximately one hour from each city. There is also a bus that runs a regular route from Manhattan to the center of Lambertville. Also, a list of local bed & breakfasts and high-end restaurants is available for the

Early Gustav Stickley sideboard, rare Limbert lamp, Weller Glossy Hudson floor vase.

David Rago Auctions
333 North Main Street
Lambertville, New Jersey
609-397-9374

New Jersey

1 ALLENTOWN

Mill House Antiques
38 S. Main St.
609/259-0659

Brown Bear's Antiques
35 S. Main St.
609/259-0177

The Artful Deposit
46 S. Main St.
609/259-3234

2 ANDOVER

Great Andover Antique Company
124 Main Street
973/786-6384
Open: Wed.-Sun. 10-5, closed Mon. & Tue.

Housed within a 2500-square-foot building constructed in 1868 and extending to two floors are the offerings of Great Andover Antique Company. The shop specializes in 18th and 19th century furniture, American pottery, textiles, jewelry, lighting, Edison players, Victrolas, radios, Victorian furniture and complete bedroom sets. A large collection of stained glass is displayed in the 1,000 square foot former carriage house located on the property.

3 Generations
1 Gristmill Lane
201/786-7000

Oriental Rugs & Antiques
Hwy. 206
201/786-6004

Scranberry Coop
Hwy. 206
201/786-6414

Red Parrot Antiques
118 Rt. 206
201/786-5007

Vintage Sam's
124 Main St.
201/786-7955

Andover Village Shop
125 Main St.
201/786-6494

Country and Stuff
127 Main St.
201/786-7086

Andover's Mixed Bag
131 Main St.
201/786-7702

3 ATLANTIC CITY

Princeton Antiques
2917 Atlantic Ave.
609/344-1943

Bayside Basin Antiques
800 N. New Hampshire Ave.
609/347-7143

4 BARNEGAT

Barnegat Antique Country
684 E. Bay Ave.
609/698-8967

Goldduster
695 E. Bay Ave.
609/698-2520

First National Antiques
708 W. Bay Ave.
609/698-1413

Federal House Antiques
719 W. Bay Ave.
609/698-5490

Lavender Hall
289 S. Main St.
609/698-8126

Babes in Barnegat
349 S. Main St.
609/698-2223

Forget Me Not Shoppe
689 E. Bay Avenue
609/698-4336

Blaze of Glory
307 Main Street S
609/597-8416

5 BARNEGAT LIGHT

Americana by the Seashore
604 Broadway
609/494-0656

The Sampler
708 Broadway
609/494-3493

6 BAY HEAD

Fables of Bay Head
410 Main Ave.
732/899-3633

7 BEACH HAVEN

Somewhere In Time
118 N. Bay Ave.
609/492-3034

Summerhouse
412 N. Bay Ave.
609/492-6420

Courts Treasure Chest
1500 Long Beach Blvd.
609/494-0910

House of Seven Wonders
7600 Long Beach Blvd.
609/494-9673

Wizard of Odds
7601 Long Beach Blvd.
609/494-9384

Age of Antiquities
8013 Long Beach Blvd.
609/494-0735

8 BELMAR

Unique Designs
809 Main St.
908/681-2060

Aajeda Antiques
1800 Main St.
908/681-2288

Belmar Trading Post
1735 State Rt. 71
908/681-3207

9 BELVIDERE

Painted Lady
16 Greenwich St.
908/475-1985

Uncommon Market
228 Mansfield St.
908/475-1460

H & H Liquidating Co.
427 Mansfield St.
908/475-4333

Major Hoops Empor. Antiques
13 Market St.
908/475-5031

10 BOONTON

Cupboard
410 Main St.
201/402-0400

Boonton Antiques
521 Main St.
201/334-4416

Claire Ann's Antiques
815 Main St.
201/334-2421

Fox Hill Exchange
900 Main St.
201/263-2270

Elizabeth's Antiques Buying Center
904 Main St.
201/263-9162

11 BRIDGEPORT

Racoon Creek Antiques
20 Main Street, Box 132
609/467-3197
Open Thurs.-Sun. 12-5 or by appointment

Directions: From the New Jersey Turnpike: Take Exit #1 and go 5 miles west on 322. Follow the signs to 20 Main Street, Bridgeport. From I-95: Raccoon Creek Antiques is 30 minutes north of Wilmington, 30 minutes south of Philadelphia, and one mile from the base of Barry Bridge, which crosses the Delaware River on the "Jersey" side.

If you are in the market for truly "old" antiques, Raccoon Creek is an absolute must on your trek. George Allen has 11 years of accumulation and selected buying savvy in the field of Americana, quilts, pottery and folk art. "I deal in items that are pre-1860s," says George. "All my stock is pre-industrial age, everything handmade— absolutely no reproductions of any kind." Examples of just some of his Americana include weather vanes, samplers and original painted furniture.

*Note: I've met up with George at several antique shows around the country. He's one of the nicest antique dealers in the business. At each of these shows, he always presents some very unusual pieces.

12 BRIDGETON

Kim Shell Gift Boutique
404 Big Oak Road
609/451-4667

Hudson House
2012 Burlington Rd.
609/433-1414

The Squirrel's Nest
680 Shiloh Pike
609/455-6594

Pony Point House
781 Shiloh Pike
609/451-6130

Dutch Neck Village
97 Trench Road
609/451-2188

13 BRIELLE

Brielle Antique Center
622A Green Ave.
908/528-8570

Chappies Antiques
406 Higgins Ave.
908/528-8989

Relics
604 Union Ave.
908/223-3452

14 BURLINGTON

H. G. Sharkey & Company
Antiques & Coffee House
306 High Street
609/239-0200
Open 8-8, seven days a week

Directions: From I-295, Exit Burlington #54, go to High Street. Located 1/2 block from the Delaware River.

Housed in an historical building, specializing in antique jewelry and collectibles. A coffee house is also located on the premises.

Antique Row
307 High Street
609/387-3050

15 CAPE MAY

John Wesley Inn
30 Guerney Street
609/884-1012
Open year round

Directions: Go to the end of the Garden State Parkway in Cape May. Take Lafayette Street to the first traffic light (at Madison Avenue). Turn left and go two blocks to Columbia Avenue. Take a right and continue down to Gurney Street (there is a monument in the center of the street) and turn left. The inn is the second building from the corner on the right.

There is a real soap-opera story behind the recent history of the John Wesley Inn. Here it is in innkeeper Rita Tice's own words: "Once upon a time in 1983, we were all very happy with our three-apartment building in Cape May - "we" being my husband John, who loves to fish; my four teenagers, who loved the beach and making money with summer jobs, and myself, who also loved the beach and touring old Victorian homes. At least we were happy for a couple of years. But everything fell in—literally—in January 1985, when an active raw sewer main collapsed under the outhouse! Following a horrible two years of work, we opened as an inn. The building was actually lifted to add a perimeter foundation. Today, it is an award-winning grand Victorian, completely restored to its 1869 splendor."

Thoroughly recovered from a horrible experience, this grand old Victorian "lady" now offers visitors six guest rooms (four with private baths) and two apartments. The entire mansion is decorated in formal Victorian style, complete with white lace curtains and all American antiques. Guests can go from Victorian formality to barefoot freedom on the beach, which is a just 1/2 block away, then come "home" and warm in front of the parlor fireplace, go to sleep in historical comfort, and wake up to an eye-opening continental breakfast and sea breezes. What a life!

Bridgetowne
523 Broadway
609/884-8107

Curious Collectibles
719 Broadway
609/884-5557

Promises Collectables
301 N. Broadway
609/884-4411

Bogwater Jim Antiques
201 S. Broadway
609/884-5558

Studio Victorian Antiques
607 Jefferson
609/884-0444

Cape Island Antiques
609 Jefferson
609/884-6028

Finishing Touches
678 Washington
609/896-0661

Antique Doorknob
600 Park Blvd.
609/884-6282

Rocking Horse Antique Center
405 W. Perry St.
609/898-0737

Hazard Sealander Antiques
479 W. Perry St.
609/884-0040

Millstone Antiques & Cllbls.
742 Seashore Rd
609/884-5155

Stephanie's Antiques
318 Washington
609/884-0289

Nostalgia Shop
408 Washington St.
609/884-7071

Midsummer Night's Dream
668 Washington
609/884-1380

16 CAPE MAY COURT HOUSE

August Farmhouse
1759 N. Rt. 9
609/465-5135

Mallard Lake Antiques
1781 N. Rt. 9
609/465-7189

Quilted Gull
1909 N. Rt. 9
609/624-1630

Village Woodcrafter
1843 N. Rt. 9
609/465-2197

17 CHESTER

Chester Antique Center
32 Grove St.
908/879-4331

Beauty of Civilization
30 Main St.
908/879-2044

Delphinium's
30 Main St.
908/879-8444

Postage Stamp
38 W. Main St.
908/879-4257

Summerfield's Antique Furn.
44 Main St.
908/879-9020

Aunt Pittypat's Parlour
57 E. Main St.
908/879-4253

Pegasus Antiques
98 Main St.
908/879-4792

The Chester Carousel
125 Main St.
980/879-7141

Marita Daniels Antiques
127 Main St.
908/879-6488

Chester House
294 E. Main St.
908/879-7856

Black River Trading Co.
15 Perry St.
908/879-6778

Spinning Wheel Antiques
76 Main St.
908/879-6080

18 CLINTON

Arts Resale
Hwy. 31
908/735-4442

Weathervane Antiques
18 Main St.
908/730-0877

Memories
21 Main St.
908/730-9096

Paddy-Wak Antiques
19 Old High #22
908/735-9770

19 COLLINGSWOOD

Ashwells Yesterdays Treasures
738 Haddon Ave.
609/858-6659

Yesteryear Shop
788 Haddon Ave.
609/854-1786

Collinswood Antiques
812 Haddon Ave.
609/858-9700

Ellis Antiques
817 Haddon Ave.
609/854-6346

Unforgettables
980 Haddon Ave.
609/858-4501

20 CRANBURY

Adams Brown Co.
26 N. Main St.
609/655-8269

Cranbury Book Worm
54 N. Main St.
609/655-1063

Cranbury Collectibles
60 N. Main St.
609/655-8568

David Wells Antiques
60 N. Main St.
609/655-0085

21 CRANFORD

Dovetails
6 Eastman St.
908/709-1638

Shirley Greens Antiques Ltd.
8 Eastman St.
908/709-0066

Not Just Antiques
218 South Ave. E
908/276-3553

Nancy's Antiques
7 Walnut Ave.
908/272-5056

Cobweb Collectibles & Ephemera
9 Walnut Ave.
908/272-5777

22 DENNISVILLE

The Henry Ludlam Inn
1336 Rt. 47
609/861-5847
Open daily year round

Directions: The inn is located on Rt. 47 in Dennisville. From Garden State Pkwy., go south to the second Ocean City exit. Turn right onto Rt. 631 and go about 2 miles. Turn left on Rt. 610 and follow the road to the end. Turn right on Rt. 47. The inn is 1 1/2 miles on right.

This National Historic Registry entry claims more than 250 years of history! Two wings of the house were built at different times, between 1740 and 1804. This Federal-style house offers guests five rooms, all with private baths. It is filled with period antiques and the Federalist style in decor helps put guests into a historical frame of mind. The inn is located near many antique shops, museums, the Cape May Zoo and county historical sites.

23 DOVER

Peddler's Shop
71 West Blackwell Street
973/361-0545
Fax: 973/366-4147
Open Wed. 2-7., Sat. 12-5, Sun. 9-5 or by appointment

Directions: The Peddler's Shop is located between Hwy. 46 and Hwy. 10. Take Exit #35 off of I-80 and take Mt. Hope Avenue. Cross Hwy. 46 and continue two blocks to Blackwell. Turn right and the Peddler's Shop is approximately five blocks on the right.

Since 1969 The Peddler's Shop has offered an unusual and rather distinctive array of items spread about its two floors of antiques. The shop is noted for its old lamps and lamp parts, furniture, glassware, dolls, trains, silver and books, and it has the largest watch fob collection in the east.

At The Hop
14 N. Morris St.
973/989-5225

The Iron Carriage Antq. Center
I-5 West Blackwell
973/366-1440

24 ENGLEWOOD

Bizet Antqs. & Unusual Finds
6 S. Dean St.
201/568-5345

Jewel Spiegel Galleries
30 N. Dean St.
201/871-3577

Chelsea Square Inc.
10 Depot Square
201/568-5911

Global Treasures
120 Grand Ave.
201/569-5532

Tony Art Gallery
120 Grand Ave.
201/568-7271

Portobello Road Antiques
491 Grand Ave.
201/568-5559

Antiques by Ophir Gallery
12 E. Palisade Ave.
201/871-0424

Crown House Antiques
39 E. Palisade Ave.
201/894-8789

Elvid Gallery
41 E. Palisade Ave.
201/871-8747

Royal Galleries Antiques
66 E. Palisade Ave.
201/567-6354

Rose Hill Auction Gallery
35 S. Van Brunt St.
201/816-1940

25 FLEMINGTON

Antiques Emporium
32 Church St.
908/782-5077

B & M Flemington Antiques
24 Main St.
908/806-8841

55 Main Antiques
55 Main St.
908/788-2605

Main St. Antique Center Inc.
156 Main St.
908/788-8767

International Show Case
169 Main St.
908/782-6640

Popkorn Antiques
4 Mine St.
908/782-9631

Furstover Antiques
505 Stanton Station Rd.
908/782-3513

26 FRANKLIN

The Munson Emporium
33 Munsonhurst Road
973/827-0409

27 FRENCHTOWN

Brooks Antiques
24 Bridge St.
908/996-7161

Jeanine-Louise Antiques
8 Race St.
908/996-3520

Frenchtown House of Antiques
15 Race St.
908/996-2482

28 GARWOOD

Classic Antiques
225 North Ave.
908/233-7667

29 HACKETTSTOWN

Family Attic Antiques Ltd.
117 Main St.
908/852-1206

Furnishings by Adam
253 Main St.
908/852-4385

Whispering Pines Antiques
77 State Rt. 57
908/852-2587

Main Street Bazaar
128 Willow Grove St.
908/813-2966

30 HADDONFIELD

General Store
37 Ellis St.
609/428-3707

Haddonfield Gallery
1 Kings Court
609/429-7722

Two in the Attic
3 Kings Court
609/429-4035

Adam's Antiques
9 Kings Hwy. E
609/770-1155

Alice's Dolls
9 Kings Hwy. E
609/770-1155

Haddonfield Antique Center
9 Kings Hwy. E
609/429-1929

Owls Tale
140 Kings Hwy. E
609/795-8110

31 HIGHTSTOWN

Olde Country Antiques
346 Franklin St.
609/448-2670

Empire Antiques
278 Monmouth St.
609/585-1266

Boat House Antiques
161 E. Ward St.
609/448-2200

Timekeeper
York Rd.
609/448-0269

32 HOBOKEN

Fat Cat Antiques
57 Newark St.
201/222-5454

Found in the Street
86 Park Ave.
201/963-6494

Sixth Street Antiques
155 6th St.
201/656-5544

Hoboken Antiques
511 Washington St.
201/659-7329

Erie Street Antiques
533 Washington St.
201/656-3596

House Wear Inc.
628 Washington St.
201/659-6009

Mission Postion
1122 Washington St.
201/222-5001

Little Cricket Antiques
1200 Washington St.
201/222-6270

33 HO HO KUS

Discovery Antiques
618 N. Maple Ave.
201/444-9170

Porreca & Chettle
620 N. Maple Ave.
201/445-7883

Camelot Home Furnishings
9 N. Franklin Turnpike
201/444-5300

Regal Antiques Ltd.
181 S. Franklin Turnpike
201/447-5066

34 HOPEWELL

H Clark Interiors
31 W. Broad St.
609/466-0738

Patsy's Antiques
33 W. Broad St.
609/466-7720

Ninotchka
35 W. Broad St.
609/466-0556

Antiques Etcetera
47 W. Broad St.
609/466-0643

Hopewell Antique Center
Hamilton Ave.
609/466-2990

Tomato Factory Antq. Center
Hamilton Ave.
609/466-9860

Your Aunt's Attic
17 Seminary Ave.
609/466-0827

Hopewell Antique Cottage
8 Somerset St.
609/466-1810

35 JERSEY CITY

RetroAntiques
3514 J F Kennedy Blvd.
201/656-6139

Cliff's Clocks
400 7th St.
201/798-7510

L & L Antiques
1170 Summit Ave.
201/656-6928

36 LAFAYETTE

Mill Mercantile
11 Meadows Rd.
201/579-1588

Ivy Antiques
Meadows Rd.
201/579-9602

Silver Willow Inc.
Meadows Rd.
201/383-5560

Lafayette Mill Antique Center
Rt. 15
201/383-6057

Lamplighters of Lafayette
156 State Rt. 15
201/383-5513

Sweet Pea's
12 Morris Farm Road
201/579-6338

37 LAMBERTVILLE

York Street House
No. 42 York Street
609/397-3007
Website: http://www.virtualcities.com

Directions: Off I-95 exit 1 Rt. 29, Downtown Lambertville off Main Street.

This gracious 13 room Manor House situated on three quarters of an acre of land was built in 1909 by George Massey as a twenty-fifth wedding anniversary gift for his beloved wife. Massey was one of the early industrialists who settled his family in the historical river village of Lambertville just after the turn of the century. In 1911, the home was featured as *House and Garden* magazine's Home of the Year, with all the modern conveniences including a central vacuum that still stands in the cellar. In 1983, the home became a designer showcase.

Today the York Street House will comfort and surround you with its elegant and comfortable atmosphere. The heart of the inn features a winding three-story staircase leading to six gracious guestrooms, some with queen size canopy beds. From matching antique Waterford crystal sconces and chandelier in the sitting room, cut glass doorknobs on the second floor to the original tile and clawfoot master bath with its leaded stained glass window, the preservation of details will delight you at every turn.

A gourmet breakfast is served in the oak-trimmed dining room with its built in leaded glass china and large oak servers, looking out over the lawn and sitting porch. Feast your eyes on original art by Gilbert Bolitho, Jack B. Yeats, Rodriguez (Blue Dog), and Autorino.

The excitement starts two blocks away with antique shops, art galleries, bookstores and fine restaurants. Walk to New Hope, Pennsylvania with its artful atmosphere, theatre and gay clubs.

Stoneman of the Delaware
Located inside Lambertville Antique Market
Rt. 29
609/397-0456
Open Wed.-Sun., 10-4

Directions: Located 1 1/2 miles south of Lambertville on Rt. 29, River Road. Next to the Golden Nugget.

Stoneman of the Delaware is located inside the Lambertville Antique Market. Specializing in Civil War, Revolutionary, Colonial, Victorian, Frontier through World War II and later; 1620-1960 historical collectibles, guns, parts, swords, bayonets, relics, coins, tokens, medals, arrowheads, marbles, old keys, jewelry, pottery, china, glassware and more. Don't Miss Museum Case #36.

Additionally, the market offers more than 100 showcases packed with all types of antiques and collectibles.

Lambertville Antique and Auction Center
333 North Main Street
609/397-9374

Directions: From Philadelphia; Take I-95 North into New Jersey. Exit at Rt. 29 North and follow 12 miles to Lambertville. Take a left at the light on Bridge Street. Take the next right onto Main Street and follow one mile to 333 North Main Street. The building will be on the left.

Year-round events including high-end arts and crafts, modern and general line auctions. Special events. Please call for information.

Perrault-Rago Gallery
17 South Main Street
609/397-1802
Open Tue.-Sun. 12-5 (usually), call to confirm

Directions: From Philadelphia; Take I-95 North into New Jersey. Exit at Rt. 29 North and follow 12 miles to Lambertville. Take a left at the light on Bridge Street. Take the next left onto South Main Street and follow one block to 17 South Main Street. The building will be on the right.

A memorable array of period furniture, decorative ceramics, metal, textiles and other accessories. Pottery, in particular, represents the finest "for sale" display in the country.

David Rago Auctions, Inc.
333 North Main Street
609/397-9374
Open Mon.-Fri. 9-5:30

Directions: From Philadelphia; Take I-95 North into New Jersey. Exit at Rt. 19 North and follow 12 miles to Lambertville. Take a left at the light on Bridge Street. Take the next right onto Main Street one mile. The building will be on the left.

Specializing in 20th century Mission, Deco, and Postwar decorative arts and furnishings. Consignments wanted.

For more information see review this section.

Jim's Antiques Ltd.
6 Bridge St.
609/397-7700

Bridge St. Antiques
15 Bridge St.
609/397-9890

Karen & David Dutch's Antqs.
22 Bridge St.
609/397-2288

Stefon's Antiques
29 Bridge St.
609/397-8609

Mill Crest Antiques
72 Bridge St.
609/397-4700

Fran Jay Antiques
10 Church St.
609/397-1571

Porkyard Antiques
8 Coryell St.
609/397-2088

Coryell St. Antiques
51 Coryell St.
609/397-5700

Center City Antqs.
11 Klines Ct.
609/397-9886

Peter Wallace Ltd.
5 Lambert Lane
609/397-4914

Charles King Ltd.
36 S. Main St.
609/397-9733

Golden Nugget Antq. Flea Mkt.
State Hwy. #29
609/397-0811

Prestige Antiques
State Hwy. #29
609/397-2400

JRJ Home
7 N. Union St.
609/397-3800

Yaroschuck Antiques
10 N. Union St.
609/397-8886

Artfull Eye
12 N. Union St.
609/397-8115

Lovrinics Fine Period Antiques
15 N. Union St.
609/397-8600

Robin's Egg Gallery
24 N. Union St.
609/397-9137

The Second Floor
29 N. Union St.
609/397-8618

Miller-Topia Designers
35 N. Union St.
609/397-9339

Garden House Antiques
39 N. Union St.
609/397-9797

Kevin Sives Antiques
43 N. Union St.
609/397-4212

Meld
53 N. Union St.
609/397-8487

Olde English Pine
202 N. Union St.
609/397-4978

Best of France
204 N. Union St.
609/397-9881

Fox's Den
7 N. Main St.
609/397-9881

38 LEBANON

Lebanon Antique Center
U.S. Hwy. 22 E
908/236-2851

39 LONG BRANCH

Antiques & Accents
55 Brighton Ave.
908/222-2274

Hyspot Antiques & Collectibles
61 Brighton Ave.
908/222-7880

Take A Gander
84 Brighton Ave.
908/229-7389

40 LONG VALLEY

German Valley Antiques
6 E. Mill Rd.
980/876-9202

Tavern Antiques
5 Will Rd.
908/876-5854

41 MANAHAWKIN

Manor House Shops
160 N. Main St.
609/597-1122

The Shoppes @ Rosewood
182 N. Main St.
609/597-7331

Cornucopia
140 N. Main St.
609/978-0099

42 MAPLEWOOD

Bee & Thistle Antiques
89 Baker St.
201/763-3166

Antiques by Greg Hawriluk
48 Courter Ave.
201/378-9036

Renaissance Consign. Btq.
410 Ridgewood Rd.
201/761-7450

Grey Swan
411 Ridgewood Rd.
201/763-0660

43 MEDFORD

Recollections
6 N. Main St.
609/654-1515

Spirit of 76
49 N. Main St.
609/654-2850

Regina's
6 S. Main St.
609/654-2521

Heather Furniture
215 Medford Mount Holly
609/654-9506

Toll House Antiques
160 Old Marlton Pike
609/953-0005

Yesterday & Today Shop
668 Stokes Rd.
609/654-7786

44 MIDLAND PARK

Brownstone Mill Antique Center
11 Paterson Avenue
201/445-3074 or 201/612-9555
Open Wed.-Sat., 10:30-5; Tuesday by appointment

Directions: Take Rt. 4 West or Rt. 287 North to Rt. 208; exit Goffle Rd./Midland Park. Continue approximately 2 miles to the corner of Goffle Road/ Paterson Avenue

Features twenty unique shops under one roof.

Tuc-D-Away Antiques
229 Godwin Ave.
201/652-0730

Time Will Tell
644 Godwin Ave.
201/652-1025

G F Warhol & Co.
18 Goffle Rd.
201/612-1010

Blue Barn
60 Goffle Rd.
201/612-0227

45 MONTCLAIR

Threadneedle Street
195 Bellevue Ave.
201/783-1336

Sablon Antiques
411 Bloomfield Ave.
201/746-4397

Americana Antiques
411 Bloomfield Ave.
201/746-2605

Past & Present Resale Shop
416 Bloomfield Ave.
201/746-8871

Gallery of Vintage
504 Bloomfield Ave.
201/509-1201

Ivory Bird Antiques
555 Bloomfield Ave.
201/744-5225

Antique Star
627 Bloomfield Ave.
201/746-0070

Buying Antiques
629 Bloomfield Ave.
201/746-7331

Milt's Antiques
662 Bloomfield Ave.
201/746-4445

American Sampler Inc.
26 Church St.
201/744-1474

William Martin Antiques
41 Church St.
201/744-1149

Garage Sale
194 Claremont Ave.
201/783-0806

Jackie's Antiques
51 N. Fullerton Ave.
201/744-7972

Earl Roberts Antqs. & Interiors
17 S. Fullerton Ave.
201/744-2232

Noel's Place
173 Glenridge Ave.
201/744-2156

Station West Antiques
225 Glenridge Ave.
201/744-9370

Way We Were Antiques
15 Midland Ave.
201/783-1111

46 MONTVALE

Antique Mall
30 Chestnut Ridge Rd.
301/391-3940

Discovery Antiques
30 Chestnut Ridge Rd.
201/391-9024

Knox Gold Corp.
30 Chestnut Ridge Rd.
201/930-0323

Lost & Found Antiques Inc.
30 Chestnut Ridge Rd.
201/391-0060

Museum Shop
30 Chestnut Ridge Rd.
201/573-8757

Treasure Finders
30 Chestnut Ridge Rd.
201/391-0006

47 MOORESTOWN

Country Peddler Antiques
111 Chester Ave.
609/235-0680

George Wurtzel Antiques
69 E. Main St.
609/234-9631

Kingsway Antiques
527 E. Main St.
609/234-7373

Monique's Antiques
400 Rt. 38
609/235-7407

Her Own Place
113 E. Main St.
609/234-2445

48 MORRISTOWN

Associated Art
31 Market St.
201/292-9203

Morristown Antique Center
45 Market St.
201/734-0900

Marion Jaye Antiques
990 Mount Kemble Ave.
201/425-0441

Robert Fountain Inc.
1107 Mount Kemble Ave.
201/425-8111

Fearicks Antiques
166 Ridgedale Ave.
201/984-3140

Bayberry Antiques
Rt. 202 (Harding Township)
201/425-0101

Coletree Antiques & Interiors
166 South St.
201/993-3011

49 MOUNT HOLLY/HAINSPORT

Country Antique Center
Rt. 38
609/261-1924
Open daily 10-5

Directions: Traveling from I-295, take Exit #40 and travel east on Rt. 38 for 4.1 miles toward Mt. Holly. At the 8th light, take the jughandle to make a U-turn on Rt. 38. The shop's driveway is 50 feet from the U-turn on the westbound side of Rt. 38. Traveling the New Jersey Turnpike, take Exit #5/Mt. Holly. After the tolls, turn right onto Rt. 541 toward Mt. Holly. At the 4th light bear right onto the Rt. 541/Mt. Holly Bypass. Continue on the Bypass to the 3rd light (Rt. 38). Turn right onto Rt. 38 west and go 3 lights. The shop's driveway is 50 feet from the 3rd light. Country Antique Center is just 30 miles from Philadelphia on Rt. 38.

The Country Antique Center celebrated its 9th anniversary in March of this year. When the "co-op" first opened its doors on March 1, 1989, it offered the wares of 28 dealers. Now, with the connection of two separate buildings into one, they are represented by more than 100 dealers from Pennsylvania and New Jersey, offering only antiques and collectibles in 8,000 square feet of browsing room. The dealers specialize in primitives, jewelry, cut glass, Depression, Heisey and Clevenger glass; Roseville pottery, dolls, furniture, postcards and paper products.

Carpet Baggers Doll Hospital
Creek Rd.
609/234-5095

Bill's Bargains
15 King St.
609-261-0096

Center Stage Antiques
41 King St.
609/261-0602

Abode Antiques
99 Washington St.
609/267-1717

50 MOUNT LAUREL

Collectors Express
104 Berkshire Dr.
609/866-1693

Creek Road Antique Cntre Inc.
123 Creek Rd.
609/778-8899

51 MULLICA HILL

The story of Mullica Hill began in the late 1600s, when English and Irish Quakers moved to the area and began establishing plantations. This Quaker community centered on the south bank of Raccoon Creek and was called Spicerville, in honor of Jacob Spicer, a prominent landowner. Originally only the north bank of the creek was known as Mullica Hill, and it was named after the town's pioneering Finnish settlers - Eric, John, Olag and William Mullica - who first purchased land here in 1704. Two of the homes the Mullica family built are still standing on North Main near the creek, nearly 300 years later!

Prior to the American Revolution, Mullica Hill was a coach town of little more than two scattered clusters of houses north and south of the creek, two taverns and a grist mill. Four of these structures still remain today. The town's first real period of growth began around 1780 and continued until the 1830s. Commercial development sprang up primarily in Spicerville (South Main) and four of the town's first churches were built here. Although a blacksmith shop, schoolhouse and one of the town's two taverns were on the north side, this neighborhood remained mostly agricultural. However, the entire village became known as Mullica Hill, probably because the hill itself was the most notable feature in the entire town. Many of the buildings from this era are still standing on Main Street today.

In the late 1800s a small mill district was established along the Raccoon Creek raceway. A woolen mill and an iron foundry operated here for several decades until fire and competition from larger industrial centers caused the area to decline drastically. Today only the 18th century gristmill remains - in a greatly altered state.

A second period of growth followed the Civil War and many noteworthy Victorian homes and public buildings were built throughout the entire village, including the town hall. Also, during this time Harrison Township established itself as one of the county's most productive agricultural areas. A railroad spur was built and very quickly the town became one of the nation's most active shipping points for agricultural commodities.

Throughout most of the 20th century Mullica Hill has served as the principal town and seat of government for Harrison Township, and its businesses catered to the needs of the surrounding farms. While agriculture today is still an important local industry, Mullica Hill's businesses are no longer so locally oriented. The town has emerged as a major antique and crafts center and is widely known for its nostalgic charm. Historic homes have been restored and the streets are now crowded with visitors from throughout the Eastern seaboard.

In 1991 the entire village of Mullica Hill was placed on the National Register of Historic Places and the New Jersey state Register of Historic Places. In 1992 Harrison Township established the village as a local historic district.

The Warehouse
2 South Main Street
609/478-4500
Open Wed.-Sun. 11-5

Directions: From U.S. 95: Take Commodore Barry Bridge and 322 East to Mullica Hill. From the New Jersey Turnpike: Take Exit #2 then 322 East to Mullica Hill. From U.S. 295: Take Exit #11 then 322 East to Mullica Hill. The Warehouse is in the middle of town on Main Street.

This interesting, large, multi-dealer shop holds several divisions: an art gallery, jewelry store, candy store, furniture store, a large showcase shop, plus a cafe and tea room where you can recover when you realize that you've spent more than you should! And it's all packaged in a Civil War-era building.

Raccoon's Tale
6 High St.
609/478-4488

Debra's Dolls
20 N. Main St.
609/478-9778

Elizabeth's of Mullica Hill
32 N. Main St.
609/478-6510

Antique Center at Mullica Hill
45 N. Main St.
609/478-4754

Kings Row Antiques
46 N. Main St.
609/478-4361

The Queen's Inn Antiques
48 N. Main St.
609/223-9433

Murphy's Loft
53 N. Main St.
609/478-4928

Carriage House Antiques
62 N. Main St.
609/478-4459

The Country Christmas Shoppe
86 N. Main St.
609/478-2250

The Old Mill Antique Mall
1 S. Main St.
609/478-9810

The Front Porch
21 S. Main St.
609/478-6556

The Sign of Saint George
30 S. Main St.
609/478-6101

Dolls, Toys, & Free Museum
34 S. Main St.
609/478-6137

Wolf's Antiques
36 S. Main St.
609/478-4992

Deja Vu Antique & Gift Gallery
38 S. Main St.
609/478-6351

Antiquities at Mullica Hill
43 S. Main St.
609/478-6773

June Bug Antiques
44 S. Main St.
609/478-2167

Sugar & Spice Antiques
45 S. Main St.
609/478-2622

Clock Shop
45 S. Main (Rear Shop)
609/478-6555

Accessories
46 S. Main St.
609/223-0100

Lynne Antiques
49 S. Main St.
609/223-9199

Jane "D" Antiques
50 S. Main St.
No Phone

The Treasure Chest
50 S. Main St.
609/468-4371

Mullica Hill Art Glass
53 S. Main St.
609/478-2552

52 NEW BRUNSWICK

French Street Antiques
108 French St.
908/545-9352

Somewhere in Time
115 French St.
908/247-3636

Aaron Aardvark & Son
119 French St.
908/246-1720

Amber Lion Antiques
365 George St.
908/214-9090

53 OCEAN CITY

Joseph's Antiques
908 Asbury Ave.
609/398-3855

Curiosity Shoppe
1119 Asbury Ave.
609/407-1251

Sutton's Antiques
1743 Asbury Ave.
609/399-0552

Only Yesterday
1108 Broadwalk
609/398-2869

B's Fantasy
11th St.
609/398-9302

54 OCEAN GROVE

Cordova Hotel
26 Webb Avenue
908/774-3084 (in season); 212/751-9577 (winter)
Open May 15 through Sept. 30

Directions: Take the Garden State Parkway to Exit #100 (from the south) or Exit #100B (from the north), then go 15 minutes on Rt. 33 East to the end. Turn left for 100 feet then make an immediate right (Broadway) to the ocean. Turn left at the ocean and go to Webb. The hotel is 1 1/2 blocks from the beach.

Here's the chance to enjoy the charm of a bygone era with the stark naturalness of the ocean. The Cordova Hotel is a grand, 120 year old Victorian hotel that is a family resort just 1 1/2 blocks from the beach. There are 20 rooms (five with private baths) and two cottages. Much of the hotel is furnished in Victorian decor, with lots of oak furniture scattered throughout. Guests are served breakfast to the pounding of the surf, and salt-scented breezes mingle with the aroma of good food at the Saturday nights wine and cheese gatherings.

55 OLDWICK

Magic Shop
60 Main
908/439-2330

Collections
Rt. 523
908/439-3736

56 PENNSVILLE

Favorite Places To Eat

Cracker Barrel Old Country Store
NJ Turnpike & SR 49, Exit 1A

57 PHILLIPSBURG

Gracy's Manor
1400 Belvidere Rd.
908/859-0928

Harmony Barn
2481 Belvidere Rd.
908/859-6159

B & B Model A Ford Parts
300 Firth St.
908/859-4856

Lil's
103 Foch Blvd.
908/454-3982

Michael J Stasak Antiques
376 River Rd.
908/454-6136

Jensen Antiques
State Hwy. #57
908/859-0240

58 POINT PLEASANT BEACH

The Time Machine
516 Arnold Ave.
732/295-9695

Fond Memories Antiques
625 Arnold Ave.
732/892-4149

Wally's Follies Antiques
626 Arnold Ave.
732/899-1840

Classy Collectibles
633 Arnold Ave.
732/714-0957

Snow Goose
641 Arnold Ave.
732/892-6929

Clock Shop & Antiques
726 Arnold Ave.
732/899-6200

Feather Tree Antiques
624 Bay Ave.
732/899-8891

Company Store
628 Bay Ave.
732/892-5353

Antiques Etc.
1225 Bay Ave.
732/295-9888

Antique Emporium
Bay Ave. & Trenton
732/892-2222

Ruddy Duck
2034 Bridge Ave.
732/892-8893

Shore Antique Center
300 High #35
732/295-5771

Bargain Outlet
2104 Rt. 88
732/892-9007

Willinger Enterprises Inc.
626 Rt. 88
732/892-2217

59 POMPTON LAKES

Charisma 7 Antiques
212 Wanaque Ave.
201/839-7779

P K's Treasures Ltd.
229 Wanaque Ave.
201/835-5212

Picker's Paradise
269 Wanaque Ave.
201/616-9500

Carrolls Antiques
326 Wanaque Ave.
201/831-6186

Sterling Antique Center
222 Wanaque Drive
201/616-8986

60 PRINCETON

Gilded Lion
4 Chambers St.
609/924-6350

Girard Caron Interiors
54 Constitution Hwy. W
609/924-1007

Eye For Art
6 Spring St.
609/924-5277

Tamaras Things
4206 Quaker Bridge Rd.
609/452-1567

Kingston Antiques
4446 Rt. 27
609/924-0332

East & West Chinese Antiques
4451 Rt. 27
609/924-2743

61 RAHWAY

Royal Treasures Antique Inc.
69 E. Cherry St.
908/827-0409

Tarnished Swan
74 W. Cherry St.
908/499-7111

Ken's Antiques
1667 Irving St.
908/381-7306

62 RED BANK

Copper Kettle Antiques
15 Broad St.
908/741-8583

Tower Hill Antiques & Design
147 Broad St.
908/842-5551

Tea & Vintage
16 West St.
908/741-6676

The Red Bank Antique Center
195 W. Front St.
908/842-3393

Antiques Associates
205 W. Front St.
908/219-0377

Gas Light Antiques
212 W. Front St.
908/741-7323

Monmouth Antiques Shoppes
217 W. Front St.
908/842-7377

Antique Gallery
27 Monmouth St.
908/224-0033

Two Broad Antiques
160 Monmouth St.
908/224-0122

Lone Arranger Outlet Store
101 Shrewsbury Ave.
908/747-9238

British Cottage Antiques
126 Shrewsbury Ave.
908/530-0685

63 RIDGEWOOD

Ridgewood Furn. Refinishing
166 Chestnut St.
201/652-5566

Irish Eyes Import
1 Cottage Place
201/445-8585

Marilyn of Monroe
39 Godwin Ave.
201/447-3123

Then and Now
419 Goffle Rd.
201/670-7090

Hahns Antiques
579 Goffle Rd.
201/251-9444

Ivory Tower Inc.
38 Oak St.
201/670-6191

64 SADDLE RIVER

Carriage House Antiques
7 Barnstable Court
201/327-2100

Baldini Ricci Galleries Inc.
24 Industrial Ave.
201/327-0890

Richard Kyllo Antiques
210 W. Saddle River Rd.
201/327-7343

65 SCOTCH PLAINS

Antique Cottage
1833 Front St.
908/322-2553

Oakwood Furniture Co.
1833 Front St.
908/322-3873

Parse House Antiques
1833 Front
908/322-9090

Gallerie Ani' Tiques
Park & Front
908/322-4600

Heritage Antiques Center
364 Park Avenue
908/322-2311

Seymour's Antiques & Cllbls.
1732 E. 2nd St.
908/322-1300

Heinemeyer's Collectibles & Antiques
1380 Terrill Road
908/322-1788

66 SOMERVILLE

Uptown Somerville Center
Division St.
908/595-1294

Somerville Center Antiques
17 Division St.
908/526-3446

Gallery
30 Division St.
908/429-0370

Incogneeto Neet-O-Rama
19 W. Main St.
908/231-1887

Country Seat Antiques
41 W. Main St.
908/595-9556

67 SOUTH ORANGE

Roberta Willner Antiques
48 Crest Dr.
201/762-8844

Aaltens Galleries Est. 1914
461 Irvington Ave.
201/762-7200

Carrie Topf Antiques
50 W. South Orange Ave.
201/762-8773

68 SPRING LAKE

Gallery III Antiques
1720 State Hwy. #71
908/449-7560

Spring Lake Antiques
1201 3rd Avenue
098/449-3322

69 SUMMIT

Plumquin Ltd.
12 Beechwood Rd.
908/273-3425

Summit Antiques Center Inc.
511 Morris Ave.
908/273-9373

The Second Hand
519 Morris Ave.
908/273-6021

Charming Home
358 Springfield Ave.
908/598-1022

Country House
361 Springfield Ave.
908-277-3400

Remmey's Consignment
83 Summit Ave.
908/273-5055

Antiques & Art by Conductor
88 Summit Ave.
908/273-6893

70 TOMS RIVER

Antique Outlet
552 Lakehurst Rd.
908/286-7788

Main St. Antique Center
251 Main St.
908/349-5764

Piggy Bank
2018 Rt. 37 E.
908/506-6133

Bulldog Glass Co.
10 W. Gateway
732/349-2742

71 TRENTON

Conti Antiques & Figurines
52 Rt. 33 (1 mile off I-295, Exit 64)
609/584-1080 or 609/586-4531
Open Mon.-Sat. usually 11-5; Sundays by appointment

Directions: Located on State Hwy. 33 between Robbinsville (Rt. 130) and Trenton. Also, Exit 64 off I-295. Two miles from Trenton, 8 miles from Bordentown, 12 miles from Hightstown, 15 miles from Princeton. Call before coming! Hours 11 a.m. - 5 p.m. unless I am on a house call or closed due to an estate appraisal. Call also for better directions.

Richard Conti has been in business twenty two years, handling lots of smalls in his 1,400 square- foot shop. Most of his stock consists of furniture and figurines, which include Royal Doulton, Hummel, Boehm, Cybis, Ispanky, Precious Moments, Goebel and others. In addition to the shop and handling appraisals, Richard also holds auctions on an "as needed" basis.

Greenwood Antiques
1918 Greenwood Ave.
609/586-6887

Armies of the Past Ltd.
2038 Greenwood Ave.
609/890-0142

Estate Galleries Ltd.
1641 N. Olden Ave.
609/219-0300

Canty Inc.
1680 N. Olden Ave.
609/530-1832

Antiques by Selmon
10 Vetterlein Ave.
609/586-0777

72 WESTFIELD

Betty Gallagher Antiques Inc.
266 E. Broad St.
908/654-4222

Westfield Antiques
510 Central Ave.
908/232-3668

Old Toy Shop
759 Central Ave.
908/232-8388

Linda Elmore Antiques
395 Cumberland St.
908/233-5443

Marylou's Memorabilia
17 Elm St.
908/654-7277

Back Room Antiques
39 Elm St.
908/654-5777

The Attic
415 Westfield Ave.
908/233-1954

Notes

New Mexico

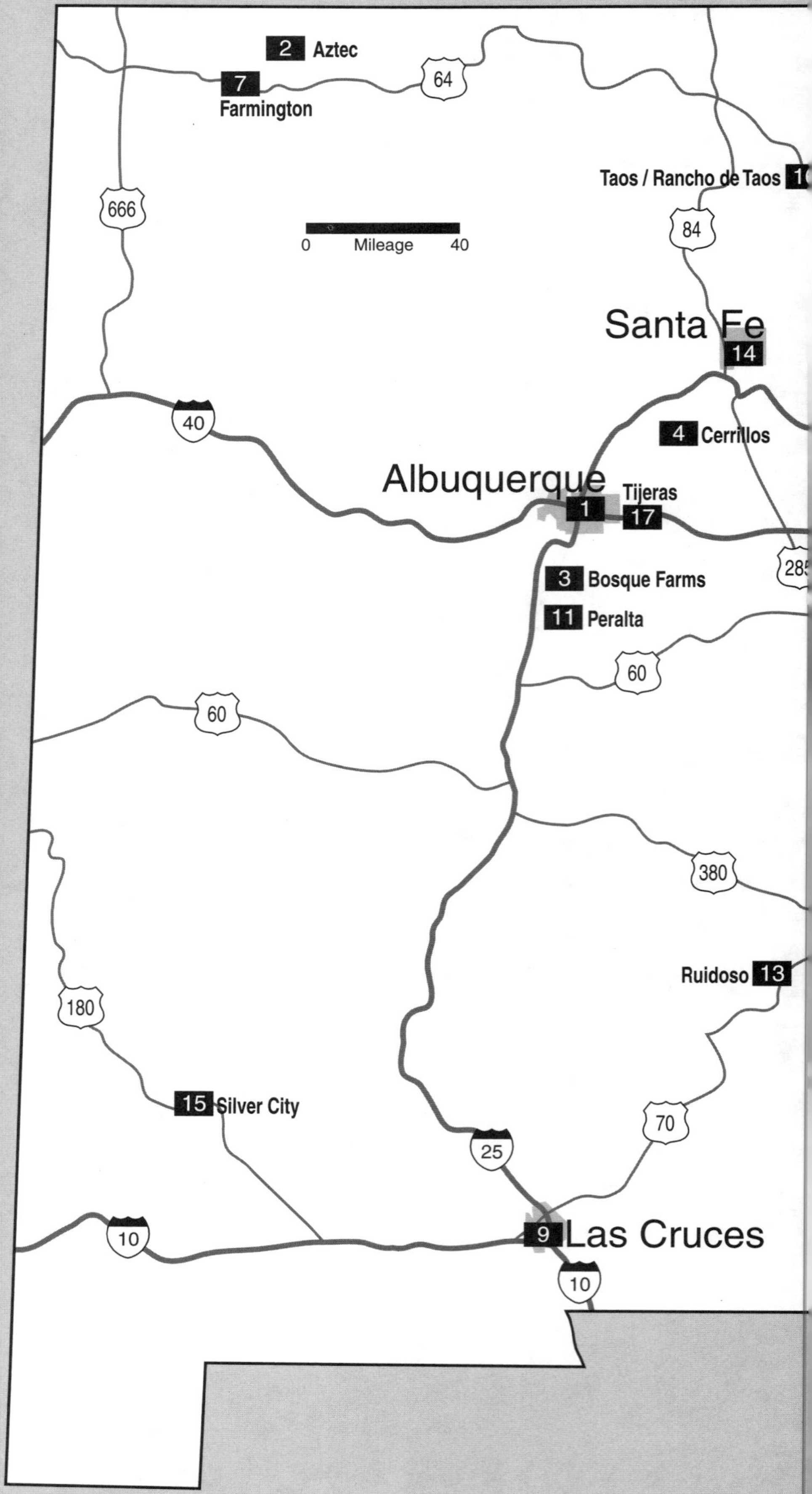

2 Aztec
7 Farmington
64
666
0 Mileage 40
Taos / Rancho de Taos
84
Santa Fe
14
40
4 Cerrillos
Albuquerque
1
Tijeras
17
3 Bosque Farms
11 Peralta
60
60
380
Ruidoso 13
180
15 Silver City
70
25
10
9 Las Cruces
10

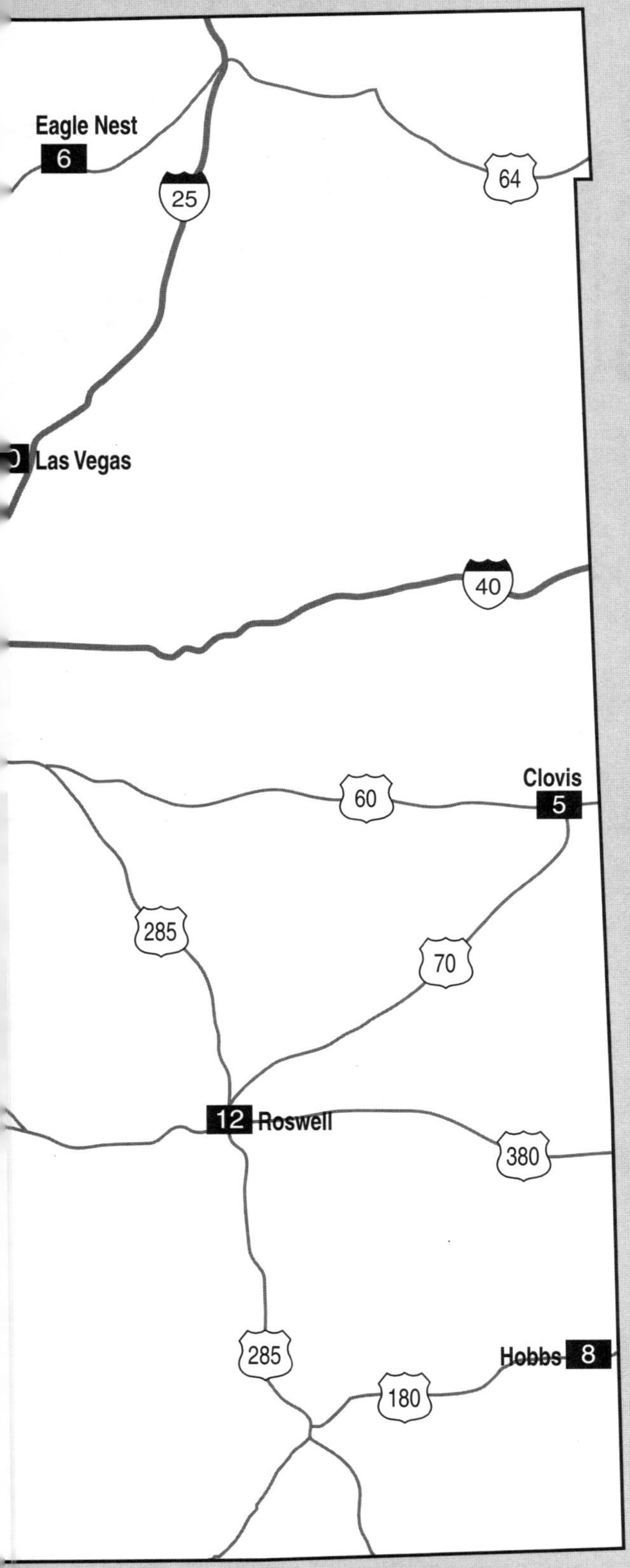
Eagle Nest
6
25
64
Las Vegas
40
Clovis
5
60
285
70
12 Roswell
380
285
Hobbs 8
180

Enchanted Circle Antiques

124 East Main Street
(Highway 64)
(505)377-3382

Eagle Nest

SILVER CITY
TRADING COMPANY

ANTIQUE MALL

205 W. Broadway
505/388-8989

Silver City

New Mexico

1 ALBUQUERQUE

Classic Century Square
4616 Central Avenue SE
505/255-1850
Open: Mon.-Sat. 10-6, Sun. 12-5; Closed Thanksgiving, Christmas and Easter

Directions: West of San Mateo

Classic Century Square is New Mexico's largest antiques and collectibles marketplace. With over 40,000 square feet of showroom space on three floors, one can only imagine the variety of treasures from which to choose. Filled to the rafters (literally), the mall has everything; music boxes, quilts and linens, glassware, pottery, advertising items, cast iron, framed prints and oils, war memorabilia, European dolls and Barbie dolls, fifties kitchen items, American Indian artifacts, furniture from every style and period, Star Wars collectibles and the list goes on and on.

An added draw to Classic Century Square has been the building's history and architectural features. Built in 1955 (art deco in design) the entire north side of the building is made of glass windows - shedding light on the spacious interior. In addition, the three story stairwell is a landmark in the Albuquerque area, and historical tidbits like the drums of sterile water stockpiled in the basement from the buildings days as a fallout shelter. A train museum located on the third floor is another popular attraction, especially for children.

Serious collectors often shop the market due to its outstanding inventory of "hot" collectibles. Decorators find it a good source for unique and interesting items not commonly found in other shops. Even set decorators, for the movie industry, have found wonderful props at Classic Century Square. Marketing to the movie industry has generated interest and numerous inquiries over the years. One of their vendor's old trunks were purchased and tossed out of a window in a scene from Billy The Kid. With so much to look at, people can sometimes get overwhelmed, but the helpful and knowledgeable staff can quickly help folks find what they are looking for. "We stress service and pleasing the customer," says owner Bob Sloan. "There is something here for everyone. We know we are the biggest, but we also think we are the best."

The Ranchette Bed and Breakfast
2329 Lakeview Rd. S.W.
505/877-5140 or 1-800-374-3230
Rates: $55-85

Directions: Call ahead for specific directions from your locations.

Just 15 minutes from historic old town Albuquerque, The Ranchette Bed and Breakfast seems a world away from the hustle and bustle of the city. With panoramic views of the Sandia and Manzano Mountains, the glorious Western sunsets, and the distant twinkle of the city lights, a sense of calm and beauty descends.

Whether you are lazing in the hot tub under the arbor, or riding the range on one of the majestic Arabian horses in residence, the atmosphere just naturally draws you in and calms you. If you like, you may bring and board your own horse. For those who prefer a more mechanical mode of transportation, walking and bicycle paths are adjacent to the property (bicycles are furnished by the Ranchette), but you'll have to bring your own Nikes!

Inside, all guest rooms are furnished with original art and antiques, writing desks, telephones, and terry robes. The living area offers a grand piano, a cozy fireplace and plenty of space to play games, plan the next day's activities, or just do nothing.

The food here is gourmet vegetarian fare, but if you have specific dietary needs, they'll be happy to accommodate you. They'll even provide picnic lunches or candlelight dinners upon request.

Whether you are on a family vacation or a romantic getaway, The Ranchette Bed and Breakfast offers its own special brand of recreation and relaxation in a smoke-free and alcohol-free environment.

Furniture on Consignment
701 Candelaria Rd. NE
505/344-1275

Old Oak Tree Antique Mall
111 Cardenas Dr. NE
505/268-6965

Lookie Loos Antiquated Furn.
519 Central Ave. NW
505/242-4740

Dans Place Antique Clocks
3902 Central Ave. SE
505/268-1010

Cowboys & Indians Antiques
4000 Central Ave. SE
505/255-4054

Morningside Antiques
4001 Central Ave. NE
505/268-0188

Antiques on Central
4009 Central Ave. NE
505/255-4800

Antique Specialty Mall
4516 Central Ave. SE
505/268-8080

Ailene's & Donna's Antq. Mall
4710 Central Ave. SE
505/255-1850

Somewhere in Time
5505 Central Ave. NW
505/836-8681

Anna's Grapevine Furniture
5517 Central Ave. NE
505/268-3427

Antique Connection
12020 Central Ave. SE
505/296-2300

Lawson's Antiques
2809 Chanate Ave. SW
505/877-0538

Good Stuff the SW Antiques
2108 Charlevoix NW
505/843-6416

Antique Manor
1701 Eubank Blvd. NE
505/299-0151

B's Antiques/Marie's Cllbls.
3107 Eubank Blvd. NE. Ste. 8
505/298-7205

Scottsdale Village Antiques
3107 Eubank Blvd. NE, Ste. 7
505/271-1522

Consignment Interiors Etc.
5850 Eubank Blvd. NE
505/293-0765

Anglo American Antiques Ltd.
2524 Vermont St. NE
505/298-7511

Seddon's Rancho Chico Antqs.
6923 4th St. NW
505/344-5201

Antiques Consortium
7216 4th St. NW
505/897-7115

Antique Co-op
7601 4th St. NW
505/898-7354

Antiques & Treasures Inc.
4803 Lomas Blvd. NE
505/268-6008

John Isaac Antqs. Rio Grande
2036 S Plaza St. NW
505/842-6656

Chatterely's Antiques
901 Rio Grande Blvd. NW D128
505/242-4430

Lawrence's
4022 Rio Grande Blvd. NW, Ste. D
505/344-5511

Adobe Gallery
413 Romero St. NW
505/243-8485

Hanging Tree Gllry.-Old Town
416 Romero St. NW
505/842-1420

Lindy's Ltd.
2035 12th St. NW
505/244-3320

Timeless Treasures
2035 12th St. NW
505/891-8183

A Perfect Setting
5901 Wyoming Blvd. NE, Ste. Y
505/821-7601

Favorite Places To Eat

Cracker Barrel Old Country Store
I-25 & San Antonio, Exit 231
505/821-8777

2 AZTEC

Rocky Mountain Antiques
107 S. Main
505/334-0004

Downtown Antiques
301 S. Main
505/334-5818

Aztec Furniture Art & More
201 E. Chaco
505/334-0033

3 BOSQUE FARMS

Behind The Barn Antiques
1435 Bosque Farms Blvd.
505/869-5212

4 CERRILLOS

What-Not Shop Antiques
15 B First Street
505/471-2744
Open 7 days a week from 10-5

Situated on the Turquoise Trail and built in 1890 by Mr. Griffith, the shop offers Native American jewelry, rugs, pottery, jewelry, pocket watches and exquisite cut glass.

5 CLOVIS

Marlene's Antiques & Gifts
1011 N. Norris Street
505/763-1396
Open Mon.-Fri. 9:30-5:30

Inside discover antique furniture, collectibles and a gift selection with limited edition collector items.

Prairie Peddler Antiques
100 S. Main Street
505/763-7392
Open Mon.-Sat., 10-5

Housed in the 1931 former Raton Creamery, you'll find antique furniture, Depression glass, primitives, Carnival, Roseville, elegant glassware, as well as cast iron pieces.

Endless Trail
201 W. Grand Avenue
505/769-1839
Open Mon.-Fri., 10-5; Sat. 10-6

For the young-at-heart collector, check out the toys, Pez and magazines.

Stitches of New Mexico — Antiques
927 N. Main Street
505/763-5018
Open Mon.-Fri., 10-5; Saturday 10-4

Inside Stitches of New Mexico, located in the Historic District of downtown, you'll find china, crystal, primitives, old books and records, RS Prussia, Carnival, cut glass, Depression glass, toys, linens, furniture, old pictures and wonderful tapestries.

Furniture Corner
123 W .Grand Ave.
505/762-1113

Endless Trail
201 W. Grand Ave.
505/769-1839

Three Keys Antique Mall
1709 Mabry Dr.
505/763-1740

Prairie Peddler Antiques
100 S. Main St.
505/763-7392

Stitches of New Mexico
927 N. Main St.
505/763-5018

6 EAGLE NEST

Enchanted Circle Co., Antiques & Accommodations
124 East Main Street (Hwy. 64)
505/377-3382
Open 10-5 daily from May 15 to October 15. Call for winter hours.

Directions: Traveling I-25 South from Raton, take Hwy. 64 West through Cimarron to Eagle Nest.

Located along The Enchanted Circle, a 100-mile scenic drive surrounding Wheeler Peak. Enchanted Circle offers antique shopping and overnight accommodations. Housed in the Main Street facility is the antique shop (the area's largest) specializing in china, silver, crystal, quilts, furniture and Southwestern artifacts. Apartments and suites on the second floor over the antique shop have antique furnishings and wood-burning stoves.

7 FARMINGTON

Browsery
1605 E. 20th Street
505/325-4885
Open Mon.-Sat., 9:30-6

In business for 21 years, featuring furnishings such as antique wardrobes, chests, dressers, pianos and a full line of new Amish-made furniture.

Antique Trove
309 W. Main
505/324-0559

Somewhere In Time
115 W. Main
505/564-2711

Dusty Attic
111 W. Main
505/327-7696

Sentimental Journey
218 W. Main
505/326-6533

8 HOBBS

Estelles Collectibles
3621 S. Eunice Hwy.
505/393-8633
Open Mon.-Sat., 9-5

This old house holds antique collectibles, furniture and primitives including irons, skillets, and churns.

Antiques Unique
2420 N. Dal Paso Street
505/392-8527
Open Mon.-Fri., 8-5

An assortment of antiques including Depression glassware, pottery, primitives (such as irons, crocks, churns), crystal and some furniture will be found in this shop.

Crafters Cottage & Antique Mall
801 E. Bender Blvd.
505/397-4481

9 LAS CRUCES

La Vieja
2230 Avenida De Mesilla
505/526-7875

Jones & Co. Jewelers
1160 El Paseo St.
505/526-2809

Main Street Antique Mall
2301 S. Main St.
505/523-0047

Things For Sale
606 W. Picacho Ave.
505/526-7876

S.O.B.'s Antiques
928 W. Picacho Ave.
505/526-8624

Coyote Traders
1020 W. Picacho Ave.
505/523-1284

Ross Bell Antiques
1144 W. Picacho Ave.
505/523-2089

High Class Junk Joint
1150 W. Picacho Ave.
505/524-4314

Favorite Places To Eat

Cracker Barrel Old Country Store
I-10 & Hwy. 28, Exit 140
505/647-0067

10 LAS VEGAS

Plaza Antiques
1805 On the Plaza
505/454-9447
Open Thurs.-Mon., 10-6; Sunday 12-4

Ten dealers display antique furniture, collectibles, vintage clothing, Western artifacts, glassware, pottery, light fixtures and more.

Virginia West-Antiques & More
150 Bridge St.
505/454-8802

Twentieth Century Store
514 Douglas Ave.
505/425-3180

11 PERALTA

Past & Present Treasures
3617 Hwy. 47
505/869-4546

12 ROSWELL

Monterey Antique Mall
1400 W. 2nd Street
505/623-3347
Open everyday from 10-6

Ten-thousand square feet and thirteen dealers provide the gamut of antique items—jewelry, furniture, dolls, coins, plus much more.

Byegones
500 W. 2nd St.
505/622-1995

Pedlar Way Uphlstry. & Antqs.
4506 W. 2nd St.
505/624-2521

13 RUIDOSO

Camel House
714 Mechem Drive
505/257-7479
Open seven days a week from 9:30-5:30

Features Southwestern artifacts, antique beds, wagons, dressers, buffets, secretaries, pie and whiskey cabinets, tobacco cases, a wide selection of clocks, as well as bronzes. The shop offers Southwestern and Western artists including G. Harvey.

House of Antiques
2213 Sudderth Drive
505/257-2839
Open 10-5 everyday except Tuesday and Wednesday

Victorian furniture, lamps, glassware and art glass are the specialties of this shop located in the walking tour section of midtown.

Yesteryear Antiques
122 N. Hwy. 7
505/378-4667

Joyce's Junque
650 Sudderth Dr.
505/257-7575

Auntie Bo's
2314 Sudderth Dr.
505/257-3683

14 SANTA FE

Guadalupe Inn
604 Agua Fria Street
505/989-7422
Office Hours; 8 a.m.-9 p.m.
Open year round

Directions: From I-25, take St. Francis Drive exit and stay on St. Francis Drive for 3.7 miles to Agua Fria Street. Turn right onto Agua Fria; proceed 3 blocks until the "604" sign then turn right.

Pampered with family hospitality, enjoy a "truly Sante Fe" experience. Built on family property, the Inn offers quiet, privacy and unique charm. Katchine, Hopi spirit dolls, enhance the local flavor of the decor. Fireplaces, patios and whirlpool tubs are available with some rooms. To the rear of the inn, a small garden makes a cozy nook for an outdoor breakfast.

The Don Gaspar Compound
623 Don Gaspar
505/986-8664
Open year round
Rates $85-220

Directions: From east & south along I-25, take the Old Pecos Trail exit and go all of the way into town. Turn left on Paseo de Peralta, then left on Don Gaspar. The Compound is 1 1/2 blocks on the left. OR from the north via 285, take St. Francis, turn left on Alameda and follow it to Don Gaspar. Turn right on Don Gaspar and go 4 1/2 blocks to the Compound.

Built in 1912 in Santa Fe's Don Gaspar Historic District, the Compound is a classic example of Mission and Adobe architecture. Six private suites offer wood and gas-burning fireplaces (one is an adobe fireplace), saltillo and Mexican-tiled floors. Step into the secluded adobe-walled garden courtyard and relax to the trickle of the fountain while breathing in the scent of brilliant heirloom flowers.

Antique Warehouse
530 S. Guadalupe
505/984-1159

Pachamama
223 Canyon Rd.
505/983-4020

Scarlett's Antiques
225 Canyon Rd.
505/983-7092

Casa Ana
503 Canyon Rd.
505/989-1781

Morning Star Gallery Ltd.
513 Canyon Rd.
505/982-8187

Claiborne Gallery
608 Canyon Rd.
505/982-8019

Kania-Ferrin Gallery
662 Canyon Rd.
505/982-8767

Tiqua Gallery
812 Canyon Rd.
505/984-8704

Architectural Antiques
1117 Canyon Rd.
505/983-7607

The Bedroom
304 Catron St.
505/984-0207

American Country Collection
620 Cerrillos Rd.
505/984-0955

La Puerta
1302 Cerrillos Rd.
505/984-8164

Pegasus Antiques & Cllbls.
1372 Cerrillos Rd.
505/982-3333

Stephen's A Consign. Gallery
2701 Cerrillos Rd.
505/471-0802

Doodlet's Shop
120 Don Gaspar Ave.
505/983-3771

Mary Corley Antiques
215 N Guadalupe St.
505/984-0863

Santa Kilim
401 S. Guadalupe St.
505/986-0340

Rio Bravo
411 S. Guadalupe St.
505/982-0230

Foreign Traders
202 Galisteo St.
505/983-6441

El Colectivo
556 N. Guadalupe St.
505/820-7205

Foxglove Antiques
260 Hyde Park Rd.
505/986-8285

In Home Furnishings
132 E Marcy St.
505/983-0808

Peyton-Wright
131 Nusbaum St.
505/989-9888

American Country Collection
620 Cerrillos Road
505/984-0955

Adams House
211 Old Sante Fe Trail
505/982-5115

Arrowsmith's Relics Old West
402 Old Santa Fe Trail
505/989-7663

James Reid Ltd.
114 E. Palace Ave.
505/988-1147

Wiseman & Gale & Duncan
940 E. Palace Ave.
505/984-8544

Susan Tarman Antqs./Fine Art
923 Paseo De Peralta
505/983-2336

Hands of America
401 E. Rodeo Rd.
505/983-5550

El Paso Import Company
418 Sandovol
505/982-5698

Dewey Galleries Ltd.
76 E San Francisco St.
505/982-8632

Things Finer
100 E San Francisco
505/983-5552

Vivian Wolfe Antiques
112 W San Francisco St.
505/982-7769

William R Talbot Fine Arts
129 W. San Francisco St.
505/982-1559

Bizaare Bazaar Company
137 W. Water St.
505/988-3999

Canfield Gallery
414 Canyon Road
505/988-4199

Economos Work of Art
500 Canyon Road
505/982-6347

Hampton Gallery
236 Delgado
505/983-9635

Moondance Gallery
707 Canyon Road
505/982-3421

Henry C. Monahan
526 Canyon Road
505/982-8750

Ron Messick Fine Arts
600 Canyon Road
505/983-9533

Reflection Gallery
201 Canyon Road
505/995-9795

Jane Smith
550 Canyon Road
550/988-4775

Umbrello Showroom
701 Canyon Road
550/984-8566

Nedra Matteucci/Fenn Galleries
1075 Paseo de Peralta
550/982-4631

Antiques on Grant
126 Grant Avenue
505/995-9701

15 SILVER CITY

The Silver City Trading Co. Antique Mall
205 West Broadway
505/388-8989
Fax: 505/388-5263
Open: Daily Mon.-Sat., 10-6, Sun. 12-4

Directions: From Lordsburg on I-10, take NM-90 north 42 miles. From Deming on I-10, take US-180 northwest 52 miles. From the north on I-25, you can take NM-152 south of Truth or Consequences, through Hillsboro, Kingston, and the Mimbres Mountains, joining US-180 eight miles east of Silver City (Inquire about road conditions in winter). The alternative is to take NM-26 from Hatch (the chile capital) to Deming and US-180. The antique mall is two blocks west of Hudson Street (NM-90) in Silver City's Historic District and near the campus of Western New Mexico University.

The Silver City Trading Co. is housed in a 12,500 square foot building erected in 1897. The pressed tin ceilings testify to its longevity. Outstanding among the offerings of the 31 dealers are objects of art, utility and decoration associated with the Old West, as well as contemporary Native American craft production from both sides of the border. Other offerings include objects associated with mining, railroading, and ranching. Collectibles include coins, currency, dolls, toys, jewelry, vintage clothing, china, pottery, and glassware.

Silver Creek Antiques
614 N. Bullard St.
505/538-8705

16 TAOS/RANCHO DE TAOS

Maison Faurie
On The Plaza
505/758-8545

Patrick Dunbar Antiques
222 Paseo Del Tueblo Norte
505/758-2511

Dwellings Revisited
10 Bent Street
505/758-3377

Horsefeathers, Etc.
109 Kit Carson Road
505/758-7457

The Barn
506 Kit Carson Road
505/758-7396

Prints Old & Rare
4155 State Road 68
505/751-4171

Annabel's Strictly by Accident
4153 State Road 68
505/751-7299

Haciendo de San Francisco
Saint Francis Plaza
505/758-0477

17 TIJERAS

Another Place N Time
Just South of I-40 on S S
505/281-1212

Notes

New York

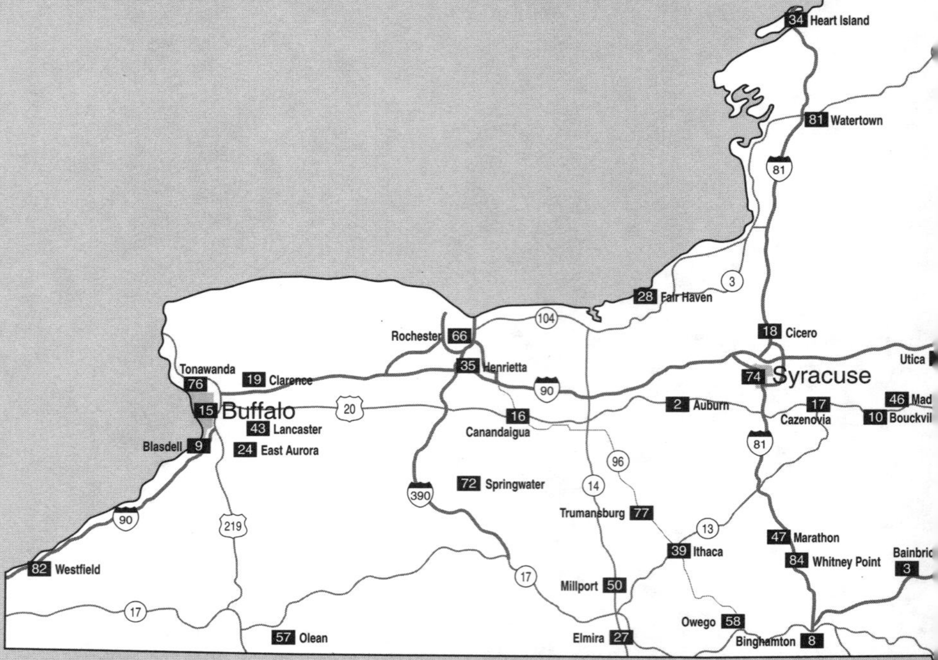

34 Heart Island
81 Watertown
81
3
28 Fair Haven
104
18 Cicero
Rochester 66
35 Henrietta
Tonawanda
76
19 Clarence
90
74 Syracuse
Utica
15 Buffalo
20
2 Auburn
17 Cazenovia
46 Mad
10 Bouckvil
43 Lancaster
16
Canandaigua
Blasdell 9
24 East Aurora
81
96
390
72 Springwater
14
90
219
Trumansburg 77
13
47 Marathon
82 Westfield
39 Ithaca
84 Whitney Point
Bainbrid
3
17
Millport 50
17
57 Olean
Elmira 27
Owego 58
Binghamton 8

Serendipity II

The little shop with the LARGE selection

3867 Route 14 *Located between Watkins Glen and Route 17*

607/739-9413

Millport

50

THE FAMILY JEWELS

Vintage Clothing
Antique Jewelry
Accessories
Linens & Textiles

832 Avenue of the Americas • (212) 679-5023

New York

54

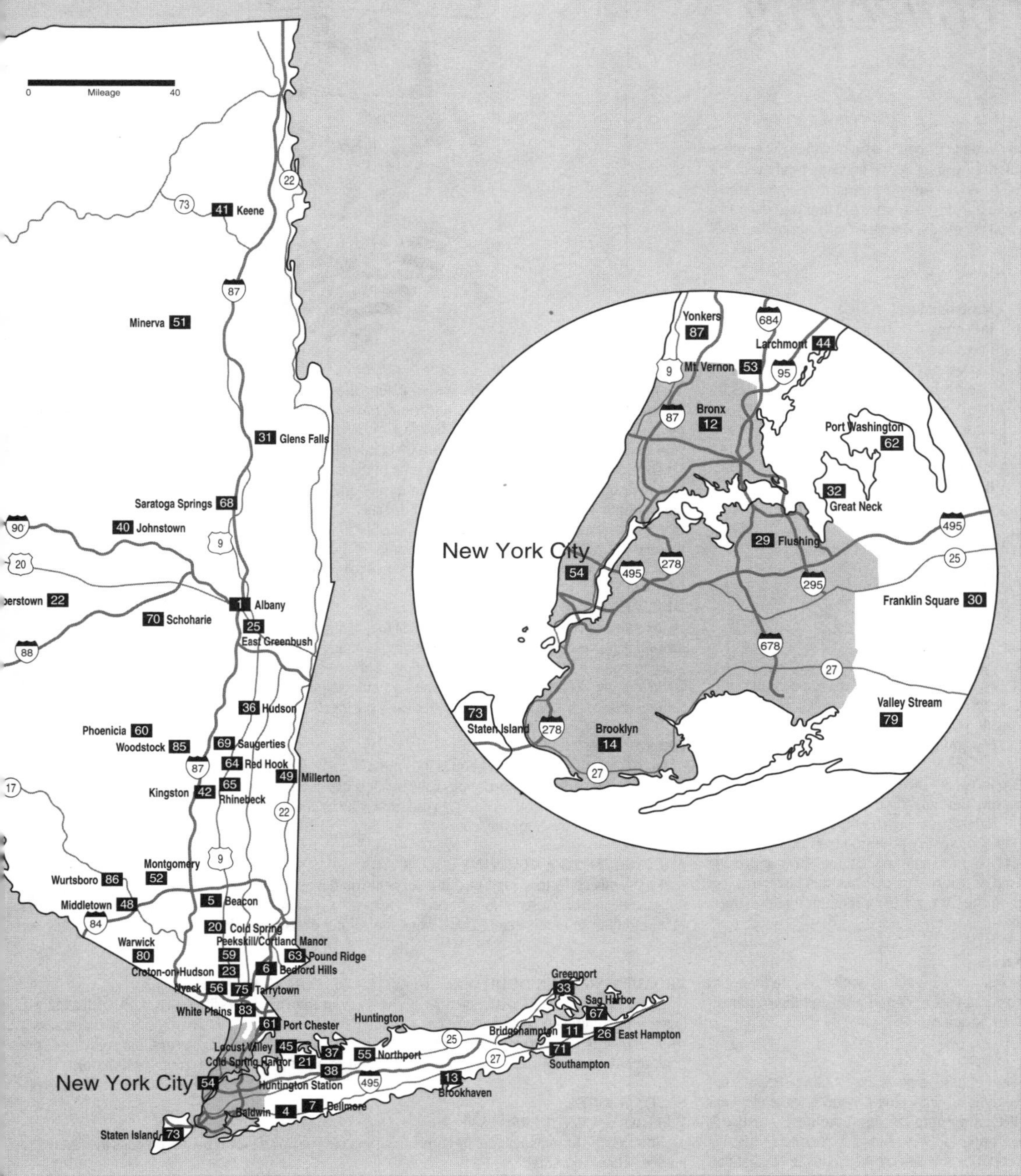

Chestnut Tree Inn

(518) 587-8681

9 Whitney Place

Saratoga Springs

68

Broadway Antiques Gallery

484 Broadway
Saratoga Springs, NY
(518) 581-8348

68

Croton-on-Hudson's

Alexander Hamilton House

Bed and Breakfast Inn

(914) 271-6737

23

di Salvo Galleries, Ltd.

Fine Art, and European Antiques
Estate Liquidation Specialists
1015 Hempstead Turnpike
(516) 326-1090

Franklin Square

30

THE BARK EATER

A True Country Inn

Nestled in the lea of the Adirondack High Peaks... at the entrance to Lake Placid's Olympic Region

Alstead Mill Road

800/232-1607

http://www.tvenet.com/barkeater

Keene

41

How to keep a level head — *at all levels of collecting*

By Bob Cahn, The Primitive Man

IDENTIFYING THE BREEDS

When it comes to variables, no one form of leisure-time activity has as many classifications as "Collecting/Antiquing." The last thing you need is another self-testing, score-keeping, grade-yourself, chart comparing, similarity-seeking, psychological profile — querying quiz (regardless of the subject matter), but we sneaked one in. There is no passing grade, but the more times you find yourself on the list, the higher your score, and the more likely you are to become a full-fledged member of the "PAP" (Preservation of Antique Pursuits) Society.

— Are you ready for the PAP test?

COLLECTOR TYPES – CAST OF CHARACTERS

( ) Garage Sale Guru
( ) Relentless Researcher
( ) Neophyte
( ) Super Collector
( ) Low Key Looker
( ) Disciplined
( ) Impulsive or Obsessive
( ) Auction Hawkshaw
( ) Ponderer
( ) Perfectionist
( ) Pack Rat
( ) Household Hoarder
( ) Casual Collector
( ) Attic Addict
( ) Frantic Frenetic Fanatic
( ) Endomorph Evaluator
( ) Museum Mogul
( ) Indecisive
( ) Enigmatic
( ) Enthusiastic Eclectic
( ) Tireless Interrogator
( ) Die-Hard Disciple
( ) Blase and Bemused
( ) Short Attention Span Spender
( ) Advanced Accumulator
( ) Beneath-the-Surface Snooper
( ) Savvy Specialist
( ) Weekend Stroller
( ) "Grandma Had One" Crowd
( ) Souvenir Selector
( ) Tire Kicker
( ) Occasional Dabbler

IT TAKES ALL KINDS

As you can see from the list, variety prevails ... and personality traits and budget are two key ingredients of an antiquers DNA. Each contributes its own subtle flavoring to the giant cauldron of collectors. Every approach is different, and combining tactics to tailor-make your personal game plan can prove extremely efficient and effective. For example, do you subscribe to local or regional periodicals, or just rely on freebie handouts? This way can keep you posted on local auctions, shows or estate sales.

If you're a gambler, auctions can prove rewarding. Do you play "auction roulette" by placing a "left bid" or participating in live telephone bidding? This can save time and effort of you're knowledgeable about the item or don't want to stay for the full auction ... but this demands having faith in the integrity of the auction house. For those with no "won't power," this route may prove too harrowing as a high blood pressure sport; you may prefer the more leisurely shop-to-shop or Antique Show approach. This way you don't have to make on-the-spot, split-second decisions. You may function better in a less intimidating, low key environment. Besides, factoring in the 10% buyer's premium could prove a hidden cost you might have overlooked.

AUCTION PREVIEW — CLANDESTINE OBSERVING

If you're an experienced collector and your reputation precedes you, if at all possible try not to touch the item you're considering for fear of alerting nearby viewers and arousing their interest. Keeping the bidding competition to a minimum is to your advantage.

UNLIKELY PLACES FOR BARGAINS

Giant flea markets are often camouflaged antique sites of hidden treasures - but persistence and frequency are key ingredients for success [also check out local thrift shops, church white elephant sales, as well as Goodwill and the Salvation Army]. It's natural to gravitate to the dealer or booth specializing in your particular category - but here's an opposing viewpoint worth considering. It's based on logic and common sense. Don't pass up a booth or sale having the opposite of what you normally seek out. The theory: whatever shows up that varies from their normal stock (in other words, a misfit), could possibly be a sleeper because it is outside their knowledge and might be underpriced.

SPREADING THE WORD ... OR DOING YOUR OWN P.R.

This advice addresses ALL three categories: beginner, intermediate and advanced.

If you are a single-purpose or theme collector, as many people as possible should know about it. Toot your own horn. Spread the word wherever and whenever you can. Register with anybody and everybody you meet. Get on lists: dealers, auction houses, tag sale specialists. Join collectors clubs. Have inexpensive cards made up. T-shirts and caps can carry your message. Want list flyers should be printed up. The more flamboyant or outrageous, the better you'll be remembered. Take out small classified ads in Antique publications and local Pennysavers. Word of mouth works, and the bigger the mouth, etc., etc.

PRICE GUIDELINES ONLY

More books on more subjects are inundating the market, but the accompanying price guides are not etched in stone. They are like quicksand, often sucking you in. No listing can be all things to all people, it's impossible. Frequently-though subconsciously-they make you feel good (or bad) about your collection. But, remember they are ONLY guidelines and seldom can reflect the current market. The minute they are published they become outdated. They should be treated like a Michael Jordan stadium hot dog—Ball Park only. When an antique is ready to change hands, guides often prove faulty, because the real test is supply and demand. The price guide is an antique Dow Jones average that has no averaging mechanism and is unable to fluctuate with a changing market. Updates are mandatory and difficult to accomplish. Because of these factors, use them as guidelines only, and take what they say with a few grains of Morton's: iodized or rock.

DISCIPLINE AND PLANNING

If time is a premium—and it is for lots of folk—plan your weekends carefully, (or your vacations) around major events. If shows are your thing, you may want to cover 2, 3 or more in a day. Check the starting time and the geographical location, and select either the one that opens first or is located farthest away. That way you've amortized your traveling in down time, eliminating a lot of wasted waiting around. You might also consider early buying. It really S-T-R-E-T-C-H-E-S your day.

GROUP SHOP ADVANTAGE

Frequenting a multi-dealer shop is the equivalent of visiting a show, and it saves you the admission price, but often does not expose you to the freshest merchandise. But let's face it, if you've never heard an old joke before, to you it's new. It's the same with antiques—if you've never seen it before, it's not tired or stale, it's fresh to your eyes.

ADDING LIFE TO A STAGNANT COLLECTION

Frequently collectors [and I'm sure some of you have been there] reach a pinnacle or plateau in their acquisitional quests, where it becomes increasingly more difficult to come up with choice pieces to add to their mini museums. That's when the painful decision to change directions sometimes occurs.

BROADENING YOUR HORIZONS: CREATIVE COLLECTING KICKS IN...

Some take a parallel path, such as branching out into pie lifters if you've been collecting pie jaggers, into cutting boards if you've centered on food choppers, or into laundry soap and powders if your focus was washboards. You get the idea. It's not that easy to change gears, but sometimes the back or side door approach can instill fresh vitality to an otherwise jaded, rundown outlook.

S.A.T.* SCORES
[*SERIOUS ANTIQUERS TEST]

Now that the term papers are in—and since you did your own grading—it's obvious that everyone passed. Happy hunting!

A FINAL WORD

Antiquing is an addiction — and we're all junkies under the skin. Technology has advanced us from main liners to on-liners — and the proverbial quick fix now ends in "dot com."

EDITOR'S NOTE: The Primitive Man caters to sophisticated collectors and specializes in — PRIMITIVES, COUNTRY & EARLY AMERICAN ACCESSORIES FEATURING DISTINCTIVE FORGED HEARTH & COOKING EQUIPMENT, UNUSUAL KITCHEN ANTIQUES, PATENT MODELS, FOOD CHOPPERS, BUTTER CHURNS, RARE WASHBOARDS, RUGBEATERS, NUTMEG GRATERS, BOOTJACKS, CORN SHELLERS, PENCIL SHARPENERS, MECHANICAL RARITIES, MOUSE TRAPS, SCALES, PIE LIFTERS, JAGGING WHEELS, EARLY LIGHTING, GADGET CANES, MEDICAL AND DENTAL ITEMS, ICE SKATES, AND OTHER WEIRD STUFF. HE CAN BE REACHED AT: 6 DARRYL LA, CARMEL, N.Y., 10512 — (914) 225-7771.

*Reprinted with permission of the *New England Antique Journal.*

Franklin Square: di Salvo Galleries

di Salvo Galleries is the brainchild of two very successful individuals who pooled their individual talents, experience and their general love for fine antiques into a thriving showroom gallery that attracts the novice collector, to the most sophisticated individuals from the tri-state area.

One partner, Rosemarie DiSalvo was formerly a legal professional specializing in estate and trust administration. For more than 20 years, Rosemarie liquidated estates with values ranging from $500,000 to millions of dollars. Through the years, Rosemarie developed close associations with appraisers, major auction houses and antique dealers. These relationships have proved invaluable as resources in obtaining wonderful selections of furniture and decorative accessories that are fresh to the market.

Annemarie DiSalvo is a designer who was formerly employed for a well-known Manhattan interior design firm specializing in residential design. Her projects included penthouse apartments in New York City, large beach-front homes in the Hamptons and country estates in New Jersey and Connecticut. Annemarie's background and experience lends itself very well in assisting clients with design projects and helping them to make the right purchasing decisions.

Annemarie is a New York University graduate with a certificate (interior design) in fine arts and antique appraisal studies; her specialty is in antique rugs and antique furniture.

The di Salvo Gallery offers such a wide variety of antique and vintage furniture, fine decorative accessories, art, porcelain, china, crystal, and antique and vintage linens. "Our inventory is selected based upon uniqueness and condition. Diversity is extremely important because our client's needs run the gamut of singles and newlyweds setting up their first home, to the baby boomers who are the biggest segment of our client base. These clients are voracious in purchasing the same furniture styles that their parents or grandparents owned," explains Annemarie.

"Catering to the interior design community is our specialty, but we also welcome the general public."

di Salvo Galleries, Ltd.

1015 Hempstead Turnpike
Franklin Square, NY 11010

(516) 326-1090

New York

1 ALBANY

Vince Kendrick Jewelers
475 Albany Shaker Rd.
518/438-6350

Daybreak Antique Clothing
22 Central Ave.
518/434-4312

Zeller's
32 Central Ave.
518/463-8221

Action Antiques & Used Furn.
85 Central Ave.
518/463-0841

S & S Antique & Used Furn. Co.
85 Central Ave.
518/462-3952

New Scotland Antiques
240 Washington Avenue
518/463-1323

Flamingo's 50s & 60s
211 Lark St.
518/434-3829

Pocket Chng Antiques & Cllbls.
4 Prospect Ave.
518/489-6413

Yankee Peddler Thrift Shop
265 Osborne Rd.
518/459-9353

2 AUBURN

Ward's Antiques
56 E. Gennesee St.
315/252-7703

Fingerlakes Antiques
104 Grant Ave.
315/252-4934

Roesch's Antiques & Cllbls.
7255 Grant Ave.
315/255-0760

Auburn Trading Post
24 McMaster St.
315/258-9492

Auburn Antiques
33 Walnut St.
315/252-9701

3 BAINBRIDGE

Berry Hill Farms Bed and Breakfast
242 Ward Loomis Road
607/967-8745 or 1-800-497-8745
Open all year
Gardens open from 8 a.m. to dusk

Directions: From I-88, take Exit 8, Bainbridge. Go west on Rt. 206 for about 4 miles to West Bainbridge. Turn right on County Road 17 toward Oxford. Go 2.3 miles. Turn right on Ward-Loomis Road. Go 1/2 mile to the top of the hill.

This secluded hilltop farm is surrounded by acres of woods and meadows. The 1820s farmhouse has been tastefully renovated, and is full of comfortable antiques. They have all the conveniences of home, and then some—flannel sheets, down comforters, extra pillows, fresh and dried flowers from the gardens and antiques everywhere.

The Berry Hill Farm gardens are already a local attraction. They are open to the public May to October. Combined with the spectacular view, you'll find them a "bit of heaven," "butterfly paradise," "food for the soul."

Guided tours are available to ensure you experience everything that Berry Hill has to offer. Altogether, there are hundreds of species of plants, so you will always find something in bloom, something to smell, and something to taste. Many of the flowers and plants are dried here on the farm to be used for herbal teas, cooking and for their dried flower business. Berry Hill Farms is conveniently located to many antique shops and auctions in the area.

Old Hickory Antique Center
Rt. 7 at Gilford Rd.
607/967-4145

Susquehanna Cafe & Antiques
Rt. 7
607/967-4100

4 BALDWIN

Joan Bogart Antiques
2398 Grand Ave.
516/223-3901

Antique Quest
87 Merrick Rd.
516/623-8351

Baldwin Antiques Centre
906 Merrick Rd.
516/867-9842

Artie's Corner
754 Sunrise Hwy.
516/867-4297

5 BEACON

Back in Time Antiques
Bloesch Originals
Located in Antiques and Uniques Antique Mall
346 Main Street
914/838-0623

Back in Time Antiques features a wonderful array of antiques and collectibles. Period furniture, unusual lamps, and a varied selection of carnival and Depression glass, books, and Limoges pieces will add to your decorative needs. For those with a taste for more youthful collectibles, choose a snow baby, circa 1800s dolls and carriages.

Bloesch Originals offers an eclectic blend of old and new gold, silver, antique diamond, and amber jewelry. They'll even repair and appraise your selections. For those jewelry buyers with a flair for the original and custom-made, choose your own beads and crystals. They'll make your piece to order.

You may also choose from an assortment of eggery, pottery, carved mechanical organ grinders, candles, and more.

All That Jazz
238 Main Street
914/838-0441

Cold Spring Galleries Inc.
324 Main St.
914/831-6800

Dickinson's Antiques
440 Main St.
914/838-1643

East End Antiques
444 Main St.
914/838-9030

Early Everything
470 Main St.
914/838-3014

Beacon Hill Antiques
474 Main St.
914/831-4577

Tioronda Antiques
15 Tioronda Ave.
914/831-3437

6 BEDFORD HILLS

Eclectic Interiors Inc.
21 Babbitt Rd.
914/241-0047

Bedford Salvage Co.
2 Depot Plaza
914/666-4595

Raphael Gallery Paintings
23 Depot Plaza
914/666-4780

Marks Time
132 Green Lane
914/242-0058

7 BELLMORE

Antiques & Antiques
111 Bedford Ave. N
516/826-9839

Rays Antiques
2962 Merrick Rd.
516/826-7129

Austern's Antiques
2970 Merrick Rd.
516/221-0098

8 BINGHAMTON

Storekeeper
95 Clinton St.
607/722-2431

China Closet
97 Clinton St.
607/724-3611

Clinton Mill Antique Center
99 Clinton St.
607/773-2036

Elysian Gems & Jewelry
99 Clinton St.
607/724-0298

Olde Breeze
173 Clinton St.
607/724-2114

Mad Hatter Antiques
284 Clinton St.
607/729-6036

Frog Alley
300 Clinton St.
607/729-6133

Silver Fox Antiques
304 Clinton St.
607/729-1342

Interiors with Claudia
310 Clinton St.
607/797-3200

Rivers Twin Antiques
352 Clinton St.
607/798-9395

For Your Listening Pleasure
368 Clinton St.
607/797-0066

World Galleries
591 Conklin Rd.
607/772-0900

Mary Websters Antq. Frames
12 Edwards
607/722-1483

Antique Exchange
22 Front St.
607/723-6921

Buyers Unlimited
140 Front St.
607/722-1725

Bob Connelly & Sallie
205 State St.
607/722-9593

9 BLASDELL

Favorite Places To Eat

Cracker Barrel Old Country Store
I-90 & Milestrip Rd., Exit 56
716/826-7487

10 BOUCKVILLE

Cobblestone Store
Corner Rt. 20 & 46
315/893-7670

Bouckville Antique Corner
Rt. 20
315/893-1828

Pinewoods Antique Shop
Corner Rt. 20 & 46
315/893-7405

Bittersweet Bazaar
Rt. 20
315/893-7229

By-Gones-Hinmans Motel
Rt. 20
No Phone

Depot Antiques
Rt. 20
315/893-7676

D & R Antiques
Rt.. 20
315/893-1801

Elvira Stanton Antiques
Rt. 20
315/893-7479

Gallery Co-Op
Rt. 20
315/893-7752

Indian Opening Antique Center
Rt. 20
315/893-7303

Jackie's Place
Rt. 20
315/893-7457

Station House Antiques
Rt. 20
315/893-7652

Stone Lodge Antiques
Rt. 20
315/893-7270

Veranda Antiques & Art
Rt. 20 & 12 B
315/893-7270

11 BRIDGEHAMPTON

Beach Plum Antiques
Main
516/537-7403

Inez G. Macwhinnie
Main
516/537-7433

Country Gear Ltd.
Main
516/537-1032

House of Charm Antiques
Montauk Hwy.
516/537-3335

John Salibello Antiques
Montauk Hwy.
516/537-1484

Kinnaman & Ramaekers
2466 Montauk Hwy.
516/537-3838

Legendary Collections
Montauk Hwy.
516/537-2211

Urban Archeology
Montauk Hwy.
516/537-0124

English Country Antiques
Snake Hollow Road
516/537-0606

Ruby Beets Antiques
1703 Montauk Hwy.
516/537-2802

12 BRONX

All Boro Estate Liquidators
45 Bruckner Blvd.
718/402-8777

Larry's Antiques
2419 Eastchester Rd.
914/779-2304

Big Apple Antiques Inc.
430 E. 188th St.
718/220-4018

F & J Furniture
1007 Tiffany St.
718/378-2038

T & I Thrift World
3980 White Plains Rd.
718/519-6724

13 BROOKHAVEN

Brook Store
378 S. Country Rd.
516/286-8503

Delancy St. East
2527 Montauk Hwy.
516/286-2956

14 BROOKLYN

Horseman Antiques Inc.
351 Atlantic Ave.
718/596-1048

Town & Country Antiques
352 Atlantic Ave.
718/875-7253

In Days of Old Limited
357 Atlantic Ave.
718/858-4233

City Barn Antiques
362 Atlantic Ave.
718/855-8566

Atlantic Antique Center
367 Atlantic Ave.
718/488-0149

Time Trader
368 Atlantic Ave.
718/852-3301

Circa Antiques Ltd.
377 Atlantic Ave.
718/596-1866

Times & Moments
378 Atlantic Ave.
718/625-3145

A Matter of Time
380 Atlantic Ave.
718/624-7867

Assaf Antiques
383 Atlantic Ave.
718/237-2912

Antiques & Collectibles Shop
483 Atlantic Ave.
718/858-6903

Antiques by Ruth
507 Avenue
718/382-3269

Easy Furniture Inc.
871 Broadway
718/574-6400

Broadway Top Class Furniture
1275 Broadway
718/452-1100

Aaa-Abbey Merchandising Co.
618 Coney Island Ave.
718/253-8830

Scottie's Gallery
624 Coney Island Ave.
718/851-8325

Antiques Plus
744 Coney Island Ave.
718/941-8805

Bernstein's
744 Coney Island Ave.
718/342-3564

Smitty's New & Used Furniture
744 Coney Island Ave.
718/854-3052

Tyler Antiques
744 Coney Island Ave.
718/331-1533

All Boro Furniture
779 Coney Island Ave.
718/272-0559

C P Galleries
779 Coney Island Ave.
718/462-3606

Northeast Furniture & Antiques
779 Coney Island Ave.
718/272-4133

Flatbush Galleries
779 Coney Island Ave.
718/287-8353

Finders Keepers Antiques
784 Coney Island Ave.
718/941-4481

Sciarrino Antiques
830 Coney Island Ave.
718/462-8134

Yava Furniture
832 Coney Island Ave.
718/693-3322

Once Upon A Time Antiques
1053 Coney Island Ave.
718/859-6295

Roy Electric Antique Light Co.
1054 Coney Island Ave.
718/434-7002

Abbey Galleries
1061 Coney Island Ave.
718/692-2421

Astor Antiques
1067 Coney Island Ave.
718/434-9200

Charlotte Nik Nak Nook Antqs.
1131 Coney Island Ave.
718/252-0088

Attic
220 Court St.
718/643-9535

Action Furniture
1171 Flatbush Ave.
718/284-2899

New You Zd
1211 Flatbush Ave.
718/856-4819

Peoples Furniture
1332 Flatbush Ave.
718/859-6850

Bibilo Furniture Store
502 5th Ave.
718/832-6696

Juke Box Class & Vintage Slot
6742 5th Ave.
718/833-8455

Colonial Global Inc.
6823 5th Ave.
718/748-4401

Abboco
8323 5th Ave.
718/238-6956

Antiques & Decorations
4319 14th Ave.
718/633-6393

South Portland Antiques
753 Fulton
718/596-1556

Park Hill Restoration
375 Atlantic Avenue
718/624-0233

Gaslight Time Antiques
5 Plaza St. W.
718/789-7185

Mel's Antique
99 Smith St.
718/834-8700

Ace New & Used Furniture
575 Sutter Ave.
718/495-5711

Grand Sterling Silver Co. Inc.
4921 13th Ave.
718/854-0623

Discoveries
8407 3rd Ave.
718/836-0583

Top Cash Antiques
2065 E. 33rd St.
718/382-4418

Dream Land Antiques
619 Vanderbilt Ave.
718/230-9142

Frank Galdi Antiques
247 Warren St.
718/875-9293

Christmas Carol's
492 Macon St.
718/919-9033

15 BUFFALO

Bailey's Furniture
3191 Bailey Ave.
716/835-6171

Scotty's Furniture
3112 Bailey Ave.
716/835-6199

Horsefeathers Arch. Antiques
346 Connecticut St.
716/882-1581

Tres Beau Interiors
489 Delaware Ave.
716/886-3514

C Markarian & Sons Inc.
3807 Delaware Ave.
716/873-8667

Lete Antiques-Carl Stone
65 Elmwood Ave.
716/884-0211

Eaton Galleries
115 Elmwood Ave.
716/882-7823

Taylor Gallery
125 Elmwood Ave.
716/881-0120

Assets Antiques
140 Elmwood Ave.
716/882-2415

Jeffrey Thier Antiques
152 Elmwood Ave.
716/883-2858

Source
152 Elmwood Ave.
716/883-2858

Mix
711 Elmwood Ave.
716/886-0141

Lots of Stuff
2703 Elmwood Ave.
716/874-1164

Dana E. Tillou Gallery
417 Franklin St.
716/854-5285

American Militaria Collector
2409 Harlem Rd.
716/891-5200

Stock Exchange
1421 Hertel Ave.
716/838-8294

Conley Interiors Inc.
1425 Hertel Ave.
716/838-1000

Just Browsin
1439 Hertel Ave.
716/837-1840

Coo Coo U
1478 Hertel Ave.
716/837-3385

Melange Vintage Clothing
1484 Hertel Ave.
716/838-9290

A to Z Auction
2150 William St.
716/896-3342

Antique Architectural Circus
86 Vermont Street
716/885-5555

Antiques Americana
5600 Main St.
716/633-2570

Jean's Creekview Antiques
5629 Main St.
716/632-2711

Erie West Antiques & Cllbls.
10 Michael Rd.
716/677-2119

Attic Antiques & Collectibles
550 Mineral Springs Rd.
716/822-0627

Antique Architectural Circus
855 Niagra
716/885-5555

Antique Jewelry Trojners
296 Roycroft Blvd.
716/839-5453

Gallery of Treasures
2180 Seneca St.
716/826-3907

16 CANANDAIGUA

Richard Cuddeback
22 Leeward Lane
716/394-4097

Petticoat Junction Antiques
103 Leicester St.
716/396-0691

Nostalgia Ltd.
238 S. Main St.
716/396-9898

Kipling's Treasures
116 S. Main St.
716/396-7270

Antiques Unlimited
168 Niagara St.
716/394-7255

Harvest Mill
40 Parrish St.
716/394-5907

Tall Pines Antiques
3257 Routes
716/394-7230

Antique Center-30 Dealers
47 Saltonstall St.
716/394-2297

Happy Clutter Antiques
3735 State Rt. 5 #-20
716/394-4199

17 CAZENOVIA

Sally's Cellar
58 Albany St.
315/655-3324

Amanda Bury
97 Albany St. Rt. 20
315/655-3326

Old Everlasting Antiques
1826 Ballina Rd.
315/655-3212

Alexandra's Attic
4010 Erieville Rd.
315/655-2146

The Old Lamplighter Antiques
3951 Number Nine Rd.
315/655-4991

Web's Country House
4031 Putnam Rd.
315/655-4177

18 CICERO

Favorite Places To Eat

Cracker Barrel Old Country Store
I-81 & NY 31, Exit 30
315/698-4311

19 CLARENCE

Christner's Antiques
10715 Clarence Center Rd.
716/741-2826

Vi & Sis Antiques
8970 Main St.
716/634-4488

Antiques at the Barn
9060 Main St.
716/632-6674

Ruth's Antiques Inc.
9060 Main St.
716/741-8001

Uncle Sams Antiques
9060 Main St.
716/741-8838

Charles M. Fisher
10255 Main St.
716/759-6433

Kelly Schultz Antqs. & Orntl.
10225 Main St.
716/759-2260

Up Your Attic Vintage Clothing
10255 Main St.
716/759-2866

Baumer Antiques
10548 Main St.
716/759-6468

Muleskinner Antiques
10626 Main St.
716/759-2661

Antique Emporium
10225 Main St.
716/759-0718

Clarence Hollow Antiques
10863 Main St.
716/759-7878

Antique Parlor
10874 Main St.
716/759-2048

Antique World & Market Place
10995 Main St.
716/759-8483

Clarence Antiques Co-op
11079 Main St.
716/759-7080

Kelly's Antique Market
11111 Main St.
716/759-7488

20 COLD SPRING

Basso Brokerage Antiques
12 Division St.
914/265-9650

38 Main
38 Main St.
914/265-3838

As Time Goes By
72 Main St.
914/265-7988

Tin Man
75 Main St.
914/265-2903

Jacquie Antiques
89 Main St.
914/265-7883

Sarabeck Antiques
91 Main St.
914/265-4414

Once Upon a Time Antiques
101 Main St.
914/265-4339

Taca-Tiques
109 Main St.
914/265-2655

Others Oldies
169 Main St.
914/265-2323

Ground Zero Antiques Inc.
290 Main St.
914/265-5275

Dew Drop Inn Antique Center
Rt. 9
914/265-4358

Rick Lawler Antiques
168 Rt. 9
914/265-2231

21 COLD SPRING HARBOR

M. Nash & Company Inc.
7 Main St.
516/692-7777

Huntington Antique Center
129 Main St.
516/692-7777

Candle Wycke Antiques Ltd.
147 Main St.
516/692-3106

Lyman Thorne Enterprises Ltd.
169 Main St.
516/692-2834

Arlene Coroaan Antiques
7 Main St.
516/692-7777

22 COOPERSTOWN

The charming village of Cooperstown sits at the foot of Lake Ostego in the heart of the area made famous by author James Fenimore Cooper (1789-1851). The streets are lined with Victorian homes and storefronts decorated with hanging baskets and window boxes. The Fenimore House Museum includes the works of famed 19th and 20th century artists along with displays of Cooper memorabilia. Nearby, the Farmer's Museum, a living history center, recreates a 19th century village. This is the setting for one of the nation's premier sports shrines—the National Baseball Hall of Fame.

This red brick facility traces its beginnings back to a discovery in a dust-covered attic near Cooperstown. Here was found an undersized, misshapen, homemade ball stuffed with cloth, believed to be the baseball used by Abner Doubleday in the first game. The baseball was purchased by Cooperstown resident Stephen C. Clark, who conceived the idea of displaying it along with other baseball objects. The one-room exhibition attracted such public interest that plans for a national museum were drawn up, and the official National Baseball Hall of Fame was officially opened in 1939 to commemorate the game's 100th anniversary.

Cooperstown Antique Center
73 Chestnut Street
607/547-2435

General line of furniture and specializing in restored electrical lighting.

23 CROTON-ON-HUDSON

Alexander Hamilton House
49 Van Wyck St.
914/271-6737
Fax: 914/271-3927

Directions: From Rt. 9, exit at Rt. 129. Go east to light at Riverside Avenue. Turn left onto Riverside for 1 block. Turn right on Grand Street. Go 1 block. Turn left onto Hamilton which interesects Van Wyck right in front of #49. Go down the drive into the parking lot. Climb the porch steps and ring the bell.

Westchester's first bed and breakfast, the Alexander Hamilton House, Circa 1889, is a stately Victorian home nestled on a cliff above the river, a short walk to the picturesque village of Croton-on-Hudson River Valley.

*Note: The Bridal Chamber at the Alexander Hamilton House was rated 4 Kisses in New York's Best Places to Kiss '92 & '94. Do you think five skylights, a king-sized bed, a Jacuzzi and a fireplace had anything to do with setting the mood?

24 EAST AURORA

Fire House Antiques
82 Elm St.
716/655-1035

Roycroft Campus Antiques
37 S. Grove St.
716/655-1565

Barn Shoppe
368 Mills Road
716/652-1099

25 EAST GREENBUSH

Favorite Places To Eat

Cracker Barrel Old Country Store
I-90 & Rt. 4, Exit 9
518/479-3646

26 EAST HAMPTON

Architrove, Inc.
74 Montauk Hwy., #3
516/329-229
Fax: 516/309-1155
Hours: 9-5, daily except Tue. & Wed. (Call for appointment on those days)

Directions: Go 2 miles east of Wainslott on Rt. 27 (Montauk Hwy.) to the Red Horse shopping Plaza.

This tasteful, upscale establishment offers the discriminating buyer the best in antique lighting fixtures, chandeliers, and sconces.

Christina Borg Inc.
41 Main St.
516/324-6997

Circle Antiques
46 Main St.
516/324-0771

Home James
55 Main St.
516/324-2307

Victory Gardens Ltd.
63 Main St.
516/324-7800

The Grand Alquistor
110 N. Main St.
516/324-7272

Antique Center of E. Hampton
251 Montauk Hwy.
516/324-9510

Lars Bolander Antqs. & Access.
5 Toilsome Lane
516/329-3400

Pantigo House
251 Pantigo Rd.
516/329-2831

Country Green Antiques
30 Race Lane
516/324-2756

Maidstone Antiques
512 Three Mile
516/329-7508

Elaine's Room
251 Partigo Road
516/324-4734

Basil
34 Park Place
516/324-4734

27 ELMIRA

AAAAAA Antiques By Proper
33 Brookline Ave.
607/734-0153

Maple Avenue Antiques
352 Maple Ave.
607/734-0332

Mark Twain Country Antiques
400 Maple Ave.
607/734-0916

Touch of Country House Shops
1019 Pennsylvania Ave.
607/737-6945

Michael Watts Antiques
558 Riverside Ave.
607/733-9126

Sturdivant Gallery
912 Southport St.
607/733-1903

28 FAIRHAVEN

Black Creek Farm Bed and Breakfast and Antique Shop

Mixer Road
315/947-5282
Hours: Bed and Breakfast open all year
Antique shop open weekends, 11-5, May 1-Sep. 15

Directions: From New York State Rt. 104, turn north on Rt. 104 A. Go approximately 6 miles to Mixer Road, and turn left. The farm is 3/4 mile down Mixer Road. From Oswego, N.Y., go west on Rt. 104 to Rt. 104 A. Continue west through the village of Fair Haven to Mixer Road (about 2 miles). Turn right and go 3/4 mile to Black Creek Farm.

This quiet, 20-acre farm is just 2 miles from Lake Ontario. Enjoy the tranquil surroundings of the fully restored 1888 Victorian farmhouse with three antique-filled, second floor rooms.

You may "help yourself to the big outdoors by strolling the lawns and gardens, playing croquet, or exploring the country lanes on a bicycle-built-for-two." You may, however, prefer to simply take a nap in the hammock under the weeping birch trees.

The adjacent antique shop specializes in Victorian furniture, accessories, and collectibles. The owners refer to Black Creek Farm as "a 20-acre slice of serenity."

Brown's Village Inn Bed and Breakfast and Antique Shop

Stafford Street
315/947-5817
Hours: 10-5, Tue.-Sun.

Directions: From Syracuse: Take Exit 34 A, Rt. 481 North off the Thruway (Rt. 90). At Fulton, go west on Rt. 3 for about 14 miles to Rt. 104 A. Take a left and follow into Fair Haven. The in is on the 2nd street on the left after passing the State Park.

Brown's Village Inn offers the perfect getaway near Fair Haven Beach. Fish the streams and lake for salmon, steel head or trout; enjoy boating, swimming and cross-country skiing in winter. The Inn's four guest rooms and two full baths offer all the comforts of home but without the responsibilities. For more private accommodations, a guest cottage is available.

Relax on the deck, walk to nearby shops and restaurants, stroll under the shade trees or enjoy the flowers in the yard.

29 FLUSHING

Auctions Room Ltd.
11641 Queens Blvd.
718/263-2274

Black Watch Rare Coins
10412 Metropolitan Ave.
718/575-9779

Comet Stamp & Coin Co., Inc.
19207 Union Turnpike
718/479-0459

Old & New Shop Inc.
7130 Myrtle Ave.
718/381-8814

Raymond's Antiques
8603 Northern Blvd.
718/335-0553

Antique Shop
15058 Northern Blvd.
718/886-8438

Ezra's Antiques
4101 162nd St.
718/353-2603

Mp Trading Co.
4117 162nd St.
718/539-7019

Feelings Antique Boutique
4217 162nd St.
718/321-1939

Queen's Collectibles
4355 162nd St.
718/445-1316

Peter Setzer Antiques
4362 162nd St.
718/461-6999

Rae's Antiques & Clocks
4366 162nd St.
718/353-5577

Antique Gallery
3563 78 th St.
718/478-1824

Golden Oldies Ltd.
13229 33rd Ave.
718/445-4400

30 FRANKLIN SQUARE

di Salvo Galleries Ltd.

1015 Hempstead Turnpike
516/326-1090
Open Tue.-Fri. 10-5, Sat. & Sun. 11-4

Directions: From Long Island Expressway: Take Exit 34 (New York Park Road); go south approximately 3 to 4 miles. Make a right on Hempstead Turnpike. Proceed 1 1/2 blocks. di Salvo Galleries Ltd. is on the left.

For specific information see review this section.

Estate Antiques
967 Hempstead Turnpike
516-488-8100

31 GLENS FALLS

Glenwood Manor Antiques Center
Glenwood & Quaker Road
518/798-4747

32 GREAT NECK

Charles Jewelers Inc.
62 Allenwood Rd.
516/482-6688

Barbara Hart Yesteryears
4 Bond St.
516/466-8748

Sabi Antiques
112 Middle Neck Rd.
516/829-1330

33 GREENPORT

Furniture Store
214 Front St.
516/477-2980

Friendly Spirits Antiques
311 Front St.
516/477-8680

Cracker Barrel Antiques
74365 Main Rd.
516/477-0843

Greenport Antique Center
74365 Main Rd.
516/477-0843

Primrose Lane
74365 Main Rd.
516/477-8876

Beall & Bell
18 South St.
516/477-8239

34 HEART ISLAND

The legacy of Thousand Island's most tragic love affair can be found in Boldt Castle, a lavish, gilded-age mansion on Heart Island that dates back to the turn of the century. The castle motif is a monument to one man's love—hearts are carved in stone throughout the building and the island itself reshaped as a heart.

George Boldt, the owner of New York City's elegant Waldorf Astoria Hotel, decided to build a castle to symbolize his devotion to his young bride Louise.

As a poor boy in Germany, George Boldt had gazed longingly at castles along the banks of the Rhine, so he commissioned workers to build a similar structure. The 120-room castle took form as the workers ferried blocks of stone and marble and exotic woods onto the island. Towns along the shoreline buzzed with excitement.

But before it was complete, the young Mrs. Boldt died suddenly. The wealthy millionaire ordered all work to come to a halt and never returned to the island. The castle that was to have been a place of great joy fell into disrepair.

In 1977, the Thousand Islands Bridge Authority acquired the property, and gradually began a restoration process that continues to this day. From the outside, the castle is an impressive structure. From the inside, parts are yet unfinished, in a sad way evocative of the affair. Visitors can walk the island, admire the carved-stone cherubs, stroll down marble hallways, examine hand-crafted tile work and pause for a moment to consider lost dreams.

Today, Heart Island, near Alexandria Bay, is accessible by private craft and tour boats. For information call 315/482-9724.

35 HENRIETTA

Wanderer's Antiques
3204 E. Henrietta Road
716/334-0224

36 HUDSON

Directions: Hudson is easily accessible from I-87 (15 minutes), I-90 (25 minutes), and the Taconic Parkway.

Take a look inside some of Hudson's unique antique shops by visiting their Web Site at http://www.regionnet.com/colberk/hudsonantique.html

With not a skyscraper or tall building in sight, Hudson is a conglomeration of architectural styles—Federal, Queen Anne, Greek Revival, Victorian and modern. It is a small city with a population of about 6,000 people. Within its downtown district over 40 antiques and collectibles shops are housed within the rich and diverse architecture of the river city. The city's grid design makes it readily accessible and its close proximity to New York draws the weekend shoppers and tourists to explore the many offerings of Hudson. Most can be found on Warren Street along with many restaurants, diners, coffee shops and the newly-renovated St. Charles Hotel.

Americana Collectibles
527 Warren St.
518/822-9026

Mark's Antiques
612 Warren St.
518/766-3937

Antiques at 601
601 Warren St.
518/822-0201

David & Bonnie Montgomery
526 Warren St.
518/822-0267

Antiquities/Antiques Etc.
415 Warren St.
518/822-1207

Vincent R. Mulford
711 Warren St.
518/828-5489

Arenskjold Antiques Art
537 Warren St.
518/828-2800

Tom Noonan Antiques
551 Warren St.
518/828-5779

The Armory Art & Antq. Gllry.
State St. at N. 5th St.
518/822-1477

Northstar Antiques
502 Warren St.
53E/822-1563

Atlantis Rising
545 Warren St.
518/822-0438

Past Perfect
4 Park Place
518/822-1083

The British Accent
537 Warren St.
518/828-2800

Pavillion Style Est. 1980
521 Warren St.
518/828-4750

The Carriage House
454 Union St.
518/828-0365

Quartermoon
528 Warren St.
518/828-0728

The Clock Man
541 Warren St.
518/828-8995

Relics
551 Warren St.
518/828-4247

Days Gone By
530 Warren St.
518/828-6109

Riverhill
610 Warren St.
518/828-2823

Doyle Antiques
711 Warren St.
518/828-3929

Jeremiah Rusconi
By Appointment Only
518/828-7531

Ecclectables
2 Park Place
518/822-1286

Savannah Antiques
521 Warren St.
518/822-1343

Fern
554 Warren St.
518/828-2886

707 Antiques
707 Warren St.
518/794-7883

Foxfire, LTD.
538 Warren St.
518/828-6281

A. Slutter Antiques/20th Cntry.
556 Warren St.
518/822-0729

Judith Harris Antiques
608 Warren St.
518/822-1371

Theron Ware
548 Warren St.
518/828-9744

The Hudson Antiques Center
536 Warren St.
518/828-9920

Townhouse Antiques
511 Warren St.
518/822-8500

Hudson Photographic Center
611 Warren St.
518/828-2178

Uncle Sam Antiques
535 Warren St.
518/828-2341

Peter Jung Art & Antiques
537 Warren St.
518/828-2698

Watnot Shop & Auction Service
525 Warren St.
518/828-1081

Kermani Oriental Rugs
348 1/2 Warren St.
518/828-4804

Benjamin Wilson Antiques
513 Warren St.
518/822-0866

Larry's Back Room Antiques
612 Warren St.
518/477-2643

K. West Antiques
715 Warren St.
518/822-1960

37 HUNTINGTON

Cracker Barrel Galleries Inc.
17 Green St.
516/421-1400

John Gennosa Antiques
51 Green St.
516/271-0355

Browsery Corner Shop
449 E. Jericho Tpke
516/351-9298

Antique & Design Center
830 W. Jericho Tpke
516/673-4079

Nannyberry's Antiques
32 Macarthur Ave.
516/421-5491

Antiques and Jewels on Main
293 Main St.
516/427-7674

Ashbourne Antique Pine
258 Main Street
516/547-5252

Estate Jewels of Huntington
331 New York Ave.
516/421-4774

38 HUNTINGTON STATION

Browsery Antiques
449 E. Jericho Tpk Rd.
516/351-8893

Yankee Peddler Antiques
1038 New York Ave.
516/271-5817

39 ITHACA

Pastimes Antiques
Dewitt
607/277-3457

Asia House Gallery
118 S. Meadow St.
607/272-8850

City Lights Antiques Inc.
1319 Mecklenburg Rd.
607/272-7010

Bogie's Bargains
608 W. Seneca St.
607/272-6016

State Street Bargain House
516 W. State St.
607/273-2303

Celia Bowers Antiques
1406 Trumansburg Rd.
607/273-1994

40 JOHNSTOWN

Homespun Memories
118 W. Main St.
518/762-2878

Pillar
222 N. Perry St.
518/762-4149

Sunshine Antiques
222 N. Perry St.
518/762-8076

Sir William Antiques
Rd. Rt. 30a A
518/762-4816

41 KEENE

The Bark Eater Inn and Stable

Alstead Hill Road
1-800-232-1607
Website: http://www.tvenet.com//barkeater
E-mail: barkeater@tvenet.com
Open all the time

Directions: From the south, take Exit 30 off I-87. Travel 17 miles west to Keene on Rt. 73. One mile west of Keene, heading toward Lake Placid, bear right onto Alstead Hill Road. The Inn is 1/2 mile on the right. From the north, take Exit 34 off I-87. Proceed 25 miles south to Keene on Rt. 9 North. Turn right on Rt. 73, heading west. Bear right at the 1 mile point onto Alstead Hill Road.

A gracious 150-year old farmhouse in the Adirondack Mountains is the setting for this unique cross country ski center and riding stable. Originally a stagecoach stopover, the rambling old inn with its 2 fireplaces, candlelight gourmet dinners, and graciously appointed accommodations offers a charming contrast to the vigorous outdoor activities that await you. Winter guests may choose cross-country or downhill skiing, bobsledding or ice climbing. If you're a beginner, Joe Pete Wilson (your host at Bark Eater) will assist you in your new adventure. You'll be in good hands, Joe Pete is a former Olympic and world competitor in nordic skiing, biathalon and bobsledding.

In summer, the inn is well known for its horseback riding program, which includes polo. Well trained horses, both English and western, are available for the rank beginner to the expert. Enthusiasts can ride for hours on miles of logging trails and back roads. For you "city slickers," riding lessons are available.

They also offer less demanding sports like shopping, dining and porch rocking (soon to be an Olympic sport!)

After a full day, you may choose one of eleven sleeping facilities, including one hand-hewn log cottage, deep in the woods.

By the way, "bark eaters" was a derisive term applied by the Mohawks to their northern neighbors, the Algonquins. Loosely translated it means, "they who eat trees."

42 KINGSTON

Boulevard Attic
400 Blvd.
914/339-6316

Skillypot Antique Center
41 Broadway
914/338-6779

John Street Jewelers
292 Fair St.
914/338-4101

Out Back Antiques
72 Hurley Ave.
914/331-4481

Catskill Mountain Antq. Center
Rt.. 28
914/331-0880

Lock Stock & Barrel
Rt.. 28
914/338-4397

Stanz Used Items & Antiques
743 Ulster Ave.
914/331-7579

Wall Street Antiques
333 Wall St.
914/338-3212

Vin-Dick Antiques
Rt. 209
914/338-7113

Keystone Arts Antiques
33 Broadway
914/331-6211

43 LANCASTER

Favorite Places To Eat

Cracker Barrel Old Country Store
I-90 & Rt. 78, Exit 49
716/635-9542

44 LARCHMONT

Dualities Galleries
2056 Boston Post Rd.
914/834-2773

Arti Antiques Inc.
2070 Boston Post Rd.
914/833-1794

Interior Shop
2081 Boston Post Rd.
914/834-6110

Briggs House Antiques
2100 Boston Post Rd.
914/833-3087

Post Road Gallery
2128 Boston Post Rd.
914/834-7568

Woolf's Den Antiques
2130 Boston Post Rd.
914/834-0066

Antiques Consign. Collectibles
2134 Boston Post Rd.
914/833-1829

Thomas K Salese Antiques
2368 Boston Post Rd.
914/834-0222

45 LOCUST VALLEY

Finer Things
24 Birch Hill Rd.
516/676-6979

Treasured Times
49 Birch Hill Rd.
516/759-2010

Early & Co Inc.
53 Birch Hill Rd.
516/676-4800

Oster Jensen Antiques Ltd.
86 Birch Hill Rd.
516/676-5454

Rena Fortgang Interior Design
27 Forest Ave.
516/759-7826

Country Cousin
302 Forest Ave.
516/676-6767

46 MADISON

Country Shop
Rt. 20
315/893-7616

Grasshopper Antiques
Rt. 20
315/893-7664

Madison Inn Antiques
Rt. 20
315/893-7639

Timothy's Treasures
Rt. 20
315/893-7008

47 MARATHON

Antiques & Accents
73 Cortland St.
607/849-3703

Riverbend Antique Center
79 Cortland St.
607/849-6305

Goldilocks
36 Main St.
607/849-6144

Village Antiques
7 Peck
607/849-6367

Crosses Antique Center
Rt. 11
607/849-6605

Yesteryear Shoppe
20 Main St.
607/849-6471

48 MIDDLETOWN

7-11 Antiques
7 W. Main St.
914/344-4289

Kaatskill Restoration & Antqs.
71 W. Main St.
914/343-6604

Attic
101 Monhagen Ave.
914/342-2252

49 MILLERTON

Old Mill of Irondale
Rt. 22 NN
518/789-9433

Country House Antqs. & Intrs.
Main St.
518/789-3630

Millerton Antique Center
Main St.
518/789-6004

Johnson & Johnson
Rt. 22
518/789-3848

Junk-Atique
Rt. 22
518/789-4718

Northeast Antiques
Rt. 22
518/789-4014

50 MILLPORT

Serendipity II
3867 Rt. 14
607/739-9413
Hours: 10-5, Mon. Through Fri., 11-4, Sat. And Sun. Open all year

Directions: Approximately 5 miles from Exit 52 North off Rt. 17. Located at the north end of Pine Valley, between Watkins Glen and Rt. 17.

Called "the little shop with the LARGE selection," this multi-dealer store offers a wide variety of glassware, especially depression and pressed glass. You'll also find an interesting assortment of furniture, lighting fixtures, books, and prints. They also offer a selection of sewing related items.

But, the most special service, and one for which they are well known, is their dedication to attention and care given to their customers.

Millport Mercantile
4268 S. Main St.
607/739-3180

51 MINERVA

Mountain Niche Antiques
Rt. 28 N
518/251-2566

52 MONTGOMERY

Clinton Shops
84 Clinton St.
914/457-5392

Olde Towne Antq. & Used Shop
110 Clinton St.
914/457-1030

Montgomery Antique Mall
40 Railroad Ave.
914/457-9339

Guns & Collectibles
1092 Rt. 17 K
914/457-9062

Marilyn Quigley-Lamplighter
70 Union
914/457-5228

Antiques at Wards Bridge
165 Wards St. Rt. (17 K)
914/457-9343

Country Corner Antiques
9 Bridge St.
914/457-5581

53 MOUNT VERNON

Westchester Furn. Exchange
78 W. 1st St.
914/668-0447

Veneque Collection
115 S. 4th Ave.
914/667-5207

Westchester Furn. & Antique
130 S. 4th Ave.
914/664-2727

Trend Antq. & Genesis Books
154 S. 4th Ave.
914/664-4478

Classic Furn. & Antqs. Inc.
5 Gramatan Ave.
914/667-1651

A Adams Unlimited
19-21 Mount Vernon Ave.
914/668-0374

54 NEW YORK CITY

The Family Jewels Vintage Clothing Store
832 Avenue of the Americas
212/679-5023
Hours: 11-7, seven days a week

Directions: Located on the southeast corner of 29th Street and 6th Avenue (a.k.a. Avenue of the Americas).

Catering to men, women, and children, this store has been named "One of the best vintage stores in the United States" by *Vogue, In Style,* and *YM* magazines.

Filled with *thousands* of unique, one-of-a-kind antique wearables, the second floor shop embraces every area from the lacy Victorian to the bell-bottomed '70s. They carry a head-to-toe, inside-out selection from sexy lingerie to overcoats, even vintage fabrics and linens.

International design houses including Dolce and Gabbana, Georgio Armani, Ralph Lauren, and Adrienne Vittadini have shopped there looking for "inspiration" for their own designs.

Costume designers, wardrobe supervisors, and photographers have dressed the likes of Cindy Crawford, Uma Thurman, David Bowie, and Rosie O'Donnell from this smashing specialty store.

Hugo, Ltd.
233 East 59th Street
212/750-6877
Fax: 212/750-7346
Hours: call for current schedule or appointment

Directions: Located in the center of Manhattan, half a block from Bloomingdale's on 3rd Avenue and 59th Street.

Hugo Ltd. offers its patrons the nation's leading collection of documented and authenticated 19th century lighting and decorative arts.

With all offerings restored in-house to museum condition, this prestigious business prides itself on being a purveyor and consultant to the United States Senate and Treasury Department in Washington, D.C., as well as to the Metropolitan Museum of Art in New York City.

Galleria Hugo
304 East 76th Street
212/288-8444
Fax: 212/570-9041

New York

Hours: By appointment or chance, call ahead
Open Monday through Friday, some Saturdays

Directions: Located in Manhattan's Upper East side, between 1st and 2nd Avenues.

This highly respected establishment, like its counterpart, Hugo Ltd.. offers the nation's leading collection of 19th century documented and authenticated lighting. All in-house restoration is done using original finishes from that period-*no plating or polishing*.

Galleria Hugo is a supplier to major collections and museums.

Cohen's Collectibles
110 West 25th, Shop 305
212/675-5300
Hours: 10-6, 7 days a week

Directions: Going north on 6th Avenue, turn left onto 25th. The building is a few hundred feet further, on the left.

Located in the Chelsea Antique Building, Cohen's is the only open shop for "ephemera" in New York City.

They buy and sell all types of airline and steamship nostalgia, sheet music, photographs, and autographs. This is also the place for Fudaica and items pertaining to Black Heritage.

Hege Steen Flowers
360 Amsterdam Ave.
212/496-2575

More & More Antiques
378 Amsterdam Ave.
212/580-8404

Portobello Antiques
190 Avenue of Americas
212/925-4067

A K F Trading Ltd. Inc.
472 Avenue of Americas
212/647-0410

Icon Jewelry And Antiques
472 Avenue of Americas
212/647-0410

David J Air
8 Beach St.
212/925-7867

Second Childhood
283 Bleecker St.
212/989-6140

Niall Smith Antiques
344 Bleecker St.
212/255-0660

Pierre Deux Antiques
369 Bleecker St.
212/243-7740

Distinctive Furnishings
370 Bleecker St.
212/255-2476

Clary & Co. Antiques Ltd.
372 Bleecker St.
212/229-1773

American Folkart Gallery
374 Bleecker St.
212/366-6566

Kitschen
380 Bleecker St.
212/727-0430

Old Japan Inc.
382 Bleecker St.
212/633-0922

Susan Parrish Antiques
390 Bleecker St.
212/645-5020

Treasures & Trifles
409 Bleecker St.
212/243-2723

Avery Home Inc.
2 Bond St.
212/614-1492

Rhubarb Home
26 Bond St.
212/533-1817

IL Buco
47 Bond St.
212/533-1932

What Comes Arnd. Goes Arnd.
351 W. Broadway
212/343-9303

B M Arts Inc.
367 W. Broadway
212/226-5808

Paracelso
414 W. Broadway
212/966-4232

Antique Addiction
436 W. Broadway
212/925-6342

Alice Underground Ltd.
481 Broadway
212/431-9067

Antique Boutique
712 Broadway
212/460-8830

William Roland Antiques
808 Broadway Aprt. 4J
212/260-2000

Agostino Antiques Ltd.
808 Broadway
212/533-3355

Blatt Bowling & Billiard Corp.
809 Broadway
212/674-8855

Jacob's Antiques
810 Broadway
212/673-4254

Turbulence
812 Broadway
212/598-9030

Abe's Antiques Inc.
815 Broadway
212/260-6424

Proctor Galleries
824 Broadway
212/388-1539

Howard Kaplan Antiques
827 Broadway
212/674-1000

Philip Colleck of London Ltd.
830 Broadway
212/505-2500

Universe Antiques
833 Broadway
212/260-9292

Hyde Park Antiques Corp.
836 Broadway
212/477-0033

David Seidenberg
836 Broadway
212/260-2810

Cheap Jack's Vintage Clothing
841 Broadway
212/995-0403

Olden Camera & Lens Co. Inc.
1265 Broadway
212/725-1234

Estelle Stranger
2508 Broadway
212/749-0393

Penine Hart
457 Broome St.
212/226-2761

Paterae Antqs. & Decorations
458 Broome St.
212/941-0880

Gray Garden
461 Broome St.
212/966-7116

Sammy's
484 Broome St.
212/343-2357

Henro Inc.
525 Broome St.
212/343-0221

Essex Gallery Ltd.
104 Central Park S
212/757-2500

Tibet West
19 Christopher St.
212/255-3416

Christopher Street Flea Market
122 Christopher St.
212/924-6118

Shady Acres Antiques
Clark St. Rd.
315/252-3740

La Belle Epoque Vintage
280 Columbus Ave.
212/362-1770

Classic Antique Iron Beds
518 Columbus Ave.
212/496-8980

Golden Treasury
550 Columbus Ave.
212/787-1411

Welcome Home Antiques Ltd.
562 Columbus Ave.
212/362-4293

Crosby Antiques Studio
117 Crosby St.
212/941-6863

Historical Materialism
125 Crosby St.
212/431-3424

A I D S Thrift Shop Inc.
220 E. 81st St.
212/472-3573

Bernard & S. Dean Levy Inc.
24 E. 84th St.
212/628-7088

Better Times Antiques Inc.
201 W. 84th St.
212/496-9001

84th St. Antiques Corp
235 E. 84th St.
212/650-1035

L J Wender Chinese Fine Art
3 E. 80th St.
212/734-3460

Steve's Antiques
206 W. 80th St.
212/721-2935

Alex's Now & Then Collectibles
256 89th Street
212/831-4825

Bijan Royal Inc.
60 E. 11th St.
212/228-3757

James Hepner Antiques
130 E. 82nd St.
212/737-4470

David George Antiques
165 E. 87th St.
212/860-3034

Heritage East Inc.
179 E. 87th St.
212/987-1901

Samuel Herrup Antiques
12 E. 86th St.
212/737-9051

Once Upon A Time Antiques
36 E. 11th St.
212/473-6424

Little Antique Shop
44 E. 11th St.
212/673-5173

Big Apple Antiques Inc.
52 E. 11th St.
212/260-5110

William Albino Antiques
55 E. 11th St.
212/677-8820

Kings Antiques Corp.
57 E. 11th St.
212/255-6455

Palace Galleries
57 E. 11th St., 3rd Floor
212/228-8800

Retro-Modern Studio
58 E. 11th St.
212/674-0530

Flores & Iva Antiques
67 E. 11th St.
212/979-5461

Metro Antiques
80 E. 11th St.
212/673-3510

Maria Whitaker Ignez
260 Elizabeth St.
212/941-6158

Zane Moss Antiques
10 E. End Ave.
212/628-7130

Hebrew Religious Articles
45 Essex St.
212/674-1770

Tucker Robbins Warehouse
366 W. 15 th St.
212/366-4427

Columbus Circle Market
58th & 8th
212/242-1217

Kermanshah Oriental Rugs
57 5th Ave.
212/627-7077

Charles G. Moore Americana
32 E. 57th St., 12th Floor
212/751-1900

Alpine Designs Inc.
230 5th Ave.
212/532-5067

Megerian Rug Gallery
262 5th Ave.
212/684-7847

Chan's Antiques & Furniture
273 5th Ave.
212/686-8668

Sadigh Gallery & Ancient Art
303 5th Ave.
212/725-7537

Aaron's Antiques
576 5th Ave.
800/447-5868

Aaron Faber Gallery
666 5th Ave.
212/586-8411

Mercia Bross Gallery, Inc.
160 E. 56th St. Gallery 8
212/355-4422

Frederick P Victoria & Son Inc.
154 E. 55th St.
212/755-2549

Sheba Antiques Inc.
233 E. 59th St.
212/421-4848

James II Galleries Ltd.
11 E. 57th St.
212/355-7040

Sheila Toma Gallery
24 W. 57th St. Ste. 803
212/757-1480

M D Flacks Ltd.
38 E. 57th St.
212/838-4575

Vojtech Blan Inc.
6th Floor, 41 E. 57th St.
212/249-4525

Dalva Brothers Inc.
44 E. 57th St.
212/758-2297

Alice Kwartler Antiques
123 E. 57th St.
212/752-3590

A. Moheban & Son Antiques
139 E. 57th St.
212/758-3900

Golden Age Antique
143 E. 57th St.
212/319-3336

Nesle Inc.
151 E. 57th St.
212/755-0515

Artifacts New York
220 E. 57th St.
212/355-5575

Iris Brown Antique Dolls
253 E. 57th St.
212/593-2882

Regal Collection
5 W. 56th St.
212/582-7695

I Freeman & Sons Inc.
60 E. 56th St.
212/759-6900

J M S. & Eva Ltd.
160 E. 56th St. Gallery 8
212/593-1113

Turner Antiques Ltd.
160 E. 56th St. G#2
212/935-1099

New Era Fine Arts & Antiques
164 E. 56th St.
212/751-3473

A Repeat Performance
156 1st Ave.
212/529-0832

R Anavian & Sons Gallery
942 1st Ave.
212/879-1234

Darrows Fun Antiques
1101 1st Ave.
212/838-0730

Tamy's Antiques
8 W. 47th St.
212/382-1112

F Namdar Jewelry & Antique
10 W. 47th St.
212/921-7990

Ira Moskovitz Estate & Antique
10 W. 47th St.
212/921-7759

Shans Premier Ancient Art
31 W. 47th St. Ste. 802
212/840-4805

Antiques Corner Inc.
608 5th Avenue
212/869-1411

Anthony Frank Antiques
124 E. 4th St.
212/477-1473

Le Fanion
299 W. 4th St.
212/463-8760

Wyeth Et Daphney
151 Franklin St.
212/925-5278

Stardust Antiques
38 Gramercy Park N
212/677-2590

Krishna Gallery Asian Arts Inc.
153 E. 57th St.
212/249-1677

Lillian Nassau Ltd.
220 E. 57th St.
212/759-6062

Fil Caravans Inc.
301 E. 57th St.
212/421-5972

Ralph M Chait Galleries Inc.
12 E. 56th St.
212/758-0937

Antique Interiors by Nushin
160 E. 56th St.
212/486-1673

John Salibello Antiques
160 E. 56th St.
212/580-9560

Windsor Antique Inc.
160 E. 56th St. G#67
212/319-1077

Newel Art Galleries Inc.
425 E. 53rd St.
212/758-1970

Charles P Rogers Brass & Iron
899 1st Ave.
212/935-6900

Raphaelian Rug Co. Inc.
1071 1st Ave.
212/759-5452

N S Allan Ltd.
Main Lobby at the Grand Hyatt
212/599-0620

Expressions by Edith
10 W. 47th St.
212/730-9584

Galerie Spektrum
10 W. 47th St.
212/840-1758

Coin Dealer Inc.
15 W. 47th St. Booth #12
212/768-7297

Euro Antiques & Gems
36 W. 47th St.
212/997-5031

Quilted Corner
120 4th Ave.
212/505-6568

Sundown & Antiques
143 W. 4th St.
212/539-1958

Urban Archeology Co.
143 Franklin St.
212/431-6969

Mobiller
180 Franklin St.
212/334-6197

Niall Smith Antiques
96 Grand St.
212/941-7354

Boca Grande Furnishings
66 Greene St.
212/334-6120

Back Pages Antiques
125 Greene St.
212/460-5998

Bars & Backbars of N.Y.
49 E. Houston St.
212/431-0600

Cobweb
116 W. Houston St.
212/505-1558

Alphaville
226 W. Houston St.
212/675-6850

Jonathan Burden Inc.
632 Hudson St.
212/620-3989

Chameleon Antiques
231 Lafayette St.
212/343-9197

Second Hand Rose
130 Duane St.
212/393-9002

Lost City Arts
275 Lafayette St.
212/941-8025

Rooms & Gardens Inc.
290 Lafayette St.
212/431-1297

Old Print Shop Inc.
150 Lexington Ave.
212/683-3950

Maximiliaan's Grand Pianos
200 Lexinton Ave. Main Floor
212/689-2177

Antique Salon
870 Lexington Ave.
212/472-0191

S. Wyler Inc.
941 Lexington Ave.
212/879-9848

Deco Deluxe Inc.
993 Lexington Ave.
212/472-7222

La Cadet De Gascogne
1015 Lexington Ave.
212/744-5925

Malvina Solomon
1021 Lexington Ave.
212/535-5200

Mood Indigo
181 Prince St.
212/254-1176

J. Dixon Prentice Antiques
1036 Lexington Ave.
212/249-0458

Tout Le Monde
1178 Lexington Ave.
212/439-8487

Alice's Antiques
72 Greene St.
212/874-3400

Charterhouse Antiques
115 Greenwich Ave.
212/243-4726

B-4 It Was Cool Antiques
89 E. Houston St.
212/219-0139

American Antique Firearms
205 W. Houston St.
212/206-1004

Uplift Inc.
506 Hudson St.
212/929-3632

Kelter-Maice
74 Jane St.
212/675-7380

A & J 20th Century Designs
255 Lafayette St.
212/226-6290

Brian Winsor Art, Antiques
272 Lafayette St.
212/274-0411

Coming to America New York
276 Lafayette St.
212/343-2968

J. Marvec & Co.
946 Madison Avenue
212/517-7665

Kim McGuire Antiques
155 Lexington Ave.
212/686-0788

The N. Y Doll Hospital Inc.
787 Lexington Ave.
212/838-7527

Lorraine Wohl Collection
870 Lexington Ave.
212/472-0191

Ellen Berenson Antiques
988 Lexington Ave.
212/288-5302

Nancy Brous Associates Ltd.
1008 Lexington Ave.
212/772-7515

Amy Perlin Antiques
1020 Lexington Ave.
212/664-4923

Bob Pryor Antiques
1023 Lexington Ave.
212/861-1601

Marckle Myers Ltd.
1030 Lexington Ave.
212/288-3288

Sylvia Pines Uniquities
1102 Lexington Ave.
212/744-5141

Garden Room
1179 Lexington Ave.
212/879-1179

F H Coin & Stamp Exchange
1187 Lexington Ave.
888 FHCoins

Lands Beyond Ltd.
1218 Lexington Ave.
212/249-6275

Jerry Livian Antique Rugs
148 Madison Ave.
212/683-2666

Bolour
595 Madison Ave.
212/752-0222

Ronin Gallery
605 Madison Ave.
212/688-0188

Macklowe Gallery
667 Madison Ave.
212/644-6400

Mayfair & Company
741 Madison Ave.
212/737-4776

Imperial Fine Oriental Arts
790 Madison Ave.
212/717-5383

Rosenblatt Minna Ltd.
844 Madison Ave.
212/288-0250

Devenish & Company Inc.
929-Madison Ave.
212/535-2888

Stair & Company
942 Madison Ave.
212/517-4400

Florian Papp Inc.
962 Madison Ave.
212/288-6770

Koreana Art & Antiques Inc.
963 Madison Ave.
212/249-0400

Leigh Keno American Antiques
980 Madison Ave.
212/734-2381

Kenneth W. Rendell Gallery
989 Madison Ave.
212/717-1776

Rafael Gallery
1020 Madison Ave.
212/744-8666

Burlington Antique Toys
1082 Madison Ave.
212/861-9708

Guild Antiques II
1089 Madison Ave.
212/717-1810

Eagles Antiques Inc.
1097 Madison Ave.
212/772-3266

Betty Jane Bart Antiques
1225 Madison Ave.
212/410-2702

Japan Gallery
1210 Lexington Ave.
212/288-2241

Las Venus
163 Ludlow St.
212/982-0608

Persian Shop Inc.
534 Madison Ave.
212/355-4643

Anita De Carlo Inc.
605 Madison Ave.
212/288-4948

F Gorevic & Sons Inc.
635 Madison Ave., 2nd Floor
212/753-9319

Lloyd Jensen Jewelers Ltd.
716 Madison Ave.
212/980-3966

America Hurrah Antiques
766 Madison Ave.
212/535-1930

Orientations Gallery
802 Madison Ave.
212/772-7705

Bardith Ltd.
901 Madison Ave.
212/737-3775

Alexander Gallery
942 Madison Ave.
212/472-1636

Antiquarium Fine Ancient Arts
948 Madison Ave.
212/734-9776

Time Will Tell
962 Madison Ave.
212/861-2663

LEO Kaplan Ltd.
967 Madison Ave.
212/249-6766

Ursus Books Ltd.
981 Madison Ave.
212/772-8787

Edith Weber Antiques
994 Madison Ave.
212/570-9668

E. Frankel Ltd.
1040 Madison Ave.
212/879-5733

Gem Antiques
1088 Madison Ave.
212/535-7399

Guild Antiques II
1095 Madison Ave.
212/472-0830

Marco Polo Antiques
1135 Madison Ave.
212/734-3775

Carnegie Hill Antiques
1309 Madison Ave. 2nd Floor
212/987-6819

New York

Wicker Garden Antique Store
1318 Madison Ave.
212/410-7000

Frank Rogin Inc.
21 Mercer Sr
212/431-6545

Barry of Chelsea Antiques
154 9th Ave.
212/242-2666

Something Else Antqs. & Cllbls.
182 9th Ave.
212/924-0006

Jan Eleni Co.
315 E. 9th St.
212/533-4396

Archangel Antiques
334 E. 9th St.
212/260-9313

Atomic Passion
430 E. 9th St.
212/533-0718

Upstairs Downtown Antiques
12 W. 19th St.
212/989-8715

Accents Unlimited
65 W. 90th St.
212/799-7490

Treasures & Gems
250 E. 90th St.
212/410-7360

John Rosselli International
523 E. 73rd Street
212/722-2137

Dixon Galleries Inc.
251 Park Ave. S.
212/475-6500

Nelson & Nelson Antiques Inc.
445 Park Ave.
212/980-5825

Chinese Porcelain Co.
475 Park Ave.
212/838-7744

James Robinson Inc.
480 Park Ave.
212/752-6166

U S E D
17 Perry St.
212/627-0730

Thomas
41 Perry St.
212/675-7296

Rural Collections Inc.
117 Perry St.
212/645-4488

Irreplaceable Artifacts
14 2nd Ave.
212/473-3300

Love Saves The Day
119 2nd Ave.
212/228-3802

Sapho Gallery Inc.
1037 2nd Ave.
212/308-0880

A A A Silver Buyer
1050 2nd Ave.
212/755-6320

Alexander's Antiques
1050 2nd Ave. Glry. 43, 44, 45, 85
212/935-9386

A R Broomer Ltd.
1050 2nd Ave. Gallery 81
212/421-9530

Paul Stamati Gallery
1050 2nd Avenue Gallery #38
212/754-4533

Estate Silver Co. Ltd.
1050 2nd Ave. Gallery 65
212/758-4858

Federico Carrera Antiques
1050 2nd Ave. Gallery 18
212/750-2870

Flying Cranes Antiques
1050 2nd Ave. Gallery 55 & 56
212/223-4600

Hadassa Antiques Inc.
1050 2nd Ave. Gallery 75
212/751-0009

Hoffman-Giampetro Antiques
1050 2nd Ave. Gallery 37
212/755-1120

John Walker Antiques
1050 2nd Ave.
212/832-9579

Kurt Gluckselig Antiques
1050 2nd Ave. Gallery #90
212/758-1805

Leah's Gallery Inc.
1050 2nd Ave. #-42
212/838-5590

LES Gallery Looms Inc.
1050 2nd Ave. Gallery #59
212/752-0995

Manhattan Art & Antqs. Center
1050 2nd Ave.
212/355-4400

Michaels Antiques & Jewelry
1050 2nd Ave. Gallery #3
212/838-8780

Natalie Bader
1050 2nd Ave. Gallery 40 A
212/486-7673

Nelson & Nelson Antiques Inc.
445 Park Avenue
212/980-5824

Rita Facks/Limited Additions
1050 2nd Avenue G#94
212/421-8132

Ostia Inc.
1050 2nd Ave.
212/371-2424

J and P Timepieces Inc.
1057 2nd Ave.
212/980-1099

Rover & Lorber NYC Inc.
1050 2nd Ave. G#27
212/838-1302

R & P Kassai
1050 2nd Ave. Gallery #1
212/838-7010

S. Elghanayan Antiques
1050 2nd Ave. Gallery #6
212/750-3344

Sidney Bell Fine Arts
1050 2nd Ave. G#16
212/486-0715

Tibor Strasser
1050 2nd Ave. G#76
212/759-2513

Suchow & Siegel Antiques Ltd.
1050 2nd Ave. Gly #-81
212/888-3489

Time Gallery
1050 2nd Ave. G#54
212/593-2323

Treasures & Pleasures
1050 2nd Ave.
212/750-1929

Unique Finds Inc.
1050 2nd Ave. G#36
212/751-1983

Robert Altman
1148 2nd Ave.
212/832-3490

A & R Asta Ltd.
1152 2nd Ave.
212/750-3364

Fairfield Antique Gallery
1166 2nd Ave.
212/759-6519

Antique Accents
1175 2nd Ave.
212/755-6540

David Weinbaum
1175 2nd Ave.
212/755-6540

Elizabeth Street
1190 2nd Ave.
212/644-6969

Oaksmiths & Jones
1510 2nd Ave.
212/327-3462

Annex Antique Fair
6th & 26th St.
212/243-5343

James Lowe Autographs Ltd.
30 E. 60th St. Ste 304
212/759-0775

Things Japanese
127 E. 60th St.
212/371-4661

Paris to Province
207 E. 60th St.
212/750-0037

Objets Trouves Ltd.
217 E. 60th St.
212/753-0221

GUY Regal Ltd.
210 E. 60th St.
212/888-2134

Victor's Antiques Ltd.
223 E. 60th St.
212/752-4100

David Duncan Antiques
227 E. 60th St.
212/688-0666

Brahms-Netski Antq. Passage
234 E. 60th St.
212/755-8307

A Smith Antiques Ltd.
235 E. 60th St.
212/888-6337

James Grafstein Ltd.
236 E. 60th St.
212/754-1290

Luxor Gallery
238 E. 60th St.
212/832-3633

Ann-Morris Antiques
239 E. 60th St.
212/755-3308

William Lipton Ltd.
27 E. 61st St.
212/751-8131

Naga Antiques Ltd.
145 E. 61st St.
212/593-2788

Dining Trade
306 E. 61st St.
212/755-2304

Epel & Lacoze Antiques Inc.
306 E. 61 St., 2nd Floor
212/355-0050

Town and Country Antiques
306 E. 61st St.
212/752-1677

Tender Buttons
143 E. 62nd St.
212/758-7004

Chrystian Aubusson
315 E. 62nd St.
212/755-2432

Marvin Alexander Inc.
315 E. 62nd St.
212/838-2320

Objects Plus Inc.
315 E. 62nd St. 3rd Floor
212/832-3386

Old Versailles Inc.
315 E. 62nd Sr
212/421-3663

Paris Antiques
315 E. 62nd St.
212/421-3340

Wood & Hogan Inc.
305 E. 63rd Street, 5th Floor
212/355-1335

Emporium Antique Shop Ltd.
20 W. 64th St.
212/724-9521

Harvey & Co. Antiques
250 E. 60th St.
212/888-7952

Schlesch & Gaza
158 E. 64th St.
212/838-3923

French & Co. Inc.
17 E. 65 th St.
212/535-3330

Rita Ford Music Boxes Inc.
19 E. 65th St.
212/535-6717

Bizarre Bazaar Antiques Ltd.
130 1/4 E. 65th St.
212/517-2100

Jean Hoffman Antiques
207 E. 66th St.
212/535-6930

Margot Johnson Inc.
18 E. 68th St.
212/794-2225

Maya Schaper Cheese & Antqs.
106 W. 69th St.
212/873-2100

Victory Gardens Ltd.
205 E. 68th St.
212/472-2472

Linda Morgan Inc.
152 E. 70th St.
212/628-4330

Leff Langham Art & Antiques
19 E. 71st St.
212/288-4030

Salander Oreilly Galleries Inc.
20 E. 79th St.
212/879-6606

George Glazer
28 E. 72nd St.
212/535-5706

Godel & Co. Inc.
39 A E. 72nd St.
212/288-7272

Oriental Decorations
253 E. 72nd St.
212/439-1573

Lantiquaire & Connoisseur
36 E. 73rd St.
212/517-9176

Hollis Taggart Galleries
48 E. 73rd St.
212/628-4000

Eric Guy Inc.
503 E. 73rd St.
212/772-2326

Elliott Galleries
155 E. 79th St.
212/861-2222

J Mavec & Co.
946 Madison Avenue
212/517-7665

Karen Warshaw Ltd.
167 E. 74th St.
212/439-7870

Judith & James Milne Inc.
506 E. 74th St.
212/472-0107

Woodard Greenstien
506 E. 74th St.
212/794-9404

Treillage Ltd.
418 E. 75th St.
212/535-2288

H M Luther Inc.
35 E. 76th St.
212/439-7919

Peter Roberts Antiques Inc.
134 Spring St.
212/226-4777

Classic Toys Inc.
218 Sullivan St.
212/674-4434

Julian Antiques Restoration
108 W. 25th St.
212/647-0305

Ultimate Erpn. Rugs & Orntl.
969 3rd Ave.
212/759-6000

Design 18 Realty Inc.
979 3rd Ave. 4th Floor
212/753-8666

Nicholas Antiques
979 3rd Ave.
212/688-3312

D & D Building/Palisander
979 3rd Ave. Ste. 818
212/755-0120

Place Des Artes Corp.
979 3rd Ave.
212/750-8092

Evergreen Antiques Inc.
1249 3rd Ave. (at 72nd)
212/744-5664

Gordon Foster Antiques
1322 3rd Ave.
212/744-4922

Ghiordian Knot Ltd.
1636 3rd Ave. Ste#-169
212/371-6390

Caldonia Antiques
1685 3rd Ave.
212/534-3307

China Importing Co. Ltd.
28 E. 10th St.
212/995-0800

Reymer-Jourdan Antiques
29 E. 10 th St.
212/674-4470

E. Époque
30 E. 10th St.
212/353-0972

Ritter-Antik Inc.
35 E. 10th St.
212/673-2213

Donzella 20th Century
90 E. 10th St.
212/598-9675

Regeneration Furniture Inc.
223 E. 10th St.
212/614-9577

Renee Antiques Inc.
8 E. 12th St.
212/929-6870

Waves
110 W. 25th Street, 10th Floor
212/989-9284

John Koch Antiques
514 W. 24th St.
212/243-8625

Tepper Galleries Inc.
110 E. 25th St.
212/677-5300

Cherubs Antiques & Cllbls.
110 W. 25th St. (11th Floor)
212/627-7097

John Gredler Antiques
110 W. 25th St. (Room 702)
212/337-3667

Lubin Galleries Inc.
110 W. 25 th St.
212/924-3777

Rocco, Vincent
110 W. 25th St.
212/620-5652

Vlasdimirs Antiques
110 W. 25th St. Ste. 207
212/337-3704

Smith Gallery
447 W. 24th St.
212/744-6171

Old Paper Archive
122 W. 25th St.
212/645-3983

Les Deux Inc.
104 W. 27th St.
212/604-9743

Sohell Oriental Rugs
29 W. 30th St.
212/239-1069

Kamall Oriental Rugs
151 W. 30th St.
212/564-7000

The Tudor Rose Antiques
28 E. 10th St.
212/677-5239

Bernard H. Goeckler Antiques
30 E. 10th St.
212/777-8209

Karl Kemp & Assoc. Ltd. Antqs.
34 E. 10th St.
212/254-1877

Martell Antiques
53 E. 10th St.
212/777-4360

Robert Gingold Antiques
95 E. 10th St.
212/475-4008

Cheapside Inc.
280 E. 10th St.
212/780-9626

Kentshire Galleries Ltd.
37 E. 12th St.
212/673-6644

Dullsville Inc.
143 E. 13th St.
212/505-2505

Forty Fifty Sixty
108 W. 25th St. 4th Floor
212/463-0980

Chelsea Antiques Building
110 W. 25th St.
212/929-0909

Cohen's Cllbls. & Ephemera
110 W. 25th St. (3rd Floor)
212/675-5300

Le Chateau
110 W. 25th St.
212/741-7570

S. Mariaschin & J. Spiller
110 W. 25th St.
212/989-3414

This N That
110 W. 25th St. Ste. 613
212/255-0727

Rene Kerne Antiques
110 W. 25th St.
212/727-3455

Garage Antique Show
112 W. 25th St.
212/337-3704

Lucille's Antique Emporium
127 W. 26th St.
212/691-1041

Metal Art Studio
150 W. 28th St.
212/229-1130

Ebison's Harounian Imports
38 E. 30th St.
212/686-4262

Joseph Solo Antiques
1561 York Ave.
212/439-1555

33rd Street Galleria
100 W. 33rd St. (16th Floor)
212/279-0462

T & K French Antiques
301 E. 38th St.
212/219-2472

Lyme Regis Ltd.
68 Thompson St.
212/334-2110

Deco Jewels Inc.
131 Thompson St.
212/253-1222

Stella Dallas
218 Thompson St.
212/674-0447

Lou Ficherea & Ron Perkins
50 University Pl.
212/533-1430

World Collectible Center
18 Versey St.
212/267-7100

Forty One
41 Wooster St.
212/343-0935

Sotheby's
1334 York Ave.
212/606-7000

Leo Design
413 Bleecker St.
212/929-8466

Second Hand Rose
130 Duane St.
212/393-9002

Garden Antiquary
724 5th Avenue, 3rd Floor
212/757-3008

Roger Gross Ltd.
225 E. 57th St.
212/759-2892

Primavera Gallery
808 Madison Ave.
212/288-1569

Pantry & Hearth
121 E. 35th St.
212/889-0026

Mary Efron Vintage
68 Thompson St.
212/219-3099

Legacy
109 Thompson St.
212/966-4827

Ellen Lane Antiques Inc.
150 Thompson St.
212/475-2988

Zero to Sixties
75 Thompson St.
212/925-0932

Pall Mall Inc.
99 University Pl.
212/677-5544

Fountain Pen Hospital
10 Warren St.
212/964-0580

Interieurs
114 Wooster St.
212/343-0800

Kendra Krienke
By Appointment Only
212/580-6516

Arts & Antique Center
160 E. 56th St. Gallery #7
212/229-0958

Regeneration Furniture, Inc.
38 Renwick Street
212/741-2102

Antiques Corner
608 5th Avenue
212/869-1411

Kendra Krienke Art
230 Central Park West
212/580-6516

Everett Collection Inc.
104 W. 27th Street, 3rd Floor
212/255-8610

55 NORTHPORT

Somewhere In Time Antiques
162 Main St.
516/757-4148

Top Notch Antiques
76 Bayview Ave.
516/754-9396

L E P Design & Consign. Shop
160 Laurel Ave.
516/754-1831

Harbor Lights Antq. Boutique
110 Main St.
516/757-4572

Wild Rose Antiques
189 Main St.
516/261-0888

Country Shop
171 Main St.
516/757-2362

Scarlett's
166 Main St.
516/754-0004

Antique Restoration By Julian
108 W. 25th Street, Ste. #208
212/647-0305

56 NYACK

Lisa's Antiques

37 South Broadway
914/358-7077
Fax: 914/358-1688
Hours: 12-6, Tue.-Sun.

Directions: From New York City and New Jersey, take Pallisades Parkway North to Exit 4 (9 West). Go north on 9 West about 6 miles to the yellow blinking light. Bear right and proceed to the south end of the Art, Craft, and Antiques area. From Upstate New York, take the NewYork Thruway South to Exit 11. Then go left on Rt. 59 (Main Street) to shopping area. From Westchester and Connecticut, cross the Tappan Zee Bridge to the first exit (10). Follow the sign for South Nyack to Clinton Avenue. Go right 1 block to Broadway, then left to the shopping area.

Part of the Hudson Valley Emporium Mall, this antique and collectibles shop specializes in oak furniture, glassware, old toys, and sterling silver. Other specialty items include postcards, metal lunch boxes, and a selection of African American prints.

Ramapo Collectors
4 N. Broadway
914/353-3019

Gene Reed Gallery
77 S. Broadway
914/358-3750

Antiques & Country Pine
41B N. Broadway
914/358-7740

Goldsmiths Treasure Mine
79 S. Broadway
914/358-2204

Arlene Lederman Antiques
142 Main St.
914/358-8616

Decorative Arts & Antiques
142 Main St.
914/353-1644

J & J Antiques
142 Main St.
914/353-3252

Jo-Antiques
142 Main St.
914/353-5154

Old Business Antiques
142 Main St.
914/358-7008

S & M Antiques
142 Main St.
914/353-4774

Bruce Anderson Intr. & Extr.
145 Main St.
914/353-3992

Elayne's Antiques & Cllbls.
6 S. Broadway
914/358-6465

Remembrances
37 S. Broadway
914/358-7226

Towne Crier Antiques
70 S. Broadway
914/358-5234

Acorn Antiques & Collectibles
142 Main St.
914/353-5897

C D Antiques
142 Main St.
914/358-1704

Hildegard's Antiques
142 Main St.
914/353-2650

Jeni Brandel's Antiques
142 Main St.
914/353-3379

Kuku Antiques
142 Main St.
914/353-1130

Room with a View
142 Main St.
914/353-4072

Vintage Gems & Antiques
142 Main St.
914/353-2264

Gloria Paul Antiques
152 Main St.
914/358-1859

Allards
167 Main St.
914/353-1884

Levesque Antiques
170-2 Main St.
914/353-4050

Ark Shop
190 Main St.
914/358-1039

Antique Center Upper Nyack
366 Rt.. 9 W.
914/358-3751

57 OLEAN

E-Lites Antiques Inc.
204 W. State St.
716/372-8661

Olean Antique Center
269 N. Union St.
716/372-8171

Jerry's Antique Co-op
1217 N. Union St.
716/373-3702

Second Time Around
126 Whitney Ave.
716/372-4308

58 OWEGO

Hand of Man
180 Front St.
607/687-2556

Sally's Place
196 Front St.
607/687-4111

Cracker Barrel Antiques & Gift
202 Front St.
607/687-0555

Heritage Antiques
36 John St.
607/687-3405

59 PEEKSKILL/CORTLAND MANOR

Toddville Antq. & Craft Center
2201 Crompond Rd.
914/736-1117

Rose Cottage
44 N. Division St.
914/737-1845

Garden Antiquary
2551 Maple Ave.
914/737-6054

60 PHOENICIA

Hernandez Edom Antiques
Rt. 28
914/688-2124

Phoenicia Antique Center
Rt. 28
914/688-2095

Bethken's Antiques
Woodland Valley Rd.
914/688-5620

Antique Store
Rt. 28
914/688-5654

61 PORT CHESTER

Simon-World Arts
168 Irving Ave.
914/934-0113

Greenberg's Antique Mall Port
27 S. Main St.
914/937-4800

Jack's Fabrics & Antiques
33 S. Main St.
914/939-3308

House of Weltz
26 Poningo St.
914/939-6513

Ninas Antiques Collectibles
191 Westchester Ave.
914/939-6806

62 PORT WASHINGTON

Port Antique Center
289 Main Street
516/767-3313
Open: Tue.-Sat. 11-5, Sun. 12-5

Directions: Long Island Expressway to exit 36 north Searingtown Rd./Port Washington. Travel 4 miles north to Main Street. Left onto Main Street and go about one and a half miles down the hill to shop on your right #289 Main. Travel time by car is 40 minutes from midtown Manhattan or 30 minutes by LIRR train.

This charming quality multi-dealer shop is located in the heart of the Port Washington Antiques District. Located one block from Port Washington Harbor this shop offers a large selection of 19th and 20th century antiques and collectables.

Twenty four dealers in the shop carry a wide variety of quality antiques including art pottery such as Roseville, Weller, Rookwood, Fulper and McCoy in addition to a wide variety of china and porcelain with a special accent on Chintz and Majolica. If glass is your passion, Port Antique Center offers a beautiful array including depression and elegant glass as well as art glass such as Tiffany and Loetz.

The store abounds in both fine and costume jewelry offering a wide selection of antique watches as well as an extraordinary collection of colorful Bakelite jewelry. Come browse and enjoy collections of silver, kitchenware, toys, vintage clothing and memorabilia. If you happen to visit during the spring, summer or fall, the shop hosts an Antique Street Fair on the last Sunday of each month from April to October. Port Antique Center is surrounded by other antique shops and restaurants all within walking distance of each other and beautiful Port Washington harbor where you can stroll and relax in this beautiful bayside setting.

Front Porch
309 Main St.
516/944-6868

Cat Lady Antiques
164 Main St.
516/883-4334

R E Steele Antiques
165 Main St.
516/767-2283

Nancy K. Banker Antiques
279 Main St.
516/883-4184

Pat Giles
287 Main St.
516/883-1104

Michael Mikiten
287 Main St.
516/944-8767

Red Door Antiques
305 Main St.
516/883-5125

Village Green
306 Main St.
516/767-3698

Baba Antiques & Collectibles
292 Main St.
516/883-6274

63 POUND RIDGE

Antiques & Tools Bus & Ktchn
Scotts Corners
914/764-0015

Petersons Antiques Ltd.
26 Westchester Ave.
914/764-5074

Antiques & Interiors Inc.
67 Westchester Ave.
914/764-4400

Strap Hinge
72 Westchester Avenue
914/764-1145

Nancy Cody Antiques
67 Westchester Ave.
914/764-4949

Objects Trouvee Inc.
69 Westchester Ave.
914/234-7600

64 RED HOOK

Broadway Antiques & Cllbls.
30 N. Broadway
914/876-1444

Cider Mill Antiques
5 Cherry St.
914/758-2599

Victorian Corner
19 W. Market St.
914/758-1011

Anntex Antiques Center
23 E. Market St.
914/758-2843

Rock City Relics Antique Center
Rt. 199 & 308
914/758-8603

65 RHINEBECK

Rhinebeck Antique Center
7 W. Market St.
914/876-8168

Hummingbird Jewelers
20 W. Market St.
914/876-4585

Gallery Shoppe
9 Mill St.
914/876-2064

Country Bazaar
14 U.S. Hwy. 9 S
914/876-4160

Old Mill House Antiques
144 U.S. Hwy. 9 N
914/876-3636

66 ROCHESTER

Treasure Hunters
1434 Buffalo Rd.
716/235-5441

Flower City Stamps and Coins
1575 Dewey Ave.
716/647-9320

Thomas Paddock Orntl. Rugs
342 East Ave.
716/325-3110

Upstate Gallery Antiques
16 Gardiner Park Dr.
716/262-2089

Antiques & Old Lace
274 Goodman St. N
716/461-1884

Village Gate Square
274 Goodman St. N
716/442-9061

Yankee Peddler Bookshop II
274 Goodman St. N
716/271-5080

Marilyn's Antiques
500 Lyell Ave.
716/647-2480

Worldwide Antqs. & Imports
631 Monroe Ave.
716/271-3217

Aries Antiques
739 Monroe Ave.
716/244-7912

James Jewelry
1315 E. Ridge Rd.
716/336-9960

Jewelry & Coin Exchange
2000 Ridge Rd. W.
716/227-6370

Antq. & Cllbl. Co-op Rochester
151 Saint Paul St.
716/232-6440

Warren Phillips Fine Art
215 Tremont St.
716/235-4060

Walt's Place
1570 Dewey Ave.
716/254-1880

Mission Oak Antiques
378 Meigs St.
716/442-2480

Eric Kase
398 Westminster Rd.
716/461-4382

Newell Distributors
39 Branford Rd.
716/442-8810

Michael Latragna
1275 Clover St.
716/442-0725

Intrntl Art Acquisitions Inc.
3300 Monroe Ave.
716/264-1440

Golden Oldies Antiques
24 Bursen Ct.
716/266-2440

Darcy's Adventures in the Past
149 Monroe Ave.
716/262-4776

Carousel Antiques
3409 Saint Paul Blvd.
716/266-3420

Adventures in Past John
149 Monroe Ave.
716/262-4776

Jack Greco's Creekside Antqs.
1611 Scottsville Rd.
716/328-9150

Hsehld Sls by Mary Kay Roden
20 Union Park
716/266-3524

Chichelli Weiss Books & Antqs.
374 Meigs St.
716/271-3980

Bettique's
1697 Monroe Ave.
716/442-2995

67 SAG HARBOR

Carriage House Antiques
34 Main St.
516/725-8004

Madison House Antiques
43 Madison St.
516/725-7242

Diana's Place
Main St.
516/725-4669

Ned Parkhouse Antiques
Main St.
516/725-9830

Sage Street Antiques
Sage Street
516/725-4036

Carriage House Antiques
34 Main St.
516/725-8004

68 SARATOGA SPRINGS

Broadway Antiques Gallery

484 Broadway
518/581-8348
Open: Daily 11-6 and extended summer hours.

Directions: Take Rt. 9 from either exit 13N or exit 15 to downtown. Broadway Antiques Gallery is 3 doors north of City Hall on the east side of Broadway in the center of downtown Historic Saratoga Springs.

A cooperative effort of ten dealers brings you a wide variety of home furnishings and accessories. Over 3,000 square feet of antiques and unique gift items may be found in this shop.

Chestnut Tree Inn

9 Whitney Place
518/587-8681
Hours: Open April through November 1

Directions: From I-87, take Exit 13 North. Take Rt. 9 North to the 5th traffic light (Lincoln Avenue) and turn right. Take the 1st left onto Whitney Place. The inn is the 2nd house on the left.

Sample a more peaceful time in Saratoga's history at this fine traditional Victorian guest house. Situated conveniently near many of the city's attractions, the inn offers 10 rooms, most with private baths.

Continental breakfast is served each morning on the porch, and during July and August, guests may congregate there in the afternoons for wine, cheese, and crackers.

Sit and relax under what is reputed to be the last living chestnut tree in Saratoga.

Ye Olde Wishin Shoppe
353 Broadway
518/583-7782

A Page In Time
462 Broadway
518/584-4876

Saratoga Antiques
727 Rt. 29 E
518/587-3153

9 Caroline Antiques & Cllbls.
9 Caroline St.
518/583-9112

Magnell's Antiques
53 Old Schuylerville Rd.
518/587-8888

Regent St. Antique Center
153 Regent St.
518/584-0107

Saratoga Antiques
727 Rt. 29 E
518/587-3153

69 SAUGERTIES

Saugerties Antiques Center
220 Main St.
914/246-8234

Fancy Flea
50 Market St.
914/246-9391

Saugerties Antiques Gallery
104 Partition St.
914/246-2323

Acanthus
112 Partition St.
914/247-0041

Peacock Antiques
2769 Rt. 32
914/246-7070

70 SCHOHARIE

Cane Shoppe Antiques
Barton Hill Rd.
518/295-8629

Patent Country Shop
Rt. 145e East Cobleskill
518/296-8000

Ginny's Hutch Antiques
Rt. 30 Mdbg Schoh Rd.
518/295-7470

Saltbox Antiques
Stony Brook Rd.
518/295-7408

Quest
Vroman Rd. Rt. 30
518/295-8805

71 SOUTHAMPTON

Southampton Antique Center
640 N. High
516/283-1006

Things I Love
51 Jobs Lane
516/287-2756

Elaine's Antiques
9 Main St.
516/287-3276

Croft Antiques
11 S. Main St.
516/283-6445

Bob Petrillos Brouserie
30 Main St.
516/283-6560

Old Town Crossing
46 Main St.
516/283-7740

Judi Boisson Antique Quilts
134 Mariners Dr.
516/283-5466

Old Town Crossing Warehouse
134 Mariners Dr.
516/287-4771

Hampton Antiques
116 N. Sea Rd.
516/283-3436

John W. Nilsson Inc.
675 North Sea Rd.
516/283-1434

72 SPRINGWATER

Canadice Farm Antiques

9034 Cratsley Hill Road
716/367-2771
Hours: 10-5, Sat. & Sun. and by chance or appointment Easter through Thanksgiving

Directions: From Rt. 390, exit at Avon/Lima. In Lima, turn right on 15 A through Hemlock, then left on Rt. 20 A. Go to County Road 37, then right and follow signs. From Rochester, go south on 65 (Clover Street). 65 becomes County road 37 at Routes 5 and 20 (West Bloomfield). Continue south to Rt. 20 A and follow signs. From Canandaigua, go west on 5 and 20 to West Bloomfield. Turn left and follow County Road 37 to 20 A in Honeoye.

Along with a full line of antiques, this store offers an appraisal service, expertise in interior design as well as landscape design. They'll even help you design the wedding of your dreams. *One Stop Shopping!*

73 STATEN ISLAND

Harborview Antiques
1385 Bay St.
718/448-4649

New Drop Village Antiques
517 & 519 Broadway
718/815-2526

Faban Gen Merch & Antique
147 Canal
718/727-2917

Hey Viv-Vintage Clothing
125 Port Richmond Ave.
718/981-3575

Rainbows End Gifts Antiques
469 Port Richmond Ave.
718/273-3124

Richmond Consignments
1434 Richmond Rd.
718/980-4333

74 SYRACUSE

Giddings Garden Bed and Breakfast

290 W. Seneca Turnpike
315/492-6389 or 1-800-377-3452
Always open

Directions: From Rt. 81, north or south, take Exit 16 A (North 481 Dewitt). Stay on Rt. 481 to Exit 1 (Brighton Avenue/Rockcut Road). Bare right onto Rockcut Road to the top of the hill. Turn left at the light onto Brighton. At the light, turn right onto East Seneca Turnpike for 1 miles. Bed and breakfast is on the right, at the corner of Milburn Drive.

This elegantly restored Federal Tavern, circa 1810, offers such tasteful amenities as in-room fireplaces, private baths, and poster beds.

Outside, the lush gardens and lily ponds offer more opportunity for peaceful pleasure.

In the morning, guests may start the day with a full gourmet breakfast followed by relaxation or antique hunting. For those who choose the latter, a local map and listings are available.

Cerenas Antqs. & Home Furn.
2111 Brewerton Rd.
315/454-5543

Antique Center of Syracuse
1460 Burnet Ave.
315/476-8270

Dacia of Ny Vintage Furn.
2416 Court St.
315/455-2651

Antique Underground
247 W. Fayette St.
315/472-5510

Lilac House
1415 W. Genesee St.
315/471-3866

Dewitt Antique Jewelry & Coin
4621 E. Genesee St.
315/445-1065

Dalton's Antiques
1931 James St.
315/463-1568

Antqs. & Jewelry on Jefferson
306 W. Jefferson St.
315/476-5926

European Gallery & Frame
201 S. Main St.
315/458-6593

Boom Babies Vintage Clothing
489 Westcott St.
315/472-1949

AAAA Antiques & Appraisals
101 Wells Ave. E
315/458-8193

Ace Enterprise
1200 Butternut St.
315/475-8006

Colella Galleries
123 E. Willow St.
315/474-6950

Jerry Bonk Enterprises
204 Rita Dr.
315/458-4649

New York

Karens Deco-Craft
2101 Brewerton Rd.
315/455-2214

Antique Exchange
1600 Blk. N. Salina
315/471-1841

Shades of Yesteryear Antiques
658 N. Salina St.
315/423-9810

Cash Corner
1101 N. Salina St.
315/475-4045

75 TARRYTOWN

Treasure Trove
19 N. Broadway
914/366-4243

Sam Said
80 S. Broadway
914/631-3368

Remember Me Antiques
9 Main St.
914/631-4080

Virginia's
13 Main St.
No Phone

Carol Master Antiques
15 Main St.
914/332-8441

Tarrytown Art & Antq. Center
19 Main St.
914/524-9626

North Castle Antiques
28 Main St.
914/631-1112

Traeger's Antiques
35 Main St.
914/631-8694

Spencer Marks
Main St.
914/332-1142

Hank's Alley
15 N. Washington St.
914/524-9895

Michael Christopher's
Main St.
914/366-4665

76 TONAWANDA

Bronstein Antiques
4049 Delaware Avenue
716/873-7000

77 TRUMANSBURG

The Archway Bed and Breakfast
7020 Searsburg Road
607/387-6175 or 1-800-387-6175
Open 7 days a week

Directions: From New York State Rt. 96 in Trumansburg, go 1/2 mile south on 227 toward Watkins Glen. The bed and breakfast is on the corner of 227 and Searsburg.

Owner Meredith Pollard relates that when they were formerly listed as simply "The Archway," they kept getting orders for cookies! They would reply, "We don't do cookies, but we make great muffins!"

This particular bed and breakfast borders a public golf course.

The Collection
9-11 Main Street
607/387-6579 or 607/273-3480
Open Tue.-Sat. 11-5, Sun. 1-5, or by appointment

Directions: The Collection is 10 miles north of Ithaca, N.Y., on Rt. 96 North, 15 miles south of New York's Thruway, Geneva Exit, Rt. 96 South.

Featuring country Americana, 18th and 19th century country and formal furniture, primitives, quilts, folk art, early lighting, decorated stoneware and samplers. Insurance and estate appraisals.

Ponzi's Antiques
9838 Congress St.
607/387-5248

78 UTICA

Antiques & Such
210 Bleecker St.
315/724-0889

Mister Jack's Antiques & Furn.
250 Genesee St.
315/735-3815

Antique Clothing Co.
252 Genesee St.
315/724-3262

AAA Vintage Furnishings
337 Genesee St.
315/738-1333

Comeskey Stamp & Coin
701 Noyes St.
315/724-9616

AA Jewelry Buyers & Swap Shp.
400 South St.
315/724-3525

79 VALLEY STREAM

Central Antiques
233 N. Central Ave.
516/825-1043

Shure Barnette Antiques Inc.
904 Rockaway Ave.
516/825-9297

80 WARWICK

Bearly Antiques
18 Beverly Dr.
914/986-1996

Antiques at the Clock Tower
65 Main St.
914/986-5199

Clock Tower Antique Center
65 Main St.
914/986-5199

Red Shutters
34 Maple Ave.
914/986-5954

1809 House
210 Rt. 94 S
914/986-1809

81 WATERTOWN

Favorite Places To Eat

Cracker Barrel Old Country Store
I-81 & State Rd. 12, Exit 46
315/782-2460

82 WESTFIELD

Lakewood Antiques
6940 Chestnut
716/326-6620

Militello's Antiques
31 Jefferson St.
716/326-2587

The Leonards Antiques
E. Main Rd.
716/326-2210

Eley Place Antiques
3 E. Main St.
716/326-2130

Antique Marketplace
25 E. Main St.
716/326-2861

Saraf's Emporium
58 E. Main St.
716/326-3590

Priscilla B Nixon Antiques
119 W. Main St.
716/326-3511

Mollard Antiques
120 E. Main St.
716/326-3521

Candelight Lodge Antiques
143 E. Main St.
716/326-2830

Notaros Antiques
161 W. Main St.
716/326-3348

Landmark Acres-Antiques
232 W. Main St.
716/326-4185

Arundel Antiques
9 Market St.
No Phone

Dorothea Bertram
53 S. Portage St.
716/326-2551

J Miller Antiques
81 S. Portage St.
716/326-6699

Vilardo Antiques
7303 Walker Rd.
716/326-2714

Monroe's Antiques & Cllbls.
69 E. Main Street
817326-3060

83 WHITE PLAINS

Vintage by Stacey Lee
305 Central Avenue, Ste. 4
914/328-0788

84 WHITNEY POINT

Days Gone By
2659 Main Street
607/692-2713
Hours: 10-5, Wed.-Mon. (Closed Tuesday)

Directions: Traveling I-81 North: Take Exit 8. Travel south on Rt. 26 to Rt. 11, and take a left. Take a right at the red light onto Main Street. Traveling I-81 South: Take Exit 8 to Rt. 11 and turn left. Turn right at 2nd light onto Main Street. The shop is in the old church between Aiello's and the Food King.

Nancy Jackson, owner of Days Gone By, is a girl "after my own heart." Her antique shop is located in an old church. I've always wanted to own such a shop myself. The shop offers 20 quality dealers situated on three floors presenting everything from glassware to furniture, and primitives to collectibles. The staff is happy to assist you in finding something here or directing you to other local antique communities nearby.

85 WOODSTOCK

While Woodstock is famous for two rock concerts, one in 1969 and one in 1996, neither took place here. The first was held in Bethel, 50 miles southwest; the second in Sougerties, 10 miles northeast.

Yet Woodstock is a delightful artists' community, with galleries, antique shops and a selection of places to stop for lunch. Reminiscent of the sixties, long skirts, long hair and tie-dye T-shirts are ubiquitous. At the center of town, you might find a reader of tarot cards, with a line of people patiently waiting a turn.

86 WURTSBORO

Wurtsboro Wholesale Antiques
203 Sullivan Street
914/888-4411

87 YONKERS

Ogrady, M
356 Riverdale Ave.
914/964-8836

Lynn's Used Furniture
26 Warburton Ave.
914/966-7075

Mitchel's Antiques
800 Yonkers Ave.
914/423-2600

Notes

North Carolina

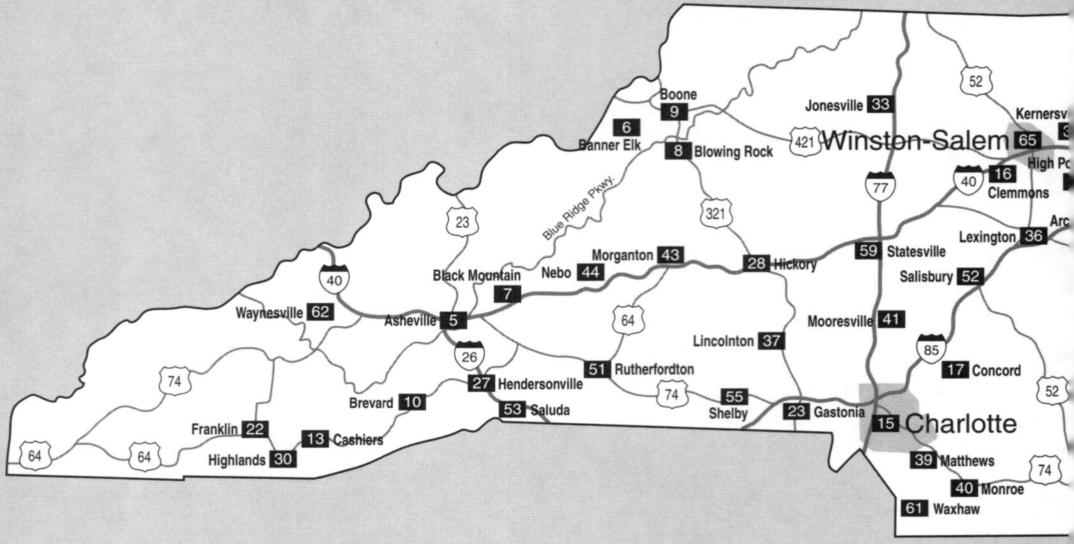

Leet Antiques, Ltd.

Direct Importer of
English & French Antiques
Gifts & Accessories
709 Hillsborough Street
(1 block east of St. Mary's College)
(919) 834-9020
Raleigh
47

Village Square Antiques & Auctions

In the
Daniel Boone Village
"Heart of North Carolina
Antique Country"

Expert Crystal Repair
& Chair Caning
126 Antique St.
(919) 732-8799
Hillsborough
31

Oakwood Antique Mall

43 PLUS DEALERS
OVER 10,000 SQUARE FEET

A Wide Variety of Furniture, Glass, Jewelry, Toys & 50's Memorabilia

Largest Selection of Antique Advertising in NC
1526 Wake Forest Road
From I-40: Take Exit 299 towards Downtown.
We are 3.7 miles on the Right.
(919) 834-5255
Raleigh
47

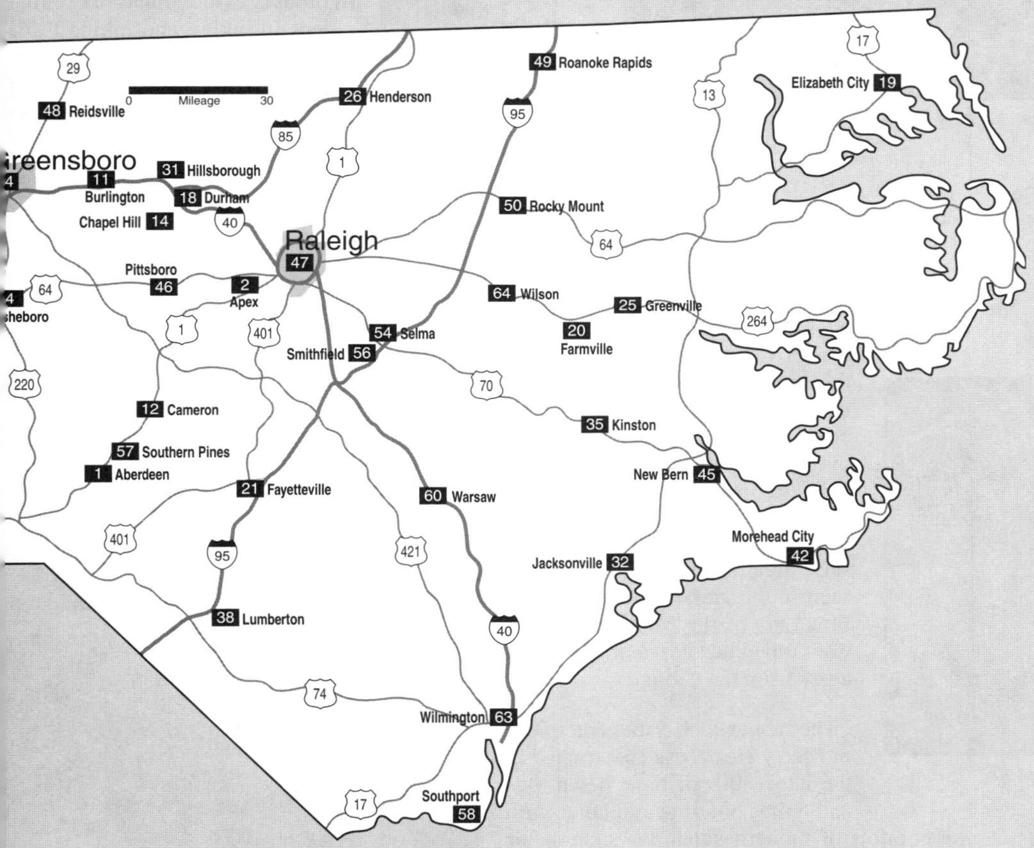

Aly Goodwin: The N.E. Horton Antique Quilt Collection

located in the
Black Mountain Antique Mall
100 Sutton Avenue
704/669-6218
Black Mountain
7

Lionheart Antiques

Located in the Historic Downtown District of Burlington. Offering an extensive collection of antiques from around the world. 120 Front St.
910-570-0830
Burlington
11

Visit
Wilson
Antique Capital of North Carolina
64

748 NC Hwy. 24 & 50
Inn-(910) 296-1831
Restaurant-(910) 296-1727
Warsaw

The Squire's Vintage Inn & The Country Squire

RESTAURANT
"Reflections of Good Taste"
60

MERRY HEART CABIN
A UNIQUE GET-AWAY VACATION

One hour east of Asheville, nestled in the Blue Ridge mountains is a place called Merry Heart Cabin.

Overlooking a forest glen, this refurbished 110-year-old log cabin is yours exclusively. Merry Heart is the perfect spot for both couples and families, the best get-away-from-it-all spot in North Carolina.

Just 8 miles north of Interstate 40 and 5 minutes away from beautiful Lake James, Merry Heart provides everything necessary for a peaceful alternative to the "hurry up and relax" syndrome often experienced during a typical vacation.

The Smarts raise a variety of animals on the farm including "babydoll" sheep.

Perfect for families desiring a quality—time environment or for couples seeking a romantic love nest, Merry Heart has it all. It is also a beautiful "safe haven" for individuals who desire a time out from life's busy pace.

Anything but a typical vacation cabin, Merry Heart recalls a simpler day in which a rich southern culture took its time to enjoy the fullness of life. It is a mood created when mankind and nature commune. Thus, Merry Heart Cabin-accented by its unique miniature animal farm including 24" sheep from England, 20" goats from Nigeria, 42" cattle from Ireland, 34" donkeys from Sardinia, and others, has become a renewal and resting spot for hundreds over the past four years.

Guests find cozy comfort in the unique sleeping loft.

Based upon the Bible scripture, "A merry heart doeth good like a medicine," the Smarts' hope to offer a dose of serenity to those who visit the cabin and farm.

Proprietors Leslie and Connie Smart state it simply, "Here at Merry Heart our desire is to offer an atmosphere of 'recreation', whether you choose to spend time at our miniature animal petting farm, horseback riding, rekindling your heart by the fire, soaking in your own private Jacuzzi or just enjoying the quiet intimacy of the quaint upstairs sleeping loft with beamed ceiling and spiral stairwell overlooking the living room with cozy fireplace."

Merry Heart is surrounded by such breathtaking scenery as was seen in the classic Michael Mann film Last of the Mohicans which was filmed just a five minute drive away from the cabin.

The cabin which is the centerpiece of Merry Heart was constructed in the late 1800s of hand-hewn logs and unites old time ambiance with the comfort of modern amenities such as air conditioning and gas heat.

From the rustic brick flooring to the high cedar-beamed ceiling, the cabin becomes a delightful home away from home.

Whether the guest have spent the day enjoying the nearby attractions or savoring a relaxing walk through the forest, a refreshing night awaits in the queen size bed in the unique sleeping loft or the two twin beds located on the lower level.

For the convenience of the guests, the cabin has a fully equipped kitchen with all staples, microwave, digital coffee maker, etc. All linens are provided as well.

Be sure to climb the knoll located at Merry Heart which provides a spectacular view over several ranges of the Appalachians, certain to enhance the peaceful mood created here. Oftentimes guests are treated to views of the gentle deer which come to feed in the glen during the early evening.

For those who enjoy the more rigorous activities, miles of exciting mountain biking and hiking trails are close by, along "Old Highway 105" winding up to and overlooking the majestic Linville Wilderness Gorge area.

Hours of sightseeing are provided by such beautiful landmarks as Table Rock Mountain, Great Smokey Mountains National Park, Blue Ridge Parkway, Shortoff Mountain, Grandfather Mountain and Pisgah National Forest to name only a few.

Located about halfway between Statesville and Asheville, off I-40 and N.C. 126, Merry Heart Cabin is ideally situated to give access to Western North Carolina's attractions and yet far enough away to provide a relaxing retreat.

Les and Connie Smart welcome you to Merry Heart Cabin.

North Carolina

1 ABERDEEN

Cameron's Antique Station
Hwy 211 E. Ashley Heights
910/944-2022

Cabbages & Kings
111 W. Main St.
910/944-1110

Honeycutt House
204 E. Main St.
910/944-9236

Town & Country Antique Mall
1369 Sandhills Blvd. N
910/944-3359

2 APEX

Freewood Antiques
541 New Hill Olive Chapel Rd.
919/362-6773

That Unique & Wonderful Place
104 N. Salem St.
919/387-9550

Creative Expressions Gallery
120 N. Salem St.
919/387-1952

Olde Barn Antiques
2708 Tingen Rd.
919/362-5266

3 ARCHDALE

The Bouldin House Bed & Breakfast

4332 Archdale Road
910/431-4909 or 1-800-739-1816
Fax: 910/431-4914
Rates: $85-95

Directions: Take Exit 111 off Interstate 85. Turn north on Rt. 311 toward High Point. Turn left on Balfour Drive. Turn right on Archdale Road. The Boulding House is 2/10 mile on your left. Located four miles from downtown High Point, 20 minutes from Greensboro and 20 minutes from Winston-Salem.

The Bouldin House offers guests a graceful version of country living on the lush, green acres of a former tobacco farm at the edge of North Carolina's bustling Piedmond Triad area. It took nearly two years to restore this fine country home to its original beauty. Today, that beauty resonates in the wainscottting of the hallways, in the finely crafted oak paneling of the dining room and in the decorative patterns and designs of the hardwood floors. Each bedroom features a fireplace, modern bath, king-size bed and large closets. The bedrooms also have personalities reflected in their names: "Warm Morning Room," "Doctor's Den," "Weekend Retreat," and "The Parlor."

The Inn is only minutes from elegant restaurants, historic sites, abundant sports and entertainment events, and America's largest concentration of furniture showrooms.

4 ASHEBORO

Nostalgia
111 N. Church St.
910/625-0644

Holly House Antiques & Cllbls.
207 E. Pritchard St.
910/625-4994

Collectors Antique Mall
211 Sunset Ave.
910/629-8105

Andorras Antiques Etc.
305 Sunset Ave.
910/626-3699

Weathervane
239 White Oak St.
910/625-2404

Cabin Creek Antiques
3574 U.S. Hwy. 64 E.
910/626-0685

5 ASHEVILLE

Fireside Antiques

30 All Souls Crescent
704/274-5977

Directions: Just one minute off I-40; take Exit 50B and the shop is located 1/4 mile on the left.

Fireside Antiques is a direct importer of European antiques featuring four galleries of fine antiques, gifts and oriental porcelain. Specializing in English Georgian mahogany, English and Irish pine, Walnut and French furniture of the 17th, 18th, and 19th centuries, this is a must stop shop when traveling through Asheville.

Pheasant on a Halfshell
36 Battery Park Ave.
704/253-3577

Lexington Park Antiques
65 W. Walnut St.
704/253-3070

King-Thomasson Antiques Inc.
64 Biltmore Ave.
704/252-1565

Village Antiques
755 Biltmore Ave.
704/252-5090

Chelsea's Gifts & Antiques
6 Boston Way
704/274-4400

Biltmore Antique Mall
30 Bryson St.
704/255-0053

Korth & Company
30 Bryson St.
704/252-0906

Pals
24 N. Lexington Ave.
704/253-0440

Catskill Antique Co.
34 N. Lexington Ave.
704/252-2611

Corner Cupboard Antique Mall
49 N. Lexington Ave.
704/258-9815

House of Alexander
54 N. Lexington Ave.
704/251-0505

Jim Knapp Antiques
503 Haywood Rd.
704/258-0031

Mac's Antiques
602 Haywood Rd.
704/255-7809

Interiors Marketplace
2 Hendersonville Rd.
704/253-2300

Old But Good
2614 Hendersonville Rd.
704/687-3890

Asheville Antiques Mall
43 Rankin Ave.
704/253-3634

Favorite Places To Eat

Cracker Barrel Old Country Store
I-40 & Rts. 19 & 23, Exit 44
704/665-2221

6 BANNER ELK

Finders Keepers
Green Mansions Village/Hwy. 105
704/963-7300

Susanna's Antiques
Hwy. 105
704/963-8685

Marjon's Antiques
10884 N. High #1055
704/963-5305

Elk River Trading Post
Hwy. 194
704/898-9477

Mill Pond Arts & Antiques
920 Shawneehaw Ave.
704/898-5175

7 BLACK MOUNTAIN

Aly Goodwin: The N. E. Horton Antique Quilt Collection

100 Sutton Avenue (inside Black Mtn. Antique Mall)
704/669-6218
Open Mon.-Sat., 10-5; Sun 1:30-5; seven days a week, year round

Directions: Located off I-40, 15 minutes east of Asheville. Headed East on I-40, take Exit 64. Turn left to Black Mountain; at St. traffic light, turn left, immediately pull to right and park. Approximately one mile from interstate.

Located in the Black Mountain Antique Mall, Aly Goodwin: The N. E. Horton Antique Quilt Collection specializes in antique quilts (c. 1780-1940) numbering over 300; as well as southern pottery and folk art, furniture, Victorian antique paintings, linens, books, tools and much more. The 7,000-square-foot Black Mountain Antique Mall is noted as being North Carolina's year-round antique show!

Treasures & Trivia
106 Broadway St.
704/669-5190

L A Glenn Co. Inc.
109 Cherry St.
704/669-4886

Hoard's Antiques
121 Cherry St.
704/669-6494

Cherry St. Antique Mall
139 Cherry St.
704/669-7942

8 BLOWING ROCK

Stone Pillar Bed & Breakfast

144 Pine Street
P.O. Box 1881
704/295-4141
Web Site: http//blowingrock.com/northcarolina
Open daily 8 to 10
Rates $65-95

Directions: From I-40, exit 123, to Hwy. 321 directly to Blowing Rock. At Sunset Drive turn left into town. At Main Street tun right to Pine Street (second street on right); turn right on Pine. Inn is located at 144 Pine Street.

Nestled in the mountains of western North Carolina, just off the Blue Ridge Parkway, the town of Blowing Rock is home to Stone Pillar Bed & Breakfast. Located just 1/2 block from Main Street, the Stone Pillar provides a relaxing home-like atmosphere in an historic 1920s house. Six guests rooms, each with private bath, offer a tasteful blend of heirlooms and antiques, accented by a few touches of modern.

A full breakfast is created daily in the house kitchen and served family style to the Stone Pillar's guests. The living/dining area, with its working fireplace, offers an opportunity to meet fellow guest.

If you want an action-packed day of frantic activity such as hiking, skiing, sight-seeing, antiquing or prefer to just relax and enjoy the peace and quiet and fresh

North Carolina

mountain air, the high country area is the ideal place to enjoy your perfect get away.

Dreamfields of Blowing Rock
Hwy. 105 Green Mt. Village
704/963-8333

Blowing Rock Antique Center
U.S. Hwy. 321 Bypass
704/295-4950

Antique Rug Buyers of Florida
999 N. Main St.
704/295-7750

Hanna's Oriental Rugs & Gifts
1123 Main St.
704/295-7073

Family Heirlooms
1125 Main St.
704/295-0090

Village Antiques
1127 Main St.
704/295-7874

Old World Galleries
1053 N. Main St.
704/295-7508

Windwood Antiques
1157 S. Main St.
704/295-9260

Mystery Hill
129 Mystery Hill Lane
704/264-2792

Possum Hollow Antiques
Opossum Hollow Rd.
704/295-3502

9 BOONE

Antiques Unlimited Mall
231 Boone Heights Dr.
704/265-3622

Wilcox Emporium
161 Howard St.
704/262-1221

Boone Antique Mall
631 W. King St.
704/262-0521

Blowing Rock Antique Center
877 W. King St.
704/264-5757

Hidden Valley Antiques
Hwy. 105 S.
704/963-5224

Marines Interiors Inc.
Hwy. 105 S.
704/963-4656

Loafer's Glory
U.S. Hwy. 321
704/265-3797

Aunt Pymm's Table Antiques
Us Hwy. 421
704/262-1041

Unique Interiors
240 Shadowline Dr.
704/265-1422

10 BREVARD

John Reynolds Antiques
6 S. Broad St.
704/884-4987

Open Door Antique Mall
15 W. Main St.
704/883-4323

Brevard Antique Mall
57 E. Main St.
704/885-2744

Carolina Connection Antiques
5 W. Main St.
704/884-9786

Whitewater Gardens
259 Rosman Hwy.
704/884-2656

11 BURLINGTON

Lionheart Antiques

120 E. Front Street
910/570-0830
Open: Mon.-Wed. by chance or appointment; Thurs.-Sat. 10-5; Sun., 1-5

Directions: Off I-40 and I-85, between Raleigh and Greensboro, North Carolina. Take Exit 145 to downtown Burlington. Turn right on Main Street and continue for 2 blocks. Turn right on Front Street. Lionheart is on the left. Look for the lions.

From its beginning at the turn of the century, the building housing Lionheart Antiques has been a showcase for fine furniture and decorative pieces for the home. Today, with the focus on antiques, the 5,000-square-foot showroom presents mahogany and glass cases displaying porcelain, crystal, boxes and scientific instruments. In the Garden and Architectural Room, a complete Columbia, S. C. post office serves as a backdrop for cast iron urns, fences, and gates from Europe. Many buying trips to Europe during the year keep the exciting and interesting pieces, from furniture to lamps and accessories, filling up the shop. Fair prices and a great variety is the reason shoppers return to Lionheart; or could it be because Boris, the Belgian Shepard greets them at the door?

Eclectic Gallery
2602 Eric Lane
910/222-1496

Robert Hodgin Antiques
346 S. Worth Street
910/229-1865

Antiques Art
309 Trollinger Street
910/229-1331

Burlwood Farm Antiques
4758 Friendship Patterson Mill
910/226-5139

Antique Collectors Showcase
1709 South Mebane St.
910/229-6499

Favorite Places To Eat

Cracker Barrel Old Country Store
I-85 & Huffman Mill Rd., Exit 141
910/584-3833

12 CAMERON

Aunt Bertie's
Hwy. 24-27
910/245-7059

Crabtree Antiques
Hwy. 24-27
910/245-3163

Cranes Creek Antiques
Hwy. 24-27
910/245-4476

Ferguson House Antiques
Hwy. 24-27
910/245-3055

McKeithen's Antiques
Hwy. 24-27
910/245-4886

McPherson's Antiques
Hwy. 24-27
910/692-3449

Old Greenwood Inn
Hwy. 24-27
910/245-7431

13 CASHIERS

Balderdash Antiques

Hwy. 107 N. (Cashiers Commons)
704/743-5499
Open April-October, Mon.-Sat., 10-5; (November) Fri. & Sat. only or by appointment

Directions: From south: I-85 to exit 1 in SC. to Rt. 11, take Rt. 11 to Walhalla to 107 north to Cashiers. From north: I-40 East to I-26. South to Hwy. 64, west through Brevard to Cashiers to Hwy. 107. Located 1/4 mile north of (only) red light on 107 north in Cashiers Commons.

Not a single word laid upon this page could ever describe Cashiers, N.C. David and I discovered it quite by accident. We had ventured off to Gatlinburg for a weekend get-a-way, when someone told us about a Flea Market in Pickens, SC. And, while it just happened to be in the middle of the night when we got this news, we decided we had better leave right away if we were going to get there by morning.

We first noticed the unusually beautiful scenery near Highlands, N.C. The road produced more curves than usual and the trees and mountains seemed to form a tunnel all around us.

In rounding a curve the glow of two tiny eyeballs beamed in the complete blackness of the night. A baby fox had wondered out to the edge of the road scavenging for food. Not intending to leave him hungry, we fed him a cookie and like any child, he devoured it.

This beauty and peaceful serenity continued for miles and miles and in this complete darkness we saw not a single light, not even a headlight of a passing car. At the crossroads of Hwy. 64 and 107 we came upon a red light and the tiny town of Cashiers. I immediately spotted Cashiers Commons to our left and noticed Balderdash Antiques. With no time to stop (not to mention it was very early in the a.m.) We proceeded on to our intended destination. The Flea Market turned out to be not as we expected and by this time I couldn't get Highlands, NC nor the antique shop in Cashiers out of my mind. It was almost a relief that the Flea Market was disappointing because I simply had to know what was inside that shop (it was one of those gut feelings). After several hours of driving back to Cashiers (once again through some of the most beautiful scenery in the world), we arrived at Balderdash Antiques. I rushed to get inside and it was just as I had expected and more. I was very impressed by the exceptional quality of their "truly" period pieces.

I tried to get David to move to Cashiers, but no such luck. But, if he ever says YES!, you can bet I'll be packed in a New York minute.

Cobbie's Interiors
Rt. 64/Near Crossroads
704/743-2585

Lyn K Holloway Antiques
Rt. 64 & 107
704/743-2524

Trove Treasure
Hwy. 64
704/743-9768

Valley Gift Shop
U.S. 64 W.
704/743-2944

Wormy Chestnut Antiques
Hwy. 64
704/743-3014

Rosemary's Antiques Etc.
Hwy. 107
704/743-9808

Cashiers East Antiques Mall
Hwy. 107 S.
704/743-3580

Not All Country Store
Hwy. 107
704/743-3612

14 CHAPEL HILL

Patterson's Mill Country Store
5109 Farrington Rd.
919/493-8149

Whitehall at the Villa Antique
1213 E. Franklin St.
919/942-3179

Countryside Antiques Inc.
9555 U.S. Hwy. 15-501 N
919/968-8375

15 CHARLOTTE

Blacklion Furniture, Gift & Design Showcases
10605 Park Road
704/541-1148

Directions: Conveniently located near SouthPark and Carolina Place Malls off I-485 at Hwy. 51.

Under one roof, in a convenient location, and in picturesque settings, Blacklion offers home decor from some of the most selective dealers in the Carolinas. A collection of distinctive show spaces feature: old world antiques, over 2,382 works of art, lawn and garden accents, lamps and rugs, as well as gifts and accessories. Twenty-three Interior Designers are available for expressing ideas, inspiration and practical solutions to your decorating needs.

Antique Kingdom
700 Central Ave.
704/377-5464

Clearing House Inc.
701 Central Ave.
704/375-7708

The Galleria Gifts & Interiors
1401 Central Ave.
704/372-1050

Crescent Collection Ltd.
2318A Crescent Ave.
704/333-7922

Circa Interiors & Antiques
2321 Crescent Ave.
704/332-1668

Tudor House Galleries Inc.
1401 East Blvd.
704/377-4748

English Room
519 Fenton Pl
704/377-3625

Consignment Corner
3852 E. Independence Blvd.
704/535-3840

Queen City Antiques & Cllbls.
3892 E. Independence Blvd.
704/531-6002

Treasure House
5300 Monroe Rd.
704/532-1613

Mary Frances Miller Antiques
1437 E. Morehead St.
704/375-9240

Treasures Unlimited Inc.
6401 Morrison Blvd.
704/366-7272

Karen's Beautiful Things
8324 Pineville Matthews Rd.
704/542-1412

Windwood Antiques
421 Providence Rd.
704/372-4577

Queen Charlotte Antiques Ltd.
603 Providence Rd.
704/333-0472

Jenko's
715 Providence Rd.
704/375-1779

Gallery Designs Ltd
739 Providence Rd.
704/376-9163

Colony Furn Shops Inc.
811 Providence Rd.
704/333-8871

Antiques on Selwyn
2909 Selwyn Ave.
704/342-2111

Le-Dee-Das
1942 E. 7th St.
704/372-9599

Perry's at Southpark
4400 Sharon Rd.
704/364-1391

Interiors Marketplace
2000 South Blvd.
704/377-6226

By-Gone Days Antiques Inc.
3100 South Blvd.
704/527-8717

Chris' Collectibles
7100 Statesville Rd. B17
704/596-1592

Metrolina Expo
7100 Statesville Rd.
704/596-4643

Dilworth Billiards
300 E. Tremont Ave.
704/333-3021

Thompson Antique Co.
7631 Wilkinson Blvd.
704/399-1405

Favorite Places To Eat

Cracker Barrel Old Country Store
I-85 & Mulberry Church Rd., Exit 33
704/393-2670

16 CLEMMONS

Favorite Places To Eat

Cracker Barrel Old Country Store
I-40 & State Rd. 113, Exit 184
910/712-9880

17 CONCORD

Irby's Antiques
244 McGill Ave. NW
704/788-1810

Clock & Lamp Shoppe
250 McGill Ave. NW
704/786-1929

Memory Shoppe
885 Old Charlotte Rd.
704/788-9443

Antique Market of Concord
14 Union St.
704/786-4296

21 Union St.-A Trading Co.
21 Union St.
704/782-1212

Six O One Trading Post
4018 U.S. Hwy. 601 S
704/782-1212

Dennis Carpenter Repro Ford
4140 U.S. Hwy. 29 S
704/786-8139

Annie's Cane Shop
5680 U.S. Hwy. 601 S
704/782-4937

Favorite Places To Eat

Cracker Barrel Old Country Store
I-85 & Earnhardt Rd., Exit 60
704/792-0277

18 DURHAM

Chelsea Antiques
2631 Durham Chapel Hill Blvd.
919/683-1865

Antiques 1
4422 Durham Chapel Hill Blvd.
919/493-7135

Orig Illusions Antqs. & Cllbls.
4422 Durham Chapel Hill Blvd.
919/493-4650

Willow Park Lane
4422 Durham Chapel Hill Blvd.
919/493-3923

Attic Treasures
2014 Granville Cr.
919/403-8639

Trash & Treasures
2911 Guess Rd.
919/477-6716

Antiques 1
947 S. Miami Blvd.
919/596-1848

James Kennedy Antiques Ltd.
905 W. Main St.
919/682-1040

White House Antiques
3306 Old Chapel Hill Rd.
919/489-3016

Twice Remembered
4109 N. Roxboro Rd.
919/471-1148

Sandpiper Antiques
5218 Wake Forest Rd.
919/596-4949

Finders Keepers
2501 University Dr.
919/490-4441

Maral Antiques & Interiors
5102 Chapel Hill Rd.
919/493-7345

Favorite Places To Eat

Cracker Barrel Old Country Store
I-85 & Cole Mill Rd., Exit 173
919/309-2888

19 ELIZABETH CITY

Pleasurehouse Antiques
608 E. Colonial Ave.
919/338-6570

Parker's Trading Post
1051 U.S. Hwy. 17 S
919/335-4896

Pasquotank Antiques
117 N. Water St.
919/331-2010

Miller Antiques
207 N. Water St.
919/335-1622

20 FARMVILLE

The Hub Mall
104 South Main Street
919/753-8560
Open Tue.-Sat., 10-5:30

Directions: Off I-95 on Hwy. 264 East between Wilson, N.C., and Greenville, N.C.

The Hub Mall is a small quaint little shop located in a restored historic building in downtown Farmville. Though small, their antiques, arts, and collectibles selections are outstanding. They accept consignments therefore they have a constantly changing inventory.

Rememberings
119 S. Main St.
919/753-7333

Jackie's Ole House
RR 1
919/753-2631

21 FAYETTEVILLE

Warpath Military Collectibles
3805 Cumberland Rd.
910/425-7000

Craft Market
5012 Cumberland Rd.
910/424-0838

Antique & Gift Center
123 Hay St.
910/485-7602

David R Walters Antique
1110 Hay St.
910/483-5832

Harris Auct. Gllry & Antq. Mall
2419 Hope Mills Rd.
910/424-0033

Eastover Trading Co. Antique
Hwy. 301 N
910/323-1121

Country Junction
Hwy. 87 S
910/677-0017

Antiques Unltd Of Eastover
1128 Middle Rd.
910/323-5439

Dimples & Sawdust Antq. Dolls
5409 Labrador
910/484-3655

Tarbridge Military Collectibles
5820 Ramsey St.
910/488-7207

A A Antique Village
5832 Ramsey St.
910/822-9822

Unique Curtains & Antiques
Stoney Point Rd.
910/424-1101

Favorite Places To Eat

Cracker Barrel Old Country Store
I-95 & Rt. 210/53, Exit 49
910/323-2025

22 FRANKLIN

Smoky Mt. Antique Mall
4488 Georgia Rd.
704/524-5293

R & S Furnishing & Antique
354 E. Main St.
704/524-8188

Friendly Village Antique Mall
268 E. Palmer St.
704/524-8200

North Carolina

23 GASTONIA

Past Time Antique Mall
401 Cox Rd.
704/867-6535

J & W Antiques
181 W. Main Ave.
704/867-0097

Willow Shoppe Ltd.
1008 Union Rd.
704/866-9611

Favorite Places To Eat

Cracker Barrel Old Country Store
I-85 & New Hope Rd., Exit 20
704/866-7069

24 GREENSBORO

Zenkes Inc.
210 Blandwood Ave.
910/273-9335

Caroline Faison Antiques
18 Battleground Ct.
910/272-0261

Carlson Antiques & Gifts
507 N. Church St.
910/273-1626

Elm Street Marketplace
203 S. Elm St.
910/273-1767

Antiques & Accessories on Elm
323 S. Elm St.
910/273-6468

Browsery Used Book Store
506 S. Elm St.
910/370-4648

Browsery Antiques
516 S. Elm St.
910/274-3231

Dramore Antiques
526 S. Elm St.
910/275-7563

Unexpected Antique Shop
534 S. Elm St.
910/275-4938

Rhynes Corner Cupboard
603 S. Elm St.
910/378-1380

Edlin's Antiques
604 S. Elm St.
910/274-2509

Knight & Elliott
909 N. Elm St.
910/370-4155

E. Freeman And Co.
420 Eugene Ct.
910/275-8487

Crumpler's Antiques & Pottery
442 N. Eugene St.
910/272-4383

Saltbox Inc.
2011 Golden Gate Dr.
910/273-8758

Posh
5804 High Point Rd.
910/294-1028

Skinner & Company
2908 Liberty Rd.
910/691-1219

Spease House of Treasures
350 McAdoo Ave.
910/275-2079

Lavene Antiques
4522 W. Market St.
910/854-8160

Gallery Antiques
801 Merritt Dr.
910/299-2426

O'Henry Antiques
3224 N. O'Henry Blvd.
910/375-0191

Tyler-Smith Antiques
501 Simpson St.
910/274-6498

Cherry's Fine Guns
3402 W. Wendover Ave. #A
910/854-4182

House Dressing
3608 W. Wendover Ave.
910/294-3900

Byerly's Antiques Inc.
4311 Wiley Davis Rd.
910/299-6510

Favorite Places To Eat

Cracker Barrell Old Country Store
I-40 & Wendover Ave., Exit 214
910/294-0911

25 GREENVILLE

Cable & Craft at Woodside
Allen Rd.
919/756-9929

Woodside Antiques
Allen Rd.
919/756-9929

Artisan's Market
2500 S. Charles St.
919/355-5536

Tried & True Inc.
924 Dickinson Ave.
919/752-2139

Dapper Dans
417 S. Evans St.
919/752-1750

Red Oak Show & Sell
264 W. Farmville Hwy.
919/756-1156

Greenville Antique Mall
E. NC Hwy. 33
919/752-8111

Now & Then Designs
801 Red Banks Rd.
919/756-8470

Johnsen's Antiques & Lamp Shop
315 E. 11th St.
919/758-4839

26 HENDERSON

Favorite Places To Eat

Cracker Barrel Old Country Store
I-85 & Ruin Creek Road, Exit 212

27 HENDERSONVILLE

Old & New Shop
3400 Asheville Hwy.
704/697-6160

Richard D Hatch & Associates
3700 Asheville Hwy.
704/696-3440

Heritage Square Antiques
Church & Barnwell
704/697-0313

Antiques & Decorative Arts
305 S. Church St.
704/697-6930

Nancy Roth Antiques
127 4th Ave. W.
704/697-7555

Antiques Etc.
147 4th Ave. W.
704/696-8255

Scottie's Jewelry & Fine Art
225 N. Main St.
704/692-1350

Days Gone By Antiques
303 N. Main St.
704/693-9056

Calico Gallery of Crafts
317 N. Main St.
704/697-2551

Fourth & Main Antique Mall
344 N. Main St.
704/698-0018

So. Comforts Antqs. & Gift
628 Shawn Rachel Pkwy.
704/693-5310

Wagon Wheel Antiques
423 N. Main St.
704/692-0992

Village Green Antique Mall
424 N. Main St.
704/692-9057

Mehri & Co. of New York
501 N. Main St.
704/693-0887

Honeysuckle Hollow
512 N. Main St.
704/697-2197

South Main Antiques
119 S. Main St.
704/693-3212

Hendersonville Antiques Mall
670 Spartanberg Hwy.
704/692-5125

JRD's Classics & Collectibles
102 3rd Ave. E.
704/698-0075

Favorite Places To Eat

Cracker Barrel Old Country Store
I-26 & Upward Rd., Exit 22
704/692-5560

28 HICKORY

Baker & Co. Antiques
227 1st Ave. NW
704/324-2334

Farm House Furnishings
1432 1st Ave. SW
704/324-4595

Collectors Cottage Antiques
4164 Henry River Rd.
704/397-6386

Norma's Antiques
327 2nd Ave. NW
704/328-8660

Southern Pride Antiques
1949 Startown Rd.
704/322-6205

Antiques and More
1046 3rd Ave. NW
704/326-9030

Hickory Antiques Mall
348 U.S. Hwy. 70 S
704/322-4004

L & L Antiques
4025 U.S. Hwy. 70 S
704/328-9373

Favorite Places To Eat

Cracker Barrel Old Country Store
I-40 & Rt. 127, Exit 125
704/261-0508

29 HIGH POINT

Deep River Antiques
2022 Eastchester Dr.
910/883-7005

Wallace Antiques
706 Greensboro Rd.
910/884-8044

Antique & Vintage Furnishings
652 N. Main St.
910/886-5126

Kathryn's Collection
781 N. Main St.
910/841-7474

North Main Antiques & Cllbls.
1240 N. Main St.
910/882-2512

Elisabeth's Timeless Treasures
1701 N. Main St.
910/887-3089

Teague Pump Co. Inc.
904 Old Thomasville Rd.
910/882-2916

Randall Tysinger Antiques
342 N. Wrenn St.
910/883-4477

30 HIGHLANDS

A Country Home
5162 Cashiers Road
704/526-9038

Country Inn Antiques
4th & Main/Highlands Inn
704/526-9380

Home & Holiday
4th St. On The Hill
704/526-2007

Mirror Lake Antiques
215 S. Fourth St.
704/526-2080

C K Swann
Hwy. 64 E.
704/526-2083

Elephants Foot Antiques
Hwy. 64 & Foreman Rd.
704/526-5451

Hanover House Antiques
Hwy. 64 E
704/526-4425

Juliana's
Main St.
704/526-4306

I'm Precious Too!
E. Main at Leonard
704/526-2754

Stone Lantern
309 Main St.
704/526-2769

Royal Scot, Inc.
318 Main St.
704/526-5917

Scudder's Galleries
352 Main St.
704/526-4111

Richard Guritz Antiques
8 Mountain Brook Center
704/526-9680

Fletcher & Lee Antiques
10 Mountain Brook
704/526-5400

Great Things
Wright Square
704/526-3966

North Carolina

31 HILLSBOROUGH

Village Square Antiques & Auction
126 Antique Street
919/732-8799
Open: Wed.-Sat. 11-5, Sun. 1-5, Mon. & Tue. Closed.

Directions: Located I-85 exit 164 & I-40 exit 261 in the Daniel Boone Village.

Located in the "Heart of North Carolina Antique Country" Village Square Antiques and Auctions is a jack-of-all-trades and master-of-ALL. The shop offers an outstanding selection of antiques such as depression glass, formal mahogany furniture, classic oak furniture, clocks, estate jewelry, carnival glass, lamps, chandeliers, old Fenton art glass, fine porcelain, Hawkes, Akro Agate children's dishes, sterling silver, cast iron and old tools, cut and elegant glass, oil paintings and prints, elegant mirrors, and this list could go on and on. All pieces are in the original finish or have been restored to its original beauty.

Village Square is both a retail and wholesale market, so dealers should definitely check this place out. L. B., the owner, has been known to give some deep discounts.

The shop also provides those "always needed" services of expert crystal repair, lamp repair and rewiring and chair caning. In addition, auctions are held periodically, but never on a set schedule.

Be sure to call ahead for auction dates.

Court Square Shop
108 S. Churton St.
919/732-4500

Goldsmith & Precious Things
116 Daniel Boone St.
919/732-6931

Gatewood Antiques
113 James Freeland Memorial Dr.
919/732-5081

Hillsborough Antique Mall Inc.
387 Ja-Max Dr.
919/732-8882

Yesterdays Treasures
361 Ja-Max Dr.
919/732-9199

House of Treasures #2
383 Ja-Max Dr.
919/732-0709

Hillside Antiques & Cllbls.
392 Ja-Max Dr.
919/644-6074

Depot Antiques & Collectibles
409 Village St.
919/732-9796

Butner Antique Barn
111 Antique St.
919/732-4606

32 JACKSONVILLE

B J's Antique Furniture
333 Bell Fork Rd.
910/346-8693

Jacksonville Antique Mall
336 Henderson Dr.
910/938-8811

Anchor Antqs. & Lamp Shades
117 S. Marine Blvd.
910/455-1900

Basement
237 S. Marine Blvd.
910/346-9833

33 JONESVILLE

Favorite Places To Eat

Cracker Barrel Old Country Store
I-77 & NC 67, Exit 82

34 KERNERSVILLE

Collective Treasures
4674 Kernersville Rd.
910/785-9886

Curiosity Shoppe
4710 Kernersville Rd.
910/785-4427

Murphy's Keepsake
231 N. Main St.
910/993-4105

Main Street Collectibles
321 N. Main St.
910/996-6969

Shouse Antiques
419 S. Main St.
910/996-5108

35 KINSTON

Just Stuff
121 E. Gordon St.
919/523-1515

Antique Market
Hwy. 70 W Bypass
919/527-8300

Claydel's Antiques
1811 N. Queen St.
919/939-1710

36 LEXINGTON

Candy Factory
15 N. Main St.
910/249-6770

Links Antique Shop
2204 S. Main St.
910/249-9590

Poor Boy Antiques
1673 Old U.S. Hwy. 52
910/249-7226

Harry's Antiques
3185 N. U.S. Hwy. 6
910/249-1716

B & D Antiques
1506 Winston Rd.
910/249-0745

Favorite Places To Eat

Cracker Barrel Old Country Store
I-85 & State Rd. 8, Exit 91
704/242-1212

37 LINCOLNTON

Antiques & Art
231 E. Main St.
704/735-5224

Antiques & Collectibles
333 E. Main St.
704/732-0500

Lincolnton Antique Mall
2225 E. Main St.
704/732-3491

Cynthia Rankin Antqs. & Intrs.
U.S. 321 Hwy. Bypass
704/735-4400

38 LUMBERTON

Antiques Limited
215 N. Elm St.
910/738-4607

Lewis Durham Furniture
307 W. 5th St.
910/739-7327

Bell's Antiques
2201 W. 5th St.
910/671-0264

Somewhere In Time Antiques
4420 Kahn Dr.
910/671-8660

Favorite Places To Eat

Cracker Barrel Old Country Store
I-95 & Rt. 211, Exit 20
910/738-1481

39 MATTHEWS

Town & Country Antiques
11328 E. Independence Blvd.
704/847-2680

Antique Alley
1325 Matthews Mint Hill Rd.
704/847-3003

Matthews Antiques & Collectibles
224 S. Trade St.
704/841-1400

40 MONROE

Bloomin Furniture
1401 N. Charlotte Ave.
704/289-4670

Crow's Nest Consignment Mall
5811 Hwy. 74
704/821-4848

Marys Country Furn. & Antqs.
2502 Old Charlotte Hwy.
704/289-2367

Austin's Collectibles
4108 Old Camden Rd.
704/282-0144

41 MOORESVILLE

Twice Treasured Antique Mall
132 S. Main St.
704/664-6255

Favorite Places To Eat

Cracker Barrel Old Country Store
I-77 & NC 150, Exit 36
704/660-6314

42 MOREHEAD

Seaport Antique Market
509 Arendell St.
919/726-6606

Cheeks Antiques
727 Arendell St.
919/726-3247

Coastal Treasures
2210 Arendell St.
919/726-1570

Ship & Shore Antiques
4660 Arendell St.
919/726-0493

Sea Pony
411 Evans St.
919/726-6070

43 MORGANTON

King's Depression
1302 Bethel Rd.
704/437-7281

Dales Antiques
Hwy. 18
704/437-4464

Possibilities Antiques
105 N. Sterling St.
704/433-0621

Dogwood Antiques
402 S. Sterling St.
704/438-4138

Old Homestead Antiques
2092 U.S. Hwy. 64
704/437-0863

Southern Legacy
106 W. Union St.
704/438-0808

44 NEBO

Merry Heart Cabin
1414 Merry Heart Lane
704/584-6174

Directions: For specific directions to Merry Heart Cabin from your location, please call the Innkeeper.

For information on the perfect get-a-way, see review this section.

North Carolina

45 NEW BERN

Jane Sugg Antiques
228 Middle St.
919/637-6985

Tom's Coins & Antiques
244 Middle St.
919/633-0615

Middle Street Antique Market
327 Middle St.
919/638-1685

Elegant Days Antiques
236 Middle St.
919/636-3689

Cherishables
712 Pollock St.
919/633-3118

Will Gorges Antiques
2100 Trent Blvd.
919/636-3039

Seaport Antique Market
504 Tryon Palace Dr.
919/637-5050

46 PITTSBORO

Beggars & Choosers Antiques
38 Hillsboro St.
919/542-5884

52 Hillsboro St. Antiques
52 Hillsboro St.
919/542-0789

Edward's Antiques & Cllbls.
89 Hillsboro St.
919/542-5649

Fields Antique Shoppe
509 West St.
919/542-1126

47 RALEIGH

Oakwood Antiques Mall

1526 Wake Forest Road
919/834-5255
Open Tue.-Sat., 10-6; Sun. 1-5; closed Monday

Directions: From I-40 at Exit 299 (Hammond Road/ Person Street) going toward downtown, go 3.7 miles to Texaco Canopy on the right side of the street. Oakwood is located in the strip with Texaco.

Inside the 10,000-square-feet of Oakwood Antiques Mall, more than 53 dealers have stuffed the aisles with a large variety of antiques and collectibles. No crafts or reproductions allowed. Marvel at the extensive collection of furniture, glass, toys, deco and '50s memorabilia. The shop is known to display the largest selection of antique advertising items in North Carolina.

Leet Antiques, Ltd.

709 Hillsborough Street
919/834-5255
Fax: 919/834-9066
Open Mon.-Fri., 10-6; Saturday 10-4

Directions: Going towards Raleigh on I-40 (East), take the Wade Avenue Exit. Go down Wade Avenue, take Exit onto Glenwood Avenue (south). Go south on Glenwood to Hillsborough St., turn right onto Hillsborough (going west). Shop sits on south side of street between Boylan Avenue and Saint Mary's Street.

Leet Antiques, Ltd. is a direct importer of English and French Period antiques. Each item is hand-picked in Europe and no "container merchandise" is found in this exquisite shop. Instead, you will find majolica and Staffordshire, Oriental, crystal, colorful antique needlepoint rugs as well as a wide variety of gifts and accessories.

City Antiques Market
222 S. Blount St.
919/834-2489

We've Lost Our Marbles Antqs.
406 Capital Blvd.
919/834-6950

Gresham Lake Antique Mall
6917 Capital Blvd.
919/878-9381

Ordinary & Extraordinary
115 W. Chatham
919/481-3955

Carolina Antique Mall
2050 Clark Ave.
919/833-8227

Antiques Emporium
2060 Clark Ave.
919/834-7250

Acquisitions Ltd.
2003 D Fairview Rd.
919/755-1110

Antiques At Five Points
2010 Fairview Rd.
919/834-4900

Highsmith Antiques
107 Glenwood Ave.
919/832-6275

Aloma Crenshaw Antiques
122 Glenwood Ave.
919/821-0705

C & T Consignments
122 Glenwood Ave.
919/828-2559

Brideshead Antiques
123 Glenwood Ave.
919/831-1926

Ad Lib
603 Glenwood Ave.
919/821-0031

Gaston Street Antiques
608 Gaston St.
919/821-5169

Carolyn Broughton Antiques
3309 Garner Rd.
919/772-8555

Memory Layne Antiques Mall
6013 Glenwood Ave.
919/881-2644

O C Cozart Ltd. Antiques
318 S. Harrington St.
919/828-8014

Elisabeth's Space
612 W. Johnson St.
919/821-2029

Shelton's Furniture Co.
607 W. Morgan St.
919/833-5548

Whitnee's Antiques
1818 Oberlin Rd.
919-787-7202

Woody Biggs Antiques
509 Dixie Trail
919/834-2287

Woodleigh Place Interiors
610 W. Peace St.
919/834-8324

Elaine Miller Collections
2102 Smallwood Dr.
919/834-0044

George R McNeill Antiques Inc.
2102 Smallwood Dr.
919/833-1415

Carolina Collectibles
11717 Six Forks Rd.
919/848-3778

Hillary's Interiors
6301 Falls Road
919/878-6633

Classic Antiques
319 W. Davie Street
919/839-8333

Park Place Antiques City Mkt.
135 E. Martin St.
919/821-5880

48 REIDSVILLE

Uptown Antiques
224 S.W. Market St.
910/349-4413

Reidsville Antique Mall
211 S. Scales St.
910/349-5060

Studebaker's of Rabbit Hill
223 S. Scales St.
910/342-9400

Settle Street Station Antiques
112 Settle St.
910/616-1133

49 ROANOKE RAPIDS

Roanoke Valley Antiques
Hwy. 158 W
919/535-4242

Past & Present Co.
125 W. 9th St.
919/537-5843

Odds & Ends
1012 Roanoke Ave.
919/308-6960

Curiosity Shop
1346 Roanoke Ave.
919/535-1532

D & R Antiques
518 Weldon Rd.
919/535-9172

Favorite Places To Eat

Cracker Barrel Old Country Store
I-95 & Hwy. 158, Exit 173
919/535-1747

50 ROCKY MOUNT

Carousel Antiques
238 S.W. Main St.
919/442-5919

Past'N Present
120 Tarboro St.
919/446-1272

Godwin's
1130 S. Wesleyan Blvd.
919/972-8972

51 RUTHERFORDTON

William & Mary Antiques
Hwy. 74 W
704/287-4507

Victorian Lace Antique Mall
202 N. Main
704/287-2820

Pastimes Antique Mall
803 S. Main St.
704/287-9288

Fiddlesticks Antique Mall
1201 Hwy. 221 S
704/286-0054

52 SALISBURY

Eighteen Thirty-Nine Antiques
218 W. Cemetary St.
704/633-1839

Livery Stable
210 E. Innes St.
704/636-2955

Salisbury Emporium
230 E. Kerr St.
704/642-0039

Beggar's Bazaar
102 S. Main St.
704/633-5315

Lillian's Library & Antiques
3024 S. Main St.
704/636-4671

53 SALUDA

The Little Store
Main St.
704/749-1258

Ryan & Boyle Antiques
Main St.
704/749-9790

The Brass Latch
23 Main St.
704/749-4200

A Gardeners Cottage
Main Street
704/749-4200

54 SELMA

TWM's Antique Mall

211 J.R. Road
919/965-6699
Open Mon.-Sat., 10-8; Sun., 10-6

Directions: Exit 97 of I-95 (Selma). Located at the junction of I-95 and U.S. 70A just south of J. R. Outlet Stores.

TWM's Antique Mall stocks a complete line of all types of antiques including furniture. Of additional interest, the mall also has a sterling silver tableware replacement service and also restores furniture.

55 SHELBY

Ken's Antiques
1671 E. Marion St.
704/482-4062

Bell's Antiques
1502 New House Rd.
704/434-2254

Antique Outlet
6300 Polkville Rd.
704/482-8542

Millie's Back Porch
1201 S. Post Rd.
704/487-4842

56 SMITHFIELD

Favorite Places To Eat

Cracker Barrel Old Country Store
I-95 & Industrial Park, Exit 95
919/989-2140

57 SOUTHERN PINES

Theater Antiques
143 N.E. Broad St.
910/692-2482

Gasoline Alley Antiques
181 N.E. Broad St.
910/692-9147

Thrifty Cobbler
240 N.W. Broad St.
910/692-3250

Down Memory Lane Cllbls.
795 S.W. Broad St.
910/693-1118

58 SOUTHPORT

Curiosity Shop
113 N. Howe St.
910/457-6118

Waterfront Gifts & Antiques
117 S. Howe St.
910/457-6496

Second Hand Rose
702 N. Howe St.
910/457-9475

Glass Menagerie Antiques
1208 N. Howe St.
910/457-9188

Antique Mall
108 E. Moore St.
910/457-4982

Northrop Antiques Mall
111 E. Moore St.
910/457-9569

59 STATESVILLE

Duck Creek Antiques & Cllbls.
2731 Amity Hill Rd.
704/873-3825

Antique Market of Statesville
114 N. Center St.
704/871-0056

Westmoreland Antqs. & Cllbls.
117 S. Center St.
704/871-1896

Shiloh Antique Mini Mall
Sharon School Rd.
704/872-2244

Riverfront Antique Mall
1441 Wilkesboro Rd.
704/873-9770

Favorite Places To Eat

Cracker Barrel Old Country Store
I-40 & Rt. 21, Exit 151
704/878-0366

60 WARSAW

The Squire's Vintage Inn
748 NC Hwy. 24 & 50
910/296-1831
Weekend Specials For Two Available
Call for Regular Rates

Directions: Located just off I-40 on Hwy. 24.

The Squire's Vintage Inn is located in the heart of Dublin County in a rural, intimate setting surrounded by nature. Beautiful gardens and lakes adorn the property while winding brick sidewalks and rustic paths, flanked by tall pines and towering oak trees, provide the perfect walk through nature.

Twenty four guests rooms are available at the Inn with one king size Bridal Suite. A continental breakfast is served to all guest in their room or can be enjoyed in the sunken patio near the fountain shaded by pines.

The Peasant House, a two-bedroom, 1 1/2 bath cottage with living room and kitchen, is also available by night, week or month. The country interior decor, brick patio, and fenced yard provide a setting for a pleasant and memorable stay.

(Also, see The Country Squire Restaurant below)

The Country Squire Restaurant
748 NC Hwy. 24 & 50
910/296-1727
Lunch: Mon.-Fri. 11:30-2, Sun. 12-2
Dinner: 5:30-until ?

The Country Squire Restaurant located next door to the Squire's Vintage Inn has been serving wonderful cuisine since 1961. Owner, Iris Lennon, has a unique way of making your dining experience a memorable one. Iris has her roots in Edinburgh, Scotland; however, she has lived many years along the coastline of Ayr where the beloved Scottish poet, Robert Burns was born. Endowed with the natural charm of her Scottish ancestry, she makes each guest feel special.

The spacious "Squire" (seating 456) creates the impression of outdoor living as decor changes with the season. The restaurant is divided into themed room settings such as the Jesters Court. In the medieval period, the court jester was summoned to entertain the manor lord and his guests around tables ladened with the best from the manor kitchens and cellars. The Jester's Court reflects this full tradition of warmth and conviviality through its rich exposed beams and traditional pine floors. The Mead Hall, a commodious room reflects the regions earliest English heritage with its brick floors, murals, tapestries, rough sawn paneling, and soft gas lighting.

Old cupboards, antiques, and fireplaces are strewn throughout the restaurant, creating a colonial dramatic setting. To every serving of food; romance, history, legend and atmosphere from all over the world has been blended. The Country Squire always welcomes guests with reflections of good taste.

61 WAXHAW

Red Barn Gallery
103 S. Church St.
704/843-1309

The Junction
100 E. South Main St.
704/843-3350

Byrum's Antiques
101 Main St.
704/843-4702

Waxhaw Antique Mart
101 W. South Main St.
704/843-3075

Ding-A Ling Antiques
103 E. North Main St.
704/843-2181

Farmhouse Antiques
103 Main St.
704/843-5500

The Rusty Hinge
107 S. Main St.
704/843-4777

Sherlock's
108 E. South Main St.
704/843-3433

Traders Path Antiques
516 E. South Main St.
704/843-2497

Victorian Lady
8511 Prince Valiant Dr.
704/843-2917

62 WAYNESVILLE

Magnolia Antique Mall
322 Branner Ave.
704/456-5054

Collector's Corner
810 Delwood Ave.
704/452-2737

Slow Lane Antiques
71 N. Main St.
704/456-3682

Antiques of Today & Tomorrow
241 N. Main St.
704/456-8832

Thad Woods Antiques Mall
780 Waynesville Plaza
704/456-3298

63 WILMINGTON

Floyd's Used Furn. Antiques
2230 Carolina Beach Rd.
910/763-8702

Good Stuff
5318 Carolina Beach Rd.
910/452-0091

Michael Moore Antiques
20 S. Front St.
910/763-0300

Antiques of Old Wilmington
25 S. Front St.
910/763-6011

Golden Goose
27 S. Front St.
910/341-7969

About Time Antiques
30 N. Front St.
910/762-9902

Unique Americana
127 N. Front St.
910/251-8859

Betty B's Trash to Treasure
143 N. Front St.
910/763-3703

Virginia Jennewein
143 N. Front St.
910/763-3703

Antiquity Ltd. of Wilmington
1305 N. Front St.
910/763-5800

Antiques & Cllbls. on Kerr
830 S. Kerr Ave.
910/791-7917

Cape Fear Antique Center
1606 Market St.
910/763-1837

Thieves Market
6766 Market St.
910/392-9194

Antiques & More
6792 Market St.
910/392-3633

Sentimental Journey Antiques
6794 Market St.
910/790-5211

Perry's Emporium
3500 Oleander Dr.
910/392-6721

Seven Seas Trading
115 S. Water St.
910/762-3022

McAllister & Solomon
4402 Wrightsville Ave.
910/350-0189

64 WILSON

Fulford's Antique Warehouse
320 Barnes Street South
919/243-7727
Open Mon.-Fri. 8-5, Sat. 8-3

Directions: Take I-95 at Hwy. 264 exit. Follow into Wilson. Continue to Lodge Street taking a left. The shop is then on the right at the corner of Lodge and Barnes

Streets.

Discover the treasures in the old Coca-Cola building now Fulford's Antique Warehouse. With 28 years of family experience, the Fulfords have stuffed 67,000-square-feet of their warehouse with an unimaginably enormous and varied collection of American, French, and English furniture, turn-of-the-century lighting, wrought iron furniture, tiger maple chests as well as a quaint selection of smalls. Across the street in the workshop, furniture repair and refinishing takes place.

Fulford's Antiques
2001 U.S. Hwy. 301 South
929/243-5581

Directions: I-95 to Hwy. 264 exit. Follow into Wilson, turn right on Forrest Hills Road at Golden Corral; continue to 301, turn left, next stop light on right.

If you don't find what you're looking for at Fulford's Antique Warehouse, then at Fulford's Antiques (2nd location) you most assuredly will. Located in the old John Deere building, this shop offers an additional 7,000-square-feet for "plowing around."

Miss Betty's Bed and Breakfast Inn
600 West Nash Street
919/243-4447 or 1-800-258-2058

Wilson, "Antique Capital of North Carolina," is home to Miss Betty's Bed and Breakfast Inn which has been selected as one of the "Best Places to Stay in the South." Four exquisitely restored homes provide guests lodging amidst Victorian elegance in downtown's historic setting. Browse for antiques at Miss Betty's or any of the other numerous shops in the area. The tranquil atmosphere of Wilson in eastern North Carolina is ideal for enjoying golf, tennis, or swimming. Don't dare leave town without sampling the famous eastern Carolina barbecue.

Albury Eagles Gallery Inc.
104 Douglas St.
919/237-9299

Bobby Langston Antiques
2620 U.S. Hwy. 301 S
919/237-8224

Antique Barn & Hobby Shop
2810 Forest Hills Rd. SW
919/237-6778

Greater Wilson Antique Market
4345 U.S. Hwy. 264
919/237-0402

Jean's Olde Store & Antiques
2007 U.S. Hwy. 301 S
919/234-7998

Marsha Stancil Antiques
2020 U.S. Hwy. 301 SW
919/399-2093

Boone's Antiques Inc.
2014 U.S. Hwy. 301 SW
919/237-1508

Boykin Antiques
2013 Hwy. 301 S
919/237-1700

Favorite Places To Eat

Cracker Barrel Old Country Store
I-95 & U.S. 264, Exit 121
919/234-7600

65 WINSTON SALEM

Pearl and Gearhart Antiques
101 N. Broad St.
910/725-2102

Extraordinary Goods
1000 Brookstown Ave.
910/773-1220

Brookstown Antiques
1004 Brookstown Ave.
910/723-5956

Memoirs Ltd.
1148 Burke St.
910/631-9595

Brass Bed Antique Company
451 W. End Blvd.
910/724-3461

Snob Consignment Shop
465 W. End Blvd.
910/724-2547

Karat Shop Inc.
420 Jonestown Rd.
910/768-3336

Cross Keys Antiques
468 Knollwood St.
910/760-3585

Timeless Treasures
3510 S. Main St.
910/785-2273

Larry Laster Old & Rare Books
2416 Maplewood Ave.
910/724-7544

Country Road Antiques
901 S. Marshall St.
910/659-7555

Marshall St. Antique Mall
901 S. Marshall St.
910/724-9007

Kim Taylor & Co.
114 Oakwood Dr.
910/722-8503

Reynolda Antique Gallery
114 Reynolda Village
910/748-0741

Village Green Antiques
114A Reynolda Village
910/721-0860

Alice Cunningham Interiors
3120 Robinhood Rd.
910/724-9667

Winston-Salem Emporium
217 W. 6th St.
910/722-7277

Oxford Antiques & Gifts
129 S. Stratford Rd.
910/723-7080

D & B Antiques
2840 Waughtown St.
190/788-4309

Notes

North Dakota

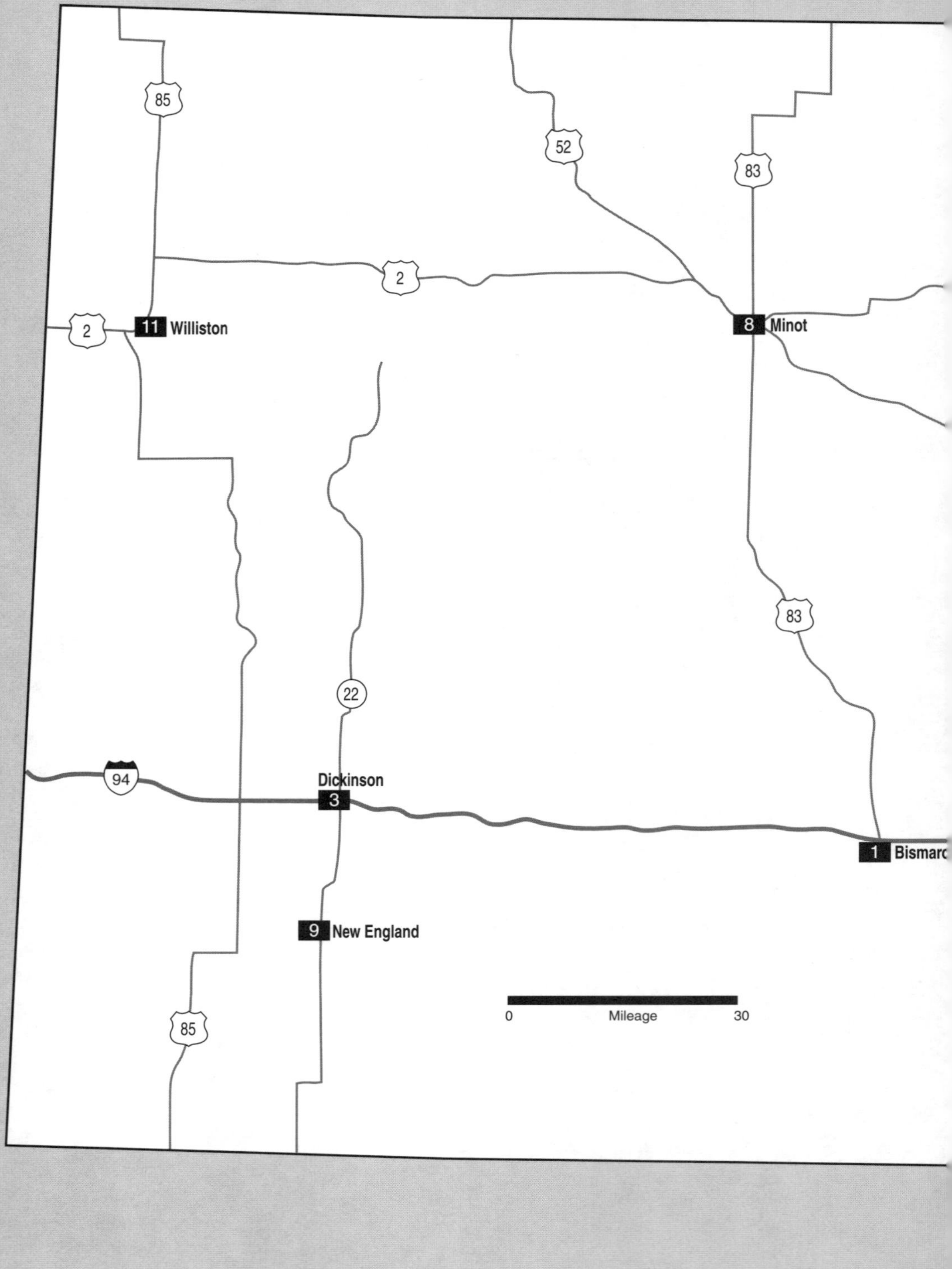

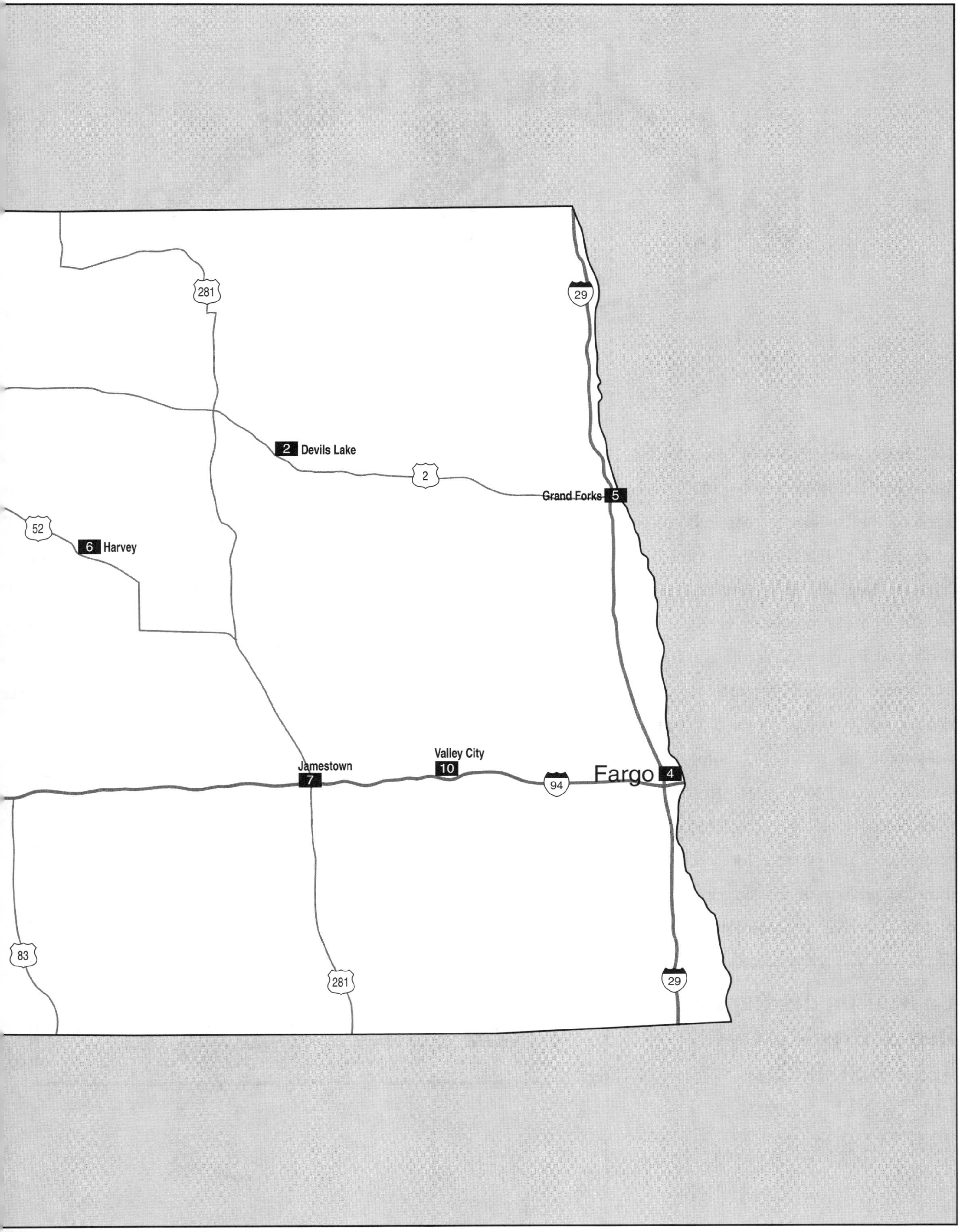

281
29
2 Devils Lake
2
Grand Forks 5
52
6 Harvey
Valley City
Jamestown
10
7
Fargo 4
94
83
281
29

La Maison des Papillons

The House of Butterflies

Bed & Breakfast

La Maison des Papillons Bed and Breakfast occupies a house built in 1899 on the Historic 8th Street South of Fargo. It is listed on the National Historic Registry. If it could talk it would share many stories of the history of Fargo such as the fire that consumed most of downtown and raged only blocks away. When walking in the front door, visitors are struck with the warmth and friendliness of days gone by. The cozy grandeur of the ground floor and the intimate privacy of the second floor bedrooms give a restful welcome invitation to the weary of mind, body, and soul.

La Maison des Papillons has four guest rooms (three of which are ready for occupancy) on the second floor. Each room is named after a butterfly that is native to North Dakota. The Monarch is a double room with a half bath located on the north side of the house for lots of quiet. The Swallowtail i double room with a beautiful stain glass window and bay window. T Fritillery is a single room overlooki the front yard and nearby park. T Admiral room will be open for use 1998. All rooms share a large o fashioned bathroom occupied by a ca iron tub/shower with clawed feet.

La Maison des Papillons
Bed & Breakfast
423 8th St. South
Fargo, ND
701/232-2041

1 BISMARCK

Antique Interiors
200 W. Main Avenue
701/224-9551
Open 10:30-5 Mon.-Sat., 1-4 Sun.

Directions: Downtown Bismarck

Located in the Historic International Harvester Building, this shop specializes in interior design through the use of antiques. Fabrics to compliment any decor are also available.

Wizard Of Odds 'N Ends
1523 E. Thayer Avenue
701/222-4175
Hours: 10-5 Mon.-Sat.

Directions: Find this shop near downtown Bismarck.

"We're off to see the wizard, the wonderful Wizard of Odd 'N Ends." Located near downtown Bismarck, this shop offers such a stunning array of antiques and collectibles, you'll think you "really" are in the Emerald City.

Antique and Coin Exchange
722 Kirkwood Mall
701/222-8859
Open Mon.-Fri. 10-9, Sat. 10-6, Sun. 12-6

Directions: Exit I-94 at State Street. Travel south on State Street. It curves to Boulevard Avenue. Go south on 7th Street to Kirkwood Mall. Shop is located in the mall.

Specializing in "pack in your car" antiques. Large selection of smalls including dishes, coins, jewelry, etc.

Antique Gallery
1514 E. Thayer Ave.
701/223-8668

Downtown Furniture Co.
117 N. 4th St.
701/255-6061

Antique Mall
200 W. Main Ave.
701/221-2594

Le Fabearge
200 W. Main Ave.
701/221-2594

Bismarck 2nd Hand Store
1612 E. Main Ave.
701/224-9467

Wood & Tiques
1514 E. Thayer Ave.
701/255-4912

Country Home Sweet Home
1144 Summit Blvd.
701/223-4897

2 DEVILS LAKE

Garden Gate
410 4th St.
701/662-6388

Antique Exchange
By Appointment
701/662-8801

3 DICKINSON

Carol's Antiques & Collectibles
14 1st St. W
701/225-4509

Barry's 2nd H "antiques"
2221 Main St. S
701/225-3701

Jackie's Antiques & Collectibles
1331 Villard E
701/227-1027

4 FARGO

Bonanzaville
West Highway 10 (Main Avenue)
701/282-2822
Open 7 days a week June 1-Nov. 1; call for museum hours

Directions: Tune into 530 AM radio for specific information.

Relive the pioneer days in Bonanzaville. Antique cars, planes, farm machinery, school, church, stores, log and sod homes, dolls, Indian artifacts, museum and much, much more.

La Maison des Papillons Bed and Breakfast
423 8th Street South
701/232-2041
Open year round
Rates $45-55

Directions: From west on I-94: Take Exit 343 to Main Avenue (downtown), follow Main Avenue to 8th Street. Take a right on 5th Avenue south. From north or south on I-29: Take Exit 65 to Main Avenue; once on Main Avenue follow previous instructions. From east on I-94: Take Exit 1 A (in Moorehead, Minnesota); follow 8th Street taking a right on 5th Avenue south.

For specific information see review this section.

Baker's Place Antiques
114 Broadway
701/235-5334

Lifetime Antique Furnishings
18 8th St.
701/235-3144

Grandpa's Antiques & Cllbls.
3041 Main Ave.
701/237-4569

Fargo Antique Mall
14 Roberts St.
701/235-1145

North Dakota Antiques Mall
1024 2nd Ave. N
701/237-4423

Gramma's Antiques & Cllbls.
314 10th St. N
701/239-4465

Market Square Mall
1450 25h St.
701/239-9814

A Place Called Traditions
1201 S. University Dr.
701/280-1864

5 GRAND FORKS

Back Porch Antiques and Gifts
205 DeMers Avenue
701/746-9369
Open Tue.-Sat. 10-6

Directions: From I-29, take the DeMers Avenue exit (140). Go east on DeMers Avenue 3 1/2 miles. The shop is 1 block from Red River.

The quaint name of the shop, Back Porch Antiques and Gifts, reveals a cozy, casual atmosphere. Potted red geraniums greet you at the door. Inside you will find a good representation of antique furniture, from headboards to foot stools; in oak, mahogany, walnut, cherry and other woods. Various periods and styles are included; such as Victorian, primitive and Art Deco. You will also discover antique linens, glassware, kitchen items, sewing implements and accessories. Fishing collectibles will catch the fancy of anglers. You can take home unusual gifts and decorative accessories as well.

City Center Antique Mall
16 City Center Mall
701/780-9076

Sannes Antiques
119 DeMers Ave.
701/772-0541

Boomerang Antiques
317 Kittson Ave.
701/772-6624

Gloria's Antiques & Collectibles
116 S. 3rd St.
701/775-7581

Yesteryears Antiques
317 S. 3rd St.
701/772-9244

Victoria's Rose Antique Shop
214 DeMers Avenue
701/772-3690

6 HARVEY

Penny Pinchers
604 Brewster St. E
701/324-2551

7 JAMESTOWN

The city of Jamestown is known as the Buffalo City, thanks to its 60-ton giant, "The World's Largest Buffalo," a sculpture standing watch on a hill over I-94. Two dozen live buffalo roam the draws below this huge statue, and the National Buffalo Museum shares the high ground at the Frontier Village Complex.

Jamestown is the birthplace for some famous folk: torch singer Peggy Lee, Anne Carlsen, renowned for her work with the disabled, and the best-selling author of all time, writer Louis L'Amour.

Treasure Chest
213 1st Ave. S
701/251-2891
Open Mon. 10-7, Tue-Sat.10-5, or by appointment.

Directions: Exit 2nd Jamestown Exit off I-94. Travel north on 1st Ave. South.

The name given to this antique shop could be considered synonymous with the name used by its former occupants in 1906, First Federal Savings "Bank." The Treasure Chest, as it is called today, holds a wealth of valuable antiques and collectibles, such as, Roseville, Rosemeade, Hull, Carnival, primitives and more.

Antique Attic
219 1st Ave. S
701/252-6733
Open Mon.- Fri.12:30-5:30, Sat. 10-4

Directions: Exit 2nd Jamestown exit off I-94. Travel north on 1st Ave. South

There are 42 dealers offering, oak furniture, fine china, lamps, books & catalogs, fine glassware, dolls, linen & silver, as well as one of a kind items.

North Dakota

On The Countryside
Hwy. 281 S & 25th St. SW
701/252-8941
Open Mon.- Fri. 10-9, Sat.10-6, Sun. 12-5.

Directions: I-94 take 2nd exit, travel south to 25th St. and.take a right.
On The Countryside specializes in antique country furnishings, primarily cupboards. Other antique pieces along with decorative accessories are also available here. The Espresso Bar serves pastries, soups, salads and ice cream.

Wilma's Antiques
221 7th St. NE
701/252-5145
Open Mon. 10-7; Tue. - Sat. 10-5 or by appointment

Directions: Exit I-94 at Jamestown. Take Main to 7th NE
Wilma's Antiques offers a large variety of antiques and collectibles specializing in everything old and wonderful.

Antiques & Uniques
Park Plaza Mall
Home Phone after 5 p.m.: 701/252-6682
(No phone in shop)

8 MINOT

Home Sweet Home
103 4th Street NW
701/852-5604
Open 9:30-5 Mon.-Sat., 12-4 Sun.

Directions: Situated near downtown Minot.
Antiques in a historic setting. Home Sweet Home is located in an old house built in 1899. They offer "everything" (as the owner says) in the way of antiques and collectibles.

Granny's Antiques & Gifts
16 Main Street S.
701/852-3644
Open Mon.-Sat. 10-5:30

Directions: Granny's is located in downtown Minot.
Granny's Antiques offers furniture, glassware and collectibles along with a nice selection of Victorian items.

Dakota Antiques
8 4th St. NE
701/838-1150

Downtown Mall
108 Main St. S
701/852-9084

Mary Norton Antiques
RR 4
701/838-3233

9 NEW ENGLAND

Country Treasures
Highway 22
701/579-4746
Hours: lives on premises and is open most of the time

Directions: Located on Highway 22 on the east end of New England.
This small, quaint shop specializes in quality smalls. Cookie jars, carnival, depression and pressed glass are represented here.

Main Attractions
709 Main Street
701/579-4419
Hours: 10-4 Mon.-Sat.

Directions: Exit from Highway 22 into New England. Located on Main Street.
At this shop, the "Main Attractions" are antique furniture, cookie jars, carnival glass and Dakota pottery.

10 VALLEY CITY

Grandma's Attic
304 Central Avenue
701/845-1441
Hours: 9-5:30 Mon.-Fri.

Directions: Grandma's Attic is found in downtown Valley City.
Grandma's Attic offers a nice collection of antiques and accents for all of your antique and decorating needs. Grandma's has another shop located in the Market Square Mall in Fargo.

E & S Antiques
148 E. Main Street
701/845-0369
Hours: 9-5 Mon.-Sat.

Directions: Located in downtown Valley City.
Located in the old 1890s Opera House in downtown Valley City, this shop prides itself on offering exceptional antique furnishings and accessories.

Unique Antiques
164 E. Main St.
701/845-3549

Kathleen's Kurio Kabinet
114 3rd St.
701/845-3569

11 WILLISTON

Collector's Corner
115 2nd St. W
701/572-9313

Larry Lynne Antiques
715 3rd Ave. E
701/572-3642

Notes

Welcome to

Ravenna

Shop, Dine,
Stay the Night

- The Added Touch
- Bello House Deli
- Copper Kettle Antiques
- Farnsworht Antiques
- Hickory Way Antiques
- Timeless Treasures
- Edie's Restaurant
- Patricia's
- Family Tradition
- Rocking Horse Inn
- The Upstairs Emporium

C & M Collectibles

Antiques Accessories & Gifts
One-of-a-Kind Collectibles
Unique, high quality and hard to find items

603 South Second St.
Bus. Phone/Fax (614) 622-6776
Coshocton

29

Drackett Designs & Antiques

9441 Main St.
(513) 561-2627
Montgomery

65

Fields of Home

Guest House

Bed & Breakfast
7278 County Rd. 201
330-674-7152

Millersburg

64

Ohio

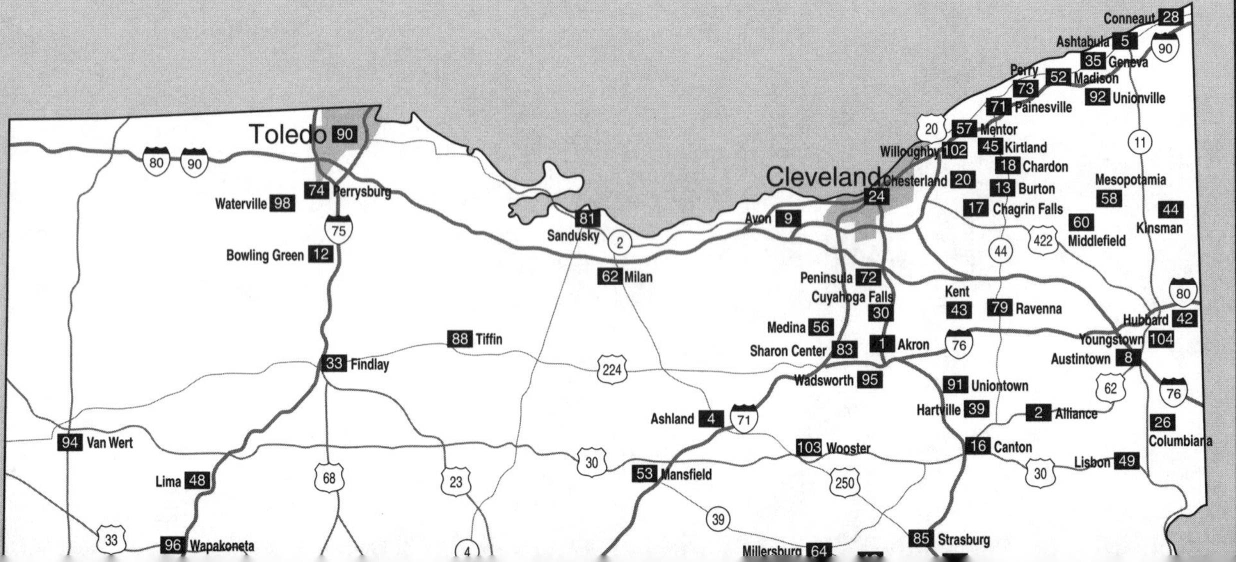

Bed & Breakfast

Quigley House

100 Market Street
New Richmond
513-553-6318

68

VISIT
AMISH
COUNTRY
in Historic
Millersburg

Yesteryear Antiques & Fine Art
268 S. Fourth Street
Columbus
27

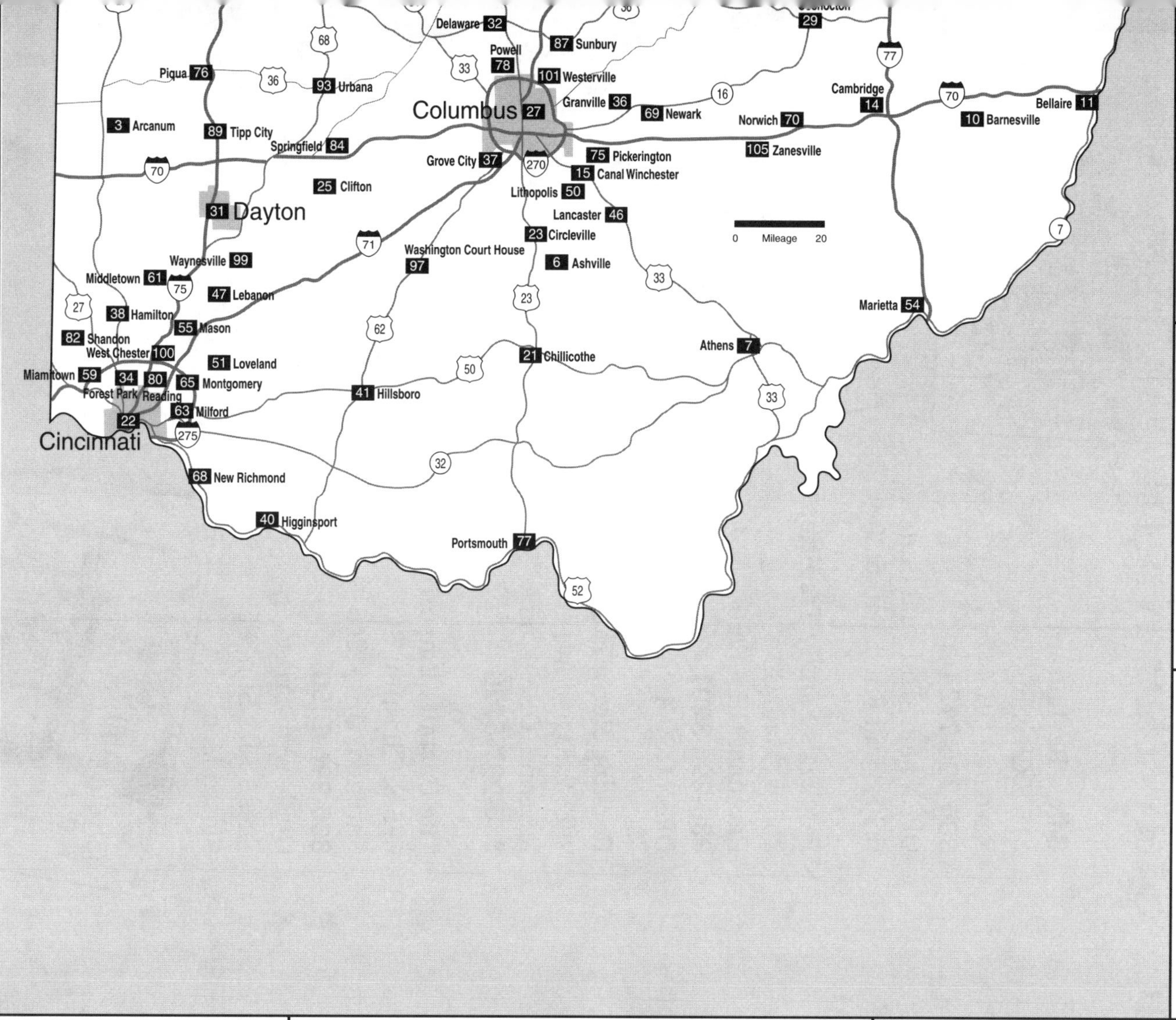

Hidden Treasures
ANTIQUES
8825 Cincinnati-Dayton Rd.
(513) 779-9908
West Chester
100

THE PORCH HOUSE
Circa 1903
A Turn-of-the Century
Bed and Breakfast
Granville
36

Lamborn's Studio
5,000 sq. ft. Gallery
19 West St.
800-244-5567
Athens
7

THE IRON NAIL
Collectibles
Crafts & Herbs
Canal Winchester
15

The Refurniture Pod
Barn Full
of Antiques
16416 U.S. RT. 50 EAST
(614) 592-1949
Athens
7

J. DUGAN
OHIO RIVER HOUSE
Bed & Breakfast & Antiques
"built in 1830"
4 Brown St. • 937-375-4395
Higginsport
40

Miller Haus
Bed & Breakfast Inn
A perfect place for *Peace & Quiet...*
Charm
19

NORTON'S ANTIQUES, etc.
Jim and Nancy Norton
State Rt. 250 in New Pittsburg
9423 Ashland Road
(330) 262-6439
Wooster
103

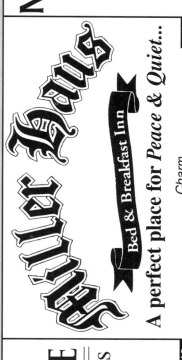

Ravenna: A haven for antiquers

Ravenna, Ohio, is a town of antique shops, bed and breakfasts, and restaurants. Start on one end of Main Street and work you way, shop by shop, through town, occasionally taking a side street to reach a special place.

Begin at **Copper Kettle Antiques.** Spend some time admiring the tin ceilings and maple floors of this 1840 building. It still has its original central staircase, giving easy access to its 38 dealers in 6,000 square feet of space on two floors. You can browse through furniture, glassware, china, pottery, advertising memorabilia, Victrolas, primitives and tools, among other collectibles. Then wander next door to **Hickory Way Antiques**. They carry a wide variety of jewelry, furniture, paper items, glassware, leaded-glass lamps, hand-painted lamp shades, Victorian lamps, primitives, and tools. Next is **Farnsworth Antiques Associates**, a 12-dealer mall featuring pottery, upscale furniture, lighting items, and a general mixture.

Fourth on your list should be **Timeless Treasures**. Owners Linda and Jeff Nicolaus specialize in glass and china, and walnut, cherry, and mahogany furniture from the mid-1800s through the 1940s, which is beautifully displayed in room settings making the shop one of the prettiest you've ever entered. Jeff designs and builds the mantels and shelves utilized in the shop and will take special requests to fill individual needs.

By this time you will probably be ready for food, so you can start with **Patricia's Family Tradition**, just down the street on Main. They serve breakfast, lunch, dinner, sandwiches, and home-baked goods at reasonable prices. Or, you can hold on a little longer and make your way to Prospect Street and **The Bello House Deli**. They offer delicious soups, salads, and special sub sandwiches, served in an Italian Villa type setting. The atmosphere is friendly and the customers are treated like family.

If you want a slightly more robust fare, visit **Edie's Restaurant** on Chestnut Street. Homestyle meals are their specialty, such as stuffed peppers, baked chicken, and baked fish for lunch and dinner. They serve the usually desired breakfast items and offer a Sunday buffet. Pricing is attractive to families.

The Upstairs Emporium is your next stop. Located on the second floor of the Ohio Trader's Mart, it is a Victorian style shop featuring one of a kind decorator items beautifully displayed amidst silk flowers, concrete statuary, and fountains. The Emporium also features a year round Holiday Shoppe overflowing with Christmas items. Move on and shop for a while at **The Added Touch**, located within an old house whose rooms are filled with the house specialty—the unusual in china, glass, and furniture.

Your final stop might be at the R**ocking Horse Inn**, where you can collapse for the night in comfort and homelike surroundings in one of its four guest rooms, complete with a private bath. This bed and breakfast sits on land that was a part of the Western Reserve and the original plat of Ravenna. After buying the land in 1867, Rev. Edward Hubbell decided to build a grand home in the then-popular Stick style. Unfortunately, the construction got out of hand and was not completed until 1875 by Quincy Cook, who also built the mill on Main Street known today as Babcock Feed Mill, the oldest continuing operation in Ravenna. Following the death of Quincy's wife Charlotte in 1920, the house had several owners. In 1954, it was purchased by Immaculate Conception Church, and the Dominican nuns used it as a convent in conjunction with the old church. As it became too expensive to maintain, the church sold the property in 1985 for use as a private nursing home for ambulatory elders. The present owners, Jim and Carolyn Leffler, purchased the property in 1991 and opened it as the Rocking Horse Bed and Breakfast.

Ohio

1 AKRON

Busy Akron gave the world Quaker Oats, Goodyear blimps, The All-American Soap Box Derby and, of course, rubber. Northeast Ohio's renowned "Rubber City" began as a nineteenth-century canal town. Within 100 years, it was a factory boom town. Dr. B. F. Goodrich's modest fire-hose plant had quietly launched Akron's rubber industry, but the burgeoning popularity of automobiles was assuring its prosperity.

Annex Antqs. & Consign. Shop
1262 S. Cleveland Massillon Rd.
330/666-5544

Wizard of Odds II
1265 S. Cleveland Massillon
330/666-1958

Antiques of Copley
1463 S. Cleveland Massillon Rd.
330/666-8170

Nanny's Antiques
125 Ghent Rd.
330/865-1250

Yellow Creek Barn
794 Wye Road
330/666-8843

Dreurey Lane Antiques
7831 Main St.
330/882-6165

Cuyahoga Valley Antiques
929 N. Main St.
330/434-3333

Coventry Antiques & Crafts
3358 Manchester Rd.
330/644-7474

Market Antiques
439 W. Market St.
330/762-7643

Stagecoach Antiques
449 W. Market St.
330/762-5422

Jerome's
451 W. Market St.
330/535-5700

West Hill Antiques
461 W. Market St.
330/762-6633

Courtyard Antiques
467 W. Market St.
330/253-3336

Fish Market Antq. Cntr. Inc.
474 W. Market St.
330/535-7799

Favorite Places To Eat

Cracker Barrel Old Country Store
I-77 & Rothrock Rd./Rt. 18, Exit 137
330/666-0279

2 ALLIANCE

Memory Lane Antiques
20515 Alliance Sebring Rd.
330/823-8568

Alliance Antiques
319 E. Main St.
330/821-0606

Attic Treasures Antqs. & More
248 E. Main St.
330/823-8920

Towne Hall Antiques
12347 Marlboro Ave. NE
330/935-0114

Mack's Barn Antiques
14665 Ravenna Ave. NE
330/935-2746

Bus Stop Antiques
6727 Waterloo Rd.
330/947-2737

3 ARCANUM

Smith's Antiques Store
109 W. George St.
513/692-8540

Stubblefield Antiques
112 W. George St.
513/692-8882

Staley's Antiques & Woodworking
7 N. Sycamore St.
513/692-8050

4 ASHLAND

The Gleaner
1488 Ashland Cty Rd. #995
419/281-2849

Antiques on Main
143 W. Main St.
419/289-8599

Willow Creek Antiques
1250 U.S. Hwy. 42
419/289-9233

5 ASHTABULA

C J's This N That
4616 Main Ave.
216/992-9479

Country Cottage
3616 North Ridge E
216/992-9620

Trash & Treasures Barn
5020 N. Ridge Rd. W
216/998-2946

The Moses Antique Mall
4135 State St.
216/992-5556

The Way We Were
1837 Walnut Blvd.
216/964-7576

6 ASHVILLE

The Barn
5201 S. Bloomfield Royalton
614/983-2238

7 ATHENS

Lamborn's Studio and Custom Framing

19 West State Street
614/593-6744; 1-800-224-5567
Open Mon.-Fri., 10:30-5:30; Sat., 10:30-5; Sun., 1-4

Directions: Downtown Athens

Located in a historically renovated building from the 1920s, Lamborn's offers fine antiques and collectibles scattered throughout the 5000-square-foot gallery that also features sculpture, prints, cards, stationery and local memorabilia.

Quality glassware, pottery and many fine old furniture pieces are available. Local artists exhibit hand painted furniture and tiles, as well as jewelry made from antique beads and glass. Photography buffs will enjoy the photography studio, which houses a private collection of old cameras. This very unique store is tucked away in the downtown area and is within walking distance of many shops and eateries.

The Refurniture Pod

16416 U.S. Rt. 50 East
614/592-1949
Hours vary, but appointments can be made by calling Lamborn's Studio at 614/593-6744.

Located just 6 miles from Athens, the Refurniture Pod is really an old barn built back in 1917. Inside, it's a furniture stripping and repair business—and a soon-to-be retail store specializing in furniture and collectibles.

As you might expect with this type of business, the hours of operation vary, but appointments may be made by calling Lamborn's Studio at the above number.

Second Rose
90 N. Court St.
614/592-4999

Random House
12 W. State St.
614/592-2464

Canaanville Antiques
16060 U.S. Hwy. 50
614/593-5105

8 AUSTINTOWN

Favorite Places To Eat

Cracker Barrel Old Country Store
I-80 & Rt. 46, Exit 223
216/652-7227

9 AVON

Country Heirs
35800 Detroit Rd.
216/937-5544

Country Side Antiques
36290 Detroit Rd.
216/934-4228

Jameson Homestead Antiques
36675 Detroit Rd.
216/934-6977

Woods & Goods
36840 Detroit Rd.
216/934-6669

Antique Gallery of Avon
36923 Detroit Rd.
216/934-4797

Sweet Caroline's
37300 Detroit Rd.
216/934-4797

Country Store
2536 Stoney Ridge Rd.
216/934-6119

10 BARNESVILLE

This Old House

118 North Chestnut Street
614/425-4444
Open Mon.-Sat., 10-5, Sun., Noon-5

Directions: Situated 6 miles south of I-70 at Exit 202, midway between Cambridge, Ohio and Wheeling, West Virginia.

This Old House, formerly known as the Smith House, was originally built in 1885 for Eli Moore, owner of the once-popular Moore's Opera House. A few years later, financial reverses forced him to sell to the Murphy family. The Murphy daughter married Carl Smith; thus the home became widely referred to as the Smith House.

This ten-room, Italianate-style brick home, listed on the National Register of Historic Places, features beautiful oak woodwork, fireplaces and ornate fretwood of the period. It provides the perfect setting for the presentation of fine antiques and gifts, such as pine furniture, lamps and shades, braided and woven rugs, Amish pictures and other wonderful decorative accessories.

Antiques on the Main
108 N. Chestnut St.
614/425-3406

Barnesville Antique Mall
202 N. Chestnut St.
614/425-2435

East Main Flea Market
511 E. Main St.
614/425-4310

11 BELLAIRE

Imperial Plaza
29th and Belmont Street
614/676-8300
Open Mon.-Sat., 9-5; Sun., 8-4

Directions: Follow Ohio Rt. 7 south to 26th Street exit. 3 miles from I-470, 4 miles from I-70.

The Imperial Glass Factory was founded in 1901 with the goal of becoming the "most modern glass factory in America." The first glass was made for the mass market: jelly glasses with tin lids, pressed tumblers with horseshoe and star designs on the bottom, and assorted tableware.

The company later expanded and produced Nuart iridescent ware and imitation "Tiffany" style lampshades. Later, Nucut Crystal, handpressed reproductions of early English cut glass pieces, was made.

Hard times plagued the company during the Great Depression, but the Quaker Oats Company saved the company by ordering a premium piece which became the forerunner to the 'Cape Cod' pattern.

In 1937, the famous Candlewick pattern was introduced. Imperial Glass was chosen by the Metropolitan Museum of Art, the Smithsonian Institution and Old Sturbridge Village to produce authentic reproductions of famous glass items for sale to discriminating collectors.

Today, though Imperial is no longer producing glassware, it has a new lease on life through the efforts of Maroon Enterprises, Inc.., the new owners. Businesses are invited to locate within the complex of Imperial Plaza. Below is a sampling of some of the shops you will find inside Imperial Plaza:

Heritage House: Handmade quilts, baskets, braided rugs, plus other samples of handicrafts people would consider themselves fortunate to own are found here. Often crafts people can be observed at work preparing the many items made on the premises.

Glass Museum: On display in this museum are many, many authentic early glass pieces from a great number of manufacturers. In the Ohio Valley, glass making thrived into the 1970s. Museum exhibits showcase local manufacturers and other famous makers.

Escott's Gallery: In addition to old and antique furniture, this gallery sells oil paintings, watercolors, sculptures in wood, bronze, terra cotta. Located in Escott's Gallery is Imperial Furniture Stripping/Refinishing. Repair services encompass resilvering mirrors, veneer, hand stripping and refinishing.

Flea Market: Each Sunday from 8:00 a.m. until 4:00 p.m. people flock to Imperial Plaza for the flea market. The selling area is a hefty 40,000 square feet. Many bargains and treasures lurk throughout the flea market.

12 BOWLING GREEN

Antique Acres
19901 N. Dixie Hwy.
419/373-0046

13 BURTON

Gordon's Antiques
Rt. 87-On The Square
216/834-1426

Spring Street Antiques
13822 Spring Street
216/834-0155

14 CAMBRIDGE

Judy's Antiques
422 S. 9th St.
614/432-5855

Tenth St. Antique Mall
127 S. 10th St.
614/432-3364

Guernsey Antique Mall
623 Wheeling Ave.
614/432-2570

Penny Court
637 Wheeling Ave.
614/432-4369

Country Bits & Pieces
700 Wheeling Avenue
614/432-7241

Favorite Places To Eat

Cracker Barrel Old Country Store
I-70 & Rt. 209, Exit 178
614/439-4599

15 CANAL WINCHESTER

The Iron Nail Collectibles, Crafts & Herbs
47 West Waterloo Street
614/837-6047
Open Mon.-Fri., 12-5:30; Sat., 11-5:30

Directions: Located 10 minutes from downtown Columbus, Ohio, from I-70 East, take Rt. 33 East to Lancaster. Exit at Canal Winchester-Gender Road. Then take a left on Waterloo Road across from Winchester Shopping Mall. Another two miles to downtown Canal Winchester. The shop is one block west of High and Waterloo in a two-story brick house.

This very diversified shop derives its name from owner, Peggy Eisnaugle, whose last name means "Iron Nail" in Dutch-German.

The selection of antique headboards, mantelpieces, chests, chairs, and tables available here are sure to impress the discriminating antique shopper. The stock, however, is varied enough to meet the needs of those looking for more collectible items as well.

You'll find Rex Bears and designer dolls by Virginia Turner. Interestingly, The Iron Nail also carries a line of fresh herbal products, edible and otherwise, many of which are from Peggy's own garden.

Canal Country Coffee Mill
154 N. High St.
614/837-4932

16 CANTON

Somewhere in Time Antiques
3823 Cleveland Ave. NW
330/493-0372

Rt. 43 Antique Mall
8340 Kent Ave. NE
330/494-9268

Oldies But Goodies
101 Nassau St. W
330/488-8008

Treasure Trove Antiques
4313 Tuscarawas St. W
330/477-9099

Andy's Antiques
5064 Tuscarawas St. W
330/477-3859

Favorite Places To Eat N. Canton

Cracker Barrel Old Country Store
I-77 & Portage St., Exit 111
330/966-1144

17 CHAGRIN FALLS

Bell Corner Shop
5197 Chillicothe Rd.
216/338-1101

Chagrin Valley Antiques
15605 Chillicothe Rd.
216/338-1800

Market
49 W. Orange St.
216/247-0733

Chagrin Antiques Limited
516 E. Washington St.
216/247-1080

Martine's Antiques
516 E. Washington St.
216/247-6421

18 CHARDON

Antiques on the Square
101 Main St.
216/286-1912

Steeplechase Antiques
111 Main St.
216/286-7473

Olden Dayes Shoppe
129 Main St.
216/285-3307

Elaine's Antqs. & Stained Glass
11970 Ravenna
216/285-8041

Bostwick Antiques
310 South St.
216/285-4701

Wedgwood Etc.
By Appointment
216/285-5601

19 CHARM

Miller Haus Bed & Breakfast Inn
P.O. Box 129
330/893-3602
Open year round

Directions: From Berlin, take State Rt. 39 East 5 miles to County Road 114; turn right on County Road 114, then right onto County Road 135. Signs will direct. From Sugar Creek, take State Rt. 39 West 4 miles to County Road 114; turn left on County Road 114, then right onto Count Road 135. Follow signs.

The unhurried atmosphere of the Amish community is charmingly captured at Miller Haus Bed & Breakfast Inn. Situated on 23 acres, it is one of the highest points in Holmes County. Needless to say, the view is spectacular.

Darryl and Lee Ann Miller, with son Teddy, and Lee Ann's mother Ann, own and operate the inn. In fact Darryl, a mason/carpenter by trade, and his uncle built the Miller Haus.

Here, you'll find all the comforts of home, and more. Each of the nine guest rooms has its own unique personality, carefully selected antiques, and a private bath. The sitting living dining room area features a cathedral ceiling and a magnificent fireplace.

From the front porch you can watch Amish neighbors plow, plant and harvest crops, using horse drawn

Ohio

equipment.

The inn is ideally situated in the country, but close enough to drive to area Amish restaurants, cheese factories, quilt shops, antique stores and other area tourist attractions.

Isn't it appropriate that the Miller Haus, which is a culmination of a love story that brought together an "English" girl and an Amish boy, came to be located in a town called Charm?

20 CHESTERLAND

The Second Time Around
11579 Chillicothe Rd. Rt. 306
216/729-6555

Antiques of Chester
7976 Mayfield Rd.
216/729-3395

21 CHILLICOTHE

Tygert House
245 Arch St.
614/775-0222

Country Peddler Store
200 Burbridge Ave.
614/773-0658

Antiques on Main Street
145 E. Main St.
614/775-4802

Cellar Room Antiques
203 W. Water
614/775-9848

22 CINCINNATI

Every Now & Then Antiques
430 W. Benson St.
513/821-1497

Special Things Antique Mall
5701 Cheviot Rd.
513/741-9127

Primitive Kitchen
9394 Butler Warren Lane Rd.
513/398-7139

Country Manor
7754 Camargo Rd.
513/271-3979

Latin Quarter
1408 Central Pkwy
513/621-2300

Wooden Nickel Antiques
1410 Central Pkwy
513/241-2985

Briarpatch
1006 Delta Ave.
513/321-0308

Markarian Oriental Rugs Inc.
3420 Edwards Rd.
513/321-5877

Acanthus Antq. & Decorative
3446 Edwards Rd.
513/533-1662

Boles Furniture
1711 Elm St.
513/621-2275

Phillip Bortz Jewelers
34 E. 4th St.
513/621-4441

Jamshid Antique Oriental Rugs
151 W. 4th St.
513/241-4004

Michael Lowe Gallery
338 W. 4th St.
513/651-4445

American Trading Co.
3236 W. Galbraith Rd.
513/385-6556

Peerson's Antiques
4024 Hamilton Ave.
513/542-3849

Mr. Furniture
4044 Hamilton Ave.
513/541-1197

Shadow Box Mini Mall
3233 Harrison Ave.
513/662-4440

Westwood Antqs. & Fine Furn.
3245 Harrison Ave.
513/481-8517

Cheviot Trading Co.
3621 Harrison Ave.
513/661-3633

Freeman Antiques
7500 Hamilton
513/921-3222

Covered Bridge Antique Mall
7508 Hamilton Ave.
513/521-5739

Teezer's Oldies & Oddities
7513 Hamilton Ave.
513/729-1500

Bartoli Antiques
7718 Hamilton Ave.
513/729-1073

Ferguson's Antique Mall
3742 Kellogg Ave.
513/321-0919

Treasures Inc.
1971 Madison Rd.
513/871-8555

M J Nicholson Antiques
2005 Madison Rd.
513/871-2466

English Traditions
2041 Madison Rd.
513/321-4730

Federation
2124 Madison Rd.
513/321-2671

Duck Creek Antique Mall
3715 Madison Rd.
513/321-0900

Greg's Antiques
925 Main St.
513/241-5487

Drackett Design & Antiques
9441 Malin
513/791-3868

Cannonball Express Antiques
77175 Mile Rd.
513/231-2200

Grosvenor Brant Antiques
3407 Monteith Ave.
513/871-1333

Parlor Antiques by Benjamin
6063 Montgomery Rd.
513/731-5550

Regarding Books
6095 Montgomery Rd.
513/531-4717

Architectural Art Glass Studio
6099 Montgomery Rd.
513/731-7336

Courtney's Corner
7124 Montgomery Rd.
513/793-1177

Heriz Oriental Rugs
9361 Montgomery Rd.
513/891-9777

Arias Oriental Rugs
9689 Montgomery Rd.
513/745-9633

A B Closson Jr. Co.
401 Race St.
513/762-5507

Farr Furniture Co.
8611 Reading Rd.
513/821-6535

Sales by Sylvia
1217 Rulison Ave.
513/471-8180

Glendale Antiques
270 E. Sharon Rd.
513/772-0663

Springdale Coin & Antiques
11500 Springfield Pike
513/772-2266

Roth Furniture Co.
1411 Vine St.
513/241-5491

Echos Past
8376 Vine St.
513/821-9696

Byrd Braman
338 Ludlow Ave.
513/872-0200

Treadway Gallery Inc.
2029 Madison Road
513/321-6742

Mount Healthy Antiques Gallery
7512 Hamiton Avenue
513/931-1880

Favorite Places To Eat

Cracker Barrel Old Country Store
Near Kings Island
I-71 & Fields Ertel Rd., Exit 19
513/683-5446

23 CIRCLEVILLE

The Country Wood Box
7979 Bell Station Rd.
614/474-6617

The Barn
5201 S. Bloomfield Royalton
614/983-2238

Brewer's Antique Mall
105 W. Main
614/474-6257

Peggy's Antiques
109 E. Mound
614/474-4578

Gateway to Yesterday
121 W. Main Street
614/474-4095

Once Upon A Time Antiques
130 W. Main Street
614/772-1164

Farm House Antiques
29483 U.S. Rt. 23 S
614/477-1092

South Bloomfield Antique Mall
U.S. Rt. 23
614/983-4300

24 CLEVELAND

Ellen Stirn Galleries
10405 Carnegie Ave.
216/231-6600

Attenson's Coventry Antiques
1771 Coventry Rd.
216/321-2515

Rastus Pl Blck Memorabilia
510 Euclid Ave.
216/687-8115

Gwynby Antiques
2482 Fairmount Blvd.
216/229-2526

Larchmere Antiques
12204 Larchmere Blvd.
216/231-8181

Paulette's Antiques
12204 Larchmere Blvd.
216/231-8181

Princeton Antiques
12628 Larchmere Blvd.
216/231-8855

Dede Moore
12633 Larchmere Blvd.
216/795-9802

Loganberry Books
12633 Larchmere Blvd.
216/795-9800

R & S Antiques
1237 Larchmere Blvd.
216/795-0408

Heide Rivshun Furniture
12702 Larchmere Blvd.
216/231-1003

Ashley's Antiques & Interiors
12726 Larchmere Blvd.
216/299-1970

Shaker Square Antiques Inc.
12733 Larchmere Blvd.
216/231-8804

Mark Goodman Antiques
12736 Larchmere Blvd.
216/229-8919

Bingham & Vance Galleries
12801 Larchmere Blvd.
216/721-1711

Bayswater Antiques
12805 Larchmere Blvd.
216/231-5055

Elegant Extras
12900 Larchmere Blvd.
216/791-3017

Bischoff Galleries
12910 Larchmere Blvd.
216/231-8313

Studio Moderne
13002 Larchmere Blvd.
216/721-2274

Blue Phoenix
13017 Larchmere Blvd.
216/421-0234

Annie's
10024 Lorain Ave.
216/961-3777

Metzgers-Ohio City
3815 Lorain Ave.
216/631-5925

Hommel's Furniture
4617 Lorain Ave.
216/631-2797

Suite Lorain Antqs. & Interiors
7105 Lorain Ave.
216/281-1959

Century Antiques
7410 Lorain Ave.
216/281-9145

Antq. Empor. Eldon Ebel Prop
7805 Lorain Ave.
216/651-5480

Artisan Antiques & Jewelry
3095 Mayfield Rd.
216/371-8639

June Greenwald Antiques
3098 Mayfield Rd.
216/932-5535

Tudor House Antique Gallery
5244 Mayfield Rd.
216/646-0120

American Antiques
3107 Mayfield Rd.
216/932-6380

Ameriflag Antiques
4240 Pearl Rd.
216/661-2608

Oriental Rug Warehouse
4925 Pointe Pkwy.
216/464-2430

Ambrose Antiques
1867 Prospect Ave. E
216/771-4874

Wolf's Gallery
1239 W. 6th St.
216/575-9653

Lee Fana Art Gallery
845 S O M Cent
216/442-7955

South Hills Antique Gallery
2010 W. Schaaf Rd.
216/351-8500

Yesterdays Treasures Antiques
4829 Turney Rd.
216/441-1920

Last Moving Picture Co.
2044 Unclid Ave. Ste. 410
216/781-1821

25 CLIFTON

Weber's Antiques Americana
Rte 343 & Clay
937/767-8581

Weber's Antique Mall
63 Clay
937/767-5060

Clifton Antique Mall
301 N. Main St.
937/767-2277

26 COLUMBIANA

Victorian Peacock
139 N. Main St.
330/482-9139

Historic Images Antiques
8 S. Main St.
330/482-1171

Philomeno's Antiques
8 S. Main St.
330/482-0004

Stray Dog Antiques
8 S. Main St.
330/482-1928

Countryside Antiques
16 S. Main St.
330/482-3259

Bunker Hill Antiques Etc.
24 S. Main St.
330/482-9004

Vivian's Antiques & Cllbls.
24 S. Main St.
330/482-3144

Columbiana Antiques Gallery
103 S. Main St.
330/482-2240

Glory Road Civil War Art
103 S. Main St.
330/482-1812

Main Street Antiques
13 E. Park Ave.
330/482-5202

27 COLUMBUS

Yesteryear Antiques & Fine Art
268 South 4th Street
614/224-4232
Fax: 614/221-6610

Directions: From I-70/71 traveling east, exit Fourth Street., turn right 4 blocks, located at Main and Fourth. Traveling west, exit Third and Fourth St., cross Third, to Fourth, turn left on Fourth, four blocks down at Main and Fourth. Fourth is one way.

Yesteryear Antiques & Fine Art is a variable treasure trove that will surely delight even the most particular shopper. Owners, John Blackburn and Gene Wagner, connoisseurs in their field, have assembled in the "full service store" a collection of merchandise that is uncompromising in quality, workmanship, and artistry.

They offer the customer superior selections of furniture and accessories from this century and the last; lighting fixtures, cut crystal, bronzes, pottery, and oil paintings are but a few of the many exceptional pieces presented here.

They also offer appraisals, furniture refinishing and restoration, upholstery, and fabric selections. Upon request, they can ship your purchases anywhere in the U.S. or abroad.

Midwest Quilt Exchange
495 S. 3rd St.
614/221-8400

All Things Considered
179 E. Arcadia Ave.
614/261-6633

Joseph M Hayes Antiques
491 City Park Ave.
614/221-8200

Minerva Park Furn. Gallery
5200 Cleveland Ave.
614/890-5235

Church on Lane Antiques Inc.
1245 Grandview Ave.
614/488-3606

Findley-Kohler Interiors Inc.
57 Granville St.
614/478-9500

Maggies Place-Buy & Sell
682 E. Hudson St.
614/268-4167

Biashara
780 N. High St.
614/297-7367

Gene's Furniture
1100 N. High St.
614/299-8162

Downstairs Attic
2348 N. High St.
614/262-4240

Alexandra Pengwyn Books
2500 N. High St.
614/267-6711

Echoes of Americana
3165 N. High St.
614/263-9600

Uncle Sam's Antiques
3169 N. High St.
614/261-0078

Clintonville Antiques
3244 N. High St.
614/262-0676

Antiques Etc. Mall
3265 N. High St.
614/447-2242

Euro Classics
3317 N. High St.
614/447-8108

Unique Treasures
3514 N. High St.
614/262-5428

Antique Etc.
3521 N. High St.
614/262-7211

Second Thoughts Antiques
3525 N. High St.
614/262-0834

Reserve Fine Area Rugs
4784 N. High St.
614/447-9955

Antique Mall on South High
1045 S. High St.
614/443-7858

Greater Columbus Antq. Mall
1045 S. High St.
614/443-7858

Pritt's Antiques and Cllbls.
3745 Karl Rd.
614/261-8187

David Franklin Ltd.
2216 E. Main St.
614/338-0833

Powell Antique Mart
26 W. Olentangy St.
614/841-9808

German Village Furniture Co.
960 Parsons
614/444-1901

Vintage Jewels
65 E. State St.
614/464-0921

Thompson's Haus of Antiques
499 S. 3rd St.
614/224-1740

G B Antique Guns
1421 Union Ave.
614/274-4121

Myra's Antiques & Cllbls. Inc.
2799 Winchester Pike
614/238-0520

Antiques & Uniques
247 W. 5th Ave.
614/294-9663

Interesting Side Trips

Travel U.S. Rt. 23 (High Street) to just north of downtown Columbus. The Short North Gallery District, bridging downtown and The Ohio State University, is Columbus's Bohemia. Here galleries sell everything from fine art to folk art to kitsch. As you explore, you'll find vintage clothing stores, coffee houses and restaurants of every description. Don't miss the Gallery Hop, the first Saturday each month, when galleries and shops hold parties and open houses.

Favorite Places To Eat

Cracker Barrel Old Country Store
I-70 & Hilliard Rome Rd., Exit 91
614/878-2027

28 CONNEAUT

Papa's Antqs. & Mltry. Cllbls.
1000 Buffalo Street
216/593-3582

Studio Antiques
242 W. Main Rd.
216/599-7614

Ferguson Antique Shop
282 E. Main Rd. Rt. 20
216/599-7162

The Furniture Doctor
314 W. Main Rd.
216/593-4121

29 COSHOCTON

C & M Collectibles
603 S. Second Street
614/622-6776
Open: 12-5:30 Mon.-Thurs., by chance or appointment Fri.-Sun.

Directions: I-77 (N&S) exit 65 (between Cleveland and Marietta), travel west approximately 20 miles, cross bridge, turn right on Second Street.

C & M Collectibles is a small Ma and Pa operation located within 1200 square feet and a basement area. Customers often comment on how they are pleasantly surprised to find such excellent collectibles at this shop. The owners are very cautious not to mislead their customers; therefore, they make every effort to offer good smalls, glassware, toys, pottery pieces, small furniture pieces and more. Additionally, they purchase items from a variety of styles and periods in hopes that they will have something to offer each and every one of their customers.

30 CUYAHOGA FALLS

House for Collectors
2128 Front St.
330/928-2844

Accent Antiques & Gifts
2204 Front St.
330/922-5411

Hidden Pearl
2206 Front St.
330/928-8230

River Walk Antiques
2237 Front St.
330/945-6898

Bill Holland & Associates
2353 N. Haven Blvd.
330/923-5300

Silver Eagle Antiques
2215 Front Street
330/929-0066

Oakwood Antique & Cllbls.
3265 Oakwood Dr.
330/923-7745

Consignment Cottage
2080 State Rd.
330/929-2080

Signature Gifts & Antiques
2208 Front St.
330/922-4528

31 DAYTON

Dayton has an extraordinary heritage of industry and invention. Daytonians devised the cash register and the automobile self-starter, which spawned the strong local presence of General Motors and NCR. The city's most clever sons were Orville and Wilbur Wright, the bicycle makers who elevated their skills to invent the airplane.

Ginger Jar Antiques
7521 Brandt Pike
513/236-6390

Taylor & Mahan Emporium
100 S. Clinton St.
513/222-0999

Then and Now
436 E. 5th St.
513/461-5859

Feathers Vintage Clothing
440 E. 5th St.
513/228-2940

Dorothy's Vintage Boutique
521 E. 5th St.
513/461-7722

Accents Antiques Etc.
635 Kling Dr. & Patterson
513/298-7666

Old World Antqs. & Est. Jwlry.
4017 N. Main St.
513/275-4488

Springhouse Antiques
49 S. Main St.
513/433-2822

Treasure Barn Antique Mall
1043 S. Main St.
513/222-4400

Purple Pig
23 Park Ave.
513/294-8197

Park Avenue Antiques
51 Park Ave.
513/293-5691

Ann's Furniture
1917 E. 3rd St.
513/254-7214

House of Marks
2025 Wayne Ave.
513/253-5100

Good Ole Stuf
621 Watervliet Ave.
513/254-9144

Arms Depot Gun Shop
746 Watervliet Ave.
513/253-4843

Barn Antiques Gallery
29 W. Whipp Rd.
513/438-1080

Favorite Places To Eat

Cracker Barrel Old Country Store
I-75 & Little York Rd., Exit 60
513/890-0047

32 DELAWARE

J & D Furniture
206 London Rd.
614/363-7575

Delaware Antiques Ltd.
27 Troy Road
614/363-3165

Corner Filling Station
3770 U.S. Hwy. 42 S.
614/369-0499

Crabtree Cottage
4 W. Winter St.
614/369-0898

33 FINDLAY

Findlay was an active Underground Railroad center. In 1860, the local newspaper editor began publishing outrageously satirical letters signed by the fictitious Southern sympathizer, Petroleum V. Nasby. These humorous Nasby Papers became so widely read that they helped sway national public opinion against slavery.

Jeffrey's Antique Gallery
11326 Allen Twp Rd. #99
410/423-7500

Antiques Establishments
3143 Crosshill Dr.
419/424-3699

Blue House Antiques
200 W. Lima St.
419/425-1507

Kate's Korner
540 S. Main St.
419/423-2653

Bowman's Antiques
303 E. Sandusky St.
419/422-3858

Am-Dia Inc.
16960 N. State Rt. 12 E
419/424-1722

Old Mill Antique Shop
10111 W. U.S. Rt. 224
419/424-4012

Favorite Places To Eat

Cracker Barrel Old Country Store
I-75 & State Rd. 224, Exit 159
419/425-2008

34 FOREST PARK

Favorite Places To Eat

Cracker Barrel Old Country Store
I-275 & Winton Rd., Exit 39
513/648-9655

35 GENEVA

Geneva Antiques
28 N. Broadway
216/466-0880

Broadway Antiques & Cllbls.
71 N. Broadway
216/466-7754

Martha's Attic
5501 Lake Road (Rte. 531)
216/466-8650

36 GRANVILLE

The Porch House

241 Maple Street
614/587-1995; 1-800-587-1995
Open year round; reservations recommended. Please do not call after 9 p.m.

Directions: From I-70, go north on Rt. 37, nine miles to Granville. Turn right on Broadway. At the second light, turn right on South Pearl. The Porch House is on the corner of East Maple and South Pearl.

The Porch House, a turn-of-the-century home in historic Granville, offers charming guest rooms with private baths. The home is adjacent to one of Ohio's most visited bike paths and within short walking distance of village shops. A full country breakfast is served.

Lynne Windley Antiques
226 Broadway E
614/587-3242

Wee Antique Gallery
1630 Columbus Rd.
614/587-2270

Greystone Cntry. House Antqs.
128 S. Main St.
614/587-2243

Cream Station Antiques
1444 Newark Granville Rd.
614/587-4814

Our Place Antiques
121 S. Prospect St.
614/587-4601

37 GROVE CITY

Favorite Places To Eat

Cracker Barrel Old Country Store
I-71 & Stringtown Rd., Exit 100
614/871-1444

38 HAMILTON

Grand Antiques
1749 Grand Blvd.
513/895-5751

Augspurger's Antiques
315 Ludlow St.
513/893-1015

Denny's Antiques
119 Main St.
513/887-6341

The Brass Pineapple
159 Millville Oxford Rd.
513/863-6166

Garden Cottage
8977 Princeton Glendale Rd.
513/942-1110

39 HARTVILLE

Hartville Antiques
Ediston St. NW
330/877-8577

Harville Coin Exchange
1015 Edison St. NW
330/877-2949

Past Memories
751 Edison St. NW
330/877-4141

Bennett's Antiques
128 Erie Ave.
330/877-4336

Bennett's Country Store
106 E. Maple St.
330/877-6044

40 HIGGINSPORT

J. Dugan Ohio River House Bed & Breakfast and Antiques

4 Brown Street
513/375-4395
B&B is open year round; call for reservations
Antique shop is open most days 9am-7pm or by appointment

Directions: 35 miles east of Cincinnati, 7 miles west of Ripley, just 1/4 mile off Hwy. 52. In Higginsport, turn South off Hwy. 52 onto Brown Street in the center of town.

Situated high on a hill in the scenic River Hills area of Brown County, Ohio, and set back from town by the expansive grounds, J. Dugan Ohio River House escorts its visitors to a quiet, secluded and exceptional river view.

J. Dugan Ohio House B & B was originally the home of J. Dugan, a merchant and river trader. The "four-brick-thick" tin-roofed house was built in 1830 from bricks handmade in the town. The adjacent all-brick warehouse which now houses the apartments and antique business once served as a coal unloading station and meat-packing house during its years of service in the river trade. The Dugan house was one of only a few houses in Higginsport that survived the "great flood of 1937." After passing through many hands, not all of which treated this grand old house with the love and care it deserved, the Dugan home was purchased by Pat and Bob Costa in 1970, at which time, to use Bob's words, "there was only one pane of glass in any of the windows." After years of hard work by the Costas, the house was restored to its original splendor. The current owners, the Lloyds, purchased the property from the Costas and are continuing the restoration.

The Lloyds encourage travelers to "stop on by" for a visit in the antique shop and a tour of the house with its antique-furnished spacious rooms and several extensive collections of turn-of-the-century glassware. A seat on the terrace to watch the river traffic or moon rise grants you the escape and vision of what life was like in a quieter time.

Bed and breakfast accommodations include outdoor riverside terrace, lovely grounds and antique-filled common and guest rooms. The J. Dugan Ohio River House also has two furnished apartments with full kitchen available for overnight or longer stays. All overnight guests savor the complimentary full country breakfast.

The area surrounding the B & B offers public boat docks, great sightseeing outings, in addition to a multitude of antique shops within an hour's drive.

41 HILLSBORO

Memory Lane Mall
116 S. High St.
513/393-8202

Fields Framg Antiques Art Gift
921 N. High St.
513/393-5357

Ayres Antiques
114 E. Main St.
513/393-1629

Old Pants Factory Mall
135 N. West St.
513/393-9934

42 HUBBARD

Liberty Bell Antiques
142 N. Main St.
330/534-3639

Hubbard-Liberty Antique Mall
5959 W. Liberty St.
330/534-9855

Antiques & Things
6138 W. Liberty St.
330/534-0880

43 KENT

Hughes Antiques
100 W. Crain Ave.
330/677-4489

Dolphin Antiques
135 Gougler Ave.
330/678-9595

City Bank Antiques
115 S. Water St.
330/677-1479

Brown & Brown
134 N. Willow St.
330/673-4396

44 KINSMAN

Market Square
6416 Kinsman-Nickerson Rd.
216/876-3178

Antiques of Kinsman
8374 Main St.
216/876-3511

The Hickory Tree
8426 State Street
216/876-3175

45 KIRTLAND

Yesteryear Shop
7603 Chardon Rd.
216/256-8293

Canterbury Station
9081 Chillicothe Rd.
216/257-0321

46 LANCASTER

Mercantile Co.
111 N. Columbus St.
614/654-2400

Guthrie Place Antiques
118 N. Columbus St.
614/654-2611

Uniquely Yours Antiques
139 W. 5th Ave.
614/654-8444

Emporium-Downtown
154 W. Main St.
614/653-5717

Priscilla's
156 W. Main St.
614/653-1355

Lancaster Antique Emporium
201 W. Main St.
614/653-1973

Po Folks Antiques
1016 Sugar Grove Rd. SE
614/681-9099

47 LEBANON

Brick sidewalks and broad avenues of fine old homes characterize this handsome southwestern Ohio town. Once a site of a Shaker settlement, Lebanon now has numerous antique and specialty shops featuring Shaker items. Collectors come from far and wide for Lebanon's January antique show and the annual holiday festival, which features a wonderful candlelight parade of horse-drawn antique carriages. (Warren County Convention & Visitors Bureau, 1-800-617-6446)

At the Warren County Historical Museum, several rooms of fascinating antiques make its Shaker collection one of the world's largest and best known. Also popular is a collection of nineteenth century storefronts assembled around a village green.

A Gentler Thyme
7 N. Broadway St.
513/933-9997

Charles Gerhardt Antiques
33 N. Broadway St.
513/932-9946

Treasurers Dust Antiques
135 N. Broadway St.
513/932-3877

Signs of our Times
2 S. Broadway St.
513/932-4435

Broadway Antique Mall
15 S. Broadway St.
513/932-1410

Oh Suzanna
16 S. Broadway St.
513/932-8246

Garden Gate
34 S. Broadway St.
513/932-8620

The Cottage
114 S. Broadway St.
513/933-9711

Miller's Antique Market
201 S. Broadway St.
513/932-8710

Grandma's Attic
9 E. Main St.
513/933-0082

Linda Castiglione Antiques
15 E. Main St.
513/933-8344

Hunter's Horn
35 E. Main St.
513/932-5688

Captain Jack's
35 E. Mulberry St.
513/932-2500

Vice's Antiques
519 Mound Ct.
513/932-7918

Main Antiques
31 E. Mulberry St.
513/932-0387

Shoe Factory Antique Mall
120 E. South St.
513/932-8300

Sycamore Tree Antiques
3 S. Sycamore St.
513/932-4567

48 LIMA

Favorite Places To Eat

Cracker Barrel Old Country Store
I-75 & Hwy. 309, Exit 125
419/222-0055

49 LISBON

Kiewall's Florist
7735 State Rt. 45
330/424-0854

Treasure Chest
119 W. Lincoln Way
330/424-3016

Treasures of Yesteryear
343 W. Lincoln N. Ave.
330/424-0102

New Lisbon Antiques
120 S. Lincoln Ave.
330/424-1288

50 LITHOPOLIS

Lithopolis Antique Mart
9 E. Columbus Street
614/837-9683

51 LOVELAND

Hole in the Wall Antiques
110 Broadway St.
513/683-7319

Antique Market of Branch Hill
392 Bridge St.
513/683-8754

Path through the Attic
122 W. Loveland Ave.
513/683-5022

Bike Trail Antiques
124 W. Loveland Ave.
513/677-1224

Loveland Antiques
204 W. Loveland Ave.
513/677-0328

52 MADISON

Colonel Lee's Antiques
120 N. Lake St.
216/428-7933

The Red Geranium
120 N. Lake St.
216/428-7933

Little Mountain Antiques
7757 S. Ridge Rd.
216/428-4264

Unionville Antiques
7918 S. Ridge Rd.
216/428-4334

Collector's Delight
5813 N. Ridge Rd.
216/428-3563

53 MANSFIELD

Cranberry Heart Inc.
1461 Ashland Rd.
419/589-0340

Mid-Ohio Antiques Mall
155 Cline Ave.
419/756-5852

Mansfield Antique Mall
1095 Koogle Rd.
419/589-5558

The Antique Gallery
1700 S. Main St.
419/756-6364

Brantina's
335 Park Ave. E.
419/524-5282

Little Journeys Bookshop
376 Park Ave. W.
419/522-2389

Cricket House
825 Park Ave. W.
419/524-7100

Yesteryear Mart
1237 Park Ave. W.
419/529-6212

Favorite Places To Eat

Cracker Barrel Old Country Store
I-71/Rt. 13 & Opossum Run Rd., Exit 169
419/774-9800

54 MARIETTA

Riverview Antiques
102 Front St.
614/373-4068

Fort Harmar Antiques
154 Front St.
614/374-3538

Stanley & Grass Vintage Furn.
166 Front St.
614/373-1556

Dollie Maude's Country Store
176 Front St.
614/374-2710

Tin Rabbit Antiques
204 Front St.
614/373-1152

Old Tool Shop
208 Front St.
614/373-9973

Dad's Advertising Collectibles
118 Maple St.
614/376-2653

55 MASON

Dupriest Antiques
207 W. Main St.
513/459-8805

Rt. 42 Antique Mall
1110 Reading Rd.
513/398-4003

Something Old Something New
4064 State Rt. 42
513/398-6036

56 MEDINA

Moon & Star Antiques
217 N. Court St.
330/723-9917

Gramercy Gallery
221 S. Court St.
330/725-6626

Heirloom Cupboard
239 S. Court St.
330/723-1010

Unique Antiques & Collectibles
602 W. Liberty St.
330/722-6666

1894 Gift Co.
1342 Medina Rd.
330/239-1311

Country Collectibles
2768 Pearl Rd.
330/723-1416

Consign. Shop in Granny's Attic
4184 Pearl Rd.
330/725-2277

Creations of the Past
44 Public Square
330/725-6979

Chuck's Antiques
7530 Tower Rd.
330/723-4406

Brothers Antique Mall
6132 Wooster Pike
330/723-7580

Medina Antique Mall
2797 Medina Road
330/722-0017

Favorite Places To Eat

Cracker Barrel Old Country Store
I-71 & State Rt. 18, Exit 218
330/725-2445

57 MENTOR

Cold Coin & Card Outlet
7292 Lakeshore Blvd.
216/946-0222

Antique Center
8435 Mentor Ave.
216/255-3315

Garage Sale Store
8510 Mentor Ave.
216/255-6296

Mentor Village Antiques
8619 Mentor Ave.
216/255-1438

Maggie McGiggle's Antiques
8627 Mentor Ave.
216/255-1623

Yesterday's
8627 Mentor Ave.
216/255-7930

Antique Dolls
8920 Mentor Ave.
216/974-8600

58 MESOPOTAMIA

Coffee Corners Antiques
8715 Parkman-Mesopotamia Rd.
216/693-4376

Beverly Tiffany Antiques
7594 South R 534
216/693-4322

Fannie Mae Emporium
8809 St. Rt. 534
216/693-4482

59 MIAMITOWN

Colonel Jim's Emporium
State Rt. 128
513/353-9323

Miamitown Antiques
6655 State Rt. 128
513/353-4598

An Added Touch
6661 State Rt. 128
513/353-4144

Vintage Antiques & Accents
6737 State Rt. 128
513/353-2945

Antiques & Things
6755 State Rt. 128
513/353-1442

Werts & Bledsoe Antique Mall
6818 State Rt. 128
513/353-2689

Merry's Go Round
6828 State Rt. 128
513/353-1119

Sweet Annie's Antqs. & Accents
6849 State Rt. 128
513/353-3099

House of Antiques & Cllbls.
6850 State Rt. 128
513/353-9776

Cade's Crossing Antiques
6868 State Rt. 128
513/353-2232

Camille's Antiques
6869 State Rt. 128
513/353-3975

60 MIDDLEFIELD

Antiques of Middlefield
14449 Old State Rd. (Rt. 600)
216/632-5221

Country Collection Antiques
15848 Nauvoo Road
216/632-1919

61 MIDDLETOWN

Favorite Places To Eat

Cracker Barrel Old Country Store
I-75 & Ohio Hwy. 122, Exit 32
513/727-4727

62 MILAN

Kelly's Antiques
32 Park
419/499-4570

Crosby's Antiques
4 Main St. N
419/499-4001

Sights & Sounds of Edison
21 Main St. N.
419/499-3093

Samaha Antiques
28 Park
419/499-4044

Betty Dorow Antiques
29 Park
419/499-4102

Milan Antique Quarters
29 Park
419/499-4646

63 MILFORD

Seibert's Antique Barn
5737 Deerfield Rd.
513/575-1311

Picket Fence Antiques
5 Main St.
513/821-1500

Village Mouse Antiques
32 Main St.
513/831-0815

Early's Antiques Shop
123 Main St.
513/831-4833

Backroom Antiques
129 Main St.
513/831-5825

Remember When Antiques
413 Main St.
513/831-6609

64 MILLERSBURG

Ever see a McDonald's drive-through window designed for buggies? You'll find one in Millersburg, in the heart of Amish Country. Ohio is proud to be home to the largest population of Amish people in the world. The Amish foreswear modern conveniences, such as automobiles and electricity, in favor of a simpler way of life. In Amish Country, women wear crisp white bonnets and long-sleeved dresses. Men wear simple black clothes and broad-brimmed hats. A few too many black buggies, and you have a traffic jam.

Most Amish in Ohio live in Geauga, Holmes, Trumbull, Tuscarawas and Wayne Counties. When you visit, keep an eye out for slow-moving buggies on the road. And be respectful of the privacy of these "plain people"—don't take close-up pictures.

For a look at Amish life firsthand, visit the Amish Farm and Home in Berlin, where you can see daily life among the Amish. Or head to Walnut Creek and Yoder's Amish Farm, an authentic working farm where you can enjoy such seasonal events as the making of apple butter. Guides at Yoder's explain the history and customs of the Amish religion, and lead you on a tour of two houses and a barn. One house is typical of an Amish home from the late 1800s, with exposed wooden floors, simple furniture and such appliances as a pump sewing machine. The other is similar to a present-day Amish home, with running water and gas floor lamps.

Kidron's Amish and Mennonite communities join together for the annual Mennonite Relief Sale the first Sunday of August. Hundreds of collectors bid for the quilts, tools and folk art presented by members of more than 100 congregations. And while you're in Kidron, don't miss Lehman's hardware store. There you'll find crockery, washboards, grist mills, copper and cast-iron kettles, water pumps—more than an acre's worth of non-electric tools and appliances. Like quilts? Head next door to the Hearthside Quilt Shoppe.

Hungry? The Amish take as much pride in their food as in their crafts. Troyer's Genuine Trail Bologna, in Trails, sells the famous bologna in a country store near the factory where it's made. Try the out-of-this-world green moon cheese at Heini's Cheese Chalet in Berlin. Heini's sells more than 50 varieties of cheeses. At Guggisberg Cheese, near Charm, you can watch as Alfred Guggisberg's famous Baby Swiss Cheese is prepared each day from a secret recipe, in a factory that resembles a Swiss Chalet. Across the road, at the Chalet in the Valley restaurant, you can sit down to a meal of Wiener schnitzel, bratwurst, freshly baked pies and Black Forest cake. As you eat, you'll be serenaded by yodelers and accordion players. If you prefer losing yourself in a nationally known peanut butter pie, try the Homestead Restaurant, where the menu of entrees also includes fried chicken and roast beef with mashed potatoes.

To soothe your sweet tooth, head for Burton and the sugar camp. You can buy candy and maple syrup from the camp at Burton Log Cabin. While you're in town, tour Century Village, a collection of historic buildings.

If you've never witnessed the Amish way of life, you may travel to Amish Country for the first time out of curiosity about a lifestyle unaffected by constantly changing surroundings. Once you've been there, you'll want to go back, again and again.

Fields of Home Guest House Bed & Breakfast
7278 County Road 201
330/674-7152
Open year round; Sundays by reservations only.
Owned & Operated by the Mervin Yoder Family
Rates $65-125

Directions: From Berlin, take SR 39 west 1/2 mile to CR 201; turn right onto CR 201 at the Dutch Harvest Restaurant. Go north on 201 for 3.8 miles.

Talk about a room with a view! Fields of Home Guest House overlooks the beautiful Amish countryside near Millersburg, Ohio. Return to a simpler time...rolling hills, spring-fed ponds, the smell of freshly plowed soil, crickets singing, the clippity-clop of horses pulling black buggies...relax and enjoy an unhurried world of gentle people, where home is a quiet retreat, peaceful and cozy, and you're secure in the trust that tomorrow will be like today. This log cabin guest house offers all the accommodations of home and more; private baths with whirlpool tubs, fireplaces, kitchenettes, a large front porch with rocking chairs and beautiful views. A wonderful place to experience the simple pleasures of life.

Antique Emporium
113 W. Jackson St.
330/674-0510

65 MONTGOMERY

Drackett Designs & Antiques
9441 Main Street
513/561-2627
Open: Tue.-Sat. 10-5 and by appointment

Directions: Interstate 71 north of Cincinnati to Cross County Parkway exit. After exiting, move to left lane and go north on Montgomery Road to Remmington Road. Turn right and we are on the corner of Remmington & Main. Parking lot behind house (also behind Montgomery Inn and across from Pomodori's Pizza.

Located in an historic home built in 1846, Drackett Designs & Antiques specializes in 18th & 19th Century English antiques and accessories. The shop also offers interior design services.

66 MOUNT VICTORY

Newland's Antiques
11262-11266 Lake View
513/842-3021

Attic Treasures
101 N. Main St.
513/354-5430

Corbin Cottage
111 S. Main St.
513/354-4330

House of Yesteryear Antq. Mall
125 S. Main St.
513/354-2020

67 NEW PHILADELPHIA

Riverfront Antique Mall
1203 Front Street
1-800-926-9806
Open Mon.-Sat., 10-8; Sun., 10-6

Directions: From I-77, take Exit 81. Go east on Rt. 39 to first light; right on Bluebell Drive, and follow to Riverfront Antique Mall.

Situated near the heart of Amish country, this mammoth antique mall proclaims itself to be "The Greatest Show in Ohio Seven Days a Week." Boasting 84,000 square feet and 350 dealers on one floor, the mall offers a 6,400-square-foot furniture showroom with another 6,000 square feet allotted to a "Rough Room," featuring unrestored and "as-is" finds.

Some of the finest dealers in the Midwest exhibit their wares in room settings or in showcases at Riverfront Antique Mall. Early advertising memorabilia, old dolls, telephones, cash registers, and toys are just a few of the collectibles offered. Elegant glassware, pottery, lighting and lots of the unusual can always be found.

68 NEW RICHMOND

Quigley House Bed & Breakfast
100 Market Street
513/553-6318
Open year round
Rates $85

Directions: Take 275 East to Exit 17, New Richmond (U.S.-52). Go 11 miles to New Richmond. Then go through 2 traffic lights. The next street to the right is Walnut. Make a right to the STOP sign, then a left onto Market. Go 1 block, and the bed & breakfast is on the corner.

Quietly situated in the heart of historic New Richmond is the village's first bed and breakfast. Unique defines this lovely turn-of-the-century home which offers four spacious guest rooms with private baths, queen size beds and decorative fireplaces. Guests will awaken to the aroma of freshly brewed coffee, served in the elegant dining room along with a deluxe continental breakfast. A lovely, large front porch invites you to reminisce and capture the nostalgia of this small river town.

Interests in the area include boating on the beautiful Ohio River with overnight mooring accommodations, restaurants, shops and golfing. Located just minutes away from River Downs Racetrack, River Bend Concert Center, Old Coney Island, Sunlight Pool, Riverfront Stadium and downtown Cincinnati.

A Loving Remembrance
204 Front St.
513/553-9756

69 NEWARK

Arcade Korner Mall
20 N. 4th St.
614/345-9176

Loewendick's
4248 Linnville Rd. SE
614/323-3127

Park Place Antiques & Collectibles
14 N. Park Place
614/349-7424

70 NORWICH

White Pillars Antique Mall
7525 E. Pike Rd.
614/872-3720

Olde Trail Antiques
7650 E. Pike Rd.
614/872-4001

Kemble's Antiques
55 N. Sundale Rd.
614/872-3507

71 PAINESVILLE

Treasure Shop
213 High St.
216/354-3552

Ye Olde Oaken Bucker
776 Mentor Ave.
216/354-0007

My Country Place
2200 Mentor Ave.
216/354-8811

Windsor Antiques
2200 Mentor Ave.
216/357-5792

A-1 Antique Buyers & Sellers
1581 N. Ridge Rd.
216/352-3038

72 PENINSULA

Antique Roost
1455 Whines Hill Rd.
216/657-2687

Innocent Age Antiques
6084 N. Locust St.
216/657-2915

Downtown Emporium
1595 Main St.
216/657-2778

Olde Players Barn
1039 W. Streetsboro Rd.
216/657-2886

73 PERRY

Main Street Antiques
4179 Main Street (Narrows Rd.)
216/428-6016

Dad's Old Store
4184 Main St. (Narrows Rd.)
216/259-5547

74 PERRYSBURG

Speck's Antique Furn
23248 Dunbridge Rd.
419/874-4272

Jones & Jones Ltd. Antiques
114 W. Indiana Ave.
419/874-2867

Perrysburg Antiques Market
116 Louisiana Ave.
419/872-0231

Favorite Places To Eat

Cracker Barrel Old Country Store
I-75 & Hwy. 12, Exit 193
419/874-7481

75 PICKERINGTON

Favorite Places To Eat

Cracker Barrel Old Country Store
I-70 & Hwy. 256, Exit 112
614/759-7799

76 PIQUA

Avenue & Alley Antiques
312 E. Ash St.
513/778-1110

Cherie's Antqs. & Fine Jewelry
317 E. Ash St.
513/773-0779

World of Oz
325 E. Ash St.
513/773-2130

Memory Lane Antiques
9277 N. County Road 25 A
513/778-0942

Apple Tree Gallery
427 N. Main St.
513/773-1801

77 PORTSMOUTH

Leading Lady Company
620 Chillicothe St.
614/353-0700

O'Neill's Antiques
215 Harding Ave.
614/776-6467

Oakery
225 Harding Ave.
614/776-7481

Ratliff's Relics
1608 Gallia St.
614/353-7409

River Bend Antiques & Gifts
440 2nd St.
614/354-3759

Shope Country
537 2nd St.
614/353-4880

Olde Towne Antique Mall
541 2nd St.
614/353-7555

Gay 90s Antiques
543 2nd St.
614/353-6111

Mr. Binn's Antique Shop
604 2nd St.
614/353-2856

Yesteryear Antiques
605 2nd St.
614/353-0007

78 POWELL

Depot Street Antiques
41 Depot St.
614/885-6034

Windsor Ltd. Antiques
9280 Dublin Rd.
614/761-7900

Powell Antiques Center
26 W. Olentangy St.
614/888-6447

Seasons Past Antiques
38 W. Olentangy St.
614/431-1265

Lane Interiors Ltd.
84 W. Olentangy St.
614/846-1007

Country Reflections
87 W. Olentangy St.
614/848-3835

Manor at Catalpa Grove
147 W. Olentangy St.
614/798-1471

79 RAVENNA

Directions: Take Ohio Turnpike Exit 13A to Rt. 44S. Follow Rt. 44S into Ravenna. From I-76, use Exit 38B, Rt. 44N, and follow Rt. 44 north into Ravenna.

Ravenna, Ohio is a town chock-full of antique shops, bed and breakfasts, and restaurants.

For specific information, see review this section.

80 READING

Every Now & Then Antq. Mall
430 W. Benson St.
513/821-1497

Millcreek Antiques
100 Mill St. (Lockland)
513/761-1512

The Furniture Craftsman
17 Pike St. (Rear)
513/554-0095

Casablanca Vintage
9001 Reading Rd.
513/733-8811

Talk of the Town
9019 Reading Rd.
513/563-8844

Grand Antique Mall
9701 Reading Rd.
513/554-1919

Amazing Grace Antiques
149 W. Benson St.
513/761-8300

81 SANDUSKY

Judee Hill Antiques & Apprsls.
809 Hayes Ave.
419/625-4442

Bay Window
223 E. Market St.
419/625-1825

Now & Then Shoppe
333 W. Market St.
419/625-1918

82 SHANDON

General Store & More
4751 Cinti Brookvl Rd.
513/738-1881

Bruce Metzger Antiques
4807 Cinti Brookvl Rd.
513/738-7256

Shandon Church Antique Mall
4825 Cinti Brookvl Rd.
513/738-3110

Red Door Antiques
4843 Cinti Brookvl Rd.
513/738-0618

83 SHARON CENTER

Country Trader
6324 Ridge Road
330/239-2104

84 SPRINGFIELD

AAA I-70 Antique Mall
4700 S. Charleston Pike
513/324-8448

American Antiquities
126 E. High St.
513/322-6281

Old Canterbury Antiques
4655 E. National Rd.
513/323-1418

Knight's Antiques
4750 E. National Rd.
513/325-1412

Central Ohio Antique Center
1735 Titus Rd.
513/322-8868

Favorite Places To Eat

Cracker Barrel Old Country Store
I-70 & State Rd. 172, Exit 54
937/325-8221

85 STRASBURG

Strasburg provides a convenient stop for antiquing travelers. Four antique shops, one mall, and one indoor Sunday Flea Market are all within one mile of Interstate 77, exit #87 on Hwy. 250.

Strasburg 77 Antiques & Collectibles
780 South Wooster
330/878-7726
Open Tue.-Sun., 11-5, and by chance or appointment

Directions: 1/4 mile west of I-77 at Exit 87, State Rt. 250.

Strasburg 77 Antiques & Collectibles is a treasure chest for those seeking interesting and unusual collectibles. The shop is packed with advertising memorabilia, old books and toys, bottles, tins, and those ever-popular Disney collectibles.

Carol's Collection
840 South Wooster
330/878-7898
Open Tue.-Sun., 11-5

Directions: 1/4 mile west of I-77 at Exit 87, State Rt. 250

Another great place to go for collectibles in Strasburg, Carol's Collection offers the usual in the way of collectibles such as bottles, advertising, books, etc. However, she loves to seek out and buy for her customers the unusual such as Indian arrowheads and relics, marbles and painted beer and soda bottles.

Yesterdays Memories Antiques
116 N. Wooster Ave.
330/878-7021

Kandle Antiques
1180 N. Woodster Ave.
330/878-5775

86 STEUBENVILLE

Pottery City Antiques
4th & Market
800/380-6933

Yesterday Antiques & Cllbls.
159 N. 4th St.
614/283-2445

Antique Emporium
2523 Sunset Blvd.
614/264-7806

87 SUNBURY

Pieces of the Past
74 E. Cherry St.
614/965-1231

Village Antiques
5 S. Columbus St.
614/965-4343

Coffee Antiques
25 E. Granvill St.
614/965-1113

Weidner's Village Sq. Antique
31 E. Granvill St.
614/965-4377

Sunberry Antique Mall
20 S. Vernon
614/965-2279

88 TIFFIN

Deerfield Station
60 Clay St.
419/448-0342

The Gallery
215 Riverside Dr.
419/447-1568

That Old Log House Antiques
1443 W. Seneca Ave.
419/447-0381

Shumway Antiques
94 N. Washington St.
491/447-8746

Tiffin Town Antiques
368 N. Washington St.
419/447-5364

Knic-Knac's Treasures
22 S. Washington St.
419/447-5922

89 TIPP CITY

Kim's Furniture Store
7505 S. County Rd. 25 A
513/667-3316

Benkin & Company
14 E. Main St.
513/667-5975

Angels Antiques
27 E. Main St.
513/667-8861

Jezebel's Vintage Clothing
15 N. 2nd St.
513/667-7566

Venkin Antique Gallery
14 E. Main
937/667-5526

90 TOLEDO

Cobblestone Antiques Mall
2635 W. Central Ave.
419/475-4561

Keta's Antqs. & Oriental Rugs
2640 W. Central Ave.
419/474-1616

Leffler's Antiques
2646 W. Central Ave.
419/473-3373

Gold & Silver Lady
5650 W. Central Ave.
419/537-9009

The Station Shop
130 W. Dudley
419/893-5674

Hyman's Red Barn
922 Lagrange St.
419/243-9409

Custer Antq. & Investment Co.
534 W. Laskey Rd.
419/478-4221

The Gift Horse
520 Madison Ave.
419/241-8547

Colour Your World
414 Main St.
419/693-5283

Frogtown Books Inc.
2131 N. Reynolds Rd.
419/531-8101

Cottage Antiques
2423 N. Reynolds Rd.
419/536-3888

Antique Barn
1598 W. Sylvania Ave.
419/470-0118

Ancestor House Antiques
3148 Tremainsville Rd.
419/474-0735

91 UNIONTOWN

Wayside Antiques
12921 Cleveland Ave. NW
330/699-2992

Colonial Antiques Arts & Crafts
13075 Cleveland Ave. NW
330/699-9878

Antique Mall Uniontown
13443 Cleveland Ave. NW
330/699-6235

Antiques of Yesteryears
13501 Cleveland Ave. NW
330/699-2090

92 UNIONVILLE

The Green Door & Red Button
6819 S. Ridge East Rt. 84
216/428-5747

Little Mountain Antiques
7757 S. Ridge East Rt. 84
216/428-4264

Unionville Antiques
Rt. 84
216/428-4334

93 URBANA

Charlie Brown's Antiques
4815 Cedar Creek Rd.
513/484-3535

Kaleidoscope
117 N. Main St.
513/653-8010

Upper Valley Antiques
3345 W. U.S. Hwy. 36
513/653-6600

94 VAN WERT

Williman's Antqs. & Used Furn.
115 S. Market St.
419/238-2282

Years Ago Antique Mall
108 W. Main St.
419/238-3362

Heritage Coin & Antique Shop
119 N. Washington St.
419/238-1671

95 WADSWORTH

Wadsworth Antique Mall
941 Broad St.
330/336-8620

Lady Sodbuster Antiques
121 E. Prospect St.
330/336-5239

Antique Design
112 Main St.
330/334-6530

96 WAPAKONETA

Take It From The Top
24 E. Auglaize St.
419/738-2421

Antique Vault
36 E. Auglaize St.
419/738-8711

Antiques Etc.
215 E. Auglaize St.
419/739-9382

Rapunzel's
115 W. Auglaize St.
419/738-3331

Auglaize Antique Mall
116 W. Auglaize St.
419/738-8004

Brick Place
202 W. Auglaize St.
419/738-5555

Ivy Haus
1321 Bellefontaine St.
419/739-9489

Log Cabin
408 S. Blackhoof St.
419/738-7578

Purple Goose
11539 Glynwood Rd.
419/738-7952

97 WASHINGTON COURT HOUSE

Past & Present Memorabilias
109 E. Court St.
614/333-3222

This Old House
427 E. East St.
614/335-8102

Storage House
153 S. Hinde St.
614/335-9267

B & D Collectibles
143 N. Main St.
614/335-8417

98 WATERVILLE

Amer. Hrtg. Antqs. Waterville
17 N. 3rd St.
419/878-8355

Waterville Antique Center
19 N. 3rd St.
419/878-3006

K & G Antiques & Etc.
36 N. 3rd St.
419/878-7778

Mill Race Antiques
217 Mechanic St.
419/878-8762

99 WAYNESVILLE

Off I-71at Exit 45, take Rt. 73 West to Waynesville, then U.S. Rt. 42 South to Lebanon. Waynesville is known for its antique shops. It is also know for its ghosts; the town's Main Street has been dubbed: "America's Most Haunted." If you visit in October, take the Not-So-Dearly-Departed Tour. One stop will be the Hammel House Inn, where antiques and apparitions converge. If there are ghosts in nearby Lebanon, it's a safe bet they'll be at Pioneer Cemetery, eternal home of Sarah, Elizabeth, Mary, and Ann Harner. According to Ripley's "Believe It Or Not", the four sisters were simultaneously killed by a ball of lightning that came down the chimney of their farmhouse and struck them all, though each was in a different room.

Highlander House
22 S. Main St.
513/897-7900

Remember When Antiques
43 S. Main St.
513/897-2438

Miscellany Collection
49 S. Main St.
513/897-1070

Bittersweet Antiques
57 S. Main St.
513/897-4580

Velvet Bear Antiques
61 S. Main St.
513/897-0709

Waynesville Antique Mall
69 S. Main St.
513/897-6937

My Wife's Antiques
77 S. Main St.
513/897-7455

Little Red Shed Antiques
85 S. Main St.
513/897-6326

Olde Curiosity Shoppe
88 S. Main St.
513/897-1755

Cranberry Corner Antiques
93 S. Main St.
513/897-6919

Bakers Antiques
98 S. Main St.
513/897-0746

Brass Lantern Antiques
100 S. Main St.
513/897-9686

Golden Pomegranate Antique
140 S. Main St.
513/897-7400

Crazy Quilt Antiques
211 S. Main St.
513/897-8181

Back in the Barn
239 S. Main St.
513/897-7999

The Rose Cottage
258 S. Main St.
513/897-1010

Tiffany's Treasures
273 S. Main St.
513/897-0116

Spencer's Antiques
274 S. Main St.
513/897-7775

Silver City Mercantile Antiques
1555 E. State Rt. 73
513/897-9000

100 WEST CHESTER

Hidden Treasures Antiques
8825 Cincinnati Dayton Road
513/779-9908
Open: Tue.-Sat. 11-7, Sun. 1-6

Directions: I-75 to Cincinnati-Dayton Road. South approximately 1/2 mile to 8825 Cincinnati-Dayton Road.

Located in a large historical home and barn, surrounded by a beautifully landscaped garden, Hidden Treasures Antiques is stacked from floor to ceiling with a fine selection of furniture, artwork, and accessories.

This family owned business prides itself in offering personal service and commitment to its' customers as well as providing - you guessed it - "Hidden Treasures!"

Van Skaik's Antiques
9355 Cinti Colmbs Rd.
513/777-6481

Memory Lane Antqs. & Repair
8872 Cincinnati Dayton Road
513/777-8565

101 WESTERVILLE

Westerville Antique Mall
34 E. College Ave.
614/891-6966

Mills Antique
3790 E. Powell Rd.
614/890-7020

Springhouse Antique Mall
2 N. State St.
614/882-2354

Heart's Content Antique Mall
9 N. State St.
614/891-6050

Allen's Jewelry
399 S. State St.
614/882-3937

Nestor's Antiques
8999 Robinhood Circle
614/882-1939

102 WILLOUGHBY

Somewhere In Time Antiques
4117 Erie St.
216/975-9409

Friend's Antiques
4119 Erie St.
216/946-1595

Tiffany Rose Antiques
4075 Erie St.
216/942-2065

Mr. Willoughby's Antiques
14 Public Square
216/951-5464

Market Square Antiques
24 Public Square
216/975-1776

103 WOOSTER

Norton's Antiques, Etc.
9423 Ashland Road
330/262-6439
Open daily by chance or by appointment

Directions: Halfway (10 miles) between Wooster and Ashland on State Rt. 250 in the village of New Pittsburg.

Inside Norton's Antiques, etc., there are a host of small possibilities. In fact, Mr. Norton refers to the majority of his stock as a collection of "smalls." From "primitives to depression," his selections are worthy of your attention. He offers pottery, china, figurines, and glassware of all varieties. A wide selection of costume jewelry is also available. Norton's Antiques, etc., located near Amish country in the village of New Pittsburgh, is an excellent reminder that, very often, good things do come in small packages.

Uptown/Downtown Antq. Mall
215 W. Liberty St.
330/262-9735

Green Room II Antiques
1357 Old Columbus Rd.
330/264-7071

104 YOUNGSTOWN

Kozak's Antqs. & Appraisals
1328 Elm St.
330/747-2775

Thomas E. Marsh Antiques Inc.
914 Franklin Ave.
330/743-8600

The Joshua Tree
4059 Hillman Way
330/782-1993

Home Classics
15 W. McKinley Way
330/757-0423

Now & Then Shoppe
2618 Mahoning Ave.
330/799-8643

Twice-Loved Books
19 E. Midlothian Blvd.
330/783-2016

Antique Alley
104 E. Midlothian Blvd.
330/783-1140

105 ZANESVILLE

Log Hollow
2825 Chandlersville Rd.
614/453-2318

Corner Cupboard Antiques
1032 Linden Ave.
614/453-3246

Allie's Antiques
524 Main St.
614/452-2280

Olde Towne Antique Mall
525 Main St.
614/452-1527

Elaine's Antique & Collectibles
531 Main St.
614/452-3627

Market St. Gallery
822 Market St.
614/455-2787

A Le Clara Belle
4868 E. Pike Rd.
614/454-2884

Seven Gables Antiques
1570 S. River Rd.
614/454-1596

Christine's Unique Antique Mall
28 N. 7th St.
614/455-2393

Notes

Oklahoma

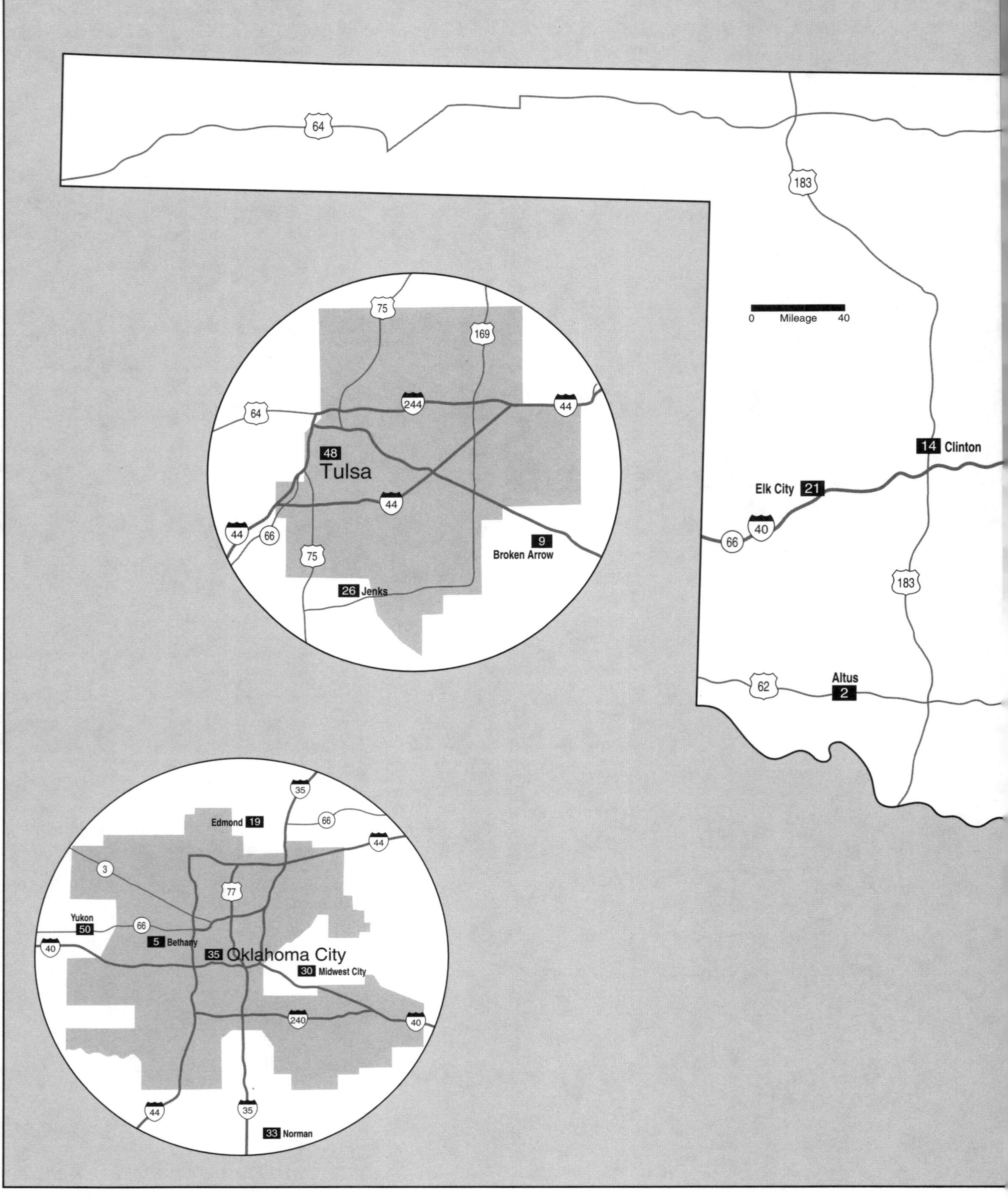

64
183
0 Mileage 40
14 Clinton
Elk City 21
40
66
183
62
Altus
2
75
169
244
44
64
48
Tulsa
44
44
66
75
9
Broken Arrow
26 Jenks
35
Edmond 19
66
44
3
77
Yukon
50
66
40
5 Bethany
35 Oklahoma City
30 Midwest City
240
40
44
35
33 Norman

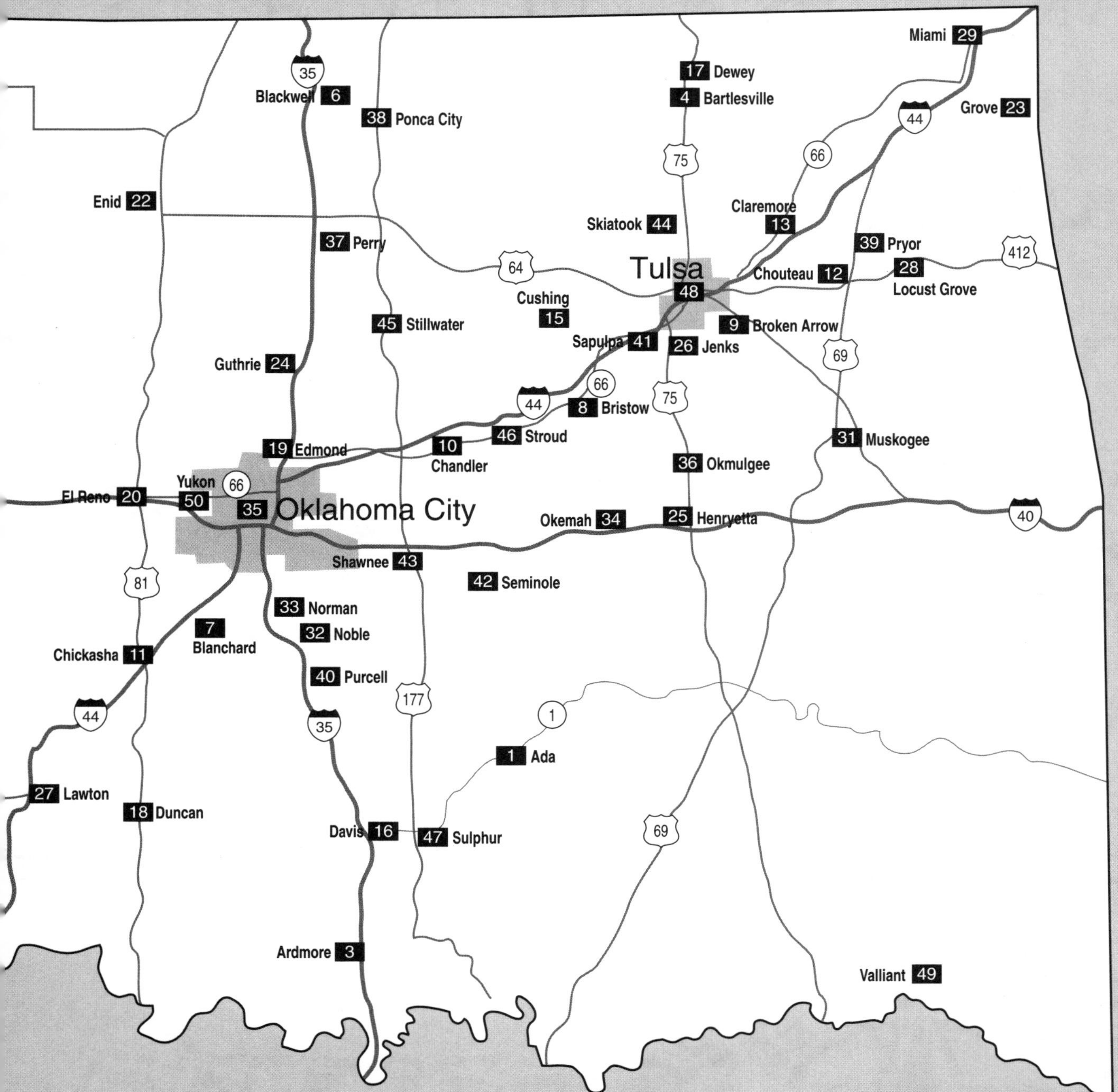

Miami 29
17 Dewey
4 Bartlesville
Blackwell 6
38 Ponca City
Grove 23
Enid 22
Claremore 13
Skiatook 44
37 Perry
39 Pryor
28 Locust Grove
Tulsa
48
Chouteau 12
Cushing 15
45 Stillwater
9 Broken Arrow
Sapulpa 41
26 Jenks
Guthrie 24
8 Bristow
46 Stroud
31 Muskogee
19 Edmond
10 Chandler
36 Okmulgee
Yukon
El Reno 20
50
35 Oklahoma City
Okemah 34
25 Henryetta
Shawnee 43
42 Seminole
33 Norman
32 Noble
7 Blanchard
Chickasha 11
40 Purcell
1 Ada
27 Lawton
18 Duncan
Davis 16
47 Sulphur
Ardmore 3
Valliant 49
35
44
75
66
64
412
69
40
81
177
1

Route 66

From its official beginning in 1926 through the heyday of auto travel in the '50s and '60s, Rt. 66 was the road for dreamers. It exemplifies the open road, beckoning adventure with the promise of freedom. It carried families, vagabonds, and untold others through bustling cities and into neon-lit small towns in the heart of America.

During the depression of the '30s, it was the road of hope for "Okies": poor Oklahoma farm families who abandoned their drought-ravaged homes and headed west for a better way of life. Their plight was made famous by John Steinbeck's novel *The Grapes of Wrath*.

Rt. 66 is "still the place to get your kicks" thanks to dozens of Rt. 66 cities who have kept their downtowns vibrant. Many today boast a diverse assemblage of shops featuring antiques, collectibles and Rt. 66 memorabilia. Movie theaters and building facades are being restored to the splendor of time past. Businesses are returning to their downtown districts, and those who remember the Mother Road during its heyday are proudly embracing their heritage. Rt. 66 is rich in Oklahoma, and it looks like the Main Street of America is here to stay.

1 ADA

Alford Warehouse Sales
217 S. Johnston St.
405/332-1026

Treasures in Time
211 E. Main St.
405/436-1200

Ada Antique Mall
222 E. Main St.
405/332-9927

Granny's Attic
715 E. Main St.
405/436-4241

2 ALTUS

The Enchanted Door
111 West Commerce
405/477-0004

The Enchanted Door offers an "enchanting" shopping experience. Here you'll find antiques, crystals, decorative accessories as well as gift baskets and specialty toys.

Granny's Antiques
905 E. Broadway St.
405/477-1565

Designs for the Goodtimes
Bunker Hill Shopping Center
405/477-0298

Yesterdaze Treasures
113 E. Commerce St.
405/482-1229

Remember When
103 N. Hudson St.
405/482-3773

Sue's Collectibles & Antiques
110 Falcon Rd.
405/482-4461

North Main Antique Mall
601 N. Main St.
405/477-1991

Catch All
1500 S. Main St.
405/482-6950

Al's Antiques
720 S. Spurgeon St.
405/482-2022

3 ARDMORE

Surrell's
318 Lake Murray Dr. E
405/223-3799

Ardmore Furniture
15 Sam Noble Pkwy.
405/226-2090

Antique Sampler
15 Sam Noble Pkwy.
405-226-7643

4 BARTLESVILLE

Lace & Such
502 S. Cherokee Ave.
918/336-8000

Apple Tree Mall
3900 E. Frank Phillips Blvd.
918/335-2485

Piper Furniture
110 S.W. Frank Phillips Blvd.
918/336-1300

Victorian Memories
310 S.W. Frank Phillips Blvd.
918/336-2952

Gans Mall
3801 S.E. Kentucky St.
918/335-1046

Hog Shooter Antiques Etc.
3922 Nowata Rd.
918/333-3333

Good Earth
101 E. Frank Phillips
918/336-6633

Country Store
Rt. 3 Box 8970
918/336-0351

Depot Corner Antiques
127 S.W. 2nd St.
918/336-9313

5 BETHANY

Before travelers even realize they've left Oklahoma City, 39th Street suddenly looks like a small- town Main Street again. It courses past old gas stations, the Rt. 66 Trading Post (boasting the "best collection in the nation" of memorabilia) and Oklahoma Southern Nazarene University. A stretch of the old highway curves by the north edge of Lake Overholser and along a rusty steel truss bridge. The old route can be followed around to the west to Yukon, where State Hwy. 66 takes over.

Judy's Antiques Cllbls. & Gifts
6722 N.W. 39th Expressway
405/787-2366

Ewok Shop
6632 N.W. 36th St.
405/495-8565

6 BLACKWELL

Ashby's Antique Mall
110 N. Main St.
405/363-4410

Rowe's Antique Mall
116 N. Main St.
405/363-2233

Larkin Gallery
201 N. Main St.
405/363-0645

7 BLANCHARD

Janet's Eats & Sweets
100 N. Main St.
405/485-2638

Yesterdays Best Antique Mall
109 N. Main St.
405/485-2550

Merctl Antiques & Collectibles
113 N. Main
405/485-3131

Main St. Antiques
114 N. Main
405/485-3688

Shade Tree Antiques
115 N. Main
405/485-9600

Aged to Perfection
114 2nd St.
405/485-3449

8 BRISTOW

Trash & Treasures
112 N. Main St.
918-367-6201

Rt. 66 Antiques & Collectibles
306 N. Main St.
918/367-5630

Joe Mounce Antiques
9th & Main St.
918/367-6492

9 BROKEN ARROW

Picket Fence
1000 N. Elm Place
918/258-2969

Medicine Man Mercantile
222 S. Main St.
918/251-1229

Antique Centre
412 S. Main St.
918/251-7092

Nailbender's
1819 S. Main St.
918/258-4644

Riverhill Antiques
19285 E. 131st St.
918/455-7530

10 CHANDLER

Chandler is headquarters for the Oklahoma Rt. 66 Association. Delightful styles of vintage gas station architecture and twelve buildings on the National Historic Register survived citywide destruction after an 1897 tornado. The museum of Pioneer History tells the story of Chandler's early days. Three miles west of town is the often-photographed metal barn advertising Meramac Caverns in Stanton, Missouri.

Treasure Barn
1112 W. 15th St.
405/258-3115

Brown Furniture
920 Manvel Ave.
405/258-1717

Fine Things On The Corner
923 Manvel Ave.
405/258-5101

Days Of Yesteryear
1214 Manvel Ave.
405/258-2217

Outskirts
1909 E. 1st St.
405/258-2902

11 CHICKASHA

Artistic Expressions Mall
309 W. Chicasha Ave.
405/224-9199

Yellow Rose Antique Mall
516 W. Chickasha Ave.
405/222-2112

Dangies Antiques
524 W. Chickasha Ave.
405/224-9019

Rocky's Ole Time Shoppe
1002 S. 4th St.
405/224-6945

Ersland Antiques
1124 S. 17th St.
405/224-2049

Collectors Corner
2001 S. 6th St.
405/224-3819

12 CHOUTEAU

Black Star Antiques
702 S. Chouteau Ave. (Hwy. 69 S)
918/476-6188
Hours: Mon.-Sat. 10-6, Sun. 12-6

Directions: Traveling Hwy. 412 take Chouteau exit. Go north 1 mile. Chouteau Avenue is Hwy. 69 South.

Space galore and jam-packed with items, this 14,000-square-foot shop houses antique clocks, tobacco tins, grocery store memorabilia, carnival chalkware (Kewpie dolls, Betty Boop, various figures). In addition, antique furniture, primitives, art and advertising collectibles are also available.

13 CLAREMORE

Claremore is home of the world-famous Will Rogers Memorial and Roger's burial site. Visitors can drive by the boarded-up Will Rogers Hotel, once resplendent with radium water baths on its top floor and a street level cafe. On the Rogers State College campus is the Lyon Riggs Memorial honoring the playwright for *Green Grows Like the Lilacs*, from which came the beloved Rogers and Hammerstein musical *Oklahoma!* Great antique browsing in dozens of shops, many of which are within expansive malls. J. M. Davis Gun Museum features more than 20,000 guns and related items, plus steins, swords, musical instruments and more.

Warden's Antique Clock Shop
105 N. Boling St.
918/341-1770

Chamwood Antique Mall
2409 N. Hwy. 20
918/341-7817

Milk Barn Antiques
220 N. Missouri Ave.
918/342-1116

Custom Frames & Collectibles
101 S. Seminole Ave.
918/341-2900

Frontier Gen. Store & Antique
318 W. Will Rogers Blvd.
918/341-3442

Shadows of Time
404 W. Will Rogers Blvd.
918/342-2633

Peachtree Antiquary
409 W. Will Rogers Blvd.
918/341-1360

Sanbear Antique Mall
508 W. Will Rogers Blvd.
918/341-6227

Hoover's Have All Mall
714 W. Will Rogers Blvd.
918/341-7878

A Place In Time Antqs. & Cllbls.
1215 W. Will Rogers Blvd.
918/343-9800

Antique Peddlers Mall
422 W. Will Rogers Blvd.
918/341-8615

14 CLINTON

In 1899, two men, waiting for a train at a station house, climbed on a box car to look over the countryside. Their eyes traveled over the Washita River Valley, and one of them said, "There's the place to build a town." The men were J. L. Avant and E. E. Blake. They were looking at the site where the town of Washita Junction would spring up, almost overnight, some four years later. However, before the dream could become a reality, there was a political fight that reached as far as the United States Congress, and the start of a feud between Arapaho and Washita Junction. The postal department refused to accept the name Washita Junction for the new town. Therefore, "Clinton" was chosen in honor of the late Judge Clinton Irwin.

Antique Mall of Clinton
815 Frisco
405/323-2486

Mohawk Lodge Indian Store
One Mile East on Old 66 Hwy.
405/323-2360

15 CUSHING

Friday Store
112 W. Broadway St.
918/225-3936

The Full Moon
120 W. Broadway St.
918/225-3936

16 DAVIS

Nelson's Cottonwood Corner
Hwy. 77 S
405/369-3836

D & D
206 E. Main
405/369-2398

Miss Sarah's
201 E. Main
405/369-2092

Honey Creek Emporium
212 E. Main St.
405/369-3524

The New Dusty Steamer Mall
222 E. Main
405/369-2959

Somethin Old Somethin New
503 E. Main St.
405/369-3418

Bric-A-Brac House
509 E. Main St.
405/369-3916

Country General
1 mile east of 1/2 Mile Rd. N
405/369-3954

Davis General Store
112 N. Third
405/369-3409

17 DEWEY

Dewey Antique Mall
202 N. Osage Hwy. 75
918/534-2660
Hours: 10:30-5:30 Mon.-Sat., 1-5 Sun.

A collector's paradise! Thirty dealers offer an amazing array of old Ertle banks, Western memorabilia, primitives, glassware and much, much more.

Treasures Are We
306 E. Don Tyler Ave.
918/534-3878

Something Different
319 E. Don Tyler Ave.
918/534-3645

Campbell's Antiques
418 Don Tyler
918/534-3068

Bar-Dew Antiques
Hwy 75 N
918/534-0222

Lighthouse
115 S. Osage
918/534-0662

Forget Me Not
305 S. Osage
918/534-3737

Linger Longer Antiques
814 N. Shawnee Ave.
918/534-0610

18 DUNCAN

Company's Comin
9 N. 8th St.
405/252-1844

Duncan Antique Mall
920 Main
405/255-2552

The Ginger Jar Antiques
1609 N. Hwy. 81
405/252-2329

Decors of Duncan
1898 N. Hwy. 81
405/252-9090

Brass Rail Antiques
5051 N. Hwy. 81
405/252-7277

Red Rose
5051 N. Hwy. 81
405/225-4925

Nancy's Antiques
Hwy 70 (Waurika)
405/228-2575

Ace High Pawn
112 E. Main
405/252-7296

Antique Market Place
726 W. Main St.
405/255-2499

2 B's Closet
806 W. Main St.
405/255-2211

K-Rider Co.
806 W. Main St.
405/255-2211

Pats Corner Mall
809 W. Main St.
405/255-4988

Aunti Msl
832 W. Main St.
405/252-3945

19 EDMOND

The city actually began in 1887 when the Santa Fe Railroad built a watering station at the highest point between the Cimarron and North Canadian rivers. The town sprang to life as homesteaders staked their claims around the station during the great Land Run on April 22, 1889.

The founders embodied the true spirit of pioneers—they were trailblazers who worked hard to ensure the best for their families and their futures. This is evident in the "firsts" they accomplished. Edmond was the first town in Oklahoma Territory to have a public school house as well as the first church. The territory's first library was organized in Edmond and the "Normal School" for teachers was established here. The Normal School is now the University of Central Oklahoma.

Country Collectibles
15 N. Littler Avenue
405/359-7210

Broadway Antique Mall
114 S. Broadway St.
405/340-8215

Edmond Antique Mall
907 S. Broadway St.
405/359-1234

Courtyard Antique Market
3314 S. Broadway
405/359-2719

Favorite Places To Eat

Cracker Barrel Old Country Store
I-35 & N.E. 122, Exit 137
405/478-7119

20 EL RENO

Motorists may notice something odd about the aged-looking broken neon sign in front of the Big Eight Motel; it boastfully proclaims the place as "Amarillo's Finest." Looks can be deceiving, though—the sign is a leftover prop from the movie *Rain Man*, which was filmed in part in Oklahoma, and Dustin Hoffman and Tom Cruise really slept here. El Reno was a major rail center for the Rock Island years ago, but a ghostly rail yard is all that remains today. Carnegie Library has archived photos of the famed Bunion Derby and paving of Rt. 66. On the west edge of town is old Fort Reno, where World War II German prisoners are among those buried in its windswept cemetery.

The Old Opera House
110 N. Bickford
405/422-3232
Hours of operation are Mon.-Sat. 10-5, Sun. 1-5

This renovated opera house features antiques and crafts. Furniture and accessories, collectibles, art and rugs offer a sampling of the items presented within the charming elegance of this massive and historic structure.

Rt. 66 Antique Mall
1629 E. State Hwy. 66
405/262-9366
Tue.-Sat. 10-6, Thurs. 10-8, Sun. 1-5, closed Mondays

On the west end of the city, 120 booths display varied and interesting pieces. Primitives are well represented. Other booths offer all types and descriptions of glassware and Americana.

Favorite Places To Eat

Old Opera House Tea Room
106 N. Bickford
405/422-3663
Open 11-2 Mon.-Sat.

Housed within the same complex of buildings as the Old Opera House, this eatery provides customers with a wide selection of meals. Soups, salads, sandwiches and hot entrees will fortify antiquers as they enjoy the shops and sights of El Reno.

21 ELK CITY

Old 66 Antique Mall
401 E. 3rd St.
405/225-9695

Kandie's Kreations & Kllbls.
2424 W. Third (Old Rt. 66)
405/225-6900

Country Creations Craft & Antique Mall
114 S. Main Street
405/225-7312

22 ENID

Mini-Mall
129 E. Broadway Ave.
405/233-5521

The Trolley Shop
910 W. Broadway
405/242-3123

Down Memory Lane Antiques
101 S. Grand St.
405/242-2100

Olden Daze Antique Mall
117 N. Grand St.
405/242-5633

Tommy's This N That
104 N. Independence
405/233-5642

Cherokee Strip Antiques
124 S. Independence
405/234-7878

Ben's Antiques
1205 S. Van Buren
405/237-5968

Enid Flea Market
S. Van Buren
405/237-5352

Cher-Dans
827 W. Maine Ave.
405/237-6880

23 GROVE

Flour Sack
307 S. Grant St.
918/786-4075

Precious Things
311 S. Grand St.
918/786-7044

Crystal's Antiques
Hwy. 59
918/786-9220

Sister's Trading Co.
Hwy. 59
918/786-9511

TBN Antiques & Uniques
3650 Hwy. 59 N
918/786-7721

Don's Swap Shop
5525 Hwy. 59 N
918/786-9590

Donna's Antiques and Cllbls.
2124 Hwy. 59 N
918/786-3534

Village Barn Antiques
Main St.
918/786-6132

Old Homestead
6 W. 3rd St.
918/786-8668

24 GUTHRIE

On a single day in April, 1889, a city was born...a new capital for a new territory. Overnight, 10,000 pioneers turned an open prairie into a sprawling array of crude tents, wagon beds, and rough-hewn wooden buildings. From that first day of chaos, an elegant Victorian city evolved with remarkable architecture and expressive character to become the capital of the 46th state, Oklahoma.

When the capital was moved south, this majesty of the plains fell by the wayside. Today, through careful restoration, this rich architectural legacy has been preserved in all its grandeur. Visitors can shop the numerous boutiques, antique malls and specialty shops downtown and also see the homes of governors, editors, law men, and outlaws in Guthrie's residential district.

Historic walking and trolley tours, jubilant festivals, cowpunching rodeos, live professional theatre, captivating museums, exquisite dining and a charming community make Guthrie a turn-of-the-century destination.

Elk's Alley
210 W. Harrison
405/282-6100

King's Antiques
107 W. Oklahoma Ave.
405/282-0534

Antiques Etc.
113 W. Oklahoma Ave.
405/282-9610

Aunt Bea's Attic
114 W. Oklahoma Ave.
405/282-4548

Recollections Antique Mall
118 E. Oklahoma Ave.
405/260-0101

89er Antique Mall
119 W. Oklahoma Ave.
405/282-2661

Vic's Place
124 N. 2nd St.
405/282-5586

Red Earth Antiques
103 S. Second
405/260-1030

25 HENRYETTA

B & Jays Antiques
214 W. Main St.
918/652-7552

Country Violet Antiques
1202 W. Main St.
918/652-4211

Attic Treasures Mall
115 N. 2nd St.
918/652-2484

26 JENKS

Jenks, like many other towns in Indian Territory originated around a railroad. It started as a Midland Valley Railroad Depot along a route between Tulsa and Muskogee.

Adhering to the provisions of the treaty concluded on February 14, 1833, between the Creek Indians and the United States of America, the final Roll of Citizens and Freedmen of the Five Civilized Tribes in Indian Territory had been completed. Those Indian citizens and Freedmen (formerly slaves) received allotments. (In 1904, the land that became the townsite of Jenks, Indian Territory was on the allotment of three Freedmen.) The Midland Valley Railroad Company purchased about 130 acres for the town. In 1907, Jenks became a town with 150 people. The city of Jenks, Ok, now consists of nearly 8,800 people.

There are various stories as to the origin of the town name. Some report that it honored a Midland Valley Railroad engineer or conductor; others say the name was that of a carpenter named Jenks who built the depot. Still others believe the town was named for Dr. Jenks who was an early day resident. The agent for the Midland Townsite Company says the name "Jenks" came from a director in the Philadelphia corporation that built the Midland Valley Railroad.

Cornerstone Memories
102 S. 1st St.
918/298-6255

A Niche In Tyme
112 S. 1st St.
918/298-1957

Linda's Things
105 N. 5th St.
918/299-5350

Main Street Antique Mall
105 E. Main St.
918/299-2806

Abbey Road Antiques
107 E. Main St.
918/299-4696

Bittersweet Antiques
108 E. Main St.
918/298-9408

Paradise Found Antiques
109 E. Main St.
918/299-2691

Kracker Box
116 E. Main St.
918/299-5353

Miss McGillicutty's
203 E. Main St.
918/298-4287

Serendipity
207 E. Main St.
918/298-5628

Jenks House
410 E. Main St.
918/299-9100

Auntie Em's Victorian Village
101 W. Main St.
918/299-7231

Ancestors Antiques
610 W. Main St.
918/298-3080

Jenkins Guild Shops
Main St.-General Info
918/299-5005

27 LAWTON

Johnson's Furn. Repair
915 S.W. A Ave.
405/357-7307

Pickering Antiques
2 S.E. B Ave.
405/357-3276

Yesterdays Antique Mall
423 S.W. C Ave.
405/353-6005

Okie's Antiques
1706 N.W. Cache Rd.
405/355-4104

Wooden Windmill
5224 N.W. Cache Rd.
405/357-9697

Pickles Antique Mall
620 S.W. D Ave.
405/353-5050

Antiques by Helen
1002 S.W. D Ave.
405/357-1375

Another Time Antiques
709 S.W. E. Ave.
405/353-0639

Antiques & Crafts by Cathy
404 S.W. 10th St.
405/355-0710

28 LOCUST GROVE

Favorite Places To Eat

Country Cottage
608 N. Hwy. 82
918/479-6439

Buffet style or changing menu. The specialty is fried chicken.

Pap's Country Market
607 N. Hwy. 82
918/479-5541

29 MIAMI

Wind along Main Street to the grand old Coleman Theater, a 1929 Spanish Mission-style structure built with profits from the Turkey Fat Mine in Commerce. The Coleman, once a regular stop on the vaudeville circuit, is now undergoing a $1.5 million renovation project. Visitors may stop by the Chamber office to arrange a tour. Miami's downtown features retail shops and a cafe, and a block away is the Dobson Museum, which houses pioneer and mining artifacts.

Ole Shoppe
301 B St. SE
918/540-2961

Gramma's Antique Mall
417 D St. NE
918/542-1585

Classy Brass Antiques
31 S. Main St.
918/542-2203

Box Office Antiques
105 N. Main St.
918/540-0557

Magnolia Manor
107 N. Main
918/542-2046

Antiques & Uniques
113 N. Main
No Phone

Charlotte's C & T Bargain Center
123 S. Main St.
918/540-0543

30 MIDWEST CITY

Favorite Places To Eat

Cracker Barrel Old Country Store
I-40 & Tinker Diagonal, Exit 156A
405/736-1202

31 MUSKOGEE

Cllbl. Corner & Antique Mall
30 W. Broadway St.
918/682-4335

Beaver's Antiques
540 Court St.
918/682-5503

Mr. Haney's Treasures
210 N. Edmond St.
918/687-6276

Yellow Brick Road
120 S. Main St.
918/686-8704

You Never Know
120 S. Main St.
918/682-8506

Old America Antique Mall
Hwy 69 S
918/687-8600

Antiques Galore
2225 W. Shawnee St.
918/683-3281

Mid-American Antique Mall
2251 S. 32nd St. W
918/683-2922

Main Street USA Antique Mall
2426 N. 32nd St. W
918/687-4334

32 NOBLE

A Point In Time
213 N. Main
405/872-8600

Vintage Village Antiques
1722 N. Main St.
405/872-7062

Remember When
119 S. Main
405/872-8484

33 NORMAN

The Company Store Antique Mall
300 East Main St.
405/360-5959
Open daily: Mon.-Fri. 10-6, Sat. 10-5, Sun. 1-5

Directions: From I-35, take the Main Street exit east. Go 2 miles. Shop located on the corner of Main and Crawford Streets.

When you reach the old green and red buckboard overflowing with colorful flowers, you've found The Company Store. This 7,000 square foot building is a local landmark (the old Palace Garage) built c. 1900. Inside, 60 dealers present an outstanding variety of distinctive antiques including Flow Blue, Roseville and Rookwood along with exceptional stained glass pieces. Superb furnishings, unusual collectibles and elegant costume jewelry are also available.

Kensington Market Antq. Mall
208 W. Gray St.
405/364-8840

Olde Town Market Place
219 E. Gray St.
405/447-8846

Whispering Pines Antiques
Hwy. 9
405/447-8297

Gallery Nouveau
1630 W. Lindsey St.
405/321-8687

Hope Chest Antqs. & Cllbls.
1714 W. Lindsey St.
405/321-8059

Lorri Ann's Antiques
3417 Sooner Fashion Mall
405/321-8633

Peddlers Shop
209 W. Main St.
405/360-1015

Theo's Marketplace
3720 W. Robinson St.
405/364-0728

Hoover Antique Galleries
210 36th Ave. SW
405/360-4488

Favorite Places To Eat

Cracker Barrel Old Country Store
I-35 & Robinson Rd., Exit 110
405/360-3117

34 OKEMAH

Pioneer Mall
215 W. Broadway St.
918/623-9124

35 OKLAHOMA CITY

The old route is sometimes hard to follow as it jogs down Lincoln Boulevard, past the State Capitol (note the oil wells on the Capitol grounds), then west along Northwest 23rd and 39th Streets. Look for a retro-style McDonald's restaurant at 23rd and Pennsylvania. Not far from the National Cowboy Hall of Fame and the Western Heritage Center on the city's northeast side, an old speakeasy once known as the Kentucky Club now welcomes all as a barbecue restaurant called the Oklahoma County Line. The eclectic Rt. 66 store at 50 Penn Place Mall injects local flavor into modern folk art, books and other symbols of the Main Street America. West on 39th Street, past Portland is Rt. 66 Bowl, the oldest still-operating bowling alley in Oklahoma City. A cool purple and green sign outside Meike's Rt. 66 Restaurant at Meridian Avenue hints of the nostalgic decor inside. A Texaco clock, old gas pump, and an assortment of metal toys give customers a feast for their eyes while they enjoy hearty home style Italian food.

A Family Tree Antique Mall
2422 S. Agnew Ave.
405/634-1159

Antique Alley
5206 N. Classen Blvd.
405/840-3514

Carolyn's Keepsakes
1116 N.W. 51st St.
405/842-1296

Colonies
1120 N.W. 51st St.
405/842-1279

Pat & Barb's Antiques
1120 N.W. 51st St.
405/840-1220

What-Not Shelf Antiques
1120 N.W. 51st St.
405/842-7176

My Daughter's Place
2648 S.W. 44th St.
405/685-5784

Michaels Antique Clocks
5920 W. Hefner Rd.
405/722-3300

Abalache Book & Antq. Shop
311 S. Klein Ave.
405/235-3288

Raggedy Anne's Market Antqs.
311 S. Klein Ave.
405/239-2273

Star Antiques
311 S. Klein Ave.
405/232-5901

Trader Jean
311 S. Klein Ave.
405/232-8044

Top of the Mart
311 S. Klein Ave.
405/239-8325

Country Temptations
4801 N. Macarthur Blvd.
405/789-8876

Bricktown Antique Shop
100 E. Main
405/235-2803

Mikes Antiques
1008 N. May Ave.
405/949-0707

Antique Co-Op
1227 N. May Ave.
405/942-1214

Buckboard Antiques & Quilts
1411 N. May Ave.
405/943-7020

May Antique Mall
1515 N. May Ave.
405/947-3800

Unique Antiques & Collectibles
2125 N. May Ave.
405/943-0404

Splvey's Antiques
2500 N. May Ave.
405/947-5454

Villa Antique Mall
3132 N. May Ave.
405/949-1185

Return Engagement
7423 N. May Ave.
405/843-6363

Apple Tree Antique Mall
1111 N. Meridian Ave.
405/947-8999

Antique House
4409 N. Meridian Ave.
405/495-2221

Pine Shop
12020 N.E. Exprwy (I-35)
405/478-0220

Antique Centre Inc.
1433 N.W. Expressway
405/842-0070

Southern Antique Mall
2196 S. Service Rd.
405/794-9898

Architectural Antiques
By Appointment
405/232-0759

Coca-Nuts Antiques
3234 E. I-240 Service Rd.
405/672-5600

Crow's Nest
2800 N.W. 10th St.
405/947-6655

Bare Necessities Mall
2842 N.W. 10th St.
405/943-2238

Apple Orchard
2921 N.W. 10th St.
405/946-3015

Apple Barrel Antique Mall
4619 N.W. 10th St.
405/947-7732

English Tea Co.
4405 S.E. 28th St.
405/672-0484

Easleys Touch of Class Antqs.
4633 S.E. 29th St.
405/672-9010

Oodles & Aah's
7622 N. Western
405/848-7099

Collectibles Etc.
1516 N.W. 23rd St.
405/524-1700

Etta's Gift Gallery
6017 N.W. 23rd St.
405/495-1048

Top Hat Antiques
4411 N. Western
405/557-1732

Antiques & Design
4512 N. Western
405/524-1969

Covington Antique Market
6900 N. Western
405/842-3030

Scranton Uniques
7512 N. Western
405/521-8715

Discoveries
7612 N. Western
405/842-9555

Jody Kerr Antiques
7908 N. Western
405/842-5951

Painted Door Gallery Ltd.
8601 S. Western
405/632-4410

Langhorne Place Antiques
9115 N. Western
405/848-3192

Sampler Antqs. & Wood Works
9201 N. Western
405/848-7007

Nothing But The Best
By Appointment Only
405/842-2545

Antique Hardware
1920 Linwood Blvd.
405/236-5662

Favorite Places To Eat

Cracker Barrel Old Country Store
I-40 & Meridian Blvd., Exit 145
405/948-1151

36 OKMULGEE

Kate's Antiques
107 S. Grand
No Phone

Ye Olde Lamp Post
113 S. Grand Ave.
918/756-4539

Starr Collectibles
100 S. Morton Ave.
918/756-0736

Legacy Antiques
218 E. 6th St.
918/756-0567

37 PERRY

Georgia's Fine Furniture
611 Delaware St.
405/336-4501

Antiques on the Square
615 Delaware St.
405/336-3327

Cherokee Strip Antique Mall
645 Delaware St.
405/336-4598

The Antique Spot
902 11th St.
405/336-5290

Memories of Yesteryear
317 N. 7th St.
405/336-5650

The Antique Station
625 6th St.
405/336-5743

Hazel's Antiques
817 Wakefield
405/336-4794

38 PONCA CITY

Terri's Toys & Nostalgia
419 S. 1st St.
405/762-8697

Early Attic
510 N. 1st St.
405/762-5142

Christy's
3005 N. 14th St.
405/765-3800

Granary
218 W. Grand
405/762-5118

39 PRYOR

Wacky Jackie
118 S. Adair St.
918/825-6125

Heritage Antique Mall
122 S. Adair St.
918/825-5714

Rustiques
207 S. Adair St.
918/825-6151

Mary's Whatnots
103 E. Graham Ave.
918/825-3757

40 PURCELL

T's Antiques Mall
116 W. Main St.
405/527-2766

Auntie Mae's Antiques
127 W. Main St.
405/527-5214

Butler Antiques
202 W. Main St.
405/527-9592

41 SAPULPA

Home of Frankoma Pottery, Sapulpa is a popular stopping-off place for travelers seeking diversion. Tours are offered weekdays, and the gift shop is open all week. In town, the Sapulpa Historical Museum is open afternoons except Sunday. Since the 1950s, locals have gathered at Norma's Diamond Cafe, and the Hickory House Restaurant serves up great barbeque and the only live music in town. A 3-mile stretch of original Rt. 66 signed as the Ozark Trail can be found west of town, where venturesome motorists will cross the steel-and-brick Ozark bridge, under an old concrete Frisco railroad bridge, and go by the Teepee Drive In, which still operates in summer.

Antiques N Stuff
15 E. Dewey Ave.
918/224-8049

Homespun Treasures
209 E. Dewey Ave.
918/227-4508

A Moment in Time
205 E. Dewey Ave.
918/224-7158

Neat Stuff
1115 E. Dewey Ave.
918/224-6097

Foote & Son Antq. Invmt. Co.
15 N. Elm St.
918/227-0250

Sara's Country Corner
1 S. Main St.
918/224-6544

Schwickerath Furniture
Main St.
918/224-5396

Favorite Places To Eat

Freddie's
1425 Sapulpa Road
918/224-4301

For more than 30 years, loyal Freddie's customers have been enjoying its famous Bar-B-Cue, perfect steaks and super seafood selections, served with Freddie's special tabouly, houmus and cabbage rolls.

This full-service restaurant is a favorite for a friendly, comfortable atmosphere, generous portions and reasonable prices.

42 SEMINOLE

Country Road Antique Market
Exit 200 I-40
405/382-1133

Memory Lane
217 N. Main St.
405/382-8200

Lil's
State Hwy. 3-1 1/2 Mi N. of Seminole College
405/382-7716

43 SHAWNEE

Crafters Showplace
115 East Main Street
405/273-7985
Hours: Mon.-Sat. 10-5:30, Jan.- March, closed Mondays

In historic Downtown Shawnee, antiques such as furniture and collectibles will catch your attention. But, the shop's main focus is smaller bric-a-brac pieces and kitchen accessories. In addition, crafts persons will enjoy the array of supplies and completed craft projects for sale.

Antiques of Distinction
111 North Broadway
405/878-9839
Open 10-5 Mon.-Sat., closed Sundays

Fine antiques with an elegant air line your stroll through this shop. Furniture stripping and refinishing are an added specialty.

Legends
124 North Beard
405/878-0066

With the name hinting fine, quality pieces, antiques and collectibles serve as the basis of the selection. Furniture and accessories are in large part responsible for the singular style of this shop.

Kickapoo Korner
1025 N. Kickapoo St.
405/275-6511

Groves
602 E. Highland St.
405/878-9919

Oliver-Hardin Antiques
313 Macarthur St.
405/273-5060

Main St. Gifts
16 E. Main St.
405/275-1088

Ok Territory Antiques Ltd. Co.
214 E. Main St.
405/878-0214

Sante Fe Trading Post
524 E. Main St.
405/275-5900

Green's Corner
723 E. Main St.
405/273-2021

Grandma Had It Antiques
36700 W. Old High #270
405/275-7766

44 SKIATOOK

Ford's Antiques & Collectibles
100 E. Rogers Blvd.
918/396-4268

Christi's Unlimited
112 E. Rogers Blvd.
918/396-0248

Third Time Around
120 E. Rogers Blvd.
918/396-3144

Rogers Blvd. Antiques
101 W. Rogers Blvd.
918/396-0065

Antique Mall of Skiatook
2200 W. Rogers Blvd.
918/396-1279

45 STILLWATER

Jeanne's Antiques
520 S. Knoblock St.
405/372-8567

Delores Antiques
4224 N. Washington St.
405/372-1455

Antique Mall of Stillwater
116 & 122 E. 9th Ave.
405/372-2322

The Myriad
119 E. 9th
405/372-6181

Mrs. Brown's Attic
211 N. Perkins Rd.
405/624-0844

Rock Barn Relics
1623 S. Perkins Rd.
405/372-2276

46 STROUD

City streets are bustling these days, thanks to the Tanger Outlet Mall that opened just a few years ago. Good restaurants are open throughout town, but the Rock Cafe is a truly Rt. 66 relic. Open since 1939, the eatery was once billed as the busiest truck stop along the old road. Its original owner paid $5 for the stones dug up during the construction of Old 66, and those stones were used to build the cafe. Tasty smoked meats, buffalo, and delectable Swiss/German cuisine are the bill o' fare, and the owner speaks German, Italian, French, English, and Swiss.

Antique Alley Mall
309 W. Main St.
918/968-3761

Memory Lane
405 W. Main St.
918/968-3491

Friends Arts & Antiques
404 W. Main St.
918/968-2568

Great Places To Stay

Stroud House Bed and Breakfast
110 East Second Street
918/968-2978 or 1-800-259-2978
Rates: $65-100

When you need a break from the hassles of life (which I do after writing this book), visit the Stroud House Bed and Breakfast, a nationally recognized historic Victorian home. The Stroud House was constructed by J.W. Stroud in 1900 and renovated by the hosts in 1992. Four beautifully decorated guest rooms offer rest and relaxation. Each guest gets a "famous" Stroud House cookie. (I need a care package sent to me now!)

47 SULPHUR

Memory Lane Antiques & Collectibles
820 W. 12th Street
405/622-2090
Open Mon.-Sat, 10-5 and Sun. 12-5

Directions: Traveling I-35 South, take Hwy. 7 East approximately 12 miles. In Sulphur, turn right 1/2 block at the traffic light on 12th Street. (If going I-35 North, take exit 51.)

A stroll among pieces from yesteryear inside this 2-building, 4,000-square-foot collector's treasure chest reveals fine porcelains such as Haviland, Limoges, Old Ivory and R.S. Prussia. Antique furniture, wall pockets, kitchen collectibles plus collector plates add to the harvest of goods.

Gettin Place
100 W. Muskogee St.
405/622-3796

Quail Hollow Depot
20 Quail Hollow Rd.
405/622-4081

Favorite Places To Eat

Bricks Restaurant
2112 W. Broadway
405/622-3125
Open Sun.-Thurs. 11-9, Fr. & Sat. 11-9:30

Specialties are barbecue and home cooking.

Quail Hollow Depot
20 Quail Hollow Rd.
405/622-4080
Open Tue.-Sat. 11-2:30 p.m.

Tea Room
The Silver Turtle
Hwy. 7 (West of Sulphur)
405/622-3500
Open Tue.-Sat.

Offering steaks and fish.

48 TULSA

Once known as "The Oil Capital of the World," Tulsa's very lifeblood from the turn of the century through the 1930s was the petroleum industry. Lavish Art Deco buildings grace the state's largest city, and walking and driving tours reveal cozy downtown eateries like Ike's Chili Hut and Jim's Coney Island Hot Wiener Shop. Rt. 66 gets quirky in town, jogging off Admiral and onto Eleventh Street, where a vintage bridge carried Rt. 66 traffic over the Arkansas River and places like the Metro Diner harken to the heyday of Rt. 66. Check out the Browsery Antiques on Eleventh for Rt. 66 momentos.

Heart of Tulsa
Exposition Center at Expo Square
1-800-755-5488
Call for dates

Over 600 exhibitors from Oklahoma and the Midwest gather to display antiques, collectibles, arts and crafts.

Great American Antique Mall
9216 E. Admiral Place
918/834-6363

Browsery
3311 E. 11th St.
918/836-4479

White Bear Antiques
1301 E. 15th St.
918/592-1914

Spectrum
1307 E. 15th St.
918/582-6480

Antiquary
1325 E. 15th St.
918/582-2897

Colonial Antiques
1329 E. 15th St.
918/585-3865

Charles Faudree
1345 E. 15th St.
918/747-9706

Sophronia's
1515 E. 15th St.
918/592-2887

Lampost Silver Co.
13012 E. 21st Street
918/438-3636

Jared's Inc.
1602 E. 15th St.
918/582-3018

Zoller Iqbal Designs & Antqs.
1603 E. 15th St.
918/583-1966

Cisar-Holt Inc.
1605 E. 15th St.
918/582-3080

Amir's Persian Imports
2204 E. 15th St.
918/744-6464

Tulsa Antique Mall
2235 E. 51st St.
918/742-4466

Kay's Antiques
2814 E. 15th St.
918/743-5653

Paula's Antiques & Estate Furn.
2816 E. 15th St.
918/742-6191

Deco to Disco
3213 E. 15th St.
918/749-3620

Glasstique
1341 E. 41st St.
918/742-3434

Sam Spacek's Antiques
8212 E. 41st St.
918/627-3021

Brass Buff
1124 S. Harvard Ave.
918/592-1717

Estate Furniture
1531 S. Harvard Ave.
918/743-3231

Side Door Antiques
1547 S. Harvard Ave.
918/742-5912

Centrum
8130 S. Lewis Ave.
918/299-3400

Snow's Consignment Store
909 S. Memorial Dr.
918/266-7446

And Then
4717 S. Mingo Rd.
918/622-9447

Flowers & Antiques by Phillip
3740 S. Peoria Ave.
918/748-9450

Consignment Treasures
3807 S. Peoria Ave.
918/742-8550

Zelda's Antiques
1701 E. 7th St.
918/583-5599

Tulsa Card Co.
4423 E. 31st St.
918/744-8020

Country Charm Antqs. & Gifts
3316 E. 32nd St.
918/743-3656

Favorite Places To Eat

Cracker Barrel Old Country Store
I-44 & 31st St., Exit 232
918-610-0414

49 VALLIANT

Vicki's Antiques, Collectibles & Crafts
Hwy. 70
405/933-5220

50 YUKON

Toward this town, the home of country music star Garth Brooks, the landscape flattens out to western prairie. The "Yukon's Best" grain mill sign can be seen for miles as it lights up nighttime skies. Across from the grain elevators lies Yukon's Best Railroad Museum, featuring restored cars containing railroad memorabilia. The famed Chisholm Trail cut through here, and a watering hole still remains for visitors to see. Residents celebrate their western and ethnic heritage with a Chisholm Trail Festival each June and Czech Festival every October.

Eagle Crest Antiques
430 W. Main St.
405/350-7474

Grandma's Treasures
453 W. Main St.
405/350-1415

Yukon's Yunique Antique
456 Main
405/354-2511

Notes

Oregon

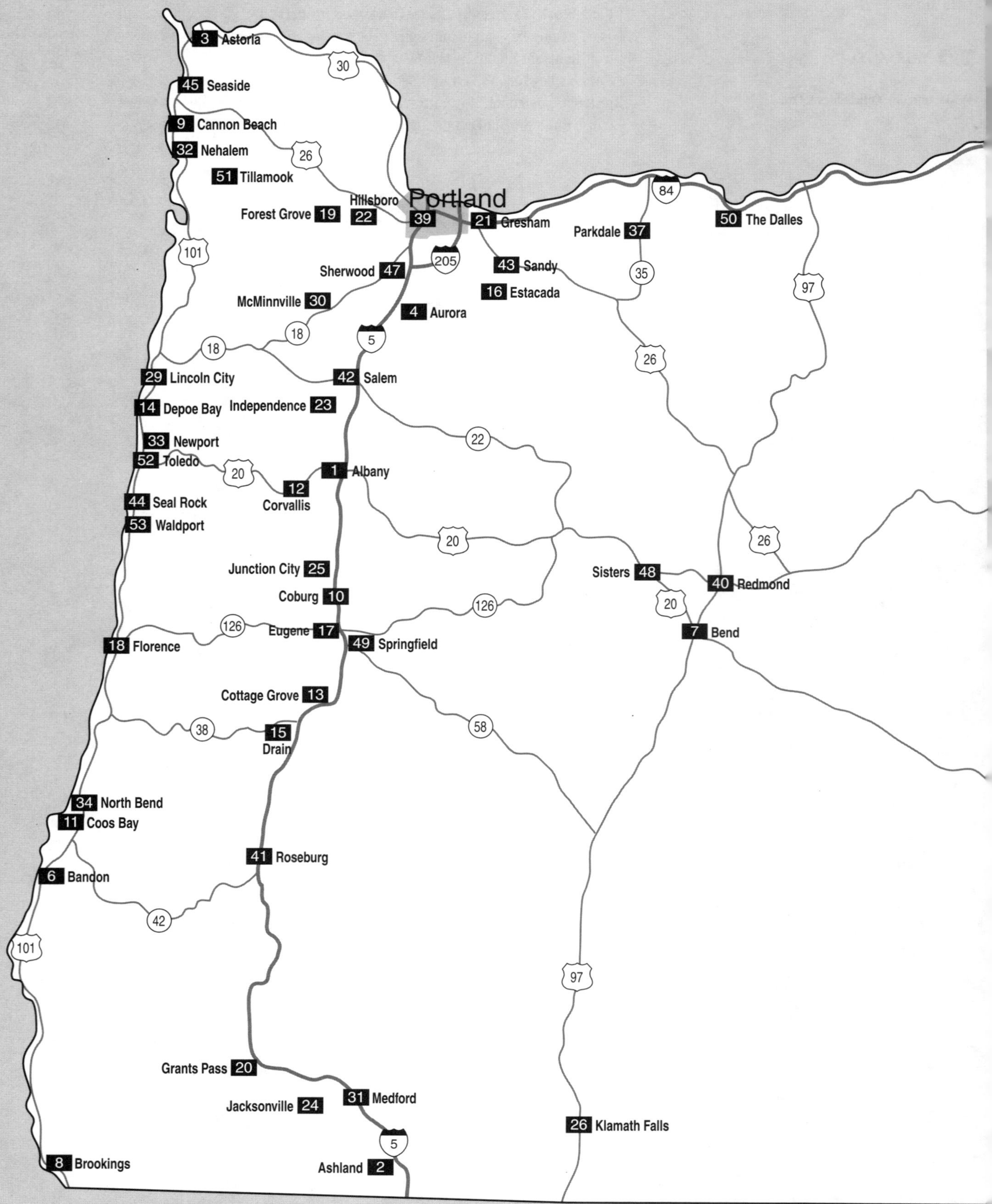

3 Astoria
45 Seaside
9 Cannon Beach
32 Nehalem
51 Tillamook
Forest Grove 19
Hillsboro 22
Portland 39
21 Gresham
Parkdale 37
50 The Dalles
Sherwood 47
43 Sandy
16 Estacada
McMinnville 30
4 Aurora
29 Lincoln City
42 Salem
14 Depoe Bay
Independence 23
33 Newport
52 Toledo
1 Albany
12 Corvallis
44 Seal Rock
53 Waldport
Junction City 25
Coburg 10
Sisters 48
40 Redmond
7 Bend
Eugene 17
49 Springfield
18 Florence
Cottage Grove 13
15 Drain
34 North Bend
11 Coos Bay
41 Roseburg
6 Bandon
Grants Pass 20
31 Medford
Jacksonville 24
26 Klamath Falls
8 Brookings
Ashland 2
30
26
84
101
205
35
97
5
18
22
20
126
58
38
42

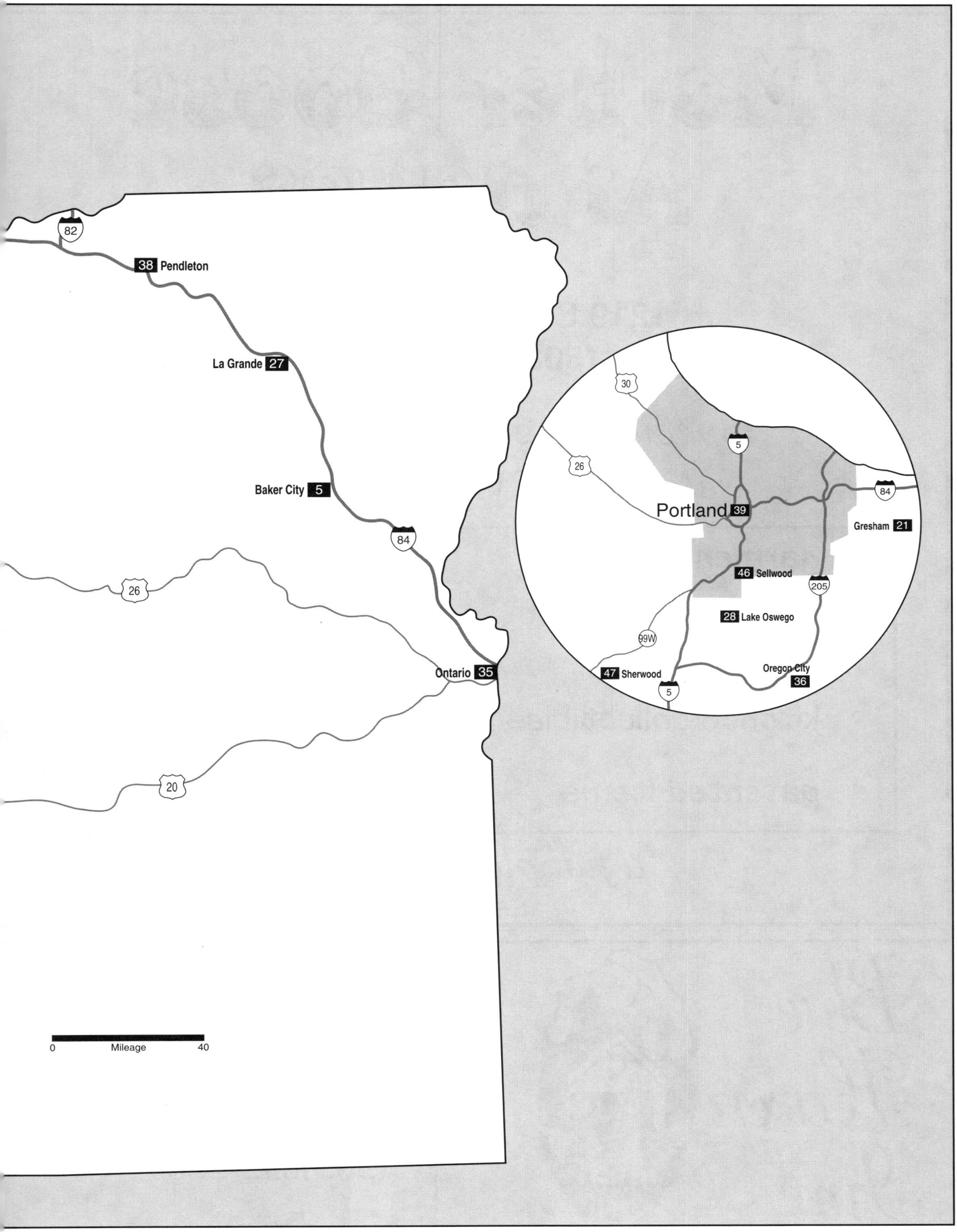

82
38 Pendleton
La Grande 27
Baker City 5
84
26
Ontario 35
20
0 Mileage 40
30
5
26
84
Portland 39
Gresham 21
46 Sellwood
205
28 Lake Oswego
99W
47 Sherwood
Oregon City 36
5

Mother Goose Antiques

1219 Soutwest 19th St.
(503) 223-4493

"Specializing in an outstanding selection of Vintage Smalls"

- garment buttons
- 50's + older dollhouse minitures
- holiday items
- costume jewelry
- kitchen collectibles
- advertising items
- patented items
- spice tins + more

"a fun place to shop'

Portland

Blue Haven Inn

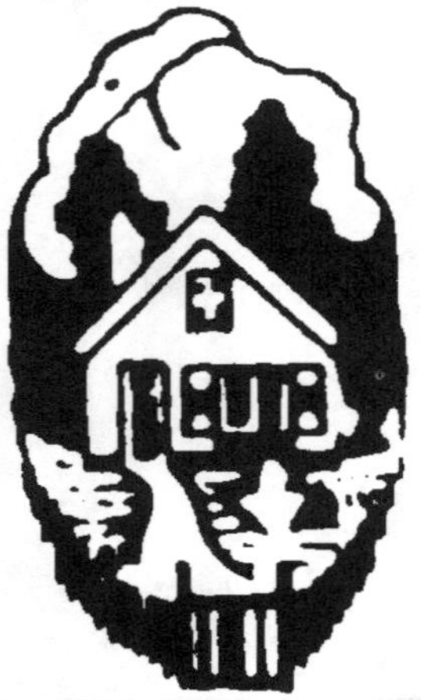

and

"Overflow Shop"

adjacent to the Inn
3025 Gienger Rd.
(503)842-2265

Tillamook

Oregon

1 ALBANY

A drive east along the Wilamette River on Hwy. 20 takes you back in time to Albany. Here, historic charm is evident in more than 700 beautifully preserved buildings, churches and homes, including the Monteith House, Albany's oldest frame-built home. While you're here discover antique shops, Victorian gardens and a farmers' market via a downtown trolley or horse-drawn wagon tour.

Feather Tree
121 Broadalbin St. SW
541/967-9381

Mitsch's Antiques
131 Broadalbin St. SW
541/926-724

Antique Traditions
122 Ferry St. SW
541/926-0380

Peabody's Antiques-Gifts
238 1st Ave. W
541/926-3654

Arlene's Victorian Rose
244 1st Ave. SW
541/928-4203

Byers Antiques
305 1st Ave. W
541/928-3195

Pastimes Antiques
317 1st Ave. W
541/926-0303

First and Ferry Antiques
343 1st Ave. W
541/928-8774

Albany Book Co.
1425 Pacific Blvd. SE
541/926-2612

Clockwise
211 2nd Ave. SW
541/926-8507

B and E Antiques & More
223 2nd Ave. SW
541/928-2174

2 ASHLAND

As the southernmost town in the I-5 corridor, Ashland is the gateway for many Oregon visitors. The main attraction is the Tony Award-winning Oregon Shakespeare Festival. From mid-February through October, it presents 11 plays on three unique stages. Tickets and bed and breakfast reservations can be hard to come by on weekends and in the summer months, so plan in advance if you can. Better yet, schedule your visit for spring or fall.

While in town, take the Backstage Tour. Visit the Exhibit Center, where you can try on old costumes, then explore some of the other features that play a leading role in the character of Ashland such as antique shops, boutiques, and unusual art galleries.

Rita's Relics
93 Oak Street
541/482-0777

Perry S. Prince Asian Antiques
349 E. Main Street
541/488-1989

3 ASTORIA

Named after John Jacob Astor, the North Coast city of Astoria, at the mouth of the Columbia, is the site of the first permanent United States settlement west of the Rockies. Its historic charm and Victorian ambiance have provided the settings for movies such as *Free Willy* and *Kindergarten Cop*.

Phog Bounders Antique Mall
1052 Commercial St.
503/325-9722

Rivers Edge Decorators
1145 Commercial St.
503/325-7040

Fort George Trading Co.
1174 Commercial St.
503/325-1690

Commercial Street Collectibles
1227 Commercial St.
503/325-5838

Marine Drive Antiques
2093 Marine Dr.
503/325-8723

Uppertown Antiques & Gallery
2911 Marine Dr.
503/325-5000

4 AURORA

Impressions of Aurora
Hwy 99 E & Main St.
503/678-5312

Old Miller Place
21358 Hwy. 99 E
503/678-1128

Aurora Crossing Antiques
21368 Hwy. 99 E
503/678-1630

Aurora Antique Mall
21418 Hy #-99 E
503/678-2139

Gary's Antiques
21627 Hy #-99 E
503/678-2616

Antique Colony
21581 Main St. NE
503/678-1010

Main Street Mercantile
21610 Main St. NE
503/678-1044

Time After Time
21611 Main St. NE
503/678-5463

Cottage Antiques
21631 Main St. NE
503/678-5911

Jacob's House
21641 Main St. NE
503/678-3078

Aurora State Bank Antiques
21690 Main St. NE
503/678-3060

Craig's Four Seasons Antiques
14979 2nd St.
503/678-2266

5 BAKER CITY

Mr. G's
2175 Broadway St.
541/523-2376

Windfall Antiques
2306 Broadway St.
541/523-7531

Baker City Collectibles
2332 Broadway St.
541/523-3592

Francis' Memory House Antqs.
1780 Main St.
541/523-6227

Do Overs Antiques
2658 10th St.
541/523-5717

6 BANDON

Country Cottage Antiques
Morrison Rd. & Hwy 42 S
541/347-3800

7 BEND

Buffet Flat
64990 Deschutes Market Road
541/389-9797
Open every day of the week from 10-6 except Christmas Day

Directions: Situated halfway between Bend and Redmond at Deschutes Junction. From Hwy. 97, travel approximately 500 feet to the northeast corner of Deschutes Junction, turn at the "Big White Wagon." heck for further directions upon arrival as a new overpass is being constructed in 1997.

Featured in *Self Magazine*, on PBS' *The Collectors* and The Learning Channel's *Neat Stuff*, Buffet Flat houses a remarkable antique, souvenir and "re-use it" store. Among the extraordinary collection of wares are pieces from the 1800s to 1950s including Victoriana, Art Nouveau, Art Deco, Moderene and Atomic. The shop serves as the jumping off point for The Funny Farm, a private park and playground which is open to the public, no admission. Mind-boggling adventure awaits as you gaze upon such sights as the Bowling Ball Garden, The Love Pond and Cupid's Arrow, or the rare Punk Flamingo to name a very few.

Icehouse Trading Post
20410 N.E. Bend River Mall Dr.
541/383-3713

Farm Antiques
838 N.W. Bond St.
541/382-8565

Homespun Antiques
856 N.W. Bond St.
541/385-3344

Enchantments Fine Antiques
1002 N.W. Bond St.
541/388-7324

Bond Street Antiques
1008 N.W. Bond St.
541/383-3386

Deja Vu Experienced Furniture
225 S.W. Century Dr.
541/317-9169

Iron Horse Second Hand Store
210 N.W. Congress St.
541/382-5175

Sally's Antiques & Collectibles
61360 S. Hwy. 97
541/385-6237

Trivia Antiques
106 N.W. Minnesota Ave.
541/389-4166

605 Antiques
604 N.W. Newport Ave.
541/389-6552

Cottage Clollectibles
210 S.E. Urania Lane
541/389-2075

8 BROOKINGS

Old Town Collectibles & Misc.
547-Chetco Ave.
541/469-0756

Van's Antiques
15714 Hwy. 101 S
541/469-3719

9 CANNON BEACH

Tolovana Antiques
3116 S. Hemlock
503/436-0261

Pat & Mike's Antiques
148 S. Monro Rd.
503/436-1843

10 COBURG

Coburg Inn Antique Shops
91108 N. Willamette St.
541/343-4550

Iron Kettle Antiques
1359 Goodpasture Island Rd.
541/683-1267

Dotson's Coburg Antiques
91109 Willamette St.
541/342-2732

Joseph's Antiques
32697 E. Pearl Street
541/345-0092

Jolene's Antiques
32697 E. Pearl St.
541/302-3310

Ages Ago
90999 S. Willamette St.
541/343-6363

Mathew House Antiques
32702 Pearl St.
541/343-3876

Ollie's Oldies
90559 Coburg Rd.
541/343-9989

Big Wheel Antiques
1091 Coburg Rd.
541/344-7300

Schram's Antiques
3699 Coburg Rd.
541/683-4965

Willow Tree Antique Mall
Coburg Rd.
541/465-4817

Cara's Antiques
155 N. Willamette
541/345-2142

Coburg Road Antiques
90934 Coburg Rd.
541/683-3310

11 COOS BAY

Auction Company of Southern Oregon
Call ahead for Auction Dates
541/267-5361

When an auction bills itself as a "full service" country auction, you never know what to expect. Anything from antiques to the family farm could be up for grabs. That's what makes it so interesting, Granny could have stuffed a lot of things away in the old barn.

Marshfield Mercantile Annex
145 S. Broadway
541/267-7706

Marshfield Mercantile Antique
145 Central Ave.
541/267-4636

Maddie's Antiques & Cllbls.
1161 Cape Arago Hwy.
541/888-9214

Charleston Mall
8073 Cape Arago Hwy.
541-888-8083

12 CORVALLIS

Finders Keepers
5820 N.W. Hwy. 99
541/745-5848

Gold Dust
1413 N.W. 9th St.
541/758-7427

Beekman Place
635 S.W. Western Blvd.
541/753-8250

13 COTTAGE GROVE

Rose Garden Mall Antique
501 E. Main St.
541/942-5064

Mike & Bev's Antiques
637 E. Main St.
541/942-3664

Apple Pie Antiques
811 E. Main St.
541/942-0057

Petersen's Antiques
818 E. Main St.
541/942-0370

Preston's Treasure Hunt
820 W. Main St.
541/942-3763

14 DEPOE BAY

What Not Shop
362 S.E. Hwy. 101
541/765-2626

Recollections
Hwy. 101
541/765-2221

15 DRAIN

The Little Pink House
116 Cedar Street
541/836-7650 or 1-800-395-8765
Open Mon.-Sat. 9:30-4:30

Directions: Traveling I-5 North, take Exit 150 to Drain and Yoncalba (Hwy. 99, part of the Applegate Trail). The shop is on the right 6 miles down, across from the Texaco gas station. OR traveling south on I-5, take Exit 162 to Drain and Elkton. Follow Hwy. 38, 6 miles, then take a left at the Texaco. The shop is across the street.

The personal touch thrives at The Little Pink House, a shop offering Tole and Folk Art. Any item purchased can be decoratively painted with your design creating one-of-a-kind pieces of singular value and beauty.

Nana's Oldies and Goodies
301 N. 1st
541/836-7363

16 ESTACADA

Petals N Treasures
398 N. Broadway St.
503/630-4411

Tole Barn
22597 S. Day Hill Rd.
503/630-4680

17 EUGENE

Fifthpearl Antiques
207 E. 5th Ave.
541/342-2733

The Antique Heart
409 High St.
541/465-1158

Antique Clock Shop
888 Pearl St.
541/683-1349

Brians Furniture Farm Antqs.
115 N. Seneca Rd.
541/689-3358

Nostalgia Collectibles
527 Willamette St.
541/484-9202

Goodness Gracious
767 Willamette St.
541/345-4517

Copper Penny Antiques
1215 Willamette St.
541/686-2104

18 FLORENCE

Bay Window
1308 Bay St.
541/997-2002

Collectors Corner
1623 15th St.
541/902-8077

Divine Decadence
129 Maple St.
541/997-7200

Old Town Treasures
299 Maple St.
541/997-1364

Fine Timed Collectibles
513 Hwy. 101
541/997-6430

19 FOREST GROVE

Sentimental Journey Antiques
2004 Main St.
503/357-2091

Acanthus Antiques
2011 Main St.
503/357-3213

Collections in the Attic
2020 Main St.
503/357-0316

Rachel's
1930 Pacific Ave.
503/357-2356

Days Past Antiques & Cllbls.
1937 Pacific Ave.
503/357-5405

Verboort Village Antiques
39690 N.W. Verboort Rd.
503/359-0454

20 GRANTS PASS

Black Swann
100 Lewis Ave.
541/474-2477

Danl Boone's Trading Post
470 Redwood Hwy.
541/474-2992

Blue Moon Antiques Gift
220 S.W. 6th St.
541/474-6666

Elegance
321 SE 6th St.
541/476-0570

6th Street Antique Mall
328 S.W. 6th St.
541/479-6491

21 GRESHAM

Antiques by Renee
17 N.W. 1st St.
503/665-4091

By Request
101 N. Main Ave.
503/661-4994

Nostalgia Antiques & Collectibles
19 N.E. Roberts Ave.
503/661-0123

22 HILLSBORO

Q's Shoppe
2437 S.E. Brookwood Ave.
503/648-4785

Heinrich's Antiques & Cllbls.
136 E. Main St.
503/693-7457

Lestuff & Floral Too
230 E. Main St.
503/640-9197

Old Library Antiques
263 E. Main St.
503/693-7324

Country Crossroads Antiques
8750 N.W. Old Cornelius Passrd.
503/645-9025

Jill's Cottage
23483 SW Rosedale Rd.
503/591-8970

Sniders Hill Theatre Antique Mall
127 N.E. 3rd Ave.
503/693-1686

23 INDEPENDENCE

Main Street Antiques
144 S. Main St.
503/838-2595

River Bend Antiques
184 S. Main St.
503/838-4555

Joni's Antiques
194 S. Main St.
503/838-5944

24 JACKSONVILLE

J Bailey's Antiques
120 W. C St.
541/899-1766

Trash Pile Antiques & Cllbls.
650 N. 5th St.
541/899-1209

Three Gables Antiques
305 S. Oregon
541/899-1891

25 JUNCTION CITY

Offering a number of excellent antique shops through which to roam, modern Junction City began with a western flavor. In 1871, the railroad had reached the settlement drawing many citizens from nearby Lancaster to relocate to Junction City. The town's name was conceived along with the notion that a west railroad line would join the main line at this point. Due to finances, no west line was constructed until 1910. Even so, the railroad town grew.

Railroad crew members found Junction City a suitable second home with its numerous rooming and boarding houses and, of course, saloons. Travelers had money to spend, and a boom time with its accompanying businesses and reputation thrived. Unfortunately, fires ravaged the business section between 1878 and 1882 with the last of the great fires burning out in 1915. The town physically changed direction after this fire as its expansion began to the west.

Today travelers return to Junction City in mid-August

as the Scandinavian Festival sprinkles downtown with the appearance of a Scandinavian village while citizens outfit themselves accordingly. Tasty Scandinavian foods are the feature of this event.

Brimhall's Antiques
595 Ivy St.
541/998-2770

Roberta's Collectibles
1480 Ivy St.
541/998-8782

Lingos Sheepbarn Antiques
27579 High Pass Rd.
541-998-2018

26 KLAMATH FALLS

Country Mercantile
1833 Avalon St.
541/882-8808

Ant Mini Antqs. & Mini Barns
1633 Division St.
541/882-9429

Linkville Antique Co.
1243 Kane St.
541/883-1285

Cat's Meow
825 Main St.
541/885-3933

Assistance League Findables
1330 E. Main St.
541/883-1721

Petri's Interiors of Yesterdays
125 N. 9th St.
541/882-8543

Carsons Old West
1835 Oregon Ave.
541/882-4188

Always Antiques & Art Gallery
915 Pine St.
541/882-8700

White Pelican Antique Mall
229 S. 6th St.
541/883-7224

Armour Antiques & Cllbls.
7341 S. 6th St.
541/882-0263

Shades of the Past
417 N. Spring St.
541/884-1188

Crafters Market
3040 Washburn Way
541/882-5270

27 LA GRANDE

Ten Twelve Adams Antiques
1012 Adams Ave.
541/962-7171

Jefferson Antiques
1114 Jefferson Ave.
541/963-9358

Hills Antiques & Refinishing
1529 Jefferson Ave.
541/963-4223

Wooden Nickel
2212 E. Penn Ave.
541/963-7507

28 LAKE OSWEGO

Frederick E. Squire III
24 A Avenue
503/697-5924

Uncle Albert's Antiques
15964 Boones Ferry Road
503/635-5535

Marquess of Granby
16524 Boones Ferry Road
503/635-3544

29 LINCOLN CITY

Portals of the Past
4250 N. Hwy. 101
541/996-2254

Vintage Corner
1520 N.E. Hwy. 101
541/994-7797

Rocking Horse Mall
1542 N.E. Hwy. 101
541/994-4647

Little Antique Store
2826 N.E. Hwy. 101
541/994-8572

Toby Torrances Pastime
545 N.W. Hwy. 101
541/994-9003

Curio Cabinet Mall
1631 N.W. Hwy. 101
541/994-9001

Jade Stone Gallery
3200 S.E. Hwy. 101
541/996-2580

Snug Harbor Antiques
5030 S.E. Hwy. 101
541/996-4021

Mouse House
6334 S.E. Hwy. 101
541/996-4127

Streetcar Village
6334 S.E. Hwy. 101
541/996-4480

Herself's
1439 S.W. Hwy. 101
541/994-9566

Bush's Antiques
5021 S.W. Hwy. 101
541/994-7363

Beachtime Antiques
5053 S.W. Hwy. 101
541/994-4001

Judith Anne's Antiques
412 S. Hwy 101
541/993-9912

Ron's Relics
1512 S.E. Hwy. 101
541/994-6788

A Change of Seasons
304 S.E. Hwy. 101
541/994-3765

30 MCMINNVILLE

Blue Angel Antique Shoppe
228 N.E. 3rd St.
503/434-5784

Old Salon Antique Shop
238 N.E. 3rd St.
503/472-8209

31 MEDFORD

Downtown Merchants Mall
117 S. Central Ave.
541/779-6640

Micellany
220 N. Fir St.
541/770-9097

Brass Horseshoe
2581 Jacksonville Hwy
541/772-8466

Mary's Dream
125 W. Main St.
541/857-1132

Jueden's Furniture
220 E. Main St.
541/772-3260

Crafters Blend
2308 Poplar Dr.
541/770-5052

L C Antiques
2312 Poplar Dr.
541/779-1115

Main Antique Mall
30 N. Riverside Ave.
541/779-9490

Jane's Antiques
308 W. 2nd St.
541/535-1315

Medford Antique Mall
1 W. 6th St.
541/773-4983

32 NEHALEM

Nehalem Antique Mall
Hwy 101
503/368-7190

Pete's Antiques
Hwy 101
503/368-6018

Three Village Gallery Inc.
35995 Hwy. 101
503/368-6924

Robin's Reliques
36025 7th St.
503/368-4114

33 NEWPORT

About halfway down the coast, the picturesque Yaquina Head Lighthouse welcomes you to Newport, a town known for its Dungeness crab and glorious harbor under the graceful Yaquina Bay Bridge. The historic Bay Front offers a mixture of shops, galleries, canneries and restaurants that serve fresh clam chowder, shrimp, oysters, crab and salmon.

Oar House
520 Southwest Second Street
541/265-9571

Formerly a boarding house, bordello, and most recently a bed and breakfast, Oar House has been serving guests since the early 1900s. This Lincoln County historic landmark situated in the beautiful Nye Beach area of Newport delights guests with its history, ghost and nautical theme. Each guest room provides a queen-size bed in addition to a view of the ocean. Be amazed by the 360 degree view of the coast area from the lighthouse.

34 NORTH BEND

Granny's Hutch
1964 Sherman Ave.
541/756-1222

Fran Carter
1966 Sherman Ave.
541/756-4333

Wagon Wheel Antqs. & Cllbls.
1984 Sherman Ave.
541/756-7023

Echoes of Time
1993 Sherman Ave.
541/756-4072

Treasures
1997 Sherman Ave.
541/756-4678

Bric Brac shack
2048 Sherman Ave.
541/756-2329

Old World Antiques
2072 Sherman Ave.
541/756-2121

Beauty & The Beast Antiques
615 Virginia Ave.
541/756-3670

35 ONTARIO

Back at the Ranch
2390 S.W. 4th Ave.
541/889-8850

Maria's Antiques
364 S. Oregon St.
541/889-3684

Grandma's Cellar Antiques & Furniture
715 Sunset Dr.
541/889-8591

36 OREGON CITY

McLoughlin Antique Mall
502 7th St.
503/655-0393

Maija's Antiques and Cllbls.
402 S. McLoughlin Blvd.
503/656-9610

Oregon City Antique Co.
502 7th St.
503/657-6527

37 PARKDALE

Parkdale Plain & Fancy
Baseline at Third Avenue
541/352-7875
Hours are Tue.-Fri. 10:30-4:30 and Sat. & Sun. 10:30-5:30, closed Jan. & Feb.

Directions: Traveling I-84, take Exit 64 at Hood River; travel south on Hwy. 35 for 15 miles to Cooper Spur Road. Take a right on Cooper Spur Road going 2 miles to Baseline. Turn right from Baseline to 3rd. OR Traveling north on Hwy. 35, turn left at Parkdale, then exit onto Baseline. Follow Baseline into downtown Parkdale to 3rd Avenue.

For a leisurely browse through the finer and everyday

Oregon

items of yesterday, the former 1930s drugstore, now, Parkdale Plain and Fancy offers its eclectic collection. Among the items overflowing in this shop are antique furniture, books, as well as glassware such as Carnival, Depression and crystal. Primitive items (plates, vases, jugs, churns) enliven the selection. Linger over the house specialty—antique bottles.

38 PENDLETON

Pendleton Antique Co.
104 S.E. Court Ave.
541/276-8172

Georgianna's
207 S.E. Court Ave.
541/276-4094

Collectors Gallery
223 S.E. Court Ave.
541/276-6697

Vintage Court Antiques
224 S.E. Court Ave.
541/276-0747

Picket Fences
239 S.E. Court Ave.
541/276-9515

Twice Nice Antiques & Cllbls.
815 SE Court Ave.
541/278-1407

Frieda N Friends Antique Mall
1400 S.W. Court Ave.
541/276-7172

Lees Antiques
813 S.E. Frazer Ave.
541/276-4158

39 PORTLAND

Mother Goose Antiques
1219 Southwest 19th
503/223-4493
Open: Mon.-Sat. Afternoons - Best to Call First

Directions: Call for specific directions.

Owner, Sigrid Clark has been in the antiques business over twenty years. Wandering through her shop you will find a wonderland of vintage smalls: garment buttons, collectible holiday items, kitchen collectibles including patented items, dollhouse minatures (50s & older), cookbooks, an impressive array of sewing items, costume jewelry, salt & pepper shakers, silver trinkets, advertising items, spice tines, matchboxes, postcards, and children's toys. As the owner puts it, "this is a fun place to shop."

General Hooker's Bed and Breakfast
125 Southwest Hooker
541/222-4435 or 1-800-745-4135
Fax: 503/295-6410
e-mail 74627.414@compuserve.com
Rates: $70-115

As the early morning's misty fog clears from town, General Hooker's Bed and Breakfast sits in the midst of its tranquil historic district. The Victorian townhouse, a stroll from downtown, displays a restrained Victorian ornamentation. Much of the casually comfortable atmosphere grows out of the 19th century family heirloom furnishings. Furniture is tasteful and cozy. In addition, Northwestern art provides an interesting flare to the decor. Throughout the house, guests move to the music of Bach and Vivaldi. Guest accommodations include four rooms, two with private baths.

Embry & Co. Antiques & Gifts
4709 S.W. Beaverton Hillsdale Hwy
503/244-1646

Quintana Galleries
501 S.W. Broadway
503/223-1729

Abacus
1224 S.W. Broadway
503/790-9303

Partners in Time
1313 W. Burnside St.
503/228-6299

Enterprises Antiques
2955 E. Burnside St.
503/223-8866

J K Hill's Antiques
7807 SW Capitol Hwy
503/244-2708

Le Meitour Gallery
7814 S.W. Capitol Hwy.
503/246-3631

Lauries and Casey's Antiques
7840 S.W. Capitol Hwy.
503/244-6775

Pagenwood Restoring
7783 S.W. Capitol Hwy
503/246-6777

Toby's Antiques & Collectibles
7871 S.W. Capitol Hwy.
503/977-2546

Really Good Stuff
3121 S.E. Division St.
503/238-1838

Family Ties
12659 S.E. Division St.
503-761-7047

Old Town Antique Market
32 N.W. 1st Ave.
503/228-3386

New Antique Village Mall Inc.
1969 N.E. 42nd Ave.
503/288-1051

Antique Alley
2000 N.E. 42nd Ave.
503/287-9848

Foster Rd. Collectibles
4932 S.E. Foster Rd.
503/788-9474

Goods Antique Mall & Empor.
5339 S.E. Foster Rd.
503/777-9919

Alameda Floral Antqs. & Intrs.
5701 N.E. Fremont St.
503/288-6149

At The Rainbow End
5723 S.E. Foster Rd.
503/788-1934

Amy's Antiques
5851 S.E. Foster Rd.
503/777-1497

Bucks Stove Palace & Antiques
6803 S.E. Foster Rd.
503/771-3374

Handwerk Shop
8317 S.E. 13th Ave.
503/236-7870

Antiques by the Wishing Crnr.
9201 S.E. Foster Rd.
503/771-1549

Wishing Corner
9201 S.E. Foster Rd.
503/771-1549

Mill Creek Crossing
9209 S.E. Foster Rd.
503/775-3141

Amsterdam Trading Co.
536 N.W. 14th Ave.
503/229-0737

Tony's Antiques & Collectibles
3709 S.E. Gladstone St.
503/788-1223

Portland Antique Co.
1211 N.W. Glisan St.
503/223-0999

Maxine Cozzettos
2228 N.E. Glisan St.
503/232-4656

End of the Trail Cllctbls
5937 N. Greeley Ave.
503/283-0419

Glass Works Gifts & Cllbls.
10105 S.W. Hall Blvd.
503/246-9897

Uncommon Treasures
3530 S.E. Hawthorne Blvd.
503/234-4813

Ruby's Antiques Fine Gift
3590 S.E. Hawthorne Blvd.
503/239-9867

Antiques Plus
6403 N. Interstate
503/289-8788

Store II
1004 N. Killingsworth St.
503/285-0747

Classic Antiques
1805 S.E. M L King Blvd.
503/231-8689

Leighton House Antiques
1226 Lexington
503/233-4248

Slot Closet Antiques
5223 N. Lombard St.
503/286-3597

Noce Antiques
8332 N. Lombard St.
503/286-3560

Milwaukie Antique Mall
10875 S.E. McLoughlin Blvd.
503/786-9950

Tyrell's Antiques
6429 S.W. Macadam Ave.
503/293-1759

Tigard Antique Mall
12271 S.W. Main St.
503/684-9550

Fanno Creek Mercantile
12285 S.W. Main St.
503/639-6963

A Child at Heart Antiques
6802 S.E. Milwaukie Ave.
503/234-3807

Stars Antique Malls
7027 S.E. Milwaukie Sve
503/239-0346

Old Friends
3384 S.E. Milwaukie Ave.
503/231-0301

Stars Antique Mall
7030 S.E. Milwaukie Ave.
503/235-5990

Timeless Memories Antiques
7048 Milwaukie Ave.
503/234-3807

Handwerk Shop
8317 S.E. 13th Ave.
503/236-7870

David H Palmrose Antiques
1435 N.W. 19th Ave.
503/220-8253

Habromania
203 S.W. 9th Ave.
503/223-0767

Palookaville
211 S.W. 9th Ave.
503/241-4751

Avalon Antiques
318 S.W. 9th Ave.
503/224-7156

Stone Fox Gallery
506 NW 9th Ave.
503/228-7949

Abundant Life Antiques
1130 S.E. 182nd Ave.
503/665-4301

Phone Company
135 S.E. 102nd Ave.
503/253-1124

Vintage Corner Antique Mall
13565 S.W. Pacific Hwy.
503/684-7024

L L Trading Post
12115 S.E. Powell Blvd.
503/761-5960

George's Antiques
640 S.E. Stark St.
503/233-7787

Antique Slot Machines Inc.
12037 S.E. Stark St.
503/253-3773

Plaid Rabbit Button Exchange
111 N.W. 2nd Ave.
503/224-0678

Arthur W. Erickson Inc.
1030 S.W. Taylor St.
503/227-4710

Polished Image
122 N.W. 10th Ave.
503/228-8347

Jerry Lamb Interiors & Antique
416 N.W. 10th Ave.
503/227-6077

Renaissance Galleries & Intrs
414 S.W. 10th Ave.
503/226-1982

Retrospection
619 S.W. 10th Ave.
503/223-5538

Richard Rife Frnch Antique
300 N.W. 13th Ave.
503/294-0276

Cubby Hole Antiques
7824 S.W. 35th Ave.
503/246-8307

Gold Door Antiques & Art
1434 S.E. 37th Ave.
503/232-6069

Geraldine's
2772 N.W. Thurman St.
503/295-5911

Andrew's Antiques
916 S.E. 20 th Ave.
503/234-9378

Stars N.W. Antique Mall
305 N.W. 21st Ave.
503/220-8180

Classic Woods
1108 N.W. 21st Ave.
503/242-1849

Shoguns Gallery
206 N.W. 23rd Ave.
503/224-0328

Jack Heath Antiques
1700 N.W. 23rd Ave.
503/222-4663

Peter M Sargent Antiques
2430 S.W. Vista Ave.
503/223-3395

N.W. Collectibles & Antique
7901 S.E. 13th St.
503/234-6061

Kathryn's Antiques & Cllbls.
7907 S.E. 13th Ave.
503/236-7120

White Parrot Antqs. & Cllbls.
7919 S.E. 13th Ave.
503/236-5366

General Store
7987 S.E. 13th Ave.
503/233-1321

Corner House Antiques
8003 S.E. 13th Ave.
503/235-3749

Den of Antiquity
8012 S.E. 13th Ave.
503/233-7334

Treasure Chest Antiques
8015 S.E. 13th Ave.
503/235-6897

Gilt Vintage Jewelry & Antiques
8017 S.E. 13th Ave.
503/231-6395

The Sellwood Collective
8027 S.E. 13th Ave.
503/736-1399

Farmhouse Antiques
8028 S.E. 13th Ave.
503/232-6757

Royal Antiques
8035 S.E. 13th Ave.
503/231-9064

Sellwood Peddler Attic
8065 S.E. 13th Ave.
503/235-0946

Spencer's Antiques
8130 S.E. 13th Ave.
503/238-1737

Sellwood Antiques Mall
7875 S.E.. 13th Ave.
503/232-3755

Consignment Gallery
8133 S.E. 13th Ave.
503/234-6606

Anomaly
8235 S.E. 13th Ave.
503/230-0734

American Country Antiques
8235 S.E. 13th Ave.
503/234-8551

Lily White
8235 13th Ave.
503/234-1630

The Green Door
8235 S.E. 13th Ave. #11
503/231-2520

Ragtime Antiques & Repairs
8301 S.E. 13th Ave.
503/231-4023

The Blue Hen & Company
8309 S.E. 13th Ave.
503/234-3197

Wood Pile Antiques
8315 13th Ave.
503/231-1145

40 REDMOND

Old Farmers Co-op Antiques
106 S.E. Evergreen Ave.
541/548-7975

Country Pleasures
502 S.W. Evergreen Ave.
541/548-1021

Rt. 97 Trading Post
2424 N. Hwy. 97
541/923-4660

The Gilbert House
203 S. 6th St.
541/548-1342

World Of Treasures
215 S.W. 6th St.
541/923-0226

Past & Presents
418 S.W. 6 th St.
541/923-0147

Memory Shoppe
422 S.W. 6th St.
541/923-6748

Country by Design Antiques
453 S.W. 6th St.
541/923-3350

The Keeping Room
528 S.W. 6th St.
541/548-7888

41 ROSEBURG

Majestic Antiques
715 S.E. Cass Ave.
541/672-1387

Woodtique
2660 N.E. Stephens St.
541/673-8385

From Days Gone By
630 S.E. Rose St.
541/673-7325

Antique Mall & Marketplace
1212 S.E. Stephens St.
541/672-8259

42 SALEM

Antique Village
211 Commercial St. NE
503/581-0318

Earle Antique Co.
223 Commercial St. NE
503/370-9666

A Part of the Past Antique Mall
241 Commercial St. NE
503/581-1004

A Touch of Nostalgia
255 Court St. NE
503/588-9123

Best Dressed Doll
385 Howell Prairie Rd. SE
503/362-6583

Gingerbread Haus Antiques
145 Liberty St. NE
503/588-2213

Engelberg Antiks II
148 Liberty St. NE
503/363-8155

Icons & Keepsakes
148 Liberty St. NE
503/370-8979

Nancy Van Zandt Antiques
1313 Mill St. SE
503/371-8612

Reid's Antiques
2625 Salem Dallas Hwy. NW
503/581-1455

Et Cetera Antiques
3295 Triangle Dr. SE
503-581-9850

Every Bloomin Thing
615 Wallace Rd. NW
503-378-1821

43 SANDY

Sandy Traders
38905 Proctor Blvd.
503/668-5749

Something Old Something New
38922 Pioneer Blvd.
503/668-0808

Treasures Antique Mall Inc.
39065 Pioneer Blvd.
503/668-9042

44 SEAL ROCK

Antiques Etc.
Hwy. 101
541/563-2242

Granny's Country Store
10261 N.W. Pacific Coast Hwy.
541/563-4899

A Part of the Past
10841 N.W. Pacific Coast Hwy.
541/563-5071

Purple Pelican Antique Mall
10641 N.E. Pacific Coast Hwy.
541/563-4166

45 SEASIDE

What was once "The End of Lewis & Clark Trail" is now Oregon's largest beach resort community. Seaside's legacy of hospitality dates back to 1873, when railroad baron Ben Holladay built the luxurious Seaside Hotel.

Wesroses Antiques
3300 Hwy. 101 N
503/738-8732

Ike & Debbies Red Barn Antqs.
3765 Hwy. 101 N
503/738-0272

Yankee Trader
4197 Hwy. 101 N
503/738-6633

Cottage and Castle
501 S. Holladay Dr.
503/738-2195

Cynthia Anderson Antiques
567 Pacific Way
503/738-8484

46 SELLWOOD

Sellwood Bazaar Antiques
7733 S.E. 13th Avenue
503/236-9110

The Raven Antiques & Military
7805 S.E. 13th Avenue
503/233-8075

Golden Girls' Antiques
7834 S.E. 13th Avenue
503/233-2160

Misty's Antiques
7825 S.E. 13th Avenue
503/233-9564

Sellwood Antique Mall
7875 S.E. 13th Avenue
503/232-3755

Leighton House Antiques, Ltd.
1226 Lexinton
503/233-4248

N.W. Collectibles & Antique
7901 S.E. 13th Avenue
503/234-4248

Kathryn's Antiques & Cllbls.
7907 S.E. 13th Avenue
503/236-7120

The General Store
7987 S.E. 13th Avenue
503/232-1321

Corner Hse./Queen Anne's Lace
8003 S.E. 13th Avenue
503/235-3749

Den of Antiquity
8012 S.E. 13th Avenue
503/233-7334

The Treasure Chest
8015 S.E. 13th Avenue
503/235-6897

Gilt Antiques
8017 S.E. 13th Avenue
503/231-6395

Farmhouse Antiques
8028 S.E. 13th Avenue
503/232-6757

The Sellwood Collective
8027 S.E. 13th Avenue
503/736-1399

Royal Antiques
8035 S.E. 13th Avenue
503/231-9064

1874 House
8070 S.E. 13th Avenue
503/233-1874

Sellwood Pedler, Attic Goodies
8065 S.E. 13th Avenue
503/235-0946

Sellwood Antiques
8132 S.E. 13th Avenue
503/236-9650

R. Soencer Antiques, Inc.
8130 S.E. 13th Avenue
503/238-1737

Anomaly, Parlor of Eclectic Art
8235 S.E. 13th Avenue
503/230-0734

American Country Antiques
8235 S.E. 13th Avenue
503/234-8551

Ragtime Antiques
8301 S.E. 13th Avenue
503/231-4023

The Blue Hen and Co.
8309 S.E. 13th Avenue
503/234-3197

Woodpile Antiques
8315 S.E. 13th Avenue
No Phone Listed

The Handwerk Shop
8317 S.E. 13th Avenue
503/236-7870

47 SHERWOOD

Inn of the Oregon Trail
416 South McLoughlin
503/656-2089

A stone's throw from the end of the Oregon Trail awaits an 1867 Gothic Revival-style home built by EB. Fellow, Inn of the Oregon Trail. Overlooking the landscaped gardens are three delightfully outfitted guest rooms on the third floor. The ground floor provides another room which offers a private entrance, bath, fireplace and wet bar. Fellows House Restaurant occupies the main floor and is open to the public weekdays, but private dinners for inn guests can be arranged with advance notice. Explore the Inn and the surrounding historic Oregon City.

Smockville Station Antiques
170 N.W. 1 St.
603/625-5866

Main Street Crossing
5 N.W. Main St.
503/625-5434

Manhattan Trade Post Antique
22275 S.W. Pacific Hwy.
503/625-7834

Bare Pockets
230 N.W. Railroad Ave.
503/625-5491

Railroad Street Antique Mall
260 N.W. Railroad Ave.
503/625-2246

Whistle Stop Antique Mall
130 N.W.. Railroad Ave.
503/625-5744

48 SISTERS

Lonesome Water Books
255 W. Cascade
541/549-2203

Treasure Trove Craft & Antique
160 S. Hoo St.
541/549-2142

Country Collections
351 W. Hood
541/549-7888

49 SPRINGFIELD

Antique Peddlers I & II
612 Main St.
541/747-1259

Rollas Relics & Reusables
868 Main St.
541/741-0838

Pretty Things For You
2142 Main St.
541/747-7718

Rose Moss
214 Pioneer Pkwy. W
541/741-2411

50 THE DALLES

Klindt's Used Books & Cllbls.
319 E. 2nd St.
541/296-4342

2nd Street Place
402 E. 2nd St.
541/296-8500

Bishop's Antiques Gift & Cllbls.
422 W. 2nd St.
541/298-1804

Old Mill Bargain Center
2917 E. 2nd St.
541/296-6706

Clem's Attic
2937 E. 2nd St.
541/296-4448

51 TILLAHOOK

Blue Haven Inn Over Flow Shop
3025 Gienger Road
503/842-2265
Rates $60-75
The inn never closes.

Directions: Turn west off Hwy. 101 at Gienger Road. The Inn is located 2 miles south of Tillamook, Ore.

Sitting in the midst of two-acres surrounded by tall evergreens, Blue Haven affords guests country serenity and seclusion. Built in 1916, the country home has been skillfully restored featuring charming antiques and limited edition collectibles throughout. Each of the 3 guest bedrooms provides a unique decor. Tara, overlooking the garden, presents a *Gone With the Wind* theme highlighted by its four poster bed, Civil War chess set and memorabilia from the movie. The queen-size brass bed in La Femme hearkens to the "feminine and frilly" ladies boudoir of earlier days. A nautical atmosphere engulfs Of The Sea, a most comfortable room, with wingback chair and ottoman in addition to a view of the garden. Enjoy a relaxing pause on the country porch to swing. Listen to music from an old radio or antique gramophone in the library/game room. In the mornings, sit down to the complimentary gourmet breakfast served in the formal dining room on fine bone china and crystal. (Dietary preferences are carefully catered to.) Step around to the "Overflow Shop" adjacent to the Inn offering antiques, glassware, limited edition plates, dolls, sewing machines, as well as clawfoot bathtubs.

Smokehouse Antiques Mall
116 Main St.
503/842-3399

Dekunsam's 2nd Hand Store
1910 2nd St.
503/842-2299

52 TOLEDO

Sherwood Antiques
112 W. Graham St.
541/336-2315

Ada's Gifts & Collectibles
123 N. Main St.
541/336-2524

Antiques N More
199 S. Main St.
541/336-4210

Main Street Antique Mall
305 N. Main St.
541/336-3477

Cedric & Christy Brown Antiques
404 N. Main
541/336-3668

53 WALDPORT

Waldport Mercantile
145 S.W. Arrow St.
541/563-4052

Old Maid New
255 S.W. Maple St.
541/563-6411

Doug and Mim's
340 N.W. Hemlock Hwy. #-34
541/563-2454

Family Tree Collectibles
1265 S.W. Range Dr.
541/563-2099

Glass Treats & Antiques
332 N. Deer Hill Drive
541/563-6282

Mim's Whims
340 N.W. Hemlock (Hwy. 34)
541/563-2454

Antiques & Reference Books
Hwy. 101
541/563-2318

Notes

Leonard's
ANTIQUES & UNIQUESS MEGA MALL

in the Chippewa Mall
"The Largest Antiques Mall In Western Pennsylvania"

all on one floor
68,000 sq. ft. under one roof
Route 60, N., Exit 15, Rt. 51 N.

Enjoy
The Grapevine Cafe

Beaver Falls 10

Creekside Inn B&B

1781 stone house in the heart of "Amish Country"

Visit our website: http://www.thecreeksideinn.com

Paradise
(Lancaster County)

106

Christopher Kratzer Hous[e]

Bed & Breakfas[t]
and
Art Gallery
Clearfield

Brownstone Corner

Situated on seven acres amid the farms and old German towns of the "Pennsylvania Dutch.

(717) 484-4460

Reinholds 117

Revisit Yesterday At
FÁILTE INN B & B
AND ANTIQUE SHOP

An elegant country inn nestled in the Susquehanna River Valley surrounded by the beautiful Endless Mountains of rural Pennsylvania. All private baths. Smoking and non-smoking. MC and Visa accepted. Innkeepers: Jim and Sarah True

RR#2, Box 323
Sheshequin
717-358-3899
Athens 7

Pennsylvania

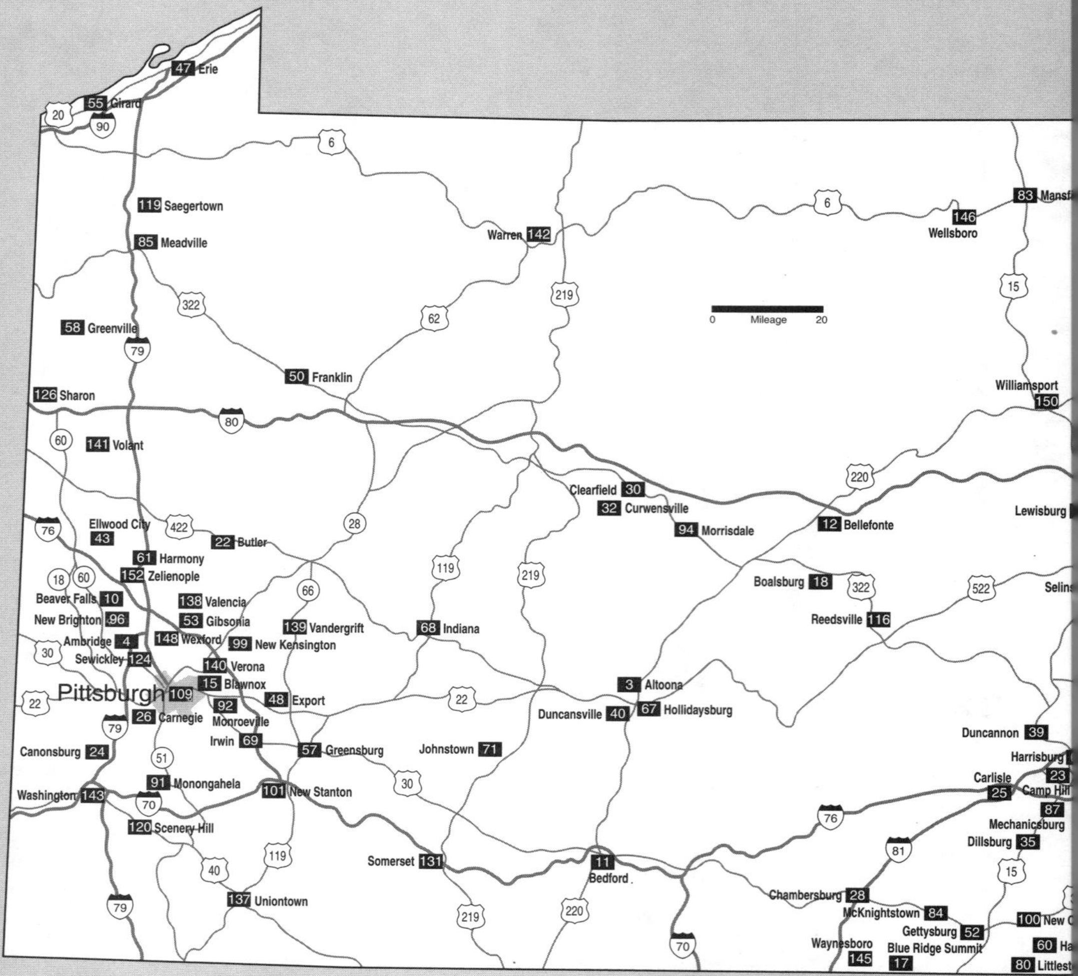

TIMELY TREASURES

Phone: (717) 226-2838
Fax: (717) 226-3943
e-mail: timely@ptd.net
www.timelytreasures.com

ANTIQUES
FURNITURE
ACCESSORIES
FEFINISHING

Hawley 64

Antique Market Place

Since 1981
Ronks 11

LARGE SELECTION
AFFORDABLE PRICES

ESTATES BOUGHT
OPEN BY APPOINTMENT

SCHMIDT'S SPRINGHOUSE ANTIQUES
•FURNITURE•

R.D. #2 • Box 164A • Route 66 at Pfeffer Rd.
(412) 325-2577
Export

48

OLD SLED WORKS
ANTIQUE & CRAFT MARKET

"History was never this much fun."
Duncannon
www.computrends.com/oldsledworks

39

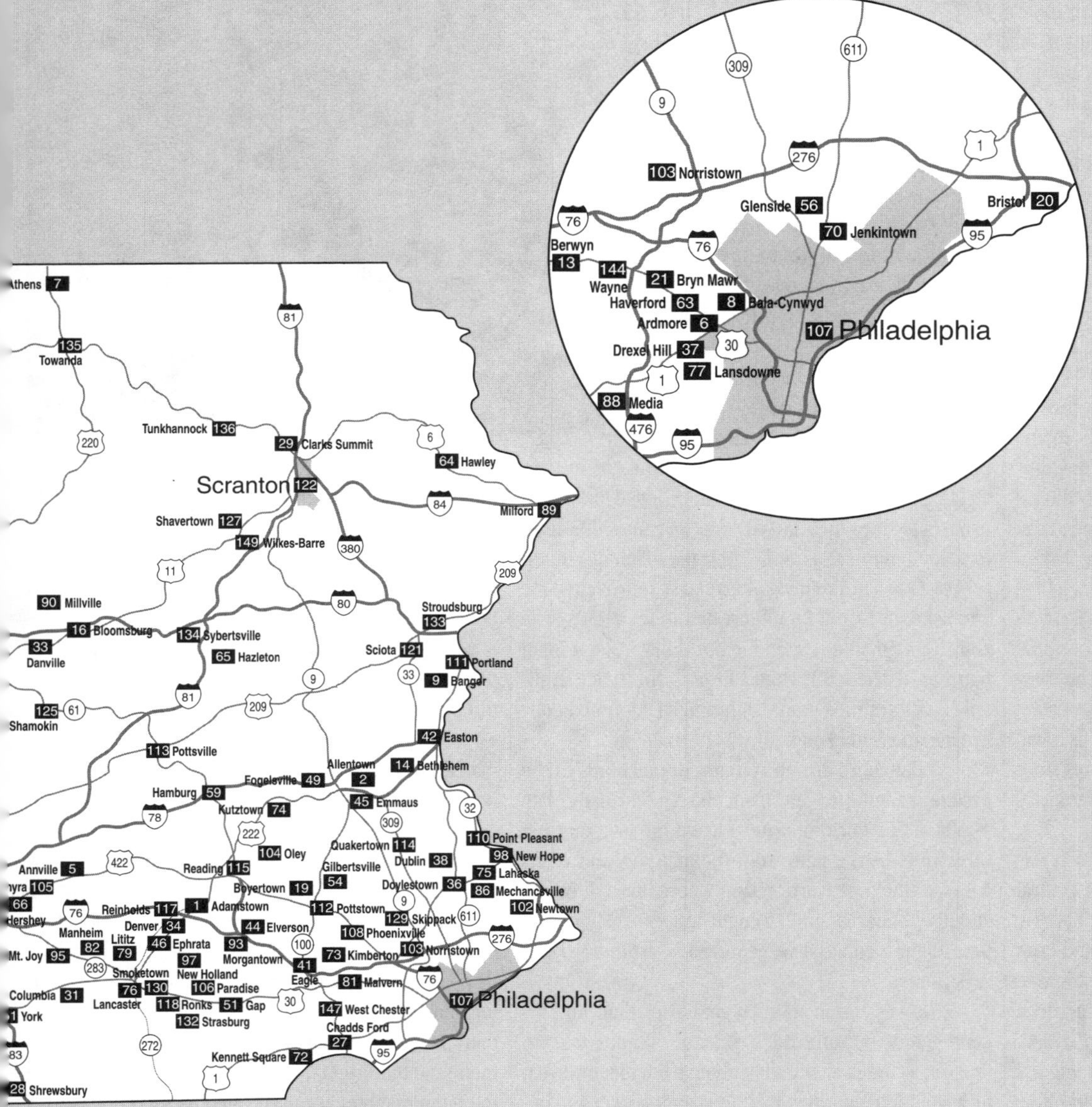

Experience the charms of a 1790 Bed & Breakfast

1324 River Road
New Hope

97

Homestead Lodging

Smoketown

130

Country Escape
275 Old Route 30 • 717-338-0611
McKnightstown

84

WOODEN HORSE ANTIQUES
FANCY OAK, WALNUT AND COUNTRY FURNITURE
(717) 794-2717
Blue Ridge Summit

17

ANTIQUES ODDS & ENDS SHOP

508 Lincoln Hwy. E. Rt. 30
(412) 863-9769
Antiques, Furniture, Glassware, Toys & Clocks
Irwin

69

Old Sled Works: Retro Duncannon

Tradition and good family memories can often be the motivating factors in our lives as we ponder the age-old question of "what do I want to do when I grow up?" These factors were precisely the motivation behind Jimmy Rosen's Old Sled Works, an enormous, old family-owned factory building in Duncannon, Pennsylvania that now houses an antique mall, crafts center, sled museum, penny arcade, and soda fountain.

Flash back, if you will, to Jimmy's childhood (he's in his early 30s now). He grew up around the old factory, which his father owned, only then it was Standard Novelty Works. The factory produced not only wooden novelties like porch gates and swings, snow scooters, and sink protectors, but it also housed the Lightning Guider Sled Factory, which manufactured sleds - hundreds of thousands of sleds - from 1904 to 1988. In its heyday, the factory was one of the busiest and best-known makers of children's sleds in the country, turning out 1,600 to 1,800 sleds a day during the 1920s and 1930s, but the whole factory closed in 1990, a victim of high-tech toys and shopping malls.

So the Rosen family was left with an empty factory, but Jimmy could not accept its demise. As his drive, ambition and memories went into high gear, an idea began to emerge. Duncannon had lots of traffic - it's near Routes 11, 15 and 322 - but it was no tourist mecca, and it didn't have an established market for anything. Rosen had to create a draw for his town, and he chose antiques. But not just any antiques store or mall would do; this is where childhood memories kicked in.

In Jimmy's words, "I wanted to distinguish this [business] from most other antique malls in central Pennsylvania. Even though I'm set up in a historic old sled factory with over 125 great antique and craft vendors, I wanted something more for my customers. As a kid, I fondly remember playing in the arcades during my family's vacations in Miami Beach . Also, we lived close to Hershey Park, which I frequented. I would dream about having my own arcade and how great it would be to have a key to each machine so you could collect all the coins or play for free as many times as you wanted. Guys would think you were cool, and the girls would swoon, I suppose. Obviously, it was just a dream back then. However, when I opened the Old Sled Works, I had some extra space so I thought, 'This is the time and place for my arcade.' I wanted only electro-mechanical machines, like those I remember, and since most of my customers are roughly 35 to 64, I knew many would remember these older machines, too, and would be thrilled to relive their childhoods."

"I began my search by reading books and subscribing to some hobby magazines. Then I began meeting people in the area and started acquiring machines: rifle games, skee-ball, pinballs, everything. I bought just about any moderately-priced machine, and customers loved it! Fathers came in to show their kids the type of games they used to play, then the dads would play the machines themselves. One day a retiring pharmacist approached me and asked if I would be interested in his 1950s-style soda fountain and related memorabilia. After a lot of figuring, I decided it would fit both the space available and the atmosphere, so Jimmy's Old-Time Penny Arcade and Soda Fountain was born."

Today there are more than 50 machines in the arcade, ranging in age from the 1920s to the late 1960s, all in working order for a dime or a quarter. Customers beat a path from the antiques and crafts areas to the 'time warp' room, where they fall on the shooting galleries and strength testers. "My cut-off time for the games I've acquired is around 1970," says Jimmy.

"Games began to go digital after that, and arcade games became video games." Jimmy tries to find out as much as possible about each machine that he installs in the arcade: the year it was manufactured, who made it, where it first appeared, etc. Each machine has its own little information card placed near it, so the arcade is not only a fun room, it's a small history lesson and museum as well.

But the old soda fountain isn't a museum, at least not in the 'look but don't touch or use' sense. Everything works just fine, and on weekends everyone crowds the fountain to get some old-fashioned ice cream goodies, like fountain drinks, banana splits, malts, and milk shakes - oh yes, and to listen to the 1950s music from the old juke box.

The complete soda fountain runs along the wall facing the games: counter, stools, freezers, ice cream dispensers, a life-sized soda jerk in full costume, signs, advertising. Everything was lifted straight from the original setup. A small seating area forms an alcove at the end of the fountain counter complete with vintage 1950s furniture of chrome, vinyl and glass table tops.

Under the glass tops are all sorts of memorabilia for customers to read and view while sipping: old photographs of area businesses, old city scenes, advertisements, old 45 records, ticket stubs, matchcovers, news clippings and other commonplace items from the 1950s and 1960s

The old sled museum is a link between this time past and time present. Jimmy wanted folks to know the history of the old factory building, which was a town landmark for nearly a century, so he put together exhibits covering the factory's 85 years. He has sleds displayed from each decade of operation, old catalogs and other advertising pieces, patent and trademark papers, tools, early printing and stenciling equipment and the original sled factory time clock. While the main displays are of the sled factory, Jimmy also has presentations of some of the other novelties that were produced in the factory.

Many of the museum pieces are owned by the Old Sled Works, but several local collectors have donated or loaned items to the museum, including a valuable watch fob, sled advertising thermometer, and miscellaneous paper advertising. In 1992, the building became a registered historic site in Pennsylvania and now boasts a blue and gold marker on the grounds.

Old Sled Works Antique and Craft Market
722 North Market Street — Duncannon
717/834-9333

Pennsylvania

1 ADAMSTOWN

What began as a temporary, stop-gap solution to a vacancy problem in a farmer's market has turned into the largest antique destination in the northeast. Adamstown, Pa., began its reign as "Antiques Capital USA" in the early 1960s when Charles Weik, an antique dealer in the area, began holding flea markets in a place called Shupp's Grove on Sundays.

Shupp's Grove had long been a favorite spot for reunions, picnics, gospel singing, get-togethers and country western music shows. The antiques offered at that time were excellent examples of Pennsylvania Dutch primitives, and there was already an established tradition of antiques shops in the area that were frequented by the Rockefellers, DuPonts, Barneses and Weygandts.

In the mid 1960s, Terry Heilman, resident manager of the former Renninger's Farmers' Market and himself an antiques collector, spent many of his Sundays at Shupp's. His farmers' market had a serious vacancy problem, so in the fall, when Shupp's Grove usually closed, Heilman began offering inside space at Renninger's to the antique dealers at Shupp's, which was all outdoors. They liked it, and by spring, the dealers wanted to stay. So Renninger's began the transformation from farmers' market to antique mall. Other ideas and things were added, and the idea grew—and grew—and grew.

Literally everything is for sale in what has become the northeast's leading year-round antiques destination that pours hundreds of thousands of shoppers and visitors into this tiny town of 3,300. The range of objects runs from 18th to 20th century, sold by a true mixed-bag of dealers; big firms, little dealers, co-ops, mom-and-pop operations, beginners, pros, you name it - indoor shops, outdoor groves, malls, farms, any and everywhere.

The anchor stores here are the original Renninger's, now called Renninger's Antique and Collector's Market, and the Black Angus Antiques Mall, both having been started over 25 years ago.

Renninger's has several hundred dealers. The Black Angus has 500. Both are open only on Sundays, and both have national reputations and followings.

Then there are the cooperatives, the fairly recent development in the antique world that has brought antiquing from its original "Sundays only" market to a daily retail-like level.

Antiques Alley in Adamstown has some of the best cooperatives on the East Coast, including South Pointe Antiques, General Heath's Antiques, Antiques Showcase at the Black Horse, and Adams Antique Market. Adamstown also has three yearly "Antiques Extravaganza" weekends that draw several thousand more dealers from all over the country. These special events are the last weekend in April, June and September.

South Pointe Antiques
Rt. 272 and Denver Rd.
717/484-1026

General Heath's Antiques
Rt. 272
717/484-1300

Adamstown Antique Mall
94 Lancaster Avenue
717/484-0464

Oley Valley Architectural Antqs.
2453 N. Reading Rd. at Rt. 272
717/484-2191

Greenwood Antique Center
2455 N. Reading Rd.
717/335-3377

Friedman & Timmons Antqs.
Rt. 272
717/484-0949

Heritage Antique Center
Rt. 272
717/484-4646

Country French Collection
Rt. 272
717/484-0200

Renninger's Antique Market
Penn. Turnpike, Exit 21, Rt. 272
717/385-0104

Schupp's Grove
Rt. 897 at Willow Street
717/484-4115

Stoudt's Black Angus
Penn. Turnpike, Exit 21, Rt. 272
717/484-4385

2 ALLENTOWN

Cottage Crafters
4636 Broadway
610/366-9222

Golden Eagle Antiques
1425 E Gordon St.
610/432-1223

Burick's Antiques
880 N Graham St.
610/432-8966

Toonerville Junction Antiques
522 W Maple St.
610/435-8697

Pete's Used Furn. & Antiques
231 N 7th St.
610/433-4481

Abe Ark Antiques
1115 N 22nd St.
610/770-1454

Camelot Collectibles & Antiques
1518 W Walnut St.
610/433-7744

3 ALTOONA

Johnny's Used Furn. & Antqs.
501 4th St.
814/944-3423

Michelle's Antiques
1546 Pleasant Valley Blvd.
814/943-6111

4 AMBRIDGE

Tom's Old Country Store
511 Merchant St.
412/266-7215

Attic Attractions
576 Merchant St.
412/266-3020

Nello's Taj Mahal
1415 Merchant St.
412/266-5656

5 ANNVILLE

Chris Machmer Antiques
146 W Main St.
717/867-4244

Meadow View Antiques
Rt. 322
717/838-9443

6 ARDMORE

En Garde Antiques & Cllbls.
24 W. Lancaster Ave.
610/645-5785

Ardmore Antqs. & Orntl. Rugs
321 W. Lancaster Ave.
610/649-4432

7 ATHENS

Fáilte Inn B&B and Antique Shop

Rt. 2
717/358-3899
Rates: $60 per night

Directions: Highway 220 to the blinking light in the village of Uster, P1. Cross over the Susquehanna River bridge and turn left at end of bridge on SR 1043. Three miles to Inn on right. From Towanda: turn left on SR 1043 after crossing James St. bridge. From Athens: turn right on SR 1043 after crossing Susquehanna River bridge in downtown Athens.

Fáilte Inn is nestled in the Susquehanna Valley surrounded by the beautiful Endless Mountains of rural Pennsylvania. You can relax in the country atmosphere of rolling farmland, away from the noise of city traffic and the stress of busy lifestyles.

Enjoy the unhurried charm of yesterday in a turn of the century farmhouse decorated in the graceful elegance of the Victorian era. Escape to a quiet, well-stocked library, listen to fine music or play and enjoy the antique baby grand piano. Relax in front of warm fires in the library or parlor on a cold winter's day. Feel the cool mountain breezes beneath the paddle fans on the wide verandahs during the lazy days of summer.

Enjoy a full country breakfast served in the elegantly appointed formal dining room or on the screened wraparound verandahs overlooking 3 acres of green lawns, apple orchards and beautiful flower gardens. (Served 8 a.m. to 10 a.m.)

Join the innkeepers for a complimentary wine or brandy, coffee or tea accompanied by cheeses or homemade pastries in the historically, restored Speak-Easy dating form the days of prohibition.

Fáilte Inn offers 5 beautifully decorated guest rooms - each with its own private bath; Susan's Room on the ground floor, Catherine's Suite with sitting room, Mama's Room with jacuzzi tub, Chelsea's Room with king side bed, and Jennifer's Room their most selected room.

8 BALA CYNWYD

General Eclectic
159 Bala Ave.
610/667-6677

Pieces of Tyme
323 Montgomery Ave.
610/664-2050

Something Beautiful to Buy
333 Montgomery Ave.
610/667-2969

9 BANGOR

Tolerico's Antiques
53 Broadway
610/588-5510

Tolerico's Past Present Future
13 N. Main St.
610/588-6981

Hartzell's Auction Gallery
521 Richmond Rd.
610/588-5831

10 BEAVER FALLS

Leonard's Antiques & Uniques Mega Mall
2586 Constitution Blvd.
412/847-2304 or 800/443-5052
Web Site: leonards.antiqueshopper.com
E-mail: leonards@timesnet.net
Open Mon.-Sat., 10-8; Sun., 10-6 (Open 362 days a year, closed Thanksgiving Day, Christmas Day and Easter Sunday, but open until midnight on New Year's Eve!)

Directions: Leonard's is located in the Chippewa Mall at the junction of Rt. 51 and Rt. 60, approximately 12 miles from the Ohio state line. From the Penn. Turnpike, take Exit #1A onto Rt. 60. Take Exit #15 off of Rt. 60 onto Rt. 51 at the Chippewa Mall.

Leonard's is the largest antiques mall in western Pennsylvania, with more than 300 dealers all under one roof, covering approximately 68,000 square feet! Inside this enormous mall, there are over a million-and-a-half items! It certainly lives up to its billing as a mega mall! Of course, as you would expect in a space this large, they carry everything from pottery to china, primitives to paper, furniture to fine and costume jewelry. And what a great idea - staying open until midnight on New Year's Eve!

Peggy Smith's Collections
621 7th Ave.
412/843-2622

Antique Emporium
818 7th Ave.
412/847-1919

Leonard's Antiques & Uniques
2586 Constitution Blvd.
412/847-2304

American & European Antqs.
601 Darlington Rd.
412/846-1002

11 BEDFORD

Founders Crossing
100 S. Juliana St.
814/623-9120

Graystone Galleria
203 E. Pitt St.
814/623-1768

Lin's Touch of Elegance
238 E. Pitt St.
814/623-2673

Thomas Antiques
Rd. 6 Box 21 Cumberland Rd.
814/623-5574

12 BELLEFONTE

Times Past Antiques & Cllbls.
141 S. Allegheny St.
814/353-1750

Hayloft Antiques
660 Benner Pike
814/355-7588

13 BERWYN

Circa Antiques & Decor
712 Lancaster Ave.
610/651-8151

McCoy
722 W. Lancaster
610/640-0433

Deja Vu
11 Waterloo Ave.
610/296-2737

And Antiques
19 Waterloo Ave.
610/644-3659

Anything & Everything Shop
36 Waterloo Ave.
610/647-8186

14 BETHLEHEM

C & D Guns Coins & Antiques
121 E. Broad St.
610/865-4355

Sir Pack Rat
99 W. Broad St.
610/974-8855

Valley Antiques Gifts & Imports
729 W. Broad St.
610/865-3880

15 BLAWNOX

Cottage Antiques
231 Freeport Rd.
412/828-9201

The Marlene Harris Collection
238 1/2 Freeport Rd.
412/828-1245

Mulberry Antiques
262 1/2 Freeport Rd.
412/828-0144

China Shop
266 Freeport Rd.
412/826-8075

Lotus Gallery
309 Freeport Rd.
412/828-7588

A Child's Heart
334 Freeport Rd.
412/826-9192

Blawnox Antiques
340 Freeport Rd.
412/828-2224

The Building Arts
340 Freeport Rd.
412/828-6876

Maple Hill Antqs. & Lighting
340 Freeport
412/826-9226

Kirk's Antiques
352 Freeport Rd.
412/828-7470

Velvet Swing Antiques
407 Freeport
412/828-4943

B Merry Interior Design
1144 Freeport Rd.
412/781-6556

16 BLOOMSBURG

Meckley's Books & Cllbls.
36 W. Main St.
717/784-3765

Red Mill Antiques
44 Red Mill Rd.
717/784-7146

Hoffman's Antiques
RR 4
717/784-9534

Liberty Antiques
RR 4
717/683-5419

17 BLUE RIDGE SUMMIT

Wooden Horse Antiques
717/794-2717 (bus. day phone)
301/241-3460 (evening phone)
Open by appointment only

Directions: If traveling on I-81, take Exit #3 (Greencastle, Pa./Rt. 16 East). Proceed east through Waynesboro (8 miles) and then to Blue Ridge Summit (6 miles). Go to the bottom of the mountain after Blue Ridge Summit. Wooden Horse is the third place on the right - there's a sign out front. If traveling Rt. 15, take the Emmetsburg/Rt. 140 West Exit and proceed into Pennsylvania, where Rt. 140 West becomes Rt. 16 West. The shop is approximately 4 miles into Pennsylvania on the left - look for the sign out front.

The folks at Wooden Horse Antiques have been wholesaling to the antique trade for 25 years. They specialize in fancy oak and Victorian furniture and accessories; also country and period furniture and estate contents. Everything is sold in "as is" condition, but these folks look for and offer the "finer" pieces. In a recent conversation with Randy Sutton (the owner), he told me that he has been doing "quite a lot" with the finer circa 1900-1930s mahogany dining room and bedroom furniture. "Mostly ball and claw," he says. "I've also been fortunate to grab some outstanding estates lately." Dealers take note - you never know what might pop up in an estate. My suggestion is to make sure you stop to see Randy when traveling through Pennsylvania.

18 BOALSBURG

Gates Antiques
805 Boalsburg Pike
814/466-6333

Serendipity Valley Farms
122 E. Main St.
814/466-7282

19 BOYERTOWN

Bashful Barn
1 E. Philadelphia Ave.
610/367-2631

Castle Hall Antiques
5 E. Philadelphia Ave.
610/367-6506

Homestead Antiques
Rt. 73
610/367-6502

Greshville Antiques
Rt. 562
610/367-0076

Boyertown Antiques
1283 Weisstown Rd.
610/367-2452

20 BRISTOL

Wilhelmina's
369 Main St.
215/945-8606

Another Time Antiques
307 Mill St.
215/788-3131

Place
5 Pond St.
215/785-1494

21 BRYN MAWR

Greentree Antiques
825 W. Lancaster Ave.
610/526-1841

Susan P Vitale Antiques
835 W. Lancaster Ave.
610/527-5653

Sandy Demaio Antique Jewelry
860 W. Lancaster Ave.
610/525-1717

22 BUTLER

Bergbigler New & Used Furn.
321 Center Ave.
412/287-0865

Fox's Antiques
160 Church Rd.
412/352-4500

Thomas Antiques Shoppe
424 S. Jackson St.
412/287-6839

Ken's Antiques
1251 Lake Vue Dr.
412/586-7271

Antiques
102 N. Main St.
412/282-2899

William Smith Antiques
102 N. Main St.
412/282-2899

Arthur's Gift Shop
126 N. Main St.
412/282-4000

Store on Main
108 S. Main St.
412/283-9923

Alley Antiques
125 S. Main St. (Rear)
412/283-6366

Butler Antiques & Collectibles
119 E. Wayne St.
412/282-7195

23 CAMP HILL

Rose Marie's Antiques
2136 Market St.
717/763-8998

Cordier Antiques
307 N. 25th St.
717/731-8662

24 CANONSBURG

Canonsburg Antique Mall I
145 Adams Ave.
412/745-1333

Treasure Lane
24 W. Pike St.
412/745-7414

Where The Toys Are
45 W. Pike St.
412/745-4599

Tri-State Antique Center
47 W. Pike St.
412/745-9116

Annabelle's Antiques
51 W. Pike St.
412/746-5950

Antique Junction
2475 Washington Rd.
412/746-5119

Rt. 19 Antique Mall
2597 Washington Rd.
412/746-3277

Canonsburg Antique Mall II
99 Weavertown Rd.
412/745-1050

25 CARLISLE

Antiques by James L Price
831 Alexander Spring Rd.
717/243-0501

Antiques on Hanover
17 N. Hanover St.
717/249-6285

Country Heritage
24 N. Hanover St.
717/249-2600

H & R Jewelry & Antiques
33 N. Hanover St.
717/258-4024

Baker's Antiques
34 N. Hanover St.
717/258-1383

Downtown Antiques
152 N. Hanover St.
717/249-0395

Northgate Antique Mall
725th Hanover Manor #726N
717/243-5802

Old Stone Tavern Antiques
2408 Walnut Bottom Rd.
717/243-6304

The Antique Quilt Source
385 Springview Rd. #D
717/245-2054

26 CARNEGIE

Heidelberg Antiques
1451 Collier Ave.
412/429-9223

Heidelberg Antiques
1550 Collier Ave.
412/429-9222

Black Swan Art & Frame Gallery
301 E. Main St.
412/276-3337

27 CHADDS FORD

Olde Ridge Village Antique Shoppes

Rt. 202 & Ridge Rd.
610/459-0960
Open: Daily 10-5, 10-8 Thurs.

Directions: Rt. 202 & Ridge Rd. One mile south of Rt. 1. Traveling on Interstate 95 in the Wilmington, DE. area, take the Wilmington/West Chester exit 8 north on Rt. 202. After crossing the PA border, travel 2 miles to the shop on the left. Coming from the PA Turnpike, take Exton Exit 23 south on Rt. 100. Exit onto Rt. 202 south and cross Rt. 1 (the shop is on the right 1 mile down).

"Olde Ridge" is a cooperative antique shop which is part of a twenty-store village of individually owned small shops and restaurants. Located in Pennsylvania's Historic Chadds Ford, the shop is a twelve room, turn of the century farm house filled with two floors of antiques and collectibles from about a dozen dealers. Displayed in room settings with country, Victorian and 30s-40s furnishings, the shop also offers a number of showcases holding incredible antiques and collectibles. China, glassware, advertising and children's items are just a few of the specialities.

Village Peddler
Baltimore Pike
610/388-2828

Antique Reflections
170 Fairville Rd.
610/388-0645

Diane's Antiques
RR 1
610/388-3956

Jane's Antiques
RR 1
610/388-6730

Pennsbury Chadds Ford Antq.
RR 1
610/388-6480

Aaron Goebels Antiques
Rt 202 & Pyle Rd.
610/459-8555

Frances Lantz Antique Shop
Rt 202 & State Line Rd.
610/459-4080

Wendy's Corner Antiques
210 Wilmington W.
610/358-4077

Joanne Rollins Antiques
Pennsbury Chadds Ford
610/388-0959

28 CHAMBERSBURG

Favorite Places To Eat

Cracker Barrel Old Country Store
I-81 & Wayne Rd., Exit 5
717/264-3311

29 CLARKS SUMMIT

Carriage Barn Antiques
1550 Fairview Rd.
717/587-5405

Heritage House Shoppes
402 N. State St.
717/586-8575

30 CLEARFIELD

Christopher Kratzer House Bed & Breakfast

101 E. Cherry Street
814/765-5024 or 1-888-252-2632
Open year round
Rates $55-70

Directions: Traveling I-80: Take Exit #19 and follow the signs to Clearfield (322W). Turn left at the light before the Nichol Street bridge onto Front Street (Rt. 153 South). Continue along the river past Pine, Locust and Market Streets to the corner of Front and Cherry, across from the park and church.

This old (pre-1840) Greek Revival house is decorated with an eclectic mix of contemporary and antique pieces, artistically intermingled by innkeepers, Bruce and Ginny Baggett. Bruce is a musician and Ginny is a printmaker, and the interior of the house reflects not only their interest in preserving history, but also their interests in art and music. Bruce has a collection of musical instruments and memorabilia of his more than 30 years in show business; he even entertains guests with songs at the piano in the music room! Ginny has filled the house with original art work for sale and has installed an art gallery on the second floor.

This is the oldest house in Clearfield, built by Christopher Kratzer, a noted lumberman, carpenter, architect, politician, and owner of the county's first newspaper. It is located in the Old Town Historic District and predates the Victorian era in which most of the other homes were built. The home overlooks the Susquehanna River and Witmer Park, and is within easy walking distance of shops, the public library, restaurants, a movie theater and the Clearfield County Historical Museum.

Guests have a choice of four rooms, two with views of the river and park, one with mahogany twin beds, the other with an antique queen-size spool bed. There is an upstairs sitting room that converts to a bedroom, and an additional bedroom with a private bath.

Carousel Antiques
404 West 7th Ave.
814/765-8518

Winter Barn Antiques
Susquehanna Bridge Rd.
814/765-5248

31 COLUMBIA

Restorations Etc.
125 Bank Ave.
717/684-5454

C A Herr Annex
35 N. 3rd St.
717/684-7850

Partners Antique Center
403 N. 3rd St.
717/684-5364

32 CURWENSVILLE

Errigo's
848 State Street
814/236-3403

33 DANVILLE

Cloverleaf Barn Antiques
120 McCracken Rd.
717/275-8838

Rising Sun Antiques
6 Mill St.
717/275-1776

Wispy Willows
419 Mill St.
717/275-1658

Fleming Antiques & Lamps
1609 Montour Blvd.
717/275-2081

34 DENVER

Antq. Showcase @ Blck. Horse
2222 N. Reading Rd.
717/336-3864

Adams Antique & Cllbls. Mkt.
Rt. 272/2400 N. Reading Rd.
717/335-3116

Heritage II
Rt. 272
717/336-0888

Covered Bridge Antiques
Rt. 272
717/336-4480

Lancaster County Antiques
Rt. 272
717/336-2701

Exit 21 Antiques & Collectibles
Rt. 272
717/336-7482

Adamstown Antique Gallery
2000 N. Reading Rd.
717/335-3435

James Maxwell/Virginia Caputo
2350 N. Reading Rd. (Rt. 272)
717/336-2185

35 DILLSBURG

B & J Antique Mall
14 Franklin Church Rd.
717/432-7353

36 DOYLESTOWN

New Britain Antiques
326 W. Butler Ave.
215/345-7282

Consignment Galleries
470 Clemens Town Cntr., Rt. 202
215/348-5244

Nejad Gallery Fine Orntl. Rugs
1 N. Main St.
215/348-1255

Dragons Den of Antiques
135 S. Main St.
215/345-8666

Y-Knot Shop
New Galena Rd. & Rt. 313
215/249-9120

Frog Pond
128 W. State St.
215/348-3425

37 DREXEL HILL

Brandywine House Antiques
1201 Cornell Avenue
610/449-5208

Fields Antique Jewelers
Landsdowne & Windsor Ave.
610/853-2740

38 DUBLIN

Kramer's Rainbow Rooms
104 Middle Rd.
215/249-1916

39 DUNCANNON

Old Sled Works
722 North Market Street
717/834-9333
Open Wed.-Sun., 10-5

Directions: Old Sled Works is located 1 mile off Rt. 11 and 15 or off Routes 22 and 322. The Works is approximately 15 miles northwest of Harrisburg.

See collector interview for information.

Cove Barn
10 Kinsey Rd.
717/834-4088

Leonard's Antique Co-op
1631 State Rd.
717/957-3536

Peggy's Antique Shop
2205 State Rd.
717/834-9379

40 DUNCANSVILLE

Duncansville Antique Depot
1401 2nd Ave.
814/696-4000

Dodson's Antique Shop
614 3rd Ave.
814/695-1901

Creekside Antiques
1031 3rd Ave.
814/695-5520

Black Kermit
1032 3rd Ave.
814/695-5909

David Donnelly Antiques
1224 3rd Ave.
814/695-5942

Don's Antiques
1324 3rd Ave.
814/696-0807

41 EAGLE

Little Bit Country
Rt. 100
(across from Historic Eagle Tavern)
610/458-0363
Open Mon.-Fri. 10-5; Sat., 11-7; Sun., 12-6

Directions: Little Bit Country is located just north, approximately 1- 1/2 miles of the Pennsylvania Turnpike Exit 23, along Rt. 100 North.

This interesting shop, with a name that sounds suspiciously like a country hit song, carries a selection of antiques and primitives that varies. They also handle fabrics and gifts.

42 EASTON

Dylan Spencer Antiques
200 Northampton St.
610/252-6766

43 ELLWOOD CITY

Marketplace on Main
402 Lawrence Ave.
412/752-1201

Into Antiques
RR 1
412/758-5127

Gramma's House
326 6th St.
412/758-4262

44 ELVERSON

Rosalind Lee's Antiques
S. Chestnut St.
610/286-9869

Tom E. Fisher
11 E. Main St.
610/286-6618

45 EMMAUS

Twin Jugs Consignments
4033 Chestnut St.
610/967-4010

Sweet Memories & Tea Room
180 Main St.
610/967-0296

The Tin Shop
161 E. Main St.
(Macungie) No Phone

46 EPHRATA

Located in the picturesque and well-known Lancaster County, home of the Pennsylvania Dutch, Mennonite and Amish communities, Ephrata was actually settled in 1732, by a German religious society under the leadership of Johann Beissel. The men and women formed the Society of the Solitary Brethren, a semi-monastic order advocating celibacy and favoring common ownership of property, although neither marriage nor private ownership was prohibited. By 1740 the self-sufficient community consisted of 36 brethren and 35 sisters housed in a single building known as the Cloisters. At the height of its prosperity, the community numbered about 300 members. The hymns and experimental melodies of founder Johann Beissel that were published here were a major influence on American hymnology.

After Beissel's death in 1768, John Miller became the head of the community and was commissioned by the U.S. Congress to translate the Declaration of Independence into several European languages. In 1745 the second printing press in Pennsylvania was set up in Ephrata, and Continental money was printed in Ephrata during the British occupation of Philadelphia. After the battle of Brandywine in 1777, the community buildings were used as hospitals. The Society of the Solitary Brethren declined after Miller's death, and today the Cloisters are maintained as a museum by the Pennsylvania Historical and Museum Commission.

Also today, the Rt. 272 corridor between Ephrata and Adamstown (in the vicinity of Exit #21 on the Pennsylvania Turnpike) is widely known as a flea market haven. Actually called "The Adamstown Antique Mile," it began as a strip of restaurants and motels easily accessible to the turnpike. This area is also the home of Pepperidge Farms, Inc.

The Inns at Doneckers
318-324 N. State Street
717/738-9502
Open year round except Christmas
Rates $59-185

Directions: From the Penn. Turnpike, take Exit #21 and take Rt. 222 South to the Ephrata exit. Turn right onto Rt. 322, which becomes Main Street in Ephrata. Go to the 4th traffic light and turn right onto State Street. The inns are about 4 blocks down on the left.

There are four individual inn properties surrounding the Doneckers community here in Ephrata, each within walking distance of Doneckers Fashion Stores for the family and home, and a gourmet restaurant. Also within walking distance in the community is an artworks complex of more than 30 studios and galleries of fine art, quilts and designer crafts, and two farmer's markets. If that is not enough for you, the inns are just minutes from Adamstown's antique markets, a short scenic drive from Lancaster County's Amish Farmland and attractions, and are convenient for a day trip to historic Gettysburg.

The four inns together offer 40 rooms (38 with private baths), each one furnished in antiques and hand-stenciled walls, and some rooms have fireplaces and jacuzzis. Guests get to choose among the Guesthouse, the Historic 1777 House, the Homestead, and the Gerhart House.

A sampling of what you'll find at the Inns at Doneckers

1777 House at Doneckers

This late Georgian-style home, which takes its name from the year of its construction, was built by Jacob Gorgas, a clockmaker in the religious Ephrata Cloister community located in Lancaster County in 1777. Later, the house served as a tavern for travelers in Conestoga wagons on their way from Philadelphia to Pittsburgh. The house has been carefully restored, and the original stone masonry, tile flooring and many other authentic architectural details have been saved.

There are 12 guest rooms in this inn (some with fireplaces), all named for brothers and sisters of the Cloister. The adjacent Carriage House offers an additional two suites with lofts.

Summer House Antiques
1156 W. Main St., Rt. 322
717/733-8989

Olde Carriage House
2425 W. Main St.
717/738-2033

Good's Collectibles
2460 W. Main St.
717/738-2033

Mother Tucker's Antiques
566 N. Reading Rd.
717/738-1297

Grandma's Attic
1862 W. Main St.
717/733-7158

Three T's Antiques
Rt. 272 South @ 322
717/733-6572

Antiques at Ephrata
1749 W. Main St.
717/738-4818

47 ERIE

Antique Attractions
202 E. 10th St.
814/459-0277

Rage
613 W. 26th St.
814/456-9931

Folly Antique Mall & Guns
654 W. 26th St.
814/459-2503

Antq. Intrs. by Dennis Pistone
1209 State Street
814/455-6992

Dempsey & Baxter
1009 E. 38th St.
814/825-6381

Sherif's Imported Rugs
3854 Peach St.
814/864-6460

Erie Antique Store
1015 State St.
814/454-6256

Dennis Pistone Antiques
1207 State St.
814/454-1510

Favorite Places To Eat

Cracker Barrel Old Country Store
I-90 & SS. 19 (Peach St.), Exit 6
814/868-2500

48 EXPORT

Schmidt's Springhouse Antiques

Rt. 66 at Pfeffer Rd.
412/325-2577, 800/771-2684
Open: Tue.-Sat. 10-5, Sunday 1-5, closed Christmas, Thanksgiving, Easter.

Directions: Located on the west side of Rt. 66, 5 miles north of Rt. 22 and 1 1/2 miles south of Rt. 366.

Schmidt's Springhouse Antiques, owned by Betty & Ed Schmidt, is dedicated to providing a large variety of ready to display quality antique furniture; country, primitives, Empire, Victorian, oak and depression. Open since 1993, the shop provides 6,000 square feet and will expand to over 10,000 square feet in 1998.

49 FOGELSVILLE

Favorite Places To Eat

Cracker Barrel Old Country Store
I-78 & State Rd. 100, Exit 14B
610/481-0055

50 FRANKLIN

Franklin Antique Mall & Auct.
1280 Franklin Ave.
814/432-8577

Haylett's
338 Grant St.
814/432-5686

Every Thing
1335 Liberty St.
814/432-4460

Angus Antiques
1581 Pittsburgh Rd.
814/432-3325

Knotty Pine Antiques
304 2nd Ave.
814/432-4193

51 GAP

Mechanical Musical Memories
5281 Lincoln Hwy.
717/442-8508

Gap Village Store
5403 Lincoln Hwy.
717/442-5263

52 GETTYSBURG

Don't ever accuse Southerners of being obsessive about the War Between the States, because there are probably not any folks more immersed in that era than the residents of Gettysburg, Pennsylvania!

There are probably only a handful of Americans who don't know something about this landmark battle of the American Civil War. It took place in July of 1863, and was the turning point of the war and the beginning of the end for the Confederacy. Here, General Robert E. Lee's Confederate army of 75,000 men and the 97,000-man Northern army of General George G. Meade met - by chance - when a Confederate brigade, sent to the area for supplies, observed a forward column of Meade's cavalry.

Of the more than 2,000 land engagements of the Civil War, Gettysburg remains the single great battle of the war. It left us with names forever connected to battle: Seminary Ridge, Cemetery Ridge, Pickett's Charge. After the battle 51,000 casualties were counted, making Gettysburg the bloodiest battle of American history. Although the war raged for another two terrible and savage years, the Confederacy never recovered from the losses at Gettysburg, and Lee never again attempted an offensive operation of such proportions. The tide had turned at Gettysburg.

T. T. & G.'s Antique Collectible Co-op

2031 York Rd.
717/334-0361
Open Mon.-Sat., 9-4:30; Sun., 12-4:30

Directions: Located on U.S. 30, 7 miles west of New Oxford Square and 3 miles east of Gettsyburg Square, on the south side of the highway.

T. T. & G.'s is 6,500 square feet of space in an old barn with 25 or more regular dealers. They carry everything from late 18th century Victorian pieces (like Eastlake) to modern. They no longer operate an upholstery shop, but are opening a reproduction room for accessories and furniture. The wood types they handle include oak, mahogany, walnut and pine.

Time Travel Antiques
312 Baltimore St.
717/337-0011

Farnsworth House Inn
401 Baltimore St.
717/334-8838

Antique & Collectibles
22 Carlise St.
No Phone

Mel's Antiques & Collectibles
103 Carlisle St.
717/334-9387

Arrow Horse
51 Chambersburg St.
717/337-2899

Maggie's Another Place & Time
52 Chambersburg St.
717/334-0325

Gettysburg Antiques & Cllbls.
54 Chambersburg St.
717/337-0432

School House Antiques
2523 Emmitsburg Rd.
717/334-4564

Keystone Country Furniture
2904 Emmitsburg Rd.
717/337-3952

Antique Center of Gettysburg
7 Lincoln Square
717/337-3669

Hope Springs Antiques
2540 Mummasburg Rd.
717/677-4695

Great Stuff
45-47 Stienwehr Ave.
717/337-0442

Magic Town
49 Steinwehr Ave.
717/337-0492

Fields of Glory
55 York St.
717/337-2837

53 GIBSONIA

Atlantic Crossing Antiques
3748 Gibsonia Rd.
412/443-5858

Allagheny Heritage Antiques
5500 Molnar Dr
412/443-6425

Jim's Antiques
Rt. 8
412/443-4866

Richland Antiques
RR 8
412/443-8090

54 GILBERTSVILLE

Shafer's Antiques
1573 E. Philadelphia
610/369-1999

Sutterby's Oak Furniture
Zern's Market - Rt 73
610/369-1777

55 GIRARD

What Not Shop
18 Main St.
814/774-4413

Westaways Antiques
21 Myrtle St.
814/774-2829

Heartland Antiques & Gifts
10100 Old Ridge Rd.
814/774-0344

56 GLENSIDE

Ludwig's Scattered Treasures
221 W. Glenside Ave.
215/887-0512

Kirkland & Kirkland
Keswick Ave.
215/576-7771

Yesterday and Today
280 Keswick Ave.
215/572-6926

57 GREENSBURG

J A Henderson Blacksmith
509 S. Main St.
412/838-7656

Antique Treasures
Rt. 22
412/837-4474

58 GREENVILLE

Iron Bridge Shoppe
108 Main St.
412/588-2455

Country Store
220 W. Methodist Rd.
412/588-9692

Country Store
133 Orangeville Rd.
412/588-5820

59 HAMBURG

Favorite Places To Eat

Cracker Barrel Old Country Store
I-78 & State Rd. 61, Exit 9B
610/562-3622

60 HANOVER

Nagengast Antiques
37 Frederick Street
717/633-1148

61 HARMONY

In Harmony
250 Mercer St.
412/452-0203

Into Antiques
280 Perry Hwy.
412/452-3210

Olde Country House
575 Perry Hwy.
412/452-0100

Finders Keepers
657 Perry Hwy.
412/452-9960

Bee Four Collectibles
Rt. 19 N.
412/452-0922

62 HARRISBURG

Antiques at Towne House Gllry.
242 North Street
717/238-4199

Doehnes Ox Box Shop
N. Progress Avenue
717/545-7930

Crafty Generations
Strawberry Square
717/234-5521

Medina
901 North 2nd Street
717/233-0115

63 HAVERFORD

Mock Fox
15 Haverford Station Rd.
610/642-4990

French Corner Antiques Ltd.
16 Haverford Station Rd.
610/642-6867

Chelsea House Ltd.
45 Haverford Station Rd.
610/896-5554

McClee's Galleries
343 West Lancaster
610/642-1661

64 HAWLEY

Natural resources have played an important part in the history of Hawley. The community was first inhabited in the late 18th century by pioneers who liked the potential of this area where three creeks converged. They settled, built a sawmill, and began sending lumber down the rivers to Philadelphia. The first child of the settlement was born in 1812; the first store opened in 1827; the Delaware & Hudson Canal, running from Honesdale to New York, was completed in 1828, and anthracite coal began moving on barges along towpaths through Hawley to the New York markets.

The area around Hawley saw great prosperity from the 1840s to the 1860s, with the economy continuing to be based around the coal industry to support businesses. In the 1920s, industries began to supplant Hawley's coal and lumber base, including fine cut glass, and silk and textile mills.

Another growth cycle began in 1925 with the introduction of hydroelectric power. The Pennsylvania Power & Light Company dammed the Wallenpaupack Creek and created the state's largest man-made lake, thus changing the focus of the area's industry. The Hawley region became an area of recreational and related business opportunities and continues in this field today.

Timely Treasures
475 Welwood Avenue
717/226-2838
Web Site: www.timelytreasures.com
Open: Thurs.-Mon. 10-5, closed Tue. and Wed.

During the late 1800s, the building which now houses Timely Treasures was the town power plant. From this building power was made available to the residents of Hawley who chose to have electricity in their homes. An appropriate site for housing wonderful antiques, the shop has six rooms of antiques from the turn of the century through the 1950s. Their speciality is furniture (1850-1950s) but, the owners also provide a nice selection of cut glass from the brilliant period, china, lamps, pottery (Roseville) and more.

Castle Antiques & Reproductions
515 Welwood Avenue
1-800-345-1667
Open Mon.-Sat., 8:30-5

Directions: Hawley is located between Scranton and Milford, about 45 minutes from Scranton and about 30 minutes from Milford. From Scranton: Take 84E to Exit 6, go left onto Rt. 507. Go to the end, make a left onto Rt. 6, and go 1.5 miles. Castle Antiques is on the right. From New York state or Milford, Pa.: Take 84W to Penn. Exit 8 (Blooming Grove). Make a right onto Rt. 402. Go 5 miles to the end, make a left onto Rt. 6, and go 5 miles. Castle Antiques is on the right.

You really cannot miss this shop - it looks like a castle! Very appropriately named, Castle Antiques & Reproductions is housed in the historic landmark known as Sherman Mill. It was constructed in 1880 and is the largest bluestone granite building in North America.

The original water-powered mill sits in the picturesque Pocono Mountains, and the unusual stone architecture gives it the appearance of a castle. It was last purchased in 1989 and has undergone extensive renovations to return it to its original beauty. Now it offers 35,000 square feet of showroom space filled with treasures from around the world.

Some of the merchandise shoppers will find at the "Castle" includes American and imported furniture, lighting fixtures, statuary, bronzes, Tiffany style lamps, and general merchandise, both old and new.

Barbara's Books & Antiques
730 Hudson St.
717/226-9021

Antiques & Collectibles
202 Main Ave.
717/226-9524

Hawley Antique Center
318 Main Ave.
717/226-8990

Decorator's Den & Resale
RR 6
717/226-0440

Loft Antiques
RR 590
717/685-4267

65 HAZLETON

Remember When
2 E. Broad St.
717/454-8465

Mariano's Furn & Gifts
1042 N. Church St.
717/455-0397

66 HERSHEY

The Hen-Apple Bed & Breakfast
409 S. Lingle Avenue
717/838-8282
Open year round
Rates $55-65

Directions: For specific directions to The Hen-Apple Bed & Breakfast, please call ahead. The innkeepers will provide excellent directions from your location.

A visit to the Hen-Apple is a chance to really enjoy the simple pleasures of country living. This bed and breakfast is a circa 1825 Georgian-style farmhouse situated on an acre of land on the edge of town. A "down home" atmosphere prevails, from the antique and reproduction furnishings to the full country breakfast. There are six guest rooms, all with private baths, plus three common rooms, a screened-in back porch, a front porch and a Wicker Room for guests to enjoy. Or take a stroll among the stand of old fruit trees, or snooze in the hammock or lawn chairs and play with the resident cat. And if and when you feel like exerting yourself, you'll be only minutes away from Hershey, Harrisburg, Gettysburg, Ephrata, Reading, antiques galore, auctions, crafts shops, Amish country, the Mt. Hope Winery, and so on and so on.

Canal Collectibles
22 W. Canal St
717/566-6940

Cocoa Curio Hist. Militaria
546 W. Chocolate Ave.
717/533-1167

Ziegler's Antique Mall
825 Cocoa Ave.
717/533-7990

67 HOLLIDAYSBURG

Remember When
1414 Allegheny St.
814/696-4638

Burkholder's Antique Shop
Rt. 22
814/695-1030

68 INDIANA

Kemp's Old Mill Antique Shop
Rt. 286 N. Box 170
412/463-0644

Denise's Log Cabin Antq. Mall
Old Rt. 119 N. & 110
412/349-4001

69 IRWIN

Antiques Odds & Ends
508 Lincoln Highway E., Rt. 30
412/863-9769
Open 11-5:30 daily

Directions: Antiques Odds & Ends is located 1/2 mile off Pennsylvania Turnpike Exit #7 on Rt. 30 East.

Antiques Odds & Ends is a husband-and-wife business. Vince and his wife have been partners for 25 years and were the "first in the State to open up an all-in-one antique shop." (I'm quoting Vince here, so figure this one out on your own.)

I've never personally met Vince, but he and I had a rather nice long chat (over the phone) about the antiques business. When he told me he had been in the "biz" for 25 years, I just had to pick his brain for some tips. This man has an incredible knowledge of antiques! We went on to discuss how sometimes it's very difficult to locate antique shops since most do not advertise. With a chuckle, Vince offered this very clever piece of advice, "A Place Of Business With No Sign, Is A Sign Of No Business."

Vince, Thanks and Here's Your Sign!

Antiques Odds & Ends
3 large buildings covering 8,000 sq. ft.
Showcasing glassware, toys, clocks, lamps, primitives and more!

Mays Antiques
624 Main St.
412/863-1840

Victoria's Looking Glass
624 Main St.
412/863-1868

Attic Treasures
Rt. 993
412/863-0338

70 JENKINTOWN

Hidden Treasure
400 Leedom St.
215/887-4150

Jeffrey Caesar Antiques
214 Old York Rd.
215/572-6040

Jenkintown Antique Guild
208 York Rd.
215/576-5044

71 JOHNSTOWN

Seven Gables Gifts & Antiques
1404 Dwight Dr.
814/266-7117

Curiosity Corner
570 Grove Ave.
814/535-5210

Greenwood's Antiques & Gifts
3549 Menoher Blvd.
814/255-5057

Always Antiques
125 Truman Blvd.
814/539-0543

72 KENNETT SQUARE

Garrett Longwood
864 S. Baltimore Pike Rd.
610/444-5257

McLiman's
806 W. Cypress St.
610/444-3876

Clifton Mill Shoppes
162 Old Kennett Rd.
610/444-5234

Antiquus
120 W. State St.
610/444-9892

Kennett Square Jewelers
123 W. State St.
610/444-5595

73 KIMBERTON

Kimber Hall
Hares Hill Rd.
610/933-8100

Corner Cupboard Antiques
Kimberton Rd.
610/933-9700

Thorum's Antiques
Prizer Rd.
610/935-3351

74 KUTZTOWN

Greenwich Mills Antiques
1097 Krumsville Rd.
610/683-7866
Open: Weekends and by appointment

Directions: 2 1/2 miles north of Kutztown along Rt. 737. Between Kutztown and I-78 (exit 12).

Greenwich Mills Antiques, located in an old 1860s stone grist mill, is filled with local country furniture, primitives, textiles, art and collectibles. (One of my favorite places to shop).

Renninger's Antiques & Cllbls.
Noble St.
610/683-6848

Louise's Old Things
163 W. Main St.
610/683-8370

Baver's Antiques
232 W. Main St.
610/683-5045

Bruce M Moyer & Karen
276 W. Main St.
610/683-9212

75 LAHASKA

Oaklawn Metalcraft Shop
5752 Rt. 202
215/794-7387

Picket's Post
5761 Rt. 202
215/794-7350

Darby-Barrett Antiques
5799 Rt. 202
215/794-8277

Choate & Von Z
Rt. 202
215/794-8695

76 LANCASTER

Chris's Buy & Sell
201 W. King St.
717/291-9133

Book Haven
146 N. Prince St.
717/393-0920

Pondora's Antiques
2014 Old Philadelphia Pike
717/299-5305

Olde Towne Interiors Inc.
224 W. Orange St.
717/394-6482

77 LANSDOWNE

Good Old Days Antiques
201 E. Plumstead Avenue
610/622-2688

Clock Services
2255 Garret Rd.
610/284-2600

Ye Olde Thrift Shoppe
213 W. Baltimore Ave.
610/623-3179

Before Our Time Antiques
54 W. Marshall Rd.
610/259-6370

Ardmart Antique Mall
State & Landsdowne
610/789-6622

Henry Gerlach Jewelers
414 S. State Rd.
610/449-7600

Attic Door
8904 West Chester Pike
610/446-6690

Spring House Antiques
4213 Woodland Ave.
610/623-8898

78 LEWISBURG

Lewis Keister Antiques
209 Market St.
717/523-3945

Rt. 15 Flea Market
Rt. 15
717/568-8080

Brookpark Farms Antiques
RR 45 W
717/523-6555

Victorian Lady
RR 45 W
717/523-8090

Lewisburg Roller Mills Mktpl.
517 Saint Mary St.
717/524-5733

Thomas K Peper Antiques
Stein Lane
717/523-8080

79 LITITZ

The Workshop
945 Disston View Dr.
717/626-6031

Hardican Antiques
34 E. Main St.
717/627-4603

House of Unusuals
55 E. Main St.
717/626-7474

Garthoeffner Antiques
122 E. Main St.
717/627-7998

Sylvan B Brandt
651 E. Main St.
717/626-4520

1857 Barn
Rt. 322 & Rt. 501
717/626-5115

Brickerville Antiques & Decoys
117 NE 28th Diivisi Dr.
717/627-2464

Heritage Map Museum
55 N. Water St.
717/626-5002

80 LITTLESTOWN

Second Chance Antiques
4895 Baltimore Pike
717/359-4038

Betty & Jack's Antiques
31 W. King St.
717/359-4809

Whitman's Country Cupboard
40 N. Queen St.
717/359-4527

King & Queen Antiques
1 S. Queen St.
717/359-7953

81 MALVERN

Conestoga Antiques
30 Conestoga Rd.
610/647-6627

King Street Traders
16 E. King St.
610/296-8818

Nesting Feathers
218 E. King St.
610/408-9377

Station House Antiques Ltd.
1 W. King St.
610/647-5193

Stevens Antiques
627 Lancaster Ave.
610/644-8282

Pennsylvania

82 MANHEIM

Noll's Antiques
1047 S. Colebrook Rd.
717/898-8677

Conestoga Auction Co. Inc.
768 Graystone Rd.
717/898-7284

Exit 20 Antiques
3091 Lebanon Rd.
717/665-5008

Country Store Antiques & Mus.
60 W. Main St.
717/664-0022

83 MANSFIELD

Country Trader
9 N. Main St.
717/662-2309

Main St. Antiques Co-op
17 N. Main St.
717/662-2444

Mansfield Antique Shop
763 S. Main St.
717/662-3624

Times Remembered
Rt. 6 W
717/662-3474

84 MCKNIGHTSTOWN

Country Escape Bed & Breakfast
275 Old Rt. 30
717/338-0611
Open year round
Rates $65-80

Directions: From the square in Gettysburg, drive west on Rt. 30. When you are 5.4 miles from the square, turn left at the small McKnightstown sign onto Old Rt. 30. Country Escape is the last house on the right in McKnightstown, just past the old post office.

As innkeeper, Merry Bush, describes it, this is a "laid back" bed and breakfast. Her idea is to get people to relax and enjoy themselves and the beautiful surroundings, but she does offer desktop publishing and faxing services for you "type A" personalities who just can't unwind!

Country Escape offers queen sized beds and all the comforts of home "amid the bucolic setting complete with mountain vistas and flower gardens." After you've refreshed yourself with a good night's sleep and a hearty breakfast, you can browse through the eclectic gift shop at the inn, soak in the hot tub, or explore the many battle sites all around the inn. The inn is located on the road where Confederate forces marched to the battle of Gettysburg.

85 MEADVILLE

Troyer's Antiques
Baldwin St. Extension
814/724-4036

Artist's Gallery
245 Chestnut St.
814/336-2792

Marcia's Mercantile
9006 Mercer Pike
814/724-8131

Pine Antique Shop
988 Park Ave.
814/336-2466

Unger's Antique Shop
1197 Pennsylvania
814/336-4262

Tamarack Treasures
Springs Rd.
814/333-2927

86 MECHANICSVILLE

Buck House Antiques
3336 Durham Rd.
215/794-8054

Howard Szmolko Antique Shop
5728 Mechanicsville Rd.
215/794-8115

87 MECHANICSBURG

Alexander's Antiques
6620 Carlisle Pike
717/766-5165

Rose's Odds & Ends
123 E. Main St.
717/766-5017

Veronique's Antiques
124 S. Market St.
717/697-4924

Mitrani & Company
6 State St.
717/766-8367

White Barn Antiques
973 W. Trindle Rd.
717/766-8727

Country Gifts N Such
5145 E. Trindle Rd.
717/697-3555

88 MEDIA

Hometown Collection
212 W. Baltimore Pike
610/565-9627

Fitzgerald Group
220 W. Baltimore Ave.
610/566-0703

Remember When Antiques
21 W. State
610/566-7411

Antique Exchange of Media
23 W. State
610/891-9992

Atelier
36 W. State
610/566-6909

89 MILFORD

Ann East Gallery
109 E. Ann St.
717/296-5166

AAA Quality Antiques
100 Bennett Ave.
717/296-6243

Schouppe's Antiques
100 Bennet Ave.
717/296-6243

Forrest Hall Antique Center
Broad & Hartford
717/296-4893

Antiques of Milford
216 Broad St.
717/296-4258

Judy's Antiques
220 Broad St.
717/296-8626

Pear Alley Antiques
220 Broad St.
717/296-8919

Elizabeth Restucci's Antiques
214 Broad St.
717/296-2118

Clockworks
319 Broad St.
717/296-5236

110 East Catharine St.
110 E. Catharine St.
717/296-4288

Pieces of Time
Rt. 663 & Allentown Rd.
215/536-3135

Milford Antiques
Rt 663
215/536-9115

90 MILLVILLE

Down on the Farm
RR 1
717/458-4956

Cats Pajamas Vintage Clothing
Rt. 42
717/458-5233

Gay Fisk Ann Antiques
RR 42
717/458-5131

91 MONONGAHELA

Longwell House
711 W. Main St.
412/258-3536

Main Street Antiques
800 W. Main St.
412/258-3560

Collectiques
808 W. Main St.
412/258-4773

92 MONROEVILLE

Flowers in the Attic
4713 Northern Pike
412/856-7001

93 MORGANTOWN

Cinnamon Stick
W. Main St.
610/286-7763

Treasure Hill
W. Main St. Rt. 23
610/286-7119

Antique Collection
238 W. Main St.
610/286-5244

Morgantown Antique Center
325 W. Main
610/286-8981

94 MORRISDALE

Chris' Collectibles
Allport Cut-off Rd. 1
814/342-3482

95 MOUNT JOY

Hillside Farm Bed & Breakfast
607 Eby Chiques Rd.
717/653-6697
Open year round
Rates $60-70

Directions: Traveling Rt. 283 (westbound), take Salunga Exit; (eastbound) take the Salunga Exit. If eastbound, turn right onto Spooky Nook Rd. Either way go 1-1/4 miles to Eby Chiques Rd. Turn right and go 1/4 mile to Hillside. Hillside Farm is the first place on the right.

Everything about this charming B&B is a tribute to the farming area and all the B&B's immediate neighbors - dairy farms! Hillside Farm B&B is housed in an old (circa 1863) farmhouse, surrounded by an old barn and outbuildings; however, today's owners do not farm and have no farm animals except the barn cats. But they are surrounded by one of the largest areas of farmland left in Lancaster County, which is why it is so peaceful here. Just a half mile down the road is one of the many Amish farms that dot the area, and a one-room schoolhouse. Innkeepers Deb and Gary Lintner can even arrange for guests to eat dinner with an Amish family (with advance reservations) and to see a modern milking at one of the other neighboring farms.

The B&B's "bottle theme" evolved from this dairy history and by an accidental discovery some few years ago. While Gary was cleaning some brush off a bank behind the barn, he noticed something shiny in the ground. Looking closer he discovered 21 unbroken antique milk bottles from different local dairies, most of which stopped operating in the late 1940s. These bottles are now displayed in the dining room.

Along with the bottles, Hillside is furnished with traditional furniture and other dairy antiques. The farmhouse is a two and a half story brick home featuring a standard design of four main rooms on each floor; although over the years, that design has been modified. Now the second floor features bedrooms, each with a view of the surrounding farmland. There are five guest rooms, three with private baths, and a hot tub for six on the porch. Guests get a full breakfast, afternoon snacks, recommendations for dinner, and directions to all the antique shops and malls in the area! Then they can come back to the inn and relax on the balcony that overlooks Chiques Creek with a view of the mill dam and an old generator house. They can listen to the owls, bullfrogs and cows and watch rabbits, squirrels and woodchucks play in the yard and drift off to sleep with the sounds of nature and the country singing their own special lullaby.

White Horses Antique Market
973 W. Main St.
717/653-6338

96 NEW BRIGHTON

Todd Antiques Plus
920 3rd Ave.
412/847-0840

Capo Furniture
928 3rd Ave.
412/846-0721

Pennypackers
1010 3rd Ave.
412/843-3336

Past and Presents
1301 3rd Ave.
412/847-3006

Our Barn Shoppe
539 Harmony Rd.
412/847-9100

97 NEW HOLLAND

Frank Cabana's Antiques
1453 Division Hwy.
717/354-6564

School House Antiques
Main St. Rt. 23
717/455-7384

Stew Country
Rt. 322
717/354-7343

98 NEW HOPE

Pineapple Hill Bed & Breakfast
1324 River Rd.
215/862-1790, 215/862-5273
Email: www.pineapplehill.com

Directions: For specific directions from your location, please call the Innkeepers.

Enjoy the charm of a beautifully restored colonial manor house built in 1790. Set on almost 6 acres, this Bucks County bed & breakfast rests between New Hope's center and Washington Crossing Park.

In the 1700s it was customary to place a pineapple on your front porch as a way of letting friends and neighbors know you were welcoming guests. Pineapple Hill continues this tradition by offering the same hospitality to their guests.

The eighteen inch walls and original woodwork at the historically registered Pineapple Hill exemplify a craftsmanship long forgotten. On the grounds, the ruins of a stone barn enclose a beautiful hand tiled pool.

Breakfast at Pineapple Hill is always the treat. A full gourmet breakfast is skillfully prepared and served in the common room each morning. Breakfast is served from 8a.m. until 10a.m. at individual candle-lit tables. This room is available to use at your leisure - to watch a movie, read a book, or just curl up on a chilly evening in front of the fireplace.

Each of the spacious guestrooms is individually furnished with locally obtained antiques, collectibles, and original artwork. For your reading pleasure, all rooms are well stocked with books and magazines. Three of the guestrooms are accompanied by a separate living room with comfortable furnishings and cable televisions. Located on the second and third floors of the inn, all guestrooms at Pineapple Hill feature private baths for your comfort and convenience.

Pineapple Hill is located deep in the heart of antiquing territory, where treasure hunting at the local shops, auctions and flea markets is readily available. There are also art galleries, theatre and speciality shops all nearby.

Pink House
W. Bridge st
215/862-5947

Hobensack & Keller
57 W. Bridge St.
215/862-2406

Bridge Street Old Books
129 W. Bridge St.
215/862-0615

Ferry Hill
15 W. Ferry St.
215/862-5335

Katy Kane Inc.
34 W. Ferry St.
215/862-5873

Don Roberts Antiques
38 W. Ferry St.
215/862-2702

Kennedy Antiques
6154 Lower York Rd.
215/794-8840

Lehmann Antiques
6154 Lower York Rd.
215/794-7724

James Raymond & Co.
6319 Lower York Rd.
215/862-9751

Francis J Purcell II
88 N. Main St.
215/862-9100

Crown & Eagle Antiques Inc.
Rt. 202
215/794-7972

Gardner's Antiques
Rt. 202
215/794-8616

Ingham Springs Antq. Center
Rt. 202
215/862-0818

Olde Hope Antiques
Rt. 202
215/862-5055

Hall And Winter
429 York Rd.
215/862-0831

Cockamamie's
9A West Bridge Street
215/862-5454

99 NEW KENSINGTON

Jolar Inc.
879 5th Ave.
412/339-4766

Gifts International
2517 Leechburg Rd.
412/339-7075

100 NEW OXFORD

Hart's Country Antiques
2 Carlisle St.
717/624-7842

Sarah's Antiques
109 Carlisle St.
717/624-9664

Rife Antiques
4415 York Rd.
717/624-2546

Fountainview Antqs. N' Things
10 Center Square
717/624-9394

Center Square Antiques
16 Center Square
717/624-3444

New Oxford Antique Mall
214 W. Golden Lane
717/624-3703

Collectors Choice Antq. Gllry.
330 W. Golden Lane
717/624-3440

Willow Way Enterprises
390 Gun Club
717/624-4920

Storms Antiques & Cllbls.
1030 Kohler Mill Rd.
717/624-8112

Adam's Apple
3 Lincoln Way
717/624-3488

Bill's Old Toys
19 Lincoln Way E
717/624-4069

KEH'R Corner Cupboard
20 Lincoln Way E
717/624-3054

Stonehouse
100 Lincoln Way E
717/624-3755

Heartland Antiques & Gifts
111 Lincoln Way E
717/624-9686

Lau's Antiques
112 Lincoln Way E
717/624-4972

Americas Past Antiques
114 Lincoln Way E
717/624-7830

Remember When Shop
4 Lincoln Way W
717/624-2426

Oxford Hall Irish Too
106 Lincoln Way W
717/624-2337

Betty & Gene's Antiques
110 Lincoln Way W
717/624-4437

Oxford Barn
330 Lincoln Way W
717/624-4160

New Oxford Antique Center
333 Lincoln Way W
717/624-7787

Barry Click Antiques
145 Newchester Rd
717/624-3185

Conewago Creek Forks
1255 Oxford Rd.
717/624-4786

Golden Lane Antique Gallery
11 N. Water St.
717/624-3800

Black Shutter Shoppes
4335 York Rd.
717/624-8766

Corner Cupboard
4335 York Rd.
717/624-4242

Weeks Antiques
4335 York Rd.
717/624-7979

101 NEW STANTON

Favorite Places To Eat

Cracker Barrel Old Country Store
I-70 & Center Ave., Exit 26
412/925-7144

102 NEWTOWN

Nostalgia Nook
591 Durham Rd.
215/598-8837

Hanging Lamp Antiques
140 N. State St.
215/968-2015

Temora Farm Antiques
372 Swamp Rd.
215/860-2742

103 NORRISTOWN

Auntie Q's
403 W. Marshall St.
610/279-8002

Stephen Arena Antiques
2118 W. Main St.
610/631-9100

104 OLEY

Shadow Brook Farm Antiques
RD. 2 Box 17C
610/987-3349

Oley Valley General Store
Rt. 73
610/987-9858

105 PALMYRA

Lenny's Antiques & Collectibles
31 N. Railroad St.
717/838-4660

106 PARADISE

Creekside Inn B&B
44 Leacock Rd.
717/687-0333, Fax 717/687-8200
http://www.thecreeksideinn.com

This 1781 stone house is centrally located in the heart of Lancaster County and "Amish Country," peacefully situated on 2 acres along the Pequea Creek. From the porch, you can listen to the sound of horse and buggy passing by as you retire from a busy day of antique shopping and sightseeing. A wide variety of dining choices are nearby, and the Innkeepers can also arrange for you to have dinner in an Amish home.

The Inn offers relaxing air-conditioned guest quarters appointed with antiques and Amish quilts. There are four second floor rooms and a first floor suite all with private in-room baths. Two of the bedrooms have working stone fireplaces. The warm and welcoming living room with its stone fireplace, or the lattice enclosed porch with rockers, offer guests a chance to socialize and enjoy this countryside inn.

A full country breakfast, featuring home baked treats, local Amish dishes, Lancaster County meats and farm fresh eggs and milk, is served each morning at 8:30 in the two dining rooms. After breakfast the Innkeepers can help you plan your day and offer advice on how to see the "Undiscovered Lancaster County."

This is a non-smoking inn. Visa, MasterCard, Discover and personal checks are accepted. They can only accommodate children over 12 and they cannot accommodate pets.

Other nearby attractions include: Adamstown ("Antiques Capital of the USA") - 10 miles, Longwood Gardens - 30 miles, Hershey - 40 miles and Gettysburg - 55 miles.

107 PHILADELPHIA

Ten Eleven Clinton
1011 Clinton Street
215/923-8144
E-mail: 1011@concentric.net
Rates $115-175

Ten Eleven Clinton is an all-apartment bed and breakfast housed in an 1836 Federal period townhouse in the heart of Philadelphia's historic, cultural and business districts. All the apartments have private baths and queen sized beds, and most have working fireplaces. Breakfast is served to each room and there is a flower-lined courtyard for guests to relax in the summer.

Although the inn is located on a quiet residential street, guests will find themselves only a five-minute walk from the Historic District and Independence Hall, the antique and jewelry districts, Chinatown, the Italian Market, South Street and the Academy of Music, just to name a few. Just a 10 to 15-minute walk brings guests to Penn's Landing Waterfront, the ferry to the New Jersey State Aquarium and Sony Entertainment Center, Rittenhouse Square, Center City shopping district and major department stores. Other area sites and attractions are only a short cab ride away.

Stoneman of the Delaware
Box 15309
Philadelphia, Pennsylvania 19111
215/322-1470

Stoneman of the Delaware is located in the Lambertville Antique Market in Lambertville, New Jersey. See listing under Lambertville, New Jersey #34. When traveling in Philadelphia, you may reach Michael Barnes at the above number.

Garden Gate Antiques
8139 Germantown
215/248-5190

Antiques at the Secred Garden
12 East Hartwell Lane
215/247-8550

Watson 20th Century Antiques
307 Arch St.
215/923-2565

Castor Furniture
6441 Castor Ave.
215/535-1500

Blum Chestnut Hill Antiques
45 E. Chestnut Hill Ave.
215/242-8877

Washington Square Gallery
221 Chestnut St.
215/923-8873

Schwarz Gallery
1806 Chestnut St.
215/563-4887

Stuart's Stamps
1103 Cottman Ave.
215/335-0950

David David Gallery
260 S. 18th St.
215/735-2922

McCarty Antiques
7101 Emlen St.
215/247-5220

Tyler's Used Furn. & Antiques
5249 Germantown Ave.
215/844-9272

Chandlee & Bewick
7811 Germantown Ave.
215/242-0375

Porch Cellar
7928 Germantown Ave.
215/247-1952

Small's Antique Market
7928 Germantown Ave.
215/247-1953

Antique Gallery
8523 Germantown Ave.
215/248-1700

Harvey Wedeen Antiques
8720 Germantown Ave.
215/242-1155

Philadelphia Antique Center
126 Leverington Ave.
215/487-3467

Niederkorn Antique Silver
2005 Locust St.
215/567-2606

Antique Mkt. Place Manayunk
3797 Main St.
215/482-4499

Ida's Treasures & Gifts
4388 Main St.
215/482-7060

Bob Berman Mission Oak
4456 Main St.
215/482-8667

Philadelphia Trading Post
4025-35 Market St.
215/222-1680

Calderwood Gallery
4111 Pechin St.
215/509-6644

Ad Lib Antiques & Interiors
918 Pine St.
215/627-5358

Classic Antiques
922 Pine St.
215/629-0211

Reese's Antiques
930 Pine St.
215/922-0796

M Finkel & Daughter
936 Pine St.
215/627-7797

Antiques & Interiors
1010 Pine St.
215/925-8600

G B Schaffer Antiques
1014 Pine St.
215/923-2263

Antique Design
1016 Pine St.
215/629-1812

Belle Epoque Antiques
1029 Pine St.
215/351-5383

Jeffrey L Biber
1030 Pine St.
215/574-3633

Schaffer Antiques Since 1906
1032 Pine St.
215/923-2949

First Loyalty
1036 Pine St.
215/592-1670

Sorger & Schwartz Antiques
1108 Pine St.
215/627-5259

Kohn & Kohn
1112 Pine St.
215/627-3909

Southwood House
1732 Pine St.
215/545-4076

Keith's Antiques Ltd.
7979 Rockwell Ave.
215/342-6556

Locks Philadelphia Gun Exch.
6700 Roland Ave.
215/332-6225

Classic Lighting Emporium
62 N. 2nd St.
215/625-9552

Architectural Antiques Exch.
715 N. 2nd St.
215/922-3669

Scarlet's Closet
261 S. 17th St.
215/546-4020

Hampton Court
6th St. @ Lombard
215/925-5321

Antiquarian's Delight
615 S. 6th St.
215/592-0256

Den of Antiquities
618 S. 6th St.
215/592-8610

Bob's Old Attic
6916 Torresdale Ave.
215/624-6382

Charles Neri
313 South St.
215/923-6669

Celebration Antiques
416 South St.
215/627-0962

Mode Moderne
111 N. 3rd St.
215/923-8536

Moderne Gallery
159 N. 3rd St.
215/627-0299

Calderwood Gallery
1427 Walnut St.
215/568-7475

Eberhardt's Antiques
2010 Walnut
215/568-1877

Urban Artifacts
4700 Wissachickon Ave.
215/844-8330

Lumiere
112 N. Third St.
215/922-6908

108 PHOENIXVILLE

Scioli's Antiques
235 Bridge St.
610/935-0118

Somogyi Antiques
129 Rt. 113
610/933-5717

Karl's Korner
843 Valley Forge Rd.
610/935-1251

109 PITTSBURGH

Dargate Galleries
5607 Baum Blvd.
412/362-3558

Jess This N That
139 Brownsville Rd.
412/381-1140

Etna Antiques
343 Butler St.
412/782-0102

Lawrenceville Antiques
3533 Butler St.
412/683-4471

Arsenal Antiques
3803 Butler St.
412/681-3002

Antiques on North Canal
1202 N. Canal St.
412/781-2710

Yesterdays News
1405 E. Carson St.
412/431-1712

Antique Parlor
1406 E. Carson St.
412/381-1412

Antique Gallery
1713 E. Carson St.
412/481-9999

Andtiques
1829 E. Carson St.
412/381-2250

Make Mine Country
190 Castle Shannon Blvd.
412/344-4141

Pittsburgh Antique Mall
1116 Castle Shannon Blvd.
412/561-6331

Mark Evers Antiques
4951 Centre Ave.
412/633-9990

East End Galleries
600 Clyde St.
412/682-6331

Caliban Book Shop
410 S. Craig St.
412/681-9111

B's South Park Antique Mall
5710 Curry Rd.
412/653-9919

Antiques on Ellsworth
5817 Ellsworth Ave.
412/363-7188

Eons
5850 Ellsworth Ave.
412/361-3368

Merryvale Antiques
5865 Ellsworth Ave.
412/661-3200

Kozloff & Meaders
5883 Ellsworth Ave.
412/661-9339

Crown Antiques & Collectibles
1018 5th Ave.
412/422-7995

Crimes of Fashion
4628 Forbes Ave.
412/682-7010

Cottage Antiques
231 Freeport Rd.
412/828-9201

Avenue Furniture Exchange
6600 Hamilton Ave.
412/441-8538

Four Winds Gallery, Inc.
1 Oxford Center (Level 3)
412/355-0998

Joys Antique & Estate Jwlry.
Clark Bldg/717 Liberty Ave.
412/261-5697

Demetrius
1420 W. Liberty Ave.
412/341-9768

Antique Exchange
2938 W. Liberty Ave.
412/341-7107

Southbery Antiques
5179 Library Rd.
412/835-4750

North Hills Antiques
1039 McKnight Rd.
412/367-9975

Tuckers Books
2236 Murray Ave.
412/521-0249

Aunt Nettie's Attic
2010 Noble St.
412/351-2688

Classiques
6014 Penn Circle S
412/361-5885

Interior Accents
6015 Penn Circle S
412/362-4511

So Rare Galleries
701 Smithfield St.
412/281-5150

Old Steuben Village
6181 Steubenville Pike
412/787-8585

Edgewood Station Antiques
101 E. Swissvale Ave.
412/242-6603

Antiques Plus
104 Swissvale Ave.
412/247-1016

Antique Prints
5413B Walnut St.
412/682-6681

Four Winds Gallery Inc.
5512 Walnut St.
412/682-5092

Antiques of Shadyside
5529 Walnut St.
412/621-4455

Angie's Antique Center
701 Washington Rd.
412/343-5503

Mastracci's Antiques
802 Wenzell Ave.
412/561-8855

Allegheny City Stalls
940 Western Ave.
412/323-8830

110 POINT PLEASANT

Jacques M Cornillon
56 Byram Rd.
215/297-5854

River Run Antiques
River Rd. (166)
215/297-5303

1807 House
4962 River Rd.
215/297-0599

111 PORTLAND

Long Ago Antiques
Delaware Ave.
717/897-0407

Portland Antiques & Cllbls.
Delaware Ave.
717/897-0129

112 POTTSTOWN

Shaner's Antiques & Cllbls.
403 N. Charlotte St.
610/326-0165

Bill's Carpet Shop
1359 Farmington Ave.
610/323-9210

113 POTTSVILLE

Dave & Julie's Then & Now
16 N. Centre St.
717/628-2838

Curious Goods
556 N. Centre St.
717/622-2173

Bernie's Antiques
313 W. Market St.
717/622-7747

114 QUAKERTOWN

Quakertown Heirlooms
141 East Broad Street
215/536-9088
Jim & Linda Roth, Owners
Open: Daily 10-5, Fri. Till 7, closed Sunday

Directions: From the PA Turnpike: Quakertown exit Rt. 663 north to 313 east about 1.5 miles. One block after railroad tracks on left corner. From I-78: Rt. 309 south to 313 east. Same as above.

Quakertown Heirlooms is an eclectic antique consortium featuring antiques, classic furniture, elegant glass, primitives, collectibles, treasured tomes, and nostalgia. Visa/MasterCard/Personal Checks accepted.

Trolley House Emporium
108 E. Broad St.
215/538-7733

Grandpa's Treasures
137 E. Broad St.
215/536-5066

Curio Corner
200 E. Broad St.
215/536-4547

115 READING

Ray's Antiques & Refinishing
401 N. 5th St.
610/373-2907

Weaver's Antique Mall
3730 Lancaster Pike
610/777-8535

Search Ends Here Antiques
RR 6
610/777-2442

Berk's County Antique Center
Rte. 222
610/777-5355

116 REEDSVILLE

Old Woolen Mill Antiques
RR 1
717/667-2173

Dairy Land Antique Center
Rt. 665
717/667-9093

117 REINHOLDS

Brownstone Corner B&B
590 Galen Hall Rd.
717/484-4460
1-800-239-9902

Directions: For specific directions from your location, please call the Innkeepers.

Located in northeastern Lancaster County, Brownstone Corner is situated on seven acres amid the farms and old German towns of the "Pennsylvania Dutch." The so-called "Pennsylvania Dutch" are not Dutch at all, but are the descendants of German (Deutsch) Mennonite and Amish settlers who emigrated here in the 1700s. It was one of these descendants who, between 1759 and 1790, built the present three-story brownstone structure.

Today, this unique house still maintains its original colonial charm. Inside, the wide plank wooden floors, lofty windows, and family antique furnishings create a warm, cozy feeling.

The house is sheltered by large, age-old sycamore trees, and the property is surrounded by mature blue spruce and fir trees which afford the guests the privacy they deserve.

Guests are invited to relax in the comfortable setting of the living room where one can read literature about the Old Order Amish, find information on local attractions and activities, or sit back and watch TV or videos.

Start your day with a full, family style breakfast in the large country kitchen with the ambiance of colonial America. Fresh fruit, juice, freshly baked quiche or souffles, home-baked breads and cakes, homemade jellies, and fresh brewed coffee and assorted teas are just an example of the country fare that awaits you after a restful night in this tranquil setting.

Lancaster and Berks Counties offer numerous diverse popular attractions. Among the many reasons people come to this area are to visit Amish farms, antique hunting, shopping at nearby discount factory outlets, or to simply get away from the hectic city life.

General Heath's Antiques
Rt. 272/Seoudeburg Rd.
717/484-1300

Clock Tower Antiques
Cocalico Rd.
717/484-2757

118 RONKS

Ja-Bar Enterprises
2812 Lincoln Highway East
717/393-0098 (business office)
717/687-6208 (shop)
Days and hours of operation vary according to the season!

Directions: Traveling U.S. Rt. 30 East out of Lancaster, Penn., cross Penn. Rt. 896. Continue 1.5 miles east to Ronks Rd. The shop is located 200 feet east of the intersection, directly across from the Miller's Smorgasbord in the heart of Pennsylvania Dutch Country.

The personalities of owners, Jack and Barbara Wolf (especially Jack's), make these shops what they are - fun! Jack is known as Mr. Fun in Lancaster County, also as Mr. Tree - he's been a top tree surgeon for almost 50 years, while Barbara keeps things climbing smoothly in the office of the tree-cutting business.

Together they now have Ja-Bar Enterprises, an eclectic place they bill as "fun shops." They divide their stock into Jack's Junque and Barb's Bric-a-brac and have it scattered about in a collection of small shops that has something for everyone: collectibles, military items, farm items, toys, household items, plus the mainstay of hats and canes. Seems like Jack started collecting hats and canes some 30 years ago and kept his collection on display in the basement of their home. When Barbara gently suggested one day that Jack sell his collection at a public sale, he decided right then that he would open an antique shop. Now he collects and sells his favorites. "I love wood," Jack says, in explanation of his passion for canes and walking sticks. "And hats always have fascinated me." When you catch Jack at the shop, you never know which hat he'll be wearing. He's been known to dress up as a clown and hand out balloons to kids of all ages; on some days he may be decked out in his chef's hat, dishing up some edible treats from the Dutch Hutch outdoor kitchenette that serves fried sweet bologna sandwiches, pork roll sandwiches, hot dogs and drinks.

The Antique Market-Place
2856 Lincoln Highway East
717/687-6345
Open daily 10-5

Directions: The Antique Market-Place is located 5 miles east of Lancaster in Soudersburg, across from Dutch Haven, and 2 miles west of Paradise! From the Pennsylvania Turnpike, go south on Rt. 22 about 18 miles to Rt. 30. Go east on Rt. 30 about 8 miles. The mall is about 5 miles east on Lancaster on Rt. 30.

This is an interesting shop, full of great pieces and knowledgeable dealers, who operate the store themselves. There are 35 dealers in this large yellow building, all of whom have been there since 1981. In fact, The Antique Market-Place was one of the first full-time antique cooperatives in the area. In the mall's 7,000 square feet you will find country and primitive furniture, glassware, linens, old tools, salts, old games, toys, miniatures, quilts, silver, lamps, china, collectibles, and antique jewelry, among other things.

Dutch Barn Antiques
3272 W. Newport Rd.
717/768-3067

Country Antiques
2845A Lincoln Hwy E
717/687-7088

119 SAEGERTOWN

Memory Lane Antqs. & Cllbls.
211 Grant
814/763-4916

McQuiston's Main St. Antiques
440 Main St.
814/763-2274

Richard J Sheakley
RR 1
814/763-3399

120 SCENERY HILL

Heart of Country Antiques
Rt. 40
412/945-6687

Little Journeys
Rt. 40
412/945-5160

Pepper Mill
Rt. 40
412/945-5155

121 SCIOTA

Halloran's Antiques
Fenner Avenue
717/992-4651
Open 12-4 Saturdays and 9-5 Sundays, open weekends year round, open daily 11-4 during July and August, also open by chance or by appointment.

Directions: Traveling I-80, take Exit #46A. Travel south approximately 9 miles and take the exit marked "Rt. 209 South Lehighton." Take the first exit (Sciota). At the bottom of the exit ramp, make a right turn, then take the second left onto Fenner Avenue. Go one block to Halloran's Antiques. Look for the two red barns on the right.

Hallroan's has two barns full...sort of like "three bags full," only larger! These folks specialize in the purchase of complete local estates and have a great selection of "the unusual" in antiques. They also offer an excellent selection of antique American brass and copper, old holiday items and kitchen gadgets. Halloran's is a family-run business that has been in its same location for over 18 years, so you know that they know what they're doing.

Collector's Cove Ltd.
Rt. 33
717/421-7439

Yestertiques Antique Center
Rt. 209 & Bossardsville
717/992-6576

Whispers In Time Antiques
Fenner Ave.
717/992-9387

122 SCRANTON

Sacchetti Enterprises
1602 Capouse Ave.
717/969-1779

Originally Yours
1614 Luzerne St.
717/341-7600

Alma's Antiques
921 S. Webster Ave.
717/344-5945

N B Levy's Jewelers
120 Wyoming Ave.
717/344-6187

Garth T Watkins Antiques
409 Prospect Ave.
717/343-1741

123 SELINSGROVE

Dutch Country Store
6B S. Hwy. 11 #15
717/743-4407

Gaskin's Antiques
300 S. Market St.
717/374-9275

Kinney's Antiques
412 W. Pine St.
717/374-1395

124 SEWICKLEY

Nickelodeon Antiques
433 Beaver St.
412/749-0525

Antiquarian Shop
506 Beaver St.
412/741-1969

Natasha's
551 Beaver St.
412/741-9484

Sewickley Traditions
555 Beaver St.
412/741-4051

125 SHAMOKIN

From a space carved out of rugged, raw wilderness, Shamokin went from a wilderness settlement to the "home" of coal in America. The current town of Shamokin encompasses 400 acres of what used to be mountain forests surrounding a narrow river valley of almost impenetrable swamp, densely covered with pine, hemlock, laurel and rocks, where a tortuously winding river flowed.

The first settlers came in the mid 1700s, with the Old Reading Rd. that opened in 1770, running through what is now Shamokin in its route between Sunbury and Reading. The town was laid out in 1835, but didn't start growing until 1838, when the western section of the Danville and Pottsville Railroad was completed. By 1839 Shamokin actually looked like a small village, and by 1890 its population was just over 14,000.

Coal was first discovered in Shamokin in 1790, when Isaac Tomlinson picked some pieces out of the earth and took them into a neighboring county for a blacksmith to try. But the ore was not put to practical use until 1810. From this small beginning coal emerged as an industrial weapon, and played a big part in the Industrial Revolution and in the industrial development of Shamokin. By 1889 more than 2.5 million tons of the black rock were being mined by 12,085 men and boys in Shamokin. At the peak of the industrial movement based on coal, Shamokin's population had grown to 16,879. But as the coal industry declined, so did the town's populace, and by the 1990 census there were only 9,184 residents in the town.

Odds & Ends Store
415 N. Shamokin Street
717/648-2013
Open Mon.-Sat. 10-5 or by appointment, closed Sundays except by appointment

Directions: From Harrisburg, Penn., go east on I-78 to I-81. Go north on I-81 to Exit #35/Rt. 901/Mt. Carmel. Go north on Rt. 901 to Shamokin, Penn (approx. 16 miles). At the second traffic light in Shamokin City, turn left onto Shamokin Street. The shop is located at 415 N. Shamokin Street.

This shop has over 8,000 square feet of show space and display area in which they offer shoppers everything from primitive and country pieces to items of the 1960s. An enormous selection of antique glassware, pottery and other various collectibles can also be found here.

126 SHARON

Honey House Antiques
71 N. Sharpsville Ave.
412/981-2208

Treasure Chest
110 S. Sharpsville Ave.
412/981-1730

Tannie's Antiques
141 E. State St.
412/347-4438

127 SHAVERTOWN

Quilt Racque
183 N. Main St.
717/675-0914

The Bay Window Shops
100 E. Overbrook Rd.
717/675-6400

128 SHREWSBURY

Shrewsbury Antique Center
65 N. Highland Dr.
717/235-6637

Antiques on Shrewsbury Sq.
2 N. Main St.
717/235-1056

Olde Towne Antqs. Shrewsbury
10 N. Main St.
717/227-0988

Sixteen N Main Antiques
16 N. Main St.
717/235-3448

Full Country Antqs. & Cllbls.
21 N. Main St.
717/235-4200

Antique Sounds
4 S. Main St.
717/235-3360

129 SKIPPACK

Remains To Be Seen
4022 Skippack Pike
610/584-5770

Thorpe Antiques
4027 Skippack Pike
610/584-1177

Nostalgia
4034 Skippack Pike
610/584-4112

130 SMOKETOWN

Homestead Lodging
184 East Brook Rd. (Rt. 896)
717/393-6927
Open all year
Tour buses available daily; children welcome; MasterCard/Visa accepted/No pets allowed.

Directions: Take Rt. 30 to Rt. 896 North. The Homestead is located one mile on the left. From the Pennsylvania Turnpike, take Exit #21 to Rt. 222 South to Rt. 30 East to Rt. 896 North. Go one mile and the inn is on the left.

Here's a place in the country where guests can enjoy clean country air, good country cooking, and interesting country company. Located in the heart of Lancaster County, the Homestead is right in the middle of Amish country. As a matter of fact, guests can hear the clippity-clop of Amish buggies as they go by. There is even an Amish farm down the lane from the inn. But that's not all that's nearby. The inn is located within walking distance of restaurants, and is minutes from farmer's markets, quilt, antique and craft shops, outlets, auctions and museums. All rooms have private baths, color TV, refrigerator, queen & double beds, individually controlled heating and cooling. Complimentary continental breakfast served each morning.

131 SOMERSET

Somerset Antique Mall
113 E. Main St.
814/445-9690

Somerset Galleries
152 W. Main St.
814/443-1369

Shoemaker's Antiques
398 W. Patroit St.
814/443-2942

Bryner's Antqs. & Clock Repair
RR6
814/445-3352

Exit 10 Antiques
RR 7
814/445-7856

132 STRASBURG

William Wood & Son Old Mill
215 Georgetown Rd.
717/687-6978

Iron Star Antiques
53 W. Main St.
717/392-5175

James W. Frey Jr.
209 W. Main St.
717/687-6722

Sugarbush Antiques
832 May Post Office Rd.
717/687-7179

Spring Hollow Antiques
121 Mt Pleasant Rd.
717/687-6171

Antiques & Uniques
1545 Oregon Pike
717/397-9119

Beech Tree Antiques
1249 Penn Grant Rd.
717/687-6881

133 STROUDSBERG

Jean Yetter's Year Round Yard Sale
R.D. #5, Box 5307
717/421-7517
Open 10-5, Fri.-Sun., hours may vary in winter, so please call first.

Directions: From I-80, take Exit #52 (Marshalls Creek Exit) and take Rt. 209 north towards Marshalls Creek, Pa., approximately 2.6 miles. Watch for signs on the right. Turn right at the signs and follow the Macadam Rd. until you see a sign against a tree. Turn right before that sign into a large parking area. Yetter's is set up on a hill a short distance from Rt. 209.

"Antiques and collectibles, trash and treasures" is how Jean Yetter Peck bills her year-round yard sale. She says she has something for everybody, and she probably does! If you don't see what you want this week, wait until next week, because Jean gets new items in weekly. Although it's billed as a "yard" sale, it's indoors, actually eight rooms and a large basement contained in two separate buildings. Shoppers will find a constantly changing assortment of antiques, furniture, books, jewelry, paper ephemera, candles, paintings, baskets, glassware, woodenware, albums, bottles, tools and much, much more.

Eleanor's Antiques
809 Ann St.
717/424-7724

Lavender and Lace
350 Main St.
717/424-7087

Ibi's Antiques
517 Main St.
717/424-8721

Olde Engine Works Mkt. Place
62 N. 3rd St.
717/421-4340

134 SYBERTSVILLE

Angie's Antiques & Collectibles
Main St.
717/788-4461

A Country Place
Rt. 93
717/788-2457

135 TOWANDA

Martin's Antiques
Bailey Rd.
717/265-8782

Foster Hall Antiques & Gifts
512 Main St.
717/265-3572

Jac's Antiques & Collectibles
417 State St.
717/265-6107

136 TUNKHANNOCK

Harry's Wood Shop
RR 6
717/836-2346

La Torres Antiques
RR 6
717/836-2021

Old Store
RR 6
717/836-6088

Village Antique Mall
RR6
717/836-8713

Country Classics Gift Shoppe
19 E. Tioga St.
717/836-2030

Bygone's Antiques & Cllbls.
8 W. Tioga St.
717/836-5815

137 UNIONTOWN

Country Stroll Antiques & Collectibles
RR 119 S
412/438-2700

138 VALENCIA

Larry Fox Antiques
124 Mekis Rd.
412/898-1114

Wagon Wheel Antiques
Rt. 8
412/898-9974

139 VANDERGRIFT

Odyssey Gallery Antiques
110 Grant Ave.
412/568-2373

Grant Ave. Express Antiques
124 Grant Ave.
412/568-2111

Vantiques
140 Lincoln Ave.
412/567-5937

140 VERONA

Allegheny River Arsenal Inc.
614 Allegheny River Blvd.
412/826-9699

Ages Ago Antiques
722 Allegheny River Blvd.
412/828-9800

Three Antiques
760 Allegheny River Blvd.
412/828-8140

141 VOLANT

Volant Mills
Main St.
412/533-5611

Leesburg Station Antiques
1753 Perry Hwy.
412/748-3040

Something Different
RR 19
412/748-4134

Wayne's World
RR 19
412/748-3072

142 WARREN

Country Loft & Glorias
7 Pennsylvania Ave. E.
814/723-8481

Antiques Kinzua Country
102 Pennsylvania Ave. W.
814/726-0298

McIntyre's Antiques
334 Pennsylvania Ave. W.
814/726-7011

Steppin Back Antiques
1208 Pennsylvania Ave. E.
814/726-9653

143 WASHINGTON

Antiques Downtown
88 S. Main St.
412/222-6800

Old Pike Antique Center
438 E. National Pike
412/228-6006

Krause's
97 W. Wheeling St.
412/228-5034

144 WAYNE

Wilson's Main Line Antiques
329 E. Constoga
610/687-5500

Golden Eagle Antiques
201 E. Lancaster Ave.
610/293-9290

Old Store
238 E. Lancaster Ave.
610/688-3344

Pembroke Shop
167 W. Lancaster Ave.
610/688-8185

Knightsbridge Antiques Ltd.
121 N. Wayne Ave.
610/971-9551

145 WAYNESBORO

Andy Zeger Antiques
32 E. Main St.
717/762-6595

Antique Market
86 W. Main St.
717/762-4711

146 WELLSBORO

Etc. Antiques Station
5 East Ave.
717/724-2733

Country Owl Florist
15 Queen St.
717/724-6355

Stefanko's Has Good Stuff
RR 6
717/724-2096

147 WEST CHESTER

Woman's Exchange
10 S. Church St.
610/696-3058

My Best Junk
622 E. Gay St.
610/429-3388

Sunset Hill Jewelers
23 N. High St.
610/692-0374

Baldwin's Book Barn
865 Lenape Rd.
610/696-0816

T Newsome & Morris Antqs.
106 W. Market St.
610/344-0657

Herbert Schiffer Antiques Inc.
1469 Morstein Rd.
610/696-1521

Fleury Olivier Inc.
708 Oakbourne Rd.
610/692-0445

Palma J Antiques
1144 Old Wilmington Pike
610/399-1210

R M Worth Antiques
1388 Old Wilmington Pike
610/388-2121

H L Chalfant Antiques
1352 Paoli Pike
610/696-1862

My Best Junk
500 N. Pottstown Pike
610/524-1116

Coldren Monroe Antiques
723 E. Virginia Ave.
610/692-5651

148 WEXFORD

Wexford Gen. Store Antq. Cntr.
150 Church Rd.
412/935-9959

North Hills Antique Gallery
251 Church Rd.
412/935-9804

Ruth Arnold Antiques
End Of Baur Rd. off English
412/935-3217

Antique Treasures of Wexford
10326 Perry Hwy. Rt. 19
412/934-8360

Scharf's Antiques
511 Wallace Rd.
412/935-3197

Red Chimney Antqs. & Millies
Warrendale Bakerstown Rd.
412/935-1990

Foster's Antique Shop
181 Rt. 910
412/935-2206

149 WILKES-BARRE

A A G International
1266B Sans Souci Pkwy.
717/822-5300

Penn Floral & Antiques
235 Scott St.
717/821-1770

150 WILLIAMSPORT

Cillo Antiques & Coins
11 W. 4th St.
717/327-9272

Harrar House
915 W. 4th St.
717/322-2900

Canterbury House Antiques
315 S. Market St.
717/322-2097

Do Fisher Antiques & Books
345 Pine St.
717/323-3573

Lycoming Creek Trading Co.
RR 4
717/322-7155

151 YORK

The York Antiques Fair
Jim Burk Antique Shows
3012 Miller Rd.
Washington Boro, Pa. 17582
717/397-7209
For information on show dates call the number listed above

York Tailgate Antiques Show
Barry Cohen, Manager
P.O. Box 9095
Alexandria, Va. 22304
703/914-1268
For information on show dates call the number listed above

Antique Center of York
190 Arsenal Rd.
717/846-1994

Bernie's What-Nots
7129 Carlisle Pike
717/528-4271

Pantry Antiques
314 Chestnut St.
717/843-5383

Antique Fishing Tackle Shoppe
133 N. Duke St.
717/845-4422

Leon Ness Jewelry Barn
2695 S. George St.
717/741-1113

Almost Anything
500 Hanover Rd.
717/792-4386

Paul L. Ettline
3790 E. Market St.
717/755-3927

Thee Almost Anything Store
324 W. Market St.
717/846-7926

Dec-Art Antiques
1419 W. Market St.
717/854-6192

Dennis's Antiques
1779 W. Market St.
717/845-2418

Kennedy's Antiques
4290 W. Market St.
717/792-1920

Wish-N-Want Antiques
4230 N. Susquehanna Trail
717/266-5961

J & J Plitt Furn & Antiques
2406 N. Sherman St.
717/755-4535

Olde Factory Antique Market
204 S. Sumner St.
717/843-2467

Favorite Places To Eat

Cracker Barrel Old Country Store
I-83 & Rt. 74 (Queen St.), Exit 6E
717/741-0938

152 ZELIENOPLE

Andrea's
110 N. Main St.
412/452-4144

Main Street Antiques
204 S. Main St.
412/452-8620

Thru Time
107 E. New Castle St.
412/452-2270

Vanwhy's Antiques
300 S. Main St.
412/452-0854

Notes

Rhode Island

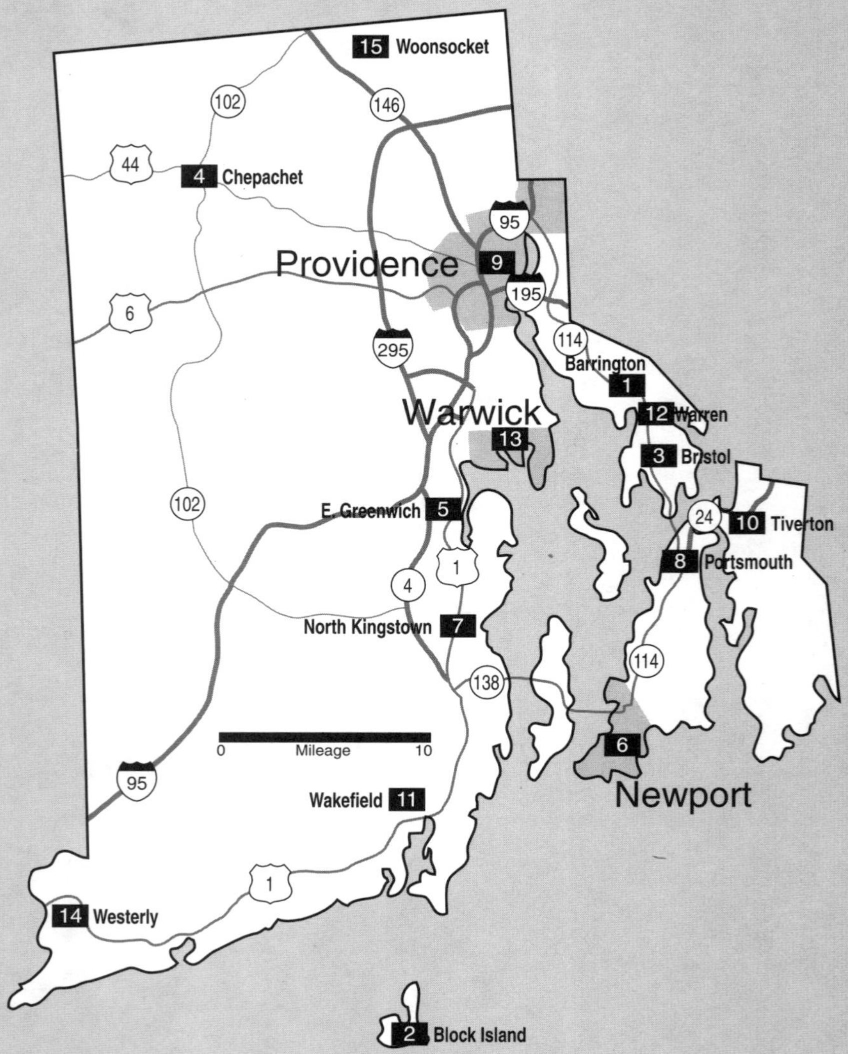

15 Woonsocket
102
146
44
4 Chepachet
95
Providence
9
195
6
114
295
Barrington
1
12 Warren
Warwick
13
3 Bristol
102
E. Greenwich
5
24
10 Tiverton
8 Portsmouth
1
4
North Kingstown
7
114
138
0 Mileage 10
6
95
Newport
Wakefield
11
1
14 Westerly
2 Block Island

A quality consignment store for fine household furnishings and antiques.

THE STOCK EXCHANGE

WE FURNISH SOLUTIONS

20th Anniversary Year

Barrington

57 Maple Avenue
Store Hours: Tues. - Sat. 10-4
Thurs. open until 7 p.m.
Sunday 12-4, Monday Closed

LINENS • BUY AND SELL • NEW AND USED • RUGS • HOUSEWARES • TOOLS

THE ISLAND EXCHANGE

Ocean Avenue across from Hardware Store

Open weekends 1-5 p.m.

Box 91 - Ocean Avenue

Block Island, RI 02807

CALL (401) 466-2093

• ANTIQUES • GLASS • FURNITURE • CHINA • LAMPS • SHADES •

1 BARRINGTON

The Stock Exchange
57 Maple Avenue
401/245-4170
Open: Tue.-Sat. 10-4, Thurs. open until 7 p.m., Sunday 12-4, Closed Mondays

Directions: From Rt. 95 North or South – Take 195 East to Barrington exit - Rt. 114 South, Follow Rt. 114 for 8 miles. Come into the center of Barrington, the Town Hall will be on you left. Take a right at the red light onto Maple Avenue. The Stock Exchange is the 5th building on the right. From Newport – Cross the Mt. Hope Bridge into Bristol, bear left after the bridge onto Rt. 114 North, pass through the center of Bristol, then the center of Warren, go over two small bridges into Barrington, at the 4th light turn left onto Maple Avenue. We are the 5th building on the right.

Owner, Jennifer LaFrance, has developed The Stock Exchange into Rhode Island's premiere consignment store for fine home furnishings and antiques. Established in 1977, The Stock Exchange has and continues to consign and sell countless household items, including, but not limited to, furniture, lamps, linens, china, silver, crystal, glassware, pictures, rugs, tools, pots and pans. Jennifer loves to keep the store interesting and diverse, so they welcome a wide range of consignable items at affordable prices. Attorneys, estate planners, trust officers and realtors have discovered what a valuable asset The Stock Exchange can be. The store specializes in buying and removing entire households/estates, accomplishing this task in one easy transaction that might otherwise take weeks of time and energy. Jennifer and her staff at The Stock Exchange invite you to visit and wander thru 3 floors of fine home furnishings and antiques, she guarantees you will be planning you next visit before you leave.

Hearts & Flowers Antiques
270 County Rd.
401/247-0770

Antique Depot
40 Maple Ave.
401/247-2006

House of Windsor
233 Waseca Ave.
401/245-7540

Barrington Place Antiques
70 Maple Ave.
401/245-4510

2 BLOCK ISLAND

Block Island is one of Rhode Island's scenic wonders. This rustic and pristine island was rated one of the twelve best unspoiled areas in the Western Hemisphere. A short ferry ride brings you to a place where you can enjoy spectacular vistas from awe-inspiring bluffs. It is ideal for visitors seeking lighthouses, delightful inns, and peace and quiet.

The Island Exchange
Ocean Avenue
401/466-2093
Open June 15-Labor Day, 7 days a week, 1-5; Labor Day-June 15, open most Saturdays, Sundays, and Monday holidays, 1-5

Directions: To reach Block Island by ferry – From Rt. 95 North, take Exit 92; turn right on Rt. 2, and proceed to Rt. 78 (Westerly Bypass). Follow Rt. 78 to end; go left on Rt. 1, and travel East to Narragausett. Exit at sign for Block Island Ferry, turn right, then right again onto Rt. 108, then right to Galilee. From 95 South, Exit 9 onto Rt. 4 South, to 1 South, to Narragausett and to Rt. 108 South, to Galilee.

This uniquely located shop brings to its customers furniture, china, glassware, collectibles and housewares. Items may be antique or merely second-hand, according to Dodie Sorenson, store owner. However, the selection is varied with new pieces arriving daily.

Dodie relates a charming story of determination regarding the shop: "Even though The Island Exchange is on an island at sea, there is always a way to get that special item home. A few years ago, a couple bought a huge spinning wheel and the matching yarn winder, but they were traveling on their sailboat. The resourceful husband had a taxi bring the items to the marina dock where he loaded them into a borrowed dinghy and then towed it behind his own dinghy out to the sailboat at its mooring in the harbor. Safely stowed away, the spinning wheel sailed away to its new home, leaving a harbor full of astonished spectators behind."

3 BRISTOL

Nana's Attic Treasures
190 High St.
401/253-4380

Joe's
278 Hope St.
401/254-1520

Jenkins & Stickney Antiques
295 Hope St.
401/254-0179

Alfred's Annex
331 Hope St.
401/253-3465

Gift Unique
458 Hope St.
401/254-1114

Dantiques
676 Hope St.
401/253-1122

Center Chimney
39 State St.
401/253-8010

Jesee-James Antiques
44 State St.
401/253-2240

4 CHEPACHET

Harold's Antique Shop
1191 Main St.
401/568-6030

Stone Mill Antique Center
Main St.
401/568-6662

5 EAST GREENWICH

Hill & Harbour Antiques
187 Main St.
401/885-4990

Shadow of Yesteryear
307 Main St.
401/885-3666

Gallery 500
500 Main St.
401/885-6711

Antique Boutique
527 Main St.
401/884-3800

Country Squire Antiques
Main St.
401/885-1044

6 NEWPORT

A Room with a View
59 Bellevue Ave.
401/847-6886

Newport Book Store
116 Bellevue Ave.
401/847-3400

Exotic Treasures
622 Thames St.
401/842-0040

Bellevue Antiques
121 Bellevue Ave.
401/846-7898

Courtyard antiques
142 Bellevue Ave.
401/849-4554

Newport China Trade
8 Franklin St.
401/841-5267

What Not Shop
16 Franklin St.
401/847-4262

John Gidley House Antiques
22 Franklin St.
401/846-8303

Patina
26 Franklin St.
401/846-4666

J. B. Antiques
33 Franklin St.
401/849-0450

Ramson House Antiques
36 Franklin St.
401/847-0555

A & A Gaines
40 Franklin St.
401/849-6844

Alice Simpson Antiques
40 1/2 Franklin St.
401/849-4252

Smith Marble, Ltd.
44 Franklin St.
401/846-7689

Lee's Wharf Eclectics
5 Lees Wharf
401/849-8786

Lamp Lighter Antiques
42 Spring St. #5
401/849-4179

Renaissance Antiques
42 Spring St. #7
401/849-8515

New England Antiques
60 Spring St.
401/849-6646

Nautical Nook
86 Spring St.
401/846-6810

Harbor Antiques
134 Spring St.
401/848-9711

Michael Westman
135 Spring St.
401/847-3091

Drawing Room
152 Spring St.
401/841-5060

Forever Yours
220 Spring St.
401/841-5290

Armory Antique Center
365 Thames St.
401/848-2398

Prince Albert's Victorian
431 Thames St.
401/848-5372

AArdvark Antiques
475 1/2 Thames St.
401/849-7233

Mainly Oak, Ltd.
489 Thames
401/846-4439

One Plus One Antiques
617 Thames
401/847-8617

7 NORTH KINGSTOWN

Lavender & Lace
4 Brown St.
401/295-0313

Wickford Antique Center II
93 Brown St.
401/295-2966

Apple Antiques
11 Burnt Cedar Dr.
401/295-8840

Antique Center
1121 Ten Rod Road
401/294-9958

Lillian's Antiques
7442 Post Rd.
401/885-2512

Mentor Antiques
7512 Post Rd.
401/294-9412

Rhode Island

Lafayette Antiques
814 Ten Rod Rd.
401/295-2504

8 PORTSMOUTH

Antique Lady
934 E .Main Rd.
401/683-3244

Caron & Co. Antiques & Decor
980 E. Main Rd.
401/683-4560

Stock & Trade
2771 E. Main Rd.
401/683-4700

Eagles Nest Antique Center
3101 E. Main Rd.
401/683-3500

9 PROVIDENCE

In Providence, scores of 18th century homes line Benefit Street's "Mile of History." The most famous are the palatial Gilded Age Newport mansions that were once the summer "cottages" of New York's wealthiest families

Benefit Street Gallery
140 Wickenden St. FL l
401/751-9109

Doyle's Antiques
197 Wickenden St.
401/272-3202

Providence Antique Center
442 Wickenden St.
401/274-5820

This & That Shoppe
236 Wickenden St.
401/861-1394

Alaimo Gallery
301 Wickenden St.
401/421-5360

Antiques at India Point
409 Wickenden St.
401/273-5550

Eastwick Antiques
434 Wickenden St.
No Phone (New Business)

Antiques & Artifacts
436 Wickenden St.
401/421-8334

Angell Street Curiosities
183 Angell St.
401/455-0450

125 Benefit St. Antiques
125 Benefit St.
401/274-6330

Boulevard Antiques
773 Blackstone Blvd.
401/273-4934

Victorian Attic
2007 Broad St.
401/781-6460

Lee Hartwell
141 Elmgrove Ave.
401/273-7433

Forgotten Garden
60 Gano St.
401/453-3650

Carole's Antiques
219 Lenox Ave.
401/941-8680

Jerry's Gallery
5 Traverse St.
401/331-0558

All Times Antiques
735 Westminster St.
401/521-7469

Robert's Gallery
777 Westminster St.
401/453-1270

10 TIVERTON

Past & Presents Tearoom
2753 Main Rd.
401/624-2890

Peter's Attic
3879 Main Rd.
401/625-5912

Country Cabin
3964 Main Rd.
401/624-2279

11 WAKEFIELD

Olde Friends Antiques
355 Main St.
401/789-1470

Dove & Distaff Antiques
365 Main St.
401/783-5714

12 WARREN

Fortier's Antiques
Rt. #136
401/247-2788

Crosstown Antiques
309 Market St.
401/245-9176

Country Antique Shop
382 Market St.
401/247-4878

Warren Antique Center
5 Miller St.
401/245-5461

Water Street Antiques
149 Water St.
401/245-6440

13 WARWICK

Clock Shop
667 Bald Hill Rd.
401/826-1212

Pontiac Mill Antiques
334 Knight St.
401/732-3969

Antique Haven
30 Post Rd.
401/785-0327

Pre-Amble Consignments
2457 Post Rd.
401/739-8886

Apponaug Village Antiques
3159 Post Rd.
401/739-7466

Golden Era Antiques
858 W. Shore Rd.
401/738-2518

Antique & Decorating Wrhse.
626 Warwick Ave.
401/461-0008

Aable Antiques
1615 Warwick Ave.
401/738-6099

Golden Heart Antiques
1627 Warwick Ave.
401/738-2243

Emporium
1629 Warwick Ave.
401/738-8824

14 WESTERLY

Old Firehouse Antiques
84 Bay St.
401/596-5650

Riverside Antiques
8 Broad St.
401/596-0266

Mary D's Antiques & Cllbls.
3 Commerce St.
401/596-5653

Frink's Collectables
271 Post Rd.
401/322-4055

15 WOONSOCKET

The Corner Curiosity Shoppe
279 Greene Street
401/766-2628

South Carolina

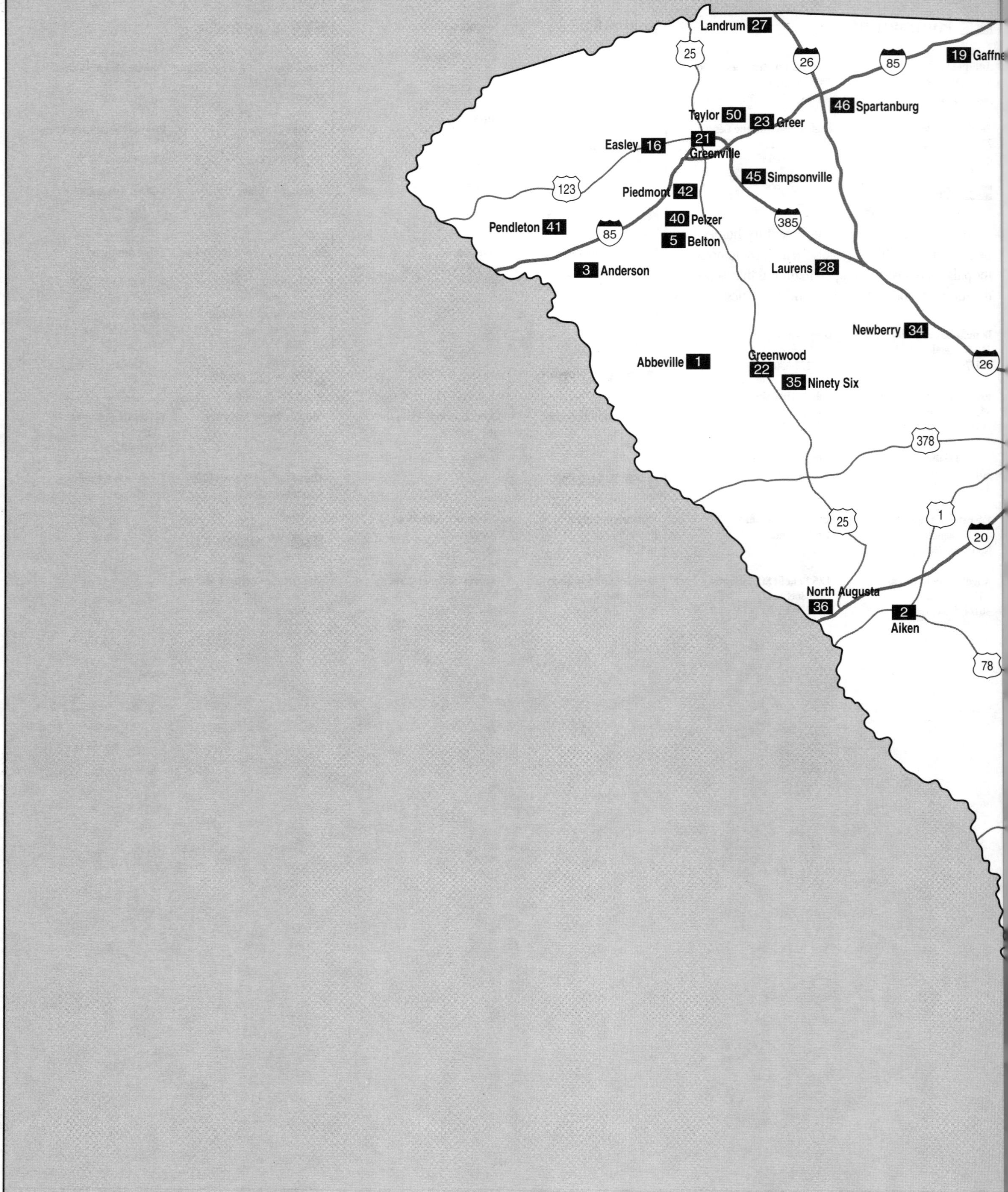

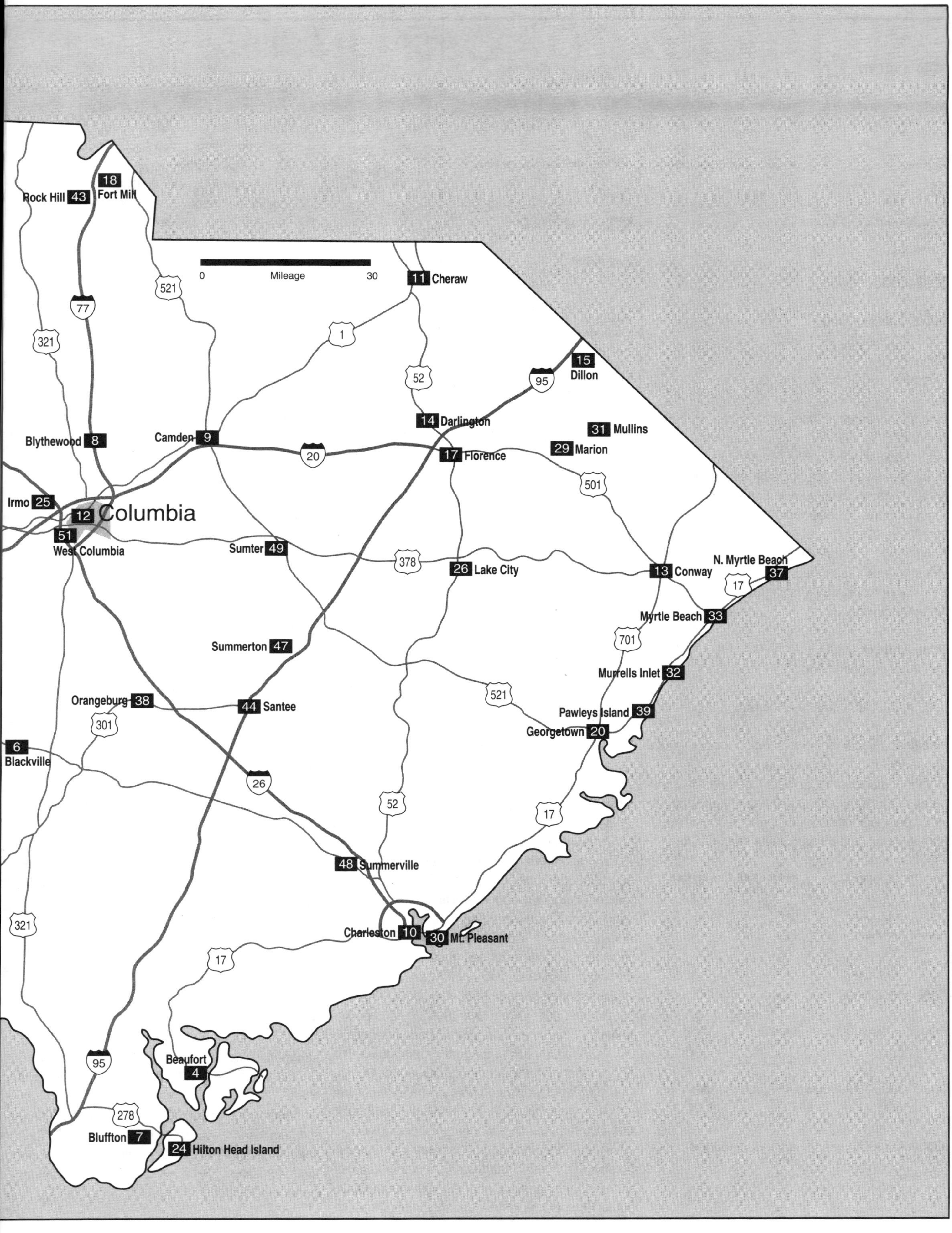

0 Mileage 30
18 Fort Mill
Rock Hill 43
77
521
321
11 Cheraw
1
52
15 Dillon
95
14 Darlington
31 Mullins
Blythewood 8
Camden 9
20
17 Florence
29 Marion
501
Irmo 25
12 Columbia
51
West Columbia
Sumter 49
378
26 Lake City
13 Conway
N. Myrtle Beach
37
17
Myrtle Beach 33
701
Summerton 47
Murrells Inlet 32
521
Orangeburg 38
44 Santee
Pawleys Island 39
Georgetown 20
301
6
Blackville
26
52
17
48 Summerville
321
Charleston 10
30 Mt. Pleasant
17
Beaufort
4
95
278
Bluffton 7
24 Hilton Head Island

1 ABBEVILLE

Edith's Decor House
Court Square
864/459-5222

Collectors Antq. Mall Abbeville
300 S. Main Street
864/459-5935

Emporium
115 Trinity St.
864/459-5388

Miriam's Southern Accents
128 Trinity St.
864/459-5995

Bagwells Furniture Warehouse
130 Trinity
864/459-5861

2 AIKEN

Aiken Antique Mall
112-114 Laurens St. SW
803/648-6700
Open Mon.-Sat., 10-6; Sun. 1-6

Directions: Two doors from the intersection of State Highways 1 and 78.

Fifty dealers fill 13,000 square feet in this old department store building. A variety of antiques such as kitchen items, period furniture, cut glass, art glass, crystal, silver, primitives, painted furniture, vintage books and Civil War relics may be found here. One dealer specializes in old hunting and fishing collectibles with a large quantity of old fishing lures. Another dealer is a local artist and historian, displaying prints and paintings that are historically correct.

Swan Antique Mall
3557 Richland Avenue West
803/643-9922
Open 10-5:30, Mon.-Sat., closed Sunday

Directions: From I-20, exit onto Hwy. 1 and go 4 miles into Aiken.

With 35 dealers and 20,000 square feet, this easily accessible mall carries all types of antiques and collectibles. They offer their customers very good prices, friendly service, and a huge parking area.

York Cottage Antiques
809 Hayne Ave. SW
803/642-9524

Antique Mall-Market Place
343 Park Ave. SW
803/648-9696

Sanford Oaks Ltd.
Laurens St. SW
803/641-1168

3 ANDERSON

Brookgreen Courts
311 N. Main St.
864/225-3126

Bee Hive
510 N. Main St.
864/225-2377

Belinda's Antique Mall & Jwlry.
711 S. Main St.
864/224-0938

Avenue of Oaks Antiques
2409 S. Main St.
864/225-8530

Highland House Interiors
1307 North Blvd.
864/226-4626

McDowell's Emporium
104 Oak Dr.
864/231-8896

Eason's Antiques & Linens
2711 Whitehall Ave.
864/226-0415

Favorite Places To Eat

Cracker Barrel Old Country Store
I-85 & Hwy. 28/76, Exit 19B
864/225-4566

4 BEAUFORT

Rhett Gallery
901 Bay St.
803/524-3339

Chitty & Co.
208 Carteret St.
803/524-7889

Michael Rainey Antiques
702 Craven St.
803/521-4532

Sturdy Beggar
900 Port Republic St.
803/521-9006

Consignor's Antique Mall
913 Port Republic St.
803/521-0660

Past Time
205 Scott St.
803/522-8881

5 BELTON

Ox Yoke Antiques
3023 Hwy. 29 N.
864/261-3275

6 BLACKVILLE

Floyd Manor Inn
111 Dexter Street, Hwy. 78
803/284-3736
Open year round

Directions: Located on Hwy. 78 between Charleston, South Carolina and Atlanta, Ga.

A stay at Floyd Manor Inn is a true step back into the luxurious "Old South" of movies and books. Located on the edge of South Carolina's famous Thoroughbred Country, Floyd Manor was built around 1886 as the manor house of an 8,000 acre plantation in the west central section of the state.

As you approach the impressive front of the mansion, you see multi-faceted reflections of leaded glass fan lights as you pass between the massive, Masonic Gothic pillars that frame the front of the house. The hallway is an amazing example of the beautiful pressed metal ceilings so popular before the turn of the century in the southern homes of South Carolina. The public rooms of the house showcase inlaid oak floors, and spacious decks overlook the back gardens and outdoor pool.

The inn offers guests a choice of five luxurious guests rooms, three with private bath. The Francis Scott Key Room is on the corner of the ground floor, directly off the main hall, with a view of the garden. It is named after Key, who was related to the original owners. The Eleanor Room has a magnificent copper tub with brass dolphin feet set in a beautiful alcove. The bedroom is rich in color and furnishings, with plush burgundy carpets and a queen size rice bed, with balloon back chairs by the fireplace.The Henry Floyd Room is named in honor of the great, great grandfather of the present lady of the house. Henry escaped religious persecution in Wales and fled to England, where he raised two sons, who were later Knighted by Queen Elizabeth. The Queen Victoria Room is named for the ruling monarch of England at the time the house was built. It holds an awesome display of Victorian pieces, with a high back bed accented with English lace and matching drapes, a high marble top dresser, and pale lime green walls that are the perfect background for the color portrait of the Queen herself. The Sam Still Room was named for Sam Still I and II. Sam I built the house and Sam II, a Citadel graduate, became an attorney and worked with President Roosevelt in Washington, and then as a Librarian of Congress.

Parrott's Antiques & Gifts
108 Lartigue St.
803/284-3670

7 BLUFFTON

Barrett L Antiques
Hayward St.
803/757-6630

Stock Farm Antiques
Hwy. 46
803/757-2511

8 BLYTHEWOOD

Blythewood Antiques
206 Blythewood Road
803/754-1116
Open Tue.-Sat., 10-6, closed Sun.-Mon.

Directions: Take Exit #27 off I-77

Blythewood Antiques is located in a house with rooms set up for show of antique furniture, glassware, collectibles, linens and more.

The Root Cellar
10500 Wilson Blvd.
803/754-7578
Open Tue.-Sat., 10-6, closed Sun.-Mon.

Directions: The Root Cellar is located at Exit #24, just 1 mile off I-77 on Hwy. 21/Wilson Road.

The Root Cellar holds 3,000 square feet of antique and collectible consignments, including furniture, dolls, china, lamps, old toys, linens, fine art, handpainted furniture and crystal.

Heart's Desire
162 Langford
803/691-8833
Open Tue.-Fri., 10-5:30; Wed., 10-1:30, Sat. 10-5, closed Sun.-Mon.

Directions: Take Exit #24 off I-77. Heart's Desire is located 3 miles from I-77 at Hwy. 21 and Langford Road.

Heart's Desire is a delightful, magical gift and antique shop housed in a spacious home built in 1875. Their antiques range from dolls to jewelry to furniture and more, while their gifts include baskets, florals and gifts for home and garden.

9 CAMDEN

Established in 1732, Camden is the oldest inland city in South Carolina and was the major British garrison of Lord Cornwallis. The Battles of Hobkirk Hill and Camden were fought in the vicinity and twelve other Revolutionary War battles took place nearby. The Camden area is also known for the fine horses trained and bred here and for its beautiful homes. The world-famous "Colonial Cup," a day of steeplechase and flat racing, takes place around Easter.

Wartime Collectibles
539 Dekalb Street
803/424-5273
Open 10:30-6, Tue.-Fri.; Mon. and Sat. By chance

Directions: From I-20, take exit #92 or 98, at the intersection of U.S. Hwy. 1 and State Rt. 521.

This shop specializes in military memorabilia, both foreign and domestic from World Wars I and II, as well as the Civil War. All items are authentic and guaranteed. You will also find included in the inventory many old toys.

Camden Antiques Exchange
818 Broad St.
803/424-1700

Camden Antique Mall
830 Broad St.
803/432-0818

Granary Antiques
830 Broad St.
803/432-8811

Timley Treasures
845 Broad St.
803/424-0171

Antiques on Broad
2513 Broad St.
803/424-1338

Dusty Bin Antiques
2606 Broad St.
803/432-3676

South's Treasures
538 Dekalb St.
803/432-7709

Fancy That Antiques
914 Market St.
803/425-5111

10 CHARLESTON

Her charm and beauty have long proven to be irrestible. You'll see it in the lacy trim of her breezy piazzas and feel it in the spirit of her rich heritage. A port city steeped in history, barely changed since its founding in 1670.

Here you'll find the very best of the South. A genteel nature, so inviting, so gracious and an indomitable strength that has proudly withstood great fires, earthquakes, pirate rouges, a Civil War and hurricanes with little more than a bat of an eye.

Indeed, the Charleston area is a place that visitors rarely want to leave. In 1995, *Glamour* magazine rated the area one of the top ten travel destinations in the U.S.., and *Conti Nast* readers rated it fourth as a destination in a list of its top ten cities. With a metro population of over 500,000, this aristocratic colonial port boasts 73 pre-Revolutionary buildings, 136 from the late 18th century and more than 600 others built prior to the 1840s. Come wander along cobblestone streets, smell the sea breezes, explore antique shops and boutiques and treat yourself to the delicious fresh seafood. Come experience the Charleston area—her streets, her homes, her people.

Period Antiques
194 King Street
803/723-2724
Open Mon.-Sat. 10-5

Directions: Take I-26 to its end in Charleston and take the King Street Exit. Turn right onto King Street and continue about a mile to the heart of downtown Charleston. Period Antiques is at 194 King Street on the left.

An interesting, unusual and changing selection of choice American and European antiques can be found at Period Antiques, including furniture, paintings, mirrors and decorative accessories - a small shop full of treasures.

Zinn Rug Gallery
269 E. Bay St.
803/577-0300

Acquisitions
273 E. Bay St.
803/577-8004

Charleston Rare Book Co.
66 Church St.
803/723-3330

Century House Antiques
85 Church St.
803/722-6248

Church Street Galleries
100 Church St.
803/937-0808

Trio Ltd.
175 Church St.
803/853-9966

Second Fling Antiques
7440 Cross Country Rd.
803/552-6604

Nazan
4501 Dorsey Ave.
803/745-0005

Goat Cart
18 E. Elliott St.
803/722-1128

Chicora Antiques Inc.
154 King St.
803/723-1711

152 A.D. Antiques
152 King St.
803/577-7042

Estate Antiques
155 King St.
803/723-2362

Ginkgo Leaf
159 King St.
803/722-0640

Moore House Antiques
161 1/2 King Street
803/722-8065

Livingston and Sons
163 King St.
803/723-9697

Helen Martin Antiques
169 King St.
803/577-6533

Decorator's Alley
177 1/2 King St.
803/722-2707

Poppe House Inc.
177 King St.
803/853-9559

D Bigda Antiques
178 King St.
803/722-0248

English Patina Inc.
179 King St.
803/853-0380

Jack Patla Co.
181 King St.
803/723-2314

John Gibson Antiques
183 King St.
803/722-0909

Joint Ventures Estate Jewelry
185 King St.
803/722-6730

Carolina Prints
188 King St.
803/723-2266

George C Birlant & Co.
191 King St.
803/722-3842

D & D Antiques
192 King St.
803/853-5266

Architrave Antiques
193 King St.
803/577-2860

The Silver Vault
195 King St.
803/722-0631

Jean Keegan
196 King St.
803/723-3953

Verdi Antiques & Accessories
196 King St.
803/723-3953

Elysia Antiques
200 King St.
803/853-8502

Petterson Antiques
201 King St.
803/723-5714

A Zola
202 King St.
803/723-3175

A'Riga IV
204 King St.
803/577-3075

Riddler Page Rare Maps
205 E. King St. Ste 102
803/723-1734

Golden & Associate Antiques
206 King St.
803/723-8886

Granny's Goodies
301 King St.
803/577-6200

Croghan's Jewel Box
308 King St.
803/723-6589

James Island Antiques
2028 Maybank Hwy.
803/762-1415

Terrace Oaks Antique Mall
2037 Maybank Hwy.
803/795-9689

Antiquities Hist. Galleries
199 Meeting St.
803/720-8771

Seymour Antique Center
1066 E. Montague Ave.
803/554-5005

Flynn's
Old Market 188 Meeting
803/577-7229

Peacock Alley Antiques
9 Princess St.
803/722-6056

D & M Antiques
4923 Rivers Ave.
803/744-6777

Brass & Silver Workshop
758 Saint Andrews Blvd.
803/571-4302

Architectural Elements
1011 Saint Andrews Blvd.
803/571-3389

Grey Goose Antique Mall
1011 Saint Andrews Blvd.
803/763-9131

Tanner's Collectibles
1024 Savannah Hwy
803/763-0199

Livingston & Sons Antiques Inc.
2137 Savannah Hwy
803/556-6162

Antique Mall
2241 Savannah Hwy.
803/766-8899

Roumilliat's Antique Mall
2241 Savannah Hwy.
803/766-8899

Shalimar Antiques
2418 Savannah Hwy.
803/766-1529

Attic Treasures
2024 Wappoo Dr.
803/762-0418

Carpenter's Antiques
1106 Chuck Dawley Blvd. (Mt Pleasant)
803/884-3411

Favorite Places To Eat
N. Charleston

Cracker Barrel Old Country Store
I-26 & Ashley Phosphate Rd., Exit 209
803/553-4232

11 CHERAW

Antique Imports Inc.
92 Powe St.
803/537-5762

Thomas Antique Co.
92 Powe St.
803/537-3422

L & M Antiques
RR 1
803/623-7307

Sentimental Journey
242 2nd St.
803/537-0461

Cheraw Furniture Refinishing
133 Second Street
803/379-3562

Expressions
129 Main St.
803/623-6668

12 COLUMBIA

Ole Towne Antique Mall
2956 Broad River Rd.
803/798-2078

Heirloom Antiques & Cllbls.
6000 Garners Ferry Rd.
803/776-3955

Amick's Bottles & Collectibles
6420 Garners Ferry Rd.
803/783-0300

Ole Towne Antique Mall
7748 Garners Ferry Rd.
803/695-1992

Past & Present Inc.
8105 Garners Ferry Rd.
803/776-6807

City Market Antiques Mall
701 Gervais St.
803/799-7722

Mais Oui Ltd.
929 Gervais St.
803/733-1704

Mary Clowney Antqs. & Intrs.
1009 Gervias St.
803/765-1280

Chic Antiques
602 Huger St.
803/765-1584

Columbia Antique Mall
602 Huger St.
803/765-1584

B & M Enterprises Inc.
3510 Phillips St.
803/799-6153

Antique Mall
1215 Pulaski St.
803/256-1420

Balloonyville USA
141 S. Shandon St.
803/771-4555

BC Treasure Barn
2515 Two Notch Rd.
803/799-7366

Ole Towne Antique Mall Inc.
8724 Two Notch Rd.
803/736-7575

Favorite Places To Eat

Cracker Barrel Old Country Store
I-20 & Bush River Rd., Exit 63
803/731-0672

13 CONWAY

Hidden Attic Antiques Mall
1014 4th Ave.
803/248-6262

Trader John Antiques
2197 Hwy. 501 E
803/248-9077

Kingston Antiques
326 Main St.
803/248-0212

14 DARLINGTON

Built around a courthouse square, the mural on the side of the courthouse is a graphic reminder of the country's colorful past. The town really comes alive on Labor Day weekend when the "Granddaddy of them all," the Mountain Dew Southern 500 stock car race is held.

Scarlett's Antiques
500 E. Broad St.
803/393-4952

H & M Plunder Shop
512 S. Main St.
803/393-4888

Fifty-Two & Main Antiques
1306 S. Main St.
803/393-4949

15 DILLON

Chris's Pack House
Hwy. 9
803/774-6144

Breeden's Old Stuff
201 Harrison St.
803/774-6321

16 EASLEY

Main Street Market
203 W. Main St.
864/855-8658

Adams Attic Antiques
223 W. Main St.
864/859-4996

King's Things Antiques
1001 Pelzer Hwy
864/859-0313

17 FLORENCE

Red Brick House
1005 S. Cashua Drive
803/669-4860
Open Thurs.-Sat. or by chance

Directions: From I-95, take Exit #157 and travel east to the first red light. Turn right on Cashua and the shop is three miles further on the left.

Owner David Robinson can help shoppers in several ways. He can sell you something from his 7,000-square-feet of antiques (mostly furniture). He can refinish a piece for you in his shop on the premises. He can help you pick out a gift from the line of gift items he carries. Is that what they mean by one-stop shopping?

Ann's Patchwork Palette
105 S. Franklin Dr.
803/665-1944

Hodges Furniture Shop
Hwy. 52 N
803/669-7391

Antique Market & Etc.
1356 James Jones Ave.
803/665-1812

Plantation Antique Mall
3979 W. Palmetto St.
803/664-8881

Grapevine Antiques Cllbls.
2138 3rd Loop
803/629-9745

Hamilton House Antiques
549 W. Evans St.
803/665-7161

Favorite Places To Eat

Cracker Barrel Old Country Store
I-95 & Hwy. 52, Exit 164
803/662-9023

18 FORT MILL

Antique Mall of the Carolinas
3700 Ave. of the Carolinas
803/548-6255

Antique & Garden Shop
229 Main St.
803/547-7822

Antiques on Main
233 Main St.
803/802-2242

19 GAFFNEY

Favorite Places To Eat

Cracker Barrel Old Country Store
I-85 & SC 105, Exit 90
864/489-3350

20 GEORGETOWN

Tosh Antiques
802 Church Street
803/527-8537
Open Mon.-Sat., 10-5; Sunday by chance

Directions: Located on Hwy. 17 in downtown Georgetown.

Everything is of fine quality here. You'll find Victorian furniture, pieces from Occupied Japan, primitives, as well as Roseville, sterling silver, and brilliant cut glass.

Hill's Used Furniture & Antqs.
4161 Andrews Hwy
803/546-6610

Clement's Carolina
803 Front St.
803/545-9000

Grandma's Attic
2106 Highmarket
803/546-2607

21 GREENVILLE

The Corner Antique Mall
700 N. Main Street
864/232-9337
Open Mon.-Sat., 10-5, closed Sundays

Directions: The Corner Antique Mall is located on U.S. Hwy. 276, where it intersects with Main Street. However, traveling I-85, take Exit #51 and travel north on I-385 to Exit #42, which is Stone Avenue. Turn right and go to the "Corner" at Stone and Main.

This 5,000-square-foot "corner" of the antique world is packed with treasures, including advertising collectibles, books and magazines, art, china, glassware, pottery, jewelry, dolls and figurines, vintage clothing, some furniture and accessories, and many more collectibles and antiques.

Little Stores of West End
315 Augusta St.
864/467-1770

Brown Street Antiques Inc.
115 N. Brown St.
864/232-5304

Penny Farthing Antiques
93 Cleveland St.
864/271-9370

Reedy River Antiques
220 Howe St.
864/242-0310

Antiques Associates
633 S. Main St.
864/235-3503

Accents Unlimited Inc.
520 Mills Ave.
864/235-4825

Greenville Furniture Exch Inc.
113 Poinsett Hwy.
864/233-3702

Bedding World Antiques
236 Wade Hampton Blvd.
864/242-0908

William Key Interiors
909 E. Washington St.
864/233-4329

Favorite Places To Eat

Cracker Barrel Old Country Store
I-85 & Woodruff Rd., Exit 50 N, 51 S
803/297-3847

22 GREENWOOD

Brewington Antiques
1215 Montague Ave.
864/229-3086

Mackey's
1728 Montague Ave.
864/223-3400

Bud's Antiques
803 Ninety Six Hwy
864/227-8999

Memories Antique Shop
626 Lowell Ave.
864/229-6353

23 GREER

Pot Luck Antiques
2013 Hwy. 101 S
864/877-1818

Coach House Antiques
401 Johnson Rd.
864/879-2616

Cooper Furniture Co.
214 Trade St.
864/877-2761

West Gerald Interiors
711 W. Wade Hampton Blvd.
864/879-2148

24 HILTON HEAD ISLAND

Ambiance
8 Wren Drive
803/671-4981
Rates $70-75

Across the street from a beautiful beach and the Atlantic Ocean, Ambiance is nestled in subtropical surroundings in Sea Pines Plantation. All the amenities of Hilton Head are offered in a contempory, congenial atmosphere. Continental breakfast is available.

Favorite Places To Eat

Cracker Barrel Old Country Store
U.S. Hwy. 278
803/785-3344

25 IRMO

Broad River Antiques
7232 Broad River Rd.
803/749-6909

Dutch Fork Antiques
1000 Dutch Fork Rd.
803/781-7174

26 LAKE CITY

Established in 1732, tobacco was introduced in the late 1800s. The market was established in 1889 and has grown to become one of the largest in the state. The crop is saluted every September during the town's Tobacco Festival. Dr. Ronald E.. McNair, one of the astronauts aboard the Space Shuttle Challenger, was born and buried here.

Gloria's Antiques & Gifts
116 E. Main St.
803/394-8360

Oakdale Antiques
3831 W. Turbeville
803/659-2210

27 LANDRUM

Landrum Antique Mall
221 Rutherford Road
864/457-4000
Open Mon.-Sat., 10-5, closed Sundays

Directions: From I-26, take Exit #1 and the shop is located 1 mile off of the interstate.

There's lots in a relatively small space here, so browse slowly and don't miss a thing! Fifty dealers have filled 10,000 square feet with early 1900s furniture, collectibles, silver, chandeliers, rugs, china and estate jewelry.

My Favorite Shop
203 E. Rutherford St.
864/457-4840

Bloomsbury Cottage Antiques
204 E. Rutherford St.
864/457-3111

Lasting Impressions
227 E. Rutherford St.
864/457-4697

28 LAURENS

This town is named for Revolutionary War statesman Henry Laurens, who was imprisoned in the Tower of London for his patriotism. The courthouse square was purchased in 1792 for two guineas (about $21). It was in this vicinity that Andrew Johnson, 17th President of the United States, once operated a tailor shop.

Treasure House Antiques
Dial Place Rd.
864/682-5915

Hall Antiques
Hwy. 221
864/984-0315

Jeff's Antiques & Furniture
Hwy 221 S
864/682-8079

Palmetto Antiques & Auction
106 E. Main St.
864/984-3011

Harper House
101 Wayside Dr.
864/984-7945

29 MARION

Antiques Dujour
231 N. Main St.
803/423-3366

Swamp Fox Antiques & Books
326 Main St.
803/423-0819

Judy's Antiques
329 N. Main St.
803/423-5227

Cuckoo's Nest
403 N. Main St.
803/423-1636

Theodosia's
724 N. Main St.
803/423-7693

30 MOUNT PLEASANT

Linda Page's Thieves Market
1460 Ben Sawyer Blvd.
803/884-9672

Carpentier's Antiques
1106 Chuck Dawley Blvd.
803/884-3411

Pleasant Antiques
616 Coleman Blvd.
803/849-7005

Lowcountry Antique Mall
630 Coleman Blvd.
803/849-8850

Victoria & Thomas Trading Co.
803 Coleman Blvd.
803/849-7230

Sweet Magnolias
976 Houston Northcutt Blvd.
803/856-9131

Mike's Antiques Inc.
401 Johnnie Dodds Blvd.
803/849-1744

Tomorrows Treasures & Antqs.
113 Pitt St.
803/881-2072

31 MULLINS

Southern Treasures
155 South Main St.
803/464-6425

Patsy's Antiques
302 South Main St.
803/464-2066

32 MURRELLS INLET

Wachesaw Row Antique Mall
4650 Hwy. 17 S.
803/651-7719
Open Mon.-Sat., 10-5

Directions: Located between Georgetown and Myrtle Beach on Hwy. 17 Bypass.

This seven-dealer mall carries a little bit of everything including American, French, and English furniture and accessories, primitives, paintings, prints, china and glassware. They also offer a selection of coins, guns, and sports memorabilia.

Golden Image Game Room
2761 Hwy. 17
803/651-0338

Legacy Antique Mall
3420 Hwy. 17
803/651-0884

Tillie's Attic
3692 Hwy. 17
803/651-1900

A & G Furniture
3974 Hwy. 17
803/651-3777

Memories Antiques
Hwy. 17 Bypass
803/651-7888

Favorite Places To Eat

Cracker Barrel Old Country Store
Hwy. 17 & Tadlock
803/357-4372

33 MYRTLE BEACH

Peggy's Antiques & Cllbls.
1040 Hwy 17 S
803/238-1442

Myrtle Beach Antiques Mall
1014 Hwy. 501
803/448-4762

Collectibles Mall
4011 Hwy. 501
803/236-1029

Fox & Hounds Antiques Mall
4015 Hwy. 501
803/236-1027

Socastee Trading Post
8569 Hwy. 544
803/236-2244

Joseph Bridger Fine Antiques
5311 N. Kings Hwy.
803/449-4171

34 NEWBERRY

Leslie's Main Street Antiques
934 Main Street
803/276-8600

Antiques and SoForths
1213 Main Street
803/276-1073

35 NINETY SIX

Burnett House
118 Main St. NW
864/543-3236

Mainly Antiques
101 Main St. NE
864/543-3636

36 NORTH AUGUSTA

In 1833, the Charleston-Hamburg Railroad ended its 138-mile rail line, then the longest steam-operated railroad in the world, at the small town of Hamburg, near the present-day town of North Augusta. Chartered by the state in 1906, North Augusta was once a foremost winter resort frequented by the very wealthy. Magnificent old Victorian cottages and imposing churches are reminders of the city's past.

Plunder Valley Antiques
207 Belvedere Clearwater Rd.
803/279-1200

Peddler's Way
4631 Jefferson Davis Hwy.
803/593-4447

37 NORTH MYRTLE BEACH

Junktique
204 Hwy. 17 N
803/249-7443

B & B Antiques
1604 Hwy. 17 S
803/361-0101

Cottage Antiques of Cherry Grove
621 Sea Mountain Hwy.
803/249-7563

Favorite Places To Eat

Cracker Barrel Old Country Store
U.S. Rt. 17 & S. 48th Ave.
803/361-2221

38 ORANGEBURG

Browsabout Antqs. & Accents
1036 Broughton St.
803/536-2182

Something Different
1041 Broughton St.
803/536-0710

39 PAWLEYS ISLAND

Elizabeth Taylor Satterfield
42 N. Causeway
803/237-8701

Mary Frances Miller Antiques
Hammock Shop/Hwy. 17
803/237-2466

Traddrock Antiques & Design
2176 S. Kings Hwy.
803/237-9232

Harrington Altman Limited
10729 Ocean Hwy.
803/237-2056

McElveen Design, Antiques & Furn.
13302 Ocean Hwy.
803/237-3326

40 PELZER

Pelzer Antique Market
19 Main St.
864/947-5558

Sue's Antiques & Collectibles
6633 Hwy. 29 N.
864/947-2039

41 PENDLETON

Pendleton Antique Co.
134 E. Main St.
864/646-7725

Pendleton Place Antiques
651 S. Mechanic St.
864/646-7673

42 PIEDMONT

P & N Antiques International
100 Piedmont Rd.
864/295-3134

Papa's Book Haven Antiques
2510 River Rd.
864/269-5700

43 ROCK HILL

In Northern York County, this rapidly-expanding city is the county's newest and largest. It was named for a cut made through white flinty rock during construction of the Columbia to Charlotte railroad. The Catawba Cultural Center at 1536 Tom Steven Rd.., in the small town of Catawba about 10 miles SE of Rock Hill, has exhibits and videos about the Catawba Indian Nation. A craft store, which features the distinctive Catawba pottery and nature trail, is also open.

Antique & Garden Shoppe
609 Cherry Rd.
803/327-4858

Upcountry Antqs. & Handcraft
1449 Ebenezer Rd.
803/324-5503

Reid Antiques
2641 India Hook Rd.
803/366-4949

Collectibles on Main
427 E. Main St.
803/366-8337

Antique Mall
104 S. Oakland Ave.
803/324-1855

Pix Designer Warehouse
147 W. Oakland Ave.
803/325-1116

Favorite Places To Eat

Cracker Barrel Old Country Store
I-77 & Dave Lyle Blvd., Exit 79
803/327-6141

44 SANTEE

Favorite Places To Eat

Cracker Barrel Old Country Store
I-95 & SC 6, Exit 98
803/854-3020

45 SIMPSONVILLE

Cudds Zoo Antiques
101 E. Curtis Street
864/963-2375
Open Mon.-Sat., 10-5 and by appointment

Directions: Located three miles off I-385 on Main Street

This shop carries mostly glass: Depression, pressed, cameo, and art. There is also a small quantity of quality furniture. The owner does chair recaning.

Hunter House Antqs. & B&B
201 E. College St.
864/967-2827

Satterfield's Antiques
106 W. Curtis St.
864/967-0955

46 SPARTANBURG

John Morton Antiques
160 E. Broad Street
864/583-0427

Directions: Follow the Spartanburg exits off either I-26 or I-85. John Morton Antiques is located in downtown Spartanburg.

This shop specializes in period, regional and country furniture and accessories, and has a furniture restoration service attached.

South Pine Antique Mall
856 S. Pine Street
864/542-2975
Open Mon.-Sat., 10-6; Closed Sundays

Directions: Take exit #585 off Interstate 85. Located five miles south of Interstate on Pine Street.

This 6,000-square-foot mall encompasses a variety of furniture, glassware, lamps, mirrors, pictures and collectibles. Several quality period pieces as well as 40s Mahoganys may also be found here.

Old Southern Trafvng Co.
1926 Boiling Springs Rd.
864/578-1025

Town & Cntry. Antqs. & Cllbls.
2929 Boiling Springs Rd.
864/578-0970

Yesterdays Treasures
2306 Chesnee Hwy.
864/542-9888

Chestnut Galleries Antiques
144 Chestnut St.
864/585-9576

C W. Trantham Trading Co.
360 Dogwood Club Rd.
864/542-2311

Ballards Sales Co.
8521 Fairforest Rd.
864/582-4852

Bye-Gone Treasures
169 E. Main St.
864/542-1590

Nan's Antiques & Collectibles
330 E. Main St.
864/585-6039

Shades of the Past Antq. Mall
512 E. Main St.
864/585-1172

Prissy's Antique Mall
914 E. Main St.
864/582-1032

Treasures of Time
155 W. Main St.
864/573-7178

Jeanne Harley Antiques
910 S. Pine St.
864/585-0386

Rickinghall Antiques Warehouse
400 Westbrook Ct.
864/583-7221

Favorite Places To Eat

Cracker Barrel Old Country Store
I-85/Business, Exit 2C
864/576-6949

47 SUMMERTON

Fishermen particularly love this town on the north shore of Lake Marion. Antique stores and beautiful historic homes and buildings enhance its charm. Stop for freshly ground grits at Senn's Grist Mill on Cantey Street on Saturdays from 8:30 to noon.

Antiques Etc.
103 Main St.
803/485-8714

Antique Mall
123 Main St.
803/485-2205

48 SUMMERVILLE

Country Store & Antiques
1106 Main Street
803/871-7548
Open Mon.-Sat., 10-5:30, Sun. 1-5 in Oct., Nov., and Dec.

Directions: Country Store is located 1/2 mile from I-26 at Exit 199A.

These folks have been in business for 13 years, and their motto is "Where Customers Are Friends." The shop's

2,000-square-feet are filled with primitives, oak furniture and pottery. They also carry a line of gifts including All God's Children by Martha Holcomb.

Missy's Memories Antiques
127 S. Main St.
803/871-5334

Carriage House Collectables
1213 S. Main St.
803/873-5704

Early Traditions
100 W. Richardson Ave.
803/851-1627

Antiques N Stuff
128 E. Richardson ave
803/875-4155

People Places & Quilts
129 W. Richardson Ave.
803/871-8872

Town Fair Antiques
131 E. Richardson Ave.
803/873-3462

Granny's Attic
71 Trolley Rd.
803/871-6838

Remember When
301 Trolley Rd.
803/821-1018

49 SUMTER

Named for Revolutionary War hero General Thomas Sumter, this progressive city was settled around 1740.

Visit Sumter's Antique Row: six shops on Broad Street less than one mile from Highways 15, 521, 378 and 76, and 15 miles from I-20 and I-95.

T. J. Player
202 Broad Street
803/778-1173

Why-Not Antiques
202 Broad Street
803/778-1173

Broadstone Manor Antiques
204 Broad Street
803/778-1890

Estate Antiques Gifts & Clocks
210 Broad Street
803/773-4214

Keepsakes and Collectibles
408 Broad Street
803/773-2235

Sumter Antique Mall
719 Broad Street
803/778-0269

50 TAYLOR

Spinning Wheel Antiques
3228 Wade Hampton Blvd.
864/244-3195

Danny's Antique Mall
4949 Wade Hampton Blvd.
864/848-7316

Buncombe Antiques Mall
5000 Wade Hampton Blvd.
864/268-4498

Way Back When Antique Mall
5111 Wade Hampton Blvd.
864/848-9839

51 WEST COLUMBIA

378 Antique Mall
620 Sunset Boulevard
803/791-3132
Open Mon.-Sat. 10-5; Sun. 1:30-5:30

Directions: From I-26, take the Hwy. 378 exit, go 2.8 miles (Hwy. 378 and Sunset Blvd. are one and the same).

With more than fifty dealers in 20,000 square feet of space, and 10 years in business, visitors can expect to find just about everything they are looking for at the 378 Antique Mall. They feature furniture from the 1800s to the early 1900s, glassware, lamps, framed art, military items, vintage jewelry, country collectables, dolls, porcelains, chandeliers, silver, art glass and cameo glass.

Harvest Moon
351 Meeting St.
803/739-0637

Rudy's Upper Deck
511 Meeting St.
803/739-9191

De Ja Vu Antiques
615 Meeting St.
803/926-0021

Boltinhouse Jewelers
3015 Platt Springs Rd.
803/794-1466

Westbank Antique Mall
118 State St.
803/796-9764

State Street Antiques
131 State St.
803/791-0008

Old Mill Antique Mall
310 State St.
803/796-4229

Treasure Aisles Bazaar
1217 Sunset Blvd.
803/791-5777

Parks Furniture Antiques
3131 Sunset Blvd.
803/791-4071

Dewey's Antiques
3740 Sunset Blvd.
803/794-9075

Eau Gallie Interiors
3937 Sunset Blvd.
803/926-9370

Notes

South Dakota

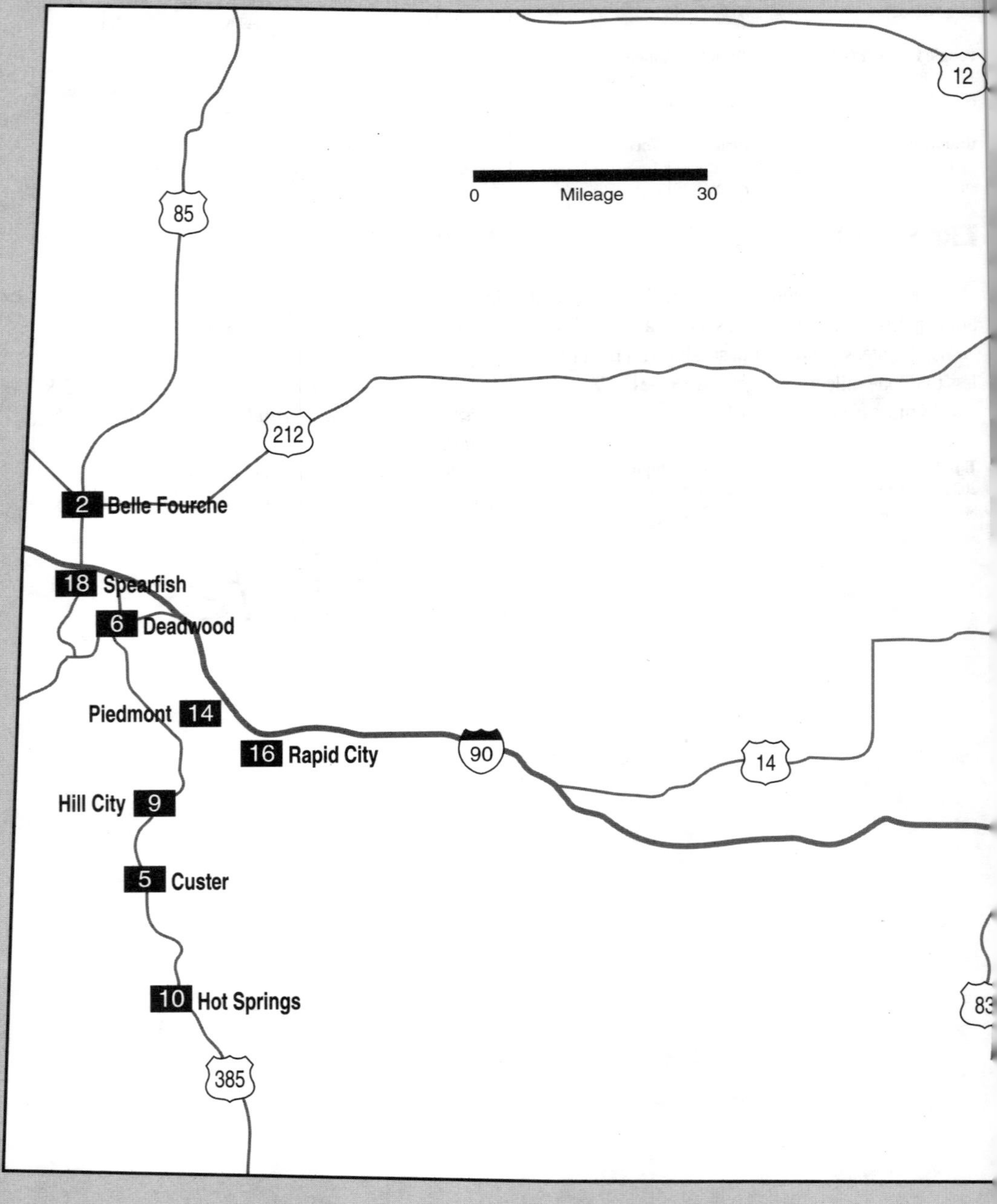

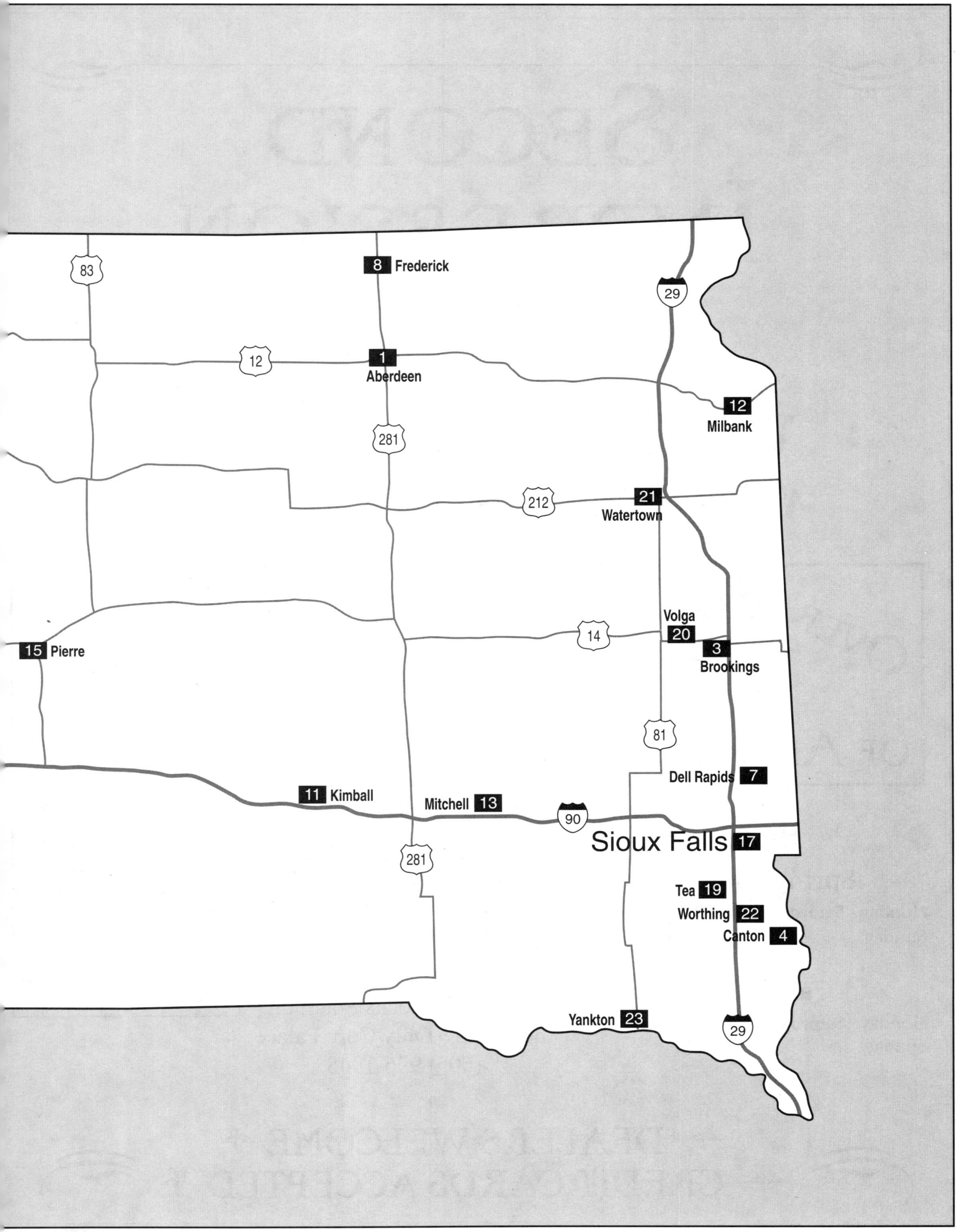

83
8 Frederick
29
12
1
Aberdeen
12
Milbank
281
212
21
Watertown
Volga
14
20
3
Brookings
15 Pierre
81
Dell Rapids 7
11 Kimball
Mitchell 13
90
Sioux Falls 17
281
Tea 19
Worthing 22
Canton 4
Yankton 23
29

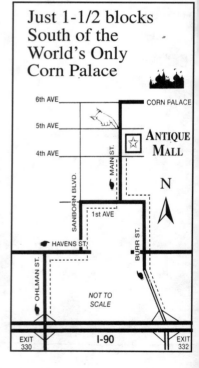

das Abend Haus Cottages & Audrie's Bed and Breakfast

· area's first and finest bed and breakfast ·blishment, family owned and operated ·e 1985.

·ering the **CRANBURY SUITE**, the mood ·ld World; deep colors and richly dark oak ·ques reminiscent of a bygone era. Sink ·p into the comfortable white sofa and ·ire the huge slate fireplace with its ancient ·ber beam stretching 14 feet across. Gently ·y in the patio swing, or relax in your hot · on your private patio.

· **HOLLAND SUITE** is bright and airy ·h a Dutch lace-covered bay window and · 1800's light oak antiques. A handmade ·n comforter covers the high back bed to ·ure a restful night's sleep. The Dutch theme ·arried throughout with tulips, wooden ·es, windmills and ice skates. This suite has ·rivate indoor hot tub, fireplace and private ·wood patio.

·the past intrigues you, then the **OLD ·WERHOUSE** is for you. This brick ·lding was built in 1910 and generated ·ctric power from a water flume into the late ·s. It features two suites.

The upstairs **CHELSEA SUITE** captures the grave of yesteryear. Pleasing to the eye at every turn, this suite emits a quiet elegance. Plush carpet, warm antique furnishings, and a hint of vanilla complete the picture. Your private outdoor hot tub sits on a redwood deck under a lattice gazebo.

An English garden comes to mind when you step into the **VICTORIAN ROSE SUITE.** Salmon pink brick, antique rose wallpaper, and a corner pedestal sink along with velvet and oak antiques bring back the plush warmth of the Victorian Era. Continue the feeling of an English garden while in your outdoor hot tub on your own brick patio. Brilliant stars, hootie owls, bubbling creek, lavender and mint included in the price.

das ABEND HAUS COTTAGE (the Evening House) is a restful creekside hide-away tucked into a mountainside. It has two suites that are designed after a German cottage in the Black Forest.

The lower **CREEKSIDE SUITE** is charmingly authentic. The minute the door opens you can feel the magical pull of the old country. Lace curtains, German steins, wooden carvings and a mahogany sleigh bed invite you in. Indoor hot tub and fireplace add to the ambience.

Your own private retreat! The exclusive upstairs suite, **BIRDSONG,** commands your attention upon entering. Luxurious comfort and enchanting atmosphere will make your stay extra special. It features a fantastic view of the surrounding hills and creek. The vaulted ceiling, crackling fireplace and private outdoor tub make you feel like you are on top of the Alps. Richly handsome antiques adorn the suite. A first class accommodation with a touch of Bavaria.

INDIVIDUAL LOG COTTAGES that overlook Rapid Creek invite you to relax in quiet. Hand-peeled lodge pole pine logs, red tile roofs and comfortable European antiques have everyone agreeing that these accommodations are unmatched in South Dakota. If you desire luxury, a romantic hideaway, or a peaceful retreat by a mountain stream, the cottages will exceed your expectations. Each cottage is tucked in the forest, surrounded by ponderosa pine and spruce. Wildlife abounds. Deer and bird watching are two favorites.

Each offers a carpet of hospitality which includes king-sized beds with cozy down comforters, large screen cable TV, VCR, stereo, refrigerator and microwave. Savor a full breakfast with homebaked breads and muffins. Brew up afternoon tea or gourmet coffee to enjoy along with hors d'oeuvres. Sooth cares away under the stars, in a private steaming spa on your redwood deck.

das Abend Haus Cottages
& Audrie's
Bed and Breakfast
23029 Thunderhead Falls Rd.
Rapid City, South Dakota 57702
(605) 342-7788

1 ABERDEEN

Aberdeen was once the home of Frank Baum, an 1890s Aberdeen newspaper editor who later wrote the all-time favorite children's story *The Wonderful Wizard of Oz.*

Mother's Antique Mall
414 S. Main St.
605/225-8992

Schmidt's Used Furn. & Antqs.
1009 S. Main St.
605/226-2782

Heirlooms Etc. at the Depot
1100 S. Main St.
605/226-3660

Lauingers Country Store
305 6th Ave. SW
605/225-0910

Remember When Antiques
504 S. State St.
605/226-3612

Court Street Lighting
123 Railroad Ave. SE
605/229-0359

Hitch'n Post Antqs. & Cllbls.
2601 6th Ave. SE
605/229-1655

Meier Antiques
State St. & Railroad Ave.
605/229-5453 or 605/225-9592

2 BELLE FOURCHE

Belle Fourche (beautiful fork) had its beginnings during the days of the dusty cattle drives when the wealth of the region attracted people such as Butch Cassidy and the Sundance Kid. The arrival of the railroad in 1890 led to the establishment of the city and the beginning of a wealthy, rowdy cattle baron dominated era. In the very early 1900s Belle Fourche became known as the largest cattle-shipping point in the world. Belle Fourche is also the center of the largest concentration of sheep in the United States, which makes it natural that it also ships more wool from its two warehouses than any other city. Belle Fourche remains to this day a "Cowtown" and its residents are proud of its history.

Love That Shoppe
515 State Street
605/892-4006
Open 9-8 Mon.-Sat., 1-4 Sun.

Directions: The shop sits in Downtown Belle Fourche at Hwys. 85 and 212.

Located in an historic 9,000-square-foot building, Love That Shoppe's 50 plus dealers' mix of Victorian, primitives, depression glass, heirloom jewelry, crockery and period furniture combine to make an enjoyable day for shopping. And when you tire of shopping, The Rocking '50s Soda Fountain located in the shop will take you back to the old drug store soda fountain days with their menu of bottled cokes, root beer floats, hot dogs, soft pretzels, ice cream sodas, sundaes and banana splits.

Tri-State Bakery Studio
705 State Street
605/892-2684
Hours: Tue.-Sat 9:30-5:30, Mon. 9:30-2

Directions: downtown Belle Fourche at Highways 85 and 212

The old Tri-State Bakery Building, dating back to 1927, is on the National and State Historical Registers and is truly representative of its early days. All the old equipment once used in creating the delicious confections, pastries and breads is still housed in the building and is available for viewing by interested customers.

Today, it has been converted to the Tri-State Bakery Studio offering a large selection of vintage advertising papers and tins and a limited amount of furniture. Also located here is the town's only Espresso Bar which features mochas and Italian sodas.

The Old Grizz Trading Post
2207 Fifth Avenue and 512 State Street
605/892-6668
Open 10-5 every day of the week

This 6,800-square-foot shop specializes in cowboy and western memorabilia, as well as a large variety of antiques and collectibles. The furniture selection mainly consists of, but is not limited to, pieces from the 1870s up through the '30s and '40s.

The Agers live on the premises at the Fifth Street location, a stately old home, dating back to 1892. They are currently in the process of restoring it to its original condition. The house still has 80% of its original wallpaper and an original 50-foot mural in the dining room.

The Agers encourage you to stop in anytime; if they're home; they're open.

Robb House Antiques
By Appointment Only
605/892-2846

3 BROOKINGS

Threads of Memories Antq.
309 4th St.
605/697-7377

Antique Treasure Co.
Rt. 1 #12
605/693-4020

4 CANTON

Canton Square Antique Emporium
121 E. Fifth St.
605/987-3152
Open Mon.-Fri. 9-8, Sat. & Sun. 9-5

Directions: Exit 62 from I-29, then 9 miles east.

Antique shop in the atmosphere of an old variety store, now a historical building. The owner says they have anything you want or ever hoped for in the way of antiques and collectibles.

Lincoln County Antique Center
123 W. 5th St.
605/987-4114
Hours: Mon.-Sat. 10-5, closed Sun.

Directions: Exit Hwy. 18 off I-29. Travel east 8 miles to Canton.

Presenting 10,000 square feet of quality Victorian furniture, art and books.

Norma's This N That Shop
109 N. Main St.
605/987-5816
Open Thurs.-Sat. 10-5 or by appointment (call 605/987-2269 for appointment)

Directions: Located 8 miles off I-29. Take Hwy. 18 east to Canton.

A general line of antiques and collectibles are featured.

5 CUSTER

Mountain Valley Antiques
3 miles W. on Rt. 16
605/673-5559

Wild Bill's Antq. Mall/Rock Shp.
2 miles W. of Custer on Hwy. 16
605/673-4186

6 DEADWOOD

Aunt Sophia's
By Appointment Only
800/377-1516

Goldbelt Mercantile & Antiques
93 Sherman St.
605/578-2202

7 DELL RAPIDS

Lambert's
428 E. 4th St.
605/428-3304

S & L Antiques & More
416/418 4th Street
605/428-4457

8 FREDERICK

Worthy Treasures Antiques
39147 105th St.
605/329-2143

Adeline Antiques
1149 300 91st Ave.
605/329-2112

9 HILL CITY

Orloske Antiques
Deerfield Road (Highways 16 & 385)
605/574-2181
Hours: 9-5, 7 days a week, year round, and by appointment

Directions: 1 1/2 miles west of Hill City on Deerfield Road and also at the intersection of Highways 16 and 385.

The total combined shopping area of these two shops is 10,000 square feet. 1800s furniture, primitives, glassware, toys, western items (saddles, tack, etc.) and Redwing Pottery are offered throughout the shop.

Big 45 Frontier Gun Shop
23850 Hwy. 385
605/574-4702

10 HOT SPRINGS

Fargo Mercantile
321 N. River St.
605/745-5189

Pioneer Trading Co.
143 S. Chicago
605/745-5252

11 KIMBALL

Red Barn Inn
Rural Rt. 2, Box 102
605/778-6332
Open year round
Rates: $32.50 up

Directions: From I-90 eastbound traffic: Take Exit 272; then travel 1/2 mile south, 7-1/2 miles east, and 3 miles south on a gravel road. From I-90 westbound traffic: Take Exit 284; then go 4 miles west and 3 miles south on a gravel road.

American know-how triumphs again in this 70-year old horse barn. No longer do steel bits, leather harnesses or hay decorate the interior. Today, a rustic decor outfitted with antique furniture and accessories celebrates the barn's reincarnation. Four rooms with separate baths serve as accommodations. Complimentary breakfast is served.

Mentzer Antiques
Box 138
605/778-6688

12 MILBANK

5th Street Antiques
902 S. 5th St.
605/432-5326

Bleser House Bed & Breakfast
311 S. 4th St.
605/432-4871

Reflections in Time
West Hwy. 12
605/432-9495

13 MITCHELL

Second Impression Palace
412 N. Main St.
605/996-1948
Spring-Summer: Mon.-Sat. 8:30-6:30, Sun. by chance; Fall-Winter: Mon.-Sat. 9-6, Sun. Closed

Directions: Located only 1 1/2 blocks south of the World's Only Corn Palace! Eastbound on I-90: Take Exit 330 north to Havens, east to Sanborn, north to 1st Avenue, east to Main Street, north to 412 North Main Street. Westbound on I-90: From Exit 332, go north to 1st Avenue, west to Main Street, north to 412 North Main Street.

This unique antique mall is a fascinating layout of old storefronts built from reassembled antique wood, glass, metal and tin. The award-winning display has been acclaimed from New York to San Francisco, and is a museum in itself.

Behind the doors of this indoor "Main Street" are over 40 dealers and 50 consignors with enough selection to satisfy everyone.

Walk down the boardwalk of time to the General Store and find trunks, dressers and Hoosier cabinets. For a more elegant variety of furniture try the Undertakers's. If vintage clothing and accessories are what you seek, you'll want to check into the Brothel. At the Sheriff's Office/Jailhouse, you'll find old tools, car accessories, and horse gear.

Cellar
400 N. Main St.
605/996-0515

14 PIEDMONT

James O Aplan Antiques & Arts
I 90 Exit 40 Tilford Rd.
605/347-5016

15 PIERRE

Capital City Antiques
819 N. Euclid Ave.
605/224-4971

16 RAPID CITY

das Abend Haus Cottages & Audrie's B&B
23029 Thunderhead Falls Road
605/342-7788
Open year round

Directions: From I-90: Take Exit 57 to light (Omaha Street and Hwy. 44). Turn right; follow Hwy. 44 west. Hwy. 44 will turn left at the next light. 7 miles west of Rapid City in the National Forest. One half mile past the Fireside Inn Restaurant, turn left onto Thunderhead Falls Road for 1/4 mile. From Hwy. 385: Turn at Junction 44; go east for 7 miles; turn right onto Thunderhead Falls Road for 1/4 miles.

Old World hospitality is thriving in the Black Hills at this enchanting retreat for couples only. Rich in the Abend Haus tradition, the spacious suites and log cottages are furnished with the largest collection of European antiques anywhere in the state.

See full page review this section.

Trader's Corner
3501 Canyon Lake Dr.
605/341-4242

Big K
805 E. Denver St.
605/343-1221

Country Est. Heritage House
2255 N. Haines Ave.
605/348-5994

Coach House Antiques
Hwy. 79
605/399-3838

Antique & Furniture Mart
1112 W. Main St.
605/341-3345

Country Lane Furn Brian Peck
2332 W. Main St.
605/343-9401

Gaslight Antiques
13490 Main St.
605/343-9276

Pawn-Derosa-Pawn
921 E. North St.
605/341-5516

Hidden Treasures
1208 E. North St.
605/342-7286

Antiques & Collectibles
225 Omaha St.
605/342-8199

St. Joe Antique Mall/Gift Shop
615 Saint Joseph St.
605/341-1073

17 SIOUX FALLS

Architectural Elements
818 E. 8th St.
605/339-9646

Antiques Gallery Midwest
1502 W. 10th St.
605/334-3051

Kolbe's Clock/Repair Shoppe
1301 S. Duluth Ave.
605/332-9662

Old House Stuff
818 E. 8th St.
605/339-9646

Eight St. Treasure Chest
1002 E. 8th St.
605/338-6878

Irish's Garage Antiques
618 S. 5th Ave.
605/334-6540

Maxwell House Antiques Inc.
612 W. 4th St.
605/334-3640

The Curiosity Shoppe
725 N. Main Ave.
605/334-1412

Recycled Treasures
801 N. Main Ave.
605/330-9473

Antique Mall
828 N. Main Ave.
605/335-7134

Koenig's Antiques
1103 N. Main Ave.
605/338-0297

Gustaf's Greenery
1020 S. Minnesota Ave.
605/334-2000

Chopping Block Antiques Ltd.
207 S. Phillips Ave.
605/334-1469

Cedar Acres Antiques
"Sebbo's" 3721 N. Cliff
605/334-8689

Cliff Ave. Flea Vendors
3515 N. Cliff
605/338-8975

Off The Hook Phone Service
"Phone First"
605/334-3151

The Patina
26th & Western Park Ridge Mall
605/357-8884

Prairie Home Antiques
5900 E. 10th
605/338-2042

The Book Shop
223 S. Phillips Ave.
605/336-8384

Dakota Weaver
5016 East 16th St.
605/336-7336

D&J Glass & Art Clinic, Inc.
46508 267th Street
605/361-7524

Packaging Store
1404 W. 41st Street
605/332-4789

18 SPEARFISH

Snowy Creek Antiques
112 West Illinois Street
605/642-2660
Open 8-5 Mon.-Fri.

Directions: Take the Spearfish exit from I-90. Shop is located in downtown Spearfish off Main Street on Illinois Street.

Oak furniture, old oak file cabinets, African art, western collectibles, primitives, toys, china, glassware are just a few of the many items offered here.

Old Mill Antiques
222 West Illinois Street
605/642-4704
Hours: (Winter) Mon.-Sat. 10-5, (Summer) Mon.-Sat. 9-6

Directions: Exit I-90. Shop is located in downtown Spearfish off Main Street.

15 dealers — a good general line of antiques and collectibles including late 1800s to '40s furniture, kitchenware, depression glass, pottery and mining and railroad collectibles.

The Browser Bin
206 Colorado
605/642-7434

Key Antiques
344 N. 5th St.
605/642-7087

Seifert's Country House
RR 1 Box 143K
605/642-4930

Kiefer Consignments
513 Spearfish Canyon Rd.
605/642-7436

19 TEA

I-29 Antiques & Collectibles Mall
46990 271st Street
605/368-5810
Mon. 9-9, Tue.-Sat. 9-5, Sun. 12-5

Directions: From I-29, take Exit 73, then 1/4 mile west.

Featuring McCoy, Fiesta, Hall pottery and Red Wing stoneware, all 10,000-square-feet of this mall have been put to good use by the 75 dealers. The curious antiquer can also find old toys, antique furniture, pictures, jewelry, glassware, and "tokens." More unusual items such as old signs plus well pumps add a touch of rustic to the collection.

Antique Furniture Company
1-29 Tea Exit #73 1/4 mi. East
605/368-2112

20 VOLGA

Red Barn Antiques
46080 U.S. Hwy. 14
605/627-5394

21 WATERTOWN

Main Street Antiques
6 E. Kemp Ave.
605/886-1919

Yellowed Pages Used Bks. V. II
10 E. Kemp Ave.
605/886-3640

Westgate
125 E. Kemp Ave.
605/882-1361

22 WORTHING

Antiques & Things
112 Main Street
605/372-4853

23 YANKTON

Kollectible Kingdom
317 West 5th Street
605/668-9353
Open daily (closed Tue.) May-Nov. 9-6, Dec.-April 11-5:30 (some Sun. 12-5)

Directions: Traveling Hwy. 81 (easily accessible from I-29 or I-90). Turn east on 5th Street which is located between Coastal convenience store and Super Lube. Shop is located behind Super Lube.

Red Wing stoneware and Depression glass are the most popular and are featured pieces in this intimate and jam-packed shop. Also notable among the diverse and plentiful selections are unusual glassware and china. For those seeking a delightful challenge, a rummage sale section allows for sifting and digging.

Dakota Antiques & Cllbls.
408 W. 11th & Broadway
605/665-7230

Gingerbread Shack
515 E. 4th St.
605/665-9924

Wright's Antique Shop
313 Mulberry St.
605/665-2003

Lewis & Clark Gallery
221 W. 3rd St.
605/665-0129

Notes

Tennessee

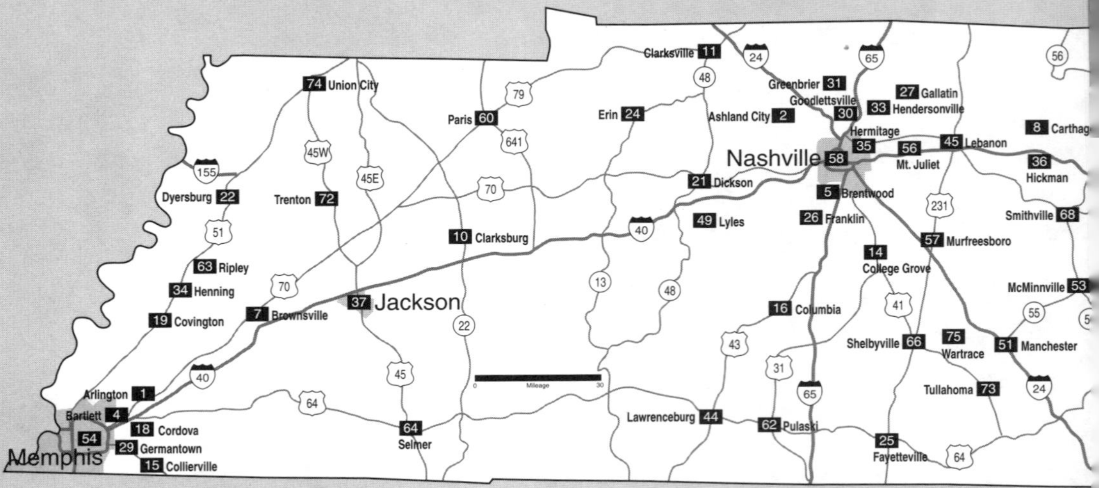
Clarksville 11
Union City 74
Paris 60
Erin 24
Ashland City 2
Greenbrier 31
Goodlettsville 30
Gallatin 27
Hendersonville 33
Hermitage 35
Carthage 8
Nashville 58
Mt. Juliet 56
Lebanon 45
Hickman 36
Dyersburg 22
Trenton 72
Dickson 21
Brentwood 5
Smithville 68
Franklin 26
Lyles 49
Clarksburg 10
Murfreesboro 57
College Grove 14
Ripley 63
Henning 34
McMinnville 53
Jackson 37
Covington 19
Brownsville 7
Columbia 16
Shelbyville 66
Wartrace 75
Manchester 51
Arlington 1
Bartlett 4
Tullahoma 73
Memphis 54
Cordova 18
Germantown 29
Collierville 15
Selmer 64
Lawrenceburg 44
Pulaski 62
Fayetteville 25
Mileage

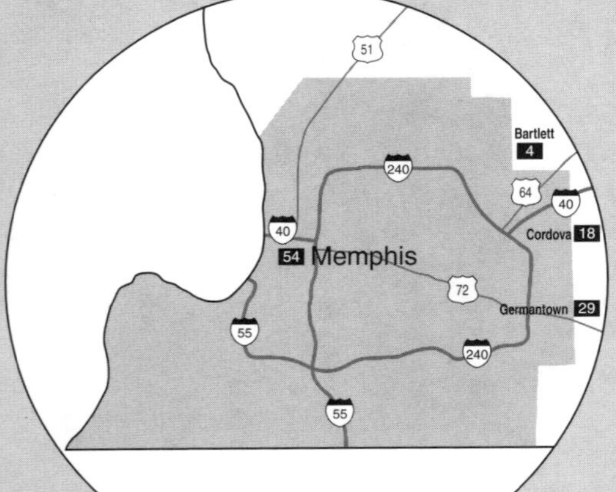
Bartlett 4
Memphis 54
Cordova 18
Germantown 29

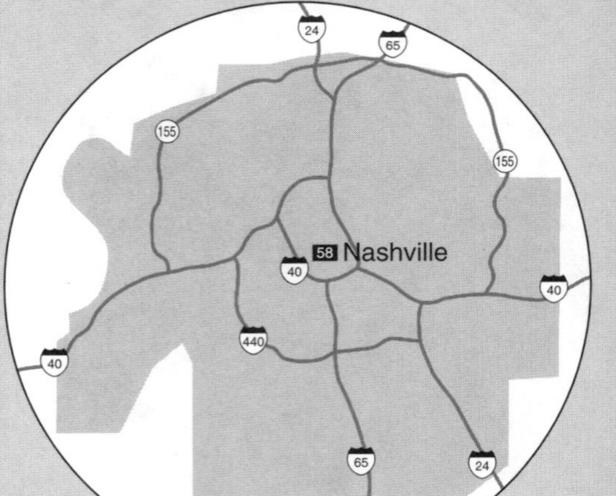
Nashville 58
Brentwood 5

Dumplin Valley Antiques & Collectibles

Lee & Jane Carson - Owners
Open Fri. 10-6
Sat, Sun 9-6

340 West Dumplin Valley Rd.
(423) 932-7713

see review this section

Kodak

42

Antique Centers I & II

TWO MALLS
I-24 EXIT 81
(615) 896-5188

Murfreesboro

57

Winner—National Trust "Great American Home Award"

HISTORIC Falcon Manor

McMinnville

Daily Tours • Group Luncheon Tours • Victorian Gift Shop
Weddings • Bed & Breakfast • Weekend Dining by Reservation

53

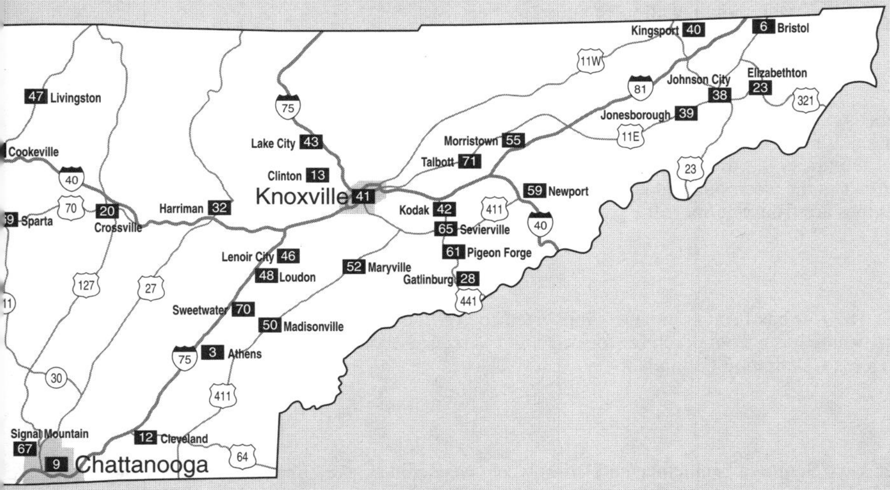

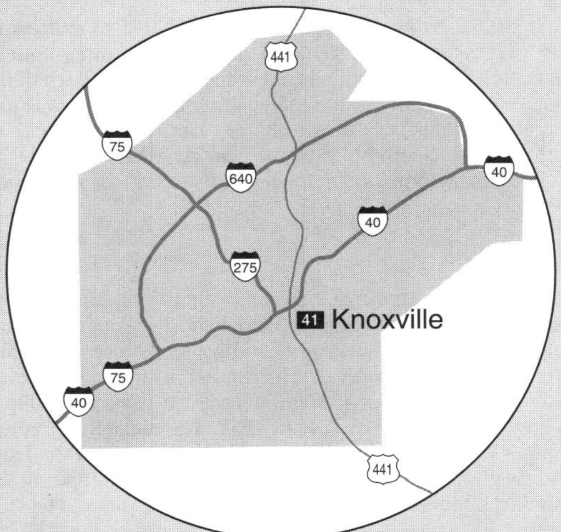

Antique Malls of Tennessee

2 Sykes Rd.
615/683-6066

Hickman

36

Farragut Antique Mall

Timeless Treasures at Affordable Prices

423-671-3630

Knoxville

41

East Town Antique Mall

Area's Largest Selection of Quality Antiques and Collectibles

30,000 Sq Ft in Two Buildings
Chattanooga, Tennessee
(423) 899-5498 (423) 490-0121

I-75 Exit 1 South or 1B North
Behind Cracker Barrel

9

Campbell Station Antiques

Antiques & Collectables

620 Campbell Station Road
(423) 966-4348
I-40 Exit 373

Knoxville

41

Antiques Plus

12,000 sq. ft
featuring upscale antiques
4500 Walker Blvd.
(423) 687-6536

Knoxville

41

ANTIQUE MARKET *of Cordova*

Upscale Group Shop for the discriminating shopper

owned by David & Kim Leggett publishers of "The Antique Atlas"

Cordova

18

Riverside *The World's Most Unique* **Antique & Collectors Mall**

1442 Winfield Dunn Parkway
(Hwy. 66)
(423) 429-0100

Sevierville

65

Homespun Craft & Antique Mall

200 Dealers
11523 Kingston Pike
423-671-3444

Knoxville

41

SHELBYVILLE & WARTRACE

JUDY'S JEWELS ANTIQUES & COLLECTIBLES 730 N. Main St., Shelbyville
Open Daily **615-685-4200**

JUDY'S JEWELS are found within her wonderful collection of antiques, a love that grew out of an affection for her mother's beautiful, old things. Among her treasures are Persian rugs, bronzes, pictures, glassware, and a fabulous collection of fine porcelain that includes R.S. Prussia, Nippon, Royal Bayreuth, and Beleek. An exquisite selection of furnishings are available as well.

THE ANTIQUE MARKETPLACE 208 Elm St., Shelbyville
Hours : Mon.-Sat. 9-5, Sun. 1-5 **615-684-8493**

The Antique Marketplace is is the largest antique mall and auction house in Shelbyville. Over 100 quality dealers occupy what once was the old Coca-Cola Bottling Plant. Come take a step back in time with Cavigny and Mike House and enjoy an old fashion bottled coke and a sample of homemade fudge. The mall offers an eclectic array of wonderful antiques from which to choose; furniture, excellent depression glassware, costume jewelry, pottery, Blue Ridge, primitives and garden accessories. Special services are also offered such as furniture stripping, sandblasting, framing, chair caning and lamp repair. A monthly auction is held on the second Friday of each month. Call to be added to their list.

CINNAMON RIDGE BED & BREAKFAST 799 Whitthorne St., Shelbyville
Open Daily 7-10 **615-685-9200**

Cinnamon Ridge is an early 1900s Colonial home that offers a relaxing, down-home stay to the Middle Tennessee traveler. Each of it's five guest rooms are complete with antique furnishings and private baths, but don't overlook the truly Southern, must-have hand sewn quilt that adorns each bed. Your stay at Cinnamon Ridge will keep you in close proximity to activities in Bedford County. It's even within walking distance of the Walking Horse Show arenas. Start your day with a full breakfast and partake of treats in the afternoon and late evening, feasting on old fashioned tea cakes, fried apple pies, or rich chocolate desserts, served with tea or coffee. All recipes are from Pat Sherrill's grandma's kitchen.

TAYLOR HOUSE BED & BREAKFAST 300 East Lane St., Shelbyville
Open Daily **615-684-3894**

The Taylor House is a three-story Victorian home built in 1890. It has been completely renovated to provide modern comforts to its guests while providing plenty of roaming room (5,300 sq. ft.). This large beauty has a front porch for rocking and a screened in back porch for late night chats. The House is only minutes away from the Tennessee Walking Horse Celebration Grounds.

THE OLD GORE HOUSE 410 Belmont Ave., Shelbyville
Open Daily **615-685-0636**

The Old Gore House presents a step back in time when men were Southern Gentlemen and ladies were considered genteel. Share in the past's elegance when you visit The Old Gore House, of true Victorian style. The home boasts double parlors and a grand formal dining room with a fireplace. The four guest rooms provide queen-size beds and bath.

THE LOG CABIN BED & BREAKFAST 171 Loop Rd., Wartrace
Open Daily **615-389-6713**

Emily Pomrenke is kinda (that's Southern for kind of) special to us. She was one of the early supporters of *The Antique Atlas*. Shortly after our commitment to this huge undertaking Emily called to express her interest and excitement in a three hour phone conversation. The conversations continued to the point that we decided to go meet her in person. The Log Cabin is out in the country on a small paved road where everybody waves when they pass. It was easy to spot - the marker on the road led us up the driveway to the cabin on the hill. It was just as I had pictured it - a wonderful get-a-way with an informal atmosphere. Each of the three guest rooms has its own theme. The Heart of Texas Room, the one most requested by horse enthusiast who stay with Emily while competing in the nearby Shelbyville Horse Shows, is decorated in Texas memorabilia. The Swing By The Window (there really is one) has a spring time appeal. The family room, synomous with its intent - to welcome a family - has plenty of sleeping space.

WALKING HORSE HOTEL AND SHOPS 101 Spring St., Wartrace
Open Daily **615-389-7050, 1-800-513-8876**

While we were in Wartrace visiting Emily, we happened upon a magnificent structure that immediately drew us in. It came as no surprise that we weren't the only ones mystified by the Walking Horse Hotel. Now owner, John Garland, was inside, steadily working on the Hotel's renovation. He, too, had happened upon the Hotel, which was in desperate need of repair, but, captivated by its history and charm, decided to purchase it and move to Wartrace from his home in Oregon. We understood his enthusiasm. The Walking Horse was, in its day, a first class hotel. In the 1930s Middle Tennessee was fast becoming "The Walking Horse Capital of the World". The Hotel's "claim to fame" was accredited to the breeding and boarding of "Strolling Jim", a high-stepping horse who won the first World Grand Championship Title in 1939. The champion trainer was Floyd Caruthers who owned both the Hotel and the stables. "Strolling Jim" is still at home as his final resting place is in the backyard of the Hotel.

Today, the Walking Horse Hotel has been re-stored to its grandeur with seven guest rooms, six occupying the third floor. Specialty shops adorn the second floor level offering a barber shop, candy shop, and framing studio, along with several gift shops. The restaurant located on the main floor serves delicious Southern cuisine.

LEDFORD MILL BED & BREAKFAST Rt. 2, Wartrace
Open Daily **615-455-2546/454-9228**

This is another story of someone who came to visit and decided to stay. In December, 1995, Dennis and Kathleen Depert bought the mill and moved from their home on an Island in Puget Sound off the coast of Washington State to the tiny town of Wartrace. The Deperts have converted the mill into a wonderful bed & breakfast inn with three special accommodations all having access to the gardens, waterfall and creek. The Mill's original machinery is highlighted in each room, where early 1900's furnishings are arranged within a spacious old factory setting. Visitors to the gift shop on the main floor are quite taken with the floor to ceiling mural in sepia tones, depicting an old mill delivery wagon. Kathleen drew her inspiration for this from an old photograph. The main floor also includes a lobby, old time kitchen and breakfast room overlooking the falls.

The Little Church That Was "Saved"

Most of us save the top of our wedding cake, the dress, or flowers as a momento of our wedding day. But Jane Carson saved the Entire Church! The little church in which Jane and her husband William were married was built in 1839. Over the past 158 years it has sheltered many members of the faith (including Jane herself) and hosted hundreds of weddings. So, when Jane heard that her little church was being torn down to build a new one, she bought it, had it moved, and opened an antique shop in it.

Today, instead of preachers and pews, you'll find depression glassware, china, pottery, lamps, late 1800s and early 1900s furniture and more. Two dealers specialize in Fostoria, china and wood and tin advertising items.

Dumplin Valley
Antiques & Collectibles
340 W. Dumplin Valley Road
Kodak, TN
(423) 932-7713

This former church is now home to Dumplin Valley Antiques . . .

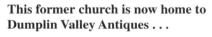

. . . no preachers, no pews . . .

. . . just antiques.

The Downtown Antique and Merchant Association

Invites you to spend the day shopping in Lebanon

In Cahoots
123 Public Square
(615) 444-8037

Cuz's Antiques
140 Public Square
(615) 444-8070

Off The Square Cafe
109 S. Cumberland
(615) 444-6217

Rainbow Relics
137 Public Square
(615) 449-6777

Southern Rose Antiques
105 Public Square
(615) 444-3308

Bonnie Blue Antiques
107 S. Cumberland
(615) 453-1158

Tennessee Treasures
109 S. Cumberland
(615) 443-2136

Coach House Antiques
Public Square
(615) 443-1905

Downtown Antique Mall
112 Public Square
(615) 444-4966

Denise's Timeless Treasures
146 Public Square
(615) 443-4996

Ophelia's Antiques
107 Public Square
(615) 443-0783

The Antique Atlas would like to make special mention of the following merchants for their support in The Downtown Antique Association.

McCullough Office Supply
108 E. Main
(615) 444-1334

Mike's Pawn Shop
107 N. Cumberland
(615) 444-3133

Wilson County Tourism
(615) 444-5503

S & B Shoe
101 Public Square
(615)443-5086

Chamber of Commerce
Public Square
(615) 444-5503

Instant Cash
124 A Public Square
(615) 449-3323

Creative Photography
106 W. Main
(615) 444-5967

Nita's Hallmark Shop
129 Public Square
(615) 444-4866

Partnership Lebanon
(615) 453-1092

Perfect Cup
104 N. Maple St.
(615) 449 7939

Advanced Sign Graphics
102 D. Hartmann Drive
(615) 443-3753

Town Pump
105 N. Cumberland
(615) 449-9947

HISTORIC DOWNTOWN LEBANON

An Exciting Discovery Around Every Corner!

LEBANON TOWN SQUARE

It's difficult to picture the now bustling public square in Lebanon, Tennessee, as once vacant, but that was the scene before its transformation. Originally, Lebanon was an active town, with business held inside its buildings and outside in the square. Time, as in many small towns, took its toll as movement to the perimeter of town, rather than the center, became the trend. Lebanon was fortunate in that, one by one, its wonderful structures in the public square area were purchased or leased and revived to become the center of activity once again. As crafters and antiquers occupied the old buildings, public interest grew, and so did that of professionals who also wanted to become a part of the newly-created, active center of town. Now the town, built in 1819, has experienced a re-birth and has undergone a facelift so that passers-by, too, can share their proud heritage.

TENNESSEE TREASURES (615) 443-2136
109 S. Cumberland Monday-Saturday, 10-5

There's no telling what you'll encounter at Tennessee Treasures, but you can be reasonably assured that if grandma had one, this shop does too! Although their specialty is kitchen items, you'll find a unique garden section with old plows, wheelbarrows, garden utensils, and gifts related to gardening. Also a part of the offerings are upscale furniture, unusual vintage clothing, and handmade Country American Christmas ornaments. There's even a birthing chair that breaks down to be carried in a bag by a mid-wife. Stop in, you never know when you'll catch a sale in progress!

IN CAHOOTS! (615) 444-8037
123 Public Square Tuesday-Saturday, 10-6; Sunday-Monday by chance

If you're searching for old drug store or five-and-dime store merchandise visit In Cahoots!. They also carry antique and vintage furniture, or for something a little different see their hand-painted children's furniture. As an added surprise, In Cahoots! includes a full-service doll shop that performs minor repairs or redresses and cleans dolls. Madam Alexander, Lee Middleton, Susan Wakeen, and antique and vintage dolls are just part of their line.

RAINBOW RELICS (615) 449-6777
37 Public Square Monday-Saturday, 9-6; Sunday 1-6

Originally a bank that was torn down then rebuilt around its old vaults in 1977, it became home to Rainbow Relics and now houses antiques, including furniture - especially oak, primitives, linens, and glassware. Also offered are collectibles of art glass by Boyd and Marble Mountain Creations, which are limited edition pieces made from Georgia marble in the shape of, for example, cars, tractors, and trains.

CUZ'S ANTIQUE CENTER (615) 444-8070
140 Public Square Monday-Saturday, 9-5; Sunday 11-5

Dubbed a "center" because it spans three buildings, Cuz's is the largest collection of merchandise in the area. Inventory includes not only fine examples of American, English, and French antiques, but also wonderful reproductions of such pieces. Cuz's also carries furniture, glassware, and bronzes. As you would expect, their selection includes oil paintings, stained glass windows, and a tremendous selection of jewelry, both estate and modern. For the pocket knife collector, Cuz's is also the home of the Fightin' Rooster Cutlery Company.

OFF THE SQUARE CAFE (615) 444-6217
109 South Cumberland Street

If all of your searching for treasures has created an appetite, stop at the Off The Square Cafe, located inside the Tennessee Treasures Antique Mall. Try one of their specialty sandwiches like the homemade apple and grape chicken salad or the cajun roasted beef. If a sandwich is a little heavy, try one of the thick and hearty homemade soups prepared daily, or have half a sandwich and a cup of soup. Whatever you choose, just save room for one of their homemade desserts!

COACH HOUSE ANTIQUES (615) 443-1905
Public Square

In the early days, Coach House Antiques was the town lawyer's office. It would be interesting to know the kinds of legal problems the town's folk had back in the 1800s. But, today throughout this historic building, the only decisions to be made are those of a "selective" nature. The shop carries a general line of antiques - everything from antique furnishings to collectibles.

BONNIE BLUE ANTIQUES (615) 453-1158
107 S. Cumberland

What once was the men's clothing store of Lebanon has now transformed into a chapter from *Gone With The Wind*. As a matter of fact, this shop with its old South theme carries *Gone With The Wind* collectibles and memorabilia. Victorian furnishings and accessories, vintage clothing and exquisite glassware are also offered at Bonnie Blue.

DOWNTOWN ANTIQUE MALL (615) 444-4966
112 Public Square

Downtown Antique Mall once sparkled with diamonds and jewels as the town jewelry shop. Today it's no different. For the past 15 to 20 years, this shop has furnished its' customers with jewels of a different nature. This 2-story building houses some of the best American furnishings in the area as well as outstanding glassware.

DENISE'S TIMELESS TREASURES (615) 443-4996
146 Public Square

For the past seventy years this store has been a favorite with women. It began life as a shoe store and now houses fine antiques, particularly from the Victorian period. In addition, the shop stocks accessories to compliment the furnishings as well as pretty stationery for your writing table.

SOUTHERN ROSE ANTIQUES (615) 444-3308
105 Public Square

Isn't it amazing how some things were just meant to be? Southern Rose was once a furniture warehouse and it still is today. This shop is filled to the brim with furniture from all styles and periods. Most likely you can spot pieces which appeared there over 100 years ago when they were sold as new.

OPHELIA'S ANTIQUES (615) 443-0783
107 Public Square

A hodge-podge, fun place to shop, Ophelia's carries antiques and collectibles covering many periods. Glassware, china, furniture, linens, prints and more can be found at this antique "stop".

East Town Antique Mall

Chattanooga, Tennessee

Area's Largest Selection of Quality Antiques and Collectibles

No Reproductions

Antiques & Collectibles Only

6503 Slater Road
Chattanooga, Tennessee
(423) 899-5498 (423) 490-0121

I-75 Exit 1 South or 1B North
Behind Cracker Barrel

30,000 Square Feet

Over 300 Booths and Show Cases

Now Open

Center Street Antiques

198 S. Center Street
Collierville, Tennessee
901-861-3711

Open Monday Through Saturday
10:00 A.M. - 5:00 P.M.
Evenings By Appointment

Come Visit Our New Shop Located
1 Block South of the Town Square
in Collierville

Browse Through Our Large
Selection of
Furniture, Collectibles, Lamps, China
Architectural Pieces, Gardenware,
Primitives, and Other Treasures!
We Also Offer Decorator Furnishings.

Quality Dealer Space Available

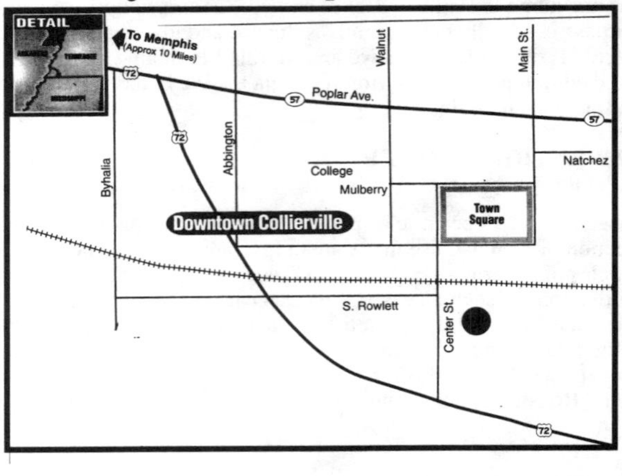

1 ARLINGTON

Lamb Crossing Antiques
11022 Highway 70
901/867-0404
Fax: 901/867-0929
Open daily, Mon.-Fri. 10-4; Sat. 10-2:30; Sun. 1-5 (closed last Sunday of the month)

Directions: Traveling I-40, take exit #20. Go north on Canada Road for 2 miles to Highway 70. Turn right and continue 3 miles. The store is on the left just after the Arlington city limits sign.

This store opened in March of last year. It's a quaint little shop, located in an old store, and filled with an eclectic blend of country and unusual items. Make sure you stop by on your way to Memphis.

Bozo's
Highway 70 (approximately 20 miles from Memphis)
901/294-3400

Bozo's menu becomes apparent about a half-mile away - barbeque! About the time you see the cloud of hickory smoke hovering over the restaurant, you start smelling all that sizzling pork. Bozo's is one of west Tennessee's landmarks, having been open every day except Sundays since 1923!

There is absolutely nothing about the decor to inspire a sense of elegance or upscale atmosphere - tired wood paneling, formica-topped tables, wooden chairs, a well-scuffed linoleum floor, pale green stools line up at gray counters, a Chevrolet-time clock on the wall. The only reason you go to Bozo's is for some of the best food you'll ever eat. They serve shrimp, chicken, salads, and steak, but the house specialty is pork, especially something called a "white and brown pulled pig plate." It's succulent white meat from the inside of the shoulder, and crustier brown meat from the outside, pulled into shreds and hunks and heaped on a plate along with saucy barbeque beans and sweet cold slaw. You can also get chopped plates and barbeque sandwiches, and sauce on the side. Nobody does it better!

2 ASHLAND CITY

B J's Attic
108 N. Main St.
615/792-7208

Saint Elsewhere Antiques
110 N. Main St.
615/792-9337

Ruth Ellen's Antiques
202 N. Main St.
615/792-1915

3 ATHENS

Ourloom
1558 County Road 561
423/745-6055

Antiques Unique
Hwy. 30 W.
423/745-5941

Gene's Olde Country Shoppe
813 S. White St..
423/745-2254

Cottage Antiques & Gifts
15 W. Washington Ave.
423/745-8528

Piedmont Antq. & Int. Design
104 N. White St.
423/745-2731

Hughes Furn. Company
316 N. White St.
423/745-2183

4 BARTLETT

Upstage Antiques
6214 Stage Road
901/385-0035
Open: Mon.-Wed. 10-6; Thurs.-Sat. 10-8;
Sunday 12-6

See color section for specific information.

The Antique Gallery
6044 Stage Road
901/385-2544
Open Mon.-Sat. 10-6; Sundays 1-5

Directions: On I-40, exit #12 and travel north on Sycamore View to Stage Road. Turn right onto Stage Road and left at the first light between McDonald's and KFC.

35,000 square feet of dealer space may seem imposing, but the only overwhelming thing about the Antique Gallery is the positive response of its visitors. From abounding friendliness to the pride expressed in the displays of the 150 dealers, shoppers delight in taking part in this group shop. Although extremely spacious, the gallery is always full, but never overcrowded, as owner Robert Bowden and manager Eric Triche strive to maintain an "airy" feeling. Booths are inviting with excellent dealer presentation of the merchandise.

Boasts Mr. Bowden, "The prices offered in the Gallery are fantastic, the best in the area, and because of the fairness in pricing, collectors are drawn here from all regions of the country." Dealers are offered even better pricing through discounts.

Within such immenseness you would not expect the diversity the Antique Gallery provides. Offerings include most any familiar name: Nippon, Hummel, Dresden, Wedgwood, Roseville, Hull, McCoy, Royal Doulton, Limoges - to name a few - and also an array of categories like depression glass, carnival glass, crystal, silver, and flow blue. The selection in furniture is equally diverse. Many other collectibles are also part of the inventory. Showcases highlight the small and often rare items.

Include the family in this stop and dine in the Serendipity Tea Room any day, except Sunday, from 11 a.m. to 2 p.m. Menu items are freshly made and include soups, salads, sandwiches, and deliciously-different biscuits. Twenty-eight specialty teas are also offered. Private parties and receptions can be held in the Serendipity Tea Room after 6 p.m. If you find any of the furnishings inviting, they, too, are offered for sale.

5 BRENTWOOD

Ivy Crest Gallery
1501 Franklin Rd.
615/377-0676

6 BRISTOL

New Hope Bed & Breakfast
822 Georgia Avenue
423/989-3343 or 1-888-989-3343
Open daily
Rates $70-130

Directions: From I-81, take exit #3 onto Commonwealth Avenue. Turn left onto State Street (downtown Bristol) and pass under the large sign. At the second light after the sign turn right onto Georgia Avenue and go five blocks. The inn is on the right, on the corner of Georgia and Pine.

The New Hope B&B is an 1892 Victorian that wraps its guests in a cloud of turn-of-the-century memories. The house exudes an atmosphere of Victorian elegance, complete with furnishings that are a mixture of antique and period. Located in an historic neighborhood, guests can stroll the streets on guided walking tours. The large wrap-around porch is the setting not only for morning or afternoon relaxation, but where breakfast is served in good weather. The private baths are large and inviting, with robes provided for after-bath enjoyment.

Oak Door Antiques
1258 Hwy. 126
423/968-7177

States Alternative Antiques
105 17th St.
423/764-3177

Vintage Antiques
24 6th St.
423/968-1090

Mary Ann Stone Antiques
610 State St.
423/968-5181

Ruth King Antiques
618 State
423/968-9062

Antiques Unlimited
620 State
423/764-4211

7 BROWNSVILLE

Mid-Town Auction
230 South Church Street
901/772-3382
Auction Dates: First Sunday of the month at 10 a.m.

Directions: Off I-40

This little country auction has some surprising results. They always manage to have something that I want. The merchandise varies from sale to sale; sometimes early primitive pieces; sometimes rough; sometimes depression. You just never know, so you have to go to find out. They usually have lots of glass and advertising items, Roseville and other potteries and old prints can almost always be found. A great dealer auction!

8 CARTHAGE

Gore Antique Mall Inc.
59 Cookeville Hwy.
615/735-9904

Massey's Country Antiques
336 Defeated Creek Hwy.
615/774-3146

Creekside Collectibles
115 Water St.
615/735-3190

Windy Hill Antiques
Hwy. 70 N
615/735-2561

The Speciality Shop
209 3rd Ave. W.
615/735-8441

9 CHATTANOOGA

East Town Antique Mall

6503 Slater Road
423/899-5498 or 423/490-0121
Open: 7 days a week 10-6 and Saturday 9-8 during daylight savings.

Directions: From I-75: Take Exit 1 or 1B one half mile south of the junction of I-24 and I-75 (one mile north of the Georgia State Line). Traveling south, take Exit 1, turn right, then turn right at the first red light. Traveling north, take Exit 1B, turn right at the second red light. The mall is behind Cracker Barrel.

This upscale mall, opened 10 years ago by John and Carol Hudson, allows antiques and collectibles only - no reproductions. "We stress quality," says Carol, "and we discourage damaged merchandise." With over 300 booths and showcases, you can imagine the diversity of items you will find here. An abbreviated list includes the area's largest selection of American art pottery, two dealers who specialize in advertising memorabilia, several depression and elegant glass dealers, one dealer who carries R.S. Prussia and art glass, one dealer who has specialized in pressed glass for over 25 years, two dealers who carry American, German, Russian and Japanese military collectibles (all authentic), several dealers whose display of American and English dinnerware includes many hard-to-find patterns, one dealer that maintains a large selection of Lenox china, three book dealers, one Life Magazine dealer, one dealer who offers a huge array of signed cast iron, including a complete set of Griswold skillets from the smallest to the largest, another dealer who specializes in Torquay and who is a past president of the collector's club, several toy and cowboy memorabilia dealers, one dealer who specializes in Nippon, another who carries many hard to find primitive items. The mall is also home to many retired modern collectibles such as Department 56, David Winter, Lladro, Royal Doulton, Wedgwood, Hummel, Disney Classics and others.

They keep a 'Want List' for customers looking for special items. And with their new expansion of 12,000 square feet, the Hudson's have added a large selection of fine furniture in all styles. There are several motels and restaurants at East Town's exit so plan to spend the night to explore all that Chattanooga has to offer.

Coates Antiques
520 Ashland Terrace
423/870-1880

Cooper's Antiques & Decor
3210 Brainerd Rd.
423/629-7411

Chase Dacus Collection
3214 Brainerd Rd.
423/622-1715

Marie's Antiques
6503 Slater Road
423/899-4607

Temple & Co. Antiques
1816 Broad St.
423/265-9339

Chattanooga Antique Mall
1901 Broad St.
423/266-9910

McCracken Bros.
2622 Broad St.
423/266-0027

High Point Antiques
3502 Broad St.
423/756-9566

Davis's Trading Post
3627 Cummings Hwy.
423/821-0061

Dacus Antiques & Fine Furn.
2422 S. Hickory
423/622-2220

Norma Jean's Antiques
3829 Hixson Pike
423/877-5719

Barnyard Antiques Etc.
7160 Lee Hwy.
423/899-3913

Furniture Barn
39 E. Main St.
423/265-1406

Berning House Antqs. & Dolls
605 Marlboro Ave.
423/624-4436

Lambs & Ivy Antiques
249 Northgate Mall
423/877-6871

Lowes Antiques
4000 Ringgold Rd.
423/633-2902

Junque Nique Shop
6009 Ringgold Rd.
423/894-7817

Cross the Years
6503 Slater Rd.
423/892-4193

Favorite Places To Eat

Cracker Barrel Old Country Store
I-75 & Ringgold Rd., Exit 1
423/899-5729

Cracker Barrel Old Country Store
I-75 & Shallowford Rd., Exit 5
423/892-0977

Cracker Barrel Old Country Store
I-24 & Hwy. 41/64, Exit 174
423/825-5885

10 CLARKSBURG

Oma's Antik Haus
3375 Hwy. 22
901/986-3018

11 CLARKSVILLE

East Gate Antiques
321 Drinkard Dr.
931/551-9572

Traditions
131 Franklin St.
931/551-9800

High Street Antique Mall
40 High St.
931/553-4040

Cherry Station Antqs. & More
212 Warfield Blvd.
931/648-4830

Ragin Cajun Antiques
210 Kraft St.
931/552-0545

The Emporium
739 Madison
931/645-1607

Pedigo's
1461 Madison St.
931/553-0420

Granny's Antiques
924 Providence Blvd.
931/648-0077

Alcocks Heritage Hill Antqs.
416 N. 2nd St.
931/648-3989

D R Marable Sales Antiques
1303 Tylertown Rd.
931/551-3259

Saint John's Antiques
128 University
931/503-1515

Favorite Places To Eat

Cracker Barrel Old Country Store
I-24 & Hwy. 79, Exit 4
931/552-4188

12 CLEVELAND

Carousel
80 Church St. NE
423/339-3934

Lace Emporium
2065 Collins Dr. NW
423/476-5836

Antiques Parlour
208 Grove Ave. NW
423/476-6921

Westside Shop
2910 Harrison Pike
423/339-9838

Treasures Forever
151 Inman St. SE
423/478-2711

Cleveland Furn. Sales
220 Inman St. SW
423/472-0099

Boardwalk Uniques & Antqs.
251 Inman St. NE
423/478-1010

Reflections Gift Shop
94 Mikel St. NW
423/559-0140

Presswood's Vintage Antiques
3350 Ocoee St. N
423/479-4460

Lamps & Things
702 17th St. NW
423/339-3963

Favorite Places To Eat

Cracker Barrel Old Country Store
I-75 & Hwy. 60, Exit 25
423/476-1577

13 CLINTON

Clinton Antique Mall
317 N. Main St.
423/457-3110

Past & Present
362 N. Main St.
423/457-1133

Market Place Antiques
333 Market St.
423/463-8635

Somebody's Treasure
364 Market St.
423/457-6947

14 COLLEGE GROVE

Leon Tywater & Sons Auction Company

Hwy. 31 A
615/790-7145, 615/368-7772
Call For Auction Dates

Directions: 30 miles South of Nashville on 31A

There are lots of reasons to attend Leon & Andy's (that's Leon's son) auction. One being, that for an auction to be located so far out in the sticks, they sure have some "good stuff." I honestly don't know where they get their merchandise, but I can tell you this, it is exceptional. If you are into early American (as I am), then this is the sale for you. The last time I attended the auction I purchased an 1800s plantation desk, a cannonball rope bed, a cherry sideboard (pegged), a mantle with original mustard paint and I let a fabulous sugar chest get away. But, if this isn't reason enough to encourage you, then this most assuredly will. Leon's wife is a wonderful cook! Leon too! They start cooking about a week in advance of the sale. Leon smokes the barbeque, and his wife makes homemade sandwiches, pies (several kinds), cakes and fried pies. But, my favorite is the chocolate cake, "it's to die for." The last time I talked to Leon he told me to call first and he would have her bake me a whole one. Well, get ready Leon, as soon as this book goes to print I'm on my way, so preheat the oven.

15 COLLIERVILLE

Collierville has over thirteen shops and malls, all within a short distance of each other. Most of the shops are located on the Historic Town Square however, two wonderful malls can be found as you enter Collierville on Poplar. These two malls are listed below.

Directions to Collierville: From I-240, take the Poplar Avenue exit for Germantown. Continue on Poplar through Germantown. Collierville is located approximately 10 minutes from Germantown.
To reach the Town Square, continue on Poplar to the third light past Abbington Antique Mall. Turn right on Main Street. An Historical Town Square marker is located in front of the bank on your right to indicate the location of the Town Square.

Sheffield Antiques Mall
708 W. Poplar
901/853-7822
Open Mon.-Sat. 10-6; Sun. 12-6

Located behind Wendy's on the left.
Sheffield Antiques Mall is Collierville's largest antique haven. With over 150 quality dealers you are sure to find many treasures here. The mall is represented by some of the best dealers in the Memphis area, offering a wonderful selection of French, English and American antiques.

Lunch in The Garden Room Cafe located within the mall. Open for lunch 11-2, Tuesday-Saturday, the Cafe features gourmet soups, salads, sandwiches and desserts. A sampling of the sumptuous menu includes; Hot Ham Delights, Crab Toasties Florentine, Faccacia Rueben, Napa Valley Chicken Salad, Shrimp and Crab Louis, Caribbean Tuna Salad and Gorgonzola Potato Salad. The dessert menu includes Sweet German Chocolate Pie (the best), Cream Cheese Clouds and Fruit Cobbler.

Abbington Antiques Mall
575 W. Poplar
901/854-3568
Open Mon.-Sat. 10-6; Sun. 12-6

Located across the street from Wal-Mart on Poplar.
Abbington Antiques, since its very beginning, has been known for exceptional antiques. Presenting distinctive pieces for the discerning customer is the desire of the dealers who make Abbington what it is today. With a focus on decorating for the home or office, an unusual offering of architectural iron, sewing collectibles, Regina music boxes, phonographs, radios, lamps, mirrors, statuary, candles, antique tools and more is available. The furnishings offered by the shop are of excellent style and quality and are often sought after by decorators from the Memphis area.

DeSheilds Lighting, Inc.
451 Hwy. 72
901/854-8691

Listed below are the shops located around the Historic Town Square.

Antique Marketplace of Collierville
88 North Main
901/854-8859

For specific information see review in color section.

Center Street Antiques
198 S. Center Street
901/861-3711
Open: Mon.-Sat. 10-5, Sunday & evenings by appointment

Directions: From I-240, take Poplar Avenue exit for Germantown. Continue on Poplar through Germantown to Collierville, take a right (east) on Hwy. 72. At the first traffic light, turn left on Center Street.
Located one block south (across the railroad tracks) of Collierville's Historic Town Square, Center Street Antiques is the newest addition to the town's growing collection of antique shops. Filled with a unique assortment of English, Continental, American, Primitive and Victorian furniture, there's something for everyone. The great selection of architectural pieces, gardenware, vintage lighting, china, antique toys and collectibles is sure to inspire the decorator in you. With each new dealer, the list of fabulous finds continues to grow.

Town Square Antique Mall
118 E. Mulberry St.
901/854-9839

Not Forgotten
94 N. Main
901/854-8859

Sentimental Journey Antiques
118 N. Main St.
901/853-9019

Liberty Tree Antiques
120 N. Main St.
901/854-4364

English Country Antiques
102 E. Mulberry St.
901/853-3170

Remember When Antiques
110 E. Mulberry St.
901/853-5470

White Church Antique Mall
Poplar (entrance to Town Square area)

16 COLUMBIA

Accents and Antiques of Columbia
Northway Shopping Center, Suite 123
119 Nashville Hwy. - Hwy. 31
931/380-8975
Fax: 931/388-5353
Open Mon.-Sat., 10-5; Sun. 1-5

Directions: From I-65: Take exit #46, then turn left onto Hwy. 412. At the end of the highway, take a left onto Hwy. 31. Follow the road until the 2nd light. Accents and Antiques is on the right.
Owner Debbie Harris has been in business three years and has over 7,000 square feet of general antiques and collectibles. She offers the very needed service of lamp repair, so when your lighting treasures burn out, you know where to go.

Sewell's Antiques
217 Bear Creek Pike/Hwy. 412
931/388-3973

Memory Shop Antiques
1564 Bear Creek Pike/Hwy. 412
931/388-4131

High Attic Antiques
216 W. 8th St.
931/381-2819

Uptown Antiques
220 W. 8th St.
931/388-4061

Moore's Antiques & Etc.
910 S. Garden St.
931/388-6926

Suite 14
808 S. High St.
931/380-2077

American Heritage Antq. Mall
Northside Plaza Shopping Center
931/388-5135

17 COOKEVILLE

A-l Clock Shop 7 Antiques
137 E. Broad
931/526-1496

Broadway Antiques
247 W. Broad St.
931/520-1978

Cookeville Antique Mall
1095 Bunker Hill Rd.
931/526-8223

Attic Window
1281 Bunker Hill Rd.
931/528-7273

Cedar Street Antiques
44 S. Cedar Ave.
931/528-9129

Cherry Creek Antiques
5589 Cherry Creek Rd.
931/526-7834

Fiesta Plus
380 Hawkins Crawford Rd.
931/372-8333

City Square Antiques
8 S. Jefferson
931/526-6939

Ailing Antiques
5441 Mt. Herman Rd.
931/526-5104

Favorite Places To Eat

Cracker Barrel Old Country Store
I-40 & Hwy. 136, Exit 287
931/372-2002

18 CORDOVA

Antique Market of Cordova
1740 Germantown Parkway
901/759-0414
Open Mon.-Sat.10-6; Sun., 1-5

Directions: Traveling I-40 just east of Memphis, take the Germantown exit which will be Germantown Parkway. Turn south and stay on Germantown Parkway through two red lights. The market is located at the third red light on the southeast corner, where Dexter Road intersects with Germantown Parkway. Look for the big red ANTIQUES sign. Turn left on Dexter Road and make an immediate right into the Dexter Ridge Shopping Center parking lot. We are located in the corner of the center. You can't miss us. We are only about 1 mile from I-40.
This 8,500-square-foot antique market also houses the offices of Rainy Day Publishing, publishers of *The Antique Atlas*. Within this quality up-scale market you'll find pieces from Victorian to Primitive to Deco. A charming shop to explore, the shop is known for its quality glassware and pristine furnishings. One dealer specializes in old radios and lamps. Garden accessories are a favorite among locals so you are sure to find wonderful pieces

available at all times.

*Note: David and I are always thrilled to meet the fellow antiquers who stop by to shop with us and to say Hello! We are always in the back working on this "atlas" so be sure to tell Danny and Julie to let us know when you come in. Thanks for all your support and we hope you enjoy antiquing as much as we do.

Sign of the Goose
9155 Rocky Cannon
901/756-0726
Open by appointment only

The Sign of the Goose is a "must see" for anyone who likes antiques, old homes, history, or just a good story.

The shop itself is located at the unique, two-story log house where Bill and Sylvia Cochran live. Sylvia actually uses her entire house as an informal showroom - but call first, because this is a by-appointment-only arrangement.

The house/shop began as an 1810 log home in Kentucky. In the 1970s a man had disassembled, tagged, numbered and hauled the logs to Tennessee, where he planned to rebuild it. But he decided not to finish the project, and that's how Sylvia first saw her family's future home: as a skeletal framework and a pile of old logs. She knew she could turn it into a wonderful home, and after much discussion with her family, Sylvia realized she would get her chance when husband Bill gave her a box of Lincoln Logs for their 16th anniversary!

The Cochrans moved the entire home - as it was - to their 20-acre homesite in Cordova near Memphis. The house was already atypical of log homes of its period, with its original 2,000 square feet and full second floor with high ceilings. And it was ideal for raising five children, who not only had a big, tough home, but acres of woods and ponds and outdoor delights to explore and enjoy. After reconstructing it, bringing it up to modern standards, adding a new porch and balcony across the front, and a kitchen addition to the back, the Cochrans had their dream house.

The rough, strikingly colored walls and plank flooring are an ideal and authentic setting for Sylvia's collection of American country furniture. She's been antiquing for 20 years, and has amassed an enormous wealth of pieces, accessories, and knowledge to share with customers.

An interesting note: During the Cochran's building process, they discovered a secret hidey-hole where an early 19th century deed of sale was found. It had been stuffed into a chink in one of the giant timbers. Now it hangs, carefully framed, on one of the log walls. Be sure to look for it as you browse through the country American antiques and architectural pieces.

19 COVINGTON

Main Street Antiques
650 U.S. Hwy. 51 S
901/475-6181

Six Oaks Antiques Inc.
1760 U.S. Hwy. 51 S
901/476-3135

*There is a great auction in Covington every third Saturday night. For information call Brad Brooks at Brooks Auction (901/475-1744) and ask to be put on his mailing list.

20 CROSSVILLE

Stonehaus Winery, Inc.
2444 Genesis Road
Exit 320, I-40
931/484-WINE (9463)
Fax: 931/484-9425
Open Mon.-Sat. 9-6; Sun. 12-5 CST
(Reduced hours during the winter months)

Directions: Stonehaus Winery is located at I-40 Exit 320 (Genesis Road), just across the interstate from Vanity Fair Shopping Mall.

Grapes, vineyards, and award-winning wines are not the things that one generally thinks of when the state of Tennessee is mentioned, but the Stonehaus Winery in Crossville, Tennessee will be producing from 80,000 to 100,000 bottles of wine this year. A wide selection of premium wines are available, including Reds, Whites, Rose and Blushes to suit the most discriminating palates.

The entire wine process is accomplished at Stonehaus, from the crushing and pressing of grapes to the fermentation, aging and bottling.

A gift shop situated in the adjoining building features many fine items from which to choose. Stroll through the shop and sample the homemade fudge. From there you can enter the cheese pantry where over 40 varieties of domestic and imported cheese, homemade bread and gourmet foods are available. From the winery you can visit the Stonehaus Antiques Shop located on the property, featuring eleven rooms of quality antiques such as quilts, glassware, furniture and more.

Antique Village Mall
I-40 Exit 320 Genesis Rd.
931/484-8664

Crossville Collectibles
314 Old Homestead Hwy.
931/456-7641

Cumberland Mt. Gen. Store
6807 South York Hwy.
931/863-3880

Little Rock House Antiques
4528 Hwy. 127 N
931/456-1032

Crossville Antique Mall
Hwy. 27 N
931/456-8768

Finders Keepers Treasures
100 West Avenue South
931/456-5533

Page's Furniture
302 Rockwood Avenue
931/456-0849

Stonehaus Antique Shop
2444 Genesis Road
931/456-5540

Rose of Sharon
2238 Peavine Road
931/484-5221

Helen & Rhoda's
1183 Miller Avenue
931/707-8654

Country Home Antiques
Hwy. 127
931/484-4229

Stonehaus Antiques & Gifts
Stonehaus Center-Genisis Rd.
931/456-5540

Past & Present Company
Hwy. 70 N
931/456-4662

The Great Upper Cumberland
58 West First Street
931/456-6270

Grandma's Attic
371 Hwy. 68
931/456-5699

Favorite Places To Eat

Cracker Barrel Old Country Store
I-40 & Hwy. 127, Exit 317
931/456-9622

21 DICKSON

Dickson can probably best be compared to some type of rubber ball or toy that keeps bouncing back every time after being flattened! The town wasn't actually chartered until 1873, although there were settlers in the immediate area long before then. In 1883, just ten years later, the town charter was revoked over some kind of argument about whiskey, and they didn't get it back until 1899. In the meantime, the town burned down! Then there was another fire in 1893 that destroyed all but three of the downtown buildings. Another fire in 1905 wiped everything out again! That's why there is very little 19th century architecture in the town today. On the other hand, Dickson is almost a perfect personification of mid-century America - the 1950s, with nighttime cruising down the main streets in 50s hot rods and classics, even down to the drive-in theater that's been open since 1950!

They also have an Old Timers Day, held the first Saturday in May since its beginning in 1958! It starts with a parade and goes on to lots of crafts, a flea market, plenty of food and entertainment that includes a liars contest and a seniors talent contest that's wide open to whatever kind of talent the old timers want to show off.

Pepper Patch Antique Mall
2699 Hwy. 46 South
615/740-0904
Open Mon.-Sat. 10-5; Sun. 12-5

Directions: From I-40, take exit #172 and go south on Hwy. 46 for 3/4 of a mile. The shop is on the right.

This upscale shop was a dream realized by its founders, Dana Martin and Yvonne Cummings, a mother-daughter team with over 50 years combined knowledge. With the addition of two capable partners, Tony Reece and Darlene Parker, this shop has grown into a unique and unusual mall with 21 dealers featuring toys, gas pumps, primitives, Continental porcelain, advertising, Americana and much, much more!

Ox-Yoke Antique & Gift
1901 Hwy. 46 S
615/446-6979
Open Mon.-Sat. 10-5 and by appointment

Directions: Take I-40 to exit #172 onto Hwy. 46. The red brick store is about 1 3/4 miles north at the red light.

Mr. and Mrs. Yates have been very busy and inventive over the last 30 years. Their building has housed four very different types of businesses - and they have owned and operated all of them! First they opened a service station in 1967: years later it became a fabric store. Then it was a steak house for the next 13 years, and in 1991, they transformed it into an antique store. Mrs. Yates, with her eye for display, carries a lot of oak, walnut and pine furniture, all kinds of collectibles including glassware, pottery, some 1950s ware, silverplate, lamps, and a nice array of jewelry.

Hamilton Place
202-210 N. Mulberry Street
615/446-5255
Open: Mon.-Sat. 9-5

Within nearly 9,000 square feet of space filled with forty-eight booths, Hamilton Place antique mall is simply packed with wonderfully unique items. Owners Jim and Ruby Reynolds remodeled and air-conditioned the historic old Roger L. Hamilton Super Market, owned by her parents, in developing the mall, which covers half a block.

Hamilton Place is filled with booths offering mostly antiques and collectibles (including "David Winter Cottages," "Hamilton Collection Dolls," and "Boyds Bears") woodcrafts, silk and dried floral items, linens, lace, brass, home accessories, "Tennessee and English" gift baskets, books, ceramics, porcelain dolls, framed prints, custom curtains and accessories and more. There is a bridal registry, layaway and an item locator service, plus all credit cards are accepted. The Reynolds also have a bed and breakfast (See below). If you like to shop, you'll love Hamilton Place—"Refreshingly Different Products at Friendly Prices."

Deerfield Country Inn
170 Woodycrest Close
615/446-3325

Directions: From Nashville, travel west on Interstate 40 approximately 35 miles to Exit 172. Exit right onto Hwy. 46. Go about two miles to the first red light. Turn left onto Pomona Road and drive to its end (about two miles) then turn left onto West Grab Creek Road. Go 1/4 mile to Woodycrest Road (first road on your right). Turn right and go to the end of the road (about 1/2 mile). Turn left onto Woodycrest Close. The inn is on your right amidst a grove of trees. From Memphis, travel east on Interstate 40 to Exit 172 - then refer to the directions above.

The Deerfield Country Inn is a newly constructed, stately, six-columnar Georgian colonial home that blends Old South charm with modern-day amenities.

Fancy yourself as Scarlet or Rhett as you saunter to the spacious front porch and enter a foyer spotlighting a grand circular staircase. Impressive antiques, oriental rugs and chandeliers augment your sense of opulence as you ramble through the main rooms. An open, airy kitchen accented with Quimper pottery and Longaberger baskets engenders a warm, welcoming ambiance.

The large first and second-story verandahs in front and two sizeable decks on the lower level at the rear entice enjoyment of a serene, rustic setting. Savor bountiful breakfasts or succumb to decadent desserts. You can always burn the calories by exploring 57 acres of shady paths and rolling hills, go bicycling or play a game of croquet.

Deerfield Country Inn is conveniently located just minutes from I-40 and downtown Dickson. Stroll along historic Main Street and exchange hearty greetings with the locals. Hunt for treasures at many area antique shops. Tap your toes to a live country music show downtown on Saturday night. Take afternoon tea and nibble on tarts at a charming area tea room. Enjoy a Southern-cooked meal or a fine dinner at one of several restaurants.

Guest Room 1 is The Susie Lucille Room. Named for the late mother of Jim Reynolds, this cozy room overlooks the field of dreams from the upstairs verandah facing southeast - the front of the house. The room is decorated with Laura Ashley wallcovering and accessories. Of special interest is the ornate double-iron bed and a dresser acquired from the estate of former Tennessee Governor Frank Clement. Guest Room 2 is The Pearl Margaret Room. This generous-sized room - named in honor of the late mother of Ruby Hamilton Reynolds - faces northwest and boasts an antique twin-bedded suite and doll collection. Guest Room 3 is The Mulberry Room. Stretch out and unwind on the carved bed in this roomy space. Sit in one of the antique chairs by the large bay window facing northwest and listen to birds singing in the trees. This room is decorated with Eastlake antiques, old-fashioned purses and a compelling collection of books, pictures and memorabilia of the Royal family - acquired during the years your hosts lived in England. This is a great get-away for those who want to experience Southern hospitality and peaceful seclusion.

Your gracious hosts at Deerfield Country Inn are well traveled and have lived abroad periodically. Since they're familiar with many cultures, you'll find them easy to talk to. As owners of an antique mall, they're happy to share their collectibles savvy. And because Jim's an accomplished carpenter and Ruby's an interior decorator, things aren't always the same at the inn!

Nana's Attic
208 W. College St.
615/441-6032

Reeder House Gallery
705 W. College St.
615/446-2603

Haynies Corner
101 S. Main St.
615/446-2993

Main St. Antiques Mall
131 N. Main St.
615/441-3633

Hamilton Place
202 N. Mulberry St.
615/446-5255

Behind Times Antiques
105 W. Railroad St.
615/441-1864

Collectors Corner
206 Sylvis St.
615/446-0552

Favorite Places To Eat

Cracker Barrel Old Country Store
I-40 & Hwy. 46, Exit 172
615/441-3353

22 DYERSBURG

Walton's Antique Mall
2470 Lake Road (Behind McDonalds)
901/287-7086
Open: Mon.-Sat. 10-5, Sunday 1-5

Directions: Exit 13 off I-155. Located behind McDonalds.

This 12,000-square-foot mall of 25 dealers, offers the antiquer an eclectic selection of antique furnishings and accessories including garden and architectural pieces, Victorian, primitive, old toys, pottery, nice glassware, linens and old books, just to name a few. But, if you miss this mall you'll be passing up on the opportunity to purchase some of the best and most unusual early collectibles around. Bill Walton, the owner, has a "nose" for finding the rare; old grape crushers, trunks and boxes, great advertising pieces (much to choose from), early toys, quilts, old coffee grinders, tools, farm tables and more. You never know what he'll find next! (I highly recommend a stop at Walton's Antique Mall)

Dyersburg Antique Gallery
2004 E. Court St.
901/285-0999

Days Gone By
913 Forrest St.
901/285-2704

Little Victorian House
5895 Hwy. 104 E.
901/285-8255

Dyersburg Trade Fair
Hwy. 51 By-Pass N.
901/285-2844

23 ELIZABETHTON

Antique & Curio Corner
441 E. Elk Ave.
423/542-0603

Antiques on Elk
509 E. Elk Ave.
423/542-3355

Duck Crossing Antique Mall
515 E. Elk Ave.
423/542-3055

Sycamore Shoals Antiques
1788 W. Elk Ave.
423/542-5423

Rasnick's Antiques
Hwy. 19 E. Bypass
423/543-2494

Antique Mall
Hwy. 19 E
423/542-6366

Maude's Antiques
Hwy. 19 E Bypass
423/543-1979

24 ERIN

Carousel Antiques & Gifts
106 Arlington St.
931/289-3057

Irish Sales
Hwy. 49 E
931/289-4400

Old Homeplace
Hwy. 13 N
931/289-5336

Shamrock Gallery
13 Spring St.
931/289-4117

25 FAYETTEVILLE

Fayetteville Antique Mall
112 College St. E
931/433-1231

Cobblestone Collectibles
209 College St. E
931/433-4778

Wyatt Antiques
301 Elk Ave. N
931/433-4241

Clark Antique & Collectibles
3011 Huntsville Hwy.
931/438-0377

Magnolia Mall Antqs. & Gifts
121 Main Ave. S
931/433-9987

Beds N' Broomsticks
127 E. Market St.
931/438-2939

Davis Antiques & Automobiles
201 Mulberry Ave.
931/433-1036

26 FRANKLIN

The town of Franklin was officially established in 1799 in Williamson County, which was one of the wealthiest counties in the state by the mid-1800s, and still is today. The town itself, as well as the surrounding area, is full of historic homes and antebellum plantations, most of which have been restored. Two in particular are often mentioned in connection with Franklin, the Carter House and Lotz House.

The Carter House had the great misfortune to be caught exactly in the middle of the battlefield of one of the worst battles of the Civil War - the Battle of Franklin. The Carter family huddled in the cellar of their house while 35,000 soldiers fought in an area roughly two miles long by one mile wide...all centered around the house. According to area historians, there were more generals (12 total) either killed or wounded here than in any other battle in the history of warfare, and the Carter House is the most battle-damaged site in the country, with evidence of over 600 cannonball and bullet holes, 203 in one structure alone! All of this damage was done in the space of a five-hour battle, two-thirds of which was fought in total darkness.

Ironically, just across the street from this amazing relic is the Lotz House. During the same battle, the Lotz family hid in the basement of the Carter house with the Carter family, but the Lotz House has no battle scars! Presumably, Mr. Lotz, who was an extraordinarily skilled woodworker, repaired the damages to his home. The house is now a museum containing the South's largest privately-owned collection of Civil War memorabilia for public display.

Franklin Antique Mall
Winner of Tennessean's Reader's Choice Award and former nominee of the Commerical Historical Preservation Award
251 Second Avenue S
615/790-8593
Open: Mon.-Sat. 10-5, Sunday 1-5

For specific information see review in color section.

Doris & Daughter
108 East Fowlkes St.
DORRISDAU@aol.com

Winchester Antique Mall
113 Bridge Street
615/791-5846

Country Charm Mall
301 Lewisburg Avenue
615/790-8908

J. J. Ashley's
119 South Margin
615/791-0011

Harpeth Antique Mall
529 Alexander Plaza
615/790-7965

Heritage Antique Gallery
527 Alexander Plaza
615/790-8115

Favorite Places To Eat

Cracker Barrel Old Country Store
I-65 & Hwy. 96, Exit 65
615/794-8195

27 GALLATIN

Antiques on Main
117 W. Main St.
615/451-0426

Our House Antiques
1765 Hwy. 109
615/452-0233

Mick's Antiques & Flea Market
803 S. Water Ave.
615/451-0878

Gallatin Antiques
913 S. Water Ave.
615/452-4373

28 GATLINBURG

Earth's Treasures
Carousel
423/436-7625

Morton's Antqs./Baseball Cards
409 Parkway
423/436-5504

29 GERMANTOWN

Anderson Mulkins Antiques
9336 Poplar Avenue (Hwy. 72)
901/754-7909
Open Tue.-Sat. 10-5

Directions: From Memphis: Take I-240 and exit at Germantown. Go 8 miles to 9336 Poplar Avenue (Poplar is also Hwy. 72 and Hwy. 57) and the shop is on the left side, at the corner of Johnson Road and Poplar Avenue. The address is on the mailbox. The shop is between Germantown and Collierville, 4 miles either way.

The Mulkins and family really know antiques. They have been in the retail business (antiques) since 1906 - 90 years!...and the business is still family owned and operated. Shoppers at Anderson's will find furniture and accessories, but they specialize in dining room chairs. Over the past 90 years they have forgotten more than most people ever know! It's worth a stop just to talk to them and hear what they have to say, not only about antiques, but about the life and times they have experienced first-hand - a life that most of us would call "antique" itself!

30 GOODLETTSVILLE

Fanny's Sugar Barrell
112 Old Brick Church Pike
615/859-7319

Main Street Antique Mall
120 N. Main St.
615/851-1704

Antique Corner Mall
128 N. Main St.
615/859-7673

Goodlettsville Antique Mall
213 N. Main St.
615/859-7002

Sweet Memories
400 N. Main
615/851-9922

Attic Treasures
429 N. Main
615/851-1377

31 GREENBRIER

Ox Yoke
2141 Hwy. 41 S.
615/643-0843

Sanders Antqs. & Restoration
2606 Hwy. 41
615/329-1017

Little Bit of Everything
2616 Hwy. 41 S
615/643-8029

32 HARRIMAN

Favorite Places To Eat

Cracker Barrel Old Country Store
I-40 & Hwy. 27, Exit 347
423/882-6636

33 HENDERSONVILLE

Tuttle Bros Antiques
691 W. Main/Hwy. 31 E
615/824-7222

Treasure Hut Antiques
115 Dunn St.
615/824-0930

Hendersonville Antique Mall
339 Rockland Rd.
615/824-5850

Sunflowers Antique Gallery
117 Marseiville Dr.
615/824-2311

Recollections & Yesterday
127 Stadium Dr.
615/822-8601

34 HENNING

A great many people know about Henning, Tennessee because of one man, his book, and the movie. The man of course is Alex Haley, and the book and movie is *Roots*. But there is more to Henning than Alex Haley. It is a town of interesting history and homes, a community intermingled with black and white, and a town that is now striving to preserve its' heritage and become a source for future generations.

Although unknown to a lot of people in the West Tennessee area, Henning is the home of a Choctaw Indian Reservation. Each fall and summer the reservation sponsors an Indian Festival. Thousands of people from across the country flock to this tiny town to participate in the celebration and to learn more about the Choctaw culture. (For information on the Choctaw Indian Festivals call Cubert Bell at 901/738-2951.)

J & A Antiques & Collectibles
236 Graves Street, Hwy. 87 East (1/2 mile off Hwy. 51)
901/738-5367

John and Aliene Richards handle the general spread of collectibles, particularly smalls, glassware and costume jewelry, but they also specialize in one item you don't find often - old marbles! They also know how to make-do in a pinch, as this funny story shows: "We loaded up to do a flea market in Arkansas and went over the evening before," say Aliene. "The van was full to within 12 inches of the ceiling. When we arrived, there were no motels available and we had to set up at daybreak, so we slept on top of the tables in the van. When we got up at daybreak to start setting up, John had lost his glasses somewhere in the van during the night, and couldn't see to begin setting up! After much searching, we finally found his glasses, but we haven't had to sleep on tables since that show, and don't plan to do so again!"

Kitty & Tony Ables
140 N. Main
901/738-2381

For specific information see review in color section.

Scoggins Collectibles
114 S. Main
901/738-5405

Peas-n-Pod
105 Moorer
901/738-2959

35 HERMITAGE

Memory Lane Antique Mall
3208 Lebanon/Hwy. 70
615/889-4257

Smorgasboard
4144 B Lebanon Rd./Hwy. 70
615/883-5789

Spring Valley Antiques
4348 Lebanon Rd./Hwy. 70
615/889-0267

J. S. Crouch Bookseller
4714 Lebanon Rd./Hwy. 70
615/316-0767

Scott's Hollow Antique Mall
Lebanon Rd./Hwy. 70
No Phone

36 HICKMAN

Antique Malls of Tennessee
2 Sykes Road (at Gordonsville Hwy.)
615/683-6066
Fax: 615/683-6067
Call ahead for hours

Directions: Approximately 45 miles east of Nashville on I-40. From I-40 take exit #258 (Carthage - Gordonsville exit). Go south (right) 2 miles to Hickman.

Larry and Penny Bartlett, owners of Antique Malls of Tennessee, opened their store in the fall of 1997. Due to their daughter living in mid-Tennessee, they decided to move from California to Hickman and establish their new antique mall in an early 1900s bank/general store building. After a considerable amount of renovation, the mall was opened. The mall consists of many collectibles of various types, as well as "antique" furniture and artifacts in the more upscaled range. No new items, and reproductions are consistently purged. The second floor of the bank is dedicated to art, from signed limited editions to fine oils, once again, of the vintage type. The art gallery also consists of various unique objects d'art and statuary. They have commissioned a famous artist in Venice, Italy to create an exclusive masterpiece to be on display. This glass artwork is beyond belief. It is worth your time to stop in Hickman to see this and the beautiful surrounding countryside.

37 JACKSON

Highland Place Bed & Breakfast
519 North Highland Avenue
901/427-1472
Fax: 901/422-7994
Open year round, 7 a.m.-10 p.m. (Office hours)

Directions: From I-40 traveling either from Memphis or Nashville, take Exit #82A onto Highland Avenue (also Hwy. 45 South). The inn is just 3.3 miles south of I-40 on Highland Avenue, between Arlington and West King Streets in the North Highland Historical District, five blocks from downtown Jackson.

There's plenty to do and see in and around Jackson, but the layout of this particular B&B suggests you carefully choose your traveling companion - it is a romantic delight and should be especially considered for those intimate little getaways you occasionally indulge in!

Highland Place has four guest rooms, with an arrangement flexible enough to have one's own multiple-room suite. The Louis Room has a sitting area, antique vanity and king size bed, with an authentic claw foot bath tub with solid brass plumbing and hand-held shower. The Butler Suite boasts a queen size cherry bed with feather mattress and a sitting area with working table (great for corporate travelers) and private bath. The Hamilton Suite offers an antique walnut dresser and a custom-built walnut queen size canopy bed, a working fireplace (very nice for romance), and just across your own private hall, a bath with a tub large enough for two. The newest addition (as of yet unnamed) is a suite with skylight, feather mattress on a queen size bed, and a private bath with a waterfall shower for two!

Yarbro's Antique Mall
350 Carriage House Drive
Temporary address: 581 Old Hickory Blvd.
901/664-6600
Open Mon.-Sat., 10-5; Sun. 1-5

Directions: Visible from I-40. Call for directions.

With its recent relocation, this mall promises even more dealers with more selections than every before. They carry a general line of antiques including Victorian furniture and accessories and many flow blue pieces. One dealer specializes in country furniture.

Brooks Shaw's Old Country Store and Casey Jones Village
Casey Jones Village
901/668-1223 or 1-800-748-9588
Fax: 901/664-TOUR
Station Inn reservations 1-800-628-2812
Open Summer 6 a.m.-10 p.m.; Winter 6 a.m.-9 p.m.

Directions: Casey Jones Village is located nearly mid-point between Nashville and Memphis on I-40 and Hwy. 45 Bypass, exit 80A, in Jackson. Look for the original 50-foot caboose sign.

At the Old Country Store and Casey Jones Village, visitors can shop, eat, sleep and get a dose of history all at the same time. An extremely popular tourist stop, the entire place is perfectly suited for little folks and big people alike, especially if they are into trains. At the Old Country Store, visitors can eat in an enormous restaurant/buffet setting, then stroll through 6,000 square feet of gifts, confections, collectibles and souvenirs, then dive into the 1890s ice cream parlor for dessert while gazing at 15,000 Southern antiques on display. If that's not enough, the historic home of Casey Jones is right next door, along with a railroad museum and train store, complete with a Lionel dealer on the premises. You can climb aboard Engine #382, then take a mini train ride and *then* play miniature golf. At this point you should be ready to fall asleep, and the Casey Jones Station Inn is conveniently right there, offering 50 train-themed rooms. You can choose to sleep in a rail car suite or a caboose. Kids of all ages will love it!

Trading Post
116 W. Chester St.
901/424-9511

Yesterdays Antiques
212 N. Liberty St.
901/427-2690

Tara Antiques
205 S. Shannon St.
901/422-3935

I-40 Antique Mall
2150 U.S. Hwy. 70 E
901/423-4448

Favorite Places To Eat

Cracker Barrel Old Country Store
I-40 & N. Highland Ave., Exit 82B
901/664-1028

38 JOHNSON CITY

Granny's Attic
200 N. Commerce St.
423/929-2205

Curiosity Shop
206 E. 8th Ave.
423/928-3322

Antiques & Heirlooms
126 W. Main St.
423/928-8220

American Pastimes Antq. Mkt.
217 E. Main St.
423/928-1611

Antique Village
228 E. Main St.
423/926-6996

Town Square Antiques
234 E. Main St.
423/929-3373

Memory Lane Antqs. & Mall
324 E. Main St.
423/929-3998

Antiques Antiques Antiques
125 W. Market St.
423/928-8697

Youngdale Antiques
214 Mountcastle Dr.
423/282-1164

Favorite Places To Eat

Cracker Barrel Old Country Store
I-181 & Boones Creek Rd., Exit 38
423/282-8113

39 JONESBOROUGH

This is Tennessee's oldest town, chartered in 1779. Its history has been colorful and exciting, and today the town is a perfect window to the past. Among the many things to do and see in Jonesborough are a stop at the Visitor's Center, where you can become acquainted with the town and its history; a visit to the Washington County History Museum; shopping in the numerous antique and specialty stores in the historic districts; and visits to the annual festivals held in July (Historic Jonesborough Days), August (Quilt Fest, with classes and exhibits), November and December (holiday arts and crafts and celebrations), and the big event in Jonesborough - the National Storytelling Festival in October. The National Storytelling Association, based in Jonesborough, has been holding this festival every year since 1973. Visitors can hear tall tales, Jack tales, Grandfather tales, anecdotes, legends, myths and more, while getting a glimpse of the oral tradition that has entertained and informed Americans for more than 200 years!

Mauk's of Jonesborough
101 W. Main St.
423/753-4648

Jonesborough Antique Mart
115 E. Main St.
423/753-8301

Old Town Hall
144 E. Main St.
423/753-2095

Trading Post Antiques
1200 W. Main St.
423/753-3661

Favorite Places To Eat

The Parson's Table
102 Woodrow Avenue
615/753-8002
Open for lunch and dinner week-days.
Sunday buffet 11:30 am-2:00 pm

Directions: From Knoxville, take I-81 to exit #23 (Hwy. 11-E). Traveling South, take 181 to the Jonesborough exit. The restaurant is behind the courthouse off Main Street.

This lovely Gothic structure that was once the First Christian Church in Jonesborough, has been a temperance hall, lecture room, and woodworking shop.

Carefully preserving its history while enhancing its Victorian origin, Chef Jeff Myron and his wife Debra have converted the architectural landmark into a soul-satisfying restaurant. The fare is Continental, or as they say, "refined South, with a little bit of French, and a whole lot of love."

The heavenly selections include crepes, Rack of Lamb Dijoinaise, Roast Duckling A'l'orange, with a choice of sinful desserts such as "Parson's Passion" and "Devilish Chocolate Ecstasy."

40 KINGSPORT

The Antique Mall
9951 Airport Pkwy.
423/323-2990

Smith Sholal's Antiques
315 Beulah Church Dr.
423/239-6280

Antiques I-81
9959 Airport Pkwy.
423/323-0808

Amanda's Antiques
115 Broad St.
423/245-1423

Anchor Antiques
137 Broad St.
423/378-3188

Haggle Shop Antique Mall
147 Broad St.
423/246-8002

Adams Company & Friends
231 Broad St.
423/247-9775

Colonial Antique Mall
245 Broad St.
423/246-5559

Country Square Antiques
635 Fairview Ave.
423/378-4130

Pittypat's Country Interiors
2633 Fort Henry Dr.
423/247-2244

Village Antiques
4993 Hwy. 11 W
423/323-2287

Toy Train Antiques
214 E. Market St.
423/245-8451

Favorite Places To Eat

Cracker Barrel Old Country Store
I-81 & State Rt. 357, Exit 63
423/323-9212

41 KNOXVILLE

Farragut Antique Mall
101 Campbell Station Road
423/671-3630
Open Mon.-Sat., 10-6; Sun., 1-5

Directions: From Knoxville: Traveling on I-40, take exit #373 and travel south 1.5 miles on Campbell Station Road. The mall is on the right, at the corner of Campbell and Kingston Pike.

This mall is located in an interesting spot - it is behind the historic Russell House a famous dairy farm in Tennessee. The actual building that houses the mall is the old creamery for the Russell Dairy Farm. There are ll dealers to "churn up" your excitement and make those dollars slide from your wallets as smooth as butter! (I'm sorry, I couldn't resist!) Farragut's displays some really fine country, Victorian, old garden accessories and lots of glass.

Campbell Station Antiques
620 Campbell Station Road
423/966-4348
Open daily, Mon.-Sat., 10-6; Sun., 1-6

Directions: From I-40 and I-75, take exit #373. Turn south and go 200 yards. The shop is on the left in Station West Center next to Cracker Barrel.

This 35-dealer mall has several specialties to tempt shoppers. In its 10,000 square feet of space you'll find vintage clothing, fine porcelains, flow blue and a large selection of rare books. Dealers in the mall specialize in period furniture and one dealer travels to Europe to buy. Additionally, they have a great mix that covers glassware, furnishings and decorative accessories for the discriminating shopper.

Homespun Craft & Antique Mall
Village Green Shopping Center
11523 Kingston Pike
423/671-3444
Fax: 423/671-0301
Open: Mon.-Fri. 10-7, Sat. 10-5, Sun., 1-5

Directions: Traveling I-40/I-75: Take exit #373 (Farragut/Campbell Station Road) south to Kingston Pike. Turn West on Kingston Pike. The Village Green Shopping Center is on the right and they are the very most center store.

Over 180 dealers are housed in this 9000 square feet facility. Find Americana, primitives, collectibles, Texaco memorabilia, wood work, ceramics, fantastic florals, jewelry, antiques, collectible bears, Howards wood products, hand crafted and one of a kind merchandise.

Antiques Plus
4500 Walker Boulevard
423/687-6536
Open Tue.- Sat. 10-5; Sun. 1-5: Closed Monday

Directions: From I-40 or I-75 take I-640 to exit #6 (Hwy. 441), turn left, the mall is 200 yards on the left - behind Buddy's Bar B Q.

Antiques Plus lives up to its name - the selection of merchandise offered is on the plus side. The 12,000 square foot upscale mall with 60+ dealers specializes in solid cherry furniture, primitives, decorative accessories, jewelry, and a wide variety of collectibles, including flow blue, cut glass, Fiesta, Jewel Tea, pocket watches, dolls, depression glass, and a good mix of other unique items.

B E L Antiques
5520 Brier Cliff Rd.
423/688-2664

Time Trader
720 Broadway
423/521-9660

Broadway Bargain Barn
1305 N. Broadway St.
423/524-5221

Attic Antiques on Broadway
1313 N. Broadway St.
423/524-2514

Marty's Antiques & Cllbls.
1313 N. Broadway St.
423/522-6466

Key Antiques
133 S. Central St.
423/546-2739

South Fork Furniture
712 N. Central St.
423/525-0513

Chances Antiques
1509 N. Central St.
423/522-0311

French Market Shops
4900 Chambliss Ave.
423/558-6065

South Knox Collectibles Mall
3615 Chapman Hwy.
423/577-6252

The Bottom Antqs. & Cllbls.
3701 Chapman Hwy.
423/579-4202

Colonial Antique Mall
4939 Chapman Hwy.
423/573-6660

Gateway Antiques
5925 Chapman Hwy.
423/573-2663

Crossroads Antiques
7100 Commercial Park Dr.
423/922-9595

Chapman Hwy. Antique Mall
7624 Chapman Hwy.
423/573-7022

Blair House Antiques
210 Forest Park Blvd.
423/584-8119

Fever
133 S. Gay St.
423/525-4771

Jackson Ave. Antq. Market
111 E. Jackson Ave.
423/521-6704

Sullivan Street Market
118 E. Jackson Ave.
423/522-2231

Carpenter Clock /Watch Repair
4612 Kingston Pike
423/584-2570

Kingston Pike Antique Mall
4612 Kingston Pike
423/588-2889

Antiques and Accents
5002 Kingston Pike
423/584-5918

Dominick's Antique Galleries
5119 Kingston Pike
423/584-1513

Garrison Collection
5130 Kingston Pike
423/558-0906

Antiques Inc.
5121 Kingston Pike
423/588-5063

Sequoyah Antiques Exchange
5305 Kingston Pike
423/588-9490

West End Antique Market
5613 Kingston Pike
423/588-1388

Calloway's Lamps & Gifts
5714 Kingston Pike
423/588-0684

Incurable Collector
5805 Kingston Pike
423/584-4371

Bearden Antique Mall
310 Mohican St.
423/584-1521

Northern Friends
1507 9th Ave.
423/546-5400

Appalachain Antiques
11312 Station West Dr.
423/675-5690

Wildwood Gallery & Frames
2924 Sutherland Ave.
423/546-3811

A True North Inc.
611 Worcester Rd.
423/675-7772

Favorite Places To Eat

Cracker Barrel Old Country Store
I-75 & Merchants Rd., Exit 108
423/688-7396

Cracker Barrel Old Country Store
I-40/I-75 & Cedar Bluff Rd., Exit 378
423/690-6060

Cracker Barrel Old Country Store
I-40 & Strawberry Plains Pkwy., Exit 398
423/522-8232

Cracker Barrel Old Country Store
Farragut (West Knoxville)
I-75/I-40 & Campbell Station Road, Exit 373
423/675-1446

42 KODAK

Dumplin Valley Antiques & Collectibles
340 W. Dumplin Valley Road
423/932-7713
Open: Fri. 10-6, Sat. & Sun. 9-6

Directions: Traveling I-40, exit 407.Turn south on Hwy. 66 toward Gatlinburg. Turn right on the first road which is Dumplin Valley Rd.. Continue 1 mile. Shop is on the right.

For specific information see review this section.

43 LAKE CITY

Favorite Places To Eat

Cracker Barrel Old Country Store
I-75 & Hwy. 25 West, Exit 129
423/426-6429

44 LAWRENCEBURG

Lawrenceburg Antq. & Auction
266 N. Military Ave.
931/762-6695

Carriage House II
34 & 38 Public Square
931/766-0428

Flea Market Shop
46 Public Square
931/762-6963

Gibbs Antqs. & Cllbls.
2310 Pulaski Hwy.
931/762-1441

Clover Leaf Antiques
4449 Waynesboro Hwy./ Hwy. 64
931/762-5658

45 LEBANON

Directions: Take I-40 to the Lebanon exit #238, go north on Hwy. 231 to find the town square area and south to find everything else.

The Lebanon area has many shops to offer
For specific information see review this section.

Favorite Places To Eat

Cracker Barrel Old Country Store
I-40 & Hwy. 231, Exit 238
615/444-4995

46 LENOIR CITY

Buttermilk Road Antiques
144 Antique Lane
423/376-5912

Allen's Antiques
103 E. Broadway
423/986-2724

John Farmer Sales
105 W. Broadway
423/986-5144

Victoria's Antique Mall
1200 W. Broadway
423/988-7957

Valley Antiques
11020 Hotchkiss Valley Rd.
423/986-6636

Twin Lakes Antiques
11827 Hwy. 321 S
423/986-8082

"Good" win's Antiques
9900 White Wind Rd./Hwy. 321
423/986-3396

47 LIVINGSTON

A Different Drummer
106 E. Broad St.
No Phone # Available

Zpast Antique Warehouse
313 S. Church St.
931/823-8888

Court Square Emporium
108 N. Court Square
931/823-6741

Antique Market
116 N. Court Square
931/823-4943

Livingston Trade Center
203 S. Goodposture St.
931/823-2898

Helen's Now and Then
521 E. Main St.
931/823-1626

48 LOUDON

Shirley's Charm Shop
407 Grove St.
No Phone

Sisters
Mulberry St.
423/458-8027

Brick Box
400 Mulberry St.
423/458-0850

General Store
411 Mulberry St.
423/458-6433

Carroll's Bargain Box
854 Mulberry St.
423/458-6320

Sweet Memories Antique Mall
930 Mulberry St., Ste 104
423/458-2331

Warehouse Antqs. & Cllbls.
1034 Mulberry St.
423/458-3412

Judy's Antiques
100 Steekee Creek Rd.
423/458-4211

49 LYLES

Old Wrigley Commissary Mall
7775 Wrigley Road
615/740-0904

50 MADISONVILLE

Ye Ole Towne Antqs. & Cllbls.
203 Tellico Street
423/442-5509

51 MANCHESTER

Top of the Hill Antiques
5751 Cathey Ridge Rd.
931/728-2610

Lester's Antiques
Gowen Rd.
931/728-2669

Antiques-A-Rama
626 Hillsboro Blvd.
931/723-4209

North Side Clocks
2032 MacArthur/Hwy. 55
931/728-4307

Somewhere In Time
324 Ragsdale Rd.
931/728-8987

Favorite Places To Eat

Cracker Barrel Old Country Store
I-24 & Paradise St., Exit 110
931/723-1358

52 MARYVILLE

Boones Barn Antqs. & Cllbls.
2408 N.W. Lamar Alexander
423/681-0877

Back In Time Antiques
504 Odell
423/983-7055

53 MCMINNVILLE

This is one of the strangest and most fun places to visit that you're likely to run across! McMinnville is the "Nursery Capital of the World," has the second largest cavern system in the country, has a bed and breakfast in a fabulous old Victorian mansion, and has one of the few remaining cheese factories still in the state. And on top of all this, it has antiques. Is this a combination or what!

There really are between 400 and 500 nursery growers (trees, plants, that kind of nursery) in the area. This is evidently the only place in the world that has such a perfect combination of climate and soil. This industry began in the 1800s when the area was widely known for its apples and especially for the apple brandy that was produced. The apple tree business grew and evolved into this enormous industry that is now world famous.

Cumberland Caverns are open to the public May through October. They were discovered in 1810 and are now a national landmark. After you've spelunked your way through the caves, you can go to the Tennessee Valley Cheese Company, in business since 1953. Their specialty is raw milk cheddar, which visitors can watch being made through windows in the shop. Sampling is encouraged!

Historic Falcon Manor
"Winner of the 1997 Great American Home Award for outstanding home restoration by the *National Trust For Historic Preservation*"
2645 Faulkner Springs Road
931/668-4444
Website: http://FalconManor.com
E-Mail: FalconManor@FalconManor.com

Directions: From I-24: Take Manchester Exit 111 east to McMinnville. DO NOT go into the business district. Keep going straight on Hwy. 70 S. Bypass. At the fifth traffic light, turn left onto Faulkner Springs Road. The mansion is at the end of the road, 1.3 miles from the

Bypass. From I-40: Take exit 273 S. And go straight through Smithville. In McMinnville, turn left onto Hwy. 70 S. Bypass, then left at the second light onto Faulkner Springs Road.

In the year 1896, wealthy entrepreneur Clay Faulkner constructed the solid brick mansion now known as Falcon Manor. He promised to build his wife "the finest home in the county" if she would move next to the mill outside McMinnville where he made Gorilla Jeans—"so strong even a gorilla couldn't tear them apart."

But the building looked more like the victim of a terrorist bombing than the finest house in the county when McGlothin bought it at auction in 1989.

Faulkner's mansion had been converted into a hospital and nursing home in the middle part of this century. In 1968, the doctor closed the medical facility and later stripped out much of the woodwork in an unsuccessful attempt to tear down the building. It was abandoned for 15 years, then a new owner began five years of restoration. After re-doing several rooms upstairs and partially demolishing hospital additions, he was unable to continue the rehabilitation.

"We had been restoring old houses for about 13 years, but the first time I showed my wife that half-dismantled disaster, she took one look at it and said, 'You put a mortgage on MY house for THIS?'" McGlothin recalled.

The couple spent 4 1/2 years completing the restoration, doing about 95 percent of the work themselves. With both the mansion's decor and their extensive collection of Victorian antiques, the McGlothins have authentically recreate Clay Faulkner's 1890s.

Today, according to local octogenarians who remember the mansion in its heyday, Falcon Manor is even more beautiful than it was in Faulkner's time.

Historic Falcon Manor took first prize in the bed and breakfast category of the eighth annual Great American Home Awards, one of four classes in which prizes were given. The National Trust added the B&B category just last year, paying tribute to "a type of establishment that has not only supported countless building rescues but also introduced their many visitors to the pleasures of living, if only temporarily, in old houses."

"I had no intention of either buying a house or opening a business when I went to that auction eight years ago," McGlothin admitted. "I just offered $50 more than the opening bid, and the auctioneer said, 'Going once, going twice, sold to that sucker over there.'"

"Having bought what looked like a big white elephant, George decided we'd would just work on restoring it as we had time and then retire there," remembers McGlothin's wife Charlien, who says she's still amazed anyone would think of 'retiring' to a 10,000-square-foot house with a three-acre lawn!

"It didn't take us long, though, to realize that this place has a friendly elegance and warmth that draws people to it. Even when we were just beginning the restoration, folks were stopping to ask for tours. We concluded this would always be a public place, whatever our intentions, so we made it official by opening Historic Falcon Manor as a bed and breakfast in 1993."

In addition to giving B&B guests an opportunity to "relive the peaceful romance of the 1890s," the mansion is open for tours each day at 1 p.m. George's rapid-fire, hour-long narration is chock full of fascinating anecdotes about the building and the people whose lives it touched, both as a private home and beloved country hospital. Church, civic and senior groups frequently combine tours with luncheons on the veranda or in the mansion. School groups round out their "trip to the 1890s" by playing old fashioned games and picnicking on the grounds.

"This is a favorite getaway for honeymooners, couples celebrating birthdays and anniversaries, and folks who just want to escape the stress of modern life," George observed. "History buffs, antique collectors, and people who've been involved in home restoration projects themselves take a special delight in experiencing the place. Of course, with the Victorian theme being so popular, we play host to lots of weddings as well."

In the three years since they opened Falcon Manor as a bed and breakfast inn, the McGlothins have hosted guests from down the road and around the world, as far away as Japan and Australia.

Six spacious guest rooms boast rich colors and museum-quality antiques. A sweeping staircase beckons guests to explore the mansion, while the 100-foot-long, wrap-around "gingerbread veranda" invites them to rock in the shade of century-old trees and sip Falcon Manor's signature pink lemonade. For more energetic travelers, McMinnville's location halfway between Nashville and Chattanooga makes it an ideal base for a Tennessee vacation. Cumberland Caverns (Tennessee's largest cave) and Fall Creek Falls and Rock Island State Parks are nearby.

Last year, the McGlothings opened a Victorian Gift Shop in the original smokehouse. It continues the 1890s theme by offering a unique variety of merchandise typical of the era to both guests and local shoppers.

The mansion was listed on the National Register of Historic Places in 1992, and it was designated as a historic site on Tennessee's Heritage Trail in 1996.

McMinnville Antique Mall, Inc.
2419 Smithville Hwy.
931/668-4735
Open Mon.-Sat. 9-5, Sun. 1-5

Directions: Take exit 111 (Manchester) off I-24, Hwy. 55, or take Silver Point exit off of I-40, Hwy. 56. The shop is one mile past McDonald's on Hwy. 56 North off of Hwy. 70 South.

Pay close attention, because this gets confusing. Barbara Oliver owns the mall, and Susan is Barbara's daughter and Charlotte is Barbara's daughter-in-law. Susan went to work at this mall, and she and Charlotte decided they wanted to own it. So they asked Barbara to buy it so they could run it. Barbara agreed, bought the mall, Susan and Charlotte manage it, and Barbara has her own shop elsewhere. Susan and Charlotte have 28 dealers in the McMinnville Antique Mall, offering a variety of furniture, Depression and other glassware, as well as pottery and a multitude of other items. It's not confusing if you're just going there to shop.

Antiques on High
301 S. High St.
931/473-0922

Main Street Antiques
205 E. Main St.
931/473-3141

B & P Lamp Supply
843 Old Morrison Hwy. 55
931/473-3016

54 MEMPHIS

Satterfield's Home Accessories
2847 Poplar Avenue, Suite 102
901/324-7312

Directions: From I-40: Take I-40 to Sam Cooper Blvd. and turn left on Tillman. Take a right on Poplar Avenue, then a left on Humes. From I-240: Exit at Poplar Avenue and then head toward downtown, West.

Satterfield's is a distinctive decorator shop filled with treasures from around the world. Some of its wares include Majolica, Spelter, porcelain and crystal. They also have a large selection of oil paintings, mirrors and bronzes.

Pinch Antique Mall
430 N. Front St.
901/525-0929

Cottage Antiques & Gifts
2330 S. Germantown Rd.
901/754-5975

Antique Mall of Memphis
3397 Lamar Ave.
901/362-7788

Crump-Padgett Antique Gallery
645 Marshall Ave.
901/522-1155

Springers Antiques
5050 Park Ave.
901/681-0025

Cottage House Mall
4701 Summer Ave.
901/761-5588

Broken Spoke Collectiques
6445 Summer Ave.
901/377-7974

Savannahs' Fine Antiques
2847 Poplar Ave., Ste. 104
901/452-7799

Chip N' Dale's
3475 Summer Avenue
901/452-8366

Chip N' Dale's
3457 Summer Avenue
901/452-5620

PALLADIO Antq. & Int. Mktpl.
2169 Central Avenue
901/276-3808

Interesting Side Trips

Ballet Memphis at the Orpheum
For Schedule Call: 901/763-0139

Founded as Youth Concert Ballet in 1975 by Artistic Director Dorothy Gunther Pugh, the company became Memphis Concert Ballet in 1985 and announced its new name, Ballet Memphis, in 1996. Now completing its tenth season as a professional company, Ballet Memphis has grown to be the largest, most successful ballet company the city has ever had. It now employs 21 full-time professional dancers on 40-week contracts and attracts a growing number of acclaimed guest choreographers and production designers each season.

Ballet Memphis presents a season of four major productions at Memphis' historic Orpheum Theatre, and also participates in several local performing arts festivals and series. In addition, the company has an extensive educational outreach program that reaches over 29,000 school children each year, and a regional touring program with performances in communities throughout Tennessee, Mississippi, and Arkansas and extending as far as Montgomery, Alabama this season.

Favorite Places To Eat

Cracker Barrel Old Country Store
I-40 & Sycamore View Rd., Exit 12
901/382-5465

55 MORRISTOWN

A-Z Repeat N More
5968 W. Andrew Johnson Hwy.
423/581-2623

Yesterday-Antiques & Uniques
128 E. Morris Blvd.
423/586-9273

Dianne's Place Antiques
1040 Buffalo Trail
423/318-0700

Johnny's Antiques
415 E. Converse Ave.
423/587-4750

Bacon's Antiques & Cllbls.
413 N. Cumberland St.
423/581-7420

Radio Center Antiques
1225 S. Cumberland St.
423/586-4337

Farm House Antiques
148 W. Main St.
423/581-1527

Olde Towne Antique Mall
181 W. Main St.
423/581-6423

56 MT. JULIET

Favorite Places To Eat

Cracker Barrel Old Country Store
I-40 & Mt. Juliet Rd., Exit 226
615/754-8300

57 MURFREESBORO

Located in the "Heart of Tennessee", Murfreesboro's location is the geographical center of the State. Home to Middle Tennessee State University and the Stones River National Battlefield. The location of the Nissan USA Motor Manufacturing plant and its close proximity to Nashville has made Rutherford County one of the fastest growing in the State.

Antique Centers I & II
2213-2219 S. Church Street
615/896-5188 (I) and 615/890-4252 (II)
Open daily, Mon.-Sat. 9-5; Sun. 10-5

Directions: From I-24 (25 miles southeast of Nashville) take exit 81-B at U.S. 231 Murfreesboro. Turn onto the access road in front of Burger King. The Centers are next to Cracker Barrel.

The Antique Center has been at the same location since its beginning in 1973. The 30,000 square foot building was divided into two shops at that time and has continued as such, therefore, giving it the name "I & II". Antique Center I has 40 dealers, three of whom have been with the center since 1973. Antique Center II has 30 dealers. Both shops carry a wide selection of furniture to meet the needs of both decorator and first-time buyers. Several dealers specialize in depression glass, elegant glassware such as Fostoria, Cambridge, Tiffin, Heisey, Carnival and Art Glass. Showcases highlight pottery such as Roseville, Hull, Weller, Watt, sterling silver, holiday collectibles, black memorabilia, toys and dolls. Antique Center II specializes in chandeliers. The chandeliers have been refurbished and are ready to go into the home. They range in size from 18" to 6 ft., and from one bulb to 12 or more as well as gas light fixtures. Delivery and shipping is available.

Chick's Antique Shop
516 S. Church St.
615/893-2459

Antiques Unlimited
2303 S. Church St.
615/895-3183

Keepsakes Antiques
2349 S. Church St.
615/890-4125

Ed's Antiques
7497 Hwy. 231
615/893-6719

Yesteryear Civil War Relics
3511 Old Nashville Hwy.
615/893-3470

Magnolias
229 River Rock Blvd.
615/848-2905

Favorite Places To Eat

Cracker Barrel Old Country Store
I-24 & Hwy. 231 South, Exit 81B
615/890-0789

Cracker Barrel Old Country Store
I-24 & Hwy. 96, Exit 78B
615/893-4980

58 NASHVILLE

Antique Merchants Mall
2015 8th Avenue South
615/292-7811
Open daily, Mon.-Sat., 10-5; Sun. 1-5

Directions: The Antique Merchants Mall is located in the heart of Nashville's "Antique District." It is five minutes south of downtown Nashville. Traveling from Memphis: follow I-40 to I-65 south, then take exit 81 (Wedgewood). Take a right and go to the traffic light and take a left at 8th Avenue South. The mall is the third business on the right. From the Opryland/Airport area, take I-40 West to I-440 West to I-65 North toward Nashville, exit 81 (Wedgewood). Take a left at the exit and go to the traffic light, which is at 8th Avenue South. At 8th Avenue South take a left, and the mall is the third business on the right.

For 20 years The Antique Merchants Mall has been Nashville's premier source for antiques and collectibles. It has been in business since 1977, making it one of the oldest antique malls in the Middle Tennessee area. It has over 40 dealers in about 6,000 square feet of space, with some dealers specializing in American, French, and English furniture. Shoppers will also find porcelains, china and crystal, as well as booths filled with pottery, silver, furniture, paintings, Depression glass, and one dealer with over 12,000 out-of-print, rare and collectible books.

Belle Meade Interiors Market
5133 Harding Road
Belle Meade Galleria
615/356-7861
Open 10-5:30, Mon.-Sat.

Directions: Belle Meade Interior Market is located in the heart of Belle Meade on Harding Road between Belle Meade Mansion and Cheekwood.

Belle Meade Interiors Market is a gallery of shops filled with American, English, French and other European fine antiques and objects d'art. Many of Nashville's premier designers are a part of Belle Meade Interiors Market and many of Nashville's talented local artists display their works there. Visitors will find a wealth of unique accessories and furnishings for the home. Belle Meade Interiors Market acts as direct importers of many one-of-a-kind pieces, wrought iron, garden and architectural elements.

Oriental Shop
2121 Bandywood Dr.
615/297-0945

The Gallery of Belle Meade
Belle Meade Shopping Cntr
615/298-5825

Antique & Flea Gallery
4606 Charlotte Pike
615/385-1055

Crystal Dragon Antqs. & Cllbls.
4900 Charlotte Pike
615/383-2189

Antiques & Things
6207 Charlotte Pike
615/356-4470

Forsyth's Antiques
2120 Crestmoor Rd.
615/298-5107

Curiosity Shop
996 Davidson Dr.
615/352-3840

White Way Antique Mall
Edgehill & Villa Place
615/327-1098

Downtown Antique Mall
612 8th Ave. S.
615/256-6616

Pia's Antique Gallery
1800 8th Ave. S
615/256-3890

Art-Deco Shoppe & Antq. Mall
2110 8th Ave. S
615/386-9373

Cane Ery Antique Mall
2112 8th Ave. S
615/269-4780

American Classical II Antqs.
2116 8th Ave. S
615/297-5514

Elder's Book Store
2115 Elliston Place
615/327-1867

Van-Garde Alt. Clothing
2204 Elliston Place
615/321-5326

Made in France Inc.
3001 W. End Ave.
615/329-9300

Ted Leland Inc.
3301 W. End Ave.
615/383-2421

Germantown Antiques
1205 4th Ave. N
615/242-7555

Temptation Gallery
2301 Franklin Rd.
615/297-7412

Courtyard Gate Antiques
2504 Franklin Rd.
615/383-0530

Little Antique Shop
6017 Hwy. 100
615/352-5190

Tony Brown Antiques
6027 Hwy. 100
615/356-7772

Marymont Plant. Antq. Shop
6035 Hwy. 100
615/352-4902

Evelyn Anderson Galleries
6043 Hwy. 100
615/352-6770

Streater Spencer
6045 Hwy. 100
615/356-1992

Spaulding Antiques
6518 Hwy. 100
615/352-1272

Calvert Antiques
6518 Hwy. 100
615/353-2879

Ro's Oriental Rugs Inc.
6602 Hwy. 100
615/352-9055

Cinnamon Hill Antqs. & Ints.
6608 Hwy. 100
615/352-6608

Pembroke Antiques
6610 Hwy. 100
615/353-0889

Polk Place Antiques
6614 Hwy. 100
615/353-1324

Harpeth Gallery
4102 Hillsboro Rd.
615/297-4300

Green Hills Antique Mall
4108 Hillsboro Rd.
615/383-4999

Antiques of Nashville
2921 Nolensville Rd.
615/831-0720

Red Wagon Antiques
6234 Nolensville Rd.
615/832-6005

Mill Creek Antiques
6367 Nolensville Rd.
615/941-1617

Cinemonde
138 2nd Ave. N
615/742-3048

A Sofa Shop
120 3rd Ave. S
615/259-0140

Tennessee Antique Mall
654 Wedgewood Ave.
615/259-4077

Wedgewood Station Antq. Mall
657 Wedgewood Ave.
615/259-0939

Favorite Places To Eat

Cracker Barrel Old Country Store
Briley Pkwy. & McGavock Pike, Exit 12B
615/883-5440

Cracker Barrel Old Country Store
I-24 & Bell Rd., Exit 59
615/731-4014

Cracker Barrel Old Country Store
I-40 & Stewarts Ferry Pike, Exit 219
615/889-4325

Cracker Barrel Old Country Store
I-65 & Harding Place, Exit 78
615/331-6733

Cracker Barrel Old Country Store
I-65 & Long Hollow Pike, Exit 97
615/859-4383

Cracker Barrel Old Country Store
I-40 & Charlotte Pike, Exit 201
615/356-5229

59 NEWPORT

Favorite Places To Eat

Cracker Barrel Old Country Store
I-40 & Hwy.. 32, Exit 435
423/623-0676

60 PARIS

Old Depot Antique Mall
203 N. Fentress St.
901/642-0222

Market Street Antique Mall
414 N. Market St.
901/642-6996

Grapevine Mall
114 W. Washington St.
901/642-7850

61 PIGEON FORGE

Favorite Places To Eat

Cracker Barrel Old Country Store
Hwy. 441
423/428-4613

62 PULASKI

Bunker Hill Antiques
145 Bunker Hill/Bryson Rd.
931/732-4500

Weeds & Seeds & Antiques
2085 Columbia Hwy./Hwy. 31
931/363-4633

Harmony Farms Antiques
211 N. 1st St.
931/424-5937

Bee-Line This & That
705 N. 1st St.
931/424-5120

Mama's Cedar Chest
Hwy. 64
No Phone Available

Kevin Walker Antiques
110 N. 2nd St.
931/424-1825

63 RIPLEY

Vandergriff's Antique Mall
567 Hwy. 51 S
901/635-3576

64 SELMER

Kennedy's Antique World
160 W. Court Ave.
901/645-6357

King's Antiques
Hwy. 45 S
901/645-5581

65 SEVIERVILLE

Volunteer Showcase Mall
1436 Winfield Dunn Parkway, Suite 2
423/429-7666
Fax: 423/428-5221
Open daily 9-6, extended summer hours

Directions: Off I-40, take exit #407 (Gatlinburg/Sevierville/Hwy. 66). Go south 5 miles and Volunteer Showcase Mall is located on the right side of Hwy. 66 in Riverside Center, next door to Riverside Antique and Collectors Mall.

Volunteer Mall, right next door to Riverside Antiques and Collectors Mall, is open the same hours, so you get two-for-one when you visit these folks. Volunteer Mall boasts 85 showcases filled with items such as the largest selection of Barbie Dolls in the area, children's dishes (including Akro Agate, Moderntone, Laurel, Doric and Pansy), carnival glass, cut glass, Nippon, fine china, graniteware, collectible toys, sterling silver, and primitive knives and weapons.

Riverside Antique and Collectors Mall
1442 Winfield Dunn Parkway (Hwy. 66)
423/429-0100
Fax: 423/428-5221
Open daily 9-6, with extended summer hours

Directions: From I-40, take exit 407 (Gatlinburg, Sevierville, Hwy. 66). Go south five miles and the mall is located on the right side of the highway. Look for the huge light gray building with a dark red roof.

I once spent four hours in this mall looking for nothing but blue and white dishes. The selection was great. One dealer had an entire wall filled with every imaginable pattern and maker. The great thing about this mall is its diverse selection. While I was looking for dishes, David was pre-occupied with the "manly things." This mall has a lot to offer for the man in your life; matchbox cars, fishing equipment, old tool boxes, sports memorabilia, Indian Relics and collectible knives.

Riverside Antique Mall encompasses 35,000 square feet so, I could burn up a lot of paper mentioning the usual hodge podge of items most malls of this size offer. Instead I think I'll tell you about some of the unusual things you'll find here. For starters, they stock over 400 reference book titles, including The Antique Atlas, (so if you've borrowed the one you're reading, stop by and get your own). They have a huge handmade basket section, row after row of showcases housing many rare items and a nice country candy counter with all sorts of varieties of candies and dried fruits (recommended for snacking on down the road). The mall is decorated with hundreds of advertising signs which really sets the mood for shopping the minute you walk in the door. And, since I've mentioned advertising signs, I probably should tell you they have much to offer in that section as well.

Memory Lane Antique Mall
1838 Winfield Dunn Parkway
423/428-0536
Open daily, 9-5:30, Mar.-Oct.; 9-5, Nov.-Feb.

Directions: From I-40, take exit 407. The mall is 4.5 miles off I-40 on the right off 66 or Winfield Dunn Parkway.

The outside of this place is deceiving. It looks much smaller than it really is and in fact even though it's larger when you get inside I still can't figure out how that much glassware could fit into that size space. (That's almost a tongue twister.) Memory Lane's unusually large glass selection consists of Tiffany, Daum, Loetz, French Cameo, along with Austria and German pieces. If you are looking to add to your depression glass collection you'll probably find it here. The various dealers who display in the shop carry a huge offering of such pieces. The furniture, though limited, is in excellent condition.

Wagon Wheel Antiques
131 Bruce St.
423/429-4007

Family Antiques
2093 Chapman Hwy.
423/428-6669

Antiques of Chapman Hwy.
2121 Chapman Hwy.
423/428-3609

Wears Valley Antique Gallery
3234 Wears Valley Rd.
423/453-5294

Tudor House Antqs. & Cllbls.
1417 Winfield Dunn Pkwy.
423/428-4400

Heartland Antqs. & Cllbls.
1441 Winfield Dunn Pkwy.
423/429-1791

Olden Days Antqs. & Cllbls.
1846 Winfield Dunn Pkwy.
423/453-7318

Action Antique Mall
2189 Winfield Dunn Pkwy.
423/453-0052

66 SHELBYVILLE

Directions: Take I-24 to the Beech Grove Road/ Shelbyville Exit #97, go west on Hwy. 64, then turn right at Hwy. 41-A/Madison Street. Hwy. 231, which intersects with Hwy. 41-A, leads to the town square.

Shelbyville is known for three things: one well-known, two almost unheard of. The first thing is its international designation as the "Walking Horse Capital of the World." The second thing is its almost unknown title of Pencil City, because the town is the center of the American pencil-making industry! The third thing is that the Shelbyville town square, laid out in 1809, was used as a prototype for town squares all over the South and Midwest.

Synonymous with Shelbyville, in most people's minds, is "The Celebration," the largest and most renowned walking horse show in the world. The show is held each year in late summer for the 10 days ending on the Saturday night before Labor Day.

Other area attractions that will be familiar to visitors are the towns of Wartrace and Bell Buckle, the Jack Daniel and George Dickel Distilleries, and perhaps unknown but worth a stop, the family-owned and operated Tri-Star Vineyards and Winery just north of Shelbyville.

For information on antiquing and for wonderful places to stay in Shelbyville, see review in this section.

67 SIGNAL MOUNTAIN

Antique Stations
1906 Taft Hwy.
423/886-7291

Aunt Polly's Parlor
3500 Taft Hwy.
423/886-4705

Log Cabin Herbs & Antiqs.
4111 Taft Hwy.
423/886-2663

Woody's Goodies
4702 Taft Hwy.
423/886-4095

68 SMITHVILLE

Fuston's Antiques

123 West Market Street
615/597-5232
Open Mon.-Sat. 9-5

Directions: Traveling I-40 east from Nashville or west from Knoxville, take exit #273 and travel south on Hwy. 56 approximately 12 miles to the first red light. At the light turn right and go two blocks to the courthouse square. Go halfway around the courthouse and turn right onto Main Street. Go to the red light and turn left onto College Street. Go one block. The shop is located on the corner of Walnut Street and South College Street.

Fuston's is a breath-taking, awe-inspiring, ocular odyssey of 25 years of accumulation. The store holds the most amazing collection of antique and collectible glassware, antique clocks and music boxes, china and lamps - both oil and electric. But the "shop" is in reality a total of five buildings all crammed with loads of furniture and everything else. Mr. Fuston has over 25,000 square feet of merchandise to choose from. Two of the buildings were, until fairly recently, the 1930s era Fuston's Five and Dime (his since the 1950s). An amazing place and an owner to match - don't miss it!

Southern Things Antiques
464 W. Broad St.
615/597-2540

69 SPARTA

Country Treasures
447 W. Brockman Way
931/836-3572

F & J's Used Merchandise
12 W. Brockman Way
931/836-3299

Liberty Square Antiques
1 Maple St.
931/836-3997

Johnny's Antqs. & Cllbls.
Old Stage Rd.
931/935-8397

Jongee's Antiques & Gifts
137 S. Young St.
931/836-2822

70 SWEETWATER

Favorite Places To Eat

Cracker Barrel Old Country Store
I-75 & Hwy. 68, Exit 60
423/337-3722

71 TALBOTT

Alpha Antique Mall
6205 W. Andrew Johnson Hwy.
423/581-2371

72 TRENTON

Carol's Antique Mall
148 Davy Crockett
901/855-0783

Virginia's Antiques
209 W. Eaton St.
901/855-0261

Bill Hamilton's Antiques
203 W. Huntingdon St.
901/855-9641

73 TULLAHOMA

Keepsake Antqs. & Cllbls.
310 S. Anderson St.
931/455-8612

Ole World Antiques
321 S. Anderson St.
931/455-7666

Memories Antique & Mall
117 West Lincoln St.
931/455-3992

Lincoln Street Antiques
212 E. Lincoln St.
931/454-9391

74 UNION CITY

Keeping Room
202 S. 1st St.
901/885-2554

Faye's Antiques
516 S. 1st St.
901/885-9507

75 WARTRACE

Directions: Take I-24 to the Beech Grove Road/ Shelbyville exit #97. Take Hwy. 64 directly to Wartrace.

This antique hamlet is known as the "Cradle of the Tennessee Walking Horse," because walking horses were first bred here in the 1930s. The town gets its name from the Native American trail that passed through the town and was used as a war path or war "trace" (the designation of wilderness roads - "traces" - during the 1600s and 1700s).

For information on the Log Cabin Bed and Breakfast, The Walking Horse Hotel, and Ledford's Mill Inn and Antique Shop, see review this section.

76 WAVERLY

You could spend a day or two here in Waverly just poking around in the various museums and odd places in town. The town was founded in 1838 and named for one of the founding families. There is a barely-changed 1948 movie house that's still operating on the square and a 1960s drive-in theater just down the highway, owned by the same family. There's Mr. Pilkington's World-O-Tools Museum just past the Farmers Co-op, be sure and call first to make sure Mr. Pilkington is there. Collecting tools was just a hobby for Mr. P in the 1950s, but now he has about 25,000 old and unique tools, primarily from the 20th century, but lots from the 1800s and even earlier. Also on the square is the Humphreys County Museum, open whenever the Chamber of Commerce is open, because they're both in the same building.

Nolan House

375 Hwy. 13 North
931/296-2511
Open March-December (office hours 9 a.m.-7 p.m.)
Rates $50-75

Directions: From I-40: Take exit 143 (Hwy. 13 North) past Loretta Lynn's Dude Ranch, approximately 14 miles. At the Waverly town center, follow Hwy. 13 North across the viaduct. At the top of the viaduct turn left at the first house. From U.S. 70 East or West: Follow the Hwy. 13 North signs across the viaduct. At the top of the viaduct run left at the first house.

The Nolan House offers a little bit o' Ireland in the rural Tennessee countryside. This National Register home was built after the Civil War by Irishman James Nicholas Nolan, who stayed in Waverly after the war and became a very successful businessman. It remained in the Nolan family for 109 years, until the last family member died in 1979. The current owners, Linda and Patrick O'Lee, are keeping the Irish legacy alive by offering spacious guests rooms, decorated with antiques. The warm ambiance of the spacious Great Room is the setting for breakfast served on fine China. Country living at its most gracious includes day trips to Nashville, Memphis, state parks with hiking, canoeing, swimming, golfing, visiting historic Civil War sites, and, of course, antique shopping.

*Legend has it Jesse James hitched his horse in front of the Nolan House.

LOS NOPALES

Antiques, Rare Books, Art

1106 W. Broadway

(915) 283-7125

Van Horn

154

Henson's Antiques

Fine Furniture • Glass • Accessories

We Specialize In American Victorian and Top Of The Line Oak

"Featured in Southern Living Magazine"

Visa, MasterCard & Layaway

230 Market Street

(915) 854-1756

Baird

9

BAIRD

The Official "Antique Capital of West Texas

On I-20, 120 miles West of Ft. Worth and 20 miles East of Abilene.

9

ANTIQUE

Mall of Lubbock

Over 24,000 Ft. • 40 Dealers

Complete Appraisal Service

- We Buy Estates - Collections "Travel Anywhere"
- We Conduct Estate Sales • Over 100 Showcases

7907 W. 19th

3 Miles West of Loop 289 on Levelland Hwy.

(806) 796-2166

Open 7 days 10AM - 6 PM

96

Memories of Munday Antiques, Etc. Mall

110 E. Main

(817) 422-5400

Mon.-Sat. 10-6

Sun. 1-5

10 Quality Dealers

Munday

110

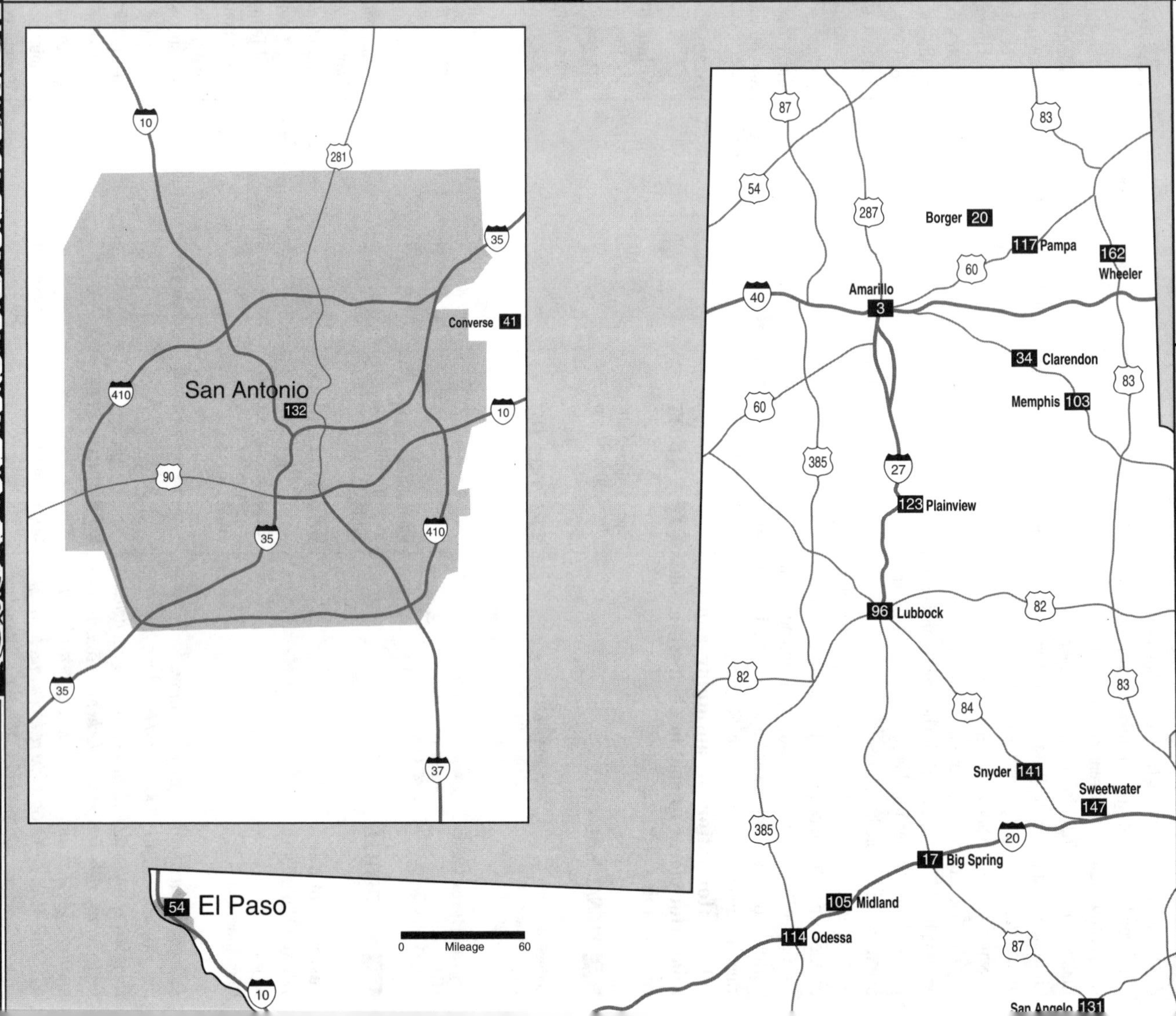

Carolyn Thompson's

ANTIQUE CENTER OF TEXAS

TEXAS' LARGEST

OVER 200 DEALERS

1001 West Loop North, Houston

(713) 688-4211

Just 2 Miles North Of The Galleria

OPEN EVERY DAY 10AM-6PM

78

The best hidden treasures in Dallas are found at

City Center

ANTIQUES & DESIGN DISTRICT

Over 100 Shops to Choose From!

FROM TOLLWAY: Go thru tollgate (head to 35 exit) to service road (Levitz on right), right on Continental, right on Industrial.

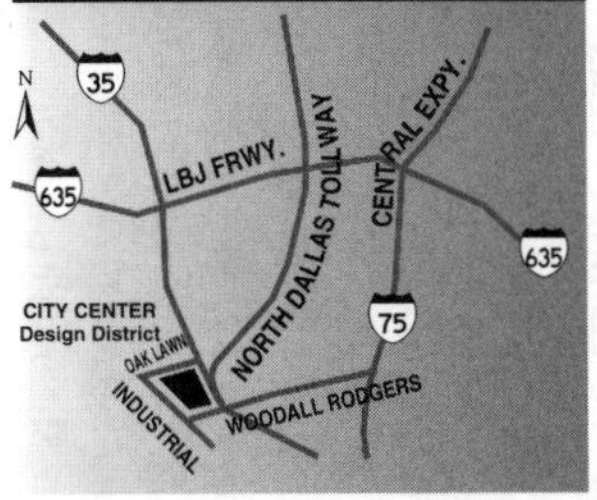

Sue's

ANTIQUE MALL

609 7TH St.

(817) 322-9552

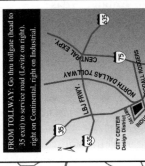

Wichita Falls

154
Van Horn
90
67
10
90

West Texas

THE COLUMNS ON ALAMO

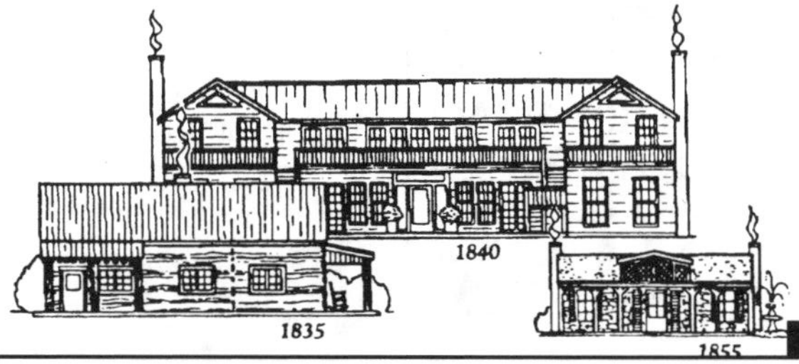
1835
1840
1855

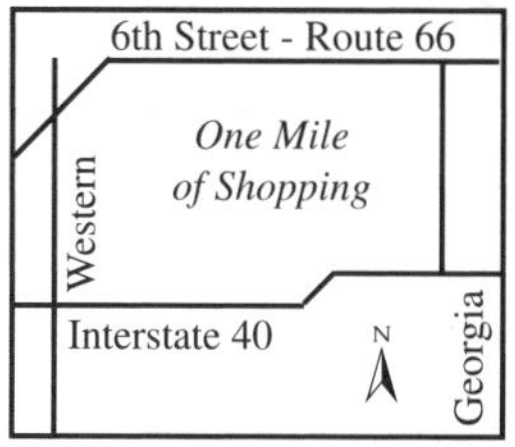
6th Street - Route 66
One Mile
of Shopping
Western
Interstate 40
N
Georgia

TRADE MART ANTIQUES

Houston's Finest Antique Mall

Over 100 Shops in
Air-Conditioned Comfort
(713) 465-2506

Open Fri., Sat. & Sun, 10 a.m.-6 p.m.
SAM HOUSTON TOLLWAY AT HAMMERLY
2 Miles North of I-10

78

Carolyn Thompson's
ANTIQUE CENTER OF TEXAS
TEXAS' LARGEST
OVER 200 DEALERS

1001 West Loop North, Houston
(713) 688-4211
Just 2 Miles North Of The Galleria

OPEN EVERY DAY
10AM-6PM

78

MAISON-BAYOU
A Creole Plantation

300 Bayou St. • (903) 665-7600 or 665-PETE
www.maisonbayou.com
Bed & Breakfast • Nature Trails
Jefferson

85

Henson's Antiques

Fine Furniture • Glass • Accessories
We Specialize In American
Victorian
and Top Of The Line Oak
"Featured in Southern Living
Magazine"
Visa, MasterCard & Layaway
230 Market Street
(915) 854-1756
Baird

9

BAIRD

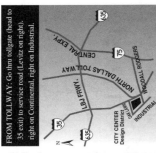

The Official "Antique Capital of West Texas
On I-20, 120 miles West
of Ft. Worth and 20
miles East of Abilene.

9

The best hidden treasures in Dallas are found at

City Center
ANTIQUES & DESIGN DISTRICT

Over 100 Shops to Choose From!

FROM TOLLWAY: Go thru tollgate (head to 35 exit) to service road (Levitz on right). right on Continental, right on Industrial.

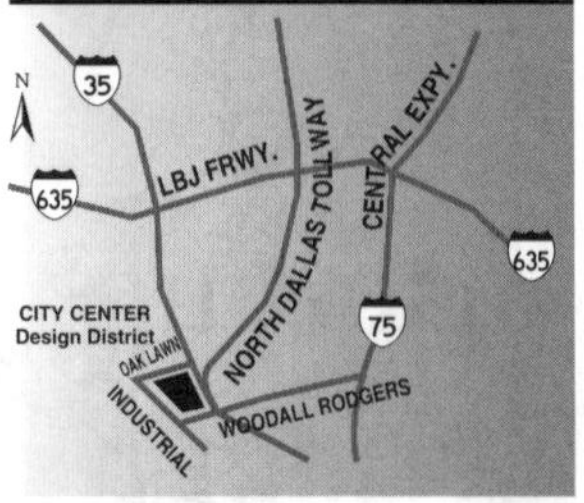

Dallas

45

East Texas

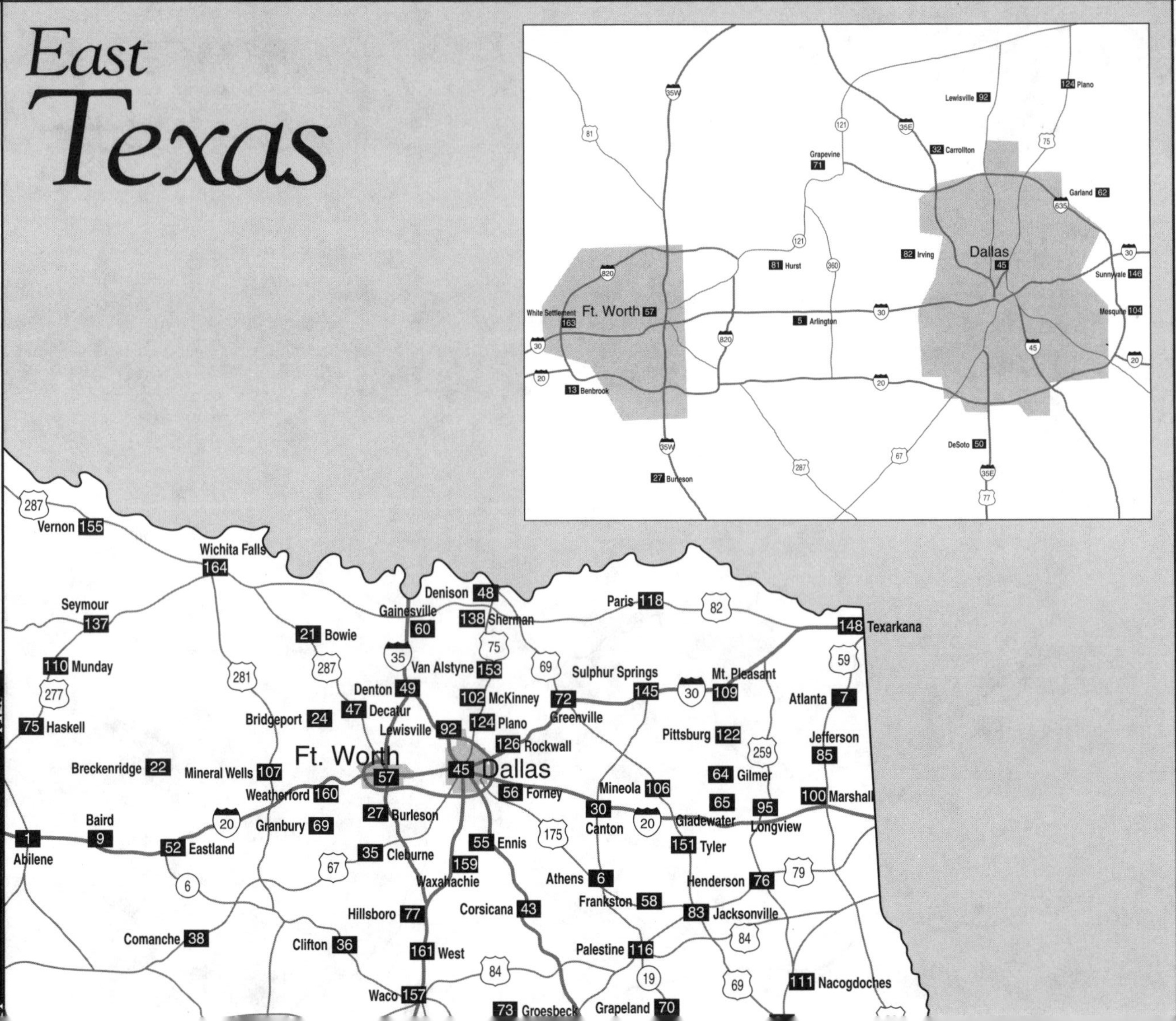

Teddie Bear's

Antiques & Collectibles

Barn full of antiques
Hwy 19 South
(409) 594-6321

Trinity

150

Antiques By Ellis

Specializing In Fine
American Furniture
1906 West Park Row
(817) 275-6761
Arlington

Courthouse Antiques Collectibles & Gifts

Treasures for all ages
from all ages!

109 S. College
(972) 938-2777
Waxahachie

While antiquing in Borger visit the

House of Coffee

at the corner of S. Main & Grand located in the old Isom Hotel built in 1926

(806) 274-7375

Borger

20

Treasure Cove Mall

2027 N. Jackson
(Hwy. 69 N.)
(903) 586-6140

Jacksonville

83

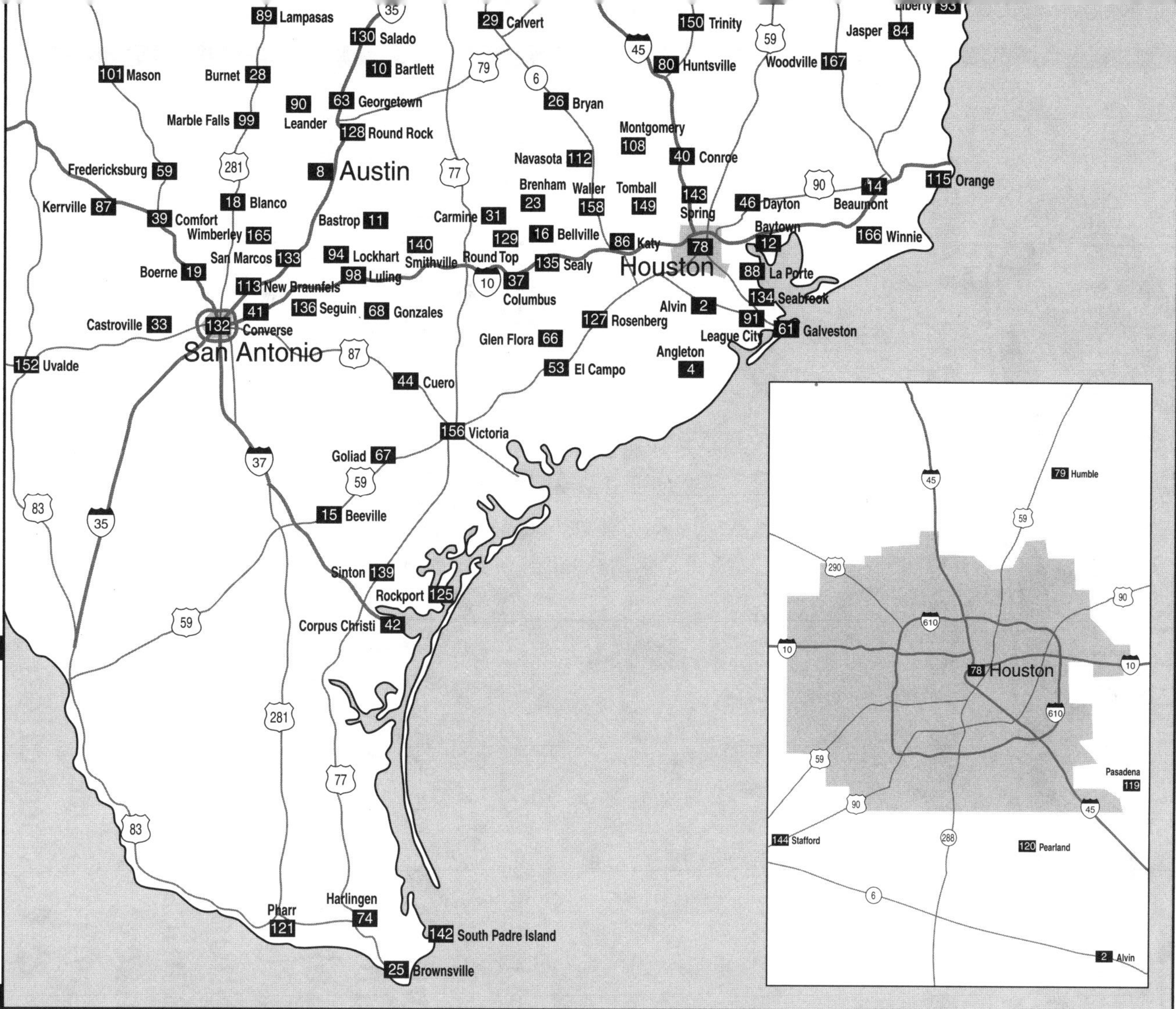

A Touch of Class

ANTIQUE MALL

118 W. Lamar
(903) 891-9379

Sherman

138

R & F Antiques

Specializing in American Antiques

912 Yale St.
(713) 861-7750
In the Historic Houston Heights District
Sun.- Tues.
by chance or appt.
Wed.- Sat. 10-5:30

Houston

78

Sand Dollar Hospitality

A BED & BREAKFAST RESERVATION SERVICE

3605 Mendenhall Dr.
1-800-528-7782

Representing a wide variety of bed & breakfast accommodations in Corpus Christi and the surrounding Gulf Coast area.

42

Visit Historic

Goliad

One of the oldest Towns in Texas

Welcome Antiquers

67

Old Fashioned Things

Antiques, Collectibles, Gifts

811 Yale Street
In the Historic Houston Heights District
(713) 880-8393

Houston

78

Come Visit

BAIRD

"on the right track"

the

"Antique Capital of West Texas"

Historic T&P Depot - Established 1891

The old Connor House B&B

ird, the Official "Antique Capital of st Texas" extends to you a warm, "West xas Welcome"! As a progressive town th a cooperative spirit, it has blossomed thin the past 6 years and is now enjoying

Area Shops offer a wide variety of antiques & collectibles

e strongest economic growth since the lroad boom of the late 1800's. The cline in railroad activity forced many sinesses to close, and Baird was left tually deserted.

The majority of the old, historic buildings left vacant in the downtown area have now been renovated and beautifully restored to house the various antique shops, antique and collectible malls, gift and craft shops, restaurants and soda fountain, candy factory, hardware stores, bank, and other retail and professional businesses. These buildings once served as boarding houses for weary travelers and railroad employees, mercantile and grocery stores, furniture and casket stores, a hatchery, banks, livery stable, hardware and dry goods stores, drug and soda shops, lodge halls, theaters, and even a hospital. These wonderful old structures are situated up and down Market Street between the Callahan County Courthouse and the old Texas and Pacific Railroad Depot. Others are located within 1 block of Market Street. Two well appointed Bed and Breakfasts provide comfort and convenience for groups and individuals visiting and shopping in Baird. An RV Park located a short distance from the downtown area offers amenities for motor homes and travel trailers.

Several Special Events are held throughout the year, including an "Art Show" in March, a "Trades Festival" with Rodeo in June, and a "Cowboy Gathering" in October. New events planned for the future will provide additional pleasure and entertainment. Please contact the Baird

Annual Cowboy Fall Reunion Parade

Chamber of Commerce at (915) 854-2003 for a schedule of events, map, and other information about Baird.

Directions: Exits 306, 307, or 308 off I-20 approximately 120 miles West of Ft. Worth or 20 miles East of Abilene.

A look inside one of the many antique shops in Baird

Courthouse Antiques, Collectibles, and Gifts

Situated in the center of Waxahachie's historic downtown district, this nine-story Ellis County Courthouse is the city's most distinctive landmark. Featuring a mixture of Romansque and Victorian architecture, this impressive 102-year-old structure is one of the most photographed and filmed courthouses in the United States.

ourthouse Antiques, Collectibles, and Gifts is situated in e very shadow of the beautiful and famous Ellis County ourthouse located in Waxahachie, TX. The 102-year old ourthouse and this charming Victorian town have been atured in numerous movies, and located right on the storic courthouse square you'll find the store. In keeping ith the surroundings, they offer vintage clothing; Haviland iina, including chocolate pots and tea sets; Wedgwood, oritake, Johnson Bros. and various European china; vintage aby items such as wicker strollers and baby scales and ramic baby feeders; furniture dating back to the early 19th ntury, some in its original ndition and some beautifully id faithfully restored; toys and olls, some dating back to the 0s and '30s and some highly ollectible like Madame lexander dolls, Gund plush ys, Ideal and Matchbox cars id planes; stained glass and her architectural pieces; ooks; linens and lace; welry and watches; clocks; assware, atomizers, decanters and bottles; bedroom and dining suites; trunks and luggage. They also buy antiques and are especially interested in buying Haviland, vintage clothing, children's items and toys.

A look inside Courthouse Antiques

Courthouse Antiques, Collectibles, and Gifts
109 S. College
(972)938-2777
Waxahachie, TX

Texas

1 ABILENE

Poppy's Antique Mall & Mus.
126 S. Access Rd.
915/692-7755

Antique Gallery
2544 Barrow St.
915/692-2422

Antique & Almost
3146 S. 11th St.
915/695-2423

Barnard's Antiques
501 Hickory St.
915/677-9076

Sharon Specialties
721 Hickory St.
915/672-1793

Yesterdaze Mall
2626 E. Hwy. 80
915/676-9030

Gizzmotique
641 Pecan St.
915/677-0041

McCloskey's
1646 N. 6th St.
915/672-6277

One Horse Sleigh Antiques
1009 S. Treadaway Blvd.
915/676-1429

Olde Abilene Treasures
2102 N. 1st Street
915/672-6493

2 ALVIN

Village Antiques & Shoppes
1200 FM 1462
281/585-1959

Once Upon A Time
1004 W. Hwy. 6
281/331-7676

Finders Keepers
312 E. House St.
281/585-0806

Country Notions
217 W. South St.
281/585-6582

Dixieland Antiques
1255 W. Hwy. 6
281/585-4085

3 AMARILLO

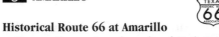

Historical Route 66 at Amarillo

Discover the magic and wonder of Sixth Street in Amarillo, Texas. Located on Historical Rt. 66 between Western and Georgia, Sixth Street offers a full range of shopping and services.

You will find Antiques and Collectibles Shops, Art Galleries, Speciality Shops and many varied service oriented businesses. You can experience wonderful food offered by several fine restaurants - from a good Texas-style hamburger with all the trimmings, smoked bar-be-que, out of this world pizza or incredible salads, sandwiches and desserts that you will never forget.

For further information about Historic Rt. 66, please write to: Historic Rt. 66, Box 4117, Amarillo, Texas 79106 (806) 372-3901. For updated information of events call the IN TOUCH INFO LINE (806)376-1000 Ext. #6150.

Town and Country Antiques Mall
2811 W. Sixth Street
806/373-3607
Open: Mon.-Sat. 10-5:30, Sunday 1-5

A wonderful place for an eclectic assortment of collectibles and antiques. They specialize in great furniture.

Alex's 66 Antique Mall
2912 W. Sixth Street
806/376-1166
Open: Mon.-Sat. 10-5, Sunday 1-5

Eighteenth and Nineteenth Century antiques plus collectibles.

Country Co-op Mall
2807 W. Sixth Street
806/372-4472
Open: Mon.-Sat. 10-5:30, Sunday 1-5

12,000 Sq. Ft. filled with antiques, collectibles and gift items. 50 plus dealers.

Webb Galleries Amarillo
2816 W. Sixth Street
806/342-4044
Open: Wed.-Sat. 11-5

Regional and Contemporary Art.

Worldwide Antiques
3218 W. Sixth Street
806/372-5288

European and American antiques. Unique antiques and gifts.

No Boundaries
Antiques, Gifts and Collectibles
602 South Carolina Street
806/371-7270
Open: Mon.-Sat. 10-5

A charming house filled with treasures.

This Olde House
3901 W. Sixth Street
806/372-3901
IN TOUCH INFO LINE 806/376-1000 #6153
Open: Weekdays 10-5:30, Sunday 1-5, Closed Tuesdays

An old craftsman style house filled with antiques, collectibles and gifts.

Red Door Antiques
3211 W. Sixth Street
806/373-0316
IN TOUCH INFO LINE 806/376-1000 #6150
Open: Mon.-Sat. 10-5:30

A complete line of American and European furniture, as well as glassware: including Fiesta and American Fostoria.

Adobe Walls Woodworks
2904 W. Sixth Street
Website: www.adobewalls.com

Handcrafted Southwest furniture, artworks and home accents.

Puckett Antiques
2706 W. Sixth Street
806/372-3075
Open: Mon.-Sat. 10-5:30

Gifts for everyone, small and large - old and new. From fine china, crystal, furniture to barbed-wire.

The Mustard Seed
3323 W. Sixth Street
806/376-9209
Open: Mon.-Sat. 10-5:30

Specializing in Primitives, both large and small. A great selection of linens and gift items.

Clay and Company
604 S. Maryland
806/376-7866

Antiques, collectibles and ladies fine clothing.

Pewter Miniatures
3120 W. Sixth Street
806/374-0488
IN TOUCH INFO LINE 806/376-1000 #6151
Open: Mon-Sat. 10-6

Handcrafted pewter sculptures by Michael Ricker, Emmett Kelly Jr. clowns, Folkstones by the Boyd Collection.

Buffalo Gals
2812 W. Sixth Street
806/374-6773
Open: Mon.-Sat. 10-6

Antiques, collectibles and gifts. An assortment of homemade fudge.

Favorite Places to Eat on Rt. 66 Amarillo

Golden Light Cafe
2908 W. Sixth Street
806/374-9237
IN TOUCH INFO LINE 806/376-1000 #6158
Serving food 10-10, beverage service until 2 a.m.

The longest continuously-operated restaurant on Historic Rt. 66. The menu features burgers, fries, chili, sandwiches and many varied beverages.

The Park on Sixth
3315 W. Sixth Street
806/374-7275
Open: Mon. 10-4, Tue.-Sat. 10-10
Dinner Menu: Thurs., Fri., and Sat.

***The Antique Atlas* would like to make special mention of the following businesses who help support Historical Rt. 66 of Amarillo, Texas.**

San Jacinto Printing
2900 W. Sixth Street
806/373-1081
Open: Mon.-Fri. 8-5

Established business since 1967. Able to handle any of your printing needs.

Disabled American Veterans Store
3913 W. Sixth Street
806/373-8501
Open: Mon.-Sat. 10-5:30, Sunday 1-5:30

A thrift store full of treasures.

Starr Body Shop
3404 W. Sixth Street
806/373-4421
Open: Mon.-Fri. 8-6

Complete collision repair service.

Texotic Pets
3100 W. Sixth Street
806/371-8505
IN TOUCH INFO LINE 806/376-1000 #6152
Open: 7 days a week, 10-6

Featuring a varied selection of exotic birds and accessories including necessities for other pets.

Anderson Agency
2722 W. Sixth Street
806/374-1159
IN TOUCH INFO LINE 806/376-1000 #6156
Open: Mon.-Fri. 11-5

A full service licensed and bonded talent agency. You can book a star or be a star with the help of this agency.

Norman Antiques & Art
1006 S. Adams St.
806/376-7115

Beauford Hill Antiques
500 W. Amarillo Blvd.
806/376-6352

Depot Antiques
500 W. Amarillo Blvd.
806/376-6352

English Rose
6203 W. Amarillo Blvd.
806/359-7905

Slesick Studio & Gallery
6666 W. Amarillo Blvd.
806/352-8823

Cornerstone Consignments
3218 Hobbs Rd.
806/356-0225

Hobbs Street Mall
3218 Hobbs Rd.
806/356-6552

Amarillo Antique Mall
3701 Plains Blvd.
806/355-4264

Phoenix & Co.
3701 Plains Blvd., Ste. 83
806/355-4264

Galaxy Toys
2461 I-40 W
806/352-0800

Maryland House Antiques
600 S. Maryland St.
806/376-7866

Antique Amarillo
2700 W. 6th Ave.
806/374-1066

Sixth Street Antique Mall
2715 W. 6th Ave.
806/374-0459

Clockworks
2725 W. 6th Ave.
806/371-7121

Carousel Antiques & Cllbls.
2806 W. 6th Ave.
806/373-9142

Scent and Fantasy Two
2818 W. 6th Ave.
806/371-0773

Timeless Accents
3020 W. 6th Ave.
806/373-5473

Antiques Plus
3119 W. 6th Ave.
806/372-3137

D & N Collectibles
3208 W. 6th Ave.
806/371-8400

Delightful Treasures
3304 W. 6th Ave.
806/379-7107

Victorianna
3300 W. 6th Ave.
806/374-6568

Rusty & Dusty Antique Shop
3302 W. 6th Ave.
806/374-6568

Don R Reid Inc.
2717 Stanley St.
806/356-0903

Favorite Places To Eat

Cracker Barrel Old Country Store
I-40 E. & Quarterhorse Dr., Exit 72A
806/372-2034

4 ANGLETON

Jeter's Old World Antiques
Hospital Dr.
409/849-5452

Kelly's Crossroads Antiques
112 W. Mulberry St.
409/849-0308

Yesterdaze
517 E. Mulberry St.
409/849-8834

The Magnolia Tree
724 W. Mulberry St.
409/848-8044

Bargain Palace
200 S. Velasco St.
409/849-4711

Gallery Antiques & Collectibles
212 N. Velasco St.
409/849-9336

County Seat Antiques
227 N. Velasco St.
409/848-1810

Attic Treasures
125 East Cedar
409/849-7307

5 ARLINGTON

Antiques by Ellis
1906 W. Park Row
817/275-6761
817/274-6879 for special appointments
Open: Tue.-Sat. 11-5:30 or by appointment Sun.-Mon. Shop is closed when on buying trips or when attending shows. Please call in advance if you are traveling.

Directions: From I-30 take Fielder exit, south 4 miles, right on Park Row, 2 blocks on the left. From I-20 take Cooper Exit, north 5 miles, left on Park Row past Fielder, 2 blocks on the left.

Located in the same spot for the past 20 years, Sue and Asa Ellis specialize in fine American antiques from 1840-1910. If you are searching for true antique furniture, accessories and lighting, then this is one antique "stop" you shouldn't pass up (no reproductions). Their speciality is furniture with an emphasis on quality and the unusual. The inventory is evenly divided between formal Victorian and fancy oak with approximately 200 exceptional pieces available at all times.

Antique Mktplace Arlington
3500 S. Cooper St.
817/468-0689

Smith's Antiques & Refinishing
3650 Garner Blvd.
817/265-7048

Antique Sampler Mall
1715 E. Lamar Blvd.
817/861-4747

D Militaria & Collectibles Shop
823 Oram St.
817/274-3515

Moth Ball
401 E. Randol Mill Rd.
817/459-2553

Helen's Antiques & Used Furn.
2307 Medlin
817/275-2064

Design Center
138 S. Bowen
817/265-0549

Antiques, Etc.
404 E. First St.
817/543-1567

Al's Antiques
1543 S. Bowen
817/548-8151

Abram Street Antiques
500 E. Abram
817/460-7250

Antiques & Moore Mall & T/room
3708 W. Pioneer Pkwy.
817/548-5931

Favorite Places To Eat

Cracker Barrel Old Country Store
I-20 & Bowen Rd., Exit 448
817/465-9583

Cracker Barrel Old Country Store
Hwy. 360 & Brown Blvd./Ave. K
817/633-5477

6 ATHENS

Olga Antiques
312 S. Carroll St.
903/677-1733

Waldenwood Country Antiques
504 E. Corsicana St.
903/675-2561

Eden Antiques
400 N. Prairieville St.
903/677-1560

Goode's Imporium
109 E. Tyler St.
903/675-9425

7 ATLANTA

Yesterdays Antique Mall
212 N. East St.
903/796-9742

Atlanta Antiques
113 E. Hiram St.
903/796-4942

Hiram St. Antique Mall
117 E. Hiram St.
903/796-9474

Memory Lane Mall
110 E. Main St.
903/796-0485

8 AUSTIN

Trails End Bed & Breakfast
The B & B Store (gift shop)
12223 Trails End Road #7
512-267-2901 or 1-800-850-2901
B&B open year round
Rates $55-170
Gift shop open year round 1-5 pm - call for appointment

Directions: From IH 35 two miles out of Georgetown, Take RM 1431 and go 11.85 miles to Trails End Road. Turn left onto Trails End and go 7/10 of a mile to the gravel road. There will be several mail boxes next to the gravel road. Turn left and go to where the road curves to the right. Keep on going around the curve and the B&B is a large gray house trimmed in white on the left. An appointment is needed. The inn is located on the north side of Lake Travis between Cedar Park, Jonestown, Austin and Leander.

This is the perfect place to go for a getaway weekend or vacation. Trails End is a country retreat located in the unique central Texas hill country. As innkeepers JoAnn and Tom Patty say, "There is nothing immediate you have to do at Trails End B&B." That means guests get to kick back and enjoy the porches, decks, the gazebo, the refreshing pool, walking in the woods or riding bikes.

Make it a family vacation - there's a private guest house for six - bring the boat or water toys for a splashing good time on nearby Lake Travis. For golfing guests, a number of golf courses are convenient. When the urge to explore hits, downtown Austin is just 35 minutes away, and Georgetown, Round Rock, Cedar Park, Lago Vista, Leander, Burnet and Salado are an easy drive.

Lelysee Antiques
5603 Adams Ave.
512/459-1727

Mona and Don's Antiques
5617 Adams Ave.
512/458-1661

Chantal's Antq. & Design Cntr.
2525 W. Anderson Lane
512/451-5705

Antique Outlet
10401 Anderson Mill Rd.
512/257-1020

Antique Marketplace
5350 Burnet Rd.
512/452-1000

Halbert Antiques
5453 Burnet Rd.
512/451-8037

The Market
701 Capital of Tx. Hwy.
512/327-8866

Now & Always Antiques
1413 S. Congress Ave.
512/707-2692

Rue's Antiques Inc.
1500 S. Congress Ave.
512/442-1775

Antigua
1508 S. Congress Ave.
512/912-1475

Uncommon Objects
1512 S. Congress Ave.
512/442-4000

Off the Wall
1704 S. Congress Ave.
512/445-4701

Armadillo Antiques & Jewelry
1712 S. Congress Ave.
512/443-7552

Turn of the Century Antiques
1703 N. Cuernavaca Dr.
512/263-5460

Tipler's Lamp Shop
1204 W. 5th St.
512/472-5007

Antiques by Grace Homan
3303 Glenview Ave.
512/472-7366

Log Cabin Antiques
9600 W. Hwy. 290
512/288-4037

House of Harriette & John
12719 W. Hwy. 71
512/263-5103

Craftown Gallery
13945 Hwy. 183
512/331-4252

Capitol Used Furn. & Antqs.
11115C N. Lamar Blvd.
512/836-1472

Accent Antiques
2200 S. Lamar Blvd.
512/441-6656

Amelia's Retro Vogue & Relics
2024 S. Lamar Blvd.
512/442-4446

Lamar Antiques
2058 S. Lamar Blvd.
512/448-3184

Corner Collectors
6539 N. Lamar Blvd.
512/453-4556

Danforth's Antiques & Gifts
1612 Lavaca St.
512/478-7808

Garner & Smith Antiques Etc.
1013 W. Lynn St.
512/474-1518

Austin Antique Mall
8822 McCann Dr.
512/459-5900

Hog Wild Vintage Toys
100A E. North Loop Blvd.
512/467-9453

Eradeco Antiques & Cllbls.
110 E. North Loop Blvd.
512/450-0861

Hurt's Hunting Grounds Inc.
712 Red River St.
512/472-7680

Robert Gage Antiques
1304 Rio Grande St.
512/472-4760

Dreyfus Antiques
719 E. 6th St.
512/473-2191

Jean's Antiques & Gifts
2 Miles South of Wimberly
512/282-1541

Fancy Finds
1009 W. 6th Street
512/472-7550

Radio Ranch
1610 W. 35th St.
512/459-6855

Bradys of Austin
1807 W. 35th St.
512/459-8929

Architects and Heroes Antiques
1809 W. 35th St.
512/467-9393

9 BAIRD

The town of Baird, Texas, is a great "come back" story. The downtown district is only three blocks long, but has five antique malls and over a dozen individual shops with either antiques or collectibles. All of the shops are located either on Market Street (the main street) or within a half block on an intersecting street.

There are several good places to eat and two bed and breakfasts, with a third in progress. More buildings are being restored all the time on the three block historic downtown strip, and the town hopes to eventually have all of them filled with shops that are either antiques or related businesses. In 1993 Baird received the designation of "Antique Capital of West Texas" from the Texas Legislature due to their revitalization efforts and the numerous antique businesses, none of which existed prior to 1991.

Before they began their revitalization program, there were only two hardware stores and a drug store in the downtown area. It's quite different now, and they draw large numbers of antique shoppers from all over.

Baird is located 20 miles east of Abilene and 120 miles west of Fort Worth.

Henson's Antiques
230 Market Street
915/854-1756
Open: Mon.-Sat. 10-5:30

If you are an advanced collector of fine quality American antique furniture and accessories or if you are a designer whose clients demand only the best, then you'll be delighted with the personally selected inventory available at Henson's Antiques. The shop specializes in American Victorian period furniture, both walnut and rosewood, ranging from gorgeous matched suites for bedroom, parlor and dining room to striking single pieces such as etageres, armoires, secretaries, marble top tables, pier mirrors and hall trees. With no intention of excluding any collectors, Henson's inventory offers styles from other periods including top of the line oak, carved front china cabinets, roll-top desks, bedroom suites and bookcases for home or office.

The shop most recently attracted the attention of *Southern Living Magazine*. An unusual tambour roll filing cabinet was featured in an article entitled "Ticket to Yesterday in Baird". It is not unusual for the elite members of the press or customers for that matter to be drawn to Henson's Antiques. Clients from as far away as New York, California, Florida and Washington flock to Henson's for the outstanding offering of quality merchandise. What is unusual, however, is that the shop is located in a tiny West Texas town.

A few years back, Baird was a railroad town but when the Texas & Pacific Railroad closed shop, the town felt its tomorrows had left the station. For years, only the rustle of leaves and whistle of wind rambled along Baird's Market Street. Then, in 1993 the tiny town of Baird received State recognition when the Texas Legislature declared it the "Antique Capital of West Texas" due to the revitalization efforts and the numerous antique shops.

Betty Henson, owner of Henson's Antiques, was a leader in the towns revitalization. She and her husband, Weldon, have been avid collectors of formal American antiques for more than 25 years. Betty first became interested in antiques while studying interior design in the late 60s. The antiques found in Betty's shop are selected using the same criteria as is used in the selection of pieces for her own home; excellent quality, condition, uniqueness, function, design, style and age are all considered.

You will often find pieces from well known American cabinet makers who took great pride in the pieces they produced. In addition to the many fine furnishings available, you'll find decorative accessories including clocks, mirrors, lamps, prints, paintings, china, glass, porcelain, silver and silverplate.

Market Street Mall
212 Market Street
915/854-1408
Open Tue.-Sat., 10-5:30; Sun., 1:30-5:30, closed Mon.

Directions: Take Business 20 to downtown Baird. Market Street intersects.

Market Street Mall is a multi-dealer mall located in a historic building in downtown Baird. With new items arriving weekly, this unique shop offers a wide array of antiques and collectibles. From Victorian through 50s; furniture and a wide variety of smalls — Market Street Mall is an antiquer's delight with wide aisles, good lighting, climate control, and handicap accessibility.

"Acquisitions"
120 West 3rd Street
(1/2 block west of Market Street in downtown Baird)
915/854-0120
Open Tue.-Sat. 10-5:30; Sun. 1-5:30; closed Mondays

"Acquisitions" is a 5,000 square foot multi-dealer mall located 1/2 block west of Market Street in Baird. Glenda Diane Buck, owner, praises her 8 dealers for handling fine European and American antiques at affordable prices. Mall policy thoroughly discourages reproductions. These dealers buy and sell on a constant basis - single items to complete estates. The mall offers the area's most complete range of estate services: appraisals, auctions, and retail sales. Off premises antique and estate auctions thru AAA Auction Associates, (Donald R. Rockhill, Jr. TX - 10367 owner/auctioneer) are conducted as scheduled. Call for dealer space availability.

The Old Shoppe
312 Market Street
(west side of Market Street between Business 20 and 3rd Street)
915/854-1911
Open Tue.-Sat., 9:30-5:30; Sun., 1-5:30; closed Mondays

The Old Shoppe is a multi-dealer mall that becomes an antiquers paradise from the moment you walk through its door. There is something for everyone in the antiques, collectibles, furniture, glassware and quality reproduction line. Owner John McClaran invites you to stop and shop this unique mall. You won't be disappointed.

The Antique Market
334 Market Street
915/854-1997

Creations by Collene
331 Market Street
915/854-5980

Em's Sweets, Eats, & Antiques
140 Market Street
915/854-5956

Flashback
234 Market Street
915/854-1410

Hughes Trading Co. & Antqs.
743 W. 4th Street
915/854-1714

Konczak Pawn
219 Market Street
915/854-1293

Antique Memories
304 Market Street
915/854-2021

Barbara's Country Tyme Antqs.
300 Market Street
915/854-2424

Cowboy Mercantile & Lonesome Dove Saddlery
124 E. 2nd Street
915/854-1265

AAA Antiques, Appraisal & Auction Associates
120 W. 3rd Street
915/893-2705

Callahan County Collectibles
209 W. 3rd Street
915/854-1782

Cha Waken Indian Crossing
201 Market Street
915/854-2575

The Corn Stalk
205 Market Street
915/854-2501

Plaza Corner
245 Market Street
915/854-5972

Primrose Lane
203 Market Street
915/854-5936

Trail's End Antiques
223 Market Street
None

Wanda's Good Stuff
341 Stella Street
915/854-1973

Bed & Breakfasts/RV Parks:

Four Seasons Guest House
425 Market Street
915/854-1565

The Old Conner House B&B
348 Vine Street
915/854-1898

Robbin's RV Park
318 E. 2nd Street
915/854-2456

10 BARTLETT

Clark St. Antique. Shop
Clark St.
817/527-3933

Mary Jane's II
Clark St.
817/527-4445

Grumbley's Antiques
Clark St.
817/527-3141

The Trellis
Clark St.
817/527-4300

Bartlett Antique Mall
110 E. Clark St.
817/527-3251

Village Antique Mall
16 E. Clark St.
817/527-3234

Rooms with a View
135 E. Clark St.
817/527-4460

Major Roome's Emporium
221 Clark
817/527-3111

11 BASTROP

Wyldwood Antique Mall
Hwy. 71 W
512/321-3280

Old Town Emporium
918 Main St.
512/321-3635

Texas Mercantile
921 Main St.
512/303-1843

12 BAYTOWN

Burns Antqs. & Trade Empor.
600 N. Alexander Dr.
713/422-7321

The Consignment
2312 N. Alexander
713/837-1061

Buford's Antiques
3716 Decker Dr.
713/424-4081

Decker Drive Antiques
3716 Decker Dr.
713/424-5211

Temptations
207 W. De Fee St.
713/422-5693

Goose Creek Emporium
219 W. De Fee St.
713/427-6690

Bea's Treasure Chest
2 N. Main St.
713/420-3494

Town & Country Sales
5215 Sjolander Rd.
713/421-1904

Schoolmarm's Attic
1504 E. Texas Avenue
713/427-3914

Favorite Places To Eat

Cracker Barrel Old Country Store
I-10 & Garth Rd., Exit 792
281/421-5091

13 BENBROOK

Favorite Places To Eat

Cracker Barrel Old Country Store
I-20 & Winscott, Exit 429B
817/249-3360

14 BEAUMONT

McCoy's Antiques
1455 Calder St.
409/835-1764

Finder's Fayre Quality Antiques
1485 Calder St.
409/833-7000

Calder House
1905 Calder St.
409/832-1955

Select Antiques & Furnishings
2694 Hazel St.
409/833-7610

Time After Time Antiques
2481 Calder St.
409/832-0016

Old Store Antiques
8319 College St.
409/866-6280

Old Store Antiques
8370 College St.
409/866-2205

Collage
2470 N. 11th St.
409/899-3545

15 BEEVILLE

Final Touch
207 W. Carter St.
512/358-5808

Delphine's
114 W. Hefferman St.
513/362-2144

McKitchen's Antiques
401 E. Houston St.
512/358-1442

The Antique Place
1101 N. Washington St.
512/358-2908

16 BELLVILLE

Bellville Antique Mall
11 N. Bell St.
409/865-9620

Andy's Candys
11 N. Bell St.
409/865-9620

Julia's Antiques
410 Centerhill Rd.
409/865-5285

Barn & Bell
854 FM 529 (Burleigh)
409/865-9648

Rafters Antiques
467 Hwy. 36 N.
409/865-3316

On The Square
4 S. Holland St.
409/865-2230

Cottonwood Cottage
8 N. Holland St.
409/865-8411

Square Trader
12 N. Holland St.
409/865-9305

Antiques Etc. Emporium
14 N. Holland
409/865-8087

Frog Hollow
22 N. Holland
409/865-3007

The Country Shop
20 E. Main
409/865-9639

Front Porch on the Park
145 N. Holland
409/865-8833

Nothing Ordinary Antiques
123 E. Main St.
409/865-8033

17 BIG SPRING

Aunt Bea's Antiques
1711 N. FM 700
915/2636923

The Country Store
Lamesa Hwy. 1/2 Mi N. Hwy. 20
915/267-8840

Antique Mall of Big Spring
110 Main St.
915/267-2631

Main Street Emporium
113 Main St.
915/263-1212

Antique Korner
217 Main St.
915/268-9580

The Country Store
209 Runnels
915/263-3093

Alamo Antiques
114 E. 2nd St.
915/264-9334

Dahmers Antiques
7309 N. Service Rd.
915/393-5537

18 BLANCO

Unique Antiques
315 Main
210/833-2201 or 1-800-460-1733
Open Thurs.-Tue. 10-5, closed Wednesdays

Directions: Unique Antiques is located on Hwy. 281, which is Main Street, on the west side of the old Blanco County Courthouse Square.

Although Unique Antiques handles antiques and collectibles, glassware and gifts in general, they particularly carry American oak furniture and a large selection of Depression glass. They also carry the largest collection of flow blue in Texas hill country. All their items are top quality and shoppers can buy just one piece or a whole estate!

Blanco Flea Market
5th & Pecan St.
210/833-5640

Blanco Trash & Treasures
313 4th St.
No Phone

A Step Back
Hwy. 281 S
210/833-4270

Nannie's Antiques
303 Main St.
210/833-9001

Merchantile
313 Main St.
210/833-2225

Cranberry Antiques
400 3rd St.
210/833-5596

Classic Antiques
317 Main St.
210/833-2216

19 BOERNE

Antiques N Things
106 S. Main St.
210/249-2313

Carousel Antiques & Pickles
118 S. Main St.
210/249-9306

Antiques & Old Lace
146 S. Main St.
210/816-2530

Boerne Emporium
179 S. Main St.
210/249-3390

The Rusty Bucket
195 S. Main St.
210/249-2288

St. George & The Dragon
210 S. Main St.
210/249-2207

Boerne Clock Co.
233 S. Main
210/249-6080

Landmark
404 S. Main St.
210/249-6002

Iron Pigtail
470 S. Main St.
210/249-8877

Heyday
615 S. Main St.
210/249-4951

20 BORGER

House of Coffee & Gifts
100 West Grand
806/274-7375

While antiquing in Borger, Texas, plan to visit the "House of Coffee" located at the corner of South Main and Grand Street in one of the first hotels built in 1926, in the original town of Isom, Texas. Isom was part of the heritage of the Texas Panhandle and the pioneering spirit that changed the Panhandle from a habitat of buffalo and cattle to a land of people.

Housed in this building is a wonderful gift shop featuring a blend of gifts: crystal, handkerchiefs, pewter frames, flower wreaths, all set in a Victorian flair with consignment antiques from Timeless Treasures.

Plan to stay for a cup of Espresso coffee, a spot of tea from 15 varieties or one of many Coco flavors. The Summer months offer frozen latte, along with 14 varieties of bagels and cream cheese toppings. If you visit in the Fall or Winter months, you could be served soup on Tuesday or Thursday at noon.

It took six months to transform the bottom area of the old hotel into this unique coffee house. The owner, Michele Nelson is a Borger native and has fond memories of when this part of the building was Barney's Pharmacy. The soda equipment in the pharmacy was taken out for the Youth Building at First Methodist Church, however, Michele still has the counter bar with the names carved on display as well as other memorabilia. Future plans for the 24 hotel rooms upstairs with original sink, heaters and transom windowed doors is undecided.

The building began as the "Isom Hotel" and was the center of Isom before it became Borger. When leased to John and Pearl Mulkey, the hotel sign read "Mulkey Hotel". They claimed it as their homestead in 1929 even though according to records, it belonged to Agnes Howe. The next owners, Light James and his family named it "St. James." The James brothers lived there until 1940.

The bottom south end of the building was sub-leased to the Hatcher Drug Co. in 1929. In the 1934 phone book it was listed "West Grand". In 1936 Byron Andress leased the space and the building housed Dr. J. R. Walker's office and a barber shop and the Hotel Isom lobby. Later the entire north end was used by Drs. W. G. & M. M. Stephens and Dr. Harvey Hayes. Mrs. Viola Stephens sold the building to Michele and she then opened for business in October 1996. You are welcome to come by and browse awhile, have a cup, and experience Isom, Texas, now known as Borger.

Season's Antiques
120 5th St.
806/274-6130

Four Sisters
416 N. Main St.
806/274-5220

Timeless Treasures
700 W. Wilson St.
806/273-6802

21 BOWIE

Nostalgia Antiques
200 N. Mason St.
817/872-6272

Days Gone By
204 N. Mason St.
817/872-2033

Antique Express
210 N. Mason St.
817/872-4717

Market Place
216 N. Mason St.
817/872-5011

Texas Pride Cards & Cllbls.
Newport Hwy.
817/872-5114

Martha's Attic
206 Smythe St.
817/872-4705

Treasure House
303 W. Wise St.
817/872-1899

22 BRECKENRIDGE

Antique Shoppe
105 W. Walker St.
817/559-1639

The Pat Rogers Collection
201 W. Walker St.
817/559-6653

Antique Depot
500 E. Walker St.
817/559-9724

23 BRENHAM

Brenham holds a special place in the hearts of romantics because of a colorful piece of history and artwork that is in the town. Brenham is home to one of only 12 antique carousels in Texas, and this particular one is the only example of a C. W. Parker Carousel with Hersehill-Spillman horses. Manufactured prior to 1910, this piece of Americana is at Fireman's Park in Brenham and visitors can ride it anytime.

Brenham is also home to Blue Bell Creameries, said to produce the best ice cream in the country. They ought to know how to do it - they've been making ice cream since 1911.

Country Co-Op
101 E. Alamo St.
409/830-0679

Today & Yesterday
101 W. Alamo St.
409/830-0707

J. H. Faske Company
114 E. Alamo St.
409/836-9282

Seek & Find Antiques
115 W. Alamo St.
409/830-1930

Somewhere in Time
204 W. Alamo St.
409/277-9511

Brenham Antique Mall
213 W. Alamo St.
409/836-7231

K & S Collectibles
Houston Hwy..
409/836-3575

Nancy's Antiques
1700 Key St.
409/836-7520

Catherine Newton's Antiques
1302 W. Main St.
409/836-2898

24 BRIDGEPORT

Serendipity House
1003 Halsell St.
817/683-3999

T & L Antique Shop
1004 Halsell St.
817/683-5545

Granny's Antiques
1010 Halsell St.
817/683-4043

Hidden Away Memories
1016 Halsell St.
817/683-8050

Our Antiques & Collectibles
1018 Halsell St.
817/683-3959

Once Again Antique Mall
1020 Halsell St.
817/683-6717

Once Again Antiques
1105 Halsell St.
817/683-6455

25 BROWNSVILLE

Pilar's Antiques & Tea Room
302 E. Adams St.
210/541-7450

Second Thought
2265 Boca Chica Blvd.
210/541-7423

26 BRYAN

Attic Antiques
118 S. Bryan Ave.
409/822-7830

Old Bryan
202 S. Bryan Ave.
409/779-3245

Gazebo Antiques
3828 S. College Ave.
409/846-0249

By Jac's
701 E. Villa Maria Rd.
409/822-2662

Plantation Shop
2024 S. Texas Ave.
409/822-6220

Tin Barn Antiques & Cllbls.
3218 S. Texas Ave.
409/779-6573

By-Mac Collections
202 W. 26th St.
409/775-7875

Brazos Trader Antiques
210 W. 26th St.
409/775-2984

Amity of Bryan
300 W. 26th St.
409/822-7717

27 BURLESON

Burleson Old Town Cllbls.
108 S. Main St.
817/295-3301

Burleson Antique Mall
2395 S.W. Wilshire Blvd.
817/295-7890

Favorite Places To Eat

Cracker Barrel Old Country Store
I-35 W. & Alsbury, Exit 38
817/295-8622

28 BURNET

Cobblestone Cottage
212 E. Jackson St.
512/756-7407

Burnet Antique Mall
206 S. Main St.
512/756-7783

A Taile of Two Antiques
212 S. Main St.
512/756-9806

Treasures on the Square
216 S. Main St.
512/756-8514

Shoppee
206 E. Polk St.
512/756-7984

29 CALVERT

Front Porch
505 S. Main
409/364-2933

Boll Weevil Antiques
508 S. Main
409/364-2835

Farmer's Wife Antiques
515 S. Main
409/364-2489

S & S Antiques
517 S. Main
409/364-2634

30 CANTON

The saying that everything is bigger and grander in Texas must have started in Canton. This town, with its regular population of just about 3,000, is the undisputed home of the granddaddy of all trade days!

Canton's First Monday Trade Days are world famous. This unbelievable "happening" dates back at least 150 years, with records existing back to the mid-1800s; most likely it's much older. First Monday Trade Days developed around the circuit court held on the first Monday of each month. In the pioneer days of East Texas, this was a time to set aside work and go into town to the county seat to hear court, buy needed supplies and sell produce and farm animals. In the mid-1960s a progressive-thinking Canton city council saw the monthly market as a potential gold mine and began purchasing land to form the First Monday Park. The park currently encompasses over 300 acres.

Through the years this gathering evolved into today's multi-acre grounds with over 6,000 booths offering literally everything: antiques, arts and crafts, clothing, toys, tools, junk, even animals from dogs to zebras! Weather is not a factor, even though a lot of the area is still outdoors. Many of the booths are now inside 14 pavilions, with an additional 35,000 square feet of building devoted strictly to antiques.

Any one of four exits off I-20 will bring you to downtown Canton.

Buffalo Village
202 N. Buffalo St.
903/567-2434

Recollections & Vintage Quilts
138 E. Dallas St.
903/567-6945

Times Past
114 E. Dallas St.
903/567-5709

Stones Antiques
Hwy. 120
903/567-6620

Timeless Treasures
111 S. Hwy. 19
903/567-6762

Marcella's Antiques
150 E. Terrell St.
903/567-6936

31 CARMINE

Antiques & Stuff
Hwy. 290
409/278-3866

Hoppe Store Antiques
Hwy. 290
409/278-3713

32 CARROLLTON

T L C Treasures
1013 S. Broadway St.
972/245-7729

Dolls of Yesterday & Today
1014 S. Broadway St.
972/242-8281

Mary Lou's
1015 S. Broadway St.
972/466-1460

Ten of Arts
1019 S. Broadway St.
972/242-3357

Pleasures Past
1105 S. Broadway St.
972/242-2084

Finishing Touch Antique Mall
1109 S. Broadway St.
972/446-3038

Classic Militaria
1810 N. Interstate 35
972/242-1957

Old Craft Store
1110 W. Main St.
214/242-9111

33 CASTROVILLE

Alice's Antiques
1213 Fiorella Street
210/931-9318

Market Place Antiques
1215 Fiorella St.
210/538-3350

Cottage
413 Lafayette St.
210/538-9713

Castroville Emporium Antiques
515 Madrid St.
210/538-3115

34 CLARENDON

Curiosity Shop
Hwy. E. 287
806/874-2409

Poor Boys Antiques
206 S. Kearney
806/874-2233

Petty's Antiques & Collectibles
222 S. Kearney
806/874-3875

My Playhouse
300 S. Kearney
No Phone

S & S Gallery
317 S. Kearney
806/874-5096

35 CLEBURNE

Butch's Treasures Chest
207 E. Henderson
No Phone

A Taste of Time
216 E. Henderson
817/558-2288

Randy's Antiques & More
204 S. Main St.
817/645-1985

Cleburne Antique Mall
215 S. Main St.
817/641-5550

Bettie's Antiques & Mall
216 S. Main St.
817/645-2723

36 CLIFTON

Clifton Antique Mall
206 W. 5th St.
817/675-2300

Hobbyhorse Gifts & Antiques
114 Main St.
817/675-7723

Bosque County Emporium
121 Main St.
817/675-8133

37 COLUMBUS

Hometown Hall
1120 Milam Street
409/732-5425

Doubletree & English Ivy
1237 Bowie Street
409/732-8802

Little of this - Little of that
1004 Milam Street
409/732-6034

38 COMANCHE

Furniture Barn
300 N. Austin
915/356-2787

Comanche Trading Post
300 W. Central Ave.
915/356-5022

Antique Country
400 E. Central
915/356-2248

Sybil's Antiques
410 E. Central
915/356-3338

Old Tyme Antiques
508 E. Central Ave.
915/356-3550

Quilts & Tops
605 E. Central Ave.
915/356-2047

Red Top Antiques
605 W. Central Ave.
915/356-2173

This Ole House Antiques
706 W. Central Ave.
915/356-2441

Martin's Antiques
804 E. Central
915/356-5711

Dee Dee's Corner
807 E. Central
915/356-2118

Culbertson's Custom Quilting
201 W. Grand
915/356-3901

Selections on the Square
127 N. Houston St.
915/356-3153

39 COMFORT

Antiquities Etc.
702 High St.
210/995-4190

Comfort Common
717 High St.
210/995-3030

Bygone Days Antiques
815 High St.
210/995-3003

Comfort Emporium
607 Hwy. 27
210/995-4000

Faltin & Company
Main & 7th
210/995-3279

Marketplatz Antique Center
405 7th St.
210/995-2000

Southwestern Elegance
509 7th St.
210/995-2297

40 CONROE

Russ Clanton Antiques
711 W. Dallas St.
409/756-8816

Antique Mall of Conroe
725 W. Davis St.
409/788-8222

Ah Collectables
920 W. Lewis St.
409/539-5122

Edith's Antiques & Gift Shop
910 Cable St.
409/756-3711

Pauline's Antiques
915 Cable St.
409/756-4762

Attic Antiques
1304 FM 2854
409/539-9116

Pamela's Antique Parlor
FM 2854
409/441-6895

Stock Exchange Antique Mall
302 N. Frazier St.
409/760-3800

Heintz Furniture & Antiques
701 N. Frazier St.
409/756-3024

Tizzie's Antiques & Collectibles
916 W. Lewis St.
409/788-2344

Golden Eagle Traders
1908 N. Frazier St.
409/441-7355

Favorite Places To Eat

Cracker Barrel Old Country Store
I-45 & League Line Rd., Exit 91
281/856-2052

41 CONVERSE

De's Oldies N Goodies
209 S. Seguin Rd.
210/658-2083

42 CORPUS CHRISTI

Sand Dollar Hospitality
3605 Mendenhall Dr.
1-800-528-7782

If you are searching for that perfect get-a-way vacation or just an exceptional place to spend the night, then I suggest contacting Sandy at Sand Dollar Hospitality. The service represents a wide variety of bed and breakfast and guest cottages in Corpus Christi and the surrounding areas.

Lee-Cunningham Inc.
3100 S. Alameda St.
512/882-4482

Emma's Arbor
4309 S. Alameda St.
512/985-8309

Betty's Trash To Treasures Too
4315 S. Alameda St.
512/993-1027

Gene's Antiques
4331 S. Alameda St.
512/994-0440

Home Sweet Home Antq. Mkt.
4333 S. Alameda St.
512/991-4001

Second Hand Rose Antiques
4343 S. Alameda St.
512/993-9626

Sister Sue's
4323 S. Alameda St.
512/992-5300

Lea's Glass Nook
1911 Ayers St.
512/884-3036

Betty's Trash To Treasures
3301 Ayers St.
512/882-9144

Country Peddlers
4337 S. Alameda St.
512/993-7237

Antiques Downtown
312 N. Chaparral St.
512/882-8865

Victorian Lady
315 N. Chaparral St.
512/883-1051

Country Peddlers Downtown
317 N. Chaparral St.
512/887-6618

Antiquity Inc.
318 N. Chaparral St.
512/882-2424

Rucker & Rucker Inc.
451 Everhart Rd.
512/994-1231

Two J's Antiques
613 Everhart
512/994-0788

Irene's Antique Flea Market
3906 Leopard St.
512/884-4467

Yesterday Peddler
3131 McArdle Rd.
512/851-2141

McLaughlin Furniture Shop
1227 12th Street
512/882-3991

Objets D'Art II
5858 S. Padre Island Dr.
512/993-2126

Odds & Ends
9841 E. Padre Island Dr.
512/937-8944

Quaint Shop
811 S. Staples St.
512/884-9541

Dragonfly Antiques
821 S. Staples St.
512/888-5442

W. Gardner
821 S. Staples St.
512/887-9351

Wild Good Chase
3509 S. Staples St.
512/851-9535

Favorite Places To Eat

Cracker Barrel Old Country Store
St. Padre Island Dr. & Weber Rd.

43 CORSICANA

This & That Antiques
101 S. Beaton St.
903/874-6941

Home Town Antiques
110 N. Beaton
903/874-8158

Carousel Crafts & Antiques
118 S. Beaton St.
903/872-4141

Merchant's
320 N. Beaton St.
903/872-6445

Jim's Clock Shop
127 W. Collin St.
903/874-5141

Traders Outpost
105 W. 7th Ave.
903/872-5392

CSL Antiques & Collectibles
106 W. 6th Ave.
903/874-8333

44 CUERO

Gallery of Memories
121 N. Esplanade St.
512/275-9226

Country Collectables
Hwy. 87
512/275-2011

45 DALLAS

Note: Certain areas of Dallas have had area code changes. Area code 972 has been added.

The Boulevard Emporium
1010 N. Industrial Blvd.
214/748-1860
Hours: Mon.-Sat. 10-5

Quality antiques and design accessories

Clements Antiques and Auction Gallery
1333 Oak Lawn Ave.
214/747-7700
Hours: Mon.-Fri. 9-5

Specializing in 18th and 19th century antiques

Country Garden Antiques
147 Parkhouse
214/741-9331
Hours: Daily 11-5 or by appt.

Furnishings for home and garden

The Estate Warehouse
905 Slocum St.
214/760-2424
Hours: Mon.-Sat. 9-6 or by appt.

Monthly estate liquidations

Farzin Designs
1515 Turtle Creek Blvd. (at The Gathering)
214/747-1511
Hours: Mon.-Sat. 10-6 or by appt.

Decorative antiques, rugs, and accessories

The Gathering
1515 Turtle Creek Blvd.
214/741-4888
Hours: Mon.-Sat. 10-6 or by appt.

Over 100 international quality antiques, art, and design dealers

Jaime Leather and Fabric Upholstery
1100 N. Industrial Blvd.
214/742-8700
Hours: Mon.-Fri. 8-6, Sat. 9-3

Specializing in the upholstery of antique furniture

Liberty and Son Designs
1506 Market Center Blvd.
214/748-3329
Hours: Mon.-Sat. 10-6, Sun. By appt.

Extensive selection of antique and decorator furnishings

Lots of Furniture
910 N. Industrial Blvd.
214/761-1575
Hours: Mon.-Sat. 10-5, Sun. 12-5

12,000 square feet of antique furniture and exotics

Mama's Daughters' Diner
2014 Irving Blvd.
214/742-8646
Hours: Mon.-Fri. 6-3, Sat. 7-3

Homemade breakfast and lunch

Parkhouse Antiques
114 Parkhouse
214/741-1199
Hours: Wed.-Sun. 11-6

For home and garden

The Rocket Restaurant
1838 Irving Blvd.
214/741-1324
Hours: Mon.-Sat. 5-2:30

Full breakfast and lunch

Sandaga Market African Imports
1325 Levee
214/747-8431
Hours: Mon.-Fri. 9-6 or by appt.

Selection of ceremonial & decorative art

Silver Eagle
1933 Levee
214/741-2390
Hours: Tue.-Sat. 10:30-5

Unusual and affordable antiques

Special Consideration by Pettigrew & Assoc.
1715 Market Center Blvd.
214/475-1351
Hours: Mon.-Fri. 9-5

New-old-odd lot furniture & decorative items

White Elephant Antiques Warehouse
1026 N. Industrial Blvd.
214/871-7966
Hours: Mon.-Sat. 10-5

18,000 square feet, 75 Dealers, & 90 Vignettes

The Wrecking Barn
1421 N. Industrial Blvd., Ste. 102 at Glass St.
214/747-2777
Hours: Mon.-Fri. 9-5, Sat. 10-3

Architectural salvage

Designing Men
4209 Avondale, Ste. 308
214/599-0029

Atrium
3404 Belt Line Rd.
972/243-2406

Antiques Antiques
5100 Belt line Rd., Ste. 218
972/239-6124

Consignment Store
5290 Belt Line Rd.
972/991-6268

The Emporium at Big Town
Big Town Mall (Mesquite)
214/320-2222

Mary Cates & Co.
2700 Boll St.
214/855-5006

Sample House
122 Casa Linda Plaza
214/327-0486

Ornaments & Heirlooms
2512 Matton Street
214/871-2020

Kornye Gallery
2200 Cedar Springs Rd.
214/871-3434

Roxy
3826 Cedar Springs Rd.
214/827-8593

Love Field Antique Mall
6500 Cedar Springs Rd.
214/357-6500

Cathy's Antiques
500 Crescent Ct., Ste. 140
214/871-3737

Ken Riney Antiques
500 Crescent Ct.
214/871-3640

Sample House & Candle Shop
9825 N. Central Expressway
214/369-6521

Beckie's Antiques & Gifts
1005 W. Davis St.
214/942-8626

Corner Shop
Decorative Center
214/741-1780

Gregor's Studios
1413 Dragon St.
214/744-3385

Joe Cooner Gallery
1605 Dragon St.
214/747-3603

Heritage Collection Ltd.
2521 Fairmount St.
214/871-0012

Les Antiques Inc.
2600 Fairmount St.
214/720-0099

Three Graces Antiques
2603 Fairmount St.
214/969-1922

Uncommon Market Inc.
2701 Fairmount St.
214/871-2775

Eagle's Antiques
2711 Fairmount St.
214/871-9301

Forestwood Antique Mall
5333 Forest Lane
972/661-0001

Sam's Antique Rugs
5333 Forest Lane
972/233-9777

Curiosity Corner
8920 Garland Rd.
214/320-1752

Trinkets & Treasures
10244 Garland Rd.
214/320-3794

Lone Star Bazaar
10724 Garland Rd.
214/324-1484

Antique Bahr
1801 Greenville Ave.
214/826-1064

A S C Deco
1805 Greenville Ave.
214/821-8288

House of Prokay Antiques
1807 Greenville Ave.
214/824-7618

Linda's Treasures & T/Room
1929 Greenville Ave.
214/824-7915

Lula B's Antique Mall
2004 Greenville Ave.
214/824-2185

Lower Greenville Antique Mall
2010 Greenville Ave.
214/824-4136

Allison Daughtry Antiques
2804 Greenville Ave.
214/823-8910

Chique & Shabby
2915 Greenville Ave.
214/828-0500

Anna's Etc.
3424 Greenville Ave.
214/828-9393

Waterbird Traders
3420 Greenville Ave.
214/821-4606

Nicole's Antiques
3611 Greenville Ave.
214/821-3740

Copper Lamp
5500 Greenville Ave.
214/521-3711

Ivy House
5500 Greenville Ave.
214/369-2411

Albert Copeland Contntl.
11117 Harry Hines Blvd.
214/241-9686

Connie Williamson Antiques
2815 N. Henderson Ave.
214/821-4134

Brant Laird Antiques
2901 N. Henderson Ave.
214/823-4100

Nick Brock Antiques
2909 N. Henderson Ave.
214/828-0624

Kent-Stone Antiques
2819 N. Henderson Ave.
214/826-7553

Canterbury Antiques
2923A N. Henderson Ave.
214/821-5265

Richard Alan Antiques
2923 N. Henderson Ave.
214/826-1588

Whimsey Shoppe
2923 N. Henderson Ave.
214/824-6300

On Consignment Inc.
2927 N. Henderson Ave.
214/827-3600

Beaux-Arts
1505 Hi Line Dr.
214/741-5555

Del Saxon Fine Arts & Antiques
1525B Hi Line Dr.
214/742-6921

Gameroom Express
141 Howell St.
214/747-3232

Market Antiques
430 North Park Center
214/369-7161

Garrett Galleries
1800 Irving Blvd.
214/742-4343

Notable Accents
8204 Kate St.
214/369-5525

Knox Street Antiques
3319 Knox St.
214/521-8888

William Little Antiques
7227 Lakehurst Ave.
214/368-8230

The British Trading Co.
4518 Lovers Lane
214/373-9071

Park Cities Antique Mall
4908 W. Lovers Lane
214/350-5983

Lover's Lane Antique Market
5001 W. Lovers Lane
214/351-5656

Le Passe
5450 W. Lovers Lane, Ste. 227
214/956-9320

Market Antiques
5470 W. Lovers Lane, Ste. 335
214/352-1220

Consignment Galleries
5627 W. Lovers Lane
214/357-3925

Silver Vault
5655 W. Lovers Lane
214/357-7115

Windsor Antique Mall
6126 Luther Lane-Preston Center
214/750-8787

Antique Galleries
2533 McKinney Ave.
214/871-1516

McKinney Ave. Antique Market
2710 McKinney Ave.
214/871-1904

El Paso Import Co.
4524 McKinney Ave.
214/559-0907

Loyd-Paxton
3636 Maple Ave.
214/521-1521

Mews
1708 Market Center Blvd.
214/748-9070

Trains & Toys
109 Medallion Center
214/373-9469

Unlimited Ltd. Antique Mall
15201 Midway Rd.
972/490-4085

Englishman's Antiques
15304 Midway Rd.
972/980-0107

Antique Shop
5616 E. Mockingbird Lane
214/823-7718

Antique Angie
603 Munger Ave.
214/954-1864

Millennium
3601 Parry Ave.
214/824-7325

China Cupboard
718 N. Paulus Ave.
214/528-6250

507 Antiques
10755 Preston Rd.
214/368-1100

HMI Architectural
1811 Rock Island St.
214/428-7774

Saint John's Silver
2603 Routh St.
214/871-2020

Drrew Ltd. Antique Gallery
2722 Routh St.
214/880-0009

Pearle Dorrace Antiques
2736 Routh St.
214/855-0008

Collage 20th Century Classics
3017 Routh St.
214/880-0020

Adam & Eve Antiques
3121 Routh St.
214/871-0225

Antiques Unique
180 Spring Creek Village
972/386-5477

Modern & Antq. Clock Repair
10435 Springhaven Dr.
972/216-9514

Southwest Gallery
4500 Sigma @ Welch
972-960-8935

Maison De France
1007 Slocum St.
214/742-1222

Gary Elam & Associates
1025 Slocum St.
214/747-4767

East & Orient Company
1123 Slocum St.
214/741-1191

Somerset Galleries Inc.
1205 Slocum St.
214/760-7065

Pittet Co.
1215 Slocum St.
214/651-7033

Oriental Treasures Inc.
1322 Slocum St.
214/760-8888

Oriental Rugs Inc.
1404 Slocum St.
214/748-8891

Le Louvre French Antiques
1313 Slocum St.
214/742-2605

Louis Rosenbach Antiques Inc.
1518 Slocum St.
214/748-0906

Y C King & Sons
1528 Slocum St.
214/698-1977

Old Wicker Garden
6606 Snider Plaza
214/373-8241

Samplers
6817 Snider Plaza
214/363-0045

Rosedale House
6928 Snider Plaza
214/369-6646

Snider Plaza Antiques
6929 Snider Plaza
214/373-0822

Remember When Shop
2431 Valwood Pkwy.
972/243-3439

Days of Olde
2901 Valley View Lane
972/247-2417

Odds and Ends Shop
210 W. Yarmouth St.
214/942-9326

Bettyann & Jimbo's Antique
4402 W. Lovers Lane
214/350-5755

Shalanes Antique Gallery
5811 S. R L Thornton Fwy.
214/374-7455

46 DAYTON

The Old School
111 West Houston
409/258-9342 or 1-800-491-9342
Open Wed.-Sat. 9:30-5:30, Mon.-Tue. by appointment

Directions: Dayton is midway between Houston and Beaumont on Hwy. 90. Houston Street is one block south of Hwy. 90. The shop is directly behind the Sonic Drive In.

Anyone care to guess why Ann Westmoreland's shop is called The Old School? I'll give you a hint: it used to house teachers and students and was a place of learning for the community. The building was constructed somewhere in the late 1800s, and was last used as a school in 1908. Ann carries furniture, glassware, primitives, jewelry, coins, some Southwestern artifacts along with other antiques and collectibles.

Charlette's Web
FM 1960
409/258-5933

Main Street Bazaar
312 N. Main St.
409/258-4049

47 DECATUR

Sisters Four Collectibles
115 W. Main St.
817/627-3177

Charles Antiques
408 W. Main St.
817/627-2485

Red Pepper Trading Post
121 N. State St.
817/627-7959

Memory Lane Antiques
104 N. Trinity St.
817/627-1121

Crossroads Antiques Mall
301 S. Washburn St.
817/627-7047

48 DENISON

Antiques & Cars by Bob Taylor
213 W. Heron St.
903/463-9924

Castaway Furniture
1500 W. Johnson St.
903/463-9855

Katy Antique Station
104 E. Main
903/465-7352

Tucker Furniture
422 W. Main
903/465-3630

Hart Place Mall
500 W. Main St.
903/463-1230

Manor House Antqs. & Cllbls.
611 W. Main St.
903/465-2601

Wright's Antiques
1030 W. Main St.
903/465-9392

49 DENTON

Memories So Special
105 Hickory
817/484-8560

Courthouse Collection
111 W. Hickory St.
817/381-1956

Downtown Mini Mall
108 N. Locust St.
817/387-0024

Cook's Red Barn Antiques
212 E. Hickory St.
817/382-5004

Favorite Places To Eat

Cracker Barrel Old Country Store
I-35 & TX Hwy. 380, Exit 469
817/382-5277

50 DESOTO

Favorite Places To Eat

Cracker Barrel Old Country Store
I-35 E. & Wintergreen Blvd., Exit 416
972/224-3004

51 DIBOLL

Quaint Shop
Rt. 3 Box 601
409/829-3466

Village Antiques
Hwy. 59 S
409/829-4500

The Dusty Attic
910 N. Temple Dr.
409/829-2743

Live Oak Antiques & Cllbls.
1443 N. Temple Dr.
409/829-3554

52 EASTLAND

House of Antiques
908 S. Bassett
817/629-1124

Hogs N Clover Antiques Gifts
109 E. Commerce St.
817/629-2755

Antiques & Uniques
114 W. Commerce St.
817/629-2143

I-20 Antiques
Exit 343
817/629-8682

Kountry Korner
112 S. Seaman St.
817/629-2214

53 EL CAMPO

Rose Garden
123 S. Mechanic St.
409/543-1097

Pararie Antiques & Collectibles
708 N. Mechanic St.
409/543-9511

54 EL PASO

Posada San Miguel
9618 Socorro Rd.
915/858-1993

Grapevine Antiques & Cllbls.
5024 Doniphan Dr.
951/584-3981

Ye Olde Antiques
5024 Doniphan Dr.
915/584-7630

Marketplace at Placita Sante Fe
5034 Doniphan Dr.
915/585-9296

Raquel's
5372 Doniphan Dr.
915/584-7861

Another Man's Treasure
6016 Doniphan Dr.
915/581-0077

Rosebud Antiques & Gifts
6016 Doniphan Dr.
915/584-7227

Ruby's
6016 Doniphan Dr.
915/581-0077

Stephen's Antiques
6016 Doniphan Dr.
915/585-0028

P & L Trading Post
6020 Doniphan Dr.
915/581-0287

A J's
6022 Doniphan Dr.
915/833-3432

Mary McNellis Antiques
6022 Doniphan Dr.
915/584-6878

Swan's Antiques
6022 Doniphan Dr.
915/585-7358

C R V Enterprises
6184 Doniphan Dr.
915/581-6416

Stars & Stripes Antiques
6458 Doniphan Dr.
915/833-6228

Antique Borderland
6465 Doniphan Dr.
915/584-3230

Caldarella's Furniture Inc.
5660 El Paso
915/859-4777

Eastside Antique Mall
7924 Gateway Blvd. E
915/594-0673

Rings Antiques & Collectibles
7924 Gateway Blvd. E
915/594-0673

Antiques Etcetera
8022 N. Mesa St.
915/833-4712

Wooden Horse Antiques
132 W. Redd Rd.
915/581-1976

Eagle's Nest
7410 Remcon Circle
915/584-0868

Mesa Street Antique Mall
7410 Remcon Circle
915/584-0868

Nana's Treasures
7410 Remcon Circle
915/585-0940

Favorite Places To Eat

Cracker Barrel Old Country Store
I-10 & N. Mesa St., Exit 11
915/581-9742

55 ENNIS

On The Corner
101 S. Dallas St.
972/875-8825

Magnolia Station Antiques
201 S. Dallas St.
972/875-7360

Deedees Antqs. Cllbls. & More
808 E. Ennis Ave.
972/875-2011

Good Time Charlies Antiques
114 W. Knox St.
972/875-9737

56 FORNEY

Pavillion Antiques
4 Forney Industrial Park
972/222-8902

Wholesale Antiques
5 Forney Industrial Park
972/564-4433

Snooper's Paradise
6 Forney Industrial Park
972/564-4214

Deridder Antiques Corp
Forney Industrial Park
972/226-8407

Star Antique Mall
Forney Industrial Park
972/564-1055

Doc's Antiques
107 Hwy. 80
972/552-4305

Philbeck's Antiques
119 E. Hwy. 80
972/564-9842

Clements Antiques of Texas
121 E. Hwy. 80
972/564-1520

Bowling Antiques
10512 West US Hwy. 80
972/564-1433

Little Red's Antiques
Hwy. 80
972/226-2304

Cotton Gin Mall
210 Hwy. 688
972/564-1220

Aires Limited
E. 125 Hwy. 80
972/564-4913

57 FORT WORTH

Cowtown Antiques The Trading Post
2400 North Main
817/626-4565
Open Tue.-Thurs., 10-5, Fri.-Sat., 11-6, Sun., 12-5, closed Mondays

Cowtown Antiques and The Trading Post are two different shops located almost together and owned by the same folks. Both are open the same hours (listed above) so you can get double your shopping time in here. The shops are in the historic Fort Worth Stockyards..."Where the West Begins," and shoppers can experience the old time atmosphere and rich heritage of this Fort Worth landmark.

With the sounds of cowboy music filling the background, shop for Western collectibles and memorabilia, pocket watches, Western wear, mounts, and hides. In addition, there is furniture, stained glass and advertising memorabilia.

Harris Antiques & Imports
7600 Scott Street
817/246-8400 or 817/246-5852
Fax: 817/246-6859

Directions: Harris Antiques & Imports is located in West Fort Worth, in a suburb called White Settlement. The shop is at I-30 West, Cherry Lane Exit (north), then right on Scott Street.

Carolyn Harris and company sells both wholesale and retail, with about 95% of their sales being to dealers, auctioneers and designers. Anyone who loves antiques should go to the showroom just to look and be impressed. Their new location is an air-conditioned mall that is the length of three football fields - a total of 440,000 square feet of antiques and accessories! Harris Antiques & Imports has been in business in Fort Worth for over 35 years, and offers merchandise to shoppers world-wide. Besides all the furniture, they offer bronzes, oil paintings, cut glass and porcelain. It's no wonder they hold the title of "the world's largest home furnishings, accessories and antiques store."

Black Orchid
3801 Camp Bowie Blvd.
871/731-8611

Flories Antiques
3915 Camp Bowie Blvd.
817/763-5380

Leigh-Boyd
4632 Camp Bowie Blvd.
817/738-3705

Fort Worth Antiques
4909 Camp Bowie Blvd.
871/731-4220

Antique Colony Inc.
7200 Camp Bowie Blvd.
817/731-7252

From The Hide
117 W. Exchange Ave.
817/624-8302

Antique Shop
5401 Jacksboro Hwy.
817/740-9966

Doll House
1815 E. Lancaster Ave.
817/332-8674

Yabba Dabba Doo Antiques
6517 E. Lancaster Ave.
817/654-4100

Drew's Antiques & Primitives
7113 E. Lancaster Ave.
817/451-8822

Antique Connection
7429 E. Lancaster Ave.
817/429-0922

Stockyard Antiques
1332 N. Main St.
817/624-2311

Lake Worth Bazaar
4024 Merrett Dr.
817/237-8064

Montgomery St. Antique Mall
2601 Montgomery St.
817/735-9685

Cornish Antiques & Cllbls.
320 S. Oakland Blvd.
817/536-9975

Choices on Park Hill
2978 Park Hill
817/927-1854

Lemon Tree Antiques Art
804 Pennsylvania Ave.
817/332-5519

Nick's Frame & Antique Shop
2616 Scott Ave.
817/534-3601

Harris' Antiques
7600 Scott St.
817/246-5852

Sample House
1540 S. University Dr.
817/429-7857

Norma Baker Antiques
3311 W. 7th St.
817/335-1152

Market
3433 W. 7th St.
817/334-0330

Butler's Antiques & Uniques
514 W. Seminary Dr.
817/921-3403

Lambert Antiques
2812 Stanley Ave.
817/926-3450

Quilter's Emporium
3526 W. Vickery Blvd.
817/377-3993

Newton's Antiques
5216 White Settlement Rd.
817/737-7009

Hidden Treasures Antiques
8906 White Settlement Rd.
817/246-8864

Favorite Places To Eat

Cracker Barrel Old Country Store
I-35 & Meacham Rd., Exit 56A
817/624-8050

58 FRANKSTON

Pandora's Box
102 West Main Street
903/876-5056
Open Mon.-Sat. 9-5:30, closed Sundays

Directions: Pandora's Box is located on the square in Frankston, one block west of Hwy. 155 and one block south of Hwy. 175.

Here's a true junque store that's not afraid to say so! That's their description of themselves: a 4,000 square foot true junque store with architectural antiques and a garden shop, all housed in an old automobile dealership building.

59 FREDERICKSBURG

Watkins Hill
608 East Creek
210/997-6739 or 1-800-899-1672
Open year round, business hours Mon.-Fri. 8-5, Sat.-Sun. 8-2

Watkins Hill Guest House is so perfectly suited for the scenic area in which it is located. Visitors are attracted to the European atmosphere, historic landmarks and the bread and pastries for which Fredericksburg is famous. Watkins Hill is conveniently accessible from Austin, San Antonio, Houston and Dallas/Fort Worth. Mr. Edgar Watkins, the innkeeper, will provide excellent directions to the Guest House from your location.

Watkins Hill, is an unusual - and unusually elegant - bed and breakfast complex in Fredericksburg, Texas.

Dreamchild of native Texan Edgar Watkins, Watkins Hill began life just a few years ago when Watkins gave up a career in product design and public relations to return to his home state and buy the 1855 Basse House, now the centerpiece of his inn.

He knew he wanted something out of the ordinary for his bed and breakfast, and he knew what he didn't like about other B&Bs, so he designed Watkins Hill with these things in mind.

One of his pet peeves is sitting down to breakfast with a group of strangers in the custom of traditional B&Bs. So he decided to serve his guests with breakfast by room service at the guest's requested time. He also doesn't like the term "bed and breakfast," instead preferring to call his accommodation a "guest house."

Another concept from the start was not to fill the inn with Texas farm furniture. Instead Watkins created an imaginary scenario, and went from there: "I fantasized that a stylish bachelor had moved here in the 1850s from the East, and had brought his family's furniture with him." Following that fantasy, the Basse House is furnished with upscale antiques from the mid-18th century to the mid-19th century, including a rare little steel bathtub from a Paris hotel.

The entire complex currently spans two acres, with seven buildings, four of which are historic 19th century structures (1835, 1840, 1855 and 1890). Twelve guest rooms are available, with a total sleeping capacity of about 40 guests.

All of this is located just two blocks from Fredericksburg's Main Street and its shops, yet longhorn cattle graze across the way on the opposite side of the street and along the creek that runs beside it.

All but two rooms have fireplaces and porches or balconies. Every room has a butler's pantry with a refrigerator stocked with complimentary wine, two kinds of coffee and several kinds of tea, distilled water, fruit juice and apples. Guests also get four kinds of snacks, current magazines, and recommendations of places to dine.

There are so many little touches of elegance, luxury and whimsey that guests could spend all their time just wandering around looking for these surprises. Beeswax tapers and potted candles glow beside a mid-19th century faux bamboo French daybed. One living room wall is covered floor to ceiling with a circa 1870 theatrical backdrop. It's a scarred canvas painting of a forest, but the creases and nicks in it fit beautifully with the combination of primitive and elegant decors that swirl throughout the house.

The frayed edges of the canvas are disguised at the top behind a pressed tin valance dipped in brass, and along both sides by a pair of 19th century pilasters from New York state. Doors at either end open onto the porches, with the open front door offering a view of a Victorian cast-cement fountain and an expansive meadow. Luxury and style with the unusual make wonderful weekend or week-long companions for guests who like to be pampered and intrigued.

Texas Trading Co.
109 N. Adams St.
210/997-1840

Room No. 5
239A W. Blvd. #5
210/997-1090

American Hiddledy Piggledy
411 S. Lincoln St.
210/997-5551

Homestead Warehouse Store
411 S. Lincoln St.
210/997-0954

Idle Hours
411 S. Lincoln St.
210/997-2908

Wild Goose Chase Antiques
105 S. Llano St.
210/997-4321

Antique Haus
107 S. Llano St.
210/997-2011

Showcase Antiques Shop
119 E. Main St.
210/997-5505

Cornerstone Market
201 E. Main St.
210/997-3204

Remember Me
203 E. Main St.
210/997-6932

Jabberwocky Antiques
207 E. Main St.
210/997-7071

Red Baron's Antiques
215 E. Main St.
210/997-6368

Lauren Bade Antiques
229 E. Main St.
210/997-9570

Main St. Antiques
234 W. Main St.
210/997-8913

Der Alte Fritz Antiques
409 E. Main St.
210/997-8249

Rustic Styles
414 E. Main St.
210/997-6219

Three Horse Trader
609 W. Main St.
210/997-6499

60 GAINESVILLE

Recollection Antiques
105 W. California St.
817/668-2170

Old West Traditions
107 W. California St.
817/665-7503

Miss Pitty Pat's Antique Porch
111 W. California St.
817/665-6540

Shady Oak Gallery
111 S. Commerce St.
817/665-0275

Lindsay House
318 E. California St.
817/665-7171

Naughty Lady Antiques
108 N. Chestnut St.
817/668-1767

Carousel Antique Mall
112 S. Dixon St.
817/665-6444

Gainesville Antique Mall Main
1808 N. IH-35
817/668-7798

61 GALVESTON

Madame Dyer's Bed & Breakfast

1720 Postoffice Street
409/765-5692
Open year round

Directions: Take I-45 South from Houston to Galveston. When you cross over the Causeway onto the island, the interstate highway becomes Broadway. Travel about 50 blocks to 18th Street. Make a left turn onto 18th Street and go 5 blocks to Postoffice Street. Turn right onto this one-way street. Madame Dyer's is the second house on the left. Park in front.

This elegant 1889 Victorian mansion is located in the East End Historic Homes District, which is one of the most beautiful and best preserved areas of Victorian homes in the country. It is within walking distance of The Strand Historic District, where restored vintage buildings house specialty shops, galleries, museums, restaurants, outlet shops and antique malls; and is two blocks away from Gallery Row, where upscale antique and gallery shops abound. In other words, it's location is perfect! Guests can even have a horse drawn carriage pick them up at the B&B's front door, or they can catch the historic trolley just two blocks away.

The ornate, two-store mansion has been faithfully restored to its turn-of-the-century glory, with two wrap-around porches, high airy ceilings, wooden floors and lace curtains. Each room is furnished with antiques, including the three guest rooms. Ashten's Room, with private bath, is furnished with a queen size bed of carved oak and antique accent pieces. Blake's Room, with a queen size bed set in a bay window, is decorated in English antiques and antique rug beaters, shoe lasts and sewing memorabilia. The private bath just down the hall holds a claw-foot tub. Corbin's Room holds a king size bed, a tiled fireplace with an oak mirrored mantel, antique dolls, whimsical old hats, and a pedestal sink and claw-foot tub in the adjoining bath.

There is a coffee/tea buffet provided each morning upstairs for early risers, a full breakfast every morning in the dining room, homemade cookies in the dining room at all times, and complimentary snacks and beverages available in the kitchen round the clock.

Jewels & Junque
2715 Broadway St.
409/762-3243

B J's Antiques
2111 Postoffice St.
409/763-6075

Collectors Gallery
2222 Postoffice St.
409/765-6443

Hendley Market
2010 Strand
409/762-2610

Old Peanut Butter Warehouse
100 20th St.
409/762-8358

Yesterdays Best
120 20th St.
409/765-1419

Somewhere In Time Antiques
124 20th St.
409/762-1094

La Maison Rouge
418 22nd St.
409/763-0717

Off The Wall Antiques
1811 23rd St.
409/765-9414

62 GARLAND

Chase & James Furniture
1817 S. Garland Ave.
214/864-0092

The Cabbage Patch
901 Jupiter
214/272-8928

Old South Antiques & Auction
1413 N. I Hwy. 30
214/240-4477

The Ritz
Main St.
214/494-0083

Treasure Chest of Antiques
115 N. 6th St.
214/276-6075

Farm House Antiques
509 W. State St.
214/487-8262

Old Garland Antique Mall
108 N. 6th St.
214/494-029

63 GEORGETOWN

Cobblestone
708 S. Austin Ave.
512/863-9607

On The Square
712 S. Austin Ave.
512/869-0448

Rust & Dust
113 E. 7th St.
512/863-6463

Georgetown Emporium
114 E. 7th St.
512/863-6845

Georgetown Antique Mall
713 S. Main St.
512/869-2088

Texas Sampler
101 River Hills Drive
512/863-7694

Poppy Hill Marketplace
820 S. Austin Avenue
512/863-8445

64 GILMER

Old Town Mall
201 Henderson St.
903/843-2359

Corner Store Antiques
203 W. Tyler St.
903/843-2466

65 GLADEWATER

Gladewater Antique Mall
100 E. Commerce Ave.
903/845-4440

Jade Junction
106 E. Commerce Ave.
903/845-3876

Now & Then Antique Mall
109 W. Commerce Ave.
903/845-5765

Bygone Tymes Mall
109 N. Main St.
903/845-2603

B & B Bygones Antiques
111 S. Main St.
903/845-2655

Old Tyme Antiques & Cllbls.
111 S. Main St.
903/845-4708

Antiques
112 S. Main St.
903/845-6493

Carlyne's Collectables
112 N. Main St.
903/845-3923

Main Street Treasures
113 N. Main St.
903/845-6671

Good Old Stuff
114 S. Main St.
903/845-8316

K D Wayside Shop
119 S. Main St.
903/845-4093

Mel's Country Classics
120 S. Main St.
903/845-2519

The Loft
121 S. Main St.
903/845-4429

Country Girl Collection
124 S. Main St.
903/845-6143

Dru's Knick Knacks
125 S. Main St.
903/845-5635

Country Carousel Mall
201 S. Main St.
903/845-4531

Studio
201 N. Main St.
903/845-6910

Bishop's Antique Mall
202 S. Main St.
903/845-7247

Saint Clair Antique Emporium
104 W. Pacific Ave.
903/845-4079

Heritage Antiques & Cllbls.
112 W. Pacific Ave.
903/845-3021

66 GLEN FLORA

Glen Flora Emporium
103 South Bridge Street
409/677-3249
Open Wed.-Sun. 10-6

Directions: Glen Flora is five miles north of U.S. Hwy. 59 at Wharton, Texas. Take the Eagle Lake exit and travel north on FM 102 until you reach the small town of Glen Flora. Bridge Street is FM 960, which intersects with FM 102. The shop is at the intersection of FM 102 and FM 960. Turn left into the parking lot. You can't miss the emporium - it's the largest building for miles.

The town of Glen Flora was founded in 1900 and is currently undergoing restoration and reconstruction. The building that houses the emporium was built in 1912. This 20 plus dealer mall handles furniture, glassware, pottery, jewelry, vintage clothing and so on.

67 GOLIAD

Goliad is one of the three oldest municipalities in Texas and was the site of the Aranama Indian village name Santa Dorotea. In 1749 the Spanish government transferred The Royal Presidio (fort) of Nuestra Senora De Loreto De La Bahia De Expiritu Santo to this location along with the Mission Nuestra Senora Del Espiritu Santo De Zuniga. A small villa grew up around the walls of the fort and was called La Bahia. This area was occupied by the Spanish until 1821 when Mexico became an independent nation. In 1829 the name "Goliad" was officially adopted. It is an anagram of the name "Hidalgo" in honor of the patriot priest of the Mexican Revolution.

In what was termed the first offensive action of the Texas Revolution, local colonists captured Goliad on October 9, 1845. The First Declaration of Texas Independence was signed here on December 20. Along with it was raised the "Bloody Arm Flag", the first flag of Texas independence. During the 1836 campaign, Col. James Fannin's Texans were defeated at the Battle of Coleto and were massacred one week later on March 27, 1836 at the Presidio La Bahia. The Goliad Massacre represents the largest single loss of life (352) in the cause of Texas independence and inspired the battle cry "Remember The Alamo - Remember Goliad."

The Honeycomb Antiques
122 N. Courthouse Square
512/645-2331

The Christmas Goose
136 N. Courthouse Square
512/645-8087

68 GONZALES

Catty Corner Antiques
501 N. Saint Joseph St.
210/672-2975

Dub's Antique Mall
517 N. Saint Joseph St.
210/672-7917

Bowden's Antiques
620 N. Saint Joseph St.
210/672-7770

Violet's Treasures
712 N. Saint Joseph St.
210/672-9744

Laurel Ridge Antiques
827 N. Saint Joseph St.
210/672-2484

Polly's House Flowers & Antqs.
830 Saint Paul St.
210/672-2013

69 GRANBURY

Brazos River Trading Co.
115 E. Bridge St.
817/573-5191

Sugar & Spice Antiques
117 W. Bridge St.
817/579-1224

Antique Emporium
116 1/2 N. Crockett St.
817/573-1939

Wagon Yard Antiques
213 N. Crockett St.
817/573-5321

Scarlet Thread
3018 Fall Creek Hwy.
817/326-3430

Antique Mall of Granbury
4303 N. Hwy. 37
817/279-1645

Classic Antiques
4316 Hwy. 377
817/579-5658

The Bazaar
4318 E. Hwy. 377
817/579-9295

Trading Company
109 N. Houston St.
817/573-3800

Hightower Antiques & Uniques
130 N. Houston St.
817/573-4488

Pearl St. Antiques & Treasures
503 E. Pearl St.
817/279-1270

Witherspoon's Antiques
600 E. Pearl St.
817/573-5254

70 GRAPELAND

Bobbye's
315 S. Market St.
409/687-4979

Echoes of Texas
924 N. Market St.
409/687-2070

Flo's Antiques
210 Main
409/687-4778

71 GRAPEVINE

Guests Main Street Antiques
201 E. Franklin St.
817/488-3647

Julia's Antiques & Tearoom
210 N. Main St.
817/329-0622

Air Nostalgia
420 S. Main St.
817/481-9005

Collectors Exchange
415 N. Northwest Hwy.
817/329-6946

Grapevine Antique Mall
415 N. Northwest Hwy.
817/329-6946

72 GREENVILLE

Better Days Antiques
2402 Lee St.
903/455-3035

Courthouse Square Antiques
2512 Lee St.
903/455-0557

Downtown Tradin Days
2801 Lee St.
903/454-9908

Billie Taggart's 1800 Shop
2417 Oneal St.
903/455-4151

Country Craft Mall
2814 Terrell Rd.
903/455-7736

73 GROESBECK

Groesbeck Antiques Mall
105 N. Ellis St.
817/729-3443

Bonds Store & Gallery
217 W. Navasota St.
817/729-5511

74 HARLINGEN

Tejas Finders
Paul C. Moon Jr.
Rt. 1, Box 695 Wilson Road
210/423-6870

He's only 20 years old, but already well on his way to establishing a solid professional name for himself in the antique trade. "He" is Paul C. Moon, Jr., and he is what's known as a "picker" in the antique world.

"I search for whatever the buyer is looking for," says Moon. "When I locate the piece, I send the buyer photographs of the piece, if possible, and, if he is completely satisfied, we come to an agreement and I expedite the deal."

Moon began his interest in antiques when he was managing an antique shop in the Harlingen, Texas area. He was fascinated by the Victorian style and era, and now specializes in Victorian pieces; however, he will search for whatever style and pieces a buyer wants to find. He's been a picker for two years, and business is good.

Working out of his home in Harlingen, Moon generally limits his travels and searches to the valley area around Harlingen. Situated in the very southeastern tip of Texas, Harlingen is conveniently located in the coastal region of east Texas, where the Victorian style abounds, left over from the influence of the steamboat and paddlewheeler days, plus the influence of changing styles that were easily accessible by water routes.

The next time you need a certain piece and style, call Moon. If it's Victorian in Texas, he probably knows right where to look.

Hilites
107 E. Jackson St.
210/412-7573

Somewhere In Time Antiques
111 E. Jackson St.
210/412-2577

Frank's Collectables & Antqs.
123 E. Jackson St.
210/423-4041

Youngblood Interiors & Antqs.
302 E. Jackson St.
210/412-1155

Antique Furniture Warehouse
2710 South F St.
210/425-3131

75 HASKELL

Nemir's Antiques
510 North 2nd Street
817/864-2258
Fax: 817/864-3124
Open Mon.-Fri., 10-5

Directions: Nemir's is located at the corner of 2nd Street and North Avenue F. From Hwy. 380, turn north 1 block west of the main red light, which is Avenue F. Go 1 block to 2nd Street and turn east. The shop is right on the corner. From Hwy. 277, turn west 1 block north of the main red light. This will be 2nd Street and the shop is on the corner.

Nemir's Antiques is a large, family-owned store with a grand selection of quality antiques and collectibles. The 5,000-square-foot store offers something for everyone including, but by no means limited to, a variety of old toys and pottery.

Peddler's Village
304 S. 1st St.
817/864-2878

Old Stuff Antiques & Gifts
300 S. Ave. E
817/864-2430

76 HENDERSON

Ms. Patty's Attic
501 Kilgore Drive
903/655-1146

Sweet Lorraine's
501 1/2 Kilgore Dr.
903/657-1163

Trunks & Treasures
123 E. Main St.
903/657-8879

Emporium on the Square
102 N. Marshall St.
903/657-3854

Nelda's Nook
112 N. Marshall St.
903/657-2332

Four Oaks Gallery
709 State Hwy. 43 E
903/657-8207

77 HILLSBORO

Veranda's Interiors & Antiques
114 S. Covington St.
254/582-9995

Old Citizens Emporium
50 W. Elm St.
254/582-1995

Dee Dee's Gifts & Tiques
106 E. Elm St.
254/582-0355

Arnold's Country Charm
110 W. Elm St.
254/582-5201

Franklin St. Antiques
55 W. Franklin St.
254/582-0055

Antique Village Inc.
116 E. Franklin St.
254/582-8632

Rainbow Gems Jwlrs.
75 N. Waco St.
254/582-8430

Hillsboro Antique Mall
114 S. Waco St.
254/582-8330

78 HOUSTON

Carolyn Thompson's Antique Center of Texas
1001 West Loop North
713/688-4211
Open: Daily 10-6

Directions: 1001 West Loop North, just 2 miles north of The Galleria.

No trip to, or near, Houston would be complete without a visit to Carolyn Thompson's Antique Center. David and I recently spent an entire day browsing throughout the store. Fortunately for us the Center has a Texas Tea Room (David is not a happy shopper when he's hungry). The food was wonderful. Our choice was the special of the day offered from a menu of soups, salads, sandwiches or hot entree (the special) along with desserts and cookies for munching as you shop.

The Antique Center is the kind of store every antique shop or mall should be. The inventory is very diverse offering something for everyone. For me this makes for a very pleasant shopping experience. My selections are usually primitive, early American painted pieces and I was thrilled to find a nice offering of such pieces amongst the exquisite formal furnishings found throughout the store. If your decor requires massive, finely crafted, artfully detailed furnishings, then look no further than Carolyn Thompson's were you'll find the absolute best in the nation. Accessories of comparable quality are also available to complete an outstanding room setting. Below is a partial listing of the items available from over 200 dealers at Carolyn Thompson's Antique Center of Texas: rugs, clocks, china, bronze, cabinets, chandeliers, art glass, French, Italian, American furnishings, stained glass, porcelain (one dealer specializes in Haviland), flow blue, silver, lace, paintings, architectural pieces, religious items, vintage hunting and fishing equipment, jewelry, dolls, and a large selection of collectibles.

See review in color section.

Trade Mart Antiques
Sam Houston Tollway @ Hammerly
713/467-2506
Open: Fri, Sat. & Sun. 10-6

Directions: Located at Sam Houston Tollway @ Hammerly, 2 miles north of I-10.

One of Houston's finest antique shopping experiences, the Trade Mart, established in 1979, houses more than 100 individual shops with a wide and diverse inventory of some of the finest antiques in East Texas. Looking for that special piece of pattern glass you haven't been able to find or the missing piece to Grandmother's old Haviland china? What about that special piece of French furniture you've been searching for? Or Oak? Or Pine? Or Mahogany? This market is a dream come true for the antiquer in all of us that desire a piece of the past. Stop in, take you time; we know you'll find something you just can't live without.

Sherry Kelley's Antiques
2323 Woodhead Street
713/520-7575
Fax: 713/520-6362
Open Mon.-Sat., 10-6

Directions: From Hwy. 59, the Southwest Freeway, exit Shepherd and go north on Shepherd to Fairview. Turn east (right) on Fairview and go to the first stop sign, which is Woodhead. Sherry Kelley's Antiques is at the corner of Fairview and Woodhead. From I-10, exit Shepherd and go south to West Gray and turn left. Go east to Woodhead and turn right. Proceed south to 2323 Woodhead and Fairview. The shop is two blocks north of Westheimer and 7 blocks east of Fairview.

Sherry Kelley is a direct importer of European antiques, making up to five trips a year to Europe, hand picking each item. Sherry specializes in mahogany Georgian style furniture, prints, books, crystal and decorative items.

Knight's Gallery
1320 W. Alabama
713/521-2785

Brian Stringer Antiques
2031 W. Alabama
713/526-7380

Lynette Proler Antq. Jewelers
2622 W. Alabama St.
713/521-1827

Almeda Antique Mall
9827 Almeda Genoa Rd.
713/941-7744

Dorothy Mostert Antiques
404Avondale St.
713/523-9165

Warren Antique Collection
2121 N. West Belt
713/465-2985

Carl Moore Antiques
1610 Bissonnet St.
713/524-2502

Gilded Monkey
2314 Bissonnet St.
713/526-8661

Silver Shop
2348 Bissonnet St.
713/526-7256

R & S Antiques
2402 Bissonnet St.
713/524-9178

Southwest Antiques & Cllbls.
6735 Bissonnet St.
713/981-6773

H Karl Scharold Antiques Inc.
5243 Buffalo Speedway
713/661-3466

Back Porch Antiques
17715 Clay Rd.
713/345-9238

Clearys Antiques
10817 Craigheard Dr.
713/664-6643

Odeon Gallery
2117 Dunlavy St.
713/521-1111

Inside Outside
510 W. 18th St.
713/869-6911

Four Roses Antiques
7979 N. Eldridge Pkwy
713/897-0507

Adkins Architectural Antiques
3515 Fannin St.
713/522-6547

Made In France
2912 Ferndale
713/529-7949

Ferndale Gallery & Antiques
2935 Ferndale St.
713/527-8358

The Market-Champion Vllge
5419 W. FM 1960
713/440-8281

French Antique Exchange
3301 Fondren Rd.
713/785-0785

Carriage House
10609 Grant Rd.
713/469-4840

T's Antiques
10609 Grant Rd.
713/890-8899

Barziza's Antiques
2121 NW Belt Dr.
713/467-0628

Simone Antique & More II
11723 W. Bellfort
713/561-7403

Madison Alley Antiques
1720 Bissonnett St.
713/526-6146

Britannia Antiques
2338 Bissonnet St.
713/529-3779

Antiques Antiques
14546 Carol Crest St.
713/527-0841

Southwest Antiques Too
6727 Bissonnet
713/981-6633

Simpson's Galleries
4001 Main St.
713/524-6751

Gabriel Galleries of Houston
7600 Burgoyne
713/528-2647

Crescent Enterprises Antiques
9229 Clay Rd.
713/462-4880

Antiques Houston
3200 W. Dallas Ave.
713/523-4705

J Silver Antiques
3845 Dunlave St.
713/526-2988

Candlelight Cottage
7979 N. Eldridge Pkwy
713/469-4210

Sanders Antiques
315 Fairview St.
713/522-0539

James A Gundry Inc.
2910 Ferndale St.
713/524-6622

Phyllis Tucker Antiques
2919 Ferndale St.
713/524-0165

McLaren's Antiques & Gifts
3225 FM 1960
713/893-0432

White & Day Antiques
6711 FM 1960
713/444-3836

Ann's Creative Frame & Antqs.
1928 Fountain View Dr.
713/781-7772

Look
5110 Griggs Rd.
713/748-6641

Burton's Antiques
9333 Harwin Dr.
713/977-5885

Cobblestone Antiques
7623 Louetta
713/251-0660

Campbell & Co. Antiques
3110 Houston Ave.
713/880-8178

Picket Fence
3010 Hwy. 146
713/474-4845

Woodlands Antique Mall
26710 N. IH 45
713/364-8111

Timely Treasures Antiques
11503 Jones Rd.
713/897-9577

Bediko Antqs. & Refinishing
3402 Laura Koppe Rd.
713/692-3008

Gillespie's Antiques
4113 Leeland St.
713/247-9604

Richard's Antiquites Inc.
3500 Main St.
713/528-5651

Once in a Life Time
12454 Memorial Dr.
713/465-8828

Thistle Antiques
12472 Memorial Dr.
713/984-2329

Happenings
4203 Montrose Blvd.
713/524-1507

Annie's Art & Antiques
1415 Murray Bay St.
713/973-6659

Old Katy Rd. Antiques
9198 Old Katy Rd. #B
713/461-8124

Market Place Antiques
10910 Old Katy Road
713/464-8023

Sitting Room
2402 Quenby
713/523-1932

Baca Antique
2121 W. Sam Houston Pkwy. N
713/984-0228

Hurta's Historics
2121 W. Sam Houston Pkwy. N
713/468-1680

Trade Mart
Sam Houston Tollway, Hammerly
713/467-2506

Antique Panache
9137 Spring Branch Dr.
713/464-2022

Country Home Antiques
14916 Stuebner Airline Rd.
713/440-1186

Silvi's Antiques Etc.
2223 Hwy. 6 S
713/597-8557

Once Upon A time
1004 W. Hwy. 6
713/331-7676

Gypsy Savage
1509 Indiana St.
713/528-0897

Meg's Cottage Inc.
2819 W T C Jester Blvd.
713/956-2229

Nelly's Porch
16300 Kuykendahl Rd.
713/893-4659

Steven's Antique Furniture
5301 Laura Koppe Rd.
713/631-3196

Antique Center of Texas
1001 W. Loop N
713/688-4211

Norbert Antiques
3617 Main St.
713/524-4334

Darby's Off-Memorial
12460 Memorial Dr.
713/465-0245

Antiques at Rummel Creek
13190 Memorial Dr.
713/461-9110

Antiques on Nineteenth
345 W. 19th St.
713/869-5030

L. R. Antiques
1919 W. Sam Houston Pkwy.
713/935-0121

C & H Antiques
10910 Old Katy Road
713/465-1120

Max Miller Antiques
10910 Old Katy Road
713/467-0450

Norman
2425 Ralph St.
713/521-1811

British Emporium
2121 W. Sam Houston Pkwy. N
713/467-3455

General Mothers Antiques
2121 W. Sam Houston Pkwy. N
713/984-9461

Studio
3951 San Felipe St.
713/961-7540

Cabin Creek Lodge
1703 Spring Cypress Rd.
713/350-5559

Mattye's This And That Antqs.
14916 Stuebner Airline Rd.
713/580-4222

Reeves Antiques
2415 Taft St.
713/523-5577

Flashbacks Funtiques
1626 Westheimer Rd.
713/522-7900

Rosen Kavalieriques
1715 Westheimer Rd.
713/527-0660

Pride and Joy Antiques
1727 Westheimer Rd.
713/522-8435

Emporium Architectural Antqs.
1800 Westheimer Rd.
713/528-3808

Howard Graetz Antiques
1844 Westheimer Rd.
713/522-5908

Kay O'Toole Antiques
1921 Westheimer Rd.
713/523-1921

Antique Pavilion
2311 Westheimer Rd.
713/520-9755

David Lackey Antiques & China
2311 Westheimer
713/942-7171

Margaret K. Reese Antiques
2233 Westheimer
713/523-8889

Wicket Antique
2233 Westheimer Rd.
713/522-0779

Brownstone Gallery
2803 Westheimer Rd.
713/523-8171

The Market
4060 Westheimer
713/960-9084

Joyce Horn Antiques
1008 Wirt Rd.
713/688-0507

Carol Gibbins Antiques
1817 Woodhead St.
713/524-9011

John Holt Antqs. & Primitives
2416 Woodhead
713/528-5065

House of Glass
3319 Louisiana St.
713/528-5289

Abelar Antiques
6008 W. 34th St.
713/683-8055

Antique Warehaus
1714 Westheimer Rd.
713/522-6858

Old Blue House Antiques
1719 Westheimer Rd.
713/521-2515

Westheimer Antique Center
1738 Westheimer Rd.
713/529-8585

Past Era Antique Jewelry
2311 Westheimer Rd.
713/524-7110

Hillingham Antiques
1848 Westheimer Rd.
713/523-4335

River Oaks Antiques Center
2119 Westheimer Rd.
713/520-8238

Crow & Company
2311 Westheimer Rd.
713/524-6055

M. J. Fine Things
2311 Westheimer
713/529-6960

Florian Fine Art
2323 Westheimer Rd.
713/942-9919

R.N. Wakefield & Co..
2702 Westheimer Rd.
713/528-4677

Lewis & Maese Arts Antiques
3738 Westheimer Rd.
713/960-1454

Belgravia Antiques
11195 Westheimer
713/785-4797

Cottage Antiques
2233 Westheimer
713/523-8889

Golden Eye
2121 Woodhead St.
713/528-3379

Las Cruces Antiques
2422 Woodhead
713/524-2422

Historical Houston Heights

Whether you are seeking affordable antiques, an outstanding playground for the kids, or turn-of-the-century showplace homes, Houston Heights is the place to come. Founded in 1887, this planned streetcar community, designed to be a rural sanctuary from Houston, is located just four miles from downtown. A

Texas

landmark for over a century, its main thoroughfare, Heights Boulevard, was modeled after Boston's Commonwealth Avenue and has been designated by the City of Houston as a "Scenic Right-of-Way." Victorian and early 20th century homes, churches, and a public library still line the Boulevard, and today an excellent walking trail exists along the esplanade where the trolley once ran. The spectacular new Heights Playground, a Robert Leathers design, complete with a depot and Victorian castle, plus Marmion Park with its majestic gazebo, and the Victorian Rose Garden are all on the Boulevard. All three are maintained by Heights' neighborhood organization, the Houston Heights Association. In addition to the beauty and historical attractions of this area, the Heights also provides shoppers with a wealth of antique stores, clothing stores, folk art shops, and casual eateries.

Old Fashioned Things
811 Yale Street
713/880-8398
713/868-7468 - Fax
Open: Mon.-Sat. 10-6 (later during holidays)

Directions: Exit off I-10 West or 610 North Loop West - From I-10W take the Yale/Heights Blvd. exit and go north. From 610 N. Loop, take the Yale St. exit and go south.

Located in the Historical Houston Heights area, Old Fashioned Things is housed in a home built in 1906. In 1996 the shop received The Community Improvement Award for renovation in the commercial property category.

Originally a part of a co-op mall for 10 years, Old Fashioned Things opened at its current location in March of 1996. The shop is filled with antiques, collectibles, and very special gift items as well as vintage and costume jewelry, furniture, glassware, linens, etc.

R & F Antiques
Specializing in American Antiques
912 Yale Street
713/861-7750
Open: Sun.-Tue. by chance of appt., Wed.-Sat. 10-5:30

Directions: Located approximately 7 blocks north of I-10 at the Heights and Yale exit.

In this "barn" red building, you will find seven rooms brimming with American furniture. For more than 25 years, Gary & Jennifer Barashi have brought the finest quality antiques to the Houston area. The shop features curved glass china cabinets, tables, chairs, secretaries, beds, chests and an outstanding collection of fireplace mantels. *Note: (I personally have not visited this shop, but I have been told by several serious collectors that it is one of the best shops in the country.)

11th Street Antiques
720 W. 11th St.
713/802-2719

Alabama Furn. & Accessories
2200 Yale St.
713/862-3035

Alboe's Antiques
718 W. 11th St.
713/861-8750

Antiques on Nineteenth
345 W. 19th St.
713/869-5030

Byers Original Finishes
115 W. 13th St.
713/868-5937

Charm of Yesteryear Antiques
355 W. 19th St.
713/868-1141

Chippendale Eastlake in Hghts.
250 W. 19th St.
713/869-8633

Country Gentlemen
221 E. 11th St.
713/880-9165

Heights Antique Co-op
321 W. 19th St.
713/864-7237

Historic Heights Antqs. & Intrs.
249 W. 19th St.
713/868-2600

Homestyle Resale
215 E. 11th St.
713/868-3400

Inside Outside
510 W. 18th St.
713/869-6911

Johns Flowers & Antiques
373 W. 19th St.
713/862-8717

Laroy Antiques & Refg., Inc.
632 W. 19th St.
713/862-5051

Sugars Collectables
249 W. 19th St.
713/868-7006

Stardust Antique
1129 E. 11th St.
713/868-1600

Twenty Second Second
611 W. 22nd St.
713/864-0261

William & Mary's Antiques
605 W. 19th St.
713/864-7605

Past Connections & Cllbls.
235 West 19th St.
713/802-1992

August Antiques
803 Heights Blvd.
713/880-3353

Heights Country Store
801 Heights Blvd.
713/862-4161

Everything Special
1906 Ashland
713/869-6906

Heights Collection
3617 White Oak Dr.
713/880-8203

Heights Station Antiques
121 Heights Blvd.
713/868-3175

On The Corner
837 Studewood St.
713/863-9143

Jubilee
242 W. 19th St.
713/869-5885

Heights Antiques on Yale
2110 Yale
Phone Not Available

Edie's Sales, Unlimited
701 E. 20th St.
Phone Not Available

Favorite Places To Eat

Cracker Barrel Old Country Store
I-10 & Barker-Cypress Rd., Exit 748
281/492-1585

79 HUMBLE

Spruce Goose Shoppes
620 2nd St.
713/540-7766

Granny Jean's Antiques
212 Charles St.
713/548-3020

80 HUNTSVILLE

Bluebonnet Square Antq. Mall
1110 11th St.
409/291-2800

Victorian House Antiques
Hwy. 19
409/295-3904

Fisher's Antiques
Hwy. 190
409/295-7661

Good Old Days
604 S. Sam Houston Ave.
409/291-8407

Scottie's
1110 Sam Houston Ave.
409/291-9414

Stone Wall Antiques
1202 Sam Houston Ave.
409/291-3422

The Raven Antiques & Gallery
1204 Sam Houston Ave.
409/291-2723

Sam Houston Antique Mall
1210 Sam Houston Ave.
409/295-7716

Avalon Antiques
1215 Sam Houston Ave.
409/291-6097

81 HURST

Antiques Et Al
208 W. Bedford Euless Rd.
817/282-8197

Country Express
245 W. Bedford Euless Rd.
817/282-9335

Hurst Antique Mall
416 W. Bedford Euless Rd.
817/282-2224

Antique Flea
431 W. Bedford Euless Rd.
817/285-8859

Whistle Stop
1350 Brookside
817/282-3224

Antique Homestead
750 W. Pipeline Rd.
817/268-1527

82 IRVING

Antiques on Main Street
105 South Main St.
972-259-1093

Ken's Discount Antqs. & Gifts
108 W. 6th Street
972/259-5505

Timeless Treasures
111 S. Main St.
972/254-9007

Irving Antique Mall
129 S. Main St.
972/254-0339

Oliver's Used Books & Things
130 S. Main St.
972/253-1299

Ye Olde Shoppe
135 S. Main St.
972/254-0615

Patsy B
136 S. Main
972/254-1086

Yesterdaze Collectibles
304 W. Pioneer Dr.
972/253-6473

Kimberley's Antiques
247 Plymouth Park
972/986-5733

Moss Rose
510 E. 2nd St.
972/579-7491

Nostalgia Etc.
1120 Senter Rd. Ste 102
972/554-6781

B & E Ventures
410 E. 6th St.
972/253-7615

Debby's Emporium
929 E. 6th St.
972/438-5895

83 JACKSONVILLE

Treasure Cove Mall
2027 N. Jackson (Hwy. 69 N)
903/586-6140
Open: Mon, Thurs., Fri., Sat., 10-6, Sunday 12-5, closed Tue. & Wed.

Directions: Located on Hwy. 69 North approximately 2 miles from the intersection of Hwys. 69 & 79.

Treasure Cove Mall is an exceptional shop in the wares that it presents and for one very unique service. For 6 years the mall has specialized in refinishing and restoring grand pianos! Three staff refinishers complete the "huge" task of turning your 1800s grand into a true masterpiece. Additionally, the shop provides caning and wicker repair. For those of you just wanting to shop, the mall offers an outstanding selection of quality antiques within its 10,000 square feet; Roseville, Weller, glassware, quilts, clocks,

Coke collectibles, Blue Ridge, old tools and furnishings from formal to primitive are just a few of the items available from the mall's 50 dealers.

Smith Barret Antiques
531 N. Bolton St.
903/586-5123

Ruffles
114 E. Commerce St.
903/586-0141

Jackson Street Merchantile
1201 S. Jackson St.
903/586-0282

84 JASPER

The Cottage
337 College
409/384-7862

Nancy Jane's
403 College
409/384-4781

Past Time Antiques
Hwy. 96 S
409/384-6440

Hwy. 63 Antiques
Hwy. 63
409/384-7324

Hearts & Flowers
209 E. Houston
409/384-2462

The Heart of Things
126 E. Lamar
409/384-9374

Hancock Drug Store
165 N. Main St.
409/384-2541

S. E. Texas Antique Mall
2034 S. Wheeler St.
409/384-7078

Treasures of Old
2573 N. Wheeler
409/384-9580

85 JEFFERSON

Maison-Bayou Bed & Breakfast Plantation

300 Bayou Street
903/665-7600
Fax: 903-665-7100
Website: www.maisonbayou.com
Open year around
Rates $59-135

This place is so wonderful we decided to use more text than usual - so therefore we opted to omit the directions. For specific directions from your location, please call Jan or Pete.

On the surface of your mind, it's sort of hard to connect Texas with Louisiana swamps and bayous - unless you live in east Texas - but if you think about it, or if you look at a map, you realize that east Texas butts right up to Louisiana and the two states sort of blur the lines between them for quite a ways into Texas. That's why you end up with such an anomaly like Maison-Bayou in Jefferson, Texas. Just over the Texas/Louisiana state line and northwest a bit from Shreveport, Jefferson itself sits on a river beside the Big Cypress Bayou.

Maison-Bayou, a Creole plantation, is located on the ancient river bed of the Big Cypress, in the middle of 55 wooded acres, yet it is only a short walk or a very short drive to the center of historic downtown Jefferson. The main house is an authentic reproduction of an 1850s Plantation Overseer's House, which features heart of pine floors, pine walls and ceilings, natural gas burning lanterns in each room, and period antiques and fabrics. A full breakfast is served in the dining room. The cabins are architecturally styled after authentic slave quarter cabins, with modern amenities carefully mixed in. All cabins have private baths, and yes, they all have indoor plumbing - although the toilets are the old fashioned pullchain variety - and individually controlled heat and air conditioning. Each cabin is located on the cypress alligator pond with a full view. Alligators are often spotted during the summer, while beaver and otters cavort in the pond during the winter.

Cabin One is the most authentically reproduced example of a slave cabin on the plantation, with cypress shake shingle roof, high pitched ceiling, wood walls and heart of pine floors. The hand-made four poster bed is full size and features a hand-made quilt. The cabin also provides a wood burning fireplace and a pier with a canoe.

Cabin Two features whitewashed walls, heart of pine floors and old-style tin roof. The Mission style full size wooden bed dates to the turn of the century and is adorned with a traditional quilt. Youth size bunk beds are included in the cabin as well. Relax in the rocking chair and watch the beaver pond from the cabin.

Cabins Three and Four are built in the "dog trot" architectural style: two independent cabins having a common roofline, sharing a full-length front and back porch, separated by a six-foot wide breezeway that runs the entire width between both cabins. Each cabin holds a primitive four poster wooden bed, rocking chairs and tables with reading lamps.

Next choice for guests is the Robert E. Lee replica steamboat paddlewheeler, moored along the bank of the cypress pond. Guests sleep in a queen size sleigh bed, and relax downstairs on the bow under a cooling ceiling fan. Or, they can climb the spiral staircase to the pilots' house and go outside for a view of the cypress pond, then stretch out for a sunbath on the deck!

Don't feel quite comfortable sleeping with the 'gators'? For all you landlubbers, there are two railroad cars and three bunkhouses still available. First is the authentic private rail car. Here guests are surrounded by beautifully varnished wood walls and ceiling, accented by 20 windows and 2 skylights, giving a panoramic view of the woods and Big Cypress Bayou.

The riverfront caboose sits directly on the banks of Big Cypress Bayou. This old Frisco line caboose offers a full size iron bed and a view of the river from the bed or from the observation windows.

The three bunkhouses are built on the old Jefferson to Marshall stagecoach road and, appropriately, overlook the corral where horses, a burrow and a llama make their homes. Buck, doe and fawns graze in nearby pastures.

As if these unusual accommodations aren't enough to hold your interest, there are a multitude of activities for guests to enjoy. On-site events and catering include pig roasts, crawfish boils, barbeques, trail rides and hayrides, weddings and receptions, company outings, family gatherings, camp and church groups and birthday parties. Wonderful nature trails and excellent fishing holes are a favorite with guest.

Maison-Bayou is a one-stop pleasure destination in a setting that's like a page out of history or a good novel. Don't miss it!

Pride House

409 Broadway
1-800-894-3526
Rates $85-110

Myth America lives in this former steamboat port of 2,200; in antique houses, behind picket fences, along brick streets and on Cypress Bayou. Step into 19th century small-town America as you walk through the doors of the finest homes in town, chug through the lillypads on the paddlewheel steamer, cheer the newlyweds leaving the church, listen to the gossip over catfish at the cafe, and find things at the hardware you haven't seen in years.

Located in the 19th century antique capital of Texas, Pride House Bed & Breakfast invites you to shop in dozens of antique shops by day and sleep in one at night!

Guests will find 10 rooms with private baths in this turn-of-the-century home with its 12-foot ceilings, stained glass windows, family steamboat memorabilia, antiques and heirlooms, original art, footed bathtubs and fireplaces. Their enticements include some statements that anyone would be hard-pressed to ignore: "Come on the weekend - we'll bake you a cake. Weekdays, we'll cut your rate. Every day we'll treat you like family - with hot or cold drinks whenever you like and breakfasts you'll never forget." These legendary breakfasts include things like their own Jefferson Pecan Coffee, Pears Praline, Not Eggsactly Benedict, Texas Bluebonnet Muffins and Strawberry Butter.

River City Mercantile
111 Austin
903/665-8270

Jefferson General Store
113 E. Austin St.
903/665-8481

Old Mill Antiques
210 E. Austin St.
903/665-8601

Liz-Beth's Antiques
216 W. Austin St.
903/665-8781

Country Corner
Hwy. 59 S.
903/665-8344

Granny Had It
114 N. Polk St.
903/665-3148

Jefferson Bottling Works
203 Polk St.
903/665-3736

Old Store II
226 N. Polk St.
903/665-2422

Three Rivers Antiques
116 N. Walnut St.
903/665-8721

Walnut Street Market
121 N. Walnut St.
903/665-8864

The Old Store I
123 N. Walnut St.
903/665-3562

Old House Antiques
304 N. Walnut St.
903/665-8852

Golden Oldies
203A N. Polk
No Phone Listed

Jefferson Arts
607 E. Broadway
903/665-3174

Petticoat Junktion
120 Polk
903/935-7322

Robbie's Music Machines
215 Polk
903/665-8533

Sweet Memories
Corner Walnut & Hwy. 49 E
903/665-3533

Turner's Place
Hwy. 59 North
903/665-2282

Choices Antiques Mall
215 Polk
903/665-8504

Cypress Cargo
120 W. Lafayette
903/665-1414

Gold Leaf
207 N. Polk
903/665-2882

86 KATY

From Rags to Riches
5714 1st St.
281/391-8200

Classic Home Furnishings
5305 Hwy. Blvd.
281/391-7515

Country Village
5809 Hwy. Blvd.
281/391-2040

Decorative Treasures
5626 2nd St.
281/391-2299

Limited Editions
2nd St.
281/391-1994

87 KERRVILLE

Corner Post
1518 Broadway
830/792-3377

Five Points Antiques
607 East Lane
830/257-8424

Grandma's House
200 S. Sidney Baker
830/896-8668

Pampell's Antiques
701 Water St.
830/257-8484

Water Street Antique Co.
820 Water St.
830/257-5044

88 LA PORTE

A Unique Store
300 W. Main St.
281/471-5551

Roelof's Antiques
301 W. Main St.
281/471-3807

Through The Ages
324 W. Main St.
281/470-6614

L & B Antiques
312 W. Main St.
281/470-8533

89 LAMPASAS

Country Collectables
1900 S. Hwy. 281
512/556-5686

Antique Emporium
406 S. Live Oak St.
512/556-6843

Ashley's Antiques & Collectibles
523 E. 3rd St.
512/556-6555

90 LEANDER

Trails End Bed & Breakfast
The B & B Store (gift shop)
12223 Trails End Road #7
512-267-2901 or 1-800-850-2901
B & B open year round
Rates $55 - 170
Gift shop open year round 1-5 - call for appointment

Directions: From IH 35 two miles out of Georgetown, take RM 1431 and go 11.85 miles to Trails End Road. Turn left onto Trails End and go 7/10 of a mile to the gravel road. There will be several mail boxes next to the gravel road. Turn left and go to where the road curves to the right. Keep on going around the curve and the B&B is a large gray house trimmed in white on the left. An appointment is needed. The inn is located on the north side of Lake Travis between Cedar Park, Jonestown, Austin and Leander.

This is the perfect place to go for a getaway weekend or vacation. Trails End is a country retreat located in the unique central Texas hill country. As innkeepers JoAnn and Tom Patty say, "There is nothing immediate you have to do at Trails End B&B." That means guests get to kick back and enjoy the porches, decks, the gazebo, the refreshing pool, walking in the woods or riding bikes.

Make it a family vacation - there's a private guest house for six - and bring the boat or water toys for a splashing good time on nearby Lake Travis. For golfing guests, a number of golf courses are convenient. When the urge to explore hits, downtown Austin is just 35 minutes away, and Georgetown, Round Rock, Cedar Park, Lago Vista, Leander, Burnet and Salado are an easy drive.

Hitching Post
18643 FM 1431
512/267-9125

91 LEAGUE CITY

Favorite Places To Eat

Cracker Barrel Old Country Store
I-45 & Hwy. 518, Exit 23
281/332-1174

92 LEWISVILLE

After Glow Antiques
417 E. Church St.
972/221-6907

Buttermilk Flats Antiques
565 E. Church St.
972/221-1993

Rare Bits Antiques
310 Lake Haven
972/420-4222

Antiques Etc.
180 Lewisville Plaza
972/436-5904

Corner Home Antq. & Gallery
101 W. Main St.
972/219-0887

Victorian Rose Antiques
102 W. Main St.
972/221-7266

String of Pearls
104 W. Main
972/436-9337

Old Red Tractor Antiques
109 W. Main
972/420-0026

Pepper Tree
112 W. Main St.
972/221-6345

Looking Glass Antique Mall
788 S. Mill
972/221-4022

Sample House
2403 S. Stemmons Frwy.
972/315-0212

Favorite Places To Eat

Cracker Barrel Old Country Store
I-35 E. & Fox Ave., Exit 451
972/436-6813

93 LIBERTY

Trinity River Trading Post
818 Commerce St.
409/336-3652

Beverly's Then & Now
1806 Sam Houston St.
409/336-9005

Liberty Bell Antique Co-Op
2040 Trinity St.
409/336-5222

94 LOCKHART

Royals Antiques
401 S. Commerce St.
512/398-6849

Archway Antiques
113 N. Main St.
512/398-7001

Lockhart Antique Emporium
119 W. San Antonio St.
512/398-4322

95 LONGVIEW

Blue Door Antiques
1311 Alphine St.
903/758-7592

George Preston's Antiques
205 N. Center St.
903/753-8041

Petticoat Lane Antiques
208 N. Center St.
903/757-8988

Turner Antiques
211 E. College St.
903/758-2562

Betty's Antiques
414 E. Cotton St.
903/753-8204

Antiques Traders
207 N. Court St.
903/758-9707

Jean's Antiques
2111 S. East Man Rd.
903/234-9011

Frederick-Nila Jewelers
306 N. 4th St.
903/753-2902

Classic Collections
409 W. Loop #281
903/663-1028

Consignments by Carolyn
1003 E. Marshall Ave.
903/758-7211

Jean's Antiques
1809 E. Marshall Ave.
903/234-9010

Linda's Best of Both Words
2713 W. Marshall Ave.
903/759-4422

Alice's Wonderland
3712 W. Marshall Ave.
903/295-1295

Gifts of Distinction
4005 W. Marshall Ave.
903/759-6055

Link to the Past
100 W. Tyler St.
903/758-6363

Treasures at Uptown Mall
106 W. Tyler St.
903/757-4425

Christie's Collectibles
113 W. Tyler St.
903/234-0816

96 LUBBOCK

Antique Mall of Lubbock
7907 W. 19th Street
806/796-2166
806/796-2164 Fax

Directions: From I-27 take Loop 289 to West 19th Street (Levelland Hwy. 114W). Continue west on 19th Street 3 miles and look for the Big Yellow Awning on the south side of the highway.

General Information: "The Source For Dealers" open 7 days a week from 10 to 6 with over 24,000 sq. ft. with 150 quality showcases and 80 fabulous booths specializing in "Hard to Find" Americana antiques and collectibles.

If you're an Antique Lover, this is one antique mall you truly don't want to miss! No brag, but they are told almost daily by dealers who travel the country that the Antique Mall of Lubbock is the BEST MALL they have ever been to. In addition, the Lubbock area has exploded with 5 malls and over 40 shops in the immediate area. Here are some of the collectibles you will find at the Antique Mall of Lubbock.

*Booth 7 - "Jennie Lee's Red Wing Shop" specializing in all types of pottery and stoneware especially some of the most fantastic pieces of Red Wing you will ever find!

*Booth 8 - "Dick Tarr's Treasures" specializes in a general line of furniture and collectibles including fine porcelain, carnival glass and one of the largest selections of Ertl banks in the Southwest!

*Booth 14 - Emma Ward's "Collectors Corner" specializes in all types of glass and dinnerware, including Depression and Elegant Glassware, Franciscan, Fiesta and Coors Rosebud.

*Booth 29 - Joyce Cheatham's "Bagladi's" booth has 1000s of small collectibles of every description imaginable.

*Booth 36 - "Chris' Collectibles" booth includes dolls of every description plus hundreds of toys and figures from the baby boom era.

*Booth 28 - "Ray Summer's Western Booth" has anything western related plus tools, farm and ranch related items.

*Booth 55 - "DR & Co.. Collectibles" carries a general line of all types of furniture, toy trains, fountain pens, tins, toys, books, sports memorabilia, black memorabilia and much more.

*Booth 59 - "RB's General Store" specializing in quality advertising, old store stock and anything unusual and hard to find. Expect to be impressed with quality and quantity! Catering to Quantity Buyers!!

*Booth 99 - "Nina's Treasures" has a HUGE quantity of general line antiques and collectibles of every description from small to large that are fabulous!

The booths listed above are just a few mentioned, but you can't miss "Papa's Pharmacy" which includes old drug store merchandise in pristine condition, "Shane's General Store" that has thousands of old store stock merchandise that are unbelievable - A MUST TO SEE, "Clay's Cowboy Hideaway", "Cory's Sport Booth", "Nina's Elegant Booth", "Kristy's Kitchen", "Logan's Blue Room", "Matt's Oil Booth", "Timmy's Coke Collectibles", and many more.

The Antique Mall has been voted by the people of Lubbock and the Lubbock area as the BEST ANTIQUE MALL four years in a row! This speaks volumes - so don't miss out!

Garden Patch
1311 Alcove Ave.
806/793-0982

Bobo's Treasures
202 Avenue S.
806/744-6449

Mandrell's Antiques & Cllbls.
5628 Brownfield Hwy.
806/799-0172

Treasure Chest Antiques
2226 Buddy Holly
806/744-0383

Carey Me Away Antiques
2309 E. 50th St.
806/765-0160

Katz in the Alley
2712 50th St.
806/795-9252

Antiques and More
3407 50th St.
806/791-1691

Finishing Touch
1401 N. Gary Ave.
806/762-2754

Flea Market
2323 K Avenue
806/747-8281

Train Station Antiques
6105 19th St.
860/788-0603

Glass Hut
7323 W. 19th St.
806/791-1260

As Time Goes By
4426 34th Street
806/795-0840

Lucky's World Antique Market
3612 P Avenue
806/744-2524

Chaparral Antique Mall
2202 Q Avenue
806/747-5431

Clark's Collectibles
2610 Salem Ave.
806/799-4747

Old Time Clock Shop
2610 Salem Ave.
806/797-8203

Vintage Rose
2610 Salem Ave.
806/793-7673

Ruth Little Art & Antiques
3402 73rd St.
806/792-0485

Antiques Galleria
1001 E. Slaton Rd.
806/745-3336

J Patrick's Antiques & Cllbls.
2206 34th St.
806/747-6731

Antiques Lubbock
2217 34th St.
806/763-5177

The Cottage
2247 34th St.
806/744-3927

Pat's Antiques
2257 34th St.
806/747-4798

Antique Marketplace
2801 26th St.
806/785-1531

As Time Goes By
4426 34th St.
806/795-0840

97 LUFKIN

Lufkin Antique Mall
118 N. 1st St.
409/634-9119

Angelina Antique Gallery
205 Herndon St.
409/634-4272

Paul Nerren's Junk Barn
4500 US Hwy. 59 N.
409/632-2580

Kinard's Antiques & Cllbls.
5151 US Hwy. 59 N.
409/634-6933

Warehouse Antiques
Hwy. 59 N
409/632-5177

Wishing Well Antiques & Gifts
901 S. John Redditt Dr.
409/632-4707

Carousel Antiques
302 N. Raguet & Frank St.
409/639-4025

98 LULING

Cripple Creek Mine
517 E. Davis St.
210/875-5062

Trinkets Treasures & Trash
519 E. Davis St.
210/875-9100

Welcome Back Antiques
711 E. Davis St.
210/875-3738

Natures Nest-Unique Gift Shop
946 E. Pierce St.
210/875-2383

99 MARBLE FALLS

Antiques Plus
1000 W. Hwy. 1431
830/693-3301

Wise Owl
3409 Hwy. 281
830/693-3844

Main Street Emporium
204 Main St.
830/693-7037

Past & Presents
700 Main St.
830/693-8877

Carol's Cottage
108 Main Street
830/693-7668

100 MARSHALL

La Trouvaille
203 W. Austin St.
903/938-2006

Antiques N Things
214 S. Lafayette St.
903/935-3339

101 MASON

Country Collectibles
Hwy. 87 N.
915/347-5249

Underwood's Antique Mall
100 N. Live Oak
915/347-5258

Antique Emporium
106 S. Live Oak
915/347-5330

P. V. Antiques
Ft. McKevett
915/347-5496

102 MCKINNEY

Iron Kettle Antiques
Hwy. 5
214/542-4903

One of a Kind
214 N. Kentucky St.
214/542-7977

Affordable Antiques & More
719 N. Kentucky St.
214/562-5551

Duffy's Antiques
202 E. Louisiana St.
214/542-5980

Antique House
212 E. Louisiana St.
214/562-0642

McKinney Antiques
112 N. Tennessee St.
214/548-8044

Remember This Antiques
210 N. Tennessee St.
214/542-8011

Victorian Corner
100 W. Virginia St.
214/548-9898

Pat Parker's Art Antiques
108 W. Virginia St.
214/562-6571

Town Square Antiques
113 E. Virginia St.
214/542-4113

Treasures from the Past
115 E. Virginia St.
214/548-0032

Antique Company Mall
213 E. Virginia St.
214/548-2929

The McAllister Collection
101 N. Kentucky
972/562-9497

103 MEMPHIS

Grandmaw's Attic
5th & Main
806/259-2575

Ivy Cottage
121 N. 5th St.
806/259-3520

Crafts & Collectibles
315 Hwy. 287 N
806/259-3817

Texas

104 MESQUITE

Antique Plus
2611 N. Belt Line Rd.
972/226-6300

Emporium @ Big Town
950 Big Town Shopping Center
214/690/6996

The Dusty Attic
3330 N. Galloway Ave.
972/613-5093

Missing Pieces
109 W. Main St.
972/288-3513

Sharon's Main St. Antiques
120 E. Main St.
972/329-3147

Favorite Places To Eat

Cracker Barrel Old Country Store
I-635 & Oates Dr., Exit 9A
972/681-9351

105 MIDLAND

ABC Antiques
110 Andrews Hwy.
915/682-4595

Cat's Meow
408 Andrews Hwy.
915/687-2004

Geri's Antiques & Fine Linens
307 Dodson St.
915/687-2660

Antiques by Josephs
325 Dodson St.
915/687-3040

Old Town Antiques
329 Dodson St.
915/570-0588

Judy Jackson's Bargain Barn
2420 W. Front St.
915/682-0227

Antiques Etc.
2101 W. Wadley Ave.
915/682-9257

Laura's Things Finer
2101 W. Wadley Ave.
915/683-4422

Motif
2101 W. Wadley Ave.
915/683-4331

Yesterday's News Antique Mall
3712 W. Wall St.
915/689-6373

Craft's Bazaar
3712 W. Wall St.
915/689-8852

106 MINEOLA

Places in the Heart
111 E. Broad
903/569-9096

Broad Street Mall
118 E. Broad
903/569-0806

Unique Mall
124 E. Broad St.
903/569-9321

Beckham Hotel Antique Mall
115 E. Commerce St.
903/569-0835

Heirloom Shoppe
119 E. Commerce St.
903/569-0835

Main Street Emporium
102 S. Johnson St.
903/569-0490

Country Girls Antiques
110 S. Johnson
903/569-6007

Roses and Relics
219 N. Newsom St.
903/569-9890

The Brownstone Mall
408 S. Pacific
903/569-6890

Durham Antiques
1823 N. Pacific St.
903/569-2916

107 MINERAL WELLS

Wynnwood Village Antiques
2502 U.S. Hwy. 180 E.
817/325-9791

Thurmon's Bargain Barn
3703 N. Hwy. 281
817/325-1695

Down Memory Lane
201 E. Hubbard St.
817/328-0609

Mama Jo's Treasures
800 E. Hubbard St.
817/328-0043

Richey's Antiques & Uniques
1201 E. Hubbard St.
817/325-5940

Sarah Janes Antiques & Crafts
115 N. Oak Ave.
817/325-3005

Wild Rose Antiques
213 N. Oak Ave.
817/325-9502

Century Corner Antiques
225 N. Oak Ave.
817/325-2525

Anita's Antiques
307 N. Oak Ave.
817/325-1455

108 MONTGOMERY

Antique Emporium
404 Eva
409/597-6903

Westlake Antiques & Old Book
25400 Hwy. 105 W
409/582-6829

Liberty Bell Antiques
207 Liberty
409/597-4606

Olde Towne Montgomery
208 Liberty
409/597-5922

The Old Post Office & Drugstore Antiques
210 Liberty
409/597-4400

109 MOUNT PLEASANT

Odds and Ends Shop
100 W. Alabama St.
903/572-2802

Brown's Country Attic
1705 W. Ferguson Rd.
903/577-9240

Classic Place
2000 W. Ferguson Rd.
903/572-6667

Antiques & Uniques
109 N. Madison Ave.
903/572-1545

Grand Nanny's Attic II Antqs.
115 N. Madison Ave.
903/572-7081

A Little Bit of Country
Union Hill Rd.
903/572-3173

Jo's Antiques
Union Hill Rd.
903/572-3173

110 MUNDAY

Memories of Munday Mall
110 East Main
871/422-5400
Open Mon.-Sat. 10-6, Sun., 1-5

Directions: Memories of Munday is located at the intersection of Hwy. 277 and Hwy. 222 in downtown Munday, Texas, which is approximately midway between Abilene and Wichita Falls (75 miles).

Located in the early 1900s community of Munday, the Memories of Munday Mall offers a varied selection of items from ten area dealers. Furniture, glassware, costume jewelry, and collectibles as well as a nice selection of vintage linens are displayed for your appeal.

Schoolmarm Antiques
210 W. Main
817/422-4474

111 NACOGDOCHES

Bremond Doll Shoppe
416 Bremond St.
409/569-9676

K H Newman Antiques
7144 Center Rd.
409/564-0820

Sparks Antiques
276 Community Rd.
409/564-4838

Nanny's Antiques
Hwy. 259
409/564-2433

Aubrey's Main Shoppe
1523 E. Main St.
409/569-7962

Squash Blossom Colony Mall
209 E. Main St.
409/560-1788

Antique Market
412 E. Main St.
409/564-8294

Sloane's Antiques
413 E. Main St.
409/559-0013

Moth Nest Vintage Clothing
2012 E. Main St.
409/560-5114

Pineapple Post
102 North St.
409/564-8285

Laurel's Antiques
4705 North St.
409/569-6290

Xavier Sanders Antiques
116 N. Pecan St.
409/560-3131

Old Pilar Street Antiques
108 E. Pillar St.
409/564-6888

112 NAVASOTA

Past & Present
119 E. Washington Ave.
409/825-7545

Downtown Antique Mall
207 E. Washington Ave.
409/825-8588

Twin Oaks Antique Mall
716 E. Washington Ave.
409/825-1837

113 NEW BRAUNFELS

Hope's Carousel
147 E. Faust St.
830/629-8113

Palace Heights Antiques Mall
1175 Hwy. 81 East
830/625-0612

Lee's Antiques
125 Hwy. 81 W.
830/629-7919

Second Time Around
870 S. State Hwy. 46
830/629-6542

Gruene Antique Company
1607 Hunter Rd.
830/629-7781

Gruene General Store
1610 Hunter Rd.
830/629-6021

Hampe House
1640 Hunter Rd.
830/620-1325

Cactus Jack's Antiques Etc.
1706 Hunter Rd.
830/620-9602

New Braunfels Log Haus Antqs.
469 IH 35 S
830/629-3774

Front Porch Antiques & Gifts
471 Main Plaza
830/629-0660

New Braunfels Emporium
209 W. San Antonio St.
830/608-9733

Good Pickins
219 E. San Antonio St.
830/625-9330

Downtowner Antique Mall
223 W. San Antonio St.
830/629-3947

Voigt House Antiques
308 E. San Antonio St.
830/625-7072

Vicky's Antiques
719 W. San Antonio St.
830/625-2837

Headrick Country Home Antqs.
697 S. Seguin Ave.
830/625-1624

Dan's Collectables
921 S. Seguin Ave.
830/629-3267

Be-Bops
1077 S. Seguin Ave.
830/625-6056

Texas

114 ODESSA

A Antique Shoppe
402 E. 8th St.
915/333-1718

D & D Antiques
2210 W. 416 46th St.
915/367-9427

Chez La Nae Fine Furnishings
5701 Austin Ave.
915/550-3106

Country Mercantile
6108 Ector Ave.
915/363-8909

The Brass Lamp
709 S. Grandview
915/332-9875

Wagon Wheel Antiques
6070 W. University Blvd.
915/381-6638

115 ORANGE

Nana & Poppie's Antiques
3834 W. Park Ave.
409/883-6941

Antiques & Uniques
2207 Macarthur Dr.
409/883-7989

Pat's This & That
2490 Martin Luther King Jr. Dr.
409/883-7215

This Ol House Co-Op
3433 Martin St.
409/883-3991

Country Porch
521 S. Hwy. 87
409/883-6503

Parlours
902 10th St.
409/886-0146

116 PALESTINE

Linda's Antiques
3913 W. Oak St.
903/729-1448

Barbara Harden's Antiques
Hwy. 84 E
903/729-6604

Vintage House
616 W. Palestine Ave.
903/729-7133

J's Music & Antiques
400 N. Queen St.
903/729-3144

Shelton Gin Antiques & Sandwich Shop
310 E. Crawford St.
903/729-7530

117 PAMPA

L & P Interiors
110 S. Cuyler
806/665-3243

Yesterdays Treasures
618 W. Francis Ave.
806/665-9449

Call Antiques
620 W. Francis Ave.
806/665-1391

J & B Antiques & Used Books
302 W. Foster Ave.
806/665-8415

Trash & Treasure Shop
1425 N. Hobart St.
806/669-6601

Collectors Corner
2216 N. Hobart St.
806/665-3246

Cottage Collection
922 W. 23rd Ave.
806/665-4398

118 PARIS

Kaufman Korner Mall
134 1st St. SW
903/784-6012

Antiques by Winona
138 Clarksville St.
903/784-4862

Curiosity
101 Grand Ave.
903/739-2716

Paris Antique Mall
Hwy. 19/Hwy. 24
903/785-0872

Blackburn's Antiques
Hwy. 82 E.
903/785-0862

Great Expectations
7 Lamar Ave.
903/784-4499

Reflections of Ducharme
6335 Lamar Ave.
903/784-3823

Reno Antique Mall
6720 Lamar Ave.
903/737-9904

Junk Lady Antiques
286 N.E. Loop #286
903/785-2513

Saffle Antique Mall
20 N. Plaza
903/785-8446

119 PASADENA

Heritage Collectables & Antqs.
3207 Preston Rd.
281/998-2775

Collector's Corner
701 Houston Ave.
281/473-9345

Stuff and Such
1615 Richey
281/473-6144

A-l Antiques
1905 Shaver St.
281/472-3777

Country Roads Antiques
1415 Southmore Ave.
281/473-2092

Antique Junction
111 W. Southmore Ave.
281/473-9824

Stephanie's Antique Furniture
5220 Spencer Hwy.
281/487-3900

120 PEARLAND

Cole's Antique Village
1014 N. Main St.
281/485-2277

A Dream Come True
2316 N. Main St.
281/997-6468

Country Merchant Antiques
14602 Suburban Garden Rd.
281/997-1319

121 PHARR

Eva's Antiques
508 N. Cage Blvd.
210/787-6457

Bygones by Guy Antiques
119 W. Park St.
210/702-4661

Socorros Antiques
620 W. Ferguson St.
210/702-0494

Memories Antiques & Mall
1311 W. Hwy. 495
210/781-4881

122 PITTSBURG

Charlotte's Market St. Antqs.
1 Market St.
903/856-2577

Rick's Antiques Safari
121 Quitman St.
903/856-6929

All Occasions Mall
122 & 128 Quitman St.
903/856-3285

123 PLAINVIEW

Old World Antiques
431 Broadway St.
806/293-3118

Horton Antiques & Collectibles
607 Broadway St.
806/293-7054

Antiques by Billie
609 Broadway St.
806/293-9407

Uniques and Antiques
615 Broadway St.
806/293-7826

Shoppe
707 Broadway St.
806/296-2201

Harman-Y House Antiques
815 Columbia St.
806/296-2505

Moore's Lantern Antiques
1406 Joliet St.
806/296-6270

Second Story Antiques & Cllbls.
403 Yonkers St.
806/296-5444

124 PLANO

Antiqueland
1300 Custer Rd.
972/509-7878

English Pine Co.
3000 Custer Rd., Ste. 220
972/596-4096

Blue Goose
1007 E. 15th St.
972/881-9295

Simple Country Pleasures
1013 E. 15th St.
972/422-0642

Main Street Gifts & Antiques
1024 E. 15th St.
972/578-0486

Ann's Place
1025 E. 15th St.
972/422-5306

Sherwood House
3100 Independence Pkwy
972/519-0194

Cobweb's Antiques Mall
1400 J Ave.
972/423-8697

History House Antiques
1408 J Ave.
972/423-2757

Nanny Granny's Antique Mus.
1408 J Ave.
972/423-3552

The Market
4709 West Parker
972/596-2699

Sample House
1900 Preston Rd.
972/985-1616

Blue Goose
3308 Preston Rd. Ste 315
972/985-5579

125 ROCKPORT

Bent Tree Galleries
504 S. Austin St.
512/729-4822

Harcrows Bluebonnet Mall
S. Hwy. 188
512/729-1724

Moore Than Feed
902 W. Market St.
512/729-4909

Mary Ann's Antiques
1005 E. Main St.
512/729-1945

126 ROCKWALL

Lakeview Lodge Antiques
706 S. Goliad St.
972/722-0219

Bountiful
708 S. Goliad St.
972/722-1313

Rockwall Antiques
212 E. Rusk St.
972/722-1280

Past Times Antiques & Cllbls.
214 E. Rusk St.
972/771-8100

127 ROSENBERG

Back When Antiques
2615 Avenue H
281/342-0601

Bakers Woods & Wares
3117 Avenue I
281/232-7733

Walger's Cottage
1030 Lawrence
281/232-6421

Old Town Antiques
828 3rd St.
281/232-2125

Memory Shoppe
931 3rd St.
281/232-7353

128 ROUND ROCK

Antique Mall of Texas
1601 S. I-35
512/218-4290

Wooten & Son
1401 Sam Bass Rd.
512/255-1447

Favorite Places To Eat

Cracker Barrel Old Country Store
I-35 & FM 3406, exit 154
512/218-0822

129 ROUND TOP

Emma Lee Turney's Antiques Productions
P. O. Box 821289
Houston, TX 77282-1289
281/493-5501
281/293-0320
E-mail: turnyshows@aol.com

Twice each year Emma Lee Turney brings outstanding antiques shows to the Round Top area. Billed as one of the largest antiques fairs in the nation, the show attracts dealers and buyers from across the United States and abroad. Emma Lee has recently written a book on her antiquing adventures. **For further information on Emma Lee's Round Top Antiques Fair and her new book see full page in the color section.**

Royers Round Top Cafe
"On the Square"
1-800-624-PIES

Cut through the backroads between Houston and Austin to find the tiny town of Round Top and one of the smallest town squares in America. Here you'll find three antique shops and Royers' Cafe which serves some of the best "sophisticated" food in the country.

My favorite—the ribs, along with buttermilk pie (the best I've ever eaten). The cafe also offers fresh salmon, grilled quail, chicken and a variety of pasta dishes.

130 SALADO

Antique Jewelry & Collectables
N. Main St.
817/947-9161

Classic Antiques
N. Main St.
817/947-0604

Fletcher's Books & Antiques
Main St.
817/947-5414

Salado Country Antiques
Main St.
817/947-8363

Hutchen's House
369 N. Main St.
817/947-8177

Salado Antique Mall
550 N. Main St.
817/947-1010

Recollection Antiques
Royal & Center
817/947-0067

Royal Emporium
Royal & Main
817/947-5718

Red Barn Antique Center
90050 B Royal
817/947-1050

Spring House Antiques
Royal
817/947-0747

Main Street Place
3 Salado Square
817/947-9908

131 SAN ANGELO

Consignments Etc.
109 S. Chadbourne St.
915/658-6480

Grammy's Corner
117 S. Chadbourne St.
915/655-8400

June's Folly
202 S. Chadbourne St.
915/655-9459

Arclight Antiques
230 S. Chadbourne St.
915/653-8832

Hard Time Post
915 N. Chadbourne St.
915/657-0905

S & R Trading Post
4736 N. Chadbourne St.
915/655-5087

Jewel of the Concho
10 E. Concho
915/653-8782

J Wilde
15 E. Concho
915/655-0878

Sassy Fox
34 E. Concho
915/658-8083

Confetti Antique Mall
42 E. Concho Ave.
915/655-3962

Cactus Patch
108 E. Concho Ave.
915/655-1456

Traders Mall
79 E. 14th St.
915/655-9617

Hodgepodge Antiques
114 Hardeman Pass
915/655-5148

American British Antiques
746 U.S. Hwy. 87 S
915/651-4873

Centerpiece Antiques
Municipal Airport Lobby
915/949-9078

Vi's Country Village
5270 Old Christoval Rd.
915/651-9088

Treasure Trunk
37 W. Twohig Ave.
915/658-6697

Washington Square
230 W. Washington
915/658-5765

132 SAN ANTONIO

The Columns on Alamo
1037 S. Alamo Street
210/271-3245 (phone and fax) or 1-800-233-3364
Open daily 8 am-9 pm

Directions: From I-37, take Exit #140B (Durango Street) at the Alamodome, and go 2 blocks from the freeway westbound on Durango to Alamo Street. Turn right and go south on Alamo five blocks to the corner of Sheridan Street and Alamo.

Innkeepers Ellenor and Art Link decided to open their elegant and stunning home as a bed and breakfast in 1994. The massive house is an 1892 Greek Revival home and they also use the adjacent 1901 guesthouse as part of the inn. Located in the historic King William District near the trolley, the inn offers 11 guest rooms, all with private baths, furnished with Victorian antiques and period reproductions. Guests can share the common areas in both houses and on the landscaped grounds.

The Links are resident innkeepers and are always ready and able to suggest excursion itineraries, dining and shopping forays for guests, and to help in planning which cultural and seasonal events to attend. They prepare their guests for the day's adventures with a full breakfast served in the main house.

When staying at The Columns, guests will be within easy walking distance to the River Walk, the Alamo, the Convention center, Southtown restaurants and shops, La Villita, German Heritage Park and Rivercenter Mall. It's only a short drive from The Columns to the Spanish Mission Trail, San Antonio Alamodome, Sea World, Fiesta Texas and the Lone Star Brewery and Hall of Horns.

Falling Pines Inn
300 West French Place
210/733-1998
Rates $100-150

This is an interesting place in an already interesting city - a purely luxurious bed and breakfast in an historic home that caters to the upscale crowd. Construction of Falling Pines began in 1911, under the plans and directions of famed architect Atlee Ayeres. Pine trees, not native to San Antonio, tower over the mansion on a one-acre, park-like setting in the Monte Vista Historic District, one mile north of downtown San Antonio.

The house itself is a combination of brick and limestone, with a green tiled roof, shuttered windows, and a magnificent limestone archway entrance and veranda on the front facade. The entry level has six rooms with quarter-cut oak paneling, wood floors, oriental carpets, fireplaces and a tiled solarium where breakfast is served. The large and elegantly appointed guest rooms are on the second level. The third level is entirely one suite, the 2,000 square foot Persian Suite that commands a grand view of downtown San Antonio and the nearby Koehler Mansion, home of a beer baron. The Persian Suite has two large, private balconies and a luxurious private bath, and is draped in miles and miles of material, reminiscent of exotic Persian tents.

Plantiques
1319 Austin Hwy.
210/824-2634

Charlott's Antiques & Clocks
2015 Austin Hwy.
210/653-3672

Pristine Peacock Estate Jwlry.
555 W. Bitters Rd.
210/494-6230

Blanco Fulton Antiques
1701 Blanco Rd.
210/737-7208

Halfmoon Antique Mall Inc.
112 Broadway St.
210/212-4401

Alamo Antique Mall
125 Broadway St.
210/224-4354

Land of Was
3119 Broadway St.
210/822-5265

Lion & Eagle
3511 Broadway St.
210/826-3483

Pat Pritchard Antiques
5405 Broadway St.
210/829-5511

Christo's
5921 Broadway St.
210/820-0424

Hugh Lackey Antiques
3505 Broadway St.
210/829-5048

J. Adelman Antiques & Art
7601 Broadway St.
210/822-5226

Marshall's Brocante
8505 Broadway St.
210/804-6320

Center for Antiques
8505 Broadway St.
210/804-6300

Chicago Connection
8505 Broadway St.
210/804-6322

San Antonio's Center for Antqs.
8505 Broadway St.
210/804-6300

Affordable Antiques
8934 Broadway St.
210/822-9600

Bobs Gifts & Antiques
3461 Fredericksburg Rd.
210/734-9007

Lasting Impressions
600 & 606 W. Hildebrand Ave.
210/737-9130

Antiques on Hildebrand
521 W. Hildebrand Ave.
210/734-9337

Abbey's Antiques
1503 W. Hildebrand Ave.
210/732-5266

Barn Haus
26610 U.S. Hwy. 281 N
210/980-7678

Antiques Downtown Mall
515 E. Houston St.
210/224-8845

Echoes from the Past
517 E. Houston St.
210/225-3714

Antique Connection
4119 McCullough Ave.
210/822-4119

Timeless Treasures Inc.
4343 McCullough Ave.
210/829-7861

J. Adelman Antiques & Jwlry.
Mengu Hotel at Alamo Plaza
210/225-5914

Main Place for Antiques
102 W. Mistletoe Ave.
210/736-4900

Gas Light Antique Shoppe
208 E. Park Avenue
210/227-4803

York's Furniture Annex
306 E. Park Ave.
210/226-1248

Dear Things
8324 Pat Booker Rd.
210/590-3003

Greenlight Antiques
13316 O'Connor Rd.
210/590-6107

River Square Antiques
514 River Walk St.
210/224-0900

Moran Antiques & Appraisals
2119 San Pedro Ave.
210/734-5668

Accents Antiques & Design
119 W. Sunset Rd.
210/826-4500

Treasures & Trifles Inc.
210 W. Sunset Rd.
210/824-9381

Different Drummer
1020 Townsend Ave.
210/826-3764

Ivy Cottage Antiques & Cllbls.
407 8th St.
210/224-2597

Favorite Places To Eat

Cracker Barrel Old Country Store
I-10 & Huebner Rd., Exit 560
210/690-3808

Cracker Barrel Old Country Store
I-35/410 & Ritman Rd., Exit 163
210/599-8080

133 SAN MARCOS

Crystal River Inn
326 West Hopkins
512/396-3739
Fax: 512/353-3248
Open year round

Directions: Crystal River Inn is located in San Marcos, off I-35 at Exit #205. Exit #205 is Hopkins Street.

With 13 guest rooms to choose from, visitors will enjoy this Texas inn that has garnered three stars in the Mobil Travel Guide. The inn itself is a romantic, luxurious Victorian mansion set in the middle of Texas hill country. It's close to the headwaters of the crystal clear San Marcos River - hence the name - and is filled with antiques, fireplaces and fresh flowers. There are gardens and fountains, a wicker-strewn veranda, and the beautiful outdoors. Gourmet breakfasts and brunches include such delectable items as stuffed French toast and bananas Foster crepes. Mystery weekends, river trips and romantic getaways are the hosts' specialty.

Ashley's Attic
2201 Hunter Rd.
512/754-0165

Centerpoint Station
3946 IH 35 S
512/392-1103

Antique Outlet Mall
4200 IH 35 S
512/392-5600

Maudie's Antiques
202 N. LBJ Dr.
512/396-8999

Paper Bear Heartworks Co.
214 N. LBJ Dr.
512/396-2283

Anchor Antiques & Iron Beds
360 S. LBJ Dr.
512/353-3995

Partin's Second Tyme Furn.
2108 RR 12
512/396-4684

Partin's II
2300 RR 12
512/396-2777

134 SEABROOK

Glory to God Antiques
1417 Bayport Blvd.
281/474-3639

Victorian Rose
909 Hall Ave.
281/474-1214

Another Era
909 Hardesty Ave.
281/474-7208

Town & Country Antiques
913 Hardesty Ave.
281/474-2779

Picket Fence
3010 Hwy. 146
281/474-4845

Carousel Antiques
1002 Meyer Rd.
281/474-4451

Old Seabrook Antique Mall
1002 Meyer Rd.
281/474-4451

Marilyn's Antiques
1402 2nd St.
281/474-4359

135 SEALY

Sealy Sampler Antiques
419 Hardeman St.
409/885-3349

Classic Collections
223 Fowlkes St.
409/885-7930

Country Antiques
121 Meyer Rd.
409/885-7976

Antique Shop
413 Meyer St.
409/885-0285

Sealy Antique Center
663 Hwy. 90 E
409/885-6556

Lilly's Antiques
502 N. Meyer St.
409/885-4040

136 SEGUIN

Art-Iques by Ken Miller
106 N. Austin St.
210/379-3209

A Wild Hare
112 W. Court St.
210/372-4822

Antique Trading Post
1530 N. State Hwy. 46
210/303-2037

Affordable Antiques
6771 N. State Hwy. 123
210/303-3135

Blue Hills Antique Mall
6832 N. State Hwy. 123
210/379-2059

137 SEYMOUR

Granny's Stuff
101 S. Main St.
817/888-2213

Hogue's
300 S. Main St.
817/888-2511

See More Antiques & Cllbls.
910 N. Main St.
817/888-2689

Classics
1620 Main St.
817/552-0672

138 SHERMAN

A Touch of Class Antique Mall
118 W. Lamar Street
903/891-9379 or 972/529-5206
903/868-3153 fax
Open Mon.-Sat., 10-5; Sun., 12-5

Directions: From Hwy. 75, take exit #58 (Lamar Street). Go to the second stoplight on the southwest corner of the downtown square, across from the Courthouse.

For specific information on A Touch of Class Antique Mall, see review in this section.

Elm House Antiques
710 N. Elm St.
903/892-4418

Donna's Corner
308 E. Houston St.
903/892-1510

Bobby Dene's Antiques & Vntg.
333 W. Jones St.
903/892-4272

Sherman Antique Mall
120 E. Mulberry St.
903/892-1225

Memory Lane Antique Empor.
1205 S. Sam Rayburn Fwy.
903/893-8894

Antiques & Brass
1617 Texoma Pkwy.
903/893-2494

Barn
309 N. Willow St.
903/892-2632

139 SINTON

Country Cornerstone Co-Op
207 W. Sinton St.
512/364-5756

Gwen's Antiques
223 E. Sinton St.
512/364-1165

140 SMITHVILLE

Alum Creek Antique Center
West Hwy. 71
512/237-3817

Cedar Chest Antiques
West Hwy. 71
512/237-3817

Silver Fox Antiques
West Hwy. 71
512/237-4825

House of Antiques
116 Main St.
512/237-4393

Century House
119 Main St.
512/237-5549

Crystal's Corner
204 Main St.
512/237-3939

Main St. Village
216 Main St.
512/237-2323

Simply Country
106 N.E. 2nd
512/237-2038

Wild Rose Antiques
108 N.E. 2nd St.
512/237-5122

141 SNYDER

Timber and Threads
1801 25th St.
915/573-4018

Nathalie's
1803 25th St.
915/573-9680

House of Antieks
4008 College Ave.
915/573-4422

142 SOUTH PADRE ISLAND

Padre Antiques & Collectibles
104 E. Hibiscus St.
210/761-7440

Peddler's Co-Op
5813 Padre Blvd.
210/761-7585

143 SPRING

Keepsakes & Kollectables
219 A Gentry
281/353-9233

The Doll Company
315 Gentry
281/350-4904

A Place in Time
315 Gentry St. Ste A
281/353-6323

Diane's Spring Emporium
324 Gentry
281/288-9202

Gentry Square Galleries
315 Gentry
281/353-5568

The Doll Hospital
419 Gentry
281/350-6722

Cobblestone Antiques
7623 Louetta Rd., Ste. 121
281/251-0660

Brenda's Attic
134 Main
281/288-0223

The Spotted Pony
202 Main
281/355-1880

Buffalo Spirit
215 Main
281/355-8100

Antiques & More on Main
302 Main St.
281/350-1214

The Wild Goose Chase
118 B Midway
281/288-9501

Friends
214 Midway St.
281/353-2255

Robyns Nest Antiques
200-1 Noble St.
281/288-7252

Southern Charm
26303 Preston E
281/288-4933

Lana Williams Gallery
26407 Preston
281/288-4043

Krystal Lain Antiques Etc.
130 Spring Cypress
281/353-7442

Granny's Odds & Engs
219 B Spring Cypress
281/288-6530

Pete & Sue's Antique Clocks
1408 Sue Ann Lane
281/288-7188

Spring Antique Mall
1426 Spring Cypress Rd.
281/355-1110

Cabin Creek Lodge Antq. Mall
1703 Spring Cypress
281/350-5559

Antique Mall
21127 Spring Town Dr.
281/350-4557

144 STAFFORD

Simone Antiques & More
11723 W. Bellfort St.
281/561-7403

Elegant Junk
Main St. (Hwy. 90)
281/242-3424

Antiques Etc.
3202 S. Main St.
281/499-9669

145 SULPHUR SPRINGS

Bright Star Antique Mall
102 College St.
903/885-4584

Granny's Attic
105 N. Davis St.
903/885-5042

Burrows Antiques
725 Davis St. N
903/885-5173

Old Town Antique Mall
101 Gilmer St. N
903/885-5646

Sanderson Antique Mall
109 Linda Dr.
903/439-0259

Victorian Rose
206 Main St.
903/885-2482

146 SUNNYVALE

East Fork Mall Antiques
613 E. Hwy. 80
972/226-2704

Jot Um Down Store
613 E. Hwy. 80
972/226-0974

Accent Antiques
616 E. Hwy. 80
972/226-9830

Fischers Antiques
536 Long Creek
972/226-1445

147 SWEETWATER

Rat Rows Antiques
113 Oak St.
915/235-8651

Second Hand Rose
122 Oak St.
915/235-1504

Arlene's Book House
124 Oak St.
915/235-1504

Raspberry Corner Antique Mall
301 Oak St.
915/235-3885

Lone Star Antiques Mall
318 Oak St.
915/235-8177

Vernon's Antiques
401 Oak St.
No Phone

148 TEXARKANA

Oak Tree
123 E. Broad
501/773-1588

M & M Antiques Mall
401 E. Broad
501/773-1871

Dun Sailin Oldes
611 Burma Rd.
903/838-9430

Jennie's Antique Mall
1901 College Dr.
903/792-2333

Red Wagon Antiques
Hwy. 59
903/832-6841

Nick's Antiques
213 Wood St.
501/772-6194

Pot Luck Antique Shop
I-30 W. Exit #218
903/832-1151

Garden Gate Antiques
603 E. 9th
501/773-1147

State Line Antique Mall
1104 State Line Rd.
501/772-8414

Green Country
1216 Trexler Rd.
903/671-2521

J Brown Antiques
817 Walnut
903/793-4114

149 TOMBALL

Whistle Stop Tearoom
107 Commerce St.
281/255-2455

Victoria Station Antiques
111 Commerce St.
281/357-0555

Precious Temptations
115 Commerce
281/351-2119

Tender Touch
115 Commerce
281/351-2119

Antique Station
119 Commerce & Walnut
281/351-7887

Maggie Mae's
121 Commerce St.
281/255-8814

Blue Caboose
104 N. Elm St.
281/255-8788

Country Harbor
106 N. Elm St.
281/255-2330

Patchwork Blue
605 Mason
281/351-5301

Tomball Antique Co-Op
208 W. Main
281/351-4160

Tomball Haus
216 W. Main St.
281/255-8282

314 East Main Antiques
314 E. Main St.
281/351-9488

Faye's Antiques
315 W. Main St.
281/255-3844

Three Sisters Antiques
330 W. Main St.
281/351-4725

The Owl's Nest
408 W. Main St.
281/351-1103

Just Passin' Time
418 W. Main
281/255-2999

J T Texas Co.
611 W. Main St.
281/351-2202

Antique Press
701 W. Main St.
281/255-8855

Past & Present
701 W. Main
281/255-8855

150 TRINITY

Teddie Bear's Antiques and Collectibles
Rt. 4
(four miles south on Hwy. 19)
409/594-6321
Open 365 days a year, 9 am to dark @ 7 pm

Directions: Teddie Bear's is located 19 miles east of Huntsville, Texas (I-45) on Hwy. 19, just across the Trinity River Bridge, or 4 miles south of Trinity, Texas on Hwy. 19.

A true country market, Teddie Bear's may just very well be the most intriguing and most fun place to visit that we've discovered! Two acres of antiques and junque to browse through is only part of the reason everybody should stop in if you are in the area. The variety of items stuffed onto these two acres range from things on outside garage sale tables to indoor, highly collectible treasures. Dealers can ask for a private tour of the huge barn full of early American primitives on the Garrison's farm just four miles away.

Ted "the Teddy Bear" and Victoria Garrison are always available to greet old and new friends alike. Ted will gladly help load things in your car or even make a free delivery if you live in the vicinity. One of the reasons people keep coming back to visit Teddie Bear's is not only the genuine friendliness they find there, but just to see what's going on at any one given time! For instance, Victoria explains it this way: "We always have something new to surprise our customers. We're a two-acre mini-flea market that keeps expanding with a life of its own! One stop leads to another, if for nothing else than to see what we've started next at Teddie Bear's!"

151 TYLER

Antiques & Uniques
433 South Vine
903/593-2779
Open Tue.-Sat. 10-5, Sun.-Mon. By chance or appointment

Directions: Traveling I-20, take the exit to Hwy. 69 and follow to downtown Tyler.

This is another shop that is very important to know. If you are into lamps, these folks can help you in every way.

Not only do they buy and sell antiques, handle appraisals and estate sales, carry gift items and reproductions, they also custom build, rewire and repair lamps, and sell lampshades. They keep over 500 lampshades in stock at all times!

John R Saul's Antiques
108 S. Broadway Ave.
903/593-4668

Tyler Square Antiques
117 S. Broadway Ave.
903/535-9994

Rose Tyler Antiques
202 S. Broadway Ave.
903/592-6711

V J's Antique Mall
236 S. Broadway Ave.
903/595-3289

Barham's Antiques
308 S. Broadway Ave.
903/593-3863

Hudson House Interiors
2301 S. Broadway Ave.
903/593-2611

Brass Lion Antiques
5935 S. Broadway Ave.
903/561-1111

Mary's Attic
417 S. College Ave.
903/592-5181

Front Street Antiques
202 W. Front St.
903/531-0008

Latif's Antiques
13819 US Hwy. 69 N.
903/882-6031

Old City Antique Mall
302 E. Locust St.
903/533-1110

Special Effects
4517 Old Bullard Rd.
903/509-0020

Crossroads Gallery Antiques
114 W. 6th St.
903/597-3021

Grey Pony
12663 State Hwy. 31 W.
903/593-8905

Glass Owl Antiques
428 S. Vine Ave.
903/595-0251

152 UVALDE

Loessberg's
524 E. Pecos St.
210/278-3958

Open House Antiques
100 W. North St.
210/278-9380

Market Square Antiques
103 N. West St.
210/278-1294

Way Out West Antiques
103 N. West St.
210/278-3648

153 VAN ALSTYNE

The Durning House B&B and Restaurant

205 West Stephens
903/482-5188
Bed & Breakfast open daily, restaurant open for lunch Wed.-Fri., 11:30-2, dinner (Fri.-Sat.only) 6-9, antiques by appointment or during restaurant hours.

Directions: From Hwy. 75, take Exit #51. After exiting toward town (east), go 6 blocks and the B&B is on the right at 205 West Stephens. If you come to a red light (the only one in town), you've gone a block too far. Van Alstyne is 50 miles north of Dallas, 15 miles north of McKinney and 15 miles south of Sherman, Texas.

When the Hixes purchased this wonderful little Victorian home, it housed their antique shop called "Elderly Things Antiques." The house is totally decorated in antiques, and some of the pieces scattered throughout the B&B and restaurant are for sale.

Guests are first greeted by three concrete pigs lolling in the front garden area, sporting hats befitting the seasons and holidays.

Diners have enjoyed the food so much that many of the recipes offered here have been included in a cookbook called Hog *Heaven - Recipes from the Durning House*. As an added incentive, if you mention *The Antique Atlas*, you will receive a 10% discount!

Yellow Rose Drug Store Antique Mall
210 E. Marshal St.
903/482-6167

154 VAN HORN

Los Nopales

1106 West Broadway
915/283-7125
Open daily 2-7 CST

Directions: Traveling I-10 East, take Exit #138 and continue 1.3 miles on Business Loop 10. Traveling I-10 West, take Exit #140B and continue 1.5 miles on Business Loop 10. From the intersection of U.S. 90, U.S. 54 and Business Loop 10, travel .8 miles west. Los Nopales is located next to Chuy's Mexican Food Restaurant.

Los Nopales is, indeed, different! They carry antiques and collectibles, art and rare books, including Texana, and there is a refinishing and upholstery shop adjoining the antique shop. They also sell Southwest native plants, and that's also connected to the name of the shop, as owner Joy Scott explains: "When I purchased a commercial lot with an abandoned building on it here in Van Horn, I was searching for an unusual business name that might truly represent our uniqueness. As we set about cleaning up the place, we discovered a prickly pear - in Spanish a "nopal" - growing on the roof amid all the debris that had accumulated there for years. There were prickly pear plants already growing in front of a fence on one part of the property. It seemed like destiny to name the business Los Nopales. For a multi-faceted business like ours, with a Southwestern flair, there just couldn't be a more appropriate name."

155 VERNON

Jailhouse Village
1826 Cumberland
817/553-4004

Hall Houseware & Furniture
1512 Fannin St.
817/552-5391

Yellow Rose Antique Mall
1516 Main St.
817/553-1511

Yesterdaze Antiques & Cllbls.
1519 Main St.
817/552-6727

PMH Enterprises
1601 Main St.
817/552-1660

156 VICTORIA

Victoria Antique Shop
804 Berkman Dr.
512/575-2203

Antique Attic
1401 S. Laurent St.
512/575-5043

Laurent Street Antique Mall
1602 N. Laurent St.
512/578-0813

Victoria's House of Lamps
1042 N. Main St.
512/575-6200

Homestead
106 W. Rio Grande St.
512/572-9666

Mundine Antiques
601 E. Rio Grande St.
512/576-9445

Blue Moon Antique Mall
1520 E. Rio Grande St. (Hwy. 59)
512/575-3233

157 WACO

Crystal Palace Antiques
618 Austin Ave.
254/756-7662

Cottage Shop
708 Austin Ave.
254/756-0988

Antiques on Austin
1525 Austin Ave.
254/753-1795

Courtyard Classic Antiques
4700 Bosque Blvd.
254/751-7077

Laverty's
600 N. 18th St.
254/754-3238

Saint Charles Shops
600 Austin Ave.
254/753-5531

Show & Tell Antiques
1525 Morrow Ave.
254/752-5372

Goodie Mill
2300 Washington Ave.
254/753-9616

Victoriana Antiques & Gifts
561 Westview Village
254/772-7704

Favorite Places To Eat

Cracker Barrel Old Country Store
I-35 & Hwy. 340, Exit 339
254/799-4729

158 WALLER

Autumn's Morn
40142 Hempstead Hwy.
409/372-5415

Clark's Collectables & Antiques
3106 Taylor
409/921-2960

Queenie's Antiques & Co-Op
2611 Washington St.
409/372-9346

Bluebonnet Antiques
2510 Hempstead Hwy..
409/931-2951

159 WAXAHACHIE

Courthouse Antiques

109 S. College
972/938-2777
Hours: Mon.-Fri. 10-5:30, Sat. 10-6, Sun. 12:30-5:30, Closed Tuesdays

Located in Historic Downtown Waxahachie.
For specific information see review this section.

Gingerbread Antique Mall
310 S. College
972/937-0968

Links to the Past
512 N. College
972/937-1421

Briarpatch
404 W. Main St.
972/937-7717

Gran's Antiques
208A S. Rogers St.
972/923-2207

Old Town Vlg Antiques
307 S. Rogers St.
972/938-9515

Waxahachie Crafters & Antqs.
315 S. Rogers St.
972/938-1222

Barbara's Antiques
113 N. College
972/935-9338

160 WEATHERFORD

Wanda's Antiques
2206 E. Bankhead Dr.
817/594-6222

On The Level Antique Mall
1716 Blair Dr.
817/594-8991

Horton House
1103 Ft. Worth Hwy.
817/599-8945

Dresser Drawer Antiques
118 S. Main St.
817/594-1191

Age Before Beauty
209 N. Main
817/596-8550

Patty's Country Memories
219 N. Main
817/594-9303

Sparks Antiques & Collectibles
220 Main St.
817/598-0089

Miss B's
311 N. Main St.
817/596-0902

The Land of Aah's
315 E. Oak
817/598-0101

Wanda's Antiques
1116 Pala Pinto St.
817/599-4112

Texas Treasures
1124 Palo Pinto St.
817/599-9505

Granny's Attic
127 York
817/613-9011

161 WEST

Molly B's Antiques
415 S. George Kacir Dr.
254/826-3052

Rasberry's Consignor Antiques
2481 I H 40 W.
254/355-5181

Huaco Antiques
20818 N. I-35
254/826-7262

Heritage Antiques
Interstate 35
254/826-3042

West Mercantile
126 N. Main St.
254/826-4461

Olde Czech Corner Antiques
130 N. Main St.
254/826-4094

Way Out West
105 E. Oak St.
254/826-3924

162 WHEELER

Antique Cupboard
103 West Texas Street
806/826-3741
Open Mon.-Sat., 9:30-5, Sundays by appointment

Directions: From I-40 at Shamrock, Texas, take Hwy. 83 North for 16 miles to downtown Wheeler.

Here's a shop that lists itself as having "a little bit of everything" including a large selection of depression glass, elegant glass, kitchen collectibles, quilts and primitives.

163 WHITE SETTLEMENT

Harris Antiques & Imports
7600 Scott Street
817/246-8400 or 817/246-5852
Fax: 817/246-6859
Open Mon.-Sat., 8:30-5:30

Directions: Harris Antiques & Imports is located in West Fort Worth, in a suburb called White Settlement. The shop is at I-30 West, Cherry Lane Exit (north), then right on Scott Street.

This store gets my vote for being the largest antique shop in America. Carolyn Harris and company sells both wholesale and retail, with about 95% of their sales being to dealers, auctioneers and designers. But anyone who loves antiques should go to the showroom just to look and be impressed. Their new location is an air-conditioned mall that is the length of three football fields - a total of 440,000 square feet of antiques and accessories! Harris Antiques & Imports has been in business in Fort Worth for over 35 years, and offers merchandise to shoppers world-wide. Besides all the furniture, they offer bronzes, oil paintings, cut glass and porcelain. It's no wonder they hold the title of "the world's largest home furnishings, accessories and antiques store."

164 WICHITA FALLS

Sue's Antique Mall
609 7th Street
817/322-9552
Open Tue.-Sat., 10-5

Directions: From I-44 and Hwy. 287, take 8th Street east to Ohio Street, turn left one block to 7th Street, then turn left again and go 1/2 block to the shop.

Few antique shops are fortunate enough to be able to display their goods in an antique building. Sue's Antique Mall occupies a 100+ year old building that is still being researched. You won't have to research the items you find here however, as there is something for everyone who has a love for antiques and collectibles.

The Hand Place
4304 Call Field Rd.
817/691-4563

Depression Glass by Bonnie
1032 Covington St.
817/855-1591

Colonial House Antiques
1510 Monroe St.
817/761-2280

The Market on Monroe
1512 Monroe St.
817/723-4997

Johnson's Junction
1514 Monroe St.
817/723-5332

Village Antique Mall
1516 Monroe St.
817/322-6255

Corner Cupboard Antiques
1518 Monroe St.
817/767-6583

Monroe Street Antique Mall
1523 Monroe St.
817/761-4151

King Albert's Antiques & Intrs.
1827 Pearl Ave.
817/761-4226

Griffis Antiques
5521 Northwest Fwy
817/855-7711

Depot Square Antiques
620 Ohio Ave.
817/766-6321

Potts Antique Shop
1310 10th St.
817/322-3488

165 WIMBERLEY

O'Neal's Antiques
100 Lange Rd.
512/847-3148

Jean's Antqs., Gifts & Boutique
11552 Ranch Rd. 12 S
512/487-2307

Old Mill Store
Wimberley Square
512/847-3068

166 WINNIE

Just What You Need
344 Broadway
409/296-3099

Old Time Trade Days
I 10 & 1663
409/296-3300

Winnie Antique Mall
Hwy. 124 & Cedar St.
409/296-2701

167 WOODVILLE

Family Tree
304 W. Bluff St.
409/283-2116

Pine Country Antiques
511 W. Bluff St.
409/283-3183

Another Time
104 Charlton St.
409/283-8222

Yvonne's Antiques
112 S. Charlton St.
409/283-2119

Family Affair Antiques
Hwy. 190 W
409/283-5685

Notes

Utah

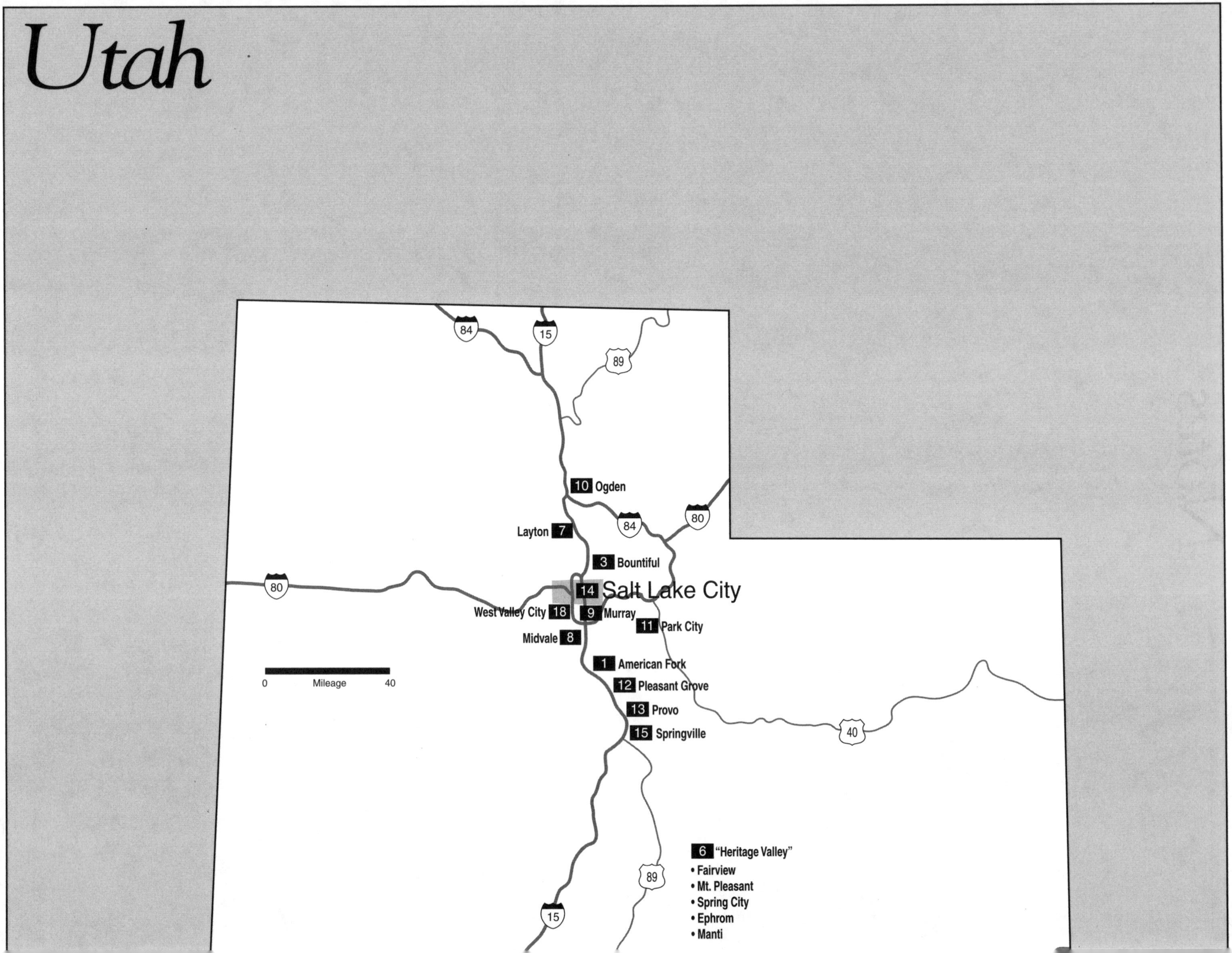

84
15
89
10 Ogden
84
80
Layton 7
3 Bountiful
80
14 Salt Lake City
West Valley City 18
9 Murray
11 Park City
Midvale 8
1 American Fork
12 Pleasant Grove
13 Provo
15 Springville
40
0 Mileage 40
6 "Heritage Valley"
• Fairview
• Mt. Pleasant
• Spring City
• Ephrom
• Manti
89
15

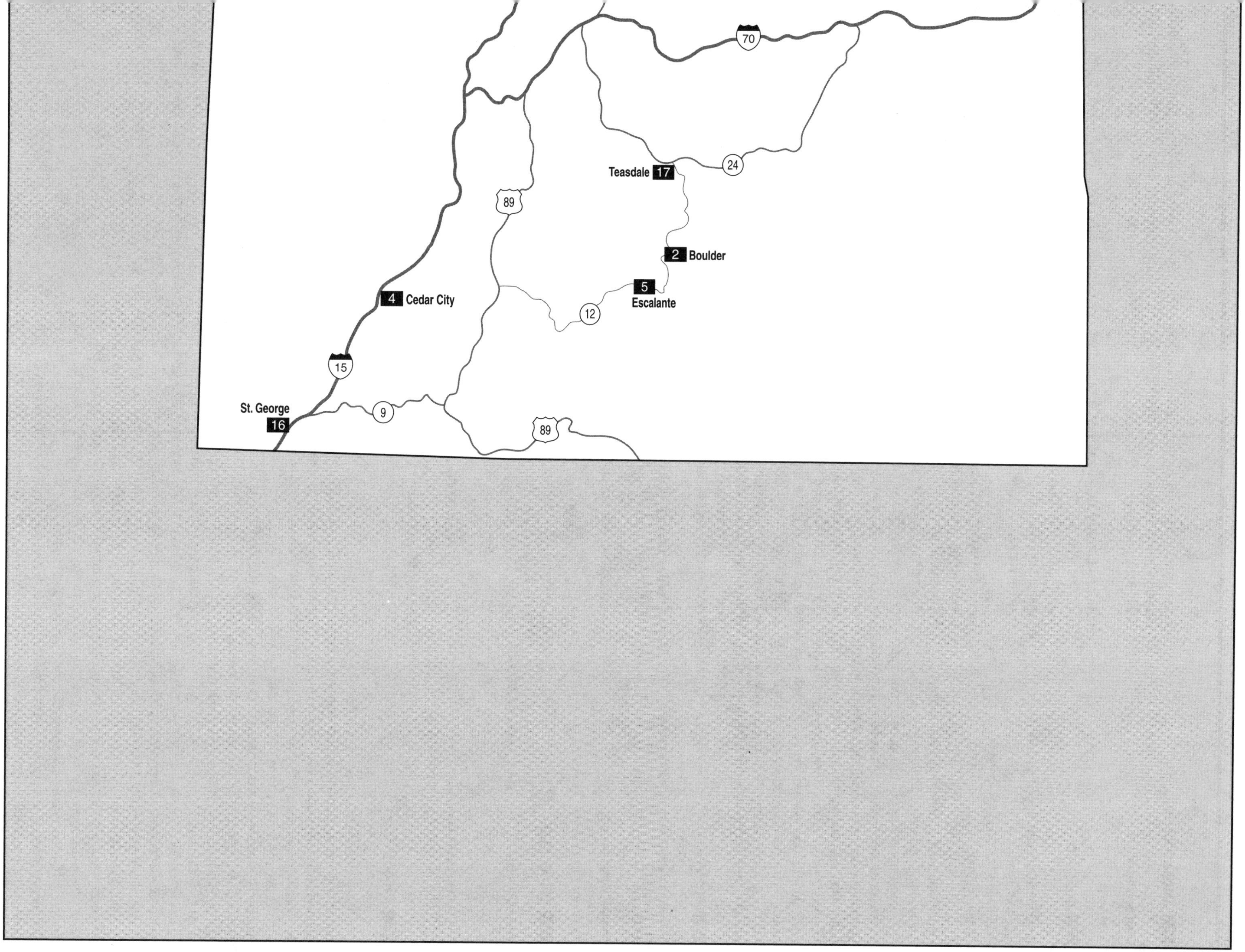

70
24
Teasdale 17
89
2 Boulder
5 Escalante
4 Cedar City
12
15
St. George 16
9
89

1 AMERICAN FORK

Lake City Antiques
143 N. 200 W
801/756-9149

2 BOULDER

Boulder Mountain Ranch and B&B
Hells Back Bone Road
801/335-7480
Open at all time

Directions: Located 3 1/2 miles off Scenic Byway 12. Just seven miles from rural Boulder.

This working cattle ranch offers the urban cowboy an opportunity to participate in the "western experience". One to six day excursions are available offering horseback riding along with other adventures for a taste of the true west. Set out on a five day ride from Bryce Canyon to the ranch along the Great Western Trail or if you're a "true-cowboy" try trail riding and cattle working. For relaxation, fish in the nearby streams. Lodge rooms or cabins are available. Breakfast is available each morning.

3 BOUNTIFUL

Newman's Antiques & Art
44 S. 400 RR 2
801/298-2884

Bountiful Antiques
399 N. Main St.
801/295-7227

Bountiful Vintage House
5 Points Mall
801/299-0588

4 CEDAR CITY

Prarie Collectibles
644 N. 800 W.
801/865-9652

Betty's Antiques & Collectibles
1181 S. Main St.
801/586-7221

Grey Wolf's Antiques & Collectibles
223 N. 100 W.
801/865-1973

5 ESCALANTE

Situated in the heart of Scenic Byway 12, Escalante and its environs were among the last frontiers to be explored in the continental United States. In the 1700s, two Spanish priests, along with their expedition, came through the area looking for a passable trail to Los Angeles. The town was eventually named for one of these priests. In 1876, Mormon pioneers settled here because of its mild climate, good grazing land, and abundance of minerals and water.

One of the few places that can still boast clean air, Escalante is surrounded by the mysteries of the past. Little is known about the civilization that lived here centuries ago, and visitors will want to explore the cliff-dwellings and artifacts left by the ancients who once occupied the mountains and canyons.The wildlife is plentiful for hunters and fishermen, and the sweeping vistas are ideal for photographers.The town itself offers modern accommodations, as well as a variety of gift and specialty shops in which to roam. The restaurant and cafes promise anything from sandwiches to steaks to satisfy even the hungriest explorer.

Rainbow Country Tours and Bed & Breakfast
586 E. 300 South
1-800-252-8824; 801/826-4567
Fax: 801/826-4557
Open every day

Directions: Located on the east end of Escalante. Turn behind the Chevron Station, go 1/4 mile to the first house on the right.

This bed and breakfast offers you an idyllic place to unwind. Comfortable and peaceful, it provides all the amenities of a traditional bed and breakfast - private rooms and hearty food - plus hot tub and wrap-around sun deck with sweeping vistas of mountain and desert.

For your entertainment, they provide off-the-beaten-path jeep and/or hiking tours, as well as overnight camping. Owner Gene Windle can also take you safely and comfortably in his 8-passenger wagon to see "some of the most beautiful, remote places in the American West." Ask him to show you the petrified forests and the 3000 year-old Indian rock art.

Serenidad Gallery - Fine Art and Antiques
360 West Main
801/826-4810
Open Mon.-Sat., 8-9; Sun., 1-8

Directions: Go 60 miles from Hwy. 89 to the West, and 65 miles from Hwy. 24 to the Northeast. The town is in the heart of Scenic Hwy. 12.

With an eye for quality, this shop carries a fine selection of art and antiques with a Western theme.

Favorite Places To Eat

Cowboy Blues Diner
200 N. Main
801/826-4251

This diner, named in honor of the true "American Cowboy" serves sandwiches, steaks, and more. Open for breakfast lunch and dinner.

6 HERITAGE VALLEY

By the time Utah became a state in 1896, the population had comfortably settled in nearly every corner of its boundaries. In fact, settlers had been colonizing likely townsites for nearly fifty years.

Such is the case with the historic towns of, Spring City, Fairview, Mt. Pleasant, Ephraim, and Manti. This string of communities was settled during the 1850s by industrious and determined Mormons from the United States and Europe.

Today, these towns form Utah's "*Heritage Valley*". In a state where history is preserved with pride, these central Utah towns stand out for their uncommon devotion to preserving their 19th century origins with architectural integrity and continuing pioneer spirit.

Spring City is one of Utah's finest examples of preservation. Laid out using the strict grid design considered ideal by early Mormons, the entire town of Spring City is on the National Historic Register. Spring City is architecturally eclectic. Some homes are styled with the Scandinavian designs favored by early settlers, and other structures are built in Greek and Romanesque Revival and classic Victorian styles. *Heritage Days*, a celebration held each spring, includes tours of historic homes, and artists' studios, wagon rides, a turkey barbecue, and much more. A self-guided walking tour is available year-round.

Fairview was settled in 1859, and many of the buildings from this era remain. The Fairview Museum of History and Art offers an excellent collection of items evocative of pioneer days including hand-crafted household implements. The museum also exhibits the remnants of ancient Pueblo cultures common to the area, and modern-day paintings and sculpture.

Mt. Pleasant was also settled permanently in 1859. Its colorful Main Street is a model of community pride and hard work. The majority of the streets' structures were built between 1880 and 1905. Mt. Pleasant's rich history includes the signing of the treaty between central Utah settlers and the Ute Indians. Mt. Pleasant hosts a pioneer Pageant each summer.

Settled by a few determined families in the 1850s, Ephraim's quiet streets are lined today with carefully preserved buildings and homes, both common and ornate. The renovated "*Ephraim Cooperative Mercantile Association*" building is one Main Street example. Guided tours of historic sites are available. Ephraim is the home of Snow College, founded in the 1880s. Today's enrollment is about 2,500 students. A *Scandinavian Festival* held each Memorial Day weekend pays homage to the Mormon convert settlers.

Manti was one of the first five towns incorporated into the *"State of Deseret"*, as early Mormons hoped their territory would someday be known. The town's most famous structure is the *Mormon Temple* constructed between 1877 and 1888, and still in use today. The grounds of the cream-colored oolite limestone edifice are the location of the *Mormon Miracle Pageant* each July. Drawing thousands of spectators nightly, it tells the story of the founding of the LDS Church, and of the early pioneers who settled this area.

For more information about ways to enjoy Utah's Heritage Valley, Contact: Sanpete Economic Development, P. O. Box 59, Ephraim, Utah 84627, 801-283-4321.

Antique Shops

Antiques Etc.
58 North Main
Manti
801/835-1122

Fairview Museum
86 North 100 East
Fairview
801/427-9216

Mt. Pleasant Museum
150 South State
Mt. Pleasant
801/462-2456

Pherson House Antiques & Bed and Breakfast
244 South Main
Ephraim
801/283-4197

Bed & Breakfast

Ephraim Homestead
135 West 100 North
Ephraim
801/283-6367

Heritage House
498 North 400 West
Manti
801/835-5050

Horseshoe Mountain
310 South Main
Spring City
801/462-2871

Larsen House
298 South State
Mt. Pleasant
801/462-9337

Legacy Inn
337 North 100 East
Manti
801/835-8352

Mainti House Inn
401 North Main
Manti
801/835-0161

Yardley Inn
190 South 200 West
Manti
801/835-1861

7 LAYTON

Favorite Places To Eat

Cracker Barrel Old Country Store
I-15 & Antelope Dr., Exit 335
801/776-3527

8 MIDVALE

Bingham Junction Antiques
23 N. Main St.
801/255-0330

Antiques Emporium
32 N. Main St.
801/565-0242

Midvale Antiques
109 N. Main St.
801/569-3204

Amusement Sales
127 N. Main St.
801/255-4731

First Class Antiques & Collectibles
7615 State St.
801/568-7878

9 MURRAY

Lyn Anne's Collectables
4844 South State Street
801/263-2293
Open 11-5:30, Mon.-Fri.; 11-5, Sat.

This is a unique shop that specializes in vintage wearables, including accessories. They also carry a selection of costume jewelry and glassware.

After Glow
4844 South State Street
801/263-2293
Open Mon.-Fri., 11-5:30; Sat., 11-5

Directions: From I-15 take the 53rd South Exit #303. Go East to State Street.

Offering the largest selection of glassware in the area, this shop also features a variety of fine china, primitives, costume jewelry, and paper.

The shop gladly offers dealer discounts and appraisal services.

Treasures Unlimited
5419 Commerce Dr.
801/268-0668

Notions
4838 S. State St.
801/263-7733

Antiquer
4203 S. State St.
801/262-9658

Rare Necessities
4967 S. State St.
801/288-0518

Sherry's Antiques
4859 S. State St.
801/266-3145

10 OGDEN

Boom Town Antiques
406 Canyon Rd.
801/621-6778

Young's General Store
109 Historic
801/392-1473

Painted Lady
115 Historic
801/393-4445

Lilt of Yesteryear
3638 Jackson Ave.
801/394-1896

Country Way Gifts & Antiques
368 10th St.
801/392-0332

Abby's Antique Mall
134 31st St.
801/394-9035

Old Time Antiques
965 28th St.
801/394-3066

Union Station
106 25th St.
801/629-8533

Curio Shop
241 25th St.
801/393-0926

Abalene Western Antiques
268 25th St.
801/399-9511

Cowboy Trading Post
268 25th St.
801/399-9511

Country Antiques
118 24th St.
801/394-4934

Ginger Jar Antiques
424 29th St.
801/399-4901

Reflections Antqs. & Cllbls.
2386 Wall Ave.
801/392-4904

Erika Martin Antiques
3480 Washington Blvd.
801/393-5963

11 PARK CITY

Angel House Inn
713 Norfolk Avenue
1-800-ANGEL-01; 801/647-0338
Open year around

Directions: From Salt Lake City, take I-80 to Rt. 224. This becomes Park Ave. At town lift, turn right on 8th Street; go two blocks, then left onto Norfolk.

Set in historic Park City, with the rugged Wasatch Mountains as a backdrop, an exquisite Victorian mansion has been transformed into the Angel House Inn. Built in 1889, during an era of elegance and service, proprietors Joe and Jan Fisher Rush have restored this historical house to its former grandeur and welcome you to experience one of its 9 romantically designed and themed rooms. Highlights of its amenities include its immediate access to Park City resorts for world class skiing in the winter and adventurous hiking and mountain biking in the summer.

Each of its 9 designer appointed rooms are named after angels who represent and embody the essence of romance and pleasure of the natural world. The inn also features an elegant sitting and breakfast area that ensures your stay is one reminiscent of the Victorian era.

Old Miners' Lodge-A Bed and Breakfast Inn
615 Woodside Avenue
1-800-648-8086; 801/645-8068
Fax: 801/645-7420
Open year around

Situated in the Historic District, this 1889 lodge was once a boarding house for fortune seeking miners. Besides the three suites and ten antique-filled guest rooms (complete with down comforters and pillows) there is a large fireplace in the living room and an outdoor hot tub available to guests all year round. Other amenities include terry cloth robes in all guest baths and a full breakfast each morning.

With the Park City ski area just a stone's throw away, this inn can easily accommodate groups or family gatherings.

Southwest Indian Traders
550 Main
801/645-9177

12 PLEASANT GROVE

Collector's Cottage
100 E. State Rd.
801/785-6782

13 PROVO

Lotus Gallery
80 W. Center St.
801/374-9201

This N That Antiques
1585 W. Center St.
801/375-3133

Kristi & Joseph Antiques
260 N. University Ave.
801/375-1211

14 SALT LAKE CITY

Wildflowers Bed & Breakfast
936 East 1700 South
801/446-0600

Built in 1891, this beautiful Victorian home is surrounded by an array of wonderful colors, one of which is evident in the blue spruce trees which surround the grounds, and more so in the wildflowers of all different shades of the rainbow. Listed on the National Register of Historic Places, the Wildflowers Bed & Breakfast is gorgeously enhanced with original chandeliers, stained glass windows, Oriental rugs, antiques, and an astonishing hand carved staircase.

A gourmet breakfast is served to the guest, making the stay at Wildflowers a complete and enjoyable one.

Brass Key Antiques
43 W. Broadway
801/532-2844

Generations Antiques
2085 S. 900 E.
801/466-0456

Beehive Collectors Gallery
368 E. Broadway
801/533-0119

Modernage
253 S. 800 Ave.
801/322-3326

Trolley Antique & Unique
602 S. 500 Ave.
801/575-8060

Distelfink Antiques
2182 Highland Dr.
801/487-5084

Temptations Plus
3922 Highland Dr.
801/272-6222

Ken Sanders Rare Books
107 Leslie Ave.
801/467-1490

Antique Shoppe
2016 S. 1100 E.
801/466-2171

Elemente
353 Pierpont Ave.
801/355-7400

Ec-Lec-Tic
380 Pierpont Ave.
801/322-4804

Ec-Lec-Tic
466 W. South Temp Circle
801/322-4813

Jitter Bug-Toy Dealers
251 S. State St.
801/537-7038

Squires Antiques
357 W. 200 S
801/363-1191

Wasatch Furniture Co.
623 S. State St.
801/521-8845

Lady Legge's China Cabinet
3838 S. State St.
801/355-8396

Bearcat Antiques
43 W. 300 South
801/532-2844

Gary Thompson Antiques & Art
43 W. 300 South
801/532-2844

Kennard Antiques
65 W. 300 South
801/328-9796

Olympus Cove Antiques
179 E. 300 South
801/532-1070

Antiques Gallery
217 E. 300 South
801/521-7055

Antoinette's
247 E. 300 South
801/359-2192

Copper Cowboy Antiques
268 S. 300 E
801/328-4401

Carmen Miranda's
270 S. 300 E
801/359-7741

Due Time
279 S. 300 E
801/521-4356

Thomson & Burrows Antiques
280 S. 300 E
801/521-0650

Briar Patch Antiques
407 E. 300 South
801/322-5234

Hidden Door Antiques
1019 E. 2100 South
801/484-1736

Cobwebs
1054 S. 2100 Ave.
801/485-9295

Honest Jon's Hills House
126 S. 200 W
801/359-4852

T C Antique Barn
2310 S. State St.
801/489-9623

Favorite Places To Eat

Cracker Barrel Old Country Store
I-15 & SR 77, Exit 263

15 SPRINGVILLE

P J's Antiques
211 N. Main St.
801/489-9137

Pioneer Antiques
391 N. Main St.
801/489-6853

16 ST. GEORGE

Holland House
70 N. 500 E
801/628-0176

Bentley's House of Antiques
46 N. 100 W
801/674-1812

Dixie Trading Post
111 W. Saint George Blvd.
801/628-7333

Butterfield's Antiques
248 E. Saint George Blvd.
801/673-8333

General Store Antiques
640 E. Saint George Blvd.
801/628-8858

Memory Lane Antique Mall
968B E. Saint George Blvd.
801/652-0447

17 TEASDALE

Cockscomb Inn Bed & Breakfast
97 South State Street
801/425-3511
Open seven days a week, year around.

Directions: Approximately five miles East of Bichnell and four miles West of Torrey (which is ten miles West of Capitol Reef National Park) on Hwy. 24, take Teasdale turnoff going South 1 1/2 miles to town center. Cockscomb Inn is on main road - center of Teasdale.

This quaint inn is only minutes from Capitol Reef National Park. The charming rooms all have private baths. Hiking and biking information is available. Excellent full breakfast is served.

18 WEST VALLEY

Favorite Places To Eat

Cracker Barrel Old Country Store
I-215 and 3500 South, Exit 18A
801/977-8221

Notes

Vermont

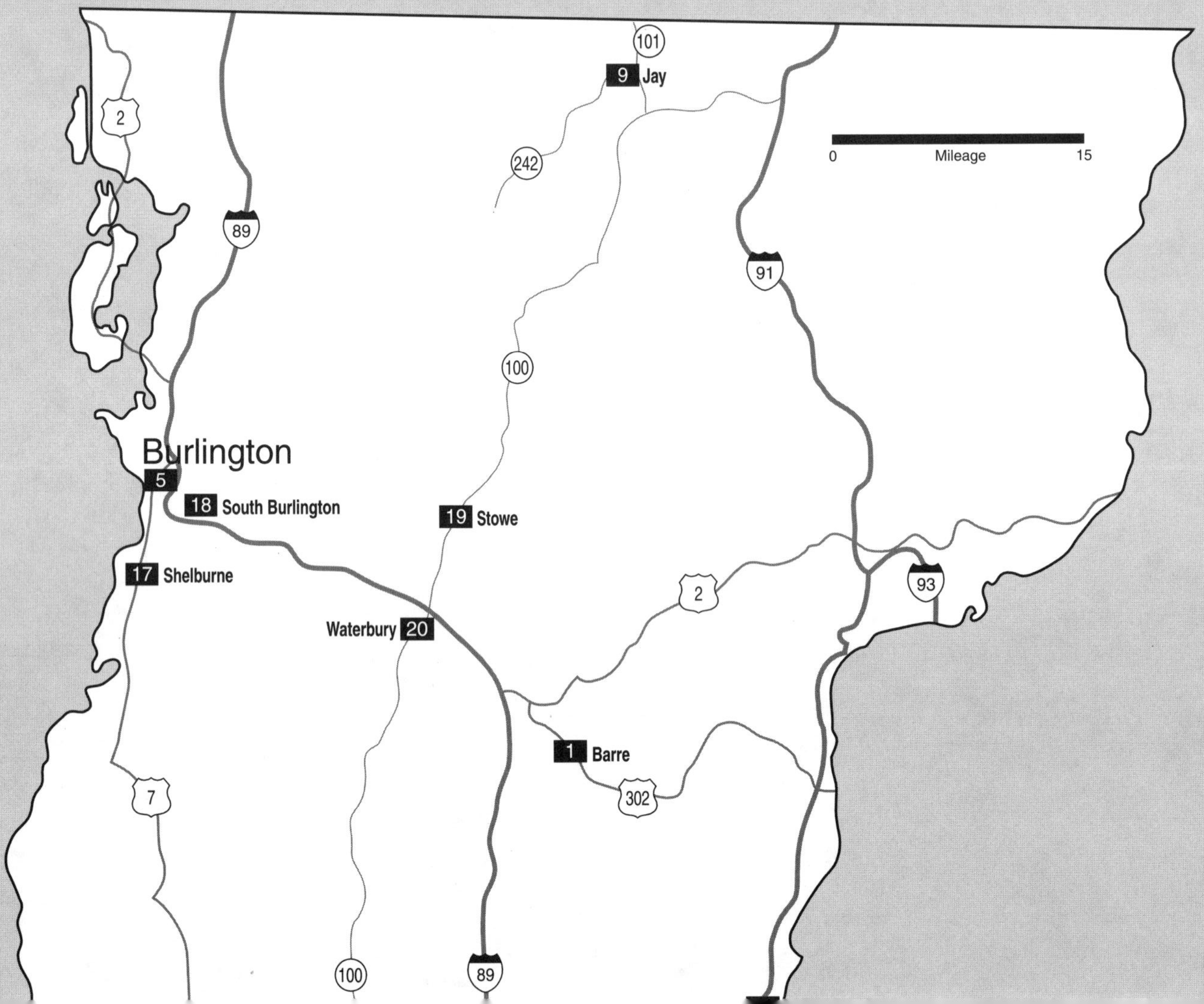

101
9 Jay
2
242
89
91
Mileage
0
15
100
Burlington
5
18 South Burlington
19 Stowe
17 Shelburne
2
93
Waterbury 20
1 Barre
302
7
100
89

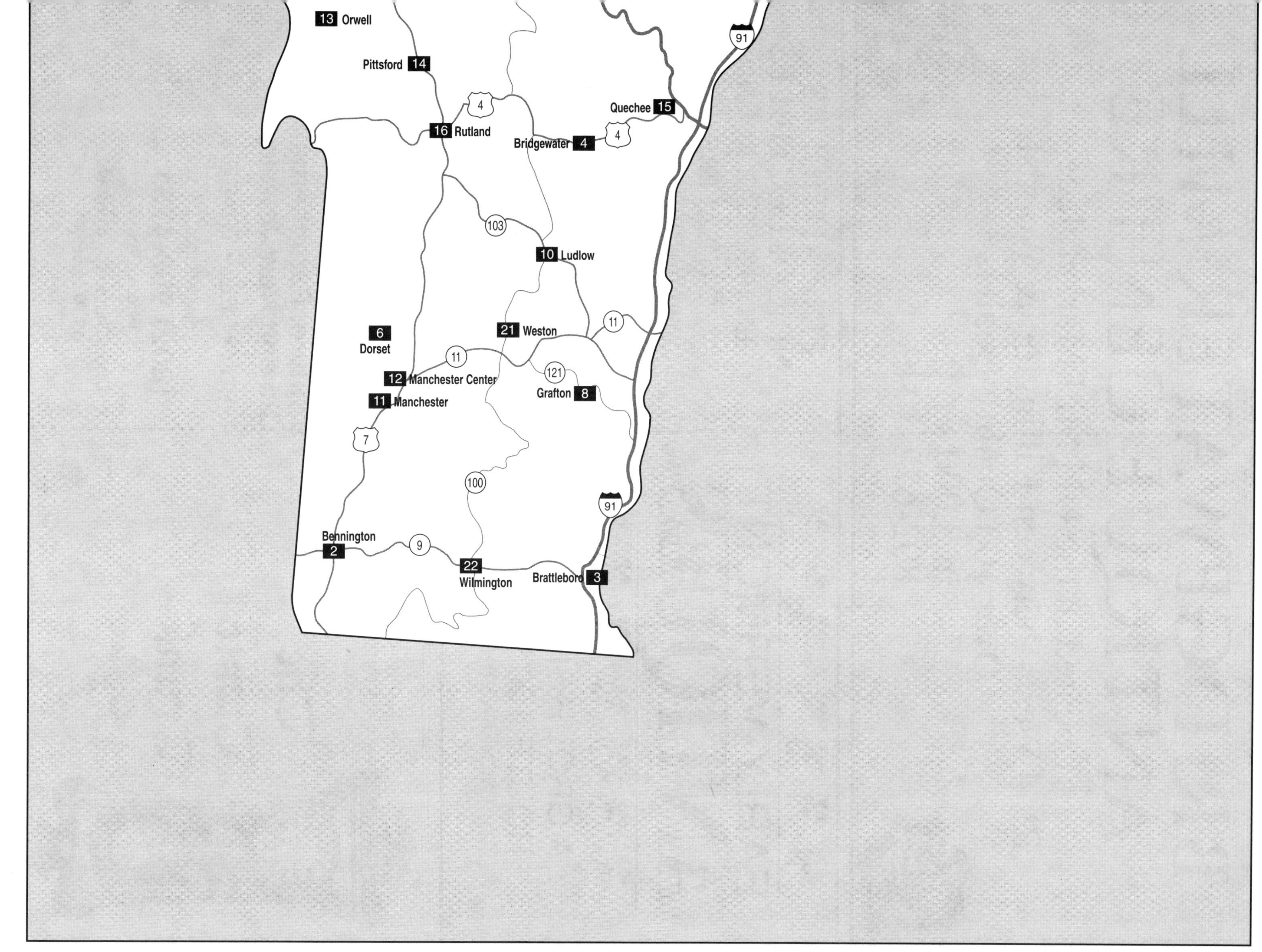
13 Orwell
Pittsford 14
Quechee 15
16 Rutland
Bridgewater 4
10 Ludlow
21 Weston
6 Dorset
12 Manchester Center
11 Manchester
Grafton 8
Bennington 2
22 Wilmington
Brattleboro 3
91
4
103
11
121
7
100
9

Vermont

1 BARRE

East Barre Antique Mall
133 Mill Street
(East Barre)
802/479-5190
Open: Daily 10-5

Directions: Located just off the junction of U.S. Rt. 302 East & Rt. 110 on Mill Street in the heart of East Barre. Bear right at the fork and up the hill.

East Barre Antique Mall is a group shop located in the center of East Barre, Vermont. Besides a general line of antiques, they offer the largest selection of antique furniture in the area, antique silver, glassware, framed prints, sports items, primitives and collectibles. The largest and cleanest shop in Central Vermont, over 12,000 square feet, the items are tastefully displayed throughout making it easy to spot your favorite pieces.

Red Wagon Antiques
1079 S. Barre Rd.
802/479-3611

Everything Under The Sun
Barre Rd.
802/479-2563

2 BENNINGTON

Pentimento
359 Main St.
802/442-8550

Thomson Mill Antiques Center
416 Main St.
802/447-2649

Four Corners East
307 North St.
802/442-2612

Antique Cntr.-Camelot Village
60 West Rd.
802/447-0039

3 BRATTLEBORO

Village Farm Antiques
Green River Village
802/254-7366

Richter Gallery
111 Main St.
802/254-1110

Black Mountain Antique Center
Rt. 30
802/254-3848

4 BRIDGEWATER

Bridgewater Mill Antique Centre
Old Mill Marketplace
Rt.4
802/672-3049
Hours: 10-6, 7 days a week

Directions: Take I-91 north to Exit 9 (Hartland). Take Rt. 12 north to Rt. 4 west, which goes to Bridgewater. The Old Mill Marketplace is situated on the left side of Rt. 4. Bridgewater is 10 miles west of Woodstock and 15 miles east of Killington.

The Bridgewater Antique Centre is located on the third floor in The Old Mill Marketplace, a 150 year old woolen mill turned antique shop. With over 100 quality dealers in 8,000 square feet, the Centre features a large assortment of antique furniture, glassware, and collectibles. They also have an impressive selection of Victorian furniture, oak dressers and tables, reconstructed pie safes, jelly and corner cupboards, dry sinks, harvest tables, and armoires. Shipping arrangements can be made in-house for delivery of large furniture anywhere in the United States. United Parcel Service (UPS) shipping is available for smaller pieces.

5 BURLINGTON

Underground Antiques
96 Church St.
802/864-5183

6 DORSET

Marie Miller American Quilts
Main
802/867-5969

Carlson Antiques
On The Village Green/Rt. 30
802/867-4510

Ex Libris
Rt. 30
802/867-0409

7 FAIRLEE

Barry Lebarron Antiques
Main
802/333-4574

Paper Americana
Main
802/333-4784

Vollbrecht Antiques
Main
802/333-4223

Conval Antique Mall
Rt. 5
802/333-9971

8 GRAFTON

Brandywine Bed and Breakfast and Antiques
Main Street
802/843-2250
Open 7 days a week

Directions: Located 8 miles off of Rt. 91, North Exit 5. Brandywine is 25 minutes from Manchester University and 30 minutes from Mount Salow as well as Straton Mountain; 45 minutes south of Ludlow, Vt., and 1 hour south of Ruthana.

For specific information see review in color section.

9 JAY

The Tickle Trunk
Jay Village
Box 132
802/988-4731
Open Thurs.-Sun., 11-5 (7 days a week at Holiday times)

Directions: One mile from Jay Peak Ski Resort. At main intersection in Jay Village on Rt. 242 and Crossroads. From I-19, Exit 27 to Newport. 30 minute drive to Jay via Rt. 105 to Rt. 101 to Rt. 242.

The Tickle Trunk, as the name implies, is noted for trunks. They also specialize in clocks, primitives, Victorian furniture, vintage clothing, costume jewelry from the '40s up, and numerous other wonderful antiques and collectibles.

10 LUDLOW

Village Barn
126 Main St.
802/228-3275

Cool-Edge Collection
Rt. 100 N
802/228-4168

Needham House
Rt. 100 N.
802/228-2255

11 MANCHESTER

Clarke Comollo Antiques
Rt. 7 A
802/362-7188

12 MANCHESTER CENTER

Center Hill Past & Present
Center Hill
802/362-3211

Cachet
Rt. 11
802/362-0058

Carriage Trade Antique Ctr
Rt. 7 A North
802/362-1125

Brewster Antiques
Rt. 30
802/362-1579

13 ORWELL

Brookside Farms Country Inn and Antq. Shop
Hwy. 22 A
802/948-2727

Listed on the National Register of Historic Places, this restored 1789 farmhouse and the 1843 Greek Revival mansion is located on a 300 acre estate. Both the farmhouse and the Mansion are decorated in 18th and 19th century furnishings. An antique shop is located on the property as well.

14 PITTSFORD

Country Barn Antique Center
Rt. 7
802/483-2846

Rutland Antiques
Rt. 7
802/483-6434

Tuffy
Rt. 7
802/483-6610

15 QUECHEE

Quechee Gorge Village
Rt. 4
802/295-1550

Antiques Collaborative
Waterman Place/Rt. 4
802/296-5858

16 RUTLAND

Park Antiques, Inc.
75 Woodstock Avenue
802/775-4184
Open daily except Monday from 10 to 5

Directions: Located 1/4 mile east on Rt. 4 from Rt. 7.

Park Antiques, Inc. is the home of an ever-changing stock of furniture (Victorian and Oak), primitives, collectibles, jewelry, stoneware, paintings, china, glassware and more.

Conway's Antiques & Decor
90 Center St.
802/775-5153

The Gallery of Antqs. & Cllbls.
Rt. 4
802/773-4940

Trader Rick's
407 West St.
802/775-4455

17 SHELBURNE

Shelburne Museum
Rt.7
802/985-3346
Hours: From late May to late Oct., 10-5 every day.
From late Oct. to late May, 1 p.m. guided tour, daily

Directions: From I-89, take Exit 13 to Rt. 7 south to Shelburne.

Described as New England's Smithsonian, Shelburne Museum is located in the heart of Vermont's scenic Champlain Valley. It was founded in 1947 by Electra Havemeyer Webb, a pioneer collector of American folk art. Mrs. Webb became captivated by the sometimes unexpected beauty of utilitarian objects that exemplified "the ingenuity and craftsmanship of the pre-industrial era".

The 37 exhibit buildings, situated on 45 scenic acres, house 80,000 objects of art, artifacts, and architecture spanning 3 centuries of American culture.

At first glance the museum looks like a well-preserved historic village, but look again: The Adirondack-style hunting lodge sits near a turn-of-the-century paddle wheel steamboat, which in turn borders a collection of community buildings and historic houses that date back to the 18th and 19th century.

The contents in some of these architectural treasures document the era of the particular building, but others serve as galleries for diverse collections to be enjoyed in a friendly and informal way.

The Shelburne Museum is a lively and intriguing combination of art and history that promises visitors a veritable patchwork of America's past.

Vincent Fernandez Oriental Rugs and Antqs.
Rt. 7
802/985-2275
Open Mon.-Sat., 10-5

Directions: On Interstate 89 take Shelburne Exit, travel south on Rt. 7, shop is six miles on the left across from the Shelburne Museum.

Rugs have been used in homes in America since the 17th century. Oriental rugs during the early periods were sometimes used on a table rather than on the floor. At Vincent Fernandez Oriental Rugs and Antiques, the offerings are spectacular. You're sure to find something to enhance any decor. This shop always carries an excellent selection of antiques.

Shelburne Village Antiques
Rt. 7-On The Green
802/985-1447
Open Mon.-Sat., 10-5; also most Sundays

Directions: Located on Rt. 7, six miles from I-89 in the heart of Shelburne Village. Within walking distance of Shelburne Museum.

A unique collection of New England furniture and decorative accessories, along with a complete line of Americana, Folk Art and primitives invitingly beckons the traveler to stop and shop.

Black Hawk
2131 Rt. 7-On The Green
802/985-8049
Open Monday through Sunday, 10-5

Directions: Traveling I-89, south to Shelburne Village. Black Hawk is a 5 minute walk from The Shelburne Museum.

Black Hawk, located in an Historic 19th century store front, is known for its American antiques and accessories.

Somewear In Time
2131 Rt. 7
802/985-3816

Burlington Center For Antiques
1966 Shelburne Rd.
802/985-4911

Champlain Valley Antq. Cntr.
1991 Shelburne Rd.
802/985-8116

Willows
6 Falls Rd.
802/985-8040

Its About Time Ltd.
3 Webster Rd.
802/985-5772

18 SOUTH BURLINGTON

Ethan Allen Antique Shop
32 Beacon St.
802/863-3764

New England Imp. Rug Gallery
930 Shelburne Rd.
802/865-0503

19 STOWE

Rosebud Antiques at Houston Farm
2850 Mountain Road
802/253-2333
Open Wed.-Sun. 9-5; closed Monday & Tuesday

Directions: Exit 10 (Stowe) off I-89. Take 100 North. At the crossroads in the village take Mountain Road (108) 2 miles. Shop is on the right.

Visiting with this shop owner by phone was quite a treat. This quaint little shop, attached to an 1850s home, is ten minutes from a ski resort. As you might surmise, they specialize in sports antiquities: skiing, fishing, snow shoes, etc. They also have a wonderful collection of children's antique sleds.

Old chocolate and ice cream molds are another hard-to-find item from the past featured in this shop.

Countryhouse Chic
1799 Mountain Rd.
802/253-8248

Stowe Antiques Center
51 S. Main St.
802/253-9875

20 WATERBURY

Early Vermont Antiques
Rt. 100 North
802/244-5373
Hours: 10-5 daily, year round

Directions: From I-89, take Exit 10, onto Rt. 100. The shop is directly across from Ben and Jerry's Ice Cream Store.

This shop is the perfect place to stop if you're "hot" because they are located directly across the street from Ben & Jerry's Ice Cream Store. Once you cool off with all that ice cream (it's absolutely wonderful, you know) then cross the street to visit Barbara at Early Vermont. This fabulous group shop offers the finest in early American antiques. Tastefully displayed throughout the shop you will find early furnishings, glass, collectibles, and accessories often native to the Vermont area.

Sugar Hill Antiques
Rt 100
802/244-7707

21 WESTON

Weston Antiques Barn
Rt. 100
802/824-4097
Open Mon.-Fri. 10-5, Sun. 11-4 during Nov.-May; Mon.-Sat. 10-5, Sun. 11-4 during June- Oct.

Directions: The Weston Antiques Barn is located on Rt. 100, 1 mile north of "Historic" Weston Village.

This twenty-five dealer shop offers a wide array of furniture, pottery, glass, paintings, books, metals and textiles. A great source for collectors, decorators, and anyone looking for something unique to treasure.

The Vermont County Store
Rt. 100
802/362-2400
Open Mon.-Sat. 9-5; closed Sundays

Known in all 50 states through *The Voice of the Mountains* mail order catalogue, here you will rediscover products you thought had long disappeared such as penny candy, Vermont Common Crackers, and floursack towels, as well as many other useful and practical items. Interspersed with the merchandise are hundreds of artifacts from the past - its like shopping in a museum. A visit you'll remember long after you get home.

22 WILMINGTON

Left Bank Antiques

Rt. 9 and 100
802/464-3224
Open Thurs.-Mon. 11-5; closed Tuesday and Wednesday

Directions: Located at the Junction of Routes 9 and 100 (at the light).

Roseville pottery, chandeliers and lighting, early 1900's furniture, old trunks and a multitude of glassware are only a few of the examples of fine antiques you will find in this eight dealer shop.

Royles Bazaar
W. Main
802/464-8093

Etcetera Shop
Rt. 9 W.
802/464-5394

Yankee Pickers
Rt. 100
802/464-3884

Pine Tree Hill Antiques
21 Warnock Rd.
802/464-2922

Notes

WRIGHT PLACE ANTIQUE MALL

Largest Antique Mall in Salem

Open seven days a week
27 W. Main Street
(540) 389-8507

Salem

58

EVERGREEN THE BELL-CAPOZZI HOUSE

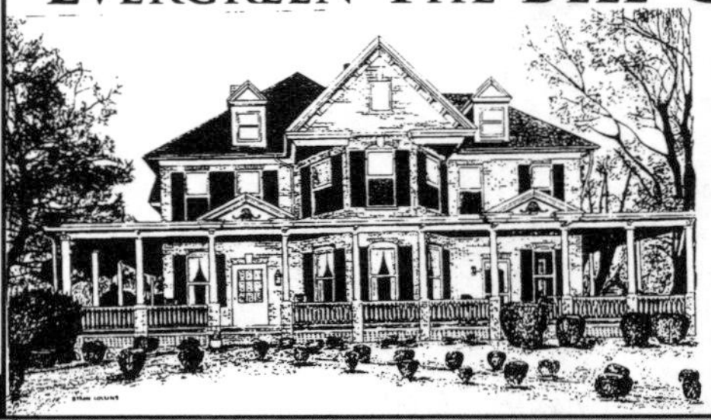

800-905-7372
http://www.bnt.com/evergreen

see review this section

Christiansburg

1

Country Shoppes of Culpeper

Antiques
Crafts
Collectibles
Furniture
Unique Gifts
Floral Arrangements
Jewelry
Gourmet Food

(703) 547-4000
10046 James Monroe Hwy.
(US 29)
2 miles South of Culpeper
(Located in the Old Gallahan Furniture Store)

Culpeper

19

Virginia

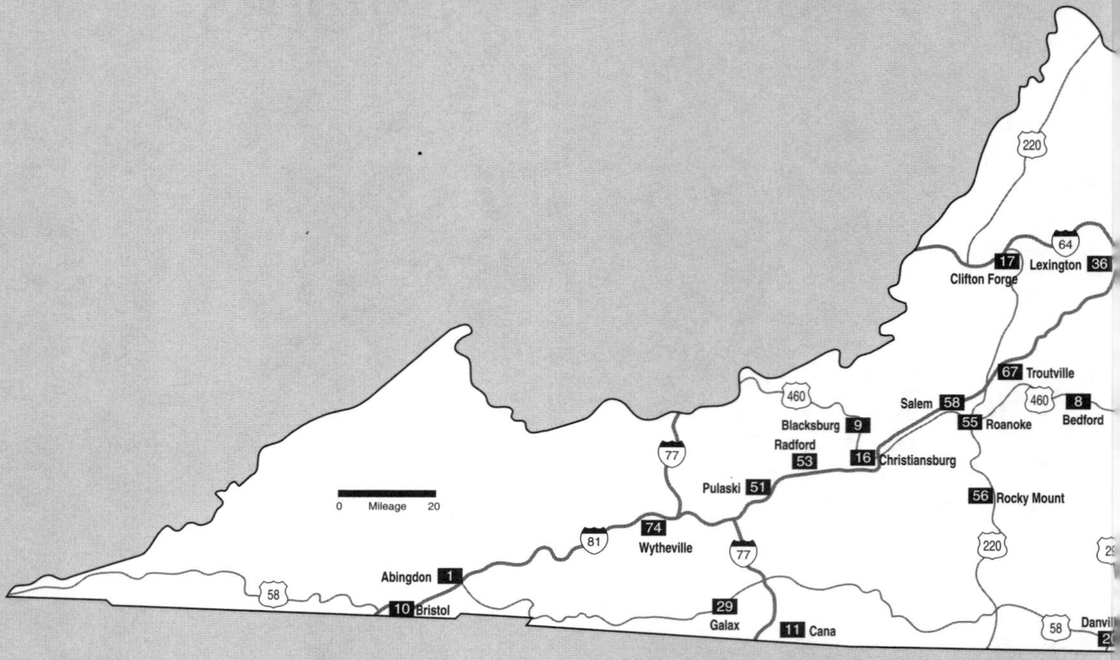

The Inn at Burwell Place

Bed and Breakfast

Built in 1907 on a summit overlooking Salem and the Southwest Roanoke Valley

601 West Main Street
1-800-891-0250
540-387-0250

Salem

58

Whitehouse Antiques

Fine American Antiques in Room Settings
Country to Formal
Appropriate Accessories

Exit 99 from I-64
(Waynesboro/Afton Exit)
Exit 107 from I-64
(Crozet Exit)
U.S. Rt. 250 to State Route 6 on the east side of Afton Mountain
2621 Greenfield Rd.
(540) 942-1194

Afton

2

CAROLINE SQUARE

Welcomes you to visit our Mini Mall in Old Town Fredericksburg, Virginia. Caroline Square is a unique court of shoppes with 50 dealers: filled with gifts, crafts, antiques, and collectibles.

Located 10 Min. from I-95 in Downtown
910-916 Caroline Street • (540) 371-4454

Fredericksburg

28

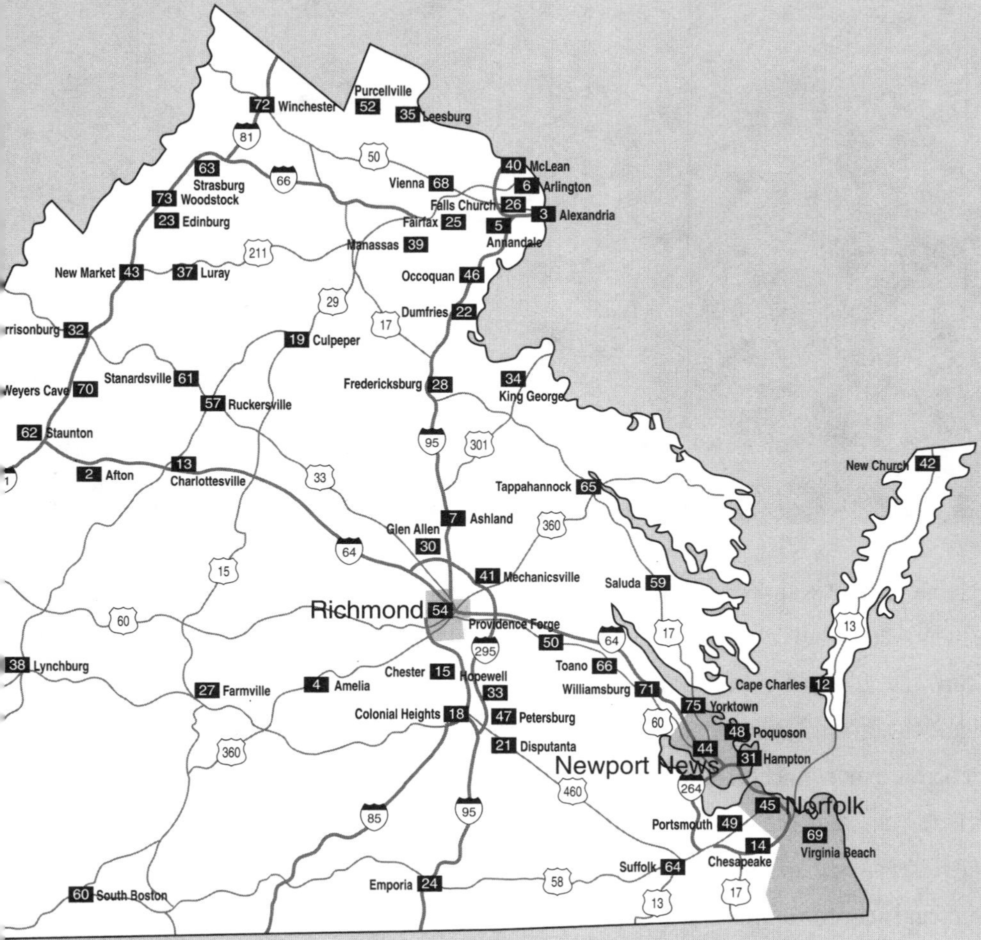

Winchester 72
Purcellville 52
35 Leesburg
81
50
66
63 Strasburg
73 Woodstock
23 Edinburg
40 McLean
6 Arlington
Vienna 68
Falls Church 26
Fairfax 25
3 Alexandria
5 Annandale
Manassas 39
211
New Market 43
37 Luray
Occoquan 46
29
Dumfries 22
17
rrisonburg 32
19 Culpeper
Stanardsville 61
Fredericksburg 28
34 King George
Weyers Cave 70
57 Ruckersville
62 Staunton
95
301
New Church 42
2 Afton
13 Charlottesville
33
Tappahannock 65
Glen Allen 30
7 Ashland
360
64
15
41 Mechanicsville
Saluda 59
Richmond 54
60
Providence Forge 50
64
17
13
295
38 Lynchburg
Chester 15
Hopewell 33
Toano 66
27 Farmville
4 Amelia
Williamsburg 71
Cape Charles 12
Colonial Heights 18
47 Petersburg
75 Yorktown
60
48 Poquoson
21 Disputanta
44
360
Newport News
31 Hampton
460
264
45 Norfolk
85
95
Portsmouth 49
14 Chesapeake
69 Virginia Beach
Suffolk 64
60 South Boston
Emporia 24
58
13
17

The Oaks in Christiansburg: Relaxing

Situated atop the highest hill in town, The Oaks is the focal point of the East Main Street Historic District in Christiansburg, Va. The home was designed by a New York architect.

Construction began in 1889 and was completed in 1893 for Major W.L. Pierce, who built the magnificent Queen Anne Victorian for his wife and seven children.

It remained in the Pierce family for 90 years, then was purchased by the Hardies in 1982. Preserving the original floor plan and elegant interior, the home was extensively restored and renovated, including the addition of modern bathrooms and other amenities.

Tom and Margaret Ray bought the home on September 21, 1989, and converted it to one of the premier bed and breakfast facilities in the nation.

The Oaks is a relaxing place – in perfect harmony with an elegant, gracious atmosphere. Guests awake to the aroma of freshly ground, perked coffee and a newspaper. All rooms have a queen or king size bed, and private bathrooms are modern and stocked with plush towels, fluffy terry robes and toiletries.

The garden gazebo houses a new hydrojet hot tub. Breakfast is always generous. Each day, the menu varies with delightful specialties such as curried eggs served in white wine sauce with Shitake mushrooms, raisin/Granny Smith apple or broccoli/lemon quiche, shirred eggs in spinach nests, rum raisin French toast or whole wheat buttermilk pancakes in praline syrup with toasted pecans and maple cream, and fluffy omelets with surprise fillings and sauces. Oven-fresh breads accompany the entree-spicy pear, French apple and banana muffins, cranberry and pumpkin teabreads and Southern buttermilk biscuits. Sausage, bacon and ginger-braised chicken breasts are favorites.

Juice, fresh strawberries (in season), orange slices, melon, kiwi or poached pears topped with special raspberry/current or orange/honey/rum sauce complete the menu.

The Oaks
Victorian Inn

311 Main Street • Christiansburg, Va.

540/381-1500

Four Diamond Award

Selected for Independent Innkeepers Association

http://www.innbook.com

1 ABINGDON

River Garden Bed and Breakfast
19080 North Fork River Road
1-800-952-4296; 540/676-0335
Open 7 days a week, year round
Rates: $60-65

Directions: Exit 17 off I-81 in Virginia following signs to Abingdon, and the road becomes Cumings Street. Continue on Cumings Street to Valley Street (dead end), and take a left on Valley Street. At Russell Road (dead end) turn right. Go to Hwy. 19 North. Turn right on 19 North (Porterfield Hwy.). At Rt. 611 (North Fork River Road) turn right. River Garden is 2-1/2 miles on the right.

The River Garden Bed and Breakfast, located on the bank of the Holston River, and seated at the base of Clinch Mountain, provides a beautiful welcome sight for travelers. Each room has its own private bath. Rooms are furnished with antique and period furniture, complete with full, queen, or king beds. To make the stay feel more homey, guests are welcome to share the kitchen area, living room, den, and dining room. Enjoy the deck from each room, which overlooks the Holston River.

With private entrances, guests are invited to come and go as they please.

Full breakfast is served each morning by the delightful hosts Carol and Bill Crump.

Court Street Collectibles
104 Court St. NE
540/628-3500

Storytellers Antiques
173 E. Main St.
540/628-8669

Highland Antique Mall
246 W. Main St.
540/676-4438

Garden Artifacts
272 W. Main St.
540/628-9686

Brandy Wine Antiques
477 W. Main St.
540/676-3944

J & R Furniture & Design
108 W. Main St.
540/628-2369

Abingdon Mercantile & Frames
130 S. Wall St.
540/628-2788

Favorite Places To Eat

Cracker Barrel Old Country Store
I-81 & U.S. Hwy. 11, Exit 39
703/628-4004

2 AFTON

Whitehouse Antiques
2621 Greenfield Road
540/942-1194
Hours: 10-5 daily, Mon.-Sun.

Directions: Exit 99 from I-64 (Waynesboro/Afton Exit). Exit 107 from I-64 (Crozet Exit). U.S. Rt. 250 to State Rt. 6 on the east side of Afton Mountain.

With a building over 100 years old as home and Virginia's famous Blue Ridge Mountains as landscape, Whitehouse Antiques presents fine American antiques in room settings. Specializing in furniture from country to formal, many pieces are local antiques selected from area estates. Decorative and accessory "smalls," also available, provide distinctive touches to any decor.

Antiques @ Afton
State Rt. 6
540/456-6515

3 ALEXANDRIA

Belgravia Fine Art
411 Cameron St.
703/548-7702

Reunions
1719 Centre Plaza
703/931-8161

Bird-In-The-Cage Antiques
110 King St.
703/549-5114

Antiques on King Street
917 King St.
703/739-9750

French Country Antiques
1000 King St.
703/548-8563

Iron Gate Antiques
1007 King St.
703/549-7429

King Street Antiques
1015 King St.
703/549-0883

Random Harvest
1117 King St.
703/548-8820

Banana Tree
1223 King St.
703/836-4317

Odds & Ends Antique Shop
1325 King St.
703/836-6722

Micheline's Antiques
1600 King St.
703/836-1893

Cambridge Classics
210 N. Lee St.
703/739-2877

Old Town Antiques
210 N. Lee St.
703/519-0009

Teacher's Pet Antiques
210 N. Lee St.
703/549-9766

Times Juggler
210 N. Lee St.
703/836-3594

Trojan Antiques
210 N. Lee St.
703/549-9766

Trojan Antiques Too
216 N. Lee St.
703/836-5410

Reflections Antiques
222 N. Lee St.
703/683-6808

Alexandria Coin Sales
6550 Little River Tpk.
703/354-3700

Presidential Coin & Antq. Co.
6550 Little River Tpk.
703/354-5454

Trojan Three
320 Prince St.
703/548-8558

Cavalier Antiques
400 Prince St.
703/836-2539

Thieve's Market Antqs. Center
8101 Richmond Hwy.
703/360-4200

Jane's Antiques
8853 Richmond Hwy.
703/360-1428

Lenore & Daughters Antiques
130 S. Royal St.
703/836-3356

Seaport Traders Arts & Antqs.
1201 N. Royal St.
703/684-2901

James Wilholt Antiques
150 N. Saint Asaph St.
703/683-6595

Icon Gallery
101 N. Union
703/739-0700

Old Colony Shop
222 S. Washington St.
703/548-8008

Brockett's Row Antiques
303 N. Washington ST
703/684-0464

Donna Lee's Collectibles
419 S. Washington St.
703/548-5830

Studio Antiques & Fine Art
524 N. Washington St.
703/548-5188

Sumpter Priddy III Inc.
601 S. Washington St.
703/299-0800

Frances Simmons Antiques
619 S. Washington St.
703/549-1291

4 AMELIA COURT HOUSE

Amelia Antique Mall
Church Street
804/561-2511

Cindy Garrett Antiques
13241 Mount Olive Lane
804/561-3999

Jodene's Antiques
12710 Patrick Henry Hwy.
804/561-3333

Emerson Antq. Mall & Cllbls.
19720 Patrick Henry Hwy.
804/561-5276

5 ANNANDALE

Heart's Desire
7120 Little River Tpk.
703/916-0361

Krueger's Antique Plus
7129 Little River Tpk.
703/941-3644

Antique Medley
7120 Little River Tpk.
703/354-6279

Bill Siaz
7120 Little River Tpk.
703/256-6688

Chris' Collectibles
7120 Little River Tpk.
703/941-0361

Christian Deschamps
7120 Little River Tpk.
703/256-6688

Chrystal Mint
7120 Little River Tpk.
703/256-6688

The Clock Works
7120 Little River Tpk.
703/256-6688

The Cottage
7120 Little River Tpk.
703/256-6688

David's Place
7120 Little River Tpk.
703/256-6688

Dloves Antiques
7120 Little River Tpk.
703/256-6688

Figaro Gallery
7120 Little River Tpk.
703/354-3200

French Connection
7120 Little River Tpk.
703/256-6688

Gene's Antiques
7120 Little River Tpk.
703/256-6688

Guinevere's Journey
7120 Little River Tpk.
703/941-0130

Henry's Antiques
7120 Little River Tpk.
703/256-6688

Joan's
7120 Little Rive Tpk.
703/256-6688

JR's
7120 Little River Tpk.
703/256-6688

Kabul Antiques & Jewelry
7120 Little River Tpk.
703/642-8260

Kim's Country House
7120 Little River Tpk.
703/256-6688

Lady Randolph's
7120 Little River Tpk.
703/750-1609

Mary's Antiques
7120 Little River Tpk.
703/256-6688

Misty Memories
7120 Little River Tpk.
703/642-1052

The Old Crank
7120 Little River Tpk.
703/256-6688

Osbourne House
7120 Little River Tpk.
703/256-6688

Past Pleasure Antiques
7120 Little River Tpk.
703/256-6688

Peggotly Antiques & Cllbls.
7120 Little Rive Tpk.
703/642-5750

Rags to Riches
7120 Little Rive Tpk.
703/941-0130

Shamma's Antiques
7120 Little Rive Tpk.
703/750-6439

Showcase Antiques
7120 Little Rive Tpk.
703/941-0130

Southerland
7120 Little Rive Tpk.
703/256-6688

Vintage Radio
7120 Little Rive Tpk.
703/256-6688

Virgilian Fine Arts Antqs.
7120 Little Rive Tpk.
703/256-6688

And Antiques
7129 Little River Tpk.
703/941-7360

Grammie's Collectibles
7129 Little River Tpk.
703/642-3999

Ken's Antiques
7129 Little River Tpk.
703/750-5453

6 ARLINGTON

Granny's Attic
3911 Lee Hwy.
703/812-0389

Consignments Umlimited
2645 N. Pershing Dr.
703/276-0051

Corner Cupboard
2649 N. Pershing Dr.
703/276-0060

Something Unique
933 N. Quincy St.
703/807-2432

Book Ends
2710 Washington Blvd.
703/524-4976

Home Artifacts
2836 Wilson Blvd.
703/812-8348

7 ASHLAND

Favorite Places To Eat

Cracker Barrel Old Country Store
I-95 & State Rt. 54, Exit 92
804/798-1542

8 BEDFORD

Elizabeth N Gladwell & Assoc.
124 S. Bridge St.
540/586-4567

Bridge Street Antiques
201 N. Bridge St.
540/586-6611

Hamilton's
155 W. Main St.
540/586-5592

Granny's Antiques & Etc.
Rt 460 E.
540/586-6861

Stoney Creek Antiques
Rt 460 W.
540/586-0166

Olde Liberty Antique Mall
802 E. Washington St.
540/586-3804

Bedford Antique Mall
109 S. Bridge St.
540/587-9322

9 BLACKSBURG

Other Times Ltd.
891 Kabrich St.
540/552-1615

Grady's Antiques
208 N. Main St.
540/951-0623

Heirloom's Originals
609 N. Main St.
540/552-9241

Whitaker's Antiques
1102 Progress St.
540/552-1186

10 BRISTOL

Antiques on Commonwealth
57 Commonwealth Ave.
540/669-1886

Bristol Antique Mall
403 Commonwealth Ave.
540/466-4064

Abe's Antiques
411 Commonwealth Ave.
540/466-6895

Frank's Antiques
413 Commonwealth Ave.
540/669-4138

Art History & Antiques
42 Piedmont Ave.
540/669-6491

Heritage Antiques
625 State St.
540/669-9774

11 CANA

Antique House
Hwy. 52
540/755-4700

Mountain Side Antiques
Hwy. 52
540/755-3875

Van Noppen T P Antiques
Hwy. 52
540/755-4382

12 CAPE CHARLES

Bay Avenue's Sunset Bed & Breakfast
108 Bay Avenue
757/331-2424
Open all year
Rates: $75-85

Directions: From Rt. 13 traffic light, go west 2 miles on Rt. 184 to Chesapeake Bay. Turn right, 4th house.

Unwind under the spell of a by-gone era in a 1915 Victorian home nestled directly on Chesapeake Bay. This recipient of AAA's 3 diamond rating and American Bed and Breakfast Association's 3 crown "Excellent" Award, offers accommodations with individual decor including the Victorian Room (period wallpaper, window seat, pedestal sink, old claw foot tub), Sheena Room (extra large contemporary with a touch of the rain forest), the Courtney Room (white wicker furniture, bay view), and the Abigail Room (colonial in decor). The common area provides a view of the bay from 3 windows. Sitting back in a rocker on the west-facing front porch is a delightful way to soak in the sunset. The nearby historic district is host to several quaint antique and specialty shops.

Charmers Antique
211 Mason Ave.
757-331-1488

13 CHARLOTTESVILLE

Aaron's Attic
1700 Allied St.
804/295-5760

Heartwood Books
59 Elliewood Ave.
804/295-7083

First Street Antiques
107 N. 1st St.
804/295-7650

Court Square Antiques
216 4 th St.
804/295-6244

Stedman House
201 E. High St.
804/295-0671

Eternal Attic
2125 Ivy Rd.
804/977-2667

1740 House Antqs. & Fine Art
3449 Ivy Rd. (Rt 250 W.)
804/977-1740

Ming-Quing Antiques
111 Main St.
804/979-8426

Consignment House Unltd.
121 W. Main St.
804/977-5527

20th Century Art & Antiques
201 E. Main St.
804/296-6818

Oyster House Antiques
219 E. Main St.
804/295-4757

Daniel Chenn Gallery
619 W. Main St.
804/977-8890

Deloach Antiques
1211 W. Main St.
804/979-7209

1817 Antique Inn
1211 W. Main St.
804/979-7353

Jefferson Coin Shop
301 E. Market St.
804/295-1765

Second Wind
1117 E. Market St.
804/296-1413

The Antiquers Mall
Rt. 29 N
804/973-3478

Renaissance Gallery
By Appointment Only
804/296-9208

14 CHESAPEAKE

American Antqs. at Blue Ridge
1505 Blue Ridge Rd.
757-482-7330

Way Back Yonder Antiques
916 Canal Dr.
757-487-8459

Cal's Antiques
928 Canal Dr.
757-485-1895

Fran's Antiques
3017 S. Military Hwy.
757-485-1656

Maria's Antiques & Cllbls.
3021 S. Military Hwy.
757-485-1799

Chesapeake House Antiques
3040 S. Military Hwy.
757-487-2219

T-N-T Treasures
3044 S. Military Hwy.
757-485-3927

Quiet Shoppe Saddlery
3935 Poplar Hill Rd.
757-483-9358

15 CHESTER

Favorite Places To Eat

Cracker Barrel Old Country Store
I-95 & Rt. 10, Exit 61
804/748-4032

16 CHRISTIANSBURG

The Oaks Victorian Inn
311 E. Main St.
540/381-1500
Open year round

Directions: From I-81, take Exit 114. At the bottom of the ramp, turn left if approaching from the south, and right if approaching from the north. You are on Main Street, so is the Oaks. Continue for approximately 2 miles to fork at Park and Main Streets, bear right on Park, then left into the Oaks' driveway. From the Blue Ridge Parkway take Rt. 8 (MP 165) through Floyd to Christiansburg. Rt. 8 becomes Main Street. Follow earlier directions.

For specific information see review this section.

Evergreen The Bell-Capozzi House
201 E. Main Street
1-800-905-7372
540/382-7372
http://www.bnt.com/evergreen
E-mail: evegrninn@aol

Directions: For specific directions from your location, please call the Innkeepers.

Fully called Evergreen The Bell-Capozzi House, this Southwestern Virginia B&B graces the hills of Christiansburg. Guest will be surprised that the house's lavish facade hides an inground heated pool in the backyard, replete with lounge chairs, gazebo, rose garden, and fish pond.

After a good workout in the pool, you can settle into comfort in a poster bed of one of the large bedrooms, each individually decorated with captivating works of talented, local artists.

Yes, there is a "Gone with the Wind" bedroom in this Victorian mansion. It features a king-size, four-poster bed along with a desk and comfortable chairs. Scarlett O'Beara and Rhett Beartler complete the makeup. Among the home's 17 rooms are five guest quarters, all with heart pine floors, original light fixtures, and private baths.

Fireplaces warm the two parlors. The formal library converts easily to a conference room that can accommodate 12 people. Innkeepers Rocco, transplanted from Corning, NY, and Barbara, a native of Virginia whose great-grandfathers fought in the Civil War, restored and decorated "for comfort" the house without altering it. Guests call it "relaxed elegance."

Your hosts cook up a traditional southern breakfast with homemade biscuits, country ham, cheese grits, eggs, silver dollar pancakes, fresh fruit, locally-made jams, jellies, and apple butter, and growing-in-fame Mill Mountain coffee and tea.

Tea time arrives in style at 5p.m. in the library during winter time with scones, cookies, cake, and small sandwiches. Summer guests are served on the porches, humming with rockers and swings.

Two blocks away are the Montgomery Museum and Lewis Miller Regional Art Center. The 204-year-old city of Christiansburg is the county seat for Montgomery County. Nearby Virginia Tech is a premier depository of American Civil War history and home base for noted Civil War historian James I. Robertson, Jr.

When you're finished scouting out the Civil War archives, you can canoe or raft the Little and New rivers, play bocce ball on Evergreen's lawn, fish Claytor Lake and the rivers, golf at Round Meadow or Virginia Tech, hike the Appalachian Trail and George Washington-Jefferson National Forest, horseback ride at Mountain Lake, or play tennis at several convenient sites. At Evergreen, when you aren't swimming, you can try your hand at puzzles, bridge, or the 1887 Bechstein concert grand piano.

Favorite Places To Eat

Cracker Barrel Old Country Store
I-81 & U.S. 460, Exit 118
540/382-2750

17 CLIFTON FORGE

Mary's Antiques & Collectibles
608 Main St.
540/863-8577

Always Roxie's
622 Main St.
540/862-2999

Dews Etc.
420 E. Ridgeway
No phone

18 COLONIAL HEIGHTS

Blue and Gray Relic Shop
2012 Boulevard
804/526-6863

T J's Corner
17100 Jefferson Davis Hwy.
804/526-3074

19 CULPEPER

Country Shoppes of Culpeper
10046 James Monroe Hwy. (U.S. 29 North)
540/547-4000
Open daily, 9-6, Mon.-Sat. And Sun., 12-5

Directions: Located on U. S. Hwy. 29 (James Monroe Hwy.) 2 miles south of Culpeper, VA., and 35 miles west of I-95/Rt. 3 Fredericksburg Exit.

One hundred dealers have stuffed this 15,000-square-foot mall full of antique furniture, accessories, collectibles, glassware, jewelry, and so much more. Unique gifts and gourmet foods enhance the selection. Daily additions to vendor's wares increase possibilities and variety.

Ace Books & Antiques
120 W. Culpeper St.
540/825-8973

Barter Post at Davis Street
179 E. Davis St.
540/829-6814

Minute Man Mini Mall
746 Germanna Hwy.
540/825-3133

Leonard's Antiques & Cllbls.
10042 James Monroe Hwy.
540/547-4104

20 DANVILLE

Pike's End Antiques
103 Franklin Tpke
804/836-2449

Judy Adkins Antiques
230 Lamberth Dr.
804/822-2257

John's Antiques
2011 N. Main St.
804/793-7961

Finders Antique House
1169 Piney Forest Rd.
804/836-6782

Majestic Interiors
127 Tunstall Rd.
804/792-2521

Antiques Cellar Engl Imports
643 Tunstall Rd.
804/792-1966

21 DISPUTANTA

Antiques Junction
10020 County Dr.
804/991-2463

Mule Shed
10026 County Dr.
804/991-2115

Kathy's Hideway Antiques
10032 County Dr.
804/991-2061

22 DUMFRIES

Favorite Places To Eat

Cracker Barrel Old Country Store
I-95 & Rt. 234, Exit 152
703/441-2764

23 EDINBURG

Richard's Antiques
14211 Old Valley Pike
540/984-4502

24 EMPORIA

Dutchman's Treasures
135 E. Atlantic St.
804/634-2267

Reids of Emporia
408 S. Main St.
804/634-6536

25 FAIRFAX

Culpeper Shoppe
11821 Lee Hwy.
703/631-0405

My Home Shop
12501 Lee Hwy.
703/631-0554

Fairfax Antique Mall
10334 Main St.
703/591-8883

26 FALLS CHURCH

Falls Church Antique Co. Ltd.
260 W. Broad St.
703/241-7074

Old Market Antiques
442 S. Washington St.
703/241-1722

27 FARMVILLE

Granny's Attic
Hwy. 15 N
804/392-8699

Suzis Antiques
235 N. Main St.
804/392-4655

Poplar Hall Antiques
308 N. Main St.
804/392-1658

Mottley Emporium
518 N. Main St.
804/392-4698

28 FREDERICKSBURG

Long before Union and Confederate cannons fired across the rolling hills, Fredericksburg was already rich in Colonial and Revolutionary history. George Washington grew up at Ferry Farm, where legend has it that he swung an axe against a cherry tree. Patriots like Thomas Jefferson and James Monroe knew Fredericksburg well. In four of the Civil War's bloodiest battles, armies under Lee and Grant fought to decide the course of our nation.

History is still alive today in more than 350 original 18th and 19th century buildings all contained within a 40-block National Historic District. The buildings house antique and gift shops as well as many fine restaurants.

Caroline Square
910-916 Caroline Street
540/371-4454
Business hours are from 10-5 Mon. - Sat., Sun. 12-5

Directions: From I-95, take the Fredericksburg-Culpeper Exit to Rt. 3 which becomes William Street in Fredericksburg. Turn right at Caroline Street. OR from I-95, take the Massaponax-Fredericksburg Exit onto Rt. 1 which jogs to the left to become Jefferson Davis Hwy., then left onto Caroline Street.

A rich collection of the past awaits you in this court of shops featuring fifty dealers. Choose from antique furniture and collectibles, quilts, dolls, as well as Shaker furniture. Most shops welcome special orders.

Neat Stuff
109 Amelia St.
540/373-7115

Picket Post
602 Caroline St.
540/371-7703

Bonanno's Antiques Inc.
619 Caroline St.
540/373-3331

Beck's Antiques & Books
708 Caroline St.
540/371-1766

Morland House Antiques
714 Caroline St.
540/373-6144

Blockade Runner
719 Caroline St.
540/374-9346

Pavilion Inc.
723 Caroline St.
540/371-0850

Future Antiques
820 Caroline St.
540/899-6229

Busy B's Treasures
822 Caroline St.
540/899-9185

Antique Corner Fredericksburg
900 Caroline St.
540373-0826

Upstairs Downstairs Antiques
922 Caroline St.
540/373-0370

Antique Court of Shoppes
1001 Caroline St.
540/371-0685

Willow Hill Antiques
1001 Caroline St.
540/371-0685

Fredericksburg Antq. Gallery
1023 Caroline St.
540/373-2961

Past and Present
5099 Jefferson Davis Hwy.
540/891-8977

Consignment Junction Ltd.
2012 Lafayette Blvd.
540/898-2344

Gold Rooster Consignment
4010 Lafayette Blvd.
540/898-4349

Antique Village
4800 Plank Rd.
540/786-9648

Amore Antiques Cllbls. & Gift
1011 Princess Anne St.
540/372-3740

Virginians Antiques Inc.
2217 Princess Anne St.
540/371-2288

Sophia Street Antiques
915 Sophia St.
540/899-3881

She-Kees Antique Gallery
919 Sophia St.
540/899-3808

Gary L Johnson Antiques
1005 Sophia St.
540/371-7141

Country Crossing
106 William St.
540/371-4588

Liberty Park Antiques
208 William St.
540/371-5309

Fredericksburg Antique Mall
211 William St.
540/372-6894

Century Shop
202 Wolfe St.
540/371-7734

Southern Heritage Antiques
107 William
540/371-0200

Favorite Places To Eat

Cracker Barrel Old Country Store
I-95 & Rt. 1, Exit 126B-N. 126 S
703/891-7622

29 GALAX

Vernon's Antiques
Hwy. 58
540/236-6390

Antique Apple
118 S. Main St.
540/236-0881

L & H Antiques
Main St.
No phone

Robert's Gift Gallery
203 S. Main St.
540/238-8877

30 GLEN ALLEN

Dixie Trading Co.
9911 Brook Rd.
804/266-6733

Treasures Inc.
9915 Greenwood Rd.
804/264-8478

Dick & Jeanette's Antqs.
10770 Staples Mill Rd.
804/672-6138

Wigwam Reservation Shops
10412 Washington Hwy.-Rt. # 1
804/550-9698

31 HAMPTON

Odessey Village & Old Village
26 S. King St.
757-727-0028

Poquoson Antique Shop
969 N. King St.
757-723-0501

Victorian Station
36 N. Mallory St.
757-723-5663

Return Engagements
18 E. Mellen St.
757-722-0617

Free City Traders
22 Mellen St.
757-722-3899

The Way We Were Antiques
33 E. Mellen St.
757-726-2300

CC & Co.
1729 W. Pembroke Ave.
757-727-0766

32 HARRISONBURG

Favorite Places To Eat

Cracker Barrel Old Country Store
I-81 & U.S. 11, Exit 243
540/574-3099

33 HOPEWELL

Bargain Bazaar
201 E. Broadway Ave.
804/458-1122

Hamilton's Civil War Relic
257 E. Broadway Ave.
804/458-6504

Curio Shop
501 N. 7 th Ave.
804/458-7990

34 KING GEORGE

End-of-Lane Antiques
9553 James Madison Pkwy.
540/755-9838

Shadyview Antiques
9294 Lambs Creek Church
540/775-0506

35 LEESBURG

Loudoun Antqs. Marketplace
850 Davis St., SE
703/777-5358

Leesburg Antique
Rt. 15, 2.5 Miles
703/777-7799

Leesburg Downtown Antique
27 S. King St.
703/779-8130

Leesburg Antique Gallery
7 Wirt St., SW
703/777-2366

Leesburg Antique Emporium
32 South King St.
703/777-3553

Spurgeon-Lewis Antiques
219 W. Market St.
703/777-6606

Loudoun Street Antiques
3 Loudoun St. SW
703/779-4009

Crafters Gallery
9 W. Market St.
703/771-9017

K & L Market St. Antiques
5 East Market Street
703/443-1827

Preston's Antiques
1 Loudoun St., SW
703/777-6055

36 LEXINGTON

Lexington Antique & Craft Mall
Hwy. 11
540/463-9511

A. Fairfax Antiques
13 W. Nelson
540/463-9885

Lexington Antiques
25 W. Washington St.
540/463-9519

37 LURAY

Wood's Antiques
Hwy. 211 E.
540/743-4406

Wanda's Wonders
Hwy. 340 S.
540/743-4197

Mama's Treasures
22 E. Main St.
540/743-1352

James McHone Antiques
24 E. Main St.
540/743-9001

Zib's Country Connection
24 E. Main St.
540/743-7394

Luray Antique Depot
49 E. Main St.
540/743-1298

P Buckley Moss Gallery
Mimslyn Inn-Main St.
540/743-5105

38 LYNCHBURG

James River Antqs. Lynchburg
503 Clay St.
804/528-1960

Dee's Antiques
1724 Lakeside Dr.
804/385-4008

Scarlett's Treasures Antq. Mall
1026 Main St.
804/528-0488

Sweeney's Curious Goods
1220 Main St.
804/846-7839

Langhorne-Stokes Antiques
1421 Main St.
804/846-7452

Redcoat Gallery & Antiques
1421 Main St.
804/528-3182

Sak's Ally
172 Norfolk Ave.
804/846-4712

Jackson's Antiques
2627 Old Forest Rd.
804/384-6411

Time & Again Antiques
2909 Old Forest Rd.
804/384-4807

Lynchburg Florist & Antqs. Inc.
3224 Old Forest Rd.
804/385-6566

39 MANASSAS

Favorite Places To Eat

Cracker Barrel Old Country Store
I-66 & Rt. 234, Exit 47B
703/369-4641

40 MCLEAN

Lilly Parker Antiques Inc.
1317 A Chain Bridge Rd.
703/893-5298

Solovey Jewelers Inc.
1475 Chain Bridge Rd.
703/356-0138

East and Beyond Ltd.
6727 Curran St.
703/448-8200

Folk Art Gallery
6216 Old Dominion
703/532-6923

Abbott Gallery & Framing
6673 Old Dominion Dr.
703/893-2010

Lights Fantastic
6825 Tennyson
703/356-2285

41 MECHANICSVILLE

Mechanicsville Antique Mall
7508 Mechanicsville Turnpike
804/730-5091
Open: Daily 10-6

Directions: Once on 295 take exit 37B; from the Main 360 take first right. (Business 360)

In August, 1997, Mechanicsville Antique Mall was voted the 2nd Best Antique Mall in Richmond by *Richmond Magazine*. This comes as no surprise since this 30,000 square foot mall is jammed packed with over 100 booths and 25 showcase galleries featuring the best in early American, Victorian, golden oak, art pottery, art glass, toys and clocks. The mall even offers clock repair. Be sure to check out Hanover Auction House - adjacent to the antique mall. For information on fine quality estate auctions, call 800/694-0759.

Antique Village
10203 Chamberlayne Rd.
804/746-8914

Favorite Places to Eat

Cracker Barrel Old Country Store
I-295 & Hwy. 360, Exit 37A
804/559-2261

42 NEW CHURCH

Bluewater Trading Co.
6180 Lankford Hwy.
757/824-3124

Worchester House
Lankford Hwy.
757/824-3847

43 NEW MARKET

Cross Roads Inn Bed and Breakfast
9222 John Sevier Road
540/740-4157
Offering year round accommodations
Rates: $55-90

Directions: Take Exit 264 (New Market) off I-81. Go east on Rt. 211 through town 3/4 mile.

Cross Roads Inn features bedrooms with English floral wallpapers and tasteful antiques, including four-poster and canopy beds with cozy down comforters. Each bedroom has a private bath.

Gourmet breakfast, included with your room, is served in the sunny breakfast room, or on the terrace. Served with your breakfast are home baked European breads and muffins as well as gourmet Austrian coffee.

Their Austrian tradition of hospitality includes your first cup of coffee in your room if you desire, and afternoon coffee/tea with Mary-Lloyd's famous strudel.

New Market Battlefield Mus.
9500 Collins Dr.
540/740-8065

B & B Valley Antiques
9294 N. Congress St.
540/740-8700

Elliot's Vly Shenandoah Antqs.
9298 N. Congree St.
540/740-3827

Benny Longs Antiques
9386 N. Congress St.
540/740-3512

Paper Treasures
9595 S. Congress St.
540/740-3135

44 NEWPORT NEWS

Lorraine's
758 J Clyde Morris Blvd.
757/596-1886

Brill's Antiques
10527 Jefferson Ave.
757/596-5333

Fine Arts Shop
10178 Warwick Blvd.
757/595-7754

Another Man's Treasure
10239 Warwick Blvd.
757/596-3739

Chameleon
10363 Warwick Blvd.
757/596-9324

Plantiques – Hilton Village
10377 Warwick Blvd.
757/595-1545

Denbigh Antique & Cllbl. Mall
13811 Warwick Blvd.
757/875-5221

Deb's Antiques & Collectibles
13595 Warwick Blvd.
757/886-0883

Favorite Places To Eat

Cracker Barrel Old Country Store
I-64 & Jefferson Ave., Exit 255
804/249-3020

45 NORFOLK

Anne Spencer Antiques
505 Botetourt St.
757/624-9156

Gale Goss Cntry. French Antqs.
1607 Colley Ave.
757/625-1211

Nero's Antiques & Appraisals
1101 Colonial Ave.
757/627-1111

Nick Nack's Cllbls. & Antiques
!905 Colonial Ave.
757/533-9545

Hollingsworth Antiques
819 Granby St.
757/625-6525

Fran's Fantasies Granby St.
1022 Granby St.
757/622-6996

Nineteenth Century Antiques
1804 Granby St.
757/622-0905

Grey Horse Antiques
1904 Granby St.
757/626-3152

Country Boy's Antiques
1912 Granby St.
757/627-3630

David's Antiques
2410 Granby St.
757/627-6376

A Touch of Mystery
2412 Granby St.
757/622-7907

Decades Art & Antiques
2608 Granby St.
757/627-0785

A Niche In Tyme
9631 Granby St.
757/588-1684

Wooden Things II
2715 Monticello Ave.
757/624-1273

Merlo's
131 W. Olney Rd.
757/622-2699

G Carr Ltd. Art & Antiques
522 W. 20th St.
757/624-1289

Carriage House Antiques
110 W. 21st St.
757/625-4504

Fairfax Shop
120 W. 21st St.
757/625-5539

Grapevine of Ghent
122 W. 21st St.
757/627-0519

Richard Levins Garfields
122 W. 21st St.
757/622-0414

International Antq. Importers
240 W. 21st St.
757/624-9658

Morgan House Antq. Gallery
242 W. 21st St.
757/627-2486

Palace Antiques Gallery
300 W. 21st St.
757/622-2733

Primrose
400 W. 21st St.
757/624-8473

Ghent Antique & Consignment
517 W. 21st St.
757/627-1900

Norfolk Antique Co.
537 W. 21st St.
757/627-6199

Scott & Company
537 W. 21st St.
757/640-1319

Monticello Antique Shop
227 W. York St.
757/622-4124

Di-Antiques
5901 E. Virginia Beach Blvd.
757/466-1717

Nautical Antiques
6150 E. Virginia Beach Blvd.
757/461-2465

A Touch of Mystery
333 Waterside Drive
757/627-9684

46 OCCOQUAN

Country Hollow
210 A Commerce St.
703/490-1877

Commerce Street Gallery
204 Commerce St.
703/491-9020

Heart of Occoquan
305 Mill St.
703/492-9158

Sisters
308 Mill St.
703/497-3131

Future Antiques
407 Mill St.
703/491-5192

Sloan's Antique Gallery
407 Mill St.
703/494-5231

Victoria's Past Tyme
308 A Poplar Alley
703/494-6134

47 PETERSBURG

Hall's Antiques
12 W. Bank St.
804/861-6060

Village Jaile Shoppe
20829 Chesterfield Ave.
804/526-7073

White Oak Antq. & Gift Shop
24118 Cox Rd.
804/861-9127

America Hurrah Antiques
406 N. Market St.
804/861-9659

Woody's Antiques
3 W. Old St.
804/861-9642

Estate Treasures & Antiques
9 W. Old St.
804/732-3032

John Reads Row
102 W. Old St.
804/732-5690

Coin Exchange
104 W. Old St.
804/861-6449

48 POQUOSON

Joanne's This That & Other
798 Poquoson Ave.
757/868-4770

Martin-Wilson House
326 Wythe Creek Rd.
757/868-7070

Antiques East
476 Wythe Creek Rd.
757/868-9976

Candlelight Antiques & Designs
499 Wythe Creek Rd.
757/868-8898

49 PORTSMOUTH

Prison Square Antiques
440 High St.
757/399-4174

Olde Towne Sales
719 High St.
757/399-4009

Mount Vernon Antique Shop
258 Mount Vernon Ave.
757/399-6550

Jems from Jennie
Poplar Hill Shopping Center
757/484-9581

Old Schoolhouse Antiques
4903 Portsmouth Blvd.
757/465-3145

50 PROVIDENCE FORGE

Jasmine Plantation Bed and Breakfast Inn
4500 North Courthouse Road
804/966-9836 or 1-800-NEW-KENT
Open 7 days a week, 52 weeks a year

Directions: Halfway between Williamsburg and Richmond, the Inn is located 2.4 miles south of I-64 at Exit 214. OR from Rt. 60, go north on State Rt. 155 for 1.4 miles.

A great place to relax between antiquing days is this 1750s farmhouse offering 6 rooms with antique decor. Enjoy the afternoons sitting on the front porch or enjoying nature along the 47 acres of walking trails. Don't pass up the complimentary full "skip lunch" country breakfast.

51 PULASKI

Upstairs Downstairs
27 Main Street W.
540/980-4809

Colony of Virginia Ltd.
61 W. Main St.
540/980-8932

Around the World Antiques
86 W. Main St.
540/980-8389

52 PURCELLVILLE

Noni's Attic
148 N. 21st St.
540/338-3489

Carousel
144 N. 21st St.
540/338-9075

Swanson & Ball Antiques
142 N. 21st St.
540/338-7077

Nick Greer Antique Restoration
Rt. 711
540/338-6607

Mary Ellen Stover
120 N. 21st St.
540/338-3823

Clark & Palmer
108 N. 21st St.
540/338-7229

Where the Attic Bird Sings
21st & Main Streets
540/338-5474

Irene Mary Antiques & Cllbls.
Corner 21st & Main Streets
540/338-1999

The Petite Emporium
105 E. Main St.
540/338-2298

End of the Rainbow
121 E. Main St.
540/338-5913

Ray E. Fields III
120 Main St.
540/338-3829

Preservation Hall
111 N. 21st St.
540/338-4233

53 RADFORD

Once Upon A Time
221 1st St.
540/633-3987

Grandma's Memories Antiques
237 1st St.
540/639-0054

Uncle Bill's Treasures
1103 Norwood St.
540/633-0589

54 RICHMOND

Midlothian Antiques Center
Coolfield Road
804/897-4913
and
West End Antiques Mall
6504 Horsepen Road
804/285-1916
Hours for both locations: 10-6, Mon.-Sat.; 12-6, Sun.

Antiques Centers, Inc., with its two locations, makes finding your treasure even easier. These centers have a combined 160 dealers and 36,000 square feet of merchandise. Choose from a huge selection of country, formal, or vintage wicker furniture, quilts, linens, glassware and books. You may also want to check their framed collectibles, woodblock prints and pewter.

Berry's Antiques
318 W. Broad St.
804/643-1044

Shamburger's Antiques
5208 Brook Rd.
804/266-8457

Antique Boutique
1310 E. Cary St.
804/775-2525

Bygone's Vintage Clothing
2916 W. Cary St.
804/353-1919

World of Mirth
2925 W. Cary St.
804/353-8991

Distinctive Consignments Ltd.
3422 W. Cary St.
804/359-3778

Johnson's Antiques
5033 Forest Hill Ave.
804/231-9727

Vintage Antique & Art Co.
5047 Forest Hill Ave.
804/233-1808

Antique Exchange
6800 Forest Hill Ave.
804/272-2990

Exile
822 W. Grace St.
804/358-3348

Kim Faison Antiques
5608 Grove Ave.
804/282-3736

Robert Blair Antiques
5612 Grove Ave.
804/285-9441

Hampton House
5720 Grove Ave.
804/285-3479

Chadwick Antiques
5805 Grove Ave.
804/285-3355

Glass Lady
7501 Iron Bridge Rd.
804/743-9811

Jahnke Road Antique Center
6207 Jahnke Rd.
804/231-5838

Robin's Nest
6925 Lakeside Ave.
804/553-1061

Bradley's Antiques
101 E. Main St.
804/644-7305

Civil War Antiques
7605 Midlothian Tpke
804/272-4570

Halcyon-Vintage Clothing
117 N. Robinson St.
804/358-1311

Tudor Gallery Estate Jewelry & Antiques
113 S. 12 th St.
804/780-0020

55 ROANOKE

12 E. Campbell Antiques
12 Campbell Ave. SW
540/343-7946

Sandra's Cellar
109 Campbell Ave. SW
540/342-8123

Continental Antiques
1809 Franklin Rd. SW
540/982-5476

John Davis Antiques
4347 Franklin Rd. SW
540/772-7378

White House Galleries
4347 Franklin Rd. SW
540/774-3529

Home Place Antiques
5348 Franklin Rd. SW
540/774-0774

Carriage House
5999 Franklin Rd. SW
540/776-0499

Sissy's Antiques
2914 Jae Valley Rd.
540/427-1712

Howard R McManus
11 S. Jefferson St.
540/344-2302

Bob Anderson Antiques
617 S. Jefferson St.
540/343-7008

BoLily Antiques
124 Kirk Ave. SW
540/343-0100

Bob Beard Antiques
105 Market Sq SE
540/981-1757

Bargain Corner Antique Shop
3804 Melrose Ave. NW
540/366-1278

Olde Window Glass Co.
4026 Melrose Ave. NW
540/362-3386

Webb's Antiques
3906 Old Garst Mill Rd.
540/774-3790

Roanoke Antique Mall
2302 Orange Ave. NE
540/344-0264

Kirk's
312 2nd St. SW
540/344-8161

Trudy's Antiques & Used Furn.
2205 Williamson Rd. NE
540/366-7898

Now & Then Shop
3133 Williamson Rd. NW
540/366-1905

Happy's
5411 Williamson Rd. NW
540/563-4473

Russell's Yesteryear
117 Campbell Ave. SE
540/342-1750

56 ROCKY MOUNT

Spinning Wheel Antiques
Rt. 220 S
540/489-5355

Blue Ridge Antique Center
Rt 220 20100 Virgil H Goode Hwy.
540/483-2362

57 RUCKERSVILLE

Archangel Antiques & Fine Art
Rt. 29 S.
804/985-7456

Country Store Antique Mall
Rt. 29
804/985-3649

Early-Time Antiques & Fine Art
Rt. 29 N
804/985-3602

Green House Shops
Rt. 29 N. & 33
804/985-6053

Red Fox Antiques
Rt. 29 N.
804/985-2080

Antique Collectors
Rt. 29 N & 33
804/985-8966

58 SALEM

Wright Place Antique Mall
27 W. Main Street
540/389-8507
Open: 7 days a week; Mon.-Sat. 10-6, Sunday 12:30-6

Step back in time at Wright Place Antique Mall located in the middle of downtown antique Salem. Enjoy a cup of coffee or a cold drink while you browse.

The mall offers a distinctive collection of beautiful furniture including: oak, walnut, mahogany, cherry & primitive. Tables, chairs, beds, kitchen cabinets, rockers, bookcases and secretaries, railroad items: dishes, lanterns, nails, locks, paper items, etc., advertising: Coke items, signs, neons, smoking items, bottles, etc, books on history, novels, civil war, science novels, books for all ages, quilts, rugs, linens, license plates, crocks, toys, dolls, clocks, cookie jars, McCoy, Hull, Watt pottery, Weller, Roseville, art, pictures, statues, jewelry, iron items, lamps: glass chandeliers, hurricane, etc., glassware: cut glass, depression, Fenton, china, carnival glass, etc.

Antique in one of the nation's most beautiful settings, and take home memories to last a lifetime. Experience a sunrise from the Blue Ridge Parkway or the Appalachian Trail, two of America's most-revered scenic byways, both winding their way through the Roanoke Valley. Enjoy the sights, sounds and smells of the farmers' markets in Roanoke, Salem and Vinton as they come to life almost every morning with their offerings of produce, flowers, baked goods and handmade items.

No visit would be complete without exploring all the shopping options which one will find at every turn. From antiques to outlets, and million-square-foot malls to boutiques in historic settings, there is something to satisfy every taste and need.

After indulging in the areas many attractions and shops, tempt your taste buds by enjoying a sumptuous meal in one of the many area restaurants. The valley has long held an excellent reputation for its wide variety of outstanding dining facilities. Delight in old-fashioned, down-home Southern cooking or a romantic candlelit dinner for two.

There's history, architecture, whimsy and excitement all over the valley. You'll meet some of the friendliest, most hospitable people in the world, who welcome the opportunity to share the area with you.

*Note: Plenty of lodging is available for over-nighters who need to spend just one more day in beautiful, historic Salem.

The Inn at Burwell Place

601 West Main Street
1-800-891-0250 or 540/387-0250
Rates include full breakfast and private bath. $70-110

Directions: From I-81 southbound, take Exit 140 (Rt. 311) south 1 1/4 miles to East Main Street; turn right on East Main Street and go through downtown Salem, 1 mile. The inn is on the right.

This spacious mansion was built in 1907 by Samuel H. McVitty, a local industrialist, on a summit overlooking Salem and the Southwest Roanoke Valley. Mr. McVitty built the mansion on land purchased from Mr. Nathaniel Burwell (pronounced Burr-ell) a prominent Salem landowner, civic leader, State Assemblyman and gentleman justice of the County Court.

In 1915, McVitty sold the mansion to Lewis E. Dawson, whose family lived there until 1971. The Dawsons made major renovations and an addition to the house in 1925. The house was home to six Dawson children and their families during this period. It was the site of many parties, weddings, and family gatherings.

During the 1970s and the 1980s the mansion was used as an architect's office and the YWCA.

Each guest-room has its own bathroom with vintage 1920s fixtures and a queen-size 4-poster bed. A wide hallway connects the second floor bedrooms. Antique walnut and cherry furnishings adorn each room.

Downstairs, the expansive common area consists of a living room, sun porch (complete with 6 x 8 foot antique carousel), two dining rooms and a massive wraparound front porch, an ideal place for reading and watching television. The common area has been the scene of many weddings, receptions, parties and business meetings reminiscent of yesteryear. Within a short walk from the Inn is a restored park and duck pond (circa 1890); historic downtown Salem, with numerous antique shops, gift boutiques, restaurants and coffee shops.

The Inn serves a full breakfast consisting of the Chef's choice of Eggs Benedict, hash browns, fruit compote, a special fruit juice blend, fresh baked muffins or fruit breads, coffee and teas. Another popular entree is French Toast prepared with fresh apple-cinnamon bread.

Chris Gladden Bookseller
211 S. College Ave.
540/389-4892

Eddy Street Antiques
1502 Eddy St.
540/389-9411

Salem Market Antiques
1 W. Main St.
540/389-8920

Virginia Showcase Antiques
4 E. Main St.
540/387-5842

Green Market-Antique Mall
8 E. Main St.
540/387-3879

Elite Antique & Consignments
17 W. Main St.
540/389-9222

Olde Curiosity Shoppe Antq.
27/29 E. Main St.
540/387-2007

Olde Salem Stained Glass Art
120 E. Main St.
540/389-9968

Auntie Em's Antiques & More
514 W. Main St.
540/389-2294

Antique Lamp Shop
1800 W. Main St.
540/389-3163

Red Barn Antiques
4506 W. Main St.
540/380-4307

Guthrie's Antiques
221 E. 6 th St.
540/389-3621

Antique Mall 50 Plus Shops
27 W. Main St.
540/389-2484

59 SALUDA

The Shops at Saluda Market
Rt. 17 & 33
804/758-2888

Trimble's Antiques
Hwy. 17
804/758-5732

Urbanna Antique Gallery
124 Rappahannock Ave.
804/758-2000

Courthouse Antiques
S.-17 Bypass
804/758-4861

60 SOUTH BOSTON

Z's Antiques
Hwy. 58 W.
804/572-6741

Van's Barnyard Antiques
Hwy. 716 Airport Rd.
804/572-4754

Miss W. & Sis Art All Nations
206 Main St.
804/575-0858

My Brother's Place Antq. Mall
234 S. Main
804/572-8888

Crystal Hill Antiques
1902 Seymour Dr.
804/575-8810

61 STANARDSVILLE

Towne Shops
121 W. Main St.
804/985-8222

Trader Mike's Antiques
313 E. Main St.
804/985-6440

J & T Antiques
317 Main St.
804/985-7299

62 STAUNTON

Turtle Lane
10 E. Beverly St.
540/886-8591

Once Upon A Time Clock Shop
25 W. Beverly St.
540/885-6064

Warehouse Antiques & Cllbls.
26 W. Beverly St.
540/885-0891

Honeysuckle Hill
100 E. Beverly St.
540/885-8261

Memory Makers
15 Middlebrook Ave.
540/886-5341

Jolly Roger Haggle Shop
27 Middlebrook Ave.
540/886-9527

Favorite Places To Eat

Cracker Barrel Old Country Store
I-81 & U.S. 250, Exit 222
703/885-7550

63 STRASBURG

Sullivan's Country Hse. Antqs.
Hwy. 55 & I 81 Exit #-296
540/465-5192

River Gallery
208 W. King St.
540/465-3527

Heritage Antiques
102 Massanutten Manor Circle
540/465-5000

Wayside of Virginia Inc.
108 N. Massanutten St.
540/465-4650

Strasburg Emporium
110 N. Massanutten St.
540/465-3711

Vilnis and Company Antiques
305 N. Massanutten St.
540/465-4405

Tiques
114 Orchard St.
540/465-4115

64 SUFFOLK

Holly Bluff Antiques
2697 Bridge Rd.
757/484-4246

Once Upon A Time Antiques
2948 Bridge Rd.
757/483-1344

Judy's Treasures
723 Carolina Rd.
757/934-7624

Southern Gun Works
109 Cherry St.
757/934-1423

Carolyn's Country Charm
3093 Godwin Blvd.
757/934-2868

Attic Trunk
167 S. Main St.
757/934-0882

Nansemond Antique Shop
3537 Pruden Blvd.
757/539-6269

Willows
800 W. Washington St.
757/934-2411

Now & Then Antiques
6140 Whaleyville Blvd.
757/986-2429

65 TAPPAHANNOCK

A to Z Antiques
608 Church Ln
804/443-4585

Antiques Place
804 Church Ln
804/443-6549

Hoskins Creek Table Co.
1014 Church Ln
804/443-6500

Mayhew's Antiques
205 Queen
804/443-2961

Queen Street Mall 2
227 Queen
804/443-2424

Nadji Nook Antiques
Queen & Cross St. Rt 360
804/443-3298

66 TOANO

Charlie's Antiques
7766 Richmond Rd.
757/566-8300

Pocahontas Trail Antiques
7778 Richmond Rd.
757/566-8050

Colonial Antique Center
7828 Richmond Rd.
757/566-8720

J & L Treasure Chest
7880 Richmond Rd.
757/566-1878

King William Antiques
7880 Richmond Rd.
757/566-2270

67 TROUTVILLE

Buffalo Creek Antiques
941 Lee Hwy. S
540/992-5288

Troutville Antique Mart
941 Lee Hwy. S
540/992-4249

Kelly's Real Deal
1411 Lee Hwy. S
540/992-5096

Harris Antiques
2240 Roanoke Rd.
540/992-5225

Favorite Places To Eat

Cracker Barrel Old Country Store
I-81 & U.S. 220, Exit 150
540/966-5438

68 VIENNA

Finders Keepers
131 N.W. Church St.
703/319-9318

Now and Then
131 N.W. Church St.
703/242-3959

Village Antiques
120 Lawyers Rd. NW
703/938-0084

Vienna Bargains
128 Maple Ave. E
703/255-6119

Twig House
132 Maple Ave. E
703/255-4985

Cameo Coins & Collectibles
444 Maple Ave. E
703/281-7053

Cabbage Rose
213 Mill St.
703/242-2051

Pleasant Street Antiques
115 Pleasant St. NW
703/938-0003

69 VIRGINIA BEACH

Colonial Cottage Antiques
3900 Bonney Rd.
804/498-0600

Mary's Attic
3900 Bonney Rd.
804/498-0600

Pat's Antiques
3900 Bonney Rd.
804/463-1252

Pelican Bay
3900 Bonney Rd.
804/481-4445

Hard Timz & Sunshine
244 London Bridge Shop
804/463-7335

Something Unique
1600 Independence Blvd.
804/363-9512

Echoes of Time Antiques
320 Laskin Rd.
804/428-2332

Shutter Door Antiques
968 Laskin Rd.
804/422-6999

La Galleria Inc.
993 Laskin Rd.
804/428-5909

Garden Gallery
1860 Laskin Rd.
804/428-8427

Chesapeake Antiques & Cllbls.
210 24th St.
804/425-6530

Rudy's Antiques
3324 Virginia Beach Blvd.
804/340-2079

Eddie's Antique Mall
4801 A Virginia Beach Blvd.
757/497-0537

70 WEYERS CAVE

Rocky's Antique Mall
Hwy. 11
540/234-9900

71 WILLIAMSBURG

London Shop
1206 Jamestown Rd.
757/229-8754

Old Chickahominy House
1211 Jamestown Rd.
757/229-4689

Shaia Orntl. Rugs Wllmsburg.
1325 Jamestown Rd.
757/220-0400

TK Oriental Antiques
1654 Jamestown Rd.
757/220-8590

Hamilton's Book Store
1784 Jamestown Rd.
757/220-3000

Quilts Unlimited
Merchants Square
757/253-0222

J L McCandlish Antiques Art
1915 Pocahontas Trl
757/259-0472

Peacock Hill
445 Prince George St.
757/220-0429

Attic Collections
2229 Richmond Rd.
757/229-0032

R & M Antiques
5435 Richmond Rd.
757/565-3344

Lamplighter Shoppe Ltd.
6502 Richmond Rd.
757/565-4676

Things Unique
6506 Richmond Rd.
757/564-1140

Favorite Places To Eat

Cracker Barrel Old Country Store
I-64 & Rt. 143, Exit 238
757/220-3384

72 WINCHESTER

Betty's Antiques
127 Morgan Mill Road
540/667-8558
Open: Wed.-Sat., 12 until 5; Sun.-Tue., by chance or appointment

Directions: Take Exit 315 from I-81 onto Rt. 7. The shop is east of Winchester.

Established in 1973, the shop specializes in refinished American oak furniture. Pieces such as bedroom suites, dressers, and round tables are just a few of the many quality antiques available here.

Past and Present
1121 Berryville Ave.
540/678-8766

Boscawen Gold & Silver Exch
41 W. Boscawen St.
540/667-6065

Kimberly's Antiques & Linens
135 N. Braddock St.
540/662-2195

Glover's Antiques
422 S. Cameron St.
540/662-3737

Stone Soup Gallery
107 N. Loudoun St.
540/722-3976

Winchester Antqs. & Cllbls.
1815 S. Loudoun St.
540/667-7411

Clay Hill Antiques
2869 Middle Rd.
540/662-3623

Millwood Crossing Shops
381 Millwood Ave.
540/662-5157

Doll House Antiques
618 S. Cameron St./By Appt.
540/665-0964

50 West Antiques
2480 Northwestern Pike
540/662-7624

Wrenwood Antique Gallery
39 W. Piccadilly St.
540/665-3055

Cecil Antiques
522 N. Sunnyside Stat
540/667-0787

Applegate Antiques & Art
1844 Valley Ave.
540/665-1933

Favorite Places To Eat

Cracker Barrel Old Country Store
I-81 & Rt. 17/50/522, Exit 313
703/722-3770

73 WOODSTOCK

River'd Inn
1972 Artz Road
540/459-5369
1-800-637-4561
Lodging available seven days a week, $150-325/night includes full breakfast.
Restaurant open Wednesday-Sunday 5-9pm, Sunday Brunch served 11am-2pm.

Directions: I-81 to Rt. 11, just north of Woodstock take SR 663 2.1 miles.

The River'd Inn offers luxurious accommodations nestled in the heart of Virginia's Shenandoah Valley. Spacious bedrooms feature antique furnishings, fireplaces and private baths with whirlpool tubs. Beautiful views from decks and porches. Gourmet restaurant, open to the public, features French-based cuisine. Fine selection of beer, wine, and spirits available. Outdoor pool with hot tub. Situated on 25 forested acres with gardens, mountain views, and paths to the Shenandoah River. Numerous attractions including Civil War sites, antique and gift shops, wineries, golf, skiing, hiking, canoeing, picnicking, and more nearby. Easy access from Interstate 81. Handicapped accessible dining and lodging.

74 WYTHEVILLE

Old Fort Antique Mall
I-81 Exit # 80
540/228-4438

Snoopers Inc.
I-81 Exit # 80
540/637-6441

75 YORKTOWN

High Cotton Ltd.
3630 G. Washington Mem. Hwy.
757/867-7132

Scot's Corner Antiques
4827 G. Washington Mem. Hwy.
757/898-1404

Galleria Antique Mall
7628 G. Washington Mem Hwy.
757/890-2950

Swan Tavern Antiques
300 Main St.
757/898-3033

Notes

Washington

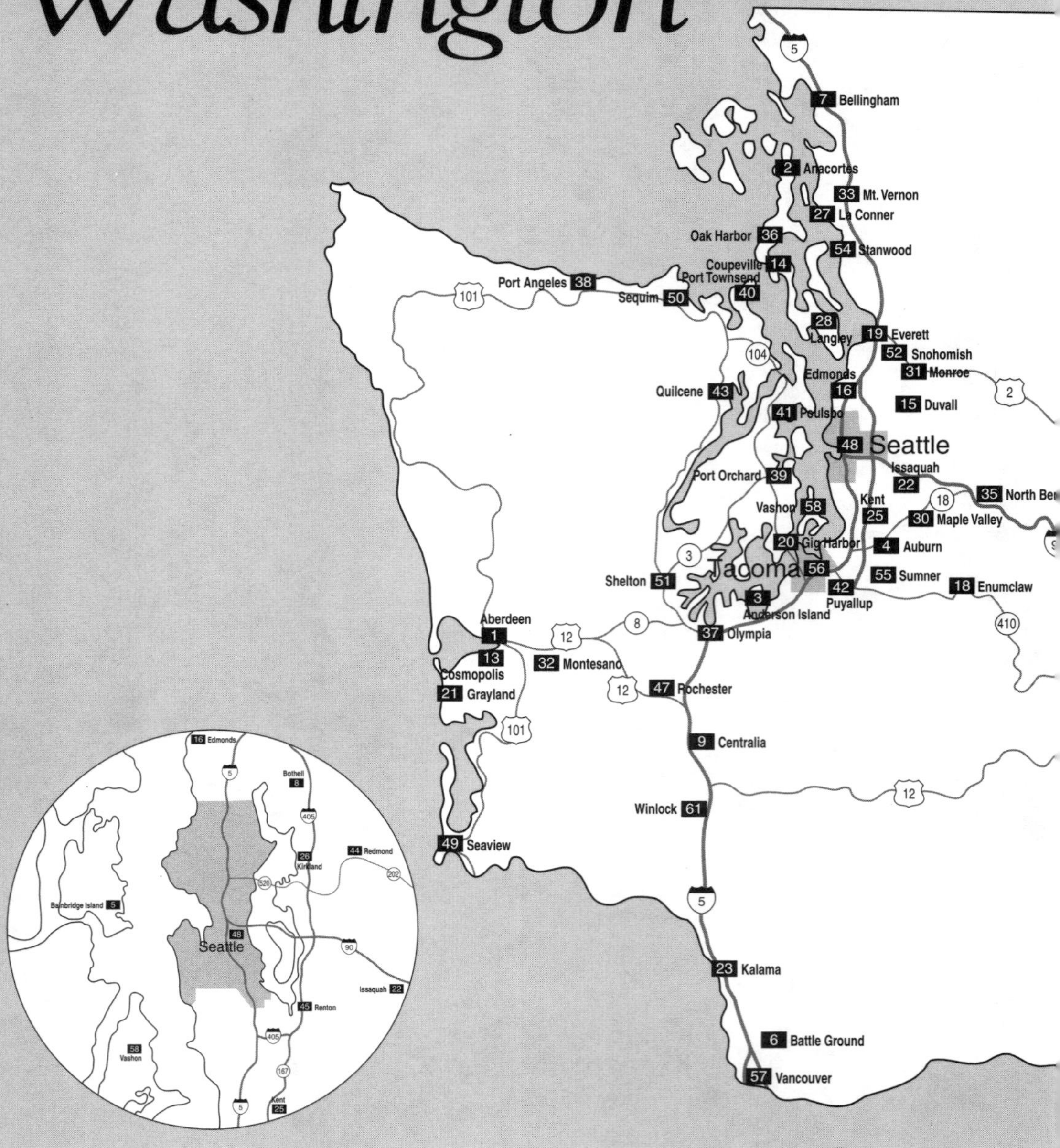

5
7 Bellingham
2 Anacortes
33 Mt. Vernon
27 La Conner
Oak Harbor 36
54 Stanwood
Coupeville 14
Port Townsend 40
Port Angeles 38
101
Sequim 50
28 Langley
19 Everett
52 Snohomish
31 Monroe
104
Edmonds 16
2
Quilcene 43
15 Duvall
41 Poulsbo
48 Seattle
Issaquah 22
Port Orchard 39
18
35 North Bend
Vashon 58
Kent 25
30 Maple Valley
20 Gig Harbor
4 Auburn
3
Tacoma 56
55 Sumner
Shelton 51
42 Puyallup
18 Enumclaw
3 Anderson Island
410
Aberdeen 1
13
8
12
37 Olympia
Cosmopolis
32 Montesano
21 Grayland
12
47 Rochester
101
9 Centralia
12
Winlock 61
49 Seaview
5
23 Kalama
6 Battle Ground
57 Vancouver
16 Edmonds
Bothell 8
5
405
26 Kirkland
44 Redmond
202
520
Bainbridge Island 5
48 Seattle
90
Issaquah 22
45 Renton
405
58 Vashon
167
Kent 25
5

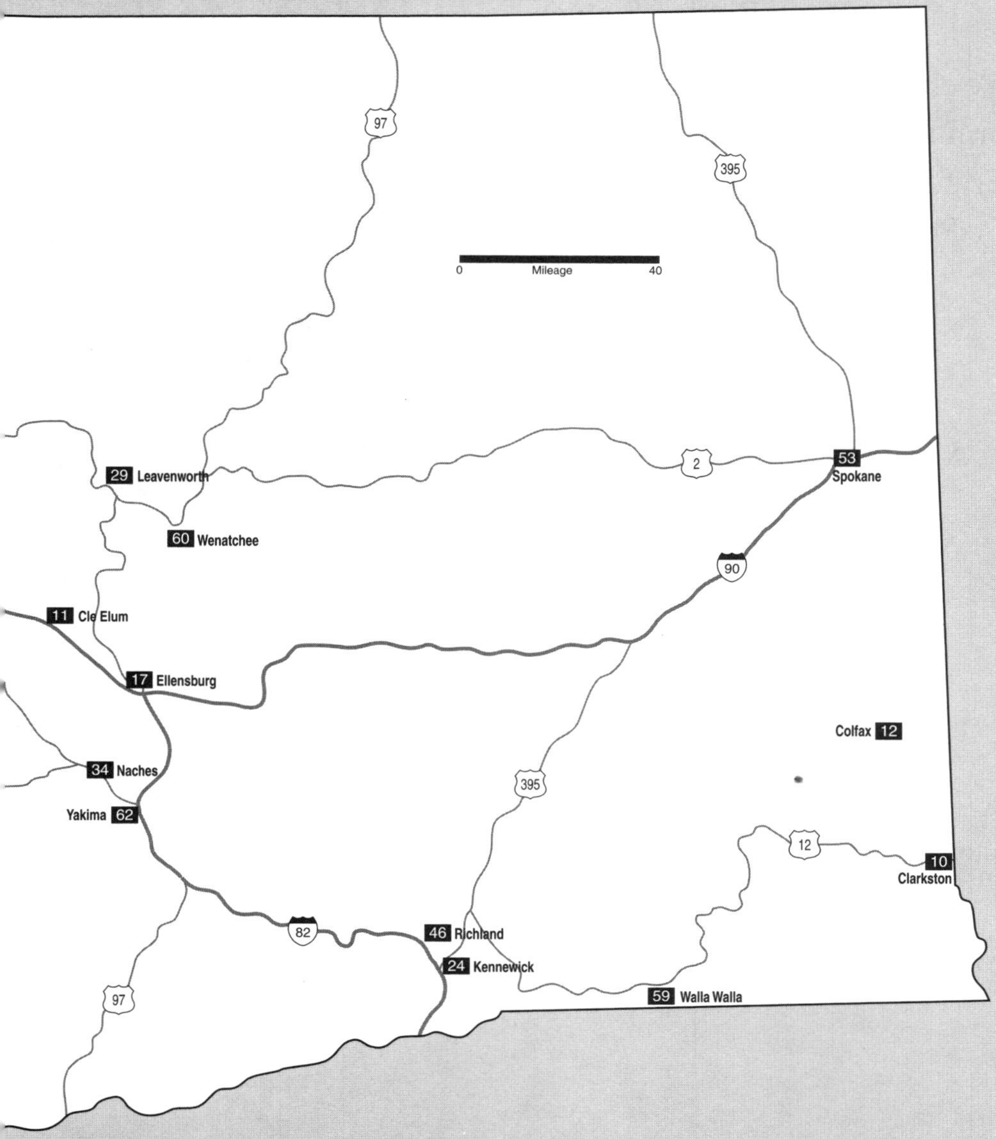
97
395
0 Mileage 40
2
53 Spokane
29 Leavenworth
60 Wenatchee
90
11 Cle Elum
17 Ellensburg
Colfax 12
34 Naches
395
Yakima 62
12
10 Clarkston
82
46 Richland
24 Kennewick
97
59 Walla Walla

The Frog Crossing

Antiques & Collectables
Bed & Breakfast

The home of The Frog Crossing Antiques & Collectables, Bed & Breakfast was built in 1913 and sets on 3/4 of an acre near old Main St. Monroe. Monstrous old maple trees and gorgeous rhododendrons surround the house giving it the feel of walking through a park. Carriage tracks from the wagon trains which crossed its path in the olden days can still be seen in the front yard.

Romantic rooms with fireplaces set the stage for the perfect get-away vacation. A beautiful Victorian bed with appropriate accessories from the same time period complete the decor.

The bed and breakfast houses an antique shop offering wonderful pieces from which to choose as a momento of your stay at The Frog Crossing.

For those of you wanting to explore, The Frog Crossing is only a hop, skip and jump away from Snohomish - The Antique Capital of the Northwest.

e Victorian bedroom at The Frog Crossing.

The Frog Crossing built in 1913 is surrounded by huge maple trees and flowering bushes.

The Frog Crossing
Antiques & Collectables
Bed & Breakfast
306 S. Lewis
Monroe, WA
206/881-7089 • 360/794-7622

1 ABERDEEN

Clevenger's Antique Mall
201 S. Broadway St.
360/533-1317

Grand Heron
200 E. Heron St.
360/532-5561

Judy's Antiques & Collectibles
401 W. Market St.
360/532-4359

Central Park Antiques
6617 Olympic Hwy.
360/538-1173

Karrie's Furnishings
110 W. Wishkah St.
360/533-7330

Antique Co-Op
112 W. Wishkah St.
360/533-6516

2 ANACORTES

The Business
1717 Commerical Ave.
360/293-9788

Left Bank Antiques
1904 Commercial Ave.
360/293-3022

Home Sweet Home Antiques
2701 Commercial Ave.
360/293-1991

Days Gone By
3015 Commercial Ave.
360/299-2222

15th St. Antiques & Gallery
1012 15th St.
360/299-3120

3 ANDERSON ISLAND

Hideaway House Bed and Breakfast
11422 Leschi Circle
253/884-4179
Fax: 253/884-2083
Open daily around the clock
Rates: $55-75

Directions: From I-5 either north or south: Take Exit 119 and follow the signs to Steilacoom. After about 3.5 miles the road leads to the ferry, with parking on the left. It is a beautiful 20 minute ferry ride to Anderson Island. Proceed west off the ferry and veer to the left at the "Y" in the road. Pass the store on the right, turn left onto West Josephine Boulevard. Go one mile, turn right onto Leschi Circle, and go to the blue house.

This description of Hideaway House and innkeepers Hank and Faye Lynn Hollenbaugh makes you appreciate that old-fashioned common courtesy and genuine desire to help others is not entirely dead.

The Hollenbaughs started their B&B unintentionally. The ferry schedule to the island is often confusing to tourists, which used to result in frequently stranded travelers. They often came to the Island General Store, where Hank works, looking for a solution. Many of them were without funds, and things only got worse when they discovered they were stranded on the island until the next morning's ferry at 6:30 a.m. Out of compassion, Hank and Faye Lynn found themselves saying, "Well, we have a room...things will look better in the morning."

And things did look better, after a good night's sleep, hot shower, hearty breakfast and directions back to the ferry dock. Unfortunately, accepting this freely given gift of hospitality from strangers was a source of embarrassment to some guests. Eventually, Hank and Faye Lynn decided to accept donations, if the guests insisted.

This happened often enough that they decided to do some major remodeling. Under the canopy of giant fir trees that surround the house, they added a large, open deck that opens into a suite decorated in garden/sunflower motif (the Sunflower Room). The focal point of the suite is a bright sunflower quilt created by Hank's 82-year-old mother in Pennsylvania. The suite includes a kitchenette and private bath, and children are welcome.

The deck also leads into the Angel Room. This suite holds a tulip quilt, created by the late, well-known islander Lois Scholl and offers a double spa tub. Both suites have access to the upstairs of the main house and to the dining area, where guest are graciously and amply fed wonderful, home-cooked meals.

Oro Bay Merchantile
12312 Eckenstam Johnson Rd.
206/884-1700

4 AUBURN

Maws Antiques & Collectibles
121 E. Main St.
206/939-3740

Auburn Main Street Antiques
124 E. Main St.
206/804-8041

Lynn's Antiques & Refinishing
130 W. Main St.
206/939-6799

Back by Popular Demand
33620 135th Ave. SE
206/939-1239

5 BAINBRIDGE ISLAND

Rose Gulch Antiques
11042 Forest Lane NE
206/842-5002

Now and Then Shoppe
901 S. W. 152nd St.
206/242-8238

Bad Blanche Antiques
133 Winslow Way E
206/842-1807

Discoveries Downstairs
155 Winslow Way E
206/842-5873

Sow's Ear & Friends
554 Winslow Way E
206/842-1203

6 BATTLE GROUND

Rock Creek Antiques
31902 N.E. Lewisville Hwy.
360/687-1892

Jo's Antiques
612 E. Main St.
360/687-0251

Main Street Antiques
706 E. Main St.
360/687-2365

Old Post Office Antique Mall
718 E. Main St.
360/687-1805

7 BELLINGHAM

Secret Treasures
186 E. Bakerview Rd.
360/734-5057

American Antiques
2330 Elm St.
360/650-9037

Fairhaven Antiques & Art
1200 Harris Ave.
360/734-7179

Urban Archeologist Antq. Mall
214 W. Holly St.
360/676-0695

Bristol Antiques & Books
310 W. Holly St.
360/733-7809

Bellingham Bay Collectibles
314 W. Holly St.
360/676-9201

Pink Flamingo
407 W. Holly St.
360/671-2789

Aladdin's Lamp Antique Mall
427 W. Holly St.
360/647-0066

Old Town Antique Mall
427 W. Holly St.
360/671-3301

Jack's by the Tracks
705 W. Holly St.
360/647-9422

Cheryl Leaf Antiques & Gifts
2828 Northwest Ave.
360/734-2880

Glass Affair
4392 Northwest Dr.
360/734-0382

I-5 Antique Mall
4744 Pacific Hwy.
360/384-5955

Wynne Associates
4744 Pacific Hwy.
360/384-5955

8 BOTHELL

Farmhouse Antiques
23710 Bothell Everett Hwy.
206/483-3354

White House Antique Mall
23712 Bothell Everett Hwy.
206/483-0676

Town Hall Antique Mall
23716 Bothell Everett Hwy.
206/487-8979

Red Barn Antq. Cllbls. & Gifts
23929 Bothell Everett Hwy.
206/486-7309

Red Barn Loft
23929 Bothell Everett Hwy.
206/485-6582

9 CENTRALIA

Common Folk Co.
125 E. High St.
360/736-8066

Q's Country Shoppe
202 W. Locust
360/330-2844

Elderly Things Antiques
918 W. Locust St.
360/736-8927

Cranberry Bog
920 W. Locust St.
360/330-0594

Centralia Square Antique Mall
201 S. Pearl St.
360/736-6406

Collectors Showcase
201 S. Pearl St.
360/736-6026

Maxine's Antiques
201 S. Pearl St.
360/736-1699

Rose Blue
111 N. Tower Ave.
360/736-0370

Irresistibles
113 N. Tower Ave.
360/330-0338

Hidden Treasures
302 N. Tower Ave.
360/736-7572

Rob Duffy's Antiques
310 N. Tower Ave.
360/736-1282

Timeless Treasures & Co.
314 N. Tower Ave.
360/736-3898

A & D Antique Mall
405 N. Tower Ave.
360/330-5240

American Antique Furn. Mkt.
120 S. Tower Ave.
360/330-0427

Centralia Antq. Furn. Market
120 S. Tower Ave.
360/736-4079

Rick's Wholesale Antiques
120 S. Tower Ave.
360/736-2529

10 CLARKSTON

Hangar Old Tyme Photos
935 Port Way
509/758-0604

Bric-A-Brac Mall
834 6th St.
509/758-7772

Dan's Antiques
823 6th St.
509/758-6223

11 CLE ELUM

Aster Inn & Antiques
521 East 1st Street
509/674-2551
Fax: 509/674-7234 (call before faxing)
Open daily 10-10 except Christmas, New Years and Thanksgiving

Directions: From the west, from I-90: Take Exit 84 straight for approximately 10 blocks (five blocks east at the only stoplight). The inn is on the left at the opposite end of the block from Cle Elum's Gourmet Bakery and Meat Market. From the east, from I-90: Take Exit 85. Turn left on Hwy. 903 and follow the signs to Cle Elum. It is exactly 1.7 miles from the freeway exit on the right.

A visit to Aster Inn & Antiques is a chance to experience firsthand some living history and hear about life early in the century in the Washington area from people who have literally experienced it. There are two interconnected parts of this living history saga: Aster Inn and Aster Antiques.

The antique store, which is attached to the inn, sells everything from collectibles to primitives, mostly in "as is" condition. This is a family-owned business, established at the turn of the century and now running continuously for more than 90 years. Innkeeper and third generation family member Patrecia Starbird says, "We can almost guarantee every shopper will be entertained by stories of the local bordellos (now extinct), coal mines, early one-room schools houses, arranged brides, etc. And the stories aren't even secondhand, but the experiences of the two proprietors!"

Those two proprietors are still working at the store and in the inn's office every summer—Theresa, age 90 and the matriarch of the family, and her brother, Dominic, age 85. The "store" has been at various times a school house, saloon, grocery store, gift shop, and for the last 30 years, an "antique" shop.

Aster Inn was built in 1934 and has been remodeled recently, retaining and maintaining a 1930s atmosphere with some "thoroughly Modern Millie" rooms!

Barnwood & Old Lace
102 N. Oakes Ave.
509/674-7611

12 COLFAX

Bryan's Antiques
Hwy. 195
509/397-3259

Whitman Mall
121 S. Main St.
509/397-2522

Quail Crossing
707 N. Main St.
509/397-6026

13 COSMOPOLIS

Cooney Mansion
1705 Fifth Street
360/533-0602

14 COUPEVILLE

Front Street Antiques
7 N.W. Front St.
360/678-7514

Country & Victorian Treasures
2531 W. Libbey Rd.
No Phone

Salmagundi Farms
185 S. State Hwy. 20
360/678-5888

San De Fuca Old Store
694 N. State Hwy. 20
360/678-3626

15 DUVALL

McCoy's Mercantile
15515 Main NE
206/788-7920

Country Collections
15525 Main St. NE
206/788-2939

Liberty's Lighthouse
15720 Main St. NE
206/788-8683

Tuxedo's Junction
15904 Main St. NE
206/788-9678

Duvall's Trading Post
15906 Main St. NE
206/788-9455

Old Memories
15925 Main NE
206/788-7508

16 EDMONDS

E & E Cllbls. at Beeson House
116 4th Ave. N
206/774-3431

Heaton House Gallery
122 5th Ave. S
206/771-7855

Edmonds Antique Mall
201 5th Ave. S
206/771-9466

Old General Store
201 5th Ave. S #12
206/771-2561

Added Touch Antqs. & Cllbls.
23428 7th Ave. W
206/778-3108

Amaryllis Antiques
18606 7th Ave. W
206/775-2252

Country Cove Antiques
527 Dayton St.
206/672-9277

Aurora Antique Pavilion Inc.
24111 Hwy. 99
206/744-0566

Rosa Mundis Antiques
318 Main St.
206/771-6598

Edmonds Sports Collectibles
508 Main St.
206/672-7892

Valhalla Antiques & Cllbls.
508 Main St.
206/771-1242

Glorious Treasures Antique
518 Main St.
206/775-5753

Wally's World
519 Main
206/774-0040

Mam's Vintage Linens & Things
537 Main
206/771-5310

Waterfront Antique Mall
190 Sunset Ave. S
206/670-0770

17 ELLENSBURG

Etcetera Shoppe
115 E. 4th Ave.
509/962-2578

Edsel Antiques
213 W. 4th Ave.
509/962-5295

Main Street Market Antq. Mall
308 N. Main St.
509/925-1762

Anchor in Time
310 N. Main St.
509/925-7067

Meadowlark Farm
606 N. Main St.
509/962-3706

Hub Antiques & Estate Sales
307 N. Pearl St.
509/925-6581

Showplace Antique Mall
103 E. 3rd Ave.
509/962-9331

Fogarty's Antiques
107 E. 3rd Ave.
509/962-3476

Attic
109 E. 3rd Ave.
509/925-7467

18 ENUMCLAW

Enumclaw Antique Mall
1501 Cole St.
360/825-4546

Delees Antiques & Accents
1717 Cole St.
360/825-9112

Country Peddler
19428 S.E. 400th St.
360/825-8313

19 EVERETT

Simply Victorian
1911 Hewitt Ave.
206/303-0760

Irene's Archives
1917 Hewitt Ave.
206/258-1881

Timeless Antiques
1922 Hewitt Ave.
206/258-9350

Country Peddler
2114 Hewitt Ave.
206/258-1557

Maxine's Antiquities & Curios
2715 Hewitt Ave.
206/252-7812

20 GIG HARBOR

Barber Shop Antiques
1617 Stone Dr. NW.
206/858-2922

Hide & Sea
3306 Harborview Dr.
206/858-8971

Pandora's Inc.
3801 Harborview Dr.
206/851-5164

Key Center Trading Post
15510 92nd St. KPN
206/884-2220

21 GRAYLAND

Ditto's Antiques & Gifts
1634 State Rt 105
360/267-4644

Olde Merchantile
1820 State Rt. 105
360/267-0121

Pregnant Onion Antiques
2399 Tokland Rd.
360/267-6914

Grandma's Treasure Chest
2190 State Rt. 105
360/267-1616

22 ISSAQUAH

Haus of Antiques
157 1/2 Front St. N
206/392-3424

Gillman Antiques Gallery
625 N.W. Gilman Blvd.
206/391-6640

Washington Antiques & Restor
685 N.W. Gilman Blvd.
206/391-7947

23 KALAMA

River Town Antique Mall
155 Elm St.
360/673-2263

Heritage Square
176 N. 1st St.
360/673-3980

Drew & Davis Antiques
222 N.E. 1st St.
360/673-4029

Columbia Antiques & Cllbls.
364 N. 1st St.
360/673-5400

Memory Lane Antique Mall
413 N. 1st St.
360/673-3663

24 KENNEWICK

Sloping M Antiques Cllbls.
W. Kennewick Ave.
509/582-1631

Nostalgia Revisted
323 W. Kennewick Ave.
509/586-7250

Carmichael's Antiques
3900 S. Oak St.
509/582-8216

Appleseed Gallery & Shops
108 Vista Way
509/735-2874

Lea's Last Place Antiques
302 N. Union St.
509/735-4305

Crown Collectibles
109 N. WashiNGTON ST.
509/586-6501

25 KENT

Robin's Antique Mall
201 1st Ave. S
206/854-6543

Lace Legacy Etc.
220 1st Ave. S
206/852-0052

The Shop
223 1st Ave. S.
206/852-5892

Fanny Jean's Antiques & Things
213 W. Meeker St.
206/852-2053

Now N Then
218 W. Meeker St.
206/852-5890

Joy's Collectables
304 W. Meeker St.
206/854-6403

Stagg's Coins & Baseball Cards
317 W. Meeker St.
206/854-6340

Mad Hatter Antiques
25748 101st Ave. SE
206/859-9293

Accrete Antiques
24526 104th Ave. SE
206/854-8916

26 KIRKLAND

Mambo
205 Kirkland Ave.
206/889-8787

Danish-Swedish Antiques
207 Kirkland Ave.
206/822-7899

Alexander McCallum Toppin
215 Lake St. SE
206/827-6593

Woodshed Antiques
5918 Lake Washington Blvd. NE
206/822-8600

Antiques at Park Lane
128 Park Lane
206/803-0136

Bettina's
128 Park Lane
206/889-0234

Kirkland Antique Gallery
151 3rd St.
206/828-4993

27 LA CONNER

Katy's Inn-A Victorian Bed and Breakfast

503 South Third
360/466-3366 or 1-800-914-7767
Open year round
Rates: $69-99

Directions: From I-5 going north from Seattle: Take Exit 221. Go west (left) over the freeway and take the first right to Conway/La Conner. Travel a country road for 10 minutes that leads to La Conner (signs are posted). Enter La Conner on Morris Street. Go left (south) on Second 1 block, then left up the hill on Washington 1 block. Katy's Inn is on the corner of Third and Washington-1 and 1/4 hours drive from Seattle; 1 1/2 hours from Vancouver, B.C.

Katy's Inn is first in several things: first-rate in location-within walking distance of everything in town, the first house in La Conner (built in 1876), and the first bed and breakfast in town (begun in 1984). This 1876 Victorian sits on a hillside two blocks above historic La Conner, which is filled with shops, galleries, antique stores, and waterfront cafes. Captain John Peck built this charming country Victorian for his wife and four daughters. It is filled with antiques, and the gardens are a blaze of Victorian glory. The inn offers five guest rooms: four upstairs (two with private baths), with French doors that open onto a wraparound porch with a beautiful view of the town and the Swinomish Channel, and a suite with private bath downstairs and a private entrance that opens into the garden.

If guests want a little activity before hot-tubbing or rocking and reading at the inn, they can feed the sea gulls on the waterfront; sail, raft or canoe down the Swinomish Channel; fish from the pier; take a cruise on the San Juan Islands ferry; ride a bike through the world-famous tulip fields of the Skagit Valley; or take a bird watching/whale watching cruise.

Nasty Jack's Antiques
103 E. Morris St.
360/466-3209

Morris Street Antiques
503 E. Morris St.
360/466-4212

Cameo Antique Mall
511 E. Morris St.
360/466-3472

28 LANGLEY

Whidbey Island Antiques
Anthes Ave. @ 2nd Ave.
360/221-2393

Lowry-James Fine Antiques
101Anthes
360/221-0477

VIrginia's Antiques & Gifts
206 1st St.
360/221-7797

Saratoga Antiques
221 1st St.
360/221-4363

29 LEAVENWORTH

Cabin Fever Rustics
923 CommerciaL ST.
509/548-4238

Country Things Antqs. & Gifts
221 8th St.
509/548-7807

Happy Wanderer
833 Front St.
509/548-6584

30 MAPLE VALLEY

Maple Valley Bed and Breakfast

20020 SE 228th
206/432-1409
Fax: 206/413-1459
Open daily-reservations required

For specific directions, please call the innkeeper who will be happy to direct you from your location.

If you have a hankering to be in the woods, in the quiet of the Pacific Northwest, this is your place. Innkeepers Clarke and Jane Hurlbut have turned their rustic cedar cottage into the Maple Valley Bed and Breakfast, complete with turret and especially built second floor suites. The hand-hewn cottage offers cedar walled guest rooms, one of which was actually built around its special bed! The bed, a handcrafted cedar piece created by Clarke out of logs cut from a nearby woods, is a prized family possession. French doors lead from each guest room onto a spacious balcony. Mint laced jugs of water and chocolate cookies await guests in each suite, and "hot babies" are quietly slipped between the sheets at night. Sounds intriguing, doesn't it? In fact, these "hot babies" have, on more than one occasion, given many guests an unexpected thrill as toes make contact with the warm, shifting lump tucked discreetly between the covers. According to the Hurlbuts, more than one person has sprung from the bed wondering if they had gotten closer to nature than they had ever intended! (Just for the record: "hot babies" are sand-filled bed warmers placed at the foot of the beds at night.)

Breakfast at the inn features Jayne's house specialty hootenanny oven pancakes, an old family recipe; or she might serve any of a number of her other specialties, like omelets, eggs benedict, or waffles. The rustic inn is not only a bed and breakfast, but an almost mythical destination for cyclists, foreign visitors and neighbors, and bed and breakfast guests mingle freely with whomever comes to share the Hurlbuts special kind of hospitality.

Maple Valley Trading Post
12400 Renton Maple Valley Rd. S
206/413-0277

31 MONROE

The Frog Crossing Antiques & Cllbls. B&B

306 S. Lewis
206/881-7089, 360/794-7622

Directions: 1/4 mile south from Hwy. 2 and directly on State Rt. 203 (Lewis St.)

For specific information see review this section.

Antique Boutique
119 W. Main St.
360/805-0325

Cobweb Antiques
21928 Yeager
360/794-4256

Antiques
110 E. Main St.
No Phone

32 MONTESANO

The Abel House Bed and Breakfast

117 Fleet Street South
360/249-6002
Open year round
Rates begin at $55

Directions: Montesana is at the intersection of State Highways 12 and 107, about 40 miles west of Olympia and 10 miles east of Aberdeen. In-town signs direct you to the Abel House Bed and Breakfast.

People should visit the Abel House just to see it! You

don't often see houses (this one built in 1908) with nine bedrooms on three of the four floors! The main floor is conveniently a common area, with the living room and library boasting "box beamed" ceilings and unique fireplaces. The entry, staircase, and dining room feature the original natural wood with a genuine Tiffany chandelier in the dining room. As the inn's brochure says, "Alas, as with many vintage homes, one bathroom per floor was considered "quite adequate." Fortunately for guests, the Abel House has recently added an addition that has eased the situation somewhat and provided some private baths. There is a game room on the upper floor, and the three lower floors are serviced by an elevator. The mansion's grounds have been lovingly and meticulously maintained and are open for guests' strolling pleasures. Breakfast and tea are served in the garden, the country English dining room, or in the privacy of the guest's room, whichever is preferred. As innkeeper Victor Reynolds says, "Eight years of repeat business indicates the house and staff are first-rate for even the most discriminating B&B goer!"

Fox's Den
124 Brumfield Ave.
360/249-5850

33 MOUNT VERNON

Old Movie House Antique Mall
520 Main St.
360/336-8919

D B's General Store
1670 Old High #99 S
360/424-5908

Posh
312 Pine St.
360/336-2728

34 NACHES

Bales Antiques
81 Locust Lane
509/653-2090

Country Kitchen Antiques
224 Naches Ave.
509/653-2008

Hobbit Shop Antiques
2450 S. Naches Rd.
509/965-0768

Wayside Antiques
10000 U.S. Hwy. 12
509/653-2120

35 NORTH BEND

Bad Girls Antiques
42901 SE. North Bend Way
425/888-1902
Open Wed.-Sat. 11-5, Sun. 12-5

Directions: From eastbound I-90: Take Exit 27, take a left off the exit, and stay on the road straight through the town of North Bend. Bad Girls is on the right, 4+ miles from the exit and 1 mile from the stoplight in town. From westbound I-90: Take Exit 32, take a right off the exit, and follow the road until you must turn. Turn left. The shop is about 1/2 mile on the left.

These "bad girls" offer a 4,000-square-foot building filled to the brim for your shopping pleasure! Browsers and buyers can take their pick from quality furniture, antique and not-so-old items, unique collectibles, art pottery, fine glass, and 1940s dinnerware.

As is common with most antique dealers, their customers often create some very funny moments. Such is the case in this story as told by Jeanne Marie Klein. "A customer came into the store one day with a lamp that she wanted to know more about. She showed it to my partner," says Jeanne Marie Klein, a Bad Girl owner, "claiming it was made (and signed) by someone named 'Art Newvoo.' 'Who was this man?' she wanted to know. My partner was quizzically examining the lamp when I entered the room. She was very puzzled and asked if I recognized the name as a designer. Frowning, I thought 'Art Newvoo??' The light dawned, and I exclaimed, "You mean Art Nouveau-that's not a person, it's a style!" The poor lady was mystified until we explained further. After she left, we had a good laugh and decided that 'Art Newvoo' must have a sister called 'Arlene Deco!'"

Zara's Collectables
401 Ballarat Ave. N
425/888-0271

Jaclyn Rose Antiques
107 W. North Bend Way
425/831-5403

Snoqualmie Valley Antique Co.
116 W. North Bend Way
425/888-5900

36 OAK HARBOR

Joseph's Antiques
28 E. Fakkema Rd.
360/679-3242

Lorenzo's Lighting & Antiques
770 W. Pioneer Way
360/675-7619

Aladdin's Antiques
780 S.E. Pioneer Way #101
360/679-4744

Oak Harbor Antique Mall
1079 W. Pioneer Way
360/679-1902

37 OLYMPIA

Mike Cook Antiques & Cllbls.
106 1/2 4th Ave.
360/943-5025

Hexen Glass
1015 4th Ave. E.
360/705-8758

Lamplight Antiques
2906 Capitol Blvd. S
360/943-9841

Homespun Craft & Antq. Mall
5729 Little Rock Rd. SW
360/943-5194

Once Upon A Time
7141 Old High #101 N
360/866-4050

R Vernon's
2724 Pacific Ave. SE
360/705-0108

Summit Lake Antiques
10724 Summit Lake Rd. NW
360/866-0580

Old Bank
404 Washington St. SE
360/786-9234

Second Hand Rose
9243 Yelm Hwy. SE
360/459-0954

Sherburne Antiques & Fine Art
100 East 4th Avenue
360/357-9177

38 PORT ANGELES

Marion's Port Angeles Antqs.
220 W. 8th St.
360/452-5411

Mouse Trap Antiques & Gifts
128 W. 1st St.
360/457-1223

Corps Shop
222 N. Lincoln St.
360/457-7041

Springtime Robins & Rainbows
719 S. Lincoln St.
360/452-4019

Waterfront Antique Mall
124 W. Railroad Ave.
360/452-3350

39 PORT ORCHARD

Side Door Mall
701 Bay St.
360/876-8631

Olde Central Antique Mall
801 Bay St.
360/895-1902

Harbor Antique Mall
802 Bay St.
360/895-1898

Great Prospects Variety Mall
1039 Bethel Rd.
360/895-1359

Owl in the Attic Antiques
5637 S.E. Mile Hill Dr.
360/871-0382

40 PORT TOWNSEND

Port Townsend Antique Mall
802 Washington St.
360/385-2590

Starrett House Antiques
802 Washington St.
360/385-2590

Ancestral Sell
830 Water St.
360/385-1475

Undertown
211 Taylor St.
360/379-8069

April Fool & Penny Too
725 Water St.
360/385-3438

Antique Company
1133 Water St.
360/385-9522

41 POULSBO

Edgewater Beach Bed & Breakfast
26818 Edgewater Blvd.
1-800-641-0955

Directions: For specific directions from your location, please call the Innkeepers.

The Edgewater Beach Bed & Breakfast is a charming and peaceful retreat ideally suited for those who want to get away from the hustle and bustle of everyday life and commune with nature. The unassuming front of this two-story cottage-style home conceals a large 4,800 square foot structure of which 3,000 square feet are dedicated to the guests.

The house was built in 1929 by Dr. Mayme MacLafferty, a Seattle physician and surgeon who selected the beautiful land to be the site of her weekend home in the country.

The guest area includes a warm, 670 square foot Great Room with surrounds an impressive, two-sided granite fireplace. Off of the Great Room is a large, bright Sun Room that opens onto an immense 2,800 square foot deck overlooking Puget Sound's fjord, (Hood Canal), an inlet of the ocean that flows in a channel carved by a glacier. The views from the Sun Room and the deck are awe inspiring. From the deck or Sun Room, the vast panoramic vista of the Olympic Mountains behind the fjord is simply breath-taking.

A family of Great American Bald Eagles lives on the edge of the fjord, and their flights are beautiful to watch. Many birds including crows and herons make their homes here; and sometimes the guests are visited by otters, sea lions and deer. On rare occasions, a whale has been spotted swimming in the fjord.

The Edgewater Beach Bed & Breakfast has accommodations for three parties. In addition to the Great Room and Sun Room, guests have access to a glass-enclosed dining room and a spacious, old-fashioned kitchen. The home is furnished in a relaxed, eclectic and sometimes whimsical manner that puts guests at ease while lightening their spirits. Many antiques and treasures from all over the United States create a delightful melange of beauty and playfulness.

Guests are treated to a bountiful breakfast basket that includes: smoked salmon, smoked turkey, cheeses, fresh fruit, pastries, cereal and sparkling beverage and juice.

Abigail's Attic Antiques
2300 NW. Vinland
360/697-7077

Hiding Place Antiques
18830 Front St. NE
360/779-7811

Bad Blanche
18890 Front St.
360/779-7788

Front Street Antiques
18901 Front St. NE
360/697-1899

Cat's Meow
18940 Front St. NE
360/697-1902

Antique Junction
122 N.E. Moe St.
360/779-1890

Granny & Papa's Antique Mall
19669 7th Ave. NE.
360/697-2221

42 PUYALLUP

Heier Echelon
107 W. Meeker
253/841-3187

Antique City
103 S. Meridian
253/840-4324

Real Oldies of Yesteryears
110 S. Meridian
253/845-4471

Pioneer Antique Mall
113 S. Meridian
253/770-0981

Traditions Antiques
202 S. Meridian
253/840-8732

Anderson's Edgewood Mall
10215 24th St. E
253/952-5295

Carnaby Antique Mall
8424 River Rd.
253/840-3844

43 QUILCENE

Granny's House of Glass
Hwy. 101 N
360/765-3230

Gay Lee's Bowser Beads
11 Old Church Rd.
360/765-3545

Ju Ju Junque
11 Old Church Rd.
360/765-3500

Quilcene Art & Antiques
11 Old Church Rd.
360/765-4447

44 REDMOND

Olde Stuff Antiques
16545 N.E. 80th St.
425/869-1697

Edwardian Antiques Inc.
7979 Leary Way NE
425/885-4433

Golden Days
8058 161st Ave. NE
425/883-0778

Washington Antiques
8309 165th Avenue NE
425/881-7627

45 RENTON

Park Avenue Antiques
101 Park Ave. N
206/255-4255

Downtown Renton Antq. Mall
210 Wells Ave. S
206/271-0511

Relics Antiques
229 Wells Ave. S
206/227/6557

St. Charles Place Antiques
230 Wells Ave. S
206/226-8429

46 RICHLAND

Carel's Antiques
1119 S.E. Columbia Dr.
509/783-1775

Collectors Emporium
1315 George Washington Way
509/943-2841

Richland Antiques Mall
1331 George Washington Way
509/943-6762

Uptown Antiques Mall
1340 Jadwin Ave.
509/943-1866

47 ROCHESTER

Up the Creek Antiques
474 Ingalls Rd.
360/736-3529

Honest Don's Antiques
19225 Joselyn Rd. SW
360/273-8114

48 SEATTLE

Eileen of China
624 S. Dearborn St.
206/624-0816
Open: Daily 10-6

This 30,000-square-foot showroom is filled with exquisite, elegant and unique Asian Antiques and Arts. Enhance your home with traditional Chinese furniture; Zitan, Haunghwali, Hardwood and Rosewood. Simplicity of workmanship.

G. C. C. Gallery
408 Occidental Avenue
206/344-5244

G. C. C. Gallery is a family opened business which has been producing top of the line replica antique furnishings in Seoul Korea since 1976. The Gallery specializes in authentic oriental styles in such finishes as oyster oliver, burr elm, zelkova, paulownia as well as veneers.

Bed and Breakfast Association of Seattle
P.O. Box 31722
Seattle, Washington 98103-1722

An association of independently owned and professionally operated bed and breakfast inns located close to downtown Seattle. For reservations or specific information, call 206/547-1020.

Lyon's Antique Mall
4516 California Southwest
206/935-9774
WebSite: http://www.lyonsam.com
Open Mon.-Sat. 10-6, Sun. 11-5

Directions: Located in the old JC Penney, one block north of Alaska Junction in West Seattle.

This large antique mall offers a wide variety of antiques and collectibles, including art deco, books, crystal, pottery, dolls and Barbies, furniture, jewelry, primitives, silver, toys, records and porcelain.

Beech Tree Manor
1405 Queen Anne Avenue North
206/281-7037
Fax: 206/284-2350
Open year round 9-8

Directions; Beech Tree Manor is located at the northwest corner of the intersection of Queen Anne Avenue North and Lee Street. It has on-street parking. Electric trolleys link the Manor to downtown Seattle and, by transfer, to the entire Metro area.

Nestled on historic Queen Anne Hill, adjacent to downtown Seattle, this turn-of-the-century mansion has been beautifully restored. Its name comes from the rare and massive Copper Beech tree on the property that has, so far, withstood nature, man, and progress. This bed and breakfast has been described as "an excellent bed and breakfast" by the New York Times, and "stunning" by Seattle's Best Places. Winning such praises as these comes from the inn's attitude about itself, which is described in its brochure as "organized for the enjoyment of those who require a genteel atmosphere for their temporary housing and special celebrations". To achieve this "genteel atmosphere", the inn offers a very proper English decor, with seven guest rooms (some with private bath). The mansion is filled with a lifetime collection of antiques and offers "all the modern amenities a seasoned traveler expects", plus a few extras, like pure white cotton sheets and a shady porch with wicker rockers. So if proper English is your style, we suggest a stay at the Beech Tree.

Antique Importers
640 Alaskan Way
206/628-8905

Antique Warehouse
1400 Alaskan Way
206/624-4683

Seattle Antique Market Inc.
1400 Alaskan Way
206/623-6115

Drager's Classic Toys
4905 Aurora Ave. N
206/545-4400

Cascade Mall
9530 Aurora Ave. N.
206/524-962

Japanense Antiquities Gallery
200 E. Boston St.
206/324-3322

Rhinestone Rosie
606 W. Crockett St.
206/283-4605

Greg Davidson Antiques
1307 First Avenue
206/625-0406

Hunter's Antiques
106 Denny Way
206/285-9172

Campbell Antiques & Cllbls.
13027 Des Moines Memorial Dr.
206/243-6807

B. Bremmer & Bradley Antqs.
8000 15th Ave. NW
206/783-7333

Mandrakes
8300 15th Ave. NW
206/781-2623

Michael Maslan Hist. Photos
214 1st Ave. S
206/587-0187

Carolyn Staley Fine Prints
313 1st Ave. S
206/621-1888

Flury & Company Ltd.
322 1st Ave. S
206/587-0260

Antiquarius
514 1st Ave. N
206/282-5489

Kagedo Japanese Antiques
520 1st Ave. S
206/467-9077

Clarke and Clarke
524 1st Ave. S
206/447-7017

Azuma Fine Art & Gallery
530 1st Ave. S
206/622-5599

Legacy Ltd.
1003 1st Ave.
206/624-6350

Asia Gallery
1220 1st Ave.
206/622-0516

Isadora's Antique Clothing
1915 1st Ave.
206/441-7711

Village Manor
17651 1st Ave. S
206/439-8842

The Junk Shop
1404 14th Ave.
206/329-4148

Fremont Antique Mall
3419 Fremond Place N
206/548-9140

Johnson & Johnson Antiques
6820 Greenwood Ave.
206/789-6489

Hobby Horse Antiques
7421 Greenwood Ave.
206/789-1574

Pelayo Antiques
8421 Greenwood Ave.
206/789-1333

Jean Williams Antiques
115 S. Jackson St.
206/622-1110

Daily Planet
11046 Lake City Way
206/633-0895

Antique Galleria
17171 Lake Forest Park NE
206/362-6845

First Hill Collectibles
1004 Madison St.
206/624-3207

Apogee
4224 E. Madison St.
206/325-2848

Stuteville Antiques
1518 E. Olive Way
206/329-5666

Auntie Shrew's Antiques
816 S.W. 152nd St.
206/242-0727

Antique Junktion Mall
23609 Pacific Hwy. S
206/878-3069

Raven's Nest Treasure
85 B Pike St.
206/343-0890

Wrinkled Bohemia
1125 Pike St.
206/464-0850

Pioneer Square Mall
602 1st Ave.
206/624-1164

Antique Elegance
1113 1st Ave.
206/467-8550

Rudy's Vintage Clothing
1424 1st Avenue
206/682-6586

Jukebox City
1950 1st Ave. S.
206/625-1950

David Weatherford Antiques
133 14th Ave. E
206/329-6533

Chelsea Antiques
3622 N.E. 45th St.
206/525-2727

Private Screening
3504 Fremont Place N
206/548-0751

Goode Things
7114 Greenwood Ave.
206/784-7572

Pelayo Antiques
7601 Greenwood Ave.
206/789-1999

Hurd's Antiques Etc.
8554 Greenwood Ave.
206/782-2405

Honeychurch Antiques
1008 James St.
206/622-1225

Gen's Antiques & Dolls
12518 Lake City Way NE
206/365-5440

Hotel Lobby Antiques
4105 Leary Way NW
206/784-5340

Veritables
2816 E. Madison St.
206/726-8047

Michael Reed Black Antiques
125 W. Mercer St.
206/284-9581

Antiques of Burien
209 152nd St. SW
206/431-0550

My Granny's Attic
901 S.W. 152nd St.
206/243-3300

Spindrifters
Pike Place Market #321
206/623-6432

B & W Antiques
311 E. Pike St.
206/325-6775

Antique Touch
1501 Pike Place Market #318
206/622-6499

Great Western Trading Co.
1501 Pike Place
206/622-6376

Old Friends Antiques
1501 Pike Place
206/625-1997

N B Nichols & Son
1924 Post Alley
206/448-8906

Curbside Collectables
7011 Roosevelt Way NE
206/522-0882

Kobo
814 E. Roy St.
206/726-0704

Ruby Montana's Pinto Pony
603 2nd Ave.
206/621-7669

Partners in Time
1332 6th Ave.
206/623-4218

Silhouette Antiques & Gifts
1516 N.E. 65th St.
206/525-2499

Cranium's Cool Collectibles
12331 32nd Ave. NE
206/364-8734

Carriage House Galleries
5611 University Way NE
206/523-4960

Fairlook Antiques
81 1/2 Washington
206/622-5130

Reba's Classic Ceramics
222 Westlake Ave. N
206/622-2459

Antique Liquidators
503 Westlake Ave. N
206/623-2740

Turner Helton Antiques
2600 Western Ave.
206/322-1994

The Antlers
15214 9th Ave. SW
206/242-3304

Mugs Antiques
1501 Pike Place
206/623-3212

Inside Out
Westlake Center/400 Pine St.
206/292-8874

Broadway Clock Shop
2214 Queen Anne Ave. N
206/285-3130

Vintage Costumers
7011 Roosevelt Way NE
206/522-5234

Shahlimar
217 2nd Ave. S
206/447-2570

Laguana Vintage Pottery
609 2nd Ave.
206/682-6162

Ageing Fancies
308 N.E. 65th St.
206/523-4556

Pacific Galleries
2121 3rd Ave.
206/441-9990

Porter Davis Antiques
103 University St.
206/622-5310

Oasis Antique Oriental Rugs
5655 University Way NE
206/525-2060

Downtown Antique Market
2218 Western Ave.
206/448-6307

222 Westlake Antique Mall
222 Westlake Ave. N
206/628-3117

Antique Distributors
507 Westlake Ave. N
206/622-0555

Madame & Co. Vintg. Fashions
117 Yesler Way
206/621-1728

49 SEAVIEW

Dory's Antiques & Collectibles
48th @ Pacific Hwy.
360/642-3005

Stagecoach Antiques
4005 Pacific Hwy. #103
360/642-4565

Sea-Tryst Antiques
48th Place
360/642-4888

Gollywobbler Antiques
4809 Pacific Hwy. S
360/642-8685

50 SEQUIM

Bramble Cottage Antiques Ltd.
305 W. Bell St.
360/683-1724

Queens Cabinet Antiques
157 W. Cedar St.
360/681-2778

Lighthouse Antique
261321 Hwy. 101
360/681-7346

Anne's Sequim Antiques
253 W. Washington St.
360/683-8287

51 SHELTON

Frontier Antiques
317 S. 1st St.
360/426-7795

Second Floor Antiques
107 S. 4th St.
360/427-9310

Carole's Jewelry
221 W. Railroad Ave.
360/426-7847

Olympic Gateway Coins/Cllbls.
106 S. 4th St.
360/426-0304

Red Rose Antiques
1209 Olympic Hwy. S
360/426-1290

52 SNOHOMISH

Redmond House Bed and Breakfast
317 Glen Avenue
360/568-2042
Rates: $85-100

Directions: Snohomish is located on Hwy. 9, just east of Everett, Was. Traveling from I-5 either north or south: use the Wenatchee-Stevens Pass exit to Hwy. 2. Cross the "Trestle" and stay to the right. The first exit will take you right into town and onto Avenue D. Turn east on 4th Street and right on Glen.

The Redmond House is another "must" for dyed-in-the-wool antique junkies. It's located in the Victorian era town of Snohomish, within easy walking distance of the "Antique Capital of the Northwest"- 400 antique dealers, gift shops, and restaurants. For the better halves who don't want to spend every minute poking through "old stuff," there are all types of outdoorsy things to do, like exploring the Centennial Trail and the walking tour of Snohomish, plus other hiking, boating, golfing, skiing, hot air ballooning, parachuting, and visits to wineries and sports events all right there in town or within easy driving distance.

The inn greets guests with wonderful gardens and a wraparound porch complete with wicker furniture and a porch swing. The house itself is furnished with period antiques and quilts for everyone's comfort. There's a sunroom with games and a hot tub, a ballroom with big band music, bedrooms with featherbeds, and some even with clawfoot tubs for soaking, plus complimentary tea or sherry at the end of a hard day.

Ranee-Paul Antiques
900 1st St.
360/568-6284

Rick's Antiques
916 1st St.
360/568-4646

Black Cat Antique Mall
923 1st St.
360/568-8144

River City Antique Mall
1007 1st St.
360/568-1155

Remember When Antique Mall
908 1st St.
360/568-0757

Old Store Antiques
922 1st St.
360/568-1919

Another Antique Shop
924 1st St.
360/568-3629

First Bank Antiques
1015 1st St.
360/568-7609

Snohomish Antiques Co.
1019 1st St.
360/563-0343

Antique Station
1108 1st St.
360/568-5034

Victoria Village
1108 1st St.
360/568-4913

Antique Palace
1116 1st St.
360/568-2644

Michael's 1st Street Antq. Mall
1202 1st St.
360/568-9735

Egelstad's Clock Shop
809 2nd St.
360/568-3444

Collectors Book Store
829 2nd St.
360/568-9455

Star Center Mall Antiques
829 2nd St.
206/402-1870

Casablanca Antiques
104 C Avenue
360/568-0308

Faded Glory Ltd.
113 C Avenue
360/568-5344

Sharon's Antique Mall
111 Glen Ave.
360/568-9854

Antique Gallery Mall
117 Glen Ave.
360/568-7644

Brenda's Antiques & Cllbls.
118 Glen Ave.
360/568-2322

Collector's Showcase
118 Glen Ave.
360/568-1339

Star Center Mall
123 Glen Ave.
206/402-1870

Louis C Wein Antiques & Art
102 Union St.
360/568-8594

53 SPOKANE

Persnickey's Antqs. & Cllbls.
408 N. Argonne Rd.
509/891-7858

Duprie's Antiques
920 W. Cora Ave.
509/327-2449

B J's Books N. Brew
1320 W. Francis Ave.
509/327-2988

Vintage Post Cards & Stamps
1908 N. Hamilton St.
509/487-5677

Luminaria & La Tierra
154 S. Madison St.
509/747-9198

Cloke & Dagger Antiques
4912 N. Market St.
509/482-2066

Aunt Bea's Antiques
5005 N. Market St.
509/487-9278

Hillyard Variety Consnmt. Store
5009 N. Market St.
509/482-3433

United Hillyard Mall
5016 N. Market St.
509/483-2647

Collectors Showcase Antq. Mall
5201 N. Market St.
509/482-7112

Benson's Antiques
5215 N. Market St.
509/487-3528

Monroe St. Bridge Antq. Mkt.
604 N. Monroe St.
509/327-6398

Antique Gallery
620 N. Monroe St.
509/325-3864

Spokane Book Center
626 N. Monroe St.
509/328-2332

Worthington Disc. China
2217 N. Monroe
509/328-7072

Vintage Rabbit Antique Mall
2317 N. Monroe
509/326-1884

Wooden Rail
818 N. Pines Rd.
509/922-3443

Spokane Valley Antique Mall
23 S. Pines Rd.
509/928-9648

Ben's Antiques
2130 E. Sprague Ave.
509/535-4368

NW Collector Arms
12021 E. Sprague Ave.
509/891-0990

Spokane Antique Mall
12 W. Sprague Ave.
509/747-1466

Larsen's Antique Clock Shop
953 E. 3rd Ave.
509/534-4994

Antiquex
28 W. 3rd Ave.
509/624-6826

Timeless Treasures Antiques
10309 E. Trent Ave.
509/928-0819

Schade Brewery Antique Mall
528 E. Trent Ave.
509/624-0272

No Place Like Home
13409 E. Wellesley Ave.
509/922-4246

54 STANWOOD

Apple Barrell Antiques
1415 Pioneer Hwy. #530
360/652-9671

Yo Mama's Attic Antiques
8617 271 St. NW
360/629-3995

55 SUMNER

The Blue Lantern
1003 Main St.
206/863-5935

Cobweb's Removed Inc.
1008 Main St.
206/863-1924

Whistle-Stop Antique Mall
1109 Main St.
206/863-3309

56 TACOMA

The DeVoe Mansion Bed & Breakfast

208 East 133rd Street
206/539-3991
Fax: 206/539-8539
Open daily 8-9
Rates: $80-90
E-mail: devoe wolfenet.com
WebSite: http://www.wolfenet.com/~devoe/

Directions: From Seattle or Tacoma: Take I-5 south (from Olympia take I-5 north) to Exit 127. Go east on Hwy. 512 approximately two miles to the Pacific Avenue exit (signs also say Mt. Rainier, State Rt. 7, Parkland, Pacific Lutheran University). Go south on Pacific Avenue approximately 2 miles, and turn left on 133rd Street South. Continue two blocks and the DeVoe Mansion is on the corner of 133rd Street and B Avenue.

Ladies, this one's for you! The 1911 DeVoe Mansion was named to the National Historic Register in 1993 in honor of a tireless pioneer in the women's suffrage movement. The home was built for John and Emma Smith DeVoe, who moved into the mansion one year after Emma had successfully helped the women of Washington State achieve the right to vote. It would be another 10 years before all women in the United States were granted that same right. Emma's home was named to the National Historic Register as a tribute to her devoted efforts to the suffrage cause on both national and state levels.

To understand and appreciate the mansion's history and decor, guests need to know a little about Emma, because Emma's life's work in the suffrage movement is the decorating basis for each of the mansion's guest rooms. Emma's dedication to the suffrage cause began when she was eight years old, when she and her sister attended a rally featuring Susan B. Anthony. When Emma came to Washington State in 1906, she found a very disorganized, unmotivated suffrage association. Her first winter on the West Coast saw her elected as president of the Washington State Equal Suffrage Association, and she spent the next four years traveling the state, rejuvenating and revitalizing the association. On November 8, 1910, Washington became the fifth state in the union to pass women's suffrage.

Each of the guest rooms is named for someone who was significant in Emma's life. The Susan B. Anthony Room features an 1880's hand-carved oak bedroom set, private sitting area and private bath. The Carrie Chapman Catt Room is highlighted by a queen-sized, four poster mahogany rice bed with an old growth Alaskan cedar tree just outside the window. The John Henry DeVoe Room is named for Emma's most devoted supporter-her husband. It holds an antique queen-size 1860s pine bedroom set. Guests are also treated to two porches for rocking and relaxing, a hot tub on the deck, landscaped grounds for strolling, and breakfast.

Abigail's Antiques
8825 Bridgeport Way SW
206/588-9712

Treasure Chest
11605 Bridgeport Way SW
206/581-2454

Victoria's
702 Broadway
206/272-5983

Mimi's Antique Furniture
3813 N. 26th St.
206/759-0506

Freighthouse Antiques Empor.
728 Broadway
206/627-8019

Sanford & Son Antiques
743 Broadway
206/272-0334

Memory Mall
744 Broadway
206/272-6476

Time Machine
746 Broadway
206/272-7254

Lily the Pad
756 Broadway
206/627-6858

Woodward's Antiques
12146 C St.
206/531-1005

Collectors Nook
213 N. I St.
206/272-9828

Bellocchio Antiques & Bistro
1926 Pacific Ave.
206/383-3834

European Antique Imports
1930 Pacific Ave.
206/272-8763

Ramlawn Antiques
1936 Pacific Ave.
206/272-5244

Pacific Run Antique Mall
10228 Pacific Ave. S
206/539-0117

Parkland Parish Antique Mall
12152 Pacific Ave. S
206/537-0978

Aries Antiques
16120 Pacific Ave.
206/582-9029

Valentino's Antiques & Books
4931 N. Pearl St.
206/759-3917

Claudia Smith's Antiques
5101 N. Pearl St.
206/759-6052

Ruston Antique Galleries
5101 N. Pearl St.
206/759-2624

Anchor Antiques Co.
5129 N. Pearl St.
206/752-1134

Curtright & Son Gallery
759 Saint Helens Ave.
206/383-2969

Teri's Curiosity Shop
760 Saint Helens Ave.
206/383-3211

Key Antiques
5485 Steilacoom Blvd. SW
206/588-0569

Museum Antiques
5928 Steilacoom Blvd. SW
206/584-3930

Mandarin Oriental Antiques
5935 Steilacoom Blvd. SW
206/582-6655

Washington

Katy's Antiques & Collectibles Mall
602 E. 25th St.
206/305-0203

57 VANCOUVER

Yesterdays Treasures
707 Grand Blvd.
360/695-2330

Vendors Outlet Mall
7907 N.E. Hwy. 99
360/574-6674

Downtown Main Antq. Mall
1108 Main St.
360/696-2253

Main Street Trader
1916 Main St.
360/695-0295

Something Nice Antiques
2310 Main St.
360/694-2948

Country Peddler
2315 Main St.
360/695-6792

Henker's
14013 S.E. Mill Plain Blvd.
360/256-5620

Jadestone Gallery
10922 N.E. St. Johns Rd.
360-573-2580

58 VASHON

Lawing's Antiques & Textiles
16619 Westside Hwy. SW
206/463-2402

Sandy's Antiques & Jewelry
17607 Vashon Hwy. SW
206/463-5807

Owens Antiques & Decorative Arts
19605 Vashon Hwy. SW
206/463-5193

59 WALLA WALLA

Bonnie's Antiques
2815 E. Isaacs Ave.
509/529-2009

General Store
211 W. Main St.
509/522-8663

Country Collectors
226 E. Main St.
509/529-6034

Antique Mall at Vintage Square
315 S. 9th Ave.
509/525-5100

60 WENATCHEE

Pretentious Antique Co.
328 N. Chelan Ave.
509/663-8221

Adams Supply Co.
509 S. Mission St.
509/662-2210

Village Mall Antiques
611 S. Mission St.
509/662-9171

Early American Light Lamps
1206 Okanogan Ave.
509/662-0386

Antique Mall of Wenatchee
11 N. Wenatchee Ave.
509/662-3671

Dimitris Antiques & Seconds
810 S. Wenatchee Ave.
509/662-2920

Collectors Gallerie
928 N. Wenatchee Ave.
509/663-5203

Treasures of the Heart
20 S. Wenatchee Ave.
509/663-8112

61 WINLOCK

Kattywampus Antique Mall
405 1st St. NE
360/785-4427

Old Hatchery
707 N.E. 1st
No Phone

62 YAKIMA

Somewhere In Time
3911 S. 1st St.
509/248-7352

Depot
32 N. Front St.
509/576-6220

Shopkeeper
807 W. Yakima Avenue
509/452-6646

Antique Alley Mini-Mall
1302 W. Lincoln Ave.
509/575-1499

Mt. Mommie's General Store
225 Naches Ave.
509/653-2556

Calico Barn Antiques
1471 S. Naches Rd.
509/966-1462

Churchill's Books & Antiques
125 S. 2nd St.
509/453-8207

Antiques & Decor Ltd.
108 S. 3rd Ave.
509/457-6949

Antiques Etc.
5703 Tieton Dr.
509/966-2513

Lantern Antiques
8507 Tieton Dr.
509/966-1396

Yesterday's Village
15 W. Yakima Ave.
509/457-4981

Green Gables
302 E. Yakima Ave.
509/577-0744

Notes

West Virginia

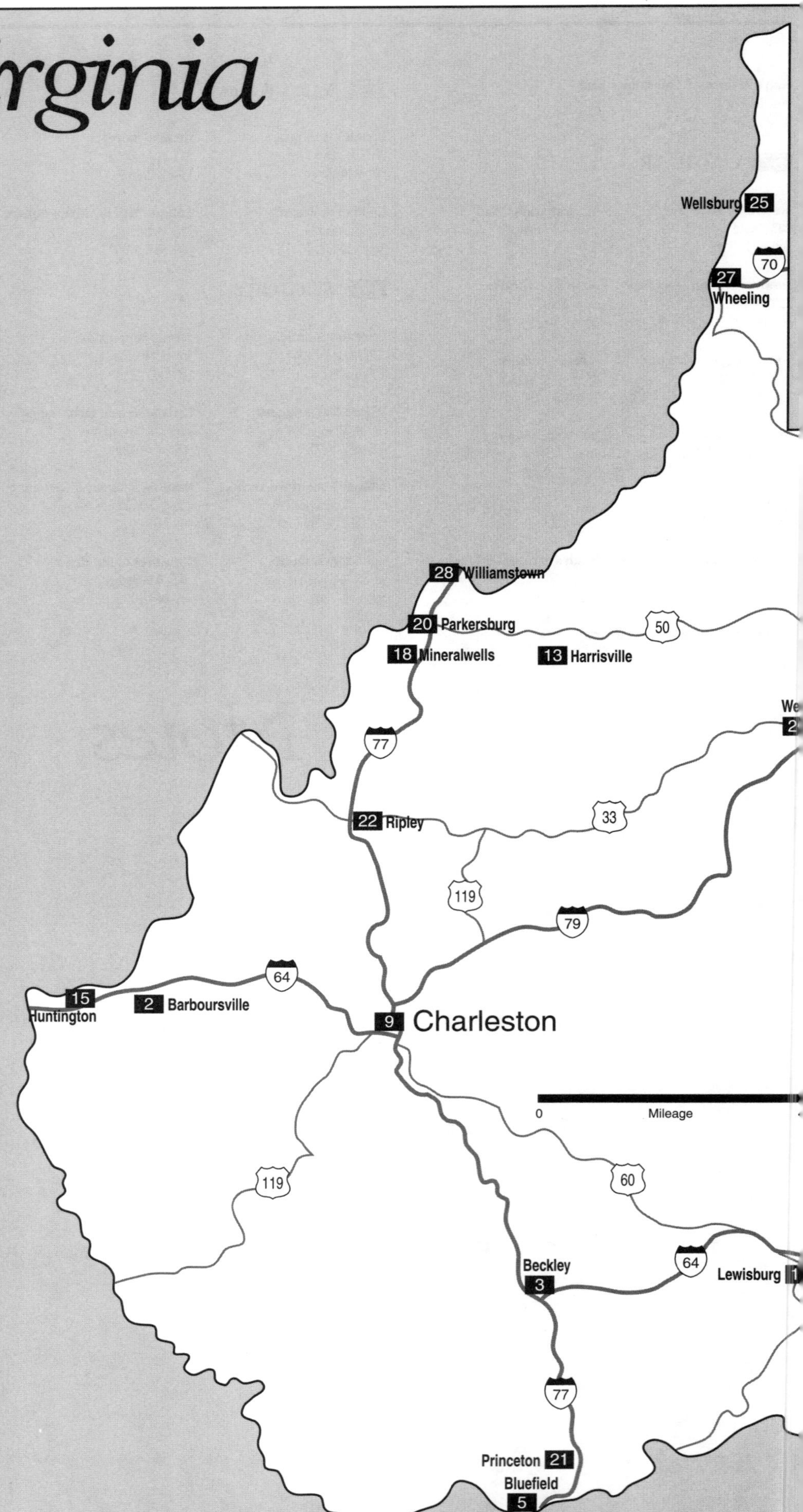

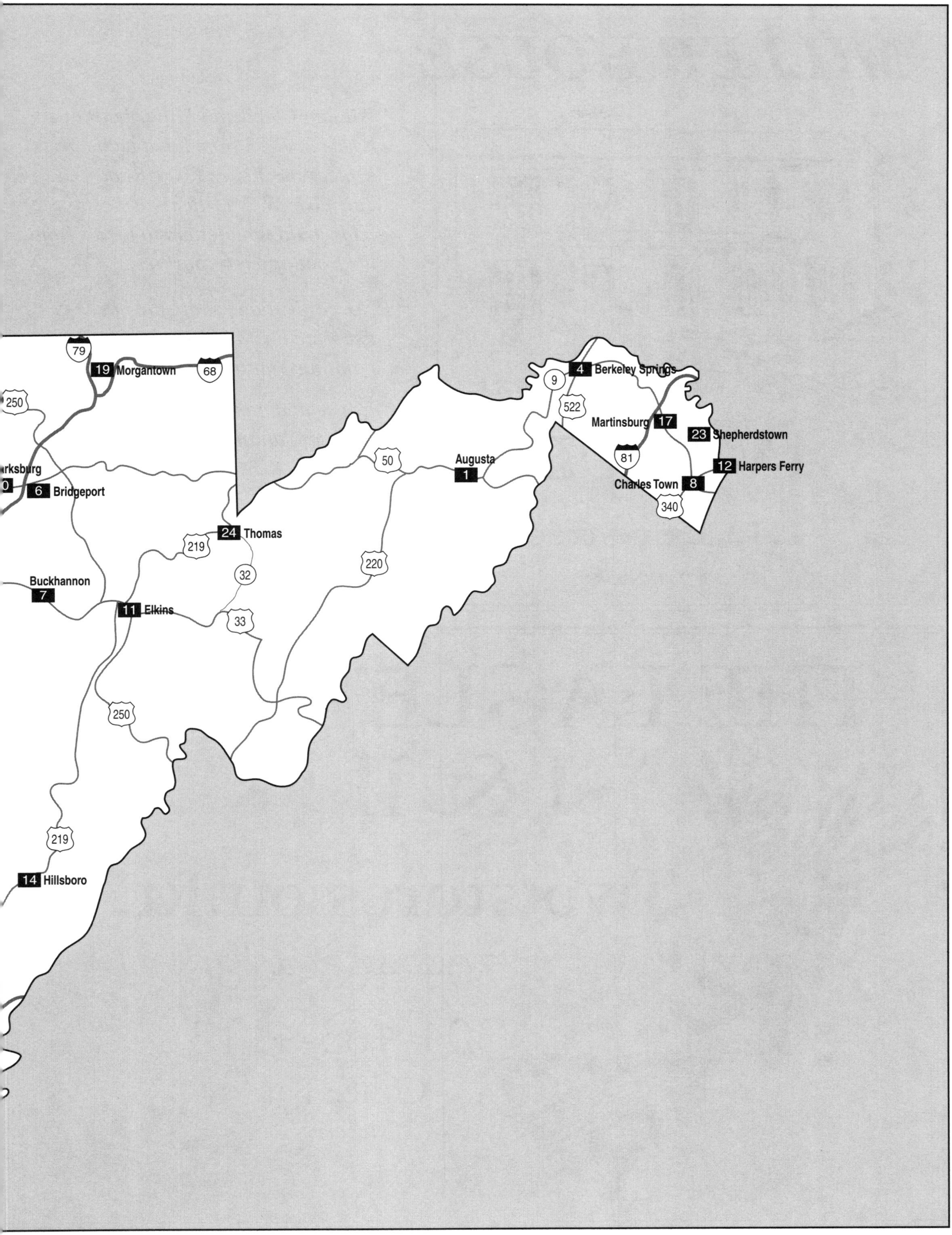
79
19 Morgantown
68
250
6 Bridgeport
4 Berkeley Springs
9
522
Martinsburg 17
23 Shepherdstown
81
50
Augusta
1
12 Harpers Ferry
Charles Town 8
340
24 Thomas
219
32
220
Buckhannon
7
11 Elkins
33
250
219
14 Hillsboro

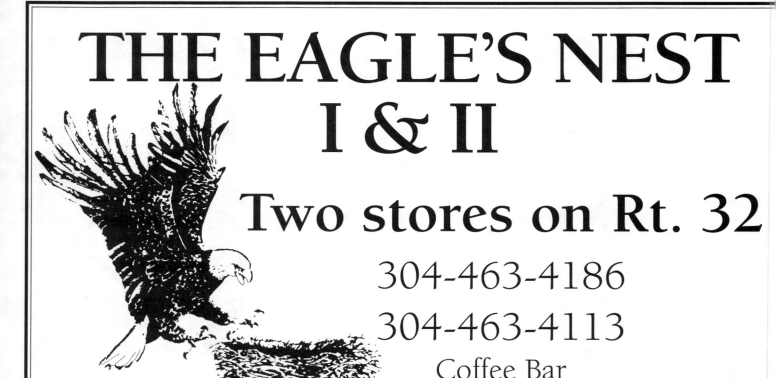

1 AUGUSTA

Dan's Antiques
Rt. 50
304/496-8187

Smith's Antiques
Rt. 50
304/496-9474

2 BARBOURSVILLE

Miller House Antiques
1112 Main Street
304/736-0845 or 304/523-6064
Open Tue.-Sat. 10-5, Sun.-Mon. By appointment

Directions: From I-64, take the Barboursville exit. Continue for 2 miles into downtown Barboursville. The shop is located on Main Street in the historic Downtown area.

The William Clendenim Miller home was built in 1852 out of "Barboursville brick," made on site. It served as the town post office from 1840 to 1860, and W.C. Miller, who was postmaster, would read letters to the townspeople from his porch or the parlor. On July 14, 1861, the Civil War's first skirmish of Barboursville took place within sight of the home, and Miller's son, John William, took a little double-barreled pistol and joined the Confederate forces. During the second skirmish the 2nd Virginia Cavalry (Union) was ordered to attack the house on rumors that it was the headquarters of Confederate Brig. A.S. Jenkins. Union Duty Sergeant, Braxton P. Reeves, was killed and his body placed on the porch of the Miller House until it could be retrieved by the Union.

In the early 1900s the home was purchased from the Miller family and used as a college boarding house.

In 1914 John W. Miller, son of the original owner, bought back his birthplace (he was born there in 1845) for obvious sentimental reasons.

Today, the house is an antique shop and is decorated with period furniture, china, paintings, quilts, etc. All are for sale. There are 11 rooms, each with a fireplace. The house is on a daily scheduled walking tour of historic Barboursville.

Favorite Places To Eat

Cracker Barrel Old Country Store
I-64 & U.S. 60, Exit 20
304/733-3450

3 BECKLEY

Favorite Places To Eat

Cracker Barrel Old Country Store
I-64/77 & SR. 3, Exit 44
304/262-3660

4 BERKELEY SPRINGS

Berkeley Springs Antique Mall
100 Fairfax Street
304/258-5676
Open Thurs.-Tue. 10-5, closed Wednesdays

Directions: From Rt. 70, take Hwy. 522 South and follow it straight for 7 miles to the heart of downtown Berkeley Springs.

Berkeley Springs offers visitors a general line of antiques from 30 dealers in 6,500 square feet of space housed in a 1910 building.

Curiosity Shop
101 N. Washington St.
304/258-1634

Old Factory Antique Mall
112 William St.
304/285-1788

Antique House
312 N. Washington St.
304/258-9420

5 BLUEFIELD

If a taste of coal culture piques your interest, head for West Virginia's southern-most border. Bluefield, off I-77, is the scene of much coal history, both past and present. The downtown overlooks an extensive network of railroad tracks, often loaded with car after car of glittering black rock. The Eastern Regional Coal Archives are housed in the Craft Memorial Library and include coal company records, diaries, oral histories and displays of miners' tools and industry artifacts.

Antiques at the Old Trade Post
1204 Augusta St.
304/325-2554

Ugly Duckling
1804 Bland St.
304/327-8900

Second Time Around
1715 Bluefield Ave.
304/325-9855

Landmark Mini Mall
200 Federal St.
304/327-9686

Interesting Side Trip

A few miles northwest of Bluefield on U.S. 52 is Bramwell, once considered the richest town in the United States. As many as 14 millionaires resided there in the early 20th century during the height of the coal boom. Tours are available in May and December, or can be pre-arranged anytime. Today the town's late 19th century fairy-tale architecture of turrets, gables, slate and tile roofs, leaded and stained glass, ornate woodwork and wide porches are a well-preserved reminder of West Virginia's Gilded Age.

6 BRIDGEPORT

Shahady's Antiques
214 East Main Street
304/842-6691 or 1-800-252-0766
Open Tue.-Sat. 10-5

Directions: Traveling I-79, take Exit 119 (Bridgeport/ Clarksburg West Virginia) to Rt. 50 East 1.5 miles to downtown Bridgeport.

Shahady's carries the largest diversified inventory in the tri-state area, with 500 pieces of furniture in stock, ranging from the 1800s to the 20th century. They also handle stoneware, lighting fixtures and glassware, plus architectural antiques, both retail and wholesale to the trade.

Grey Fox Farm Antiques
R.R. 1, #39 A
304/842-4219
Open Mon.-Sat. 11-3

Directions: From I-79, take exit 119. Turn left and go east on Rt. 50 for several miles. Turn right onto Rt. 58 and go a half-mile to the stop sign. Turn left on Rt. 26. The shop is located 2.9 miles farther on the right.

The shop is actually located in the barn of Grey Fox Farm. They (the shopkeepers) specialize in carefully selected 18th and 19th century furniture, as well as offering a wide selection of decorative accessories and gifts.

7 BUCKHANNON

Buckhannon Antique. Mall
Clarksburg Rd.
304/472-9605

Franklin Trash & Trsry. Antqs.
Clarksburg Rd.
304/472-8738

Antiques Etc.
4 E. Main St.
304/472-1120

8 CHARLES TOWN

Wooden Shoe
222 W. Washington St.
304/725-1673

Grandma's Treasures
615 E. Washington St.
304/728-2199

9 CHARLESTON

Hale St. Antiques & Collectibles Mall
213 Hale Street
304/345-6040
Open Tue.-Sun. 11-5

Directions: From I-64 East, take the Lee Street exit and turn right onto Hale Street.

This antique mall is located in a historic hardware and paint store, and is the largest antiques shop in Charleston. Its three floors are filled with a variety of furniture, glassware and collectibles.

Alex Franklin Ltd.
1007 Bridge Rd.
304/342-8333

B & L Antiques
300 Crestview Dr.
304/343-7941

Attic Antiques
313 D St.
304/744-8975

D L Jackson Antiques
215 Hale St.
304/344-9840

South Charleston Antq. Mall
4800 MacCorkle Ave. SW.
304/766-6761

Art Works Plus Inc.
4849 McCorkle Ave. SW
304/768-8111

Vagabond House Fine Cllbls.
4851 MacCorkle Ave.
304/766-6982

Tiny Tim's
5206 MacCorkle Ave. SE
304/925-3398

Trophy Design
418 Virginia St. W
304/346-3907

Tiki's Antique. Gallery
1312 Watts St.
304/346-6160

Belle's Antiques
4270 Woodrums Ln.
304/744-5435

Kanawha Coin/Antiques
707/712 Fife
304/342-8081

Split Rail Antiques
2580 Benson Dr.
304/342-6084

10 CLARKSBURG

Clarksburg, the birthplace of General Thomas "Stonewall" Jackson, was the adopted home of thousands of immigrant laborers after the Civil War and, thanks to the discovery of gas and oil, a manufacturing center for glass, tin and zinc.

Two monuments mark the town's heritage. A likeness of "Stonewall" sits astride a bronze horse on the courthouse plaza and nearby, a heroic sculpture represents the Belgian, Czech, Greek, Hungarian, Irish, Italian, Romanian and Spanish immigrants who flocked to the region beginning in the 1880s.

Kollage
1625 Buckhannon Pike
304/622-8137

West End Antiques
97 Milford St.
304/624-7600

Red Wheel Antiques.
600 Southern Ave.
304/622-2192

Carney's Fine Antiques
315 Spring Ave.
304/622-1317

11 ELKINS

Bittersweet Books & Antiques
212 Davis Avenue
304/636-6338 or 1-800-417-6338
Open Mon.-Sat. 10-5, Sundays by appointment or chance

Directions: Bittersweet is accessible from Highways 250, 33 and 219, all of which lead to historic downtown Elkins.

Bittersweet Books and Antiques specializes in paper, as well as carrying a general line of antiques. Their paper goods include sheet music, postcards, magazines, trade cards, and old and rare books.

The Warfield House Bed & Breakfast
318 Buffalo Street
304/636-4555
Open year round
Rates begin at $65

For specific directions to The Warfield House Bed and Breakfast call the innkeepers.

Guests get to choose from four rooms in this grand "Old Colonies Style" house, each furnished in antiques of a specific wood indigenous to the area: oak, pine, maple and walnut. This shingle and brick house, built in 1901, has been faithfully restored with turn-of-the-century reproduction carpets and wallpapers, and furnished with antiques. The house features spectacular stained glass, an ornately carved staircase, an abundance of oak and cherry appliqued molding, and a massive terra-cotta fireplace.

After a hearty breakfast of fresh fruit, home-baked breads and pastries, and a hot entree, guests can go hiking, biking, rafting, bird watching, mountain climbing, horseback riding, downhill and cross-country skiing, antiquing, or visiting battlefields and festivals. When you get tired, return to the house and relax with a glass of lemonade on the 70-foot wrap-around porch.

S and S Company
204 Findley St.
304/636-2366

Granny's Attic
427 Kerens Ave.
304/636-4121

Justine's Antiques. Etc.
Old Seneca Rd.
304/636-2891

12 HARPERS FERRY

The town of Harpers Ferry is perhaps livelier today than it was in 1859, when abolitionist John Brown staged his raid on the United States Arsenal there, setting off a chain of events that resulted in the Civil War. Undoubtedly more beautiful than ever, its historic section is polished and maintained as a national historic park, and is part of the Civil War Discovery Trail.

Hodge Podge
144 High Street
304/535-6917
Open Mon.-Fri. 10-5, Sat.-Sun. 10-6

Directions: Hodge Podge is located on Hwy. 340 in downtown historic Harpers Ferry.

Hodge Podge handles small antiques, gifts, collectibles, and Civil War items—a true "hodgepodge" of merchandise!

Stone House Antiques
108 Potomac St.
304/535-6688

Washington St. Antiques
1080 Washington St.
304/535-2411

Interesting Side Trip

Wind along the cobblestone streets of Harpers Ferry to the town of Bolivar, where shops feature a remarkable collection of antiques including Civil War memorabilia and local crafts.

13 HARRISVILLE

A short detour off U.S. highway 50 south on West Virginia Rt. 16 takes you to quaint Harrisville, where Berdine's 5 & Dime, the nation's oldest five and dime, still operates after 80 years on Court Street. Its solid oak cabinets and glass bins offer penny candy, small toys and practical household items.

Connard Collectibles His & Hers Corner
201A E. Main St.
304/643-2599

14 HILLSBORO

On the literary front, Hillsboro is the birthplace of Pearl S. Buck, one of the world's best loved authors. Her family home, the Stulting House, is open for tours, and contains original furnishings and memorabilia. Among its annual events is *Author's Day* in August, dedicated to keeping the Nobel and Pulitzer Prize writer's spirit alive.

While in Hillsboro, step back in time at the Hillsboro General Store, and stop for a bite to eat at the popular little Country Roads Cafe.

Hillsboro General Store
Rt. 219
304/653-4414

Favorite Places To Eat

Country Roads Cafe
Rt. 219
304/653-8595
Open 11-9 Tue.-Fri., 8-9 Sat. & Sun.

The modern occupation of Country Roads Cafe is serving up home-cooked meals with fresh-baked desserts. Breakfast, lunch and dinner specials are regular features. This 100-year-old establishment still possesses a ladder from its earliest years as a general store. Furnishings are antique, and visitors can buy antique wire-made frames, mirrors, and numerous other small delights.

15 HUNTINGTON

Antique Center, Inc.
610 14th St. W
304/523-7887

Adams Avenue Antique Mall
1460 Adams Ave.
304/523-7231

Collectors Store Antique Mall
1660 Adams Ave.
304/429-3900

Stouffer's Shady Business
845 8th Ave.
304/697-8905

Bus Barn Antiques Mall
402 18th St. W
304/429-8207

Hattie & Nan's Antique Market
521 14th St. W.
304/523-8844

Mark's Antiques
600 14th St. W
304/525-3275

Pieces of the Past
606 14th St. W
304/522-7892

Bob's Second Hand
619 14th St. W
304/523-6854

Old as the Hills Antiques
705 14th St. W
304/697-0633

Lewis' Antiques & Collectibles
720 14th St. W
304/522-0444

Memories of the Heart
720 14th St. W
304/697-5301

A Touch of Country
418 9th St.
304/525-2808

Mimmi's Collectors Dolls
544 6th Ave.
304/522-4841

Central City Antique Mall
611 14th St. W
304/523-0311

16 LEWISBURG

Antiques
120 E. Washington St.
304/647-3404

Peddlar's Alley Antiques
123 E. Washington St.
304/645-4082

Great Places To Stay

Lynn's Inn Bed & Breakfast
Rt. 4, Box 40
1-800-304-2003
Open year round
Seasonal rates

Directions: Lynn's is located 1.5 miles north of I-64 (Exit 169) on U.S. Hwy. 219.

This is a switch from the majority of bed and breakfasts because, instead of being a former farm, this is a *working* farm—they actually raise beef cattle. The inn itself is a former tourist home built in 1935 and furnished with original antiques. There are four guest rooms, all with private baths and two sitting rooms. Guests are served a full country breakfast, and there is a large porch with rockers and ferns to help folks enjoy a true country weekend.

17 MARTINSBURG

Incorporated in 1778, Martinsburg later flourished as a railroad town, home to the B & O Railroad engine shop. Coveted by both sides in the Civil War, the Union army held it for 32 months, the Confederate for 16.

Old Town Martinsburg offers a variety of antique shops specializing in primitives, Victoriana, dolls, linens and unusual accessories.

Olde Kilbourne Antq. Gallery
616 W. John St.
304/263-2900

Blue Ridge Country Antiques
204 S. Queen St.
304/263-4275

Manor House Antiques
242 S. Queen St.
304/263-5950

Affordable Antiques & Furn.
556 N. Queen St.
304/263-9024

Little Shop Antiques
563 N. Queen St.
304/267-1603

Favorite Places To Eat

Market House Grill
100 North Queen Street
304/263-7615

To dine at the historic Market House Grill is considered an "eating adventure," with both Continental and Cajun fare their specialty—quite out of the ordinary for the location.

Cracker Barrel Old Country Store
I-81 & Foxcroft Ave. North, Exit 13
304/262-3660

Interesting Side Trips

The Apollo Civic Theatre
128 East Martin Street, P.O. Box 519
304/263-6766

The Apollo Civic Theatre has the distinction of being the oldest live performance stage in West Virginia. Call for a complete listing of shows, times and ticket prices.

18 MINERAL WELLS

Favorite Places To Eat

Cracker Barrel Old Country Store
I-77 & Rt. 14, Exit 170
304/489-2382

19 MORGANTOWN

Bittersweet Antiques
431 Beechurst
304/296-4602

Dale's Oldtiques
Stewartstown Rd.
304/599-9074

20 PARKERSBURG

Antique shops in the region frequently carry a broad selection of vintage regional glass. Maher's Antiques in Parkersburg offers glass, plus a selection of crocks with A.P. Donagho's Excelsior Pottery signature, recalling the days when homes throughout the Midwest stored food in the Parkersburg Company's pots.

Maher's Antiques
1619 Saint Mary's Avenue
304/485-1331

21 PRINCETON

Hobby Shop Antiques
305 Mercer St.
304/487-1990

Olde Towne Shoppe
929 Mercer St.
304/425-3677

Ealy's This & That Shop
1201 Mercer St.
304/487-2879

A-Z Trading Center
509 Roger St.
304/425-4365

Favorite Places To Eat

Cracker Barrel Old Country Store
I-77 & U.S. Hwy. 460, Exit 9
304/425-4003

22 RIPLEY

Blue Ribbon Antiques
Rt. 33
304/372-5006
Open Tue.-Sat. 9-4, closed Sun.-Mon.

Directions: Take Exit 138 off I-77. The shop is 2 miles west of the Ripley exit on Rt. 33.

Here's one for a rainy day or for the serious browser. Housed in a 200-year-old seven-room farmhouse, the shopkeeper describes Blue Ribbon Antiques as being "floor to ceiling, wall to wall; the old house is literally bulging with antiques and glassware."

Country Place
111 Court St. S
304/372-5048

Millie's Antiques
1 Starcher Place
304/372-1859

Antique Junction
1 Railroad St.
304/372-3742

23 SHEPHERDSTOWN

Just a few miles northeast of Martinsburg lies Shepherdstown, one of the oldest towns in West Virginia, established in the 1730s as Mechlenberg. Today, it's a quaint town of wooden storefronts and tree-lined streets, where specialty shops, charming restaurants, small inns and cultural programs of Shepherd College fill the town with visitors.

The eclectic 1930s Yellow Brick Bank, The Olde Pharmacy Cafe, complete with original pharmaceutical trappings, and Ye Olde Sweet Shoppe offer historic settings and good food.

Matthews & Shank Antiques
139 West German
304/876-6550

24 THOMAS

Eagle's Nest I & II
Rt. 32
304/463-4186 or 304/463-4113
Open daily 10-5

Directions: Both Eagle's Nests are located on Rt. 32 in Thomas, 37 miles from Elkins.

These two stores carry collectibles, antiques and good junque. They also claim to have the best selection of handmade dolls and crafts in West Virginia. After you're through admiring the familiar, the strange and the remarkable, have a refreshment at their coffee bar while you decide what to take home from the shop.

25 WELLSBURG

True to its beginnings as a late 18th century port, Wellsburg's downtown wharf still welcomes vintage riverboats such as the *Mississippi Queen* in July and the *Delta Queen* in October. For each visit, the town puts on a party, with bands, food, artisans and boat tours.

Wellsburg's downtown National Historic District features specialty shops, riverside greens and restaurants. A short drive from downtown you'll find Drover's Inn, an authentic 1848 country inn with handcrafted furnishings, an Old English-style pub and a restaurant famous for its home-cooked buffet.

Wellsburg Flower Shop, Inc.
600 Charles St.
304/737-3380

Federman's Country Co-op
642 Charles St.
304/737-1518

Watzman's Old Place
709 Charles St.
304/737-0711

26 WESTON

Ethel's Antiques & Collectibles
107 Main Ave.
304/269-7690

A Penny Saved Antq. & Cllbls.
230 Main Ave.
304/269-3258

27 WHEELING

Wheeling is the historical and commercial hub of the Northern Panhandle. From its earliest days as a pre-Revolutionary outpost and stop along the National Road's path to the western frontier, to its 18th and 19th century role as a port of entry, through its boom and bust Victorian Era as the center of glass, steel and textiles, Wheeling has preserved and persevered.

Independence Hall in downtown Wheeling has served as an 18th and 19th century customs house, as the capitol of the Restored Government of West Virginia, and later as the state capital for the new state of West Virginia. Today, it serves as a center for art and a showcase for the state's history, and is part of the Civil War Discovery Trail.

The city's most distinctive historic landmark, the 1849 Wheeling Suspension Bridge, dazzles visitors at night with its brilliant necklace of decorative lights. The oldest major long span suspension bridge in the world, the bridge is a designated National Historic Landmark.

Just blocks from downtown, Wheeling's Centre Market district is listed on the National Register of Historic Places. It's also high on the list for shoppers seeking antiques, traditional crafts, gourmet and specialty food items and unique gifts. Restaurants and a Victorian-style confectionery will rejuvenate the weary shopper.

The Old Town neighborhood on Main Street in north Wheeling also offers shoppers the opportunity to visit another era. Shops located in historic townhouses and mansions offer fine works of art, antiques and Victorian decorations and accents. Unique restaurants provide a relaxing respite.

Northgate Antiques & Intrs.
735 Main St.
304/232-1475

Outdoor Store
1065 Main St.
304/233-1080

Downtown Wheeling Antiques
1120 Main St.
304/232-8951

Antiques on the Market
2265 Market St.
304/232-1665

28 WILLIAMSTOWN

Since 1905, Williamstown's Fenton Art Glass Company has been producing the finest in original art glass. On a free plant tour, you'll see molten glass born in fiery hot furnaces begin its unique journey on the way to becoming tomorrow's heirlooms. Under the persuasion of master craftsmen using century-old tools and techniques, beautiful Fenton Glassware takes shape amidst a constant, roaring baptism of fire. For a nominal fee, visit the company's glass museum to view one-of-a-kind glass pieces, including Fenton's original carnival glass, and to watch a video on the history of Fenton Glass.

Williamstown Antique Mall
439 Highland Avenue
304/375-6315

Notes

Wisconsin

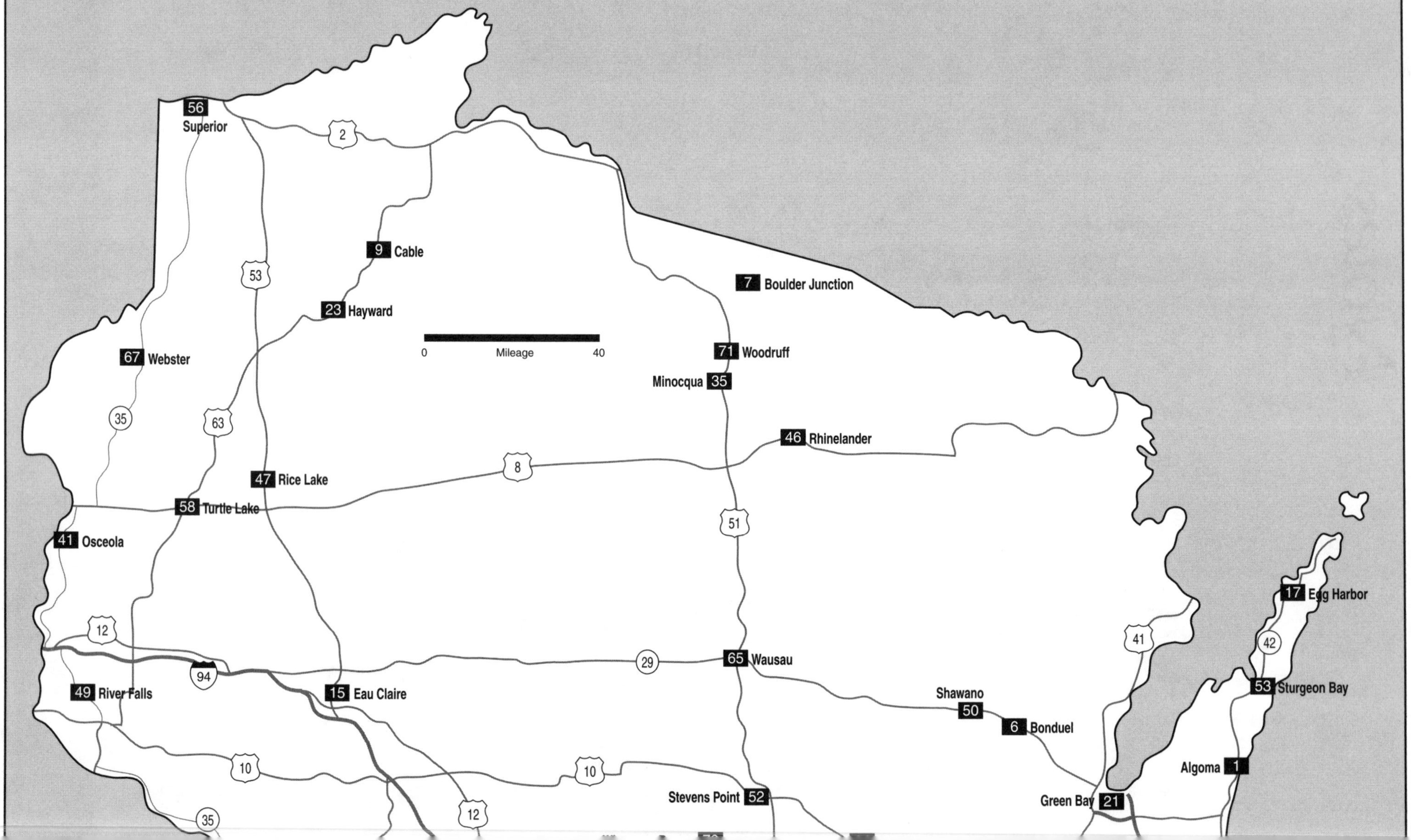

56 Superior
2
9 Cable
53
23 Hayward
7 Boulder Junction
0 Mileage 40
67 Webster
71 Woodruff
Minocqua 35
35
63
46 Rhinelander
8
47 Rice Lake
58 Turtle Lake
51
41 Osceola
17 Egg Harbor
12
41
42
29
65 Wausau
94
49 River Falls
15 Eau Claire
Shawano 50
53 Sturgeon Bay
6 Bonduel
10
10
Algoma 1
Stevens Point 52
Green Bay 21
35
12

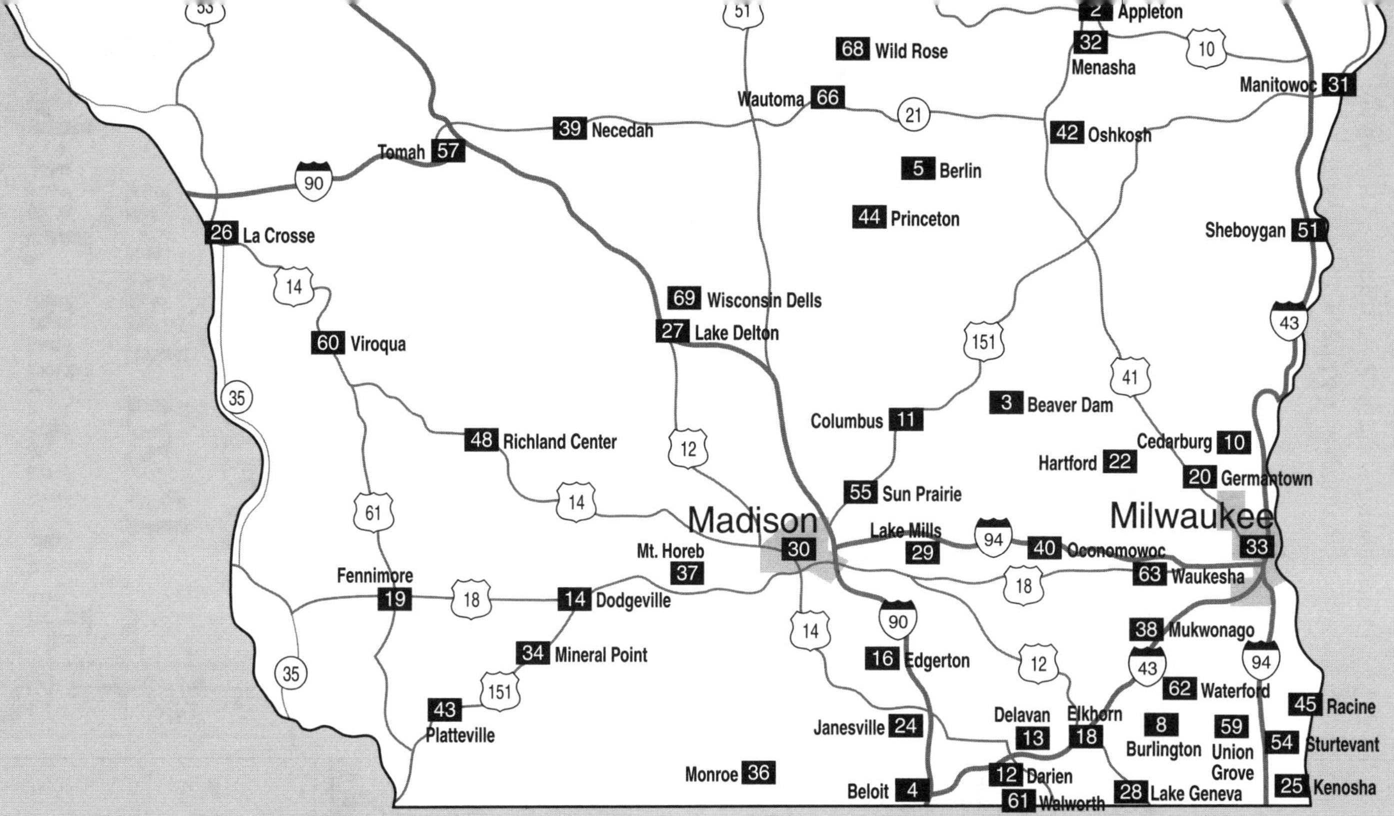
Appleton
Menasha
Manitowoc
Wild Rose
Wautoma
Necedah
Oshkosh
Tomah
Berlin
Princeton
Sheboygan
La Crosse
Wisconsin Dells
Lake Delton
Viroqua
Beaver Dam
Columbus
Richland Center
Cedarburg
Hartford
Germantown
Sun Prairie
Madison
Milwaukee
Lake Mills
Oconomowoc
Mt. Horeb
Fennimore
Waukesha
Dodgeville
Mukwonago
Edgerton
Mineral Point
Waterford
Racine
Delavan
Elkhorn
Burlington
Union Grove
Sturtevant
Janesville
Platteville
Darien
Monroe
Beloit
Lake Geneva
Kenosha
Walworth

Craftmaster
ANTIQUES
& Restoration

Variety at a reasonable "take home" price!

Three floors full of restored furniture, stripped furniture, and stuff in the ruff.

2034 North 15th Street

920-452-2524

Sheboygan

51

Carousel Collectibles & Antiques

• Handpainted Carousel Horses
• Carousel gift items • Antiques • Glassware
• Primitives • Paper Collectibles

121 N. Iowa

Dodgeville

608-935-5196

Fax 608-935-5025

E-mail: carousel@mhtc.net

14

The Jordan House

Bed and Breakfast

Relax in ... Country Charm

81 South Main Street

414-673-5643

Hartford

22

ANTIQUE MALL OF TOMAH

Specializing in "smalls"
60 plus dealers
I-94 & Hwy 21 East
(608) 372-7853

Tomah

57

NORTHLAND COLLECTORS MART

(ACROSS FROM THE GAZEBO)

211 Main St.

608/565-3730

Necedah

39

ANTIQUES

About Time Red Barn Menasha Jack

3 SHOPS IN 1

68 Racine

920-725-4880

ANTIQUES

Menasha

32

Wisconsin

1 ALGOMA

Algoma Antique Mall
300 4 th St.
414/487-3221

Gaslight Antiques
1000 Freemont
414/487-5705

Granny's Attic Antiques
1009 Jefferson St.
414/487-3226

White Pine Antiques
720 3rd St.
414/487-7217

2 APPLETON

Audio's Antiques
1426 N. Ballard Rd.
414/734-2856

American Heritage Antique
6197 W. City Tk. Kk
414/734-8200

Avenue Coins & Jewelry
303 E. College Ave.
414/731-4740

Harp Gallery Antiques & Furn.
2495 Northern Rd.
414/733-7115

Memories Antique Mall
400 Randolph Dr.
414/788-5553

Fox River Antique Mall
1074 S. Van Dyke Rd.
414/731-9699

3 BEAVER DAM

Added Touch
108 Front St.
414/887-2436

Tree City Antiques
114 Front St.
414/885-5593

4 BELOIT

Nest Egg Ltd.
816 E. Grand Ave.
608/365-0700

Riverfront Antiques Mall
306 State St.
608/362-7368

5 BERLIN

Abe Old Antiques
166 Huron St.
414/361-0889

6 BONDUEL

Hearthside Antique Mall
129 S. Cecil St.
715/758-6200

7 BOULDER JUNCTION

Joan's Antiques
10377 Main
715/385-2600

Fisherman's Wife
10382 Main
715/385-9205

8 BURLINGTON

Gingham Dog Antiques
109 E. Chestnut St.
414/763-4759

Gingham Dog Antiques
120 E. Chestnut St.
414/763-2348

Antique Alley Mall
481 Milwaukee Ave.
414/763-5257

9 CABLE

Cottage Shop
Box #-113
715/798-3077

Nordik Sleigh Antiques
Hwy. M
715/798-3967

Honey Creek Antiques
RR 1 #-73
715/798-3958

10 CEDARBURG

Creekside Antiques
N69 W6334 Bridge Rd.
414/377-6131

Cedar Creek Antiques
N70 W6340 Bridge Rd.
414/377-2204

Robins Nest Antiques & Gifts
N70 W6340 Bridge Rd.
414/377-3444

Spool N Spindle Antiques
N70 W6340 Bridge Rd.
414/377-4200

Antiquenet
6920 Kingswood Dr
414/375-0756

Don's Resale & Antique Shop
N57 W6170 Portland Rd.
414/377-6868

Antique Loft
576 62 Ave.
414/377-9007

Crow's Nest
6404 66 St.
414/377-3039

American Country Antiques
W61 N506 Washington Ave.
414/375-4140

Heritage Lighting
W62 N572 Washington Ave.
414/377-9033

Nouveau Antique & Jewelry
W62 N594 Washington Ave.
414/375-4568

Patricia Frances Interiors
W62 N634 Washington Ave.
414/377-7710

11 COLUMBUS

Antq. Shops of Columbus Mall
141 W. James St.
414/623-2669

Antique Shops of Columbus
902 Park Ave.
414/623-3930

12 DARIEN

Ice Cream Shoppe
18 S. Beloi St.
414/724-5060

13 DELAVAN

Geneva Lk. Imprts. & Antqs.
2460 N. Cty. Tk. O S.
414/728-8887

Treasure Hut Florist
6551 State Rd. 11
414/728-2020

Antiques of Delavan
229 E. Walworth Ave.
414/728-9977

Beall Jewelers
305 E. Walworth Ave.
414/728-8577

14 DODGEVILLE

Carousel Collectibles & Antiques
121 North Iowa Street
608/935-5196
May-Dec. 7 days a week, Jan.-Apr., Mon.-Sat. Call ahead to be sure shop is open, Hours vary.

Directions: Traveling north from Dubuque on Hwy. 151, exit to Hwy. 23 North into Downtown Dodgeville. Traveling west from Madison on 151-18, take Exit 60 (18 West) to Hwy. 23. At stoplight turn left to Downtown Dodgeville. From Spring Green, stay on Hwy. 23 South to Downtown Dodgeville.

Carousel Horses have been a big part of the Reynolds family's lives for the past 20 years. Virginia Reynolds began painting carousel horses at The House On The Rock. She learned a very unique method of painting, and after five years passed this knowledge on to her daughter Cherie. During the next 15 years, the two worked together painting hundreds of carousel horses in all sizes. The painting of each horse is one-of-a-kind. In 1985 Carousel Collectibles and Antiques was opened. Through her creativity and artistic talents, Virginia passed on her love of carousels to many people who came to the shop. Virginia died unexpectedly in January 1995, which was a great loss to all those who knew her and admired her work. Cherie continues the painting of carousel horses with the hopes of carrying on her mother's memory and her love of carousels.

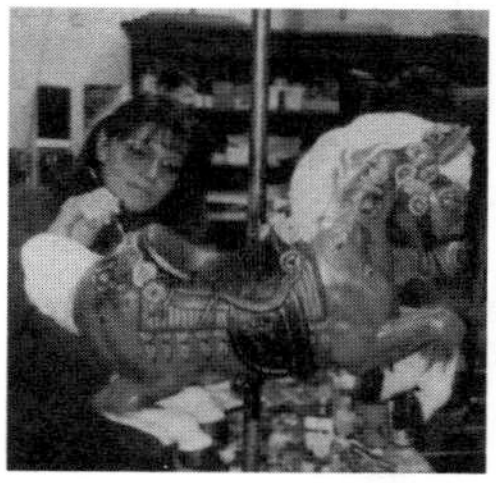

In addition to beautifully handpainted carousel horses, the shop carries a wide variety of collectibles - stunning glassware, handpainted dishes, pottery, primitives, furniture, paper collectibles, pictures, books and more. The shop also carries many carousel gift items including the handpainted carousel horses ranging from 12 to 60 inches in size.

Rustic Floweral Antiques
101 W. Leffler St.
608/935-5564

Woodshed
RR 1
608/935-3896

15 EAU CLAIRE

Rice's Antiques
202 S. Barslow St.
715/835-5351

Piney Hills Antiques
5260 Deerfield Rd.
715/832-8766

Antique Emporium
306 Main St.
715/832-2494

16 EDGERTON

Mildred's Antiques
4 Burdick St.
608/884-3031

Antiques & Art Gallery
104 W. Fulton St.
608/884-6787

Sisters Act
114 W. Fulton St.
608/884-6092

Edgerton Resale Mall
204 W. Fulton St.
608/884-8148

17 EGG HARBOR

Basil Sweet Ltd.
7813 Egg Harbor Rd.
414/868-2300

Country Bumpkin
6228 State Hwy. 432
414/743-8704

Door County Antiques
7150 State Hwy. 42
414/868-2121

Bay Trading Co.
7367 State Hwy. 42
414/868-2648

Olde Orchard Antique Mall
7381 State Hwy. 42
414/868-3685

CJ's Antiques Etc. & CJ's Too
7899 State Hwy. 42
414/868-2271

Shades of the Past
8010 State Rd. 42
414/868-3800

18 ELKHORN

Powell's Antique Shop
14 W. Geneva St.
414/723-2952

Front Parlor Antiques
6696 Millard Rd.
414/742-3489

Twin Pines Antique Mall
5438 State Road 11
414/723-4492

Bits of the Past & Present
5691 State Road 11
414/723-4763

Loveless Antiques
7091 U.S. Hwy. 12
414/742-2619

Heirlooms
12 S. Wisconsin St.
414/723-4070

19 FENNIMORE

Tuckwood House
1280 10th St.
608/822-3164

20 GERMANTOWN

Favorite Places To Eat

Cracker Barrel Old Country Store
U.S. Hwy 41 & County Line Rd., Exit 52
414/253-4188

21 GREEN BAY

American Antiques & Jewelry
1049 W. Mason Street
414/498-0111

Meadow Suite
630 E. Walnut St.
414/432-1733

Towne Trader Antiques
914 Main St.
414/435-8070

Red's-Shirley Antiques
1344 Main St.
414/437-3596

Yesteryears Antique Mall
611 9 th St.
414/435-4900

Packer City Antiques
712 Redwood Dr.
414/490-1095

22 HARTFORD

Jordan House Bed and Breakfast
81 South Main Street
414/673-5643
Open year round. Reservations required
Rates: $55 Private Bath, $45 Shared bath

Directions; From Hwy. 41, take Hwy. 60 exit west 7 miles to Downtown Hartford (intersection of Highways 60 and 83). Turn left on Main Street, go 1 1/2 blocks.

Built at the turn-of-the-century for Mr. Bruno Jordan, a prominent businessman and one of the city's first aldermen, the Jordan House was designed and built by Mr. Jacob Jacobi, a noted Milwaukee architect. The original building plans are still intact and illustrate the substance of the construction. The care in design is reflected in the front foyer, complete with built-in bench and a beautifully preserved staircase.

The four guest rooms, located upstairs, are decorated with antique furnishings from the turn-of-the-century.

Your choice of a continental or hearty country breakfast is served each morning.

Sharron's Antiques
135 N. Main St.
414/673-2751

Hartford Antique Mall
147 N. Rural
414/673-2311

Erin Antiques
1691 State Rd. (Hwy. 835)
414/673-4680

23 HAYWARD

Red Shed Antiques
County Rd. #-B
715/634-6088

Remember When
114 N. Dakota Ave.
715/634-5282

Hill's Antiques
RR 2
715/634-2037

Nelson Bay Antiques
RR 3
715/634-2177

24 JANESVILLE

Carousel Consignments
31 S. Main St.
608/758-0553

Foster Lee Antiques
218 W. Milwaukee St.
608/752-5188

Pipsqueak & Me
220 W. Milwaukee St.
608/756-1752

Franklin Stove Antiques
301 W. Milwaukee St.
608/756-5792

General Antique Store
8301 N. U.S. Hwy. 1 St.
608/756-1812

Yesterdays Memories Antique
4904 S. U.S. Hwy. 51
608/754-2906

Another Antique Shop
419 W. Milwaukee St.
608/754-5711

Favorite Places To Eat

Cracker Barrel Old Country Store
I-90 & Milton Rd., Exit 171A
608/752-7750

25 KENOSHA

Sara Jane's Antiques & Cllbls.
627 58th St.
414/657-5588

A Miracle on 58th Street
706 58th St.
414/652-3132

Cypress Tree
722 50th St.
414/652-6999

Country Cove Antiques
710 57th St.
414/654-0738

Dairy Land Antiques
5220 120th St.
414/857-6802

Greta's
4906 7th Ave.
414/658-1077

Laura's Resale & Collectibles
6013 Sheridan Rd.
414/657-1810

Red Barn Antique
12000 Sheridan Rd.
414/694-0424

Hyden Seec Antiques
5623 6th Ave.
414/654-8111

Helen's Remember When Antqs
5801 6th Ave.
414/652-2280

Memory Lane Antiques
1942 22nd Ave.
414/551-8452

Favorite Places To Eat

Cracker Barrel Old Country Store
I-94 & Hwy. 50, Exit 344
414/857-2995

26 LA CROSSE

Caledonia Street Antique Mall
1213 Caledonia Street
608/782-8443

Plantique
115 7th St. S
608/784-4053

Hornet's Nest Antiques
1507 Caledonia St.
608/785-2998

Wild Rose
1507 Caledonia St.
608/785-2998

4th St. Antique Gallery
119 4th St.
608/782-7278

Manon's Vintage Shop
535 Main St.
608/784-2240

27 LAKE DELTON

Old Academy Antiques & Gift
Hwy. 12
608/254-4948

Our Gang Antique Mall
Hwy. 23
608/254-4401

Braun's Happy Landing Antique Shop
30 N. Judson
608/253-4613

28 LAKE GENEVA

Sign of the Unicorn
233 Center St.
414/248-1141

Antiques International
611 W. Main St.
414/248-1800

Steffen Collection
611 W. Main St.
414/248-1800

Cedar Fields
755 W. Main St.
414/248-8086

Lake Geneva Antique Mall
829 Williams St.
414/248-6345

29 LAKE MILLS

Old Mills Market
109 North Main Street
414/648-3030
Hours: Winter—10 to 5 Sunday through Saturday, Tuesday by chance; Summer—10 to 5 Sunday through Saturday, Tuesday by chance, Thursday until 7

Directions: Located 24 miles east of Madison on I-94 OR 64 miles west of Milwaukee on I-94. From I-94, exit onto Hwy. 89 South; go 3/4 mile. In Lake Mills, shop is located across from the Commons Park.

Tucked inside the turn-of-the-century historic Luetzow Meat Market building, the expansive selection of antiques includes furniture, vintage clothing, jewelry, collectibles, heirlooms, gifts, and linens. Appraisal, by on-staff qualified appraiser, and estate services are provided. A treat for the tummy while shopping comes in the shop's delightful "special" hand-dipped chocolates. Also, the coffee pot is always on.

Opera Hall Antique
211 N. Main St.
414/648-5026

30 MADISON

Broadway Antiques Mall
115 E. Broadway
608/222-2241

Bethel Parish Shoppe
315 N. Carroll St.
608/255-9183

Antiques Mall of Madison
4748 Cottage Grove Rd.
608/222-2049

Janet's Antiques
815 Fern Dr.
608/238-4474

Hopkins & Crocker, Inc.
807 E. Johnson St.
608/255-6222

Florilegium
823 E. Johnson St.
608/256-7310

Vintage Interiors
2615 E. Johnson St.
608/244-3000

Antique Gallery
6608 Mineral Point Rd.
608/833-4321

Chris Kerwin Antqs. & Intrs.
1839 Monroe St.
608/256-7363

Mapletree Antique Mall
1293 N. Sherman Ave.
608/241-2599

Kappel's Clock Shop
2250 Sherman Ave.
608/244-6165

Favorite Places To Eat

Cracker Barrel Old Country Store
I-90/94 & Hwy. 151, Exit 135A
608/242-0560

31 MANITOWOC

Ebert's Antiques
5712 Country Trunk JJ
414/682-0687

Washington St. Antique Mall
910 Washington St.
414/684-2954

Antique Mall of Manitowoc
301 N. 8 th St.
414/682-8680

Viking Antiques
314 N. 8 th St.
414/682-0100

Pine River Antiques
7430 Hwy. Cr.
414/726-4440

Larco Resale & Antiques
2204 N. Rapids Rd.
414/682-9066

Medley Resale & Antiques
1114 S. 10th St.
414/682-8400

Wheeler on the River Antiques
436 N. 10th St.
414/682-3069

Timeless Treasures
112 N. 8th St.
414/682-6566

32 MENASHA

About Time/Red Barn/Menasha Jack's Antiques
68 Racine
920/725-4880
Open: Tue.-Sat. 10-4:30, March through January; 10-4:30 Saturday only in February

Directions: Take Hwy. 441 to Menasha, exit at Racine Street. Go south approximately 1 mile.

Three stores in one offer not only a wide variety, but also a large quantity of antiques such as furniture, fixtures, lamps, jewelry, primitives, graniteware, stoneware and pottery. In addition to great selections, the shops buy and appraise antique pieces.

Anderson Resale Shop
922 Appleton Rd.
920/725-5599

Country Goose My
1018 Appleton Rd.
920/722-1661

Not New Now
212 Main St.
920/725-5545

Wood-Shed
746 3rd St.
920/725-3347

33 MILWAUKEE

Wishful Things
207 E. Buffalo St.
414/765-1117

Time Traveler Book Store
7143 W. Burleigh St.
414/442-0203

Noah's Ark
7153 W. Burleigh St.
414/442-1588

Chattel Changers Inc.
2520 E. Capitol Dr.
414/961-7085

Capital City Comics
2565 N. Downer Ave.
414/332-8199

Village Bazaar
2201 N. Farwell Ave.
414/224-9675

Fifth Avenue Antiques
422 N. 5th St.
414/271-3355

Brass Light Gallery
131 S. 1st St.
414/271-8300

Antique Center-Walkers Pt.
1134 1st St.
414/383-0655

Carters on Delaware
2466 Graham St.
414/482-0014

Architectural Antiques
804 W. Greenfield Ave.
414/389-1965

Collectors Toystop
6026 W. Greenfield Ave.
414/771-7622

Past Presence Collectibles
7123 W. Greenfield
414/774-7585

Celebrity Coin & Stamp
4161 S. Howell Ave.
414/747-1888

Peter Bentz Antqs. & Apprsls.
771 N. Jefferson St.
414/271-8866

American Estates
2131 S. Kinnickinnic Ave.
414/483-2110

Milwaukee Antique Center
341 N. Milwaukee St.
414/276-0605

D & H Antiques Toys & Trains
501 W. Mitchell St.
414/643-5340

Echols Antiques & Gfts
6230 W. North Ave.
414/774-5556

Military Relics Shop
6910 W. North Ave.
414/771-4014

Eileen's Warehouse Antiques
325 N. Plankinton Ave.
414/276-0114

Legacies Ltd.
7922 N. Port Washington Rd.
414/352-8114

Town & Country Shop Inc.
8822 N. Port Washington Rd.
414/352-6570

Colonel's Choice
2918 S. 13th St.
414/383-8180

Tony's Resale
949 N. 27th St.
414/931-0949

American Victorian
203 N. Water St.
414/223-1130

Lights of Olde
203 N. Water St.
414/223-1130

Water St. Antiques
318 N. Water St.
414/278-7008

Centuries Antiques
326 N. Water St.
414/278-1111

D & R International Antiques
137 E. Wells St.
414/276-9395

Antique Cupboard Matching
3712 N. 92nd St.
414/464-0556

Elizabeth Bradley Antiques
1115 W. Greentree Road
414/352-1521

Shorewood Coin Shop
4495 N. Oakland Ave.
414/961-0999

34 MINERAL POINT

Livery Antiques
303 Commerce St.
608/987-3833

Green Lantern Antiques
261 High St.
608/987-2312

35 MINOCQUA

Island City Antique Market
8661 Hwy. 51 N
715/356-7003

Hildebrand's Antiques
7537 U.S. Hwy. 51 S
715/356-1971

Finders Keepers
7 Hwy. W
715/356-7208

36 MONROE

New Moon Antiques
1606 11th St.
608/325-9100

Garden Gate Floral & Antiques
1717 11th St.
608/329-4900

Bev's Attic Treasures
1018 17th Ave.
608/325-6200

Breezy Acres Li Antiques
1027 16th Ave.
608/325-1201

It's a Bunch of Crock Antqs.
1027 16th Ave.
608/328-1444

Luecke's Diamond Center Inc.
1029 16th Ave.
608/325-2600

37 MOUNT HOREB

First Street Antiques
111 S. 1st St.
608/437-6767

Hoff Mall Antique Center
101 E. Main St.
608/437-4580

Main Street Antiques
126 E. Main St.
608/437-3233

Isaac's Antiques
132 E. Main St.
608/437-6151

Lucy's Attic
520 Springdale St.
608/437-6140

Yapp's Antique Corner
504 E. Main St.
608/437-8100

38 MUKWONAGO

Country Junction
101 N. Rochester St.
414/363-9474

Indian Creek Antiques
214 S. Rochester St.
414/363-7015

39 NECEDAH

Northland Collectors Mart
211 South Main Street
608/565-3730
Open: Spring/Summer 10-5 Mon.-Sat., 10-4 Sun.; Nov. & Dec. 10-4, 7 days; Jan.-Mar., Thurs.-Sun. 10-4

Directions: Necedah is situated at the intersection of Highways 21 and 80.

Across from the town gazebo sits a collector's haven crammed with antiques and collectibles. Among the extraordinary array of styles, periods, textures, and functions, antiquers roam among furniture, glassware, figurines, pottery, jewelry and artifacts. Consignments accepted.

40 OCONOMOWOC

Mapleton Antiques
W360 8755 Brown Street
414/474-4514

Ye Old Antqs.-Rural
N880 W38726 McMahon Rd.
414/474-4380

Old Homestead Lighting
514 Silver Lake St.
414/567-6543

Gathering Place
5780 359 St.
414/567-5123

Marsh Hill Ltd.
456 N. Waterville Rd.
414/646-2560

41 OSCEOLA

Osceola Antiques
117 Cascade Street
715/294-2886
Open everyday year-round, Mon.-Sat. 10-5, Sun. Noon-5

Directions: Downtown Osceola is on Wisconsin Hwy. 35. From I-94, go north at Hudson on Hwy. 35.

Osceola Antiques is Northwest Wisconsin's largest antique shop. With over 11,000 square feet for prime antique hunting you're sure to find just what you're looking for here. The shop displays furniture of all eras, linens to accent, art, jewelry, loads of glassware and more. For collectors and the curious, over 800 antique reference books are available. Enjoy ice cream, homemade candy or cappuccino while you shop.

42 OSHKOSH

A Blend of the Past Antiques
738 N. Oakwood Rd.
414/235-0969

Cat's Meow Antiques & Cllbls.
807 Ohio St.
414/231-6369

Wagon Wheel Antiques
2326 Oregon St.
414/233-8518

Originals Mall of Antiques
1475 S. Washburn St.
414/235-0495

Impressions-Antiques Etc.
1773 S. Washburn Street
414/235-3899

43 PLATTEVILLE

Marilee's Main Street Mall
70 E. Main St.
608/348-6995

Platteville Antiques
5924 State Road 80 #-81
608/348-4533

Milly McDonnell's
5946 U.S. Hwy. 151
608/348-8500

44 PRINCETON

River City Antique Mall
328 S. Fulton St.
414/295-3475

Parkside Antique Mall
501 S. Fulton St.
414/295-0112

Melchert's Antiques
605 S. Fulton St.
414/295-4243

Merry's Little Toy Shop
615 W. Water St.
414/295-6746

Victorian House Antiques
330 W. Water St.
414/295-4700

Princeton Antique Mall
101 Wisconsin St.
414/295-6515

45 RACINE

Fair Trader
1801 Douglas Ave.
414/637-2222

Ace & Bubba Treasure Hunters
218 6 th St.
414/633-3308

Travel Through Time Antiques
1859 Taylor Ave.
414/637-7721

Another Man's Treasure
1354 Washington Ave.
414/633-6869

Now & Then Gifts & Antiques
1408 Washington Ave.
414/634-8883

D & J's Junque
1428 Washington Ave.
414/633-9884

Avenue Antiques
1436 Washington Ave.
414/637-6613

46 RHINELANDER

Jane's Country Cottage
3961 Indian Lake Rd.
715/272-1444

Demitra Lane Antiques & Gifts
432 Lincoln St.
715/362-2206

Second Hand Rose Antiques
1309 Lincoln St.
715/369-2626

47 RICE LAKE

Country Antique Shop
1505 Fencil Ave.
715/234-4589

Bits of Yesteryear Antiques
2237 Lakeshore Dr
715/234-4641

Victorian Cottage
601 N. Main St.
715/234-3482

Portals to the Past
613 N. Main St.
715/234-7530

48 RICHLAND CENTER

Valley Antiques
186 S. Central Ave.
608/647-3793

Antiques & Etc.
194 E. Court St.
608/647-4732

Memory Lane Antique Mall
177 E. Haseltine St.
608/647-8286

Ray's Trading Post
RR 1
608/536-3803

49 RIVER FALLS

Chicken Coop Antiques
7086 N. 820th Street
715/425-5716

Little River Antiques
363 Cemetery Road
715/425-5522

Homestead Antiques
208 N. Main St.
715/425-9522

County Line Antiques
RR 3 #-148A
715/425-9118

50 SHAWANO

Zurko's Midwest Promotions
211 W. Green Bay St.
715/526-9769

Yesterdays Antique Mall
712 E. Green Bay St.
715/524-6050

A-C Antiques
RR 2
715/524-5254

51 SHEBOYGAN

Craftmaster Antiques & Restoration
2034 N. 15th Street
920/452-2524
Open: Mon.-Sat. 10-5, Closed Sunday

Directions: Take Hwy. 23, exit east to 14th St. Make a left turn on 14th St., Make a right turn on 15th St. or exit Hwy. 42 into Sheboygan. Make a left turn on Geele Ave., make right turn on 15th St.

Enjoy an old mill setting and browse on three floors full of antiques and collectibles. Discover fine furniture, primitives, china, glassware, stoneware, light fixtures, collectibles and a little bit of everything for everyone. The shop holds true to its slogan: *Variety at a reasonable "take home" price!*

Sheboygan Antiques
336 Superior Avenue
414/452-6757

Treasure Gardens
1327 N. 14 th St.
414/458-8232

Sheridan Park General Store
632 S. 14th St.
414/458-5833

Three Barns Full-Two
7377 State Rd. 42
414/565-3050

52 STEVENS POINT

Downtown Antiques Shops
1100 Main St.
715/342-1442

Memory Market
2224 Patch St.
715/344-2026

Second Street Antiques
900 2nd St.
715/341-8611

53 STURGEON BAY

Cottage Antiques and Quiltry
820 Egg Harbor Road
414/746-0944

Westside Antiques
22 S. Madison Ave.
414/746-9038

Antiques of Institute
4530 State Hwy. 57
414/743-1511

54 STURTEVANT

Revival
9410 Durand Ave.
414/886-3666

Carridge House Antiques
9525 Durand Ave.
414/886-6678

School Days Mall
9500 Durand Ave.
414/886-1069

Antique Castle Mall
1701 S.E. Frontage Rd.
414/886-6001

Tree of Life
2810 Wisconsin St.
414/886-1601

55 SUN PRAIRIE

Circa Victoriana
104 E. Main St.
608/837-4115

Coffee Mill Antique Mall
3472 Hoepker Rd.
608/837-7099

56 SUPERIOR

Superior Collectible Inv.
1709 Belknap St.
715/394-4315

Port of Call Superior Mktplace.
4101 E. 2 nd St.
715/398-5030

Berger Hardware & Antiques
525 Tower Ave.
715/394-3873

Curious Goods
1717 Winter St.
715/392-7550

57 TOMAH

Antique Mall of Tomah
I-94 and Hwy. 21 East
608/372-7853
Open 7 days a week: Apr.-Dec., Mon.-Sat. 8-8, Sun. 9-5; Jan.-Mar. 9-5 daily

Directions: From I-94 and Hwy. 21 East, take Exit 143 to Tomah.

The 60-plus dealers of quality antiques and collectibles

specialize in "smalls." Primitives, jewelry, glassware, plates and dishware, in addition to a large assortment of lamps make up the pleasing selection. The stock of furniture is limited but offers fine workmanship and good condition.

Oakdale Antique Mall
RR 3
608/374-4700

Esther's Antiques
RR 4
608/372-6690

58 TURTLE LAKE

Memories Antiques & Cllbls.
231 W. U.S. Hwy. 8
715/986-4950

Country Side Antiques
12 W. US Hwy. 8
715/986-2737

59 UNION GROVE

Remember When
20715 Durand Ave.
414/878-4101

Ye Olde Red Barn Antiques
20816 Durand Ave.
414/878-2044

Storm Hall Antique Mall
835 15 th Ave.
414/878-1644

House on Main
1121 Main St.
414/878-1045

60 VIROQUA

Golden Comb & Etc.
124 W. Court St.
608/637-7835

Main Street Antique Mall
207 N. Main St.
608/637-8655

Etc. Antiques & Collectibles
124 W. Court Street
608/637-6429

Antiques Cellar
205 N. Main St.
608/634-2749

Lam's Ear Country Gifts
608/637-2099

Small Ventures
608/637-8880

61 WALWORTH

On The Square Antique Mall
109 Madison
414/275-9858

Bittersweet Farm
114 Madison
414/275-3062

Van's Antiques
1937 U.S. Hwy. 14
414/275-2773

62 WATERFORD

Freddy Bear's Antique Mall
2819 Beck Dr
414/534-2327

Heavenly Haven Antique Mall
318 W. Main St.
414/534-4400

Afternoon Tea Antqs. & Furn.
411 E. Main St.
414/534-3664

Dover Pond Antiques
28016 Washington Ave.
414/534-6543

63 WAUKESHA

Mill Creek Farm Bed and Breakfast
S47 W22099 Lawnsdale Road
414/542-4311
Office hours: 7-11pm, 7 days.
Rates: $65-75

Directions: From I-43 going west, take Racine Avenue (Exit 54) north 2 miles to County 1 (Lawnsdale Road). Turn left on County 1, go 1.6 miles. The farm is on the left. Located 7 miles southeast of Waukesha, 20 miles southwest of Milwaukee.

Located on 160 acres in Waukesha County, you'll find one of the area's loveliest, private retreats. Mill Creek Farm offers two special rooms adorned with fine linens and all the amenities to make your stay a pleasant one. Guests share a fully renovated, skylit bath, elegantly decorated for comfort and convenience right down to the heated towel rack! The reading/television room offers a subdued atmosphere for curling up with a good book or watching a romantic movie.

This wooded Shangri-la offers a variety of outdoor activities to help you escape. You can head out on a paddle boat and absorb the serenity of Mill Creek Pond, or fish for bass and bluegills in this one-acre spring fed pond.

For the more active relaxer, there are 3 miles of groomed trails to hike, jog, or cross country ski.

This amusing anecdote was submitted by the Mill Creek Farm Bed and Breakfast: "Last summer we had as our guests a young family from the Chicago area. Mother, father, and two sons came for a three-day period planning to enjoy the Milwaukee Zoo, Wisconsin State Fair, Old World Wisconsin, and several other attractions in the area. However, when they got here they discovered our pond for which we provided them with fishing poles and paddle boat. The boys began to catch fish, frogs, and all manner of pond life. As the first day progressed, they decided to stay on the farm and not venture out for other sights. The second day, the same decision. Third day, same decision. So it turned out, they never left the farm for the whole three-day stay! And as they were leaving on the morning of the fourth day, Noah, who is 7, turned to his father and said, 'Dad, how much would it cost to buy this place?' We concluded that Noah was the youngest sale prospect we've ever had!"

Just a Little Bit of Country
N4 W22496 Bluemont Rd.
414/542-8050

Babbling Brook
416 E. Broadway
414/544-4739

Store
301 N. Grand Ave.
414/547-2740

James K Beier Antique Maps
2312 N. Grandview Blvd
414/549-5985

Susan H Kruger Antiques
401 Madison St.
414/542-7722

Gift Sampler
275 W. Main St.
414/544-1343

Bix Stripping & Refinishing
850 Martin St.
414/542-3185

Fortunate Finds
124 E. Saint Paul Ave.
414/542-8110

A Dickens of a Place
521 Wisconsin Ave.
414/542-0702

64 WAUPACA

Grey Dove Antiques & Resale
118 S. Main St.
715/258-0777

Danes Home
301 N. Main St.
715/256-0693

65 WAUSAU

Kimberly's Old House Gallery
1600 Jonquil Lane
715/359-5077
Open 10-5 Thurs., Fri., Sat., and by chance or appointment

Roam 10,000-square-feet packed with antique architectural pieces. Fireplaces, lighting, plumbing, and millwork represent some of the finds. Building salvage, cross-country delivery and locating services also available.

Kasen's Bittersweet Antique
8705 Bittersweet Rd.
715/359-2777

Rib Mt. Antique Mall
3300 Eagle Ave.
715/848-5564

Stoney Creek Antqs. & Jwlry.
4307 State Hwy. 52
715/842-8354

Ginny's Antiques & Consign.
416 3rd St.
715/848-1912

66 WAUTOMA

Coach's Corner Antiques
2192 Hwy. 152
414/787-3845

Silver Lake Antique Mall
W. 7853 State Rd. 21
414/787-1325

Finishing Touch Antiques
502 W. Main Street
414/787-2525

67 WEBSTER

Lake Country Mall
Hwy. 35
715/866-7670

Old House Antiques
7419 Airport Road
715/349-7289

68 WILD ROSE

Finders Keepers Antiques
526 Front
414/622-3077

Sampler
N6571 State Rd. 22
414/622-4499

69 WISCONSIN DELLS

Antique Mall of Wis. Dells
720 Oak St.
608/254-2422

Days Gone By Antique Mall
729 Oak St.
608/254-6788

70 WISCONSIN RAPIDS

Kellner Pioneer Shop
8620 Cty. Trk. W.
715/424-2507

Antique Heaven
3620 8th St.
715/423-3599

Whetstone's Antiques
322 State Hwy. 73 S
715/325-5139

Aunt Nancy's Antiques Cllbls.
6421 State Hwy. 13 S
715/325-2800

71 WOODRUFF

Mill
1405 1st Ave.
715/356-5468

Roxane's Antiques & Gifts
189 U.S. Hwy. 51 N
715/356-7718

Town N Travel Antique Shop
237 U.S. Hwy. 51 N
715/358-2535

Wyoming

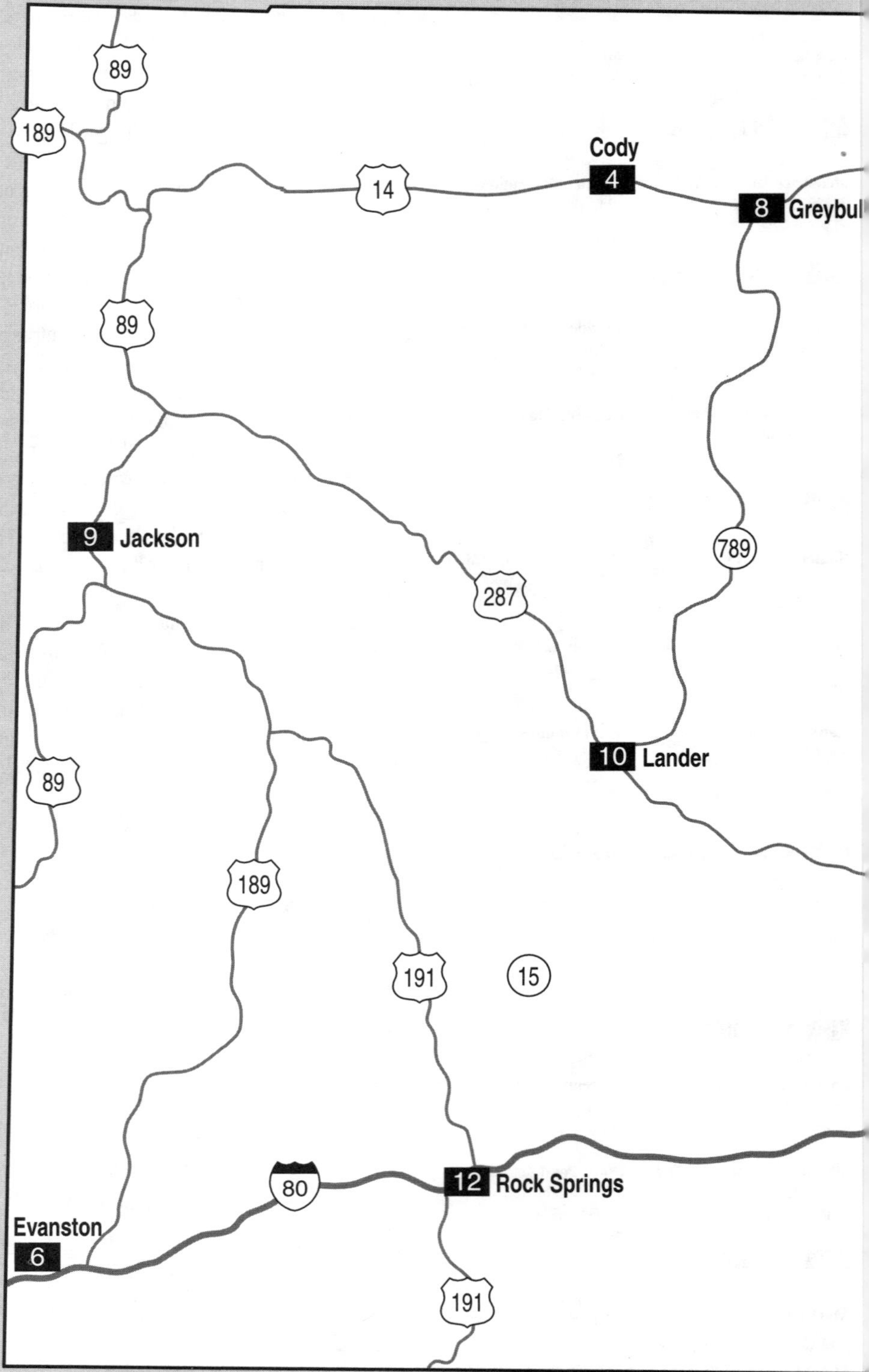
89
189
Cody
4
14
8 Greybul
89
9 Jackson
789
287
10 Lander
89
189
191
15
80
12 Rock Springs
Evanston
6
191

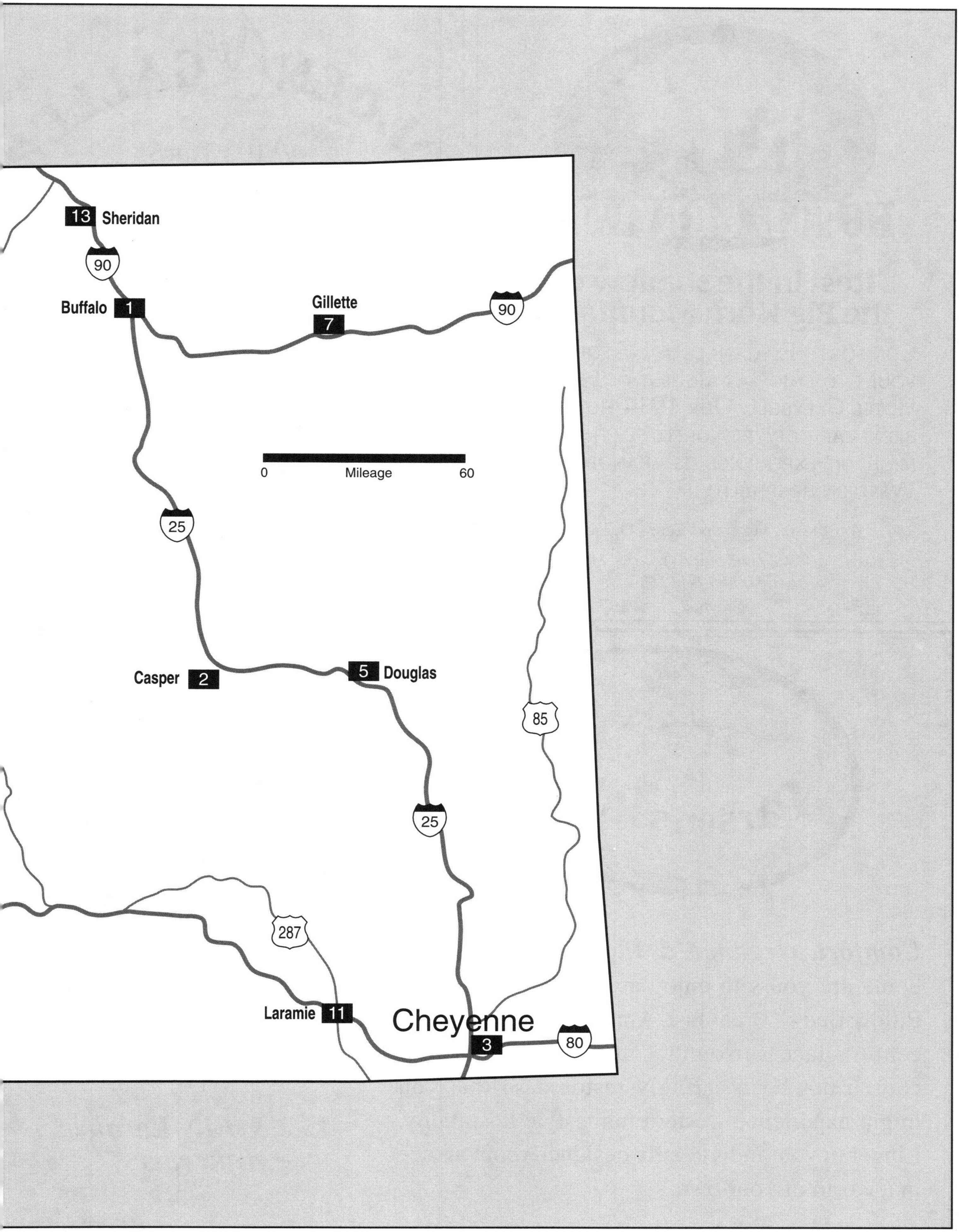
13 Sheridan
90
Buffalo 1
Gillette
7
90
0 Mileage 60
25
Casper 2
5 Douglas
85
25
287
Laramie 11
Cheyenne
3
80

1 BUFFALO

Yesterdays Treasures
100 E. Hart St.
307/684-7318

Rock Bottom Country Store
29448 Hwy. 196
307/684-2364

Heritage Antiques
22 S. Main St.
307/684-2326

2 CASPER

Doubletree Antiques & More
146 South Elk
307/472-4858
Open Tue.-Sat., 10-5, closed Sunday and Monday

Directions: Exit off I-25 at McKinley Street. Go south on McKinley to First Street. Turn east on first then south on Elk.

This shop has a constantly changing inventory, which means business is good. On a regular basis, they stock 1800s through Art Deco furniture, a wide selection of oak furniture, glassware such as Depression, carnival and much more. An additional bonus; there is a furniture refinisher on site who gives free estimates. What more can you ask for?

Carriage House Antiques
830 W. 15th Street
307/266-2987
Open Tue.-Sat., 10-5; Fri. 11-5; closed Sunday and Monday

Directions: Take Poplar Street Exit off I-25. Travel south on Poplar to CY Avenue. Turn left on CY then immediately right on 15th Street.

Carriage House has a complete line of antiques including glassware, pottery, jewelry, toys, Cowboy and Indian collectibles.

Mary's
341 W. Yellowstone Hwy.
307/577-5206

What's In Store
211 W. Collins Dr.
307/237-8137

Antique Warehouse
2080 Fairgrounds Rd.
307/234-2034

Antique Lighting Inc.
1514 S. Kenwood St.
307/265-4614

3 CHEYENNE

Sidekick Antique Mart
1408 S. Greeley Hwy.
307/635-3136
Open 7 days a week, 10-6

Directions: Exit south on Greeley Hwy. off I-80. Located one to two miles on the right.

This multi-dealer market (70-80 dealers) with its 10,000 square foot of space is filled with primitives, old tools, barnwood furniture, 1800s to 1950s oak, walnut and mahogany furniture, Fenton, Cambridge and Imperial glassware, porcelains, black powder guns, brewery, Coke, sports and Indian memorabilia and Persian rugs. The inventory is limitless. If you can't find it here, you'll probably have a hard time finding it anywhere.

Porch Swing Bed and Breakfast
712 East 20th Street
307/778-7182
Rates: $43-66

The Porch Swing Bed and Breakfast in its charming authentically restored 1907 two-story cottage is filled with antiques. Handmade quilts are on every bed. Summer gardens are fragrant with flowers and herbs. Edible flowers are served as well as a full breakfast by the fire in the winter and on the back porch in the summer. Located within walking distance is downtown Cheyenne where you may enjoy museums and restaurants as well as other forms of entertainment. Not far from the bed and breakfast, mountain parks for hiking, bicycling, and cross-country or downhill skiing are available.

Old Gold Antiques
1309 W. 18 th St.
307/632-8557

Odds & Ends
3208 S. Greeley Hwy.
307/635-8535

Tomorrow's Treasures Antqs.
903 W. Lincoln Ave.
307/634-1900

Bart's Flea Market
Lincolnway & Evans
307/632-0063

Royce's Releques
1020 E. Pershing Blvd.
307/634-8324

Treasures from the Heart
1024 E. Pershing Blvd.
307/638-6736

Collectibles Corner
2622 Pioneer Ave.
307/634-7706

Antiques Central
2311 Reed Ave.
307/638-6181

Grandma's Attic
113 W. 17th St.
307/638-6126

Frontier Antiques
216 W. 17th St.
307/635-5573

Downtown Flea Market
312 W. 17th St.
307/638-3751

The Avenue Flea Market
315-1/2 E. 7th Ave.
307/635-5600

The Bargain Barn
2112 Snyder Ave.
307/635-2844

4 CODY

Parson's Pillow Bed & Breakfast
1202 14th Street
307/587-2382

Directions: Located just off Hwys 14, 16, 20 and 120. For specific directions from your location please call the Innkeepers, Lee & Elly Larabee.

Put on your boots and amble down "Main Street" Cody, visiting fine restaurants, shops, and galleries. After a hard day on the antique trail, have an old fashioned ice cream soda...or saddle up old tin lizzy and head out to the Cody Nite Rodeo, Old West Trail Town or visit the Buffalo Bill Museum.

Then, after a short ride out of town watching the buffalo roam and the antelope play, knock the dust off your boots at Parson's Pillow Bed and Breakfast, a wood framed church dedicated in 1902 as a Methodist Episcopal Church. Prior to that, Mr. Beck, one of William F. Cody's closet friends who helped Buffalo Bill in the founding and building of Cody, was involved in a poker game one evening. The pot grew to a whopping $500!!! At that point, Mr. Beck and his opponent agreed that the winner would use the money to build Cody's first church building. Mr. Beck won and built an Episcopal Church. However, even in losing, the Methodists built their own church at the corner of 14th and Beck Avenue! The former bell tower with its magnificent bell, which was donated by a cousin of Buffalo Bill's (herself an Episcopalian), was the envy of Mr. Beck and all the Episcopalians!

Today, comfort, elegance and the sense of coming home are yours to enjoy as a guest of Parson's Pillow B & B. Filled with antiques and turn of the century lace, this 1902 former church has been caringly restored so that all who enter it might experience western homestyle hospitality. Choose from four themed guest rooms; the Rose - filled with Barbara Cartland novels to enhance your romantic fantasies; the Garden - provides a private vintage pedestal tub; the Western - rustic simplicity with your own private oak framed prairie tub; and the Memories - featuring an antique bed with fluffly feather pillows.

Breakfast is served in the guests dining room.

Olde General Store
1323 Sheridan Avenue
307/587-5500
Open Summer 9-9 (7 days a week), June-August; Winter 9-6, Mon.-Sat., 12-4 Sun.

Directions: Hwy. 14 is the main street in Cody. Shop is located on Hwy. 14 which is also Sheridan Avenue.

The two floors of this shop specialize in mostly oak furniture including a few pieces of Mission oak. They also have added a line of handmade Wyoming log furniture. Throughout the store, you'll find primitives, collectibles, western memorabilia as well as gifts and decorative accessories.

Old West Antiques
1215 Sheridan Ave.
307/587-9014

The Wiley House
913 Sheridan Ave.
307/587-6030

Cottage Antiques
1327 Rumsey Ave.
307/527-4650

5 DOUGLAS

Antiques Etc.
404 S. 4th St.
307/358-2253

Country Touch
421 S. 4th St.
307/358-3641

6 EVANSTON

The story of Evanston is largely a story of the Union Pacific Railroad, which was, at that time laying track through the country at a rate of seven miles per day. By November, the graders had reached Bear River City, about 90 miles west of Green River.

The Bear River City Riot of November 21, 1868 was instigated by the rough element which preyed on the railroad workers. The riot has served as the prototype for nearly every Western movie ever made—the good guys against the bad guys. Soldiers from Fort Bridger were called to quell the disorder, but the good guys had things well in hand by the time they arrived.

Bear River City eventually grew into Evanston, which was named for the surveyor who platted the town, and Evanston became the commercial and shipping center of the area.

Sheila's Memories Antiques and Collectibles
900 Main St.
307/789-0638
Mon.-Sat., 10-5

Directions: Take Front Street exit off I-80. Go 3 blocks; turn left at 9th Street. Go one block to Main. Located at the corner of 9th and Main. An alternative: Exit I-80 at Harrison Drive. Go to Main Street; turn left and store is at the corner of 9th and Main.

Collectors listen up! Inside this 7,200 square foot shop, boasting to have a large selection of everything, sit two rare and in good condition 1950s pinball machines. Hummel figurines grace tabletops as well. Grandeur and beauty increase with prints from Parrish, Fox and Thompson. Additional pieces include Victorian furniture and accessories, old dolls and toys, as well as vintage jewelry. Appraisal services are offered.

Eliza Doolittle's
944 Main St.
307/789-5656

7 GILLETTE

Deer Park Bed and Breakfast and Cobweb Shoppe Antiques
2660 Bishop Road
307/682-9832 OR 800/565-9713

Directions: Exit Hwy. 59 South from I-90. Travel 10 miles. Turn east on Bishop Road and continue 8 miles.

Step back in time as you imagine the luxury of the Victorian era. You may relax in the Victorian antique furnishings in the large, luxurious rooms with private baths. Gaze out on the peaceful countryside and watch the deer in the meadows. Take a stroll through the Cobweb Shoppe, the on site antique shop, where you will find Victorian furniture, hand painted china, all types of lamps and much, much more.

Doc's Swap Shop Antiques
950 Chandler Lane
307/682-1801

Flower Boutique
1001 S. Douglas Hwy.
307/682-4569

8 GREYBULL

Established in 1909 as a railroad town, Greybull is named for the Greybull River which itself was derived from; a legendary grey bison bull said to be sacred to the Indians. Currently a center for bentonite mining, Greybull is also a region rich in Indian relics, fossils and semiprecious stones. The Greybull Museum (free admission) is just one block east of the Post Office on Greybull Avenue. Displayed are Indian apparel and artifacts, old weapons and pioneer utensils. There are outstanding agate collections dating back millions of years. Don't miss the largest fossil ammonite in the world.

Historic Hotel Greybull
602 Greybull Avenue
307/765-2012, 800/417-1115

Directions: Located at the crossroads of Hwys. 14, 16, 20 and 789. For specific directions from your location please call the hosts, Jason and Laura DeTullio.

Built in 1914 during the boom days of the railroad in the Old West, this historic hotel offers the opportunity to experience the grandeur of the olden days. Enter under the awning and find eleven upstairs rooms, each with its own personality and grandeur in decor and color to fit your every mood. Join fellow guest in the "Gathering Room" for a sumptuous breakfast buffet, beverages and snacks.

9 JACKSON

Samuel's Continental Imports
745 West Broadway
307/733-4794
Open Mon.-Sat., 10-9; Sunday by appointment only

Directions: Jackson Hole is considered the kick off point when approaching the Grand Tetons and Yellowstone National Park from the south, Samuel's is easy to find. Just follow the signs on I-80 or I-15 and you will arrive at the doorsteps at 745 West Broadway as you enter the town of Jackson, Wyoming, Samuel's is the large green building just opposite the Virginia Lodge. You can't miss it. The American and Italian flags are always flying outside the door.

Samuel's Continental Imports had its beginning in 1993, when two people, Sam Galano and Molly Morgan, with a love for fine old European and American furniture felt that there was a lack of the same in the ever increasing number of antiques and designer stores in Jackson Hole, Wy., and the surrounding areas. So they decided to bring "the stuff" they loved to this western town through overseas buyers in addition to their own finds in barns, estate sales, auction houses, and private homes. They imported the graceful lines of many eras and styles and rejoiced in the warm patinas of the quality wood that European and American craftsmen have used to create decorative and practical furniture for generations. They even have an "in house doctor" for the pieces. Sam Galano, part owner of the business, has a highly trained eye and years of knowledge and expertise in restoration. Samuel's Continental Imports also offers custom framing and uses only conservation materials to preserve the quality of each piece being framed. Sam is responsible for this work and takes an artistic approach to insure the art work is complimented, not overwhelmed. They haven't ignored the smalls, offering everything from art glass and fine china to nail kegs and horseshoes. The store carries an extensive line of antique lighting fixtures and showcases the original artwork of wonderful artists.

Showcase Antiques
115 W. Broadway Ave.
307/733-4848

Bear Print
140 N. Cache
307/733-1558

Fighting Bear Antiques
35 E. Simpson
307/733-2669

Beyond Necessities Antiques
335 S. Millward
307/733-7492

Back Porch
145 E. Pearl Ave.
307/733-0030

Cheap Thrills
250 W. Pearl Ave.
307/739-9266

10 LANDER

Village Store
23 Shrine Club Road
307/332-2801

Charlotte's Web
228 W. Main Street
307/332-2801

Annie's Attic
523 Garfield
307/332-2279

11 LARAMIE

The city of Laramie is noted as playing a definite role in the testing of many of Wyoming's unique laws. Reporters flocked to the Gem City of the Plains to witness the first woman in the world to serve on a jury in March, 1870. In the fall of 1871, another first occurred in Laramie when "Grandma" Louiza Swain went to the polls and was the first woman in the world to vote in a general election.

Golden Flea Gallery
725 Skyline road
307/745-7055
Open daily, 10-6

Directions: On the south side of Laramie near the Holiday Inn and Motel 6. Once on Skyline Road, go 4/10 mile as it bends to the left, Golden Flea is on the left side of the Street. Getting to Skyline Road: From I-80 heading east: take Exit 313 (Third Street). Turn left onto Skyline Road (at Holiday Inn). From I-80 heading West: take Exit 313 (Third Street). Turn left onto third Street. Go 2/10 mile then turn left as though to get on I-80 East, but then immediately turn right onto Service Road (Skyline Road) by Holiday Inn. From Hwy. 287 North from Fort Collins, Colo.: turn right as if to get on I-80 East, then immediately turn right onto Service (Skyline) Road.

The "great wide open" of Wyoming has come indoors at this 20,000 square foot gallery. Inside, among the wares of over 140 dealers, you can wander among antique furnishings and accessories, collectibles, old records and books. An interesting and surprising assortment of gift items adds to the greatness of this showcase named after such a small creature (the flea).

Country Antiques 2nd Story
105 E. Ivinson Ave.
307/745-4423

Curiosity Shoppe
206 S. 2nd St.
307/745-4760

Antique Attic
207 S. 2nd St.
307/721-3134

Granny's Attic
1311 S. 3rd St.
307/721-9664

Under One Roof
1002 S. 3rd St.
307/742-8469

12 ROCK SPRINGS

Olde Towne Antiques
426 South Main Street
307/382-3207
Hours: Mon.-Sat. 10 to 5

Directions: Exit I-80 at Elk Street. Travel south to old downtown Rock Springs.

This eight-dealer shop offers a large selection Depression glass, pottery, kitchen collectibles, advertising and railroad items, 1920s and '30s furniture, stoneware and toys. Big Selection, Great Prices!

Antique Mall
411 N. Front Street
307/362-9611

Tynsky's Rock Shop
706 Dewar Drive
307/362-5031

13 SHERIDAN

Raven's Nest Antiques
1617 N. Main Street
307/672-8171
Open Mon.-Sat. 10-5, closed Sunday

Directions: Traveling east on I-90 exit Sheridan Main Downtown. Shop is about eight blocks from I-90 across from Kentucky Fried Chicken.

This five dealer, 3,000 square foot shop features High Boys, oak and pine Hoosiers as well as other fine pieces of furniture. From days of yore you will find elegant glassware, fiesta, sheet music, vintage clothing, costume jewelry and Western memorabilia.

Pack Rat
157 W. Brundage St.
307/672-0539

Interior Images
200 W. Brundage St.
307/674-7604

Best Out West Antqs. & Cllbls.
109 N. Main St.
307/674-5003

Q Man Music & Antiques
528 N. Main St.
307/672-9636

North Main Antiques
1135 N. Main St.
307/672-3838

Notes

Shows & Auctions

Below is a listing of shows and auctions throughout the U.S. The information was provided by promoters and auctioneers who called to have their show or auction listed. Since show and auction dates change, it would be best to call the particular show or auction of interest and have them place you on their mailing lists. Some shows and auctions are listed in more detail throughout *The Antique Atlas*. Those particular ones are indicated with an asterisk *.

Alabama

Auctions

***Pell City Auction Co. #39**
Highway 231 South
Pell City, Alabama
205/525-4100

Arizona

Shows

Acorn Antique Guild
Scottsdale, Arizona
602/258-5700

Jack Black Enterprises
Mesa, Arizona
1-800-678-9987

The Brass Armadillo Antique Mall
Phoenix, Arizona
1-800-965-7117

Arkansas

Shows

Antique Toy & Doll Show
Eureka Springs, Arkansas
501/253-2244

Buchannan Productions
Little Rock, Arkansas
405/478-4050

David B. Yust
Little Rock, Arkansas
417/782-2687

California

Shows

Laughing Whale Productions
714/367-1222

South Coast Shows, Inc.
714/840-9649

Americana Enterprises, Inc.
213/655-5703

Sy Miller Productions
760/930-0731

Northridge Antique Market
562/633-3836

Monthly Antique Market
Glendale, California
213/380-2626

Bill Weinstein Productions
Healdsburg, California
707/578-7772

MCM Productions
Santa Fe, California
505/995-9678

Canning Attractions
San Bernardino, California
213/560-SHOW Ext. 12

R & N Postcard Productions
Foster City, California
818/287-6066

Bullock Productions
Pomona, California
310/430-5112

Miller Productions, Inc.
Ventura, California
619/930-0731

South Coast Shows, Inc.
Santa Barbara, California
714/840-9649

Golden Gate Shows
San Raphael, California
415/459-1998

Lois Over Productions
(Dolls & Bears)
Hayward, California
510/581-0223

Antique Productions
Modesto, California
209/527-3401

Sy Miller Productions
San Diego, California
619/930-0731

Postcard Productions
Buena Park, California
818/287-6066

Bustamante Enterprises, Inc.
Santa Clara, California
209/358-3134

Auctions

Santa Margarita Auction Barn
P. O. Box 702
San Margarita, Ca. 93453
805/438-5395

Early American Auctions
P. O. Box 3341
La Jolla, California 92038

Butterfield & Butterfield's
San Francisco, California
1-800-596-3146

Colorado

Shows

Gemini Productions
Glenwood Springs, Colorado
303/430-9771

Peak Promotions
Denver, Colorado
1-800-333-3532

Continental Shows Ltd.
Durango, Colorado
1-800-423-6846

GPL Productions
Steamboat Springs, Colorado
208/939-4422

World Wide Antique Shows
Denver, Colorado
1-800-525-2729

Auctions

Pettigrew Auction Co.
Colorado Springs, Colorado
719-633-7963

Atomic Antiques Auction
Denver, Colorado
303/722-0530

Connecticut

Shows

The Maven Co.
Berlin, Connecticut
203/758-3880

Cord Shows Ltd.
New Milford, Connecticut
914/273-4656

F & B Sports Cards Inc.
Danbury, Connecticut
718/667-9588

Revival Promotions
Farmington, Connecticut
508/839-9735

Little Rigger Toy Shows
Bristol, Connecticut
860/589-8037

***Marilyn Gould Antiques**
Promotions Inc. #75
203/762-3525

Florida

Shows

Piccadilly Promotions
West Palm Beach, Fla.
813/345-4431

King Antique Shows
Tallahasse, Fla.
904/269-2431

Dolphin Promotions, Inc.
Ft. Lauderdale, Fla.
954/563-6747

Palm Coast Productions
Daytona, Fla.
904/673-3178

Weather Vane Antique Shows
North Miami Beach, Fla.
813/895-2492

Auctions

Enterprise Auction
Holly Hills, Fla.
904/255-9191

Georgia

Shows

Lakewood Antiques Market
Atlanta, Ga.
404/622-4488

The Nelson Garretts, Inc.
Athens, Ga.
803/849-1949

Scott Antiques Market
Atlanta, Ga.
614/569-4112

Auctions

***Big Shanty Antiques & Auctions #35**
Kennesaw, GA.
770/795-1704

Idaho

Shows

Alee Leighton
Hailey, ID.
208/788-9292

Illinois

Shows

Four Star Group Shows
Moline, Illinois
309/757-1858

Frank J. Galati Promotions
Collinsville, Illinois
573/775-2308

Trend Studios
Rosemont, Illinois
630/837-0482

Zurko Pormotions
Mt. Prospect, Illinois
715/526-9769

Sherry's Teddy Bears, Inc.
Westmont, Illinois
773/594-1710

Marilyn Sugarman Shows
Wheaton, Illinois
847/455-6090

Lake County Promotions
Grayslake, Illinois
847/223-1433

Mid America Promotions, Inc.
Springfield, Illinois
816/220-2870

Brymax Enterprises, Inc.
Niles, Illinois
708/851-6023

Dolphin Promotions, Inc.
Rosemont, Illinois
954/566-1982

Auctions

Leslie Hindman Auctioneers
Chicago, Illinois
312/670-0010

Indiana

Shows

Brymax Enterprises
Merrilville, Indiana
708/851-6023

Stewart Promotions
Indianapolis, Indiana
502/456-2244

Collectors Carnival, Inc.
Evansville, Indiana
812/471-9419

Heartland Promotions
Kokomo, Indiana
614/759-9614

Hoosier Antiques Expo
317/862-3865

231 Expo Center
812/937-7188

Iowa

Shows

The Brass Armadillo Antique
Des Moines, Iowa
1-800-965-7117

Zurko Promotions
715/526-9769

Heartland Promotions
1-800-232-8334

Stookey Companies
515/277-8958

Iowa Show Productions, Inc.
319/232-0218

Midwest Antique Guild
507/368-9343

Kansas

Shows

Advantage Productions, Inc.
Overland Park, Kansas
913/681-9800

Continental Shows
Wichita, Kansas
1-800-423-6846

Heart of America Toys
913/451-7622

Gemini Productions, Inc.
303/430-9771

Shows

Woody Auction
Kansas City, Kansas
316/747-2694

Kentucky

Shows

Stewart Promotions
502/456-2244

Rex Roger Productions
502/366-3828

Auctions

Hays & Assoc. Inc.
502/584-4297

***Diamond D Auctions #35**
Russellville, Kentucky
502/726-7892

Louisiana

Shows

Continental Shows Ltd.
1-800-423-6846

Larry Brown Promotions
1-800-437-1516

Auctions

***Louisiana Purchases Auction Co. #2**
Baton Rouge, Louisiana
504/346-1803

Maine

Shows

Forbes & Turner Antiques Shows
207/767-3967

Auctions

***Houston Brooks Auction #10**
Burnham, Maine
1-800-254-2214

Maryland

Shows

Bellman Collectors
410/329-2188

Bill Peters Productions, Inc.
717/671-8220

Sha-Dor Inc.
301/738-1966

Tobacco Barn Show
301/627-8469

Auctions

Greenberg Shows, Inc.
410/795-7447

Massachusetts

Shows

Malden Bridge Productions
508/636-3382

***Brimfield Antique Shows #11**
(See Brimfield Mass. for info)

Drummer Boy Antiques Show
Bernice &David Bornstein Shows
P. O. Box 2204
Marblehead, Massachusetts 01945
508/744-2731

Central Park Antiques Show
413/596-9257

J & J Promotions
413/245-3436

Lori Faxon - Dealers Choice
508/347-3929

Greenburg Shows
410/795-7447

New England Antiques Market
413/245-3348

Atlantic Group
508/379-9733

Michigan

Shows

***Michigan Antqs. Festival #42**
Midland, Michigan
517/687-9035

***Margaret Brusher #3**
Ann Arbor, Michigan
313/662-9453

M & M Enterprises
810/469-1706

Wood & Fulkerson
616/453-8780

Heartland Promotions
614/759-9614

R. R. Promotions, Inc.
313/455-2110

Auctions

Recycled Time Antiques & Auctions
616/258-3494

Minnesota

Shows

Carol's Dollhouse
612/755-7475

Zurko's Promotions
715/526-9769

Prime Promotions
612/771-3476

Midwest Antique Guild
507/368-9343

Townsend Promotions
507/288-0320

Heartland Promotions
614/759-9614

Auctions

Smith Auctions
612/434-4038

Mississippi

Shows

Emery Exibitors Inc.
1-800-246-2858

B & B Promotions, Inc.
601/878-6600

Bagwell Antiques Show & Trail
601/856-8948

Auctions

Gold Coast Antiques & Auctions Gallery
601/364-1196

Missouri

Shows

Jeff Williams Productions
816/228-5811

Mid America Productions Inc.
816/220-2870

Peak Promotions
1-800-333-3532

Heartland Promotions
614/759-9614

Jeanne Fisherman Shows
810/548-9066

Auctions

Meadows Auction Center
816/313-2104

Nebraska

Shows

Gemini Promotions Inc.
303/430-9771

David Yust
417/782-2687

Barbara Lupton
402/346-6111

Heartland Promotions
614/759-9614

Jack Lawton Webb
International Shows
417/781-4000

Devine Promotions
712/323-5233

Nevada

Shows

Piccadilly Promotions
813/345-4431

Meadows Lane
702/870-2078

New Hampshire

Shows

***New England Antique Show #8**
Center Sandwich, New Hampshire
603/539-1900

Auctions

Garry Wallace Auction Gallery
Rt. 16
Ossipee, New Hampshire
603/539-5276

New Jersey

Shows

Nadia Promotions Inc.
215/643-1396

Stella Show Management Co.
212/255-0020

Bellman Collectors
410/329-2188

F & B Sports Cards, Inc.
718/667-9588

Auctions

***David Rago Auctions #37**
Lambertville, New Jersey
609/397-9374

New Mexico

Shows

Ameri West Shows
1-800-355-4264

Whitehawk Association
505/992-8929

Auctions

The Wright Auction Co.
505/881-4567

New York

Shows

Cord Shows Ltd.
914/273-4667

Memory Lane Promotions
718/428-0829

Sanford Smith's Shows
212/777-5218

Peddler Inc.
716/287-2777

Larry Stowell Promotions
716/924-4530

Paul DeCarlo
516/289-7398

Shows by Ruth
516/499-7586

Elias PeKale Shows
516/868-2751

Strawberry Hill Shows
607/785-5058

Malden Bridge Productions
508/636-3382

Gloria Rothstein Shows Inc.
914/782 SHOW

North Carolina

Stewart Antiques Show
1-800-869-0636

Metrolina Expo
1-800-824-3770

Terry & Brenda Merritt
904/781-9684

Piccadilly Promotions
813/345-4431

King Antique Shows, Inc.
904/269-2431

Auctions

***Village Square Auctions #31**
Hillsborough, N.C.
919/732-8799

North Dakota

Shows

Bruce Skogan
701/223-6185

Ohio

Shows

Marion Coblentz
330/877-9860

Sha Dor Inc.
301/738-1966

Columbus Productions
614/781-0070

Jen & Job Stofft
812/547-5707

Luck Promotions, Inc.
330/867-6724

Antiques Show & Market
937/325-0053

Heartland Promotions
614/759-9614

Bruce Metzger
513/738-2577

Auctions

Treadway Gallery
513/321-6742

Norton Auctioneers
517/279-9063

Oklahoma

Shows

Buchanan Productions
405/478-4050

Roy L. Baker
918/749-4707

Heartland Promotions
1-800-232-8334

Jack Lawton Webb Int'l Shows
417/781-4000

Fiesta Club of America, Inc.
815/282-2585

David B. Yust
417/782-2687

Continental Shows Ltd.
1-800-423-6846

Heart of Tulsa
1-800-755-5488

Oregon

Shows

Collectors Market
503/283-2940

Auctions

***Auction Co. of Southern Oregon**
541/267-5361

Pennsylvania

Shows

***Jim Burke Antq. Shows #151**
York, Pa.
717/397-7209

***York Tailgate Antqs. #151**
York, Pa.
703/914-1268

Great Eastern Productions
215/529-7215

Marilyn Gehman
717/484-4115

Renninger's Promotions
717/385-0104

Carlisle Productions
717/243-7855

Bellman Collectors
410/329-2188

Raab Enterprises, Inc.
216/237-3424

Heritage Promotions
717/620-2422

Greenberg Shows, Inc.
410/795-7447

The Old Show
412/228-3045

Rhode Island

Shows

Malden Bridge Productions, Inc.
508/636-3382

South Carolina

Shows

Terry Brenda Merrit
904/781-9684

The Nelson Garretts Inc.
803/849-1949

Jeff Stewart Antiques Shows
941/627-9805

South Dakota

Barbara Lupton
402/346-6111

Tennessee

Shows

***Heart of Country Antqs. #58**
Nashville, Tennessee
1-800-862-1090

Jack Lawton Webb
International Shows
417/781-4000

Esau's Inc.
1-800-588-ESAU

Auctions

Stephen Shutt's Auctions
P.O. Box 1124
White House, TN. 37118

***Mid-Town Auction #7**
Brownsville, Tennessee
901/772-3382

***Leon Tyewater Auctions #14**
College Grove, Tennessee
615/790-7145

***The Antique Marketplace #66**
Shelbyville, Tennessee
615/684-8493

Texas

Shows

***Emma Lee Turney #129**
Round Top, Texas
281/493-5501

Continental Shows Ltd.
1-800-423-6846

Larry Brown Promotions
1-800-437-1516

Calvert Antique Guild
409/364-2933

International Shows
417/781-4000

Ollie Maye West
817/752-5179

Auctions

Diamond Star Auctions
2721 N. Jackson
Palastine, TX 75801
903/729-2711

Billy Miles Auction
Katy Hockley Cut Off
Katy, Texas
281/371-9766

Bud Burton Auction
Houston, Texas
713/789-9333

Flagship Enterprises
P.O. Box 205
Leona, TX. 75850

Tom Keilman & Son Auctioneers, Inc.
512/251-4236

Utah

Shows

Acorn Antique Guild
602/258-5700

Vermont

Shows

Forbes & Turner Antiques Show
207/767-3967

Virginia

Shows

The Joe & Marl Shows
941/751-6275

Renaissance Promotions, Inc.
804/462-6190

Presentations by Ginny
1-800-659-8190

D'Amore Promotions
804/431-9500

Sha-Dor Inc.
301/738-1966

Greenberg Shows
410/795-7447

Auctions

Old American Auction Gallery
8 W. Main Street
Pulaski, VA 24301
540/980-8404

Green Valley Auctions
540/434-4260

Washington

Shows

Jim Custer Enterprises, Inc.
509/924-0588

Palmer/Wirfs & Associates
503/282-0877

Michele Karl Promotions
206/744-0983

Milette Enterprises
509/292-8286

Wisconsin

Shows

C & J Promotions
715/588-3665

Zurko Promotions
715/526-9769

Badger Military Show
608/752-6677

Generation Promotions
608/362-2844

Wyoming

Shows

Traylor Antique Shows
1-800-571-6615

Specialties

Below is a listing of shops/malls/markets which specialize in particular antiques and collectibles.

ADIRONDACK

GA, Lakemont	THE LAKEHOUSE on Lake Rabun	# 37	pg.# 127

ADVERTISING

AZ, Cornville	Eight Ball Antiques	# 2	pg.# 22
CA, Chowchilla	Gray Duck Antique Mall	# 29	pg.# 49
IL, Evanston	Eureka	# 32	pg.# 142
KS, Augusta	White Eagle Antique Mall	# 4	pg.# 176
KS, Emporia	Wild Rose Antique Mall	# 12	pg.# 177
MO, Hannibal	Mrs. Clemens Antique Mall	# 23	pg.# 270
NE, Grand Island	Country Trader	# 5	pg.# 292
NC, Raleigh	Oakwood Antiques Mall	# 47	pg.# 356
NH, Nashua	House of Josephs Antiques & Cllbles.	# 30	pg.# 306
OH, Strasburg	Strasburg 77 Antiques & Collectibles	# 85	pg.# 378
PA, Chadds Ford	Olde Ridge Village Antique Shoppes	# 27	pg.# 407
PA, Duncannon	Old Sled Works	# 39	pg.# 408
TN, Chattanooga	East Town Antique Mall	# 9	pg.# 448
TN, Dickson	Pepper Patch Antique Mall	# 21	pg.# 450
TN, Knoxville	Homespun Antique Mall	# 41	pg.# 454
TN, Kodak	Dumplin Valley Antiques	# 42	pg.# 455
TN, Sevierville	Riverside Antique Mall	# 65	pg.# 458
TX, Fort Worth	Cowtown Antiques The Trading Post	# 57	pg.# 477
TX, Lubbock	Antique Mall of Lubbock	# 96	pg.# 484

AIRLINE NOSTALGIA

NY, New York City	Cohen's Collectibles	# 54	pg.# 340

AMERICAN ANTIQUES

AL, Ashville	Antique Warehouse	# 3	pg.# 12
AL, Pell City	David Tims Wholesale Antiques	# 39	pg.# 16
AZ, Glendale	The Apple Tree	# 5	pg.# 23
AR, Keo	Morris Antiques	# 19	pg.# 35
CA, Exeter	Exeter Antiques	# 45	pg.# 50
CA, Laguna Beach	Wild Goose Chase-Sweet William	# 76	pg.# 54
CA, Solvang	Solvang Antique Center	# 175	pg.# 76
CT, East Hampton	Old Bank Antiques	# 17	pg.# 94
FL, Deerfield Beach	A Moment In Time Antiques & Clltbles	# 18	pg.# 110
LA, New Orleans	Didier, Inc.	# 17	pg.# 199
ME, Wells	MacDougall-Gionet Antiques	# 33	pg.# 209
OH, Montgomery	Drackett Designs & Antiques	# 65	pg.# 377
SC, Spartanburg	John Morton Antiques	# 46	pg.# 430
TX, Arlington	Antiques by Ellis	# 5	pg.# 469
TX, Houston	R & F Antiques	# 78	pg.# 480
VT, Waterbury	Early Vermont Antiques	# 20	pg.# 504
VA, Mechanicsville	Mechanicsville Antique Mall	# 41	pg.# 513
VA, Winchester	Betty's Antiques	# 72	pg.# 516
WV, Bridgeport	Grey Fox Farm Antiques	# 6	pg.# 533

AMISH

NM, Farmington	Browsery	# 7	pg.# 327

ANTIQUE HARDWARE

CA, Murphys	D.E.A. Bathroom Machineries	# 108	pg.# 58
GA, Chamblee	Eugenia's Authentic Antique Hardware	# 15	pg.# 125
IN, Indianapolis	Colonial Antiques	# 29	pg.# 158

ARCHITECTURAL

AR, Mountain Home	Earl's Antiques	# 23	pg.# 36
CA, Murphys	D.E.A. Bathroom Machineries	# 108	pg.# 58
CA, Santa Monica	Santa Monica Antique Market	# 167	pg.# 74
CA, Visalia	Spit n Polish	# 199	pg.# 78
CO, Denver	Architectural Salvage Inc.	# 11	pg.# 84
CO, Denver	Do-it-ur-self Antique Plumbing	# 11	pg.# 84
IL, Chicago	Salvage One Architectural Artifacts	# 17	pg.# 141
IN, Indianapolis	Colonial Antiques	# 29	pg.# 158
NE, Lincoln	Conner's Architectural Antiques	# 9	pg.# 293
TN, Collierville	Center Street Antiques	# 15	pg.# 449
TX, Dallas	The Wrecking Barn	# 45	pg.# 475
WI, Wausau	Kimberly's Old House Gallery	# 65	pg.# 545

ART

AL, Ashville	Antique Warehouse	# 3	pg.# 12
CT, Westport	George Subkoff	# 74	pg.# 100
FL, Deerfield Beach	A Moment In Time Antiques & Clltbles	# 18	pg.# 110
FL, Plant City	The Olde Village Shoppes Mini Mall	# 69	pg.# 116
GA, Macon	Village Antique Mall	# 40	pg.# 128
MD, Bethesda	Grapevine of Bethesda	# 7	pg.# 214
NJ, Lambertville	David Rago Auctions, Inc.	# 37	pg.# 317
TN, Hickman	Antique Malls of Tennessee	# 36	pg.# 453
TX, Amarillo	Webb Galleries Amarillo	# 3	pg.# 468

ART GLASS

CA, Pomona	Swan Song	# 132	pg.# 67
ME, Auburn	Orphan Annie's Antiques (Tiffany, Stuben, Quezal, Galle, Daum Nancy, D'Argental, Loetz)	# 2	pg.# 206
MD, Bethesada	Grapevine of Bethesada	# 7	pg.# 214
MD, Hanover	AAA Antiques Mall	# 28	pg.# 216
MI, Chesang	Fancy That Antiques	# 13	pg.# 239
MS, Ridgeland	Antique Mall of the South (Fenton)	# 35	pg.# 262
SC, Simpsonville	Cudds Zoo Antiques	# 45	pg.# 430
TN, Chattanooga	East Town Antique Mall	# 9	pg.# 448
TN, Murfreesboro	Antique Centers I & II	# 57	pg.# 457
VA, Mechanicsville	Mechanicsville Antique Mall	# 41	pg.# 513

BANKS

OK, Dewey	Dewey Antique Mall	# 17	pg.# 386
TX, Lubbock	Antique Mall of Lubbock	# 96	pg.# 484

BARBER SHOP

AR, Mountain Home	Earl's Antiques	# 23	pg.# 36

BLACK MEMORABILIA

IL, Evanston	Eureka	# 32	pg.# 142
MD, Hanover	AAA Antiques Mall	# 28	pg.# 216
TN, Murfreesboro	Antique Centers I & II	# 57	pg.# 457

Specialties

BOOKS

CO, Denver	The Gallagher Collection	# 11	pg.# 85
IL, Geneva	Findings of Geneva Antiques	# 40	pg.# 143
IL, Lemont	Antique Parlour	# 58	pg.# 145
MO, Kennett	Bank of Antiques & Special Finds	# 31	pg.# 274
NH, Fitzwilliam	Rainy Day Books	# 19	pg.# 305
OH, Strasburg	Strasburg 77 Antiques & Collectibles	# 85	pg.# 378
TN, Knoxville	Campbell Station Antiques	# 41	pg.# 454
TN, Nashville	Antique Merchants Mall	# 58	pg.# 457
WV, Elkins	Bittersweet Books & Antiques	# 11	pg.# 534

BOTTLES

MI, Chesang	Fancy That Antiques	# 13	pg.# 239
OH, Strasburg	Strasburg 77 Antiques & Cllbles	# 85	pg.# 378
OR, Parkdale	Parkdale Plain & Fancy	# 37	pg.# 397

BRONZE

AL, Ashville	Antique Warehouse	# 3	pg.# 2
AL, Pell City	David Tims Wholesale Antiques	# 39	pg.# 16
NM, Ruidoso	Camel House	# 13	pg.# 327

CANDLES

DE, Wilmington	Sheepish Grin, Inc.	# 13	pg.# 105

CARNIVAL

OK, Chouteau	Black Star Antiques	# 12	pg.# 385

CAROUSELS & REPAIR

IL, Somonauk	House of Seven Fables	# 106	pg.# 149
WI, Dodgeville	Carousel Antiques & Collectibles	# 14	pg.# 541

CHAIRS

CT, East Hampton	Old Bank Antiques	# 17	pg.# 94
IN, Atlanta	The Wooden Indian Antiques	# 3	pg.# 156
TN, Germantown	Anderson Mulkins Antiques	# 29	pg.# 452

CHINA/PORCELAIN

AZ, Mesa	Carole & Maxine's Antiques (flow blue)	# 10	pg.# 24
CA, Chowchilla	The Glasstique Shoppe (flow blue)	# 29	pg.# 49
CA. Solvang	Solvang Antique Center	# 175	pg.# 76
CO, Englewood	Van Dyke's Antiques (flow blue)	# 13	pg.# 86
CO, Littleton	Colorado Antique Gallery (R.S. Prussia, Royal Bayreuth)	# 23	pg.# 87
CT, East Hampton	Old Bank Antiques	# 17	pg.# 94
GA, Macon	Village Antique Mall	# 40	pg.# 128
MD, Bethesada	Grapevine of Bethesada (China, Sets of 12)	# 7	pg.# 214
MS, Ridgeland	Antique Mall of The South (flow blue)	# 35	pg.# 262
MO, Ozark	Antique Emporium	# 46	pg.# 274
NH, Stratham	Compass Rose Antiques (1800s China)	# 41	pg.# 307
NH, Chichester	Teacher's Antiques at Thunder Bridge (flow blue)	# 9	pg.# 304
NM, Eagle Nest	Enchanted Circle Co. Antiqs. & Accom.	# 6	pg.# 327
NE, Lincoln	Conner's Architectural Antiques (China matching service)	# 9	pg.# 293
NE, Nebraska City	Peppercricket Farm Antiques (flow blue)	# 13	pg.# 294
OK, Norman	The Company Store Antique Mall (flow blue)	# 33	pg.# 388
PA, Chadds Ford	Olde Ridge Village Antique Shoppes	# 27	pg.# 407
TN, Chattanooga	East Town Antique Mall (Lenox, R.S. Prussia, Wedgewood, Nippon, Torquay)	# 9	pg.# 448
TN, Jackson	Yarbrough's (Blue Willow)	# 37	pg.# 453
TN, Knoxville	Antiques Plus (Jewel Tea)	# 41	pg.# 454
TN, Knoxville	Campbell Station Antiques (flow blue)	# 41	pg.# 454
TN, Kodak	Dumplin Valley Antiques (Fostoria)	# 42	pg.# 455
TN, Murfreesboro	Antiques Centers I & II (Fostoria)	# 57	pg.# 457
TX, Blanco	Unique Antiques (flow blue)	# 18	pg.# 472
TX, Houston	Carolyn Tompson's Antique Center Of Texas (Haviland)	# 78	pg.# 480

CLEVENGER GLASS

NJ, Hainsport/Mt. Holly	Country Antique Center	# 49	pg.# 318

CLOCKS

CA, Solvang	Solvang Antique Center	# 175	pg.# 76
CT, East Hampton	Old Bank Antiques	# 17	pg.# 94
FL, Plant City	Bay Antiques & Clock Repair	# 69	pg.# 116
FL, Sarasota	Mark of Time	# 74	pg.# 117
IL, Lemont	Lemont Antiques	# 58	pg.# 145
IN, Flora	Bill's Clock Works	# 22	pg.# 157
IN, Terre Haute	Hoosier Antiques & Clocks	# 72	pg.# 161
NH, Exeter	Peter Sawyer Antiques	# 18	pg.# 305
NM, Ruidoso	Camel House	# 13	pg.# 327
VT, Jay	The Tickle Trunk	# 9	pg.# 503
VA, Mechanicsville	Mechanicsville Antique Mall	# 41	pg.# 513

COINS

KS, Leavenworth	Caffee's Leavenworth Antique Mall	# 22	pg.# 178

COPPER/BRASS

AZ, Mesa	Carole & Maxine's Antiques	# 10	pg.# 23
PA, Sciota	Halloran's Antiques	# 121	pg.# 416

COUNTRY FURNISHINGS & ACCESSORIES

CT, East Hampton	Old Bank Antiques	# 17	pg.# 94
DE, Wilmington	"sweet potato cabin"	# 13	pg.# 105
FL, Deerfield Beach	A Moment In Time Antiques & Clltbles	# 18	pg.# 110
FL, Ocala	Frazer Coal Co. Antiques	# 59	pg.# 115
IL, Lemont	Antique Parlour	# 58	pg.# 145
IN, Roanoke	Antiques From BC At Lonsdale	# 63	pg.# 160
KY, Paducah	American Harvest Antiques	# 32	pg.# 190
ME, Thomaston	David C. Morey American Antiques	# 31	pg.# 209
MA, Great Barrington	The Coffman's Country Antiques Mkt.	# 29	pg.# 226
NE, Grand Island	Lana's Antique Mall	# 5	pg.# 292
NH, Richmond	The Yankee Smuggler Antiques	# 38	pg.# 307
NJ, Bridgeport	Racoon Creek Antiques	# 11	pg.# 314
TN, Henning	Kitty Ables	# 34	pg.# 453
VA, Afton	Whitehouse Antiques	# 2	pg.# 509

Specialties

COUNTRY STORE

AR, Mountain Home	Earl's Antiques	# 23	pg.# 36
OK, Chouteau	Black Star Antiques	# 12	pg.# 385

CRYSTAL

NM, Eagle Nest	Enchanted Circle Co., Antiques	# 6	pg.# 327

CUT GLASS

NJ, Hainsport/Mt. Holly	Country Antique Center	# 49	pg.# 318
TN, Knoxville	Antiques Plus	# 41	pg.# 454

DECO

CA, Chowchilla	The 2nd Frontier	# 29	pg.# 49
CA, Santa Monica	Santa Monica Antique Market	# 167	pg.# 74
FL, West Palm Beach	Boomerang Modern (Blonde Streamline Heywood Wakefield)	# 89	pg.# 119
KS, Lawrence	Quantrill's Antique Mall	# 21	pg.# 178
KY, Hazel	Retro-Wares	# 18	pg.# 189
NJ, Lambertville	David Rago Auctions, Inc.	# 37	pg.# 317

DEPRESSION GLASS

MO, Ozark	Ozark Antique Mall	# 46	pg.# 276
NE, Waterloo	Venice Antiques	# 18	pg.# 295
NJ, Hainsport/Mt. Holly	Country Antique Center	# 49	pg.# 318
NY, Millport	Serendipity II	# 50	pg.# 339
SC, Simpsonville	Cudds Zoo Antiques	# 45	pg.# 430
SD, Yankton	Kollectible Kingdom	# 23	pg.# 438
TX, Blanco	Unique Antiques	# 18	pg.# 472
TX, Lubbock	Antique Mall of Lubbock	# 96	pg.# 484

DOLLS

FL, Plant City	The Olde Village Shoppes Mini Mall	# 69	pg.# 116
NJ, Hainsport/Mt. Holly	Country Antique Center	# 49	pg.# 318
NM, Albuquerque	Classic Century Square	# 1	pg.# 326
TN, Knoxville	Antiques Plus	# 41	pg.# 454
TN, Murfreesboro	Antique Centers I & II	# 57	pg.# 457
TN, Sevierville	Volunteer Showcase Mall	# 65	pg.# 458

ELEGANT GLASSWARE

GA, Atlanta	Cheshire Antiques (Fostoria)	# 4	pg.# 124
MO, Ozark	Antique Emporium (Candlewick, Heisey)	# 46	pg.# 276
NJ, Hainsport/Mt. Holly	Country Antique Center (Heisey)	# 49	pg.# 318
TX, Lubbock	Antique Mall of Lubbock	# 96	pg.# 484

FIGURINES

MS, Ridgeland	Antique Mall of the South (Hummels)	# 35	pg.# 262
NJ, Trenton	Conti Antiques & Figurines (Goebel, Precious Moments, Ispanky, Cybis, Hummel, Royal Doulton)	# 71	pg.# 320
TN, Chattanooga	East Town Antique Mall (Hummels, Royal Doulton, Lladro, David Winter, Dept. 56)	# 9	pg.# 448

FOLK ART

AR, Ozark	Stu's Web Antiques & Ozark-Abillia	# 25	pg.# 37
OR, Drain	The Little Pink House	# 15	pg.# 396

FORMAL FURNISHINGS

AL, Ashville	Antique Warehouse	# 3	pg.# 12
AR, Keo	Morris Antiques	# 19	pg.# 35
CA, Santa Monica	Santa Monica Antique Market	# 167	pg.# 74
CA, Solvang	Solvang Antique Center	# 175	pg.# 76
CT, Westport	George Subkoff	# 74	pg.# 100
CT, Woodbury	Wayne Pratt	# 78	pg.# 101
GA, Roswell	Roswell Antique Gallery	# 53	pg.# 129
IN, Roanoke	Antiques From BC At Lonsdale	# 63	pg.# 160
MD, Bethesada	Grapevine of Bethesada	# 7	pg.# 214
NY, Franklin Square	Di Salvo Galleries	# 30	pg.# 337
NC, Asheville	Fireside Antiques	# 5	pg.# 351
PA, Blue Ridge Summit	Wooden Horse Antiques	# 17	pg.# 406
TX, Houston	Carolyn Thompson's Antique Center of Houston	# 78	pg.# 480
TX, Houston	Sherry Kelley's Antiques	# 78	pg.# 480
VA, Afton	Whitehouse Antiques	# 2	pg.# 509

JEWELRY

CA, Redlands	Ila's Antiques & Collectibles	# 139	pg.# 68
CA, Solvang	Solvang Antique Center	# 175	pg.# 76
CA, Tehachapi	Mom & Apple Pie Antiques	# 187	pg.# 77
CO, Littleton	Colorado Antique Gallery	# 23	pg.# 87
CT, East Hampton	Old Bank Antiques	# 17	pg.# 94
CT, Hartford	The Unique Antique	# 27	pg.# 94
MO, Columbia	Columbia Emporium	# 11	pg.# 269
NJ, Burlington	H.G. Sharkey & Co.	# 14	pg.# 314
NJ, Hainsport/Mt. Holly	Country Antique Center	# 49	pg.# 318
NY, Beacon	Back in Time Antiques	# 5	pg.# 334
OH, Wooster	Norton's Antiques, Etc.	# 103	pg.# 380

LAMPS/LIGHTING

CA, Solvang	Solvang Antique Center	# 175	pg.# 76
CT, East Hampton	Old Bank Antiques	# 17	pg.# 94
FL, Plant City	The Olde Village Shoppes Mini Mall (Victorian Lamps)	# 69	pg.# 116
IL, Lemont	Main Street Antique Emporium (Lamps & Repair)	# 58	pg.# 145
IL, Somonauk	House of Seven Fables (Lighting & Repair)	# 106	pg.# 149
IN, Bloomington	The Garrret	# 6	pg.# 156
IN, Indianapolis	Colonial Antiques	# 29	pg.# 158
NY, East Hampton	Architrove, Inc.	# 26	pg.# 336
TX, Tyler	Antiques & Uniques	# 151	pg.# 490
WY, Jackson	Samuel's Continental Imports	# 9	pg.# 550

LIGHTERS

MO, Hermitage	H. Bryan Western Collectibles	# 25	pg.# 272

LUNCH BOXES

NY, Nyack	Lisa's Antiques	# 56	pg.# 343

Specialties

MARBLES

OH, Strasburg	Carol's Collection	# 85	pg.# 378
TN, Henning	J & A Collectibles	# 34	pg.# 452

MILITARY

CA, Chowchilla	Gray Duck Antique Mall	# 29	pg.# 49
FL, Monticello	Southern Friends Antique Mall	# 52	pg.# 114
FL, Seminole	Cobweb Antiques	# 76	pg.# 117
GA, Summerville	Cherokee Antique Market (Civil War Documents)	# 58	pg.# 130
IL, Geneva	Findings of Geneva Antiques	# 40	pg.# 143
KY, Corbin	Past Times Antique Mall	# 7	pg.# 186
MD, Hanover	AAA Antiques Mall	# 28	pg.# 216
MS, Vicksburg	Yesterday's Treasures Antique Mall (Civil War)	# 39	pg.# 262
NH, Stratham	Compass Rose Antiques	# 41	pg.# 307
NJ, Lambertville	Stoneman Of The Deleware (Revolutionary, Civil War)	# 37	pg.# 316
SC, Camden	Wartime Collectibles	# 9	pg.# 427
TN, Chattanooga	East Town Antique Mall (American, German, Russian, Japanese)	# 9	pg.# 448
TN, Sevierville	Riverside Antique Mall	# 65	pg.# 458

MISSION

CA, Santa Monica	Santa Monica Antique Market (Stickley, Limberts, etc.)	# 167	pg.# 74
CA, Solvang	Solvang Antique Center	# 175	pg.# 76
GA, Macon	Village Antique Mall (Limbert, Stickley)	# 40	pg.# 128
NJ, Lambertville	David Rago Auctions, Inc.	# 37	pg.# 317

MOVIE MEMORABILIA

AR, Ozark	Stu's Web Antique & Ozark-Abillia	# 25	pg.# 37
FL, Plant City	The Olde Village Shoppes Mini Mall	# 69	pg.# 116

MUSIC BOXES

CA, Solvang	Solvang Antique Center	# 175	pg.# 76

MUSICAL INSTRUMENTS

MD, Baltimore	Antique Amusments A-1 Jukebox & Nostalgia Company (Jukeboxes including parts)	# 2	pg.# 213
MO, Grubville	Grubville Guitars (Vintage Guitars)	# 22	pg.# 270
NJ, Andover	Great Andover Antique Company (Edison Players, Victrolas, Radios)	# 2	pg.# 314
TX, Jacksonville	Treasure Cove Mall (Grand Pianos)	# 83	pg.# 482

ORIENTAL

NH, Nashua	House Of Josephs Antiques & Cllbles.	# 30	pg.# 306
WA, Seattle	Eileen of China	# 48	pg.# 526
WA, Seattle	GCC Gallery	# 48	pg.# 526

PAPER

CA, Chowchilla	Village Antiques	# 29	pg.# 49
CA, San Juan Capistrano	Yesterday's Paper	# 156	pg.# 73
CA, Sunland	Adventure In Postcards (Postcards)	# 184	pg.# 77
IL, Evanston	Eureka	# 32	pg.# 142
IL, Geneva	Findings of Geneva Antiques	# 40	pg.# 143
NE, Grand Island	Great Exchange Flea Market	# 5	pg.# 292
NJ, Hainsport/Mt. Holly	Country Antique Center	# 49	pg.# 318
NY, Nyack	Lisa's Antiques (Postcards)	# 56	pg.# 343
TN, Chattanooga	East Town Antique Mall	# 9	pg.# 448
WV, Elkins	Bittersweet Books & Antiques	# 11	pg.# 534

POST OFFICE

AR, Mountain Home	Earl's Antiques	# 23	pg.# 36

POTTERY

AL, Heflin	The Willoughby Street Mall (Hull, Roseville, Shawnee)	# 22	pg.# 14
AR, Mountain Home	The Farm House Antique & Craft Mall (Franciscan Pottery)	# 23	pg.# 36
CA, Carlsbad	AANTEEK Avenue Mall (California Pottery)	# 22	pg.# 47
CA, Chowchilla	The Parrott Shop (California Pottery)	# 29	pg.# 48
CA, Lockeford	Foxglove Antiques (Roseville)	# 84	pg.# 55
GA, Atlanta	Cheshire Antiques (Hull, Fiesta, Roseville, McCoy)	# 4	pg.# 124
GA, Macon	Village Antique Mall (Van Briggle, Niloak)	# 40	pg.# 128
ME, Auburn	Orphan Annie's Antiques (Roseville)	# 2	pg.# 206
MI, Chesang	Fancy That Antiques (Rookwood, Roseville)	# 13	pg.# 239
MO, Ozark	Antique Emporium (Roseville)	# 46	pg.# 276
MO, Ozark	Ozark Antique Mall	# 46	pg.# 276
NJ, Hainsport/Mt. Holly	Country Antique Center (Roseville)	# 49	pg.# 318
NM, Clovis	Prarie Peddler Antiques (Roseville)	# 5	pg.# 326
OK, Norman	The Company Store Antique Mall (Rookwood, Roseville)	# 33	pg.# 388
SD, Hill City	Orloske Antiques (Red Wing)	# 9	pg.# 436
SD, Yankton	Kollectible Kingdom (Red Wing)	# 23	pg.# 438
TN, Chattanooga	East Town Antique Mall (American Pottery	# 9	pg.# 448
TN, Knoxville	Antiques Plus (Fiesta)	# 41	pg.# 454
TN, Murfreesboro	Antique Centers I & II (Roseville, Hull, Weller, Watts)	# 57	pg.# 457
TX, Lubbock	Antique Mall of Lubbock (Red Wing, Franciscan, Fiesta)	# 96	pg.# 484
VA, Mechanicsville	Mechanicsville Antique Mall (Art Pottery)	# 41	pg.# 513

PRIMITIVES

NJ, Hainsport/Mt. Holly	Country Antique Center	# 49	pg.# 318
TN, Chattanooga	East Town Antique Mall	# 9	pg.# 448
TN, Dickson	Pepper Patch Antique Mall	# 21	pg.# 458
TN, Dyersburg	Walton's Antique Mall	# 22	pg.# 451
TN, Henning	Kitty Ables	# 34	pg.# 453
TX, Amarillo	The Mustard Seed	# 3	pg.# 468

PRINTS

NY, Nyack	Lisa's Antiques (African American)	# 56	pg.# 343

QUILTS

CA, Santa Monica	Santa Monica Antique Market	# 167	pg.# 74
IN, Goshen	Carriage Barn Antiques	# 25	pg.# 157
NE, Omaha	Kirk Collection	# 16	pg.# 294
NM, Eagle Nest	Enchanted Circle Co., Antiques	# 6	pg.# 327
NC, Black Mountain	Aly Goodwin: The N.E. Horton Antique Quilt Collection	# 7	pg.# 351

RAILROAD

KY, Corbin	Past Times Antique Mall	# 7	pg.# 186
MS, Ridgeland	Antique Mall of the South (Old Trains)	# 35	pg.# 262
SD, Spearfish	Old Mill Antiques	# 18	pg.# 437
TN, Jackson	Casey Jones Museum (Trains)	# 37	pg.# 453

RUGS

MI, Birmingham	Hagopin World of Rugs	# 9	pg.# 238
VT, Shelburne	Vincent Fernandez Oriental Antq. Rugs	# 17	pg.# 504

RUSTIC FURNISHINGS

GA, Lakemont	THE LAKEHOUSE on Lake Rabun	# 37	pg.# 127

SHAKER

CA, Santa Monica	Santa Monica Antique Market	# 167	pg.# 74
CA, Solvang	Solvang Antique Center	# 175	pg.# 76

SILVER

CT, East Hampton	Old Bank Antiques	# 74	pg.# 94
NM, Eagle Nest	Enchanted Circle Co., Antiques	# 6	pg.# 327
NY, Nyack	Lisa's Antiques	# 56	pg.# 343
NC, Selma	TWM's Antique Mall	# 54	pg.# 356

SPORTING EQUIPMENT

IL, Joliet	Uniques Antiques, Ltd. (Hunting, Fishing)	# 51	pg.# 144
MO, Ozark	Ozark Antique Mall (Fishing)	# 46	pg.# 276
SC, Aiken	Aiken Antique Mall (Fishing, Hunting)	# 2	pg.# 426
VT, Stowe	Rosebud Antiques at Houston Farm (Sporting Equipment)	# 19	pg.# 504

STAINED GLASS

FL, Plant City	The Olde Village Shoppes Mini Mall	# 69	pg.# 116
OK, Norman	The Company Store Antique Mall	# 33	pg.# 388
TX, Fort Worth	Cowtown Antiques The Trading Post	# 57	pg.# 477

STEAMSHIP NOSTALGIA

IL, Lemont	Pacific Tall Ships	# 58	pg.# 145
NY, New York City	Cohen's Collectibles	# 54	pg.# 340

TEXTILES

AL, Fairhope	Bay Antiques & Collectibles (Antique Linen & Lace)	# 14	pg.# 14
CA, Santa Monica	Santa Monica Antique Market	# 167	pg.# 74
CA, Solvang	Solvang Antique Center	# 175	pg.# 76
IL, Geneva	Findings of Geneva Antiques	# 40	pg.# 143
NE, Omaha	The Kirk Collection	# 16	pg.# 294

TOYS

AZ, Cornville	Eight Ball Antiques (Small scale collectible cars)	# 2	pg.# 22
GA, Atlanta	Cheshire Antiques	# 4	pg.# 124
IL, Geneva	Findings of Geneva Antiques	# 40	pg.# 143
MI, Midland	Michigan Antiques Festival	# 42	pg.# 242
NM, Albuquerque	Classic Century Square (Star Wars collectibles)	# 1	pg.# 326
NY, Nyack	Lisa's Antiques	# 56	pg.# 343
OH, Strasburg	Strasburg 77 Antiques & Collectibles (Disney Collectibles)	# 85	pg.# 378
PA, Duncannon	Old Sled Works (Old Sleds)	# 39	pg.# 408
SC, Camden	Wartime Collectibles	# 9	pg.# 427
TN, Chattanooga	East Town Antique Mall	# 9	pg.# 448
TN, Dickson	Pepper Patch Antique Mall	# 21	pg.# 450
TN, Murfreesboro	Antique Centers I & II	# 57	pg.# 457
TN, Sevierville	Riverside Antique Mall	# 65	pg.# 458
TX, Lubbock	Antique Mall of Lubbock	# 96	pg.# 484
VA, Mechanicsville	Mechanicsville Antique Mall	# 41	pg.# 513

TRUNKS

MI, Ionia	Grand River Antiques	# 29	pg.# 240
VT, Jay	The Tickle Trunk	# 9	pg.# 503

VICTORIAN

AR, Keo	Morris Antiques	# 19	pg.# 35
CA, Pomona	Swan Song	# 132	pg.# 67
CA, Santa Monica	Santa Monica Antique Market	# 167	pg.# 74
CA, Tehachapi	Mom & Apple Pie Antiques	# 187	pg.# 77
IL, Lemont	Antique Parlour	# 58	pg.# 145
KS, Emporia	Wild Rose Antique Mall	# 12	pg.# 177
MO, Florissant	Gittemeir House Antiques	# 16	pg.# 269
NE, Lexington	Bargain John's Antiques	# 8	pg.# 293
NE, Nebraska City	Peppercricket Farm Antiques	# 13	pg.# 294
NJ, Andover	Great Andover Antique Company	# 2	pg.# 314
NY, Fairhaven	Black Creek Farm Bed & Breakfast and Antique Shop	# 28	pg.# 337
PA, Blue Ridge Summit	Wooden Horse Antiques	# 17	pg.# 406
SC, Georgetown	Tosh Antiques	# 20	pg.# 428
TX, Baird	Henson's Antiques	# 9	pg.# 470
VA, Mechanicsville	Mechanicsville Antique Mall	# 41	pg.# 513

VINTAGE CLOTHING

NY, New York City	The Family Jewels Vintage Clothing	# 54	pg.# 339
UT, Murray	Lyn Anne's Collectables	# 9	pg.# 497

WATCHES/WATCH FOBS

MS, Ridgeland	Antique Mall of the South	# 35	pg.# 262
MO, Hermitage	H. Bryan Western Collectibles	# 25	pg.# 272
NJ, Dover	Peddler's Shop (Watch Fobs)	# 23	pg.# 315

WESTERN MEMORABILIA

AZ, Wickenburg	Head-West Barber & Antique Shop	# 21	pg.# 27
CA, Chowchilla	Frontier Towne	# 29	pg.# 48
CA, San Juan Capistrano	Sentimental Journey West	# 156	pg.# 73
MO, Hermitage	H. Bryan Western Collectibles	# 25	pg.# 272
NM, Albuquerque	Classic Century Square	# 1	pg.# 326
NM, Eagle Nest	Enchanted Circle Co., Antiques	# 6	pg.# 327
NM, Ruidoso	Camel House	# 13	pg.# 327
OH, Strasburg	Carol's Collection (Arrowheads)	# 85	pg.# 388
OK, Dewey	Dewey Antique Mall	# 17	pg.# 386
SD, Belle Fourche	The Old Grizz Trading Post	# 2	pg.# 436
TN, Chattanooga	East Town Antique Mall	# 9	pg.# 448
TX, Fort Worth	Cowtown Antiques The Trading Post	# 57	pg.# 477

WICKER

CT, East Hampton	Old Bank Antiques	# 17	pg.# 94
IL, Somonauk	House of Seven Fables (Wicker Repair)	# 106	pg.# 149
MA, Marblehead	Wicker Unlimited	# 39	pg.# 227

WORLD FAIR ITEMS

IL, Evanston	Eureka	# 32	pg.# 142
IL, Geneva	Findings of Geneva Antiques	# 40	pg.# 143

A Final Note....

The Station

by Robert J. Hastings

Tucked away in our subconscious minds is an idyllic vision in which we see ourselves on a long journey... We're traveling by train, and from the windows, we drink in the passing scenes of cars on nearby highways, of children waving at crossings, of cattle grazing in distant pastures, of smoke pouring from power plants, of row upon row of cotton and corn and wheat, of flatlands and valleys, of city skylines and village halls.

But uppermost in our minds is our final destination — for at a certain hour and on a given day, our train will finally pull into the station with bells ringing, flags waving and bands playing. And once that day comes, so many wonderful dreams will come true. So restlessly, we pace the aisles and count the miles, peering ahead, waiting, waiting, waiting for the station.

"Yes, when we reach the station, that will be it!" we promise ourselves. "When we're 18...win that promotion...put the last kid through college...buy that 450 SL Mercedes-Benz—pay off the mortgage...have a nest egg for retirement."

From that day on, we will all live happily ever after.

Sooner or later, however, we must realize there is no station in this life, no one earthly place to arrive at once and for all. The journey is the joy. The station is an illusion — it constantly outdistances us. Yesterday's a memory; tomorrow's a dream. Yesterday belongs to history; tomorrow belongs to God. Yesterday's a fading sunset; tomorrow's a faint sunrise. Only today is there light enough to love and live.

So, gently close the door on yesterday and throw the key away. It isn't the burdens of today that drive men mad, but rather the regret over yesterday and the fear of tomorrow.

"Relish the moment" is a good motto, especially when coupled with Psalm 118:24: "This is the day which the Lord hath made; we will rejoice and be glad in it."

So stop pacing the aisles and counting the miles. Instead, swim more rivers, climb more mountains, kiss more babies, count more stars. Laugh more and cry less. Go barefoot more often. Eat more ice cream. Ride more merry-go-rounds. ***Go Antiquing.*** *Watch more sunsets. Life must be lived as we go along.*